International Conference on Electronic Information Technology and Computer Engineering (EITCE 2017)

MATEC Web of Conferences Volume 128 (2017)

Zhuhai, China
23 - 24 September 2017

Editor:

Yansong Wang

ISBN: 978-1-5108-5049-1

Printed from e-media with permission by:

Curran Associates, Inc.
57 Morehouse Lane
Red Hook, NY 12571

CURRAN ASSOCIATES INC. proceedings.com

Some format issues inherent in the e-media version may also appear in this print version.

Printed by Curran Associates, Inc. (2017)

For additional information, please contact EDP Sciences – Web of Conferences at the address below.

EDP Sciences – Web of Conferences
17, Avenue du Hoggar
Parc d'Activité de Courtabœuf
BP 112
F-91944 Les Ulis Cedex A
France

Phone: +33 (0) 1 69 18 75 75
Fax: +33 (0) 1 69 28 84 91

contact-edps@webofconferences.org

Additional copies of this publication are available from:

Curran Associates, Inc.
57 Morehouse Lane
Red Hook, NY 12571 USA
Phone: 845-758-0400
Fax: 845-758-2633
Email: curran@proceedings.com
Web: www.proceedings.com

TABLE OF CONTENTS

THE SOFTWARE DESIGN OF SIBCN TEMPERATURE SENSOR WIRELESS SWEEP SIGNAL RECEIVING AND DISPATCHING SYSTEM BASED ON FPGA 1
Jiang Chengzhi, Li Tianli, Zhang Xiaojie, Zhang Jiyue, Yan Li

DESIGN OF WIRELESS SWEEP SIGNAL RECEIVING AND DISPATCHING HARDWARE SYSTEM BASED ON SIBCN TEMPERATURE SENSOR 5
Wei Huayu, Li Tianli, Yan Li, Zhang Jiyue, Zhang Xiaojie

SPEECH DENOISING IN WHITE NOISE BASED ON SIGNAL SUBSPACE LOW-RANK PLUS SPARSE DECOMPOSITION 9
yuan Shuai, Sun Cheng-li

THE RESEARCH ON WLAN TECHNOLOGY OF CHAIN NETWORK BASED ON MONITORING INFORMATION TRANSMISSION OF CATENARY 13
Chunmei Wu, Guilin Li, Shaowei Wang, Xueyan Lan

RESEARCH ON DISPLACEMENT CALCULATION OF DYNAMOMETER CARD BASED ON KAIMAN FILTER AND DISCRETE NUMERICAL INTEGRATION 19
Yan Nan, Shu Dai Jia

INVESTIGATION ON MEASURING TOTAL PERIPHERAL RESISTANCE OF HUMAN BODY BY MEANS OF RECONSTRUCTED IMPEDANCE CARDIOGRAM 24
Shi-jiang Kuang, Hui Zhao, Zi-min Wang, ming-xing Kuang

RESEARCH ON ESTIMATION OF WHEAT CHLOROPHYLL USING IMAGE PROCESSING TECHNOLOGY 28
Zhou Liya, Yuan Yingchun, Song Yufei, Wang Bin

RESEARCH AND IMPLEMENTATION OF DIGITAL IMAGE ENHANCEMENT ALGORITHMS 33
Yue Liu, Meishan Li, Dandan Ma, Desheng Liu

ADAPTIVE SCALE COMPRESSIVE TRACKING WITH FEATURE INTEGRATION 37
Luo Mingqi, Wang Tuo, Zhou Bin

ADAPTIVE MULTI-PART TARGET REPRESENTATION FOR TRACKING 41
Luo Mingqi, Wang Tuo, Zhou Bin

TXCP: A COPROCESSOR FOR LTE-A 45
Huang Xin, Liu QingBin, Wu JunNing, Du XueLiang, Wang DongLin

RESEARCH ON HIGH-TECH AMMUNITION TRAINING SYSTEM BASED ON VIRTUAL REALITY TECHNOLOGY 49
Meng Zhang, Lutie Xu, Weibo Yu, Hongbo Liu

DIRECTION-OF-ARRIVAL AND RANGE ESTIMATION OF WIDEBAND SOURCES IN THE NEAR FIELD 54
Lin Wen-Feng, Ma Wei-Dong, Xie Min, Xu Li-Xing, Wei Ping

A NEW METHOD BASED ON TWO-STAGE DETECTION MECHANISM FOR DETECTING SHIPS IN HIGH-RESOLUTION SAR IMAGES 59
Xu Yongli, Xiong Wei, Lv Yafei, Liu Hengyan

NUMERICAL SIMULATION OF UNDERWATER ACOUSTICAL FIELD WITH DIRECTIONAL SOURCES BASED ON THE NORMAL MODES MODEL 67
Jihui Wang, Zhenshan Wang, Bing Jia

TIBETAN INFORMATION EXTRACTION TECHNOLOGY INTEGRATED WITH EVENT FEATURE AND SEMANTIC ROLE LABELLING 71
Wan Fucheng, Xia Jianhua

THE APPLICATION STUDY ON THE IMPROVED CANNY ALGORITHM FOR EDGE DETECTION IN STRAIN GAUGE IMAGE 76
Wei Qin, Juan Li

RESEARCH ON MODELING METHOD OF POWER SYSTEM KEY COMPONENTS FOR E-REV 81
Niu Jigao, Shi Xiaoli, Xu Chunhua, Li Chenxu

SIMULATION AND ANALYSIS OF PASSIVE ROLLING COMPENSATION OF HIGH SEA SALVAGE SYSTEM 86
Lin Liqun, Chen Zhixin

MULTI-OBJECTIVE PARTICLE SWARM OPTIMIZATION BASED IMAGE WATERMARKING SCHEME 91
Fu YongGang, Wang HuiRong, Chen Lizhen, Jiang Yunfei

OPTIMIZATION OF WEAPON-TARGET ASSIGNMENT PROBLEM BY INTUITIONISTIC FUZZY GENETIC ALGORITHM 95
Jinshuai Yang, Jin Li, Yi Wang, Tong Wen, Zhanqiang Liu

ANALYSIS AND SIMULATION OF MULTI-TARGET ECHO SIGNALS FROM A PHASED ARRAY RADAR 100
Jia Zhen, Zhou Rui

DESIGN, SIMULATION AND VALIDATION OF HMC833 LOOP FILTER BASED ON MATLAB 105
Hu Shachang, Li Tianli, Zhang Jiyue, Yan Li, Zhang Xiaojie

SIMULATION ON TEMPERATURE AND AMPACITY OF MINING FLAME-PROOF HIGH VOLTAGE CABLE CONNECTOR 109
Li Haiying, Xue Zhuocheng, Song Jiancheng

RESEARCH ON FAULT TOLERANCE ENHANCEMENT OF ARRAY ERASURE CODES 113
Tang Dan, Xiao Feng, Fan Di

A SEPARATION AND DECODING ALGORITHM FOR QPSK SIGNALS WITH LOW COMPLEXITY 121
Pan Baijun, Tu Shilong

RESEARCH ON PEPPER DISEASE DIAGNOSIS MODEL BASED ON GENETIC NEURAL NETWORK 125
Wei Qingfeng, Sun Sufen, Luo ChangShou

THE MASSIVE REMOTE SENSING DATA ORGANIZATION AND MANAGEMENT STRATEGIES 128
Wei Hou, Yuheng Zhang

DEVELOPMENT OF A HARDWARE-IN- LOOP SIMULATION PLATFORM FOR NPP MAIN CONTROL SYSTEMS 132
Liu Pengfei, Bi Chunyu, Yu Yang, Lin Meng, Song Xinli, Wu Guoyang, Su Zhida

NUMERICAL INVESTIGATION ON THE EFFECT OF LABYRINTH SEAL CONFIGURATION ON LEAKAGE 137
Zhang Tianlu, Zhang Xi, Chen Xuemei, Jia Yifan

DESIGN OF REAL TIME DATA ACQUISITION SYSTEM FRAMEWORK FOR PRODUCTION WORKSHOP BASED ON OPC TECHNOLOGY 141
Yue-xina Yang, Gong-chang Ren

AN UPDATED PROJECTION TWIN SUPPORT VECTOR MACHINE FOR CLASSIFICATION 144
Hua Xiaopeng, Xu Sen

APPLICATION OF DATA ARCHITECTURE MODEL IN ENTERPRISE MANAGEMENT 148
Shi Song, Ji Yalin

FAULT DETECTION BASED BAYESIAN NETWORK AND MOEA/D APPLIED TO SENSORLESS DRIVE DIAGNOSIS 152
Zhou Qing, He Ling, Lu PengFei

METHOD OF MULTI-SENSOR DATA ASSOCIATION BASED ON LARGE SCALE 156
Xu-hui Lan, Ling-zhi Li, Yong-ming Guo

A PLAGIARISM DETECTION ALGORITHM BASED ON EXTENDED WINNOWING 159
Duan Xuliang, Wang Mantao, Mu Jiong

RESEARCH OF A SCHEDULING OPTIMIZATION ALGORITHM BASED ON HASH ADAPTER 164
Yang Wenchuan, Fu Zhen, Zuo Wen

LARGE SCALE FACE DATA PURIFICATION BASED ON CORRELATION FUNCTION AND MULTI-PHASE GROUPING 168
Zhang Xiangxiang, Fang Zhijun, Xi Zhenghao, Liu Xiaoshuang

DISCRETE TEACHING-LEARNING-BASED OPTIMIZATION ALGORITHM FOR TRAVELING SALESMAN PROBLEMS 172
Wu Lehui, Zoua Feng, Chen Debao

IMPACT OF PACKET SIZE ON PERFORMANCE OF TCP TRAFFIC WITH SMALL ROUTER BUFFERS 177
Zhang Bo, Li Yu, Liang Yanlei

STRUCTURE AND MICROSCOPIC WEAR ANALYSIS OF LINING MATERIAL BASED ON EDEM 181
Wang Zhongsheng, Wang Rujie, Fei Qiou, Li Jianguo, Tang Jiachen, Shi Boqiang

A BRIEF SURVEY ON NONLINEAR SURFACE PLASMONICS 185
Liang Yizeng

AN EXTRUSION DIE WITH TWIN CAVITIES FOR SEMI-HOLLOW AL-PROFILES 190
Huang Xuemei, Deng Rurong

SIMULATION ON THE THERMAL PROPERTIES OF POLYMER COMPOSITES REINFORCED BY BUCKYPAPER 195
Zhang AYing, Li ZhengHong
THERMAL PROPERTIES OF BUCKYPAPER ENABLED POLYMER COMPOSITES 199
Zhang AYing, Li ZhengHong
MICROSTRUCTURE AND MECHANICAL PROPERTIES OF 304L STEEL FABRICATED BY ARC ADDITIVE MANUFACTURING 203
Ji Lei, Lu Jiping, Liu Changmeng, Jing Chenchen, Fan Hongli, Ma Shuyuan
STRUCTURE AND MECHANICAL PROPERTIES OF TIO2/UHMWPE NANOCOMPOSITE MONOFILAMENTS 209
Wen YU Wen, Gao SHI Jian, WANG Lei, Li LIU Yong, Xue CHEN Xiao
INFLUENCE OF MATERIAL WITH MEDIUM AND HIGH MOLECULAR WEIGHT REPLACING POLYETHYLENE ON TRAWL PERFORMANCE 212
Liu Yongli, Wang Lei, Wen Yu Wen, Shi Jiangao, Zhou Ai zhong, Wang Lu min
FABRICATION AND CHARACTERIZATION OF 5 VOL.% $(AL_2O_3)_P$ + 8 VOL.% $(AL_2O_3)_F$/A336 HYBRID MICRON AND NANO-COMPOSITES 216
Ren Luyang, Zhang Qiang, Hu Henry
STUDY ON INDENTATION EXPERIMENTS AND MECHANICAL BEHAVIOR OF RB-SIC 220
Cheng Fan, Shijie Zhang, Qizhi Zhao, Lei Zhang
STUDY ON PROCESSING TECHNOLOGY AND QUALITY OF MORINGA OLEIFERA LEAVES WITH Y - AMINOBUTYRIC ACID 226
Wei Zhou, Qian Li, Changqing Guo, Yupo Cao, Shaodan Peng, Wei Jing, Jihua Li
STUDY ON HOT DIAPHRAGM FORMING PROCESS OF CCF300/5228A COMPOSITES 233
Yan Li, An Xuefeng
OPTIMIZATION ON TRAJECTORY OF STANFORD MANIPULATOR BASED ON GENETIC ALGORITHM 238
Han Xi
EVALUATION AND STUDY ON RELATIONSHIP BETWEEN SITTING POSTURE AND WORK EFFICIENCY 245
Xuesheng Pei, Liyingi Tian
A NOVEL RELIABILITY EVALUATION METHOD BASED ON RBD AND AHP FOR INDUSTRIAL NETWORK SYSTEMS 250
Li Yongni, Li Zhenxing, Li Baiyi, Hu Song
COMBINING THEOREM PROVING AND MODEL CHECKING IN THE SAFETY-CRITICAL SOFTWARE DEVELOPMENT THROUGH TRANSLATING EVENT-B TO SMV 256
Sen Liang, Xiangyu Luo, Zuxi Chen
A PRACTICAL J2EE APPLICATION STATIC ANALYSIS METHOD BASED UPON TAINT PROPAGATION 262
Hu Jian Jun, Wen Qiaoyan, Guo Dai Fei
INVESTIGATION AND ANALYSIS ON THE CONSTRUCTION SITUATION OF "THREE LINKS AND TWO PLATFORMS" OF EDUCATION FOR NATIONALITIES IN YUNNAN PROVINCE IN CHINA 266
Zhilin Zhao, Jianhou Gan
MEASUREMENT METHOD AND PRINCIPLE FOR THORACIC IMPEDANCE GRAPH 270
Hui Zhao, Shi-jiang Kuang, Bai-qing He, Zi-min Wang, Xiao-ling Cheng
AN IMPROVED SEQUENTIAL SMOOTHING PARTICLE FILTERING METHOD 274
Cao Shijie
THE DESIGN OF NONLINEAR CHIRP BASED ON THE DSP BUILDER TECHNIQUE 278
Zhang Dong, Yang Shou-liang, Zhang Yang
SIMPLIFIED CASING PROGRAM FOR DEVELOPMENT WELLS IN MAHU WELL BLOCK 282
Lu Zongyu, Chen Weifeng, Li Sihao, Zhang Yingjin
IMPROVING CO-RUNNING PROGRAM'S PERFORMANCE ON CMP 286
Tian Dawei, Li Hongkui, Niu Wenhui, Deng Ying, Li Fujian
A METHOD OF INITIAL VELOCITY MEASUREMENT FOR ROCKET PROJECTILE 290
Zhang Jiancheng, Zhang Tianle, Cai Zhengyu
RESEARCH ON COLLABORATIVE ACQUISITION OF MULTIDIMENSIONAL MASSIVE WEB BASED ON FUSION CREDIBILITY 294
Ya-juan Zhang, Wen-qing He
DESIGN OF A DISTRIBUTED FOOD TRACEABILITY PLATFORM AND ITS APPLICATION IN FOOD TRACEABILITY AT GUANGDONG PROVINCE 298
Luo Haibiao, Li Yin, Liu Dongcheng, Ouyang Yunxiong, Yuan Feng

FINGER VEIN RECOGNITION BASED ON CONVOLUTIONAL NEURAL NETWORK 305
Meng Gesi, Fang Peiyu, Zhang Bao
ENSURING THE FAIRNESS OF PROGRAM'S PERFORMANCE ON CMP 310
Wang Qilong, Gao Jun, Hou Guangsong, Li Hongkui, Xu Ke
RESISTANCE REQUIREMENTS OF THRESHOLD SWITCHING SELECTORS IN 1S1R CROSSBAR ARRAY 314
Lin Chenglong, Li Gaosheng, Jia Xueqing
DESIGN AND IMPLEMENTATION OF THE AUTOMATIC ASSESSMENT SYSTEM FOR THE COMMAND AND CONTROL SPECIALTY IN SHIPS 318
Zhang Hao, Wang Zheng-yi, Yin Wei
DESIGN AND IMPLEMENTATION OF TERMINAL LOGISTICS DISTRIBUTION SYSTEM BASED ON IOS PLATFORM 322
Zhuang Yufeng, Huang Rong
RESEARCH ON TEST SYSTEM FOR DISEASE AIDED DIAGNOSIS 328
Wei Chen, Zhangxiong Wen, Lin Chen, Fengwen Sun
EXPERIMENTAL VERIFICATION OF NEW FUNCTION THEORIES OF PARTICLES (1)-EXPERIMENTAL VERIFICATION OF NEW KINETIC ENERGY THEOREM OF RIGID BODY FIXED AXIS ROTATION 332
Yong Yang, Wei-Ping Zhao, Xiao-Gang Guo, Zheng-Qiang Jing
SURVEY OF OPTIMIZATION METHODS FOR BIW LIGHTWEIGHT DESIGN 336
Zheyun Wang
EFFECT OF BEVEL ANGLE OF THREE-LAYER PARALLEL PLATE ON HYDRODYNAMIC PERFORMANCES OF OTTER-BOARD 340
Wang Lei, Wang Lu Min, Zhang Yu, Zhong Zhou Ai, Li Liu Yong, Wen Yu Wen, Zhang Xun
EFFECT OF DEFLECTOR ANGLE ON HYDRODYNAMIC PERFORMANCES OF A DOUBLE-SLOTTED CAMBERED OTTER-BOARD 345
Wang Lei, Wang Lu Min, Shi Jian Gao, Zhang Yu, Liu Yong Li, Wen Yu Wen, Zhang Xun
INVESTIGATION ON MECHANICAL PROPERTIES' ANISOTROPY OF ROD UNITS IN LATTICE STRUCTURES FABRICATED BY SELECTIVE LASER MELTING 349
Jing Chenchen, Zhou Yong, Jiping Lu, Fan Hongli, Ji Lei, Li Penglin
THE BAFFLE INFLUENCE ON SOUND RADIATION CHARACTERISTICS OF A PLATE 353
Bao Liu, Yuchen Sun, Deshi Wang
EFFECT OF COMBINED TENSILE, BENDING AND TORSION DEFORMATION ON MEDIUM CARBON STEEL WIRE 359
Polyakova Marina, Gulin Aleksandr, Golubchik Eduard
STUDY ON ASSEMBLY PRECISION RELIABILITY ASSESSMENT FOR INDUSTRIAL SENSING DEVICES 364
Fan Tian, Tao Wei, Hu Hanxian, Liu Wei
EFFECT OF TOOL-PATH ON MORPHOLOGY AND MECHANICAL PROPERTIES OF TI-6AL-4V FABRICATED BY WIRE AND ARC ADDITIVE MANUFACTURING 368
Fu Jie, Qiu Kun, Gong Lin, Liu Changmeng, Wu Qianru, Lu Jiping, Fan Hongli
REFORM AND PRACTICE OF MULTIMEDIA TECHNOLOGY AND APPLICATION FOR APPLIED UNDERGRADUATES 372
jiaming Zhong, geng Zhu
RECOGNITION OF AIRCRAFT ENGINE SOUND BASED ON GMM-UBM MODEL 376
Yuan Shuai, Sun Chengli, Yang Haoge
AN INNOVATIVE CELLULAR AUTOMATA TECHNIQUE FOR MAPPING CRACKING PATTERN OF AIRPORT PAVEMENT 380
Yin Fucheng, Zhou Guangchun, Guo Edward, Zhang Shuang
FACTORY-LIKE OPTIMUM DRILLING DESIGN OF CLUSTER WELL IN JIMSAR WELL BLOCK 385
Liu Yingbiao, Zhang Wenbo, Lin Han, Zhu Zhongxi
MULTIPLE SYNERGISTIC DRILLING FLUID SYSTEM APPLICATION IN AIHU OILFIELD 389
Liu Yingbiao, Lu Zongyu, Dang Wenhui, Zhu Zhongxi
FAULT DIAGNOSIS FOR CONSTANT DECELERATION BRAKING SYSTEM OF MINE HOIST BASED ON PRINCIPAL COMPONENT ANALYSIS AND SVM 393
Li Juan-Juan, Hu Liang, Meng Guo-Ying, Xie Guang-Ming, Wang Ai-Ming, Wang Shuai, Jia Yi-Fan
MEASUREMENT OF ARGON EMISSION SPECTRAL OF ICP PLASMA USING A DIAGNOSTIC SYSTEM BASED ON PHOTOMULTIPLIER TUBES ARRAY 398
Liu Weifeng, Yang Yiyong, Han Chuankun, Cheng Jia, Ji Linhong
INDIVIDUAL DRILLING BIT DESIGN AND OPTIMIZATION IN MAHU AREA 403
Zhang Wenbo, Dang Wenhui, Chen Weifeng, Zhang Yingjin

RESEARCH AND IMPLEMENTATION OF INSTRUMENT SYSTEM ON A LIGHT-DUTY ELECTRIC AIRCRAFT SIMULATOR 407
Tian Feng, Sun Yonggang, Meng Guanglei, Yu Yongtao
Author Index

EITCE 2017 Preface

The 2017 International Conference on Electronic Information Technology and Computer Engineering (EITCE 2017) was successfully held from September 23-24, 2017 in Beijing Normal University, Zhuhai Guangdong, China. The conference addressed recent development in the following,

(1) Signal & Image Processing
(2) Simulation Model and Algorithm
(3) Electronic Material
(4) Computer Programming
(5) Electromechanical Technologies

The technical program consisted of 4 international keynote speakers, 19 invited speakers, 30 oral presentations, and a poster session with more than 30 posters.

This volume of MATEC Web of Conferences is a compilation of the accepted papers in EITCE 2017 and represents important results that were presented in the conference. The electronic submission and handling of the manuscripts via the conference website, including the selection of reviewers and evaluation of manuscripts, were identical to the procedures applied to manuscripts submitted as regular contributions for publication in peer reviewed journals.

The organization of this conference and the preparation of proceedings volume would have been impossible without the tremendous efforts and dedication of many individuals. Prof. Yansong Wang oversaw the organization of the Conference. We would like to acknowledge a large team of reviewers for their timely submission of quality reports. Without this support, the conference could not have been successful. We sincerely hope that EITCE 2017 will serve as an ideal forum for academia, industrial practitioners and government agents.

Prof.Yansong Wang
Shanghai University of Engineering Science, China
General Chairman of EITCE 2017

Organizing Committees

Conference Chair

Prof.Yansong Wang, Shanghai University of Engineering Science, China (Dean of Automotive Engineering College)

Local Committee

Assoc.Prof.Hao Chen, Shanghai University of Engineering Science, China
Prof.Hengyun Zhang, Shanghai University of Engineering Science, China
Prof.Xiao Yan, Shanghai University of Engineering Science, China
Prof.Yanfeng Xing, Shanghai University of Engineering Science, China
Assoc.Prof.Wei Liang, Shanghai University of Engineering Science, China
Assoc.Prof.Hui Guo, Shanghai University of Engineering Science, China

Technology Program Committee

Dr.David Chua Sing Ngie, University Malaysia Sarawak, Malaysia
Prof.Sanam Shahla Rizvi, Department of Computer Sciences, Preston University, Pakistan
Dr.Ahmad Kadri Junoh, Institute for Engineering Mathematics,Universiti Malaysia Perlis,Malaysia
Prof.Dr.Taha Elsayed Taha, Menoufia University, Egypt
Dr.Xiaozhou Du, Communication Engineering Design and Research Institute, China
Prof. Dr.Ha Duong Ngo, University of Applied Sciences Berlin/Fraunhofer Institute IZM, Germany
Dr.Guiyuan Jiang, Nanyang Technological University, Singapore
Dr.Jiangling Yin, Data scientist At Apple Inc., USA
Prof.Hossein Nezamabadi, Shahid Bahonar University of Kerman, Iran
Assoc.Prof.Cheung-Chieh Ku, National Taiwan Ocean University, Taiwan
Prof.Jack Luo, University of Bolton, School of Engineering, UK
Dr.Gang Qin, University of Electronic Science and Technology of China, China
Assoc.Prof.Xiaoxia Wang, North University of China, China
Dr.Guanjun Wang, China University of Mining and Technology, China
Dr.Pan Su, Hunan University, China
Prof.Yifei Shi, National University of Defense Technology, China
PhD.Jozef Martinka, Slovak University of Technology, Slovakia
Dr.Ali Boroumandnia, Tehran Azad University, Iran
Prof.Yong-Lin Kuo, Industrial Technology Research Institute, Taiwan/National Taiwan University of Science and Technology, Taiwan
Prof.Farah Bouakrif, University of Jijel, Algeria

Technical Program Secretary-General

Dr.Yulin Zhong, South China University of Technology, China

MATEC Web of Conferences **128**, 01001 (2017)
EITCE 2017
DOI: 10.1051/matecconf/201712801001

The Software Design of SiBCN Temperature Sensor Wireless Sweep Signal Receiving and Dispatching System Based on FPGA

Chengzhi Jiang, Tianli Li*, Xiaojie Zhang, Jiyue Zhang and Li Yan

Shenzhen Key Laboratory of Electromagnetic Control,Shenzhen University,Shenzhen 518060,China

Abstract. SiBCN (silicon boron carbon nitrogen) wireless passive microwave resonant cavity temperature sensor is a new type of sensor under the development trend of radio frequency microwave technology. Based on the working principle of the sensor, the software design of SiBCN temperature sensor wireless sweep transceiver system based on FPGA is carried out on the basis of the existing wireless sweep signal transceiver system hardware. Let the signal source send the 11.0GHz ~ 11.6GHz range sweep signal to the sensor. The feedback signal of the sensor is filtered and the resonant frequency is obtained. The detection of temperature is based on the correspondence between the resonant frequency and the temperature.Through the analysis of the measured results, the system software design meets the requirements, and the temperature and frequency change rate is about 421.2KHz / °C.

1 Introduction

Temperature is a physical quantity prevalent in scientific experiments and industrial production, and temperature monitoring is required in many areas. However, in environments where the environment is extremely poor, such as in the aerospace industry, the temperature of the motor rotor and the aircraft turbine is extremely high and the conventional temperature sensing device can not detect it. Therefore, the design of a new type of high temperature temperature sensor detection system for many harsh environments temperature detection is of great significance.With the development of materials science, a temperature sensor based on SiBCN (silicon boron carbonitride) ceramic material was developed. The sensor is a new type of sensor under the development trend of radio frequency microwave technology, which has good high temperature thermal stability and anti-oxidation [1]. Figure 1 shows a top view and a side cross-sectional view of a SiBCN ceramic sensor.

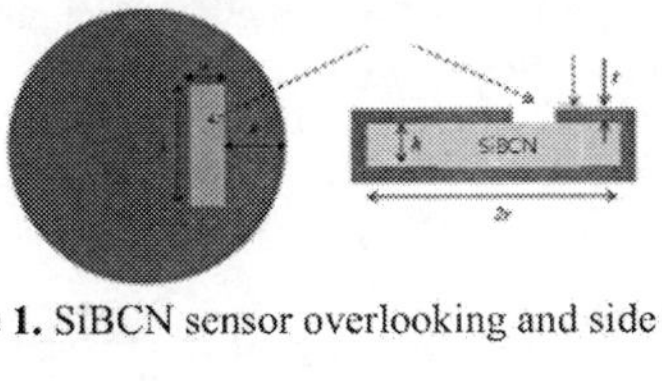

Figure 1. SiBCN sensor overlooking and side view[1].

SiBCN temperature sensor resonant frequency will change according to the temperature shift, so the sensor works can be described as:The sensor in the full range of constant amplitude microwave scanning signal under the continuous excitation conditions, when the sensor contact temperature changes, the sensor dielectric constant will follow the change, causing the cavity resonant frequency point offset[2].Figure 2 shows the SiBCN sensor temperature principle demonstration.

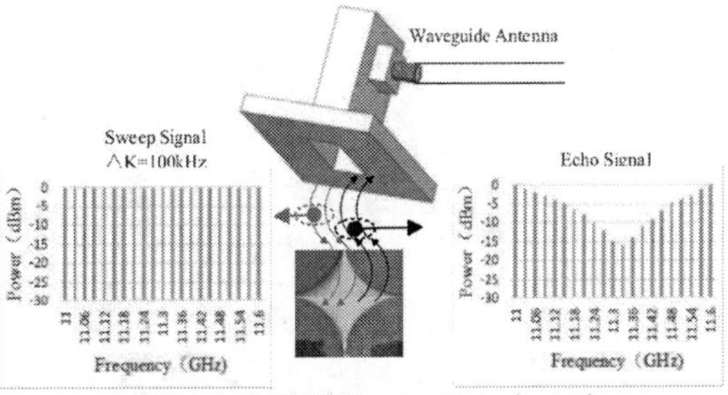

Figure 2. SiBCN sensor test schematic.

2 Introduction to system software

The software design scheme uses the programmable logic device FPGA as the main control chip of the system. All peripherals of the control system, as well as the realization of digital signal filtering processing, all external device pins are connected to the FPGA and the FPGA unified allocation settings. FPGA software development using modular design, as shown in Figure 3 for the overall framework of the system software design. The software design mainly includes the following modules: HMC833 signal source module to control the transmission of the sweep signal; A/D module to complete the acquisition and processing of echo signals; SD card module to achieve data storage; host computer

[a] Corresponding author: ltl988@gmail.com

communication module, touch screen interactive module for the final system data waveform display.

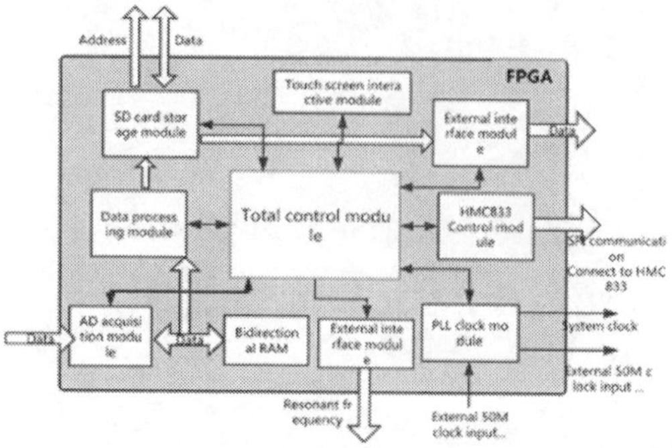

Figure 3. Software module block diagram.

Figure4 shows the system software design process. After the system is started, the modules are initialized first. Then the control signal source generates the RF signal to sweep the sensor. The data of the sensor feedback is collected by the AD acquisition card and the median value filtering is carried out. When all the sweep ends After the series of mean values obtained by filtering, drawing the S11 curve, find the lowest point of the curve that is the minimum value of the feedback power to determine the corresponding resonant frequency point; and then the resonant frequency point into the corresponding temperature value, and through the touch screen to display.

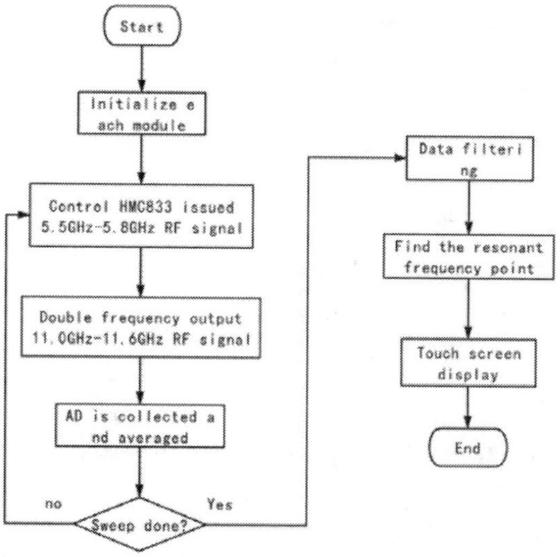

Figure 4. System software design process

3 FPGA software design

According to the performance index and demand analysis of the sensor, the system software is mainly divided into two aspects: the sweep signal generating module and the echo signal acquisition and processing module.

3.1 Software Design of Sweep Signal Generation Module

The design of the signal source chip used by the Hittite company to produce a low phase noise, wide bandwidth fractional frequency-locked loop VCO chip HMC833. FPGA and HMC833 through the SPI interface protocol to communicate, to achieve the HMC833 internal register read and write control, control the signal source frequency of the launch, and by setting the relevant registers to achieve frequency automatic calibration function to ensure the accuracy of the transmission frequency [3].The output of the chip is:

$$f_{out} = \frac{f_{VCO}}{k} \quad (1)$$

$$f_{vco} = \frac{f_{xtal}}{R}(N_{int} + N_{frac}) = f_{int} + f_{frac} \quad (2)$$

Type R: the reference branch frequency coefficient is set to 1 of the system; fxtal:the system reference frequency is set to 52MHz for phase;Nint:for integer frequency coefficient, Nfrac: fractional coefficient, software programming is achieved by changing the sweep frequency of integer frequency and fractional coefficient.

The software design of SPI communication is the prerequisite for controlling the signal source. Figure 5 shows the SPI bus write HMC833 internal register timing diagram. First, the master pulls high enable pin SEN while clearing SDI to enable SPI communication; then pull the SDI selection write operation when the first clock SCK comes; then send the next 30 clock falling edge 6-bit address bits and 24-bit data bits; finally pulled down. SEN to indicate that the write operation is complete.

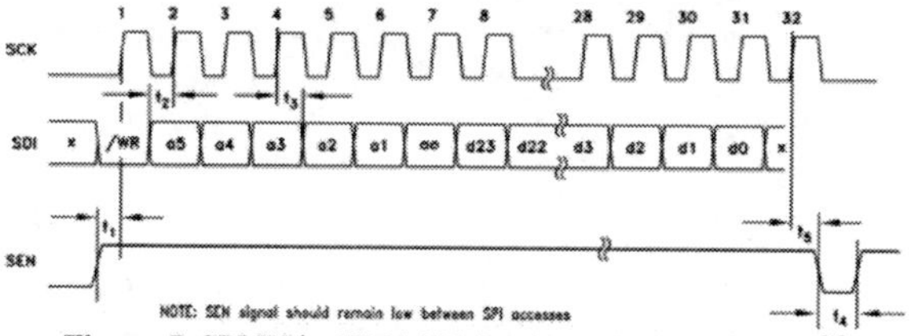

Figure 5. SPI Write HMC833 Register Timing Diagram[3]

After the completion of the SPI read and write communication function, the successful completion of the HMC833 chip internal VCO and PLL two sets of registers configuration, you can achieve the output of the RF signal. The REG 05H controls all the VCO register, for the output frequency setting signal source chip ratio and output power; while the PLL register is mainly used to control the signal source chip mode, which includes mode setting, fractional ratio coefficient setting[4]. As shown in Table 1, when the 5GHz signal is emitted by the signal source, the reference table of the register parameter value of the HMC833 in fractional frequency mode is given.

Table 1. HMC833 control register method table

Register number	Register value	Register number	Register value
REG 00h	0x0a7975	REG 0Bh	0x07c021
REG 01h	0x000002	REG 0Fh	0x000001
REG 02h	0x000001	REG 05h	0x000188
REG 03h	0x000060	REG 05h	0x00a090

REG 06h	0x200b4a	REG 05h	0x002898
REG 07h	0x00014d	REG 05h	0x0060a0
REG 08h	0xc1beff	REG 05h	0x001628
REG 09h	0x547fff	REG 05h	0x000000
REG 0Ah	0x002046	REG 04h	0x276276

As shown in Figure 6, the RTL view of the main program of the HMC33 signal source module. The float for the floating point processing module mainly realizes the register REG 03h and REG 04H (integer divider) (fractional) calculation, the hmc833_tx value of the hmc_833 internal register control module is used to configure the HMC833 chip register value,Spi_module is the communication module of SPI. It mainly realizes the function module of communication between FPGA and hmc833, and completes the writing of each register value.

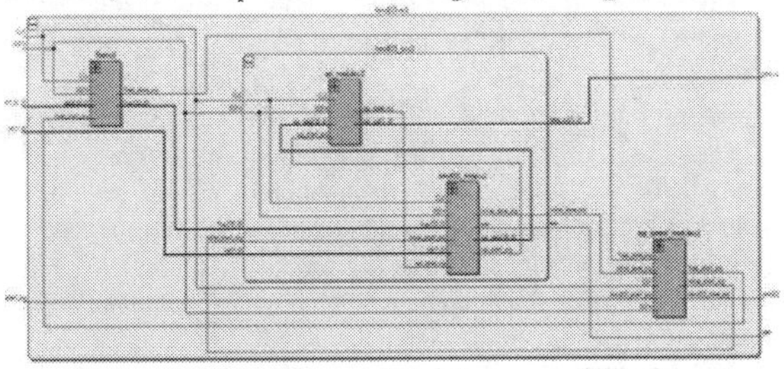

Figure 6. HMC833 module total program RTL view

3.2 Software Design of Echo Signal Acquisition and Data Processing Module

The chip used for collecting echo signals is a precision AD9226 with 12 bits. The echo signal returned by the sensor is collected at the 1MHz sampling frequency, and the median filtering method is used to filter the collected data to obtain the valid mean value for each frequency. The final resonant frequency is determined by the three-stage sweep-frequency design.

Figure 7 for the AD9226 data acquisition timing diagram. The AD9226 uses a single clock signal to control the internal data conversion of the chip. It can be seen from the timing diagram that a sample value is acquired at the rising edge of each clock, and the sampling result is output after seven clock cycles. Programming control only need to provide the AD chip clock signal, no need for data communication to control it,and easy to use, the hardware only need to the 12-bit data pin and the clock foot and the FPGA corresponding to the pin connected, can achieve data acquisition [5].

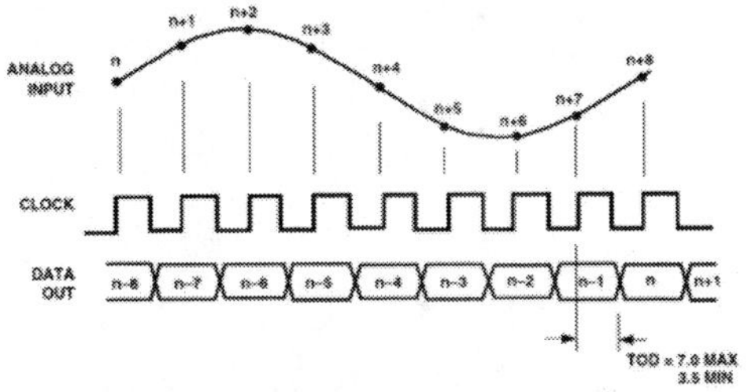

Figure 7. AD9226 timing diagram [5]

In order to improve the validity of data acquisition, this design selects the median average filtering algorithm for the digital filtering of ad data based on the actual situation of the system. The implementation process is first to sort the sampling sequencesto generate sequences, and according to the actual data acquisition of the sequence of intermediate segmentlocation value as the valid data region mean. The sorting algorithm is the key to achieve median mean filtering algorithm [6].In view of the FPGA chip in the system has a sufficient amount of logic resources, the design uses a fully parallel sorting algorithm, using a large number of logic resources in exchange for the rate of sorting algorithm. Parallel four main steps are as follows: first of all the data synchronization algorithm are compared between each other, and according to the comparison result output 0 (small) or 1 (high); and then compare the results of steps to accumulate data on all data calculated for each sort of value; then the ranking values assigned to the corresponding sorting space; the final output results. In the 4 clock cycle, it can be completed all the data sorting process. As shown in Figure 8, the debugging results of the median value filtering algorithm based on full parallel sorting.

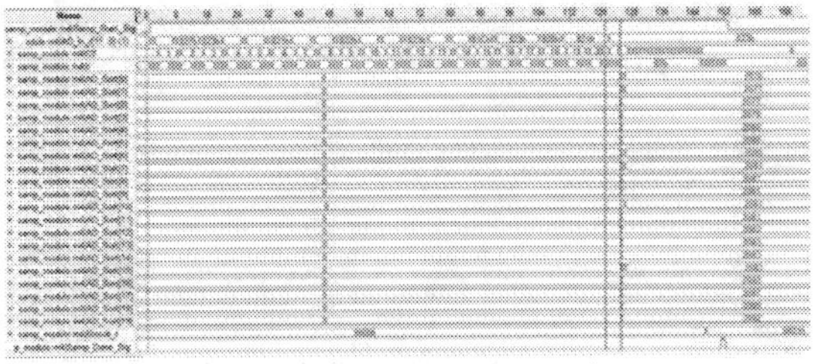

Figure 8. Data processing results

Three-stage sweep program specific process is to first sweep a large interval (3MHz), the number of 200 full-range sweep excitation. The starting frequency is 11.0GHz and the termination frequency is 11.6GHz. After the sweep, the data returned by the sensor is obtained by detecting the detector, and the corresponding frequency of the lowest point of the S11 curve is obtained by data processing, and the frequency is about 15MHz A small interval (300KHz), the number of points of 100 for the second sweep, reducing the resonant frequency point of the search range; with the first paragraph of the sweep is similar to the detector by detecting the sensor to return the signal, and then determine a frequency, and here The frequency is about 5MHz for 3 times the small interval (100KHz), the number of points of the third paragraph of the sweep of the third paragraph of the three sweep is completed, the three sweep calculated by the S11 curve of the lowest point corresponding to the frequency value .The frequency value obtained by the mean value is the resonant frequency at the current temperature determined by the final temperature, and then the current temperature value is obtained by the correspondence between the sensor temperature and the frequency. Fig. 9shows a graph of the three-step sweep S11, where (a) shows the first segment sweep S11, Fig. 2 (b) shows the second segment, and Fig. 3 (c) shows the third segment.

DOI: 10.1051/matecconf/201712801001

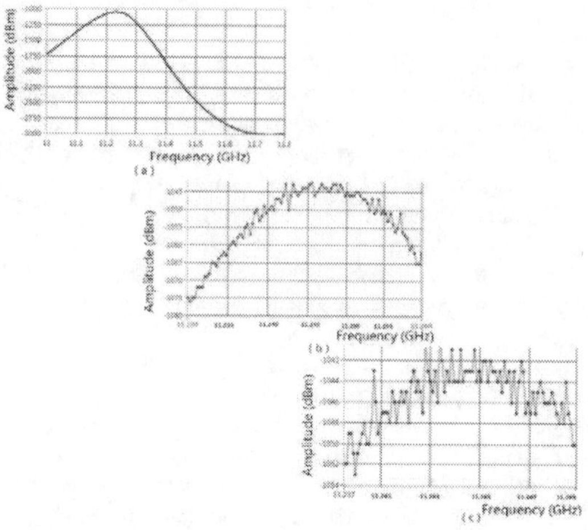

Figure 9. Three-stage sweep-frequency S11 graph

4 Analysis of system software performance and measured results

The performance of the system software is analyzed from the perspective of resource usage. As shown in Figure 10, an analysis of the use of resources after the system is compiled. A detailed description of the system using FPGA chip model and internal logic resources, pins, memory cells, embedded multiplier and clock management PLL consumption.

Flow Summary	
Flow Status	Successful - Tue Feb 28 15:07:41 2017
Quartus II 64-Bit Version	13.1.0 Build 162 10/23/2013 SJ Full Version
Revision Name	freq
Top-level Entity Name	freq
Family	Cyclone IV E
Device	EP4CE15F17C8
Timing Models	Final
Total logic elements	12,063 / 15,408 (78 %)
Total combinational functions	11,339 / 15,408 (74 %)
Dedicated logic registers	3,723 / 15,408 (24 %)
Total registers	3723
Total pins	33 / 166 (20 %)
Total virtual pins	0
Total memory bits	181,632 / 516,096 (35 %)
Embedded Multiplier 9-bit elements	4 / 112 (4 %)
Total PLLs	1 / 4 (25 %)

Figure 10. Analysis of the use of system resources

The temperature of the sensor is continuously changed from 25°Cto a temperature of 350°C, and a temperature mark is selected at intervals of 25°C. Figure 11 shows the relationship between the resonant frequency and temperature. The results show that when the temperature increases, the resonance frequency decreases, and vice versa, the measurement curve is consistent with the characteristic curve of the sensor itself, which verifies the feasibility of the design.

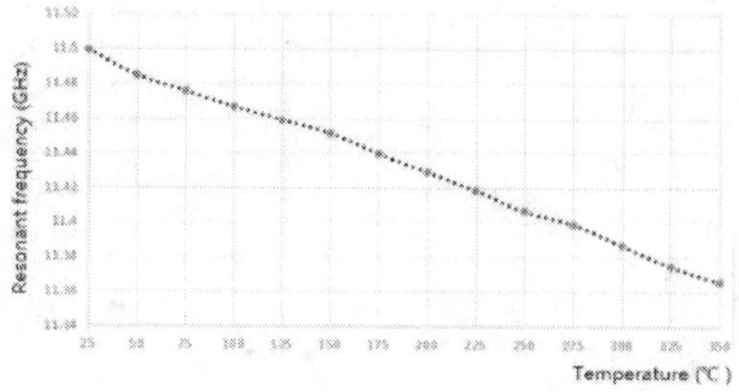

Figure 11. The relationship between temperature and frequency

Conclusion

Based on the above software design, this paper designs a temperature detection system to achieve the temperature detection. Through the measurement, the system is in the temperature of 30~350°C, the frequency temperature change rate is about 421.2KHz/°C, the temperature update period 0.35s, in line with the expected requirements. But it still needs to be improved in accuracy. The system has good practical value and wide application prospect in the field of high temperature detection.

References

1. J. Lee, D.P. Butt, R.H. Baney, et al. Synthesis and pyrolysis of novel polysilazane to SiBCN ceramic, J. Non-Cryst. Solids, 351.37–39(2005).
2. A. Müller, J. Peng, H.J. Seifert, et al. Si−B−C−N Ceramic Precursors Derived from Dichlorodivinylsilane and Chlorotrivinylsilane. 2. Ceramization of Polymers and High Temperature Behavior of Ceramic Materials, Chem. Mat, 2002, 14(2002): 3406-3412.
3. J.K. Tian, J.K. Yan, T. Chu, H.Z. Chen. Programming and analysis of wideband frequency synthesizer, Electronic Measurement Technology (2014).
4. T. Li, Y. Chen, G. Xu, et al. Design of low phase noise and low stray frequency source based on FPGA+HMC833, International Conference on Electrical, Mechanical and Industrial Engineering, 2016:1301-1305.
5. P. Chen, L.U. Zhenyang, J. Liu, et al. FPGA-based synchronous acquisition system of image and analog signal, Modern Electronics Technique (2015).
6. D. Goldberg. Using collaborative filtering to weave an information tapestry, Commun. ACM, 1992, 35(12):61-70.

MATEC Web of Conferences **128**, 01002 (2017)
EITCE 2017
DOI: 10.1051/matecconf/201712801002

Design of Wireless Sweep Signal Receiving and Dispatching Hardware System Based on SiBCN Temperature Sensor

Huayu Wei, Tianli Li[a], Li Yan, Jiyue Zhang and Xiaojie Zhang

Shenzhen Key Laboratory of Electromagnetic Control,Shenzhen University,Shenzhen 518060,China

Abstract. Based on the working principle of SiBCN temperature sensor and the principle of perturbation method, a wireless sweep signal transceiver system based on SiBCN temperature sensor covering 10 ~ 12GHz is designed to measure the temperature in harsh environmental such as high temperature, high oxidation and strong corrosion. Through the joint test of the system, the experimental results show that the resonant frequency and temperature of the sensor are negatively correlated at 25 ~ 350 °C, that is, the temperature is increased and the frequency decreases, which is consistent with the formula.The temperature and frequency change rate is about 421.2kHz / °C,which achieve the performance indicators of the SiBCN temperature sensor on the hardware system.

1 Introduction

In industrial production, for measurements of temperature under harsh environmental conditions such as high temperature,oxidation and corrosion,ordinary temperature sensors has been unable to meet the requirements. Therefore,this paper uses a temperature-sensitive SiBCN ceramic materials based on microwave resonant wireless passive Temperature sensor [1],to measure the temperature of the harsh environment.SiBCN temperature sensor is a wireless passive microwave resonant cavity temperature sensor, belonging to Transverse Magnetic mode (TM010) resonator[2]. Based on the working principle of SiBCN temperature sensor and the principle of perturbation measurement, this paper designs a hardware system based on SiBCN temperature sensor wireless sweep signal transmission and reception.

2 Sensor working principle

The SiBCN temperature sensor is wrapped with a layer of metal platinum, which is made of SiBCN ceramic material.The cavity wall is filled with dielectric and connected with the slot antenna.The slot antenna is used to receive the sweep frequency signal and transmit the echo signal ,shown in Figure 1.

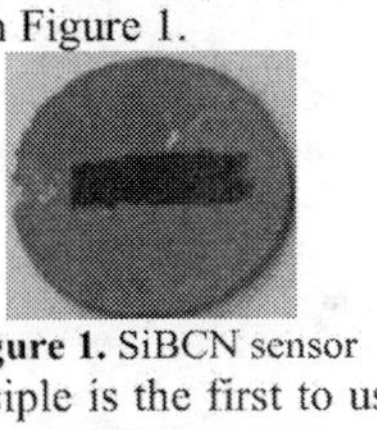

Figure 1. SiBCN sensor

Its working principle is the first to use the waveguide antenna transmit constant power sweep signal excitation sensor.Then, the sensor slot antenna receives the sweep signal and a certain frequency point of the sweep signal resonates with the resonant cavity.After a response period, the slot antenna sends different power amplitude echo signal received by the waveguide antenna, and the lowest amplitude point appears. When the ambient temperature of the sensor rises, the dielectric constant increases,which eventually leads to the sensor resonant frequency reduced.Finally, the lowest amplitude of the echo signal is shifted to the left.As shown in Figure 2:

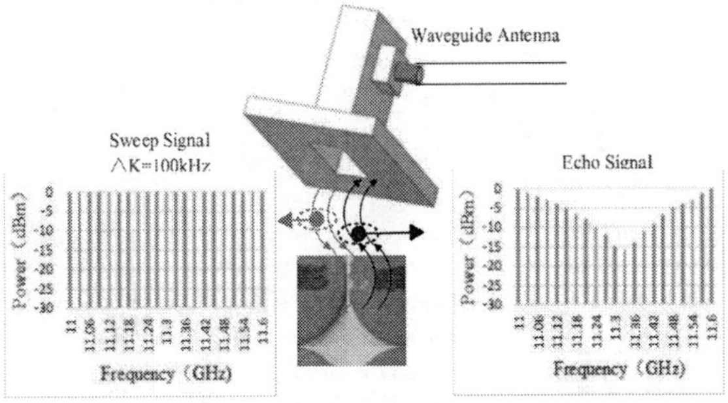

Figure 2. SiBCN sensor test schematic

The relation between the resonant frequency and the dielectric constant of a sensor is represented by a formula (1)as follows:

$$f_r = \frac{P_{01}}{\pi a \sqrt{u_0 \varepsilon_0 \varepsilon_r}} \qquad (1)$$

The fr is the resonant frequency of the resonant cavity

[a] Corresponding author: LTL988@gmail.com

DOI: 10.1051/matecconf/201712801002

of the SiBCN temperature sensor,and the u_0 is the vacuum permeability which is a constant.The ε_0 is the vacuum permittivity, which also known as the vacuum dielectric constant is a constant.The a is the sensor radius which is a fixed value. P_{01} is the first the Bessel function of the firstkind which the first solution is a constant. And the εr is the dielectric constant of the SiBCN temperature sensor which is a variable.

With the temperature change The dielectric constant will change.The following formula shown in equation (2)

$$\alpha_\varepsilon = \frac{1}{\varepsilon}\cdot\frac{d\varepsilon}{dt} \tag{2}$$

The αε is the temperature coefficient of the ε at the t temperature. The ε is the dielectric constant at the t temperature, among them:

$$d\varepsilon = \varepsilon_r - \varepsilon_1$$
$$dt = t_r - t_1 \tag{3}$$

formule(1), (2) and (3) are simplified as follows:

$$f_r = \frac{P_{01}}{\pi a\sqrt{u_0\varepsilon_0\cdot(\alpha_\varepsilon\varepsilon_1\cdot(t_r - t_1) + \varepsilon_1)}} \tag{4}$$

Among (4),in addition to the tr which is variable,other parameters are known for the fixed value. It can be seen that the temperature tr and the frequency fr are inversely proportional to the relationship, that is, with the temperature increasing, the frequency decreases, the temperature decreases, the frequency increases. The different temperature values correspond to different frequencies.Using this principle,a measuring system for measuring the resonant frequency of a sensor can be designed to measure the environmental temperature.

3 Perturbation method of measurement

The measuring method of SiBCN temperature sensor is perturbation measurement method [4]in this paper. The principle of the perturbation method is related to the dielectric constant of the medium in the resonator of the SiBCN temperature sensor. The dielectric constant of the dielectric in the above equation (1) corresponds to the resonant frequency.

When the resonant cavity is externally excited, the excitation signal input the inner cavity of the metal SiBCN temperature sensor , reflected and superimposed. At this point, if the external excitation signal and the resonant cavity resonance occurs, it will form a standing wave in the cavity and the excitation signal energy is absorbed in the sensor.The energy reflected back at the resonant frequency point is minimum. Therefore, as long as the energy value of the echo signal is detected,the resonance of the sensor will be judged.According to this characteristic, the reflection coefficient (S11 parameter) which stand for the output signal and input signal ratio of the sensor slot antenna can be used to evaluate:

$$S = \frac{\text{Output signal}}{\text{Input signal}} \tag{5}$$

The SiBCN temperature sensor is excited by the swept signal sent by the excitation source.The slot antenna receives the swept signal and sends the echo signal.The signal frequency will not change, instead of the energy value of the signal is changed before and after stimulation. In this paper, the corresponding S11 curve is obtained by collecting the data, the ordinate of the curve represents the gain (dB), and the abscissa represents the frequency (GHz).

4 System design

Design system hardware program shown in Figure 3. The program is divided into five modules which are the controller module, the sweep signal generation module, the transmission channel conversion module, the signal conversion acquisition module and the external interface module respectively.

The controller module uses a field programmable gate array (FPGA) as a control chip. It control the HMC833 signal source to adjust the frequency range of the sweep signal, step and sweep points.It outputs the system required base frequency signal and control AD analog converter to collect analog signals, and converted into digital signals, data processing, drawing S11 curve and displaying. The sweep signal generating module obtains the frequency signal required for the system by double-frequency the fundamental frequency signal outputted from the signal source. The function of the transmission channel conversion module is to isolate the transceiver channel and send the sweep signal to receive the echo signal. The signal conversion acquisition module converts the power value to the voltage and collects it. The external interface module outputs data to the upper computer or the display screen.

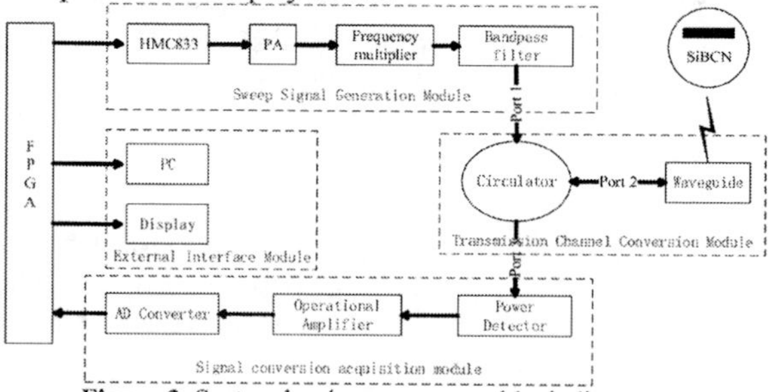

Figure 3. System hardware program block diagram

5 Design of HMC833 Signal Source

The signal source chip used in this system is a low phase noise (<-170dBc / Hz) produced by Analog Devices, broadband, integrated fractional frequency divider PLL HMC833 chip [5], as shown in Figure 4.The chip is internally integrated with voltage controlled oscillator (VCO), charge pump (CP), integrated phase detector (PFD), Σ-Δ modulator, and N or R frequency division doubler (DIV). The VCO has a base frequency range of 0.015 to 3GHz. The PFD and modulator give the external loop filter (LF) a wider bandwidth while suppressing external noise to improve the output signal immunity and stability. By frequency division or frequency doubling of the reference signal, HMC833 output frequency range reaches 0.025 ~ 6GHz. FPGA controls HMC833 chip registers of fractional-N frequency,which can achieve 5.5 ~ 5.8GHz frequency output.Then, after multiplying the frequency doubler ,the frequency output of the 11.0~11.6GHz can be theoretically obtained to meet the system requirements.

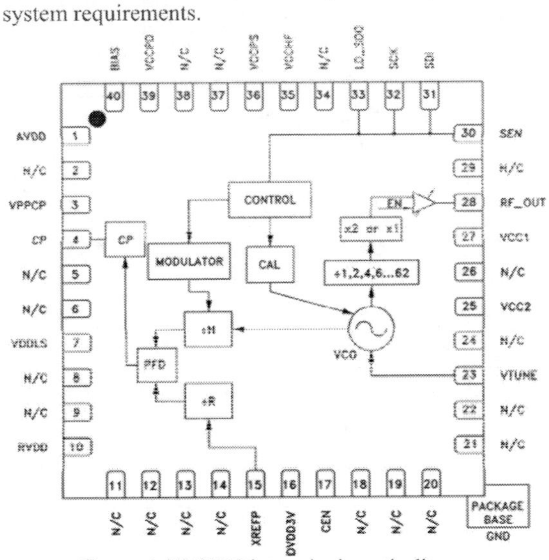

Figure 4. HMC833 internal schematic diagram

Program of frequency synthesis of HMC833 signal source is designed by PLL principle, which is called charge pump phase locked frequency synthesis. As shown in Figure 5:

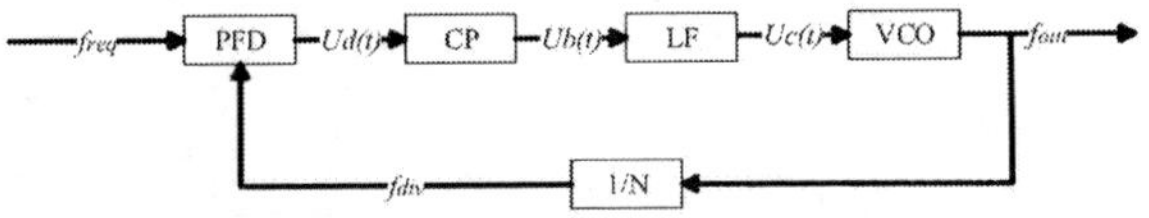

Figure 5. HMC833 signal source block diagram

The HMC833 chip integrates VCO, CP and PFD.A loop filter (LF) is designed on the periphery of the chip to form a complete PLL. Phase-locked loop operating principle[6]: firstly suppose the VCO output frequency fout = 0GHz. Phase difference of reference frequency f_{req} and divider output frequency f_{div} is large, which makes $U_d(t)$ maximum. Through CP and LF, signal of controling VCO that has been output to make the VCO oscillate with a large frequency. The frequency of the VCO output is passed through the N frequency division, and the frequency is compared with the reference signal frep. When there is a steady phase difference between the fdiv and the freq, the output signal that is $U_d(t)$ stabilize. PLL implements the VCO output to follow the reference signal.

6 System results test

The hardware of the system is in the right of Figure 6, and the heating platform is on the left. The temperature range is at 30~350 C. The waveguide is placed the heating platform above, and the sensor is placed at the bottom of the waveguide, as shown in Figure 6:

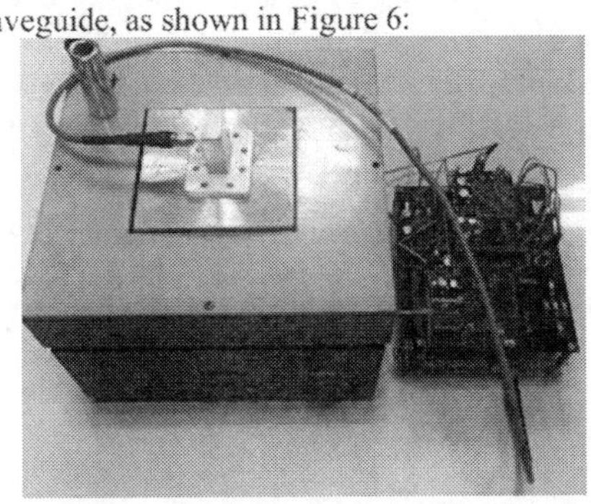
Figure 6. System hardware physical and heating platform

Figure 7 is a sensor S11 curve at 50℃, 100℃, 150℃, 200℃, 250℃, 300℃ and 350℃, and each S11 curve has the lowest point. Its abscissa corresponds to the resonant frequency of sensor at the temperature and its ordinate corresponds to the S11 value of the sensor. On the whole, in the several S11 curves at 50~350℃,the minimum value of the corresponding S11 is -27.53dB, and the maximum value is -20.8dB. Within the resolution range of S11 curve resonance frequency, the hardware requirements are met.

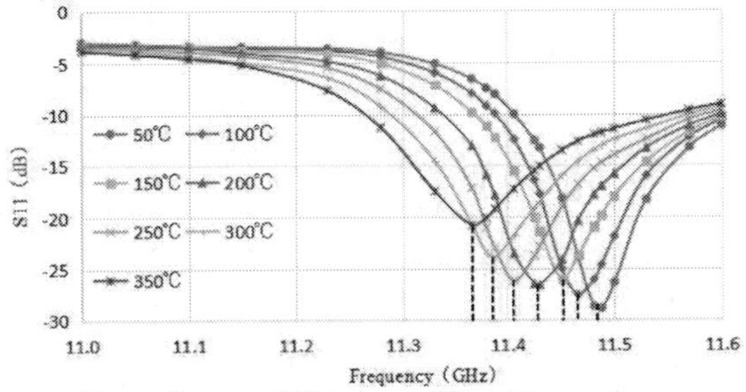

Figure 7. sensor S11 curve at different temperatures

According to the experiment, the temperature of the sensor is increased from 50 to 350 degrees by the heating platform, and the average value of the 14 data is taken every 25 degrees, as shown in figure 8. The resonant frequencies of the sensors at 50 and 350 degrees are 11.488 GHz and 11.360 GHz, respectively.The experimental results show that the resonant frequency decreases with the increase of the temperature of the sensor in the 50~350 degrees range ,and vice versa.The experimental results accord with the theoretical deduction which is negative correlation.The temperature-frequency change rate is about 421.2kHz/℃.

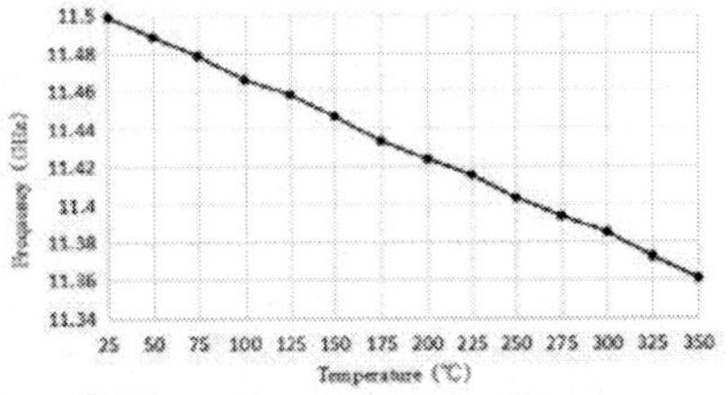

Figure 8. Temperature and resonant frequency curve

DOI: 10.1051/matecconf/201712801002

7 Conclusion

Based on the principle of SiBCN temperature sensor and the principle of perturbation measurement, a hardware system of wireless frequency sweep signal receiving and transmitting based on SiBCN temperature sensor is designed. The system has good stability and high integration. When the temperature is 30~350℃,the resonant frequency of the sensor is negatively correlated with the temperature, and the temperature and frequency change rate is about 421.2kHz/℃.

References

1. H. Cheng, X. Ren, S. Ebadi, et al. Wireless Passive Temperature Sensors Using Integrated Cylindrical Resonator/Antenna for Harsh-Environment Applications, IEEE Sens. J, 2015, 15(3):1453-1462.
2. Z.X. Xia, Y.J. Cheng, Y. Fan. Frequencyreconfigurable TM010-mode reentrant cylindrical cavity for microwave material processing, J. Electromagn. Waves Appl, 2013, 27(5):605-614.
3. C.P. Wang, Y.E. Liu, L.I. Ai-Xia, et al. Measurement of complex permittivity of NiZn-ferrite by resonant cavity perturbation method, Journal of Anhui University, 2012.
4. G.J. Wang. Application of the micro-disturbance method in microwave resonant-cavity analysis, Journal of Ningxia University, 2002, 23(1):50-52.
5. T. Li, Y. Chen, G. Xu, et al. Design of Low Phase Noise and Low Stray Frequency Source Based on FPGA+HMC833, International Conference on Electrical, Mechanical and Industrial Engineering. 2016.
6. W. Zhao, F. Guan, Q.I. Youguang. Implementation and Application of S-Band Frequency Synthesizer Based on Fractional N Phase-Locked Loop, Journal of Spacecraft Tt & C Technology, 2011.

MATEC Web of Conferences **128**, 01003 (2017) DOI: 10.1051/matecconf/201712801003
EITCE 2017

Speech Denoising in White Noise Based on Signal Subspace Low-rank Plus Sparse Decomposition

Shuai yuan[1], Cheng-li Sun[2,a]

[1]*Science and Technology on Avionics Integration Laboratory, Shanghai, China*
[2]*Nanchang Hangkong University, Nanchang, 330063 China*

Abstract—In this paper, a new subspace speech enhancement method using low-rank and sparse decomposition is presented. In the proposed method, we firstly structure the corrupted data as a Toeplitz matrix and estimate its effective rank for the underlying human speech signal. Then the low-rank and sparse decomposition is performed with the guidance of speech rank value to remove the noise. Extensive experiments have been carried out in white Gaussian noise condition, and experimental results show the proposed method performs better than conventional speech enhancement methods, in terms of yielding less residual noise and lower speech distortion.
Keywords- speech enhancement; subspace method; low-rank plus sparse decomposition.

1. Introduction

Speech enhancement refers to the improvement in quality and intelligibility of noise corrupted speech signals by using supervised or unsupervised speech enhancement methods. It is widely used as a pre-processing block in a lot of applications like automatic speech recognizer and other communication systems.

Over the last fifty decades, many algorithms have been proposed about for speech enhancement. The typical algorithms including spectral subtraction[1], minimum mean square error (MMSE) estimation [2-4], Wiener filtering [5-8], and subspace methods [9-13]. Spectral Subtraction and Wiener filtering have been widely used for enhancing speech because of their simplicity and ease of implementation in single channel systems but they suffer from the production of musical noise after enhancement and is one of their major drawbacks. Signal subspace approach [9-13], have shown to give a better compromise between less residual noise and signal distortion of the output signal, compared to the other existing techniques.

Signal subspace approach was firstly proposed by Ephraim Y, et al. The principle of this method is to separate the noisy speech observation space into a signal subspace and a noise subspace, and the enhanced speech was constructed using only the components of the signal within the signal subspace. In the subspace-based algorithms, subspace decomposition is a critical step for subspace separation, which is often performed via Karhunen-Loeve transform (KLT)[10] or singular value decomposition (SVD) [9]. The main issue in developing a subspace-based model is the way of splitting and refining the signal and noise subspace in an optimal way. In [14], variance of the reconstruction error criterion was introduced to optimize the subspace selection for speech enhancement. In [15], to optimize the subspace decomposition model, human auditory psychoacoustic properties are incorporated into the subspace filter to reconstruct the enhanced signal. Although many efforts were conducts to improve the subspace methods, the existing subspace-based speech enhancement methods still suffer from the problem of low decomposition accuracy in the presence of large noise, resulting in a high remainder noise within enhanced speech in strong noise cases.

In this paper, we propose a new subspace-based method for speech enhancement based on the principle of low-rank and sparse decomposition (LSD). The main idea behind our method is motivated by the recent development of low-rank and sparse theory [16]. According to this theory, if a given corrupted data matrix Y has an underlying low-rank structure, yet corrupted by sparse additive noises. The underlying low-rank component L can be effectively recovered by solving a convex optimization problem, even if the noise is arbitrary in magnitude. In the time domain, owing to the short-time stability of human speech, speech signals can be assumed to have a low-rank structure. On the other hand, due to the randomness of noise, background noise is more variable and thus can be viewed as sparse and high-rank. Thus LSD theory can be exploited to recover the underlying speech from corrupted speech signals.

The rest of the paper is organized as follows. We first briefly review the previous works in Section 2. In Section 3, we describe the LSD based signal subspace speech enhancement method. Section 4 presents the experiments and results. Finally, we give the concludes and future work in section 5.

2. Related work

The goal of principal component analysis (PCA) technique is to determine the most significant basis to re-express a

[a] Corresponding author: sun_chengli@163.com

DOI: 10.1051/matecconf/201712801003

noisy speech set [17]. This new basis will filter out the noise and reduce a multidimensional speech to lower dimensions by avoiding redundant data.

Let us consider the problem of the enhancement of a speech signal contaminated by an independent additive noise. Let $x(t)$ and $d(t)$ denote the sampled clean speech and noise signal, respectively. The observed noisy speech signal $y(t)$ is

$$y(t) = x(t) + d(t). \quad (1)$$

Suppose $y(t)$ was framed with the length N. Arranging the N-dimensional vectors into a $(M\text{-}l\text{+}l)\times l$ Toeplitz structure matrix, we can get

$$Y = X + D. \quad (2)$$

Assuming that the rank of matrix Y is r, the optimal enhanced speech matrix $\hat{X}$ can be estimated according to the following least-square criterion

$$\min_{\hat{X}} \left\| Y - \hat{X} \right\|_F^2, \ \operatorname{rank}(\hat{X}) \le r \ , \quad (3)$$

where symbol $\|\cdot\|_F$ denotes the Frobenius norm of a matrix and $\|X\|_F = \sqrt{X_{ij}^2}$.

If $d(t)$ is a white Gaussian noise, it satisfies the conditions $D^T D = \sigma_d^2 I$ and $X^T D = 0$. Where σ_d^2 is the variance of noise. The optimal solution of (4) can be obtained by applying singular value decomposition (SVD) of Y.

$$Y = U \Sigma V^T$$

$$\hat{X} = \sum_{i=1}^{r} \lambda_i U_i V_i^T . \quad (4)$$

Here, U and V are two orthogonal matrices holding the left and right (approximate) singular vectors of given matrix, and Λ is a diagonal matrix holding the singular values: $\lambda_1 \ge \lambda_2 \ge \cdots \lambda_{r-1} \ge \lambda_r$.

The above low-rank matrix $\hat{X}$ represents the original speech matrix X in the sense of least-square minimization. This may get the optimal estimate when the noise is small, independent, and identically distributed Gaussian.

However, PCA is highly sensitive to the presence of large corruptions. Even a single outlier in the data matrix can render the estimation of the low-rank component arbitrarily far from the true model. In [16], a new theory called Robust PCA was developed for this shortcoming. The basic idea of Robust PCA is to decompose the data matrix M as M=L+S, where S Î ¡ $^{N' K}$ is a sparse matrix with a sparse number of non-zero coefficients with arbitrarily large magnitude. RPCA can be solved by minimizing the following convex program

$$\min \|L\|_* + \lambda \|S\|_1 , \text{ s.t. } M = L + S, \quad (5)$$

where $\|\cdot\|_*$ denotes the matrix nuclear norm, which is defined as the sum of all singular values and is suggested as a convex surrogate to the rank function [18]. $\|\cdot\|_1$ denotes the l_1-norm of a matrix, which is defined as the sum of the absolute values of matrix elements. This problem is known to have a stable solution provided L and S are sufficiently incoherent [19], i. e., the low-rank matrix is not sparse and the sparse matrix is not low-rank. More recently, RPCA theory was introduced into the speech enhancement task in [20], where a constrained low-rank and sparse matrix decomposition (CLSMD) algorithm is designed for noise reduction.

3. LSD based speech denoising method

In this work, we propose a new subspace decomposition algorithm based on the LSD, which is less sensitive to the large noise interferences.

Firstly, we formulate the speech enhancement problem as the following optimization problem,

$$\min_{L,S} \|Y - L - S\|_F^2 , \qquad \text{s.t. } rank(L) \le r, \ |S|_0 \le h. \quad (6)$$

The above formula can be solved by alternatively solving the following two formulas until convergence

$$\begin{cases} L_i = \arg\min\limits_{\operatorname{rank}(L)\le r} \|Y - L - S_{i-1}\|_F^2 & \text{(a)} \\ S_i = \arg\min\limits_{|S|_0 \le h} \|Y - L_i - S\|_F^2 & \text{(b)} \end{cases} \quad (7)$$

Given an estimate of sparse matrix S_{i-1}, the minimization in (7-a) over L is to learn a rank-r low-rank matrix from partial observations. This is a fixed-rank approximation problem, we can solve it use bilateral random projections (BRP) based fast low-rank matrix approximation.

$$L_i = M_1 (A_2^T M_1)^{-1} M_2^T \quad (8)$$

Where $M_1 = YA_1$, $M_2 = Y^T A_2$. Both $A_1 \in R^{n\times r}$ and $A_2 \in R^{m\times r}$ are Gaussian random matrices.

The minimization in (7-b) over S is to learn a sparse matrix from partial observations. This can be computed via entry-wise hard thresholding function [21],

$$\varphi_T(x) = x \cdot 1(|x| > u), \quad (9)$$

which keeps the input if it is larger than the threshold; otherwise, it is set to zero. In summary, we have following optimization algorithm for LSD.

Algorithm 1. Optimization algorithm for LSD

Given r, T, ε, t_{maxiter};
Initialize $Y_0 = Y$, $S_t = [0]_{N\times K}$, t=0;

while not converged do
  %Update of low-rank matrix L
  $A_1 = randn(n, r)$;
  $A_2 = randn(m, r)$
  $M_1 = Y_t A_1$,
  $M_2 = Y_t^T A_2$
  $L_t = M_1 (A_2^T M_1)^{-1} M_2^T$;
  %Update of sparse matrix S
  $X_t = Y_t - L_t + S_t$;
  $S_t = X_t \otimes (X_t > T)$;
  % Stopping criteria
  If $\|Y - L_t - S_t\|_F^2 / \|Y\|_F^2 \le \varepsilon$ or $t == t_{\text{maxiter}}$
    break;
  end
  $Y_t = L_t + X_t - S_t$
  $t = t + 1$;

DOI: 10.1051/matecconf/201712801003

end while
output: $L = L_t$, $S = S_t$

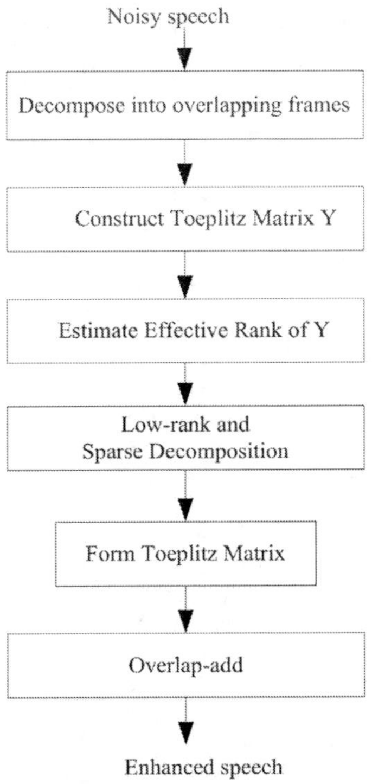

Figure 1. The scheme of LSD based speech enhancement method

Figure 1 shows the scheme of LSD based speech enhancement method. At first, the noisy speech signal is divided into frames in the time domain. Then we arrange each frame of the noisy speech into a Toeplitz matrix. After we estimated the effective rank r with the analysis-by-synthesis approach [22], the noisy speech matrix Y is decomposed into the low-rank matrix L with the rank r using the LSD algorithm. Since L is not a Toeplitz matrix, we average all the diagonal elements of L to let it became a Toeplitz matrix form. Finally, the enhanced speech is constructed by taking the inverse transform of Toeplitz matrix followed by least-squares overlap-add synthesis [23].

4. Experimental results

For evaluation of the proposed JLSMD method, we choose a total of 30 sentences (sp01~sp30) taken from NOIZEUS database. Both speech and noise were sampled at 8 kHz 16 bits. Time frame length is 264 sample points with 50% frame overlap. White Gaussian noise was added to clean speech at various levels. We use segSNR and PESQ ((Perceptual Evaluation of Speech Quality) scores for performance measure. four conventional speech enhancement methods: spectral subtraction (SSboll [1]), Subspace SVD based subspace decomposition algorithm (SSVD) [9], Wiener filter based method (Wiener [8]), minimum mean-square error algorithm (MMSE [24]), KLT [12] and CLSMD [20]).

Tables 1 and 2 show the comparison of performance in terms of PESQ and segSNR scores. The larger the PESQ-MOS and segSNR scores are, the better the performances are. We can see the proposed method LSD has got the highest PESQ-MOS and segSNR scores among all the compared methods, except at 0 dB where CLSMD has the highest segSNR score.

Table 1. PESQ scores in the white noise case at different SNRs

Methods	**0 dB**	**5 dB**	**10 dB**	**15 dB**
KLT	1.100	3.529	5.937	8.058
MMSS	-0.464	0.787	2.119	3.374
SSboll	-3.519	-2.213	-1.061	0.051
SSVD	0.4106	2.9652	5.4880	7.9579
CLSMD	2.146	3.685	4.856	5.640
LSD	1.468	3.970	6.596	9.074

Table 2. PESQ scores in the white noise case at different SNRs

Methods	**0 dB**	**5 dB**	**10 dB**	**15 dB**
KLT	1.994	2.397	2.744	3.078
MMSS	1.455	1.710	2.140	2.498
SSboll	1.651	1.943	2.179	2.462
SSVD	1.713	2.194	2.596	2.972
CLSMD	2.009	2.384	2.587	2.720
LSD	2.055	2.478	2.844	3.198

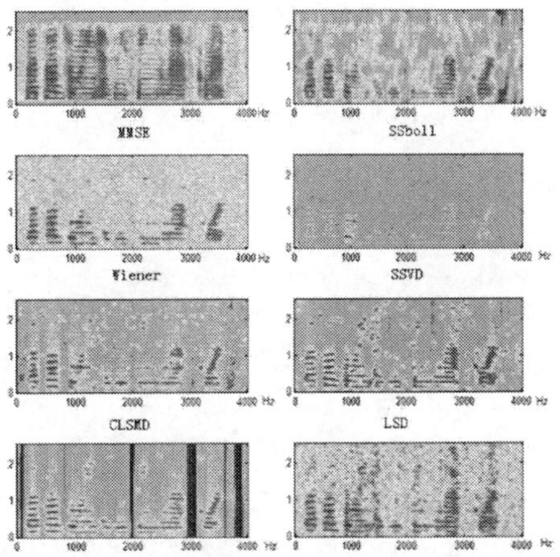

Figure 2. Comparison of the spectrograms for speech enhanced by different methods

Fig. 2 presents spectrogram comparisons for various speech enhancement methods in the 10 dB SNR. We can see from these enhanced speech spectrograms. Along with the high levels of noise reduction, the proposed LSD based method is still able to preserve most of the low-energy speech components compared with the seven speech enhancement methods.

5. Conclusions

In this paper, we presented a LSD based signal subspace speech enhancement method. The proposed method is less sensitive to the large interferences as compared with traditional algorithms, and can significantly reduce noise. Experiments demonstrate that the proposed method is good at improving the overall enhanced speech quality, especially in low SNRs. It should be pointed out that LSD method has improved the original subspace method based on SVD and can wipe out more residual noise. In the future research work we will devote more efforts to improving the noise reduction performancein the colored noise.

Acknowledgements

This work was supported by China's Aviation Science fund (No. 20145556011).

References

1. Boll, S.F., Suppression of acoustic noise in speech using spectral subtraction. IEEE Trans. Acoust. Speech Signal Process, 1979. 27(2): p. 113-120.
2. Ephraim, Y. and D. Malah, Speech enhancement using a minimum mean square error log-spectral amplitude estimator. IEEE Trans. Acoust., Speech, Signal Process, 1985. SSP-33,(2): p. 443–445.
3. Ephraim, Y. and D. Malah, Speech enhancement using a minimum mean square error short-time spectral amplitude estimator. IEEE Transactions on Acoustics, Speech, and SignalProcessing, 1984. vol. ASSP-32(6): p. 1109-1121.
4. Stark, A. and K. Paliwal, Use of speech presence uncertainty with MMSE spectral energy estimation for robust automatic speech recognition. Speech Communication, 2011(53): p. 51-61.
5. Soon, I.Y. and S.N. Koh. Low distortion speech enhancement. in Inst. Elec. Eng. 2000.
6. Wiener, N., Extrapolation, Interpolation, and Smoothing of Stationary Time Series. 1949, New York: Wiley.
7. Plapous, C., C. Marro, and P. Scalart, Improved Signal-to-Noise Ratio Estimation for Speech Enhancement IEEE Transactions on Acoustics, Speech, and SignalProcessing, 2006. 14(6): p. 2098-2108.
8. Scalart, P. and J. Vieira-Filho, Speech enhancement based on a priori signal to noise estimation, in Proc. 21st IEEE Int. Conf. Acoust. SpeechSignal Processing. 1996: Atlanta, GA. p. 629-632.
9. Moor, B.D., The singular value decomposition and long and short spaces of noisy matrices. IEEE Trans. on Signal Processing, 1993. 41(9): p. 2826-2839.
10. Ephraim, Y. and H. Van Trees, A signal subspace approach for speech enhancement. IEEE Trans. Speech Audio Process., 1995. 3(4): p. 251-266.
11. Doclo, S. and M. Moonen, GSVD-Based Optimal Filtering for Single and Multimicrophone Speech Enhancement. IEEE Transactions on signal processing, 2002. 50(9): p. 2230-2242.
12. Hu, Y. and P.C. Loizou, A Generalized Subspace Approach for Enhancing Speech Corrupted by Colored Noise. IEEE Transactions on Audio, Speech and Language Processing 2003. 11(4): p. 334-342.
13. Hermus, K., P. Wambacq, and H.V. hamme, A Review of Signal Subspace Speech Enhancement and Its Application to Noise Robust Speech Recognition. EURASIP Journal on Advances in Signal Processing, 2007: p. 1-15.
14. Saadoune, A., A. Amrouche, and S.-A. Selouani, Perceptual subspace speech enhancement using variance of the reconstruction error. Digital Signal Processing, 2014. 22: p. 187-196.
15. Surendran, S. and T.K. Kumar, Variance normalized perceptual subspace speech enhancement. International Journal of Electronics and Communications, 2017. 74: p. 44-54.
16. Wright, J., Y. Peng, and Y. Ma, Robust Principal Component Analysis: Exact Recovery of Corrupted Low-rank Matrices by Convex Optimization. In NIPS, 2009.
17. Jolliffe, I.T., Principal Component Analysis. Springer Series in Statistics. 2002, New York: Springer.
18. Candes, E.J. and T. Terence, The power of convex relaxation: near-optimal matrix completion. IEEE Transactions on Information Theory, 2010. 56(5): p. 2053-2080.
19. Candes, E.J., et al., Robust Principal Component Analysis? Journal of the ACM, 2011. 58(3): p. 1-37.
20. Sun, C., Q. Zhu, and M. Wan, A novel speech enhancement method based on constrained low-rank and sparse matrix decomposition. Speech Communication, 2013. 60(12): p. 44-55.
21. Chang, S.G., B. Yu, and M. Vetterli, Adaptive Wavelet Thresholding for Image Denoising and Compression. IEEE Transactions on Information Theory, 2000. 9(9): p. 1532-1547.
22. Loizou, P.C., Speech Enhancement: Theory and Practice. 2007, New York: Taylor & Francis.
23. Quatieri, T., Discrete-Time Speech Signal Processing: Principles and Practice. 2002, Prentice Hall, Upper Saddle River, NJ.
24. Cohen, I., Speech Enhancement Using a Noncausal A Priori SNR Estimator. IEEE Signal Processing Letters, 2004. 11(9): p. 725-728.

The Research on WLAN Technology of Chain Network Based on Monitoring Information Transmission of Catenary

Wu Chunmei[a], Li Guilin, Wang Shaowei and Lan Xueyan

College of electrical information, Dalian Jiaotong University, Dalian 116028, Liaoning Province, China

Abstract. The structure of railway catenary line is "long chain". Considering each catenary as a wireless node, it will form the chain wireless network that solves the transmission problem of monitoring data on railway catenary line. Using token method to manage the distribution of channel resources can optimize the structure of "long chain". The local system decomposes several subnet class units which consist of one or more nodes. Then the token is transmitted in denomination of subnet. The system structure is composed of multiple subnets connected in series, making the route more flexible. The network can self-repair and prevent system breakdown due to node failures. The stability of system will be enhanced. The monitoring data can be sent in parallel, and the network efficiency becomes higher. Using token as control information, nodes will not interfere with each other, thus achieving orderly utilization of the channel.

1 Introduction

The catenary line is composed of a group of poles and two ends of power supply workshops, electric power communication covers only the power supply workshops, but the whole transmission line corridor is the blank of coverage, as shown in figure 1. In order to transmit the monitoring information to the power supply workshops, it is necessary to construct the communication channel of transmission line corridor.

Because of long distance and high-voltage of the catenary line, it is very difficult to set up the monitoring communication network by laying cables, and the economy could not afford, so wireless communication is usually adopted[1]. The wireless communication technology for on-line monitoring device of transmission line includes WiFi, WiMax, wireless Mesh network technology and wireless pubic network. WiFi and ZigBee are not suitable for the long chain structure of transmission lines. At present, the public network transmission is feasible, however, due to the limited coverage of the public network and the high running cost of the system, it is difficult to meet the requirements of the power system too[2].

Chain transmission network based on the wireless Mesh has the characteristics of dynamic self-organization, self-repairing and self-balance[3]. On-line monitoring access points of catenary line require a wide coverage, and communication equipment should operate in harsh environments. However, the communication bandwidth and real-time of data transmission requirements are not high. This makes wireless Mesh technology become the mainstream technology of transmission line on-line monitoring communication. Using the advantages of wireless Mesh network technology, transmit monitoring data to power supply workshops, then transmit the data to monitoring center through the optical communication system. This method avoids the complexity of communication line wiring, and could also be installed in harsh environments[4].Wireless chain network is suitable for transmission line communication system, the network mode and points access are flexible. This provides a data transmission channel for power network monitoring. The transmission efficiency is improved, the network security is strengthened, and the reliability of the power communication network is ensured. It is a great significance to the safe operation of railway power supply[5-6].

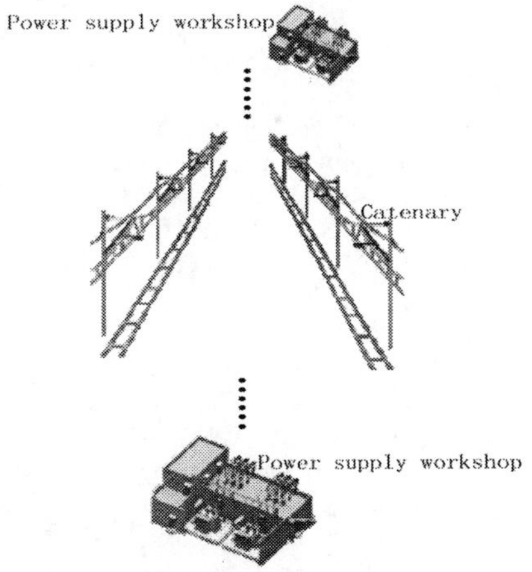

Figure 1. Catenary line's diagram of distribution

[a]Corresponding author: m18524406315@163.com

 DOI: 10.1051/matecconf/201712801004

2 Physical structure of chain wireless network

The distance between the poles of the catenary line is about 50 meters, and it is linear distribution, which provide a natural condition for short distance wireless multi hop transmission. This paper uses the scheme of catenary line monitoring communication based on wireless Mesh: The monitoring devices collect the relevant state information of catenary line and transfer to the wireless Mesh routing node, then the Mesh nodes transmit the information to the sink (power supply workshop) through wireless multi hop. Finally, upload the information to the monitoring center.

The backbone line data transmission module uses 802.11a standard of 5.8GHz, which has 12 non overlapping channels to facilitate the deployment of large-scale networks. Monitoring device information access module is configured as 802.11b/g standard of 2.4GHz[7]. Physical structure of the chain wireless network is shown in figure 2.

In practice, we can adjust the transmitting power of wireless module to control the coverage of nodes and reduce the interference of the neighbor nodes. In chain wireless network, we control the transmitting power of nodes and make the coverage is two hop nodes, which means that the nodes can only listen to the idle condition of the channel within two hops and the nodes outside the two hop range can transmit information without producing interference simultaneously.

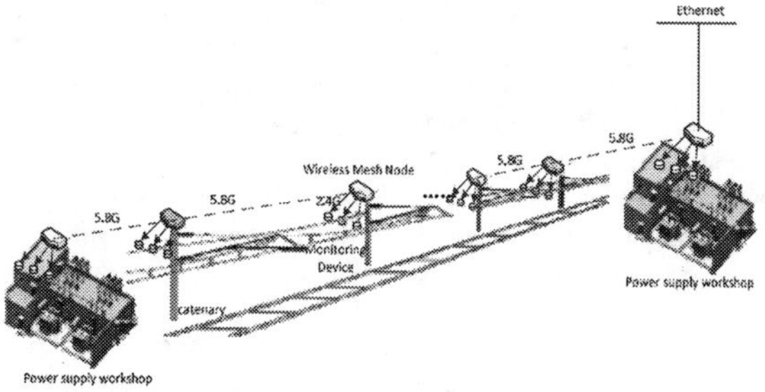

Figure 2. Physical structure of chain wireless network

3 The topological structure of chain wireless network based on token

In this paper, a special topological structure of multi subnet in series for "chain structure" is presented, which belongs to the type of Mesh and is composed of a plurality of wireless communication networks that are connected in series, each sub network including one or more peer wireless monitoring nodes[8].

The chain wireless network consists of the initial power supply workshop, the main node of the token-ring which has data to transmit, the next main node, the common nodes and terminal power supply workshop. A main node of token-ring and two common nodes forms a wireless communication subnet. A plenty of subnets in series connection form a long chain. The initial power supply workshop completes the procedure of initialization, so that each node knows its predecessor and successor nodes; the main node of token-ring is the node which has monitoring data to transmit. Before transmission, it listens to the idle condition of channel within two hop range, and declares to be the main node of token-ring, then it makes up a token ring to transmit the monitoring data; The next main node is the main node of the next sub token-ring network, which is similar to the main node of the token-ring which has data to transmit; The common node plays a role of relay in the information transmission, it is the intermediate node in the transmission process; The terminal power supply workshop is the node at the end of catenary line, and the data information on the line will be collected to the power supply workshop and be handled finally.

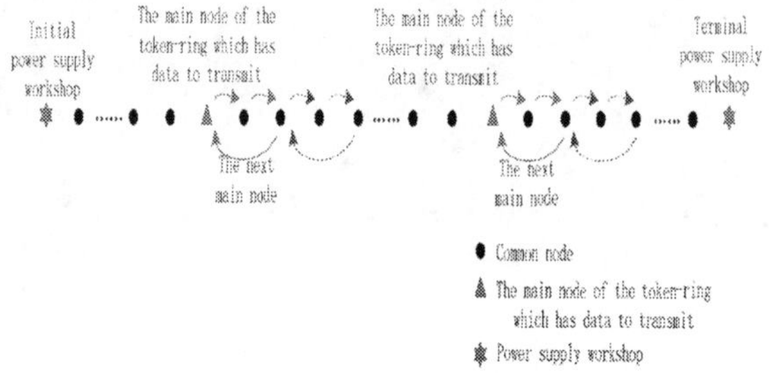

Figure 3. The topological structure of chain wireless network based on token

4 Working mode of token in wireless network

4.1 Initialization, make nodes know their predecessor and successor nodes

Power supply workshop monitoring center nodes (the two ending nodes of the long chain) are responsible for the generation, taking back and management of tokens. Each node is assigned a unique address of the whole network as its own identity, and has an initial neighbor table which is used to determine the destination address of the next hop. The center node receives the remote command to start and generate a "Neighbornode-detection" token. The token carries the address information of the current node. In the form of single hop, the token is transmitted along the nodes of initial path. The nodes read the value of SA when they receive the token[9], and record it as their predecessor node. When the token arrives at the terminal of the line, nodes transmit the detection token back according to the original path and the token will be token back by center node[10].Complete the initialization, and form a neighbor node table for future node operation.

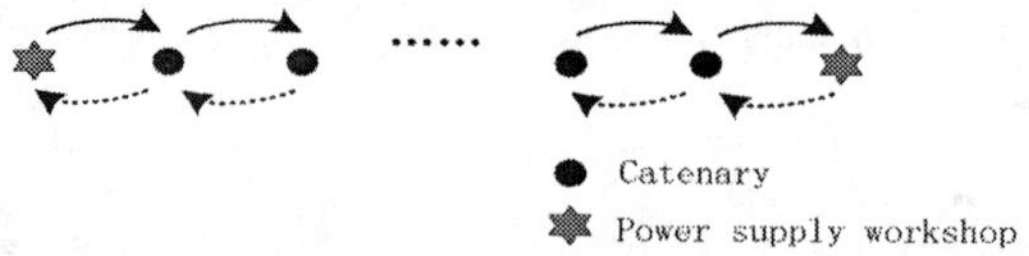

Figure 4. Initialization process of nodes access to electricity

4.2 When node has data to transmit, the procedure of creating a logical ring

DOI: 10.1051/matecconf/201712801004

After initialization, the node enters the FLT state. If the node needs to transmit data and the channel of its adjacent two hop range is idle, then the node enters the SFR state and keeps on listening, if the channel is still idle, it declares to be the main node of the token-ring and sends a solicit_successor token to invite its next hop node to join the token-ring. Then the node enters SEK state, waiting for the response of other nodes. When the next hop node receives the solicit_successor token sent by the node, then it enters the SRP state for random back-off. If it receipts the information of the existence of other token ring during the back-off time, then it returns to the FLT state and waits for the next opportunity to join; If there is no response of other nodes, then it replies the set_successor token to respond and receives the token with right to send data which is sent by the invitation node. The one hop successor node which join the token ring successfully has the right to invite the two hop successor node of the main node to join the token ring. With the token passing periodically, it makes the nodes of the two hop range of main node join the token ring orderly.

When the data frame is transmitted to the two hop successor node of the main node, the two hop successor node sends common token to the main node, then the main node reads the value of GenSeq of the frame. When the value of GenSeq is 1 (the token is transmitted one circle on the ring), the main node will take back the token and send the set_successor token to the successor node of its two hop. After its two hop successor node receives the confirmation signal and the channel of its two hop range is idle, it declares to be the new main node of the token ring. In accordance with the above steps, a subnet is established. A plurality of subnets which are connected in series realize the transmission of data to the power supply workshop.

Because the data transmission is random, there may be multiple tokens on the whole line, that is, there may be multiple subnets on the whole line to transmit data at the same time. However, the channel of the main node's adjacent two hop range is idle as the logical ring is set up, so there is no interference during each subnet transmitting the data. This not only ensures the correctness of data transmission, but also reduces the delay of data transmission.

4.3 The process of nodes joining the token-ring

The process of nodes joining the token-ring is based on the four steps handshake mechanism.

After a node holds the token, it sends a solicit_successor token and asks for the nodes whose address is between the current node and the next node in the logical order to join the token-ring.

Node A broadcasts the solicit_successor token that contains the address information of Node C. In order to avoid the collision of the plurality of application nodes' joining responses, after Node B hears the solicit_successor, it will choose a random back-off time. If Node B hears the set_successor token that is sent by other nodes during the back-off time, it will give up this application. Otherwise, when the back-off time is over, the joining application will be issued immediately, and Node C will be recorded as its probable successor node. After Node A receives the set_successor token sent by Node B, it will record Node B as its probable successor node and send the set_predecessor token. After Node B receives the set_predecessor token, it will record Node A as its probable predecessor node and send the set_predecessor token to Node C in order to close the token ring.

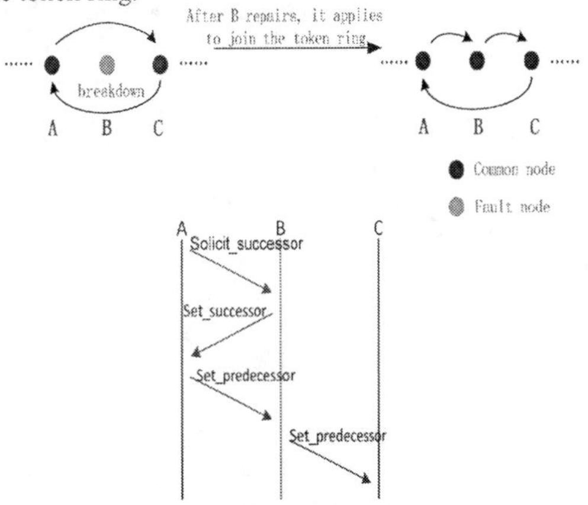

Figure 5. Nodes join token ring

4.4 The process of nodes leaving the token-ring

The protocol needs to support the recovery mechanism of token ring network, because the nodes on the token ring may break down. The process of node leaving the network is shown in figure 6. If Node B needs to apply to leave the token ring, it will wait for the token being held and notify its predecessor node spontaneously. Specific steps are as follows: Node B sends the set_successor token to its predecessor node (Node A), which contains the MAC address of its successor node (Node C), and declares it will leave the token ring. Node A sends the set_predecessor token to Node C, enters the listening state and starts the token transfer timer. If the timer does not overflow and Node A hears the implied confirmation signal, it is considered that the token ring is closed successfully. And nodes will upload their local connection table.

Figure 6. Nodes leave token ring

5 The maintenance of token ring network

5.1 Fault handling

(1) One hop successor node of the main node breaks down

If the main node of token ring (Node C) does not hear valid message, it will send the token again to the same successor node (Node D). After two successive failures,

DOI: 10.1051/matecconf/201712801004

Node C considers Node D is broken-down and then sends a solicit_successor packet in order to find the address of Node E which is the successor node of the broken-down Node D. If Node C receives the set_successor response, it shows that the next node of Node D (Node E) can work normally, so Node C skips the broken-down point Node D, and connects with the new successor Node E. If Node C doesn't receive the set_successor response, it can retry. If it fails again, it indicates that the network node is broken-down or the receiver of the node broken-down. Node C will stop working right now, and listen to the condition of the bus.

If the main node of token ring (Node C) connects with its two hop successor node (Node E), Node C will take the token back after one circle of token passing, and send a confirmation signal to Node E. After Node E receive the confirmation signal, if it hears the channel of its adjacent two hop range is idle, then it declares to be the new main node of token ring and forms a new token ring with Node F and Node G.

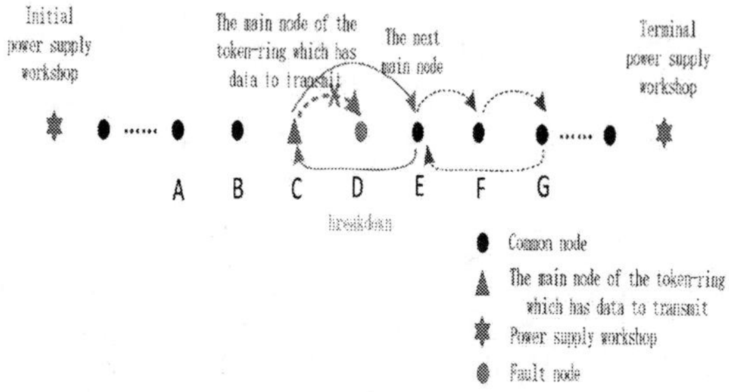

Figure 7. Main node's one hop successor node breaks down

(2) Two hop successor node of the main node breaks down

If one hop successor node (Node D) of the main node (Node C) works normally, and Node C can hear a valid message, then Node C convers to the state of listening. And the token is passed by Node D, if Node D which sends the token doesn't hear the valid message, it will send the token to the same one hop successor node (Node E) again. After two successive failures, Node D considers Node E is broken-down and send a set_predecessor packet which contains its own address. Node C and Node D form a new token ring which contains two nodes.

If the main node of token ring (Node C) and its one hop successor node (Node D) form a token ring which has two nodes successfully, Node C will take the token back after one circle of token passing and send a confirmation signal to Node D. After Node D receives the confirmation signal, if it hears the channel of its adjacent two hop range is idle, then it declares to be the new main node of token ring, skips the broken-down point Node E and forms a new token ring with node F.

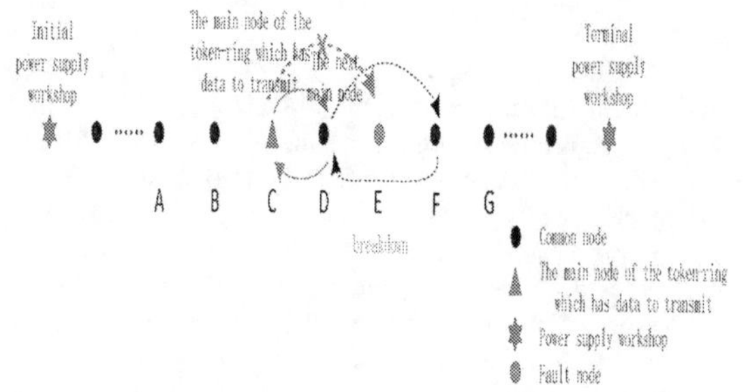

Figure 8. Main node's two hop successor node breaks down

5.2 The elimination of multiple tokens

The chain wireless transmission protocol should be able to detect the situation of multiple tokens existing in each subnet, and could take some measures to eliminate multiple tokens. Use the priority of the token to eliminate the low priority token, so that only one token is passed in a token ring. The more nodes, the higher priority of the token ring. If the number of nodes of the ring is the same, the older age of token ring, the higher priority. In the case of token loss, the age of the regeneration token will be added 2 based on the age of local ring. So the priority of new token will be higher than original token, thus the old token will be eliminated.

6 Performance analysis of the chain wireless network

Literature[11] analyze the data flow of digital substation communication network and simulate the network performance. Literature[12] analyzes and simulates the performance of the wireless token ring protocol and proposes the optimization algorithm. According to the transmission process and characteristics of the power supply workshop communication network monitoring data flow, in this paper, the traditional token ring protocol is improved. The system is decomposed into several subnets which connect in series, based on that, we mainly analyze the network performance indexes such as the information transmission delay, the information throughput and the number of nodes that can be accommodated by the system.

In the electric power monitoring system, the length of the monitoring data depends on the negative exponential distribution. Usually the monitoring data is loaded in the message segment of frame whose length is less than or equal to b_0, in this case, it can be transferred effectively.

Assume that the length of the message segment is a random variable X, and its density function is $f(x) = \mu e^{-\mu x}$. The length of frame follows a negative exponential distribution and a fixed length of service time, it is a random variable L, and its density function is $f(l)$. That is, some frames in the range of $h \sim h + b_0$ depends on the negative exponential distribution and their density functions are $f_1(l)$, while the other frames whose length are fixed values $h + b_0$, their density functions are $f_2(l)$.

$$f(l) = (1 - e^{-\mu b_0}) f_1(l) + e^{-\mu b_0} f_2(l) \qquad (1)$$

where

$$f_1(l) = \begin{cases} \frac{\mu e^{-\mu(l-h)}}{1-e^{-\mu b_0}}, & h < l < h + b_0 \\ 0, & l < h or l > h + b_0 \end{cases} \quad (2)$$

$$f_2(l) = \delta(l - (h + b_0)) \quad (3)$$

The length of frame L to loop bandwidth C ratio is the frame transmission time S. The expressions are obtained by calculation as follow:

$$\mathrm{E}(S) = \frac{1+\mu h - e^{-\mu b_0}}{\mu c} \quad (4)$$

$$\mathrm{E}(S^2) = \frac{1+(1+\mu h)^2 - 2(1+\mu b_0+\mu h)e^{-\mu b_0}}{(\mu c)^2} \quad (5)$$

The wireless chain transmission network is composed of m subnets which connect in series, and each subnet consists of three nodes. The token is passed on the token ring nodes one by one in one way in each power supply workshop. After the information frame arrives at the node, it participates in the queue and waits for the token. The node which acquires the token can send only one information frame and follow the principle of first come first served. Assume that the information frame which arrives at node i depends on Poisson distribution, and the average arrival rate is $\lambda_i (i = 0,1,2)$. Then token ring is M/G/1 queue system. Assume that each subnet has the same performance, so we first analyze the performance of a single subnet.

Average waiting time of information frame in subnet:

$$\mathrm{E}(D) = \frac{\lambda E(S^2)}{2(1-\rho)} \quad (6)$$

Where $\lambda = \lambda_0 + \lambda_1 + \lambda_2$, $\rho = \lambda E(S)$ is loop busy probability.

The transmission delay of the information frame of the subnet is the time interval form the information frame reaching a node to being sent out, its mathematical expectation is:

$$\mathrm{E}(W) = E(D) + E(S) \quad (7)$$

The time of one circle of token passing on the ring:

$$B_r = \sum_{i=0}^{2}[\rho_i S + (1-\rho_i) l_t] = \rho S + (1-\rho)\, l_t \quad (8)$$

Where $\rho_i = \lambda_i E(S)$ is the busy probability of node i, l_t is the passing time of idle token.

Define the number of information bits transmitting on the subnet in unit time as the information throughput of subnet.

$$\mathrm{H} = \frac{\frac{(1-e^{-\mu b_0})\rho_i}{\mu}}{\rho E(S) + (1-\rho) l_t} \quad (9)$$

According to IBM TOKEN RING frame format, the length of monitoring segment is 336bit and idle token is 18bit. Assume that average length of user information is $\frac{1}{\mu} = 1376$bit and loop bandwidth is 25Mb/s.

According to the above formula, simulate with matlab, the performance analysis curves of the protocol of chain wireless network which consists of multi subnets in series are as follow.

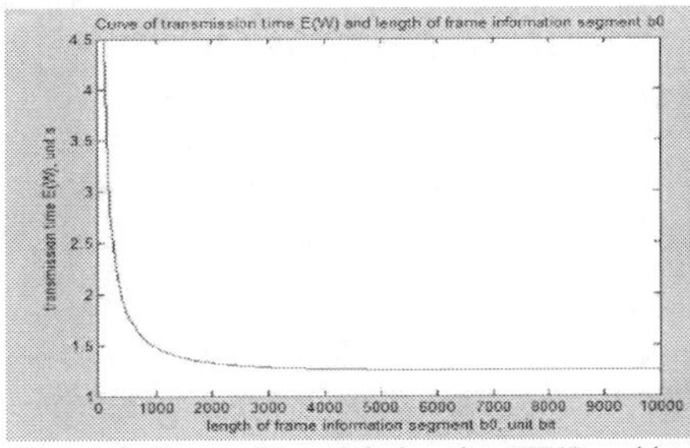

Figure 9. Curve of transmission time E(W) and length of frame information segment b0

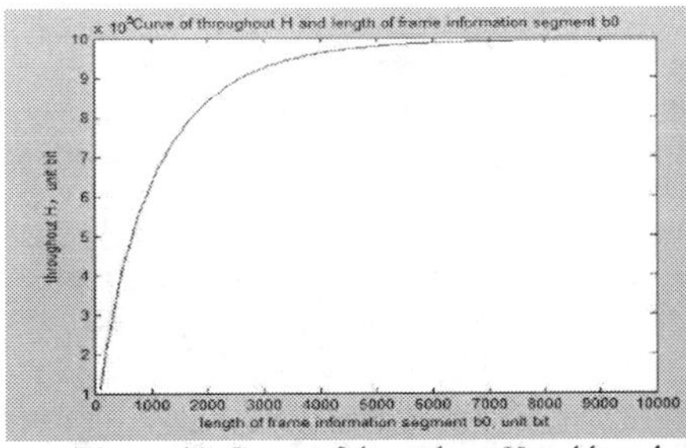

Figure 10. Curve of throughout H and length of frame information segment b0

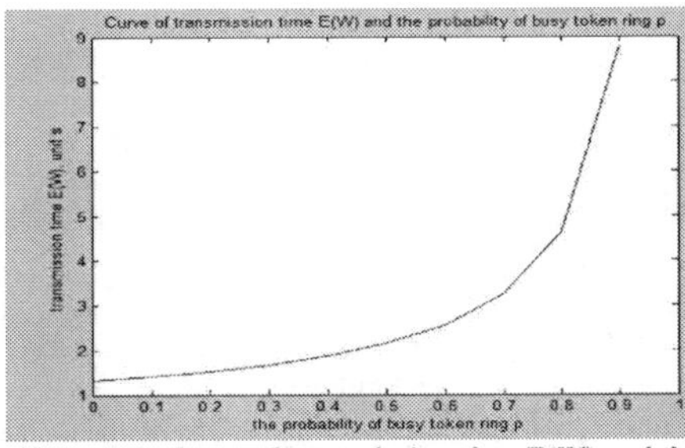

Figure 11. Curve of transmission time E(W) and the probability of busy token ring ρ

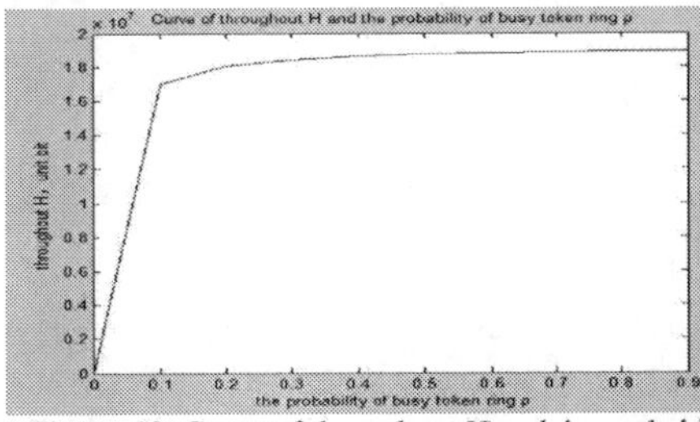

Figure 12. Curve of throughout H and the probability of busy token ring ρ

As it is shown in Figure 9 and Figure 10, for the maximum information throughout H and the minimun transmission delay E(W), the optional maximum length of message segment is different, and the latter is often less than the former. When $b_0 > 2000\ bit$, the growth rate of information throughout has a sharp decline, while the transmission delay E(W) no longer reduces. b_0 should take account of these two parameters, in order to obtain the smaller transmission delay and the larger information throughout. Therefore, the length of information segment of the frame b_0 should not be greater than 200 bit.

As it is shown in Figure 11 and Figure 12, when the loop busy probability ρ is bigger than 0.8, the transmission delay E(W) grows rapidly. Compromise the transmission delay E(W) and the information throughout H, the ideal value of ρ is in the range of 0.5~0.8. The relation of the number of nodes N and ρ is as follow: N=3m, $\rho=3m\rho_0$. Therefore, Figure 12 also reflects the relationship of the number of nodes N and the transmission delay E(W). For example, when ρ_0=0.005 and N=160, already make $\rho = N\rho_0 = 0.8$. So when the number of nodes increases, it will lead to the rapid increase of transmission delay E(W).

Because the chain network is made up of m subnets which connect in series, the transmission delay of the whole line is m times of the subnet transmission delay. When the number of nodes N in the chain network reaches a significant degree, the transmission delay of the network will increase dramatically. So there is a maximum capacity of the number of nodes in the network N. Because it is necessary to monitor that the states of all the nodes in its two hop range are idle when the node has data to transmit, so in the network, the maximum number of nodes is five, the nodes form a transmission subnet, and then form a transmission chain. Therefore, the number of tokens in the network should not exceed N/5, otherwise there will be interference.

7 Conclusion

In this paper, the network node and the corresponding transport protocol of the chain network which is suitable for power monitoring data transmission are proposed. The network-forming is convenient and costs little. The protocol is simple and easy to implement. Because the power of wireless node is limited, in the whole line, there can be multiple subnets to transmit information at the same time, and subnet will not interfere with each other, thus greatly improves the transmission efficiency, decreases the delay and reduces the bit error rate. At the same time, the token carries control information to each node, so that the nodes will not interfere with each other and realize the orderly use of the channel.

About the author

Wu Chunmei (1992), female, Master graduate student, the main research direction is communication theory and its key technology.

References

1. Li Xin. Research on Online Monitoring System of The Catenary Security Status Based on Catenary Tension and Wire Temperature[J]. Beijing Jiaotong University. 2015.
2. Li Lifen, Zhu Yongli, Yu Yonghua. Transmission of power line on-line monitoring data based on long-chain tree-like wireless sensor network[J]. Power System Technology, 2011, 35(6):199-203(in Chinese).
3. Yin Hua, Wang Fa. Application of Wireless Mesh Technology in Power Transmission Line Monitoring[J]. Telecommunications for Electric Power System, 2010, 39(12) : 3609-3614.
4. LIU Yaoxian, SUN Yi, WU Xin, WEI Lei, DUAN Quansheng. A Reliable WSN Routing Method for Distribution Network Fault Detection[J]. Power System Technology, 2015, 39(12): 3609-3614(in Chinese).
5. Zhao Ziyan, Liu Jianming. A new service risk balancing based method to evaluate reliability of electric power communication network[J]. Power System Technology, 2011, 35(10): 209-213(in Chinese).
6. Zhou Jing, Lü Tianguang, Chen Xi, et al. Study on bandwidth analysis and capacity planning of provincial dispatching digital network[J]. Power System Technology, 2012, 36(5): 173-177(in Chinese).
7. Zhang Huafangzi. Research on Monitoring Communication System for High Voltage Transmission Lines Based on Mesh[D]. North China Electric Power University. 2013.
8. Xia Heng. Research of Wireless Streetlight Control System[D]. Harbin Institute of Technology. 2011.
9. Yang Bin, Ren Ping, Liu Yi. A Self-adaptive Token Passing Algorithm for the WTRP Network[J]. Ship Electronic Engineering. 2015, 5:47-50.
10. Li can. The Research and Application of Token Ring Protocol In The Network Communication With High-Frequency[D]. China Ship Research and Development Academy. 2014.
11. Zhang Zhidan, Huang Xiaoqing, Cao Yijia. Comprehensive data flow analysis and communication network simulation for virtual local area network-based substation[J]. Power System Technology, 2011, 35(5) :204-209(in Chinese).
12. Taner Kurtulus, Improvement and development of High-Frequency wireless token-ring protocol, Middle East Technical University, Dec 2010.

MATEC Web of Conferences **128**, 01005 (2017) DOI: 10.1051/matecconf/201712801005
EITCE 2017

Research on Displacement Calculation of Dynamometer Card Based on Kalman Filter and Discrete Numerical Integration

Nan Yan[a], Jia Shu Dai

School of Computer and Information, Anhui Polytechnic University, 241000 Wuhu, China

Abstract: In order to calculate the dynamometer card of oil well using acceleration sensor, the algorithm which combined by Kalman filter and discrete numerical integration is proposed. It can be applied to calculate the displacement and precipitation displacement period of oil well dynamometer card. The Kalman filter not only filters out the noise of the acceleration signal, but also maintains the original shape feature. The accurate precipitation of the displacement period ensures the correctness of displacement. The discrete numerical integration algorithm can make the relative error of displacement measurement less than 1%, which meets the requirement for dynamometer card accuracy. It is suitable for different types of oil wells.

1 Introduction

The dynamometer card is a graph that reflects the change rules of polished rod load of pumping unit with its displacement. The real-time dynamic of oil well and the rationality of pumping unit device can be known through the analysis of dynamometer card. The dynamometer card is one of the important basis for the fault diagnosis of the pumping unit, and the displacement is the horizontal ordinate of the graph. The products for measuring dynamometer cards by acceleration sensors have been developed at abroad, but few of them are still available in china. At present, the modes of measuring the displacement and stroke which used in oil field are mainly wired and wireless. The wired measurement mode has high precision and good reproducibility. However, there are some shortcomings, such as heavy equipment, high breakage rate, serious local wear and so on, these resulting in a lot of inconvenience to field operations [1]. The wireless measurement mode is mainly measured by the inclination sensor and the acceleration sensor. The inclination and the acceleration sensor measure the displacement with the advantages of legerity and convenient, and are not interfered by the external environment. However, due to excessive vibration and resistance during the movement process of pumping unit, these caused the collected digital signals have a lot of noise and singular points (too large or too small signal). At present, the smoothing filter is used to calculate the displacement of acceleration signal in oil industry. This method is difficult to filter out the noise signal and remove the signal singular points, the calculated displacement measurement accuracy is low, the repetition rate is poor and the error is large [2]. How to obtain an accurate and small error displacement is the key to solve the problem of dynamometer card. Therefore, the algorithm which combined by Kalman filtering and discrete numerical integration is proposed to calculate the displacement and the precipitation displacement period of oil well dynamometer card, as follows.

2 Filtering Processing

The filtering algorithm is used to de-noise the original acceleration data so as to make the acceleration signal as smooth as possible. The vibration of pumping unit and resistance of downhole will cause the acceleration signal a lot of noise in the acceleration acquisition process. Thus, the displacement after second order integral will produce a great error. Therefore, filtering is essential before integration. The incoming interface of the acceleration signal will plus 0.1 uF filter capacitor for hardware filtering. The Kalman filter is the first time applied to the displacement calculation of the dynamometer card after comparing the common 7-point smoothing filter and Kalman filter.

2.1 The principle of 7-point moving average filtering

The measurement data storage in the 7- point moving average filtering is the queue. The first seven points of the queue (length N) to be processed is divided into a group, the results after processing is putted to the end of the queue while the header of the original queue is discarded. Then the latest N data remains in the queue. When the average is calculated, the arithmetic average of the seven data in the queue produces a new arithmetic mean. The new arithmetic averages can be obtained after

[a] Corresponding author: 16417442@qq.com

each time processing until the end of the queue. The three times 7-point moving average filtering is carried out on the RAM which stored 400 acceleration signals. The formula is as follows:

$$X_k = (X_{k-3}+X_{k-2}+X_{k-1}+X_k+X_{k+1}+X_{k+2}+X_{k+3}) \quad (3 \le k \le N-3) \quad (1)$$

Where, X_k is the k-th acceleration data, N is the number of data which collected in the entire process.

2.2 The principle of Kalman filter and its modeling realization

Kalman filter has been applied to robot control, sensor data fusion, navigation and other fields. It has also been widely used in image processing, and has the advantages of fast speed and high computational precision. Kalman filter is an iterative algorithm, while the minimum mean square error estimation is the best criterion [3]. The basic idea of Kalman filter is to use the signal and noise state space as the model under the best estimation criterion. The estimated values are obtained by update the state variable estimation using the last estimated value and current measured value. The discrete process systems and the measurement equations of the data to be processed are established to satisfy the best criteria. The Kalman filter modeling method is as follows.

Step 1 The discrete control process system is introduced which can be represented by a linear stochastic differential equation:

$$X(k) = A\,X(k-1) + B\,U(k) + W(k) \quad (2)$$

The measured values of the system

$$Z(k) = H\,X(k) + V(k) \quad (3)$$

In the formula (2) and (3), X (k) is the system state at time k, U (k) is the control variable of the system at time k, A and B are the system parameters. Z(K) is the measured value at time k, H is the measurement system parameter. W (k) is the process noise, V (k) is the measurement noise, assuming these are Gaussian white noises, their covariance is Q, R (here we assume that they do not change with the state of the system).

Step 2 Predict the current state. The Kalman filter is the most suitable algorithm for the Gaussian white noise system. The optimized output estimates are according to the covariance of the system. Set k is the current system state, the current state estimate value can be predicted by the system's previous state, the current estimate state is:

$$X(k \mid k-1) = A\,X(k-1) + B\,U(k) \quad (4)$$

In the formula (4), X (k | k-1) is the previous state prediction result. U (k) is the current state control variable, when there is no control variable, it is 0. The system results are updated here, but the covariance of X (k | k-1) is not updated. P is the covariance; the current error is predicted by:

$$P(k \mid k-1) = A\,P(k-1)\,A^T + Q \quad (5)$$

In the formula (5), P (k | k-1) is the covariance of X (k | k-1), P (k-1) is the covariance of X (k-1), A^T is the transposed matrix of A, the covariance of system process is Q.

Step 3 Get the optimal estimate value X (k). X (k) is the current optimal estimate value (current state k), the present state prediction results in step 2 can be obtained by combine the measured values and the previous predicted values;

The current optimal estimate value is:

$$X(k) = X(k \mid k-1) + Kg(k) * (Z(k) - H\,X(k \mid k-1)) \quad (6)$$

Kg is the Kalman gain,

$$Kg(k) = \frac{P(k \mid k-1)\,H^T}{(H\,P(k \mid k-1)\,H^T + R)} \quad (7)$$

Here, X (k) is the optimal estimate value in the state k, P(k) is updated (the covariance of X (k)) so that the Kalman filter can be run continuously before the end of the system:

$$P(k) = ((I - Kg(k)\,H)P(k \mid k-1) \quad (8)$$

The matrix I in formula (8) is 1(Single measurement of single model, I=1). When the system is updated to state k + 1, P(k)=P(k-1) (formula (5)). Keep running in an autoregressive manner.

The basic model of Kalman filter can be realized through the above three steps. The formulas (4), (5), (6), (7) and (8) are the five basic formulas of the Kalman filter, it is easy to code implement with these five formulas [4]. From the above, the current optimal estimate value X (k) and the error value P (k) can be obtained through the initial state X_0 and the initial error P_0, and the current observation value Z (k). Figure 1 is the original acceleration data which collect from acceleration sensor, Figure 2 and Figure 3 are the effect comparison of Kalman filter and three times 7-point moving filter.

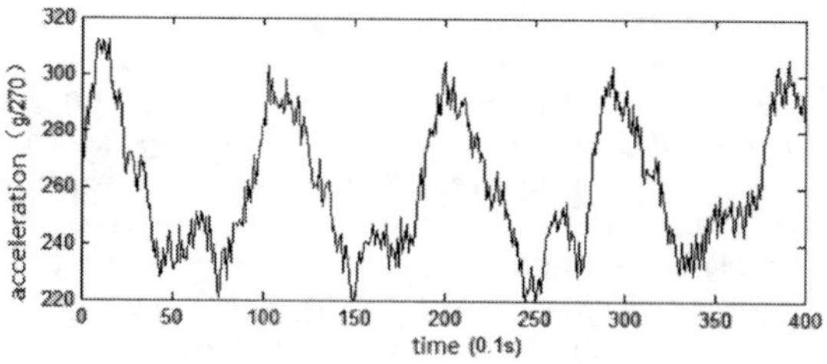

Figure 1. The original data of acceleration.

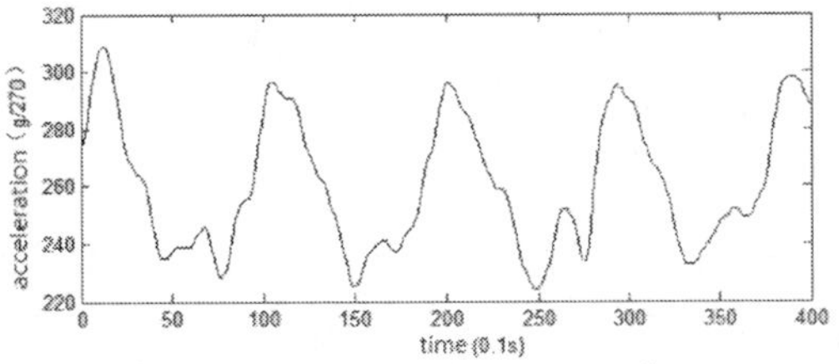

Figure 2. The data after Kalman filter.

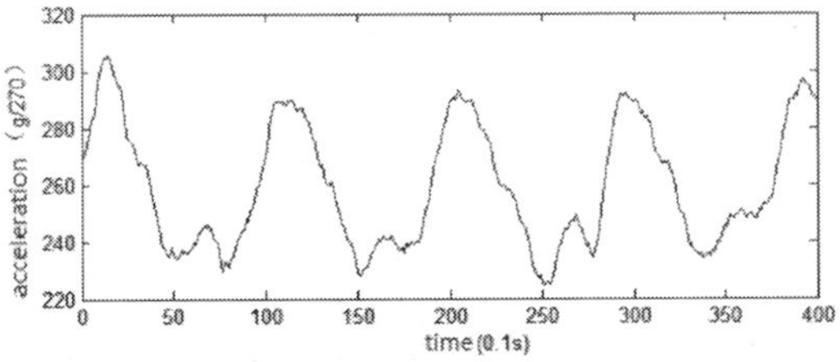

Figure 3. The data after 7-point moving filter.

By comparing Figure 2 and Figure 3, the Kalman filter described in Figure 2 is better to reflects realistic acceleration signal, the stroke measurement has a good repeatability in the same oil well. It can eliminate the singular points in the acceleration noise. The most outstanding advantage is that fast real-time processing and saving memory capacity.

3 The displacement period is precipitated by the acceleration after filtering

According to the periodic characteristics of sucker rod movement, the acceleration of 400 points are collected at a time, the acquisition interval is controlled at 100 ms. In order to obtain at least one period of acceleration raw data of pumping unit at different speeds, once acquisition per 40s. Since the pumping rod of pumping unit makes periodic reciprocating motion, assuming that the movement period is T, the movement regulation satisfies the following three formulas:

$$a(0) = a(T) \tag{9}$$

$$v(0) = v(\frac{T}{2}) = v(T) \tag{10}$$

$$d(0) = d(T) \tag{11}$$

Among them, a(t) is the acceleration of sucker rod, v (t) is the speed of sucker rod, d (t) is the relative displacement of the sucker rod.

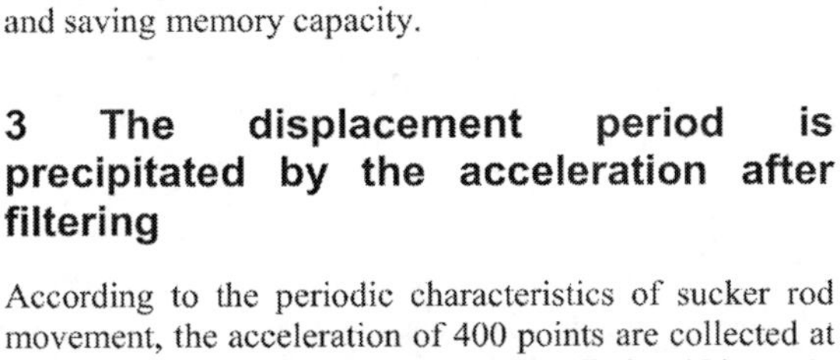

Figure 4. The period analysis chart.

In the process of pumping up and down, the speed at the maximum and minimum acceleration is 0. As can be seen from Figure 4, the MAX set of acceleration is the highest point at the displacement of the pumping unit which is the zero point of relative displacement. Among them, MIN is the maximum point of relative displacement, and the two adjacent local maximum or minimum point is a displacement period. The algorithm for calculating the period is divided into the following four steps to ensure the correctness of the period.

Step 1 Look for the maximum and minimum values of the previous 2/3 periods (this step ensures that the complete period can be found in the case of very little acceleration)

Step 2 Compare the subscripts of the maximum and minimum, if the subscript of the maximum value is close to 0, go to (step 3), otherwise, go to (step 4).

Step 3 The begin point of the maximum acceleration subscript is recorded. As the MAX1 in figure, look backward for the nearest absolute maximum value to the local maximum value can obtain the MAX2, the determination of MAX2 is based on the difference between the maximum and the minimum according to step 2.

$$\text{Period} \quad T = [MAX_{[n+1]} - MAX_{[n]}] * 0.01 \tag{12}$$

Step 4 The begin point of the minimum acceleration subscript is recorded. As the MIN1 in figure, look backward for the nearest absolute minimum value to the local minimum value can obtain the MIN2, the determination of MIN2 is based on the difference between the maximum and the minimum according to step 2.

$$\text{Period} \ T = [MIN_{[n+1]} - MIN_{[n]}] * 0.01 \tag{13}$$

4 Gravity acceleration calibration

The acquired acceleration signal value is the sum of the longitudinal acceleration and the gravity acceleration (or longitudinal component) of the sucker rod, it can be represented as:

$$A(t) = a(t) + g \tag{14}$$

Where, A (t) is the acceleration value, a (t) is the longitudinal acceleration of the sucker rod, and g is the gravity acceleration.

Due to differences in sensors and deviations in installation, there are differences of g in the different oil wells [5]. This difference will be magnified after second order integral, thus affecting the final accuracy. Therefore, the acceleration must be zero point corrected. The static storage g has been tested, but due to the use of static g zero-point correction will still result in residual, and can not be changed according to different pumping units, so that the final calculation of the displacement has a greater error. According to the movement characteristics of the pumping unit, the method of dynamic zero-point correction is proposed.

This method can dynamically adjust the calculated gravity acceleration according to the types of pumping units. v (t) is the speed of the sucker rod, the time is t, and the integral of a (t) in one period is

$$v(T) = v(0) + \int_0^T a(\tau)d\tau \qquad (15)$$

From the formula (14), (15), we can get

$$v(T) = v(0) + \int_0^T [A(\tau) - g]d\tau \qquad (16)$$

From the formula (10), (16) , we can get

$$g = \frac{1}{T}\int_0^T A(\tau)d\tau \qquad (17)$$

The gravity acceleration g of an oil pumping unit is the average value of a periodic acceleration signal.

5 The displacement is obtained by discrete numerical integration

According to the determined period, the acceleration signal is discretized by numerical integration to obtain displacement [6]. The speed is calculated by integrating the acceleration of a complete period at one time, and the displacement is obtained by integrating the speed. There are many methods of discrete numerical integration, the Simpson formula is used in second order integral to obtain displacement as shown in the following formula [7].

$$\int_a^b f(x)dx \approx \int_a^b P_2(x)dx = \frac{b-a}{6}[f(a)+4f(\frac{a+b}{2})+f(b)] \qquad (18)$$

The speed is obtained by first order integrating the acceleration through Simpson formula according to formula (18), the speed after further integration is obtained by zero points correct to it, then integrating the speed once again.

$$v(t) = v(0) - \frac{1}{T}\int_0^T v(\tau)d\tau \qquad (19)$$

V (0) is the initial value of the speed, the beginning point of the relative displacement is zero, the relative displacement can be obtained by integrating V (T) with Simpson formula:

$$d(t) = \int_0^t v(\tau)d\tau \qquad (20)$$

Figure 5 is the displacement graph calculated according to the above formula, the practice measured displacement is 3.3 m. The displacement calculated from the acceleration is 3.28 m. In order to increase the persuasiveness, a series of experimental measurements have been carried out by this method, the data are shown in Table 1.

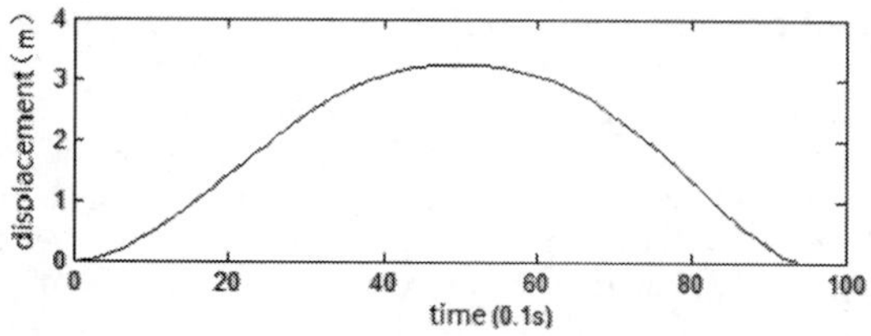

Figure 5. The Periodic displacement diagram.

Table 1. The displacement of Kalman filter measurement analysis
(displacement unit is m; Scale measurement3.3m)

Measured times	The measured displacement	The relative error
1	3.28	0.60%
2	3.29	0.30%
3	3.31	0.30%
4	3.33	0.90%
5	3.28	0.60%
6	3.32	0.60%
7	3.31	0.30%
8	3.27	0.90%

Table 2. The displacement of 7-point moving filtering measurement analysis
(displacement unit is m; Scale measurement3.3m)

Measured times	The measured displacement	The relative error
1	3.34	1.20%
2	3.199	3.30%
3	3.31	0.30%
4	3.43	33.90%
5	3.38	2.40%
6	3.42	3.60%
7	3.32	0.60%
8	3.24	1.80%

6 CONCLUSION

Compared with the most commonly used 7- point moving filtering, the field experiment results show that the Kalman filtering algorithm owns smaller maximum error and higher repeatability, which satisfies the requirement of relevant accuracy of oil well dynamometer card.

The displacement period searching method which proposed in this paper provides a reliable and basis method for the calculation of displacement, and improves the accuracy of displacement calculation. The zero point correction to the dynamic acceleration sensor data acquisition not only eliminates the residual of gravity acceleration, but also can be dynamically adjusted according to the different pumping unit and installation environment, this method is more suitable for different types of oil pumping unit. The displacements computed by the discrete numerical integral through the Simpson formula have smaller relative errors and higher accuracy.

Acknowledgements

This research is supported by National Natural Science Foundation of China under Grants 61501005, the Program of Educational Commission of Anhui Province under Grants KJ2017A104 and Science and Technology Projects of Production under Grant No.2015cxy03, which are gratefully acknowledged.

References

1. PENG Jian, XU Zhi qiang, ZHOU Zhi quan. Design of Dynamometer Based on Sensor Technology[J]. Chinese Journal of Sensors and Actuators,2012,25(12):1701-1705.
2. WU Xin-sheng, TANG Ping, QIN Han. The application of digital filtering technique in signal acquisition of weighing system[J].Transducer and Microsystem Technologies,2010,29(09):131-134
3. Han Ping, Sang Wei lin, Shi Qing yan. Novel nonlinear Kalman filtering method[J]. Chinese Journal of Scientific Instrument,2015,36(03):632-638
4. Jian min Duan, Hui Shi, Dan Liu, Hong xiao Yu. Square Root Cubature Kalman Filter-Kalman Filter Algorithm for Intelligent Vehicle Position Estimate[J]. Procedia Engineering,2016, 137:.
5. Kailei Liu, Zhi jia Li, Cheng Yao, Ji Chen, Ke Zhang, Muhammad Saifullah. Coupling the k -nearest neighbour procedure with the Kalman filter for real-time updating of the hydraulic model in flood forecasting[J]. International Journal of Sediment Research, 2016,:.
6. Peter Matisko, Vladimír Havlena. Optimality tests and adaptive Kalman filter[J]. IFAC Proceedings Volumes,2012,45(16):.
7. Simo Särkkä,Arno Solin. On Continuous-Discrete Cubature Kalman Filtering[J]. IFAC Proceedings Volumes,2012,45(16):.

Investigation on Measuring Total Peripheral Resistance of Human Body by Means of Reconstructed Impedance Cardiogram

Kuang Shi-jiang, Zhao Hui [a], Wang Zi-min and Kuang ming-xing

Department of Electronic Engineering, Nanchang Institute of Technology, Nanchang 330044, China

Abstract. Objective The purpose in this article is to investigate the measurement method and normal values of the total peripheral resistance (TPR) and total peripheral resistance index (TPRI) measured by the reconstructed impedance cardiogram (RICG). **Methods** The cardiac output and cardiac index of 180 normal adults is measured by means of the RICG. The computed formula of the TPR and TPRI are deduced, and the TPR and TPRI are calculated. The subjects are divided to the different groups according to the sex and age. The TPR and TPRI are calculated statistically. **Results** The TPR and TPRI are increased with the increase of the age, and there is significant difference between the young and elder groups (P<0.05). In the same age group, the TPR of the female group is higher than that of the male group (P<0.05), but the TPRI of the male and female groups is basically the same (P> 0.05). The normal value of the TPR is less than 1650 $dyn.s.cm^{-5}$, and that of the TPRI is less than 2650 $dyn.s.cm^{-5}.m^2$. **Conclusion** The TPR and TPRI measured by the RICG can reflect the hemodynamic changes of the normal or abnormal body.

1 Introduction

The total peripheral resistance (TPR) of the human body is the total flow resistance of the blood in the systemic circulation system. The TPR is a parameter which reflects the effect of the blood flow obstruction in the blood vessels, and it is an important hemodynamic data to study the diseases such as hypertension and heart failure. Now the TPR is usually measured by the Kubicek' method (or Sramek' method) in the measurement of the cardiac function of Impedance cardiogram (ICG)[1,2]. But many studies have confirmed that the ICG measured by the above methods is a kind of the mixed impedance signal, which mainly evokes from the volume changes of the aorta, blood vessels in lung and ventricles[3,6]. Thus the measurement results obtained with this mixed signal include not only the left heart effects, but also include the right heart effects. This method lacks the uniqueness for evaluating the cardiac function. Many scholars raised disagreement on its theoretical rationality. In order to avoid the above difficulties, the TPR is measured by the reconstructed impedance cardiogram (RICG) and are analyzed statistically for 180 normal adults in this paper.

2 Methods and Materials

2. 1 Calculated method

It is known from the medical physics that the flow rate Q of the fluid is proportional to the pressure difference ΔP at both ends of the pipe and is inversely proportional to the flow resistance R[7], i.e.

$$Q = \frac{\Delta P}{R} \tag{1}$$

If the above formula is used to the circulation system of the human body, the Q should be replaced by the cardiac output, the ΔP is approximately replaced by the mean blood pressure P_m, the R is the total peripheral resistance, so Equation (1) can be rewritten as

$$TPR = \frac{P_m}{CO} \tag{2}$$

It is known from the physics that

$$1mmHg = \frac{1}{10}cm \times 13.6g \cdot cm^{-3} \times 980cm \cdot s^{-2}$$
$$=1332.8g \cdot cm \cdot s^{-2} = 1332.8dyn \cdot cm^{-2}$$
$$1L \cdot min^{-1} = \frac{1000cm^3}{60s} \,\square\, 16.67cm^{-3} \cdot s^{-1}$$

Substituting the above unit conversion relationship into Equation (2) obtaining

$$TPR \,\square\, 80\frac{P_m}{CO} \tag{3}$$

This is the practical formula used to calculating the total peripheral resistance of the systemic circulation of the human body. The coefficient 80 is introduced in the unit conversion. The total peripheral resistance index (TPRI) is also commonly used in clinical practice, and it is equal to the radio of the mean blood pressure P_m to the cardiac index (CI), i.e.

$$TPRI = 80\frac{P_m}{CI} = TPR \cdot BSA \tag{4}$$

[a] Corresponding author: 79481914@qq.com.cn

DOI: 10.1051/matecconf/201712801006

In which the CI= CO/BSA, the BSA is the body surface area, and its unit is m^2.

The average blood pressure P_m in the above equations (2), (3) and (4) can be computed by the followed formula, approximately

$$P_m = \frac{1}{3} \cdot P_s + \frac{1}{3} \cdot P_d \tag{5}$$

In which the P_s is the systolic pressure, and the P_d is the diastolic pressure. The cardiac output CO is the blood volume which is fed to the aorta by left ventricle in one minute, and it is equaled to the product of the stroke volume (SV) and heart rate (HR),

$$CO = SV \times HR \tag{6}$$

2.2 Subjects

The subjects are 180 normal adults aged between 18 and 69 years, and they are divided into three age groups: the youth group (18 to 35 years); middle group (36 to 49 years) and Elder group (50 to 69 years). There are 30 males and 30 females in each age group. All the subjects by asking the medical history, as well as the ECG, blood pressure, heart rate and other tests are normal. The blood pressure requirements: the diastolic pressure, ≤ 85mmHg for the youth group, ≤ 90mmHg for the middle and elder groups; the systolic pressure, ≤ 130mmHg for the youth group, ≤ 140mmHg for the middle and elder groups. In addition, the diastolic pressure is not less than 65mmHg, the systolic pressure is not less than 95mmHg.

2.3 Measurement methods

The impedance signal on the chest surface is detected by means of six leads consisting of 15 electrodes [8], as shown in Fig.1. In which there are 3 cureent electrodes and 12 voltage electrodes.

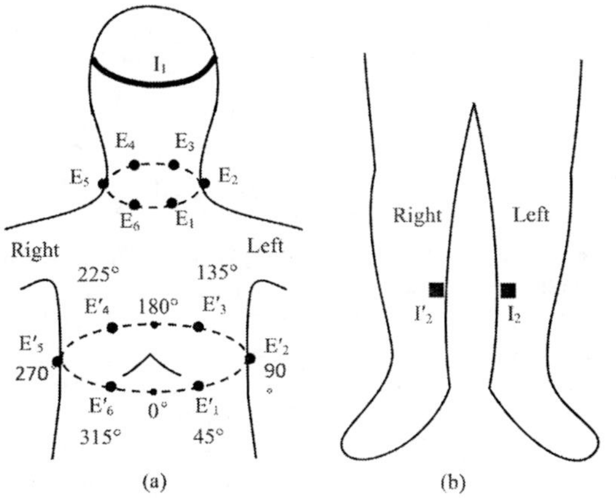

Fig. 1 Placement method of the sening electrodes

The weak high frequency current I_0, with a constant root-mean-square (rms) current, is fed into the human body by means of the current electrodes I_1, I_2 and I_2'. In which the I_1 is located on the forehead, the I_2 and I_2' are located on the left and right lower leg, and the I_2 and I_2' are connected by wires. The voltage sensing electrodes are used for detecting the impedance signals on the chest surface, and all they are the disposable Ag/AgCl electrodes. In which the E_1, E_2, E_3, E_4, E_5 and E_6 are applied to the neck root, and the E_1', E_2', E_3', E_4', E_5' and $E_6'$are applied to the chest surface at the xiphoid level. In addition, the electrodes for sensing the electrocardiogram (ECG) are attached to the right upper arm and to left and the right lower legs. The transducer for sensing the phonocardiogram (PCG) is placed at the position of the cardiac apex on the chest surface.

The instrumentation used in this study was developed by the research group. As shown in Fig. 2, its main parts consist of: an alternating current source, six impedance detection circuits with same structure, an amplifier for the ECG, an amplifier for the PCG, an A/D transform circuit, an isolated source, a computer, each electrodes, as well as the measurement software.

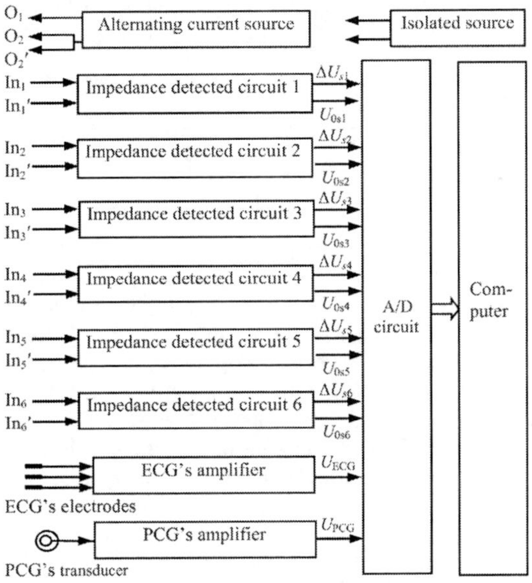

Fig. 2 Block diagram of instrumentation

The subject' body height, body weight, neck circumference, chest circumference, blood pressure and other parameters are measured before the measurement, then they are entered into the computer. The supine position of human body is adopted for the measurement. The subject is asked to hold his/her breath for the duration of the measurement. Then the thoracic impedance changes and base impedances of six leads, as well as the ECG and PCG are collected and displayed simultaneously by the computer. After the waveform collection is ended, the Q wave starting point of four continuous heart beat cycles in the ECG and the corresponding second heart sound S2 of the PCG are selected by means of the artificial operation. The waveform reconstruction of the impedance cardiogram is automatically completed through simplifying and solving the thoracic impedance equations. The waveform parameters of the impedance change components are

DOI: 10.1051/matecconf/201712801006

measured. The TPR and TPRI, as well as other cardiac function data are computed.

3 Results

The TPR and TPRI measured by the above method are computed statistically according to the sex and age groups. The results are shown in Table 1 (In order to analyze expediently, the measured results of the CO, CI and P_m are also listed). It can be seen from Table 1 that:

(1) The TPR and TPRI of the normal adults are increased along with the age augmentation, and there is the significant difference between the young and elder groups (P<0.05).

(2) In the same age group, the TPR of the female group is higher than that of the male group (P<0.05), but the TPRI of the male and female groups is basically the same (P> 0.05).

Table 1 The measurement results of the total peripheral resistance for 180 normal adults ($\bar{x} \pm s$)

Groups	Sex	number	TPR (dyn .s.cm^{-5})	TPRI (dyn .s.cm^{-5}.m^2)	CO (L.min^{-1})	CI (L.min^{-1}.m^{-2})	P_m (mmHg)
Youth	Male	30	1135 ± 130	1882 ± 204	6.17 ± 0.54	3.72 ± 0.34	86.8 ± 5.4
	Female	30	1253 ± 169	1823 ± 248	5.42 ± 0.66	3.72 ± 0.40	83.8 ± 5.5
Middle	Male	30	1183 ± 131	2105 ± 232	6.00 ± 0.61	3.37 ± 0.28	88.0 ± 6.1
	Female	30	1349 ± 163	2044 ± 249	5.15 ± 0.63	3.40 ± 0.39	85.9 ± 5.7
Elder	Male	30	1313 ± 165	2280 ± 249	5.72 ± 0.63	3.29 ± 0.25	93.1 ± 8.4
	Female	30	1457 ± 203	2241 ± 278	5.08 ± 0.50	3.30 ± 0.29	91.6 ± 6.7
Total	/	180	1282 ± 194	2060 ± 301	5.59 ± 0.72	3.47 ± 0.38	88.2 ± 7.1

4 Discussion

The blood is an uneven viscous fluid, and the blood vessels show a certain degree of the resistance when the blood is flowed. This resistance effect is denoted by the flow resistance. The flow resistance R of the vessels are mainly generated from two aspects[9]: First is the friction between the blood and wall of the vessel, and second is the friction caused from the inner relative movement of blood.

According to Poiseuille's law, the flow resistance of the pipe is proportional to the length L of the pipe and the viscosity η of fluid, while is inversely proportional to the fourth power of the pipe radius r. If Poiseuille's Law is used in the systemic circulation of the human body, the flow resistance is the total peripheral resistance TPR (note that it is not an interaction force in the physics and does not have also a force dimension). For a particular individual, the change of the vessel length is very little, so the TPR is mainly determined by the viscosity η of the blood and the radius of the vessel. The physiology shows that the peripheral arteries are the main part of the blood blockage[9], because the flow resistance of the vessel is inversely proportional to fourth power of the pipe radius, and a small change of the inner diameter of the small arterials can make a large peripheral resistance. Therefore, the size of the inner diameter of the small arterials is the main factor affecting the total peripheral resistance. However, the total peripheral resistance cannot be measured directly by means of the vessel length, inner diameter and blood viscosity, and it is usually calculated using the mean blood pressure P_m and the cardiac output CO according to Equation (3).

From the above equations (2) and (3), we know that the TPR is calculated using the mean blood pressure P_m and the cardiac output CO, but the effect of the individual size on the CO is large; hence the total peripheral resistance is also affected by the size of the individual. Generally large the size of an individual is, the lower the TPR is, while the smaller the size of an individual is, the higher the TPR. Thus it is appeared that the TPR of the female group is higher than that of the male group for the normal adults in Table 1. In order to facilitate the comparison between the different individuals, this paper uses Equation (4) to calculate the total peripheral resistance index TPRI. It can be seen from Table 1 that in the same age group, the difference between the TPRI of the male and female groups is small, and the difference of the TPR is large. Thus it can be concluded that using the TPRI is more reasonable than using only the TPR to compare the blood flow resistance in the systemic circulation between the different individuals.

It can be seen from Table 1 that the CO and CI of the population decrease along with the increase in the age, and the average blood pressure P_m increases along with the increase in age, so the TPR and TPRI calculated by Equations (3) and (4) are increased along with increase in the age. These results is consistent with the change laws of the human physiology. In the same age group, there is not the significantly difference between the mean blood pressures of the male and the female groups, but the CO of the female group is significantly lower than that of the male group. Therefore, in the condition that the TPR is calculated by means of the equation (3), the TPR of the female group is higher than that of the male group.

According to the measurement results of the TPR and TPRI in Table 1 and the calculation method of the normal value in the medical statistics, it can be obtained that the normal value of the TPR is less than 1650 $dyn.s.cm^{-5}$, and that of the TPRI is less than 2650 $dyn.s.cm^{-5}.m^2$.

References

1. Kubicek W.G., WG, Karnegis JN, Patterson RP, et al. Development and evaluation of impedance cardiac output system [J]. Aerospace Med., 37: 1208, 1966.
2. Sramek BB, Rose DM and Miyamoto A. Strove volume equation with a linear base impedance model and its accuracy, as compared to thermodilution and magnetic flowmeter techniques in humans and animals [C]. Proceeding of 6th ICEBI, Zadar, Yugoslavia, 38-41, 1983.
3. Baker LE and Mistry GD. Assessment of cardiac function by electrical impedance [M]. Proceeding of 5th ICEBI., Tokyo, Japan, 7-10, 1981.
4. Patterson RP, Kubicek WG, Witsoe DA, et al. Studies on the effect of controlled volume change on the thoracic electrical impedance [J]. Med. Biol. Eng. Comput., 1978: 531-536, 1978.
5. Sakamoto K, Muto K, Kanai H, et al. Problems of impedance cardiography [J]. Med. Biol. Eng. Comput., 17: 679-709, 1979.
6. Patterson RP. Sources of the thoracic cardiogenic electrical impedance signal as determined by a model [J]. Med. Biol. Eng. Comput., 23(5): 411-417, 1985.
7. Hu Xinminr. Medical Physics, Fifth Edition [M]. Beijing: People's Health Publishing Company, 37-39, 2001.
8. Kuang Ming-Xing, Xiao Qiu-Jing, Kuang Nan-Zhen, et al. Studies on separating the impedance change components of blood vessels and ventricles in thorax from mixed impedance signals on chest surface[J]. Med. Phys., 38: 3270-3278, 2011.
9. Yao Tai. Physiology, 6th Edition [M]. Beijing: People's Health Publishing Company, 101-203, 2004.

Research on Estimation of Wheat Chlorophyll Using Image Processing Technology

Liya Zhou [1, a], Yingchun Yuan[1], Yufei Song[1] and Bin Wang[1]

[1]*Hebei Agricultural University, School of Information Science and Technology, 071001, China*

Abstract. In the field environment, the chlorophyll values of wheat leaves are estimated based on image processing. The estimation model of wheat color features and SPAD(chlorophyll value) is established. The model is tested by applying them into five different nitrogen fields, and the experimental results show that the actual value and the estimated value of the model are correlated with high significance.

1 Introduction

As a big agricultural country, China has a lot of different kinds of crops. Wheat is one of the most important economic crops so that the researching on its nutritional status is of great significance [1]. At different nitrogen levels, the color characteristics of wheat leaves are different, so the nitrogen nutrition characteristics of the crop could be judged by leaf color, and the fertilization was instructed to alleviate the waste of fertilizer and the phenomenon of land plate [2]. For a long time, the wheat experts and growers often evaluate the depth of leaf color on their naked eyes [3].This method is time consuming and laborious. The evaluation results are often qualitative and no quantitative indicators, and they are also affected by the experience of the observers. In contrast, computer recognition is more accurate than the human eyes [4]. Guo Wenchuan et.al [5] extracted the corn leaf color characteristics, the green standard value G / (R + G + B) was chosen to characterize the nitrogen content of maize leaves. Zhang yan'e et.al [6] used the digital image technique to obtain the color characteristics (R, G, B, H, I, S) of the cucumber leaf image under natural light. The results show that the color components G and H are related to the nitrogen content under the same light, and the method can be used to predict the nitrogen content of cucumber, but the model is affected by the light intensity. Zhu Hong et.al [7] extracted the color characteristics of the wheat canopy image, and evaluated the nutritional status of the wheat on the low, medium and high nitrogen levels by the histogram calculation of the RGB and HIS systems. In actually, wheat's growth is affected by the natural environment, so the research results are only a trend, which cannot accurately evaluate wheat nitrogen nutrition. Shi lei et. al [8] established an estimation model between wheat color characteristics and chlorophyll. The results show that the chlorophyll status of wheat populations could be estimated effectively by wheat color characteristics. The disadvantage of this estimation model is that the extraction of color features is not as accurate as it should be owing to the growth period and the light effects.

It is found that the jointing period of wheat is the most obvious period of the relationship between color characteristics of wheat and SPAD [9]. Therefore, in the jointing period of wheat, using the image processing technology to extract the color characteristics of wheat leaf in the field environment, the estimation model between color and SPAD was established.

2 Experimental data collection

The experiment was carried out in the Huangtuo Village (Qingyuan County, Baoding city) between the years of 2016 and 2017. In the field environment, selecting Ji Mai 22 as experimental varieties, and selecting 15 test sites numbered block from 1 to 15. Experimental urea (containing 46% N) is used as nitrogen fertilizer. In this study, five nitrogen levels were selected, respectively as N255 (pure N, 255 kg / hm2), N330 (pure N, 330 kg / hm2), plots and N-level (N), N180 (pure N, 180 kg / hm2). The corresponding relationship between plots and N levels is shown in Table 1.

[a] Corresponding author: 18730286229@163.com

Table 1. The map of block and the level of nitrogen application .

Block number	Nitrogen level / (kg/hm2)				
	0	**100**	**180**	**255**	**330**
1,8,10				※	
2,9,13		※			
3,5,12					※
4,7,14			※		
6,11,15	※				

In the jointing period of wheat, the data were collected on May 6, 2017 which included the acquisition of wheat chlorophyll value and image acquisition of wheat leaf. The leaf image was taken after the SPAD value was measured, that is, the blade image is in one-to-one correspondence with the SPAD value.

The SPAD value of wheat was obtained by chlorophyll meter [10]. Fifteen representative wheat canopy leaves were selected from each of the 15 experimental sites, with a total of 450 sample data. Take leaf from the leaf base 1/3 and measure the SPAD value, then repeat the measurement 3 times, eventually, take the average as the leaf chlorophyll content.

The wheat leaf image is captured with the Sony FDR-AXP35 4K HD camcorder and stored in BMP format. Pictures are taken when the weather is clear (to avoid the light being too strong or too dark) and without wind. The photo time is fixed within 12 am given or within 2 hours. When the lens is at the position of 100cm perpendicular to wheat leaf, the image can be taken. When taking the pictures, put a piece of pure A4 paper closer to the wheat leaves, in order to get a better extraction of the wheat leaf color. Before taking pictures, fix the camera internal parameters first, and set the exposure speed at about 1/650 s, the aperture value about F6.0. Get the picture shown in Figure 1A.

A) The Original Image B) The Normalized Image C) The Segmented Image

Figure.1 The picture before and after image processing

3 Modeling

3.1 Image Preprocessing

After the wheat leaf image is collected, it is preprocessing first. The order operation includes normalization, color segmentation and morphological processing, in which the particularly important operations are normalization and color segmentation.

3.1.1 Normalization

The light effects on the extraction of color features are very significant. Given one piece of wheat leaf, its color information is recorded under different lights, which are shown in Table 2.

Table2. Color characteristic values under different lights.

I	G	B
0.3	23	12
0.55	60	26
0.70	80	39
0.85	97	52
1.0	112	65
1.15	124	76
1.3	135	88
1.45	144	97
1.6	151	106

In table 2, the symbol I indicates the ratio between the brightness and darkness of the light, and R, G, B respectively stand for the values in the red channel, the green channel, and the blue channel of a leaf. I = 1 represents the ideal light.From table 2, the values of R, G and B are positively correlated with the light. However, the changes of I are not the same as the change of R, G and B. Therefore, the results show that the light has an effect on the color feature extraction.

As the leaf image is carried out in the field environment, the light impact on it cannot be avoided [11]. To avoiding the light impact on the color feature extraction, all the images need to be normalized, which can be achieved by using the formula (1) as follow.

$$\begin{cases} r = \frac{R}{\sqrt{R^2+G^2+B^2}} \\ g = \frac{G}{\sqrt{R^2+G^2+B^2}} \\ b = \frac{B}{\sqrt{R^2+G^2+B^2}} \end{cases} \quad (1)$$

Where, the R, G, B respectively represents the color components of the original image, and r, g, b stands for the normalized color components. The normalized image is shown in Figure 1B.

DOI: 10.1051/matecconf/201712801007

3.1.2 Color Segmentation of lages

Threshold segmentation can be divided into gray scale and color segmentation. Color segmentation is adopted in this paper in order to preserve better color information. Color segmentation can affect the accuracy of color feature extraction. Segmentation technologies have edge segmentation technology, threshold segmentation technology and regional segmentation technology. Among them, the threshold segmentations include global threshold segmentation, Otsu threshold segmentation and iterative threshold segmentation [12]. This study uses iterative threshold segmentation. Its procedure is described as follows:

(1) Set the parameters, find the minimum gray value Z0 and the maximum gray value Z1 in the image, and select the initial estimation parameter T1 = (Z0 + Z1) / 2.

(2) The image is divided by the threshold value T1. The image is divided into two parts: the gray value is greater than T1 for the C1 part, less than the T1 part of the C2.

(3) Find the average gray values u1 and u2 for the C1 and C2 pixels, and the new threshold T2 = (u1 + u2) / 2.

(4) If | T2-T1 | <T0, then T2 is the optimal threshold; otherwise, T1 = T2, and repeat steps (2) ~ (4) until the optimal threshold is obtained.

(5) The threshold image is multiplied by the RGB image to obtain a split image.

The image after color division is shown in Fig. 1C.

3.2 Color features selection

The color features can be described the surface characteristics of the image area, so the color features are widely used in image recognition. The related literatures has shown that SPAD is closely related to the color features. In this paper, 12 characteristic parameters are required to study the relationship between SPAD and color characteristics. They are the first moments(R, G, B), the second moments(SR, SG, SB), the normalized first moments(r, g, b), and the normalized second moments(Sr, Sg, Sb). Table 3 shows the results of the 12 characteristic parameters extracted from 450 samples (where id shows the leaf number and avg is the mean value).

Table 3. Color characteristic values.

id	R	G	B	SR	SG	SB	r	g	b	Sr	Sg	Sb
1	72	97	57	15	12	22	136	187	104	5	11	24
2	69	89	58	15	12	20	138	180	115	5	9	20
3	46	65	36	15	13	22	129	191	98	10	13	40
4	56	77	45	16	12	27	132	189	100	7	10	38
5	39	52	36	15	13	16	130	181	123	8	8	12
6	54	81	36	16	15	19	130	199	86	8	9	30
7	38	51	30	13	12	15	134	187	106	9	10	24
8	47	64	39	15	13	19	133	187	107	7	11	23
…	…	…	…	…	…	…	…	…	…	…	…	…
443	65	90	66	20	16	24	126	180	127	9	12	16
444	46	58	38	13	12	14	139	179	115	6	11	15
445	36	49	32	13	12	14	133	183	115	8	10	16
446	42	60	40	16	13	18	126	184	119	10	10	22
447	57	80	48	21	18	24	130	190	105	10	14	27
448	37	52	32	14	12	15	131	188	110	8	11	18
449	30	40	30	13	11	15	127	180	125	8	10	20
450	55	77	52	17	13	23	127	185	117	8	11	25
avg	53	72	39	15	13	19	134	188	100	8	11	26

The first moments R, G, B and normalized r, g, b are the components representing the color information, and the second moments SR, SG, SB and the normalized second moments Sr, Sg, Sb indicate whether the distribution of color information is uniform.

From Table 3, the first moment of the R, G, B values become larger after normalization, whereas the second moments of Sr and Sg become smaller. The results show that the influence of light reflection and shadow on the image is significant in different images. After the normalization, its color distribution span becomes smaller, and the color information is more stable, more suitable for the color diagnosis.

3.3 SPAD prediction model

The correlation between the 12 color characteristics of Table 3 and SPAD was analyzed by SPSS22.0 data analysis software, and the correlation was established as shown in Table 4.

 DOI: 10.1051/matecconf/201712801007

Table 4. Correlation between color features and SPAD value.

Number	Color feature	Correlation coefficient
1	R	-0.545
2	G	-0.589
3	B	0.183
4	SR	0.009
5	SG	-0.191
6	SB	-0.247
7	r	-0.704
8	g	-0.619
9	b	0.794
10	Sr	0.391
11	Sg	0.065
12	Sb	-0.441

Table 4 lists the correlation between color characteristics and SPAD, and the higher correlation color features are selected to establish the regression model. Experiments show that the correlation of the color eigenvalues of r, g, b and SPAD is notable. So the regression equation is described as follow (2), and its coefficient R equals to 0.85.

$$SPAD = 59.098 - 0.432r + 0.100g + 0.275b \quad (2)$$

4 Model test

The independent samples test the above estimation equation between color feature and SPAD value. Three parameters are selected to evaluate it such as the relative error of the estimated results(E), root mean square error (ERMS), and accuracy (R2). The samples are 100. The corresponding test results are shown in Table 5 below.

Table 5. Test results.

Number	Relative error	Root mean square error	Accuracy
1~20	0.043-0.137	1.7263	0.8935
21~40	0.041-0.135	1.7132	0.9100
41~60	0.042-0.139	1.6745	0.8973
61~80	0.044-0.137	1.6851	0.8896
81~100	0.046-0.137	1.6737	0.8965

From table 5, the estimated values of the model are significantly correlated with the measured values. The average of corresponding mean square error is less than 1.8, the average of relative error is between 4.3% and 13.7%, the average of accuracy is 0.8974. So all the results indicates that the estimate model has achieved a high accuracy.

5 Conclusion

In this study, image processing technology has been used to establish the estimation model of wheat color characteristics and chlorophyll. First, the color characteristics information of wheat leaf has been extracted by using color segmentation. Then the relationship between the color characteristics of wheat leaf and SPAD are also analyzed. At last, the estimation model is established ant it can achieve higher accuracy by testing in 450 image samples. However, this study is still inadequate; SPAD and partial color characteristics of the low correlation still need further study for the reason that the images are collected in the field environment, and the leaf color information collection is affected by the light impact. Otherwise, the normalized operation can remove some darker colors, so the collected color information is incomplete.

References

1. Fusuo. Zhang, Kuiqing.Wang, Weifeng. Zhang, etc., *Acta Pedologica Sinica*, 45(5), 915-92, (2008).
2. Funing Wu. Beijing, *China Agricultural University*, (2004).
3. Yuanyuan. Shi,Jinsong. Deng, Lisu. Chen, etc., *Sp ectr-oscopy and Spectral Analysis*, 30, 214-219, (2 010).
4. Tao. Liu, Xiaochun. Zhong, Chengming. Sun, etc., Scie-ntia AgriculturaSinica, 47 (4), 664-674, (201 4).
5. Wenchuan. Guo, Chaochao. Zhou, Wenting. Han, *Tra-nsactions of the Chinese Society of Agricultura l Machinery*, 42 (1),275-280, (2014).
6. Yanye. Zhang, Minzan. Li,*Transaction of the Chin -ese Society of Agricultural Machinery*, 21, 102-10 5, (2005).
7. Hong. Zhu, Limin. Zheng, Jianling. Yin, Fu'ning. Wu, *Transactions of the Chinese Society of Agricu ltural Machinery*, 26 (2), 16-20, (2010).

8. Lei. Shi, Xiaodan. Pang, Cheng. Qian, etc., *Journal of Taiyuan University of Technology,* 47(2016).
9. Zhongbo. Xiao, Liangliang. Jia, Xinping. Chen, *Chinese Agricultural Science Bulletin,*24 (8),448-453, (2008).
10. Tiancheng. Ai, Fangmin. Li, Zhian. Zhou, etc., *Journal of Hubei Agricultural College,* 20(1), 6-8, (2000).
11. Jiayue. Chen, Xia. Yao, Fen. Huang, etc., *Transactions of the Chinese Society of AgriculturalMachinery,* 32 (4), 163-170, (2016).
12. Zhibin. Zhang, Xiwen. Luo, Ying. Zang, etc., *Transa-ctions of the Chinese Society of Agricultural Machinery* ,27(7), 183-189, (2011)

 DOI: 10.1051/matecconf/201712801008

Research and Implementation of Digital Image Enhancement Algorithms

Liu Yue, Li Meishan, Ma Dandan and Liu Desheng*

College of Information Science & Electronic Technology, Jiamusi University Jiamusi,154007, China

Abstract. From the viewpoint of technique orientation, this article has realized several image enhancement techniques, which have been proved to be effective, by means of Delphi8.0 language. The experiment indicated that this procedure may be fast and accurately carried on the gradation transformation to the gradation picture and center the value filter and that can make the picture contrast gradient strengthened, the noise eliminated and the picture quality was improved.

1 Introduction

Image enhancement processing is related with a series of techniques to improve information of the focused region, weaken or remove the unnecessary information, or even to convert the whole image into more suitable information model for human and machine post-processing such as perception, analysis and recognition in the special application fields. Given that various external factors like illumination and sensor resolution have an impact on images, the original image obtained may suffer from blurred edges or reduced local or global contrast to a certain degree [1]. Thus, a good image enhancement algorithm should be able to deblur edges, improve the contrast, and effectively suppress noises of images so that the processed images are made more suitable for human eye observation or machine analysis processing.

2 Digital Image Enhancement Algorithm

2.1 Gray Transformation

Gray transformation, as an important image enhancement method, enjoys the advantage of accentuating image features by broadening the dynamic range of the image and increasing the contrast while maintaining spacial relations in the image [2]. Gray scale transformation can be denoted by g(x,y)=T[f(x,y)].

2.2 Linear Transformation

Increasing contrast is a relatively simple method which can be achieved through the linear transformation of tonal range. Suppose the gray scale range of the original image f(x,y) is [a,b] and the gray scale range of the image obtained after transformation is expected to be enlarged to [c,d]. Then, the following linear transformation can be used to achieve this target:

$$g(x, y) = c + \frac{d - c}{b - a}[f(x, y) - a] \tag{1}$$

This linear transformation is able to forcibly transform pixels whose gray scale values are smaller than a into ones with the gray scale value of b and transform pixels whose gray scale values are larger than b into ones with the gray scale value of d.

Implementation steps of the algorithm are described as follows. First, define the original image fxy and the obtained image gxy after linear transformation as a two-dimensional array, respectively [3].Then, call the image gray scale solving procedure and linear transformation procedure:

procedure initfxy;
procedure initxbh;

During the linear transformation, a = 65, b=100, c=0, d=255 are used; both rows and columns start looping from 0 to 255. If the tonal range of the original image is in a≤fxy≤b, then the image gxy=c+[(c—d)/(b—a)][f(x, y)—a] is the output; if fxy<a, then gxy=c; if fxy>b, then gxy=d. Finally, the transformed image gxy is displayed. Figure 1 is the original image. Figure 2 is the image obtained after linear transformation.

Figure 1. Original image.

* Corresponding author: zdhlds@163.com

 DOI: 10.1051/matecconf/201712801008

Figure 2. Image obtained after linear transformation.

2.3 Piecewise Linear Transformation

Piecewise linear transformation can be used to accentuate the tonal range where the interested object resides in and suppress the uninterested tonal range. Suppose that the original image f(x,y) is in [0,Mf], the tonal range of the interested object is [a,b] which is expected to be enlarged to [c,d]. The mathematical expression of this transformation is as follows:

$$g(x, y) = \begin{cases} (c / a)f(x, y) \\ [(d - c) / (b - a)f(x, y) - a] + c \\ [(Mg - d) / (Mf - b)f(x, y) - b] + d \end{cases} \quad (2)$$

First, define the original image fxy and the obtained image gxy after piecewise linear transformation as a two-dimensional array, respectively. [3] [4]:

Then, call the image gray scale solving procedure and piecewise linear transformation procedure. During the piecewise linear transformation, a=55, b=100, Mf =255, c=15,d=225, Mg =255 are used; rows and columns start looping from 0 to 255. If fxy is in [0,a], then gxy=(c/a)f(x,y); if fxy is in [a,b], then gxy=[(d-c)/(b-a)f(x,y)-a]+c; if fxy is in [b, Mf], then gxy=[(Mg-d)/(Mf-b)f(x,y)-b]+d. The image obtained after piecewise linear transformation gxy is shown in Figure 3.

Figure 3. Image obtained after piecewise linear transformation.

Figure4. Image obtained after nonlinear transformation.

2.4 Nonlinear Transformation

Certain nonlinear functions like exponential functions and logarithmic functions can be used as mapping functions to implement nonlinear transformation of image gray scale [5].

2.4.1 Logarithmic Transformation

The general expression of logarithmic transformation is

$$g(i, j) = a + \frac{\ln[f(i, j) + 1]}{b \bullet \ln c} \quad (3)$$

where a, b and c are parameters introduced for adjusting the position and shape of the curve. When the lower gray scale area is expected to be significantly stretched while higher gray scale area is expected to be compressed, logarithmic transformation can be used to make the gray scale distribution compatible with human visual characteristics.

2.4.2 Exponential Transformation

The general expression of exponential transformation is

$$g(i, j) = b^{c[f(i,j)-a]} - 1 \quad (4)$$

Parameters a, b and c are used to adjust the position and shape of the curve. This transformation is able to significantly stretch the higher gray scale area of an image. Figure 4 shows the image obtained after nonlinear transformation.

2.5 Histogram Equalization

Histogram equalization is one of the most frequently used and important image enhancement spatial domain methods. Histogram equalization revises the histogram of the original image into one with evenly distributed gray scale by using the gray scale transformation function and then revises the original image according to this obtained histogram[6-8].

Histogram equalization is a histogram modification method based on cumulative distribution function transformation. Suppose that the transformation function is

$$s = T(r) = \int_0^r p_r(\omega)d\omega$$

where ω is the integration variable while T(r) is r's cumulative distribution function. The cumulative distribution function here is a function of r, which monotonically increases from 0 to 1. So this transformation function meets the condition that the monodromy of T(r) monotonically increases in $0 \le r \le 1$. It can be proved that using the cumulative distribution function of r as the transformation function can produce an image with evenly distributed gray scale and probability density. As a result, the dynamic range of pixel values has been expanded. The image enhancement technology for the purpose of obtaining an even histogram is called histogram equalization processing or histogram linearization processing. The cumulative distribution function can be expressed in the discrete form as:

$$S_k = T(r_k) = \sum_{j=0}^{k} \frac{n_j}{n} \quad \text{k=0,1,2,...l-1} \quad (5)$$

2.6 Median Filtering

Noise jamming of a certain degree exists in any original image. Eliminating these noises is known as image filtering. The purpose of image filtering is to improve the image quality and to make it ready for feature extraction [8-10]. Median filtering is an edge-preserving algorithm with excellent performance. Median filtering replaces local average with the local median. Suppose that [f(x,y)] represents a digital image array, the value of f(x,y) represents gray scale. Then, the image obtained after median filtering is [g(x,y)], where g(x,y) is the median of gray scales of all pixels covered by the N×N window with (x,y) as its center point.

The distribution of gray scale values of the first small area in the image is shown as follows:

a1 a2 a3
a4 a5 a6
a7 a8 a9

The new value of Point a5 after median filtering is equal to the fifth numerical value after the sequencing. The image processed by median filtering is then displayed. Figure 6 is an example of median filtering.

Figure5. Image obtained after histogram equalization.

Figure 6. Image obtained after median filtering.

3 Conclusion

Image enhancement is an essential link in image processing. The three image enhancement methods discussed above are fundamental. In practice, the problems of images must be analyzed first before deciding which method or group of methods should be used for image enhancement.

Acknowledgment

The work was financially supported by the key scientific and research projects of Jiamusi University(12Z1201520, 13Z1201576) and Scientific and technological innovation team construction project of Jiamusi University (Cxtdpy-2016-03)

References

1. Sheng, Yu, and W. Wang. "Design and Implementation of Compression Algorithm Comparator for Digital Image Processing Based on Component." The, International Conference for Young Computer Scientists IEEE Computer Society, 2008:1337-1341.
2. Jia, Tong, C. D. Wu, and D. Y. Chen. "Research and implementation of a digital image processing education platform." International Conference on Electrical and Control Engineering IEEE, 2011:6719-6722.
3. Lorenzo, Jorge Gonz, et al. A MapReduce Implementation of the Spreading Activation Algorithm for Processing Large Knowledge Bases Based on Semantic Networks. IGI Global, 2017.
4. Seng, Cheong Loke, K. A. Kasmiran, and S. A. Haron. "A Software Application for Survey Form Design and Processing for Scientific Use." IEEE Access PP.99(2017):1-1.
5. Alareqi, Mohammed, et al. "An Efficient FPGA Implementation of Real Time Hardware Co-Simulation for Digital Image Enhancement Algorithms Using Xilinx System Generator." The International Conference on Wireless Technologies Embedded and Intelligent Systems Wits-2016 Ensa of Kenitra 21-22 April 2016.

6. Stuchilin, Vladimir Valerievich, V. A. Rumyantseva, and I. S. Svirin. "The Use of Digital Signal Processing Algorithms for Electrophysiological Diagnostics of Cardiovascular Diseases." Biomedical & Pharmacology Journal (2017):119-128.
7. Deng, Xiaojun, et al. "Research and Implementation of a Scalable Automatic Enhancement Technique for DR Image." Recent Advances in Electrical & Electronic Engineering (2016).
8. Zoican, Sorin, R. Zoican, and G. Dan. "METHODS FOR REAL TIME IMPLEMENTATION OF IMAGE PROCESSING ALGORITHMS." Upb Scientific Bulletin 77.2(2015):137-148.
9. Singh, Manvendra, et al. "FPGA based implementation of real-time image enhancement algorithms for Electro-Optical surveillance systems." International Conference on Electrical Engineering/electronics, Computer, Telecommunications and Information Technology IEEE, 2015:1-6.
10. Feng, Yutian, et al. "Research and implementation of remote gas meter direct reading based on image processing." Electronic Measurement Technology (2016).

MATEC Web of Conferences **128**, 01009 (2017) DOI: 10.1051/matecconf/201712801009
EITCE 2017

Adaptive Scale Compressive Tracking with Feature Integration

Mingqi Luo[1,a], Tuo Wang[2] and Bin Zhou[1]

[1]*The school of Electronic and Information Engineering, Xi'an Jiaotong University, Xi'an, Shanxi, China*
[2]*Xi'an Jiaotong University Suzhou Academy, Suzhou, Jiangsu, China*

Abstract. Compressive tracking (CT) is utilized to cope with real-time tracking, which use a very sparse measurement matrix to compressive samples of targets and background, then a classifier is trained to distinguish foreground and background. However, this algorithm suffers from the drifting problem, and used the fixed size tracking box to detect, recognize, and update the samples and classifier. In order to solve these problems, we adopt a different way to extracted positive samples, and employ powerful features to exploit the advantages of feature fusion to describe target, a scale pyramid is used to realize adaptive scale tracking. Experimental results on various benchmark video sequences demonstrate the superior performance of our algorithm.

1 Introduction

Object tracking is one of the most important subjects in computer vision for its various applications in video surveillance, robotics, human computer interaction and driver-less vehicle. The job of tracking is to estimation the target states in subsequent frames under the condition that the initialized state of the target in the start frame has been know via a sequence of measurements made on the object. Despite significant progress has been made in recent years, the problem is still a tough difficult due to partial occlusion, geometric deformation, motion blur, illumination changes, background clutter and scale variations [1]. Tracking methods with fixed models of target usually fail because of the unavoidable changes of appearance. This is why the online learning methods are used to handle the variations in appearance. The learning methods that used by the online tracking can be divided into generative and discriminative methods. In generative online learning methods, the appearance of model for target is updated adaptively in response to appearance variations [2, 3, 4]. The discriminative methods utilize information about the target and the background simultaneously and tracking is treated as a classification problem [5, 6].

The sparse representation and compressed sensing techniques have attracted a great deal of attention in visual tracking. These algorithms represent target as a sparse combination of target templates. Zhang [7]proposed an effective tracking algorithm with a discriminative model, named compressive tracking, known as CT, adopts a very sparse measurement matrix to efficiently extract the features for the appearance model which makes is possible for real-time tracking and achieves relatively good results on some challenging video sequences. However, the algorithm suffers from the drifting problem because it just using a single feature to represent target, we can employ various powerful features to exploit the advantages of feature fusion. Secondly, the CT algorithm used the fixed size tracking box to detect, recognize and update the samples and classifier. Obviously, in practical, the target scale usually changed with the target moving. The fixed size tracking box easily caused the target lost when the target changed significantly in scale and it was not suitable in practical application. In [8], authors present a multi-scale compressive tracker. This tracker integrates an improved appearance model based on normalized rectangle features extracted in the adaptive compressive domain into the bootstrap filter. The compressive features of a particle in special scale were achieved by the projection via a modified adaptive random measurement matrix. This matrix is updated based on the initial matrix and the corresponding particle's current scale value. A 2-order transition model which considers two previous statuses has been used to estimate the current position and scale status for each particle. In [9], presents a novel enhanced compressive tracking. It not only utilizes the instances at the current frame, but takes the appearance of target in previous frames into account, experiments proved this way can obtain a much more effective classifier to detect object at each frame. In order to deal with the target appearance change, in [10], constructed a feature template using online vector boosting, because it filtering the noisy, this algorithm can deal with target appearance change. In [11], the motion estimator was introducing into appearance model in compressive space.

In this paper, we have proposed an effective and efficient tracking algorithm. The key contribution of this work can be summarized as follows. Firstly, we employ various powerful features to exploit the advantages of feature fusion. There are two types of features used in our

[a] Corresponding author: lmq232x@163.com

proposed tracker. Secondly, when the tracking window determined, a certain number of positive samples are extracted by the Gaussian distribution around the point of the canter of the tracking window. Thirdly, in order to estimation the scale accurately, a scale pyramid is used.

2 Compressive tracking

The compressive sensing (CS) theory states that an original high-dimensional sparse or compressible signal can be reconstructed from a low-dimensional signal, that is to say, 'random projection' and the 'random measurement matrix' are two important concepts involved with compressive sensing. From the compressed sensing theory[12], for a measurement matrix $R \in R^{n \times m}$, $n << m$ if we want to use R to compress high-dimensional signals (high-dimensional signals are compressible, such as image, video, audio, etc.) to low signals, while the low-dimensional signal can contain almost all the information, R should satisfy the sparse and restricted isometry property(RIP). Baraniuk et al. [13] proved that the random matrix satisfying the Johnson-Lindenstrauss lemma also holds true for the restricted isometry property in compressive sensing. Therefore, if the random matrix in (1) satisfies R the Johnson-Lindenstrauss lemma, it can reconstruct x with minimum error from v with high probability if x is compressive such as audio or image.

$$v = Rx \tag{1}$$

In CT, in order to tackle scale problems, a set of rectangle filters at multiple scales $\{h_{1,1}, \ldots, h_{w,h}\}$, defined as

$$h_{i,j}(x, y) = \begin{cases} 1, 1 \le x \le i, 1 \le y \le j \\ 0, otherwise \end{cases} \tag{2}$$

Where i and j are the width and height of a rectangle filter, respectively, is used to convolve z , $z \in R^{w \times h}$. Thus, a high-dimensional multi-scale image feature vector $x = (x_1, x_2, \ldots, x_n) \in R^n$, where $n = (wh)^2$ can be obtained. In [14], a random Gaussian matrix $R \in R^{n \times m}$, which is a typical matrix satisfying restricted isometry property(RIP), is utilized to reduce the dimensionality. The entries in R are defined as

$$r_{ij} = \sqrt{s} \times \begin{cases} 1 \quad with \quad probability \dfrac{1}{2s} \\ 0 \quad with \quad probability \dfrac{1}{2s} \\ -1 \quad with \quad probability \dfrac{1}{2s} \end{cases} \tag{3}$$

In compressive tracking algorithm, the random measurement matrix is computed only once offline and remain fixed throughout the tracking process. Then the feature vector which is projected onto lower-dimensional space would be computed efficiently.

After calculating the features, updating the classifier with these features is followed. Diaconis and Freedman [15] showed that the random projections of high dimensional random vectors are almost always Gaussian. Therefore μ and σ can be used to simulate the random features of rectangular distribution after projection using the equation (4), where $y = 1$ means positive samples, $y = 0$ means negative samples.

$$\begin{cases} p(v_i \mid y = 1) \sim N(\mu_i^1, \sigma_i^1) \\ p(v_i \mid y = 0) \sim N(\mu_i^0, \sigma_i^0) \end{cases} \tag{4}$$

The scale parameters in(4) are incrementally updated

$$\begin{cases} \mu_i^1 \leftarrow \lambda \mu_i^1 + (1 - \lambda)\mu^1 \\ \sigma_i^1 \leftarrow \sqrt{a} \end{cases} \tag{5}$$

Where

$$a = \lambda(\sigma_i^1)^2 + (1-\lambda)(\sigma^1)^2 + \lambda(1-\lambda)(\mu_i^1 - \mu^1)^2 \tag{6}$$

$$\begin{cases} \sigma^1 = \sqrt{\dfrac{1}{n} \sum\limits_{k=0|y=1}^{n-1} (v_i(k) - \mu^1)^2} \\ \mu^1 = \dfrac{1}{n} \sum\limits_{k=0|y=1}^{n-1} v_i(k) \end{cases} \tag{7}$$

$$H(v) = \log\left(\frac{\prod_{i=1}^{n} p(v_i \mid y = 1) p(y = 1)}{\prod_{i=1}^{n} p(v_i \mid y = 0) p(y = 0)}\right) = \sum_{i=1}^{n} \log\left(\frac{p(v_i \mid y = 1)}{p(v_i \mid y = 0)}\right) \tag{8}$$

By integrating the equation (5) and (7) to update the classifier, the $\lambda > 0$ is a learning parameter.

The process of searching the target is first to sample some samples around the target in the previous frame. The extracted sample features with different dimensions of the rectangle to convolution filter is every sample of high dimensional feature vector x , and then use the sparse measurement matrix R to do projection to the low dimensional vector v on compressed domain. And v can be calculated by generalized Haar-like features [16]. A naïve Bayes classifier is adopted to classify object as shown in Equation (8). The maximum value of the corresponding sample in $H(v)$ is the target of the next frame image.

3 The tracker

When a target is determined by a rectangle in the first frames, let point $X = (x_0, y_0)$ be the center of the rectangle, the number of positive samples center extracted around the center point with Gaussian distribution $N(\mu, \sigma)$, all of these samples have same size of the current tracking rectangle window.

Color histogram[17] which is used in this paper has been widely used to represent, analyze, and characterize images. They allow for significant data reduction, and can be computed efficiently. Color histograms are robust to noise and local image transformation. In the target tracking domain, color histogram are a popular form of target representation, because of their independence from scaling and rotation, and robust to partial occlusions. Denote by $\{x_i\}_{i=1,\dots,n}$ the normalized pixels in target region. The probability of the feature $u(u=1,\dots,m)$ in the target model is computed as[18]:

$$\begin{cases} q=\{q_u\}_{u=1,2,\dots,m} \\ q_u = C_h \sum_{i=1}^{n} k(\left\|\frac{x_i}{h}\right\|^2)\delta(b(x_i)-u) \end{cases} \tag{9}$$

Where q is the target model, q_u is the probability of the uth element of q , δ is the Kronecker delta function, $b(x_i)$ associates the pixel x_i to the histogram bin and $k(x)$ is an isotropic kernel profile. Constant C_h is a normalization function defined by:

$$C_h = \frac{1}{\sum_{i=1}^{n_h} k(\left\|\frac{x_i}{h}\right\|^2)} \tag{10}$$

Similarly, the probability of the feature u in the target candidate model from the candidate region centered at position y is given by:

$$\begin{cases} p(y)=\{p_u(y)\}_{u=1,2,\dots,m} \\ p_u(y) = C_h \sum_{i=1}^{n} k(\left\|\frac{y-x_i}{h}\right\|^2)\delta(b(x_i)-u) \end{cases} \tag{11}$$

$$C_h = \frac{1}{\sum_{i=1}^{n_h} k(\left\|\frac{y-x_i}{h}\right\|^2)} \tag{12}$$

Where $p(y)$ is the target candidate model, $p_u(y)$ is the probability of the uth element of $p(y)$, $\{x_i\}_{i=1,\dots,n_h}$ are pixels in the target candidate region centred at y , h is the bandwidth and C_h is a normalization function.

In order to calculate the likelihood of the target model and the candidate model, a metric based on the Bhattacharyya coefficient[19] is defined by using the two normalized histograms q and $p(y)$ as follows

$$d(y)=\sqrt{1-\rho[\hat{p}(y),\hat{q}]} \tag{13}$$

Where

$$\rho(y) \equiv \rho[\hat{p}(y),\hat{q}] = \sum_{b=1}^{m} \hat{p}_b(y)\hat{q}_b \tag{14}$$

Histogram of oriented gradient (HOG) is one of the most popular visual features in vision community, since it is very effective in practical applications and can be computed efficiently. HOG feature was extracted on the distribution of the edge of targets in local region; it is a good representation of object shapes.

Because the HOG puts emphasis on the image gradient while color histogram focuses on the color information, that is to say, the two features are complementary to each other. The overall algorithm is summarized into Algorithm1.

Algorithm 1 ASFICT

Input t-th video frame

Step1. A certain number of positive samples whose center of those samples obeys the Gaussian distribution around the center point of the previous tracking window are extracted, randomly crop some negative samples far away from the target box, and extracted the features of color histogram and HOG feature.

Step 2. Use the Naïve classifier to each feature vector and find the tracking location with the maximal classifier response.

Step 3. Building the scale pyramid on the current location, extracted the color histogram and HOG feature on each scale pyramid, find the most similarity scale whose features have the most similarity with the previous features.

Step 4. Extracted samples as step1 to updated the classifier just as the CT algorithm.

Output: tracking location and the scale parameters.

4 Experiments

In this section, we implement our method on 7 challenging sequences, compared with the latest three algorithms (CT[7], WMIL[20], and FCT[14]). All the video clips are publicly available (all of the sequences can be download on visual tracking benchmark). For fair comparison, we use the source or the binary codes provided by the authors with tuned parameters for the best performance. Our MATLAB implementation currently runs on an Intel(R) 3.30GHz CPU with4.00GB RAM. All the challenging sequences were showed in Table 1.

Sequence	Main challenge
David2	scale, illumination and pose changes
Sylvester	pose changes
walking	self-occlusions
faceocc2	particle occlusions
tiger1	comprise illumination and pose variations
Tiger2	motion blur and particle occlusion
Lemming	clutter

Table 1 The challenging sequences

We use two metrics to evaluate the performance of our tracking method, that is success rate (SR) and center location error (CLE) which are used in FCT tracking algorithm. The success rate is used in the PASCAL VOC challenge [21] defined as,

$$score = \frac{area(ROI_T \cap ROI_G)}{area(ROI_T \cup ROI_G)} \tag{15}$$

where ROI_T is the tracking bounding box and ROI_G is the ground truth bounding box. If the $score$ is larger than 0.5 in one frame, the tracking result is considered as success. In this paper, the ROI_T and ROI_G are present by its area.Table2 shows the tracking results in terms of success rate. The center location error is defined as the Euclidean distance between the central locations of the tracked objects and the manually labeled ground truth. Table 3 shows the average tracking errors of all methods.

Sequence	TF	ASFICT -FF	CT-FF	WMI L-FF	FCT-FF
Tiger1	353	3	77	32	3
Tiger2	364	20	48	28	18
Walking	411	80	68	50	116
David2	536	40	10	3	58
Sylvester	1000	7	9	63	15
Faceocc2	813	0	0	2	0
Lemming	299	20	29	0	21
A-SR	--	24.2	34.4	25.4	33

Table 2

Sequence	TF	ASFICT -FF	CT-FF	WMIL-FF	FCT-FF
Tiger1	353	22	37.0	24	22.4
Tiger2	364	27	47.4	31	37.7
Walking	411	30.1	22.5	38	28.9
David2	536	15.9	20	7.1	16.9
Sylvester	1000	8.6	9.0	9.1	8.5
Faceocc2	813	16.3	7.3	16	16.3
Lemming	299	30.3	22	39	24.3
A-SR	--	21.4	23.6	23.4	22.1

Table 3

Where TFrames is the total frames of single sequences, FF is the number of failed tracking frames, A-SR it the average success rate, A-CLE is the average CLE. We note that our method has lower fail tracking frames and less average CLE.

Fig1 shows the error plots of OUR algorithm, compressive tracking algorithm, fast compressive tracking algorithm, and weighted multiple instance learning tracking algorithm applied to the lemming, tiger2 and walking tested sequences.

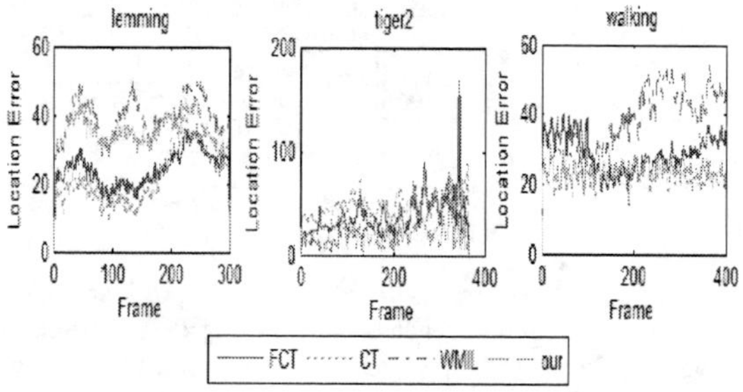

Fig 1

According to the experimental results showed by Table2, Table3, we can observe that our algorithm achieves the superior performance for most of test sequences in terms of the illumination, clutter and blurs motion. Compared with other state-of-art algorithm, ASFICT algorithm is more robust and effective.

5 Conclusions

In this paper, we proposed an effective and efficient tracking algorithm based on CT algorithm. In order to exploit the advantages of feature fusion, we choose the color histogram and HOG feature to descript target. Because in practical, the target scale usually changed with the target moving, then we use the scale pyramid to achieve adaptive compressive tracking. Experimental results on many challenge video clips, showed superior performance of our algorithm.

Acknowledgment

Research supported by National Natural Science Foundation of China (No.61071217) and Jiangsu Science and Technology Program Foundation (No.BK20141216)

References

1. Yilmaz,O.Javed,M.Shah, ACM, Computing Surveys **38**(2006).
2. Ross, D., Lim, J., Lin, R., Yang, M.-H. IJCV **77**(2006)
3. Li, H., Shen, C., Shi, Q.CVPR(2011)
4. Mei, X., Ling, H.,PAMI,33(2011)
5. Grabner, H., Grabner, M., Bischof,(2006)
6. Babenko, B., Yang, M.-H., ,PAMI**33**(2011)
7. K. Zhang, L. Zhang, and M. Yang,ECCV(2012)
8. Yunxia Wu · Ni Jia · Jiping Sun,31(2015)
9. Rui Xu, Xiaodong Gu,IAPR(2013)
10. Qingshan Liu, IEEE Trans Cybern,**1**(2016)
11. Eric Wang, Jorge Silva, 2009 IEEE/SP
12. D. Donoho. IEEE Trans. Information Teory,**4**(2006)
13. Diaconis, P., Ann. Stat.**12**(1984)
14. K. Zhang, L. Zhang, IEEE transactions on pattern analysis and machine intelligence.**36**(2014)
15. E.J. Candes and T. Tao. IEEE Transactions on Information Theory, 12(2005).
16. Viola P, Jones M,CVPR(2001)
17. P.Perez, C.Hue, J.Vermaak,ECCV**1**(2002)
18. D.Coumaniciu, V.Ramesh, IEEE Trans. on Pattern Analysis and Machine Intelligence, **25**(2003)
19. Kailath,T., IEEE Trans. Commun.Technol.,**1**(1967)
20. K. Zhang, H. Song. Pattern Recognition, **46**(2013)
21. Yi Wu , Jongwoo Lim. CVPR,(2013)

MATEC Web of Conferences 128, 01010 (2017) DOI: 10.1051/matecconf/201712801010
EITCE 2017

Adaptive Multi-part Target Representation for Tracking

Mingqi Luo[1,a], Tuo Wang[2] and Bin Zhou[1]

[1]The school of Electronic and Information Engineering, Xi'an Jiaotong University, Xi'an, Shanxi, China
[2]Xi'an Jiaotong University Suzhou Academy, Suzhou, Jiangsu, China

Abstract. In this paper we propose and evaluate an effective approach based on multiple colour histograms. The target is adaptively divided into non-overlapping regions. The proposed partition does not weaken the robustness of the colour histogram representation; it can be used to any class targets. Experimental results show that the proposed representation improve the tracking accuracy and decrease the number of iterations.

1 Introduction

Visual localization and tracking plays a central role for many applications like intelligent video surveillance, smart transportation monitoring etc. Localization and tracking algorithms aim to find the most similar region to the tracking in image sequence. One of the most crucial difficulties in robust tracking is the construction of representation models that can accommodate the illumination variations, deformable appearance changes, partial occlusions, etc.

Colour histograms have been widely used to represent, analyse, and characterize images. They allow for significant data reduction, and can be computed efficiently; moreover colour histograms are robust to noise and local image transformation. In the target tracking domain, colour histogram are a popular form of target representation, because of their independence from scaling and rotation, and robust to partial occlusions [1]. Nevertheless the robustness of such a model is weakened in challenging tasks due to the lack of spatial information. This problem can be limited by computing more than one histogram on different parts of the target [2], but there is no generally accepted solution for a generic division.

In this paper we propose and evaluate an effective approach based on a multi-part model. The target is divided into non-overlapping regions in order to increase the tracking sensitivity to rotations and anisotropic scale changes. The proposed partition does not weaken the robustness of the colour histogram representation; it can be used to any class targets.

2 Mean shift tracking algorithm

Mean shift algorithm war first proposed by Fukunage and Hostetler [3] in 1975. Coumaniciu[4]employed the MS algorithm successfully in feature space analysis. MS algorithm was also used in image smooth and image segmentation, and got good performance.

2.1 Target representation

In object tracking domain, a target is usually defined as a rectangle or an ellipsoidal region in image. Currently, a widely used target representation is the color histogram because of its independence of scaling, rotation and partial occlusion. Denote by $\{x_i\}_{i=1,\dots,n}$ the normalized pixels in target region. The probability of the feature $u(u=1,\dots,m)$ in the target model is computed as [1]:

$$\begin{cases} q=\{q_u\}_{u=1,2,\dots,m} \\ q_u = C_h \sum_{i=1}^{n} k\left(\left\|\frac{x_i}{h}\right\|^2\right)\delta(b(x_i)-u) \end{cases} \quad (1)$$

Where q is the target model, q_u is the probability of the uth element of q, δ is the Kronecker delta function, $b(x_i)$ associates the pixel x_i to the histogram bin and $k(x)$ is an isotropic kernel profile. Constant C_h is a normalization function defined by:

$$C_h = \frac{1}{\sum_{i=1}^{n_h} k\left(\left\|\frac{x_i}{h}\right\|^2\right)} \quad (2)$$

Similarly, the probability of the feature u in the target candidate model from the candidate region centered at position y is given by:

$$\begin{cases} p(y)=\{p_u(y)\}_{u=1,2,\dots,m} \\ p_u(y) = C_h \sum_{i=1}^{n} k\left(\left\|\frac{y-x_i}{h}\right\|^2\right)\delta(b(x_i)-u) \end{cases} \quad (3)$$

[a] Corresponding author: lmq232x@163.com

DOI: 10.1051/matecconf/201712801010

$$C_h = \frac{1}{\sum_{i=1}^{n_h} k(\left\|\frac{y-x_i}{h}\right\|^2)} \qquad (4)$$

Where $p(y)$ is the target candidate model, $p_u(y)$ is the probability of the uth element of $p(y)$, $\{x_i\}_{i=1,\dots,n_h}$ are pixels in the target candidate region centred at y, h is the bandwidth and C_h is a normalization function.

In order to calculate the likelihood of the target model and the candidate model, a metric based on the Bhattacharyya coefficient [5] is defined by using the two normalized histograms q and $p(y)$ as follows

$$d(y) = \sqrt{1-\rho[\hat{p}(y),\hat{q}]} \qquad (5)$$

$$\rho(y) \equiv \rho[\hat{p}(y),\hat{q}] = \sum_{b=1}^{m} \hat{p}_b(y)\hat{q}_b \qquad (6)$$

2.2 Mean shift

Minimizing the distance $d(y)$ in (5) is equivalent to maximizing the Bhattacharyya coefficient $\rho[\hat{p}(y),\hat{q}]$ in (6). The optimization process is an iterative process and is initialized with the target position, denoted by y_0, in the previous frame. By using the Taylor expansion, the linear approximation of the Bhattacharyya coefficient $\rho[\hat{p}(y),\hat{q}]$ can be obtained as:

$$\rho(y) \approx \frac{1}{2}\sum_{u=1}^{m}\sqrt{p_u(y_0)q_u} + \frac{C_h}{2}\sum_{i=1}^{n}\omega_i k(\left\|\frac{y-x_i}{h}\right\|^2) \qquad (7)$$

$$\omega_i = \sum_{u=1}^{m}\delta(b(x_i)-u)\sqrt{\frac{q_u}{p_u(y_0)}} \qquad (8)$$

Since, the first term in (7) is independence of y, to minimize the distance in (5) is to maximize the second term in (7). In the mean shift iteration, the estimation target moves from y to a new position y_1, defined as

$$y_1 = \frac{\sum_{i=1}^{n}\omega_i x_i g(\left\|\frac{y-x_i}{h}\right\|^2)}{\sum_{i=1}^{n}\omega_i g(\left\|\frac{y-x_i}{h}\right\|^2)} \qquad (9)$$

3 Adaptive target representations

3.1 Adaptive partition

Since the colour histogram is the whole statistical characteristics of the target, its lack of spatial information, as it depends on the colour feature, it cannot give good performance when an object and its background have similar colours.

In the case of rectangle-based trackers the adaptive partition is as follows.

$$k = \frac{w}{h} \qquad (10)$$

Where w h are the width and height of the rectangle, respectively. Defined $k_0 = 2$. The adaptive partition is as Fig1:

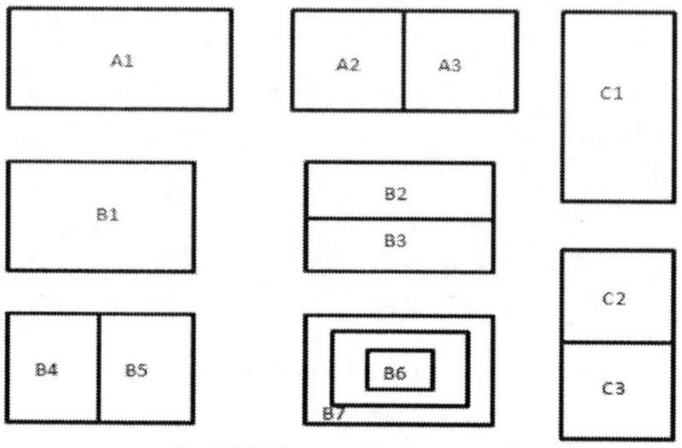

Fig.1 Multi-part representation

When $k > k_0$, that is $w > 2h$, the moving target is partition into A1, A2 and A3; when $0.5k_0 < k < k_0$, the moving target is partition intoB1, B2, B3, B4, B5, B6 and B7; when $0 < k < 0.5k_0$, the moving target is partition into C1, C2 and C3, where B6 have half width and height of the original rectangle, B7 have double width and height of the original rectangle.

3.2 The weighted Bhattacharyya coefficient

The Bhattacharyya coefficient is used to calculate the likelihood of the target model and the candidate model. Emilio Maggio and Andrea Cavallaro [6] using the average Bhattacharyya coefficient as the finally coefficient. They do not consider that the different parts have difference impact to the whole likelihood. In this paper, we adopt that the more likelihood of the same sub-part of the rectangle, the bigger weights. A commonly used weight is calculated as follow:

$$\omega'(i) = \frac{BC(p_i(y),q_i)}{\sum_{j=1}^{C} BC(p_i(y),q_i)} \qquad (11)$$

$$\rho(y) = \sum_{i=1}^{C}\rho(\hat{p}_i(y),\hat{q}_i)\omega'(i) \qquad (12)$$

Where $\omega(i)$ denote the weight of $i-th$ sub-part, $BC(p_i(y),q_i)$ is the Bhattacharyya coefficient between $p_i(y)$ and q_i, C is the number of the sub-part, $p_i(y)$ and q_i are the probability distribution of target model and the candidate model, respectively, $\rho(y)$ is the finally Bhattacharyya coefficient between target model and candidate model.

3.3 The algorithm

Given:

The target model $\{q_u^i\}_{u=1,2,...,m}$, $i=1,2,...,C$, and its location y_0 in the previous frame. The width w and height h of the external rectangle.

Step1. Using the width and height decide the adaptive partition, and calculate the sub-part target model.

Step 2. Initialize the location of the target in the current frame with y_0, computer $\{p_u^i(y)\}_{u=1,2,...,m}$, $i=1,2,...,C$, and evaluate the Bhattacharyya coefficient $\rho[q, p(y_0)]$ between each same sub-part by(10) and (11).

Step 3. Derive the weights $\{\omega(i)\}_{i=1,2,...,m}$ according to (8).

Step 4. Find the next location of the target candidate according to (9).

Step 5. Compute $\{p_u^i(y)\}_{u=1,2,...,m}$, and the Bhattacharyya coefficient $\rho[q, p(y_1)]$ of each sub-part between $\{p_u^i(y)\}_{u=1,2,...,m}$ and $\{q_u^i\}_{u=1,2,...,m}$.

Step 6. While $\rho[q, p(y_1)] < \rho[q, p(y_0)]$

Do $y_1 = 0.5(y_1 + y_0)$

Evaluate the $\rho[q, p(y_1)]$

Step 7. If $\|y_1 - y_0\| < \varepsilon$, then stop.

Otherwise set $y_0 = y_1$ and go to step3.

4 Implementation of the algorithm

In order to select the most appropriate color feature, Emilio Maggio [6] described and evaluated eight representations. The eight representations are derived from seven color spaces: RGB, rgb, rg, CIELab, XYZ, YCbCr, and two representations based on HSV (HSV-D, HSV-UC) [7]. After the evaluating eight different color, they conclude that the RGB-based representation outperformances the others. In this paper, the RGB feature space is selected.

The parameters are the same for all test sequences, and are described in the following. The Epanechnikov profile is accepted in these experiments. To satisfy the low-computational cost imposed by read-time processing discrete densities, $16\times16\times16$ -bins histograms used in RGB feature spaces. Maximum number of iterations is 10. The results presented in this section are based on a dataset of targets extracted from 6 different test sequences, including faces, vehicles and pedestrian. All of these test sequence is download on [8] and [9]. Fig2 showed the target initialization.

Fig.2. Target initialization

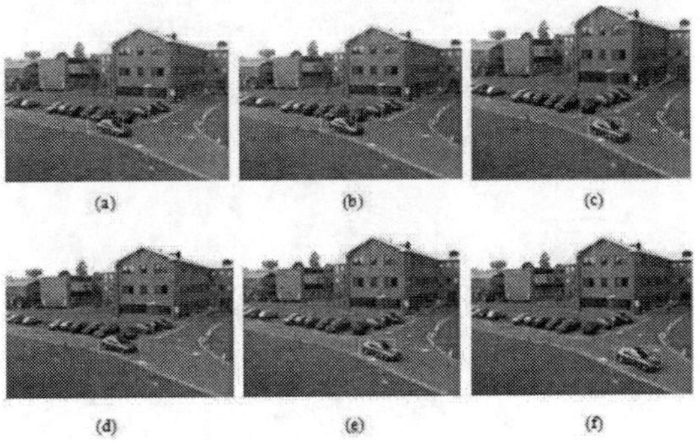

Fig.3. The tracing results

Fig.3. showed the car's tracking results. (a), (b) and (c) are the results of the traditional single-histogram tracking algorithm. (d), (e) and (f) are the results of the adaptive multi-part representation tracking results; all of the results are initialization with the same. They are the 24th, 39th and 51th, respectively. By analyzing these results, it is possible to notice that the multi-part representation improves in average the performances. Apparently, compare the frame of 39th, the single-histogram tracking algorithm does not contain the whole car, but the multi-part representation does. However, this algorithm is still some problems as single-histogram algorithm. Apparently, the scale is remaining the same throughout the tracking process.

Fig4 showed the curve of the number of iterations of different multi-part representation on faces sequences as showed in the middle of top row of the Fig2.

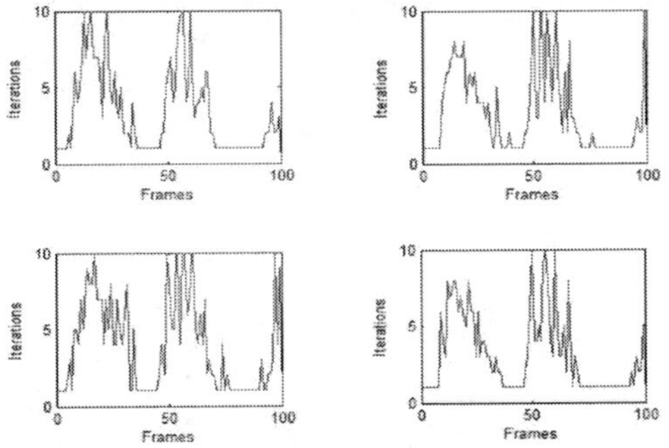

Fig.4. The number of iterations

DOI: 10.1051/matecconf/201712801010

In the left of the top row is the single-histogram, the right is the two-part partition representations, the left bottom is the seven-part partition representations, the right is the two-part partition representations as the series of the A,B and C showed in Fig1, respectively. The average number of iterations is 3.96, 3.15, 3.18 and 2.91, obviously, the number of iteration is decrease.

5 Conclusions

To summarize, we have proposed an adaptive multi-part target representations methods for tracking. Its adaptive decides the ways that divided the target by the size of external rectangle. The weighted Bhattacharyya coefficient is used to calculate the likelihood of the target model and the candidate model. Experimental results showed that the proposed adaptive multi-part representation is more accurate than the single histogram, and achieves better results in predicting the correct orientation. Future work includes investigating an adaptive scale change.

Acknowledgment

Research supported by National Natural Science Foundation of China (No.61071217) and Jiangsu Science and Technology Program Foundation (No.BK20141216).

References

1. D.Coumaniciu, V.Ramesh. IEEE Trans. on Pattern Analysis and Machine Intelligence,**125**,(2003)
2. P.Perez, C.Hue, J.Vermaak, ECCV,**1**(2002)
3. K.Fukunage and L.D.Hostetler, IEEE Trans.on Information Theory,**1**(1979)
4. D.Coumaniciu and P.Meer, IEEE trans.on Pattern Analysis and Machine Intelligence,**5**(2002)
5. Kailath,T., IEEE Trans. Commun.Technol.,**15**(1967)
6. Emilio Maggio and Andrea Cavallaro, Proc IEEE Int Conference on Image Processing. Genoa,(2005)
7. http://www.poynton.com/PDFs/coloureq.pdf.
8. http://www.iipl.fudan.edu.cn/~zhangjp/Dataset/fd_pede_dataset_intro.htm.
9. http://www.elec.qmul.ac.uk/staffinfo/andrea/MP.html.

TxCP: A Coprocessor for LTE-A

Xin Huang[a], QingBin Liu, JunNing Wu, XueLiang Du and DongLin Wang

Institute of Automation, Chinese Academy of Sciences, University of Chinese Academy of Sciences, 95 Zhongguancun East Road, 100190, Beijing, China

Abstract. With the widely use of 4G network, the corresponding bandwidth processing has become a critical issue. The current recognized 4G network is LTE-A. In the baseband processing for LTE-A, the processing of its physical layer algorithm is the biggest bottleneck for current processors. The use of application specific integrated circuit (ASIC) design has become necessary. This article will introduce a communication dedicated coprocessor (TxCP), specifically for LTE-A physical layer uplink shared/control channel (PUSCH/PUCCH) algorithm for bit-level acceleration. Its internal support for PUSCH/PUCCH CRC, Turbo encoding, equation definable convolutional encoding, data channel and control channel rate matching, channel interleaving, scrambling and modulation supporting QPSK, 16QAM and 64QAM. And in order to ensure that the coprocessor has a certain degree of flexibility, its internal controller design will support a variety of modes to ensure that some of the algorithm modules can be run separately. The programming model of the processor is relatively simple, and the user does not need to go through a complicated design.

1 Introduction

In the physical layer processing flow of LTE-A, the encoding process involves many small bitwidth bit-level processing, such as the characteristics of high density data operations (channel estimation), small bitwidth data interleaving characteristics (rate matching, channel interleaving), and some specific complex algorithms (Turbo decoding, Viterbi decoding). In different channels, these algorithms will have different application modes. The coding channels in LTE/LTE-A are also divided into various types, such as PUSCH, PUCCH, and PRACH [1]. In this article, we mainly support the PUSCH and PUCCH for coding and modulation process.

There is a high demand for peak rates in LTE physical layer solutions. LTE requires the downlink peak rate to reach 100Mbps, the uplink peak rate to reach 50Mbps [2]. This may be relatively easy for baseband processing designs. However, in LTE-A, the downlink peak rate requirements of 1Gbps, uplink peak rate requirements of 500Mbps [3]. This brings a lot of challenges to baseband processing.

At present, baseband processing is mainly based on general purpose processor (GPP), FPGA, digital signal processor (DSP) and coprocessor. But for the bit-level processing of the physical layer coding processing, GPP and DSP are difficult to achieve the desired speed requirements. For large-scale application solutions, the cost of FPGA is a problem, and FPGA will bring a lot of power problems. In this case ASIC solutions become a very good choice. In the article [4], we can see that ASICs have been specifically designed for hardware acceleration of PDSCH, PBCH and PMCH.

In this article, we present a coprocessor (TxCP) design specifically for PUSCH and PUCCH. The coprocessor specifically accelerates the encoding process for PUSCH and PUCCH. The entire acceleration process involves the cyclic redundancy check (CRC), turbo encoding, convolutional encoding, data information and control information rate matching, channel interleaving, and scrambling and modulation supporting for three modulation modes. In addition, in order to ensure that the operation modes of TxCP have some flexibility, TxCP internal parts of the algorithm modules can be separately scheduled.

The rest of this paper is organized as follows. Section 2 describes the overall architecture, internal modules, and the internal operations of the controller of TxCP. Section 3 introduces the results of the TxCP performance evaluation, including the synthesis results provided by Synopsys's DC tools. Finally, we summarize our work in section 4.

2 TxCP Architecture

The TxCP is internally composed of six configurable submodules for the LTE/LTE-A physical layer algorithm (CRC, TEC, CCE, RM, CIM, SMC). The configuration of each submodule is controlled by a unified top-level controller.

2.1 Overall Architecture

The TxCP is divided into three main parts: the controller, the memory, and the algorithm modules. The TxCP is

[a] Xin Huang: huangxin2015@ia.ac.cn

DOI: 10.1051/matecconf/201712801011

internally controlled by a controller. The memory is responsible for storing the input data of the TxCP and the intermediate processing result of the algorithm modules. The algorithm modules accelerate PUSCH algorithms, a total of six modules. The overall architecture is shown in Figure 1.

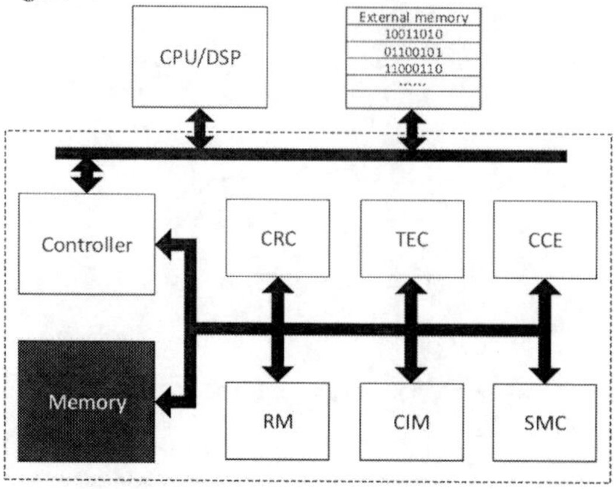

Figure 1. TxCP overall architecture.

2.2 Cyclic Redundancy Check

The Cyclic Redundancy Check module completes the CRC check in 4G communication. The module consists of CRC-8, CRC-16, CRC-24a, CRC-24b four basic modules and control module. CRC-8 is mainly used for checking CQI information. CRC-16 is mainly used for downlink control channel and broadcast channel data transmission verification. CRC-24A and CRC-24B are mainly used for the verification of PUSCH data. CRC supports big/little-endian two different storage methods. And for multi-code block check, CRC supports both CRC-24A and CRC-24B. As the input interface is 8-bit width, CRC complements 0 in high bit for the code blocks which its bit length is not an integral multiple of 8-bit. And the check information is appended into the data information to output.

2.3 Turbo Encoding Coprocessor

The turbo encoding coprocessor (TEC) implements the turbo encoding of data information. In accordance with the requirements of the LTE-A protocol [5], this module has three-way information output, respectively, the original information, direct check information, and information interleaved in the memory and then encoded. The original information is essentially obtained by directly outputting the input data. The direct check information is obtained by encoding the input data. So the original information in this module and the direct check information is output in parallel. The third path information is obtained by interleaving all the data read into memory and then encoding the information after the interleaving is completed. This completes the 1/3 rate turbo coding function.

2.4 Convolutional Coding Engine

The convolutional coding engine (CCE) applys a more general solution. CCE can not only solve the LTE-A scenario, but also contain all the 1/4 bit rate, 1/3 rate and 1/2 rate of the constraint length of 7 convolutional coding, while supporting non-tail-biting and tail-biting convolutional coding. To meet these solutions, CCE allows the user to configure the equations required for convolutional coding through the registers in the TxCP. Therefore, in the LTE-A solution, only need to apply coding rate 1/3 to CCE. Figure 2 shows the convolutional coding solution in LTE-A with three-way convolution constraints of 133 (octal), 171 (octal), and 164 (octal). In order to achieve 1/3 rate, the fourth convolutional encoding of the configuration register is set to 0, the other three in its corresponding register can be configured in the corresponding value.

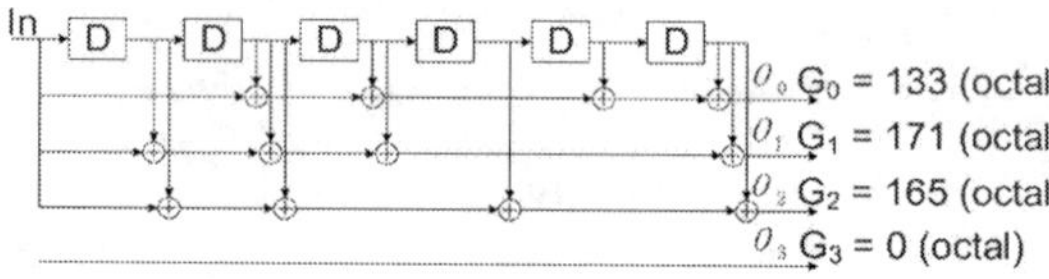

Figure 2. CCE configuration in LTE-A.

2.5 Rate Matching

The rate matching module supports the rate matching of the data channel and the control channel, and also has the function of code block concatenation. The rate matching module first needs to interleave the three sets of data streams from the turbo encoder or the convolutional encoder separately (the data channel and the control channel are interleaved differently) and are filled with null bits, and then the data is passed to the rate matching of the bit collection, selection and transmission module. The bit selection module is responsible for entering 3-way data streams into a circular buffer. The null bits are then deleted when selecting bits, and the result is output according to the start bit and length in the configuration [5].

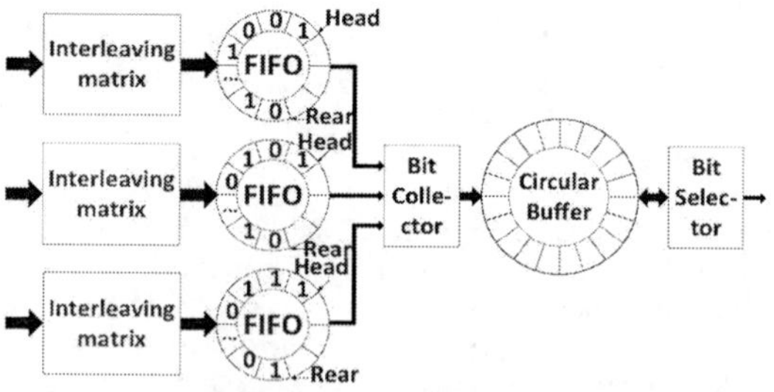

Figure 3. RM module diagram

The above is an implementation scheme in LTE-A. In this design, a first-in first-out queue (FIFO) will be added between the interleaving matrix and the bit collector, as shown in Figure 3. This operation affects the order of bits entering the circular buffer. Therefore, in addition to receiving the three sets of data from FIFO after interleaved, the bit collection and selection module will receive empty bit location information to ensure the correctness of the data entering the circular buffer.

 DOI: 10.1051/matecconf/201712801011

2.6 Channel Interleaving Module

Channel interleaving module (CIM), to achieve the RI, CQI, DATA, ACK four different information intertwined [6]. Channel interleaving module needs to support QPSK, 16QAM, 64QAM three different modulation methods, support different loop prefix mode, support different information of different interweaving. The module uses 6-bit bitwidth 10K memory as the physical mapping of the interleaving matrix, mapping the interleaved matrices of different number of columns (9,10,11,12) into memory. Using 8-bit output interface, the use of travel listed in the way, the output information to the lower module. For RI, ACK, and CQI information for some modules, cyclic fetches are made from 32-bit registers, reducing the dynamic power consumption of information in memory and reducing overall power consumption.

2.7 Scrambling and Modulation Coprocessor

The scrambling and modulation coprocessor (SMC) mainly scrambles and modulates the data outputted by the channel interleaver. SMC supports the generation of pseudo-random sequences, generating random sequences in a specific way according to the initial sequence set. And then the generated random sequence and input data XOR to scramble the data. Finally, the results of the scrambling are modulated. In this design, the modulation supports three modes, QPSK, 16QAM and 64QAM. In LTE-A, the placeholder X/Y will be used in the ACK and RI information. In the scrambling process, the position of the placeholder X/Y needs to be judged in order to obtain the correct symbol for modulation. So the mechanism used to determine the ACK and RI information is added to the SMC. The judgment process is based on the information provided by the CIM module.

2.8 TxCP Controller

The controller is responsible for the overall control within the TxCP, including the entire PUSCH channel encoding process and the control of the modulation process. TxCP supports up to seven operating modes through a finite state machine: Data only mode, Data + UCI mode, UCI only mode, CRC mode, TEC mode, CCE mode, CIM mode. The first three modes are the control modes for the PUSCH channel encoding process, which will schedule all the modules within the TxCP. The remaining four modes are for a single module within the TxCP.

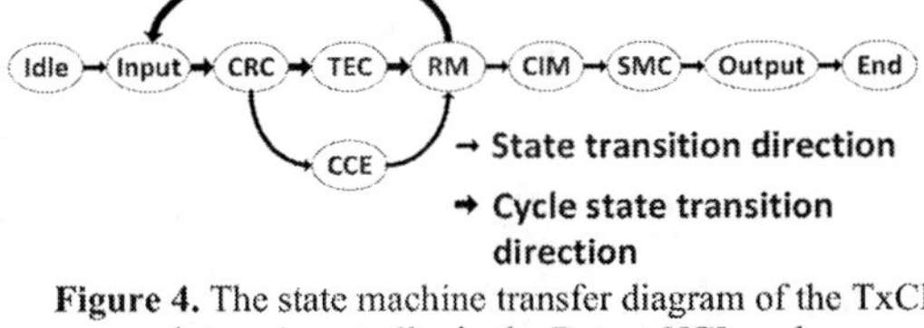

Figure 4. The state machine transfer diagram of the TxCP internal controller in the Data + UCI mode

Take the Data + UCI mode as an example, as shown in Figure 4 for the TxCP controller internal state machine transfer diagram in this mode. The thick lines in the figure represent the transition paths that need to be cycled in the case of multi-code blocks. In our design, TxCP supports a total of 13 code blocks, so the maximum number of loops is 13. In each loop, the RM is responsible for concatenation of the multi-code blocks. After the above cycle, the controller controls the TxCP to continue reading CQI information from the outside, via CRC, CCE, RM, and finally completing channel interleaving and scrambling and modulation, and eventually outputting the result.

There are 81 registers in the TxCP, 72 of which are configured for the internal algorithm module, and the rest is the overall configuration of the TxCP configuration. One of the registers is used to start TxCP. There is also a register that is responsible for storing the memory address where the data resides. After TxCP is started, the controller will determine the operating mode according to the contents of the configuration register, and reads the data into the internal memory of the TxCP according to the configured address. Then the controller will write the configuration registers of each submodule to the corresponding module. When multiple blocks are present, some modules have multiple sets of configurations. The controller of the TxCP will configure the algorithm module according to the number of blocks that should be handled at present. These internal registers of the TxCP are configured by writing to a Slave port of the TxCP via an external CPU or DSP.

After the algorithm module has been executed, TxCP will transfer the result data to the data output address specified by the configuration register. After doing the above, the controller sends an interrupt request to indicate that the task is completed. The CPU can write to one of the registers inside the TxCP to cancel the interrupt.

3 TxCP Performance evaluation

TxCP is designed to work at 600MHz frequency. So TxCP simulation test is also carried out in this frequency. In the current TxCP test, TxCP throughput performed well. Especially in the face of more data volume, TxCP can play the best performance. As shown in Table 1, it is the maximum throughput for the three operating modes for PUSCH. The throughput Thp_{in} is calculated as shown in equation (1), where D_{in} is the total input data and T is the total time from TxCP startup to sending interrupt request:

$$Thp_{in} = D_{in}/T \quad (1)$$

The output data in unit time Thp_{out} is calculated as shown in equation (2), where D_{out} is the total output data of the test case:

$$Thp_{out} = D_{out}/T \quad (2)$$

As shown in the table, TxCP has a high throughput in Data-only mode and Data + UCI mode. One of the main reasons why TxCP perform bad in UCI-only mode is that the input data in this mode is quite small, and the rate matching module and the channel interleaving module interleave and reuse the data multiple times, resulting in a large amount of output data. So the throughput in this mode will be very low. The corresponding Thpout has a high value. We can conclude that the test case that produces the maximum throughput multiplexed the data so many times.

Table 1. TxCP Maximum throughput in different operating mode.

TxCP operating mode	Maximum Thp_{in} (Mbps)	The Thp_{out} of corresponding test cases (Mbps)
Data-only	297.44	1866.30
Data+UCI	289.64	1769.27
UCI-only	0.39	5128.78

Table 2. The synthesis results of TxCP.

Technology	TSMC 28nm
Area	25
Power	20
Frequency	19

TxCP not only has a high throughput, its area and power consumption on the same good performance. The TxCP synthesis is carried out under the DC tool provided by Synopsys. The results obtained are shown in Table 2.

4 Summary

As a solution for LTE-A PUSCH/PUCCH, TxCP has six modules for the communication physical layer algorithm. Part of the algorithm modules use a common design, to ensure that the TxCP has a certain degree of scalability and compatibility. The TxCP is controlled by an internal controller. The controller can support seven operating modes. There are three modes dedicated to the PUSCH of LTE-A, and the remaining four modes can individually schedule the sub-modules within TxCP to cope with more application scenarios. TxCP has a good performance, running at 600MHz under the maximum throughput of up to 297.44Mbps. TxCP also has a very good area and power performance.

Acknowledgments

This work is supported by the Strategic Priority Research Program of Chinese Academy of Sciences (under Grant XDA-06010402).

References

1. 3GPP TS36.211, Evolved Universal Terrestrial Radio Access (EUTRA); Physical Channels and Modulation (Release 11).
2. S. Sesia, I. Toufik, and M. Baker, LTE-The UMTS Long Term Evolution: From Theory to Practice, Wiley Publishing ,7 (6): 437-440 (2009).
3. A. Ghosh, R. Ratasuk, B. Mondal, N. Mangalvedhe, T. Thomas, LTE-advanced: next-generation wireless broadband technology, Wireless Communications, IEEE, **17**(3) :10-22 (2010).
4. K. G. Digish, R. Thilagavathy, ASIC Implementation of Physical Downlink Shared Channel for LTE, ICCICCT, IEEE:370-376(2014).
5. 3GPP TS36.212, Evolved Universal Terrestrial Radio Access (EUTRA); Multiplexing and channel coding (Release 11).
6. FaTang Chen, Yan Chen, Research and DSP realization of uplink channel interleaver and deinerleaver in LTE system, AET, **37**(5):60-63. (2011).

 DOI: 10.1051/matecconf/201712801012

Research on High-tech Ammunition Training System Based on Virtual Reality Technology

Zhang Meng, Xu Lutie, Yu Weibo, Liu Hongbo

Abstract. With the development of computer technology, the virtual reality technology has become more and more widely used in military field. The training of high-tech ammunition has the problems of low efficiency, high cost, poor security and inconsistent working mechanism. This paper fully analyzes the construction objectives and main contents of the high-tech ammunition virtual training, and applies virtual reality technology and Vega Prime to achieve the simulation of the process of a rocket weapon system to combat the target. This paper also makes further research on the technology of rocket trajectory calculation, real-time collision detection, etc., and achieves the whole process of combat simulation of the weapon system. The establishment of the system opened a new dimension of the military ammunition combat training .

1 Introduction

Currently, there are several methods of the training of large complex ammunition equipment system as follows: Firstly, learning the relevant theories through pictures, videos, animation or multimedia resources,etc.; Secondly, strengthening the theoretical understanding and securitying skills via internship and practical training such as manipulating ammunition models and their main components; Thirdly, understanding the combat applications and combat security of ammunition by observing in troops .Due to the limitations of equipment, cost, safety risk and other teaching conditions, there are only scant chances for students to carry on live warfare program training[1]. Although certain training effect can be obtained from this kind of training mode, its defects in many aspects, such as reproducing the training process, simulating small probability events, showing the actual scene and self-training still exist. Students can not correct cognitive errors on their own initiative, besides, their abilities to deal with emergencies and psychological endurance for harsh battlefield environment can’t get equipped or improved[2]. Solving the various problems and contradictions mentioned above has become problems that need to be solved urgently for ammunition combat operations and combat security research institutions.

The application of virtual reality technology in ammunition training is a new way to solve the contradictions above. Since the technology possesses abilities to simulate ammunition combat environment and smoke light effects and sense the relative position and attitude of the operator/ammunition in the characteristic environment, it is very suitable for the combat operation and security training of ammunition equipment. This technique not only allows the trainees to master the equipment theory and combat skills before training for confrontation[3-5], but also minimizes the actual operation accident caused by personal factors, holding great potential to achieve the ideal training effect and the best military economic benefits.

2 Function and Composition of Ammun-ition Virtual Reality System

2.1 The goal of the system

The objective of this system is to complete a integrated dynamic simulation system of the structure, component status, ammunition emission, ammunition movement of a rocket weapon system. Data and status are graphically described entirely, which can be tested, improved, and evaluated for technical and tactical performance[6].

2.2 Function of the system

The main function of the system is to simulate the whole process of a rocket weapon system to hit the target with the command car commanding the launch vehicle to aim and launch after locating the target position under the command of the simulation control node. Here are the specific processes:

1) The simulation control node is responsible for controlling the signal generation;

2) It generates a control signal and transmits it to the weapon system;

3) Completing the simulation of the process includes rocket loading, barrel lift, gunpowder burning and launch, etc. based on the control command and physical model.

[a] Corresponding author: Zhang Meng, E-mail: 1027032562@qq.com, Tel: 18031441240

4) Completing the rocket shooting under the comman-d of control signal;

5) Completing the simulated scenes and effects display of all the process;

6) Carrying out the dynamic observation process of profile;

7) It possesses multi-window display function.

The system performer is the user and the simulation control node, which provide the information or issue instructions to the system respectively, and the system provides operational results based on them[7-9].

2.3 The composition of the system

The logical structure of a rocket weapon system simulation based on Vega Prime is shown in Fig.1, and the diagram includes a simulation control node and a simulation demonstration node, which communicate by UDP protocol communication via the network connection. The simulation demonstration node consists of network management and transmission module, analog signal simulation module, visual simulation module, physical simulation module, database processing module and result visualization module.

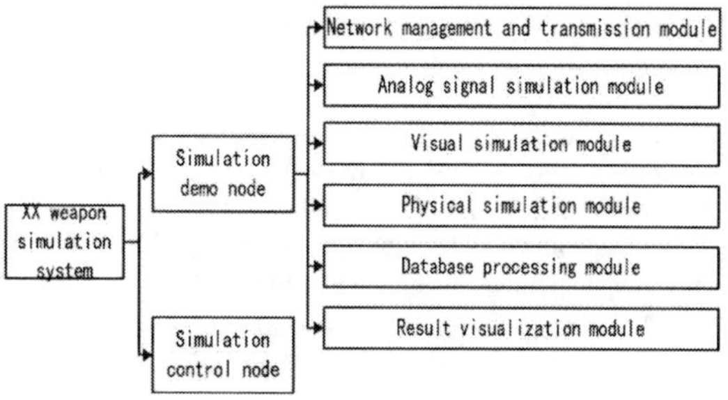

Figure 1. The structure of system

3 The key technology of the system

The effect of the simulation system depends mainly on the authenticity of the system motion model. The motion model of the system mainly includes rocket flight and collision detection, etc[10].

3.1 Trajectory model

3.1.1 Coordinate system and conversion relationship

For the convenience of the theoretical research and simulation of the rocket's motion in the inertial space, this paper establishes the emission coordinate system $oxyz$, the missile coordinate system $ox_1y_1z_1$, the quasi-missile coordinate system $ox_4y_4z_4$, the quasi-velocity coordinate system $ox_vy_vz_v$ and the trajectory coordinate system $ox_2y_2z_2$. And the Earth coordinate system $o_ex_ey_ez_e$ and 84 coordinate system WGS-84 are also be utilized in order to meet the need of guidance simulation[11].

For the convenience of analysis, coordinates need to be converted, commonly used are:

(1) The conversion matrix from $o_ex_ey_ez_e$ to $oxyz$

$$C_e^f = \begin{bmatrix} -\cos\lambda_0\sin B_0\cos A_0 - \sin\lambda_0\sin A_0 & -\sin\lambda_0\sin B_0\cos A_0 + \cos\lambda_0\sin A_0 & \cos B_0\cos A_0 \\ \cos\lambda_0\cos B_0 & \sin\lambda_0\cos B_0 & \sin B_0 \\ \cos\lambda_0\sin B_0\sin A_0 - \sin\lambda_0\cos A_0 & \sin\lambda_0\sin B_0\sin A_0 + \cos\lambda_0\cos A_0 & -\cos B_0\sin A_0 \end{bmatrix} \quad (1)$$

Then conversion relationship of the speed vector from $o_ex_ey_ez_e$ to $oxyz$ is:

$$\begin{bmatrix} V_x \\ V_y \\ V_z \end{bmatrix} = C_e^f \begin{bmatrix} V_{xe} \\ V_{ye} \\ V_{ze} \end{bmatrix} \quad (2)$$

The transformation of the position coordinate component from $o_ex_ey_ez_e$ to $oxyz$ is:

$$\begin{bmatrix} x \\ y \\ z \end{bmatrix} = C_e^f \begin{bmatrix} x_e - R_{xe0} \\ y_e - R_{ye0} \\ z_e - R_{ze0} \end{bmatrix} \quad (3)$$

Where:

$$\begin{cases} R_{xe0} = (N + h_0)\cos B_0 \cos\lambda_0 \\ R_{ye0} = (N + h_0)\cos B_0 \sin\lambda_0 \\ R_{ze0} = (N(1-e^2) + h_0)\sin B_0 \end{cases} \quad (4)$$

$$N = a_e / \sqrt{1 - e^2 \sin^2 B_0} \quad (5)$$

R_{xe0} 、 R_{ye0} 、 R_{ze0} ——The component of the geocentric vector at launch point in the earth coordinate system;

x_e 、 y_e 、 z_e ——The component of geocentric vector at the centroid of the rocket in the earth coordinate system;

N ——The radius of prime circle of launch point.

(2) The conversion matrix from $ox_1y_1z_1$ to $oxyz$ is:

$$C_1^f = \begin{bmatrix} \cos\phi\cos\psi & -\sin\phi\cos\psi\cos\gamma + \sin\psi\sin\gamma & \sin\phi\cos\psi\sin\gamma + \sin\psi\cos\gamma \\ \sin\phi & \cos\phi\cos\gamma & -\cos\phi\sin\gamma \\ -\cos\phi\sin\psi & \sin\phi\sin\psi\cos\gamma + \cos\psi\sin\gamma & -\sin\phi\sin\psi\sin\gamma + \cos\psi\cos\gamma \end{bmatrix} \quad (6)$$

(3) The conversion matrix from $oxyz$ to $ox_4y_4z_4$ is:

$$C_f^4 = \begin{bmatrix} \cos\phi\cos\psi & \sin\phi & -\cos\phi\sin\psi \\ -\sin\phi\cos\psi & \cos\phi & \sin\phi\sin\psi \\ \sin\psi & 0 & \cos\psi \end{bmatrix} \quad (7)$$

(4) The conversion matrix from $ox_4y_4z_4$ to $ox_1y_1z_1$ is:

$$C_4^1 = \begin{bmatrix} 1 & 0 & 0 \\ 0 & \cos\gamma & \sin\gamma \\ 0 & -\sin\gamma & \cos\gamma \end{bmatrix} \quad (8)$$

3.1.2 Rocket dynamic equation

(1) The kinematic equation of centroid motion of the rocket established in the emission coordinate system is:

$$\begin{bmatrix} \frac{dx}{dt} \\ \frac{dy}{dt} \\ \frac{dz}{dt} \end{bmatrix} = \begin{bmatrix} V_x \\ V_y \\ V_z \end{bmatrix} \quad (9)$$

(2) The angular velocity equation of the rocket in the quasi-missile coordinate system is:

$$\begin{bmatrix} \frac{d\gamma}{dt} \\ \frac{d\psi}{dt} \\ \frac{d\varphi}{dt} \end{bmatrix} = \begin{bmatrix} \omega_{x4} - \omega_{y4} tg\varphi \\ \frac{\omega_{y4}}{\cos\varphi} \\ \omega_{z4} \end{bmatrix} \quad (10)$$

(3) The kinetic equation of centroid motion in the coordinate system is:

$$\begin{bmatrix} \frac{dV_x}{dt} \\ \frac{dV_y}{dt} \\ \frac{dV_z}{dt} \end{bmatrix} = \frac{1}{m} \begin{bmatrix} F_x + F_{rkx} + F_{cx} + F_{gx} + R_x \\ F_y + F_{rky} + F_{cy} + F_{gy} + R_y \\ F_z + F_{rkz} + F_{cz} + F_{gz} + R_z \end{bmatrix} + \begin{bmatrix} g_x \\ g_y \\ g_z \end{bmatrix} + \begin{bmatrix} a_{cx} \\ a_{cy} \\ a_{cz} \end{bmatrix} + \begin{bmatrix} a_{ex} \\ a_{ey} \\ a_{ez} \end{bmatrix} \quad (11)$$

(4) The kinetic equation of the centroid rotation established in the quasi-coordinate system is:

$$\begin{bmatrix} J_{x4}\frac{d\omega_{x4}}{dt} \\ J_{y4}\frac{d\omega_{y4}}{dt} \\ J_{z4}\frac{d\omega_{z4}}{dt} \end{bmatrix} = \begin{bmatrix} M_{x4} + M_{rkx4} + M_{cx4} + M_{gx4} \\ M_{y4} + M_{rky4} + M_{cy4} + M_{gy4} \\ M_{z4} + M_{rkz4} + M_{cz4} + M_{gz4} \end{bmatrix} - \begin{bmatrix} 0 \\ (J_{x4} - J_{z4})\omega_{x4}\omega_{z4} \\ (J_{y4} - J_{x4})\omega_{x4}\omega_{y4} \end{bmatrix} + \begin{bmatrix} 0 \\ -J_{z4}\omega_{z4}\frac{d\gamma}{dt} \\ J_{y4}\omega_{y4}\frac{d\gamma}{dt} \end{bmatrix} \quad (12)$$

(5) Geometric relationship equation. Assuming the vertical component of wind is 0, the Mach number equation of the rocket relative to the atmospheric speed and dynamic pressure is:

$$\begin{bmatrix} W_x \\ W_y \\ W_z \end{bmatrix} = \begin{bmatrix} -W\cos(A_0 - A_w) \\ 0 \\ W\sin(A_0 - A_w) \end{bmatrix} \quad (13)$$

$$\begin{bmatrix} V_{xw} \\ V_{yw} \\ V_{zw} \end{bmatrix} = \begin{bmatrix} V_x \\ V_y \\ V_z \end{bmatrix} - \begin{bmatrix} W_x \\ W_y \\ W_z \end{bmatrix} \quad (14)$$

$$V_w = \sqrt{V_{xw}^2 + V_{yw}^2 + V_{zw}^2} \quad (15)$$

$$M_{aw} = \frac{V_w}{\sqrt{1.4 \times 287.053 T_H}} \quad (16)$$

$$q = \frac{1}{2}\rho_H V_w^2 \quad (17)$$

Convected acceleration and Coriolis acceleration due to the objective existence of the earth rotation when the rocket is launching:

$$\begin{bmatrix} a_{ex} \\ a_{ey} \\ a_{ez} \end{bmatrix} = \begin{bmatrix} \omega_e^2 - \omega_{ex}^2 & -\omega_{ex}\omega_{ey} & -\omega_{ex}\omega_{ez} \\ -\omega_{ex}\omega_{ey} & \omega_e^2 - \omega_{ey}^2 & -\omega_{ey}\omega_{ez} \\ -\omega_{ex}\omega_{ez} & -\omega_{ey}\omega_{ez} & \omega_e^2 - \omega_{ez}^2 \end{bmatrix} \begin{bmatrix} R_{xd} \\ R_{yd} \\ R_{zd} \end{bmatrix} \quad (18)$$

$$\begin{bmatrix} a_{cx} \\ a_{cy} \\ a_{cz} \end{bmatrix} = \begin{bmatrix} 0 & 2\omega_{ez} & 2\omega_{ey} \\ 2\omega_{ez} & 0 & 2\omega_{ex} \\ 2\omega_{ey} & 2\omega_{ex} & 0 \end{bmatrix} \begin{bmatrix} V_x \\ V_y \\ V_z \end{bmatrix} \quad (19)$$

In the formula above: F is the engine thrust; Rx4、Ry4、Ry4 is the aerodynamic; gx、gy、gz is the gravity; Frkx、Frky、Frkz is the Coriolis force of the gas stream; Fcx1、Fcy1、Fcz1 is the pulse control force; Fgx、Fgy、Fgz is the interference force;Mx4、My4、Mz4 is the aerodynamic moment;Mrkx4、Mrky4、Mrkz4 is the Coriolis moment of gas flow;Mcx1、Mcy1、Mcz1 is the control torque; Mgx4、Mgy4、Mgz4 is the interference torque;

3.2 Collision detection model

BUMP is a collision detection method based on the bounding box. In the simulation system, Since Vega Prime is a frame-based operation, the rocket motion trajectory is a motion curve composed of many discrete points. When the flight speed exceeds the threshold value, the target may locate between the two points, and the system can not detect the collision. Therefore, the BUMP method must be improved. First, it is necessary to calculate the shape change of the bounding box, and transform matrix T.

$$T = T_{rx}T_{ry}T_{rz} = \begin{bmatrix} 1 & 0 & 0 & 0 \\ 0 & \cos\theta & \sin\theta & 0 \\ 0 & -\sin\theta & \cos\theta & 0 \\ 0 & 0 & 0 & 1 \end{bmatrix} \bullet \begin{bmatrix} \cos\phi & 0 & -\sin\phi & 0 \\ 0 & 1 & 0 & 0 \\ \sin\phi & 0 & \cos\phi & 0 \\ 0 & 0 & 0 & 1 \end{bmatrix} \bullet \begin{bmatrix} \cos\varphi & \sin\varphi & 0 & 0 \\ -\sin\varphi & \cos\varphi & 0 & 0 \\ 0 & 0 & 1 & 0 \\ 0 & 0 & 0 & 1 \end{bmatrix} \quad (20)$$

In order to improve efficiency and accuracy, the method used in this system is: No collision detection is performed before hitting the target. If the distance vector angle between current frame and next frame is greater than right angle, take several points on the track for bounding box collision detection. If there is no collision, target is not hitted. This method needs less amounts of computation and is relatively accurate[12].

S_h is the centroid of the rocket, $b(S_h)$is bounding box of object, A is the vector from the rocket to target, The algorithm is as follows:

1) Calculating the current frame vector A_c

2) Calculating the next frame vector A_n according to the frame interval

3) If $A_c \cdot A_n \leq 0$, take several points on the track between the two frames and calculate the $b(S_h)$

4) If (exist b(Sh)!=Φ), turn on effects

5) Else do not turn on special effects (Did not hit the target)

6) If $A_c \cdot A_n \geq 0$, then $A_c = A_n$

7) Goto 2)

During the flight of the missile, the system compares the methods before and after the improvement. The results show that the possibility of detecting the collision by the former method is inferior in the state of high-speed flight. In 50 experiments, crossing phenomenon was happened. While using the improved methods, crossing phenomenon did not occur in all the 50 experiments, which means the success rate was 100%.

4 Design and implementation of the system

4.1 Realization of rocket flight process

Rocket flight process can be divided into several stages include uncontrolled section, free flight section, closed-loop display guidance, proportional guidance, etc. The simulation of the rocket on the trajectory is shown in Fig.2 and Fig.3.

Figure 2. The process of rocket movement

Figure 3. The process of rocket movement

In order to observe the battlefield thoroughly, the simulation system used the form of picture-in-picture to monitor. Users can switch between different windows as needed. Flight attitude and trajectory of rocket can be obtained from rocket tracking window. The target tracking window is mainly responsible for monitoring the trajectory of the target, the collision between the rocket and the target, and the degree of damage after the target is hitted.

4.2 Realization of hitting target

Rocket gun simulation is the key part of the weapon system simulation, The initial state, flight trajectory, placement of every rocket projectile should be calculated separately. In order to standardize the movement of rockets, the system defines a structure that contains the spatial motion attributes and control parameters of the bomb.

```
typedef struct gun_ shot |
    double timeout;                 //rocket life
    double flight_ time;            //flight duration
    float x0, y0, z0, h0, p0, r0; //position
    float Vx, Vy, Vz;               //the speed of the rocket
    float az;                       //rocket Acceleration
    float starttime;                //starting time
    int state;                      //status
    vpIsector * los;                //impact checking
    vpCommon*handle;                //rocket handle
    vpPosition* pos;                //Position parameter
| Shot;
```

As the rockets hit different targets with different exploding effects and destructive consequences, the system sets different eigenvalues to islands and trees, etc. In the rocket collision detection, the system will determine the special effects and damage results caused by eigenvaluse based on the results.

Figure 4. The simulation of rocket trajectory

Figure 5. The effect of blast damage

5 Concluding remarks

Under the new situation, how to break the traditional teaching mode, focus on actual combat, adapt the training of ammunition talents to the requirement of construction and development at information age and carry out experimental teaching reformation of ammunition technology as well as combat utilization is an important project faced by military ammunition applications and security work. This paper bases on the virtual reality technology, and utilizes standardized software and hardware to construct a simulation platform which combines the technology and tactics to present the rocket action process. Results show that the simulation model of the platform is authentic and efficient, and the visualization effect is good, besides, the results possess high degree of simulaiton. The system has laid a solid foundation for the establishment and development of teaching resources and application abilities for virtual simulation teaching platform aiming at follow-up model rockets.

References

1. Guida M., Lanzotti A.Improving design validation of playground equipment in virtual reality[J].Internatio -al Journal on Interactive Design and Manufacturing, 2013,7(3):191-201.

DOI: 10.1051/matecconf/201712801012

2. Lim C.K., Chen I.M., Yeo S.H.A virtual reality syste -m for arm and hand rehabilitation [J].Frontiers of M echanical Engineering,2011,6(1):347-354.
3. J Rigelsford.Virtual Reality Technology[J].Presence, 2015,12(6):663-664.
4. ZM Aghajan, L Acharya, JJ Moore.Impaired spatial selectivity and intact phase precession in two dimensional virtual reality[J].Nature Neuroscience, 2015,18(1):121
5. W Wang, Z Lv, X Li, W Xu.Virtual Reality Based GIS Analysis Platform[J].International Conference on Neural Information, 2015:638-645
6. C Chou, H Hsu, Y Yao.Construction of a virtual reality learning environment for teaching structural analysis[J].Computer Applications in Engineering Education,2015,5(4):223-230
7. RI Garcíabetances, MTA Waldmeyer, G Fico.A Succinct Overview of Virtual Reality Technology Use in Alzheimer's Disease[J].Frontiers in Aging Neuroscience,2015,7:80
8. E Ronchi, D Nilsson.A Virtual Reality Experiment o n Flashing Lights at Emergency Exit Portals for Roa d Tunnel Evacuation[J].Fire Technology,2016, 52(3): 623-647
9. A Moglia, V Ferrari, L Morelli.A Systematic Review of Virtual Reality Simulators for Robotassisted Surgery[J].European Urology,2016,69(6):1065-1080
10. Castelvecchi, Davide.Low-cost headsets boost virtual reality's lab appeal[J].Nature,2016,533:153
11. A Alaraj, CJ Luciano, DP Bailey.Virtual Reality Cer e-bral Aneurysm Clipping Simulation With Real Tim e Haptic Feedback[J].Neurosurgery,2015,11,2(1):52
12. Webel.Evaluating virtual reality and augmented reality training for industrial maintenance and assembly tasks[J].Interactive Learning Environments, 2015,23(6):778-798

 DOI: 10.1051/matecconf/201712801013

Direction-of-arrival and Range Estimation of Wideband Sources in the Near Field

Wen-Feng Lin[1,a], Wei-Dong Ma[1],Min Xie[1], Li-Xing Xu[1]and Ping Wei[2]

[1]*Institute of Electronic Engineering, China Academy of Engineering Physics, Mianyang 621900, China*
[2]*Department of Electronic Engineering, University of Electronic Science and Technology of China, Chengdu, Sichuan, China*

Abstract. In this letter, we address the problem of wideband sources localization in the near field of the sensor array. It is shown that the spatial sampling rate can be considered as a function of temporal frequency so that wideband sources can be represented in the spatial frequency domain. A computationally efficient localization method is then developed based on the Toeplitz matrices constructed from the frequency-dependent cross-correlation between sensors. This allows us to resolve near field sources with quite a few numbers of sensors. Indeed, the sources can be located with fewer sensors. Finally, the simulation results are presented to validate the performance of the proposed method.

1 Introduction

The localization of radiating sources using sensors arrays is a problem of considerable importance, occurring in a variety of fields ranging from radar, sonar, wireless communication, and radio astronomy to seismology[1-4]. Therefore, this problem has received considerable attention in the literature, resulting in a plethora of estimation algorithms [5-7]. However, the majority of such algorithms have been restricted to DOA estimate of narrowband sources in the far-field. Recently, there has been growing interest in developing sources location estimators in the near-field, in which case, both the angle and the range are required to be estimated simultaneously. Huang and Barkat[8] presented two techniques, i.e., two-dimension (2-D) MUSIC method and the maximum likelihood estimator (MLE), to determine the range and the angle of sources, which can be considered to be the modified versions of far-field cases. In [9-12], a series of ESPRIT-like methods are proposed, where higher order statistics is involved. Lately, some computationally simple second-order statistics-based methods have been proposed in the literature, such as the cyclic-based method [13], the weighted linear prediction method [14], the generalized ESPRIT method [15-16], the CRB-Based method[17-18] ,the NF-DSPE and the JADSSE method [19] etc. Recently, mixed near-field and far-field sources localization are proposed[20-21]. Significantly, most of the aforementioned methods rely on the narrowband assumption, therefore, to deal with wideband signals, e.g., acoustic or seismic, in [22-23] the authors provided some schemes to solve the problem of joint range and DOA estimation for multiple wideband near field sources. However, these methods have been designed under the assumptions that the number of the sources can be estimated is less than or equal to the number of antenna elements. This is a central problem in some environments and situations in which the number of sensors is limited by physical or economical considerations.

Therefore, the objective of our letter is to propose a novel scheme to simultaneously estimating the DOA and sensor location using fewer sensors, possibly less than the number of wideband sources in the near-field. Like the conventional methods for wideband sources[24-26], the received data is transformed to the frequency domain firstly, and each frequency bin can be represented by the narrowband model. Secondly, we make use of the fact that the relative distance between different elements (i.e. the physical size measured in wavelengths) is a function of the temporal frequency. Therefore, the Toeplitz matrices including the angle and the range information can be obtained by the frequency-dependent cross-correlation between sensors[27]. Then, we can employ the traditional subspace-based methods to estimate the angle and the range of wideband near field sources. Finally, the simulation results show that our proposed technique can improve greatly the detection and estimation capability for wideband near field sources.

2 Problem Formulation and Proposed Method

Consider K near field, wideband, and uncorrelated radiating sources observed by a passive nonuniform antenna array of five sensors indicated in Figure1,

[a] Corresponding author: linwenfeng_job@163.com

DOI: 10.1051/matecconf/201712801013

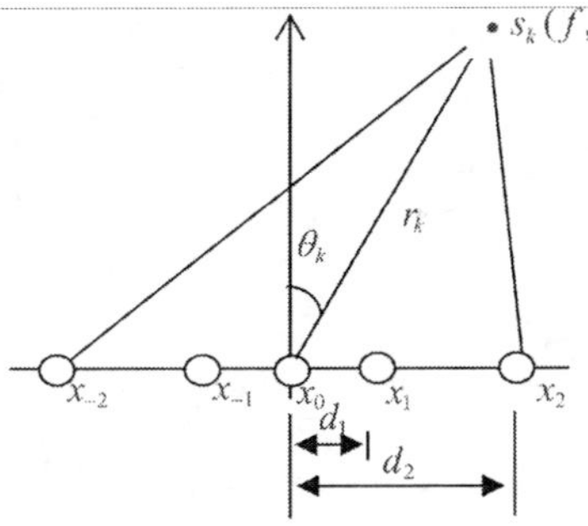

Figure 1. Near-field, wideband sources observed by a five nonuniform linear array which is symmetric about the original element.

where the array center is the origin and the phase reference point. Since we consider wideband sources in the near field, the array signal model in the frequency domain can be given by

$$x_p(f)=\sum_{k=1}^{K}s_k(f)e^{j\tau_{pk}(f)}+N_p(f)\quad p=0,\pm1,\pm2 \tag{1}$$

where $s_k(f)$, $N_p(f)$, and $\tau_{pk}(f)$ denote the kth source signal spectrum, the additive noise, and the delay associated with the kth source signal propagation time between the original sensor at the pth sensor in the f frequency band ,respectively. The noise $N_p(f)$ is a zero-mean spatially white process uncorrelated with the signal sources, and $\tau_{pk}(f)\approx\omega_{pk}(f)+\phi_{pk}(f)$ [14] and ω_{pk} and ϕ_{pk} are given by

$$\omega_{pk}(f)=\begin{cases}-p2\pi fd_1\sin(\theta_k)/c & p=\pm1\\ -p\pi fd_2\sin(\theta_k)/c & p=\pm2\\ 0 & p=0\end{cases} \tag{2}$$

$$\phi_{pk}(f)=\begin{cases}\pi fd_1^2\cos^2(\theta_k)/cr_k(f) & p=\pm1\\ \pi fd_2^2\cos^2(\theta_k)/cr_k(f) & p=\pm2\\ 0 & p=0\end{cases} \tag{3}$$

where c is the speed of the signal propagation in the considered medium, and $r_k(f)=r_kc/f$ is a frequency dependent value.

In addition, the wideband sources are assumed to be the same power spectrum over a given frequency band $[f_{\min},f_{\max}]$ provided with symmetric characteristic with respect to the central frequency $f_0=\dfrac{f_{\min}+f_{\max}}{2}$, i.e., $s_k(f_0+n\Delta f)=s_k(f_0-n\Delta f)\ k=1,\cdots,K,\ n=1,\cdots,N$, without loss of generality, where we can make the following assumptions that each wideband source can be decomposed into $2N+1$ frequency bins with inter-frequency bin difference $\Delta f=\dfrac{f_{\max}-f_{\min}}{2N}$.

Next, making use of the assumptions mentioned above, we can define the cross-correlation between $x_1(f_0+n\Delta f)$ and $x_{-1}(f_0+n\Delta f)$ or $x_2(f_0+n\Delta f)$ and $x_{-2}(f_0+n\Delta f)$ as

$$\begin{aligned}&r_p(f_0+n\Delta f)\triangleq E\{x_p(f_0+n\Delta f)x_{-p}^*(f_0+n\Delta f)\}\\ &=E\left\{(\sum_{k=1}^{K}s_k(f_0+n\Delta f)e^{j(\omega_{pk}(f_0+n\Delta f)+\phi_{pk}(f_0+n\Delta f))})(\sum_{k=1}^{K}s_k(f_0+n\Delta f)e^{j(-\omega_{pk}(f_0+n\Delta f)+\phi_{pk}(f_0+n\Delta f))})^*\right\}\\ &\quad+E\{N_p(f_0+n\Delta f)N_{-p}^*(f_0+n\Delta f)\}\\ &=\sum_{k=1}^{K}P_k(f_0+n\Delta f)e^{j2\omega_{pk}(f_0+n\Delta f)}\qquad p=1,2\ \ n=-N,\cdots,-1,0,1,\cdots,N\end{aligned} \tag{4}$$

where $E\{\bullet\}$ and $(\cdot)^*$ denote the statistical expectation and the complex conjugate , respectively. Additionally, $P_k(f_0+n\Delta f)=E\{s_k(f_0+n\Delta f)s_k^*(f_0+n\Delta f)\}$ is the power spectral of the kth source at frequency $f_0+n\Delta f$. To simplify the descriptions, we will consider the scenario as in [28] where the power spectral is constant in different frequency in the subsequent section.

Thus, the cross-correlation in (4) can be rewritten by

$$r_p(n)\triangleq r_p(f_0+n\Delta f)=\sum_{k=1}^{K}P_{kf_0}e^{j2\omega_{pk}(n\Delta f)}\triangleq\sum_{k=1}^{K}P_{kf_0}e^{jn\alpha_{pk}} \tag{5}$$

where $P_{kf_0}\triangleq P_ke^{j2\omega_{pk}(f_0)}$, $\alpha_{pk}\triangleq 2\omega_{pk}(\Delta f)$, and $p=1,2\ n=-N,\cdots,-1,0,1,\cdots,N$, then we can construct the following Toeplitz matrixs $\mathbf{R}_{p,1}$ [27] and by the cross-correlations $\{r_p(n)\}_{n=-N}^{N}$,

$$\begin{aligned}\mathbf{R}_{p,1}&=\begin{bmatrix}r_p(0) & r_p(1) & \cdots & r_p(N)\\ r_p(-1) & r_p(0) & \cdots & r_p(N-1)\\ \vdots & \vdots & \ddots & \vdots\\ r_p(-N) & r_p(-N+1) & \cdots & r_p(0)\end{bmatrix}\\ &=\mathbf{A}_{p,1}\mathbf{D}(\mathbf{P})\mathbf{A}_{p,1}^H\end{aligned} \tag{6}$$

where $(\cdot)^H$ denotes the complex conjugate, and $\mathbf{A}_{p,1}=[\mathbf{a}_{p,1}(\theta_1),\mathbf{a}_{p,1}(\theta_2),\cdots,\mathbf{a}_{p,1}(\theta_K)]$ with $\mathbf{a}_{p,1}(\theta_k)=[1,\exp(-j\alpha_{pk}),\cdots,\exp(-jN\alpha_{pk})]^T$ and $\mathbf{D}(\mathbf{P})\triangleq diag(\mathbf{P})=diag\{P_{1f_0},P_{2f_0},\cdots,P_{Kf_0}\}$.

Since $\mathbf{A}_{p,1}$ is a $(N+1)\times K$ Vandermonde matrix [29] with full column rank when $\theta_i\neq\theta_j(i\neq j)$, the columns are linearly uncorrelated matrix. From the expression of P_{kf_0} $k=1,2,\cdots,K$ in (5), we can see that $P_{kf_0}\neq0$ and $\mathbf{D}(\mathbf{P})$ has a rank of K. Therefore, the rank of $\mathbf{R}_{p,1}$ equals to the number of wideband sources and the signal subspace or noise subspace can be obtained by singular value decomposition (SVD). Finally, the traditional narrowband subspace-based DOA techniques [30] are applicable to $\mathbf{R}_{p,1}$ in (6) to obtain $\{\alpha_{pk}\}_{k=1}^{K}$, and the DOAs are estimated by the simple operation.

Then we also define the cross-correlation between $x_1(f_0+n\Delta f)$ and $x_{-1}(f_0-n\Delta f)$ or $x_2(f_0+n\Delta f)$ and $x_{-2}(f_0-n\Delta f)$ as

$$\begin{aligned} r_p(n\Delta f) &\triangleq E\{x_p(f_0+n\Delta f)x^*_{-p}(f_0-n\Delta f)\} \\ &= E\left\{\left(\sum_{k=1}^{K} s_k(f_0+n\Delta f)e^{j(\omega_{pk}(f_0+n\Delta f)+\phi_{pk}(f_0+n\Delta f))}\right)\left(\sum_{k=1}^{K} s_k(f_0-n\Delta f)e^{j(-\omega_{pk}(f_0-n\Delta f)+\phi_{pk}(f_0-n\Delta f))}\right)^*\right\} \\ &\quad + E\{N_p(f_0+n\Delta f)N^*_{-p}(f_0-n\Delta f)\} \\ &= \sum_{k=1}^{K} P_k(n\Delta f)e^{j(\omega_{pk}(f_0+n\Delta f)+\omega_{pk}(f_0-n\Delta f))}e^{j(\phi_{pk}(f_0+n\Delta f)-\phi_{pk}(f_0-n\Delta f))} \\ &= \sum_{k=1}^{K} P_k(n\Delta f)e^{j2\omega_{pk}(f_0)}e^{j\pi d_p^2\cos^2(\theta_k)4f_0 n\Delta f/c^2 r_k} \quad p=1,2\ n=-N,\cdots,-1,0,1,\cdots,N \end{aligned} \tag{7}$$

where $P_k(n\Delta f)\triangleq E\{s_k(f_0+n\Delta f)s_k^*(f_0-n\Delta f)\}$ $=P_k(f_0+n\Delta f)=P_k(f_0-n\Delta f)=P_k$, then Eq.(6) can be rewritten as

$$r_{p\Delta f}(n)\triangleq r_p(n\Delta f)=\sum_{k=1}^{K} P_{kf_0}e^{j\pi d_p^2\cos^2(\theta_k)4f_0 n\Delta f/c^2 r_k}\triangleq\sum_{k=1}^{K} P_{kf_0}e^{jn\beta_{pk}} \tag{8}$$

where $p=1,2$, $n=-N,\cdots,-1,0,1,\cdots,N$,

$P_{kf_0}\triangleq P_k e^{j2\omega_{pk}(f_0)}$, $\beta_{pk}\triangleq\pi d_p^2\cos^2(\theta_k)4f_0\Delta f/c^2 r_k$.

In the similar way to (6), we can construct the following Toeplitz matrixs $\mathbf{R}_{p,2}$,

$$\begin{aligned} \mathbf{R}_{p,2} &= \begin{bmatrix} r_{p\Delta f}(0) & r_{p\Delta f}(1) & \cdots & r_{p\Delta f}(N) \\ r_{p\Delta f}(-1) & r_{p\Delta f}(0) & \cdots & r_{p\Delta f}(N-1) \\ \vdots & \vdots & \ddots & \vdots \\ r_{p\Delta f}(-N) & r_{p\Delta f}(-N+1) & \cdots & r_{p\Delta f}(0) \end{bmatrix} \\ &= \mathbf{A}_{p,2}\mathbf{D}(\mathbf{P})\mathbf{A}_{p,2}^H \end{aligned} \tag{9}$$

where $\mathbf{A}_{p,2}=[\mathbf{a}_{p,2}(\theta_1,r_1),\mathbf{a}_{p,2}(\theta_2,r_2),\cdots,\mathbf{a}_{p,2}(\theta_K,r_K)]$ with $\mathbf{a}_{p,2}(\theta_k,r_k)=[1,\exp(-j\beta_{pk}),\cdots,\exp(-jN\beta_{pk})]^T$ and $\mathbf{D(P)}\triangleq diag(\mathbf{P})=diag\{P_{1f_0},P_{2f_0},\cdots,P_{Kf_0}\}$ .Similarly, we can also obtain $\{\beta_{pk}\}_{k=1}^{K}$ and then the ranges of wideband sources can be estimated by

$$r_k=4\pi d_p^2\cos^2(\theta_k)f_0\Delta f/c^2\beta_{pk}\quad k=1,\cdots,K \tag{10}$$

Remark: It is worth noting that for unique estimation of the DOA and the range, we need to make the following assumption

$$d_p\le c/2\Delta f \text{ and } d_p\le c\sqrt{r_{\min}/f_0\Delta f}/2 \tag{11}$$

where $r_{\max}$ denote the minimum value in the set $\{r_k\}_{k=1}^{K}$. Without loss of generality, we can employ $\mathbf{R}_{2,1}$ and $\mathbf{R}_{1,2}$ to estimate the DOA and the range respectively due to a tradeoff between the estimation performance and the phase ambiguity in the following simulations.

3 Simulations

We now evalutate the performance of the proposed method in estimating the DOAs and the range of wideband near-field sources. The spectral range of the wideband sources is taken to be the normalized frequency interval [0.8,1.2] with respect to the central frequency f_0, that is a bandwidth of 40% of f_0, where we decompose the wideband sources into 21 frequency bins with $\Delta f=0.02$. The element spacing $d_1=c\sqrt{r_{\min}/f_0\Delta f}/2$ and $d_2=c/2\Delta f$ is considered.

Firstly, we examine the estimation performance of the proposed method. The impinging source signals are two wideband sources signals located at $[\theta_1,r_1]=[-10^\circ,4]$ and $[\theta_2,r_2]=[5^\circ,2]$, respectively. The performance is measured by the normalized root mean square error (RNMSE) for the range and the root mean square error (RMSE) for the DOA defined in [12]. The results shown below are based on 1000 independent trials. Figure 2 and Figure3. show the RMSE and RNMSE of the estimated source angles and ranges with respect to the SNR from -3dB to 15dB. It is observed that the RMSE of DOA estimation is very small even at low SNR; for example, the RMSE is only 0.2 degree for SNR = −2 dB. In addition, we also see that the smaller the range is, the better estimation performance is.

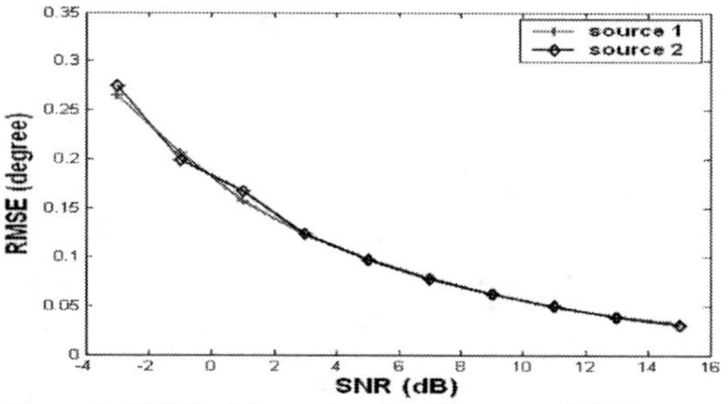

Figure 2. RMSE of the angle estimation versus SNR for two wideband near field sources.

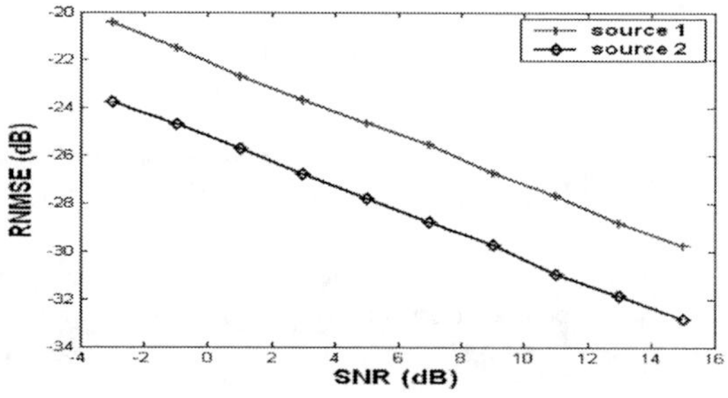

Figure 3. NRMSE of the range estimation versus SNR for two wideband near field sources.

Next, we examine the estimation capability for multiple sources of the proposed method shown Figure4(a) and (b) show that the DOA of five and six near-field uncorrelated wideband sources are placed at $[-20^\circ\ -10^\circ\ 0^\circ\ 10^\circ\ 20^\circ]$ and $[-30^\circ\ -20^\circ\ -10^\circ\ 0^\circ\ 10^\circ\ 20^\circ]$. It can be seen from Figure 4 that we can estimate much more wideband near field sources than the number of sensors while it is impossible for the conventional methods to deal with more sources than sensors.

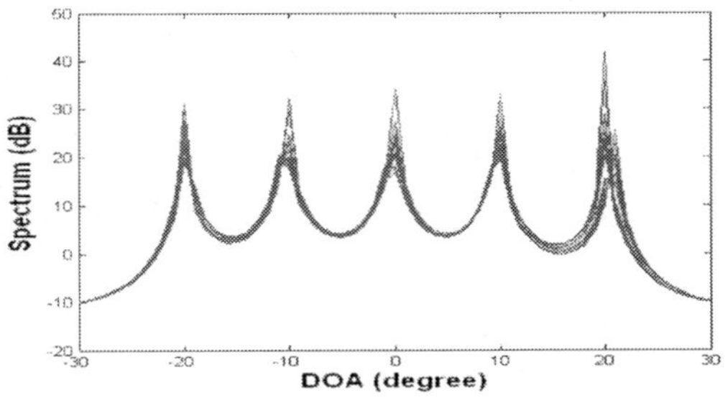

(a)

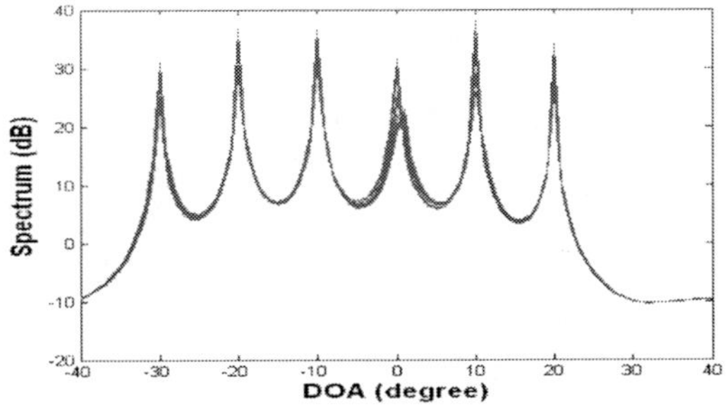

(b)

Figure 4. DOA estimation of uncorrelated wideband sources by the proposed algorithm, (a) five sources $[-20^{\circ}\ -10^{\circ}\ 0^{\circ}\ 10^{\circ}\ 20^{\circ}]$ at SNR=5dB, (b) six sources $[-30^{\circ}\ -20^{\circ}\ -10^{\circ}\ 0^{\circ}\ 10^{\circ}\ 20^{\circ}]$ at SNR=10dB.

4 Conclusions

We have presented a novel joint DOA and range estimation algorithm for wideband near field sources to deal with the scenarios in which there are more sources than sensors. This method takes advantage of the characteristics of wideband sources and obtains cross-correlation between sensors at each frequency bin to form Toeplitz matrixs that contains all DOA and range information. As a result, DOA and range estimation can be achieved using the conventional narrowband signal subspace techniques. Simulation results have demonstrated the effectiveness of the proposed method.

References

1. S. Haykin, *Adaptive Radar Signal Processing*, John Wiley & Sons, Hoboken, NJ(2007)
2. P. S. Naidu, *Sensor Array Signal Processing*, CRC Press LLC(2001)
3. T. K. Sarkar, M. C. Wicks, M. Salazar-Palma, and R. J. Bonneau, *Smart Antennas*, John Wiley & Sons, Hoboken, NJ(2003)
4. J. Capon, "High-resolution frequency-wavenumber spectrum analysis," *Proc. IEEE*, vol. **57**, pp. 2408–2418(1969)
5. J. Krim and M. Viberg, "Two decades of array signal processing research: The parametric approach," *IEEE Signal Processing Mag.*, vol.**13**, pp. 67–94(1996)
6. L.Gan, W.F. Lin, X.Y. Luo , P. Wei, "Estimation 2-D angle of arrival with a cross-correlation matrix," *Journal of the Chinese Institute of Engineers*,vol.**36**, pp.667-671(2013)
7. L.Gan, X.Y. Luo, "Direction-of-arrival estimation for uncorrelated and coherent signals in the presence of multipath propagation," *IET Microw. Antennas Propag.*, vol.**7**, pp.746-753(2013)
8. Y. D. Huang and M. Barkat, "Near-field multipe source localization by passive sensor array," *IEEE Trans. Antennas Propag.*, vol. **39**, no. 7, pp. 968–975, (1991)
9. Y. Wu, L. Ma, C. Hou, G. Zhang, and J. Li, "Subspace-based method for joint range and DOA estimation of multiple near-field sources," *Signal Process.*, vol.**86**, pp:2129-2133(2006)
10. R. N. Challa and S. Shamsunder, "High-order subspace-based algorithms for passive localization of near-field sources," in Proc. *29th Asilomar Conf. Signals, Syst., Comput., Pacific Grove, CA*, pp. 777–781 (1995)
11. M. Haardt, R. N. Challa, and S. Shamsunder, "Improved bearing and range estimation via high-order subspace based Unitary ESPRIT," in Proc. *30th Asilomar Conf. Signals, Systems, and Computers, Pacific Grove, CA*, pp. 380–384 (1996)
12. Y.H. Xu, A.G. Wang, W. Leng and Z.E. Nie, "Joint Frequency, 2-D DOA and Range Estimation of Near Field Sources," *Third International Conference on Measuring Technology and Mechatronics Automation*, pp. 455–458(2011)
13. J-H. Lee and C-H. Tung, "Estimating the bearings of near-field cyclostationary signals," *IEEE Trans. Signal process.*, vol. **50**, pp: 110-118(2002)
14. E. Grosicki, K. Abed-Meraim and Y. Hua, "A weighted linear prediction method for near-field source localization," *IEEE Trans. Signal process.*, vol. **53**, pp: 3651-3660(2005)
15. W. Zhi and M. Y-W Chia, "Near-field source location via symmetric subarrays," *IEEE Signal Process. Lett.*, vol.**14**, pp:409-412(2007)
16. J. Xie, H.H. Tao, X. Rao and J. Su, "Efficient Method of Passive Localization for Near-Field Noncircular Sources," *IEEE Antennas and Wireless Propag.*, vol. **14**, pp. 1223–1226(2015)
17. H. Gazzah and J.P. Delmas, "CRB-Based Design of Linear Antenna Arrays for Near-Field Source Localization," *IEEE Trans. Antennas Propag.*, vol. **62**, no. 4, pp. 1965–1974(2014)
18. J.P. Delmas, M.N.E. Korso, H. Gazzah and M. Castella, "CRB analysis of planar antenna arrays for optimizing near-field source localization," *Signal Processing*, pp. 117–134(2016)
19. J.A. Chaaya, J. Picheral, and S. Marcos, "Localization of spatially distributed near-field sources with unknown angular spread shape," *Signal Processing*, pp. 259–265(2015)
20. J. Xie, H.H. Tao, X. Rao and J. Su, " Localization of mixed far-field and near-field sources under

unknown mutual coupling," *Digital Signal Processing*, pp. 229–239(2016)
21. J.J. Jiang, F.H. Duan, J. Chen, Y.C. Li and X.N. Hua, "Mixed Near-Field and Far-Field Sources Localization Using the Uniform Linear Sensor Array," *IEEE Seneors Journal*, pp. 3136–3143(2013)
22. J. C. Chen, R. E. Hudson and K. Yao, "Maximum-Likelihood source localization and unknown sensor location estimation for wideband signals in the near-field," *IEEE Trans. Signal process.*, vol. **50**, pp: 1843-1854(2002)
23. C. Serap, C. Erdinc, and C. Hakan Ali, "Location estimation of wideband Sources with expectation maximization algorithm," *Signal Processing and Communications Applications*, 2007. SIU 2007. IEEE 15th, pp:11-13(2007)
24. M. Wax, T-J. Shan and T. Kailath, "Spatio-temporal spectral analysis by eigenstructure methods," *IEEE Trans. ASSP*, Vol. ASSP-**32**, No.4,pp:817-827(1984)
25. F. Sellone, "Robust auto-focusing wideband DOA estimation," *Signal Processing*, Vol. **86**, pp:17-37(2006)
26. Y-S Yoon, L. M. Kaplan and J. H. McClellan, "TOPS: New DOA estimator for wideband signals," *IEEE Trans. Signal Process.*, Vol.**54**, pp:1977-1989 (2006)
27. J.-F. Gu, N.-J. Li, P. Wei and H.-M. Tai, "Wideband DOA estimation using two sensors," *2010 International Conference on Measuring Technology and Mechatronics Automation*, pp:1095-1098(2010)
28. S. Valaee and P. Kabal, "Estimation of directions of arrival of wideband and wideband spread sources," *Signal Processing*, Vol. **87**, pp:614-622(2007)
29. C. D. Meyer, "Matrix Analysis and Applied Linear Algebra", *SIAM*(2000)
30. A. J. van der Veen, E.F. Deprettere, and A.L. Swindlehurst, "Subspace-based signal analysis using singular value decomposition," *Proc. IEEE*, vol. **81**, pp. 1277-1308(1993)

A New Method Based on Two-Stage Detection Mechanism for Detecting Ships in High-Resolution SAR Images

Yongli XU[1,*], Wei XIONG[1], Yafei LV[1], Hengyan LIU[1]

[1]*Institute of Information Fusion, Naval Aeronautical and Astronautical University*

Abstract. Ship detection in synthetic aperture radar (SAR) remote sensing images, being a fundamental but challenging problem in the field of satellite image analysis, plays an important role for a wide range of applications and is receiving significant attention in recent years. Aiming at the requirements of ship detection in high-resolution SAR images, the accuracy, the intelligent level, a better real-time operation and processing efficiency, The characteristics of ocean background and ship target in high-resolution SAR images were analyzed, we put forward a ship detection algorithm in high-resolution SAR images. The algorithm consists of two detection stages: The first step designs a pre-training classifier based on improved spectral residual visual model to obtain the visual salient regions containing ship targets quickly, then achieve the purpose of probably detection of ships. In the second stage, considering the Bayesian theory of binary hypothesis detection, a local maximum posterior probability (MAP) classifier is designed for the classification of pixels. After the parameter estimation and judgment criterion, the classification of pixels are carried out in the target areas to achieve the classification of two types of pixels in the salient regions. In the paper, several types of satellite image data, such as TerraSAR-X (TS-X), Radarsat-2, are used to evaluate the performance of detection methods. Comparing with classical CFAR detection algorithms, experimental results show that the algorithm can achieve a better effect of suppressing false alarms, which caused by the speckle noise and ocean clutter background inhomogeneity. At the same time, the detection speed is increased by 25% to 45%.

1 Introduction

Synthetic aperture radar (SAR) is known as a kind of advanced active microwave sensors, with its all-weather, all-day, multi-polarization, multi-band advantage, has been increasingly paid attention to by all countries seeking to detection technology in remote sensing. Compared with optical and infrared sensors, SAR is not affected by lighting, climate and other conditions, the imaging patterns are rich, SAR can satisfy the different requirements of ships detection [1]. Target monitoring based on SAR has developed into a common detection technology in remote sensing images. Currently, the spaceborne SAR has gradually become the first choice of ships monitoring because of its all-day, all-weather work capacity and wide-area detection capability [2].

As the basis of its classification and identification, ship detection in SAR images is always an important aspect of SAR application [3]. The principle of ship target detection in SAR images is to segment and extract objects from the input image based on the difference between the scattering characteristics of target areas and background areas. At present, a large number of ship target detection algorithms for SAR images have been developed. However, with the successful launch of TerraSAR-X (TS-X), Radarsat-2, Mark three and other next-generation SAR sensors, SAR is gradually evolving towards higher resolution, larger width, and more multi-polar directions. Traditional detection system in low-resolution SAR images can not interpret and analysis complex features of high-resolution SAR images timely and effectively. Common as traditional CFAR detection method in complex ocean can not meet the real-time detection requirements due to the high false alarm rate [4,5]. For high-resolution SAR images showing characteristics different from the low-resolution SAR images, ship target detection method is now widely used statistical models based on distributed targets [6], such as CFAR detection algorithm and its improved algorithm, including CA-CFAR, SO-CFAR, GO-CFAR, OS-CFAR, etc. However, these detection algorithms have a strong pertinence, the current research lacks detection models and detection algorithms with versatility and robustness.

At present, the main problems in the field of ship target detection in SAR images are: Firstly, as the size of the images grows, the processing speed of the algorithm based on point-by-point calculation in images becomes slow, and it is difficult to achieve the requirement of real-time processing [7,8]. What's more, there is a contradiction between the large information amount of SAR image and the limited computer processing power, there is an urgent need to find a fast detection method [9].

[a] Corresponding author: xuylhjhy@126.com

DOI: 10.1051/matecconf/201712801014

Finally, the quality of SAR images is getting closer to the same kind optical images, and the characteristics of the image is more prominent. Therefore, more and more learning methods can be used to classify the SAR images with different characteristics [9,10].

To solve above questions, we proposes a ship detection algorithm in high-resolution SAR images based on two-stage detection mechanism.

2 Detective Theory Based on Improved SR Visual Attention Model

Although the research of computer vision has made great progress in recent years, a series of achievements have been obtained. However, the ability of human eye to process and analyze information on the realistic scene is still more efficient. Consequently, scholars continue to study human visual perception system, and try to put forward the mathematical model to simulate human visual perception system. Currently, commonly used visual model [11]: ITTI model and AIM model and spectral residual model.

Considering the computational complexity of the first two visual models is high, it is not conducive to the construction of real-time application system, especially when it is applied to high-resolution SAR images, it is difficult for the models to get saliency maps quickly.

In general, it is necessary to adopt a global search method to obtain a better real-time detection algorithm. This method also reduces the search cost of local traversal [12]. In [13], a method extracting visual salient regions based on image frequency domain is proposed, which is spectral residual (SR). Compared with other visual models, the SR method is a global pattern of visual salient regional extraction, the processing of the model is based on the frequency domain, and is implemented by fast Fourier transform, which has the advantages of simple and fast calculation. The basic idea of the method is that: the logarithmic amplitude spectrum of most natural images has approximately identical shape, Therefore, in the spectrum of an image, the parts that are different from the identical shape is the spectral residual parts that contain the target information.

Assuming $I(x)$ is an image, the spectrum of the image is decomposed into two parts: amplitude spectrum $A(f)$ and phase spectrum $P(f)$.

$$A(f) = \mathrm{Amp}\{\mathrm{FFT}[I(x)]\} \quad (1)$$

$$P(f) = \mathrm{Pha}\{\mathrm{FFT}[I(x)]\} \quad (2)$$

A low-pass filter and the logarithmic amplitude spectrum of the image are convolved to calculate, and the amplitude spectrum is smoothed. and subtracts the logarithmic amplitude spectrum of the original image, and the spectral residual value is obtained.

$$L(f) = \log[A(f)] \quad (3)$$

$$R(f) = L(f) - h_n(f) * L(f) \quad (4)$$

Combining the spectral residual and phase spectrum that have been obtained, we can get the saliency map of original image. The spectral residual is calculated as:

$$S(x) = g(x) * |\mathrm{FFT}^{-1}[\exp(R(f) + i \cdot P(f))]|^2 \quad (5)$$

Among them, FFT and FFT^{-1} represent the fast Fourier transform of the image and its inverse transform; $h_n(f)$ is a low-pass filter in the frequency domain, such as a mean filter; $g(x)$ is a low-pass filter in the time domain, a Gaussian smoothing filter can be used; $A(f)$, $P(f)$, $L(f)$ are the amplitude spectrum, the phase spectrum, and logarithmic amplitude spectrum of original image, respectively; $R(f)$ is the spectral residual; $S(x)$ is the saliency map.

We can see that, when calculating spectral residuals, the phase spectrum of original image is a key factor. Relative to the logarithmic amplitude spectrum, the phase spectrum is a real contribution to the saliency map, based on this, the SR method is improved. The new visual attention calculation model is:

$$P_N(f) = \mathrm{FFT}[I(x)] / |\{\mathrm{FFT}[I(x)]\}| \quad (6)$$

$$R_N(f) = BP(f) \cdot P_N(f) \quad (7)$$

Where: $BP(f)$ refers to band-pass filter; $P_N(f)$ is the phase spectrum of original image; $R_N(f)$ is the spectral residual.

$$BP(f) = \exp[-\frac{(f - f_0)^2}{2\Delta f^2}] \quad (8)$$

In this paper, in the selection of the filter $BP(f)$, a Gaussian filter with center frequency (f_0) and cutoff frequency (Δf) is selected.

$$S_N(f) = \mathrm{FFT}^{-1}[R_N(f)] \quad (9)$$

$S_N(x)$ is the saliency map. The calculation of improved spectral residual model mainly includes two steps: normalization of the original spectrum and band-pass filtering in the frequency domain.

Compared with the previous SR method, the improved SR method does not need to do calculation of logarithmic amplitude spectrum and low-pass filtering, also does not need to do the exponential operation in the frequency domain and the Gaussian filtering in the time domain, thus this can greatly improve the computational speed. The improved method consists of two control parameters f_0 and Δf, the parameters can be adjusted according to the characteristics of targets, so this visual model has a certain adaptability. Finally, the original SR model and the improved SR model are compared and analyzed through the experiment.

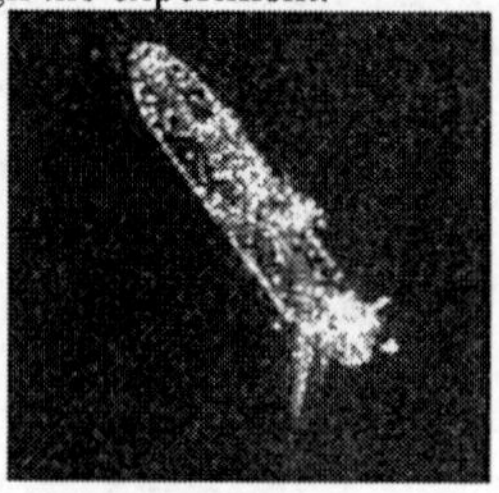

DOI: 10.1051/matecconf/201712801014

a. The original image①

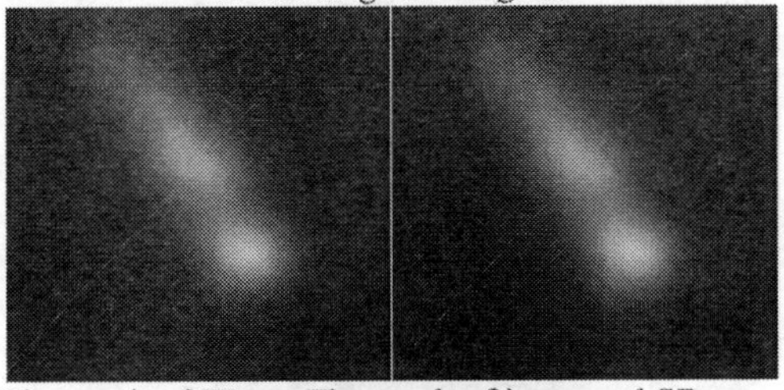

b. The result of SR c. The result of improved SR

c. The original image②

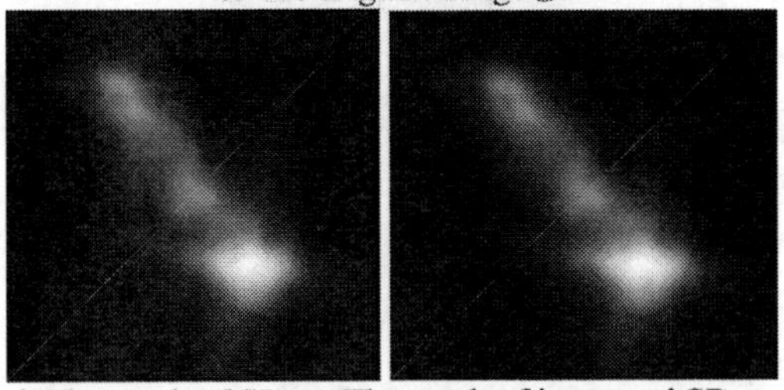

d. The result of SR e. The result of improved SR

Fig 1. Comparison of the details of saliency maps

It can be seen in Fig. 1 through the human eye observation from experimental data: The saliency maps obtained after the improvement are very similar with the saliency maps of original SR method in visual perception. It is further verified by Fig. 2 that: The subtraction values of the two salient maps are randomly distributed in the intervals [-1,3]. Thus, the similarity of the two salience maps is further illustrated, and it is found that the gray scale difference near the coordinates of the ships is more prominent. Therefore, it can be concluded that the new spectrum calculation model increases the signal-to-noise ratio of targets to a certain extent.

In general, the gray value of targets in SAR images are higher than the gray value of the pixels of background in their adjacent area. Therefore, the potential area of the ship targets is generally included in visual salient regions that have been obtained in the previous step, the method of extracting this salient regions can greatly reduce the amount of data in the subsequent local traversal detection, but also to a certain extent, improve the practical performance of the detection algorithm [14].

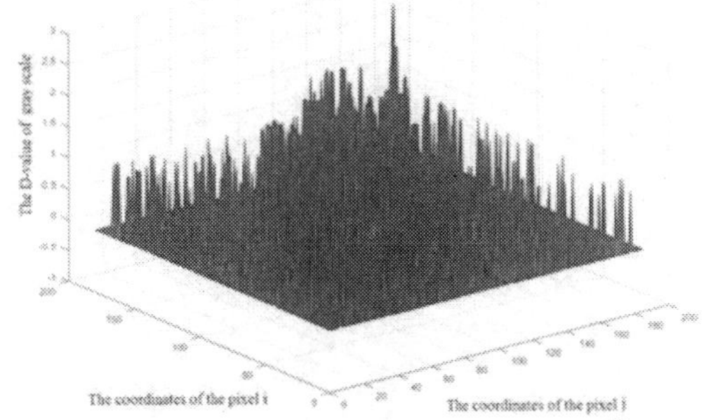

a. The gray scale contrast in image slice①

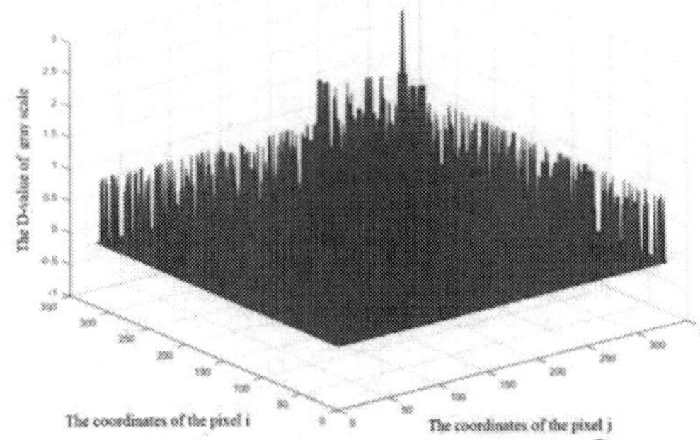

b. The gray scale contrast in image slice②

Fig 2. Comparison of gray difference of image slices

3 Design of Algorithm for Detecting Ships in SAR Images

This paper analyzes the characteristics of the clutter in background and target in high-resolution SAR images, and we consider the visual attention detection theory, A ship target detection algorithm in SAR images is proposed. The first step designs a pre-training classifier based on improved spectral residual visual model to obtain the visual salient regions that contain ships quickly, then achieve the purpose of probably detection of ship targets; In the second stage, considering the binary hypothesis tests in Bayesian theory, a local maximum posterior probability (MAP) classifier is designed for the classification of pixels, After the parameter estimation and judgment criterion, the classification of pixels are carried out in the target areas to achieve the classification of two types of pixels in the salient regions. The flow chart is shown in Fig. 3.

3.1. Extraction of Region of Interest Based on Improved Visual Model

In most cases, ships are sparsely distributed on the sea.

DOI: 10.1051/matecconf/201712801014

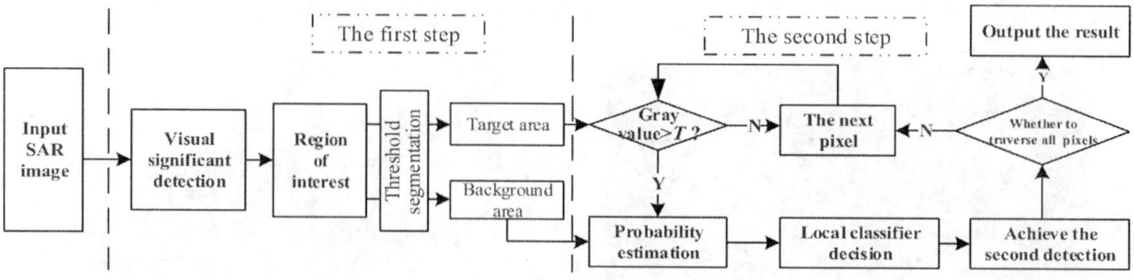

Fig 3. The flow chart of the two-stage detection algorithm proposed in this paper

When dealing with SAR images, the general detection algorithms usually spend much time in sea areas, which reduce the efficiency of detection. Thus we consider the idea of visual attention mechanism in frequency domain of image: frequent information in the image does not have visual saliency, compared to these frequent information, ships and other new information can catch more attention of human eye [15,16]. Thus, visual saliency detection is used for ship detection to achieve rapid extraction of visual salient regions in the image. The first stage of the algorithm is the extraction of the region of interest under the visual attention mechanism, and the saliency map is obtained and processed by the improved SR method. In the process, we mainly carry out two steps: one is the extraction of the region of interest; and the other is the binarization of saliency map.

Thus, we perform two threshold segmentation operations. Firstly, the visual salient regions are segmented by T_0, in order to screen out the significant areas that contain potential ships.

$$x(i,j) > T_0, \text{The pixel belong to the region of interest} \quad (10)$$

The second threshold segmentation is done by setting two thresholds T_1, T_2, ($T_1 < T_2$), pixels in the saliency map are segmented, so as to complete the approximation of gray scale histogram in target areas and background areas more accurately.

$$\begin{aligned} &x(i,j) > T_2, \text{The pixel belongs to the target area} \\ &x(i,j) < T_1, \text{The pixel belongs to the background area} \end{aligned} \quad (11)$$

3.2 Ship Detection Based on Local MAP Classifier

From the perspective of classification, the problem of ships detection is a classification of two categories of targets. In order to achieve further work on the detection of ship targets in visual salient regions of image, this paper designs a local MAP classifier.

3.2.1 Local MAP Classifier

According to Bayesian theory, the object detection is actually a binary hypothesis test of the data vector x, so as to detect whether the target exists. Data samples are divided into two categories, The categories of samples are ω_1 and ω_0, Assume that $P(\omega_i)$ is the prior probability that the input pixel belongs to ω_i. Therefore, what we can get from the Bayesian criterion for binary hypothesis test is that:

$$P(\omega_1 \mid x) = \frac{P(x \mid \omega_1)\cdot P(\omega_1)}{P(x)} \quad (12)$$

$$P(\omega_0 \mid x) = \frac{P(x \mid \omega_0)\cdot P(\omega_0)}{P(x)} \quad (13)$$

Where: $P(\omega_1|x)$ and $P(\omega_0|x)$ refer to the posterior probability of the detected pixel belongs to the target and the background, respectively; $P(x|\omega_i)$ is the conditional probability under given class ω_i; $P(x)$ refers to the probability of acquiring the pixel. According to the Bayesian criterion and the MAP criterion, our classifier can be defined as:

$$Y(i) = \arg\max_i \left(P(\omega_i \mid x)\right) \quad (14)$$

When the target exists, the condition is met:

$$\frac{P(\omega_1 \mid x)}{P(\omega_0 \mid x)} > 1 \quad (15)$$

The criterion of the Local MAP classifier is:

$$\frac{P(x \mid \omega_1)}{P(x \mid \omega_0)} \underset{0}{\overset{1}{\gtrless}} \frac{P(\omega_0)}{P(\omega_1)} \quad (16)$$

In order to be able to use the Local MAP classifier for target detection, The conditional probability of the input pixels in a given category ($P(x|\omega_i)$), and the prior probability of the corresponding category of the input pixels ($P(\omega_i)$) must be obtained.

3.2.2 Parameter Estimation of The Classifier

Calculate the conditional probability of the input pixels in the given two categories $P(x|\omega_i)$, that is, the probability density function of the target areas and the background. In high-resolution SAR images, ship targets present the morphological characteristics of distributed targets, the salient regions of the saliency map also present a distributed characteristic, The more significant the pixels are, generally, the more likely the target pixels are. Thus, a larger division threshold T_0 is set to split the saliency map. Then extract pixels larger than the division threshold (The segmentation threshold for this step is T_2) in the region, and obtain the probability distribution of their gray histogram, finally fit distribution of ships. Correspondingly, we extract the pixels that is smaller than the threshold T_1, and the histogram of their gray value is used as the approximation of the background probability density.

In general, the local CFAR detection methods require to calculate the distribution of all local regions in background areas. In this paper, the use of this global approach is better approached the actual distribution of the target and background areas, but also reduces the amount of calculation. Under normal circumstances, methods complete the target detection based on the difference of target and background, we need to calculate the distribution of the background to obtain an adaptive division threshold. In this paper, we use a sliding window to obtain the prior probability of the input pixels belongs to ω_i, so as to complete local adaptive detection. The prior probabilities $P(\omega_i)$ are defined as:

$$P(\omega_i)=\begin{cases} c\cdot\left|x_t-\dfrac{1}{N}\sum_{j=1}^{N}x_j\right|, i=1 \\ 1-c\cdot\left|x_t-\dfrac{1}{N}\sum_{j=1}^{N}x_j\right|, i=0 \end{cases} \tag{17}$$

Where: x_t is the gray value of the detected pixel currently, and x_1, x_2,...,x_N are the pixels that belongs to background areas in the sliding window; $c=a/G$, G is the maximum gray scale of the image; $0<a\leq1$, a is an empirical parameter for adjusting the prior probability.

Combining with the prior probabilities and conditional probabilities, the algorithm performs secondary detection on the potential target areas.

4 Experimental Analysis

This section carries out the target detection experiment on the basis of visual saliency and local classifier theory. Considering TS-X image is a typical high-resolution SAR image, several representative TS-X images are selected. Compared with classical detection algorithms, the advantages and disadvantages of this algorithm are analyzed.

4.1. Evaluation Index of Detection Results

In order to verify whether the algorithm is valid to SAR images with a wide range of complex ocean conditions, strong speckle noise, A TS-X image was selected as the experimental data, whose pixels is 5517×3712. the imaging area is Strait of Gibraltar, the sampling rate of this image is 1.25 meters, the polarization mode is HH polarization, the distribution of sea in this area is complex and there are a lot of ships and strong speckle noise. Where contains a certain area of non-uniform ocean background. In this area, the comparative analysis of optical remote sensing satellite data in this region, combining with GPS and AIS data analysis, we collect and sort out the geographical information of the Strait of Gibraltar, and determine the number and location of ships in SAR image data, and improve the objectivity of evaluation in experimental results. For better evaluation of detection algorithms, define the quality factor [17]:

$$FoM=\frac{N_{tt}}{N_{fa}+N_{gt}} \tag{18}$$

Among that, N_{tt} is the number of targets detected by the algorithm; N_{fa} said the number of false alarm; N_{gt} is the number of actual targets.

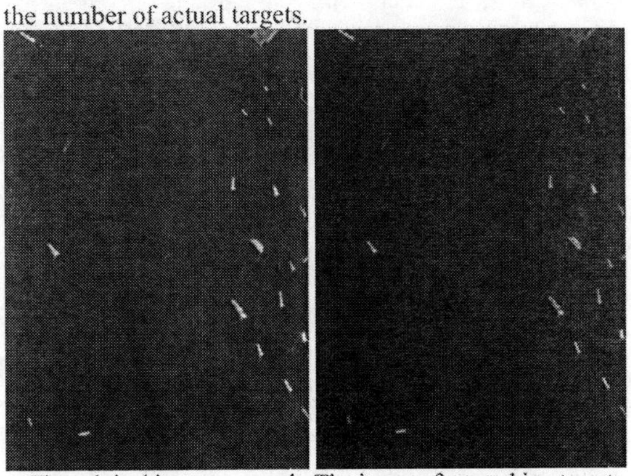

a. The original image b. The image after marking targets
Fig 4. Experimental simulation image

4.2 Experimental Results and Evaluation Analysis

In order to analyze the detection performance of the algorithm, the classical two-parameter CFAR detection algorithm and the CFAR detection algorithm based on the local K distribution are selected respectively.

The simulation experiment data used in this paper is shown in Figure 4 (a), which contains a large number of non-uniform sea background and different sizes of ship targets, and there is still a certain area of land area. Figure 4 (b) is the image after marking targets, and the actual number of ships in the experimental image is 19.

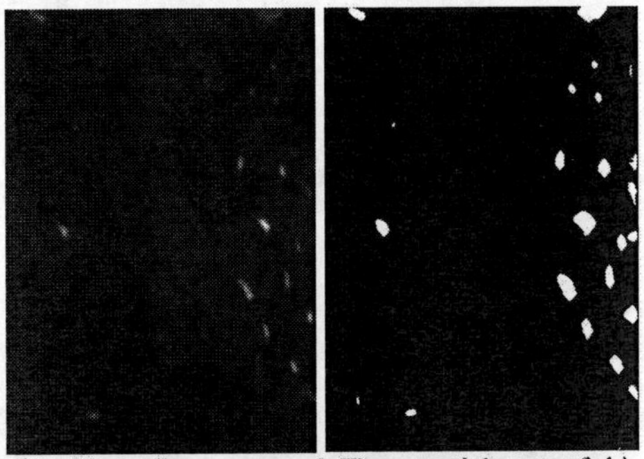

c. Significant figure d. The potential areas of ships

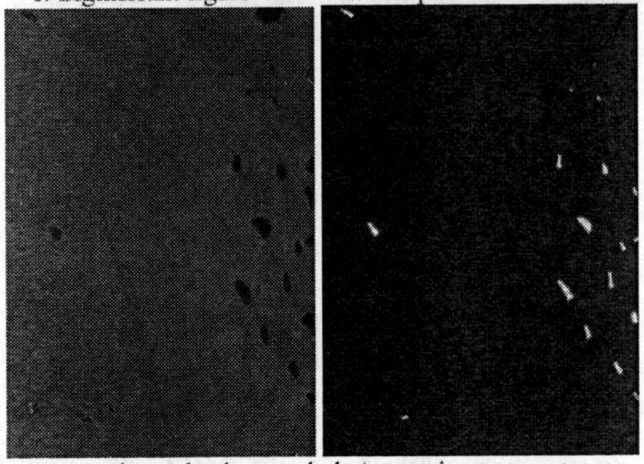

c. Approximate background d. Approximate target areas
Fig 5. Area extraction based on visual attention

Firstly, a saliency map is calculated using the improved spectral residual method. Figure 5 (a) is a saliency map of the experimental image, for the detected image in the experiment, the variance parameter of Gaussian filter is set to 0.25. It can be seen from the figure that the saliency map retains the obvious target of visual cognition, and also eliminates the big land areas. Through the two threshold segmentation operations in the saliency map, the potential region extraction of the ship target is completed, and the fitting of the histogram in the background and the target areas is completed, the simulation results are shown in Figure 5. In this paper, when completing the global approximation extraction operation in the background and target areas, two thresholds are used to segment the signal to achieve more accurate approximation. When the saliency map is divided by the thresholds, the thresholds are adjusted according to the image. For the experimental image, the first threshold T_0 is set to 28, to complete potential target areas extraction from the original image. The second threshold combination contains two thresholds, The larger threshold T_1 is set to 50, and the smaller threshold T_2 is set to 65. The approximate background area is obtained by segmenting the image by threshold value T_1, and similarly, the approximate target region is obtained by segmenting the image by threshold value T_2.

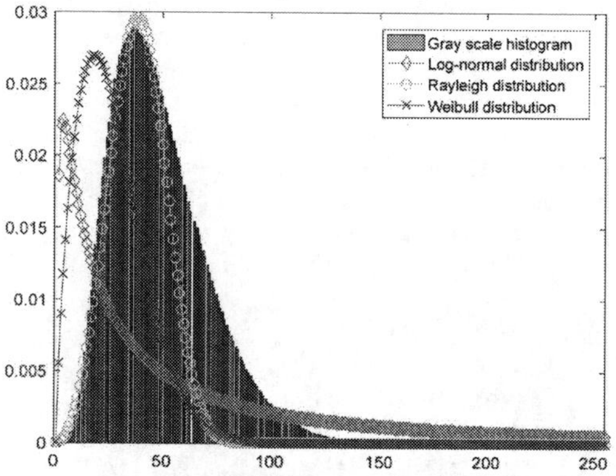

a. Fitting of background areas

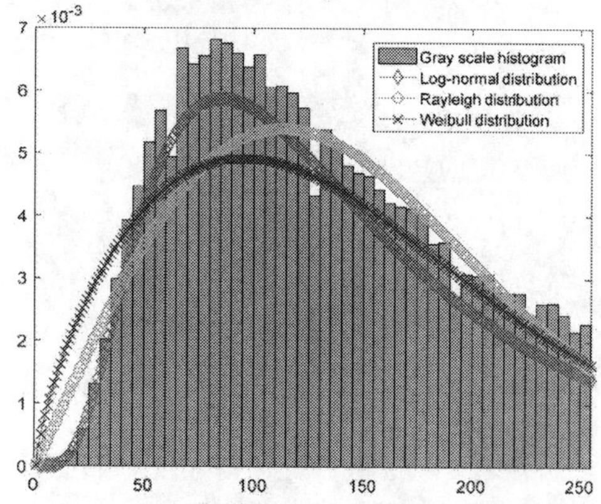

b. Fitting of target areas

Fig 6. Fitting of target and background distribution

Figure 6 (a) and (b) are the histogram fitting results of background and target, the logarithmic normal distribution, the Rayleigh distribution are used to fit the distribution of target areas and background, and the conditional probability density is obtained in the local MAP classifier. Then, a sliding window is used to calculate the prior probability of potential ship regions. The design of the sliding window need to consider the pixel count, size and distribution of ship targets in SAR images, For the experimental image in this paper, the size of the window is set to 180×180, the window slides in steps of 90 pixels, the empirical parameter c takes 4×10-6. Fig. 7 shows the final results by local classifier detection.

Fig 7. The detection results of the experimental images

The two-parameter CFAR algorithm is based on the assumption that the sea clutter obeys the Gaussian distribution. At present, a large number of studies have confirmed that: To some extent, the Gaussian distribution can effectively simulate the background variation of marine clutter, and its sliding window technology has a good adaptability to the local variation of marine clutter background. The CFAR ship detection algorithm based on the logarithmic normal distribution is a CFAR detection algorithm which assumes that the sea clutter obeys the logarithmic normal distribution. The radar imaging mechanism explains the good fitting effect of the logarithmic normal distribution used for the statistical model of sea clutter. These two algorithms are representative, are used in the existing mature detection system relatively.

Experiments were performed by using experimental image, table 1 shows the comparison of these three different algorithms, They are the two-parameter CFAR algorithm and the CFAR algorithm based on logarithmic normal distribution and the algorithm proposed in this paper. the false alarm rate of the two-parameter CFAR detection algorithm is 10^{-4}, the false alarm rate of CFAR detection algorithm based on logarithmic normal distribution is set to 10^{-6}.

Table 1. Comparison of three results in TerraSAR images

Detection algorithm	**Missed number of targets**	N_{tt}	N_{fa}	**Detection time**	***FoM***
Two-parameter CFAR	1	18	7	92.63s	0.720

DOI: 10.1051/matecconf/201712801014

Log-normal CFAR	0	19	5	130.13s	0.792
The proposed algorithm	0	19	4	46.24s	0.826

It can be seen from the table: two-parameter CFAR detection algorithm missed some ship targets, and existed seven false alarm targets, the algorithm runs for a longer time. The advantages of the two-parameter CFAR algorithm are the relatively simple parameters estimation for Gaussian distribution. However, The fitting degree of Gaussian distribution to sea clutter is not high when the sea surface is complex, Moreover, although the parameters are simple to estimate, but it also take a lot of time; The CFAR ship detection algorithm based on logarithmic normal distribution detected all the real ships, but there are five false alarm targets, and ran the longest time. Although the fitting degree of logarithmic normal distribution to the sea clutter is improved, the time spending on the parameters estimation and the calculation of the probability distribution function is relatively long. Compared with the above two methods, The experimental results show that the proposed algorithm is very fast and effective. The reason is that, in visual attention calculation, the frequency of the land is higher relative to ship targets. Therefore, this paper does not need to pretreat the land and sea segmentation, but use the visual model gets regions of interest in image directly, Then through a MAP classifier, this has a higher detection efficiency and a lower false alarm rate than the target detection on the original image.

Figure 8 shows the details of ship detection results. (a) is the partial slices of ship detection results based on local logarithmic normal distribution, and (b) is the result of partial slices of the algorithm presented in this paper. The results of the local log-normal algorithm are ambiguous in the edge of ships, and there are more "small false alarms", so it is difficult to describe the ship contour accurately in the morphological bridging operation. The pixels in detail slices generated by our algorithm are relatively concentrated, it is conducive to maintaining the shape of ships.

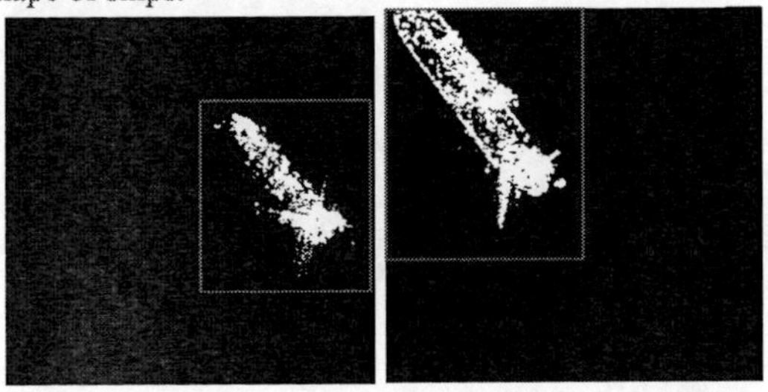

a. The detail slices of Log-normal CFAR detection results

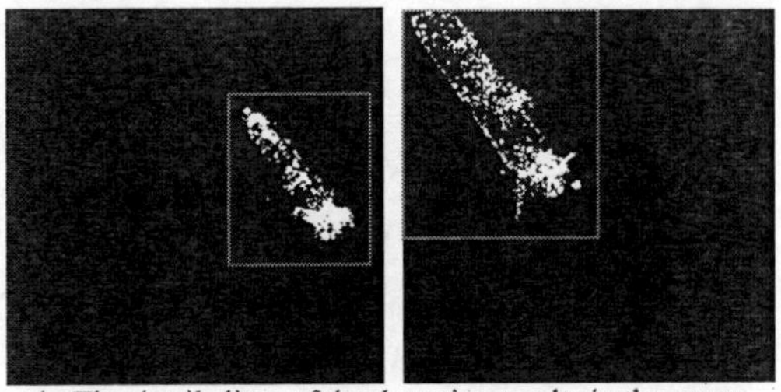

b. The detail slices of the detection results in the paper

Fig 8. Comparison of detection results

5 Conclusions

This paper analyzed the statistical characteristics of sea clutter and the basic theory of targets classification under different sea conditions, The performance of common detection classifiers was simulated and analyzed in the uniform clutter environment and interference target environment. The paper focuses on the problem of their poor performance when the classical CFAR detection algorithms are applied to high-resolution SAR images with complex background, A new method based on two-stage detection mechanism for detecting ship targets in high-resolution SAR images is presented in the paper. In the end, a number of detection experiments were performed in TS-X images with a complex background, The results show that the proposed algorithm has a good balance between the false alarm rate and the leakage alarm rate in the detection, and has a great advantage in the detection of ship targets in SAR image.

The next phase of research is: (1) If there are many smaller islands and land areas in the detection scenario, pretreatment of land removal is required. In summary, the elimination of land areas is another important focus of research; (2) When carrying out the calculation of visual vision saliency in the frequency domain, it is necessary to further improve the parameter setting of the band-pass filter according to the image characteristics of the ships, to find the filter with relatively strong applicability; (3) In the next stage, we will learn from the ideas of biological awareness, machine learning, and design and improve the performance of ship detection algorithm.

Acknowledgments

Received funds for covering the costs to publish in open access: National Natural Science Foundation of China: Basic Theory and Key Technology of Spatial Information Network for Continuous Observation of Sea Target. (Number: 42511133N)

References

1. Moreira A, et al.. A tutorial on synthetic aperture radar[J]. IEEE Geoscience and Remote Sensing Magazine, 2013 1(1):6-43.
2. Deng Yun-kai, Zhao Feng-jun, Wang Yu. Development trend and application of spaceborne SAR Technology[J]. Journal of Radar, 2012 1(1):1-9.

 DOI: 10.1051/matecconf/201712801014

3. • Chong Jin-song, Ouyang Yue, Zhu Min-hui. Detection of ocean target in synthetic aperture radar imagery[M]. Ocean Publishing Firm, 2006.
4. • Xing Xiang-wei, Ji Ke-feng, et al.. Review of ship surveillance technologies based on high-resoluion wide-swath synthetic aperture radar imaging[J]. Journal of Radar, 2015 4(1):107-121.
5. • He You, Guan Jian, Peng Ying-ning. Automatic radar detection and constant false alarm rate processing[M]. Tsinghua University Press, 1999.
6. • L. Gagnon, H. Oppenheim and P. Valin. R & D activities in airborne SAR image processing/analysis at Lockheed Martin Canada[C]. Proceeding of SPIE 998-1003.
7. • Kazuo Ouchi, Shinsuke Tamaki, Hidenobu Yaguchi and Masato Iehara. Ship Detection Based on Coherence Images Derived From Cross Correlation of Multilook SAR Images[J]. IEEE Geoscience and Remote Sensing Letters, 2004 1(3):184-187.
8. • Xing Xiang-wei, Ji Ke-feng, Zou Huan-xin, et al.. Feature selection and weighted SVM classifier based ship detection in PolSAR imagery[J]. International Journal of Remote Sensing, 2013, 34(22): 7925-7944.
9. • Gao Gui. A parzen-window-kernel-based CFAR algorithm for ship detection in SAR images. IEEE Geoscience and Remote Sensing Letters, 2011 8(3): 557–561.
10. • Wang. C, Jiang S F, Zhang H, et al.. Ship detection for high-resolution SAR images based on feature analysis[J].IEEE Geoscience and Remote Sensing Letters, 2014 11(1):119-123.
11. • Jiao Li-cheng, Zhang Xiang-rong, Hou Biao, et al.. Intelligent SAR image processing and interpretation [M]. Science Press, 2007.
12. • Gao D, Han S, Vasconcelos N. Discriminant saliency, the detection of suspicious coincidences, and applications to visual recognition[J]. Pattern Analysis and Machine Intelligence, IEEE Transactions on, 2009 31(6): 989-1005.
13. • Hou X and Zhang L. Saliency detection: a spectral residual approach[C]. Proceedings of the 2007 IEEE Conference on Computer Vision and Pattern Recognition (CVPR 2007), Minneapolis, Minnesota, USA, 2007: 1-8.
14. • Wang Juan, Ci Lin-lin, Yao Kang-ze. Research of feature selection methods[J]. Computer Engineering and Science, 2005 27(12): 68-71.
15. • Harm G. Developments in detection algorithms at JRC[C].The Third Meeting of the DECLIMS Project, Vancouver, BC, 2004: 1-7.
16. • Achanta R, Estrada F, Wils P, et al.. Salient region detection and segmentation[C]. Proceedings of the 6th International Conference on Computer Vision Systems (ICVS 2008), Santorini, Greece, 2008: 66-75.
17. • Zhang Zhi-long, Yang Wei-ping, Zhang Yan, et al.. Ship Detection in Infrared Remote Sensing Images Based on Spectral Residual Transform[J]. Journal of Electronics & Information Technology, 2015 2(3):15-24.A. Mecke, I. Lee, J.R. Baker jr., M.M. Banaszak Holl, B.G. Orr, Eur. Phys. J. E **14**, 7 (2004)

Numerical simulation of underwater acoustical field with directional sources based on the normal modes model

Wang Jihui*, Wang Zhenshan, Jia Bing

Science and Technology on Underwater Test and Control Laboratory, 116000, Dalian, China

Abstract. In this paper, beamforming and normal modes method are combined to calculate the underwater acoustical field. Firstly, beamforming technology is used to form directional sources by controlling the phase and relative amplitude. Secondly, considering the ocean speed, surface and bottom boundary, the point source sound field is calculated based on the normal modes model. Then underwater acoustical field with directional sources is achieved by adding all point source field. Taken the 11 elements vertical linear array as an example, the special directional source is formed by chebyshev amplitude weighting, and then underwater acoustical field is calculated in the Munk profile of different grazing angles. The results indicate that beam grazing angle is very essential to its sound field, and changing the grazing angle can enhance the sound intensity of the shadow zone correspondingly.

1 Introduction

The operating range of active sonar is decided by target characteristics and underwater sound channel in ocean environment. The propagation loss of active sonar signal can be derived with hydrology and bottom material parameters. In order to assess sonar performance, the operating range can be predicted combined with typical target scattering characteristics. Due to outstanding anti-reverberation ability, directional source is widely used in underwater active detection.

A beamformer is a spatial filter and can be used to increase the signal-to-noise ratio by blocking most of the noise outside the directions of interest. As practical engineering application, the signal phase is arranged at specific positions to enhance signal-to-reverberation ratio[1,2]. The sound field in complicated ocean channel by sonar beams propagation is the concerned problem in this thesis.

Acoustic Toolbox program is created by Maggi and Duncan of Curtin University of Technology in Perth, Australia. We can use the Acoustic Toolbox for the underwater environment modelling, which includes versions of BELLHOP, KRAKEN, and SCOOTER, etc. Users can select proper parameters of grazing angles for their simulation work[3-6]. However, optimization of the transmitting pattern function is weak. In order to design the transmitting acoustic beam in detail but not have the grazing angle only, acoustic propagation field simulation method is established based on vertical line array directional source and typical models are simulated in this paper.

2 NUMERICAL METHODS

Using the phase-shift beamforming technique, frequency is fed to the individual array element with the correct phase relationship so that it produces directional source in a desired direction.

2.1 Phase-shift beamforming

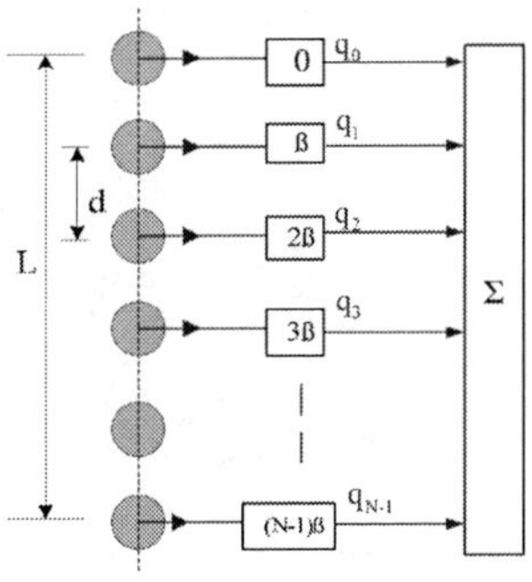

Figure 1. The structure of the perpendicular linear array.

Figure 1 shows the structure of the linear array. Each element is multiplied by the weights to form the array output signal[7]. Consider a linear array with N elements, L is the length, d is the spacing, the linear array with initial direction angle ϕ, $(N-1)\beta$ is compensation phase of each element and q_n is corresponding weight function. Based on the mathematical model of a far-field plane

* Corresponding author: wangjihuihgc@163.com

 DOI: 10.1051/matecconf/201712801015

wave, the transmitted signal is given by the following Equation 1 by adding the result of each element.

$$R(\theta) = q_0 + q_1 \cos(\varphi - \beta) + q_2 \cos(2(\varphi - \beta)) + \ldots q_{N-1} \cos((N-1)(\varphi - \beta)) \tag{1}$$

The array factor q_i is obtained using the method proposed by Dolph, which is based on the approximation to the Chebyshev polynomials of order n. The Chebyshev polynomials of order n are defined as:

$$\mathrm{T}_n(x) = \cos(n \arccos x), |x| \leq 1 \tag{2}$$

While $x = \cos\phi$, and then Equation 3 becomes:

$$T_n(x) = \cos(n\phi) \tag{3}$$

It can generate a chebyshev-type amplitude distribution with a total number of elements N and the ratio of lobes[8].

2.2 Normal modes method

As actual ocean environments are usually complex, sound fields calculating is influenced by the factors including the sea surface roughness, typical SSP, layered media and so on. Normal modes method has been used for many years in underwater acoustics. On the assumption that the sound field is range independent, the normal modes method calculates an isolated point source in acoustic medium, which is based on separation of variables. The solution is governed by the acoustic helmholtz equation:

$$\frac{1}{r}\frac{\partial}{\partial r}\left(r\frac{\partial p}{\partial r}\right) + \frac{\partial^2 p}{\partial z^2} + \frac{\omega^2}{c^2(z)} p = -\frac{\delta(r)\delta(z - z_s)}{2\pi r} \tag{4}$$

Assume that the surface is pressure release boundary and the bottom at depth D. is the perfect rigid boundary. The free surface condition is an approximation for the surface boundary condition. For the surface yields perfectly free boundary:

$$p(0) = 0 \tag{5}$$

The perfectly rigid assumption enjoys some popularity for a bottom boundary. For a purely acoustic problem, this becomes

$$p'(D) = 0 \tag{6}$$

Solved by separation of variables, the pressure field is:

$$p(r,z) = \frac{i}{4\rho_0} \sum_{m=1}^{N} \psi_m(z_s)\psi_m(z) H_0^{(1)}(k_{rm} r) \tag{7}$$

Where $r = \sqrt{(x_P - x_Q)^2 + (y_P - y_Q)^2}$, $H_0^{(1)}$ is the Hankel function of the first kind of order zero. The equation has N eigenvalues k_{rm} and corresponding eigenvectors ψ_m, z_s is the depth of the source[9].

Many ways can compute the equation numerically, and the finite difference method is chosen. The interval depth $0 < z < D$ is divided into N equal intervals. Once the eigenvalues are found, the eigenvectors are computed using inverse iteration. The inverse iteration is given by equation 8.

$$A(k^2)\mathrm{Z} = 0 \tag{8}$$

Here, A is a symmetric tridiagonal matrix defined, and Z is the vector with components Z_0, Z_1,... Z_N. KRAKEN normal modes code in the Acoustic Toolbox is used in this thesis to model the sound field transmitted from the point source. KRAKEN normal mode model is robust, accurate, and efficient[9,10]. A version of KRAKEN with a MEX wrapper is used so that it can easily be called from Matlab software, and the Python Scripts source code is used for reading/writing input/output the sound field calculation results.

3 Model simuliting and analysis

3.1 Computating model

In the simulation, we consider classical chebyshev and uniform linear array of 11 elements with half wavelength spacing. The centre of the linear array is 1300 meters, the frequency value of the transmitted signal is 100Hz, and the ratio of lobes is 30 dB. Figure 2 shows different simulation results using the uniform and chebyshev weights. We can observe that the peak side lobe with chebyshev weight is same -30dB.

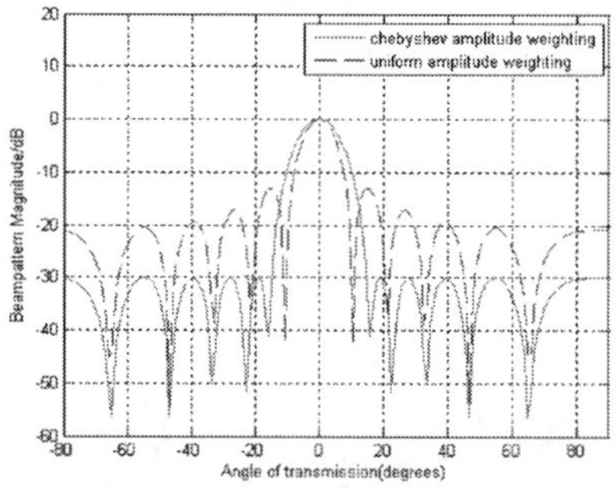

Figure 2. The rectangular plot of beam pattern magnitude of with uniform and chebyshev amplitude distribution.

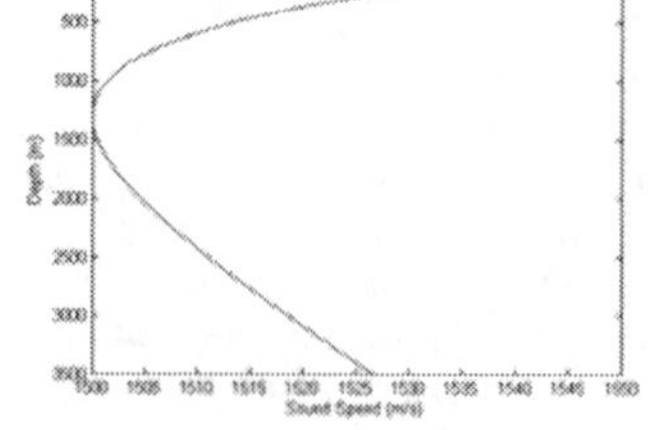

Figure 3. Munk profile.

 DOI: 10.1051/matecconf/201712801015

The Munk profile is an idealized sound speed profile but it can illustrate typical features of deep water SSP[11]. Consider the depth is 3500 meters, and the resulting profile is plotted in figure 3.

3.2 Sound field simulation

3.2.1 point source sound field simulation

Figure 4 shows the selected modes 1, modes 20, modes 60 and modes 100 of the Munk profile with the surface pressure released and the bottom is perfect rigid boundary. Lower order modes in particular mode 1 is zero in the position near the sea surface and bottom, and all modes make contribute to the sound field.

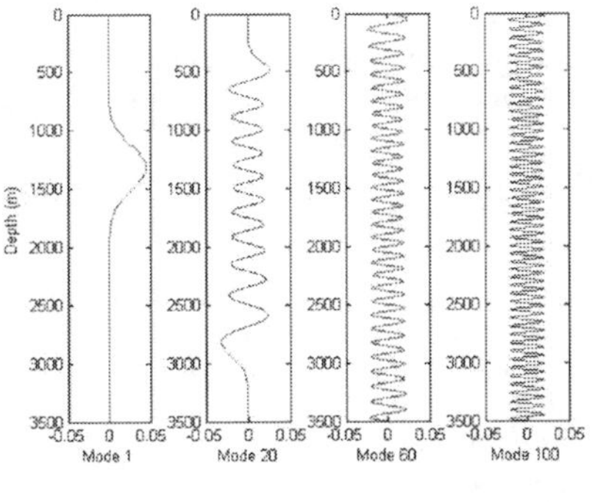

Figure 4. Selected modes in the Munk profile.

The transmission loss TL is calculated by Equation 9:

$$TL = 10log\frac{I(1)}{I(r)} \tag{9}$$

Where $I(1)$, $I(r)$ is the sound intensity at 1 meters and r meters far away from the equivalent sound center respectively.

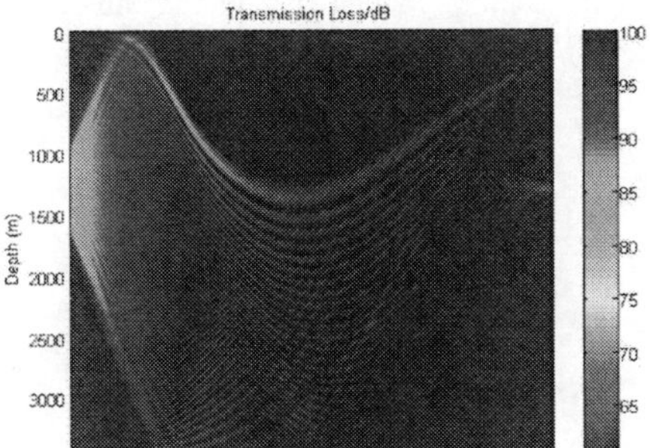

Figure 5. Horizontal range-depth sound field transmission loss distribution of point source.

Figure 5 shows the sound field transmission loss distribution generated by the point source. The horizontal range is 1-50 kilometers, and the depth is from 0 to 3.5 kilometers. There is shadow zone clearly where nearly no sound wave reach.

3.2.2 directional sources sound field simulation

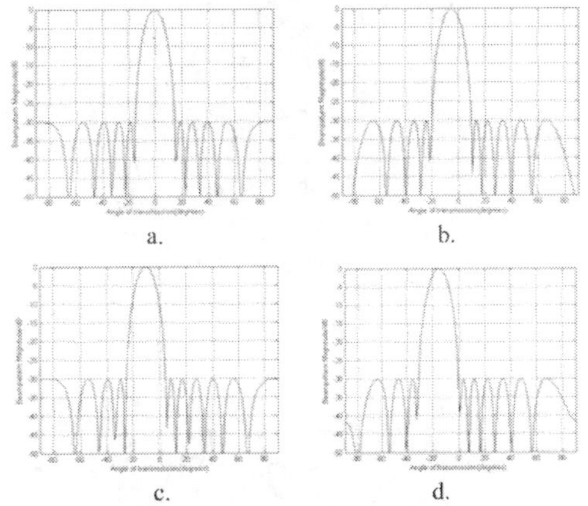

Figure 6. Beam pattern magnitude of different direction angle is 0°, 5°10°15°in proper order a-d.

Figure 6 shows the beam pattern magnitude of different direction angles with chebyshev amplitude weight.

The point source sound field is calculated based on the normal modes model. Add the sound field generated by each point source and at last the underwater acoustical field with directional sources is achieved.

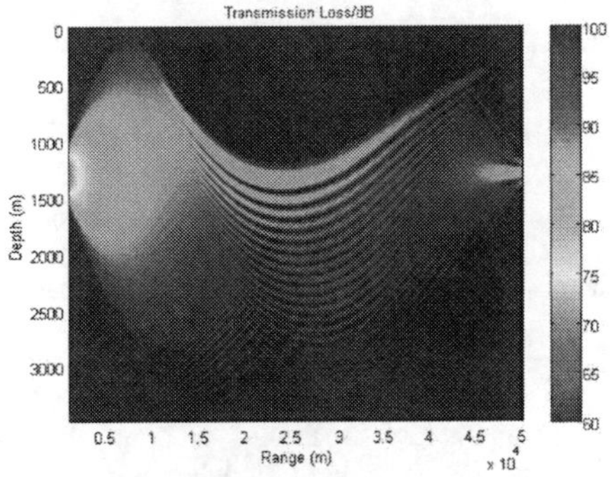

a. Grazing angle 0°

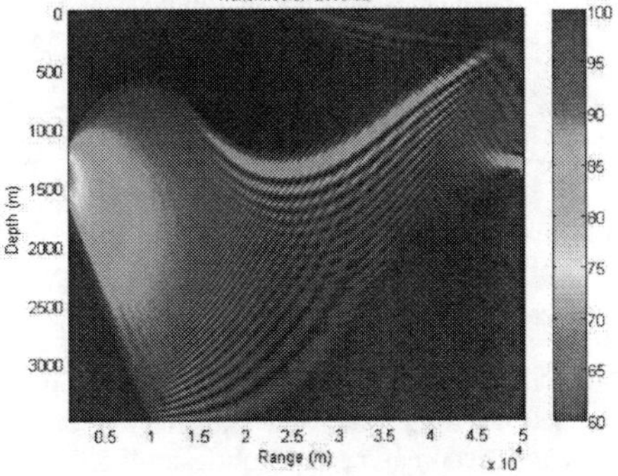

b. Grazing angle 5°

 DOI: 10.1051/matecconf/201712801015

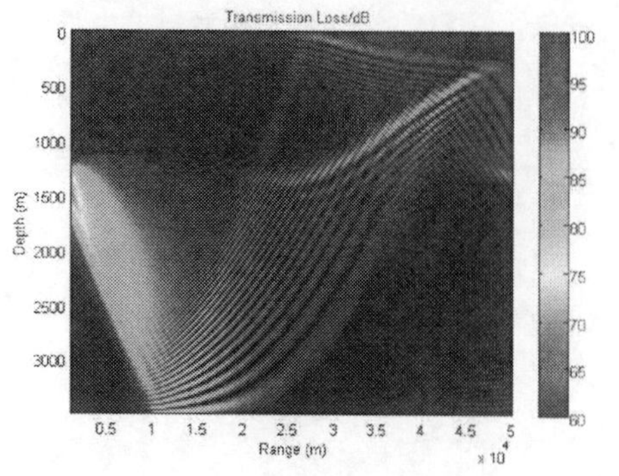

c. Grazing angle 10°

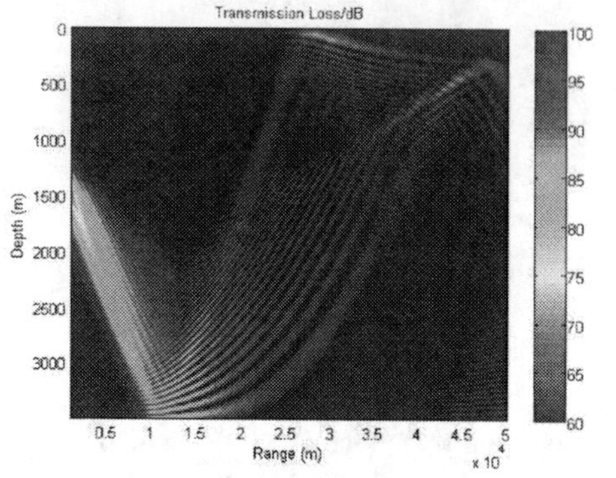

d. Grazing angle 15°

Figure 7. Horizontal range-depth transmission loss distribution of different grazing angles.

Figure 7 shows that the transmission loss has a convergence zone near the sound source, but the energy rapidly decline under the influence of the ocean sound speed profile and the reflection of the interface. Also it exists obvious shadow zone where the sound wave cannot reach.

There is the similar transmission loss distribution of grazing angle 0°to the point source sound field when the grazing angle is low, see Figure 7a. Contrasting on figure 7b, figure 7c and figure 7d, when the grazing angle increases, the energy of the ocean bottom reflection is stronger and stronger. It can reveal that the directional beam may enhance the sound intensity of the shadow zone for the reason that the sound wave can be reflected by the bottom.

4 Conclusion

Beamforming is spatial filtering, a means of transmitting sound preferentially in some directions over others. Instead of computing the sound field supported by the Acoustic Toolbox program directly, beamforming and *KRAKEN* normal modes method are combined to calculate the underwater acoustical field. This article provide a convenient method for designing the directional sources and researching its sound field generated in the oceanic waveguide.

Sound field of directional sources in deep sea has been investigated. The results indicate that it exists shadow zone where direct and reflect sound wave cannot reach, but the sound intensity can be enhanced by varying the grazing angle of the directional sources. If the target places in the shadow zone, the traditional method has many difficulties, but this method can be probably helpful for underwater target detection and may have some significance for active sonar system.

References

1. M A Ainslie, Principles of Sonar Performance Modeling, Springer (2010)
2. J. Benesty, J. Chen, and Y. Huang, Microphone Array Signal Processing, M (2008)
3. Mieheal B. Porter. The BELLHOP Manual and User's Guide:PRELIMINARY DRAFT.Heat, Light, and Sound Research, Inc(2010)
4. M.B.Porter.(2011,Jan.).The BELLHOP manual and user's guide:PRELIMINARY DRAFT. Heat, Light, and Sound Research,Inc (2012)
5. DA Lianglong, Modeling and Application of Underwater Acoustic Environmental Effect[M]. Beijing, Science Press(2012)
6. Alec J Duncan, Iain M Parnum and Peter J Henley. Efficient modeling of mid to high frequency underwater acoustic propagation[J].Proceedings of Acoustics(2013)
7. Shafqat U K, Ijaz M Q, Bial S and Aqdas N, Recovery of failed element signal with a digitally beamforming using linear Symmetrical array antenna, J. Journal of information science and engineering. 32 (2016)
8. R. E. Blabut, W. Millerm, and C. H. Wilcox, Radar and Sonar, Part I, Springer-Verlag, New York(1991)
9. Jensen F B, Kuperman W A, Porter M B, Schmidt Henrik, Computational Ocean Acoustics(2011)
10. L.M. Brekhovskikh and Yu P. Lysanov, Fundamentals of Ocean Acoustics, Springer-Verlag (2003)
11. W.H.Munk, Sound channel in an exponentially stratified ocean with applications to SOFAR, J. Acoust. Soc. Am. 55(1974)

 DOI: 10.1051/matecconf/201712801016

Tibetan Information Extraction Technology Integrated with Event Feature and Semantic Role Labelling

Fucheng Wan[1] Jianhua Xia[2]

[1] *(Key lab of China's National Languages Information Technology, Northwest University for Nationalities, Lanzhou, China)*
[2]*College of Computer and Information, Hohai University, Nanjing, China*

Abstract: we integrate with semantic information which is based on syntactic analysis for extracting the Tibetan information. For Tibetan language information extraction, through experiments analyzed, syntactic analysis model which is integrated with information of semantics, as well as the evaluation of program can be used in Tibetan language information extraction task successfully.

1 Introduction

Information extraction refers to automatic extraction of main information from the text, displayed in a structured form. Information extraction [1], as a key technology in the field of information processing, has been widely used in information retrieval [2], automatic question and answer [3], text mining and so on. Tibetan information extraction algorithm of syntactic information and semantic parsing can be used the information security system such as the Tibetan public opinion surveillance, Tibetan text link detection, Tibetan hot topic recognition and tracking, etc., with good academic value and broad application prospect. It has positive significance in automatic generation of Tibetan database and knowledge base, Tibetan question and answer system, Tibetan information retrieval research, etc.

2 Related Research

In the late 1950s, Zellig Hams put forward the related information extraction and indexing of the literature of science and technology [4], and since 2000, the ACE evaluation meeting and information extraction have developed through decades of years.

In foreign countries, the researches on information extraction have developed from particular field to the open field, enabling the extraction information to be more comprehensive. Data format has developed from regular standard text to irregular common text. Data type has developed from news report and scientific paper to various website texts, Weibo, etc. Method has developed from manual modeling to automatic modeling of machine learning. The information extraction has obtained more notable achievements [6]. Heng Ji et al. [7] studied the cross-document event extraction and tracking, as well as its evaluation standard. Alan Ritter, et al. [8] studied the event extraction facing the open field such as Twitter, applying event extraction technology to real-time and irregular social media space, which makes event extraction technology further practical.

In China, Chinese information extraction technology was started relatively late, but it has made some research achievements. Yuan Yulin [9] studied to semantic resources construction of even extraction. Zhao Yanyan, Liu Ting et al. [10] s proposed event type recognition based on trigger word and binary classification technology. Xu Ronghua, Zhu Qiaoming et al. [11] defined an event fusion framework, TEFF, and made theme event displayed in the hierarchical form according to the role of all kinds of meta events in the theme events. Ding Xiao, Qin Bing, Liu Ting et al. [12] researched event extraction in the field of music, and applied research results in the platform of Harbin industrial university language technology (LTP) [13].

The research foundation on Tibetan information processing is weak, and the information extraction research still stays on the lexical analysis. Xu Tao et al. [14] Researched automatic parsing model by combining the rules of sentence analysis and MEM based on the research of Li Xiang, Liu Qun, et al. [15]. Jin Ming, et al. [16] conducted Tibetan named entity recognition through rules and dictionary method. Zhu Hongzhi et al. [17] used the co-occurrence frequency of named entities to calculate the relationship between Tibetan entities, but in the open field, there are a fewer researches on Tibetan event extraction at home and abroad.

3 Analysis of Tibetan functional semantics

3.1 Tibetan part-of-speech tagging and syntactic

rule

Tibetan sentence components include subject, predicate, object, attributive and adverbial. The sentence is mainly predicate sentence as the core with subject-predicate structure. Tibetan word order is as follows: subject, object (direct object, indirect object), predicate, belonging to SOV syntactic structure, which is different from Chinese. When adjectives, numerals, demonstrative pronoun are taken as modifier, they are put after the center word. When personal pronoun and noun are taken as modifiers, they need to add utterances in front of central word. Verb adjective modifiers are generally before the central word. For example, the characteristic form of Tibetan of verb phrases includes V + UT + UM + UE (UT as tense auxiliary, UM as modal auxiliary, UE voice end utterances). The order and quantity of case-auxiliary word (grammatical function is equal to postpositive preposition); the connection relation between case-auxiliary word and front nouns reflects the grammar characteristics of the Tibetan language.

In order to construct syntax treebank of Tibetan phrase, the Tibetan notional word and function word are respectively refined and tagged, shown as in figure 1:

Table 1 collection of part-of-speech tagging of Tibetan phrase treebank

Common noun --NN	Name --NR	Noun of time --NT	Name of organization --NO	Name of place --NS	Rhetoric word --NE
Buddhist Sanskrit --NF	Numeral --CD	Quantifier --M	Adverb --AD	Conjunction --CC	Noun of locality --LC
Interjection --IJ	Personal pronoun --RR	Demonstrative pronoun --RZ	Interrogative pronoun --RY	Indefinite pronoun --RB	Closing speech -E
Mimetic word --ON	Idiom --I	Dialect --L	Abbreviation --J	Case-auxiliary word --P	Verb--VV

3.2 Examples of Tibetan phrase treebank integrated with semantic information

According to the labelling in table 1, with the use of labeling specification about phrasal level of Chinese tree from university of Pennsylvania library (university of Pennsylvania, Chinese tree CTB), this paper constructs the Tibetan phrase syntax treebank for Tibetan event. The phrase syntax treebank is as shown in figure 1

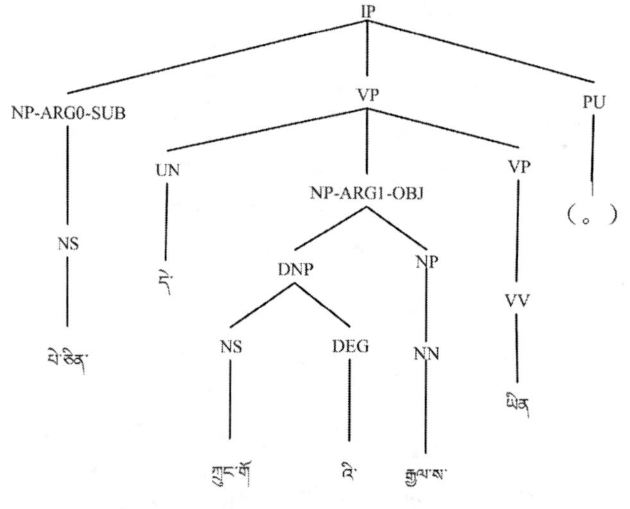

Figure. 1 sample 1 of phrase syntax treebank for Tibetan event

In the current construction of Tibetan syntax treebank, there are more relying on the syntax, but what is interdependent on syntactic withdrawal is the word dependencies. This paper focuses on Tibetan phrase syntax, with the samples in figures 1 and 2 as the standard, to manually label the Tibetan content words and function words respectively. The corpus with 2000 sentences is taken the training corpus, to decrypt test corpus, and then it is assisted with artificial proofreading, adopting the method of bootstrapping to gradually expand the Tibetan phrase syntax treebank.

4 Sample of Tibetan information extraction integrated with semantic feature

4.1 Trigger word recognition

Information extracting must identify the trigger word in the sentence firstly. Tibetan verbs are generally at the end of the sentence, and the core of the whole sentence; from the aspect of position, the Tibetan language identification is relatively easier than other components. Many verbs do not appear in the training corpus, and are non-record words. (respect for teachers, for example), assuming (respect teacher; assuming (respect) does not appear in the training corpus as trigger word, it is easier to identify this event. However, the meaning of (respect) and (esteem) is close; based on this, this paper semantic similarity calculation based on Tibetan verb dictionary, and trigger word dictionary, automatically extends event trigger word, and cover all types of event trigger word as much as possible. For Tibetan word's semantic similarity, the word vector space model and the Tibetan vocabulary context words are used to describe, and the context can provide abundant linguistic information for words. First, a group of feature words are selected, and then according to the frequency of this set of words in the corpus and TF-IDF value, the relevance between a group of words and every word is calculated to get a featured vector; finally, the similarity between vectors is used as the similarity of two words. Root trigger word and its information category form a binary set (trigger, type), for example, (chairman, Person/Respect), to build the binary comparison table of "Tibetan root trigger word - information category"; the binary table has two columns of event trigger words and information categories.

Table 2 comparison table of "root trigger word-information category"

Root trigger word	Information category
(Close down)	Business/Declare-Bankruptcy
(Resist)	Conflict/Attack
(Escape)	Movement/Transport
(Demonstrate)	Conflict/Demonstrate
...	...

The first column is root trigger word; the second column represents the information category of each trigger; each trigger word corresponds to the only one information category, and the trigger words in this table will cover the entire information category. The information category is labelled as the different symbols, with maximum likelihood probability algorithm to get parameters for identification model, and the state transition matrix parameter is

$$Ta_{ij} = \frac{TC_{i,j}}{\sum_{i=1}^{N} TC_{i,k}}, 1 \leq i, j \leq N,$$

$TC_{i,j}$ is the corresponding state of all symbols, TS_i is the number of times to reach the state TS_j., representing the frequency of root trigger word in the corpus to the information category.

$$Tb_j(V_K) = \frac{TE_j(V_K)}{\sum_{i=1}^{N} TE_j(V_i)}, 1 \leq j \leq N, 1 \leq i \leq M$$

$TE_j(V_K)$ is V_K sending frequency in the state of TS_i, $Tb_j(V_K)$ is the proportion of sum of sending probability. $Init(i)$ is the total number in the state of i.

$$TP_i = \frac{Init(i)}{\sum_{j=1}^{N} Init(j)}, 1 \leq i \leq N$$

4.2 Semantic role labelling

The frame semantics of C.J.Fillmore upholds that the case of proposition includes: (1) Agentive; (2) Instrumental; (3) Dative; (4) Factitive; (5) Locative; (6) Objective; (7) Benefactive; (8) Source; (9) Goal; (10) Commutative. On the basis of the Tibetan syntax rule, with the reference of the classification of frame semantics about case, this paper takes five Tibetan function semantics clues including agent, object, time, place, way as the study content.

Chinese Proposition Bank (CPB) of University of Pennsylvania is the resource of Chinese superficial semantic labelling based on Penn Chinese Treebank. The labelled data of Penn Chinese Treebank mainly comes from Xinhua news, Smorama news and magazine and Hong Kong news. CPB contains more than 20 semantic roles; the same semantic role has different semantic meanings for different target verbs. The core semantic role is from Arg0 to Arg5. Arg0 usually means the action of agent; Arg1 usually shows the effect of action and so on. The remained semantic roles are additional semantic role, with the prefix ArgM to express, followed by some additional tags to represent semantic category of these parameters, for example, ArgM2LOC represents location, and ArgM2TMP represents time, etc.

With the structure of "predicate -argument role", for each predicate in the sentence (verbal predicate or nominal predicate, etc.), the corresponding semantic roles of the predicate in the sentence are marked, and the main argument role is the agent AGR0-SUB, object ARG1-OBJ, auxiliary argument role, time ARGM - TEMP, place ARGM-LOC, way AGRM - MNR, as shown in table 3. This integrates semantic information into the syntactic structure tree, as shown in figure 1 and figure 2 at phrasal level; for training and syntax analyzer, Berkeley Parser is used.

Table 3 Corresponding table of semantic labeling

Agent	ARG0-SUB	object	AGR1-OBJ	Time	AGRM-TMP
Place	AGRM-LOC		Method	AGRM-MNR	

5 Experiment and assessment

5.1 Experiment setting

 DOI: 10.1051/matecconf/201712801016

(1) corpus selection: Tibetan text categorization corpus, including 1200 texts of 6 major categories including history, literature, religion, rhetoric, philosophy, politics, etc. among which there are 1000 are the training texts, and 200 are test texts.

Table 4 experiment corpus setting (unit: piece)

Training corpus	Test corpus
1200	200

(2) Result assessment scheme

In this paper, the results of Tibetan information are compared with the standard library for analysis; F value of accuracy (P), and recall rate (R) is used for comprehensive evaluation.

P=number of correct sampling attribute/ number of actual sampling attribute x100%

R= number of correct sampling attribute/ number of imposed sampling attribute x100%

$$F = \frac{2 \times P \times R}{P + R} \times 100\%$$

5.2 Experimental method and results

This experiment compares the methods of part-of-speech tagging, trigger word recognition, part-of-speech tagging integrated with trigger word, and semantic role labelling integrated with trigger word.

(1) Part-of-speech tagging: the part-of-speech method of only using Tibetan words, for example, verb is labelled as vv, and noun is labelled as NN.

(2) Trigger word recognition: taking the results of model recognition as the input of information extraction model to get the results of information extraction

(3) Part-of-speech tagging integrated with trigger word: combing the former two methods, and comparing it with single method

(4) Semantic role labelling integrated with trigger word: namely, the method used in this paper, trigger word as event feature, semantic role information as the text feature of Tibetan, as shown in figure 1 and 1, and labeled in treebank.

The experiment results are shown in table 5

Table 5 result analysis of Tibetan information extraction

Method	P	R	F
Part-of-speech tagging	60.52	57.63	59.04
Trigger word recognition method	65.34	53.26	58.68
part-of-speech tagging+trigger word	68.74	62.34	65.38
trigger word+semantic role labeling	76.78	75.32	76.04

Comparison of the methods of Tibetan information extraction

5.3 Result analysis

From table 5, it can be seen that when only using part-of-speech tagging method (method 1), and only using the trigger word recognition method (method 2), the F value is low; thus, only using dictionary information and part-of-speech tagging method have low contribution rate for Tibetan information extraction. The reason is that both dictionary and part-of-speech tagging method more focus on the objective knowledge, but not to integrate the Tibetan linguistics into the model.

F value of the former two methods have not significantly improved, which also proves the a priori knowledge or artificial model has no good effect on increasing efficiency.

Semantic role labeling information fusion trigger word, that is, the method used in this paper, has improved overall accuracy and recall rate for the Tibetan extraction, thus, integrating Tibetan syntactic and semantic information of linguistics also helps Tibetan information processing of tasks. In addition, information extraction also has a lot to do with the accuracy of the syntactic analysis. The Tibetan information extraction model based on semantic role labeling relies on the accuracy of syntax analysis model of Tibetan language phrase, especially syntactic analysis of long sentences.

6 Conclusion and following work

Tibetan information extraction model integrated with semantic information is integrating semantic information for training on the basis of Tibetan language phrase syntax, so as to provide support for Tibetan information extraction. This paper provides a solution for the Tibetan information extracting on the aspect of semantic information, including the Tibetan semantic information classification, Tibetan semantic information labelling and the syntax analysis of phrases in the Tibetan language, etc. It contributes to providing an information extraction solution for other languages, including Mongolian, Uygur and other ethnic minority languages.

The next step is to strengthen research in the lexical syntactic level to study and Tibetan lexical and syntactic integration model, so as to realize Tibetan language information extraction model without, namely, Tibetan language syntax analysis model based on syllable sequences, serving the Tibetan information extraction.

Acknowledgement

This work is supported by "the National Natural Science Foundation of China (Grant: 61602387)", and "the Fundamental Research Funds for the Central Universities(2014B33014)"

References

1. Liang Han, Chen Qunxiu, Wu Pingbo, Information Extraction System based on Event Framework. Journal of Chinese Information Processing, 2006, Vol.20No.2:40-46.
2. Naomi Daniel, Dragomir Radev and Timothy Allison. Sub-event based Multi-document Summarization [C]. In: Proceedings of the

DOI: 10.1051/matecconf/201712801016

HLT-NAACL Workshop onText Summarization. 2003. pp9-16.
3. Jiang Jifa. Question and Answer Method of Chinese Knowledge in Open Field, computer engineering, 2005.06, 31(11):1-3.
4. W. W. Cohen, A. McCallum. Information Extraction and Integration: an Overview[C].KDD 2003 Tutorial, Washington DC, U.S.A, 2003:pp1-89.
5. Tan Yehong. Research on Key Technology of Chinese Event Extraction. Harbin: Harbin Institute of Technology, 2008.06.
6. S. G Soderland. Building a Machine Learning Based Text Understanding System[C]. Proceedings of workshop on Adaptive Text Extraction and Mining (ATEM-2001), USA, 2001: pp133-154.
7. Heng Ji, Ralph Grishman, Zheng Chen and Prashant Gupta. 2009. Cross-document Event Extraction and Tracking: Task, Evaluation, Techniques and Challenges[C]. Proc. RANLP, 2009: pp162-172.
8. Alan Ritter, Mausam, Oren Etzioni and Sam Clark. Open Domain Event Extraction from Twitter[C]. In SIGKDD'12. 2012.
9. Yuan Yulin. Research on semantic knowledge resources of information extraction. Journal of Chinese Information Processing, 2002, 16(5): 8-14.
10. Zhao Yanyan, Qin Bing, Che Wanxiang, Liu Ting. Research on Extraction Technology of Chinese Event. Journal of Chinese Information Processing, 2008, 22(1): 3-8.
11. Xu Ronghua, Wu Gang, Li Peifeng, Zhu Qiaoming. Research on theme event fusion based on event framework. Application Research Of Computers, 2009, 12, 12(26):4542-4545.
12. Ding Xiao, Song Fan, Qin Bing, Liu Ting, Research on extraction method of typical event in music field. 5th national youth computer language seminar (YWCL 2010). 2010, 7: 431-437.
13. Wanxiang Che, Zhenghua Li, Ting Liu. LTP: A Chinese Language Technology Platform[C]. In Proceedings of the Coling 2010: Demon strati on s. 2010.08:pp13-16.
14. Xu Tao, Jia Yangji, Ding Hongzhi. Automatic punctuation of Tibetan in combination of statistics and rule. Journal of Yunnan University (natural science), 2012Vol.34(6):653-657, 663.
15. Li Xiang, Cai Zangtai, Jiang Wenbin, Lv Yajuan, Liu Qun. Tibetan sentence boundary recognition method in combination of maximum entropy and rule
16. Jin Ming, Yang Huanhuan, Shan Guangrong. Research on Tibetan identity of named entity. Journal of Northwest University for Nationalities (natural science)
17. Hongzhi Yu, Tao Jiang, Bing Zhang. Relation Discovery by Named Entity Recognition from Tibetan Websites[C]. IEEE SWS, 2009: pp177-179.

The Application Study on the Improved Canny Algorithm for Edge Detection in Strain Gauge Image

Qin Wei[1,a], Li Juan[2]

[1]Shaanxi University of Technology, School of Physics and Telecommunication Engineering, Hanzhong, Shaanxi, 723000, china
[2]Shaanxi University of Technology, School of Electrical Engineering, Hanzhong, Shaanxi, 723000, china

Abstract. In order to realize automatic cutting of strain gauge diaphragm, it is needed to detect and identify strain gauge edge. Though classic canny algorithm can detect the edge of strain gauge, it has such problems as low accuracy, being easily influenced by light, random noise. This paper proposes an improved canny algorithm, replacing Gauss filtering of classic canny algorithm with median filtering, improving gradient magnitude calculation method, and selecting threshold with iteration. Compared to classic canny algorithm the method can improve the ability to resist random noise while detecting strain gauge edge more accurately. Application of the method to strain gauge edge detection will lay foundation for realization of strain gauge automatic cutting.

1 Introduction

Resistance strain gauge is a strain measuring device used most widely and most effective in strain measuring technology of engineering structure. Resistance strain type weighing sensor made of various resistance strain gauge plays vital role in electronic industry. The diaphragm of strain meter in strain gauge production process is 115mm long, 100mm wide, with total 150 strain units. Currently domestic producers still adopt manual cutting, with lower quality, yield and production efficiency than automatic cutting, and strain gauge image edge detection is the key technology that needs to be resolved for strain meter diaphragm automatic cutting. Recently as mathematical theory and AI develop, many new modern edge detection methods emerge, Canny approximately replaces optimal algorithm with first derivative of Gauss function, proposing Canny algorithm, empirically testing effectiveness of the algorithm in detection, positioning and single edge response[1-3]. So far, among existing edge detection algorithms, Canny edge detection is still the most important detection algorithm[4]. But classic canny algorithm has some flaws, such as the problem of response to random noise and fuzzy image boundary. This paper uses median filtering to detect strain gauge image, increasing anti-noise capacity of canny algorithm, meanwhile selects appropriate threshold to eliminate weak edge, increasing accuracy of edge detection.

2 Canny Principle and realization procedure of Canny algorithm

Classic edge detection algorithm realizes edge positioning based on original image, by solving differential of location with obvious gray variation in the image, in brief, uses gradient variation between brightness and darkness. Its biggest advantage is simplicity, and effectiveness. Canny finds that optimal algorithm can be approximately replaced with first derivative of Gaussian function, so he proposes Canny algorithm based on it, and empirically tests the effectiveness of the algorithm in detection, positioning and single edge response. Realization of Canny algorithm mainly includes the following procedures:

(1) Gray processing of source image

Canny algorithm mostly processes gray image, processing color image needs gray processing of image. Gray processing of color gram is to sample red, green, blue channel of image and take weighed mean of sampled value. In terms of RGB format, gray processing often uses the following methods, as shown in equation 1 and 2.

$$Gray = (R+G+B)/3 \quad (1)$$

$$Gray=0.299R+0.587G+0.114B; \quad (2)$$

Where parameters in equation 1 are set mainly considering physical characteristics of human eyes, the color image of other format can also be transformed to RGB format according to corresponding relation before gray processing.

(2) Gaussian filtering processing of image

Filtering operation of image can be achieved by two differential weighing processing of 2 one-dimensional Gaussian cores or one convolution of 1 two-dimensional Gaussian core.

Realization of Gaussian core

$$K = \frac{1}{\sqrt{2\pi}\sigma} e^{\frac{x^2}{2\sigma^2}} \quad (3)$$

[a] Corresponding author: Qin Wei@rain301@126.com

Equation 3 is discrete form of one-dimensional Gaussian function, where σ is the variance of the function, when the parameter is determined, the one-dimensional core vector is known.

$$K = \frac{1}{2\pi\sigma^2} e^{\frac{x^2+y^2}{2\sigma^2}} \quad (4)$$

Equation 4 is discrete form of two-dimensional Gaussian function, where σ is the variance of the function, when the parameter is determined, the two-dimensional core vector is known.

Gaussian filtering operation of image is essentially a weighing mean operation following specific rules based on gray value of pixel points to be filtered and every point within neighbourhood, which is very useful to filter out high frequency noise mixed in the image.

(3) Calculation of gradient amplitude and direction

Use first differential algorithm to solve partial derivatives of center pixel point in X and Y direction G_x and G_y respectively, and the amplitude and direction of gradient can be obtained, its expressions of first partial derivative, gradient amplitude and direction are shown in equation 5, 6, 7 and 8.

$$G_x = \frac{f[i,j+1] - f[i,j] + f[i+1,j+1] - f[i+1,j]}{2} \quad (5)$$

$$G_y = \frac{f[i,j] - f[i+1,j] + f[i,j+1] - f[i+1,j+1]}{2} \quad (6)$$

$$G = \sqrt{{G_x}^2 + {G_y}^2} \quad (7)$$

$$\theta = arctan\frac{G_y}{G_x} \quad (8)$$

In equation 5, 6, 7 and 8, f[i, j] is center pixel point, G_x and G_y are first partial derivatives of center pixel point, G is its gradient amplitude, θ is direction derivative.

(4) Non-maximum suppression of gradient amplitude

Only global gradient is not enough to determine edge, so in order to determine edge, the point with max local gradient must be retained, and use the direction of gradient to suppress non-maximum, discretize gradient angle into one of four sections of circumference, so as to use a 3 x 3 window to conduct suppression operation. Mark numbers of 4 sections are 0 to 3, corresponding to 4 possible combinations of a 3 x 3 domain, at every point, the center pixel of domain M[x,y] compares with 2 pixels along gradient line. If the gradient value of M[x,y] is not greater than gradient values of two neighbouring pixels, then let M[x,y]=0.

After maximum suppression of image, we will obtain a binary image, but the image still contains many false edges resulting from noise or other causes, so the image needs further processing.

(5) Edge detection and connection of dual-threshold algorithm

The typical method to reduce number of false edge is to use a threshold to N[i, j], giving zero value to all values less than the threshold. Select a threshold using dual-threshold algorithm. Dual-threshold algorithm applies 2 thresholds T_h and T_l to non-maximum suppression image, and $T_h \approx 2T_l$, so 2 threshold edge image $N_1[i,j]$ and $N_2[i,j]$ are obtained. Because $N_2[i,j]$ is obtained using higher threshold, it contains very few false edge, but contains discontinuity (non-closure) [5]. Dual-threshold algorithm will connect edges to contour in $N_2[i,j]$, when arriving at end points of the contour, the algorithm will locate the edge able to connect the contour at the location of 8 neighbouring points of $N_1[i,j]$, as such, the algorithm continuously collects edge in $N_1[i,j]$ till connecting with $N_2[i,j]$. when connecting edges, use array to simulate realization of queue, conducting 8 connected domain search.

3 Improvement of Canny edge detection algorithm

3.1 Improve image filtering method

Median filtering is a nonlinear smoothing technique, setting gray value of every pixel point as mid-value of gray value of all pixel points in a neighbourhood window of the point. Median filtering is based on sequence statistical theory, effectively suppressing noise[6]. The paper uses 3 x 3 two-dimensional rectangle filter. Its operating procedure is: first, rank pixel value in neighbourhood according to gray value. Then, take pixel mid-value of ranked sequence as output mid-value. Finally, compare gray value of surrounding pixel with output mid-value, modify the pixel value with greater difference to a value close to surrounding pixels to realize elimination of noise point[7]. In traditional median filtering, every pixel in filtering zone influences the result equally, without considering the important factor of distance between them and the center, so the proposed median filtering with weighing value distributes an independent weighing value for every location in filtering zone, and distribution of weighing value is decided by the matrix $W(i,j) \in N$. During filtering calculation, every pixel value $I(u+i, v+j)$ is inserted in extended pixel vector, times of insertion id its weighing value $W(i,j)$, extended pixel vector is shown in equation 9.

$$Q = (p_0, \cdots, p_{L-1}) \quad (9)$$

Where, length $L = \sum_{(i,j \in R)} W(i,j)$

Then rank the pixel vector, with a pixel as the center, select a 3 x 3 two-dimensional rectangle neighbourhood, rank the pixel vector according to gray value of every pixel in the neighbourhood. Calculate mid-value y according to equation 10, next further conduct median filtering processing according to mid-value.

$$y = Med\{f_1, \cdots, f_n\} = \begin{cases} x_{i((n+1)/2)} & \text{n is odd} \\ \frac{1}{2}\left(x_{i(n/2)} + x_{i((n+1)/2)}\right) & \text{n is even} \end{cases} \quad (10)$$

Where, y is mid-value, $f_1, \cdots, f_n$ is pixel points in 3 x 3 square neighbourhood, x_i is the value of the array after pixel points in 3 x 3 square neighbourhood are ranked, i is the location of every value in the array, n is the length of the array.

3.2 Improved gradient amplitude calculation method

Canny algorithm calculates gradient amplitude by solving finite difference in 2 x 2 neighbourhood, considering sensitivity of the method to noise, it easily detects false edge, missing real edge. The improved method uses first partial derivative within a 3 x 3 neighbourhood to solve gradient amplitude and direction[8]. First calculate the first partial derivative in the direction of x, y, 45° and 135°, as shown in equation 11, 12, 13 and 14.

X: $F_x(x,y) = I(x+1,y) - I(x-1,y)$ (11)

Y: $F_y(x,y) = I(x,y+1) - I(x,y-1)$ (12)

45°: $F_{45^\circ}(x,y) = I(x-1,y+1) - I(x+1,y-1)$ (13)

135°: $F_{135^\circ}(x,y) = I(x+1,y+1) - I(x-1,y-1)$ (14)

Then, use partial derivatives in the four directions to solve the difference in vertical and horizontal direction, as shown in equation 15, 16:

$$M_H(x,y) = F_x(x,y) + \frac{F_{45^\circ}(x,y) + F_{135^\circ}(x,y)}{2} \quad (15)$$

$$M_V(x,y) = F_y(x,y) + \frac{F_{45^\circ}(x,y) - F_{135^\circ}(x,y)}{2} \quad (16)$$

Finally use equation 17 and 18 to solve gradient amplitude g and gradient direction θ.

$$g = \sqrt{M_V(x,y)^2 + M_H(x,y)^2} \quad (17)$$

$$\theta = arctan\frac{M_V(x,y)}{M_H(x,y)} \quad (18)$$

Where, $F_x(x,y)$、$F_y(x,y)$、$F_{45^\circ}(x,y)$、$F_{135^\circ}(x,y)$ are first partial derivatives in the direction of x, y, 45° and 135°, $I(x,y)$ is the pixel point in 3 x 3 neighbourhood.

3.3 Selection of image segmentation threshold

Threshold segmentation, in brief, is to segment the target of image from background with threshold, and require to minimize the probability of improper segmentation of target from background. When dealing with practical problem, however, due to adverse influence of noise and other inevitable factors on selection of threshold, it is very difficult to determine a threshold meeting requirement. Using iteration algorithm to determine threshold, not only reduces interference of noise and other factors with selection of threshold, but also determines optimal threshold more easily[9].

Mean value T of minimum Z_{min} and maximum Z_{max} of gray value is obtained through histogram statistics and is used as initial threshold, then use the T to divide gray value - part H_0 above T and part H_1 below H, solve mean value TL of H_1, then again solve mean value of T_H and T_L as threshold, and the threshold is new threshold obtained after our first iteration, compare obtained new threshold with the initial threshold. It their value is the same or their difference meets the condition we set, the iteration ends, T_H and T_L are required optimal high, low threshold. If condition is not met, use the threshold obtained this time to divide all gray value again, continue the process of iteration till new threshold meets requirement[10]. New threshold calculated through multiple iteration will be much better than initial threshold, minimizing probability of improper segmentation of image. Specific procedure of iteration algorithm is as follows:

(1) Make statistic of histogram of image, use equation 19, 20 to calculate initial threshold T of image

$$T = \{T_k | k = 0\} \quad (19)$$

$$T = \frac{Z_{min} + Z_{max}}{2} \quad (20)$$

Where K is times of iteration, Z_{max} represents max gray value, Z_{min} represents min gray value.

(2) Divide image into part H_0 above T and part H_1 below H, as shown in equation 21, 22.

$$H_0 = \{f(i,j) | f(i,j) \geq T\} \quad (21)$$

$$H_1 = \{f(i,j) | f(i,j) < T\} \quad (22)$$

(3) Calculate gray mean value T_H ,T_L of H_0 and H_1, as show by equation 23, 24.

$$T_H = \frac{\sum_{f(i,j)\geq T} f(i,j)}{\sum_{f(i,j)\geq T} N_0(i,j)} \quad (23)$$

$$T_L = \frac{\sum_{f(i,j)<T} f(i,j)}{\sum_{f(i,j)<T} N_1(i,j)} \quad (24)$$

Where f(i, j) is gray value of pixel point (i, j), $N_0(i,j)$, $N_1(i,j)$ meet conditions of equation 25, 26 respectively.

$$N_0(i,j) = \begin{cases} 1, f(i,j) \geq T \\ 0, \quad \text{else} \end{cases} \quad (25)$$

$$N_1(i,j) = \begin{cases} 1, f(i,j) < T \\ 0, \quad \text{else} \end{cases} \quad (26)$$

(4) Calculate mean value of T_H and T_L as new threshold TT, as shown in equation 27.

$$TT = \frac{T_H + T_L}{2} \quad (27)$$

(5) If TT and initial threshold have same value or meet the condition we set, then iteration is completed, if TT obtained this time fails to meet requirement, then continue iteration till TT meeting requirement is found.

(6) Iteration completes, use the result of calculation TT - T_H and T_L meeting condition as optimal high, low threshold for detection.

4 Result of strain gauge image edge detection

4.1 Experimental test of edge detection method

The key for Canny algorithm to detect image edge is selection of Gaussian filtering function σ and threshold. Fig. 1 a is the image of original strain gauge, Fig. 1 b is the image of edge detected by classic canny algorithm, Fig. 1 c Image of filtering and gradient solution improved Canny algorithm edge detection, Fig. 1 d Image of threshold obtaining method improved Canny algorithm edge detection

To test processing effect of improved canny algorithm on Gaussian noise, add Gaussian noise to strain gauge original image. Fig. 2 a is Gaussian noise added original image, Fig. 2 b is classic canny algorithm detected edge image, Fig. 2 c is filtering and gradient amplitude solution improved canny algorithm detected edge image, Fig. 2 d is threshold improved canny algorithm detected edge image.

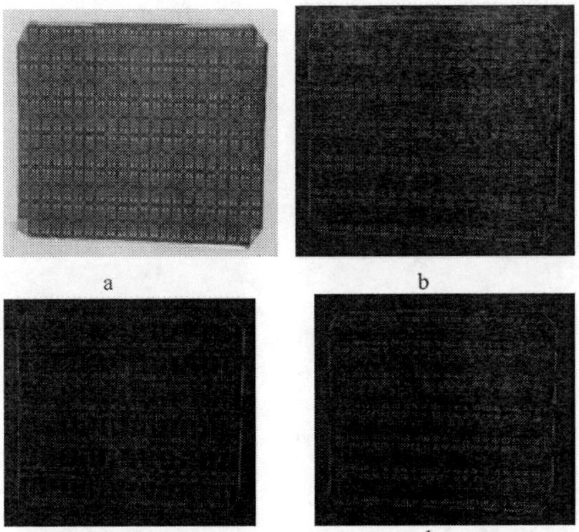

Figure 1. Result of detection without noise edge

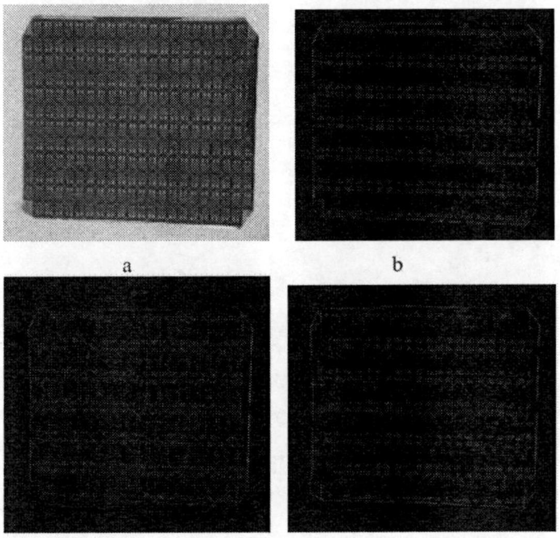

Figure 2. Result of edge detection when adding Gaussian noise

4.2 Analysis of experimental result

1. Without adding noise, compare edge detection results of different Canny algorithm in Fig. 1, it can be found that compared to edge characteristics detected by classic Canny algorithm, threshold obtaining method improved algorithm detect more real edges when automatically selecting threshold, and filtering and gradient solution improved algorithm detects most complete edge characteristics among three algorithms when selecting very good threshold.

2. When adding Gaussian noise, compare detection results of Fig. 2, it can be found that the algorithm using Gaussian filtering almost filter out all false edges produced by noise, but it also filters out many real edges, especially when using traditional algorithm of manually setting threshold, and the algorithm using median filtering keeps most real edges though, it also keeps many false edges resulting from noise.

5 Conclusion

There are many image edge detection methods, but precision and time of strain gauge cutting need to be guaranteed during strain gauge edge detection. Aiming at these requirements, based on classic canny algorithm, during canny algorithm edge detection processing, the design optimizes Gaussian filtering processing and threshold selection. Experimental result shows that the optimization method proposed in the paper has obvious effect on increasing accuracy of strain gauge edge detection and anti-noise capability, as well as certain reference value for application of strain gauge visual detection cutting.

Acknowledgment

The Special Scientific Research project of Education Department of Shaanxi Province(NO.17JK0139).

References

1. Li Hong Dong; Peng Bing Zhao.Application of Improved Canny Edge Detection Algorithm in Coal-Rock Interface Recognition[J].Applied Mechanics and Materials. 1279-1283(2012).
2. Ranita Biswas; Jaya Sil.An Improved Canny Edge Detection Algorithm Based on Type-2 Fuzzy Sets[J].Procedia Technology.820-824(2012).
3. Mingjie Wang; Jesse S. Jin; Yifei Jing;Xianfeng Han;Lei Gao;Liping Xiao.The Improved Canny Edge Detection Algorithm Based on an Anisotropic and Genetic Algorithm[J].Advances in Image and Graphics Technologies.115-124(2016).
4. Tao Sun; Chang Zhi Gao.An Improved Canny Edge Detection Algorithm[J].Applied Mechanics and Materials.2869-2873(2013).
5. Yupeng Wang; Jiangyun Li.An Improved Canny Algorithm with Adaptive Threshold Selection[J].MATEC Web of Conferences.(2015)
6. Alejandro Díaz-Sánchez; Jaime Ramírez-Angulo;Javier Lemus-Lopez.Analog Adaptive Median Filters[J].Analog Integrated Circuits and Signal Processing. **36**,3,207-213(2003).
7. A. I. Kravchonok (1); B. A. Zalesky (1);P. V. Lukashevich (1).An algorithm for median filtering on the basis of merging of ordered columns[J].Pattern recognition and image analysis. **17**,3,402-407(2007).
8. Yang, Tao; Qiu, Yue-hong.Improvement and implementation for Canny edge detection algorithm[J].Proceedings of the SPIE.(2015)
9. Dan Dan Han; Tian Chi Zhang;Jing Zhang.Research and Implementation of an Improved Canny Edge Detection Algorithm[J].Key Engineering Materials.566-569(2013).

DOI: 10.1051/matecconf/201712801017

10. Wei Qing Wang; Hua Feng Ding;Xing Jiang Xiao;Jun Xu;Yuan Zhang.The Improved Algorithm of Edge Detection Based on Canny Operator[J].Advanced Materials Research.97-102(2011).

Research on Modeling Method of Power System Key Components for E-REV

Jigao Niu[1,a], Xiaoli Shi[1], Chunhua Xu[1] and Chenxu Li[1]

[1]*Zhongyuan University of Technology, School of Mechanical & Electronic Engineering, Zhengzhou 450007, China*

Abstract. Aiming at the modeling problem of power system key components for an Extended-Range Electric Vehicle (E-REV), the co-simulation platform based on AVL-Cruise and Matlab/Simulink software is introduced, and the modeling methods of E-REV engine, driving motor and battery are studies by the method of mixing the theoretical modeling with the experimental modeling. Off-line simulation results with chosen driving cycles indicate that the proposed vehicle model has better simulation precision and can meet the simulation specification of the E-REV dynamic performance.

1 Introduction

Through its charging device, the E-REV can get electric energy from power grid. It not just dramatically decreases the human dependency on petroleum, but effectively reduces air pollution. Because of these merits, E-REV has become an alternative development and research direction of clean energy vehicles [1-3]. By building reasonable and effective simulation model of power train components in the process of E-REV development, the effects of power train parameters matching to the vehicle performance can be quantitatively evaluated. Moreover, under the promise of vehicle performance and driving range, the optimal scheme of power train parameters matching can be obtained conveniently and quickly. In addition, the energy management strategy (EMS) of the E-REV can be developed by using the simulation platform, which can verify the advantages and disadvantages of various control strategies quickly, and reduce the unnecessary vehicle manufacture and test.

Firstly, a co-simulation platform of AVL-Cruise and Matlab/Simulink is introduced. Secondly, the modeling methods of the E-REV power train key components including the engine, driving motor and power battery are studied by adopting the way of mixing the theoretical modeling with the experimental modeling. Finally, the model precision is verified by off-line simulation.

2 E-REV co-simulation platform

AVL Cruise is a software tool developed by AVL LIST GmbH, which could simulate vehicle dynamics, fuel economy performance and emissions [4]. The graphical modeling method and friendly interface function with Matlab/Simulink make it more popular in the modeling and simulation of traditional automobile and hybrid electric vehicle. Cruise model elements include vehicle, battery, motor, engine, clutch, wheels, cockpit, monitor, brakes, electrical components, mechanical components, etc., and using these elements, E-REV simulation platform can be established. Among them, the EMS and fuel economy calculation models are built in Matlab/Simulink software. Figure 1 shows the co-simulation platform of the E-REV.

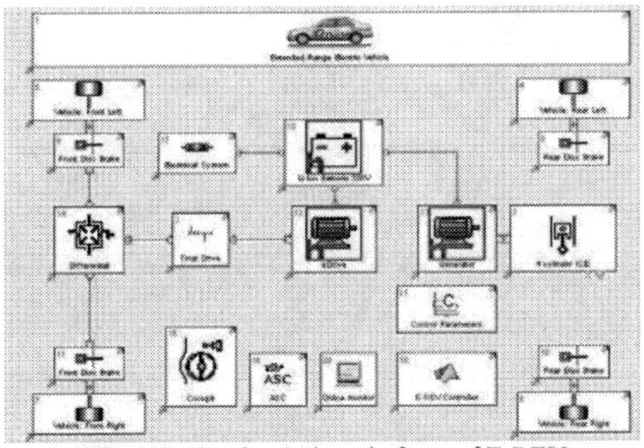

Figure 1. Co-simulation platform of E-REV

3 Key components modeling of power system

The key components of the E-REV power system include engine, driving motor and power battery, the modeling method of these components are described as follows.

3.1. Engine model

Under the range-extended mode, the engine is the main power source of E-REV, and the engine model accuracy has a great influence on the vehicle performance

[a] Corresponding author: jigaoniulucky@163.com

 DOI: 10.1051/matecconf/201712802001

simulation. At present, there are two modeling methods, namely theoretical modeling and experimental modeling. Because the lookup method has a series of advantages, such as simple process, high precision and easy realization, therefore, this paper uses the lookup method to establish the engine model, which includes the engine torque characteristics and throttle opening relationship model, and the engine fuel consumption and emissions model.

3.1.1 Output torque model

According to the universal characteristics experimental data of the engine, Figure 2 shows the torque figure of the engine, which describes the engine torque relationship with throttle opening and speed. By using the lookup and interpolation method, the engine output torque can be obtained as

$$T_e = f_{T_e}(n_e, \alpha_e) \qquad (1)$$

where T_e is the engine output torque in N·m, n_e is the engine speed in rpm, α_e is the throttle opening from the vehicle controller unit (VCU).

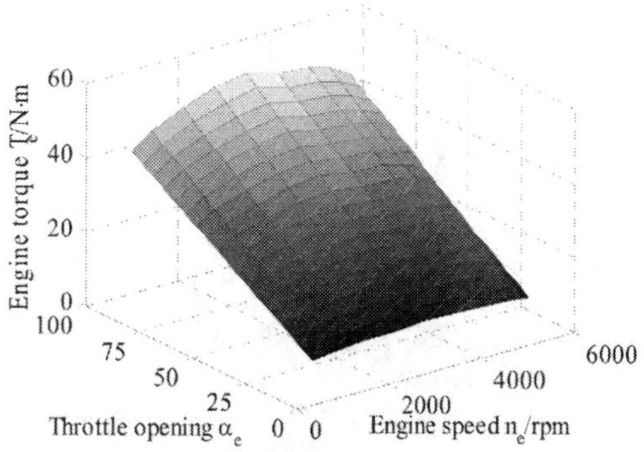

Figure 2. Engine steady torque characteristic

It is well known that the output torque of the engine is decreased because of the friction torque T_{ef}, which is increased with the increasing engine speed. Therefore, the friction torque should be considered when the engine is modeled. Based on factors mentioned above, the post-correction output torque of the engine can be expressed as

$$T_e = \begin{cases} T_{ef}(n_e) + \alpha_e\left[T_{e\_max}(n_e, \alpha_e) - T_{ef}(n_e)\right], & \alpha_e \in [0,1] \text{ and } n_e \geq n_{idle} \\ 0, & \text{others} \end{cases} \qquad (2)$$

where T_{ef} and T_{e_max} are the friction torque and maximum output torque of the engine in N·m at the speed n_e, respectively.

3.1.2 Fuel consumption model

Based on universal characteristics experimental data of the engine, the characteristic diagram of the specific fuel consumption is shown in Figure 3, which describes the engine fuel consumption relationship with the engine torque and speed.

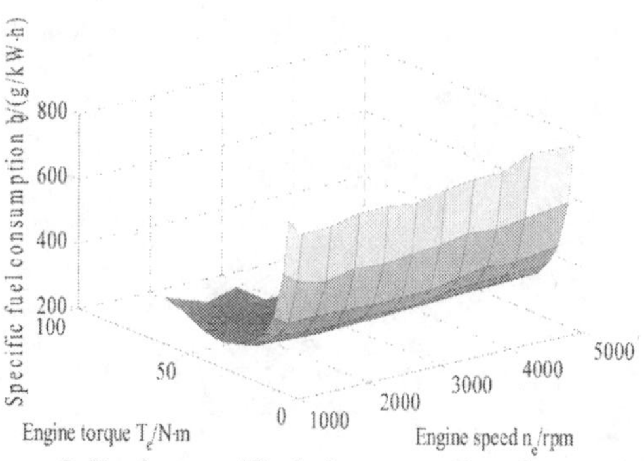

Figure 3. Engine specific fuel consumption characteristic

According to the specific fuel consumption of the engine operating point (Figure 3) and the output power, the engine fuel consumption of per hour can be obtained, and then the engine fuel consumption can be calculated by the integral operation. The calculation formulas are given by

$$b_e = f_b(n_e, T_e) \qquad (3)$$

$$q = \frac{P_{ice} b_e}{1000} \qquad (4)$$

$$Q = \frac{1}{3600 \rho_{fuel}} \int_0^T q dt \qquad (5)$$

where b_e is the engine specific fuel consumption in g·(kW·h)$^{-1}$, q is the fuel consumption of per hour in kg·h^{-1}, P_{ice} is the output power of the engine operating point in kW, Q is the fuel consumption of the engine in L, ρ_{fuel} is the fuel density in kg·L^{-1}, and T is the running time in s.

Simultaneously, according to the parameters of P_{ice} and q, the efficiency of the engine operating point can be calculated as

$$\eta_e = \frac{3600 P_{ice}}{q H_{fuel}} \qquad (6)$$

where H_{fuel} is the fuel heat value in KJ·kg^{-1}.

The modeling methods of the engine exhaust such as CO, HC and NO_x are similar to the fuel consumption as discussed above.

3.2 Motor model

The motor model adopts generally the theoretical model or the quasi-steady model based on the motor efficiency chart, but the former needs to obtain the motor physical parameters, and the simulation speed is slower, therefore, it is generally used to evaluate the motor dynamic characteristics. The latter is the most commonly used in the motor model, which is similar to the engine model, and its advantage is that when the accurate motor physical parameters cannot obtained, the motor performance can be intuitively evaluated according to the motor characteristics parameters. Therefore, it is suitable for various types of motor models.

Based on the experimental data of the motor external characteristic, Figure 4 shows the 3D curved surface figure, which describes the relationship of the motor steady torque measured with the load signal (i.e., motor throttle signal) and the motor speed. The output steady torque of the motor can be obtained by using the lookup method. Moreover, the motor output steady torque can be modified by introducing one order inertial link, and the dynamic output torque of the motor is given by the following equations.

$$T_{m\_s} = f_{T_{m\_s}}(n_m, \beta_m) \tag{7}$$

$$T_m = T_{m\_s}\frac{1}{K_t s + 1} \tag{8}$$

where T_{m_s} and T_m are the output steady torque and dynamic torque of the motor in N·m, respectively, n_m is the motor speed in rpm, β_m is the load signal of the motor from the VCU in %, K_t is the time constant, and S is the laplace transform factor.

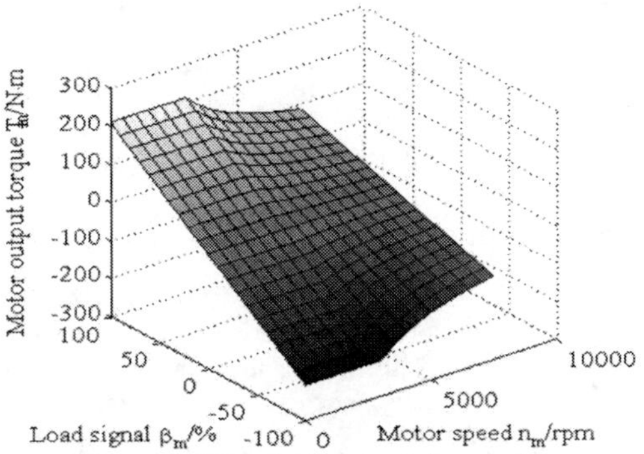

Figure 4. Motor steady torque characteristic

According to the experimental data of the motor efficiency characteristic, Figure 5 shows the motor efficiency relationship with the motor speed and torque.

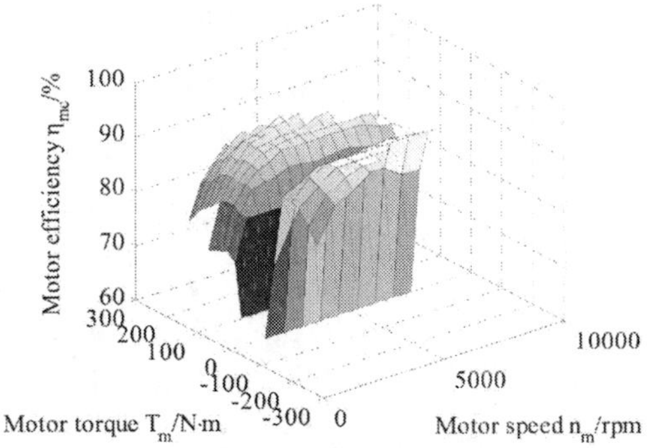

Figure 5. Motor efficiency characteristic

By the way of lookup, the motor efficiency η_{mc} can be expressed as

$$\eta_{mc} = f_{m\_\eta}(n_m, T_m) \tag{9}$$

From Equations 8 and 9, the motor current is calculated by using the method of lookup and interpolation as follows

$$I_{m\_net} = \begin{cases} (1000 T_m n_m)/(9550 \eta_{mc} U_{m\_net}), & electric\ \text{mode} \\ (1000 T_m n_m \eta_{mc})/(9550 U_{m\_net}), & generating\ \text{mode} \end{cases} \tag{10}$$

where I_{m_net} is the motor current in A, U_{m_net} is the motor voltage in V.

The effective output torque of the motor is given by

$$T_{m\_out} = T_m - J_m \omega_m \tag{11}$$

where J_m is the rotational inertia of the motor rotor in kg·m^2, ω_m is the motor angular acceleration in rad·s^{-2}.

3.3 Battery model

The battery charge-discharge is associated with the complex electrochemical reaction, and its performance parameters are greatly affected by temperature, consistency and other factors, therefore, it is difficult to describe the dynamic characteristics of the power battery by the accurate mathematical model [5]. There are two equivalent circuit models (i.e. Rint and RC) in Cruise, and Rint model is adopted in this paper. In this model, the battery is equivalent to an ideal voltage source U_{ocv}, which is series with the battery internal resistance R_{batt}. Rint circuit model is shown in Figure 6.

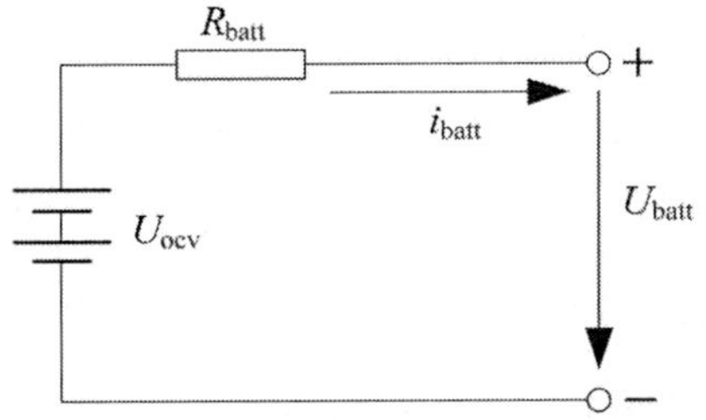

Figure 6. Equivalent circuit of Rint model

According to the Kirchhoff Law, the output voltage of the battery model (see Figure 6) can be written as

$$U_{batt} = U_{ocv} - i_{batt} R_{batt} \tag{12}$$

where i_{batt} is the battery charge and discharge current in A, R_{batt} is the battery charge and discharge internal resistance in Ω.

The state of charge (SOC) of the battery reflects its capacity state, and the SOC can be expressed as

$$SOC = C_r / C_{I\_max} \tag{13}$$

where C_r and C_{I_max} are the residual capacity and actual capacity of the battery when discharging with the constant current in A·h, respectively.

According to the total capacity C_{I_max} and initial capacity C_i of the battery, the input or output electric quantity C_{re} can be calculated by using the adding method. The current SOC is given by the equations (14) ~ (16).

$$C_i = SOC_i C_{I\_max} \tag{14}$$

DOI: 10.1051/matecconf/201712802001

$$C_{re} = \frac{1}{3600}\int_0^t i_{batt}\,dt \tag{15}$$

$$SOC = \frac{C_i - C_{re}}{C_{I\_max}} \tag{16}$$

where C_i is the initial SOC, i_{batt} is the charge and discharge current in A, t is the charge and discharge time in s, the unit of the battery capacity and electric quantity is A·h.

The battery discharge efficiency is represented with the energy efficiency η_{batt} , which is the ratio of the discharge total energy $E_{T,I}$ and the nominal energy E_n. η_{batt} can be expressed as

$$\eta_{batt} = \frac{E_{T,I}}{E_n} \times 100\% \tag{17}$$

where η_{batt} is the discharge energy efficiency of the battery, E_n is the nominal energy of batteries in W·h, and $E_{T,I}$ is the total discharge energy of the battery under the condition of temperature T and current I, W·h.

In order to get the battery experimental data, the $LiFePO_4$ power battery pack (320V/50 A·h) is taken as the testing object in this paper. The open circuit voltage (OCV) and charge-discharge internal resistance of the battery are tested at normal temperature, respectively. Moreover, the hybrid pulse power characterization is used in the test for the charge-discharge internal resistance.

Figure 7 shows the SOC-OCV curve, which is obtained in the process of the battery charging and discharging at normal temperature. From Figure 7, it can be observed that the OCV curve is not coincident, and the charging curve is always slightly higher than the discharging.

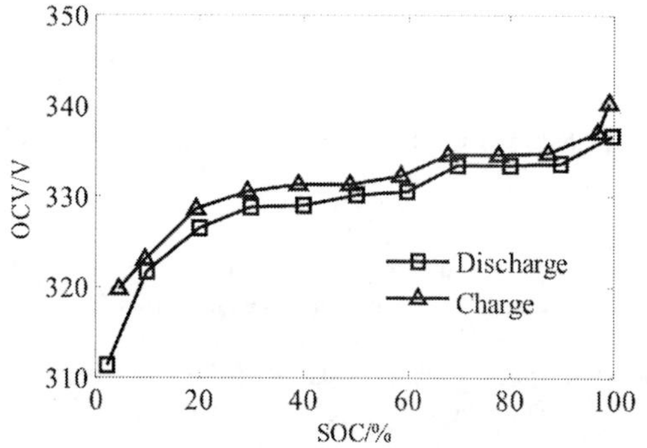

Figure 7. OCV -SOC charging and discharging curve (25◦C)

Figure 8 and Figure 9 show the relationships between the internal resistance of the discharge and charge with the SOC at normal temperature, respectively. It can be seen that when the SOC is located at low region, the internal resistance of the battery discharge and charging is increased drastically, and in other relatively wide SOC ranges, the internal resistance curve of the battery becomes gentle.

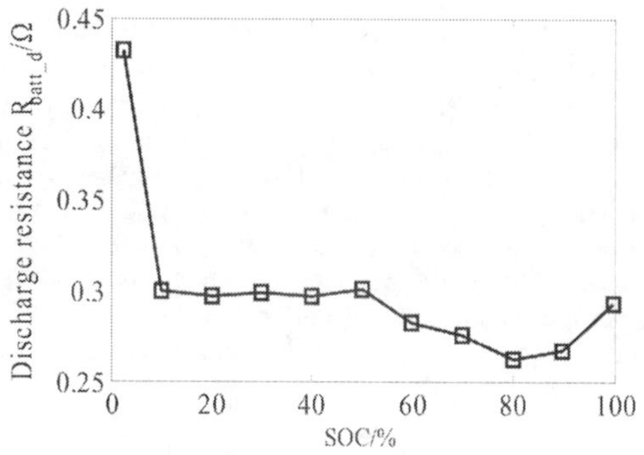

Figure 8. Battery discharge resistance curve

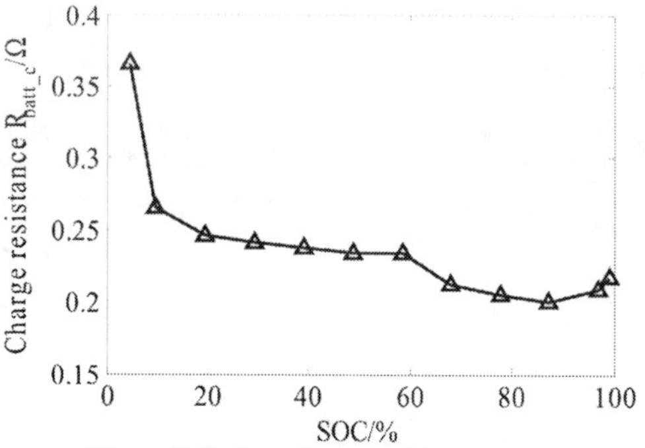

Figure 9. Battery charge resistance curve

4 Simulation results analysis

In order to verify the model precision, the vehicle data and model mentioned above are embedded into the E-REV simulation platform and the simulation calculation of the dynamic performance with a chosen driving cycle are conducted. Figure 10 shows the vehicle speed simulation result in an NEDC drive cycle, and Figure 11 shows the tracking error of the vehicle speed. Off-line simulation results indicate that the simulation speed can follow the driving cycles speed appropriately, and the parameters matching of the E-REV power train can meet the requirements of speed and acceleration. Therefore, the model precision of the key components above mentioned can meet the design requirements.

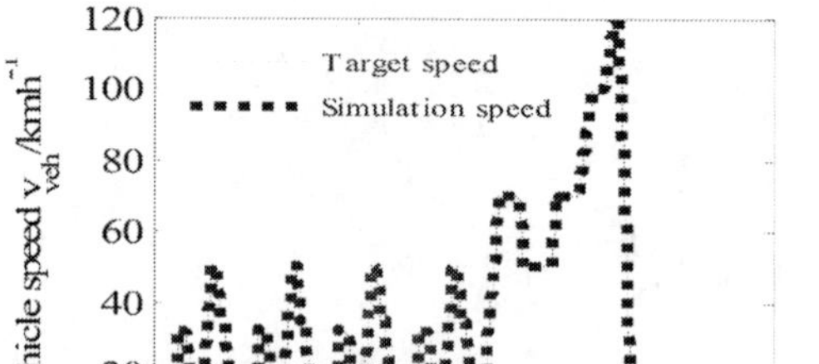

Figure 10. Results comparison of vehicle speed

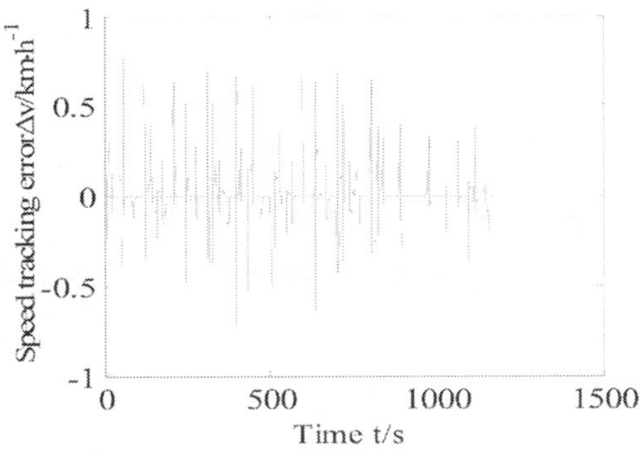

Figure 11. Tracking error of vehicle speed

5 Conclusion

The modeling methods of E-REV power train key components including the engine, driving motor and power battery are studied by adopting the way of mixing the theoretical modeling with the experimental modeling in this paper. Off-line simulation results with chosen driving cycles indicate that the proposed vehicle model has better simulation precision and can meet the simulation specification of the E-REV dynamic performance.

Acknowledgment

The work is supported by Key Research Projects of Henan Higher Institution "Optimization and Control Research of Energy Management Strategy for E-REV" (Item Number: 17A460006).

References

1. G. Fontaras, Z. Samaras. *A quantitative analysis of the European automakers' voluntary commitment to reduce CO_2 emission from new passenger cars based on independent experimental data.* Energy Policy. J. **35** 2239-2248 (2007)
2. J Guanetti, S Formentin, S M. Savaresi. *Energy management system for an electric vehicle with a rental range extender: a least costly approach.* IEEE T INTELL TRANSP. J. **17**, 3022-3034(2016)
3. Y. Wang, B. Meng, Y P. Shen, et al. *Researches on power systems of extended range electric vehicles.* Proceedings of the CSEE. J. **34**, 4629-4639 (2014). (in Chinese)
4. S. Yang, B. Qiu, L. Ta, et al. *A Study on Simulation of Energy Management Strategy of Extended Range Hybrid Bus Based on Cruise.* Automobile Technology. J.7 37-42 (2017) (in Chinese)
5. L. Ramotar, G L. Rohrauer, R. Filion, et al. *Experimental verification of a thermal equivalent circuit dynamic model on an extended range electric vehicle battery pack* [J]. Journal of Power Sources, J **343**, 383-394 (2017)

MATEC Web of Conferences 128, 02002 (2017) DOI: 10.1051/matecconf/201712802002
EITCE 2017

Simulation and Analysis of Passive Rolling Compensation of High Sea Salvage System

Liqun Lin [1,2,a], Zhixin Chen [1,2]

[1]Fishery Machinery and Instrument Research Institute, Chinese Academy of Fishery Science, Shanghai200092, China.
[2]Joint Research Laboratory for Deep Blue Fishery Engineering Equipment Technology, Qingdao National Laboratory for Marine Science and Technology, Qingdao266237, China.

Abstract: Method and device of a flexible interception and salvage system was introduced in this paper. In order to study the effect of wave motion on salvage operation, we proposed a passive wave compensation scheme that utilizes a combination of variable-pitch cylinders and accumulators, and established the mathematical vibration model of the rolling motion of the salvage compensation system. With the relationships between the stiffness coefficient and the accumulator parametric of passive compensated gas-liquid system, we determined the effective compensation stiffness range through Mathematica simulation analysis. The relationship between the roll displacement of the salvage arm and the initial volume V_0 of the accumulator has been analysed. The results show that the accumulatorV_0 in a certain range has a great influence on the passive compensation. However, when the volume is greater than 20m^3, the compensation effect is weakened, and tend to a certain value, irrespective of the passive system accumulator volume capacity, it does not achieve full compensation. The results have important guidance on the design and optimization of rolling passive compensation of the practical high sea salvage system.

1 Introduction

At present, China's salvage rescue system is better in the coastal waters or low sea conditions. They generally use close-up salvage methods, or through auxiliary work boats for salvaging. However, in the high sea conditions, personnel or work boats can't leave the mother ship to operate. Because in the process of salvaging important objects, the salvage equipment is affected by the great movement of the mother ship, causing a sharp swing of the salvage object, so that the salvage efficiency is relatively low, the safety is poor, and even the salvage operation can't be carried out [1]. Therefore, it is of great significance to develop salvage equipment with wave compensation function for high sea salvage operation efficiency and safety.

Wave compensation device is mainly divided into active and passive modes, and the compensation purpose is to effectively suppress the impact of wave on offshore operation. At present, the passive wave compensation system is relatively mature, and has been widely used in marine engineering at home and abroad, the compensation principle is almost similar [2-5]. However, the wave compensation equipment for different operation modes and compensation needs is different in structure, and there are different requirements for compensation variables, control methods and compensation precision. In this paper, we have studied a passive compensation technique for the salvage system of a marine rescue vessel, and introduced a method of flexible net salvage system .In order to improve the success rate of salvage and safety of lifting process in high sea conditions, we have presented a kind of passive composite wave compensation scheme with variable amplitude cylinder as the actuator, and established the mathematical vibration model of the rolling motion of the salvage compensation system. With the relationships between the stiffness coefficient and the accumulator parametric of passive compensated gas-liquid system, we have determined the effective compensation stiffness range through mathematica simulation analysis. The relationship between the roll displacement of the salvage arm and the initial volume V_0 of the accumulator has been analysed.

2 Salvage and wave compensation principle

Flexible salvage with professional salvage ship method under high sea conditions is a new integrating salvage method which based on marine fishery boom trawl technology, by using side crane boom to support and open the flexible fishing nets to salvage and lift objects [6-7]. The salvage system structure shown in Figure 1, mainly includes salvage crane, flexible nets, winch, variation cylinder, anti-shake device, tension rope, etc.

[a] Corresponding author: linliqun@fmiri.ac.cn

DOI: 10.1051/matecconf/201712802002

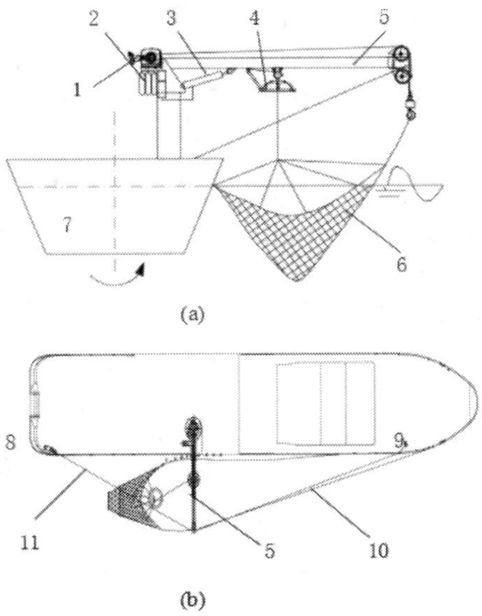

1、8、9. Winch, 2. Accumulator, 3. Variation Cylinder, 4. Anti-sway device, 5. Interception arm of salvage crane, 6. Flexible net, 7. Salvage, 10、11. Tension rope

Figure 1 Schematic diagram of the salvage system structure

As for the motion compensation design of the salvage system, we only take into account the compensation method of the lateral rolling, according to the characteristics of its own motion and operation requirements. The passive roll compensation system consists of hydraulic cylinders, gas-liquid accumulators and air cylinders. We propose a gas-liquid passive compensation system, the hydraulic cylinder is used to bear the weight of the load, the accumulator is used to store and release the ship movement energy. The rodless cavity of the cylinder is connected with the liquid chamber of the gas-liquid accumulator, and the cylinder rod is connected to the atmosphere or the tank which pressure is the same as the atmospheric pressure, and the gas chamber of the accumulator is connected with the air bottle. In order to make the size of the compensation cylinder is not too large, the system pressure is not too high, two compensation cylinders are designed. When the ship is stationary in the equilibrium position, or the compensation system is locked to work, the compensation lift generated by the hydraulic cylinder is equal to the total weight of the salvage system. The torque of the hydraulic cylinder is equal to the total load torque of the salvage system, and the working pressure of the system depends on the total load torque. When the ship counterclockwise swing, the fixed base of the salvage crane along with the ship rose, but the interception arm of the crane (connected with the piston rod of the compensating cylinder) has the tendency to stay in the balance position due to the inertial action, the oil in the rodless chamber is compressed into the accumulator and the gas in the accumulator is compressed. Otherwise, in the rodless chamber, the oil is sucked in from the accumulator, the gas in the accumulator expands, compensating for the falling displacement and releases energy, thus achieving roll compensation. It can be seen that the compensating power of the passive compensation system is derived from the waves and the system does not need to provide additional power.

3 Mathematical model

3.1 Assumption

The salvage system is a spring damping system. According to the actual situation, the actual factors are simplified as the following basic assumptions.

(1) The wave is regarded as sinusoidal waves, the ship rolling with the wave during salvaging, α_0 is roll angular displacement of the salvage ship, α_1 is the interception arm's roll angular displacement, x is the cylinder displacement. Do not consider the reaction force of the salvage device to the ship.

(2) The base of the salvage crane, rodless side of the cylinder, the accumulator are seen as rigid bodies following the boat movement, we do not discussed the force of the rigid bodies as a sinusoidal roll excitation for the interception arm, its motion excitation function is $\alpha_0 = \alpha_m \sin(2\pi t / T)$.

(3) The oil in the cylinder and the gas in the accumulator are regarded as massless substance, the stiffness coefficient is k, the viscosity resistance coefficient is c.

(4) The compensation system is divided into two parts, that is, intercepting salvage compensation and lifting compensation. The former mainly maintains the relative displacement of the intercept arm and the sea to keep the best intercept net shape, the latter is mainly to ensure the lifting safety. This article only consider the intercepting salvage compensation, so as no need to consider the lifting load. Regardless of the wind load on the interception arm.

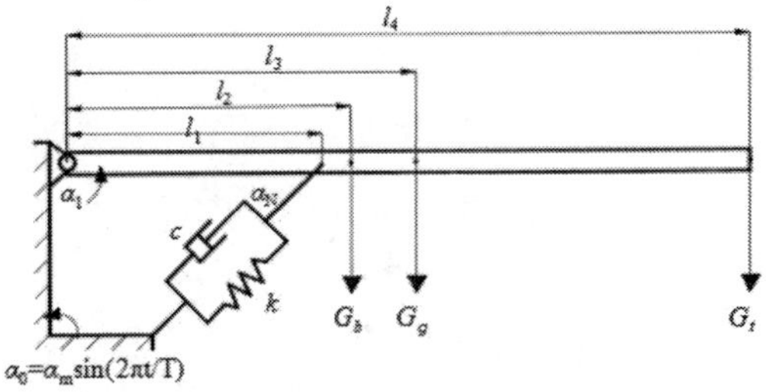

Figure 2 Mathematical model of the interception arm rolling compensation system

3.2 Mathematical model of salvage system

Through the above assumptions and simplification, the interception arm rolling compensation system can be simplified as shown in Figure 2, the intercept salvage system compensation dynamics equation is as:

$$J\ddot{\alpha}_1 + c(\dot{\alpha}_1 - \dot{\alpha}_0)\sin^2\alpha_N l_1^2 + k(\alpha_1 - \alpha_0)\sin^2\alpha_N l_1^2 = 0 \quad (1)$$

DOI: 10.1051/matecconf/201712802002

It is simplified as follows:

$$J\ddot{\alpha}_1 + c\sin^2\alpha_N l_1^2\dot{\alpha}_1 + k\sin^2\alpha_N l_1^2\alpha_1 = \frac{2\pi}{T}\alpha_m c l_1^2\cos(\frac{2\pi}{T}t) + \alpha_m k l_1^2\sin(\frac{2\pi}{T}t) \quad (2)$$

Where, J is total inertia of intercept arm, anti-sway device and net weight, $J = m_b l_2^2 + m_g l_3^2 + m_t l_4^2$, m_b is the interception arm weight, kg. m_g is lifting anti roll device, weight, kg. m_t is the weight of the nets, kg. l_1 is the distance between hinge joint of the cylinder and the point O, m. l_2 is the intercept arm inertial radius, m. l_3 is distance between anti sway device installed and the point O, m. l_4 is distance from the points of nets on intercept arm to point O, equal to the length of intercept arm, m. T represents the ship's rolling period with the wave, s .Let

$$H = \frac{\sin^2\alpha_N l_1^2}{J} \quad (3)$$

From equation (2), we can know that the salvage system inherent frequency ω_n, relative resistance coefficient ξ, ship roll vibration frequency$\omega$and frequency ratio$\lambda$are respectively as follows

$$\omega_n = \sqrt{\frac{k}{J}}l_1 = \sqrt{kH} \quad (4)$$

$$\zeta = \frac{c}{2}\sqrt{\frac{H}{k}} \quad (5)$$

$$\omega = \frac{2\pi}{T} \quad (6)$$

$$\lambda = \frac{\omega}{\omega_n} \quad (7)$$

Turn the equation (4) ~ (7) into equation (2) as:

$$\ddot{\alpha}_1 + 2\zeta\omega_n\dot{\alpha}_1 + \omega_n^2\alpha_1 = Hk\alpha_m\sin(\omega t) + Hc\omega\alpha_m\cos(\omega t) \quad (8)$$

Equation (8) can be solved by the complex method [8]. By using the linear superposition principle, it is obtained.

$$\alpha_1 = \frac{Hk\alpha_m}{\omega_n^2}\frac{1}{\sqrt{(1-\lambda^2)^2+(2\zeta\lambda)^2}}\sin(\omega t-\theta_1) + \frac{Hc\omega\alpha_m}{\omega_n^2}\frac{1}{\sqrt{(1-\lambda^2)^2+(2\zeta\lambda)^2}}\cos(\omega t-\theta_1) = \alpha_m\sqrt{\frac{1+(2\zeta\lambda)^2}{(1-\lambda^2)^2+(2\zeta\lambda)^2}}\sin(\omega t-\theta_1+\theta_2) \quad (9)$$

Where $\theta_1 = \arctan[2\zeta\lambda/(1-\lambda^2)]$, $\theta_2 = \arctan(2\zeta\lambda)$. The salvage crane interception arm rolling amplitude B_0 is:

$$B_0 = \alpha_m\sqrt{\frac{1+(2\zeta\lambda)^2}{(1-\lambda^2)^2+(2\zeta\lambda)^2}} \quad (10)$$

The amplitude magnification factor of the roll angle displacement β is:

$$\beta = B_0/\alpha_m = \sqrt{\frac{1+(2\zeta\lambda)^2}{(1-\lambda^2)^2+(2\zeta\lambda)^2}} \quad (11)$$

3.3 Mathematical model of gas liquid passive compensation system

During the expansion or retraction of the hydraulic cylinder of the passive compensation device, the gas is compressed or expanded by the free piston of the accumulator to change the inner volume of the cylinder, causing the pressure inside the accumulator to change. Passive compensation cylinder and accumulator system model shown in Figure 3.

Ignoring the accumulator piston mass and oil compression, compensation cylinder and accumulator pressure equal. According to the ideal gas state equation, the definition of the gas spring stiffness coefficient can be obtained as.

$$p_0V_0^n = p_1V_1^n \quad (12)$$

$$V_1 = V_0 - A_a x_{\max} \quad (13)$$

$$kx_{\max} = (p_1 - p_0)A_a \quad (14)$$

Where, V_1 is the minimum gas volume of the accumulator cylinder, m^3. V_0 is the initial gas of the accumulator, m^3. P_1 is the pressure in the accumulator when the gas volume turns to V_1, MPa. P_0 is the pressure in the accumulator when the gas volume turns to V_0, MPa. $x_{\max}$ is the maximum displacement of the accumulator piston, m. n is Gas polytropic index, due to its short heat exchange time, it can be considered as an adiabatic process, and the polytropic index n=1.4. A_a is the accumulator piston area, m^2.k is the stiffness coefficient, kN/m. The stiffness coefficient k can be solved by equation (12)-(14):

$$k = \frac{p_0A_a}{x_{\max}}\left[\left(\frac{V_0}{V_0 - A_a x_{\max}}\right)^n - 1\right] \quad (15)$$

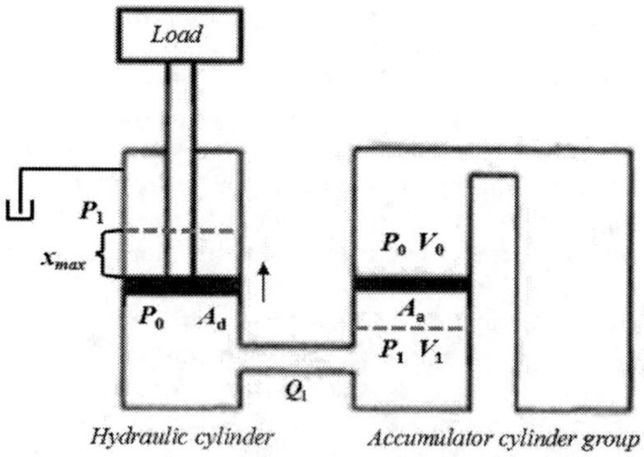

Figure 3 Passive compensation model for gas and liquid systems

3.4 Design requirements

In high sea conditions, the ship roll amplitude α_m=15°, The period T=10s. Interception arm roll angle is designed within ± 8 °, other relevant parameters are as follows:

Table 1 Calculation conditions

No.	Parameters	Value
1	G_b	90kN
2	G_g	12kN
3	G_l	10.6kN
4	l_1	4.8m
5	l_2	5.6m
6	l_3	8.8m
7	l_4	16.8m
8	α_N	26°
9	c	1700N/(m/s)
10	P_0	16MPa
11	x_{max}	0.6m
12	A_a	0.126m^2

4 Simulation results and analysis

The rolling amplitude B_0 of the intercepting arm depends on the amplitude α_m of the supporting mother ship, the frequency ratio λ and the relative resistance coefficient ξ. The effect of the frequency ratio λ and the relative resistance coefficient ξ on the amplification factor β is shown in Figure 4. It shows that when λ<1, the interceptor salvage arm roll amplitude is greater than the mother ship roll amplitude. When λ=1, that is, when the vibration frequency of the interceptor arm is equal to the frequency of the ship rolling, the interception arm resonates, the amplification factor β increases greatly with the decrease of the relative resistance coefficient ξ. However, when $\lambda=\sqrt{2}$, No matter what the relative resistance coefficient ξ value is, amplification factor β is equal to 1, that means the amplitude of the intercepting arm is equal to the ship amplitude. When $\lambda>\sqrt{2}$, $\xi<1$, the amplitude of the intercepting arm is less than B_0. As the frequency ratio increases, the amplification factor approaches 0, and the larger the relative resistance coefficient is, the smaller the amplitude is. From the above analysis, in order to make the amplitude of the intercepting arm lower than the mother roll, we need to design the frequency ratio and resistance ratio of the system reasonably, satisfy this inequality $\lambda>\sqrt{2}$.

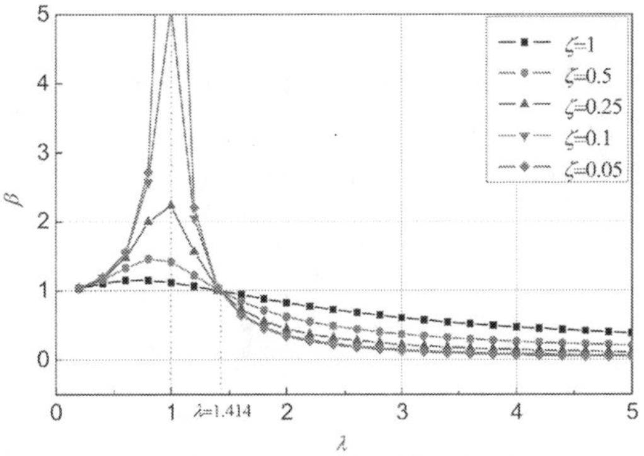

Figure 4. Relationship of $\beta - \zeta - \lambda$

The simulation curve of the interception arm is shown in Figure 5, corresponding to the initial volume of the accumulator V_0 = 8m^3, 13m^3, 20m^3. After the installation of gas-liquid passive compensation, the interception arm roll angle amplitude was significantly lower than the salvage ship's roll angle amplitude. In the different initial volume conditions, the amplitude of the roll is significantly different. When V_0 = 8m^3, the interception arm roll angle amplitude is 10 °, V_0= 13m^3, the interception arm roll angle amplitude is 5 °, V_0 = 20m^3, interceptor arm roll angle amplitude is 2.5 °.

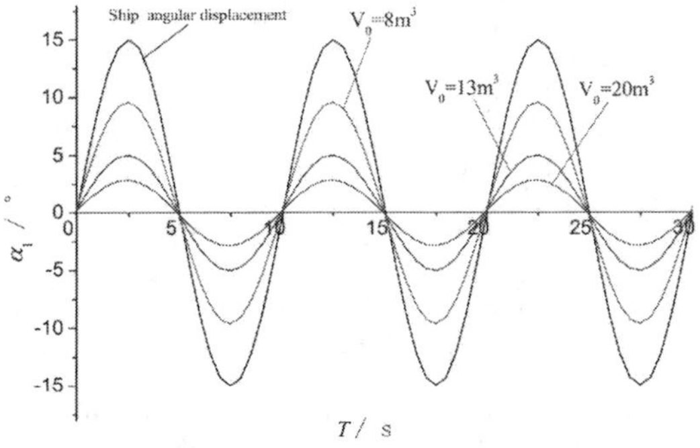

Figure 5. Passive roll compensation curve

The relationship between the compensation effect and the initial volume is shown in Figure 6. It shows that passive compensation system with accumulator is not necessarily compensated. When the accumulator volume V_0 is less than 6.5m^3, the angle amplitude of the interceptor arm is greater than 15 °, the compensation effect is negative, which can't be compensated. When the accumulator volume V_0 is greater than 6.5m^3, the system compensation is shown to be effective. In this range, increasing the capacity of the accumulator can effectively improve the compensation effect, but the improvement of the compensation effect is not proportional to the V_0. As the volume increases, the compensation effect increases rapidly, and then the change gradually tends to be gentle, and finally tends to a certain value. However, no matter how large the volume of the passive system accumulator is, it does not achieve complete compensation.

DOI: 10.1051/matecconf/201712802002

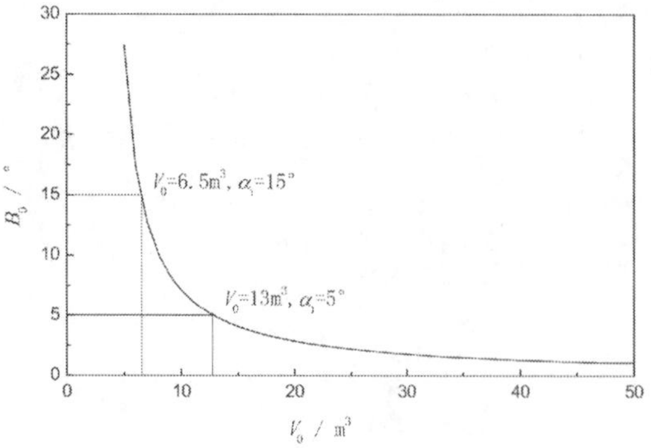

Figure 6. Curve of intercepting arm roll amplitude changing with accumulator volume

5 Conclusion

Aiming at ship salvage under high sea conditions, we introduced method and device based on flexible interception and salvage, and proposed a passive wave compensation scheme that utilizes a combination of variable-pitch cylinders and an accumulators, and established the mathematical vibration model of the rolling motion of the salvage compensation system. With the relationships between the stiffness coefficient and the accumulator parametric of passive compensated gas-liquid system, we determined the effective compensation stiffness range through Mathematica simulation analysis. The relationship between the roll displacement of the salvage arm and the initial volumeV_0 of the accumulator has been analysed. Results show that increasing the capacity of the accumulator can effectively improve the compensation effect, but the improvement of the compensation effect is not proportional to the V_0. As the volume increases, the compensation effect increases rapidly, and then the change gradually tends to be gentle, and finally tends to a certain value. However, no matter how large the volume of the passive system accumulator is, it can't achieve complete compensation. The results have important guidance on the design and optimization of rolling passive compensation of the practical high sea salvage system.

Acknowledgments

This work was financially supported by two project, one is Qingdao Ocean Science and Technology National Laboratory Aoshan Science and Technology Innovation Project No.2016ASKJ10, another is Chinese Academy of Fishery Sciences Basic Scientific Research Project No.2016YJS011.

References

1. Zhenggu Xu, Zhixin Chen, Zhongxin Wang, et al. Equipment for salvaging floating objects [P]. **CN200410024783.3** (2005)
2. Lumeng Huang, Yanting Zhang, Lei Zhang, et al. Semi-active drilling drawworks heave compensation system [J]. Petroleum Exploration and Development, **40 (5)**, p 620-624 (2013)
3. Haibo Wang, Qingfeng Wang. Design and Internal Model Robust Control of Underwater Towed Heave Compensation System [J]. JOURNAL OF MECHANICAL ENGINEERING, **46 (8)**, p 128-132 (2010)
4. Xiaoyan Tang, Shaojun Liu, Gang Wang. Modeling of heave compensation system for deep-ocean mining and its simulation of fuzzy logical control[J].JOURNAL OF CENTRAL SOUTH UNIVERSITY, **39 (1)**, p 128-134 (2008)
5. Jinbo Wu, Yucheng Song. Design and Analysis of Active Heave Compensation System for Offshore Cranes [J]. China Mechanical Engineering, **27 (15)**, p 1989-1995, 1996 (2016)
6. Zhixin Chen, Tong Zhou HaoXu. Electric hydraulic integration controlling system for salvage equipment of aircraft returning cabin in terrible ocean environments [J]. FISHERY MODERNIZATION, **34 (6)**, p 55-59 (2007)
7. Liqun Lin, Zhixin Chen, Ping Liu,et al. Experimental study on high sea floating object fishing net [J].FISHERY MODERNIZATION, **43 (5)**, p 34-39 (2016)
8. Zhenghua Ni, Wenliang Chen, Liqun Chen.Vibration mechanics [M]. Higher Education Press (1998)

Multi-objective Particle Swarm Optimization Based Image Watermarking Scheme

YongGang Fu[1], HuiRong Wang[2], Lizhen Chen[1a], Yunfei Jiang[1]

[1]*College of computer engineering, Jimei University, Xiamen, 360121, China*
[2]*College of Chinese Literature, Jimei University, Xiamen, 361021, China*

Abstract. A novel image watermarking scheme based on the statistics of the blocked DCT coefficients. The watermark is embedded into the middle frequency of those DCT coefficients by modulating the number of those positive and negative coefficients. In order to achieve better robustness and imperceptibility, multi-objective particle swarm optimization (MPSO) has been used in the watermark embedding and extracting procedure. The particle swarm optimization is applied to obtain optimum multiple scaling factors and the embedding strength. The experimental results show that the proposed scheme has significant improvement in term of imperceptibility and robustness under various general attacks.

1 Introductions

Computer and networks have been a significant way to exchange information in this era. Various digital multimedia products are spread on the Internet. Nowadays, people can copy, alter, and transmit multimedia properties easily, including texts, images, audios, videos, and so on. Modern information technology brings not only convenient and cheap digital transmission services, but also various challenges. One of the most important is how to protect the properties of the legal owner [1]. In this case, digital watermarking is proposed, which means hiding information or anti-counterfeit mark into the host image to protect copyright. It will be flourishing in the next decades with the urgent market demand. It is the digital watermarking technology that may be utilized as a supplement for cryptography encryption and scrambling technology [2].

During the last decade, many robust image watermarking algorithms have been proposed, which can be divided into three categories according to the domain what the watermark can be embedded: spatial domain watermarking, transform domain and hybrid domain watermarking. The spatial domain watermarking algorithms [3, 4]mainly embed the watermark by modulating the image pixels or altering its gray values directly, such as the least significant bit (LSB) and so on. These algorithms are fragile to manipulations, but they have little computation work and can be easily implemented. The transform domain watermarking schemes are mainly concentrated on some signal transforms such as DCT(Discrete Cosine Transform) [5, 6], DFT(Discrete Fourier Transform) [7] and DWT(Discrete Wavelet Transform) [8-10], etc. The watermark is embedded into the host by modifying some or all frequency domain coefficients, especially middle frequency coefficients. These methods have better robustness and can resist common attacks [11-13]. The hybrid domain can employ the advantages in two or more domain. The typical scheme is based on two transform domains. The first transform may have some good characteristics to some common attacks, and the second transform can be robust to geometric attacks. The hybrid domain algorithms can achieve good performance, but they are complex in implementation. It may be a future development direction because computer performance is strengthening on calculation. Now, most of the proposed watermarking schemes are based on the transformation domain. In this paper, the proposed algorithm can effectively resist some geometrical attacks.

The paper is organized as follows. In section II, the particle swarm optimization is reviewed. Section III describes the proposed watermarking scheme in detail. The experimental results are shown in section VI. And section VII conclude the paper.

2 The particle swarm optimization

The particle swarm optimization is a meta-heuristic swarm based algorithm widely used in parameter optimization, which is proposed by Kennedy and Eberhart [14]. The particle swarm optimization mimics the simplified social models such as fish schooling and bird flocking. A swarm is defined as a set of mobile agents that collectively carry out problem solving in a distributed manner. Each agent is called one particle. In a swarm, each particle keeps track of their own attributes.

[a] Corresponding author: f_rock@163.com

Initially, the position $x_{(i,j)}(k)$ and the velocity $v_{(i,j)}(k)$ of each particle p are randomly created. Each particle represents a candidate solution to optimize problem by calculate its fitness. The fitness of each particle is evaluated by an objective function. During iteration, the best location visited by each particle is kept as the local best position $P_{best(i,j)}$, while the best location visited by all particles is kept as the global best position $G_{best(i,j)}$.

Therefore, a new population is created based on a preceding one and the particles are updated by the following equations:

$$\begin{cases} v_{(i,j)}(k+1) = \omega v_{(i,j)}(k) + c_1 r_1 [P_{best(i,j)}(k) - L_{(i,j)}(k)] \\ \qquad + c_2 r_2 [G_{best(i,j)}(k) - L_{(i,j)}(k)] \\ L_{(i,j)}(k+1) = L_{(i,j)}(k) + v_{(i,j)}(k+1) \end{cases} \quad (1)$$

Where those parameters can be depicted as follows: (i,j): index of the position in the particle; k=1,2,…P , is the iteration number; $v_{(i,j)}(k)$: velocity of the particle in the swarm at the position index (i,j); $L_{(i,j)}(k)$ is the current position of the particle at the position index (i,j); r_1 and r_2 are random values uniformly distributed in range [0,1]; c_1 and c_2 are positive acceleration coefficients, which control the influence of $P_{best(i,j)}$ and $G_{best(i,j)}$; ω : inertia weight, usually with in $0.8 \le \omega \le 1.4$.

The detail procedure of PSO algorithm can be depicted as follows:

Algorithm 1. Particle Swarm Optimization(PSO)
1) Create a population, P of random particles.
2) For each particle calculate the fitness value and find the local best P_{best}.
3) Calculate the global best, G_{best} for the swarm.
4) Update each particle's velocity and position using Eq.1.
5) If termination condition is not met, goto step 2).

3 Proposed watermark embedding and extracting scheme

The block DCT coefficients can be divided into DC coefficient and AC coefficients. The DC coefficients of mth block can be expressed $F_m(0,0)$ and the rest may be divided into low, middle and high frequency coefficients. Since tiny modification of the DC or low frequency coefficients may degrade image subjective quality, embedding watermark into the DC or low frequency coefficients should not be adopted. The watermark information embedded into high frequency coefficients can be easily removed during the general image

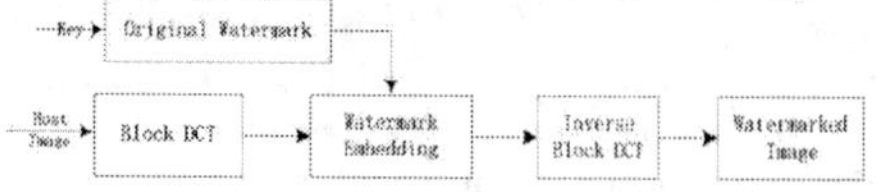

Fig.1. Block diagram of watermark embedding

processing. So the middle frequency coefficients may be a better choice according to the necessity of compromise between robustness and invisibility. In this paper, the watermark is embedded into the middle frequency coefficients. Watermark embedding and extracting block

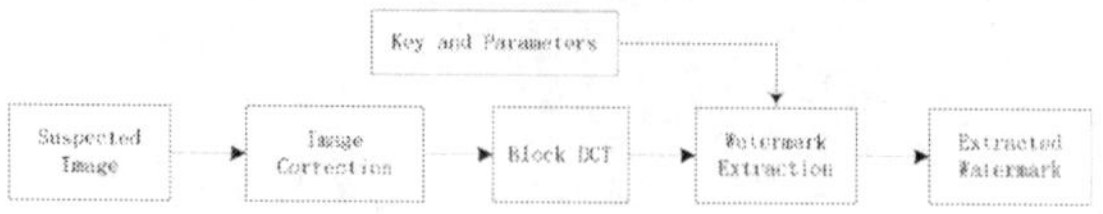

Fig.2 Block Diagram of Watermark Extraction

diagrams are shown in Fig. 1 and Fig. 2 respectively:

Firstly, the host image is divided into disjoint blocks and then transformed to frequency domain by block-DCT. And mid-frequency DCT coefficients are selected for watermark embedding. The Zigzag scanning of 8×8 coefficients and embedding positions can be shown in Fig. 3:

Since slight modification of the 1st, 2nd and 3rd coefficients may affect the image quality serious, middle frequency coefficients are selected for watermark embedding. The proposed watermark embedding and extraction procedure can be depicted as following steps:

1) Watermark embedding procedure

(1) Divide the original image into 8×8 blocks denoted as $f_m(i,j)$, and then they are transformed to DCT domain coefficients $F_m(u,v)$. The logo watermark is denoted as $watermark\ (k)$;

(2) $F_m(u,v)$ is scanned into $F_m(s)$ with zigzag scanning, and those coefficients between k_1^{th} and k_2^{th} are selected. The positive and negative numbers among these coefficients can be denoted as $Tp(i,j)$ and $Tn(i,j)$, respectively.

(3) Modify the coefficients and getting modified coefficients $F_m'(u,v)$ as following:

(i) If $watermark(k) = 1,\ Tp(i,j) = \alpha(p,q)Tn(i,j)$

(ii) If $watermark(k) = 0,\ Tn(i,j) = \alpha(p,q)Tp(i,j)$

Those selected coefficients are modified by changing the sign of the least coefficients in ascending order of their absolute values until the numbers of positive or

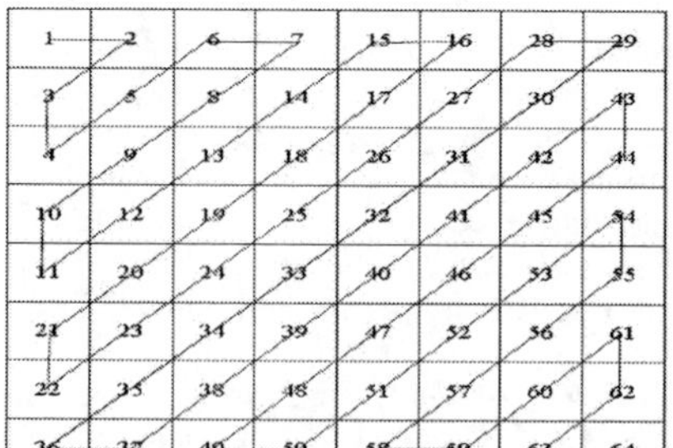

Fig.3. The zigzag scanning of the 8×8 DCT

negative coefficients to be Tp or Tn ,respectively.

(4) Every block $F_m'(u,v)$ is transformed by inverse block DCT and merged into the watermarked image I'.

Where the parameters are as follows: $0 \le i, j, u, v \le 8$, $0 \le k_1 \le k_2 \le 63$, $m = M * N / 64$, M*N is the original host image size.

In a word, every watermark bit can be embedded in each block. The total watermark capacity may be 1024 bits.

After analyzing the characteristics of middle frequency coefficients, it can be found that the absolute values are very close, so we introduce an embedding strength factor, which can not only adjust the compromise between robustness and invisibility, but also eliminate rounding error from the function uint8. This error may affect the watermark extraction.

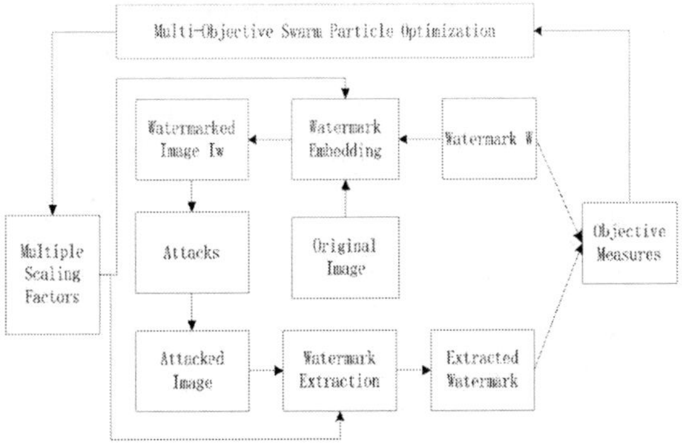

Fig.4 Block Diagram of multi-objective optimization

2) Determining multiple scaling factors:

A parameter $\alpha(p, q)$ which is used to control the trade-off between the imperceptibility and robustness, generally used as scaling factor, should be decided firstly. If the scaling factor is different in each watermark bit to be embedded, α can be a matrix, i.e. multiple scaling factors. To determine the optimal values of these multiple scaling factors can be viewed as an optimization problem. Multi-objective particle swarm optimization may be applied.

The block diagram of multi-objective optimization is a closed-loop control system. The system input is multiple scaling factors and objective measure as system output. This measure is calculated from original image I, watermarked image I_w, watermark W and the (T+1) extracted watermarks.

The steps for applying a multi-objective particle swarm optimization into the proposed watermarking scheme are enumerated.

3) Watermark extraction procedure:

(a) Divide the suspected image into 8×8 blocks and perform the DCT transform on each block. The m-th block coefficients are denoted as $F_m'(u,v)$;

(b) Scan $F_m(u,v)$ into $F_m(s)$ with zigzag scanning, and select those coefficients between the $k_1 th$ and $k_2 th$. The positive and negative numbers of them are counted as $Tp'(i,j)$ and $Tn'(i,j)$, respectively.

(1) If $Tp'(i,j) \ge \alpha(p,q) Tn'(i,j)$, $ewatermark(k) = 1$

(2) If $Tp'(i,j) < \alpha(p,q) Tn'(i,j)$, $ewatermark(k) = 0$

(c) Merge those extracted bits $ewatermark$ into logo image.

Where the parameters are as follows: $0 \le i, j, u, v \le 8$, $0 \le k_1 \le k_2 \le 63$, $m = M * N / 64$, M*N is the original host image size.

4 Experimental results

In order to evaluate the performance of the proposed method, some experimental results are done on MATLAB Ra2008. The experiments are carried out on several images including "Lena", "Pepper", "Plane", "Baboon", which represent different texture complexity. Due to the limitation of space, here only demonstrate the experimental results on Lena with size 256 × 256 Lena gray image. Fig. 5 shows the original image, watermarked image, logo watermark and the extracted watermarked.

4.1 Objective image visual quality evaluation

Image visual quality evaluation methods can mainly be divided into two categories which are subjective ones and objective ones. The subjective ones are the methods of grading subjective quality or video expert group, etc. The objective one are the methods of the mean square error (MSE), the signal-to-noise ratio (SNR), the peak signal-to-noise ratio (PSNR), the structure similarity (SSIM), and other methods based on human visual characteristics. Here mainly uses the mean square error (MSE) and the peak signal-to-noise ratio (PSNR) to measure the image quality.

Suppose the host image $f(i,j)$ being the gray value of L-level image whose size is $N \times N$, $f'(i,j)$ is the gray value of the watermarked image, and $0 \le i, j \le N-1$, MSE and PSNR are defined as follows:

$$MSE = \frac{1}{N \times N} \sum_{i=0}^{N} \sum_{j=0}^{N} | f(i,j) - f'(i,j) |^2 \quad (6)$$

$$PSNR = 10 \log_{10} \frac{(L-1)^2}{MSE} \quad (7)$$

The smaller MSE is, the distortion is less and the PSNR is larger; the larger MSE is, the distortion is more serious and the PSNR is smaller.

4.2 Extracted watermark quality evaluation

The original watermark and the extracted watermark can be denoted as $watermark(i,j)$ and $ewatermark(i,j)$ respectively, whose size is $N/8 \times N/8$. The bit error ratio (BER) is used to evaluate the quality of extracted watermark. The BER can be defined as follows:

$$BER = \frac{64}{N \times N}\sum_{i,j} ewatermark(i,j) \neq watermark(i,j)$$

Where $\sum_{.}$ is the sum on all the bit errors, and $0 \le i, j \le N/8$.

4.3 Experimental results

We choose five 256×256 gray images (Lena, Cameraman, Couple, Peppers, and Barbara) to do the simulation experiments. The block size is 8×8. The results are shown in Table 2. The watermark embedded is 1024 bits. The strengths are set to $d = k_1 - k_2 + 1 = 28 - 7 + 1 = 22$. The PSNR and the BER result of watermark extraction non-using MPSO and using MPSO method are shown in Table 1.

Table 1 Experimental result of Proposed Scheme

Attacks	PSNR (dB)		BER (Bit Error Rate)	
	Non-PSO	Using PSO	Non-PSO	Using PSO
JPEG (75%)	29.472	33.4573	0.772	0.8573
JPEG (85%)	32.5443	34.6574	0.8443	0.8874
Gaussian noise (2%)	31.5785	32.6342	0.8785	0.9342
Scaling (25%)	31.3235	33.5343	0.8235	0.9343
Salt&pepper (2%)	30.5241	32.7645	0.8241	0.9545
Noisy (2%)	31.5363	32.6465	0.8563	0.9465
Cropping (10%)	29.4232	31.5433	0.8632	0.9533
Blurring (4×4)	30.3423	33.4554	0.8423	0.9154
Sharpening (4×4)	32.2136	34.5765	0.9136	0.9365
Rotation (3°)	29.5712	31.6357	0.8712	0.9457

5 Conclusions

A novel block DCT based image watermarking scheme is proposed in this paper. MPSO is used to optimize the embedding scaling factors to achieve a good compromise between the invisibility and robustness. The experimental results show that the proposed method based on MPSO is robust to general attacks and resilience to some geometric attacks.

Acknowledgments

This work was partly supported by the Soft Science Foundation of Fujian Province of China (No. 2016R0067), and Special Foundation of Fujian Province Educational Program (No.Z816239).

References

1. I.J. Cox, et al., Secure Spread Spectrum Watermarking for Multimedia[J]. IEEE transactions on image processing, 1997. 6(12): p. 1673-1687.
2. H.Berghal and L.O.Gorman, Protecting ownership rights through digital watermarking[J]. IEEE Computer, 1996. 29(7): p. 67-72.
3. C.-K. Chan and Cheng, L.M., Hiding data in images by simple LSB substitution[J]. Pattern Recognition, 2004. 37: p. 469-474.
4. D.P. Mukherjee, Maitra, S., and Acton, S.T., spatial domain digital watermarking of multimedia objects for buyer authentication[J]. IEEE transactions on multimedia, 2004. 6(1): p. 1-15.
5. S. Alyammahi, et al. A new multiple watermarking scheme for copyright protection and image authentication. in IEEE International Midwest Symposium on circuits and systems. 2016. Abu Dhabi, UAE.
6. C. Li and Qin, Z. A blind digital image watermarking algorithm based on DCT. in IET International conference on smart and sustainable city. 2013.
7. V. Solachidis and Pitas, L., Circularly symmetric watermark embedding in 2-D DFT domain[J]. IEEE transactions on image processing, 2001. 10(11): p. 1741-1753.
8. K. Zebbiche and Khelifi, F., Efficient wavelet-based perceptual watermark masking for robust fingerprint image watermarking[J]. IET Image Process, 2014. 8(1): p. 23-32.
9. C.M.Namratha and S.Kareemulla. Multi image watermarking using Lagrangian support vector regression. in IEEE International Conference on recent trends in electronics information communication technology. 2016. India.
10. C. Mingzhi, et al., A combined DWT and DCT watermarking scheme optimized using genetic algorithm[J]. Journal of Multimedia, 2013. 8(3): p. 299-305.
11. E.Esen and A.A.Alatan, Robust video data hiding using forbidden zone data hiding and selective embedding[J]. IEEE transactions on circuits and systems for video technology, 2011. 21(8): p. 1130-1137.
12. Y. Fu, Robust oblivious image watermarking scheme based on coefficient relation[J]. Optik - International Journal for Light and Electron Optics, 2013. 124(6): p. 517-521.
13. L. An, et al., Robust lossless data hiding using clustering and statistical quantity histogram[J]. Neurocomputing, 2012. 77: p. 1-11.
14. J. Kennedy and Eberhart, R.C., Particle swarm optimization[D], in Proceedings of IEEE International conference on neural networks. 1995. p. 1942-1948.

Optimization of weapon-target assignment problem by intuitionistic fuzzy genetic algorithm

Yang Jinshuai [a], Li Jin, Wang Yi, Wen Tong, Liu Zhanqiang

Air and Missile Defense College, Air Force Engineering University,710051, Xi'an, China

Abstract. Aiming at the shortcoming of precocity and slow convergence in the application of traditional algorithms to solve the Weapon-Target Assignment (WTA) problem, this paper proposed an intuitionistic fuzzy genetic algorithm that combined with simulated annealing Meta-Lamarckian learning strategy and adaptive mutation to improve the efficiency and speed of solving WTA problem. Firstly, it considered the various constraint functions of WTA problem, in which make the threat of remaining targets minimum and the damage from attacks maximum, established the mathematical model. Next, it defined the membership and non-membership functions of object and constraint function, and built the intuitionistic fuzzy WTA model on the basis of the "min-max" operator. Then, this paper designed a strategy of Meta-Lamarckian learning for simulated annealing and adaptive mutation to enhance the capability of local search and the speed of upper convergence for the algorithm. Finally, this method is effective via the simulation and the analysis of comparison with GA, PSO.

1 Introduction

Weapon target assignment (Weapon-Target Assignment WTA) is a key problem for battlefield command and decision, is a NP complete problem, the size of the solution space with the number of defensive weapons and targets to increase the number of exponential growth. To solve the WTA problem, the heuristic search algorithm[1] such as genetic algorithm (GA), particle swarm optimization (PSO), Yi Qun algorithm (ACO) has a certain effect.

The paper [2] combine the genetic algorithm and ant algorithm to solve the WTA, shorten the reaction time of weapon system, but increase the complexity; the paper [3] proposed a discrete differential evolution algorithm, widely search the solution space to obtain good convergence performance; the paper [4] presented a particle focusing distance adaptive particle swarm algorithm for solving various WTA problem; the paper [5] design a chromosome encoding scheme to meet the constraints, solving the problem into a combinatorial optimization problem without constraints of the form; the paper [6] use genetic algorithm to solve WTA, being fast convergence but can't fundamentally solve the premature convergence of genetic algorithm. Genetic algorithm has the advantages of strong global optimization and fast convergence speed, which can search robustly the WTA problem, but it has a long iterative time and is easy to fall into the local best[7].Aiming at the shortcoming, many scholars embed local search as a kind of learning mechanism into the genetic algorithm to enhance the performance of the algorithm, which depend on the choice of initial point and need to traverse all of the individual, affect learning efficiency and even lead to fall into the local optimum. Therefore, this paper presents an intuitionistic fuzzy genetic algorithm (IFGA) with learning capacity.

2 Mathematical model of WTA problem

Assuming n targets, m weapon platforms, the threat coefficient of target j is V_j, the kill probability of weapon i to kill target j is p_{ij} $(i = 1,\ldots,n; j = 1,\ldots,m)$, and target survival probability is $q_{ij} = 1 - p_{ij}$, the platform i can launch W_i weapons at most, and kill x_{ij} weapons. if $x_{ij} = 1$, the target j is assigned to the weapon i, else $x_{ij} = 0$ .The goal of solving WTA problem is to determine the allocation scheme of the weapon platform for the incoming target, which can make the threat of the remaining target minimum and the maximum damage value, so building model:

$$\begin{aligned} &\min f_1(x) = \min\Big(\sum_{j=1}^{n} V_j \prod_{i=1}^{m} q_{ij}^{x_{ij}}\Big) \\ &\max f_2(x) = \max\Big(\sum_{j=1}^{n} \Big[1 - \prod_{i=1}^{m} q_{ij}^{x_{ij}}\Big]\Big) \end{aligned} \quad (1)$$

Constraint condition:

1. $\sum_{j=1}^{n} x_{ij} \le W_i$: the number that weapons platform i

[a] Corresponding author: Yang Jinshuai, youngjinshuai@163.com

fire incoming targets j is W_i at most;

2. $\sum_{i=1}^{m} x_{ij} \le \sum_{i=1}^{m} W_i$, the total number of allocated weapons does not exceed the total number of existing weapons;

3. $\sum_{j=1}^{n} V_j = 1$, for the high threat of target can be assigned many weapons.

Without considering the dynamic factors, in order to meet the three constraints of the number of weapons, the number of enemy targets, the choice of the priority to combat, the objective function is solved, that is to solve the WTA problem.

3 WTA problem optimization model based on intuitionistic fuzzy sets

3.1 Fuzzy WTA problem optimization model

The WTA problem is a multi-objective and multi constraint problem, show commonly as (2):

$$\begin{aligned} &\min \quad f_i(x), \quad i = 1,2,\ldots p \\ &s.t. \quad g_j(x) \ge 0, j = 1,2,\ldots,q \end{aligned} \tag{2}$$

Bellman and Zadeh combine the fuzzy set theory, the formula (2) is transformed into the fuzzy constraint[8], and the mathematical model of the fuzzy optimization problem is established:

$$\begin{aligned} &\widetilde{\min} \quad f_i(x), \quad i = 1,2,\ldots p \\ &s.t. \quad g_j(x) \tilde{\le} 0, j = 1,2,\ldots,q \end{aligned} \tag{3}$$

$\widetilde{\min}$ is shown as fuzzy minimum, $\tilde{\le}$ is shown as fuzzy less than and equal to. $m_{f_i(x)}$ and $m_{h_j(x)}$ are defined as fuzzy objective function and constraint function:

$$m_{f_i(x)} = \begin{cases} 1, & f_i(x) \le f_i^{\min} \\ \dfrac{f_i^{\max} - f_i(x)}{f_i^{\max} - f_i^{\min}}, & f_i^{\min} < f_i(x) < f_i^{\max} \\ 0, & f_i(x) > f_i^{\max} \end{cases} \tag{4}$$

$$m_{g_j(x)} = \begin{cases} 1, & g_j(x) \le 0 \\ \dfrac{d_j - h_j(x)}{d_j}, & 0 < g_j(x) \le d_j \\ 0, & g_j(x) > d_j \end{cases} \tag{5}$$

$f_i^{\max}$ is maximum value, $f_i^{\min}$ is minimum value in the domain U, d_j is maximum deviation of the constraint function. The mathematical model of fuzzy multi-objective optimization is given by the "Min- Max" operator:

$$\begin{aligned} &\max \quad m \\ &s.t. \quad m \le m_{f_i}(x), i = 1,2,\ldots,p \\ &\qquad\; m \le m_{g_j}(x), j = 1,2,\ldots,q \\ &\qquad\; 0 \le m_A(x) \le 1 \end{aligned} \tag{6}$$

3.2 Intuitionistic fuzzy WTA problem optimization model

$f_i(x) = \{< x, m_{f_i}(x), g_{f_i}(x) >, x \in U\}$, which equal to the intuitionistic fuzzy objective function, and the non-membership function of the objective function is defined as:

$$g_{f_i(x)} = \begin{cases} 0, & f_i(x) \le f_i^{\min} \\ \dfrac{f_i(x) - f_i^{\min}}{a_i \cdot f_i^{\max} - f_i^{\min}}, & f_i^{\min} < f_i(x) < f_i^{\max} \\ 1, & f_i(x) > f_i^{\max} \end{cases} \tag{7}$$

a_i could adjust the $p_{f_i(x)}$, when $a_i = 1$, $p_{f_i(x)} = 0$,and $a_i \to \infty$, $g_{f_i(x)}$ is 0, $p_{f_i(x)} = 1 - m_{f_i}(x)$. Non-membership dominant optimization at the early stage, to take a_i a smaller degree of hesitation, generally [1,1.3].

$g_j(x) = \{< x, m_{g_j}(x), g_{g_j}(x) >, x \in U\}$, which equal to the intuitionistic fuzzy constraint function, and the non-membership function of the constraint function is defined as:

$$g_{g_j(x)} = \begin{cases} 0, & g_j(x) \le 0 \\ \dfrac{g_j(x)}{d_i + b_i}, & f_i^{\min} < f_i(x) < f_i^{\max} \\ 1, & g_j(x) > d_i \end{cases} \tag{8}$$

$b_i \ge 0$ could adjust $p_{g_i}(x)$, when $b_i = 0$, $p_{g_i}(x) = 0$,and $b_i \to \infty$, $p_{g_j}(x) \to 1 - m_{g_j}(x)$. Membership dominant optimization at the later stage, to take a smaller degree of hesitation, generally b_i take [0,10][9]. A mathematical model of intuitionistic fuzzy multi-objective optimization based on formula (6), (7) and (8):

$$\begin{aligned} &\min \quad b \\ &s.t. \quad b \ge g_{f_i}(x), i = 1,2,\ldots,p \\ &\qquad\; b \ge g_{g_j}(x), j = 1,2,\ldots,q \end{aligned} \tag{9}$$

Getting"Min"operator from the objective function and the constraint function:

$$M = \bigcap_{i=1}^{p} f_i(x) = \{< x, m_{M_i}(x), g_{M_i}(x) >, x \in U\} \tag{10}$$

$$S = \bigcap_{j=1}^{q} g_j(x) = \{< x, m_{S_j}(x), g_{S_j}(x) >, x \in U\} \tag{11}$$

Among, $m_M(x) = \bigcap_{i=1}^{p} m_{f_i}(x)$, $g_M(x) = \bigcup_{i=1}^{p} g_{f_i}(x)$; $m_S(x) = \bigcap_{j=1}^{q} m_{g_j}(x)$, $g_S(x) = \bigcup_{j=1}^{q} g_{g_j}(x)$.

Getting"Min"operator from the objective function and the constraint function:

$$D = M \cap S = \{x, m_D(x), g_D(x), x \in U\} \tag{12}$$

Among, $m_D(x) = m_M(x) \cap m_S(x)$, $g_D(x) = g_M(x) \cup g_S(x)$. Getting ''Max'' operator in the domain U of intuitionistic fuzzy sets:

$$\begin{array}{ll} \max & m_D(x) \\ \min & g_D(x) \end{array} \quad (13)$$

Therefore, the form of intuitionistic fuzzy optimization:

$$\begin{array}{ll} \max & a - b \\ s.t. & a £ m_f(x) \\ & a £ m_k(x) \\ & b ^3 g_f(x) \\ & b ^3 g_g(x) \\ & 0 ? a \quad b ? 1 \end{array} \quad (14)$$

It is clear that $a_i = 1, b_i = 0$ in the formula (7), (8), then $a - b = 1 - 2b$, the intuitionistic fuzzy multi-objective is reduced to the fuzzy multi-objective optimization. Therefore, the mathematical model of WTA and the constraint conditions can be transformed into intuitionistic fuzzy optimization model, which is intuitionistic fuzzy WTA problem, could describe the assignments.

4 Solving WTA problem based on intuitionistic fuzzy algorithm

4.1 Simulated annealing Meta-Lamarck ian learning strategy

The genetic algorithm iterative evolution mainly through selection, crossover and mutation, only children participate in the competition in every generation, there is no competition between children and parent, leading to lack of excellent individual parent, premature convergence and weak local search ability[10]. The simulated annealing algorithm (SA) convergence with probability 1 to the optimal individual[11] in the process of iteration, which can accept the optimal solution, but also can accept inferior solutions in accordance with the Metropolis standards, and with the decrease of temperature, the acceptance probability gradually tends to zero. This is helpful for the algorithm to jump out of local minimum and avoid local optimum. In view of this, this paper adopts simulated annealing Meta-Lamarckian learning strategy[12], the parent of the best individual to join the offspring competition, choose the most suitable for the current search structure for local search from multiple fields in the structure. The steps are as follows:

Step1: uses n different field structures, the best individual in the population local search n (n-1) step based on simulated annealing at the initial temperature;

Step2: calculating value for each field:

$$\eta_i = (pf - cf_i)/(n(n-1)) \quad (15)$$

Among, the x_{best} before the local search is pf, the optimal objective function values obtained by local search of the i(i=1,2,…,n) domain structure;

Step3: calculating the probability of choice in various fields according to the reward value η_i:

$$p_{ut,i} = \eta_i \Big/ \sum_{j=1}^{n} \eta_j \quad (16)$$

Step4: Based on the probability of selection, a domain structure is determined by the roulette wheel selection strategy, and then the best individual of the population is searched locally at the current temperature;

Step5: updating bonus value, if the Step4 select the i domain structure, then update the reward value $\eta_i = \eta_i + \Delta\eta_i$, the formula as above is $\Delta\eta_i$.

The initial temperature of simulated annealing affects the performance of local search, which uses the function $t_{k+1} = at_k, k = 0,1,2,....$ to balance the global and local search speed.

4.2 Adaptive mutation

The direction and magnitude of mutation directly affects the efficiency of the algorithm and the convergence speed[15], but the mutation in a GA generally, gene position determined randomly using regular mutation probability, resulting in a large number of similar individuals filled the entire search space at later, reducing the population diversity, slow convergence speed.

This paper adopts adaptive mutation method: to adapt to the variable value is higher than the average fitness of the individual, the mutation probability is low, enabling the individual to protect the next generation; to adapt to the value is lower than the average fitness of individuals, the mutation probability is high, the individual is eliminated. Adaptive mutation probability formula is as follows:

$$p_m = \begin{cases} \dfrac{k_1(f_{max} - f)}{f_{max} - f_{avg}}, & f \geq f_{max} \\ k_2, & f < f_{max} \end{cases} \quad (17)$$

f_{max} is the maximum fitness value of the population, f_{avg} is the average fitness value of the population, f is the individual fitness value, k_1 and k_2 is a constant, and $k_1 < k_2$.

4.3 IFGA algorithm to solve the WTA problem steps

The steps that solving the WTA problem by IFGA are as follows:

Step1: initialization. Initialize the population size, the maximum number of iterations to generate the initial population;

Step2: calculating $m_{f_i(x)}$, $m_{h_j(x)}$, $g_{f_i(x)}$, $g_{h_j(x)}$ from formula (4), (5), (7), (8)and the fitness value of the individual from formula (14), selecting the best individual;

Step3: calculating learning capacity of the individual and the population, if the individual learning ability is greater than or equal to the average of the population learning ability, then next step, if the average of the

 DOI: 10.1051/matecconf/201712802004

population, then stop the search;

Step4: using the simulated annealing Meta-Lamarckian learning, selecting and replacing the new generated solution according to the Metropolis standard, and then down the temperature;

Step5: bring the new individual into the iterative evolutionary population, crossover and adaptive mutation;

Step6: end judgment. Whether the algorithm searches for the global optimal value or the maximum number of iterations is to stop, output the optimal allocation scheme, or return to Step2.

4.4 Time complexity analysis

The time complexity of the IFGA is analyzed according to the solving steps. The number of chromosomes in the population is N, M is the number of iterations, and the iteration time is T. In the standard GA, all the individuals in the population are iterative and the wasted time is $N \cdot M \cdot T$, the time complexity is $O(N \cdot M \cdot T)$. On the basis of the standard GA, the local search strategy and adaptive mutation are added to the IFGA, which increase the wasted time. The probability that the best individual conduct simulated annealing Meta-Lamarckian learning strategy is PML_i (when $PML_i = 1$, implementing learning strategies, $PML_i = 0$, no learning strategies), the average cost is T_{PML}, then consuming time of IFGA is:

$$N \cdot M \cdot (T + \sum_{i}^{N} PML_i \cdot T_{PML}) \qquad (18)$$

Because the individual of the Meta-Lamarckian learning strategy for simulated annealing is the best individual in the population, the number is small and the time is small, so it is not enough to improve the order of time complexity. Therefore, the complexity of the IFGA is consistent with the standard GA, which does not increase the computational overhead.

5 Simulation Analysis

This paper conducted many simulation and calculation by using the Matlab programming language to verify the performance of the algorithm in solving the WTA problem, which achieve a good result. Assuming a total of 10 batches of threat targets, we have 8 different types of weapons platforms can be used to intercept, known to each target threat to us and our success probability of interception of the target, as shown in table 1:

Table 1. Interception probability and threat of targets

Weapon	Target									
	1	2	3	4	5	6	7	8	9	10
1	0.81	0.71	0.26	0.66	0.51	0.26	0.64	0.12	0.92	0.73
2	0.73	0.14	0.83	0.55	0.12	0.82	0.57	0.59	0.71	0.38
3	0.92	0.66	0.34	0.76	0.48	0.39	0.74	0.86	0.63	0.56
4	0.16	0.82	0.77	0.53	0.22	0.75	0.51	0.43	0.86	0.94
5	0.51	0.49	0.85	0.90	0.35	0.76	0.84	0.59	0.61	0.46
6	0.87	0.30	0.58	0.78	0.89	0.60	0.81	0.39	0.78	0.79
7	0.59	0.89	0.49	0.69	0.78	0.51	0.44	0.96	0.88	0.59
8	0.84	0.69	0.78	0.92	0.54	0.81	0.59	0.67	0.32	0.66
V_j	0.57	0.41	0.37	0.69	0.43	0.36	0.29	0.54	0.47	0.24

Set the parameters of the IFGA, the number of population is 100, the maximum number of iterations is 100, $k_1 = 0.01$, $k_2 = 0.02$ which is adaptive mutation probability constant, the initial temperature of 90, the temperature ratio of $a = 0.97$.

The IFGA in the above settings, repeating experiments 20 times, getting the weapon target allocation scheme, as shown in Table 2, the best allocation of benefit value of 3.9365, takes time 1.068s.

Table 2. Program of WTA

Target	1	2	3	4	5	6	7	8	9	10
Weapon	3	7	5	8	6	2	5	7	1	4

Comparing this paper IFGA in best allocation of benefit value for solving the WTA problem with GA-ACO in [2], DDE-MRR in [3], improved PSO in[4], a GA in [5], the results are shown in figure 1.

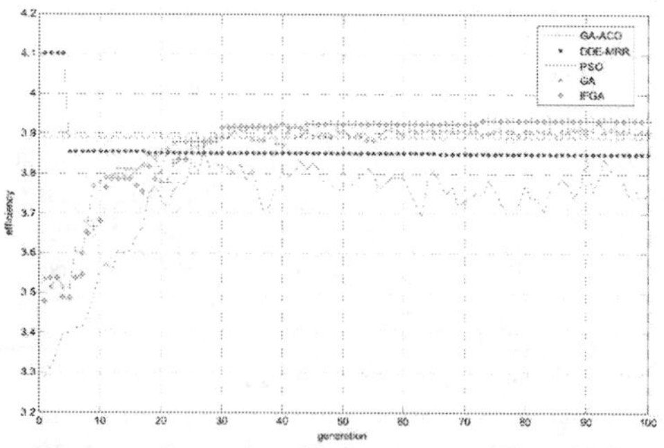

Figure 1. Comparing efficiency that solving WTA

The IFGA achieve the best benefit value of 3.9365to solve the WTA at 50 iteration; the best benefit GA-ACO achieved with stable value 3.89; the DDE-MMR achieve the best fitness value of 3.86at 60 iteration; the convergence performance of the improved PSO in iterations is poor, it is difficult to get the best benefit value; the best benefit GA to get the value of 3.9365, but the convergence effect is poor. The IFGA proposed in this paper is superior to GA-ACO, DDE-MMR and improved PSO. Compared with GA, the IFGA can obtain faster convergence rate and get the best benefit value, thanks to the introduction of non-membership function, clearly describe the solution WTA fitness function; Meta-Lamarckian learning strategy using simulated annealing, local search, jump out of the local minimum, avoid premature; the mutation probability adaptively to balance the global and local search ability to accelerate the convergence speed.

In order to verify the performance of the IFGA in solving WTA problems of large size, simulation of the attacking target and weapon platform respectively (10, 8), (20, 16) and (40, 20), the same intercept probability of success and threat targets, the population size is 100, the maximum number of iterations is 200 setting, were repeated 20 times, record the maximum and minimum value of the intercept efficiency and average time algorithm is the fastest and the slowest and the average value, and obtain the iterative optimal solution, get the table 3.

Table 3. Efficiency and time of WTA

Target	Weapon	Intercept Efficiency			Time /s			Generation
		Max	Min	Ave	Max	Min	Ave	
10	8	3.936	3.908	3.933	1.07	1.31	1.25	50
20	16	7.869	7.748	7.811	1.33	1.67	1.60	80
40	20	180.05	173.42	176.97	1.582	1.883	1.785	130

It can be found that with the increase of the number of incoming targets and the number of weapons platforms, the interception benefit value will increase, but the change of time is small, only between 2~3s. The IFGA proposed in this paper can effectively solve the problem of large scale WTA, and can meet the requirements of fast and accurate air defense operation.

6 Conclusions

It is of great military significance to study the problem of weapon target assignment. In this paper the intuitionistic fuzzy genetic algorithm, by introducing the non-membership function, clearly describes the objectives and requirements of the WTA problem and the constraint conditions, the simulated annealing Meta-Lamarckian learning strategy and adaptive mutation probability, effectively enhance the ability of local search algorithm to speed up the convergence, and to solve the problem of WTA has larger scale good effect.

References

1. Yu Lianfei, Liu Jin, Zhang Weiming, et al. Review of Weapon-Target Assignment Problem Algorithm [J]. Mathematics in Practice and Theory, 2016, 46(2):26-32.
2. Wu Congmeng, Wang Gongbao. Application of Genetic Ant-Colony algorithm in Target Assignment problem [J]. Ordnance Industry Automation, 2014, 33(4):8-11.
3. Zhang Chunmei, Chen Jie, Xin Bin. A Discrete Differential Evolution Algorithm for the Weapon Target Assignment Problem [J]. Transactions of Beijing Institute of Technology, 2014, 34(3): 289-293.
4. Li Xinran, Fan Yongsheng. An Improved Particle Swarm Algorithm for Weapon Target Assignment Problem Solving [J]. Fire Control & Command Control, 2014, 39(12):58-61.
5. Wang Wei, Cheng Shuchang, ZHANG Yuzhi. Research on approach for a type of weapon target assignment [J]. Systems Engineering and Electronics, 2008, 30(9):1708-1711.
6. Yang Shanliang, Huang Jian, Liu Yang, et al. Analysis of Weapon Target Assignment Problem in Joint Fire Strike Solving by Genetic Algorithm [J]. Computer Simulation, 2012, 29(3):61-63.
7. Wu Kunhong, Zhan Shixian. Optimization for Target Assignment in Fire Strike Based on Distributed Genetic Simulated Annealing Algorithm [J]. Fire Control & Command Control, 2016, 41(3):89-92.
8. ANGELOV P P. Optimization in an intuitionistic fuzzy environment [J]. Fuzzy Sets and Systems, 1997, (86): 299-306.
9. Xu Xiaolai, Lei Yingjie, Dai Wenyi. Weighted Intuitionistic Fuzzy Multi-object Programming Based on Improved Particle Swarm Algorithm [J]. Journal of System Simulation, 2009, 21(11):3280-3282.
10. LI Kangping, WANG Pengjun, ZHANG Huihong. The Search of the Best Power Polarity of Ternary FPRM Circuit Based on Simulated annealing Genetic Algorithm[J], Journal of Zhejiang University(Science Edition),2016,43(2):190-194,199.
11. Lin Lingjuan, Liu Xiyu. Rapid partical swarm optimization combined simulated annealing algorithm [J]. Computer Engineering and Applications, 2011, 47(8):27-29.
12. Liu Bo, Wang Ling, Jin Yihui. An effective hybrid PSO-based algorithm for flow shop schedualing with limited buffers [J]. Computers & Operations Reasearch, 2008, 35(9): 2791-2806.
13. Luan Zhibo, Huang Qitao, Jiang Hongzhou, et al. Mixed application of two learning mechanisms in genetic algorithm [J].Systems Engineering and Electronic, 2009,31(8):1985-1988.
14. Wei Zhen, Wu Lei, Ge Fangzhen, et al. Hybrid PSO Algorithm Based on Memetic Framework [J]. Pattern Recognition and Artificial Intelligence, 2012, 25(2):213-219
15. Zhang Xian, Yaofeng Ren, Wang Runpeng. Research on path planning [J]. Journal of China Ordnance search in continuous time optimal adaptive genetic algorithm based on 2015, 36 (12): 2386-2395.

MATEC Web of Conferences 128, 02005 (2017)
EITCE 2017
DOI: 10.1051/matecconf/201712802005

Analysis and Simulation of Multi-target Echo Signals from a Phased Array Radar

Zhen Jia[1,a], Rui Zhou[2]

[1]Jiangsu Automation Research Institute, 222061 Lianyungang, China
[2]Zhengzhou Technical College, 450121 Zhengzhou, China

Abstract. The construction of digital radar simulation systems has been a research hotspot of the radar field. This paper focuses on theoretical analysis and simulation of multi-target echo signals produced in a phased array radar system, and constructs an array antenna element and a signal generation environment. The antenna element is able to simulate planar arrays and optimizes these arrays by adding window functions. And the signal environment can model and simulate radar transmission signals, radar internal noise, clutter and jamming signals. These signals are combined linearly to generate the radar echo signal. The simulation results indicate that multi-target echo signals are completely overwhelmed by other signals, satisfying the needs of subsequent signal processing and data processing.

1 Introduction

In recent years, many countries have been generalizing the phased array radar technology vigorously. Compared to other radars, the phased array radar has unique advantages: rapid scan of antenna beams, varieties of beam shapes, composition of space powers, and powerful data processing system, as well as tracing multiple targets simultaneously. In the real application, performance evaluation of a radar system is known to be significantly important. However, the evaluation implemented with traditional methods become more difficult now, and the semi-physical or all-digital simulation method can therefore be employed to fulfill design and evaluation of the radar system [1].

The generation of radar echo signals is of great importance to radar simulation systems. There are some studies on simulating the radar echoes by combining different kinds of signals. Cui *et al.* [2] investigated the modeling and simulation of the target echo and *K*-distributed clutter echo for each radar member, and simulated radar echo signals by combining the target echo with Gauss noise or clutter echo. Zhao *et al.* [3] presented a radar video signal simulation method based on the pre-recorded radar video signal, and radar video signals were consist of target echo signals, clutters and noises. Generally, the number of targets searched by radar is more than one, *i.e.* the simulated radar echo signal always contains several targets. Qin *et al.* [4] investigated the radar echo waveform and analyzed the performances of the target and sea clutter signals, reporting that the compound signal waveform could simulate the radar system's echo signal well, by superposing the targets, K distribution clutter and white Gaussian noise signals. Wang *et al.* [5] studied and simulated the phased array radar system by using Simulink as the simulation platform, and their radar echo signal is the linear combination of target echo, Rayleigh distribution clutter and Gaussian white noise signals. However, few researches have been done on including jamming signals in the radar echoes.

In this paper, a signal generation environment is built as the front-end of a phased array radar simulation system. The target echo signal are investigated in detail, and noise, clutter and jamming signals are analyzed and simulated respectively. These four signals are ultimately combined to create radar echo signals, approximating the true radar returns.

2 Target Echo Signal

When a radar works, its signal transmitter will transmit a series of high-frequency and repeated periodic signal towards some specific space. If the signal encounters any target during the propagation course, the radar receiver will receive a return reflected by the target. Meanwhile, the receiver's internal noise will be mixed in the echo signal inevitably. The linear frequency modulated (LFM) signal is commonly used as the transmission signal. Because the matched filter used later is insensitive to the Doppler shift. Even if the echo signal has a larger frequency shift, the same filter can be applied to accomplish the pulse compression.

2.1 Phase Array Antenna

The reason why this radar is called the "phased array" radar is that its work basis is a phase-controlled array

[a] Corresponding author: zjia1987@gmail.com

DOI: 10.1051/matecconf/201712802005

antenna. The array antenna has diversified forms, such as a linear array and a planar array. The planar array antenna can realize the antenna beam scan at the azimuth or pitch angle direction [7]. Both rectangular and circular array antennas can be simulated, and the rectangular array antenna is modeled here.

$$E(\theta,\varphi)=\left|\frac{\sin\left[\left(Nkd_x\sin\theta\cos\varphi\right)/2\right]}{\sin\left[\left(kd_x\sin\theta\cos\varphi\right)/2\right]}\right|\left|\frac{\sin\left[\left(Nkd_y\sin\theta\cos\varphi\right)/2\right]}{\sin\left[\left(kd_y\sin\theta\cos\varphi\right)/2\right]}\right| \quad (1)$$

Where N is number of antenna array elements, k is wave number, d_x is vertical spacing between array elements, d_y is horizontal spacing between array elements, and θ is azimuth angle of the antenna beam pointing, as well as φ is pitch angle of the antenna beam pointing. When simulating, all supposed parameters of the radar antenna are listed in Table 1, where λ is the radar working wavelength. The simulation results are shown in Figure 1.

Table 1. Total parameters of the phased array antenna

Parameter	Value	Parameter	Value
N	30×30	k	2π/λ
d_x	0.5λ	θ	30°
d_y	0.5λ	φ	45°

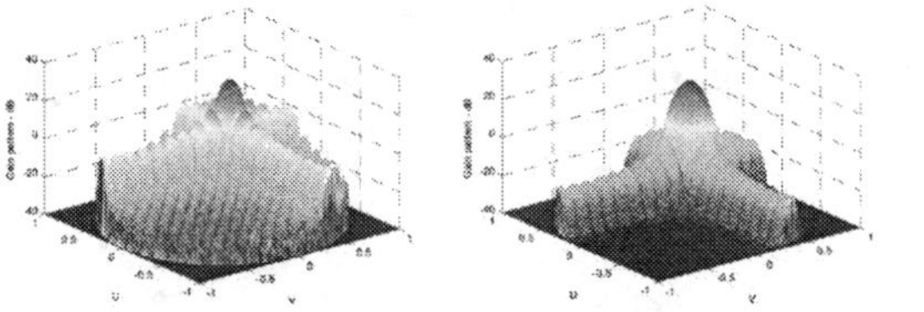

(a) (b)

Figure 1. Antenna direction pictures of the rectangular array. (a) without adding a window; (b) after adding a Kaiser window.

Seen from Figure 1(a), the first side lobe is about 13dB lower than the main lobe. This is far from adequate for most radar applications, but window functions can be added to reduce the side lobe level. The common window functions are rectangular, Bartlett, Blackman, Hamming, Hanning and Kaiser windows [7]. Here the Kaiser window is added, and its effect is demonstrated in Figure 1(b). It is clear that, the side lobe amplitude is reduced and the main lobe is widened.

2.3 Radar Noise

In the simulation process, the noise of the phased array radar itself is treated as a Gaussian white noise. And this noise should also be added to the received echo signal, which can be produced through a built-in random function of MATLAB.

In the paper, three point targets are supposed to be searched by the phased array radar. Table 2 lists their own initial movement parameters. The target range can be transformed to a range gate, and the target velocity conversed to a Doppler shift. Figure 2(a) shows the simulated multi-target echo signal, and Figure 2(b) is the echo signal mixed by the radar's internal noise.

Table 2. The initial parameters of three targets

Parameter \ No.	1	2	3
Power(1)	1	1	1
Range(m)	15000	20000	13000
Radial velocity (m/s)	300	-100	-200

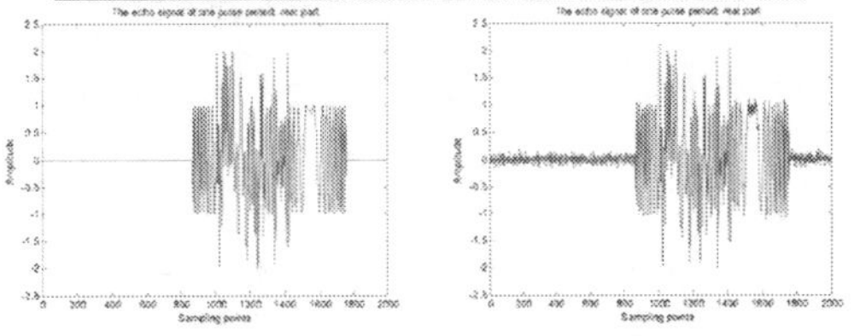

(a) (b)

Figure 2. Time domain waveform of target echo signals. (a) without the white noise; (b) with the white noise.

3 Clutter

The clutter in a resolution unit contained a number of scatterers. The phase and amplitude of these scatterers are stochastic, and probability distribution functions can therefore be leveraged to describe the clutter statistically [7-9]. The types of these functions are determined by characters of the clutter itself, grazing angle and radar operating frequency.

3.1 Rayleigh Distribution Clutter

If a sea or ground clutter contains a lot of scatterers, and the probability of one scatterer receiving the return is not relevant to that of another scatterer, the clutter can be modeled with the Rayleigh distribution:

$$f(x)=\frac{x}{\sigma^2}\exp\left(-\frac{x^2}{2\sigma^2}\right),\quad x\geq 0 \qquad (2)$$

where σ is standard error of the clutter.

3.2 Lognormal Distribution Clutter

The lognormal distribution is good at describing the ground clutter with a low grazing angle, as well as depicting the high-resolution radar sea clutter [4]. It can be expressed as:

$$f(x)=\frac{1}{\sqrt{2\pi}\sigma_c x}\exp\left[-\frac{\ln^2(x/u_m)}{2\sigma_c^2}\right],\quad x>0,\sigma_c>0,u_m>0 \quad (3)$$

where u_m is scale parameter, representing the distribution mean; δ_c is form parameter, meaning the distribution gradient.

3.3 Weibull Distribution Clutter

The Weibull distribution can model the clutter whose frequency is between 1~10GHz and grazing angle below 5° [5]. This model lies between the Rayleigh distribution and the lognormal distribution, and its formula is as following:

 DOI: 10.1051/matecconf/201712802005

$$f(x)=\frac{p}{q}\left(\frac{x}{q}\right)^{p-1}\exp\left[\left(-\frac{x}{q}\right)^{p}\right],\quad x\geq 0 \tag{4}$$

where p is form parameter, with a value $0<p\leqslant 2$; q is scale parameter. Noting that the Weibull distribution will turn into the Rayleigh distribution when $p=2$.

3.4 K Distribution Clutter

A large number of analyses on actual measurement data indicate that, the sea clutter not only is a simple stationary stochastic process, but also has some fast and slow modulated variables [6]. By curve fitting, it was proved that the correlated K-distribution is able to describe the high-resolution radar sea clutter, whose probability density function is:

$$f(x)=\int_0^{\infty}p(y)p\left(\frac{x}{y}\right)dy=\frac{2c}{\Gamma(v)}\left(\frac{cx}{2}\right)^{v}K_{v-1}(cx) \tag{5}$$

where $K_{v-1}(\cdot)$ is $(v-1)$ order second revised Bessel function; c is proportion coefficient, with a value $\sqrt{\frac{v\pi}{E(y^2)}}$, in which $E(y^2)$ is average clutter power.

There are three steps to generate the above-mentioned four clutters: (1) Generating a Gaussian white noise sequence; (2) Processing the white noise via a linear filter, and gaining a correlated Gaussian sequence; (3) Generating a correlated random sequence with arbitrary distribution, by adopting the zero memory nonlinearity (ZMNL) or spherically invariant random processing (SIRP) method [7]. The simulation results of these clutters are shown in Figure 3.

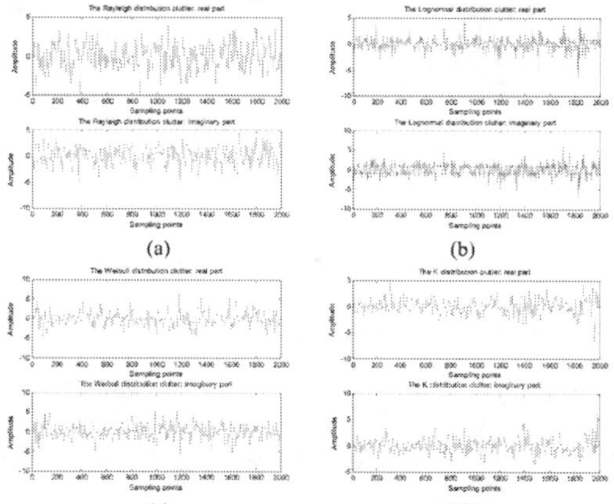

Figure 3. Time domain waveform of clutter signals. (a) Rayleigh distribution; (b) Lognormal distribution; (c) Weibull distribution; (d) K distribution.

4 Jamming

As one of the important radar countermeasure's components, radar jamming is the technical name of destroying and hindering normal operation of the enemy' electronic and radar equipments. It makes the radar unable to detect and trace the true targets correctly, in order to disturb the radar's working. In terms of jamming energy source, radar jamming falls into unintentional and intentional jammings. And intentional jamming is divided into active and inactive jammings based on transmitting electromagnetic signals or not. Moreover, active jamming splits into masking and deception jammings [7,10-12].

4.1 Masking Jamming

Masking jamming can overwhelm or cover the target signals by using noise or noise-like jamming signals, to hinder the radar to detect target information. Its basic principle is use the radar to detect the target echo between external and internal noises, and the detecting process can be carried out with certain guidelines: If the SNR exceeds the detection threshold, targets were considered to exist; if not, there are no targets. According to producing way of the masking noise signals, active masking jamming can be classified into four kinds below.

4.1.1 RF Noise Jamming

The jamming that magnifies and transmits the narrowband Gaussian noise directly is RF noise jamming, also called direct noise amplifier (DINA). The expression of narrowband Gaussian noise is:

$$J(t)=U_n(t)\cos\left(\omega_j t+\varphi\right) \tag{6}$$

where envelope function $U_n(t)$ obeys the Rayleigh distribution; phase function $\varphi(t)$ obeys the $[0,2\pi]$ uniform distribution, independent of $U_n(t)$; carrier frequency is a constant and much larger than the bandwidth of $J(t)$, and $J(t)$ is generally formed through filtration and amplification of a low-power noise.

4.1.2 Noise AM Jamming

The carrier's oscillation amplitude varies with the change of modulated noise, and this modulation process is called noise AM. The signal's expression is:

$$J(t)=\left[U_j+U_n(t)\right]\cos\left(\omega_j t+\varphi\right) \tag{7}$$

where U_j is a constant.

4.1.3 Noise FM Jamming

If the carrier's instant frequency changes with modulation voltage, while the amplitude holds the line, this circumstance is referred to as noise FM. The signal expression is:

$$J(t)=U_j\cos\left[\omega_j t+2\pi k_{FM}\int_0^t U_n(t)dt+\varphi\right] \tag{8}$$

where k_{FM} is FM slope.

4.1.4 Noise PM Jamming

The expression of a generalized stationary random noise PM process is:

$$J(t)=U_j\cos\left[\omega_j t+k_{PM}U(t)+\varphi\right] \tag{9}$$

where k_{PM} is a constant, meaning PM slope. Figure 4 represents time domain waveform and frequency

 DOI: 10.1051/matecconf/201712802005

spectrogram of the above-mentioned masking jamming signals.

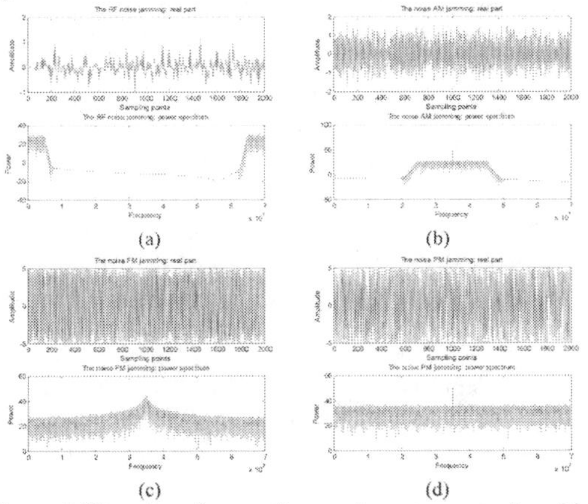

Figure 4. Time domain waveform and spectrogram of masking jamming signals. (a) RF noise jamming; (b) noise AM jamming; (c) noise FM jamming; (d) noise PM jamming.

4.2 Deception Jamming

The basic principle of deception jamming is produce one jamming signal to act on the radar, which has similar features as the transmission signal, in order to interrupt the enemy to detect the true targets' signal parameters. This way will disturb the radar system on an information level. Here, range and velocity deception jammings are studied by theoretical analysis and simulation.

4.2.1 Range False Target Jamming

The main theory of range false target jamming is delay and amplify the received radar transmission signal, aimed to disturb the target detection. Suppose the distance between a true target and the radar is R, and time delay of the received echo is $\tau=2R/c$; the distance between a false target and the radar is Rf, and time delay is $\tau=2R_f/c$. If

$$\left|R_f - R\right| > \varepsilon R \tag{10}$$

Then this false target is a range false one. If using the jamming theory of range false targets, and adopting the pulse delay stacking technique, many false targets will be produced to interrupt the radar to detect the true targets normally.

4.2.2 Range Pull-off Jamming

The false target range function $R_f(t)$ of range pull-off jamming can be expressed as:

$$R_f(t) = \begin{cases} R & 0 \le t < t_1 \quad \textit{Stop} \\ R + v(t-t_1) \text{ or } R + a(t-t_1)^2 & t_1 \le t < t_2 \quad \textit{Pull off} \\ \textit{Jamming Shutoff} & t_2 \le t < T_j \quad \textit{Closed} \end{cases} \tag{11}$$

where R is target distance; v is velocity when pulled off at a constant speed, and a is acceleration when pulled off at a constant accelerated speed.

Under the self-defense jamming condition, in which R is also target distance, the equation above can be converted into time delay of the received radar project signal retransmitted by the jammer. The retransmitted time delay of range pull-off jamming Δt_f is

$$\Delta t_f(t) = \begin{cases} 0 & 0 \le t < t_1 \quad \text{Stop} \\ \dfrac{2v(t-t_1)}{C} \text{ or } \dfrac{2a(t-t_1)^2}{C} & t_1 \le t < t_2 \quad \textit{Pull off} \\ \textit{Jamming shutoff} & t_2 \le t < T_j \quad \textit{Closed} \end{cases} \tag{12}$$

Here the uniform pull-off way is utilized to disturb the true targets, and Figure 6(b) shows the time domain waveform of range pull-off jamming.

4.2.3 Velocity False Target Jamming

The typical velocity false target jamming is the frequency-shift stacking jamming, whose principle is that the target's Doppler frequency measured by radar is influenced by the jamming radar's receiver. Learning from Fourier transform, frequency shift is time domain of the original signal multiply $e^{-j2\pi ft}$. The following jamming signal can be generated from the LFM signal.

$$J(t) = Au(t)\sin\left\{2\pi\left[\left(f_0 + \Delta f\right)t + \frac{1}{2}kt^2\right]\right\} \tag{13}$$

If the shift frequency is positive ($\Delta f>0$), the false target is ahead of the true target; otherwise, the false target falls behind.

4.2.4 Velocity Pull-off Jamming

The basic theory of velocity pull-off jamming is retransmit the jamming signal with the same Doppler frequency f_d as the target return, and the energy of the jamming signal is higher than that of the target return, to enable the radar's speed tracking circuit to capture the Doppler frequency fd. Because the jamming energy is higher, the speed tracking circuit will follow by the jamming's Doppler frequency, resulting in velocity information errors. In the velocity pull-off jamming, Doppler frequency f_{dj} of the jamming signal is expressed as following:

$$f_{dj}(t) = \begin{cases} f_d & 0 \le t < t_1 \quad \textit{Stop} \\ f_d + v_f(t-t_1) & t_1 \le t < t_2 \quad \textit{Pull off} \\ \text{Jamming shutoff} & t_2 \le t < T_j \quad \textit{Closed} \end{cases} \tag{14}$$

where v_f is change rate of the interfering frequency, namely the separation velocity, whose plus or minus depends on acceleration direction (*i.e.* pull-off direction) of the velocity pull-off jamming. The time domain waveforms of the above-mentioned deception jamming signals are shown in Figure 5.

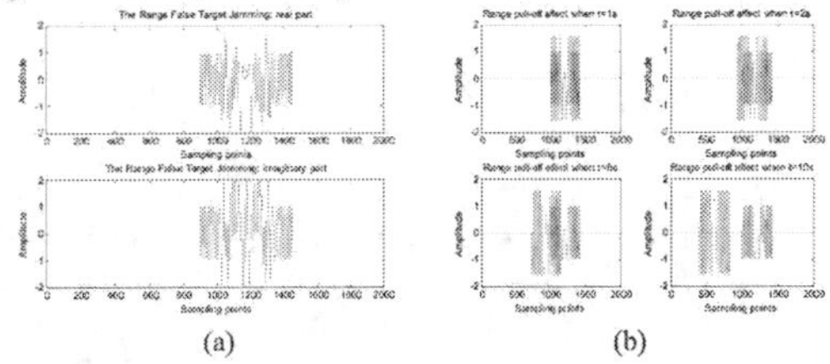

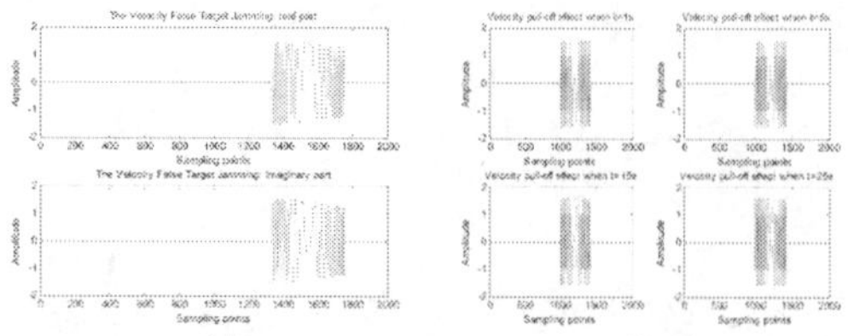

(c) (d)

Figure 6. Time domain waveform of deception jamming signals. (a) range false target jamming; (b) range pull-off jamming; (c) velocity false target jamming; (d) velocity pull-off jamming.

5 Radar Echo Signal

The radar echo signal is achieved by superposing the target echo signal, noise, clutter and jamming linearly, as shown in Figure 6. There are several types of clutter and jamming signals simulated in the paper, therefore two optional combinations are used to construct the multi-target echo signal. The first one is the combination of radar transmission signal, Gaussian white noise, Rayleigh distribution clutter and noise AM jamming. The second one is the combination of radar transmission signal, Gaussian white noise, K distribution clutter and range false target jamming. These two combinations are respectively shown in Figure 7.

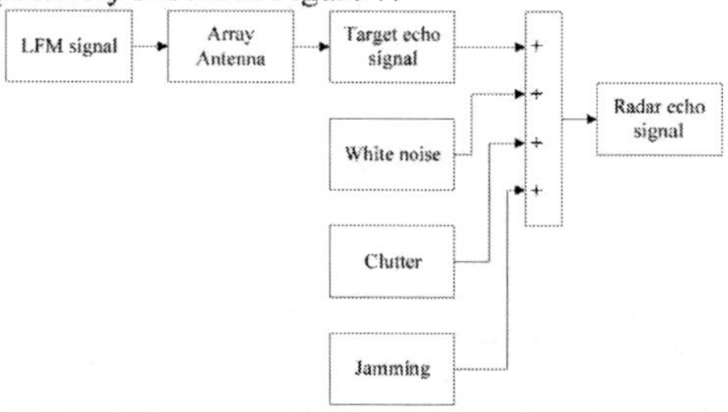

Figure 6. Linear combination for the radar echo signal.

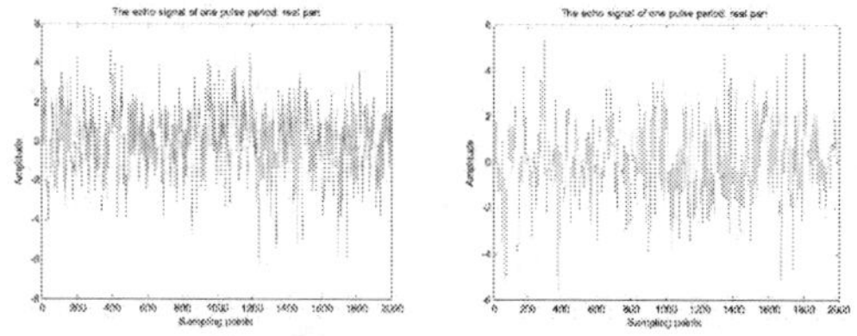

(a) (b)

Figure 7. Time domain waveform of the radar echo signal. (a) first combination; (b) second combination.

Comparing with Figure 2, it can be seen that target signals are totally overwhelmed by noise, clutters and jammings, and they cannot be distinguished intuitively. Therefore, the signals are considered to approximate the true radar returns.

6 Conclusion

In the paper, with the purpose of attaining multi-target radar echo signals, the transmission signal, noise, clutter and jamming are analyzed theoretically and simulated in MATLAB. After superposing these four signals, the resulting return signal is significantly different from the transmission signal. In the future, signal processing and data processing modules of the phased array simulation system will be constructed, in order to complete range and velocity information measurements, and display multi-target movements on the radar search interface.

References

1. S.H. Talisa, K.W. O'Haver, T.M. Comberiate, *et al.* Benefits of Digital Phased Array Radars. Proceedings of IEEE, 2016, 104(3): 530-543.
2. Xiaohai Cui, Tao Zeng, Teng Long. Radar Target Echo Signal and Clutter Simulator Based on HLA. 2004
3. Jianhe Zhao, Guoqing Qi, Xianying Song. Simulation of Marine Radar Video Signal. IEEE International Conference on Instrumentation and Measurement, Computer, Communication and Control, 2014: 805-808.
4. Hua Qin, Hao Cha, Mo Zhou, *et al.* Simulation and Modeling of Radar Echo Signal. IEEE International Conference on Fuzzy Systems and Knowledge Discovery, 2012: 1954-1957.
5. Taotao Wang, Xiaodong Wan, Jie He. Simualtion of Phased Array Radar Systems. Computers and Modernization, 2014, 2(47): 209-218.
6. M.U. Afzal, A.A. Qureshi, M.A. Tarar, *et al.* Analysis, Design, and Simulation of Phased Array Radar Front-end. Emerging Technologies (ICET), 2011, (7): 1-6.
7. B.R. Mahafa. Radar Systems Analysis and Design Using MALAB, Third Edition. 2013: 559-586.
8. Fuchun Zhang, Yanzhong Hao, Yongxue Liu, *et al.* Studies of Modeling and Simulation of Phased-Array Radar System. IEEE Internationl Conference on Cyber Technology in Automation, Control, and Intelligent Systems, 2012: 415-418.
9. C.D. Curtis, M. Yeary, J.L. Lake. Adaptive Nullforming to Mitigate Ground Clutter on the National Weather Radar Testbed Phased Array Radar. IEEE Transactions on Geoscience and Remote Sensing, 2016, 54(3): 1282-1291.
10. Kelei Wei, Ning Tai, Lei Huang, *et al.* Shift-frequency jamming against pulse compression radar. 2016 Progress in Electromagnetic Research Symposium (PIERS), Shanghai, 2016: 2251-2254.
11. F. Novillo, J.R. Arguello, E. Guerrero, *et al.* Performance Evaluation of Radar Systems in Noise Jamming Enviroments. 2016 IEEE Ecuador Technical Chapters Meeting (ETCM), Guayaquil, 2016: 1-6.
12. S. Lu, G. Cui, W. Yi, *et al.* Radar Waveform Design against Signal-dependent Jamming. 2017 IEEE Radar Conference (RadarConf), Seattle, WA, USA, 2017: 1075-1080.

MATEC Web of Conferences **128**, 02006 (2017) DOI: 10.1051/matecconf/201712802006
EITCE 2017

Design, Simulation and Validation of HMC833 Loop Filter Based on Matlab

Shachang Hu, Tianli Li*, Jiyue Zhang, Li Yan and Xiaojie Zhang

Shenzhen Key Laboratory of Electromagnetic Control, Shenzhen University, Shenzhen 518060, China

Abstract. In the light of the complexity of the conventional research and design of HMC833 wideband PLL, this paper studies a design method of HMC833 loop filter based on Simulink modeling in Matlab. The dynamic parameters of loop response, such as maximum overshoot, regulation time and steady-state error, are analyzed to verify the feasibility of HMC833 loop filter design.

1 Introduction

High temperature ceramic sensor detection system based on FPGA control needs to use FPGA as the master chip to control the high frequency signal of 5.42GHz-5.5GHz produced by the HMC833 chip. Then the high temperature ceramic passive wireless sensor is used for feedback collection to obtain the reflected resonant frequency, and then the real-time temperature is obtained by the relationship between resonant frequency and temperature parameters. Finally, the time curve of the resonance frequency, the real-time temperature, the S11 waveform and the temperature are displayed on the touch screen.

In order to ensure the stability of HMC833 chip to send 5.42GHz-5.5GHz high frequency signals, broadband PLL is used to lock frequency.

2 Principle of HMC833

The HMC833 chip uses a surface mount package with 40 pins, including power and ground pins, signal control pins, high frequency signal pins, low frequency signal pins, and idle pins. From the Figure 1,you can see the HMC833 internal resources and function of each module.

The external reference clock is brought into the chip by the pin XREFP.The pin CP turns the error signal of the discriminator into a current pulse, and then outputs it to an external loop filter.The filtered signal enters the on-chip VTUNE from the pin VCO. Finally, the VCO outputs a high frequency signal [1] by the pin RF-OUT through a programmable frequency division doubler.

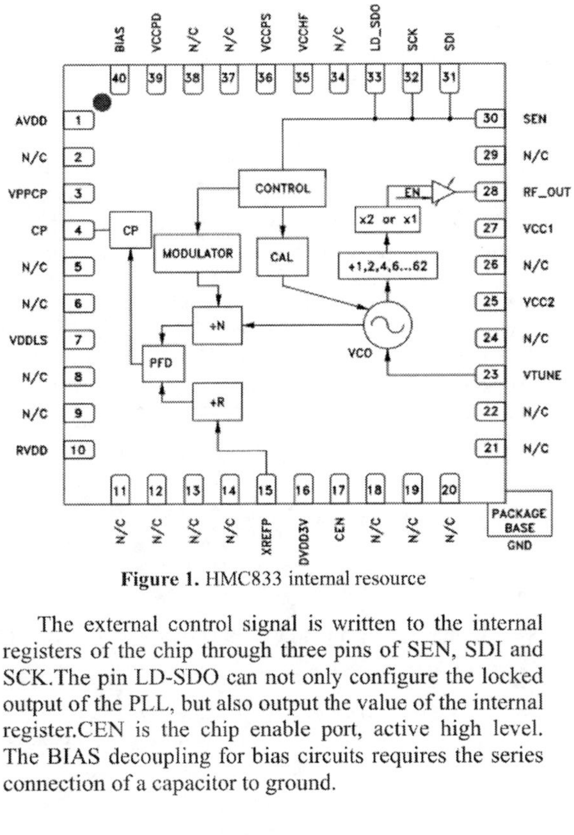

Figure 1. HMC833 internal resource

The external control signal is written to the internal registers of the chip through three pins of SEN, SDI and SCK.The pin LD-SDO can not only configure the locked output of the PLL, but also output the value of the internal register.CEN is the chip enable port, active high level. The BIAS decoupling for bias circuits requires the series connection of a capacitor to ground.

3 Phase-locked loop

The charge pump phase locked loop is an automatic controlled closed-loop negative feedback system. It automatically tracks the phase and frequency of the input signal. The phase of the output signal can also be locked. The principle of automatic control is its theoretical basis.

[a] Corresponding author: LTL988@gmail.com

DOI: 10.1051/matecconf/201712802006

Phase frequency detector (PFD), charge pump (CP), loop filter (LPF), voltage controlled oscillator (VCO), frequency divider (N frequency divider, NFD) are its basic components.It is shown in Figure 2.

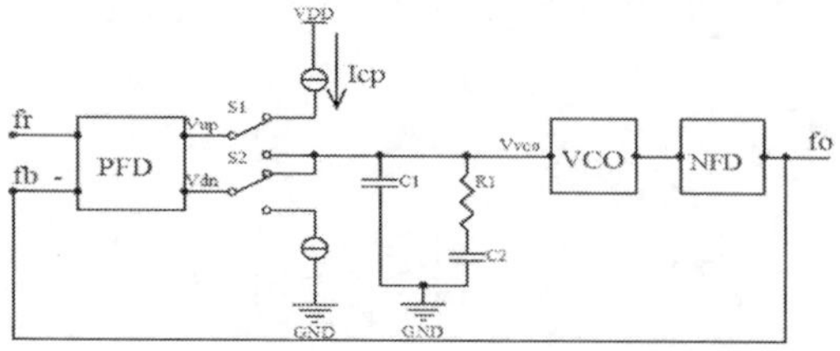

Figure 2. Schematic diagram of PLL

The complete working flow of the charge phase-locked loop is that the input f_r and the feedback voltage f_b are controlled by PFD to generate the control voltage to control the opening and closing of the S1 and S2 in the CP, thus changing the charge pump current I_{cp}.The I_{cp} is filtered by LPF to produce a control voltage V_{vco}, to control the output frequency of the VCO. The frequency signal generated by VCO is divided into PFD by NFD and compared with the input f_r. So cycle until f_r equals f_b.

4 Design of loop filter

The higher order loop filter model is evolved from the two order model. It adds two stage capacitor resistance combinations at the back of the 2 order model [2]. In the actual circuit, the first two stage filter plays a major role in the parameters of PLL, loop bandwidth, damping coefficient and phase noise. In contrast, the third and fourth stage filters in the back end are designed to optimize phase noise and improve output performance. The Simulink model in Matlab is shown in Figure 3.

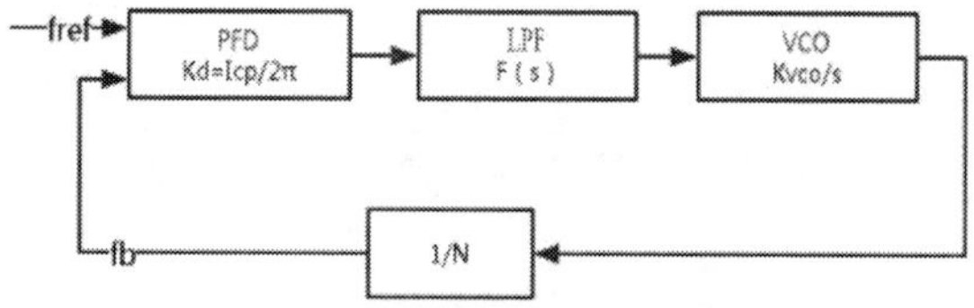

Figure 3. Simulink model

Assume the gain of the PFD is K_d, the transfer function of the LPF is F(s), the gain of the VCO is K_{vco}, and N is the frequency division of the FD. The open-loop transfer function of the phase-locked loop can be obtained as shown in the equation [4].

$$G(s) = K_d \cdot F(s) \cdot \frac{K_{vco}}{s} \cdot \frac{1}{N} \qquad (1)$$

The quality of the loop filter directly affects the output characteristics of the PLL. This section is based on the maximum tuning voltage of HMC833 in the VCO chip of 5V, so the passive two order loop filter is adopted.

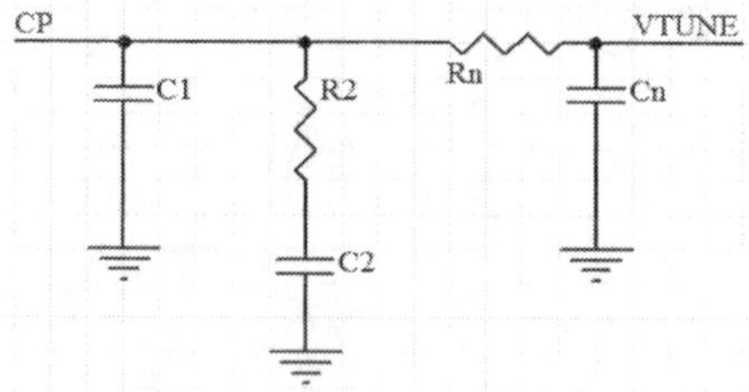

Figure 4. Passive loop filter model

According to figure 4 shows that the main elements of the second-order loop filter are C1, C2, R2. The ts transfer function is shown in the following formula.

$$F(s) = \frac{1 + T_2 s}{Ct \cdot s(1 + T_1 s)} \qquad (2)$$

T_1=C1C2R2/Ct, T_2=C2R2,Ct=C1+C2.The T_1 and the T_2 are loop time constant.The Ct is the total capacitance of the loop.

The time constant can be obtained by the phase margin equation and its partial differential equation[5]. The phase margin expression is shown below.

$$\phi = 180^o + \arctan(2\pi f_c T_2) - \arctan(2\pi f_c T_1) \qquad (3)$$

The f_c is the Loop bandwidth.

The partial differential of the angular margin diagonal frequency:

$$\frac{d\phi}{dw}\Big|_{w=w_c} = \frac{w_c T_2}{1 + w_c^2 T_2^2} - \frac{w_c T_1}{1 + w_c^2 T_1^2} = 0 \qquad (4)$$

$$T_1 = \frac{\sec(\phi) - \tan(\phi)}{w_c} \qquad (5)$$

$$T_2 = \frac{1}{w_c^2 \cdot T_1} \qquad (6)$$

The value of Ct can be approximated by the loop gain of 1, so there are the following formulas.

$$Ct \approx \frac{K_d K_{vco}}{N w_c^2} \cdot \sqrt{\frac{1 + w_c^2 T_2^2}{1 + w_c^2 T_1^2}} \qquad (7)$$

The K_d is phase detector gain.The I_{cp} is charge pump output current. The relation between K_d and I_{cp} is shown in the following formula.

$$K_d = I_{CP} / 2\pi$$

The calculation of the capacitance resistance parameter can be obtained by the above method. According to the above formula, in the calculation, we need to know the gain of PLL detector, the gain and the frequency division ratio of VCO, and the expected(1) performance parameters such as phase margin and loop bandwidth. Then the corresponding circuit element value can be estimated. If the phase margin of the phase locked loop is generally between 40 and 60 degrees, the system has better stability. The loop bandwidth is taken between one percent and 1/10 of the reference frequency, and the

 DOI: 10.1051/matecconf/201712802006

phase noise of the system can be better suppressed without losing the response speed.

The actual parameters of HMC833 VCO are shown in Table 1.

Table 1. VCO Parameters

Parameter	value
Frequency Range	1.5GHz~3.0GHz
Reference frequency	5MHz
Charge pump current	2.54mA
VCO tuning voltage	5V
Phase margin	50°
Loop bandwidth	500kHz
Integer division ratio	53

According to table 1, the component values of the two order loop filter can be obtained, as shown in Table 2.

Table 2. Component value

Parameter	value
C1/pF	26.45
C2/nF	1.9702
R2/KΩ	4.4389

5 Simulink modeling and simulation

Using Matlab Simulink to build the model shown in Figure 5.

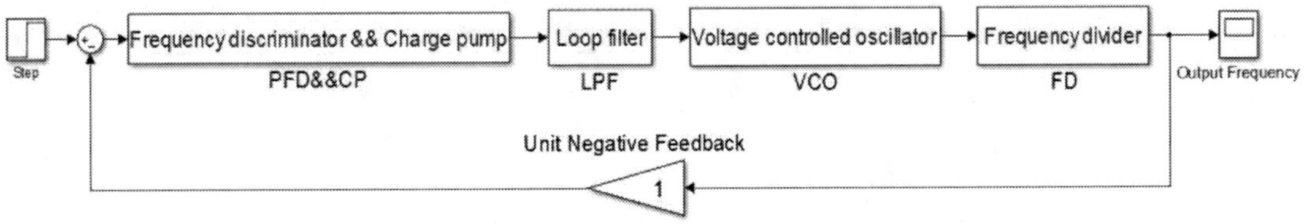

Figure 5. Simulink model.

In the Matlab simulation, the step signal is used instead of the input frequency signal fr, the frequency division ratio is 53, and the step signal initial frequency is 4000000kHz.As shown in Figure 6, the target output frequency is 5512028kHz. For ease of observation, the image is magnified at the time axis 20us. In Figure 6, ordinates represent frequency values, and abscissa indicates time.

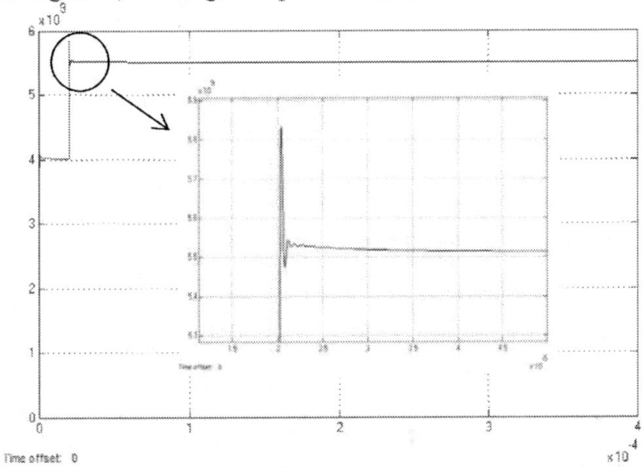

Figure 6. Time domain response

For accurate index analysis, the input signal is set to the unit step signal in Matlab simulation. The time domain step response curve and the open-loop response in the frequency domain are shown in Figure 7, Figure 8.

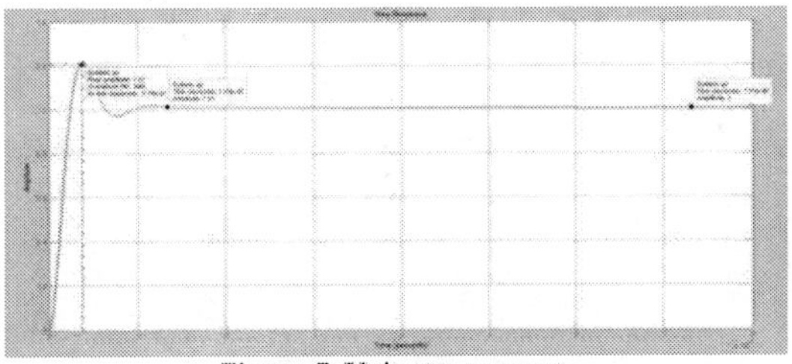

Figure 7. Unit step response

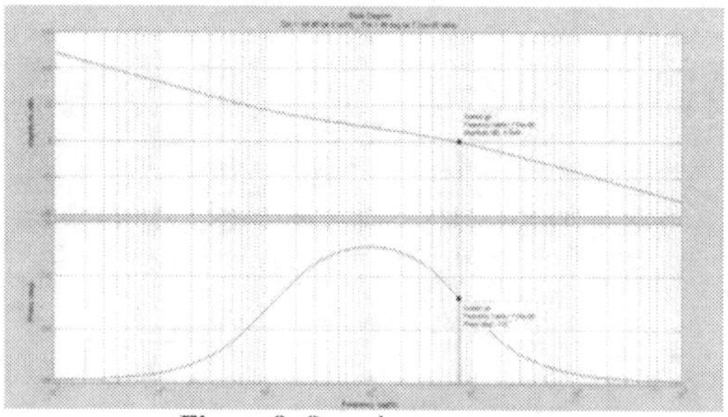

Figure 8. Open-loop response

6 Simulation results analysis

Figure 6 shows the two oscillations, the first oscillation that frequency from 0Hz jump to the starting frequency of 4000000kHz process.And the second oscillation that frequency from 4000MHz jump to the target output frequency 5512028kHz process. Figure shows that the system maximum overshoot is 5.82%, the system reach the steady-state value of 5512028kHz at 0.35us.

When the unit step signal is used as input, the responses obtained are shown in Table 3.

Table 3. Response indicator

Index	Value
Steady state error	0
Maximum overshoot	20.96%
Rise time/us	0.247
Adjustment time/us	0.845
Peak time/us	0.382
PM Frequency/(rad/s)	7.5463e+06
Phase Margin/(°)	47.9678
Delay Margin/(rad/s)	1.1094e-07
Stable	1

From the above results, it can be analyzed that the maximum overshoot of the system is 20.96%, the regulation time is 0.845us, and the steady-state error is zero. This system has faster response speed, higher precision and meet the performance requirements of PLL frequency. Thus, it is proved that the design method of HMC833 loop filter is feasible.

7 Experimental verification

The experimental platform and the real-time output frequency display are shown in Figure 9.

Figure 9. Real-Time output frequency

The HMC833 is controlled by FPGA with an output frequency of 551208Khz. The output frequency error curve that runs for 10 minutes is shown in Figure 10.

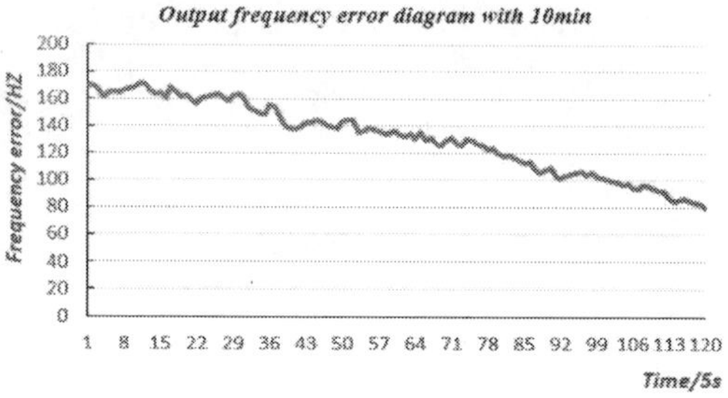

Figure 10. Output frequency error

The output frequency jump margin is 12Hz and the frequency lock accuracy is 1kHz. It has the characteristics of good stability and high steady-state precision. It satisfies the performance requirements of CPPLL for locking frequency, which verifies feasibility of the design method of HMC833 loop filter.

References

1. J.K. Tian, J.K. Yan, T. Chu, H.Z. Chen. Programming and analysis of wideband frequency synthesizer, Electronic Measurement Technology (2014).
2. F.M. Gardner. Charge-Pump Phase-Lock Loops, IEEE Trans. Commun, 28.11(1980):1849-1858.
3. J.J. Yao, et al. Design and analysis of VCO in PLL Circuit, Electron. Des. Eng (2011).
4. S. Mirabbasi, K. Martin. Design of loop filter in phase-locked loops, Electron. Lett, 35.21(2002):1801-1802.
5. J.B. Lan, et al. A nonlinear phase frequency detector for fast-lock phase-locked loops, IEEE, International Conference on Asic IEEE, 2009:1117-1120.

MATEC Web of Conferences **128**, 02007 (2017)
EITCE 2017 DOI: 10.1051/matecconf/201712802007

Simulation on Temperature and Ampacity of Mining Flame-proof High Voltage Cable Connector

Haiying Li[1,a], Zhuocheng Xue[1] and Jiancheng Song[2]

[1]*Department of Electrical Engineering, University of Shanghai for Science and Technology, Yangpu District, Shanghai 200093, China*
[2]*College of Electrical and Power Engineering, Taiyuan University of Technology, Taiyuan 030024, Shanxi Province, China*

Abstract. To investigate the accident causes of mining flame-proof high voltage (F-HV) cable connector, the temperature and ampacity of LBG1-200/6 high voltage cable connector are analyzed. At first, the material properties and structure of connector are introduced from the aspects of electrical, insulation and thermal. Then the electromagnetic field and thermal field coupling model of cable connector are established by the finite element method. Finally, in the numerical examples, temperature distribution and ampacity change caused by power harmonics, dielectric loss and slight structure change are quantitatively plotted and analyzed. The paper provides great insight into the security operation of F-HV cable connector.

1 Introduction

F-HV cable connector is used in 6-10kV mining transmission line per 300~500m. These connectors experience power harmonics, insulation aging and slight structure change in operation. In addition, F-HV cable connectors are enclosed with limited volume. Heat accumulation easily leads to explosion. The proportion of cable connector accidents is up to 70% of cable accidents [1]. The temperature and ampacity of cable connectors are important parameters to evaluate the potential vulnerability.

Numerous thermal behaviors on enclosed space have been reported. Gas isolated switchgear (GIS) is an enclosed equipment. Its heat issues and power losses are analyzed by combining the electric-magnetic field and thermal-fluid field [2]. The air flow on temperature distribution is further discussed [3]. Joint bay of high voltage cables in power systems is another kind of enclosed equipment. Its temperature rise is studied by the finite element method [4]. The above research lays the foundation for temperature and ampacity analysis of F-HV cable connector. However, F-HV cable connectors have many unique features. ① Mining cable is flame retardant with special shielding layers to resist crush and hit. Its structure is different from power cable, so the structure of connector is unique. ② Load fluctuates frequently in mining activities. The connector expands with heat and contracts with cold, which causes slight structure change. Additional heat is generated. ③ Wide application of inverters in the mine brings high proportion harmonics. The extra temperature rise by harmonic currents can't be ignored [5]. ④ Connectors run in the environment with 100% relative humidity all year round. Insulation aging is common due to the interaction among electricity, heat and humidity. The extra temperature rise by dielectric losses should be considered [6].

[a] Corresponding author: sh_lhy@163.com

In this paper, temperature and ampacity of F-HV cable connector are investigated with consideration to power harmonics, dielectric loss and slight structure change. Electric-magnetic-heat coupling method and ANSYS software are adopted. It will provide great insight into the design, type selection and fault analysis of cable connector.

2 F-HV cable connector

LBG1-200/6 F-HV cable connector is widely used in the mine. Its geometry size is shown in Table 1.

Table 1. Geometry size of the high voltage cable connector.

Materials	Thickness (mm)	Thermal conductivity (W/(°C•m))
Brass core[b]	10	109
DMC layer	5	2.5
DMC insulator	/	2.5
Internal air gap	3	0.026
External air gap	4	0.026
Cast iron shell	10	32

[b] Diameter of brass core.

Brass core is the conductor of cable connector with low resistivity, cheap price, high hardness and good anti-oxidation. It is insulated by dough molding compounds (DMC). DMC is dyed red to warn high voltage.

LBG1-200/6 F-HV cable connector using DMC makes itself with fine insulation property. Compared with other resin-composite, DMC has better characteristics [7]. ① Withstanding voltage is up to 36kV. ② Resistivity is 10^{12} Ω•m, even in high humidity condition. ③ Flame retardation and anti-arc capacities are advanced. Thermal deformation temperature (TDT) is high. It's the best choice in the environment with high density gas. Its detail physical properties are shown in Table 2. In addition, to enhance the insulation, internal air gap is employed to ensure the creepage distance.

Table 2. Physical properties of DMC.

Properties	Value	Units
Resistivity	10^{12}	Ω·m
Conductivity	2.5	W/(°C·m)
Anti-arc	180	s
Work temperature	130	°C
TDT	220	°C

To meet the technical requirements of thermal performance, air gap is designed. ① Internal and external air gap can prevent the heat from transferring to the outer layer. The temperature difference between the connector shell and the cable is avoided. ② Air gap can act as heat buffer when transient peak currents pass. The temperature rise of the shell is constrained to avoid fire accidents. Simplified cross-section is shown in Figure 1.

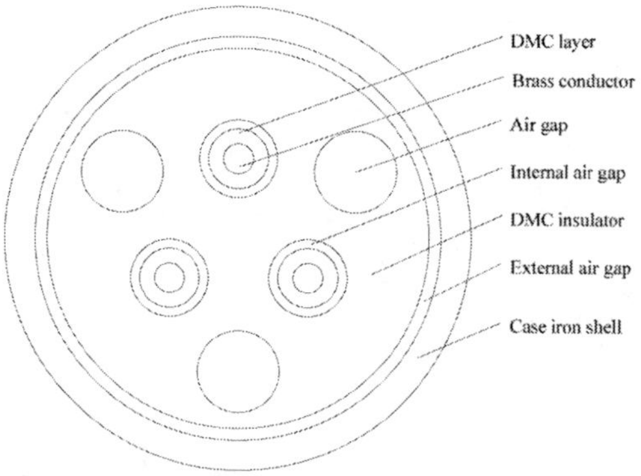

Figure 1. Simplified cross-section of F-HV cable connector.

DMC and cable connector combine many advantages, but their physical properties still may change irreversibly due to contacting with AC currents in its long service period. Slight structure change, insulation aging and harmonic currents happen frequently in manufacture or in operation. Slight structure change increases heat accumulation. Insulation aging in DMC causes dielectric losses. Harmonics bring extra power losses. Extra temperature rise and reduced ampacity make the connector vulnerable.

3 ANSYS simulation

Electromagnetic-thermal coupling model [8] in ANSYS software is adopted to analyze the temperature rise and ampacity of LBG1-200/6 F-HV cable connector. The impacts of harmonics, dielectric loss and slight structure change are incorporated.

3.1 Electromagnetic-thermal coupling model

Physical environment method [9] is selected to build the electromagnetic field and thermal field. The current is loaded in the electromagnetic field. The relative parameters, such as power and electric-magnetic distribution, are obtained. These results treated as thermal sources are loaded in the thermal field. The temperature distribution is gotten. The solver for electromagnetic field is unit Plane53. The solver for thermal field is unit Plane77. Unit Plane230 is used to analyze insulation aging via dielectric permittivity and dissipation factor parameters. The resistivity of the conductor is varying with temperature, so the temperature is determined by iteration method.

3.2 Key instructions in simulation

① Concentric circles in the model overlap together. Before define the material property for every layer of the model, overlap instruction should be used to make the concentric circle separated. Otherwise mistakes by overlap will happen. ② To plot the finite elements, more elements will result in slow calculation speed, fewer elements will affect the accuracy. In practice, increase the number of elements until the results will not change obviously. The number of finite elements in this model is set to 20. ③ The voltage degrees of freedom in the model require coupling to ensure the conductor integrated. Then select one finite element to load the current, the integrated conductor is loaded simultaneously. Three phase angular differences are 120°. ④ In insulation aging analysis, result file (.rst) can't be generated in electric field. To couple with thermal field, heat generation rate is output by instruction *get. Command flow is programmed to calculate the temperature distribution.

4 Numerical examples

4.1 Ampacity analysis

Ampacity is the current in amperes when the steady temperature of electrical conductor reaches 90°C based on standard IEC 60287 [10]. Load rated current 200A to LBG1-200/6 F-HV cable connector in ANSYS software, the temperature distribution by electromagnetic-thermal analysis is shown in Figure 2. We can see the highest temperature is 90.2°C, so its design fits for the security standard.

4.2 Harsh environments analysis

Harsh Environments refer to harmonic currents and dielectric losses. Harmonics in the mine are brought by powerful equipments [11, 12]. Harmonic currents proportions are {200, 0.3125, 0.1563, 0.09375} obtained from the investigation. That means fundamental current is 200A, the third harmonic current is 62.5A, the fifth harmonic current is 31.26A and the seventh harmonic

 DOI: 10.1051/matecconf/201712802007

current is 18.75A. The temperature distribution in harmonic environment is shown in Figure 3.

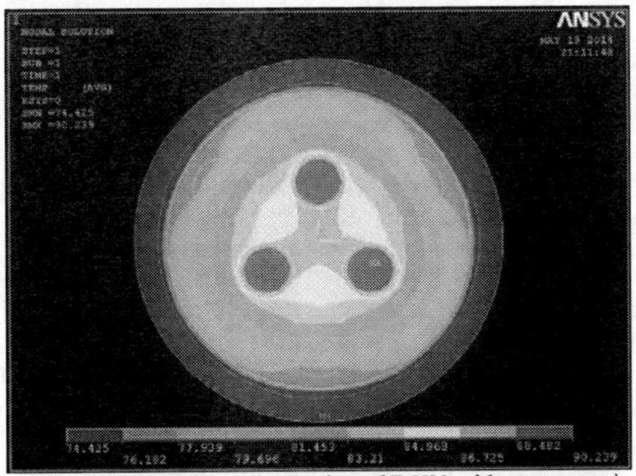

Figure 2. Temperature distribution of F-HV cable connector in rated condition.

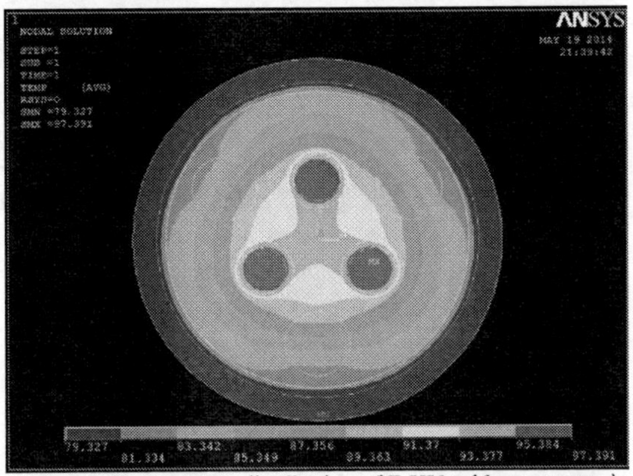

Figure 3. Temperature distribution of F-HV cable connector in harmonic environment.

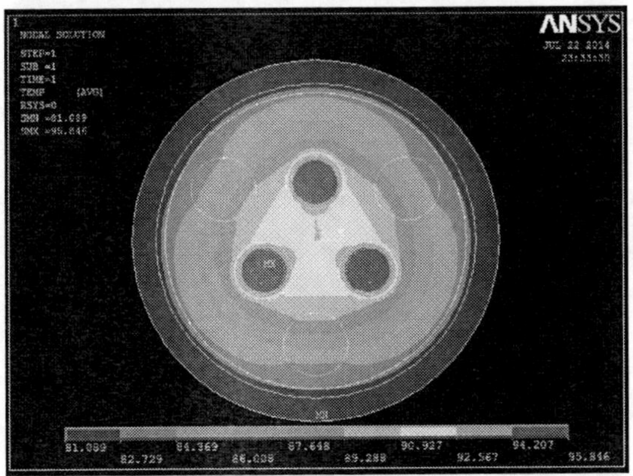

Figure 4. Temperature distribution of F-HV cable connector in aging environment.

From Figure 3, we can see the temperature of conductor is up to 97.4°C and the temperature of shell is 79.3°C affected by the harmonic currents. The temperature is far beyond the security temperature. If the connector works long in such case, the accidents easily happen.

In addition, dielectric losses can't be ignored since DMC properties change in its long service period. In normal case, the relative dielectric constant is 3.6~4.3 and dielectric loss tgδ is 0.0129. In aging case, the relative dielectric constant increases to 5.0 and dielectric loss tgδ increases to 0.03 [13]. The temperature distribution in aging environment is shown in Figure 4.

From Figure 4, we can see the temperature of conductor is up to 95.8°C and the temperature of shell is 81.1°C affected by the insulation aging. Emphasize here the temperature difference exists between the connector and the cable in this case. The insulation breakdown will happen.

4.3 Slight structure change analysis

Air gap has great effect on heat radiation. However, external air gap can't keep the design size even in manufactory process [14].

4.3.1 Effect on temperature

The initial design size of external air gap is 4mm. To discuss its impact, load rated current but adjust the thickness of air gap. The air gaps are varying from 3 mm to 6mm. The temperature distributions for the conductor and the shell are shown in Figure 5 and Figure 6.

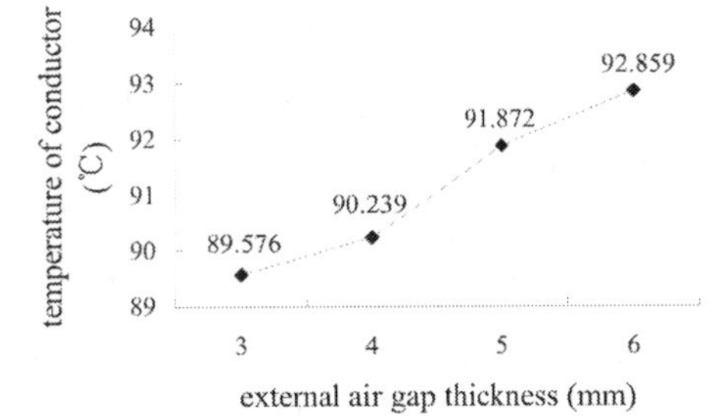

Figure 5. Temperature distribution of the conductor.

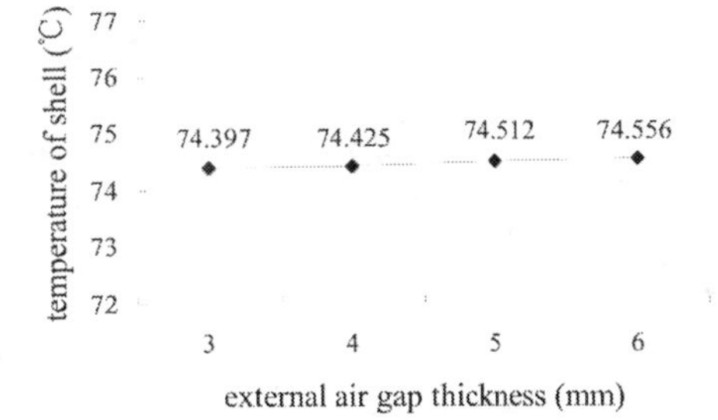

Figure 6. Temperature distribution of the shell.

From Figure 5, we can see the thicker the air gap, the higher the temperature. High thermal conductivity of air gap prevents the internal heat from transferring. The temperature rise is about 2.6°C (92.859°C-90.239°C).

DOI: 10.1051/matecconf/201712802007

Structure change incorporating the harmonics and aging makes the temperature higher. These phenomena explain the reason that some connector accidents happened in non-full load case.

From Figure 6, we can see the temperature of the shell increases only 0.16°C. This is because the heat accumulates in the air gap layer. The effect of structure change mainly acts on the temperature of conductor.

4.3.2 Effect on ampacity

Structure change constrains heat transfer, thus it will affect the ampacity directly. The ampacities with different thickness are shown in Table 3.

Table 3. Relationship between air-gap thickness and ampacity under safe temperature.

Thickness (mm)	Ampacity[c] (A)	Difference ration of ampacity and rated current
3	203.1	+1.55%
4	200.0	/
5	196.6	-1.7%
6	193.4	-3.3%

[c] RMS of current.

From Table 3, we can see the thicker the air gap, the lower the ampacity. To ensure the security, reducing operating current is the common measure. Improving ventilation and monitoring temperature are also necessary for the connector in such harsh environments.

5 Conclusion

The research on LBG1-200/6 F-HV cable connector shows the conclusions as follows. In rated condition, internal air gap design keeps the temperature of connector and cable identical. When harmonics are superposed, RMS value increases and temperature rise is up to 7.4°C. Dielectric loss of DMC will bring additional 5.8°C temperature rise, even temperature difference with the cable. Slight structure change will further intensify the condition. The ampacity decreases obviously. The research provides insight into accident causes and ampacity analysis of other type connectors.

Acknowledgments

This work was financially supported by Key Laboratory of Mining Electrical Equipment and Intelligent Control (Taiyuan University of Technology), Shanxi, China (MEI201601).

References

1. JW Qi and JC Song, *Industry and Mine Automation*, **12**, 32 (2009) (In Chinese)
2. H K Kim Y H Oh and S H Lee, *T and D Asia* (NJ: IEEE Computer Society, 2009)
3. J Lei, JY Zhong, SJ Wu, Z Wang, YJ Guo and XY Qin, *Journal of Electrical Engineering and Technology*, **11**, 781(2016)
4. J A Pilgrim, D J Swaffield, P L Lewwin, S T Larsen and D Payne, *IEEE Trans. on Power Delivery*, **24**, 1029(2009)
5. CY Li, J Chen, LB Hu and JY Cao, *12th IET Int. Conf. on AC and DC Power Transmission* (Institution of Engineering and Technology, 2016)
6. B Zhu, ZD Jia, Y Yuan, G J Lu, W N Fang and Z C Guang, *IEEE 11th Int. Conf. on the Properties and Applications of Dielectric Materials* (Institute of Electrical and Electronics Engineers Inc., 2015)
7. W L Wu and Y S Feng, *Int. Conf. on Advanced Fibers and Polymer Materials* (Chemical Industry Press, 2009)
8. HY Li, YC Liu and JC Song, *High Voltage Apparatus*, **50**, 82(2014) (In Chinese)
9. A Sedaghat and D L Francisco, *IEEE Transactions on Power Delivery*, **29**, 2306(2014)
10. S Dubitsky, G Greshnyakov and N Korovkin, *IEEE Int. Energy Conf.* (Institute of Electrical and Electronics Engineers Inc., 2016)
11. A Hiranandani, *IEEE Industry Applications Magazine*, **4**, 42(1998)
12. D Charis, P L Dimitris, S D Petros and G Kostas, *IEEE Transactions on Power Delivery*, **22**, 584(2007)
13. DH Wu, *Fiber Reinforced Plastics/Composites*, **6**, 19(1996) (In Chinese)
14. Y Kong, *Engineering Plastics Application*, **28**, 21(2000) (In Chinese)

DOI: 10.1051/matecconf/201712802008

Research on Fault Tolerance Enhancement of Array Erasure Codes

Dan Tang[1,a], Feng Xiao[1] and Di Fan[1]

[1]*Software Engineering Institute, Chengdu University of Information Technology,610225Chengdu, P. R, China*

Abstract. Array erasure coding technology is one of the most desirable methods to enhance the reliability of storage systems, but fault tolerance is always the bottleneck to the use of array codes. There are several improvement schemes for fault tolerance of array codes now, such as graph theory method, hybrid layout method, and so on. But improvement of the fault tolerance is pretty small, and always cost too much. In view of this, the paper presents a new method to improve fault tolerant ability of array erasure codes. The new method has a highly computing efficiency because all calculations are binary XOR operations, and it is convenient to implement because of its simple construction. Using this new method, we can model a horizontal array code with the optimal updating expenses. Although MDS array codes cannot be modeled by the new method, but storage efficiency can be improved by increasing the strip size. The most important contribution of this paper is that, this new method can construct an array erasure code which has the unconstrained fault tolerant ability in theory.

1 Introduction

At present, the data generated by all sectors of industries is growing explosively. To deal with the storage reliability problem caused by the rapid growth of the data quantity, an effective method is to build a storage system using multiple independent storage nodes together besides the simple expansion of the storage node capacity. This method can effectively increase the storage capacity, enhance the system reliability, improve the data parallel access efficiency and reduce the cost of storage system construction. In this case, we use the number of storage nodes to represent the scale of a storage system. At present, storage systems with more than 100 nodes have become more popular, some companies such as Google and Facebook even already have many storage systems with node quantity between 3000 to 4000[1]. However, under the condition that the average failure probability of a single node is certain, the increasing amount of nodes means that the number of nodes that may fail simultaneously in any time period would increase. In addition, earthquake, flood, fire, debris flow, and other natural disasters, hacker attacks, terrorist attacks, operational mistakes, intentional or unintentional destruction, and other emergencies may also cause multiple storage nodes to fail simultaneously. Therefore, it is extremely important to research the fault tolerant technology of storage systems for ensuring data security.

Replication is the most concise and intuitive fault tolerant method, which stores multiple copies of the same data to different storage nodes, and redundant data are copies of the original file. Because any copy in a node is equal to the original data, so when a node failure occurred, all data in the failure node could be recovered by any other normal node. This replication method is easy to implement and is convenient to deploy and expand dynamically. However, as the method which core idea is to enhance the reliability of the storage system, replication has great defects. The biggest problem is that it will lead to the low efficiency of storage space utilization. Using replication strategies to build a f fault tolerant storage system where f is a positive integer, it needs to copy each data to $f+1$ different storage node, in other words, the storage efficiency of the entire system is only $1/(f+1)$, and this is clearly unacceptable to a large scale storage system. In addition, the high updating expenses is another problem of replication strategy, any one of the smallest unit of data changes will involve all storage nodes which have the data duplicate. If the update operations occurred frequently, the operation efficiency of the whole system would be greatly affected.

The fault tolerant method based on erasure codes is a kind of storage reliability enhancement method which has attracted more and more attention in recent years. Compared with the fault tolerant method based on replication, in a storage system, erasure codes based methods can effectively balance fault tolerance, storage efficiency, repair bandwidth, updating expenses, and so on, so it has become an important approach to enhance the storage reliability. At present, erasure codes used in the storage reliability enhancement include RS erasure codes, LDPC erasure codes, array erasure codes, etc...

At present, the RS erasure code is the only one known MDS code which can correct any number of faults. It has achieved the Shannon bound, so the fault tolerant scheme based on RS codes has the advantages of unrestricted

[a] Corresponding author: tangdan@foxmail.com

fault tolerant capability and optimal storage efficiency. However, because of the complexity of RS codes over finite field operations, its computational cost is hard to be accepted by any large-scale practical system. In view of this, scholars have put forward some useful modified methods to improve the computing efficiency[2~3]. In recent years, scholars have made some great work on the efficiency improvement of operations over the finite field, in which the most typical is the GF-Complete proposed by professor Plank[4]. In spite of this, the operational efficiency of the RS code still cannot completely meet the needs of the storage system, especially the large-scale storage system. The LDPC(Low Density Parity Check) erasure code is a kind of erasure codes which encoding and decoding process are all based on XOR operations, so compared with RS codes, its operational efficiency is much higher. The LDPC erasure code is not a MDS code, but with the same fault tolerant capability, its code rate can be close to the MDS code rate. Although the LDPC code has many advantages, but it still faces a lot of problems when face to the storage system, including the irregularity of the code structure and the probability of successful decoding. And these features have greatly hindered the utilization of LDPC codes. And nowadays, the application of LDPC codes in the storage system is few[5].

Only simple binary XOR operations are used in the encoding and decoding process of array erasure codes (simply as array codes) , so it has a high computational efficiency. In addition, which has many other advantages such as simple realization, two-dimensional coding structure. These features make array codes suitable for being used in the storage system with multiple nodes. According to the storage efficiency, array codes can be subdivided into MDS codes and non MDS codes. Among them, 2 fault tolerance codes such as EVENODD codes[6] and X codes[7], 3 fault tolerance codes such as Star codes[8] and extended X codes[9] are all typical MDS array codes. However, the research work of MDS array codes with higher fault tolerance has not made a breakthrough. Researchers have modeled some array codes that have higher fault tolerance by giving up some storage efficiency, including Weaver code[10], Hover code[11], Grid code[12], and E code[13], and so on. The fault tolerant capability of these array codes has a certain improvement compared to the MDS array code, but it can only reach 10 or more, and such fault tolerant ability is still difficult to fully meet the application requirements.

This paper focuses on methods to improve the fault tolerant capability of array codes, and gives a method to effectively improve the fault tolerance. The new method can balance some important performance of the storage system. And it is proved that the proposed method can make the array code have the theoretically unrestricted fault tolerance. The organizational structure of this paper is as follows: In the first chapter, some general concepts in the fault tolerant area are given, and some common methods of improving the fault tolerance of array codes are presented. The second chapter will give a new method to improve the fault tolerance of array codes, as well as restrictions. In the third chapter, some important properties of the new method are analyzed. The last chapter is the summary of this article.

2 Basic concepts and related works

2.1 Basic concepts

Data, parity, element, stripe, strip, and other common terms can refer[6]-[13], while some of the symbols and concepts given below are prepared to explain the new method. It is important to note that the fault tolerance enhancement method proposed by this paper is based on the horizontal data layout.

Coding chain and slope: The data elements array of the storage system can be regarded as a two-dimensional coordinate system, the element at the first row and the first column be the origin of the coordinates, the horizontal rightward axis be the positive X axis, the vertical downward axis be the positive Y axis, and all data elements can be seen as a point in the coordinate system, so all data elements that need to calculate one parity can be considered as a chain on the coordinate system. What needs to explain specially is that, the coding chain is not first proposed in this paper, and such concepts have been mentioned in several previous research papers of array codes, for example, the X code call the coding chain as decoding chain[7]. Supposing the coordinates of all elements of a coding chain are (x_1, y_1), (x_2, y_2) … (x_m, y_n), then these coordinates must meet the following conditions:

$$\begin{aligned}&(y_2 - y_1)\%n/(x_2 - x_1)\%n\\&= (y_3 - y_2)\%n/(x_3 - x_2)\%n\cdots\\&= (y_m - y_{m-1})\%n/(x_m - x_{m-1})\%n\end{aligned} \qquad (1)$$

And the slope of the coding chain can be defined as $s = (y_m - y_1)\%n/(x_m - x_1)\%n$. In the process of encoding and decoding, the coding chain is used as a basic unit to participate in. Obviously, the XOR sum of all elements in a coding chain will produce a parity element(or check element). This parity element will also be involved in the encoding and decoding process as data elements in a coding chain, so it can be called as coding chain tail. When deploying a coding chain, it is just need to select a location from the parity array section in a certain sequence to store the parity element, namely the XOR sum of all data elements in a coding chain. For example, Figure 1 shows selections of corresponding parity elements when deploying a coding chain with the slope 1, while the XOR sum of all elements with the same texture is zero. In addition, if there were only one failure element in a coding chain and its tail, this failure element can be recovered obviously, so this coding chain can be called as the valid decoding chain.

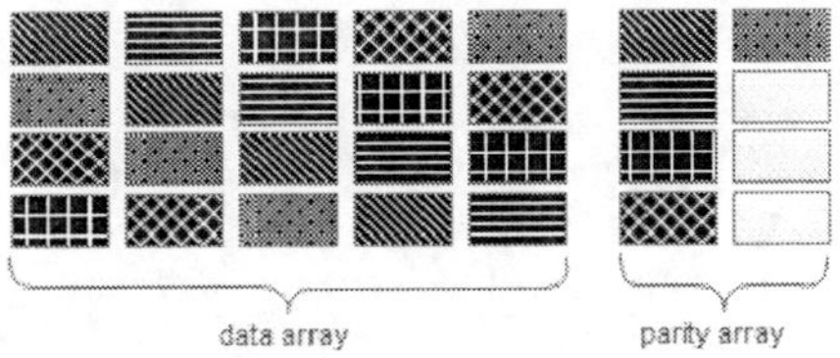

Figure 1. The coding chain of slope 1 and parity elements.

$El(i,j)$: The arithmetic expression $El(i,j)$ denotes the element of i-th row and j-th column, where i and j are all positive integers. When there are a number of elements that need to be represented, the symbol ':' can be used to show a range, such as $El(i,1:4)$ represents the element collection of i-th row and 1st to 4th column in the storage array, and $El(i,:)$ represents all elements of i-th row.

$Chain^{s}_{El(i,j)}$: The coding chain which includes the element $El(i,j)$ and has the slope s. The superscript and subscript of that expression can be omitted according to the actual situation. For example, $Chain_{El(:,j)}$ represents a collection of coding chains with any slopes and contains any element of the column j, $Chain^{s}$ refers to all coding chains with the slope s, while s can be a certain number or a collection.

D^{i}_{j} : D^{i}_{j} represents the distance from the column i to the column j in a storage array, and which definition is as below: $D^{i}_{j}=(j-i-1)\%n+1$, where n is the number of columns of the storage array. In the research of array codes, a column of a storage array is usually used to represent a node in the actual storage system, and node failure that means all elements lost in the corresponding column. A special note is the distance between failure columns, if one or more failure columns existed between the failure column i and j, there were no distance from column i to j, that is denoted as $D^{i}_{j}=0$.

R: Symbol R indicates that failure elements can be recovered with a coding chain or a set of coding chains. For instance, $R(EL(i,j))=Chain^{s}_{El(i,j)}$ indicates that the failure element $El(i,j)$ can be recovered by one or more coding chains which contain the element $El(i,j)$ itself and have the slope s, and can be denoted as the expression $R(EL(i,j))=Chain^{s}$ simply. Using multiple R expressions, the recovery process for failures can be displayed clearly.

2.2 Review of related works

Low fault tolerance is one of the most important factors that restrict the development of array codes, so how to improve the fault tolerance of array codes is an important research subject. At present, main methods to improve the fault tolerance of array codes can be summarized as follows.

1. Graph theoretical method. All data and parity elements in the same stripe are used as nodes, connections among these elements are used as edges, then an undirected graph set up. In the establishment of relationships among elements, namely adding edges among nodes should strictly control the out-degree and in-degree to meet some conditions, and based this to find approaches to improve the fault tolerance of array codes. If constraint conditions of the elements in the graph were reasonable, array codes that could tolerate 10 or more erasures can be constructed. However, this method is usually unable to construct a general fault tolerant capability model, which restricts the application range of which using this kind of array codes. In addition, using this method to improve fault tolerance will pay a high cost of storage efficiency. The weaver code is a typical representative of using graph theory to improve fault tolerance, the fault tolerant ability of weaver codes can be up to 12 or even higher. But when the weaver code is used to construct a 10 fault-tolerant storage system, the storage efficiency will be less than 20%, which is only slightly higher than the replication strategy[10].

2. Hybrid layout method. As previously mentioned, according to the layout relation of parity elements and data elements in a storage array, array codes can be divided into the vertical array code and the horizontal array code. For the vertical array code and horizontal array code, the layout relationship between the parity elements and the data elements is fixed. The hybrid layout method refers to a combination of vertical and horizontal data layout in the design of array codes to achieve the purpose of improving the fault tolerant ability. Compared with the Graph theoretical method, using the hybrid layout method to model array codes has a smaller cost of storage efficiency, and the fault tolerant ability can be proved in theory. However, this method usually has strict restrictions for stripe and stripe size, so it is not easy to extend, nor fully consider the update penalty and other factors. The grid code is a typical representative of using hybrid layout method to improve fault tolerance, and the fault tolerant ability can be up to 15 or even higher[12]. However, the array size is subject to the traditional horizontal and vertical codes used in the construction of a grid code, and a write operation of a minimum unit involves data access of all storage nodes, so it is hard to apply to large scale storage systems.

3. Random parities method. To improve fault tolerance while maintaining the balance of many other performance of the storage system, the random parity method gives up the practice of establishing the linear relationship between the data and the parity, and the stochastic method is used to establish connections between the data and the parity elements. At present, a number of array codes constructed by this method can tolerate 30 or even higher failures. However, there are more problems in the random parities method, the fault tolerant ability of array codes constructed by this kind of method has not obtained a mathematical proof, it is just gotten by the computer experiment usually, confirmed by the exhaustive method, or using a sampling method to prove the fault tolerant ability can achieve in a high probability, so these make this method difficult to apply

in various practical applications. The E code and GE code are typical representatives of using the random parity method to improve fault tolerance, and experiments prove that the fault tolerant ability of E codes or GE codes can be up to 30 or even higher in a high probability, but the fault tolerant ability is less than 10 under certain conditions, so this feature greatly limits the popularization and application of this kind of method[13].

3 Fault tolerance enhancement method based on coding chains

This chapter will propose a new method to improve the fault tolerant capability of array codes. In order to ensure the high efficiency of encoding and decoding process, all operations in the new method are XOR operations over the binary field. On the data layout of the vertical array codes, data elements and parity elements exist in the same strip, storage nodes can have a good load balance, but elements in different nodes are highly dependent on each other, and it's not easy to extend. This new method uses the typical horizontal data layout. At present, most array codes with similar technical routes organize the relationship between data elements and parity elements by using horizontal, diagonal and negative diagonal three kinds of coding chains, but the maximum fault tolerance of that strategy is not more than 3 in theory. Even more serious is that, in order to adapt to the large scale storage system, the horizontal coding chain is no longer applicable, otherwise, a minimum unit data update on one node will involve read operations of all the other data nodes. Thus, in order to improve the fault tolerance of array codes, this paper builds the correlation between data elements and parity elements by using coding chains with multiple disparate slopes.

3.1. Basic encoding and decoding method

As mentioned before, in order to reduce the correlation strength among data and parity elements, the article uses a typical horizontal data layout. Assuming that the fault tolerant ability of storage nodes is *f*, the number of rows of the storage array is *m*, the number of columns of the data array portion is *n*, and the number of columns of the parity array portion is *t*, then the size of the entire storage array can be expressed as $m\times(n+t)$, obviously, *f*, *m*, *t* are all positive integers, and $m\geq 2$. If there is no special description, these symbols *m*, *f*, *n*, *t* in later sections have the same meanings as described here.

Deploying f coding chains in the $m\times n$ data array portion, and there are two situations will be discussed respectively. When *f* is odd, deploying coding chains with slopes $\pm 1,\pm 2\cdots\pm\lfloor f/2\rfloor,\lceil f/2\rceil$ in the data array portion, and when *f* is even, deploying coding chains with slopes $\pm 1,\pm 2\cdots\pm\lceil f/2\rceil$ in the data array portion. The XOR sum of all elements in a coding chain is placed in the parity array as the column-major sequence. As noted above, the size of the data array portion is $m\times n$, all elements in the data array can be denoted as $El(:,1:n)$, namely, the symbolic representation $El(i,j)$ can denote every element of the data array portion when $1\leq i\leq m, 1\leq j\leq n$. Similarly, all elements of the $m\times n$ parity array portion can be denoted as $El(:,n+1:n+t)$, or as $El(i,j)$ when $1\leq i\leq m, n+1\leq j\leq n+t$. Each parity element is derived from XOR sum of *m* data elements, now still assuming that *f* is the maximum fault tolerant ability, then every parity element can be expressed and calculated by formula (2).

$$El_{check}=\sum_{row=1}^{m}El(row,((row-1)\cdot sign\cdot slope+1+beta)\%n) \quad (2)$$

In the formula (2), the symbol El_{check} represents any parity element, the symbol *sign* indicates that the slope of the current coding chain is positive or negative, the absolute value of the current coding chain is represented by the symbol *slope*, and the symbol *beta* represents the increment value between the column number of the current data element in a coding chain and the column number of the previous element. And all these symbols are defined as follows.

$$slope=\lceil i/2\rceil,\ beta=j-1, \quad (3)$$

$$sign=\begin{cases}-1\ ,i\%2=0\\ 1\quad i\%2=1\end{cases}, \quad (4)$$

In above definitions, symbols *i* and *j* indicate that the *j*-th coding chain of maximum *i*-fault-tolerance is deploying, where $1\leq i\leq f$, $1\leq j\leq n$. Therefore, all parity elements can be derived through the formula (2).

The above shows that, the fault tolerant capability of the storage system increased by 1, you need to deploy *n* more coding chains, and to increase *n* more parity elements correspondingly, so the number of parity nodes is $t=\lceil f\cdot n/m\rceil$.

Array erasure codes with unrestricted fault tolerance can be constructed by the above method according to the application environment. Then we will explain how to recover failure elements on failure nodes. This paper only considers the storage node failure, namely all elements lost in a failure nodes, not consider partial data loss in a node. Node failures can be divided into three categories according to the type of failure nodes, including all failures occurred in the parity array portion, all failures occurred in the data array portion, the data array and the parity array all have failures. All failures occurred in the data array portion is most difficult to recover, so assuming all failures occur in the data array portion. The core idea of this method is to find valid decoding chains to recover the loss elements on failure nodes, which is similar to the Zig-Zag decoding method[8] but a more concise valid decoding chains searching algorithm.

Supposing there are *f* failure nodes in the data array portion, and each node in a storage system can correspond to one column in a storage array, so label all *f* failure columns as $1,2\cdots f$ sequentially. The distance between column *f* and column 1 can be denoted as D_1^f, then supposing D_1^f is maximum among all distance values of adjacent failure columns. The core idea of this algorithm describes as follows: searching a coding chain and its corresponding tail which have only one lost element, namely a valid decoding chain, then XOR sum of all the other elements of this coding chain and its tail is just the lost element value. As stated earlier, all deployed coding chains have the slope symmetry property, and using this property, the search range of valid decoding chains can be reduced greatly. For example, if $Chain^{s}_{El(i,j)}$ was a valid decoding chain, then $Chain^{-s}_{El(m+1-i,j)}$, $Chain^{-s}_{El(i,f+1-j)}$ and $Chain^{s}_{El(m+1-i,f+1-j)}$ are all valid decoding chains, where $1 \le i \le \lfloor f/2 \rfloor$, $1 \le j \le \lfloor m/2 \rfloor$. In other words, if the loss element $El(i,j)$ can be recovered by the coding chain $Chain^{s}_{El(i,j)}$, the loss elements $El(i,f+1-j)$, $El(m+1-i,j)$ and $El(m+1-i,f+1-j)$ can be recovered by coding chains $Chain^{-s}_{El(m+1-i,j)}$, $Chain^{-s}_{El(i,f+1-j)}$ and $Chain^{s}_{El(m+1-i,f+1-j)}$ respectively.

Example 1. A storage array, supposing the size of the data array portion is 4×7, and maximum fault tolerant ability requirement is 2, then 2 coding chains need to be deployed obviously. A total of 14 parity elements will be generated, so 4 parity columns are also needed. The deployment of two coding chains is showed in Figure 2, all elements with the same texture constitute the coding chain and its corresponding tail, and the XOR sum of those elements is zero.

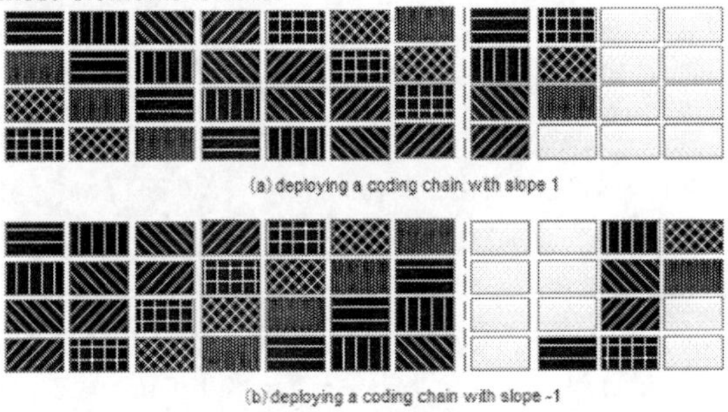

Figure 2. The deployment of coding chains to tolerate 2 failures.

In example 1 above, the second and fourth nodes are assumed to be failure, namely all elements in the second and fourth column lost. According to the data recovery method described in this chapter, all loss element can be recovered completely, and details of the recovery process are shown in Figure 5. An important point to be explained is that, the parity array portion is leaved out because all failures are in the data array portion. Furthermore, in subfigures of Figure 3, all elements with the same flag are coding chains used to recover loss elements.

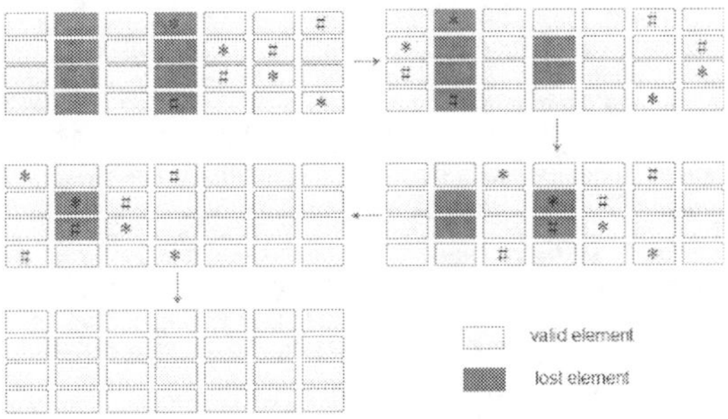

Figure 3. The recovery process of lost data.

In example 1, the size of the data array portion is 4×7, all lost data in column 2 and 4 are recovered successfully. Supposing the size of the data array portion is 4×5, the second and fourth nodes are also assumed to be failure, and two coding chains are deployed as before, shown in Figure 4, but now, any coding chain and its tail with only one lost element can not be found, all lost data can not be recovered. And more, another conclusion can be drawn from the experiment, deploying coding chains like this chapter, if the size of data array portion is 4×5, all lost data cannot be recovered if two or more nodes are failure.

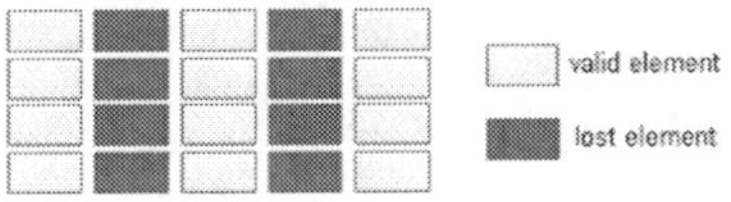

Figure 4. All lost data can not be recovered..

3.2 Constraint conditions of the data array size and fault tolerance

Place the figure as close as possible after the point where it is first referenced in the text. If there is a large number of figures and tables it might be necessary to place some before their text citation. If a figure or table is too large to fit into one column, it can be centred across both columns at the top or the bottom of the page.

From descriptions of loss data recovery of previous section, an intuitive conclusion can be drawn, just deploying coding chains cannot ensure the fault tolerant capability of array codes, the size of the storage array is also a constraint factor of fault tolerance. In other words, with the same number of rows, reducing the number of columns of the data array portion will decrease fault tolerant ability of array codes. Extending example 1 again, another conclusion can be obtained through exhaustive testing, in the case of 4 rows, 2 node failures can be recovered as long as the number of columns is equal or over 7. So using the method proposed in this paper to improve the fault tolerance of array codes, a prerequisite is that the size of the data array and the number of fault tolerance need to satisfy a certain relationship.

Symbols *m* and *n* still represent the number of rows of the storage array and the number of columns of the data array portion, for a *f*-fault-tolerant storage system, assuming that *f,m,n* satisfy the following constraints: $n \ge m \cdot f - f + 1$, where *m*, *n* and *f* are positive integers, and $m \ge 2$. Now we discuss fault tolerant ability of array codes under that condition.

 DOI: 10.1051/matecconf/201712802008

As mentioned before, the symbol t is denoted as the column number of parity array portion, then $t = \lceil f \cdot n / m \rceil$, thus $n > m$ and $t > m$. For horizontal array codes, the occurrence of failures can be divided to three types as follows: all failures occurred in the parity array portion, both data array portion and parity array portion have failures, and all failures occurred in the data array portion. The following will discuss these three cases respectively.

All f failures occur in the parity array portion is the simplest case of data recovery, all lost elements can be recovered by simply recalculating the parity elements. The case that both data array portion and parity array portion have failures is also easy to deal with. From the deployment of coding chains, in an array code with f fault tolerant capability, each data element belongs to f coding chains, the XOR sum of all elements is corresponding to only one parity element, so one data element is associated with f parity elements. The row-major sequence is used in coding chains deployment, and the column-major sequence is used when arranging the corresponding parities, and by the aforementioned restriction $n \geq m \cdot f - f + 1$, n is strictly larger than m, so two parity elements that associated with the same data element be not in the same column affirmatively. Supposing there were i failures in data array portion, and $f - i$ failures in parity array portion, in other words, $m \cdot (f - i)$ data elements and $m \cdot i$ parity elements are failure. Then for any data element, there are $f - 1$ correlation parity elements lost at most. Thus all failures occurred in the data array portion can be recovered, and then other failures occurred in the parity array portion can be recovered. The following discussion is the most difficult case of data recovery, this is the case that all failures occurred in the data array portion.

Using the mathematical induction to analysis, for convenience, assuming all discussions of this article below will follow the following conditions: all f failure columns are sequential denoted as $E_1, E_2 \cdots, E_f$ respectively, denote the distance between failure column as E_i and its right failure column as d_i, namely $D^{E_i}_{E_{(i-1)\%f+1}} = d_i$. Supposing $\max(d_1, d_2 \cdots, d_f) = d_f$, $i = 1,2 \cdots, f$. because of $n \geq m \cdot f - f + 1$, the inequality $d_f \geq m$ is established according to the pigeonhole principle.

Denote the only failure column as E_1 when $f = 1$, because of $n \geq m \cdot f - f + 1$, $n \geq m$ can be obtained. By the deployment of coding chains, a coding chain with slope 1 is deployed in the data array portion, so every failure element is passed through by a coding chain with slope 1. There is only one failure element on every coding chain contained failures, so each failure element can be recovered, namely the expression $R(El(:, E_1)) = Chain^1$ is established. Thus a conclusion can be drawn, all failures can be recovered when $f = 1$.

Denote two failure columns as E_1 and E_2 when $f = 2$, because of the precondition $n \geq m \cdot f - f + 1$, $n \geq 2m - 1$ can be obtained. All distances among columns are all positive integers, so expressions $R(El(1, E_1)) = Chain^{-1}$, $R(El(1, E_2)) = Chain^1$ hold. Then all failures in the first row of the storage array can be recovered, namely the expression $R(El(1,:)) = Chain^{\pm 1}$ holds. Repeat steps above, all failures can be recovered. Thus a conclusion can be drawn, all failures can be recovered when $f = 2$.

Supposing all failures can be recovered when $f = 2k$ .The following is a discussion about $f = 2k + 1$ and $f = 2k + 2$. Denote all $2k + 1$ failure columns as $E_1, E_2 \cdots E_{2k}, E_{2k+1}$ when $f = 2k + 1$. The distance $d_{2k+1} \geq m$ is the maximum among all distances of failure columns from the prerequisite. When $d_1 \geq \lceil m/2 \rceil$ holds, the equality $R(El(:, E_1)) = Chain^{\pm 1}$ has been obtained. For the same reason, when $d_{2k} \geq \lceil m/2 \rceil$ holds, the equality $R(El(:, E_{2k+1})) = Chain^{\pm 1}$ has been obtained. From two cases above, all failures can be recovered when $d_1 \geq \lceil m/2 \rceil$ or $d_{2k} \geq \lceil m/2 \rceil$. While inequalities $d_1 < \lceil m/2 \rceil$ and $d_{2k} < \lceil m/2 \rceil$ holds, these equations can be obtained obviously, $R(El(1, E_1 : E_k)) = Chain^{-1 \geq s \geq -k}$, $R(El(1, E_{k+2} : E_{2k})) = Chain^{1 \leq s \leq k}$, $R(El(1, E_{k+1})) = Chain^{k+1}$. So all failures in the first row of the storage array can be recovered, repeat the same steps above, all failures can be recovered when $f = 2k + 1$. Denote all $2k + 2$ failure columns as $E_1, E_2 \cdots E_{2k+1}, E_{2k+2}$ when $f = 2k + 2$. The distance $d_{2k+1} \geq m$ is the maximum among all distances of failure columns because of the prerequisite. When $d_1 \geq \lceil m/2 \rceil$ holds, the equality $R(El(:, E_1)) = Chain^{\pm 1}$ has been obtained. For the same reason, when $d_{2k+1} \geq \lceil m/2 \rceil$ holds, the equality $R(El(:, E_{2k+1})) = Chain^{\pm 1}$ has been obtained. From two cases above, all failures can be recovered when $d_1 \geq \lceil m/2 \rceil$ or $d_{2k+1} \geq \lceil m/2 \rceil$. While inequalities $d_1 < \lceil m/2 \rceil$ and $d_{2k+1} < \lceil m/2 \rceil$ holds, these equations can be obtained obviously, $R(El(1, E_1 : E_k)) = Chain^{-1 \geq s \geq -k}$, $R(El(1, E_{k+3} : E_{2k})) = Chain^{1 \leq s \leq k}$, $R(El(1, E_{k+2})) = Chain^{k+1}$, $R(El(1, E_{k+1})) = Chain^{-k-1}$. So all failures in the first row of the storage array can be recovered, repeat the same steps above, all failures can be recovered when $f = 2k + 2$.

Thus we can conclude that, there are f failures in a $m \times n$ storage array, if f, m, n can satisfy the restrictive condition $n \geq m \cdot f - f + 1$, f failures can be recovered under the array coding scheme proposed in this chapter, where f, m, n are positive integers and $m \geq 2$.

3.3 Colour illustrations

You are free to use colour illustrations for the online version of the proceedings but any print version will be printed in black and white unless special arrangements have been made with the conference organiser. Please check with the conference organiser whether or not this is the case. If the print version will be black and white only, you should check your figure captions carefully and remove any reference to colour in the illustration and text. In addition, some colour figures will degrade or suffer loss of information when converted to black and white, and this should be taken into account when preparing them.

4 Performance analysis

Equations should be centred and should be numbered with the number on the right-hand side.

$$T_s(l,t) = T_g(l,t) \quad (1)$$

$$T_s(l,t) = T_g(l,t)\, T_b(x \qquad , t) = 0 \quad (2)$$

Use italics for variables (u) and bold (**u**) for vectors. The order for brackets should be {[()]}, except where brackets have special significance.

This paper proposes a new improvement scheme for a class of array code tolerance ability, and the specific implementation steps and some restrictions are described above. However, for the entire storage system, it is undesirable to pursue only high fault tolerant capacity and ignore other performance. The previous article has demonstrated that this method can effectively improve the array code fault tolerance, and a chapter of the restrictions of ranks of the array codes on using the new method after are described. This chapter will describe the major performance costs overhead resulting from the use of new fault tolerance enhancement method.

4.1 Operational workload

About fault tolerance, compared with replication method, a major disadvantage of encoding method is that operations is necessary when storing data, just like RS erasure codes with so many advantages can not be applied to large-scale storage systems, one of the most direct reason is the high computational complexity required for encoding and data reconstruction. For storage systems, especially a large-scale storage system, the practicability of erasure codes largely depends on the operational workload. And the calculation load of encoding and decoding is an important indicator of erasure codes. For most non-MDS array codes, their structures are not normative usually, so it is difficult to use a certain formula to express calculations load of encoding or data recovery. Thus the number of binary XOR operations which are needed to generate a parity element is used to measure the complexity of encoding, and the number of binary XOR operations which are needed to recover a lost element is used to measure the complexity of data recovery.

From the previous chapter, based on the code-string array fault tolerance enhancement method, the amount of XOR operations required to generate a single parity element, and the amount of XOR operations required to recover a single lost element are all $m-1$, where m is the number of rows of the storage array, namely the strip size. With the most important prerequisite $n \geq m \cdot f - f + 1$ described in the previous chapter, when m is a given value, the more fault tolerance number means that the more parity elements need to be generated. In the case of m is 8, Figure 5 shows the amount of XOR operations required to store a 100M file when f is from 2 to 50. It is not difficult to see from this figure, the required binary XOR operations to store a 100M file is less than 13×10^8 even when the fault tolerant ability is as high as 50, and all of these operations can be completed by a most common computing node soon.

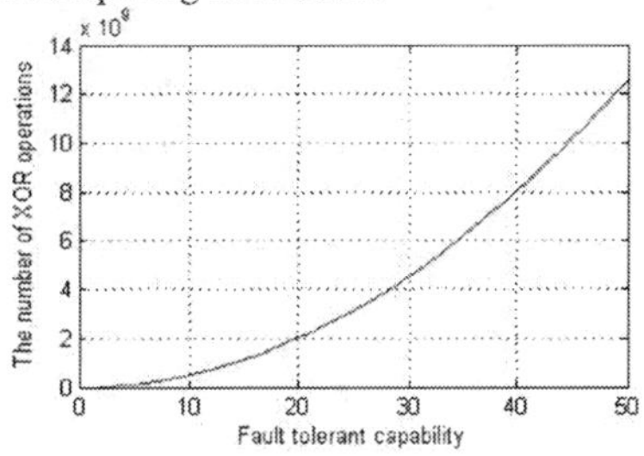

Figure 5. Relationship between fault tolerance and calculations.

4.2 Update penalty

The update penalty of an erasure coding scheme is the number of parity nodes whose contents must be changed when a minimal change is made in the contents of a given information node. Because parallelism is the reason we want to use storage arrays, the number of storage nodes of access required to effect a small data update must be minimized. By information theory, at least f parity nodes are involved when a minimum data update of a f-fault-tolerant array code with horizontal data layout, namely the minimum update penalty is f.

From steps of the new method, in using this method to model a f-fault-tolerant array code, any data element is belong to just f coding chains, namely every data element is interrelated to f parity elements, and these f parity elements are in different nodes certainly from proof of the previous chapter, it would result access operations in just f different parity nodes when a minimum data update, achieve The theoretical minimum update penalty.

4.3 Storage efficiency

A biggest drawback of the fault tolerant method based on replication strategy is the extremely low storage efficiency, the waste of storage space will be unacceptable especially when the storage scale becomes large. While the erasure codes based fault tolerant method can improve storage efficiency under the condition of the same fault tolerant ability. Storage efficiency is an important performance indicator of fault

DOI: 10.1051/matecconf/201712802008

tolerant codes. Under the equivalent fault tolerance, if the codes based method had an approximate or even lower storage efficiency, the coding scheme is fail, at least from the perspective of that computational cost versus storage efficiency.

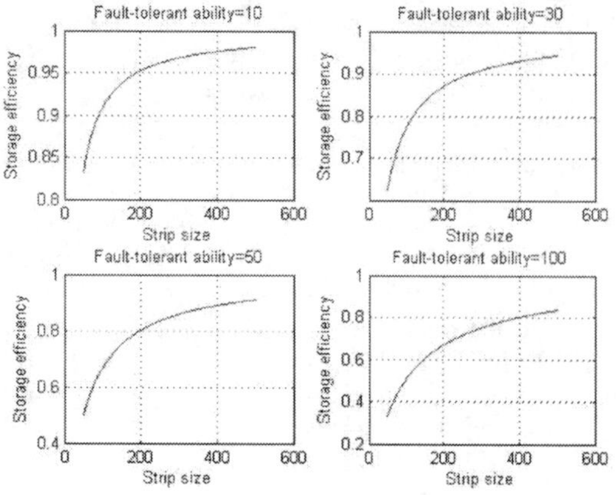

Figure 6. Correlation between the strip size and the storage efficiency.

MDS array codes cannot be modeled by the new method proposed in this paper, so an optimal storage efficiency can not be obtained. And even worse, increased fault tolerance can also lead to a decrease of storage efficiency. How to improve storage efficiency while ensuring fault tolerance is also a key point in the process of constructing array codes based on the new method. Under the new method, there are $f \cdot n$ data elements and $m \cdot n$ parity elements, in addition, the inequation $n \geq m \cdot f - f + 1$ must satisfy, so the storage efficiency can be improved by increasing *m*. Figure 6 shows the correlation between strip size and the storage efficiency.

5 conclusions

Low fault tolerance is one of the most important factors that restrict practical applications of array codes. However, considering the failures recovery time, internal communication mechanism between nodes, the operational efficiency of the entire storage system, and many other factors, for a fault tolerant scheme of a storage system, it can not be said that a higher fault tolerance array code has a higher practical value certainly. The starting point of this paper is to find a method to improve the fault tolerance of array codes, in other words, following this method, an array code which fault tolerance number can be preestablished. This method can also avoid strong constraint conditions that are needed for most array codes, and limit performance costs paid for the fault tolerance in an acceptable range. The work in this paper achieve these targets, the method proposed in this paper is also the first one that model array codes can tolerate arbitrary number of failures from the current known literature and reference materials. Therefore, it is reasonable to assume that our work will play a positive role in improving the range of application and practical value of array codes.

References

1. Sathiamoorthy M, Asteris M, Papailiopoulos D, et al. Xoring elephants: Novel erasure codes for big data. In: Proceedings of the VLDB Endowment. VLDB Endowment, 2013, 325–336.
2. Zheng Z, Sinha P. XBC: XOR-based buffer coding for reliable transmissions over wireless networks. In: Proceedings of Broadband Communications, Networks and Systems, Raleigh, 2007. 76–85.
3. Plank J S, Xu L. Optimizing Cauchy Reed-Solomon codes for fault-tolerant network storage applications. In: Proceedings of Network Computing and Applications, Massachusetts, 2006. 173–180.
4. Plank J S, Greenan K M, Miller L. Screaming fast Galois field arithmetic using Intel SIMD instructions. In: Proceedings of 11th USENIX Conference on File and Storage Technologies (FAST 13), San Jose, 2013. 298–306.
5. Harihara G, Janakiram B, Chandra M G, et al. SpreadStore: a LDPC erasure code scheme for distributed storage system. In: Proceedings of the 2010 International Conference on Data Storage and Data Engineering, Bangalore, 2010. 87–93.
6. Blaum M, Brady J, Bruck J, et al. EVENODD: an efficient scheme for tolerating double disk failures in RAID architectures. IEEE Trans Comput, 1995, 45: 192–202.
7. Xu L, Bruck J. X-code: MDS array codes with optimal encoding. IEEE Trans Inform Theory, 1999, 45: 272–276.
8. Huang C, Xu L. STAR: an efficient coding scheme for correcting triple storage node failures. IEEE Trans Comput, 2008, 57: 889–901.
9. Meng Q C. Research of erasure codes applied in distributed storage system. Dissertation for Ph.D. Degree. Beijing: Graduate University of the Chinese Academy of Sciences, 2007.
10. Hafner J L. Weaver codes: highly fault tolerant erasure codes for storage systems. In: Proceedings of Usenix Conference on File and Storage Technologies, San Francisco, 2005. 16–16.
11. Hafner J L. Hover erasure codes for disk arrays. In: Proceedings of International Conference on Dependable Systems and Networks, Philadelphia, 2006. 217–226.
12. Li M Q, Shu J W, Zheng W M. Grid codes: strip-based erasure codes with high fault tolerance for storage systems. Acm Trans Stor, 2009, 4: 15–22.
13. Chen Z. A class of array erasure codes and their applications. Dissertation for Ph.D. Degree. Beijing: Graduate University of the Chinese Academy of Sciences, 2009.

A Separation and Decoding algorithm for QPSK Signals with Low Complexity

Baijun Pan[1,a], Shilong Tu[2]

[1]*Science and Technology on Blind Signal Processing Laboratory, Chengdu, china*
[2]*Science and Technology on Blind Signal Processing Laboratory, Chengdu, china*

Abstract. In this paper, we consider separation and decoding for two QPSK signals, which have the same symbol rates. However, the complexity of the present method is too high. To solve this question, an algorithm based on lattice reduction and joint iteration is proposed to enhance the separation performance. The complexity is greatly reduced while retains considerable performance. Simulation results are provided to illustrate the performance of the proposed algorithm.

1 Introduction

PCMA is a new type of satellite communication multiple access technology[1], which can not only increase the frequency utilization ratio of satellite channel, but also improve the anti-interception capability of communication. So, during the past decades, it has become the research focus of signal processing. In the communication of PCMA, the third party obtains the mixed signal of the same frequency band, and the target signal can not be demodulated by the traditional method. There are two effective methods in the separation of PCMA signal at present. One is the separation of time-frequency mixing signals based on particle filter, which has good separation performance and good error performance, but in order to guarantee the performance of the algorithm, it requires increasing the number of particles, so the computational complexity is large, and the complexity increases exponentially with the modulation order of the signal. The second is the PSP algorithm, which is also of high complexity and is not suitable for processing high order modulation signals. In recent years, the development of lattice reduction techniques in the field of wireless communication is more and more widely used. Lattice reduction technology is originally used in MIMO detection[2]-[5], which enhance the symbol detection performance while reduce the complexity of the algorithm.

In this paper, we propose a low complexity iterative separation and decoding algorithm based on lattice reduction[6]. The remaining part of this paper is organized as follows. The reception model of coded PCMA signals is given in the next section. The section 3 describes the low complexity PCMA joint iterative separation and decoding algorithm. The simulation results are provided in Section 4. Finally, conclusions are drew in Section 5.

2 Basic signal model

PCMA is the superposition of two identical frequency modulated signals. The signal model at encoding is shown in Fig. 1

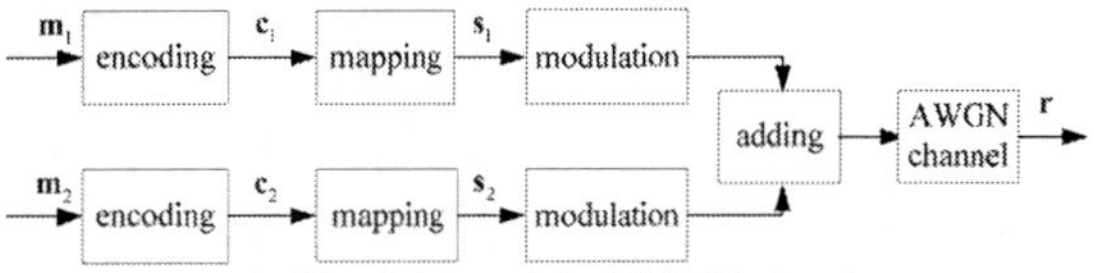

Fig. 1 the model of PCMA signal

The received signal may be expressed as
$r(t) = h_1 e^{j(\Delta\omega_1 t+\theta_1)} x_1(t) + h_2 e^{j(\Delta\omega_2 t+\theta_2)} x_2(t) + v(t)$ (1) where h_1 and h_2 are amplitude fading of two signals respectively, $\Delta\omega_1$ and $\Delta\omega_2$ are carrier offsets of two signals, θ_1 and θ_2 are the carrier phase of two signals, $v(t)$ is the additive Gauss white noise, with the mean value is zero and the single power spectrum density is N_0, and the $x_i(t)$ is a baseband digital modulation signal that can be represented as

$$x_i(t) = \sum_{n=-\infty}^{+\infty} s_{i,n} g_i(t - nT + \tau_i(t)) \; (i = 1, 2) \qquad (2)$$

where $s_{i,n}$ is the transmitted modulation symbol sequence of the i th signal, $g_i(t)$ is the pulse responses of the equivalent channel filters which consist of shaping filters, a physical transmission channel, and a receiving filter, T is the symbol period, and $\tau_i(t)$ are the relative

[a] Corresponding author: 18689676684@163.com

time delays between the two received modulated signals and the local clock reference.

Sampling the received signal at rate $2/T$, we can write the discrete-time baseband signal as

$$r_{2k+m} = h_1 e^{j(\Delta\omega_1(kT+mT/2)+\theta_1)} x_{1,2k+m} + h_2 e^{j(\Delta\omega_2(kT+mT/2)+\theta_2)} x_{2,2k+m} + v_{2k+m} \quad (3)$$

where $r_{2k+m} = r(kT+mT/2)$, $x_{i,2k+m} = x_i(kT+mT/2)$, $v_{2k+m} = v(kT+mT/2)$, $k = 0,1,2,\cdots$ stands for symbolic moments, $m = 0,1$ represents the two sampling times at the same symbolic moment.

Assuming that $g_i(t)$ affects only a total of L symbols before and after, the expression is

$$x_{i,2k+m} = \sum_{n=1-L_1}^{L_2} s_{i,k+n} g_i(-nT+\tau_{i,2k+m}) \quad (4)$$

where $\tau_{i,2k+m} = \tau_i(kT+mT/2)$, $L_1 + L_2 = L$.

Bring the formula(4) into the formula(3), and

$$f_{i,2k+m}(n) = h_i e^{j(\Delta\omega_i(kT+mT/2)+\theta_i)} g_i(-nT+\tau_{i,2k+m}) \quad (5)$$

Then we can get

$$r_{2k+m} = \sum_{n=1-L_1}^{L_2} s_{1,k+n} f_{1,2k+m}(n) + \sum_{n=1-L_1}^{L_2} s_{2,k+n} f_{2,2k+m}(n) + v_{2k+m} \quad (6)$$

In the first separation, we use decision feedback equalization(DFE) based on lattice reduction to detect symbol. Firstly, the channel matrix is extended, that is

$$\underline{\boldsymbol{H}}_f = \begin{pmatrix} \boldsymbol{H}_f \\ \sigma I_{K(r+1)} \end{pmatrix} \quad (7)$$

where $\boldsymbol{H}_f$ is feedback channel matrix, σ^2 is the variance of $v(t)$, and $I_{K(r+1)}$ is the identity matrix. $\boldsymbol{G}_f = \underline{\boldsymbol{H}}_f \boldsymbol{U}$ is the transformed channel matrix, $Y = \boldsymbol{G}_f \bar{\boldsymbol{S}}_f + \boldsymbol{n}$, then we can get $\bar{\boldsymbol{S}}_f(n) = \boldsymbol{U}^{-1}\boldsymbol{S}_f(n)$, where $\boldsymbol{U}$ is unimodular[7]. By conducting pseudo inverse on matrix $\boldsymbol{G}_f$, then we obtain

$$\bar{\boldsymbol{S}}_f = \boldsymbol{G}_f^+ Y \quad (8)$$

where $\boldsymbol{G}_f^+$ is the pseudo inverse matrix of $\boldsymbol{G}_f$. Once $\bar{\boldsymbol{S}}_f$ is determined, the desired estimation result $\boldsymbol{s}(n-k)$ can be obtained from $\boldsymbol{S}_f(n)$ by

$$\hat{\boldsymbol{S}}_f(n) = q_\Phi\left\{\boldsymbol{U}\hat{\bar{\boldsymbol{S}}}_f(n)\right\} \quad (9)$$

Finally, we implement the decision on $\hat{\boldsymbol{S}}_f$, which means that the part ISI is eliminated and the results are more reliable.

3 Joint iterative separation and decoding algorithm

The prior information of symbol is helpful to improve the separation efficiency. Fig. 2 is a block diagram of joint iterative separation and decoding, and iteration is performed by constantly interacting soft information between the blind separation and decoding modules. In order to reduce the computational complexity, we use the separation algorithm based on lattice reduction at the first time and then the separated symbols are fed into the decoding module. In the latter iteration, the separation is performed using the PSP algorithm. The blind separation module is processed according to the received mixed signal $\mathbf{r}$ and a priori information of symbol $L_s^a(s_{i,k})$, and calculates bit information $L_d^a(c_{i,kJ+j})$ that is output to the decoding module. The decoding module calculates the posterior information $L_d(c_{i,kJ+j})$ of each bit according to the decoding algorithm, and then subtracts the prior information $L_d^a(c_{i,kJ+j})$ to obtain the external information $L_d^e(c_{i,kJ+j})$. After mapping, a priori information $L_s^a(s_{i,k})$ is formed, which is fed back to the blind separation module and the next iteration is started.

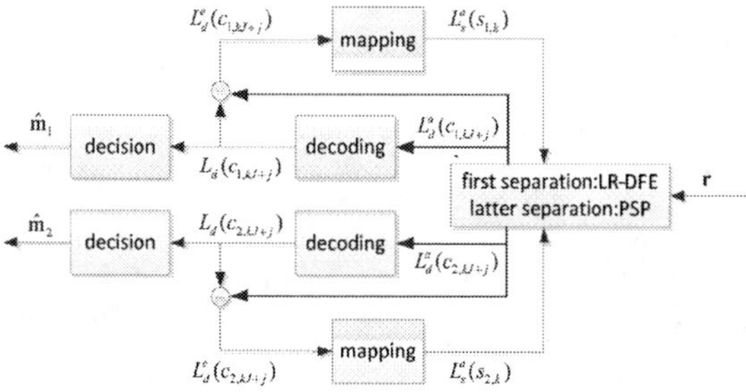

Fig. 2 block diagram of joint iterative separation and decoding

In the above block diagram, blind separation and decoding are two key modules. The decoding module can adopt the existing mature algorithm, and the blind separation module will be described below.

In order to iteration, the separation here requires the soft input values and provides soft output. Using the bit likelihood metric, the bit information of the output can be represented as

$$L_d^a(c_{i,kJ+j}) = \ln \frac{p(c_{i,kJ+j} = 1 \mid r_{0:2K-1})}{p(c_{i,kJ+j} = 0 \mid r_{0:2K-1})} \quad (10)$$

where K is the total number of symbols for the data segment to be processed. We take $r_{2k:2k+3}$ four points, then the formula (10) can be rewrite to

$$L_d^a(c_{i,kJ+j}) = \ln \frac{p(c_{i,kJ+j} = 1 \mid r_{2k:2k+3})}{p(c_{i,kJ+j} = 0 \mid r_{2k:2k+3})} \quad (11)$$

We can futher write the formula(10) into

$$
\begin{aligned}
L_d^a(c_{i,kJ+j}) &= \ln \frac{p(c_{i,kJ+j}=1 \mid r_{2k:2k+3})}{p(c_{i,kJ+j}=0 \mid r_{2k:2k+3})} \\
&= \ln \frac{\sum_{S_k : c_{i,kJ+j}=1} p(S_k \mid r_{2k:2k+3})}{\sum_{S_k : c_{i,kJ+j}=0} p(S_k \mid r_{2k:2k+3})}
\end{aligned} \tag{12}
$$

where S_k is the sequence of symbols corresponding to $r_{2k:2k+3}$, then we can get

$$
\begin{aligned}
p(S_k \mid r_{2k:2k+3}) &\propto p(r_{2k:2k+3} / S_k) \cdot p(S_k) \\
&= \prod_{l=2k}^{2k+3} p(r_l / S_k) \cdot \prod_{l=k+1-L_1}^{k+L_2+1} p(s_{1,l}) p(s_{2,l}) \\
&= \prod_{l=2k}^{2k+3} \frac{1}{\sqrt{\pi}\sigma} \exp\left(-\frac{|r_l - \hat{r}_l|^2}{\sigma^2}\right) \cdot \prod_{l=k+1-L_1}^{k+L_2+1} \prod_{j=0}^{J-1} p(c_{1,lJ+j}) p(c_{2,lJ+j})
\end{aligned} \tag{13}
$$

where σ^2 is the noise variance, and $\hat{r}_l$ is the reconstructed value of r_l, which is calculated as following according to the formula(6)

$$
\hat{r}_{2k+m} = \sum_{n=1-L_1}^{L_2} s_{1,k+n} \hat{f}_{1,2k+m}(n) + \sum_{n=1-L_1}^{L_2} s_{2,k+n} \hat{f}_{2,2k+m}(n) \tag{14}
$$

where $s_{i,k+n}$ is derived from sequence S_k, and $\hat{f}_{i,2k+m}(n)$ is the estimate of $f_{i,2k+m}(n)$, which can be tracked using the LMS algorithm.

Bring the formula(13) into the formula(12) and use the approximate formula

$$
\ln(e^x + e^y) \approx \max(x, y) \tag{15}
$$

Then we can get

$$
\begin{aligned}
L_d^a(c_{i,2k+j}) \approx & \max_{S_k : c_{i,2k+j}=1} \Big(-\frac{1}{\sigma^2} \sum_{l=2k}^{2k+3} |r_l - \hat{r}_l|^2 \\
& + \sum_{l=k+1-L_1}^{k+L_2+1} \sum_{j=0}^{J-1} (c_{1,lJ+j} L_d^e(c_{1,lJ+j}) + c_{2,lJ+j} L_d^e(c_{2,lJ+j}))\Big) \\
& - \max_{S_k : c_{i,2k+j}=0} \Big(-\frac{1}{\sigma^2} \sum_{l=2k}^{2k+3} |r_l - \hat{r}_l|^2 + \\
& \sum_{l=k+1-L_1}^{k+L_2+1} \sum_{j=0}^{J-1} (c_{1,lJ+j} L_d^e(c_{1,lJ+j}) + c_{2,lJ+j} L_d^e(c_{2,lJ+j}))\Big)
\end{aligned} \tag{16}
$$

Obviously, limiting the range of the S_i can reduce the amount of calculation with some performance loss. In the first separation, we use decision feedback algorithm based on the lattice reduction, which is achieved by fixing the symbol of the preceding time. In the latter separation, we can fix the symbol before and after target symbol because the entire sequence of symbols has been estimated. The amount of calculation in blind separation brought from iterative process can be negligible, thus greatly improve the detection performance.

4 Simulation results

This section presents the performance of the algorithm which is evaluated through simulation using two QPSK modulated signals. We first compare the performance of the two methods of separation. We suppose that LDPC encoding is adopted.

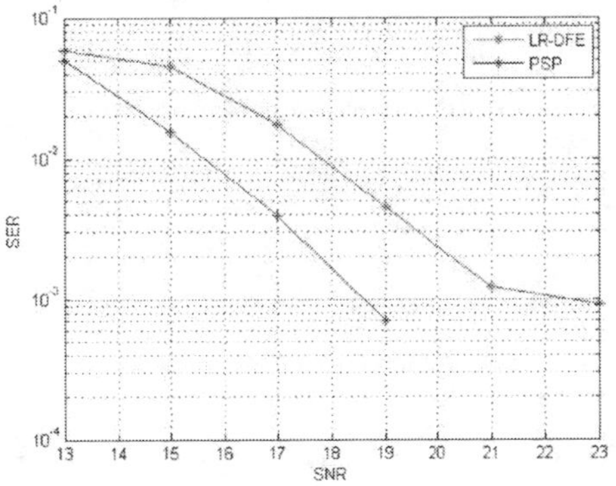

Fig. 3. The separation performance of LR-DFE algorithm comparing with PSP

As can be seen from Figure 3, when the bit error rate is 10^{-3}, LR-DFE has a 2.2db performance penalty relative to the PSP algorithm, but the computation is reduced by 10 times[8], so it can be used to process higher order modulation signals, such as 8QAM, 16QAM, so the LR-DFE algorithm has better engineering applicability.

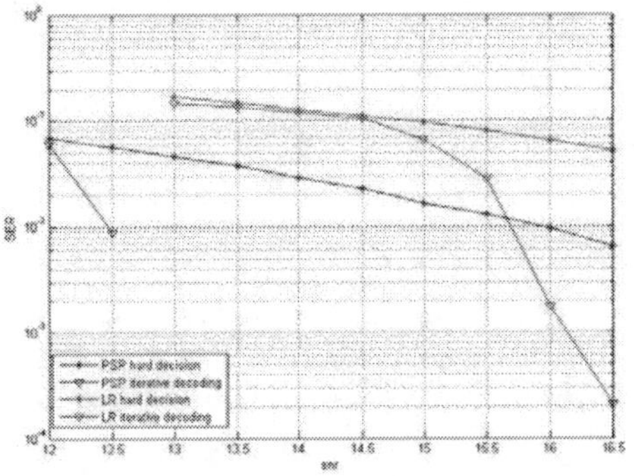

Fig. 4. The performance of joint iterative separation and decoding algorithm

Last, the performance of joint iterative separation and decoding algorithm is investigated. As mentioned earlier, in the first separation, we fix the symbol before the target symbol and in the later separation, we fix the symbol before and after the target symbol. In the first separation, we use different separation methods, one is LR-DFE, and the other is PSP. As can be seen from the diagram, the iterative decoding brings huge improvement to the performance of separation, and the maximum bit error rate can be reduced from 9.62E-2 to 6.55E-2 at an iteration, and achieve generally error free at two iteration.

5 Conclusion

A low complexity joint iterative and decoding algorithm is proposed in this paper, It's complexity is 10 times lower than that of PSP iterative decoding, so it has good practicability. Simulation results show that under the same number of iterations, the performance loss is 2.2db

Compared with PSP. However, iterative decoding can bring 1.5-1.2db gain, so the effectiveness of the algorithm is proved.

References

1. Mark D. Paired carrier multiple access(PCMA) for satellite communication[C]. Pacific Telecommunications Conference, Honolulu, Hawaii, 1998: 787-791.
2. H.Yao,G.W.Wornell.Lattice-reduction-aided detectors for MIMO communication systems[C].IEEE Global Telecommunication Conference,Taipei,2002,424-428.
3. C.Windpassinger,R.F.H.Fischer.Low-complexity near-maximum-likelihood detection and precoding for MIMO systems using lattice reducation[C].IEEE Information Theory Workshop(ITW),Paris,2003,345-348.
4. D. Wubben,R.Bohnke,V.Kuhn,et al..Near-Maximum-Likelihood Detection of MIMO Systems Using MMSE-Based Lattice Reduction[C].IEEE International Conference on Communication(ICC),Paris,2004,798-802.
5. Qin X B, He G H, Ma J. The application of Lattice Reduction Algorithm in MIMO detection[J]. Chinese scientific papers, Vol.10, No.14, 2015.
6. Liao C H, Tu S L, Wan J. Single channel blind separation/decoding Algorithm based on iterative mixed frequency signals[J]. Journal of communications, 2011, 32(8): 111-117.
7. Zhao Y F, Cao Y J, Dai X C. Single Antenna Interference Cancellation Algorithm Based on Lattice Reduction[J]. Journal of Communications,2015:93-100.
8. C. P. Schnorr and M. Euchner, "Lattice basis reduction:Improved practical algorithms and solving subset sum problems,"Mathematical programming, vol. 66, no. 3, pp. 181-199, 1994.

MATEC Web of Conferences **128**, 02010 (2017) DOI: 10.1051/matecconf/201712802010
EITCE 2017

Research on Pepper Disease Diagnosis Model Based on Genetic Neural network

Qingfeng WEI[1,2], Sufen SUN[1,2], ChangShou LUO[1,2]

[1]*Institute of Agricultural Information and Economics. Beijing Academy of Agriculture and Forestry Sciences, Beijing, China*
[2]*Beijing Research Center of Engineering Technology on Rural Distance Information Service, Beijing, China*

Abstract. To explore the effective method of the pepper diseases, using the method of combining the genetic algorithm and BP neural network, the establish neural network diagnostic model for pepper diseases is established to improve the model convergence rate and accuracy. The experimental results show that the model is convergent effectively and the diagnostic accuracy is improved by 12%.

1 Introduction

Pepper is rich in vitamins.It can enhance the physical strength, dispel cold and clear damp, and has been one of the daily necessities of vegetable species. Pepper industry is one of the most important vegetable industries in china. Pepper disease is an important factor restricting high quality production. If the disease can not be diagnosed effectively, the best prevention and control time will be delayed, the quality of agricultural products will be reduced and the losses will be greater.

Resent years, BP neural network is widely used in diagnosis, which provides a new way for the diagnosis of plant diseases. But throughout the current study, there are major problems: Firstly, the traditional method (additional momentum and adaptive learning rate method) for performing neural network performance optimization is an iterative search process which the optimal solution is obtained from an initial point in the solution space. The search information provided by a single search point is not much, so the search efficiency is not high in the intention to obtain the global optimal solution. Secondly, these algorithms often use deterministic search methods. Namely, one search point to another, there is a definite transfer method and transfer relationship. This kind of certainty often makes the search process fall into the local optimal solution and stagnates, and even makes it impossible to reach the optimal solution forever.

In view of the existing problems in the application of the model, the genetic algorithm is used to optimize the weights of the neural network in order to improve the model and improve the accuracy of diagnosis.

2 BP neural network model construction

2.1.1 Input matrix construction

Pepper disease symptoms are mainly reflected in the whole plant of seedling stage, and 5 parts of roots, stems, vines, leaves, flowers, fruit. Therefore, the input vectors are divided into 6 units. The contribution of different symptoms to disease diagnosis is different. Some of the obvious symptoms are often the important basis for the identification of certain diseases. Invite 5 experts, according to the contribution of disease symptoms to disease diagnosis, making in the root, stems, leaves, flowers, fruit, seedlings, and take the average value to build input vector.

Table 1 symptom types and scores

Type	Score	Explain
Typical symptom	1	The type of disease can be determined by this type of symptom.
Main symptom	0.7	Through the comprehensive expression of several symptoms, can determine the type of disease.
General symptoms	0.3	The symptoms only serve as an auxiliary judgment, and can not determine the disease types.

2.1.2 Hidden layer neuron determination

The hidden layer is the value map that is input to output. The output formula of hidden layer neuron is as follows:

$$y = f(\sum_i w_{ji} x_i - \theta_j)$$

Among them, "y" is the hidden layer node value, "wji" is the weight between the input point and the hidden layer neuron node, and "θ" is the threshold value.

DOI: 10.1051/matecconf/201712802010

The activation function is as follows:

$$f(x) = \frac{1}{1+e^{-x}}$$

The number of neurons in the hidden layer is determined as follows:

$$l = \sqrt{n+m} + a \quad 0 < a < 10$$

Among them, "l" is the number of neurons in the hidden layer, "n" is the input layer neuron number, "m" is the output layer neuron number, and "a" is the constant value between 0 and 10.

2.1.3 Output matrix construction

The output vector is a matrix of n*n. It constructed by binary encoding of "1 in n". Among them, n is the length of coding, that is, the total number of diseases. Each set of codes represents a kind of disease. Only 1 of them were 1, and the other N-1 was 0. The location of 1 is different. The types of diseases are different. The closer the maximum of the element in the vector to 1, the greater the likelihood that the disease will occur, and the closer it is to 0, the smaller the likelihood of the disease.

3 Optimization of initial weights of neural networks based on Improved Genetic Algorithm

A genetic algorithm is based on real number coded generally. The range of cross coefficient is [0, 1]. When it is used to optimize the weights of the neural network model, it will cause the chromosome individuals to contract or diverge in the search space. Therefore, the optimization ability is reduced, which is not conducive to global optimization. For variability, if the variability is too low, the search is too narrow and the evolution rate is slow. If the amount of variability is too large, the search will oscillate near the target point, and the optimization goal can not be achieved. To those problems, the improvement method is: To the parent chromosome individual in an initially uniform distribution, increase the dispersion degree of the population after the crossover operation to generate new search space. At the same time, the offspring are distributed evenly in the search space. In the search space, neither contraction nor divergence, and ensure that individuals with excellent patterns are not completely destroyed by crossing operation, so as to improve the global optimization ability. For mutation operators, when the evolutionary process is smooth, the rate of variability is maintained at a low level. When evolution is not successful, the search range is increased by increasing mutation rates. When the evolutionary algebra reaches a set threshold, it is assumed that the population has reached an early maturity. Forcing the population out of an early maturing state by forced mutation. The step is as followed:

Step1: The chromosome gene coding is based on the structure of the neural network model and the solving problem.

Step2: Randomly generated initial and uniform chromosomes population.

Step3: According to the problem, calculate the fitness values of individuals in a population. Use training sample to train the neural network represented by the individual in the group, calculate the learning error of each individual, and then determine the fitness value. Learning error E is calculated by the lower form:

$$E = \sum_{k=1}^{n} E_K \text{ , } E_k = \sum_{j=1}^{q} (y_j^k - C_j^k)^2 / 2$$

Among them, "n" is the training sample number. "q" is the number of output units. The represents the difference between the actual output and expected output of the k sample training the j output unit. "fs=1/E" is fitness function. It ensures that the smaller the error, the greater the fitness value.

Step4: Genetic manipulation of individuals in a population, including selection, crossover, and variation.

Selection: Roulette method is used to select the operation.

Cross: If x1, X2 are the parent individuals, and uniformly distributed random numbers in V=[xmin, xmax] , then, the uniformly distributed random numbers Z1 and Z2 on the interval [xmin, xmax] after cross is calculated by the following formula:

y1=ax1+(1-a)x2, y2=ax2+(1-a)x1

z1=MOD(y1,V),z2=MOD(y2,V)

Z1 and Z2 are the offspring after crossover, in which, a is integer and MOD is modulo operator.

Variation: the rate of variation Pm is defined by the following:

Pm=0.001+NG*cof

Among them, Pm represents the rate of variability of the current algebra. NG is an algebra that has not evolved since the last evolution. COF is the coefficient that determines the threshold of chromosome variation (100% variation). The variance quantity Var is defined as:

var = rand * w * dyna

In the formula, rand is the random number between [0, 1]. "w" is a fixed value within the value range of the weight. "dyna" is the dynamic parameters of Var. Initial dyna= 1.0. If "counter" > "nochange", "dyna"= "dyna0.1" and "counter"= 0. Among them, "counter" is an algebra that has not evolved since the last evolution until the present generation. "nochange" is a constant, is the threshold to decide whether to change the "dyna".

Step5. Calculate fitness value again.

Step6 If the stopping search condition is satisfied, the iteration stops and the output solution is the optimal solution. Otherwise, the steering step D. At the same time, In order to ensure that individuals with the best patterns are not damaged by genetic manipulation, the optimal individual retention strategy is adopted. That is, the individuals with the greatest current fitness value are genetically transmitted to the next generation without genetic manipulation. The improved genetic algorithm guarantees the stability and convergence of the optimized neural network model, and makes the improved genetic algorithm always have higher optimization efficiency in the optimization of the neural network model.

4 Model test

Take 15 kinds of diseases as an example, such as scab, powdery mildew, leaf blight etc. 6 dimensional input vectors and 15 dimensional output vectors are constructed by the above method.In Matlab, the hidden layer units is 10, the target error is 0.0001, and the loop 1000 times, and the Levenberg-Mar quardt algorithm is used to train, and statistical accuracy of diagnosis.

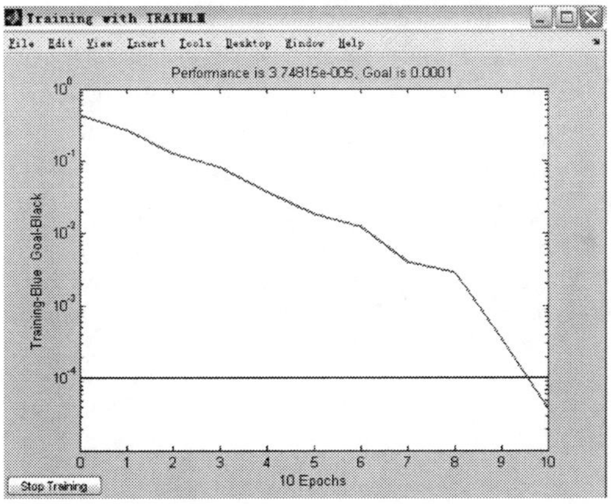

Fig.1 Test data convergence

Table 7 The test results of different models

Models	Diagnostic accuracy		Average accuracy
	Laboratory test sample data	Field application data	
BP neural network	73.70%	58.20%	66%
Genetic neural network	82.60%	73.40%	78%

The accuracy of this model is compared with BP neural network. The test data consists of two types: Laboratory test sample data, farmers generated data according to field symptoms. Test statistics show that, Whether laboratory data or household data, the diagnosis method based on genetic neural network is better than the BP neural network in correct rate. It shows that the improved genetic algorithm is more effective in improving the accuracy of the model. And the result of laboratory data test is better than that of peasant data. The reason is that, laboratory data reflect the relationship between a disease and a class of symptoms. In the field of actual production, there are many diseases at the same time, and a kind of symptoms corresponding to many diseases. When this happens, the diagnostic accuracy is influenced. It also shows that efforts in this regard can further to improve the usefulness of the model.

5 Conclusion

In this paper, the crossover mutation operator of genetic algorithm is improved, the improved genetic algorithm is used to optimize the weights of the neural network, and then, a pepper disease diagnosis model based on Genetic Neural Network is established. Tests were carried out on 15 kinds of pepper diseases, the accuracy of the model is improved by 12% compared with the general BP neural network model.

Acknowledgment

The research work was supported by Beijin science and technology plan project: Beijing science and technology correspondent resources service platform construction and demonstration, the fund for agriculture of Beijing municipal commission of rural affair: The application of APP and "zixuntong" products in the management and service of general agricultural technicians, the young scientist fund of BAAFS: Research on agricultural scientific technical online counseling system based on the knowledge map (NO.QNJJ201534), the innovation fund of BAAFS: Agricultural water-saving technology training and counseling service demonstration project (NO.KJCX20151409). The correspondence author: Sufen SUN(Sunsf@agri.ac.cn).

References

1. J.C. LAI, B. MING, S.K. LI ect. Agricultural Sciences in China Vol.8(2010), p.1222
2. Mansin gh G, Reichgelt H, Bryson K-MO. CPEST: Expert Systems with Applications Vol.32(2007),p. 185.
3. Ghosh I, Samanta R K. Teapest: Applied Engineering in Agriculture Vol.19(2003), p. 620
4. Y.F. CUI, S.P. WANG:Journal of shanghai jiaotong university Vol.29(2011),p.80
5. Li-feil YOU, Xiao-qinZHONG, Chang-yuan LI. Study of the Evaluation Method of Management Diagnosis Scheme Based on Modified Artificial Neural Network. Journal of Guangzhou Maritime College. Vol 2(2017), p 35-38.
6. ZHU Lizhong, CHENG Nan. Fault Diagnosis of SCADA System for Artificial Neural Network. Transactions of Shenyang Ligong University. Vol 2(2017), p102-106.
7. ZHANG Wen-jing, ZHANG Lei, LIU Ming.Fault Diagnosis of Wind Turbine Gearbox Based on Wavelet Transform and BP Neural Network. Techniques of Automation and Applications. Vol 6(2017), p1-4.
8. Lv Shenglin, Jiang Hongjun, Yu Sidong. Optimization Analysis of Automobile Plastic Part CAE Based on BP Neural Network and Genetic Algorithm. Modern Plastics Processing and Applications. Vol 2(2017), p 55-59.
9. SUN Xianping YANG Bing LIU Qiangqiang etc. Warm Extrusion Die Wear Optimization Design Based on BP Neural Network and Genetic Algorithm. Lubrication Engineering. Vol 4(2017), p 84-88.
10. WANG Li-min,QIAO Ling-ling,WEI Lin-jing. Optimal convolutional neural networks learning method combined with genetic algorithm. Computer Engineering and Design. Vol 7(2017), p1945-1950.

The Massive Remote Sensing Data Organization and Management Strategies

Hou Wei[1], Zhang Yuheng[1]

[1]*Harbin space star data system technology Co., Ltd., 150028 HARBIN, CHINA*

Abstract. With the continuous development of earth observing technology of China, Remote sensing image data has characteristics of large volume, multisource, multi-type and multi-resolution, finding a way to store, manage, and publish the data is a big challenges. This paper proposes a massive Remote sensing tile data organization and management strategy based on spatial database, design a data distribution and node management strategy to solve the massive remote sensing data organization and management problem.

1 Introduction

With the continuous development of earth observing technology of China, Earth Observation System (EOS) will form the characteristic of temporal and spatial coordination, all-weather, all-time, and it can also obtain massive remote sensing imagery[1-2]. Remote sensing image data has characteristics of large volume, multisource, multi-type and multi-resolution, finding a way to store, manage, and publish the data is a big challenges. The research on the storage of massive remote sensing image data presents a new research trend: First, the storage architecture of data present smaller and denser and the way of data storage present more discretization. The scale of data storage is gradually developed from the original single storage mode to the large-scale cluster. In addition, the research presents a special-purpose Remote Sensing Data management system according to the characteristics of remote sensing image, which can gradually replaces the leading role of the Relational database management system (RDBMS) in the area of massive data management. In this development trend, the method of distributed and high performance parallel processing will be the first solution to the comprehensive management of massive spatial information data[3-4].

2 Current Situation on the Research of Massive Image Data Management System

The representative massive image data storage management systems mainly contain Google Earth/Maps[5], the open-source geographical science software World Wind[4] launched by NASA, the online map service Bing Maps[6] released by Microsoft, online public atlas TerraServer[7-9], and national geographic information public service platform Map World[1].

Table 1. CPMPAROSPM OF EACH IMAGE STORAGE MANAGEMENT SYSTEM.

Management system	Data storage organization	Physical storage architecture	Spatital reference	Data format	Data storage management
Google maps	Quadtree-based tile layer	Distributed server cluster storage and cloud computing	Mercator Projection	JPEG, PNG	BigTable and GFS
World Wind	Tile layer based on the spherical grid	Centralized server cluster storage	Plate caree projection	JPEG, PNG	Distributed file system
Bing Maps	Quadtree-based tile layer	Distributed server cluster storage and cloud computing	Mercator projection	JPEG, PNG	Windows Azure and SQL Azure
TerraServer	UTM zone division and data tile	Centralized server cluster storage	UTM	JPEG, GIF, TIFF	Blob-based SQL Server database
Map World	Pyramid tile based on equal intervals of the latitude and longitude	Distributed server cluster storage	CGCS2000	JPEG, PNG	Commercial database and file

[a] HouWei: 892118874@qq.com

Comparison of each image storage management system is shown in Table 1. The management of tile data mainly base on multi-resolution pyramid of spherical coordinate system, physical storage is classified as distributed and centralized storage sever cluster, general data format supports TIFF, JPEG and PNG, data storage has file storage and BLOB of relational database.

Based on current remote sensing data organization format and the development trend, organizing massive global remote sensing data with latitude and longitude to establish a geographic Lat/Lon projection spherical subdivision system , is an effective way to unitedly store massive global remote sensing data. Meanwhile, as tile data stored by relational database, storage capacity is restricted to DBMS, database technology will reach bottleneck once the data is too big, and relational database is not suitable for unstructured big data due to characteristic; if using pure file system, remote sensing data will be stored in file format to meet the demand of mass storage, but the organization strategies of massive tile file will directly affect the storage and retrieval efficiency.

3 The Massive Remote Sensing Data Organization and Management Strategies

To resolve PB-level remote sensing data organization and application, proposes a massive Remote sensing tile data organization and management strategy based on spatial database, establish distribution rules for date between multiple nodes,and the multisource heterogeneous remote sensing data management.

3.1 Data Organization and Management

This paper designs the Multi-scale organization management model for Remote sensing spatial data guided by the "horizontal multi elements, vertical multi-level and multi-scale". As shown in figure 2-1,it means the horizontal uses high-resolution remote sensing data as the basic unit to realize the data organization of different spatial geographic resource types and the vertical manages with multilevel resolution. Which achieves horizontal and vertical management functions for different levels of different types of resources. The management of spatial data resources at the national, provincial and municipal levels takes the county as the basic unit, and the logical relation of the national, provincial and municipal levels is managed by the regional characteristics. Different types of resources are established at the county level according to the spatial region. A resource builds different types of galleries according to scale, time, etc..That is the basic geographic spatial spatio-temporal data at the county level visit the five granularities(the resource, the map depot, the layer, the layer set and the surface features) which are divided by the resource authorization granularity to mange data.

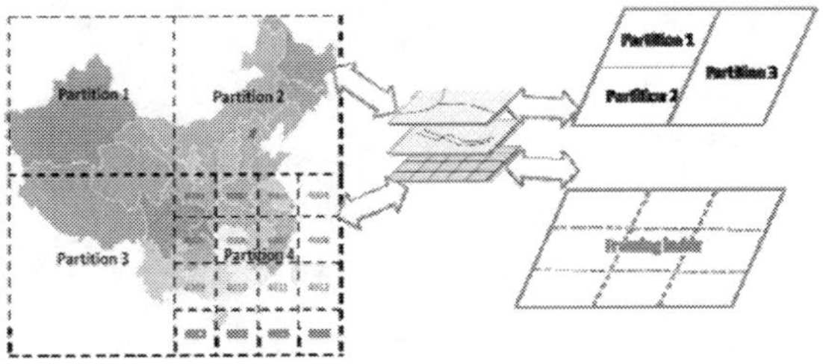

Figure 1. Multi - scale organization and management model of remote sensing spatial data resources.

3.2 Storage Strategy

3.2.1 Distributed Strategy

For remote sensing data users, each query's performance due to the dispersion and equilibrium of remote sensing data distribution. So we should require the data fragmentation as high as possible and satisfy the load balancing requirements by satisfying the data volume of each node. In this way, we can ensure each node machine retrieves the same amount of data as the same amount of data in parallel retrieval, and it can store almost the same amount of data for each node machine.

Use hash functions to do data fragmentation is a common method as hash functions have excellent dispersion to assures the load balance.

Hashing algorithm use hash functions to modulus operator on the key, and put the result as the key's Hash table entry address. If we need to map an object key uniform mapping to nodes, we should use the result of Hash (key)%N to make sure which node to storage.

This paper's distributed strategy draw lessons from hashing algorithm, the formula is:

$$H(key) = (3*row + col)\%K \quad (1)$$

H(key) is Split space number, K is Maximum number of virtual nodes, K>H(key)>0, row is the row number of the lower left corner of the tile, col is the column number of the lower left corner. Split space number was at the top of the tile file tree structure.

This gives you any 3 * 3 tile requests, 9 of which have different space Numbers. At last, using fixed pixel size (e.g. 512*512) tile image to correspond each grid tile under each level.

For the mapping of the split space number with the actual physical node, for example, the number of actual physical nodes is n (n < = K), the number of fragments allocated by each node should be between (INT) K/n and (INT) K/(n + 1) and the difference between each node is n. In this paper we design the max number(K) of storage nodes is 255, n is 9, the split space number information is shown in the following table

Table 2. Space sharding example

Physical node number	Application server	Split space number
1	192.168.1.1	0,9,18,27,36,45,…,243,252

DOI: 10.1051/matecconf/201712802011

2	192.168.1.2	1,10,19,28,37,46,...,244,253
3	192.168.1.3	2,11,20,29,38,47,...,245,254
4	192.168.1.4	3,12,21,30,39,48,...,246
5	192.168.1.5	4,13,21,31,40,49,...,247
6	192.168.1.6	5,14,23,32,41,50,...,248
7	192.168.1.7	6,15,24,33,42,51,...,249
8	192.168.1.8	7,16,25,34,43,52,...250
9	192.168.1.9	8,17,26,35,44,53,...251

When K is 255, each tile's store split space number like 3 table.

Table 3. The tile spacer

0	1	2	3	4	5	6	7	8	···	250	251	252	253	25
3	4	5	6	7	8	9	10	11	···	253	254	0	1	2
6	7	8	9	10	11	12	13	14		1	2	3	4	5
9	10	11	12	13	14	15	16	17	···	4	5	6	7	8
12	13	14	15	16	17	18	19	20	···	7	8	9	10	11
15	16	17	18	19	20	21	22	23	···	10	11	12	13	14
18	19	20	21	22	23	24	25	26	···	13	14	15	16	17
21	22	23	24	25	26	27	28	29	···	16	17	18	19	20
24	25	26	27	28	29	30	31	32	···	19	20	21	22	23
···	···	···	···	···	···	···	···	···	···	···	···	···	···	···
242	243	244	245	246	247	248	249	250	···	237	238	239	240	24
245	246	247	248	249	250	251	252	253	···	240	241	242	243	24
248	249	250	251	252	253	254	0	1	···	243	244	245	246	24
251	252	253	254	0	1	2	3	4	···	246	247	248	249	25
254	0	1	2	3	4	5	6	7	···	249	250	251	252	25

The whole table is like a remote sensing data, each of them represent a tile image data, just like the remote sensing is divided and processed to large number of tile image data. We can find that for any 3*3 request, the 9 tiles data involved are stored in different pieces space and the space number is continuous. In this way, we can ensure the uniformity to each node is the highest and most efficient. Even n*n requests, the nodes of each tile distribution are scattered, not concentrated in some nodes, so we can guarantee the efficiency. From the point of each line, each line includes all continuous shard space (0-254), each shard space to store the number of tiles are equal, then each physical node actually stored almost approximate equal number of tiles. So the whole picture of remote sensing image data are processed data generated by the tiles according to the hash distribution strategy of this research will be evenly dispersed to different storage nodes, each tile data volume of a storage node is approximately equal to meet the needs of the query efficiency and load balancing.

3.2.2 Redundancy Strategy Distributed Strategy

Even the distributed strategy based on hashing algorithm have excellent ability to ensure the load balancing of the system, but lack of design for system security and reliability. When one storage node invalid, the node's tile data will lose causing great loss to the system.

Most of the current distributed storage system tend to use fault-tolerant to increases the system reliability. Fault-tolerant means allow the system to fail and requires that relevant functions and services not be invalidated when the fault occurs.

The basic idea of this paper redundancy strategy is design a new method "copy of spatial data fragmentation" based on hashing algorithm to set up the distributed redundant deployment solutions. This method increase the redundant slice space to the physical node to increase the copy of the system, the fault tolerance of the system can be effectively improved, thus ensuring the reliability and security of the distributed system. The specific method is: add two copies of the spatial lamination number obtained by the hashing model, placing two copies in the previous node and the last node. Then each tile data will be stored in three node, two of them is copy data. When the primary physical node malfunction, the others alternate physical node can provide tile data, each node spatial lamination number have three list to record it.

Table 4. the spatial lamination number corresponding to the i physical storage node

Copy node of i-1	I node	Copy node of i+1
(i-1)-1	i-1	(i+1)-1
(i-1)-1+n	i-1+n	(i+1)-1+n
(i-1)-1+2n	i-1+2n	(i+1)-1+2n
(i-1)-1+3n	i-1+3n	(i+1)-1+3n
...	...	...
(i-1)-1+kn	i-1+kn	(i+1)-1+kn

3.3 Data Organization and Management

The final data that the cloud storage master transmits to the user is the integration of data from the various storage nodes, as the dynamic and autonomous nature of the resources, each node allows self-maintenance of the current situation and correctness of the data, which is bound to cause the data inconsistencies between the nodes. So users need a certain scheduling mechanism when they need data.

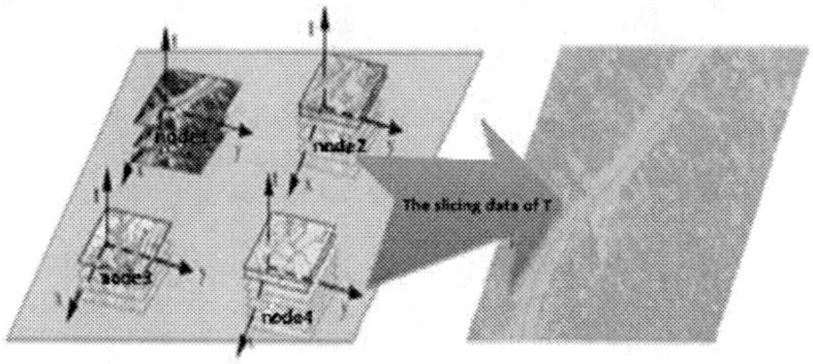

Figure 2. Inter - point spatial - temporal data integration.

As shown in Figure 2, the grid consists of off-site distribution of each network, each network has its own data resources and data organization, storage format. Over time, the frequency of changes of each node data inconsistency. As shown in the figure, the update of the image data is slower in the same time interval, and the updating of the vector data varies depending on the frequency of the change of each node element. So different time points can be formed at different time slices. When the central node needs to provide users with a time slice of the integrated data, the need for the node of the data time cutting, projection, and finally integrated in the same reference, the formation of a time and space data provided to the user.

4 Conclusions

This paper proposes a massive Remote sensing tile data organization and management strategy based on spatial database, design a data distribution and node management strategy to solve the massive remote sensing data organization and management problem. Not only ensures that each node machine stores almost the same amount of data, but also makes the amount of tile data retrieved by each node machine in the same way, which effectively improves the system's concurrent query performance and load balancing. Taking into account the reliability and availability, the design of the "fragment space copy" redundancy strategy, effectively guarantee the system tile data security and system reliability.

References

1. X. F. Lv, C. Q . Cheng, J. Y . Gong, —Review of Data storage and Management Technologies for Massive Remote Sensing Data.‖ Science China Technological Sciences, vo.54, pp.3220-3232, 2011.
2. Jian Shen, —Research on Object-Oriented Relational Image Database Technology Based on XML Metadata.‖ Nanjing Normal University, 2008.
3. M. Gibin, A. Singleton, R. Milton, —An Exploratory Cartographic Visualization of London Through the Google Maps API. — Appl Spat Anal Pol, vol.2, pp.85-97, 2008.
4. D. G. Bell, F. Kuehnel, C. Maxwell, —NASA World Wind: Open source GIS for Mission Operations.‖ In Proceedings of IEEE Aerospace Conference. Big Sky, MT, pp.1-9, 2007.
5. B.KARP(2006). The Google File System. [Online]. Available:http://wenku.baidu.com/view/3e4ba4efaea ad1f346933f9f.ht ml
6. I. Foster and C. Kesselman—Globus: A Meta-computing Infrastructure Toolkit.‖ International Journal of High Performance Computing Applications,Vol.15,pp. 359-374,2001.
7. T. Barchlay, W. Chong, J. Gray, —TerraServer Bricks– a high availability cluster alternative.‖ Microsoft Technical Report, MSR-TR- 2004-107, 2004.
8. T. Barchlay, W. Chong, J. Gray, —TerraServer SAN-Cluster architecture and operations experience.‖ Microsoft Technical Report, MSR-TR-2004-67, 2004.
9. T. Barchlay, W. Chong, J. Gray, —Microsoft TerraServer: a spatial data warehouse." In: Proceedings of the ACM SIGMOD International Conference on Management of Data. Dallas, Texas: ACM, 29(2): 307– 318,2000.

 DOI: 10.1051/matecconf/201712802012

Development of a hardware-in- loop simulation platform for NPP main control systems

Pengfei Liu[1,a], Chunyu Bi[1], Yang Yu[1], Meng Lin[1], Xinli Song[2], Guoyang Wu[2] and Zhida Su[2]

[1] *School of Nuclear Science and Engineering, Shanghai Jiao Tong University, Shanghai 200240, China*
[2] *China Electric Power Research Institute, Beijing 100192, China*

Abstract. The simulation technology of the nuclear power plant are gradually applying to the nuclear power industry. However, most of the research on nuclear power plant simulation system only focus on pure computerized simulation at present, and it is difficult to fully display the characteristics of the simulating objects. In order to simulate the response characteristics of control system more really, a hardware-in-loop simulation platform of main control systems in the nuclear power plant has been developed in this paper. This simulation platform consists of thermal-hydraulic model, control and protection system model, physical DCS system and real-time interactive database. A physical industrial DCS system has been coupled to this platform to simulate the main control systems in the NPP, which makes the simulation result much closer to the actual control systems. The devoloped simulation platform has been validated by some steady and transient cases in this paper. This hardware-in-loop simulation platform can be used in the simulation and optimal design of NPP control systems. Furthermore, it can be used in the failure mode and effect analysis of the instrumentation and control systems in the nuclear power plant.

1 Introduction

The nuclear power plant systems have the characteristics of high construction cost, the professionalism of operation and the risk of improper handling of the incident. Therefore, simulation tests shall be done before a nuclear power plant system or a new reactor is put into operation, including the power up and down in normal operation, the response of the parameters during transient operation, and the action of controlling and protection and so on. However, most of the research on nuclear power plant simulation system only focus on pure computerized simulation at present, which means the whole models are realized by computer codes. Pure computerized simulation is difficult to simulate the characteristics of the simulation objects perfectly, especially the simulation of digital instrumentation and control systems. The digital instrument control system is widely used in the new nuclear power plants or the upgrade. This new technology has produced many benefits as well as new problems in the safety and reliability of nuclear power plants[1].In order to simulate the real characteristics of control systems, it is necessary to develop a set of the hardware-in-loop simulation platform of NPP control system.

A pure computerized simulator of NPP has been developed in our laboratory, and this simulator has been used in the verification and validation of the digital I&C systems and reactor protection system in the CPR1000-type nuclear power plants of China, such as Ling Ao, Hong Yan He, Yang Jiang nuclear power plants[2-5]. Based on this NPP simulator, a physical DCS system has been coupled to the NPP simulator to form a hardware-in-loop simulation platform in this paper. By the real-time database and synchronization control, the presented simulation platform can reach real-time operation. After the design of the hardware-in-loop simulation platform, corresponding verification works have also been carried out.

2 Framework of hardware-in-loop simulation platform

The presented hardware-in-the-loop simulation platform consists of a physical DCS system, modules of NPP simulator and real-time interactive database. The general framework is shown in Figure 1.

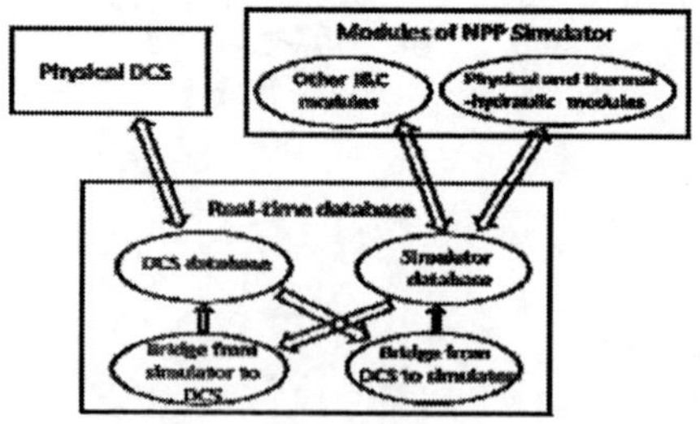

Figure 1. General framework of hardware-in –loop simulation platform

[a] Corresponding author: pfliu@sjtu.edu.cn and bichunyu@sjtu.edu.cn

Because of the difference between the two databases of DCS and simulator, we develop two bridges to achieve data conversion and delivery. Due to the limitations of the simulation scale and I/O numbers of the physical DCS system, the DCS is only used to develop main control systems in the nuclear power plant. Other auxiliary control systems are simulated in the NPP simulator by Matlab/Simulink tools.

2.1 Physical and thermal-hydraulic modules

Physical and thermal-hydraulic modules in the NPP simulator are developed by RELAP5. RELAP5 is a one-dimensional, unbalanced and two-phase thermal hydraulic system program developed by Idaho National Engineering Laboratory. It is widely used in nuclear industry for numerical simulation and safety analysis. Figure 2 shows thermal-hydraulic nodalization scheme of the primary loop of a CPR1000-type nuclear power plant in this simulation platform. It includes a reactor vessel, a pressurizer, three loops (which each has a steam generator and circulating pump) and other auxiliary systems. The secondary loop and other auxiliary systems are also included in the simulation platform.

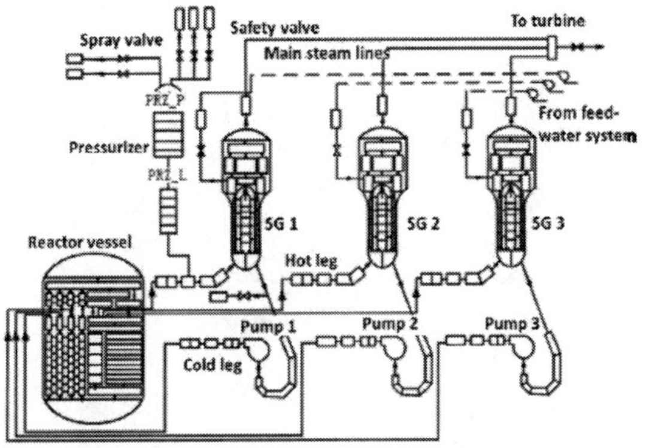

Figure 2. The thermal-hydraulic node diagram of primary loop

2.2 Physical DCS and control systems

A distributed control system named XDC800 of Xinhua Company is used in the hardware-in-loop simulation platform, which has been shown in Figure 3. It is made up of three DCS cabinets and a computer server. The DCS cabinets have configured I/O modules and controllers, which is to realize the signal acquisition, processing and logic control. The computer server has configured DCS software, which is to realize channel configuration, logical configuration and human-machine interface. The DCS server has also be used as the server of NPP simulator. XDC800 uses redundant communications and controller strategies to improve reliability. Ethernet is used as communication networks in the platform. The physical DCS in the simulation platform can achieve analog-to-digital signal conversion from the DCS to simulator, and digital-to-analog conversion from the simulator to DCS, and real-time transmission and control of data.

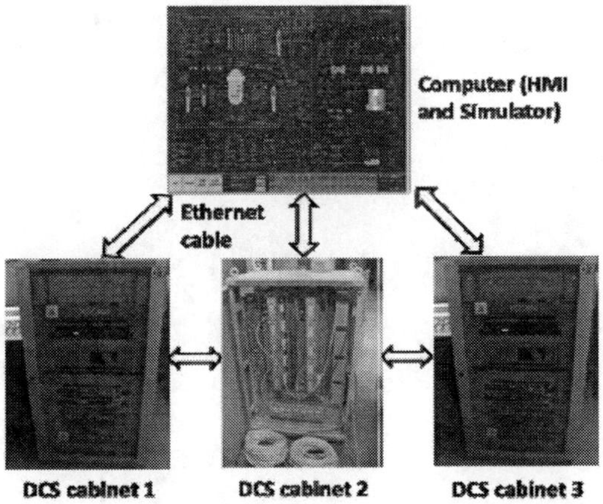

Figure 3. Physical DCS system

This physical DCS has more than 400 I/O points and it can meet the simulating requirement of main control systems in the nuclear power plant. The developed control systems include main control system of NPP, such as reactor power control system, pressurizer pressure and water level control system, and water level control system of the steam generator, and load control system of the turbine, steam dump control system, and so on. By taking pressurizer pressure control system as an example, we will introduce the modelling progress of the control system in the DCS.

The main function of the pressurizer pressure control system is to maintain the pressure at its nominal value of 15.5MPa (absolute pressure) in the primary loop. The executive structure is spray valves at top of pressurizer and heaters at the bottom. The control system schematic is given as Figure 4. By taking pressure differential between the measured value and reference value as input signal, a PID controller will regulate the opening of two spray valves and heating power. There are three low-level alarm and two high-level alarm to protect the pressurizer. In general, if the pressure is higher than reference value, the controller will increase the opening of spray valve and decrease the heating power. This ensures that the normal transient will not cause an emergency shutdown of the reactor, nor will the safety valve open.

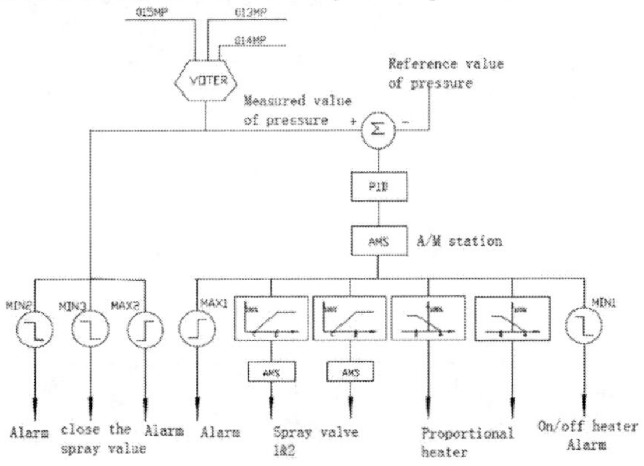

Figure 4. Pressurizer pressure control system schematic

According to the pressure control schematic, the control logic can be realized as shown in Figure 5 by DCS configuration tools.

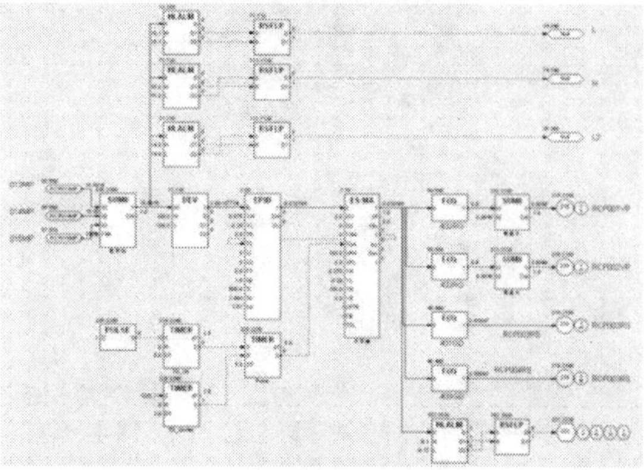

Figure 5. Logic configuration of pressurizer pressure control system in DCS

2.3 Real-time database and synchronization

Real-time operating and synchronization control are key characteristics in the hardware-in-loop simulation. The DCS system and database can achieve operation in real-time very easily. Most of the important is how to achieve the real-time operation of the NPP simulator. As we know, the simulation time is up to the scale and algorithm of the simulation platform. Because the physical and thermal-hydraulic modules of nuclear power plant are very large and complex, the RELAP simulation would cause the run-time failure of the simulation in a real-time mode. Our solution is to divide the whole RELAP5 model into parts and use two or more RELAP5 modules to perform the same simulation. This parallel calculating mode can increase the calculating speed to achieve operation in real-time of the simulator. The method of time synchronization control has been described in detail at [6]. As shown in the Figure 6, we set a synchronization time Δt_{syn} before simulation, when the simulation start, the fast modules (like DCS processing) will wait until the synchronization time finishes at a step. Therefore, the developed hardware-in-loop simulation platform can operate in real-time as long as the calculating time step of RELAP modules is small enough. The calculating time step of RELAP modules can be set to 100ms or less in this simulation platform.

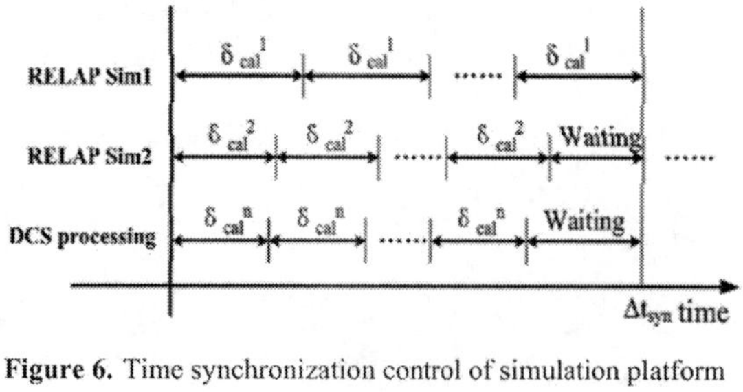

Figure 6. Time synchronization control of simulation platform

3 Validation of the simulation platform

After the hardware-in-loop simulation platform has been developed, much validation works should be done. As we mentioned in the introduction, we have developed a pure computerized NPP simulator from 2005, and it has been used to V&V of digital control and protection systems in Chinese CPR1000-type nuclear power plants. Here we use pure computerized NPP simulator as the reference to validate the hardware-in-loop simulation platform.

The validation work include steady state at different power level and all kinds of normal transients in the nuclear power plant. Here we just give the two examples as follows.

3.1 Steady state at full power

The simulation platform should achieve steady states at the different power stage firstly. Figure 7 gives history of main parameters of the primary loop at 100%FP steady state. The simulation results show that the designed hardware-in-loop simulation platform can achieve and keep the steady state at 100%FP. The main parameters are very close to nominal value and the steady state error is less than 0.2%.

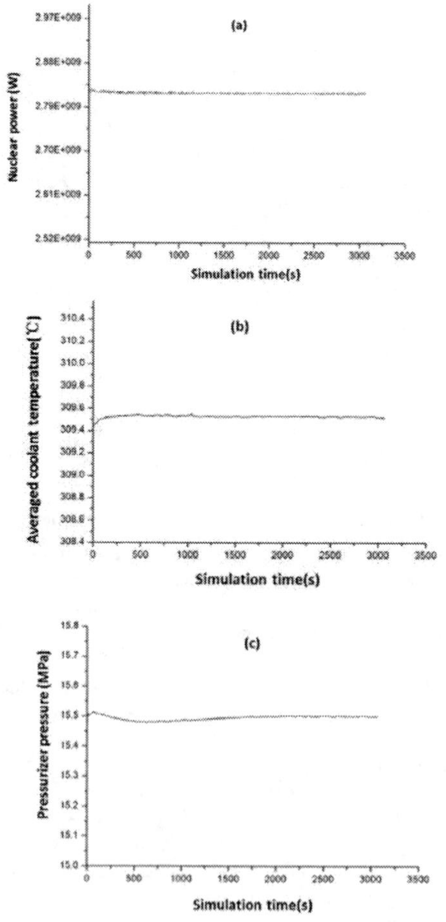

DOI: 10.1051/matecconf/201712802012

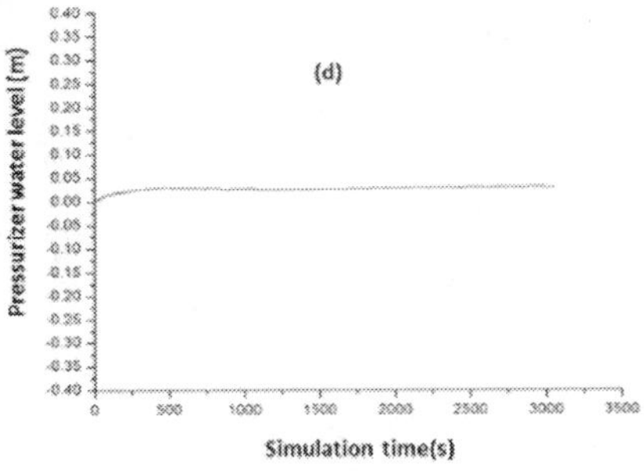

Figure 7. History of main primary loop parameters at 100%FP steady state

3.2 Load ramp transient from 100%FP to 15%FP

To verify the load tracking ability and the adjustment ability of the hardware-in-the-loop simulation platform, some step load and linear load change tests have been carried out. A load ramp transient from 100%FP to 15%FP at 5%FP/min rate is given as an example.

Figure 8 shows the history of main parameters during the load ramp transient. From the figure, we can see that the turbine load changes firstly, and then nuclear power tracks the load change by regulating the reactor power control system. The steady value of nuclear power will be bigger than turbine load, this is due to activate of the final power setting value. After transient fluctuations, coolant averaged temperature, pressure and water level of the pressurizer are eventually stabilized at the nominal values corresponding to the 15%FP. The results indicate that all the main control systems have play roles. The comparison results between the hardware-in-loop simulation platform and pure computerized simulator show that the overall trend of the transient and the final steady value are consistent, but there are some differences. For example, the overshoot of hardware-in-loop platform is a little bigger than that of pure computerized simulator. The simulation result of the hardware-in-loop also shows some characteristic of the digital system, such as fluctuations caused by signal interference and resolution.

4 Conclusions

In this paper, the industrial DCS configuration and cabinet are applied to the NPP control systems simulation platform, and this can improve the simulation results by considering the response characteristic of the digital I&C systems in the nuclear power plant. The presented validation shows that this hardware-in-loop simulation platform can simulate all kinds of steady state and transient of plants. It means that this simulation platform can be used to the simulation and optimal design of NPP digital control systems. Furthermore, due to a physical DCS including in this platform, it can also be applied to reliability analysis of digital systems in the future.

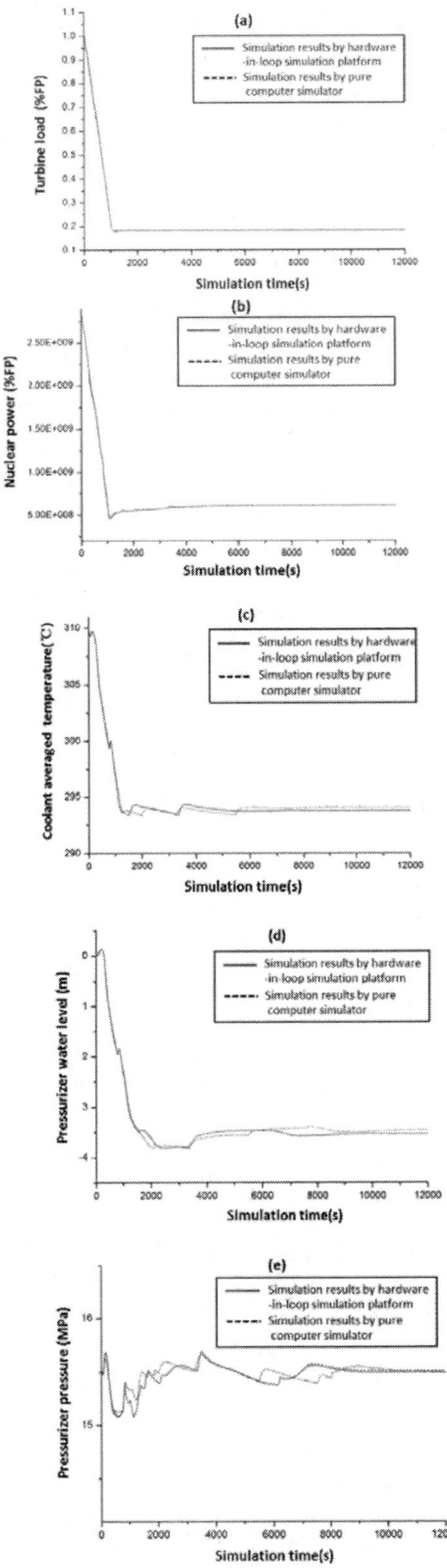

Figure 8. Historyof main parameters at load ramp transient

DOI: 10.1051/matecconf/201712802012

Acknowledgment

Authors are grateful to State Grid Corporation Science and Technology Project of China (No: XT71-15-060) and China Electric Power Research Institute Innovation Fund Project (No: XT83-15-002) for providing the financial support for this study.

References

1. National Research Council, *Digital Instrumentation and Control Systems in Nuclear Power Plants: Safety and Reliability Issue.*(National Academy Press, 1997)
2. Liu P., Lin M., Hou D., et al., Research on engineering eimulator for function validating of DCS in nuclear power plant. Nucl. Power. Eng.,**30(5s)**,48-51(2009)
3. Lin M., Su Y., Hu R., et al., Development of a thermal-hydraulic system code for simulators based on RELAP5 code. Nucl. Eng. Des.,**235 (6)**, 675–686(2005)
4. Lin M., Hou D., Liu P., et al., Main control system verification and validation of NPP digital I&C system based on engineering simulator. Nucl. Eng. Des. ,**240**, 1887-1896(2010)
5. Hou D., Lin M., Xu Z., et al., Development and application of an extensible engineering simulator for NPP DCS closed-loop test. Ann. Nuc. Energy, **38**,49–55 (2011)
6. Li Y., Lin M., Yang Y., Coupling methods for parallel running RELAPSim codes in nuclear power plant simulation. Nucl. Eng. Des. ,**297**, 1-14(2016)

Numerical investigation on the effect of labyrinth seal configuration on leakage

Tianlu Zhang[1,a], Xi Zhang[1], Xuemei Chen[1] Yifan Jia[1]

[1]*School of Mechanical Electronic & Information Engineering, China University of Mining & Technology (Beijing), Beijing 100083, P. R. China*

Abstract. Labyrinth seals have been widely used in rotating machines. In this paper, labyrinth seals with rectangular tooth used in seawater pump with axial flow distribution were studied. The effects of structure parameters of labyrinth seals on sealing performance were numerically studied by the commercial computational fluid dynamics (CFD) software. The sealing length was considered as a constant, while the cavity width, cavity depth, tooth width and pressure ratio were varied. A large number of models were calculated to study the effects of various variables on leakage of labyrinth seals. Firstly, the results show that the effects of the cavity depth on leakage could be ignored compared with that of the cavity width and sealing length. Secondly, the optimal labyrinth seals with lowest leakage can be obtained with the appropriate values of cavity widths. Furthermore, for a certain pressure ratio, the optimal cavity widths resulting in the lowest leakage were demonstrated to be stable irrespective of the values of cavity depth and sealing length. Finally, increasing pressure ratio gives rise to an increase in the optimal cavity width. It reveals that the higher the pressure ratio is, the longer the cavity width is needed to reduce the leakage.

1 Introduction

Seawater pump is the key component of the SWRO (reverse osmosis seawater desalination) system[1-3]. Seawater pump with axial flow distribution has the advantage of simplicity, reliability and tolerance. However, this structure has an inherent problem of leakage, which deteriorates the volumetric efficiency of the pump seriously[4]. The labyrinth seal featured by non-contacting structure has been widely used in rotating machines for dynamic seal over the years[5-8]. In marine environment, however, the labyrinth seal shows the benefits of low maintenance and reduced particulate contamination. Therefore, the labyrinth seal structures with rectangular cavities have been designed in seawater pump with axial flow distribution for reducing leakage.

For the labyrinth seal, both the shape and structural parameters of cavities have effects on leakage. For example, straight-through seals[6, 8, 9], stepped seals[1, 6, 10], honeycomb seals[10-13], interlocking seals[1, 14, 15] have different sealing performance. Furthermore, the structural parameters of cavities also influence the leakage of labyrinth seals, such as cavity width, cavity depth, cavity numbers and clearance size, etc.[1, 13, 16]. Actually, the sealing length is always fixed for a specific equipment. Therefore, it is significant to optimize the structure parameters of labyrinth seals considering the fixed sealing length.

In this paper, the effects of structure parameters of labyrinth seals on sealing performance were numerically studied by CFD software. To begin with, the sealing length was considered as a fixed value. Moreover, the cavity width, cavity depth, tooth width and pressure ratio were defined as a constant. Then, a large number of models were calculated to try to find the changing rules between the leakage and structure parameters of labyrinth seals. Finally, effects of these parameters on leakage were obtained, which is helpful to the design of labyrinth seals with low leakage.

2 Method

2.1 Computational model

Generally, increasing numbers of cavities can result in leakage reduction[10,17]. Thus, to exclude the effects of cavity numbers, the model with single cavity was performed, as shown in Fig. 1 (b). Wherein, the sealing length L was set to be 3 mm, 5 mm, 10 mm, respectively. The parameters of cavity width, cavity depth and clearance size were defined as B, h and c, respectively. There was differential pressure between the input and output of labyrinth seals.

2.2 Computational method

The numerical study presented in this paper was conducted by CFD software. Water was chosen as the working fluid. The typically standard k-ε model was used for turbulence. The pressure of the inlet and outlet was set to be 3 and 1 atmospheres, respectively. The effect of

[a] Corresponding author: zhangtianlu123@126.com

 DOI: 10.1051/matecconf/201712802013

grid density on simulation results was checked and then the total computational cells were set to be about 1×10^5.

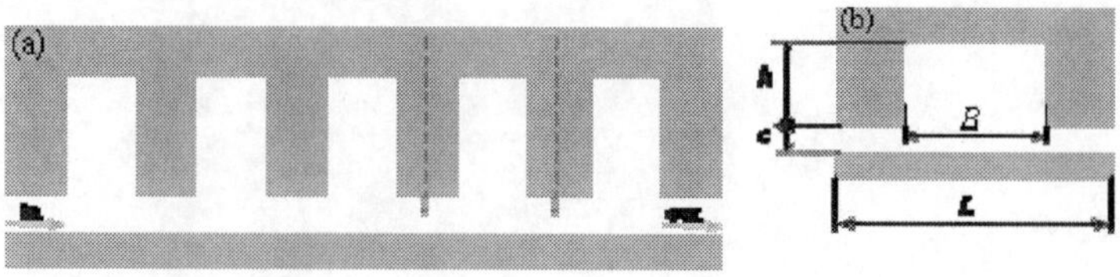

Figure 1. Labyrinth seal with rectangular structures, (a) the sketch of Labyrinth seal, (b) the model with single cavity, sealing length *L*, cavity width *B*, cavity depth *h*, clearance size *c*.

3 Results and discussion

Fig. 2 depicts the influences of the cavity depth, cavity width and sealing length on leakage of labyrinth seals. Firstly, it can be seen from Fig. 2 that the longer the sealing length is, the lower the leakage is in labyrinth seals. To be specific, labyrinth seals with the sealing length of 10 mm have a lower leakage than that with shorter sealing length of 5 mm and 3 mm. Secondly, for a fixed sealing length, both the cavity width and depth have influences on the leakage of labyrinth seals. Obviously, the effect of changing cavity depth is smaller than that of cavity width and sealing length. As shown in Fig. 2, for the same value of *L*, the leakage Q is nearly equal with the different cavity depth, *h*, 0.5 mm, 0.75 mm, 1.0 mm and 2 mm, respectively. Finally, it is clearly seen that the leakage firstly decreases and then increases with the increasing of cavity width *B*. It is obvious that the lowest leakages could be obtained with the changing of cavity width *B*. It should be noted that all the labyrinth seal models with different parameters almost acquire their lowest leakage in the same value of *B*. In other words, the optimal labyrinth seal model with the lowest leakage can be found by the nearly constant value of *B* irrespective of the values of cavity depth and sealing length. These results could contribute to the optimal design of labyrinth seals with rectangular structures.

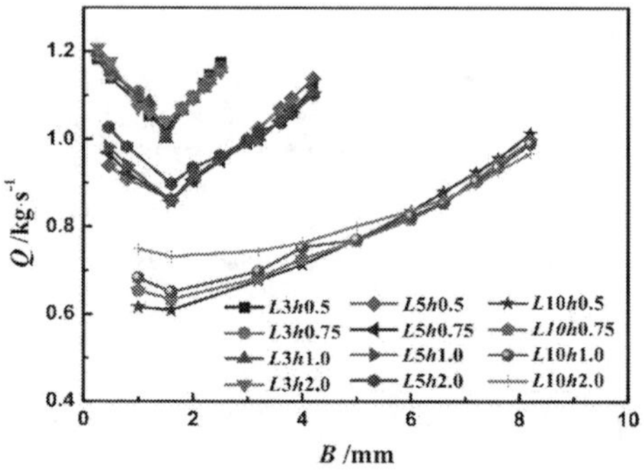

Figure 2. Effects of labyrinth seals structure parameters on leakage

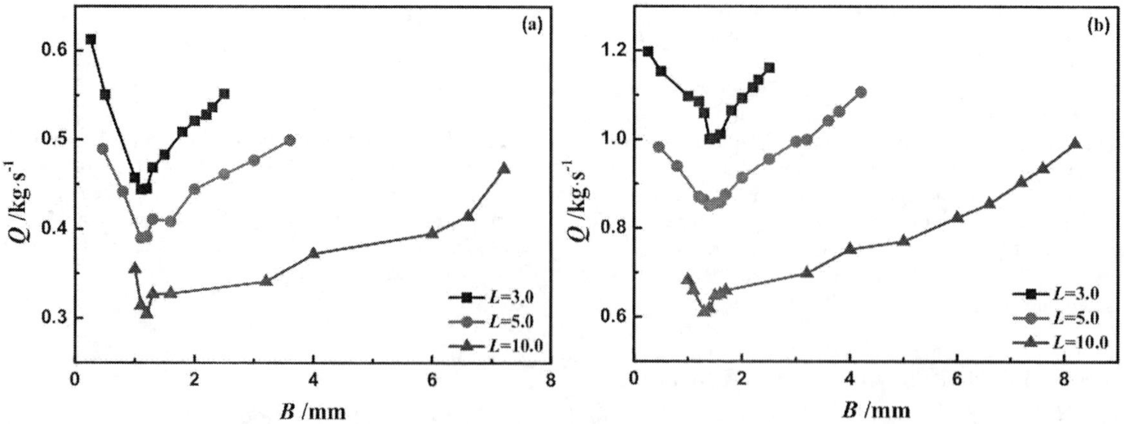

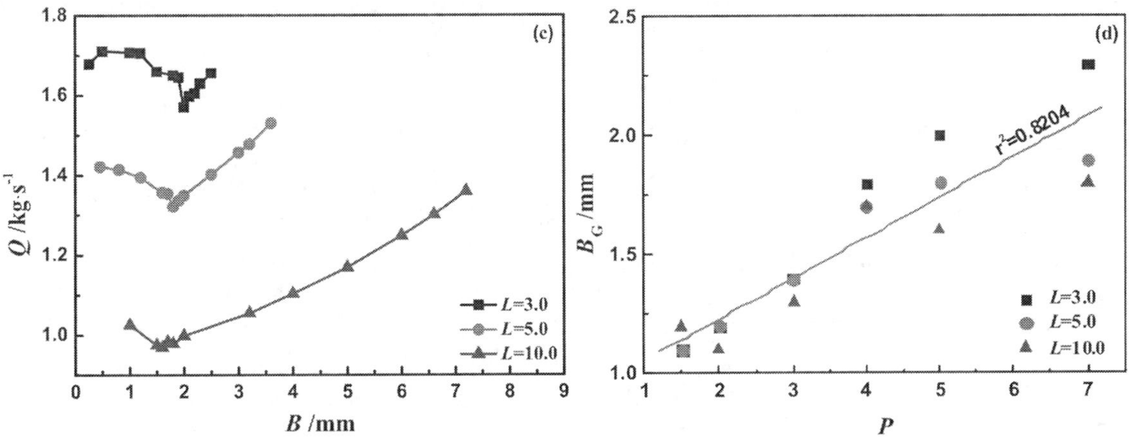

Figure 3. Effects of pressure ratios on optimal cavity width, (a) h=1.0 mm, P=1.5, (b) h=1.0 mm, P=3.0, (c) h=1.0 mm, P=5.0, (d) h=1.0 mm, various values of P.

The results show that the optimal labyrinth seal models were mainly decided by the cavity width has been obtained. The pressure ratio was another important factor which influences the leakage of labyrinth seals. Therefore, the value of cavity width B for optimal labyrinth seal models in different pressure ratio situation was studied further. As shown in Fig.3, three different pressure ratio was considered with the value of 1.5, 3.0 and 5.0 and the results were shown in (a), (b) and (c), respectively. For the reason that cavity depths have small effect on leakage, models with the value of 1 mm for cavity depth were typically carried out. On one hand, it depicts that there are different values of B, where the leakage of labyrinth seals come to the lowest value, for various pressure ratio. On the other hand, the almost equal values of B were obtained in a certain pressure ratio regardless of the values of sealing lengths. Finally, more values of pressure ratios were calculated to try to find the rule between pressure ratio and optimal cavity widths B_G, where acquire the lowest leakage. Fig. 3 (d) reveals that increasing pressure ratio increases the value of optimal cavity width B_G. It means that with the higher pressure ratio in actual conditions, longer cavity width is needed to reduce the leakage irrespective of the values of sealing length and cavity depth. Furthermore, the fitted curve was obtained to provide supports for more operating conditions, as followed equation:

$$B_G = 0.89 + 0.17P \quad (1.5 \leq P \leq 7) \qquad (1)$$

4 Conclusion

In this paper, labyrinth seals with rectangular teeth were studied. Firstly, labyrinth seals with longer sealing length have lower leakages than that with shorter sealing lengths. Secondly, when the sealing length comes to a constant value, the effect of cavity width on leakage follows the trend that decreasing at first and then increasing. In addition, cavity depths have smaller influence on leakage than cavity width. Finally, the value of optimal cavity width resulting in the lowest leakage does not change over the cavity depth and sealing length, but changes over the pressure ratio. The increasing pressure ratio increases the value of optimal cavity width. It means that the higher pressure ratio is, the longer cavity width was needed to reduce the leakage irrespective of the value of sealing length and cavity depth. The results is valuable for the optimal design of rectangular labyrinth seals with low leakage adapt to the given operating conditions with various pressure ratios and sealing lengths.

Acknowledgements

The supports from the National Natural Science Foundation of China (Grant No. 51475197) are acknowledged.

References

1. Greenlee LF, Lawler DF, Freeman BD, Marrot B, Moulin P. Reverse osmosis desalination: water sources, technology, and today's challenges. *Water research*, **43**, 2317-2348 (2009).
2. Fosselard G, Wangnick K. Comprehensive study on capital and operational expenditures for different types of seawater desalting plants (RO, MVC, ME, ME-TVC, MSF) rated between 200 m3/d and 3,000 m3/d. *Desalination*, **76**, 215-240 (1989).
3. Wang D, Li Z Y, Zhu Y Q. Lubrication and tribology in seawater hydraulic piston pump. *Journal of Marine Science and Application*, **2**, 35-40(2003).
4. Jibin H, Yunfei Z, Xinjun Z, Shihua Y. Balancing characteristics of flow divider pintle in ball piston pump. *Transactions of the Chinese Society of Agricultural Engineering*, (2008).
5. WANG W Z, LIU Y Z, JIANG P N, CHEN H P. Numerical analysis of leakage flow through two labyrinth seals. *Journal of Hydrodynamics*, **19**, 107-112 (2007).
6. Kim TS, Cha KS. Comparative analysis of the influence of labyrinth seal configuration on leakage behavior. *Journal of Mechanical Science and*

Technology, **23**, 2830-2838 (2009).

7. Schramm V, Denecke J, Kim S, Wittig S. Shape optimization of a labyrinth seal applying the simulated annealing method. *International Journal of Rotating Machinery*, **10**, 365-371 (2004).
8. Zhao W, Nielsen T, Billdal J. Effects of cavity on leakage loss in straight-through labyrinth seals. *25th IAHR Symposium on Hydraulic Machinery and Systems 2010* (2010).
9. Rhode DL, Adams RG. Rub-groove width and depth effects on flow predictions for straight-through labyrinth seals. *Journal of Tribology*, **126**, 781-787 (2004).
10. Braun E, Dullenkopf K, Bauer H-J. Optimization of labyrinth seal performance combining experimental, numerical and data mining methods. *Proceedings of ASME Turbo Expo*, Copenhagen, Denmark (2012).
11. Chochua G, Shyy W, Moore J. Computational modeling for honeycomb-stator gas annular seal. *International journal of heat and mass transfer*, **45**, 1849-1863 (2002).
12. FrÄ D, Bochon K. Influence of Honeycomb Rubbing on the Labyrinth Seal Performance. *Journal of Engineering for Gas Turbines and Power*, **139**, 012502 (2017).
13. Li J, Kong S, Yan X, Obi S, Feng Z. Numerical investigations on leakage performance of the rotating labyrinth honeycomb seal. *Journal of Engineering for Gas Turbines and Power*, **132**, 062501 (2010).
14. Gao R, Kirk G. CFD study on stepped and drum balance labyrinth seal. *Tribology Transactions*, **56**, 663-671 (2013).
15. Wang W, Liu Y, Meng G, Jiang P. Nonlinear analysis of orbital motion of a rotor subject to leakage air flow through an interlocking seal. *Journal of Fluids and Structures*, **25**, 751-765 (2009).
16. Marsis E, Morrison G. Leakage and Rotordynamics Numerical Study of Circular Grooved and Rectangular Grooved Labyrinth Seals. *Proceedings of ASME Turbo Expo 2013: Turbine Technical Conference and Exposition*, San Antonio, Texas, USA, (2013).

 DOI: 10.1051/matecconf/201712802014

Design of Real Time Data Acquisition System Framework for Production Workshop Based on OPC Technology

Yang Yue-xin[a], Ren Gong-chang

Shaanxi University of Science and Technology, Xi'an Shaanxi 710021, China

Abstract. In this paper, the low level of production management information in a hydraulic torque converter enterprise is presented. It is needed to develop a digital assembly shop MES to solve this problem. There is a high demand for the real-time data acquisition of the production line in the digital assembly shop MES. According to the actual needs of MES in digital assembly workshop, a real time data acquisition system framework based on OPC technology and database technology is proposed. The framework can be used to meet the actual needs of the real time monitoring system and production business information processing in MES.

1 Enterprise Status

The enterprise concerned in this paper is a hydraulic torque converter manufacturer. It produces more than 200 types of torque converters, which are used in construction machinery, industrial vehicles and automobiles..The products produced by this enterprise have entered the domestic market in China. However, the enterprise still collects the production line information through manual acquisition and manual input, the accuracy and timeliness of these two methods are inadequate. Manual input mode can only be carried out regularly, and can not update the production data in the system. This is not only detrimental to the smooth progress of production, but also restricts the further improvement of production capacity. Therefore, the enterprise is faced with a bottleneck problem: the data in the production process can not be collected in real time[1-4].

The enterprise's workshop information level is weak, production information is difficult to timely feedback to the management of enterprises, resulting in the management of enterprises can not make timely and correct decisions.. Data in the process of production include data of workshop personnel, materials, processing equipment, work tickets, tooling, processing and so on. How to obtain production data in time and analyze it plays an important role in production management, planning, scheduling, equipment maintenance, raw material procurement, parts storage and so on[5].

Therefore, the development of a digital assembly workshop MES can combine the actual needs of the enterprise production workshop, serve the production of enterprises, and improve the economic efficiency and technical and economic indicators of enterprises. Real time data acquisition system of workshop is an important part of digital assembly workshop left MES system, which is responsible to provide personnel, production line materials, products and equipment status information for the MES system[6-9].

2 Introduction to OPC Technology

The full name of OPC is OLE for Process Control. The emergence of OPC has built a bridge for Windows based applications and field process control applications. In the past, in order to access the data information of various devices on the production line, special interfaces were needed for different types of devices. Due to the wide range of equipment and the continuous upgrading of the product line, users and software developers often have a huge burden. And this does not meet the actual needs of the production line, so system integrator and developers urgently need a universal and efficient device driver. In this case, the OPC standard is generated.

The OPC standard is based on Microsoft Corps OLE technology, and its formulation is accomplished by providing a standard OLE/COM interface. OLE 2 technology is used in OPC technology. OPC technology uses the OLE/COM mechanism as the communication standard for applications. OLE/COM is a client / server model with the advantages of language independence, code reusability, and easy integration. After the adoption of OPC technology, applications use a unified way to access different types of equipment on the production line, thus ensuring the transparency of the software for customers and reducing the burden on enterprises.

3 System Framework

The framework of real-time data acquisition system in production workshop based on OPC technology is shown

[a] Corresponding author: yangyuexin2012@126.com

in figure 1. The real-time data of the sensors in the workshop and the material, personnel and other information on the production line are collected by means of PLC, DCS, HMI and other equipment. Each data is marked as a OPC entry, which is uploaded to the OPC Server through the standard OPC DA protocol.

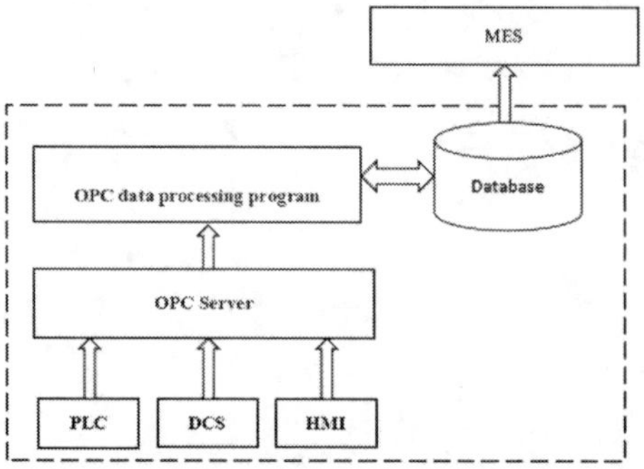

Figure 1. Real time data acquisition system framework of production workshop

The direct interaction between the data acquisition end and the OPC Server is adopted by some real-time data acquisition systems based on OPC technology, which will result in slower response to data collection due to network and OPC Server reasons. In the system designed in this paper, a OPC data processing program is developed through C# to access the OPC entries in OPC Server. When the value of a OPC item changes, the OPC data processing program finds and updates the latest value of the OPC item to the OPC item information table in the relational database. In the digital assembly workshop MES, the production line real-time monitoring system or the production information processing business module can obtain the real-time production information of the production line by accessing the OPC item information table in the relational database.[10-13].

4 System implementation

4.1 The naming and grouping of OPC Items

The torque converter production line is divided into 5 production areas. In order to facilitate the processi ng of information points by the OPC data processing program, all the OPC Item on the production line a re divided into 5 OPC groups. The five OPC groups are Pump_Island, Turbine_Island, Coverwheel_Island, Guide_Island, and Final_Assembly. Each OPC Item corresponds to a station on the production line, so ea ch OPC Item item is named in the form of Figure 2.

OPC group name.station number_device name_status point name

Figure 2. OPC Item item naming rules

As shown in Figure 2, the OPC group name is the name of the production area to which the OPC item belongs;the station number is the number of stations in which the OPC Item is located (numbered from 1 in the order of the stations on the production line); the device name is the name of the device under which the OPC Item item belongs to; the status point name is called the specific information name represented by the OPC Item.

4.2 Design of OPC data processing program

The OPC data processing program is used to connect to OPC Server. When a OPC Item value changes, the program modifies the current value, historical value, and the latest update time in the OPC Items table of the relational database. The overall flow of the handler is shown in figure 3.

According to the access rules of the OPC DA protocol, the flow of the OPC data processing program is described as follows:

The first step is to create the OPC Server object representing the actual OPC server;

The second step connects the actual OPC server through the computer name and IP address of the actual OPC server to be connected;

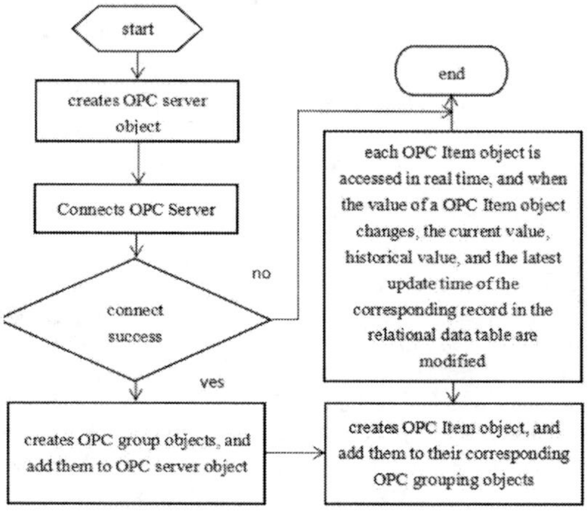

Figure 3. the overall flow of the handler

The third step if the connection is successful, read all the information from the OPC packet in a relational database, create a OPC group object for each packet, the packet is created before adding all objects to create a OPC Server object;

The fourth step to obtain OPC information of a OPC packet from a relational database, create a the OPC Item object for each OPC, and each OPC Item object to the OPC object in group.

The fifth step registers the Data-Change event for each OPC group object.

```
String serIp = "192.168.0.1";//define the IP for the OPC server
String serverName = "MES_OPC_Server";//define the name of OPC Server
OPCServer   server = new OPCServer();//creats a OPC server object
server.Connect(serverName, serIp);//connects to the OPC server object
if (server.ServerState == (int)OPCServerState.OPCRunning)
//determine whether the OPC server is running
{

      String[] OpcGroups=OPCControl.getAllGroups();//get all the OPC groups
      for(int i=0;i<OpcGroups.length;i++)
      {
            OPCGroup group=Groups.Add(OpcGroups[i]);//add all OPC groups
            group.UpdateRate = 250;
            group.IsActive = true;
            group.IsSubscribed = true;
            ......
            group.DataChange += new Group_DataChangeHandler(Group_DataChange);
            OPCItems items = group.OPCItems;
            ......
      }
}
```

Figure 4. some of the key code

After the Data-Change event is registered, once the value of a OPC Item item changes, the record value in the OPC Item table in the relational database is modified (modifying the current value, the historical value, and the last update time).Some of the key code is shown in figure 4.

5 Summary

The real time data acquisition system framework of production workshop designed in this paper adopts mature OPC technology. Through this framework, the production workshop MES does not need to write different types of interfaces for different types of equipment on the production line to obtain production data. Enterprise managers can obtain production data in real time through the system developed by this framework, and adjust production in a timely manner. This framework can greatly improve the level of enterprise informatization.

Acknowledgments

This work was financially supported by Shaanxi province of China science and technology research and development project (No.2014 GY2-04).

References

1. Koutroulis E, Kalaitzakis K. Development of an integrated data-acquisition system for renewable energy sources systems monitoring[J]. Renewable Energy, 2003, 28(1):139-152.
2. Miller M, Mi B, Kita A, et al. Development of automated real-time data acquisition system for robotic weld quality monitoring[J]. Mechatronics, 2002, 12(9–10):1259-1269.
3. Morley R E, Richter E J, Klaesner J W, et al. In-shoe multisensory data acquisition system[J]. IEEE Transactions on Biomedical Engineering, 2001, 48(7):815.
4. Benghanem M. Measurement of meteorological data based on wireless data acquisition system monitoring[J]. Applied Energy, 2009, 86(12):2651-2660.
5. Belmili H, Cheikh S M A, Haddadi M, et al. Design and development of a data acquisition system for photovoltaic modules characterization[J]. Renewable Energy, 2010, 35(7):1484-1492.
6. Omata K, Fujita Y, Yoshikawa N, et al. A data acquisition system based on a personal computer[J]. IEEE Transactions on Nuclear Science, 2002, 39(2):143-147.
7. Sheng B, Su J, Lu Q, et al. Study on Data Acquisition System of Production Line for MES[J]. Computer Measurement & Control, 2015.
8. Cleary F, Mcgrath M J, Gaiser M, et al. Development of a Low Cost Data Acquisition System for Milk Powder Production Line Monitoring[J]. Journal of Dairy Science, 1999, 82(9):2039-2048.
9. Duan R H. Development and Design of Supervisory Control and Data Acquisition System of Tobacco Leaf Production Line[J]. Mechanical Engineering & Automation, 2013.
10. Zhang C X, Jin L H. Production Line Data Acquisition and Interlock System[J]. Applied Mechanics & Materials, 2013, 310:409-412.
11. Subramaniam S, Husin S, Yusop Y B, et al. Real time shop floor monitoring system for a better production line management[C]// Applied Electromagnetics, 2007. APACE 2007. Asia-Pacific Conference on. IEEE, 2008:1-4.
12. Li X, Wang X, Jing S. Research and Design of Energy Data Acquisition System in Cement Enterprise[C]// International Conference on Information Technology and Management Innovation. 2015.
13. Huang P. Scheme of product line information based on data acquisition[J]. Electronic Measurement Technology, 2008.

MATEC Web of Conferences **128**, 02015 (2017) DOI: 10.1051/matecconf/201712802015
EITCE 2017

An Updated Projection Twin Support Vector Machine for Classification

Xiaopeng Hua[1,a] and Sen Xu[1]

[1]*School of Information and Engineering, Yancheng Institute of Technology, 224001 Yancheng, China*

Abstract. Based on projection twin support vector machine (PTSVM) and its extensions, this paper describes an updated PTSVM (UPTSVM) for classification. Compared with existing PTSVMs, UPTSVM has its own advantages. First, similar to the standard support vector machine (SVM), UPTSVM maintains the consistency of the optimization problems in the linear and nonlinear case, which results in the nonlinear formulations can be directly turned into the linear ones. Nevertheless, the existing PTSVMs lose the consistency because of using empirical kernel to construct nonlinear formulations. Second, UPTSVM avoids the inverse of kernel matrixes in the course of solving dual problems, which indicates it can not only reduce computing time but also save storage space. Third, UPTSVM can be practically proved equivalent to the PTSVM with regularization (RPTSVM). Experimental results on lots of data sets show the virtue of the presented method.

1 Introduction

Recently, proposed projection twin support vector machine (PTSVM) [1], which is on the base of multi-weight vector support vector machine (MVSVM) [2] and twin support vector machine (TWSVM) [3], has got the attention of increasing researchers. For binary classification problems, PTSVM has the intension of searching two projection axes same as MVSVM and formulates two small scale optimiaztion problems similar to TWSVM. Experimental results in [1] indicatie that PTSVM has comparable generalization ability than MVSVM and TWSVM in some aspects.

For the objective of improving the generalization ability of PTSVM furtherly, a method named as PTSVM with regularization term (RPTSVM) is proposed in [4]. Compared with PTSVM, RPTSVM has better classification capability because of considering the minimization of the structual risk similar to standard SVM [5]. For furthering the local learning ability of PTSVM, a weighted PTSVM (WPTSVM) [6] is proposed by adding the weight of each sample to the primal formulations of PTSVM. Experimental results validate WPTSVM can obtain better classification performance in dealing with manifold data sets. Shao et al. proposed a least squares PTSVM (LSPTSVM) [7], which can reducing the compiting time to a great extent by changing the inequality constrains in PTSVM to the equality ones and turning the L1 norm in the objective functions of PTSVM into L2 norm. Just like WPTSVM improves PTSVM, Hua et al. present a weighted LSPTSVM with local information, termed as (LIWLSPTSVM) [8], to improve the local learning ability of the LSPTSVM.

However, PTSVM and its extensions can not avoid the inverse of kernel matrixes in the course of training, which indicate they need more computing time and storage space in solving their dual problems. In addition, existing PTSVMs use empirical kernel to construct nonlinear formulations, which leads to the inconsistency of linear and nonlinear optimization problems. For the intention of overcome the above two defects, we propose an updated PTSVM (UPTSVM) in this paper.

The rest of this paper is organized as follows. In section 2 we overview RPTSVM briefly. Section 3 describes our new model, and section 4 shows the experiment results. In section 5 we give a summary of this paper.

2 Projection twin support vector machine with regularization term

Let us consider the classification problem with two classes of training samples, which are organized as a $l_1 \times n$ matrix A with positive samples (class 1) and a $l_2 \times n$ matrix B with negative samples (class 2). Define $E = A - e_1 e_1^T A / l_1$, $F = B - e_2 e_1^T A / l_1$, $G = A - e_1 e_2^T B / l_2$, and $H = B - e_2 e_2^T B / l_2$. For the linear classification problem, the formulations of the RPTSVM are

$$\begin{aligned} \min \quad & \frac{1}{2} w_1^T E^T E w_1 + C_1 e_2^T \xi_2 + \frac{C_2}{2} \| w_1 \|^2, \\ \text{s.t.} \quad & -F w_1 + \xi_2 \ge e_2, \quad \xi_2 \ge 0, \end{aligned} \tag{1}$$

and

[a] Corresponding author: xp_hua@163.com

$$\min \quad \frac{1}{2} w_2^T H^T H w_2 + C_3 e_1^T \xi_1 + \frac{C_4}{2} \| w_2 \|^2, \qquad (2)$$
$$\text{s.t.} \quad G w_2 + \xi_1 \geq e_1, \quad \xi_1 \geq 0,$$

where $C_1 \sim C_4$ are positive parameters, ξ_1 and ξ_2 are slack vectors. The dual problems of Eqs. (1) and (2) are

$$\min \quad \frac{1}{2} \alpha^T F (C_2 A^T A + I)^{-1} F^T \alpha - e_2^T \alpha, \qquad (3)$$
$$\text{s.t.} \quad \mathbf{0} \leq \alpha \leq C_1 e_2 .$$

and

$$\min \quad \frac{1}{2} \beta^T G (C_4 H^T H + I)^{-1} G^T \beta - e_1^T \beta, \qquad (4)$$
$$\text{s.t.} \quad \mathbf{0} \leq \beta \leq C_3 e_1 .$$

Two projection axes are given by

$$w_1 = (C_2 E^T E + I)^{-1} F^T \alpha , \qquad (5)$$

and

$$w_2 = (C_4 H^T H + I)^{-1} G^T \beta . \qquad (6)$$

The decision function is

$$label(x) = \arg\min_{i=1,2} \left(\left| \frac{w_i^T}{\| w_i \|} (x - m_i) \right| \right), \qquad (7)$$

where x is a new sample, m_i is the mean of the ith class samples, and $|\cdot|$ is the 1-norm.

3 Updated projection twin support vector machine (UPTSVM)

3.1. Linear UPTSVM

In the linear case, the optimization problems of UPTSVM are formulated as

$$\min \quad \frac{1}{2} \| w_1 \|^2 + \frac{C_2}{2} \eta^T \eta + C_1 e_1^T \xi, \qquad (8)$$
$$\text{s.t.} \quad E w_1 \leq \eta, \quad -E w_1 \leq \eta, \quad -F w_1 \geq e_2 - \xi, \quad \xi \geq \mathbf{0},$$

and

$$\min \quad \frac{1}{2} \| w_2 \|^2 + \frac{C_4}{2} \tilde{\eta}^T \tilde{\eta} + C_3 e_2^T \tilde{\xi}, \qquad (9)$$
$$\text{s.t.} \quad H w_2 \leq \tilde{\eta}, \quad -H w_2 \leq \tilde{\eta}, \quad G w_2 \geq e_1 - \tilde{\xi}, \quad \tilde{\xi} \geq \mathbf{0},$$

where ξ, η, $\tilde{\xi}$, $\tilde{\eta}$ are slack vectors.

Consider the formulation (8). Compared with the formulation (1), the only change is taking the upper bounds $\eta^T \eta$ instead of $w_1^T E^T E w_1$, where $| E w_1 | \leq \eta$. Obviously, we can easily prove the equivalence between the formulations (1) and (8). The formulation (9) has similar conclusion.

In order to gain the solutions of (8), we need to construct the Lagrangian function given by

$$L(w_1, \xi, \alpha, \gamma) = \frac{1}{2} \| w_1 \|^2 + \frac{C_2}{2} \eta^T \eta + C_1 e_1^T \xi + \alpha^T (E w_1 - \eta) - \alpha^{*T} (E w_1 + \eta) + \beta^T (F w_1 + e_2 - \xi) - \gamma^T \xi, \qquad (10)$$

where α, α^*, β and γ are Lagrangian multipliers. Then the KKT conditions for (8) are given by

$$\frac{\partial L}{\partial w_1} = \mathbf{0} \Rightarrow w_1 = (\alpha^* - \alpha)^T E - \beta^T F , \qquad (11)$$

$$\frac{\partial L}{\partial \eta} = 0 \Rightarrow \eta = \frac{\alpha + \alpha^*}{C_2} , \qquad (12)$$

$$\frac{\partial L}{\partial \xi} = 0 \Rightarrow \mathbf{0} \leq \beta \leq C_1 e_2 , \qquad (13)$$

Substituting (11) and (12) into (10) and combining with (13) can generate the dual problem described as

$$\min \quad \frac{1}{2} (\alpha^* - \alpha)^T (E E^T + \frac{1}{2C_2} I)(\alpha^* - \alpha) - (\alpha^* - \alpha)^T E F^T \beta + \frac{1}{2} \beta^T F F^T \beta - \beta^T e_2, \qquad (14)$$
$$\text{s.t.} \quad \alpha^*, \alpha \geq \mathbf{0}, \quad \mathbf{0} \leq \beta \leq C_1 e_2 .$$

Furthermore, define

$$\pi = (\alpha^{*T}, \alpha^T, \beta^T)^T , \qquad (15)$$

$$\kappa = (\mathbf{0}, \mathbf{0}, e_2^T)^T , \qquad (16)$$

$$C = (+\infty e_1^T, +\infty e_1^T, C_1 e_2^T)^T , \qquad (17)$$

and

$$Q_1 = (E E^T + \frac{1}{2C_2} I), \; Q_2 = E F^T, \; Q_3 = F F^T , \qquad (18)$$

and

$$M_1 = \begin{pmatrix} Q_1 & -Q_1 \\ -Q_1^T & Q_1 \end{pmatrix}, M_2 = \begin{pmatrix} -Q_2 \\ Q_2 \end{pmatrix}, M_3 = Q_3 , \qquad (19)$$

$$\Lambda = \begin{pmatrix} M_1 & M_2 \\ M_2^T & M_1 \end{pmatrix}, \qquad (20)$$

the dual problem (14) can be reformulated as

$$\min \quad \frac{1}{2} \pi^T \Lambda \pi - \kappa^T \pi, \qquad (21)$$
$$\text{s.t.} \quad \mathbf{0} \leq \pi \leq C.$$

Similarly, the dual problem of (9) can be generated as

$$\min \quad \frac{1}{2} (\hat{\alpha}^* - \hat{\alpha})^T (H H^T + \frac{1}{2C_4} I)(\hat{\alpha}^* - \hat{\alpha}) - (\hat{\alpha}^* - \hat{\alpha})^T H G^T \hat{\beta} + \frac{1}{2} \hat{\beta}^T G G^T \hat{\beta} - \hat{\beta}^T e_1, \qquad (22)$$
$$\text{s.t.} \quad \hat{\alpha}^*, \hat{\alpha} \geq \mathbf{0}, \quad \mathbf{0} \leq \hat{\beta} \leq C_3 e_2,$$

where $\hat{\alpha}$, $\hat{\alpha}^*$, and $\hat{\beta}$ and are Lagrangian multipliers. It can also be described as

$$\min \quad \frac{1}{2} \hat{\pi}^T \hat{\Lambda} \hat{\pi} - \hat{\kappa}^T \hat{\pi}, \qquad (23)$$
$$\text{s.t.} \quad \mathbf{0} \leq \hat{\pi} \leq \hat{C},$$

where

$$\hat{\pi} = (\hat{\alpha}^{*T}, \hat{\alpha}^T, \hat{\beta}^T)^T , \qquad (24)$$

$$\hat{\kappa} = (\mathbf{0}, \mathbf{0}, e_1^T)^T , \qquad (25)$$

$$\hat{C} = (+\infty e_2^T, +\infty e_2^T, C_3 e_1^T)^T , \qquad (26)$$

and

$$\hat{\Lambda} = \begin{pmatrix} \hat{M}_1 & \hat{M}_2 \\ \hat{M}_2^T & \hat{M}_1 \end{pmatrix}, \qquad (27)$$

$$\hat{M}_1 = \begin{pmatrix} \hat{Q}_1 & -\hat{Q}_1 \\ -\hat{Q}_1^T & \hat{Q}_1 \end{pmatrix}, \hat{M}_2 = \begin{pmatrix} \hat{Q}_2 \\ -\hat{Q}_2 \end{pmatrix}, \hat{M}_3 = \hat{Q}_3 , \qquad (28)$$

and

DOI: 10.1051/matecconf/201712802015

$$\hat{Q}_1 = (HH^T + \frac{1}{2C_4} I),\ \hat{Q}_2 = HG^T,\ \hat{Q}_3 = GG^T. \quad (29)$$

After solving the dual problems (21) and (23), we can obtain the solutions of w_1 and w_2. A new point x can be predicted according to

$$label(x) = \arg\min_{i=1,2}(|\, w_i^T (x - m_i)\,|), \quad (30)$$

where m_i is the mean of the ith class samples.

3.2 Nonlinear UPTSVM

In order to solve linearly inseparable problems, we extend the linear UPTSVM to the nonlinear one. Different from existing PTSVMs, we directly formulate the nonlinear dual problems using the kernel function $K(\ ,\ )$ according to the linear formulations (14) and (22), which is similar to the standard SVM. The formulations of nonlinear UPTSVM are

$$\min\ \frac{1}{2}(\alpha^* - \alpha)^T (K(E,E) + \frac{1}{2C_2} I)(\alpha^* - \alpha)$$

$$-(\alpha^* - \alpha)^T K(E,F)\beta + \frac{1}{2}\beta^T K(F,F)\beta - \beta^T e_2, \quad (31)$$

$$\text{s.t.}\ \alpha^*, \alpha \ge 0,\ 0 \le \beta \le C_1 e_2,$$

and

$$\min\ \frac{1}{2}(\hat{\alpha}^* - \hat{\alpha})^T (K(H,H) + \frac{1}{2C_4} I)(\hat{\alpha}^* - \hat{\alpha})$$

$$-(\hat{\alpha}^* - \hat{\alpha})^T K(H,G)\hat{\beta} + \frac{1}{2}\hat{\beta}^T K(G,G)\hat{\beta} - \hat{\beta}^T e_1, \quad (32)$$

$$\text{s.t.}\ \hat{\alpha}^*, \hat{\alpha} \ge 0,\ 0 \le \hat{\beta} \le C_3 e_2.$$

3.3 Comparision of UPTSVM with RPTSVM

Consider the linear UPTSVM. Compared with the dual problems (3) and (4) in RPTSVM, the dual problems (14) and (22) in UPTSVM avoid the inverse of kernel matrixes in the course of training, which can not only reduce computing time but also save storage space. The nonlinear UPTSVM has the same advantage.

Comparing the dual formulations in nonlinear UPTSVM with ones in linear UPTSVM, we can find that the only difference is the kernel function $K(\ ,\ )$ taken instead of inner product. That is to say UPTSVM maintains the consistency of linear and nonlinear primal formulations in addition to using different kernel functions. However, RPTSVM use empirical kernel to construct nonlinear formulations [4], which leads to the inconsistency of linear and nonlinear optimization problems.

4 Experimental results

For the intention to compare the performance of our NPTSVM with PTSVM and RPTSVM, we conduct experiments on lots of standard datasets used in [13], [14], [15]. All of the classification methods are implemented on a computer with Matlab 7.0. The computer is equipped with Intel P4 processors (2.3 GHz) and 2 GB RAM. For the sake of brevity, $C_1=C_2$ is set for PTSVM, and $C_1=C_3$ and $C_2=C_4$ are set for RPTSVM and our UPTSVM. For the parameter values, we select them from the range $\{2^i|i= -8,-6,\ldots,+8\}$. Table 1 shows the average 10-fold cross-validation results. It discloses that the classification ability of our UPTSVM is comparable than PTSVM and RPTSVM. However, UPTSVM has higher computing complexity, although it does not need to compute the large inverse matrices. This is mainly because UPTSVM has more variables (number of $2l_1+l_2$ or $2l_2+l_1$) than PTSVM and RPTSVM (number of l_1 or l_2) during the learning process.

We also conduct experiments on benchmark datasets in nonlinear case. The RBF kernel $\exp(-\|x_i-x_j\|2/\delta)$ is choosed for all of the methods, the value of δ is selected from the set $\{2^i|i= -1,0,\ldots,+7\}$. Table 2 lists experimental results in nonlinear case. It reveals that the generalization ability of our UPTSVM is better than PTSVM and RPTSVM because of adopting different kernel tricks in constructing nonlinear formulations. It also disclose that UPTSVM is little slower than RPTSVM and PTSVM in terms of training time.

Table 1. Experimental results in linear case.

Datasets	PTSVM Accuracy % Time (s)	RPTSVM Accuracy % Time (s)	UPTSVM Accuracy % Time (s)
hepatitis (155×19)	83.88±6.75 0.0094	84.00±13.06 0.0078	**84.17±12.59** 0.0562
sonar (208×60)	**68.71±14.31** 0.014	67.07±13.42 0.0125	65.71±13.72 0.1123
haberman (306×3)	**74.94±5.48** 0.0265	73.94±5.38 0.0281	74.83±4.25 0.3152
Cleve (296×13)	**82.48±3.87** 0.0218	82.42±5.66 0.0187	82.48±4.16 0.2621
spectf (267×44)	80.05±3.64 0.0281	76.50±12.82 0.0234	**80.51±6.92** 0.2246
glass_7 (214×10)	87.77±6.71 0.0156	**96.77±9.71** 0.0172	91.09±12..56 0.1264
heart (270×13)	82.96±4.74 0.0109	84.82±5.35 0.0172	**84.82±1.99** 0.2059
p_gene (106×57)	62.50±11.24 0.0047	**77.88±10.87** 0.0078	**77.88±10.87** 0.0218
wpbc (198×33)	77.51±6.28 0.0156	77.78±5.67 0.0249	**78.93±7.48** 0.1014
monks3 (432×6)	76.93±9.93 0.0312	80.95±14.75 0.0437	**81.35±11.43** 0.8159
parkinsons (195×22)	**83.59±8.34** 0.0125	83.59±12.24 0.0140	82.73±9.56 0.0952
spect (267×22)	80.87±11.15 0.0250	78.26±17.71 0.0234	**82.88±10.96** 0.2231
votes (435×16)	95.79±2.64 0.0499	**96.03±2.47** 0.0452	94.90±3.07 0.8424
bupa_liver (345×6)	59.40±7.45 0.0265	64.06±4.51 0.0265	**64.28±7.51** 0.4290
australian (690×14)	86.28±5.53 0.1404	86.11±5.72 0.1357	**86.81±4.74** 2.9453
breast (699×9)	96.38±2.92 0.1716	96.23±3.68 0.1700	**97.12±2.26** 3.1559

DOI: 10.1051/matecconf/201712802015

Table 2. Experimental results in nonlinear case.

Datasets	PTSVM Accuracy % Time (s)	RPTSVM Accuracy % Time (s)	UPTSVM Accuracy % Time (s)
hepatitis (155×19)	83.33±4.47 0.1701	85.17±10.23 0.1607	**85.67±7.61** 0.1825
sonar (208×60)	**73.29±16.95** 0.6536	69.07±20.32 0.6552	70.86±18.13 0.7098
haberman (306×3)	74.56±3.77 0.6427	74.83±5.19 0.6443	**75.17±2.63** 0.8097
Cleve (296×13)	82.48±4.44 0.6178	**84.78±6.00** 0.6131	83.57±4.77 0.7316
spectf (267×44)	80.96±7.81 1.0015	83.18±8.08 1.0218	**83.35±6.80** 1.1248
glass_7 (214×10)	95.32±4.95 0.3011	95.71±5.12 0.312	**96.91±3.38** 0.3713
heart (270×13)	82.22±7.55 0.5008	**84.44±4.32** 0.5101	84.44±4.63 0.5881
p_gene (106×57)	77.13±11.04 0.1591	78.13±14.02 0.1701	**83.88±11.30** 0.1778
wpbc (198×33)	82.83±7.11 0.2746	80.19±6.68 0.2683	**83.41±5.00** 0.3214
monks3 (432×6)	**98.68±2.95** 1.3541	93.83±5.02 1.3853	94.97±3.78 1.7893
parkinsons (195×22)	90.25±11.79 0.2558	89.70±11.71 0.2589	**92.53±9.24** 0.3089
spect (267×22)	84.25±8.33 0.5039	**85.49±5.83** 0.5023	85.49±6.55 0.6053
votes (435×16)	94.6±3.62 1.4227	95.08±2.80 1.4056	**95.79±2.17** 1.8798

5 Conclusions

In this paper, an updated PTSVM (UPTSVM) is presented for improving the performance of existing PTSVMs. Compared with existing PTSVMs, UPTSVM avoids the inverse of kernel matrixes in the course of training and maintains the consistency of linear and nonlinear primal problems. In addition, UPTSVM can be practically proved equivalent to RPTSVM. However, although UPTSVM does not have to compute the large inverse matrices as existing PTSVMs do, it has higher computing complexity. So improving the computational efficiency is our further research goal in the future.

Acknowledgment

This work is partly funded by Jiangsu Provincial Science and Technology Support Project of China (Nos. BY2016065-05, BY2016065-01).

References

1. X. Chen, J. Yang, Q. Ye, J. Liang, Pattern Recogn. **44** 2643 (2011)
2. Q. Ye, C. Zhao, N. Ye, Y. Chen, Pattern Recogn. **31** 2006 (2010)
3. Jayadeva, R. Khemchandai, S. Chandra, IEEE Trans. Pattern Anal. Mach. Intell. **29** 905 (2007)
4. Y.H. Shao, Z. Wang, W.J. Chen, N.Y. Deng, Knowl-Based Syst. **37** 203 (2013)
5. C. Cortes, V.N. Vapnik, Mach. Learn. **20**, 273 (1995)
6. X. Hua, Y. Sun, S. Ding, CAAI Trans. Intell. Syst. **11** 384 (2016)
7. Y. Shao, N. Deng, Z. Yang, Pattern Recogn. **45** 2299 (2012)
8. X. Hua, S. Ding, Neurocomputing **160** 228 (2015)
9. Y. Xu, Z. Yang, X. Pan, IEEE Trans. Neural Netw. and Learn. Syst. **28** 359 (2017)
10. M. Carrasco, J. Lopez, S. Maldonado, Expert Syst. Appl. **54** 95 (2016)
11. X. Peng, D. Xu, L. Kong, D. Chen, Inform. Sci. **340/341** 86 (2016)
12. R. Khemchandani, P. Saigal, S. Chandra, Neural Netw. **79** 97 (2016)
13. F. Alamdar, S. Ghane, A. Amiri, Neurocomputing **186** 8 (2016)
14. F. Dufrenois, J.C. Noyer, Pattern Recogn. **52** 96 (2016)
15. H. Wang, Z. Zhou, Knowl-Based Syst. **128** 125 (2017)

DOI: 10.1051/matecconf/201712802016

Application of Data Architecture Model in Enterprise Management

Song Shi, Yalin Ji

Ordnance Engineering College, Shijiazhuang, 050003, China

Abstract. Today is in the era of rapid development of information, data volume of high-speed expansion, it is difficult in the previous system for communication, sharing and integration. In order to integrate data resources, eliminate the "information island", build enterprise development blueprints, people gradually realize the importance of top design. Many enterprises for their own development to establish their own enterprise architecture of the top design, and as its core data architecture model is also reflected in different industries according to different development. This paper mainly studies the data architecture model, expounds the role of data architecture model and its relationship.

1 Introduction

Data and information is the economic lifeline of the 21st century. In the information age, the data is considered to be an important corporate asset. Often a company has long accumulated a lot of demand, description, database, data model, procedures and a variety of information technology finished components, but the lack of an "overall design."

This is not to say which information system, database or database management system (DBMS) is wrong or misleading, but said that the current generation of a large number of information technology (Information Technology, IT) components, and the urgent need to establish a " General structure "to its specification, optimization or even standardization.

In the previous data warehouse project, the concept and methodology of the system data model usually focuses on how to design and build a data warehouse rationally, but rather an application system (OLTP system) models design without the need for effective methodological guidance.The application system are different in different periods by different manufacturers in the design and development,and lack of communication between each other, resulting in data scattered and repeated, inconsistent caliber and poor data compatibility. As the data warehouse in the overall enterprise information planning belongs to the downstream system, it can only passively receive data generated by the application system, data warehouse. Due to inconsistent caliber, poor compatibility, it brings great difficulties in data integration. Enterprises in a lot of manpower, material and capital to promote information technology, but there are still a lot of "information island" phenomenon.

This paper argues that the success of enterprise information construction depends largely on the rationality of the system model and the consistency of the concept of different systems. The enterprise data model is the core of enterprise information. Through the enterprise data model to define the entire enterprise information system of data standards, and gradually unify the internal data standards. It will also guide the application system data model unified design, and can fundamentally guarantee the data onto the system compatibility and consistency. Enterprise data model can eliminate data fragmentation, inconsistency, and information islanding due to the design and development of the application system. It can promote the integration of various applications within the enterprise and data sharing, and comprehensively enhance the business decision-making, operations management, business development , customer service and other aspects of support capabilities.

2 Definition of enterprise data architecture model

2.1 Basic definition of data architecture model

Enterprise-level data architecture models, is a method used to define the regular representation of information. By using the information model, we can use different applications to reuse, change, and share the data that is being managed. Enterprise data architecture can help enterprises to eliminate information island, and build a shared, generic, consistent and extensive enterprise data infrastructure platform. [1]

The enterprise data model can not be equated with the data warehouse model. The enterprise data model is the perspective of the whole enterprise business, and the whole description of the whole enterprise data (including production data and consumption data). Enterprise-level data model is the business and IT staff to communicate the media, but also within the enterprise and external communication.

2.2 Data model structure

A reference model for an enterprise's data architecture includes:

- Data element model
- Conceptual data model
- Database logic model
- Database physical model
- A view model that connects physical databases and application information systems

The five data structures above form a core, and around the core of a large number of information technology support can be interconnected, interoperable, and non-redundant. All the information technology products, including data structure reference model of those are drawn in a map inside, you will get as shown in Figure 1.

We need an application information system with a "meta-database" cores. The data model for this "metabase" is highly engineered, and it really supports interrelated, interoperable, and non-redundant. [2]

3 Data architecture reference model

The data architecture of the enterprise and its accompanying data models have always been seen as important assets. Figure 1 of the preceding article illustrates how important this asset is. This importance is not only reflected in the fact that the data model forms the basis of the corporate strategy, and the data model is the ultimate "intersection" of all information technology products.

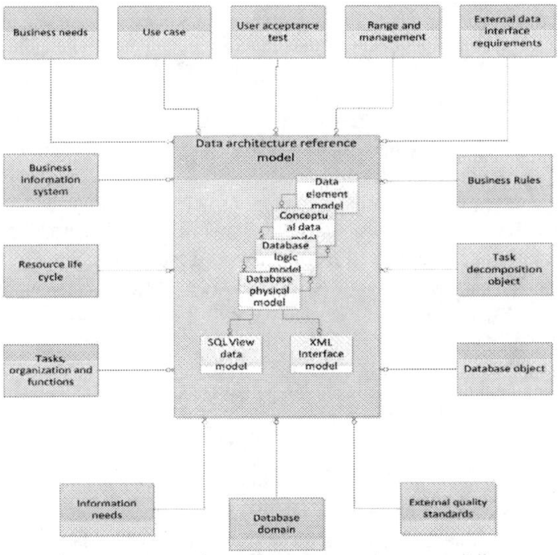

Figure 1. Enterprise architecture product set and data architecture reference model

The separate data models in the data architecture are independent of each other and handle different data separately. These architectures promote model integrity, interoperability, and non-redundancy. In addition, a "more advanced" model can be used as a template for creating "low" models.

Once the reference model of the data architecture has been completed, it can serve as a framework to help understand the scope and interrelationship of the component model. [3]

This model is useful for communication between component instances in the data architecture model.

Our understanding of the natural concepts of data, database deployment, and business information systems has evolved over the years, and on this basis, we can see that the data structure reference model (Figure 2) has six separate models. The six models are:

- Data element model
- Concept data model
- Logical database model
- Physical database model
- SQL view model
- XML document structure model

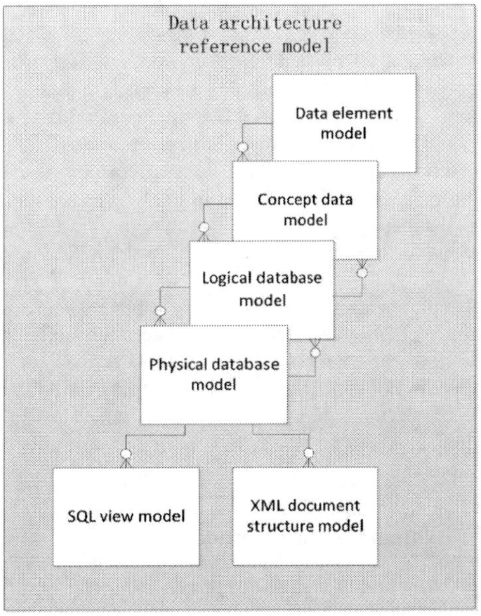

Figure 2. Data architecture reference model

4 The role of each model in the data architecture reference model

4.1 Data element model

The data element is the essence of the enterprise and is used as the semantic basis of the entity attribute in the conceptual data model. It supports the columns of the database model required by the business and is implemented in the database management system. [4] It is used in the business information system (view Data model), to achieve the enterprise resources required for the database object, and to support the completion of corporate tasks.

 DOI: 10.1051/matecconf/201712802016

4.2 Concept database model

The conceptual data model consists of the subject, the entity, the relationship between the attribute and the entity. Relationships can reflect the interrelationships among multiple subjects. Each data model should correspond to only one concept, such as a person's name, or an address. The conceptual data model can be used as a template when creating a database model (logical data model or physical data model). Each entity attribute should be mapped to its parent data element. Semantics and data usage modifiers can be attributed to each entity attribute. The key components are themes, entities, attributes, and relationships.

The conceptual data model can be expressed as a container, such as a student, a school, an organization, or an address. These containers (such as students or schools) must be described in detail before they can be implemented in one or more different database tables, and eventually become objects that can be operated by a database management system such as Oracle. [5]

4.3 Logical database model

The logical data model is a data model that is independent of the database of the database management system. The data structure components that make up the model includes: patterns, tables, columns, and the relationship between tables. The relationship is limited to a single schema table. Although each implementation of the database model can correspond to multiple descriptive data models, but each implementation of the database model should only correspond to a problem. Each column of the table should be mapped to a parent attribute. Semantics and data usage modifiers can be attributed to each column. There are many-to-many relationships between the description data model and the implementation of the database model. The key components are patterns, tables, columns, and relationships.

4.4 Physical database model

The data model is a data model that is bound to a database of a particular database management system. The data structure components that make up the model include: database management system model, database management system table, database management system column and the relationship between the database management system tables. The database management system relationship is limited to a single schema in the database management system table. Each physical database model can correspond to multiple logical database models. Each column of the database management system should be mapped to a parent column. There is a many-to-many relationship between the logical database model and the physical database model. The key components are database management system model, database management system table, database management system and database management system relationship. [6]

If the data model is dependent on the state of a particular database management system and a particular software application performance, the data model is called "physical", and the data model is a physical database model that is bound to the application business information system through a view data model. Operating the database model inside the database management system table is to achieve the database model inside a single table in a single column deployment.

4.5 View data model

The view data model represents the interface between the physical database model and the business information system. The column of views and views can be characterized as input / output. [7] In addition, these views can be mapped to each other on a column basis, and the process can be specified to define arbitrary data value conversions.

The view data model is bound to a specific database management system by its definition. The view data model enables an application system to select, apply, or update a database system based on its physical data model, without having to include details of the physical data model in the application system. [8]

5 Conclusion and outlook

Enterprise architecture is a strategic information asset. It describes the current and expected relationship between an organization's business, mission, management process, and supporting infrastructure. The data architecture is the core of the enterprise architecture. It evolves business or mission into a more efficient, more efficient, and more popular fashion. It enhance the interoperability, and the sharing of information. At the same time, it improve business processes, and promote major decision-making planning.

Many enterprise systems have the same architectural approach, although an organization can have many different genres and practices in the implementation of enterprise data architecture. This demonstrates a variety of technical patterns and designs that are independent of a particular application area , are effective against generating responsive, scalable, flexible, and unified enterprise applications. The development of enterprises can not be separated from the enterprise data architecture, and reasonable data architecture applications may be the future of information society enterprises to survive the key.

References

1. Hailan Yu. Enterprise architecture. [M]. (2009)
2. Libo Xu. Model Design of Data Warehouse in Book Chain Enterprise. [J]. (2011)
3. Chengliang Lin. Power supply enterprise data model analysis and design
4. Genbao Zhang. Enterprise Informatization. [M]. (1999)

5. Enterprise architecture. Www.wiscorp.com/sp/sp08.pdf
6. Jijiang Yang,Wei He,Chunxiao Xing. Construction of e-government general data model [J]. E-government .1.(2001)
7. Engineering and Management Information System Planning www.wiscorp.com/sp/sp11.pdf
8. Adamson, Christopher and Michael Venerable. Data Warehouse Desgn Solutions. John Wiley & Sons, 544(1998)

Fault detection Based Bayesian network and MOEA/D applied to Sensorless Drive Diagnosis

Qing Zhou[1,a], Ling He[2] and PengFei Lu[1]

[1]*Wuhan University of Technology, School of Automation, 122 Luoshi Road, Wuhan, China*
[2] *Wuhan University of Technology, School of Management, 205 Xiongchu Road, Wuhan, China*

Abstract. Sensorless Drive Diagnosis can be used to assess the process data without the need for additional cost-intensive sensor technology, and you can understand the synchronous motor and connecting parts of the damaged state. Considering the number of features involved in the process data, it is necessary to perform feature selection and reduce the data dimension in the process of fault detection. In this paper, the MOEA / D algorithm based on multi-objective optimization is used to obtain the weight vector of all the features in the original data set. It is more suitable to classify or make decisions based on these features. In order to ensure the fastness and convenience sensorless drive diagnosis, in this paper, the classic Bayesian network learning algorithm-K2 algorithm is used to study the network structure of each feature in sensorless drive, which makes the fault detection and elimination process more targeted.

1 Introduction

The complexity of automation systems is steadily increasing, especially in process engineering. These are usually made up of individual autonomous subsystems, and their failure can have a serious impact on the overall system. Usually, this can lead to loss of production, which can lead to considerable economic losses.The sensorless monitoring of synchronous motors is based on the analysis of the current data in the process of operation, so as to obtain the damage state of synchronous motors and connecting components [1].Considering the number of features involved in the process data, if the characteristics of all measurements are taken directly, the amount of calculation will be larger in the process of fault detection. Moreover, due to the interference of redundant features, the classification of fault states is not very accurate, so feature selection(FS) is needed to reduce the data dimensionality. There have been some studies in this field. For example, the generalised Rayleigh coefficient [2] computed using LDA is applied to choose suitable feature combinations among all possible combinations optimised with respect to compactness and separability of the classes [3]. But most feature selection algorithms focus only on selection rather than selection and weighting, where the later has the potential to further enhance the classifier performance [4].

In this paper, we use the Dataset for Sensorless Drive Diagnosis to select and weigh the 48 features in the data set based on the MOEA/D algorithm [5]. The feature vectors are selected and weighted or scaled simultaneously to project the data points to such a hyper space, where the distance between data points of non-identical classes is increased, thus, making them easier to classify.

At the same time, in order to quickly troubleshoot in the fault detection problem, you need to know the relationship between the variables. There are many methods for this, such as neural networks [6], Petri nets [7,15], fault tree [8], decision tree [9], etc., but there are some deficiencies in all respects. In this paper, the classical Bayesian network learning algorithm (K2 algorithm [11]) for fault detection [10] is applied to learn the sensorless drive network structure according to the data after the feature selection and weighting. The network structure is closely related to the causal relationship between the various features, and more targeted in the process of sensorless drive.

2 Dataset

The data set has 48 consecutive features, is about the current signals of the motor, shaft, bearing and load sensors in the motor running process. The data set also includes a category column, which has 11 possible values, describing the different failure modes of the various components of sensorless drive [1].

Features are extracted from electric current drive signals. The drive has intact and defective components. This results in 11 different classes with different conditions. Each condition has been measured several times by 12 different operating conditions, this means by different speeds, load moments and load forces. The current signals are measured with a current probe and an oscilloscope on two phases.

[a] Qing Zhou: qingzhou@whut.edu.cn

The Empirical Mode Decomposition (EMD) was used to generate a new database for the generation of features. The first three intrinsic mode functions (IMF) of the two phase-currents and their residuals (RES) were used and broken down into sub-sequences. For each of those sub-sequences, the statistical features mean, standard deviation, skewness and kurtosis were calculated. More information about the measurement procedure and a detailed description of the demonstrator's mechanical part can be found in [1].

3 Fault Detection Based Bayesian Network and MOEA/D

3.1. MOEA/D Algorithm

The fewer features are required for distinction, the more efficient is the decision making. A dimension reduction results in a better interpretability as well as in a reduced complexity of the information to be analysed. This leads to less learning effort for classification and a faster reaction time which is an important criterion for future implementations in industrial applications.

3.1.1 Algorithm principle

MOEA/D is a feature selection and weighting method aided with the decomposition based evolutionary multi-objective algorithm. the formulated inter-class and intra-class distance measures are maximized and minimized simultaneously by using a Multi-Objective Evolutionary Algorithm based on Decomposition (MOEA/D). The population of MOEA/D comprises of vectors containing the candidate feature weights, which are varied according to the algorithm to optimize the inter-class and intra class distance measures discussed subsequently. A repair mechanism is used to increase the probability of choosing lesser number of features. Also, a penalty function is augmented with the fitness functions to reduce the number of features selected. After convergence to optima using MOEA/D, a fuzzy membership based technique [12] is incorporated to choose only a single feature subset (representing the best compromise solution) out of the Pareto optimal solution set.

In the process of multi-objective evolutionary iteration, there are two objective functions, which are the distance between classes and the distance within the class. The individual of the evolutionary population is the weight vector of the weight of all the features.

3.1.2 Algorithm flow

The goal of evolution is to find a feature weight vector which maximizes the inter-class and minimizes the intra-class and the specific algorithm flow is as follows:

(1) Input the training dataset;

(2) Normalize the training dataset;

(3) Compute inter-class and intra-class distance;

(4) Randomly initialize Feature Selecting-Weighting vector (W) which comprise the population of MOEA/D, Repeat (4) to (8) for every individual of the MOEA/D population;

(5) Crossover and Mutation to create new feature selecting-weighting vectors;

(6) Repair the newly generated selecting-weighting vectors;

(7) Compute the Objective values;

(8) Update solutions;

(9) Judgment of iteration termination criteria If termination criterion not reached, return to (4), else go to (10) end if;

(10) Use Best Compromise Solution technique to find the optimal feature selection-weighting vector (W^*) from the Pareto optimal set.

In the process of obtaining the optimal feature selection-weighting vector (W^*), according to its processing of the data, we can get the data with selection and weighting, as the input data to learn the relationship between the various characteristics.

3.2. Fault detection base Bayesian network

A Bayesian Network (BN) is a probabilistic graphical model [13], which provides an elegant way to express probabilistic relationships between random variables. Edges of the graph represent dependence between linked nodes. A formal definition is given here:

A Bayesian network is a triplet $\{G,E,D\}$ where:

$\{G\}$ Is a directed acyclic graph, $G=(V,A)$, with V the set of nodes of G, and A the set of edges of G,

$\{E\}$ Is a finite probabilistic space (Ω,Z,p), with Ω a non-empty space, Z a collection of subspace of Ω, and p a probability measure on Z with $p(\Omega)=1$,

$\{D\}$ Is a set of random variables associated to the nodes of G and defined on E. Such as:

$$p(V_1,V_2,...,V_n)=\prod_{i=1}^{n} p(V_i|C(V_i)) \qquad (1)$$

with $C(V_i)$ the set of causes (parents) of V_i in the graph G.

In the network, although the relationship between the parent node and the child node does not require causality, this representation can accurately reflect the dependency relationship between them in the fault diagnosis. Bayesian network structure (directed graph) expresses the relationship between the characteristics and the degree of influence. The node variables represent features, the directed edge of the connected node represents the association between the features, the conditional probability represents the degree of influence between the features. The Bayesian network has the following characteristics:

(1) Bayesian network is an uncertain causal relationship model. The Bayesian network is a kind of probabilistic knowledge representation and reasoning model which visualizes the multivariate knowledge, and

more closely implies the causal relationship and the conditional relation between the node variables [14].

(2) Bayesian networks have powerful ability to deal with uncertain problems. The Bayesian network uses conditional probabilities to represent the correlations among the information elements. It can learn and reason under limited, incomplete and uncertain information.

(3) Bayesian network can effectively perform multi-source information representation and fusion. The Bayesian network can integrate various information related to fault detection into the network structure, and can be unified according to the way of nodes, and can be effectively fused according to the correlation of the information.

The appeal Bayesian network characteristics are consistent with the requirements of fault detection. It can be seen that the Bayesian network-based fault detection method is more superior and qualitatively and quantitatively represents the relationship between variables and Visualization. Here we use the classic K2 algorithm, based on data learning to obtain the relationship between the various characteristics of the Bayesian network.

4 Experimental results

Before the feature selection, the size of the data set is 50000 * 49, where the first 48 columns are different for the synchronous motor operation. The last column is the label of each sample, indicating which class the sample belongs to, a total of 11 classes. Since the data given is about the synchronous motor's various current characteristics, it is continuous data. Firstly, the data is pretreated and normalized and discretized. Each feature is divided into 15 classes, each of which is valued as an integer between $[1\ 15]$. Without the application of feature selection, the 40000 sets of data are based on the classical K2 algorithm to study its network structure, and the resulting Bayesian network structure is shown in Figure 1.

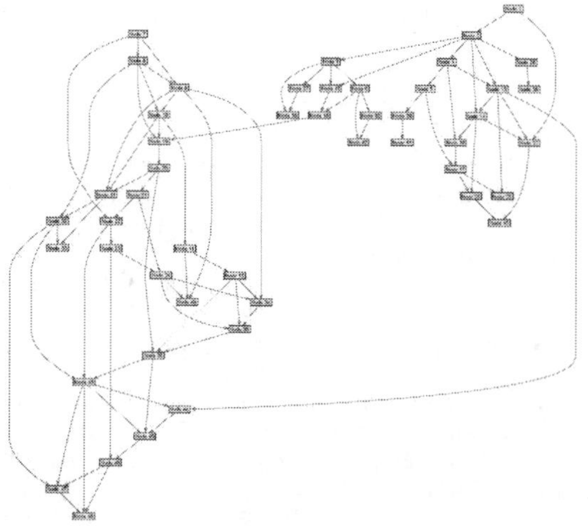

Figure 1. Bayesian network structure before feature selection.

Based on the first 10000 sets of samples, the MOEA/D algorithm is used to iterate the 150 generation to get the feature weight vector W^* with the highest accuracy, as shown in Table 1. According to the eigenvector W^*, the data is dimensioned down to obtain a data set with a size of 50000 * 29, and then the normalized and discretized processing is carried out. The Bayesian network structure obtained by K2 algorithm is shown in Figure 2.

Table 1. feature weight vector W^* .

W							
10	0	1.668	0	8.702	1.211	9.995	10
10	9.474	9.884	10	0	0	6.100	0
0	0	0	0	0	0	1.201	0
10	10	10	10	0	0	10	1.381
3.282	1.424	10	1.470	5.559	0	6.247	5.835
0	2.512	0	0	2.575	0	3.808	0

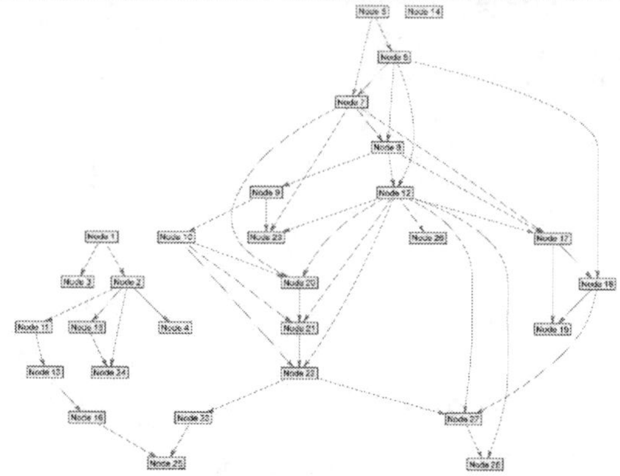

Figure 2. Bayesian network structure after feature selection.

Before and after the FS, the parameters of the network structure learning are shown in Table 2, where the accuracy is calculated as

$$\eta = \frac{N_{true}}{N_{test}} \times 100\% \qquad (2)$$

Where N_{test} is the number of samples in the test data and N_{true} is the number of samples correctly classified. It can be seen that the time required for learning the Bayesian network structure (T_{train}) is significantly shortened, and the accuracy of classification is not reduced. In this way, the feature selection of the data reduces the computational complexity and reduces the time required for training. The fault detection method based on Bayesian network can visualize the relation among each feature, so that the fault can be eliminated quickly.

Table 2. Before and after FS.

	Feature number	Training data number	Training time	Test dataset number	accuracy
Before FS	48	38000	467.099	2000	88.25%
After FS	28	38000	110.688	2000	88.30%

DOI: 10.1051/matecconf/201712802017

5 Conclusion

In this paper, the MOEA/D algorithm based on multi-objective evolution is applied to the feature selection and weight calculation of Sensorless Drive. Under the premise of accurate classification and decision-making, we choose the least possible features to reduce the computational complexity. The classical K2 algorithm is applied to study from the data before and after FS, to get the network structure which characterizes the relationship between features. Through the above experiments, we can find that under the action of MOEA/D algorithm, the number of features is obviously reduced, the time required for training is reduced, and the accuracy of classification is not reduced. This kind of network relationship is more practical, in the actual fault detection and elimination process more quickly and efficiently.

Acknowledgment

This work was supported in part by the National Natural Science Foundation of China (Grant No. 71603197, 71371148), Junior Fellowships for CAST Advanced Innovation Think-tank Program (DXB-ZKQN-2016-013), China Postdoctoral Science Foundation (2016M592403, 2017T100588), Special Project of Technology Innovation of Hubei Province -Soft Science (No. 2016ADC094) Fundamental Research Funds for the Central Universities (175211006).

References

1. Lohweg, Volker, Paschke, Fabian, Bayer, Christian. Sensorlose Zustandsüberwachung an Synchronmotoren[J]. 2013.
2. Bator M, Dicks A, Mönks U, et al. Feature Extraction and Reduction Applied to Sensorless Drive Diagnosis[C]// 22. Workshop Computational Intelligence. 2012.
3. Duda, R. O.; Hart, P. E.; Stork, D. G.: Pattern classification. New York: Wiley, 2 Aufl. ISBN 9780471703501. 2001.
4. Raymer M L, Punch W F, Goodman E D, et al. Dimensionality reduction using genetic algorithms[J]. IEEE Transactions on Evolutionary Computation, 2000, 4(2):164-171.
5. Paul S, Das S. Simultaneous feature selection and weighting - An evolutionary multi-objective optimization approach[M]. Elsevier Science Inc. 2015.
6. Mechefske C K, Li L. Induction Motor Fault Detection and Diagnosis Using Artifical Neural Networks[C]// ASME 2005 International Design Engineering Technical Conferences and Computers and Information in Engineering Conference. 2005.
7. Tazaki E, Yoshida K. A fuzzy Petri net model for approximate reasoning and its application to medical diagnosis[C]// IEEE International Conference on Systems, Man and Cybernetics. IEEE, 1992:627-631 vol.1.
8. Andow P K. Difficulties in Fault-Tree Synthesis for Process Plant[J]. IEEE Transactions on Reliability, 2009, R-29(1):2-9.
9. Zhao Y, Yang L, Lehman B, et al. Decision tree-based fault detection and classification in solar photovoltaic arrays[C]// Applied Power Electronics Conference and Exposition. IEEE, 2012:93-99.
10. Matsuura J P, Yoneyama T. Learning bayesian networks for fault detection[C]// Machine Learning for Signal Processing, 2004. Proceedings of the 2004, IEEE Signal Processing Society Workshop. IEEE, 2004:133-142.
11. Herskovits E, Herskovits E. A Bayesian Method for the Induction of Probabilistic Networks from Data[M]. Kluwer Academic Publishers, 1992.
12. Abido M A. A novel multiobjective evolutionary algorithm for environmental/economic power dispatch[J]. Electric Power Systems Research, 2001, 65(1):71-81.
13. Lenz H J. Finn V. Jensen, Thomas D. Nielsen (2007): Bayesian Networks and Decision Graphs[J]. Statistical Papers, 2011, 52(1):235-237.
14. Genesereth M R, Nilsson N J. CHAPTER 8– Reasoning with Uncertain Beliefs[J]. Logical Foundations of Artificial Intelligence, 1987:177-206.
15. Gao Meimei Wu Zhiming. Fuzzy Reasoning Petri Net and its Application to Fault Diagnosis[J]. Acta Automatica Sinica, 2000, 26(5):677-680.

DOI: 10.1051/matecconf/201712802018

Method of multi-sensor data Association based on large scale

LAN Xu-hui [a], Li Ling-zhi, Guo Yong-ming

No.4 Department, Air Force Early Warning Academy, Wuhan 430019, China

Abstract. In the multi-sensor fusion system, great difference of detection information accuracy results high uncertainty of heterogeneous information correlation. This paper proposes a multi-sensor data correlation method basing on large scale which combines evidence theory and multi-factor fuzzy integrated decision theory in information correlation. For solving the problem of uncertainty of information correlation and obtaining evidence difficultly, the method first combines uncertain information evidence, and then obtains evidence from multi-factor fuzzy integrated decision membership degree function. The test results that heterogeneous information correlation using this method can conquer uncertainty of evidence combination and reduce the error and miss correlation rate.

1 Introduction

For a single sensor, it is difficult to detect the target correctly because of single detection means,limited data and failure detection probably. Multi-source heterogeneous data fusion can solve the problem. Multi-sensor heterogeneous data correlation is the base of multi-source data fusion.

Now, traditional data correlation algorithm is mainly based on statistics and fuzzy mathematics [1-2]. Weighting method, sequential method, dual-threshold, the nearest-neighbor method, K-NN method, and amended K-NN method are based on statistics. Fuzzy mathematics method, fuzzy dual-threshold method, fuzzy integrated function method and multi-factor fuzzy integrated decision method are based on fuzzy mathematics. Membership degree function of fuzzy mathematics can express fuzzy factors well, which brings high correlation rate[3]. These traditional methods are better for similar sensors data correlation. But there is high error correlation rate and miss correlation rate for uncertain heterogeneous data correlation.

This paper proposes a method of large scale for multi-sensor heterogeneous data correlation. Evidence theory that has preponderance for uncertain data, is used to multi-factor fuzzy integrated decision theory which can obtain evidence well from membership degree function[4]. Improved method step based on evidence theory and fuzzy decision theory is provided in this article. Simulation proves the method can reduce the error and miss correlation rate effectively for heterogeneous data correlation.

2 Related theory

2.1 Multi-factor fuzzy integrated decision data correlation algorithm

1) Determination of the fuzzy factors set

Taking Euclidian distances of target location and orientation angle of two different type of sensor to the factors set, that is fuzzy set $U=\{u_k\}=\{u_1,u_2,\cdots u_n\}$ with $n=2$ .Where u_1 is the target location, u_2 is orientation angle, then:

$$\begin{cases} u_1(l)=\left[\left(x_r(l)-x_a(l)^2\right)+\left(y_r(l)-y_a(l)^2\right)\right]^{1/2} \\ u_2(l)=\left|\arctan[y_r(l)/x_r(l)]-\arctan[y_a(l)/x_a(l)]\right| \end{cases} \quad (1)$$

Where $u_1(l)$ is the diameter distance difference of two targets for time l, $u_2(l)$ is the orientation angle difference of two targets for time l, $x_r(l)$ is X location component of sensor 1 for time l, $x_a(l)$ is X location component of sensor 2 for time l, $y_r(l)$ is Y location component of sensor 1 for time l, $y_a(l)$ is Y location component of sensor 2 for time l. The right angle coordinate is used in calculation process.

2) Determination of the fuzzy judgments set

If the associated result of two sensors'data is divided into m Level, the set consisted by these results is called the judgments set, and denoted $V=\{v_l\}=\{v_1,v_2,\cdots,v_m\}$, where $v_l, l=1,2,\cdots,m$ is the judgment results of lth level. Any judgment result of two sensors' data is a fuzzy subset of V actually.

We only concern about whether the target data association. Therefore, from the point of view of practical applications and simplifying the process, the judgments set is selected $V=\{v_1,v_2,\cdots,v_m\}$ with m=3, where v_1

[a] LAN Xu-hui: 4517665@qq.com

denotes correlation, v_2 denotes non-correlation, v_3 denotes uncertainty,that is $V=\{\text{correlation, non-correlation, uncertainty}\}$. Of course, the judgments set can be easier, that is $V=\{\text{correlation, non-correlation}\}$.

3) Determination of single factor fuzzy judgment matrix

Single factor fuzzy judgment matrix is defined $R=(r_{kl})_{n\times m}$ from U to V in direct product set $U\times V$, where r_{kl} denoted the probability of the lth result of two sensors' data when the kth factor is congsidered.

According to the characteristics of fuzzy data correlation factors, memberships can be used with normal distribution, Cauchy distribution, middle distribution, etc. The paper selects normal distribution membership function. When $m=2$, the normal distribution membership degree based on the kth factor judgment is:

$$r_{k1}=\exp[-\tau_k(x^2/\sigma_k^2)];k=1,2 \qquad (2)$$

$$r_{k2}=1-\exp[-\tau_k(x^2/\sigma_k^2)];k=1,2 \qquad (3)$$

Where τ_k is the adjustment coefficient; σ_k^2 is the variance. Therefore, the single factor fuzzy judgment matrix as follows:

$$R=\begin{bmatrix} r_{11} & r_{12} \\ r_{21} & r_{22} \end{bmatrix}$$

4) Criterion of multi-factor fuzzy judgment

The factor weight fuzzy set is $A=(a_1,a_2)$ with $a_1=0.7$, $a_2=0.3$ in the paper considering that distance precision is higher than orientation precision of sensor. Factor weight coefficients can be adjusted through a large number of experimental statistics.

Integrated decision of two sensors' data is compound effect of the factor weight fuzzy set A and fuzzy judgment matrix R, which is the composition operation. The fuzzy set B of correlation probability of two sensors' data in V compositing by A and R is following:

$$B=A\cdot R=(b_l)=(b_1,b_2)$$

$b_l(l=1,2)$ is the membership degree of v_l which is an element of judgments set. Composition operation has three kinds of algorithm, which are "weighting average", "subjective factor" and "hybrid". In order to equalize all factors based on weight, "weighting average" is used as follows:

$$b_l=\sum_{k=1}^{2}a_k r_{kl}, l=1,2$$

If data correlation probability of two sensors' for level l is judged bythe maximum membership degree principle, the result is following:

$$b_l=\max\{b_1,b_2\}$$

However, the reliability is poor by above method. Because so long as the condition is $b_1>b_2$, the judgment is correlation. The composition operation is simple, but the result is not accurate.

2.2 Evidence theory

D-S evidence theory defined a space Θ which is called frame of discernment. It is composed of mutual exclusive and exhaustive elements. Any proposition A of the problem domain is belonged to powers set 2^Θ. Basic probability assignment function is defined in 2^Θ set: $m:2^\Theta\rightarrow[0,1]$ .m satisfies three conditions, which are: (1) $m(\Theta)=0$; (2) $0\le m(A)\le 1$; (3) $\sum_{A\subset\Theta}m(A)=1$.

$m(A)$ denotes a true subset which supports proposition A by evidence but not any A. If A is a subset of Θ, and satisfies $m(A)>0$, it is called focus element of evidence. Interval $[Bel(A),Pl(A)]$ is used to describe event A in evidence theory, where Bel is called belief function and Pl is called plausibility function.

D-S evidence theory provides a very useful composition formula. It can compose evidences from multiple evidence sources. The formula is defined as follows (an example for two evidences):

$$m(A)=\frac{1}{1-K}\sum_{A_i\cap B_j=A}M_1(A_i)M_2(B_j) \qquad (4)$$

With $k=\sum_{A_i\cap B_j=\Phi}M_1(A_i)M_2(B_j)$ .Its value reflects conflict degree of evidence. The coefficient $1/(1-k)$ is called normalization factor. Its role is to avoid that non-zero probability is assigned to the null set when composing evidences.

3 Improved correlation method based on evidence theory

Frame of discernment for evidence is Θ = (correlation, non-correlation, uncertainty) .The factors set influencing the decision is $U=\{u_1,u_2,\cdots u_n\}$. Supposing that the basic probability of the main two factors influencing data correlation is assigned as following:

m_1(correlation)=0.6 m_1(non-correlation)=0.3
m_1(uncertainty)=0.1
m_2(correlation)=0.4 m_2(non-correlation)=0.5
m_2(uncertainty)=0.1

The basic probability is obtained by membership degree functions of multi-factor fuzzy integrated decision data association algorithm.

Synthesizing evidence by evidence theory:

Table 1. calculation of evidence synthesis

Assignment m_2	**Evidence synthesis calculated values**		
	m_1(correlation) 0.6	m_1(non-correlation) 0.3	m_1(uncertainty) 0.1
m_2(correlation) 0.4	0.24	0.12	0.04
m_2(non-correlation) 0.5	0.3	0.15	0.05
m_2(uncertainty) 0.1	0.06	0.03	0.01

k= m_1(non-correlation)× m_2(correlation)+ m_1(uncertainty) × m_2(correlation)+ m_1(correlation) × m_2(non-correlation)+ m_1(uncertainty) × m_2(non-correlation)+ m_1(correlation) × m_2(uncertainty)+ m_1(non-correlation) × m_2(uncertainty)=0.4

Integrated probability after evidence synthesis is assigned:

m(correlation)=0.6 m(non-correlation)=0.375 m(uncertainty)=0.025

If data correction decision rules are:

Table 2. Data Association guidelines

Decision	Rules
correction	m(correlation)> m(non-correlation) and m(correlation)> m(uncertainty)
non-correction	m(non-correlation)≥m(correlation) and m(non-correlation) ≥m(uncertainty)
Uncertainty	m(uncertainty)> m(correlation) and m(uncertainty)> m(non-correlation)

By combination rules of evidence, the result is data correction.

4 Simulation analysis

$\Theta = \{A, B, \theta\}$,Initial evidence formed by decision factor that two weights are 0.7 and 0.3 is:

$a_1(\text{weit}) = 0.7 \quad m_1(\text{A}) = 0.7 \quad m_1(\text{B}) = 0.3 \quad m_1(\theta) = 1\text{-}a_1 = 0.3$

$a_2(\text{weit}) = 0.3 \quad m_2(\text{A}) = 0.1 \quad m_2(\text{B}) = 0.9 \quad m_2(\theta) = 1\text{-}a_1 = 0.7$

Evidences are obtained by multi-factor fuzzy integrated decision method. The result using multi-factor fuzzy integrated decision membership degree synthesis data correction algorithm is following

$$\begin{cases} m(A) = a_1 m_1(A) + a_2 m_2(A) = 0.52 \\ m(B) = a_1 m_1(B) + a_2 m_2(B) = 0.48 \\ m(\theta) = m_1(\theta) + m_2(\theta) = 1 \end{cases}$$

After normalization:

$$m(A) = 0.26 \quad m(B) = 0.24 \quad m(\theta) = 0.5$$

The evidences combination result is that

$$\begin{cases} m(A) = m_1 \oplus m_2(A) = 0.23 \\ m(B) = m_1 \oplus m_2(B) = 0.31 \\ m(\theta) = m_1 \oplus m_2(\theta) = 0.46 \end{cases}$$

Data correction algorithm using multi-factor fuzzy integrated decision, although can choose A as the final decision according to new evidences. Obviously, the trust degree difference for A and B is only 0.02, but uncertainty degree is 0.5, that is unreasonable and is not conformity with algorithm rule. Using evidences combination, the trust degree difference for A and B is 0.08, but uncertainty degree reduces to 0.046, and the result is B. Therefore data correction algorithm using evidence theory can reduce uncertainty degree effectively, obtain better reasonable correction result, and reduce error correction rate.

5 Conclusions

Multisource heterogeneous data correction exits high uncertainty degree, but evidence theory can depose the problem well. It is difficult to obtain evidence, but it is easy to obtain evidences by multi-factor fuzzy integrated decision membership degree function. Therefore, for high uncertainty degree of heterogeneous data correction, combining evidence theory and multi-factor fuzzy integrated decision can reduce error correction rate and leak correction rate. In addition, evidence theory gets some beneficial progress in disposing evidence conflict, calculation complexity and evidence combination explosion etc. The dependability of evidence theory becomes better in engineering. As a result, it is a useful expand that evidence theory is used to heterogeneous data correction.

References

1. he you , Wang Guohong , Guan Hin . . The theory of information fusion and its application [M]. Beijing : Publishing House of electronics industry ,2010:178.
2. Han Chongzhao , Zhu Hongyan , overcome . Source new information fusion [M]. Beijing : Tsinghua University Press , 2006: 290.
3. he you , land , Peng Yingning , and so on . Tracks correlation algorithm based on fuzzy synthetic function [J]. Journal of Naval Engineering College ,1999 ,89 (4):1-11
4. Dezert J. Foundations for a New Theory of Plausible and Paradoxical Reasoning, Information & Security [J]. An Int Journal, 2002, 45 (9):13-57.
5. Dezert J, Smarandache F. Advances and Applications of DSmT for Information Fusion [M]. American Research Press, Rehoboth, 2009:15-20.
6. Wei-Ping Huang , Xu Yu , Wang Jie . Comprehensive utilization of various information of / Data Association of radar [J]. Chinese Journal of sensors ,2009,22(6) : 216-821.
7. Dong Hongbo , busy hero Liu Jin , Zhang Chunmei , and so on . Research on airborne fuzzy track correlation algorithm with dissimilar sensors [J]. Sensors and Microsystems ,2010,29 (7): 8-10.
8. Chen Shiyou , xiaohou , Liu Hao . Representation of uncertainty in track correlation [J]. Electronics ,2011,39 (7) : 1589-1593.
9. A. Mecke, I. Lee, J.R. Baker jr., M.M. Banaszak Holl, B.G. Orr, Eur. Phys. J. E **14**, 7 (2004)
10. M. Ben Rabha, M.F. Boujmil, M. Saadoun, B. Bessaïs, Eur. Phys. J. Appl. Phys. (to be published)

A Plagiarism Detection Algorithm based on Extended Winnowing

Xuliang DUAN[1,a], Mantao WANG[1], Jiong MU[1]

[1]*College of Information Engineering, Sichuan Agricultural University, Ya'an 625014, China*

Abstract. Plagiarism is a common problem faced by academia and education. Mature commercial plagiarism detection system has the advantages of comprehensive and high accuracy, but the expensive detection costs make it unsuitable for real-time, lightweight application environment such as the student assignments plagiarism detection. This paper introduces the method of extending classic Winnowing plagiarism detection algorithm, expands the algorithm in functionality. The extended algorithm can retain the text location and length information in original document while extracting the fingerprints of a document, so that the locating and marking for plagiarism text fragment are much easier to achieve. The experimental results and several years of running practice show that the expansion of the algorithm has little effect on its performance, normal hardware configuration of PC will be able to meet small and medium-sized applications requirements. Based on the characteristics of lightweight, high efficiency, reliability and flexibility of Winnowing, the extended algorithm further enhances the adaptability and extends the application areas.

1 Introduction

Plagiarism detection, also known as duplicate or copy detection is to detect whether the contents of one file copy from one or more others. Strictly speaking, plagiarism means more than intact copy, and also includes the transformation of transposing, synonym substitution and restatement of original ideas without reference [1]. Plagiarism detection is an important method for academic misconduct, author identification and digital products intellectual property protection. The PAN (Plagiarism Detection Author Identification Author Profiling) founded by EU digital library project hold the annual competition on plagiarism detection, author identification and author profiling which involves the most advanced method and technology in this field [2]. In China, several major bibliographic databases such as CNKI, Wan Fang Data, CQVIP constructed their own plagiarism detection system that effectively prevent the occurrence of academic misconduct.

Plagiarism is an unavoidable topic in digital age. "In surveys, nearly 70% of college students admit to having taken material from the internet without properly crediting its source" [3]. And in recent decades, various forms of plagiarism and plagiarism are increasing year by year [4]. In terms of financial and time costs, the commercial detection system is hard to meet the demand of lightweight, real-time, and normalization for students' assignments plagiarism detection. In recent years, plenty of research in this field has been done and some results are obtained. Zhong et al. transformed the C source code to XML document and then extracted the XML structure information to detect code block and statement rearrangement etc. [5]. Qin et al. presented an algorithm based on local word-frequency fingerprint and improved the simple digital fingerprinting and word frequency based algorithms [6]. Zhang et al. compared the Winnowing fingerprint algorithm and the dynamic programming in assignment plagiarism detection and found that the Winnowing has better anti-interference ability for noise words and it is more effective and reliable [7-8].

This paper presents an approach to extend the Winnowing fingerprint algorithm, for each text fragment in a document, the location and length are preserved while generating the fingerprint. The fingerprint extra information is used to locate and mark plagiarism text in source documents that extends the application field and practicability of the Winnowing algorithm.

2 Related Technologies

2.1 Plagiarism detection

The research of text copy detection can be traced back to the code similarity detection which is used to prevent the large-scale program copying in 1970s. Natural language copy detection technology appeared in the 1990s. Till now, the plagiarism detection research is broadly classified into two categories: the internal and external plagiarism detection. The internal plagiarism detection aims to determine whether the text is plagiarism mainly based on the author's writing style model, while external algorithms compare the suspicious document with a closed documents setting to check the similarity whether

[a] Corresponding author: duanxuliang@sicau.edu.cn

over a certain threshold. The general meaning of plagiarism detection refers to the external detection.

According to the text feature extraction, there are mainly three kinds of methods of plagiarism detection [9]: 1) Grammar based methods. These algorithms focus on document grammatical structure and measure the document similarity based on string matching, such as the LCS (Longest Common Substring), Karp-Rabin string matching algorithm [10], and the MOSS text block fingerprint detection algorithm. The grammar based methods have higher efficiency and precision for direct replication. 2) Semantic based methods. Based on vector space model, these methods first construct document feature vector using term frequency or TF-IDF (Term Frequency–Inverse Document Frequency), and then calculate vectors' similarity using dot product or the cosine of vector angle. While it's generally not easy for these approaches to determine the location of the plagiarism text. 3) The hybrid of semantic and grammatical. Integrate the above two methods in order to complement one another and achieve better results.

The Winnowing [11] algorithm is a fingerprint based text similarity detection method, proposed by Schleimer et al in 2003. The basic idea of Winnowing comes from the Karp-Rabin algorithm which using overlapping k-gram and moving window for string matching. Winnowing chooses the minimize hash value in each window to compose the document fingerprint, and then compares documents' fingerprints using pair-wise method to find the copied text. Winnowing is a lightweight and flexible similarity detection method, it is robust for sentence and text block rearrangement, and the influence of interference words can be effectively reduced through reasonable parameter setting.

There are three parameters, t, k, w, used to control the detection granularity and fingerprints density, adjustment of these parameters makes Winnowing be capable of different detection requirements. Parameter t is the guarantee threshold, any substring match at least as long as t would be detected, and any matches shorter the noise threshold k will not be detected. Bigger k value means longer k-gram substring and once detected plagiarism the result is more irrefutable, but larger k may reduce the detection sensitivity. Parameter w is the scan window size, smaller w will lead to higher detection sensitivity, but more hashes causes greater storage requirements and the processing efficiency will be reduced. Schleimer et al. proved that the expect selected density is $d = \frac{2}{w+1}$, and parameters can be adjusted according different application requirements.

The basic process of Winnowing fingerprint selection algorithm is as follows:

a. Text preprocessing, including the case conversion, and removal of blank characters, stop words, meaningless symbols, etc.;

b. Using k-gram method to segment the text and calculate the hash of each block, so there will be a hash sequence representing the document;

c. Using the w width window to sample the document hashes. The selection principles are as follows: in each window select the minimum hash value, if there is more than one hash with the minimum value, select the rightmost occurrence;

d. Save all selected hashes as the document fingerprint for further processing.

2.2 Plagiarism Text Location

Text location is an important components of plagiarism detection technology. The purpose of plagiarism detection is not only to calculate document similarity, but also to get the copied text location and be marked in original documents. At present, copied text location is largely based on character comparison method, such as the longest common subsequence. For example, Zaslavsky et al. constructed MDR (Match Detect Reveal) [12] system for Spanish similar text location, Sediyono et al. proposed the LCCW (Longest Commonly Consecutive Word) [13] algorithm to find and locate similar contents of a document. In order to improve the efficiency, the character comparison method is mostly indexed by words. But for Chinese text, there are few clear separators between words, word segmentation must be proceeded before indexing so the processing efficiency is relatively low.

3 Extended-Winnowing Algorithm

Winnowing is a high flexibility algorithm, the detection sensitivity and fingerprints density could be adjusted to different application scenarios. However, in practice, due to the lack of location information, the similar text matching and marking are costly. This paper presents a method of keeping the original text block location to extend the basic Winnowing algorithm, which can locate anyone fingerprint in original document and improve the adaptability of the detection algorithm.

3.1 Extracting Fingerprints with Location Information

The first step in Winnowing is to remove irrelevant features from source text, such as punctuation, spaces, control characters, stop words. After cleaning, seg_i indicates the i-th k-gram text block, and the fingerprint is the hash value of this text block, that is $h_i = hash(seg_i)$. It could be seen that from the above process, text length has been changed and the location of segment hash is lost as well.

In extended Winnowing, in order to accurately locate the text segment in source document, any preprocessing that may change text length will not execute any more and the text cleanup operation is implemented in processing the k-gram segment. The ith k-gram text segment seg_i contains k useful characters, as the meaningless characters are removed so the length of text segment in origin document is not less than k, therefor $len_i \geq k$. The extended fingerprint is made up of triples

$h_i = \{hash(seg_i), loc_i, len_i\}$

In which loc_i is the start location of text segment seg_i in origin document, and the len_i is the source length of seg_i in origin document.

After obtaining the hash sequence of a document, the next step is to select the "proper" hashes according to a certain rule and then generate a new sequence of hashes which represents the origin document. Algorithm 1 gives an extension method to calculate all the *k*-gram fingerprint sequences of a document. Algorithm 2 describes the process of winnowing and selecting the fingerprints sequence.

Algorithm 1. Fingerprint extraction algorithm of extended Winnowing

INPUT: the *text* in document, *stopwords* List, length of *k*-gram(value of *k*)

OUTPUT: the *k*-gram hashes list *H*[ ] (without Winnowing)

```
Function GetTextFingers(text, stopwords, k)
 for (loc = 0; loc < text.length - k; loc++) do
   len ← k;    //the default length of k-gram is k
   kgram ← substring(text, loc, len);   //get k-gram substring
   kgram ← replace(kgram, stopwods, '');
   //clear stop word characters
   while length(kgram) < k do
   //the length of k-gram may less than k,
   //continue until the length is k
     len ← len + ( k - length(kgram) );
     kgram ← substring(text, loc, len);
     kgram ← replace(kgram, stopwods, '');
   endwhile
   H[ ].add(<hash(kgram), loc, len>);
   //calculate each k-gram hash,
   //and record the location and length
 endfor
 return H[ ]    //return all k-gram hashes list
endfunction
```

Algorithm 2. Fingerprints Sampling algorithm for extended Winnowing

INPUT: all *k*-gram hashes list *H*[ ], threshold *t*, *k* of *k*-gram

OUTPUT: sampled hashes list *HS*[ ]

```
Function SamplingFingers(H[ ], t, k)
 w ← t + 1 - k;    //scan window width
 n ← H[].count;  //all hashes count
 minIndex ← -1;
 preMinIndex ← -1;
 tmpMin;
 for (i = 0; i ≤ H[].count - w; i++) do
   tmpMin = -1;
   for ( j = i; j < i + w; j++ ) do
     if H[j].hash ≤ tmpMin then
     //if there are more than one minimum in a window,
       minIndex ← j;    // take the rightmost one
       tmpMin ← H[j].hash;
     endif
   endfor
   if minIndex ≠ preMinIndex then
   //the same value only select once
     preMinIndex ← minIndex;
     HS[ ].add( H [minIndex] );
   endif
 endfor
 return HS[ ]    //return sampled hashes list
endfunction
```

3.2 Text Similarity and Plagiarism Rate

After Winnowing, the document is represented as a series of discrete hashes, and Jaccard distance [14] can be used to measure the similarity between documents. There are many variants of Jaccard for practical application, the basic definition for two sets X and Y is the quotient of intersection elements number and union elements number, as shown in formula (1):

$$J(X,Y)=\frac{|X\cap Y|}{|X\cup Y|}=\frac{|X\cap Y|}{|X|+|Y|-|X\cap Y|} \quad (1)$$

In practical, too much difference between text size may lead an inaccurate result for Jaccard distance, for example, if A is a proper subset of B, although A is totally plagiarized while the Jaccard distance will less than 1.

In order to improve the precision and recall ratio, we set the minimum elements number of A and B as the denominator, as shown in formula (2), where $F(A)$ and $F(B)$ are the fingerprints set of documents A and B:

$$sim(A,B)=\frac{|F(A)\cap F(B)|}{\min(|F(A)|,|F(B)|)} \quad (2)$$

TF-IDF (Term Frequency–Inverse Document Frequency) could also be introduced to compute the documents similarity. Documents are presented by vectors in VSM (Vector Space Model), and the angle cosine value indicates similarity of two vectors.

Since the fingerprint weight calculated by the TF-IDF increases in proportion to the number of occurrences it appears in the file and decreases inversely with the frequency it appears in all documents, so the similarity results are more reasonable. For example, assuming that each document has a fingerprint corresponding to the string "*int main ()*", the term frequency *tf* of this fingerprint is 1, and the inverse document frequency *idf* is 0, so the TF-IDF weight $w = tf{\cdot}idf$ is 0, which means that the string fragment "*int main ()*" will not be considered in computing documents similarity. The TF-IDF results are more accurate, while in the case of large documents the corresponding VSM may be very sparse and facing very low processing efficiency.

As each document is represented by a discrete hash sequence, the document plagiarism rate is also relatively simple, formula (3) shows the calculation method, $F(A)$ represents all fingerprints of a document, $F'(A)$ represents the fingerprints also appear in other documents (suspected plagiarism fingerprints):

$$P(A)=\frac{|F'(A)|}{|F(A)|} \quad (3)$$

3.3 Location and Marking

Essentially, the plagiarism detection is to calculate the intersection of a specific document from each file in source documents. In processing, for every same hash value (suggest the copied text fragment) there will be a plagiarism hash index generated,

p-index ={*pid*, *ploc* , *plen*, *sid*, *sloc*, *slen*}

where *pid* is the current detection document ID and *sid* is the source document ID, *ploc* and *plen* are respectively the location and length of copied text fragment in current detection document, correspondingly *sloc* and *slen* are parameters in source document.

Plagiarism text marking separately processing in current detection document and source document, the principle is basically the same, the marking implementation process is as follows:

1) Sorting. Sort the plagiarism hash index ascending order by *ploc*;

2) Merging. If two adjacent plagiarism hash index are derived from a same source document and the interval is less than a certain threshold, the two indexes could be merged. Algorithm 3 describes the detail processing of the merging adjacent plagiarism hash index;

3) Marking. According to the position and length information in plagiarism hash index, respectively mark plagiarism text segments in detection and source documents.

Algorithm 3. Merging Adjacent Plagiarism Hash Index

INPUT: plagiarism indexes *P*[ ] of a document, the interval threshold *spacer*

OUTPUT: merged plagiarism indexes *P*[ ]

```
Function MergeFingerIndex( FI[ ], spacer)
P[ ] ← sort( P[ ] )  //sort by p_loc in ascending order
for ( i= P[ ].count -1; i > 0; i-- ) do
//check the adjacent indexes from behind
//if the two adjacent indexes have the same document id
//and the interval is less than threshold, merge the two into one
  if P[i].pid = P[i - 1].pid && P[i].sid = P[i - 1].sid then
    if P[i - 1].ploc + P[i - 1].plen + spacer≥ P[i].ploc && P[i-1].sloc + P[i-1].slen + spacer ≥P[i].sloc then
      P[i - 1].plen= P[i].ploc- P[i - 1].ploc+ P[i].plen;
      // update the length
      P[i - 1].slen= P[i].sloc- P[i - 1].sloc+ P[i].slen;
      // update the length
      delete P[i];
      //merging, update the previous one and delete the after one
    endif
  endif
endfor
return P[ ];
endfunction
```

Figure 1 describes the merge process of adjacent fingerprints with an example. The first 3 indexes have the same *pid* and *sid*, and the interval is less than threshold, so they are combined into one index; the interval between 3rd and 4th indexes is greater than threshold and will not be processed; the 4th and 5th are merged; although interval between 5th and 6th is less than threshold, but as the *sid* is different, skip the merge process. It should be noted that, as the algorithm skips the space and other stop words in the fingerprint extraction process, the *plen* and *slen* is not necessarily exactly the same in one fingerprint index. The merged fingerprint index contains the plagiarized text source and its exact location in the original document, which can be used for marking and positioning.

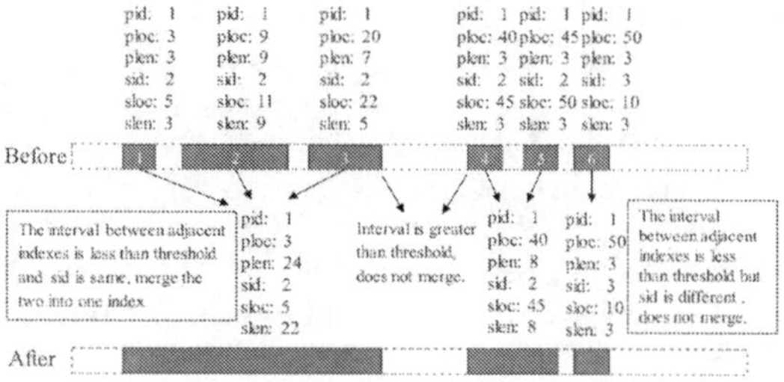

Figure 1. An example of merging neighboring fingerprint indexes

4 Experiment and Analysis

The data used in the experiment are derived from the PAN2013 corpus, there are total 3230 source text documents, and the file size ranges from 1KB to 507KB, in total 13.8MB. There are 1827 documents waiting to be checked, the file size ranges from 1KB to 101KB, in total 15.1MB. We run a PC with Intel E7500 2.93GHz CPU and 2GB physical memory and WIN7 for test platform. The algorithms are implemented by C#.

Winnowing algorithm as a highly efficient and flexible plagiarism detection algorithm, many scholars have confirmed its effectiveness in plagiarism detection [8, 15]. The extended Winnowing algorithm does not change the principle of the algorithm itself, therefore, the precision and efficiency are not affected.

The extended Winnowing algorithm performance is first tested. According to the fingerprint sampling method described above, the 3230 source documents are first *k*-gram hashed, then process the fingerprint sampling, and then get time-consuming according to the average file size. Figure 2 shows the relationship between file size time-consuming. The abscissa represents the text file size (KB), and the ordinate indicates the average time-consuming in milliseconds(ms). In order to preserve the text location information, the stop words removing is processed in the *k*-gram splitting stage, which is the main reason for the decrease of the algorithm efficiency. Before extending, the efficiency is about 270KB/s, and the extended algorithm efficiency is reduced to about 200KB/s, that is, about 200,000 characters per second.

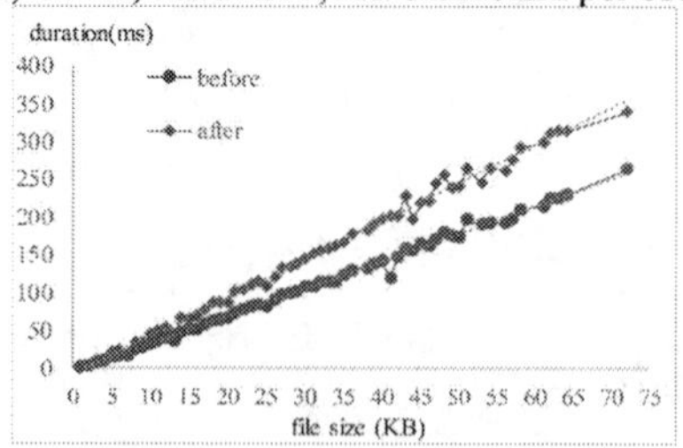

Figure 2. Relation between file size and time-consuming of original/extended finger computing algorithm

Operational efficiency test shown in Figure 3, the figure can be seen, time-consuming and overall file size linear relationship.

The following test is about plagiarism detection algorithm. For the 1827 waiting checked documents, each file is examined to determine whether it is suspected plagiarism from the 3230 source documents, and then collect statistics of average time-consuming for each file. Figure 3 shows the efficiency, the abscissa is the file size (KB), and the vertical axis represents the average time-consuming (ms). It can be found that time-consuming and file size overall show a linear trend. Checking a file of 100KB with all 3230 documents in source takes about 1 second.

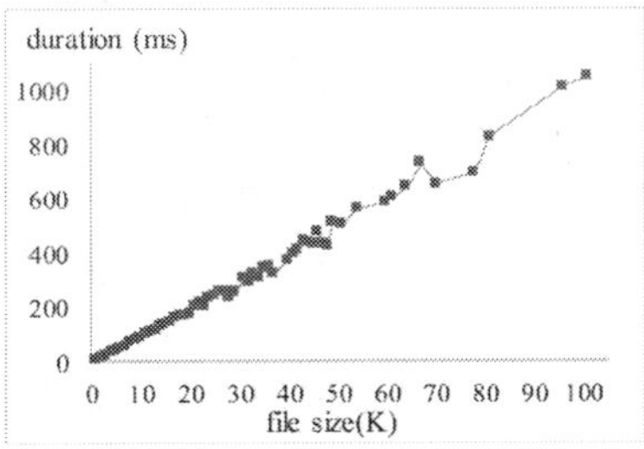

Figure 3. Relation between file size and time-consuming of plagiarism detection

Figure 4 shows the testing result of the file "suspicious-document00119.txt" in PAN2013 corpus. The result is displayed as a web page, and the plagiarism text sections are highlighted. When the mouse hover over the plagiarism text above, the source document will be displayed.

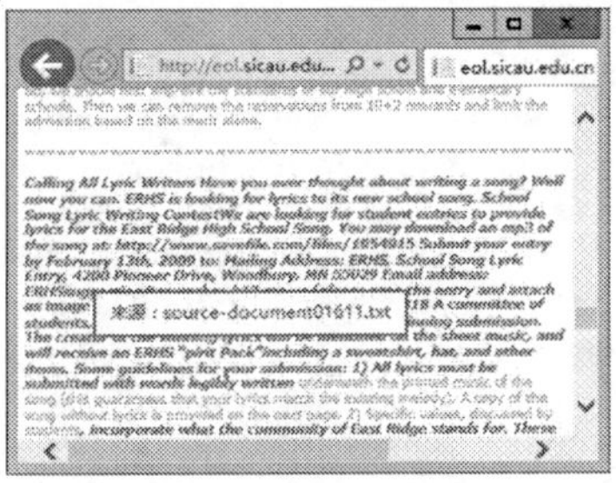

Figure 4. Marking of plagiarism text in html page

5 Conclusion

This paper introduces the basic principles and methods of extending the Winnowing algorithm. Based on the characteristics of the original lightweight, high efficiency, reliability and flexibility of the algorithm, the extended algorithm well reserve the position information of plagiarized text in detecting process, improves the algorithm function and further expand the adaptability and usability of the algorithm. Experiments show that the extended algorithm has no significant effect on the performance of the original algorithm, and the execution efficiency can meet the requirements of small and medium-sized applications in general hardware configuration, and has certain practical value.

The algorithm has been running over 3 years in our learning platform, some algorithms implement and parameters can be further optimized, and the fingerprint index space occupancy remains to be further optimized. In the future work, we will further optimize and improve the algorithm, and constantly enhance the algorithm adaptability, in order to achieve better results.

Acknowledgements

The research is supported by the Sichuan Provincial Department of Education natural science project of "Construction of Big Data Hierarchical Storage Model for Agricultural Internet of Things" (15ZB0017).

References

1. Junpeng Bao, Junyi Shen, Xiaodong Liu, et al. Journal of Software, **14**,1753-1760 (2003)
2. PAN 2015, Overview of the 6th international competition on plagiarism detection, http://www.uni-weimar.de/medien/webis/events/pan-15/pan15-web/index.html
3. Blum S. D. *My word! Plagiarism and college culture* (New York: Cornell University Press, 2009)
4. Martin D F. Journal of Education for Business, **80**,149-152 (2005)
5. Mei Zhong, Liping Zhang, Dongsheng Liu. Computer Engineering and Applications, **47**,215-218 (2011)
6. Yuping Qin, Qiangkui Leng, Xiukun Wang, et al, Computer Engineering, **37**, 193-194 (2011)
7. Huidong Ma, Guohua Liu, Xu Li, et al. Computer Engineering and Science, **29**,63-64(2007)
8. Liang Zhang, Xiumin Liu, Xiujuan Liu. Computer Engineering and Science, **31**,147-149(2009)
9. Wang T, Fan X Z, Liu J. *2008 International Conference on Machine Learning and Cybernetics*, 2574-2579(2008).
10. Karp R M, Rabin M O. IBM Journal of Research and Development, **31**,249-260 (1987)
11. Schleimer S, Wilkerson D S, Aiken A. *2003 ACM SIGMOD International Conference on Management of Data*, 76-85(2003)
12. Zaslavsky A, Bia A, Monostori K. *The 5th European Conference on Research and Advanced Technology for Digital Libraries*, 103-114(2001)
13. Sediyono A, Ku-Mahamud K R. *International Conference on Digital Information Management*, 253 - 259(2008).
14. Wikipedia. Jaccard index, https://en.wikipedia.org/wiki/Jaccard_index
15. Zou D, Long W J, Ling Z. *2010 International Conference on Internet Technology and Applications*, 1-5(2010)
16. Chuanbo Huang, Xiaoqin Hu, Xiaoxu Ma, et al. Journal of Sichuan University (Natural Science Edition), **49**,535-542(2012)

Research of a Scheduling Optimization algorithm based on Hash Adapter

Wenchuan Yang[1,a], Zhen Fu[2] and Wen Zuo[3]

[1]*Beijing University of Posts and Telecommunications;*
[2]*Beijing University of Posts and Telecommunications;*

Abstract. The performance of hash-based Scheduling optimization algorithm for network flow cannot be bounded under the worst-case because of hash conflicts. To make up for the shortage of the above algorithm, a multiple-hash algorithm based on counting Hash Adapter, which stores the digest of flow needed to be adjusted in the Exact Stream Hash Adapter(ESHA) structure, is designed. Compared with the basic hash table, the integrity of the conversation is maintained and the query performance is improved due to the lower probability of conflict. An example is given as a validation of this method and the result data reflect the practical effect.

1 Introduction

The current network security applications, such as intrusion detection system and the firewall technology needs to flow through each IP packet inspection.

With the rapid development of Internet, network bandwidth growth rate far exceeds the rate of growth of processors. According to the Gilder law, communication bandwidth doubles every 6 months, the growth rate of network bandwidth faster 3 times than the computer's performance. On the other hand, the processor will develop into multiple nuclear age calculation, which brings new opportunities to the IP packet processing.

This paper presents an efficient Do Hash selection algorithm. Scheduling optimization algorithm is mainly divided into the message level scheduling and stream scheduling. Message based Scheduling optimization algorithms, such as Round-Robin load scheduling algorithm with low cost, high efficiency characteristics, is not able to keep the stream (flow) IP packets in the sequence.

Flow based Scheduling optimization algorithm is mainly based on hash algorithm. Jaccob[1] proposed an adaptive scheduling optimization algorithm for session, and the work of this paper is based on 2 points: To redefine the concept of session; and to do a depth research on the performance of Hash and algorithm.

2 Optimization Algorithm

Herein we use some acronyms such as DA SA DP SP, which present the destination address, source address, destination port and source port.

Definition 1 a stream

A stream which has the same <DA, SA, DP, SP> packet is consists of a collection data.

Definition 2 total flow

<DA, SA, DP, SP> identifies semi flow and <SA, DA, SP, DP> identifies another semi flow.

Definition 3 session

<DA, SA, DP, SP> identifies the total flow and the dynamic analysis of the new four tuple <DA ', SA ', DP ', SP ' > identifies the total flow.

Hash based Scheduling optimization algorithm which belong to the same 1.5 stream of data packets are distributed to the same processing nuclear, This is not only to maintain the message sequence but also beneficial to use Cache. But the Hash algorithm can not adapt to the change in the height of network flow.

By researching on statistical stream length, flow characteristics of a heavy tail distribution, the Scheduling optimization algorithm based on the Hash need to adjust to different mapping flow core. In addition, the paper analyzed most of the multimedia protocol signaling and data transmission which used in a different port.

Traditional Scheduling optimization algorithms cannot guarantee the multimedia session to map to a core. Therefore, there is need to adjust the map location according to the flow of information dynamically. This paper achieve it by adjusting the total flow identifier and generating corresponding to the summary information on Digest and then saving it to the exact flow matching Hash Adapter (ESBF). For each incoming IP packet, we extracts <DA, SA, DP, SP> logo and the generation of Digest, and then for querying ESBF structure we can do it based on the <DA, SA, DP, SP> and Digest.

By saving the flow identification to the hash tables, it can dynamically specify a full flow to the corresponding processing nuclear.

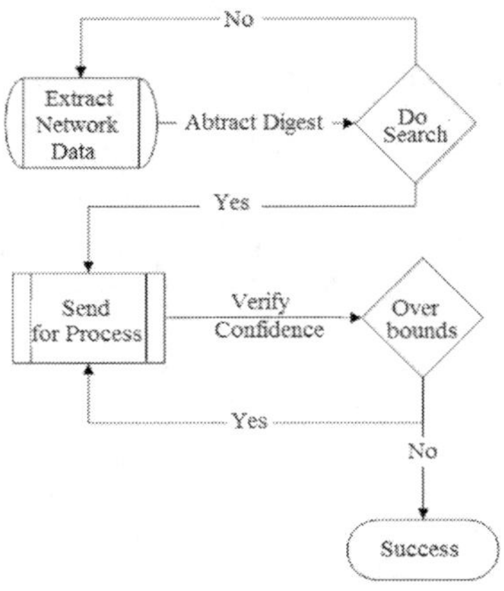

Fig 1. Processing Workflow

Back-end processing send nuclear add rule request (<DA, SA, DP, SP>, ID) according to the processed information, the <DA, SA, DP, SP> identification stream is sent to the designated processing nuclear ID.

3 Full Flow Digest Generation Algorithm

As shown in Figure 1, the majority of Miss rule packets directly mapped the Digest modulus to each core, Digest algorithm randomness and the performance of the Scheduling optimization algorithm has a strong effect.

Wilsley[3] proved that the bit between XOR and displacement operation can improve the hash values of the random character, and it has a very good performance, so this paper uses the XOR and shift to realize the generation of Digest.

Let bdip present DA 16 bit, adip present DP 16 bit, bsip present SA 16 bit, asip present 16 SP 16 bit.

Algorithm use OR (|), XOR (a), right (> >) and left (< <) operation. And hash1, hash2 use 16 bit unsigned integer. N for processing nuclear number.

Digest is a full flow <DA, SA, DP, SP> summary information. Algorithm DIGEST_HASH as following:

```
DIGEST_HASH(<DA , SA , DP , SP>){
    hash1 =asip<<3|asip>>(16-3);
    hash2 =bsip<<3|bsip>>(16-3);
    hash =hash1∧hash2∧dport;
    hash1 =adip<<3|adip>>(16-3);
    hash2 =bdip<<3|bdip>>(16-3);
    digest=hash1∧hash2∧sport;
    return digest;
}
```

Through the DIGEST_HASH algorithm, which belongs to the same total flow will generate the same Digest and map to the same core, thus it preserve the integrity of the conversation.

Table 1 to 4 based on Hash function operands are compared

Table 1. Hash function operands and its evaluative info

Network	Evaluative info	Hash optimzer factor
low	worst	(0,0,0,0.25)
low	worse	(0.2,0.3,0.3,0.4)
low	bad	(0.25,0.35,0.45,0.6)
medium	general	(0.3,0.5,0.5,0.7)
high	good	(0.5,0.65,0.75,0.8)
high	better	(0.7,0.8,0.8,1)
high	best	(0.7,1,1,1)

4 Exact Match of the Hash Adapter Algorithm

Adjusting mapping to different core needs to realize the precise flow matching. It can use basic Hash table to realize the precise flow matching, but due to a conflict exists, it cannot guarantee worst case performance.

Next serveral section are designed to support the Hash Adapter algorithm ESBF of accurate flow matching, it can satisfy the high-speed link to high speed flow classification requirements, and ensure the low collision probability.

5 Hash Adapter algorithm

First we introduced the Hash Adapter[4] (Hash Adapter, BF), which give a global U, BF a n bit vector B[i] ($1<i<n$) that set S, |S|=m, initialization time for all i, $B[i]=0(1<i<n)$.

The filter also needs to introduce k independent hash functions $h_1, h_2, \ldots h_k$,each function has the range for {1,2, ... , n}. hash function elements use the U as input, the elements in the U uniformly mapped to the range of function space.

For each element $h_x \in S$, set the $B[h_i(x)]=1$ (the same location may be repeatedly placed 1); thus, Hash Adapter can indicate the collection S.

Query for the elements of Y, if for any I ($1<i<k$), $h_i(y)=1, y \in S$, otherwise $y \notin S$.

From the above description it can be seen that for an element of Y, if $y \in S$, then return true conclusion.

But if $y \notin S$, it may also return a true conclusion, namely the false positive cases.

In the M members are Hash to the Hash Adapter, the one is for 0's probability.

$$p=(1-\frac{1}{n})^{km} \approx e^{-km/n} \quad (1)$$

False positive probability for

$$f=(1-(1-\frac{1}{n})^{km})^k \approx (1-e^{-km/n})^k=(1-p)^k \quad (2)$$

When m and n are a constant, we get the derivative for (2) as

$$f_{\min}=\left(\frac{1}{2}\right)^k \quad k=\lfloor \ln 2(n/m) \rfloor \quad (3)$$

Hash Adapter will get the lowest false positive rate at this time.

6 ESBF structure

Hash Adapter based on bit vector does not support elements removed, so the Increment Hash Adapter (Increment Hash Adapter, CBF) appeared later.

CBF standard BF digit group expansion for a small counter (Counter) each, if it inserts an element to the corresponding K (k is the Hash function a number) ,counter value plus 1, Counter value minus 1 if it deletes elements to the corresponding K.

CBF gives BF a delete operation through multiple occupancy of several times the storage cost. In this section the design of the ESBF algorithm is based on CBF, it use CBF multiple Hash functions to ensure the algorithm has lower conflict probability[5], its structure is shown in figure 2.

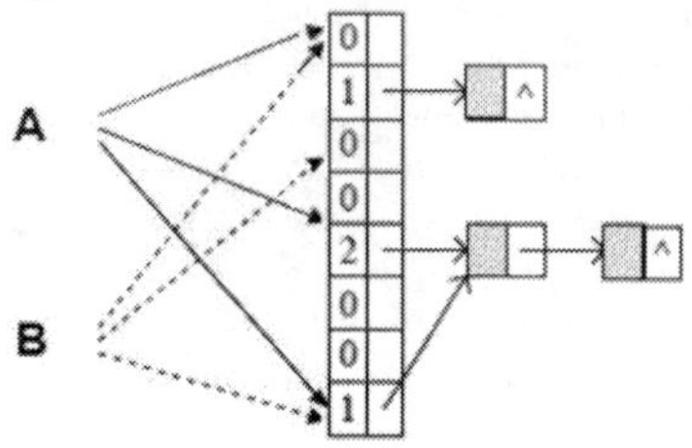

Fig 2. ESBF data structure

$h_i(x)$ is for k independent Hash function, the data structure in the CBF change into a chain list header node, the node is defined as follows:

```
Class Linknode{ //Linked list node
unsigned short digest; //Full flow Abstract
int id; // Specified number of processing cores
Linknode next;};
Class Linkhead { //Chain Header node
unsigned int counter; //counter
Linknode next;};
```

we take CBF as the vector length of 65536, and the CBF of each dimension is LinkHead structure. Input algorithm x=<DA,SA,DP,SP>.

The insertion algorithm code is as follows

Procedure Insertion Algorithm Insertelem(x, id)

```
{ Digest ← DIGEST_HASH(x)
Create Linked list node and assign digest & id
for i=Lm-1 downto 1 do{
if(LHEAD(L1,...,Lm).sup[i]<=sup(LHEAD(L1,...,Lm))
and LHEAD(L1,...,Lm).conf[i]>= min_α{
COUNTER[++length]=item(i);
output COUNTER and LHEAD(L1,...,Lm).count[i]/n;
build LHEAD(L1,...,Lm,i) on LHEAD(L1,...,Lm);
If(there is an linked headin LHEAD(L1,...,Lm,i))
add(LHEAD(L1,...,Lm,i)); }
length--;}
```

Digest which was generated by Insertion algorithm were inserted into the K list. In order to save space, if the nodes are added to a linked list tail, K list can share a single linked list node.

7 ESBF Time Complexity Analysis

Because the algorithm memory access time is longer, so here it used the memory access times as its main operation to estimate the time complexity of algorithm.

The first analysis algorithm of query time complexity, for a total of MK into ESBF, average each counter value is mk/n, the query is always traverse the K (hash function number) counter in the smallest list corresponding to the mk/n item.

Therefore, the average time complexity is mk/n, and for optimization of the Hash Adapter $k=\lfloor \ln 2(n/m) \rfloor$, so the time complexity is O(k). Similarly, add and delete elements operate time complexity is O(k).

From the theoretical analysis of ESBF and basic hash table the average chain length is shown as follows in the same probability of cases.

For the basic hash table, length L is i probability when hit after needs to query the list

$$P(L=i \mid L>0)=\frac{P(L=0,L>0)}{P(L>0)}=\frac{\binom{m}{i}\left(\frac{1}{n}\right)^{i}\left(1-\frac{1}{n}\right)^{m-i}}{1-\left(1-\frac{1}{n}\right)^{m}} \tag{4}$$

For ESBF, with K Hash function, by the above analysis, the length L for i probability when hit after needs to query the is equivalent to finding the minimum value of K counters for the I probability $P(L_{smallest}=i)$.

$P(L=i)$ is a counter in a value for the i probability, $P(L>i)$ is K counter value which is greater than the probability of i. It can be:

$$P(L=i)=\binom{mk-k}{i-1}\left(\frac{1}{n}\right)^{i-1}\left(1-\frac{1}{n}\right)^{[(mk-k)-(i-1)]} \tag{5}$$

$$P(L>i)=1-\sum_{h=1}^{i}P(L=h) \tag{6}$$

$$P(L_{smallest}=i)=\sum_{j=1}^{k}\left[\binom{k}{j}\left(P(L=i)^{j}\times P(L>i)^{(k-j)}\right)\right] \tag{7}$$

Data in Table 2 and 3 show the result with or without Optimzer. In table 2 the n=65 536, m=5 000, k=5 calculated the 2 list length probability distribution.From table 3 we can find, ESBF chain lengths of 2 and 3 probability is much smaller than the underlying hash table hash table.

The basic chain length of 2 probability is 3.67%, ESBF is 0.32%, the latter as 1/11 less than; List length was 3 and the probability of the basic hash table is 0.09%, and ESBF 0.Thus, ESBF conflict probability is much lower than the underlying hash table, which ensure that the ESBF query performance.

Table 2. Probability distribution of chain length for Normal Hash

Length for	Probability				
	0	0	0	0	1
2	0	1	0	0	0
3	1	0	0	0	0
4	0	0	0	0	1

Table 3. Probability distribution of chain length for Hash with Optimizer

Length for	Probability				
	0.005	0.01	0.02	0.03	0.0
2	1	0	0	0	0
3	0	0	1	0	0

8 Experiments

Packet classification performance testing tools ClassBench simulation meet the heavy tail distribution flow accord with the actual traffic characteristics. Flow in the flow is assumed according to the back-end processing need or according to the systems of various nuclear load conditions need to be forwarded to the designated processing nucleus of the flow.

The flow of Digest and specify the processing of nuclear ID hash table and inserted into the basic structure of ESBF. on the basic of hash table and ESBF structure list length statistics, Table 4 in m=65 536, k=3 conditions,We get comparison table based on basic hash table and ESBF list length statistical. Among them, n is to simulate the resulting stream number, each of which is divided into 2 rows. The length of statistical data is shown as follows which was based on the behavior of basic hash table list and behavior under ESBF list length statistics

Table 4. Statistc for Chain length for various data

Chain	Number for Data						
	1000	2000	3000	4000	5000	6000	7000
1	966	1920	2855	3702	4621	5531	6134
2	15	32	55	121	231	311	427
3	0	0	3	5	7	18	24
4	0	0	0	0	3	0	3

The evaluation for complaint variables must be compatible, and it should fit for both quantitative and qualitative information. So the quantitative information must be properly transformed into a dimensionless value before expressed as the fuzzy numbers.

Because of experimental data is used to meet the heavy tail distribution of flow, which exist in the same Baotou, so the table in the same row list length statistics may be smaller than the test data set n. From the watch 2 in can see, 1 for n 000~4 000, ESBF no length is 3, and the ratio of length 2 is far less than the underlying hash table. When n is 5000, ESBF is 3 of the length ratio of only basic hash table 1/2. In the case of small n, ESBF list length was significantly shortened basic hash, and worst case time complexity is smaller than the underlying hash table.

As n is greater than 4000, although the two worst case time complexity equivalent, but ESBF algorithm meet the worst case that probabilities is below the basic hash table. So ESBF algorithm performance is better than the basic query hash table.

But it should be noted that, because ESBF uses multiple Hash functions, it will be the same as a key value is mapped to the K position, which makes the ESBF the load factor become the basic Hash table K times, on the other hand it led to conflict probability.

This section can be obtained by experiments, the load factor is lower, ESBF effectively specify the full stream which sent to the corresponding processing nuclear according to the system processing nuclear load condition and requirement of application. It meets the growing IP packet processing applications.

Compared to the underlying hash table, the algorithm for the conflict has better probability constraints, the Scheduling optimization algorithm has higher performance. Because of its simple and efficient, how to reduce the conflict has yet to be further studied and solved.

9 Conclusions

According to the characteristics of network streaming media application protocol and network security application needs, this paper put forward load balance based on CBF algorithm, this algorithm is mainly composed of a full flow abstract algorithm and ESBF algorithm. It Focuses on the research of Scheduling optimization algorithm based on Hash performance problems, and committe to reducing what would function conflict brought negative effect for the entire algorithm performance, and from the theoretical and experimental results it verify the algorithm's advantages.

References

1. G. Jaccob, A. C. Kay, S. J. Spencer, Loving those who justify inequality: The effects of system threat on attraction to women who embody benevolent sexist ideals. Psychological Science, 19, pp.**20-21**, (2008).
2. S. Levin, Intergroup biases as a function of social dominance orientation, ingroup status, and ingroup identification. Unpublished master's thesis, University of California, Los Angeles,pp.**121-127**,(1992).
3. S. Wilsley, C. M. Federico, J. Sidanius,J. L. Rabinowitz, Social dominance orientation and intergroup bias: The legitimation of favoritism for high-status groups. Personality and Social Psychology bulletin, 28,pp.**144-157**, (2002).
4. C. Oishi, F. Yoshida, Black sheep effect and ingroup favoritism in social identity perspective.Shinrigaku kenkyu, 73, pp.**405-411**, (2002).
5. J. L. Rabinowitz, Go with the flow or fight the power The interactive effects of social dominance orientation and perceived injustice on support for the status quo. Political Psychology, 20, pp.**1-24**,(1999).
6. K. J. Reynolds, J. C. Turner, S. A. Haslam, M. K. Ryan, B. Bizumic, E. Subasic, Does personality explain in-group identification and discrimination Evidence from the minimal group paradigm. British Journal of Social Psychology, 46, pp.**517-539**, (2007).

 DOI: 10.1051/matecconf/201712802021

Large Scale Face Data Purification based on Correlation Function and Multi-Phase Grouping

Xiangxiang Zhang[1], Zhijun Fang[1,a], Zhenghao Xi[1] and Xiaoshuang Liu[1]

[1]*School of Electronic and Electrical Engineering, Shanghai University of Engineering Science*

Abstract. Recent advances in deep learning technologies enable high performance artificial intelligence, which is an equivalence of human capability or higher for various application. However, deep learning is highly resorted to the large scale training data, which typically contains large number of outlier samples that are difficult to remove. In this paper, we proposed a face image purifying algorithm, which combines the correlation function of deep features with multi-phase grouping technique. A correlation function was proposed to determine the principal class by measuring the similarities between all different samples. The principal class was further used as a prior for the multi-phase grouping algorithm to purify the face data by multiple thresholds. The experimental results demonstrate that the proposed algorithm has significant improvement than the primitive cluster algorithm, such as K-Means.

1 Introduction

Artificial intelligence and machine vision are the frontier of modern industrial and information science, and face recognition technology is one of the earliest implementations of machine vision. Recently, with the development of artificial intelligence in the dynamic face recognition and facial portrait differentiation technology, the face recognition technology has found a new research direction again [2-3]. Furthermore, combining the traditional face recognition technology with the large data technology, training the face features with a large number of samples, and improving the face recognition at the performance has been an issue problem in the field of machine vision research.

However, there are lots of non-target images in the collected face training samples. We define the non-target images in the same kind of face images as the noisy samples, which have the similar features with the target images. The sample noise has seriously affects the training results. At present, how to remove the sample noise in a large number of training samples has become a new focus of face recognition technology [4].

Many recent researchers proposed some approaches for this problem: Fitzgibbon and Zisserman [5] proposed a sample purification method based on Joint Manifold Distance (JMD), this method treats a group of face data as a subspace, and performs face clustering by calculating JMD. Wu B et al. [6] established a clustering model using the probabilistic constraint conditions of the hidden Markov random field, they classified all face sample images into K disjoint clusters, and the K should be given in advance. Because they cannot obtain the accurate K value in advance, the results are very unstable. In [7], Zhang et al. clustered the shape of the face to seven classes. Then, they continue to subdivide the smaller classes according to the facial features extracted by the ASM method. This method relies on the facial contour, but the facial expression is varied, and the influence of light, occlusion and other factors, the deep feature of human face is not easy to extract. Therefore, the method has some limitations.

In addition, some researches combine intelligent algorithm with clustering method. [8] first extracted the deep characterization features of face images using convolution neural network (CNN) algorithm, then they combined the feature with the clustering method (e.g. K-MEANS and hierarchical clustering method) to achieve clustered the face images. However, the problem of this method is similar with [6], the K-MEANS needs to estimate the number of clusters in advance, and the clustering results are more sensitive to the initial values. The hierarchical clustering with different types of feature similarity can classify the data into different clusters, but it cannot be re-classified, the result of cluster purification is not satisfactory. Even so, compared with the method only using clustering algorithm, the methods combined intelligent algorithm and clustering algorithm improves the accuracy and efficiency of sample purification to a certain extent.

In this paper, we proposed an algorithm that combines the correlation function of deep features with multi-phase grouping technique to solve the problems of sample purification. Firstly, we use the VGG Face [1] network to extract the high-level feature information of face images, and we define the correlation function used to compute the principal class. Then, we choose the appropriate multiple thresholds to divide the data into

[a] Corresponding author: zjfang@sues.edu.cn

groups. Finally, we remove the noisy data and get the purification of the sample images by filtering noisy samples in each group.

The remainder of the paper is organized as follows. Section 2 describes feature extraction of face images and similarity measure. The proposed face image purifying algorithm is introduced in detail in section 3, which includes definition of the correlation function、analysis of principal class、multi-phase grouping and setting thresholds. Section 4 shows the experimental results.

2 Face Feature Extraction

2.1 Feature Extraction

CNN is an efficient intelligent algorithm, which has been developed rapidly recent years. Because of its deep structure, strong learning ability and hierarchical nonlinear mapping, CNN has been widely used in facial feature extraction [1-3], and it becomes the main method of face recognition [9]. In this paper, we establish the face feature extraction network by the CNN of VGG FACE [1], and the CNN with 13 convolution layers, each convolution layer contains a linear operator, which followed by one or more nonlinear operator, such as ReLU. The last three blocks are fully connected layers (FC). This paper uses the fc7 FC layer to extract the face image features, [1] shows that the face recognition accuracy rate is 97% using this method in the Youtube Faces Dataset. So, we combine it with our proposed face image purification algorithm to refine the face data.

2.2 Similarity measure

We use the CNN method to extract high-level feature $\mathbf{X}=\{\mathbf{x}_1,\mathbf{x}_2,...,\mathbf{x}_j,...,\mathbf{x}_n\}$, where, $\mathbf{x}_j$ is the feature vector of the jth image sample. $j=1,2,3,...,n$. Then the distance between any two samples can be expressed as $dist(\mathrm{x}_i, \mathrm{x}_j)$, and the similarity between them is

$$eachsim(\mathbf{x}_i,\mathbf{x}_j)=1-dist(\mathbf{x}_i,\mathbf{x}_j) \quad (1)$$

where, $dist(\mathbf{x}_i,\mathbf{x}_j)$ is the Euclidean distance after $\mathbf{x}_i,\mathbf{x}_j$ are normalized.

3 Face image purifying algorithm

3.1 Defining the correlation function

Let the face data set as $\boldsymbol{R}=\{c_1,c_2,c_3,...,c_i,...,c_m\}$, where, c_i is the image samples of the ith category, $i=1,2,3,...,m$. The number of the images in c_i is a_i, $i=1,2,3,...,m$. The proportion of the ith category image in the face data set is

$$P(c_i)=a_i/\sum_{k=1}^{m}a_k \quad (2)$$

When $P(c_i)$ is the maximum, c_i is the target sample, and the other category images are taken as noisy samples.

In order to automatically and unsupervised find the face image samples, which distributed densely in the current data set, we define the correlation function, which is the accumulation of similarity of each sample with the other samples, the correlation function for any $\mathbf{x}_i$ is

$$Correlation(\mathbf{x}_i)=\sum_{j=1}^{n-1}eachsim(\mathbf{x}_i,\mathbf{x}_j) \quad (3)$$

where, $i\neq j$, $eachsim(\mathbf{x}_i,\mathbf{x}_j)$ is the similarity between the two feature vector x_i and x_j.

The data can be divided into several different classes by pre-setting the number of clusters, but this method may cause the data which in a same class to be divided into several categories, or be classified into other cluster so that they become noise. Once the number of clusters is pre-determined, the data samples of the misclassified categories will not be able to be back. This will affect the effect of data purification. The correlation function can reflect correlation of each sample in the global situation, and can estimate principal class among the sample classes. This avoids splitting the same samples into other classes, reduces the misclassification probability of the samples.

3.2 Analysis of principal class

Let $\mathbf{S}=\{\mathbf{f}_1,\mathbf{f}_2,...,\mathbf{f}_i,...,\mathbf{f}_N\}$, $1\le i\le N$ as the set of feature vectors for training samples set, where, $\mathbf{f}_i$ is the feature vector of the ith face image in training samples, N is the number of the samples in the training samples set. We get the similarity $eachsim(\mathbf{f}_i,\mathbf{f}_j)$ of any two different training feature vectors by Eq. (1), where $i\neq j$. The correlation function $Correlation(\mathbf{f}_i)$ of each training feature vector by Eq. (3), and we can get the main component sample by maximizing the $Destin(\mathbf{f}_i)$ as follows

$$\mathbf{f}_{\max}=Max\{Correlation(\mathbf{f}_i)\} \quad (4)$$

where, $\mathbf{f}_{\max}$ is the training feature vector of face images and the target sample vector when the correlation function is maximized.

3.3 Multi-phase grouping

In the dataset $\boldsymbol{R}$, we classify the main component samples by $\mathbf{f}_{\max}$, and let the classified main component samples set be $\boldsymbol{A}$, the rest of the samples will belong to set $\boldsymbol{B}$, $\boldsymbol{R}=\boldsymbol{A}+\boldsymbol{B}$, $\boldsymbol{A}$ and $\boldsymbol{B}$ both are the proper subsets of the data set.

Let the threshold as T_1, we compare the similarity between $\mathbf{x}_i$ and $\mathbf{f}_{\max}$ by Eq. (1), if the similarity is greater than T_1, then the sample will belong to $\boldsymbol{A}$, if not, it will belong to $\boldsymbol{B}$, which can be expressed as

 DOI: 10.1051/matecconf/201712802021

$$eachsim(\mathbf{x}_i, \mathbf{f}_{max}) = \begin{cases} \geq T_1, \mathbf{x}_i \in \boldsymbol{A} \\ < T_1, \mathbf{x}_i \in \boldsymbol{B} \end{cases} \quad (5)$$

We initially purify samples of the principal class by T_1, and divide the $\boldsymbol{R}$ into $\boldsymbol{A} = \{\mathbf{f}_{A_1}, \mathbf{f}_{A_2}, \mathbf{f}_{A_3}, ..., \mathbf{f}_{A_i}, ..., \mathbf{f}_{A_G}\}$, and $\boldsymbol{B} = \{\mathbf{f}_{B_1}, \mathbf{f}_{B_2}, \mathbf{f}_{B_3}, ..., \mathbf{f}_{B_j}, ..., \mathbf{f}_{B_D}\}$, and $\boldsymbol{A}$ is the principal class and $\boldsymbol{B}$ is the group to be filtered, where $\mathbf{f}_{A_i}$ $1 \leq i \leq G$ is the feature vectors which are divided into the principal group of $\boldsymbol{A}$, and f_{B_j} $1 \leq j \leq D$ is the feature vectors which are divided into the group to be filtered of $\boldsymbol{B}$, $G + D = N$. However, the face change or an unclear image will lead to diversification of face images, which makes it be more difficult to comprehensively characterize multiple principal samples. In this paper, we use the centroid of the feature vectors, and the strict thresholds to solve the problem of multi-features fusion when deciding whether each sample is a main component target sample. Let $\mathbf{O}_1$ be the centroid of $\boldsymbol{A}$, then, $\mathbf{O}_1$ can be expressed as

$$\mathbf{O}_1 = \frac{1}{G}\sum_{i=1}^{G}\mathbf{f}_{A_i} \quad (6)$$

To minimize the loss of the number of samples of principal class as much as possible, we check for the principal sample images that may be left in the set $\boldsymbol{B}$, and we purify the $\boldsymbol{B}$ group again. Let the threshold as $T_2 T_3$, then we compare $\mathbf{O}_1$ with each of feature vectors in the set $\boldsymbol{B}$, and filter the target samples, which can be expressed as follows

$$eachsim(\mathbf{O}_1, \mathbf{f}_{B_j}) = \begin{cases} \geq T_2, \mathbf{f}_{B_j} \in A \\ < T_2, \mathbf{f}_{B_j} \in B \end{cases} \quad (7)$$

Let the set of the second purifying principal class be $\mathbf{A}' = \{\mathbf{f}_{A'_1}, \mathbf{f}_{A'_2}, \mathbf{f}_{A'_3}, ..., \mathbf{f}_{A'_i} ..., \mathbf{f}_{A'_E}\}$, $1 \leq i \leq E, G \leq E \leq N$. We purify the group of principal class and update the centroid to $\mathbf{O}_2$. Then, let the threshold as T_3, the principal class will be purified as follows

$$eachsim(\mathbf{O}_2, \mathbf{f}_{A'_i}) = \begin{cases} \geq T_3, \mathbf{f}_{A'_i} \in A' \\ < T_3, \mathbf{f}_{A'_i} \in B \end{cases} \quad (8)$$

We divide the samples into different groups by the different thresholds to be purified, and classify the samples of principal class from each group, so that the purity of the samples is improved continuously. The multi-phase grouping does not only extend the interclass distance, but also minimizes distance within the class. The flowchart of the proposed algorithm is shown in Figure 1.

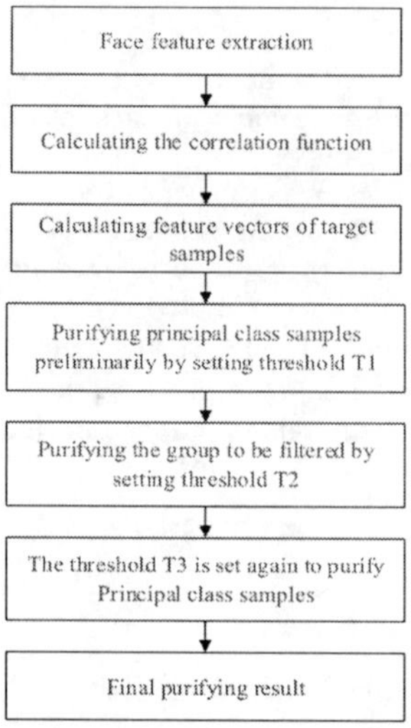

Figure 1. Flowchart of our face purifying algorithm.

3.4 Thresholds setting

Our thresholds can strictly filter the noisy data, and prevent the noisy data from contaminating the target samples. Figure 2 shows the distribution of similarity between each two samples. The horizontal axis represents the similarity values, and the vertical axis represents the number of samples. When the threshold is below 0.6, the similarities of samples are low, this part represents most of the noisy data. When the threshold is above 0.7, the similarities of samples are high, this part represents target samples. In this paper, we get the threshold between 0.7 and 0.8 by the experience.

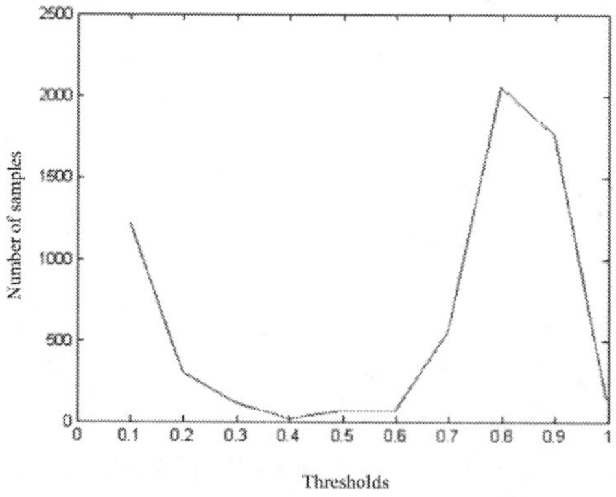

Figure 2. The distribution of similarity between each two samples.

4 Experimental results and analysis

The effect of the proposed algorithm is evaluated using precision and recall of [9]. The precision and recall of class i in the jth cluster are defined as follows

$$P = precision(i, j) = N_{ij} / N_i \quad (9)$$

$$R = recall(i,j) = N_{ij} / N_j \quad (10)$$

where, N_{ij} is the number of class i in the jth cluster, N_j is the number of the samples, N_i is the number of target samples in class i, the F-measure of the class i is

$$F(i) = 2PR/(P+R) \quad (11)$$

The experimental database was selected from the opened face data MS-Celeb-1M [10], which is provided by Microsoft Research Institute and includes images of 1,000,000 celebrities. In our experiment, we randomly select 10,000 face images of the data.

In our experiment, we keep the T_1 unchanged, adjust T_2 and T_3 to obtain the satisfactory purification results. Figure.3 shows the F-measure results using different thresholds.

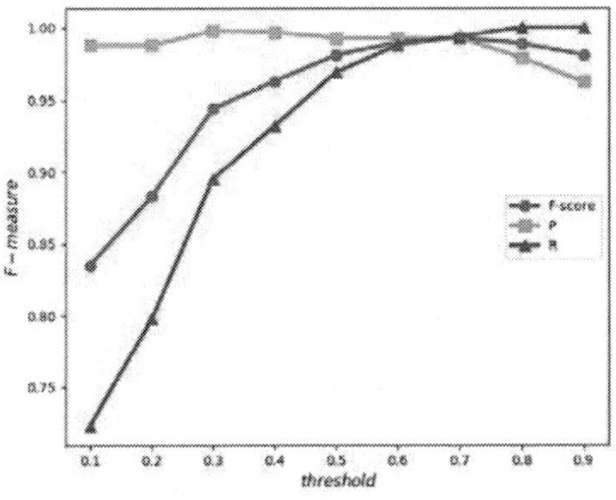

Figure 3. The F-measure results using different thresholds

The F-score reflects the result of the face images purification, recall reflects the purity of the data, and precision reflects the number of target samples loss. However, the result of the purification is the best when the threshold is increased to about 0.7.

We select part of the samples whose similarities are so high to compare with K-MEANS method, and to calculate recall rate of principal samples, the result is shown in Figure.4.

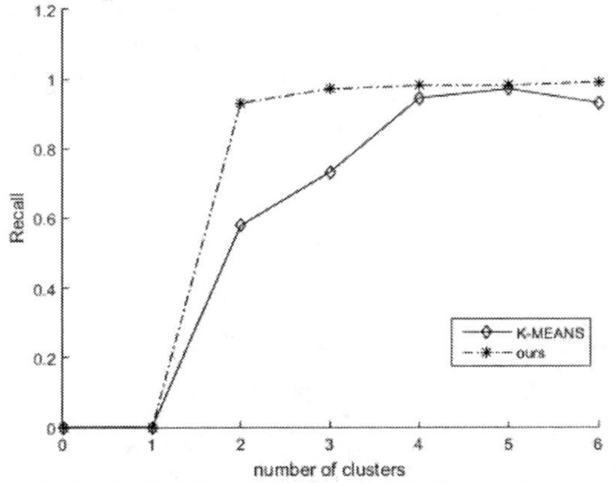

Figure 4. Recall rate of different clustering results

5 Conclusion

Data purification is an important method for big data analysis and application. To reduce the data loss and purify face images as much as possible, we proposed a simple yet effective purification algorithm for face data. We used this novel algorithm to purify the target face samples in big data samples by selecting the appropriate thresholds. The experiment results indicate that the proposed algorithm is helpful for improving the rates of precision and recall. The highlights of this paper are that the proposed algorithm is more accurate and stable than traditional clustering algorithm.

References

1. Parkhi O M, Vedaldi A, Zisserman A. Deep Face Recognition[C]// British Machine Vision Conference. 2015:41.1-41.12.
2. Taigman Y, Yang M, Ranzato M, et al. DeepFace: Closing the Gap to Human-Level Performance in Face Verification[C]// Computer Vision and Pattern Recognition. IEEE, 2014:1701-1708.
3. Schroff F, Kalenichenko D, Philbin J. FaceNet: A Unified Embedding for Face Recognition and Clustering[C]// Computer Vision and Pattern Recognition. IEEE, 2015:815-823.
4. Frénay B, Verleysen M. Classification in the presence of label noise: a survey[J]. IEEE Transactions on Neural Networks & Learning Systems, 2014, 25(5):845-869.
5. Fitzgibbon A W, Zisserman A. Joint manifold distance: a new approach to appearance based clustering[A].Fitzgibbon A W. IEEE Conference on Computer Vision and Pattern Recognition[C]. Madison: IEEE, 2003.
6. Wu B, Zhang Y, Hu B G, et al. Constrained Clustering and Its Application to Face Clustering in Videos[C]// IEEE Conference on Computer Vision and Pattern Recognition. IEEE Computer Society, 2013:3507-3514.
7. Zhang S C, Fang B, Liang Y Z, et al. A face clustering method based on facial shape information[C]// International Conference on Wavelet Analysis and Pattern Recognition. IEEE, 2011.
8. Hu Y, Dong Y. Face clustering using high-level feature based on deep learning[J]. 2015.
9. STEINBACH M, KARYPIS G, KUMAR V. A comparison of document clustering techniques[C] / /Proc of KDD-2000 Workshop on Text Mining. 2000.
10. Guo Y, Zhang L, Hu Y, et al. MS-Celeb-1M: A Dataset and Benchmark for Large-Scale Face Recognition[C]// European Conference on Computer Vision. Springer, Cham, 2016:87-102.

MATEC Web of Conferences **128**, 02022 (2017) DOI: 10.1051/matecconf/201712802022
EITCE 2017

Discrete Teaching–learning-based optimization Algorithm for Traveling Salesman Problems

Lehui Wu, Feng Zou[a], Debao Chen
School of Physics and Electronic Information, HuaiBei Normal University, Huaibei, 235000, China

Abstract. In this paper, a discrete variant of TLBO (DTLBO) is proposed for solving the traveling salesman problem (TSP). In the proposed method, an effective learner representation scheme is redefined based on the characteristics of TSP problem. Moreover, all learners are randomly divided into several sub-swarms with equal amounts of learners so as to increase the diversity of population and reduce the probability of being trapped in local optimum. In each sub-swarm, the new positions of learners in the teaching phase and the learning phase are generated by the crossover operation, the legality detection and mutation operation, and then the offspring learners are determined based on greedy selection. Finally, to verify the performance of the proposed algorithm, benchmark TSP problems are examined and the results indicate that DTLBO is effective compared with other algorithms used for TSP problems.

1 Introduction

The traveling salesman problem (TSP) is the most used and famous optimization problem within the kind of combinatorial optimizations [1]. The main aim of TSP is to obtain the shortest tour that starts from one city and visits each of the other cities once before returning to the starting city. This is one of the most fundamental NP-complete optimization problems [2]. Since the TSP problem belongs to the class of NP complete problems, its solution grows exponentially with the increase in distribution points. Thus, exact algorithms [3-4] are not capable of solving problems with large dimensions. On the other hand, heuristics [5-6] are thought to be more preferable and efficient for a complex TSP problem and have become very popular with researchers.

Although heuristic methods can be used to solve complex TSP problems, they are easy to be trapped into local optimum and cannot obtain the optimum solution. As a result, a new kind of optimization algorithms named meta-heuristics has been proposed in recent years and these relevant meta-heuristics have been proposed to solve complex problems [7-8]. In contrast to heuristic algorithms, meta-heuristic algorithms make use of the randomization of the search space, effectively explore and exploit some promising solution regions. Hence, meta-heuristic algorithms have many advantages of implementation simplicity, adaptability, flexibility and robustness, and the algorithms can obtain a more better or near-optimal solution of higher quality in relatively low time. Here many meta-heuristic algorithms have been developed to solve complex TSP problems [9-10].

Recently, a meta-heuristic algorithm called Teaching–learning-based optimization algorithm (TLBO) has been developed [11]. TLBO and its variants have shown significant performance for combinatorial optimization problems [12, 13]. In this paper, we present a new discrete version of TLBO to solve TSP problems. In the proposed method, the learner representation scheme is redefined based on the characteristics of TSP problem, and the updating rules for learners are also redesigned. Finally, to verify that our proposed DTLBO algorithm is a promising method, 7 different TSP problems are examined. The results indicate that DTLBO is effective compared with other algorithms used for TSP problems.

[a] Corresponding author: Feng Zou zfemail@163.com

2 Teaching–learning-based optimization

Teaching–learning-based optimization algorithm (TLBO) is a population-based optimization algorithm inspired from the philosophy of teaching and learning. The learners correspond to the individuals of evolutionary algorithms. The teacher is the learner with the best fitness and she/he can share her/his knowledge to all the learners, thus enhancing the average grade of the class in teaching phase. Each learner also learns knowledge from another randomly selected learner in the class, thus enhancing the average grade of the class in learning phase.

2.1 Learner initialization

In the initial phase, all learners in the class are randomly initialized. The i-th learner $X_i = (x_{i1}, x_{i2}, \cdots, x_{id})$ in the class can be generated as follows.

$$X_i = X_i^{min} + rand \cdot (X_i^{max} - X_i^{min}) \quad (1)$$

where X_i^{min} and X_i^{max} are the lower and upper bounds of the control variables respectively, $rand$ is a random vector within the range [0, 1].

 DOI: 10.1051/matecconf/201712802022

2.2 Teaching phase

During the teaching phase, the task of learning is to increase the mean marks of the class. In this phase, all learners update their positions according to the difference between the current teacher and the mean position of the class. The updating formula of the i-th learner X_i in the class is expressed as follows.

$$newX_i = X_i + r g(Teacher - TF g Mean) \tag{2}$$

where, $newX_i$ is the new positions of the i-th learner X_i, $Teacher$ is the best learner of the class and $Mean = \frac{1}{NP}\sum_{i=1}^{NP} X_i$ is the mean position of the class. $TF = round[1 + rand(0,1)]$ is a teaching factor that decides the value of mean to be changed, the typical value of it is either 1 or 2. r is a random number in the range [0, 1].

2.3 Learning phase

Learners also can increase their knowledge by means of group discussions, presentations, formal communications, and so on. In this phase, each learner update their positions learns something new if the other learner has more knowledge than him or her. The updating formula of the i-th learner X_i in the class is expressed as follows.

$$newX_i = \begin{cases} X_i + r□(X_i - X_k) & if\ f(X_i) < f(X_k) \\ X_i + r□(X_k - X_i) & otherwise \end{cases} \tag{3}$$

where, $newX_i$ is the new positions of the i-th learner X_i, X_k is a randomly selected learner from the class, r is a random vector in the range [0, 1], $f(X_i)$ and $f(X_k)$ is the fitness value of the learner X_i and X_k, respectively.

After the new candidate learner has been generated in the teaching and learning phases, the greedy selection is executed to determine the offspring learners. That is, if the value $f(newX_i)$ is better than the value $f(X_i)$, then replace X_i with $newX_i$.

3 The proposed DTLBO

In this section, the discrete variant of TLBO is presented. First, initialize a population with N individuals based on a problem-specific strategy. Then, all learners are randomly divided into several sub-swarms with equal amounts of learners. Moreover, the best individual and the mean individual in each sub-swarm are determined, and the crossover operation, the legality detection and mutation operation are performed to generate a candidate learner for each learner in the teaching and learning phases. Finally, the learner is updated by performing a comparison of the current learner and the candidate learner. The above process ends when the termination criterion is met; otherwise, the next iterative process is performed. The detailed description of the DTLBO algorithm is as follows.

3.1 Individual representation and initialization

For a TSP problem, the goal is to obtain a city sequence of with the shortest path. Therefore, it is natural and intuitive to code the solution as a set of real integer values based on the number of cities, whose length is the same as the number of total cities and where each real integer value corresponds to a unique city number. For a TSP problem with 7 cities, the learner can be represented as shown in Figure 1.

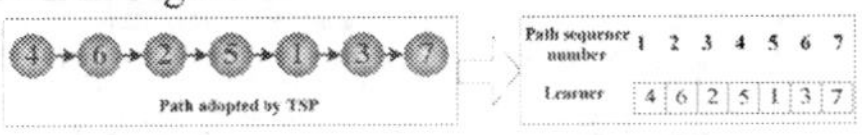

Figure 1. Individual representation of learners

Based on the above individual representation method, the learners of population can be generated by random initialization method. Assume that the population size is NP, the city size of the TSP problem is N, and then a matrix of $NP \times N$ is generated after initialization. The i-th row of the matrix corresponds to the i-th learner individual, and each column of the i-th row represents a city. The column order represents the order of visiting cities. Concretely, the initialization of the learner can be shown as follows:

$$X_i = randperm(N) \tag{4}$$

where the $randperm(N)$ representation yields a random permutation of the integers from 1 to N.

3.2 The determination of teachers and mean individuals

In the original TLBO algorithm, the teacher tries to disseminate knowledge among learners, which in turn helps learners to achieve good grades and increases the knowledge level of the entire class, thus improving the mean results of the class. The updating of the learner is implemented based on the teacher and the mean individual. However, all learners learn from the random difference between the teacher and the mean individual, and this easily causes learners to become trapped in local optima. To avoid this situation, the multi-swarm mechanism is introduced to maintain the diversity of the population. That is, all learners are randomly divided into several sub-swarms with equal amounts of learners in each iterative process. Suppose that there are K (K=4 in this paper) learner individuals $X_{i_1}, X_{i_2}, \cdots, X_{i_K}$ in the i-th sub-swarm, and $NTeacher_i$ and $NMean_i$ are the best individual and the mean individual respectively in the i-th sub-swarm, which can be respectively given as follows:

$$NTeacher_i = Best(X_{i_1}, X_{i_2}, \cdots, X_{i_K}) \tag{5}$$

$$NMean_i = \left(\sum_{k=1}^{K} x_{i_k,1}, \sum_{k=1}^{K} x_{i_k,2}, \cdots, \sum_{k=1}^{K} x_{i_k,D}\right) \tag{6}$$

Different from the original TLBO algorithm, in our approach, $NTeacher_i$ and $NTeacher_i$ are all integer vectors in which each element corresponds to a unique city number. However, there are the same elements in the mean individual according to Eq.(6). For example, the mean individual may be expressed as follows:

NMean$_i$	3	6	6	5	4	3	4

Obviously, there are duplicate elements in the learner $NTeacher_i$, and they are illegal. Hence, the legality detection for the learner individual must be executed.

Generally, the executing process of the legality detection for the individual $NMean_i$ is given as follows:

Step 1: Count the number of times each city appears. For the above individual $NMean_i$, cities marked 3, 4 and 6 appears 2 times, and the city marked 5 appeared once. It can be expressed as a vector A. In the vector A, if a city appeared more than once, the number of times this city appears is written into the last appeared location of this city; otherwise, the other locations are set to 0.

Step 2: Determine the cities that did not appear. For the above individual $NMean_i$, cities marked 1, 2 and 7 have not appeared. It can be expressed as a vector B. In the vector B, the order number of a city that did not appear is written into the associated location of this order number, and the other locations are set to 0.

Step 3: Find out the last location of a city that has appeared more than once. In the vector C, if a city appeared more than once, the order number of this city is written into the last appeared location of this city; otherwise, the other locations are set to 0.

Step 4: Determine the location of cities that did not appear in the individual. For the above individual $NMean_i$, in the vector C, the order numbers of cities that did not appear is written into the locations with the values of zeroes, and then the final $NMean_i$ can be obtained.

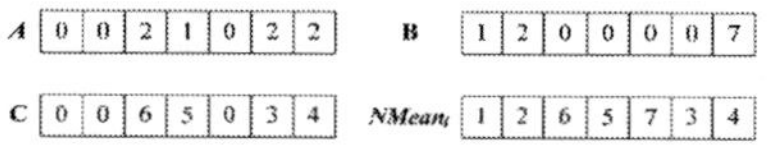

Figure 2. The legality detection for the learner individual

3.3 Teaching phase of DTLBO

In the original TLBO algorithm, the updating of the learner is implemented according to Eq.(2) and it is used to deal with continuous optimization problems. For discrete TSP problems, it needs to redefine the updating strategy of learners.

As a result, assume that there are four learners $X_{i_1}, X_{i_2}, X_{i_3}, X_{i_4}$ in the i-th sub-swarm. Their updating strategies can be given as follows:

$$TX_{i_1} = X_{i_1} \otimes Teacher \tag{7}$$

$$TX_{i_2} = X_{i_1} \otimes NTeacher_i \tag{8}$$

$$TX_{i_3} = X_{i_1} \otimes NMean_i \tag{9}$$

$$TX_{i_4} = NTeacher_i \otimes NMean_i \tag{10}$$

where $\otimes$ represents the crossover operation.

Generally, the crossover operation $\otimes$ can be described in detail as follows. Assume that there are two learners A and B shown as follows:

$$A = 2\ 3\ |7\ 5\ 1|\ 4\ 6 \quad B = 1\ 7\ |4\ 6\ 5|\ 2\ 3$$

Then, randomly select two gene loci and exchange the corresponding elements between two gene loci in A and B:

$$AA = 2\ 3\ |4\ 6\ 5|\ 4\ 6 \quad BB = 1\ 7\ |7\ 5\ 1|\ 2\ 3$$

Due to existing duplicate elements in AA and BB, they need to be revised by means of the legality detection to obtain $newA$ and $newB$ as follows:

$$newA = 2\ 3\ |4\ 6\ 5|\ 7\ 1 \quad newB = 6\ 4\ |7\ 5\ 1|\ 2\ 3$$

After the crossover operation has been completed, the legality detection is executed so that the duplicate elements in the learner are revised. And then, the mutation operation is executed to generate the candidate learner shown as follows:

$$newX_i = \Theta TX_i \tag{11}$$

where Θ represents the mutation operation.

In this paper, the reverse mutation is performed and it is given as follows: randomly select two gene loci in the order of visiting cities, and then reverse the elements between two gene loci to generate the new mutation individual. For example, two gene loci in $newAA$ is 3 and 5, the new mutation individual $newAA$ can be obtained by the mutation operation:

$$newA = 2\ |3\ 4\ 6\ 5|\ 7\ 1 \quad newAA = 2\ |5\ 6\ 4\ 3|\ 7\ 1$$

3.4 Learning Phase of DTLBO

In the learner phase of the original TLBO algorithm, the learner is updated according to the difference between the current learner X_i and the current random selected learner X_j. In the learning phase of the DTLBO algorithm, the current learner individual X_i is updated as follows:

$$TX_i = X_i \otimes X_j \tag{12}$$

where, $\otimes$ represents the crossover operation, and it is as same as the crossover operation in the teaching phase.

Just like the learning rules in the teaching phase, when the crossover operation is completed, the duplicate elements in the learner are revised, and then the mutation operation is executed to generate the candidate learner shown as follows:

$$newX_i = \Theta TX_i \tag{13}$$

where Θ represents the mutation operation.

Just like the original TLBO algorithm, the greedy selection is executed to determine the offspring learners. That is, after the candidate learner has been generated in the teaching and learning phases, if the value $f(newX_i)$ is better than the value $f(X_i)$, then replace X_i with $newX_i$.

4 DTLBO algorithm for solving TSP

In this section, in order to verify the validity and correctness of the algorithm, we have compared the effectiveness and efficiency of our proposed algorithm on 7 classic benchmark problems for the TSP in comparison with several other meta-heuristic algorithms.

4.1 Parameter setting

The algorithms are tested on several sample instances of TSPLIB [14] with different cities. Every algorithm requires appropriate parameter settings to get proper outcome. For all population-based algorithms, the size of population on the test problems is set to 100, and the maximum number of iteration on the test problems is set to 500 for fair comparison.

4.2 Comparison of simulation result

The simulated experimental results are listed in Table 1. In the table, KOS denotes the known optimal solution as reported in TSPLIB. Best denotes the best solution found by each algorithm and Mean denotes the average value of all solutions by running independently 20 times.

Table 1. Comparison of test results

TSP	KOS	ACO[15]	ABC[16]	PSO	GA	DTLBO
Oliver30	420	**423.74**	432	464.71	455.45	**423.74**
Chn31	15377	15602	15942	17097	16646	**15397**
Att48	33522	33536	33541	37882	36458	33524
rand50	5553	—	—	6788	5848	5555
Eil51	426	435	426	563.03	460.48	434.67
rand75	7054	—	—	16544	8506	7170
Eil76	538	555.7	541	1083.91	685.59	565.21

As shown in Table 1, for Oliver30, DTLBO and ACO have the best performance in terms of the average value of 423.74 in all of 20 runs, and the average values obtained by ABC, GA and PSO are 432, 455.45 and 464.71 respectively. For Chn31, DTLBO obtains the average value of 15397, and those of ACO, ABC, PSO and GA are 15602, 15942, 17097 and 16646. It can be clearly seen that DTLBO is closer to the known optimal solution 15397 than the other four algorithms. For Att48, the average value obtained by DTLBO is 33524, while the other four algorithms are worse than the DTLBO. For Eil51 and Eil76, ABC has the best performance in terms of the average value and DTLBO is better than ACO, PSO and GA, While ABC can reach the known optimal solution of 426 for Eil51. For rand50 and rand75, DTLBO performs better than PSO and GA.

To demonstrate the effectiveness of the new DTLBO algorithm, the convergence curves and route tracing obtained by PSO, GA and DTLBO are given in Figure 3. However, we are only able to show convergence graphs for the proposed algorithm DTLBO, SPO and GA because the data of ACO and ABC were taken from literature and this information was unavailable. It can be concluded from Table 1 and Figure 3 that the DTLBO has a good performance for the most of all TSP problem instances in this paper.

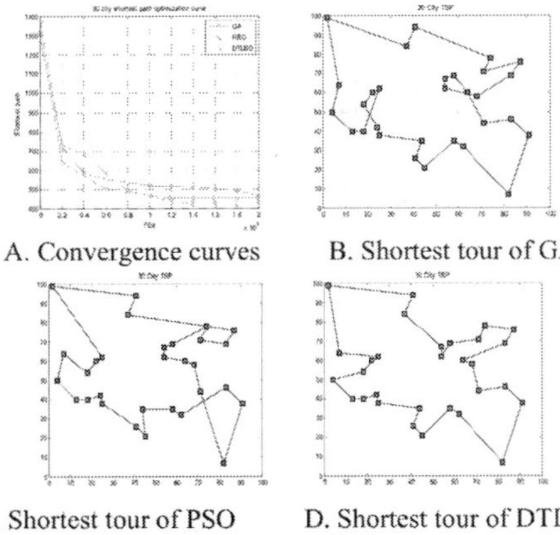

A. Convergence curves B. Shortest tour of GA

C. Shortest tour of PSO D. Shortest tour of DTLBO

Figure 3. Oliver 30 city TSP optimization curve and path

5 Conclusion

In this paper, a new discrete teaching–learning-based optimization algorithm (DTLBO) is proposed for solving the traveling salesman problem. The proposed approach used multi-swarms mechanism to maintain the diversity of the population and reduce the probability of being trapped in local optimum and introduced the new crossover operation, legality detection and mutation operation into the teaching phase and the learning phase. The numerical simulation tests were carried out on 7 different TSP problems, and the results show that the DTLBO algorithm is a promising method for TSP problems. However, it can also be seen from the results that, the performance of DTLBO is also decreased with the increasing of city size. Hence, future work will concentrate on how to improve DTLBO's performance for TSP problems with large scale cities.

Acknowledgements

This work is partially supported by the National Natural Science Foundation of China (Grant Nos.61572224, 41475017 and 11504121) and the National Science Fund for Distinguished Young Scholars (Grants No.61425009). This work is also partially supported by Anhui Provincial Natural Science Foundation (Grant No.1708085MF140), the Major Project of Natural Science Research in Anhui Province (Grant No.KJ2015ZD36) and the Natural Science Foundation in colleges and universities of Anhui Province (Grant No.KJ2016A639).

Reference

1. A. Philip, A. A. Taofiki, O. Kehinde. *International Journal of Advanced Computer Science & Applications*, 2(1): 26-29(2011).
2. M. Mavrovouniotis, F. M. Muller, S. Yang. *IEEE Transactions on Cybernetics*, 47(7):1743-1756(2016).
3. V. Mak, N. Boland. *Discrete Applied Mathematics*, 155(16):2093-2110(2007).
4. J. F. Cordeau, M. Dell'Amico, M. Iori. *Computers & Operations Research*, 37(5):970-980(2010).
5. W. Malika. *Operations Research Letters*, 35(6):747-753(2007).
6. A. I. Vakhutinsky, B. L. Golden. *IEEE World Congress on Computational Intelligence*. 7, 4535-4540(1994).
7. D. Simon. Biogeography-based optimization. *IEEE Transactions on Evolutionary Computation*, 12(6): 702-713(2008).
8. J. Knox. *Computers & Operations Research*, 21(8): 867-876(1994).
9. B. Akay, D. Karaboga. *Information Sciences*, 192(1): 120-142(2012).
10. A. Ouaarab, B. Ahiod, X. S. Yang. *Neural Computing & Applications*, 24(7-8):1659-1669(2014).
11. R. V. Rao, V. J. Savsani, D. P. Vakharia. *Information Sciences*, 183(1):1-15(2012).
12. A. Baykasoğlu, A. Hamzadayi, S. Y. Köse. *Information Sciences*, 2014, 276(C):204-218(2014).
13. X. Ji, H. Ye, J. Zhou, et al. *Applied Soft Computing*, 57, 504-516(2017).

DOI: 10.1051/matecconf/201712802022

14. http://comopt.ifi.uni-heidelberg.de/software/TSPLIB95/
15. Liu Yin, Ma Liang. *Application Research of Computers*, 9: 2694-2696(2013).
16. Zhonghua Hu, Min Zhao. *Transactions of Beijing Institute of Technology*, 11:978-982 (2009).

 DOI: 10.1051/matecconf/201712802023

Impact of Packet Size on Performance of TCP traffic with Small Router buffers

Bo Zhang[1,a], Yu Li[2] and Yanlei Liang[2]

[1,2]*Faculty of Science and Technology, Communication University of China, China*

Abstract. In this paper, we research the impact of packet size on the performance of TCP traffic with small router buffers. First of all, we established a simple model which had two TCP flows, combined with the queue management mechanism in a router and analyzed the effect on TCP packet loss performance of variable packet sizes. Secondly, the corresponding network topology was established based on the NS2 simulation software. And the correctness of the model was verified by experiments.

1 Introduction

Network technology develops rapidly and the scale of the Internet continues to expand. It put forward higher requirements on the network quality of service, and as the router is a hub to connect the different network, its performance directly determines the quality of service in network communication. The main performance indicators of the router include the throughput, delay, utilization and packet loss rate and so on. The router buffer is essential for network data exchange. The buffer can reduce the packet loss by absorbing the burst traffic, but it also causes the queuing delay and jitter. So, how to set the buffer size to make various performance parameters of the network achieve the best compromise will be a very important issue. It has been researched for a few years and some different conclusions are obtained. However, until now, there is still no unified conclusion on the research of router buffer requirement.

Currently commercial router buffer is still in accordance with the rule-of thumb [1] to design. It was proposed by Villamizar and song in 1994, namely $B = \overline{RTT} \times C$, where B was the size of the buffer, RTT was the average round-trip time of a TCP connection, C was the bandwidth of the bottleneck link. But it was questioned by the Stanford Rule [2]. It proposed that if the number of TCP flows in the network was large enough, the transmission of TCP flows was tends to the non-synchronization, and buffer size could be reduced to $1/\sqrt{N}$times, where N was the number of the long TCP flows. Through extensive researches, some other rules had been put forward, like buffer sizing for congested Internet links [3] and tiny buffer rule [4]. It was pointed out that buffer size could be further decreased, even about dozens of packet groups would be able to meet the demand. Obviously, with the increasing of multimedia services in future network, the demand for bandwidth is increasing, and the rapid development of optical network determines the importance of the research of small buffer.

At the same time in studying the small buffer, it found that the network packet size was a very important factor for the performance of a router. Different packets sizes had different effects on the packet loss rate and the throughput. According to the needs of the link layer, usually in the Internet, packet size has been clearly defined, such as Ethernet. In the Ethernet the maximum packet size is 1500bytes [5]. However, a lot of applications (such as VoIP applications) usually use a small packet flow in order to minimize the delay time [6]. In another paper [7], the authors presented the result of simulation experiment on wireless IPv6 network by implementing TCP Vegas with the packet spacing adaption. Packet spacing improved the performance of TCP Vegas. In the simulation experiments, it controlled the flow packet interval uniform to minimize the burstiness of flow at the bottleneck link. Different sizes of FTP packets were sent in a wireless IPv6 environment. The experimental results showed that the data packets of different sizes leaded to different network performance. When FTP packet size was set 512bytes, it had smaller packet loss rate, lower queue delay, higher link utilization. Therefore, when the packet was transmitted in wireless IPv6 network, they suggested that the packet size is 512bytes. However, no more useful information in papers suggested that the impacts of different packet sizes on the TCP flow were not fair. In order to study the effects of different packet sizes on the performance of TCP, we have done some research.

The rest of the paper is organized as follows. In Section II, we introduced the theoretical model to analyze the impact of packet size. In Section III, we made simulation and observed the performance impact of various packet sizes with different buffer capacity. We analyzed the experimental phenomenon and discussed its non-accidental. We summarized our work and obtained the

[a] Corresponding author: zhangbo86108@163.com

experimental conclusions, and pointed out directions for future work in Section IV.

2 Theoretical model

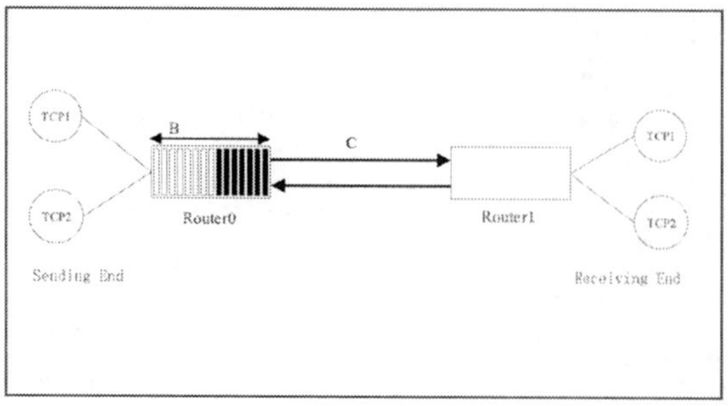

Figure 1. Theory Architecture of the Topology

As shown in Figure 1, we set up a simple dumbbell topology. We establish two TCP flow links. Among them, the bandwidth of bottleneck link is C_{out}, the bandwidth of each TCP flow access link is C_{in}. Assume the packets size of first flow TCP is l_1, the other is l_2, and $l_1 > l_2$. At the same time we assumed some related parameters as shown in Table 1.

Table 1. The Presentations of Parameters

Parameters	Presentation
d_1	The amount of TCP1 loss packet
d_2	The amount of TCP2 loss packet
N_1	The amount of TCP1 packet
N_2	The amount of TCP2 packet
P_1	The probability of a TCP1 packet reaching to Router0
P_2	The probability of a TCP2 packet reaching to Router0
p_1	The probability of a TCP1 packet lost
p_2	The probability of a TCP2 packet lost

In the paper [8], it was pointed out that the router buffer capacity had a very important impact on the arrival process of the TCP flows. If the buffers was too large, it could cause the synchronization between the TCP flows, which could cause a burst. But when the buffer became small, the distribution of the TCP flows could be approximated by the Poisson distribution. For us, the buffer was very small in experiments, so it could be considered that the TCP packets arrival obeyed Poisson distribution.

In our model, we assume that arrival rate of TCP1 is λ_1, arrival rate of TCP2 is λ_2, $\lambda_1 = \lambda_2 = \lambda$, and the rate of flow packets from the router to the bottleneck link is C_{out}. According to the length of router queue management strategy of Drop Tail, when the router queue is full, then the arrival packets will be discarded. Assuming the header packets in router buffer queue is a packet of TCP1, then the time that packet transferred from the router to the bottleneck link is:

$$t_1 = \frac{l_1}{C_{out}} \quad (1)$$

Similarly, if this packet is TCP2's packet, then the time that packet from the router to the bottleneck link is:

$$t_2 = \frac{l_2}{C_{out}} \quad (2)$$

Because of $l_1 > l_2$, $t_1 > t_2$.

Assuming that the router buffer capacity is full, in a very short period of time t, $t < t_2 < t_1$, the probability that there is at least one TCP flow packet arriving to the router at this time according to the principle of Poisson distribution is:

$$P = 1 - \frac{(\lambda t)^0 e^{-\lambda t}}{0!} = 1 - e^{-\lambda t} \quad (3)$$

At the same time, P also denotes the probability of the packet lost in the time t.

According to the Equation (3), the probability of a TCP1 or a TCP2 packet lost can be expressed in the following Equation:

$$P_1 = 1 - e^{-\lambda_1 t}, \ P_2 = 1 - e^{-\lambda_2 t} \quad (4)$$

Furthermore, the ratio of the probability of a TCP1 packet lost to the probability of a TCP2 packet lost R_p was:

$$R_P = \frac{P_1}{P_2} = \frac{1-e^{-\lambda_1 t}}{1-e^{-\lambda_2 t}} \quad (5)$$

In the period of time t, it is equal between the traffic of TCP1 and the traffic of TCP2. So the ratio of the amount of TCP1 to the amount of TCP2 R_N was:

$$R_N = \frac{N_1}{N_2} = \frac{\frac{S}{l_1}}{\frac{S}{l_2}} = \frac{l_2}{l_1} \quad (6)$$

The ratio of TCP1 packet loss rate to TCP2 packet loss rate R_{loss} could be expressed in the following Equation:

$$R_{loss} = \frac{\frac{d_1}{N_1}}{\frac{d_2}{N_2}} = \frac{d_1}{d_2} \times \frac{N_2}{N_1} \quad (7)$$

Through the above analysis,

$$\frac{d_{TCP1}}{d_{TCP2}} \approx \frac{P_1}{P_2} = R_P \quad (8)$$

According to Equation (5) (6) (7) (8), R_{loss} could be expressed as:

$$R_{loss} = \frac{1-e^{-\lambda_1 t}}{1-e^{-\lambda_2 t}} \times \frac{l_1}{l_2} \quad (9)$$

According to Equation (9), it could be obviously found that:

$$l_1 > l_2, \ R_{loss} > 1 \quad (10)$$

That is to say when the packet size of TCP1 was larger than the packet size of TCP2, the probability of TCP1 packet loss rate was larger than the probability of TCP2 packet loss rate either. So it can be drew that it's more easily discarded when the packet size is large.

3 Simulation and Findings

3.1. The experiment topology and settings

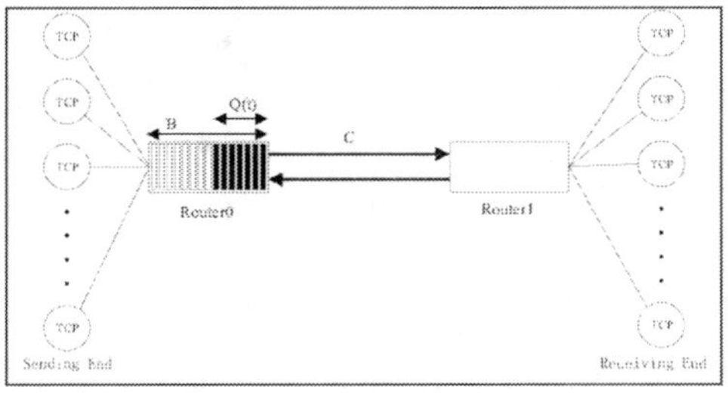

Figure 2. NS-2 simulation topology

In the last section of the theoretical analysis, we analyzed the simplest case, but there are a lot of TCP flows in the actual network, and there will be a certain impact between the flow and flow. So then we will validate our theoretical model through simulation experiments. The NS-2 simulation topology is shown in Fig.2. The classical dumbbell topology is commonly used. In the experiment, we used 100 TCP flows, so that each TCP flow can be approximately independent and not synchronized. Furthermore, we use TCP-Reno in all our simulations, consistent with the TCP version used in most of the Internet nowadays, and employ FIFO (First In First Out) queue with drop-tail queue management, which is commonly used in most routers today. We set the bottleneck link at 20 Mbps and TCP access links at 5 Mbps The propagation delay on the TCP access link is distributed between [1,25]ms. The propagation delay on the bottleneck link (r0, r1) is 50ms; thus RTT (Round-Trip Time) vary between 104ms and 200ms. All TCP sources start at random times between [0, 10] s. The simulation duration is 600s and performance measurements are recorded after 100s, to allow for the stabilization of all TCP flows. In our experiment, we fix the buffer size, change the packet size of the TCP traffic, and measure the packet loss rate and throughput. According to the Stanford Rule, the best buffer size is $B = \frac{\overline{RTT}\times C}{\sqrt{n}} \approx 40\text{KB}$, so we set the buffer size close to 40KB, including 20 KB, 30 KB, 40 KB and 50 KB. The packet size is between $200byte$ and $1500byte$, and the step length is 100byte.

3.2 The Results

Figure 3 shows the packet loss rate of the TCP traffic. Figure 4 shows the throughput of the TCP traffic.

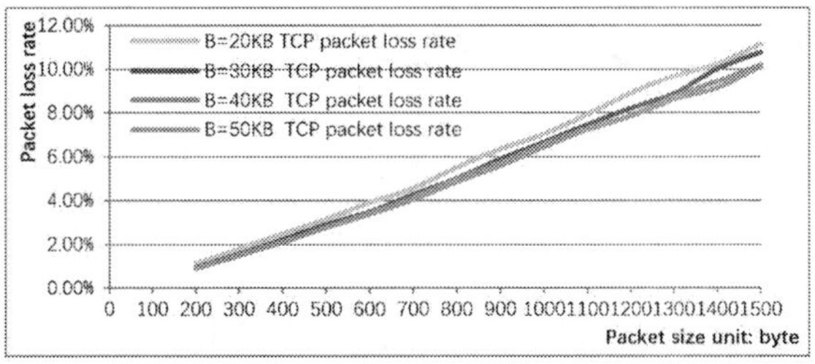

Figure 3. Packet loss rate of TCP traffic with different buffer sizes

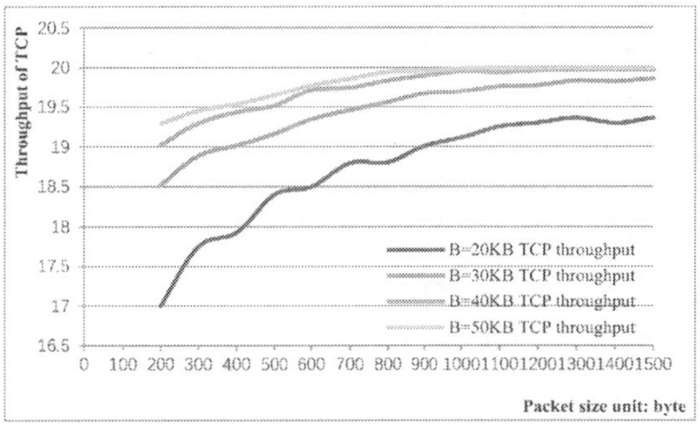

Figure 4. Throughput of TCP traffic with different buffer sizes

Figure 3 shows that when the buffer size is 20 KB, 30 KB, 40 KB and 50 TCP, the packet loss rate of TCP traffic is changing with the various packet size. Obviously, with the increase of the buffer size, the packet loss rate of TCP is gradually decreased. For a fixed buffer size, the larger the packet size is, the greater the packet loss rate of the TCP traffic would be. This is consistent with the derivation of our theoretical model. Figure 4 shows the throughput of the TCP traffic with different buffer size and various packet size. It can be found longitudinally that when the buffer is set to 20 KB, the queue space can not meet the requirements of the network, resulting in low throughput; when the buffer is 40 KB, the queue space is large enough and the size of the buffer is not a factor limiting the throughput of TCP. At the same time, we can find that the impact of packet size on the throughput of TCP is not remarkable when the buffer is set reasonably. When the packet size increases gradually from the 200byte, the throughput of TCP flows increases slowly; when the packet size is up to1000byte, the throughput of TCP reaches a maximum and keep stable, so the TCP packet size is often set to 1000byte in the experimental process.

According to the formula that the expression of the classic TCP throughput [9], the average throughput of a single flow can be expressed as:

$$R_L = \frac{kL}{T\sqrt{p}} \tag{11}$$

Assuming there are n streams, the total throughput can be expressed as:

$$R_L = n \times \frac{kL}{T\sqrt{p}} \tag{12}$$

Where k is constant, T represents the average round-trip time of TCP stream, L denotes the length of the packet, and p is the packet loss rate. For the same network environment, it can be seen that:

$$R_L \propto \frac{L}{\sqrt{p}} \tag{13}$$

It can be seen from Fig.4 that the throughput of TCP traffic has a slow upward trend with the packet increasing, but this phenomenon deviated with our intuitive understanding. Theoretically, the throughput decreases with the increasing of the packet loss rate. In addition, from the Equation (13) it can be seen that the throughput has a relationship between packet length and packet loss rate, and the trend is changed by the packet length and packet loss rate. As seen from Fig.3, packet loss rate grows approximately in straight line with packet length. The growth rate of the packet is obviously faster than the square-root of the growth rate of the packet loss rate. So it has an upward trend of throughput of TCP traffic.

In conclusion, the larger size packets of the TCP stream are more likely to have behavior of packet loss, but large packets are more likely to get higher throughput, so a rational choice of packet size plays a critical role in performance of TCP flows.

4 Conclusion

This paper mainly studied the effect of TCP flow packet size on the performance of TCP. It included two aspects. In the first part, we established a simple model used two flows, which theoretically analyzed that bigger packets were likely to have greater packet loss rate. And in the second part, we carried out experiments on the network simulation platform to verify the conclusion of the network was applicable to multiple streams, mainly considering two aspects of TCP traffic: packet loss rate and throughput. The experimental results showed that the packet size had different effects on the packet loss rate and the throughput of the TCP stream. The larger the packet size was, the greater the packet loss rate and throughput would have. That was to say, it needed reasonable choice of the size of the packet in order to make the performance of TCP to reach the optimal. At the same time, it was pointed out that the impact of the unfairness of the packet size was only a qualitative study of the trend of the packet loss rate and throughput. And the paper only studied the unfairness effect on TCP performance by TCP packet size, and ignored open-loop flows in the network. These could be used as future research directions.

ACKNOWLEDGMENT

This work was supported in part by College Student Research and Career-creation Program of Beijing City.

References

1. C. Villamizar, C.Song, "High Performance TCP in ANSNET," ACM SIGCOMM Computer Communication Review, vol.24, no.5, Oct. 1994, pp.45–60
2. G. Appenzeller, I. Keslassy, N. McKeown, "Sizing Router Buffers," ACM SIGCOMM Computer Communication Review, vol.34, no.4, Oct. 2004, pp.281–292
3. A. Dhamdhere, H. Jiang, C. Dovrolis, "Buffer Sizing for Congested Internet Links," the 24th Annual Joint Conference of the IEEE Computer and Communications Societies, Miami, Florida, USA, Mar. 13-17, 2005, pp.1072–1083
4. M. Enachescu, Y. Ganjali, A.Goel, N. McKeown, T. Roughgarden, "Part Part III: Routers with very small buffers," ACM SIGCOMM Computer Communication Review, vol.35, no.2, July 2005, pp.83–89
5. J. Nieminen, J. Karvo, P. Lassila, M. Peuhkuri, "Impact of Heterogeneous Packet Sizes on Flow Fairness," the 16th international conference on Telecommunications, Marrakech, Morocco, May 25-27, 2009, pp.248-253
6. A. Lakshmikantha, C. Beck, and R. Srikant, \Impact of file arrivals and departures on buffer sizing in core routers," IEEE/ACM Transactions on Networking, pp. 347 -358, April 2011
7. B.S. Yew, B. L. Ong, and R. B. Ahmad, \Optimizing TCP Vegas performance with packet spacing and effect of variable FTP packet size over wireless IPv6 network," International Journal of Computer and Communication Engineering, vol. 6, pp. 89-97, February 2012
8. A. Vishwanath, V. Sivaraman, and D. Ostry, \How poisson is TCP traffic at short time-scales in a small buffer core network?," IEEE 3rd International Symposium on Advanced Networks and Telecommunication Systems, April 2009
9. M. Mathis, J. Semke, J. Mahdavi, T. Ott, "The Macroscopic Behaviors of the TCP Congestion Avoidance Algorithm," ACM SIGCOMM Computer Communication Review, 1997, pp.67-82.

MATEC Web of Conferences 128, 03001 (2017) DOI: 10.1051/matecconf/201712803001
EITCE 2017

Structure and Microscopic Wear Analysis of Lining Material Based on EDEM

Zhongsheng Wang[1,a], Rujie Wang[1,b], Qiou Fei[1,c], Jianguo Li[2,d], Jiachen Tang[2,e] and Boqiang Shi[2,f]

[1]*Anshan Iron and Steel Group Mining Co., Ltd. equipment manufacturing branch, China*
[2]*School of Mechanical Engineering, University of Science and Technology Beijing, China*

Abstract. The microscopic influence of sliding distance and load on the wear of cone crusher liner is studied. The main factors that affect the hardness of the liner and the material are clearly put forward, and the hardness of the liner is verified according to the national standard to ensure the correctness of the lining and the ore material. Simulation experiments were carried out with EDEM. When the material was certain, the positive pressure and sliding distance between the ore and liner were changed, and the micro wear of the liner was quantitatively calculated by the number of bond keys of the lining plate. The results show that when the liner moves at the same distance, the pressure is greater and the lining plate is seriously worn. When the lining plate is subjected to the same pressure, the moving distance increases, and the lining plate is seriously worn. This method has some reference value for cavity design of new crusher and other material wear research.

1 Introduction

When the cone crusher breaks the ore, the movable cone liner is worn by the squeezing action of the ore, so the movable cone liner needs to be replaced regularly. For large crushing equipment, replacing the lining of the frequency, crushing efficiency and, business efficiency is closely related. Therefore, the research on the wear of the movable cone liner is very important. It has been found that the wear of the movable cone liner depends on the wear properties of the liner material and, on the other hand, the mechanical action, such as the sliding distance between the movable cone liner, the ore and, the load of the movable cone liner [1]. In this paper, the effect of different sliding distance and load on the wear of the movable cone liner under the dry friction condition is studied by using the discrete element method to study the effect of the composite material and the crushing cavity type Provide reference.

2 Cone liner material and ore material structure

In order to study the wear of the movable cone liner, it is necessary to construct the dynamic cone liner material and the ore material. The material of the liner is set according to the microscopic parameters (shear modulus, Poisson's ratio, particle radius, particle stiffness, bonding bond strength, etc.) of the actual material, which makes the material model consistent with the mechanical properties of the material. The main component of the material is ZGMn13Cr2, the main component of the ore material is limestone, assuming that the material particles are uniform, the main parameters of the lining material and the ore material are shown in Table 1:

Table 1 Basic parameters of liner material and ore material

	Poisson's ratio	Elastic modulus (GPa)	Compressive strength (Mpa)	Particle radius (mm)
Liner	0.26	200	1500	1
ore	0.3	41	140	1

In the EDEM Hertz-mindlin with bonding contact model, the normal stress and tangential stress limits between the particles are:

$$\sigma_{\max} < -\frac{F_n}{A} + \frac{2M_t}{J} R_b \quad (1)$$

$$\tau_{\max} < -\frac{F_t}{A} + \frac{M_n}{J} R_b \quad (2)$$

F_n is the normal force between particles; F_t is the

[a]1993962830@qq.com, [b]as_wangrujie@sina.com, [c]8815587@qq.com, [d]guo-email@163.com,[e]1357273236@qq.com, [f]ustb1007@163.com

tangential force between particles; M_n is the normal moment between particles; R_b is the intergranular bonding radius. $A=\pi R_b^2$, $J=\pi R_b^4$, The normal compressive strength of the material σ_{max} can be found by the data.

In the EDEM model, because the particle size is mostly macroscopic state, the cohesive force between the particles is often neglected to influence the tangential force [2]. From the formula (1) and (2), it can be seen that the hardness and the normal stiffness of the material k_n, the tangential stiffness k_t are related to the bonding radius after the particles are completely bonded.

$$k_n=\frac{\sqrt{2rE}}{3\left(1-\mu^2\right)}=\frac{\sqrt{2\times0.001}\times2\times10^{11}}{3\left(1-0.26^2\right)}=1.01\times10^9$$

Since the calculation of k_t is very complex, according to Mindlin [3] analysis results, the elastic entity in the event of contact, the oval contact area ratio $k_t/k_n=[2/3,1]$, here take

$$k_t=\frac{2}{3}k_n=0.673\times10^9$$

The maximum compressive strength of ZGMn13Cr2 can reach 1500MPa, cohesion can be ignored, particle radius is 0.1mm, the bonding radius is 0.15mm.After the material is constructed, it is necessary to measure the hardness of the material. According to the national standard GB / T230.1-2004 [4], Rockwell hardness in the range of 20HRB ~ 100HRB, the pressure head with a diameter of 1.5875mm carbide ball. The main test force $F_0=98.07N$, the main test force $F_1=882.6N$, the total force $F=980.67N$ points in two steps into the sample surface, after a specified time, the removal of the main test force, measured at the initial test force Of the residual indentation depth h , the Rockwell hardness is H:

$$\text{H}=130-\frac{h}{0.002} \tag{3}$$

To measure the depth of the indenter material, the ram was applied at a rate of 0.1 m/s. The pressure of the indenter changes with time as shown in Fig.1.The least squares method is used to fit a 4-step [5] smooth curve.

$$\text{F}=1.5943\times10^{14}\text{t}^4-4.4013\times10^{13}\text{t}^3+4.4560\times 10^{12}\text{t}^2-2.0959\times10^{11}\text{t}+3.6153\times10^9 \tag{4}$$

Formula (4) is the relationship between the force of the indenter F and the time t. According to the experience of material rebound [6], We can measure indentation $h=\left(0.07047-0.06829\right)\times100\times0.85=0.1853mm$, According to equation (3), the Rockwell hardness is 37.35 .

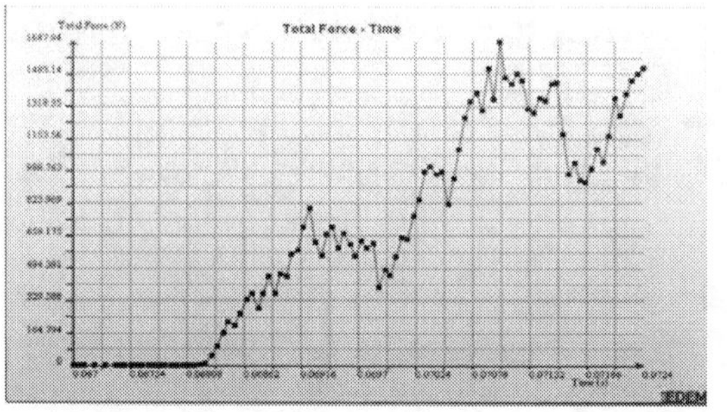

Fig.1 The pressure of the indenter changes with time

In order to verify the correctness of the liner hardness measurement, by measuring the liner strength, according to the national standard GB / T1172-1999 steel strength and hardness of the conversion value, you can indirectly get hardness.

The particles having a radius of 0.05 mm were bonded into $4mm\times1mm\times0.7mm$ blocks with the same bonding parameters as measured in Fig. 1, the left half of the block was fixed in the housing and the other end was extended into the housing. From the middle of the block 1.5mm, with a pressure plate at a constant rate of pressure to the block, as shown in Fig.2. The strength of the material can be obtained by force in the vertical direction by the platen. Fig. 3 shows that the pressure plate at 62.8304N, the block broken, according to formula (6), the block of the tensile strength is 1154Mpa.We can see that the hardness of the material is 36. And the direct hardness measured by the error:

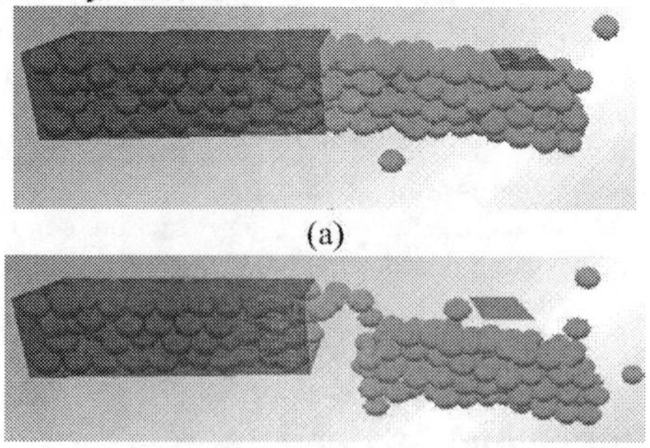

(a)

(b)

Fig. 2 Strength measurement model

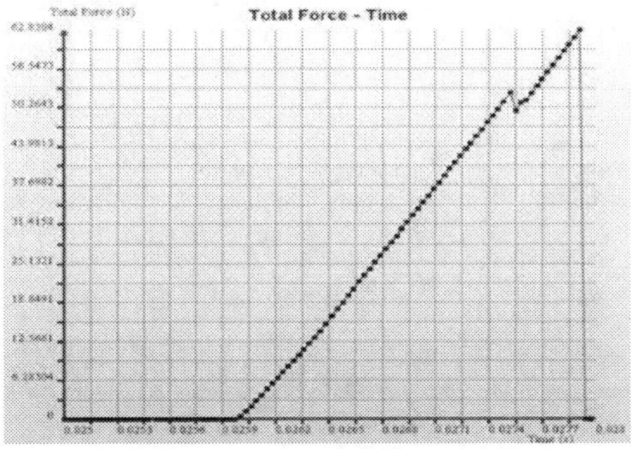

Fig. 3 Pressure plate with time variation

We change the value of k_t、 k_n in equal proportion, we can get different hardness of the material, through the simulation experiment can be obtained between the hardness and stiffness of the material. When other factors remain unchanged, k_t、 k_n in a certain range increases, the hardness first increased and then reduced. When too large or too small, the particles will not bond. By selecting different parameters, you can construct different hardness of the material. Similarly, the same method used to construct limestone materials.

3 Study on the Factors Affecting Wear of Conical Liner

For the liner wear, domestic and foreign scholars have carried out experimental research, and the establishment of the corresponding wear model, given some wear calculation formula [7].Archard in the study of gear meshing sliding, considering the contact stress, sliding speed, plastic deformation contact area and other factors, put forward the classic wear equation [8-9], and is widely cited so far, the wear calculation formula:

$$\omega = Ks\frac{P}{P_m} \quad (5)$$

ω is the wear loss; s is the slip distance ; P is contact surface load; P_m is the softer material hardness; K is wear coefficient.

We can derive from equation (5) that wear is related to wear coefficient, load, slip distance and material hardness. Because the wear coefficient and the hardness of the material are related to the degree of lubrication and the material itself, the positive pressure and the sliding distance between the ore and the liner are changed when the material is constant. The liner wear simulation process is shown in Fig. 4.

Fig. 4 Simulation of liner wear

In Fig. 4, the upper material is limestone, the lower material is the liner, the ore material is long, wide and high, respectively 12mm, 1mm, 2mm, the movement displacement is 1mm. Since EDEM can not directly set the positive pressure between the ore and the liner, through the fixed liner, change the vertical movement speed of the ore, so that the pressure between the two changes. Figure 6 shows the vertical velocity of the ore v = 0.001m / s, frequency f were 40HZ, 60HZ, 80HZ liner bond bond breaking number.

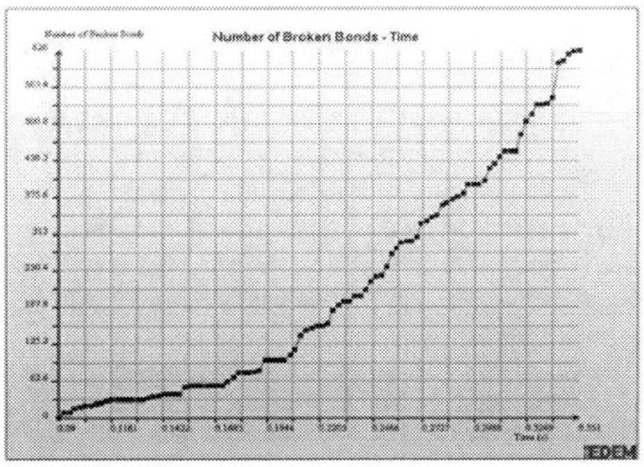

(a) The amount of liner material wear when f = 40HZ

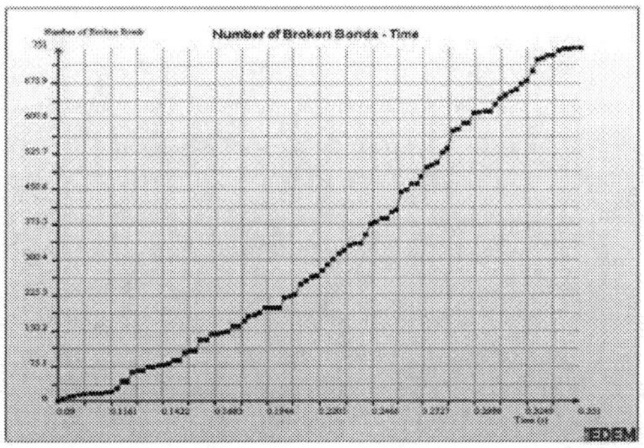

(b) The amount of liner material wear when f = 60HZ

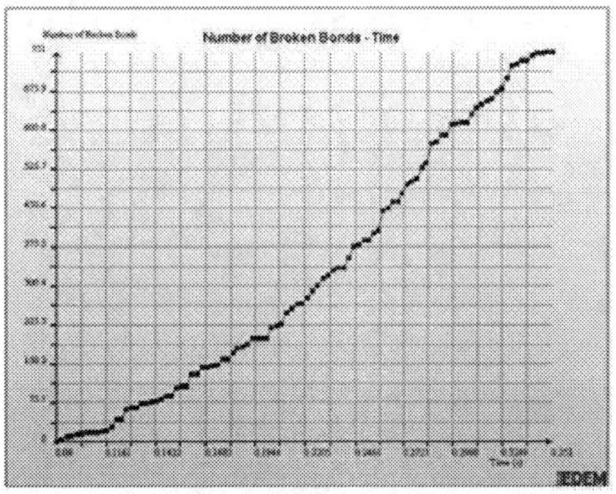

(c) The amount of liner material wear when f = 80HZ

Fig. 5 different ore movement frequency under the liner material wear

The following conclusions can be drawn from Fig. 5:

(1) For the same frequency, as time increases, that is, the movement distance increases, the liner bond bond number increases, that is, liner wear increases;

(2) For different frequencies, take a certain moment, the frequency of the liner bond bond number broken, that is, high frequency, the same time the distance of movement, liner wear serious.

4 Conclusions

This paper mainly studies the influence of ore slipping distance and load on liner wear. First study the factors that affect the hardness of the cone material and the ore material, and then construct the dynamic cone liner and ore material. According to the national standard to verify the hardness of the material to ensure the correctness of the material structure. Secondly, the effects of different materials on the wear and tear of the cone are studied. The method reduces the physical test and saves the material cost. Plate material selection and research has important reference value.

References

1. Chao Wang, Yahui Hu, Yanqing Tan, etc.2014.Study on wear rate prediction model of sliding guideway based on Archard wear theory [J], Lubrication and Sealing, **39** (8): 73-76.
2. Qiang Lei. 2011. Research on material breakage mechanism based on discrete element [D]. Jiangxi University of Technology.
3. Mindlin R D. Compliance of elastic bodies in contact. 1949.Journal of Applied Mechanics, 16: 259-268.
4. China Institute of Metrology Science. 1999.GB/T 1172-1999 hardness and strength conversion value of ferrous metals [S]. Beijing: China Standard Press, 2.
5. Hui Ni. 2010. Research on some problems in the fitting of moving least squares data [D]. Hangzhou: Zhejiang University of Technology.
6. Lin Jingyu. 2015. Evaluation of Uncertainty of Metal Rockwell Hardness Measurement [j], Technology and Enterprise, 09:176-177.
7. Guobin Li,Delin Guan,Mingxing Zhang. 2008. Study on friction and wear behavior of surface nanometer carbon steel in dry friction condition [J], Journal of Tribology, 28 (1): 39-43.
8. Changlin Gui. 1990. Archard wear design calculation model and its application method [J], Lubrication and Sealing,(1): 12-21.
9. Challen J M, Oxley P L. 1986.Prediction of Archard wear coefficient for metallic sliding friction assuming a low cycle fatigue wear mechanism [J]. Wear, (111): 275-288.

MATEC Web of Conferences 128, 03002 (2017) DOI: 10.1051/matecconf/201712803002
EITCE 2017

A Brief Survey on Nonlinear Surface Plasmonics

Yizeng Liang[1,a]

[1] *Zhejiang Normal University, School of Mathematics and Information Engineering, Jinhua, China, 321000*
[a] *ZSDliangyz@163.com*

Abstract. With the rapid development of optical nonlinearities, the study of nonlinear surface plasmonics becomes more popular. Due to the huge potential application value of surface plasmonics, lots of researches in this field become the hotspot. This paper reviewed the history and basic researches of nonlinear plasmonics and focused on several hot topics attracting global attentions. In addition, we introduced the application status of nonlinear surface plasmonics and draw a conclusion. Meanwhile we outlooked the future developments.

1 Introduction

Over the past decades, nonlinear optical effects have been proved to be useful for many different applications, including nonlinear microscopy [1], ultrafast laser systems [2], optical frequency conversion [3], and all-optical switching [4]. In fact, the optical nonlinearities are inherently weak, because they are governed by photon-photon interaction enabled by materials. Nonlinearities are superlinearly dependent on the electromagnetic field and they can be strengthened in material environment that provide mechanism for field enhancement. An increased effective nonlinear optical response can be achieved through plasmonic effects.

Recently, there has been much interest in studying these phenomena at the nanoscale, particularly in plasmonic structures [5]. Such structures typically incorporate nanoscopic metallic features that enable enhanced nonlinear effects modified by surface plasmon polaritons (SPPs), which are electromagnetic excitations propagating at the interface between a metal and a dielectric and evanescently confined in the perpendicular direction [6]. These electromagnetic surface waves arise via the coupling of the electromagnetic fields of incident light to oscillations of the metal's electron plasma. Because of their capacity to concentrate intense fields over subwavelength scales, SPPs can enhance nonlinear optical processes in metallic nanoparticles as well as at extended metal surfaces by modifying the refractive index near the metal surface which results in significant modifications of the plasmonic resonance [7].

There are many ways of exciting SPPs using either electron beams or photons on planar, rough, or grating surfaces. Historically, electron beam excitation was first used, with optical excitation being introduced in the late 1960s [8]. By far the most versatile technique of exciting SPPs in planar geometries is the method of attenuated total reflection (ATR), which was independently demonstrated by Otto et al. [9].

The nonlinear response of SPPs propagating along different types of plasmonic wave guides has been theoretically investigated by several groups [10-13]. In most of these studies it is assumed that the nonlinearity results from a Kerr-type nonlinear dielectric bounding the metal, while the metal is taken as a linear medium. However, SPPs are intrinsically nonlinear even in the absence of a nonlinear dielectric as the metal exhibit strong and ultrafast third-order nonlinear response at optical wavelengths [14]. Calculation of the intrinsic nonlinear propagation of SPPs supported by two typical plasmonic waveguides: a metallic slab and a semi-infinite metal bounded by linear dielectrics have been shown by Israel [15].

The excitation of a surface plasmon can cause optical signal enhancement which is dipole allowed, including second-harmonic generation (SHG) [16] and third-harmonic generation (THG) [17]. And the SHG and THG depend on the square and cube of the incident intensity. Even the formation of a novel hybrid-vector spatial plasmon-soliton in a Kerr slab embedded in-between metal plates can be predicted and analyzed with a modified NLSE, encompassing hybrid vector field characteristic [18].

This paper is arranged as follows. In Section 2, the basic researches in nonlinear plasmonics are introduced. In Section 3, we reviewed several hot topics attracting global attention. Some latest developments are presented in Section 4. Finally, in Section 5, we draw a conclusion and our expectation in this field.

2 Basic researches in nonlinear plasmonics

In 1957, Ritchie, investigated that loss phenomena associated with interaction taking place at metallic surfaces were recorded via the diffraction of electron beams at thin metallic foils, which was then linked with the original work on diffraction gratings in the optical domain in the 1960s. By that time, Kretschmann et al. had achieved the excitation of Sommerfeld's surface waves with visible light using prism coupling in 1968. And then a unified description of all these phenomena in the form of surface plasmon polaritons was established [19].

When light interacts with nanostructures, it can couple to free-electron excitation near the metal surface. The electromagnetic resonances associated with these surface plasmons depend on the details of the nanostructures, opening up opportunities for controlling light confinement on the nanoscale. The resulting strong electromagnetic fields allow weak nonlinear processes, which depend superlinearly on the local field, to be significantly enhanced. In addition to providing enhanced nonlinear effects with ultrafast response times, plasmonic nanostructures allow nonlinear optical components to be scaled down in size [20]. Nonlinear optical effects arise when electronic motion in a strong electromagnetic field cannot be considered harmonic. Expansion of the anharmonicity as power series in the field strength mixes the incident fields and produces new fields that oscillate at the sums and differences of the incident frequencies and can propagate in various directions.

For applications, the most important effects occur at second and third order. The second-order response typically gives rises to wave-mixing effects that lead to frequency conversion, the most common example being second-harmonic generation(SHG), its second harmonic, 2ω . New frequencies arise also from third-order nonlinearities. More importantly, however, the third-order response contains terms at the incident frequencies. This is known as the optical Kerr effect and results in nonlinear modification of the refractive index, allowing all-optical switching and modulation of light. By combining Kerr nonlinearities with optical cavities or other systems with feedback, it is possible outputs. For optical beams with finite transverse size, diffraction and nonlinear effects can balance each other, giving rise to optical solitons.

The plasmonic structure can enhance nonlinear effects in two main ways. First, such structures provide field enhancement near the metal-dielectric interface, associated with the excitation of either SPPs or LSPs. This is characterized by the frequency-dependent local-field factor $L(\omega,r)=|E_{loc}(\omega,r)/E_0(\omega)|$, where r is the position vector, $E_{loc}(\omega,r)$ is the local field at frequency ω associated with the plasmonic excitation, and $E_0(\omega,r)$ is the incident field. The resulting strong fields enhance the nonlinear response locally and, when carefully designed, even whole the response is integrated over the whole sample. This concept is equally applicable to increasing the nonlinearity of the metal itself (intrinsic response) or of a material adjacent to the metal (extrinsic response). Second, the plasmonic excitation parameters, including the SPP wavevector and the LSP or metamaterial resonance frequency, are very sensitive to the refractive indices of the metal and the surrounding dielectric. A nonlinear change in the index of either material can therefore significantly modify plasmonic resonances and associated reflection, transmission or absorption of light.

3 Hot topics in nonlinear plasmonics

Surface-enhanced nonlinear effects. Surface-enhanced SHG [16] was first studied using electrochemically roughened silver surfaces. The SHG signal was found to be diffuse, but increased by four orders of magnitude relative to a flat reference surface when integrated over all detection directions. The results suggested that the signals are incoherent and enhanced by LSP resonances of the nanoscale surface features.

More-recent work has addressed surface-enhanced SHG from a number of viewpoint. Near-field SHG measurements have been performed using near-field detection and excitation, the latter also correlated with surface topography. Far-field SHG microscopy has emphasized the spatial overlap of the local fundamental and SHG modes. These and additional studies show that the SHG signals depend on the polarization of the fundamental field even if the light is focused down to the achievable resolution of a few hundreds of nanometers.

LSP resonances can also enhance nonlinear processes other than SHG. In particular, surface-enhanced third -harmonic generation has also been observed and its different symmetry rules, relative to those of SHG, discussed.

Enhancement of SHG by propagating SPPs was also demonstrated early on, and SPPs have been used to enhance four-wave mixing (FWM). Very recently, the roles of photonic and plasmonic modes in SHG from metal films have been addressed by momentum-space spectroscopy.

Many scientists believe that the future of signal processing and computing lies not within electronics but in the field of sub-wavelength optics. Controlling light at sub-wavelength scale, forbidden by traditional far-field optics, relies on surface plasmon techniques [21]. SPPs are electromagnetic waves that exist on the surface of metals such as gold or silver. The interaction between the electromagnetic field and the free electrons in the metal helps confine SPPs tightly to the surface. The behavior of this wave can be manipulated by nanostructuring either the surface or a nearby dielectric. By contrast, metallic particles (or nanoscale dielectric voids in a metallic host) can enhance the field by supporting localized plasmonic excitation that create superior field confinement. Both mechanisms can locally control the electromagnetic field, a pre-requisite for the development of such light-based circuity and devices.

In order to directly make plasmonic components, scientists commonly propose two approaches, both based on the modification of the refractive index near the metal surface. The firs uses the electro-optic effect exhibited, for example, by liquid crystal molecules. Here, the refractive index depends on the molecular alignment, which can be modulated using an electronic and photonic signals can be transferred, processed, and interconnected in the same metallic circuitry. A second method relies on dielectric materials with a large Kerr nonlinearity, or a refractive index that depends on the intensity of the illuminating light. Wayne Dickson got a result of making plsmonic components with his cooperators, as shown in Fig.1.

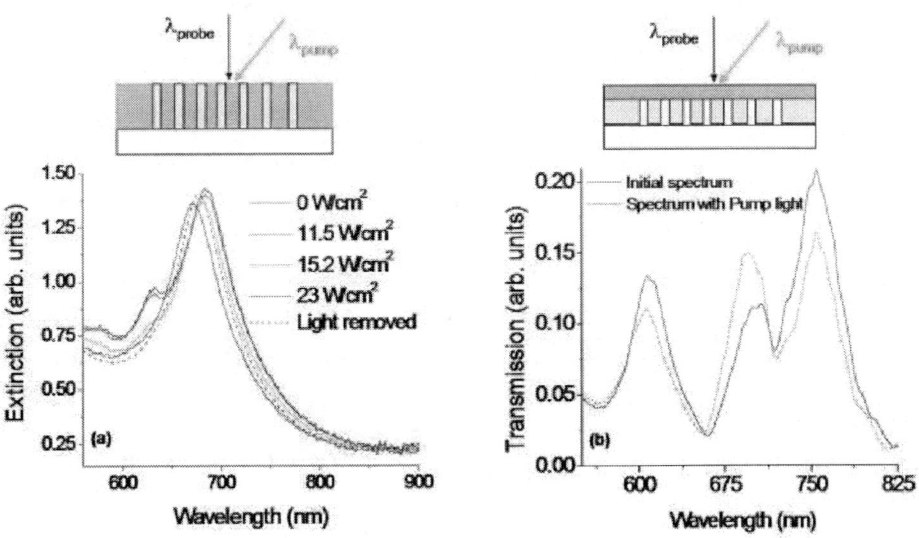

Figure 1. Modulation of transmission by an array of gold nanorads (left) and a whole array in a thin gold film (right). Both were coated with poly-3BCMU (blue in schematic) and pumped with control light at 514nm.

To modulate and switch SPP signals by optical means in a waveguiding geometry, changes can be included in the real or imaginary part of the permittivity by control light, and these changes can occur in the metal or the adjacent dielectric. Light-induced absorption modulation has explored with the intrinsic metal (Au and Ga) nonlinearity [22-23] as well as the dielectric component in a plasmonic waveguide [24].

The intrinsic nonlinearity of gold is related to the interband excitation of non-equilibrium electrons and results in small changes in the real part of the permittivity but in more considerable changes in the imaginary part. The associated relaxation time is on the picosecond scale [25], and terahertz-rate direct modulation of SPP signals in plasmonic gold waveguides is thus possible. The variation of SPP modes via modification of their wave. To convert this to intensity modulation. Various phase-sensitive configuration, including Mach-Zehnder interferometers and Waveguide-ring resonators, are needed.

Periodically structured metal films and surfaces, the so-called plasmonic or surface plasmon polaritonic crystals (SPPCs), provide considerable versatility for tailoring the wavelength-dependent plasmonic resonances and the electromagnetic field enhancement in devices a few tens of wavelengths in size [26]. SPPCs have optical properties analogous to those of two-dimensional photonic crystals. The spectral positions of their resonances, their dispersion, and the phase and group velocities of SPP Bloch modes can be engineered by controlling the size and shape of the unit cell and its period. In particular, relatively flat SPP modes with low group velocity are possible, resulting in the high field enhancement beneficial for high effective nonlinearity. These effects have been demonstrated using the nonlinearity of gold gratings to control SPP excitation at speeds determined by the subpicosecond response time of the gold nonlinearity.

4 Latest developments in nonlinear plasmonics

The method of calculating the nonlinear propagation of surface plasmon polaritons in one-dimensional planar waveguides consisting of a metal slab or a semi-infinite metal bounded by linear dielectrics, starting with an assumed third-order nonlinearity that characterizes the nonlinear response of the metal has been demonstrated by Israel. With this approach he model the self-phase-modulation of surface plasmon polaritons. Expressions relating the complex nonlinear parameter of these surface wave with the third-order nonlinear susceptibility of the metal are provided. We present and discuss results pertaining to the self-phase-modulation of the symmetric and antisymmetric surface plasmon polaritons supported by a thin gold slab in vacuum and of the surface plasmon polaritons supported by the single gold-vacuum interface [15].

The expression for the complex nonlinear parameter that characterizes the self-phase-modulation in term of the structural properties of the wave guide, and use it to construct a differential equation that describes the evolution of the SPP's complex amplitude can be derived.

DOI: 10.1051/matecconf/201712803002

Solving this differential equation provides us with a self-consistent way to estimate the nonlinear phase and nonlinear loss experienced by the SPP upon propagation. Israel De Leon and his cooperators got the result of estimating the nonlinear phase and nonlinear loss experienced by the SPP upon propagation as shown in Fig.2.

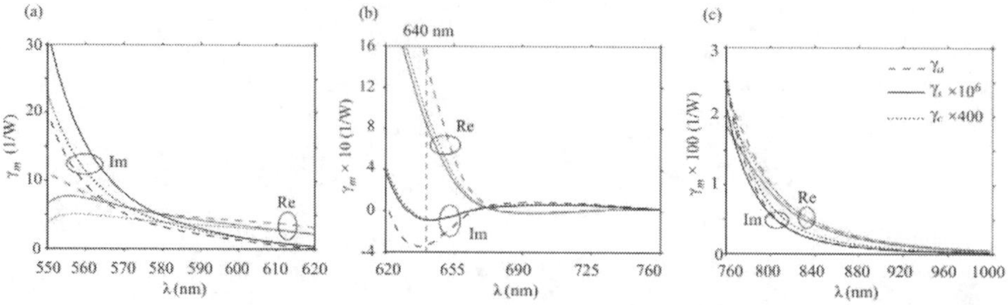

Figure 2. Complex nonlinear parameter of the various SPP modes m=(s, a, c), calculated over three different wavelength ranges. The values of γ_s and γ_c have been multiplied by a factor of 10^6 and 400, respectively, before plotting. (Color online) Plasmon-Soliton

The derivation of a hybrid vector NLSE describing slab confined TM modes which are self-trapped in the free (in-plan) dimension by the Kerr effect [27]. A nonlinear slab sandwiched between metal layers supports a hybrid plasmon-soliton, and exhibits high confinement with lower effective beam size than the conventional diffraction limit-although practically the soliton self-trapping dimension is not reduced below the diffraction limit with available nonlinear material. Assisted by the transverse plasmonic effect, the self-trapping dimension of the plasmon-soliton was substantially compressed when reducing the slab width. The practical limitation of the plasmon-soliton size reduction is determined by available nonlinear materials and metal loss. A novel dispersion characteristic-the nonlinear index dispersion, exhibits saturation at small gap width-while the linear effective index keeps increasing indefinitely.

The field of nanophotonics is finding myriad applications in information technology, health care, lighting, sensing and national security. The scientific community's interest in this area was recently sparked with the discovery of enhanced light transmission through nanoholes in an array or with surrounding surface corrugations. Even with a hole far below the cutoff of the enhanced fields, due to the resonant SPP excitation, the amount of light scattered through the holes was several times larger than expected for an isolated subwavelength hole [28]. The excitation and visualization of ultrafast dynamics of SPP modes can be achieved in experiments by coupling the optical field into and out of the metallic film using a 2D array of nanoholes etched in the metallic film on a dielectric substrate. By measuring the transmittance for a number of samples with various periods, one can gain a better understanding of the modal structure of SPP fields. The spectra are dominated by asymmetric, Fano-type lineshapes at the various SPP excitation conditions. There are two components to this transmitted field: one that passes through the small, subwavelength holes directly, and one that is a product of the excited surface mode. The interference between these two components results in various maxima and minima.

5 Conclusion

In this article, we reviewed the basic researches of nonlinear of plasmonic, which is still a young research field. And its basic concepts have been demonstrated in a wide variety of ways. Also we reviewed the hot topics and the latest developments in nonlinear plasmonics. The role of plasmonics in nonlinear optics is threefold. First, by enhancing the effective nonlinearity, plasmonic nanostructures contribute to conventional photonics by allowing nonlinear effects to be utilized with reduced optical power. Second, they make it possible to scale down nonlinear components in size, which is important for the development of integrable photonic devices. Third, the response time of plasmonic excitations is ultrafast, allowing optical signals to be manipulated on femtosecond timescales. The field of plasmonics offers several research opportunities. To fulfill the promise offered by plasmonics, more research needs to be done in these areas. Some of the challenges that face plasmonics research in the coming years are as follows: (i) demonstrate optical frequency subwavelength metallic wired circuits with a propagation loss that is comparable to conventional optical waveguides. (ii) Develop deep subwavelength plasmonic nanolithography over large surfaces.

Reference

1. Y. Wang, C.-Y. Lin, A. Nikolaenko, V. Raghunathan, and E. O. Potma, Adv. Opt. Photon. 3, 1 (2011).
2. G. Cerullo and S. De Silvestri, Rev. Sci. Instrum. 74, 1 (2003).
3. M. Fejer, phys. Today 47, 25 (1994).
4. D. Cotter, R. Manning, K. Blow, A. Ellis, and A. Kelly, Science 286, 1523 (1999).

5. M. Kauranen and A. V. Zayats, Nat. Photon. 6, 737 (2012).
6. H. Raether, Surface Plasmons on Smooth and Rough Surfaces and on Gratings (Springer, Berlin, 1988).
7. J. A. Schuller, E. S. Barnard, W. Cai, Y. C. Jun, J. S. White, and M. L. Brongersma, Nat. Mater. 9, 193 (2010).
8. H. RAETHER, physics of Thin Films 9 (1977) 145.
9. A. OTTO, Z. phys. 216 (1968) 398 and Phys. Stat. Solidi. 26 (1968) 199.
10. D. Mihalache, G. I. Stegeman, C. T. Seation, E. M. Wright, R. Zanoni, A. D. Boardman, and T. Twardowski, Opt. Lett. 12, 187 (1987).
11. H.Yin, C. Xu, and P. M. Hui, Appl. Phys. Lett. 94, 221102 (2009).
12. J.-H. Huang, R. Chang, p.-T. Leung, and D. P. Tsai, Opt. Commun. 282, 1412 (2009).
13. A. R. Davoyan, I. V. Shadrivov, and Y. S. Kivshar, Opt. Express 16, 21209 (2008).
14. F. Hache, D. Ricard, C. Flytzanis, and U. Kreibig, Appl. Phys. A 47, 347 (1988).
15. I. D. Leon, J. E. Sipe, and R. W. Boyd, Phys. Rev. A 89, 013855 (2014).
16. R. M. Corn, M. Romagnoli, M. D. Levenson and M. R. Philpott, Chemical. Phys. Lett. Vol 106, Number 12 (1984).
17. T. Y. F. Tsang, Opt. Lett. Vol 21. No 4 (1996).
18. E. Feigenbaum and M. Orenstein, Opt. Lett. 32, 674 (2007).
19. S. A. Maier, Plasmonics: Fundamentals and Applications, 2006.
20. M. Kauranen and A. V. Zayats, Nature. Photo. Vol 6, (2012).
21. W. Dickson, A. Krasavin, G. Wurtz, and A. Zayats, Newsroom, 10.1117.
22. Rotenberg, N. Betz, M. & van Driel, H. M. Ultrafast all-optical coupling of light to surface plasmon polaritons on plain metal surfaces. Phys. Rev. Lett. 105, 017402 (2010)
23. Krasavin, A. V. & Zheludev, N. I. Active plasmonics: controlling signals in Au/Ga waveguide using nanoscale structural transformations. Appl. Phys. Lett. 84,1416-1418 (2004).
24. Pacific, D. Lezec, H. J.& Atwater, H. A. All-optical modulation by plasmonic excitation of CdSe quantum dots. Nature Photon. 1, 402-406 (2007).
25. Baida, H. et al. Ulfast nonlinear optical response of a single gold nanorod near its surface plasmon resonance. Phys. Rev. Lett. 107, 057402 (2011).
26. Wurtz, G. A. & Zayats, A. V. Nonlinear surface plamon polaritonic crystals. Laser Photon. Rev. 2, 125-135 (2008).
27. E. Feigenbaum and M. Orenstein, Opt. Lett. 32, 674 (2007).
28. Y. Fainman, K. Tetz, R. Rokitski and P. Lin, Optics & Photonics. 17, 24-29 (2006).

MATEC Web of Conferences 128, 03003 (2017) DOI: 10.1051/matecconf/201712803003
EITCE 2017

An Extrusion Die with Twin Cavities for Semi-hollow Al-Profiles

Xuemei Huang[1,a], Rurong Deng[2,b *]

[1,2]Guangzhou Vocational College of Science and Technology, Guangzhou, 510550, China
[a]Email: 41784402@qq.com, [b]Email: SQF6410@163.com
[*] The corresponding author

Abstract. The importance of extrusion die with multi-cavities was elaborated. Through an actual case. A new structure for the semi-hollow Al-profiles was introduced. The structure named substituted type to solve the cantilever strength was presented. And the selection and the optimization of structure parameters were described in detail. Including the determination of extrusion machine ability, the layout for the die holes, the use of computer simulation software for analysis and comparison to determine the arrangement of portholes, the structure of chamber in female die, the selection of bearing etc. It was shown that the structure with twin cavities for semi-hollow profiles is effective, the structure can greatly improve the production efficiency and reduce the cost. It is worth promoting. The purpose is to provide reliable data and reference for the further research and development of this technology on the extrusion die with multi-cavities in a die.

1 Introduction

In recent years, aluminum products have been widely used, and the field of application is more widely. The types and specifications of aluminum alloy products are more and more. The profile of the profiles becomes more and more complex. And in these kinds and specifications, many products are the semi hollow profiles. The design of dies for semi hollow profile is complicated, and the key problem is to solve the die strength. While modern manufacturing technology keeps improving, especially in recent years, the total cost of the enterprises was rising, the enterprises are facing some pressure so that the extrusion technology of multi-cavities in a die is being studied in order to improve production efficiency and reduce costs .

2 Determination of die structure parameters

2.1 The structure form

This is a substituted type extrusion die structure to make a cut in a reasonable position of the cantilever of semi hollow section. The cantilever is divided into two parts, one part is used as a fake core to design the male die instead of the cantilever in extrusion process, while the other is designed as a die hole of female die. When the male and female die are fitted together and composed of porthole extrusion die, the fake core and die hole recombine in cutting position and reform the integrity of the cantilever, it improves the stress state of the cantilever, the immediate force to the cantilever is changed from the original cantilever to hollow bridge, it greatly improves the strength of the die. For the extrusion die with twin cavities in a die, because each of die core position in the male die is not in the center of the die same as the single hole in the equilibrium of the force around without creating additional pressure difference due to core elastic offset. Therefore, this factor must be taken into account in the die of twin cavities. Otherwise, the offset of the die core will change the wall thickness of the profile. Figure 1. shows a typical semi hollow profile and a schematic diagram for cutting the cantilever into two parts. The section area of the profile is 120mm^2, and its tongue ratio is 5.4.

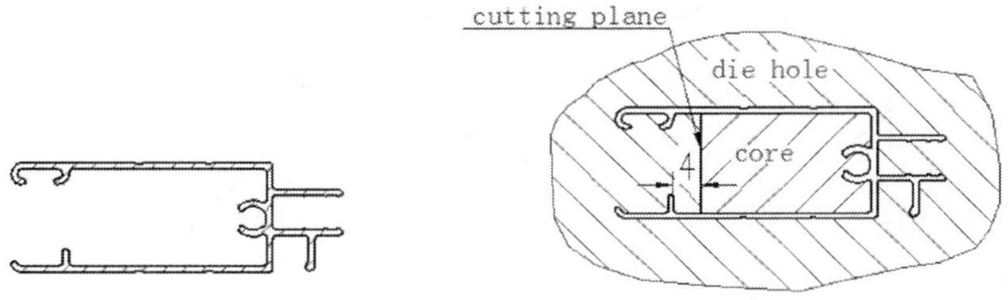

(a) The profile section (b) The signal of cantilever cutting

Figure 1. The sketch of section and cantilever division

2.2 Determination of extrusion machine capacity

To determine the extrusion machine is to select the proper size of the inner diameter of the extrusion container and the proper pressure of the extrusion machine on the section of the extrusion cylinder. The size of the inner diameter of the extrusion container determines the degree of deformation of the extrusion named extrusion coefficient. The extrusion coefficient is too large, the extrusion force will increase, the extrusion forming will be difficult, and the force that the die will endure will also increase, and the strength of the die will be reduced. The extrusion coefficient is too small, which will affect the mechanical properties and surface quality of the profile. The specific pressure of the extrusion machine is to meet the working pressure for extrusion forming. If the pressure is too small, extrusion forming will be difficult, and the pressure is too high, it will increase the force of the die and reduce the life of the die. Based on the experience, the extrusion coefficient is the most suitable in the range of 40～80, while the relative pressure is most favorable at 650 ～ 800MPa. Based on these considerations, for the profiles shown in Figure 1,the choice of 10MN extrusion machine is made, the extrusion cylinder diameter is up to 130mm. By calculation, the extrusion press is 753MPa. If the single hole extrusion is adopted, the extrusion coefficient is 110.6, which is obviously not suitable, it is suitable for twin cavities with the extrusion coefficient of 55.3.

2.3 Arrangement of die holes

Determining the die hole arrangement of twin cavities means to determine the discharge mode of extrusion. The principle of selecting the discharging way is as follows:

One is to ensure that the two hole does not occur interweave, twist, or rub each other in the extrusion process. Two is to consider the choice of die parameters can give full play the potential of the extrusion cylinder. The three is to consider the strength and rigidity of the die.

As a substituted type extrusion die structure with twin cavities, because the core is false, so we must consider the position and direction of the cutting plane in the die, in order to make it possible to cut away from the die center. The layout of the die holes is shown in figure 2.

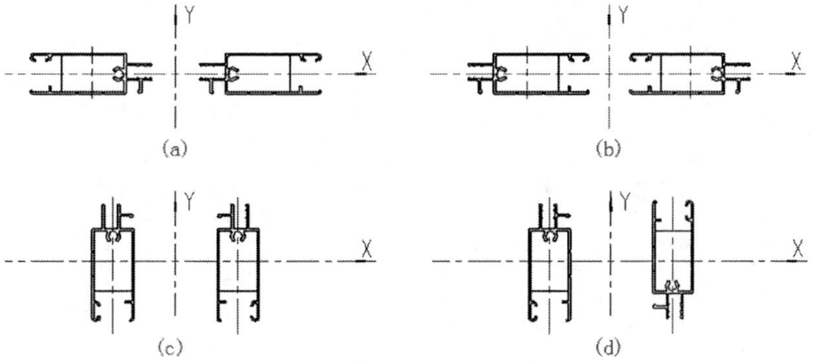

Figure2. The layout of die hole

The Figure 2- (a) is the most reasonable of the four methods in the diagram. In this way, the large surface of the profile is selected and the contact mode is introduced so as to realize the smooth extrusion. Due to the cutting plane is arranged away from the center, so that when the male and female die reset together, the elastic offset of the core will make the gap of the cutting plane be smaller. According to the plastic forming minimum resistance law, the metal is less likely to enter the joint gap. Thus, the drawing or reinforcing bar of the section can be avoided.

Figure 2-(b) is just the opposite. For the die of multi cavities, an elastic deviation is caused by the additional pressure difference due to the pressure gradient in the radial direction of the extrusion cylinder, as shown in figure 3. The force F1 in the diagram is greater than the force F2, while the force F3 is equal to the force F4.

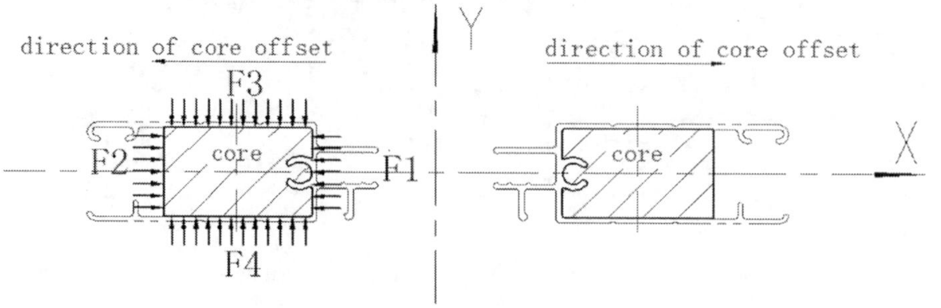

Figure3. The diagram of elastic deviation of die core

2.4 Determination of design parameters of male die

The parameters of male die include the design of the portholes, the determination of the diversion ratio, and the size selection of the bridge etc.

The arrangement of the feeder ports is shown in figure 4.

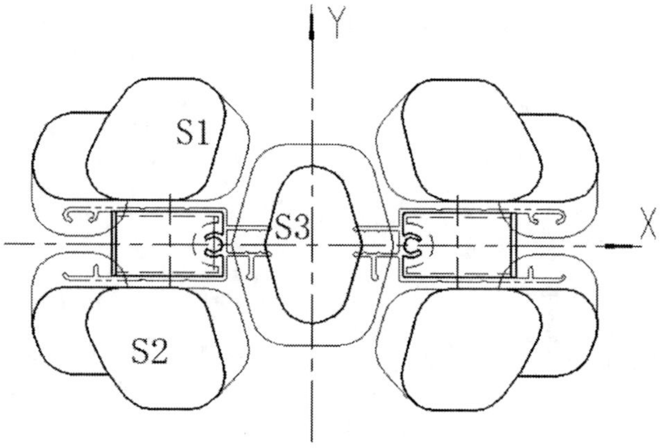

Figure4. The signal of portholes

To design a common feeder port in the die center is to consider that the screw hole in the core is a difficult part of metal forming, It is necessary to ensure that there is sufficient metal flow supply.

The main parameters are as follows:

1. The feeding ratio is 14.5.

Considering the surface quality of the profiles and the extrusion force during the extrusion process, the experience shows that The most appropriate is that the ratio is (25~35)% of the extrusion ratio. Therefore, using computer simulation software and personal experience, the final feeding ratio value is appropriate.

2. The width of hollow bridge are 20mm and 16mm respectively.

3. The height of the hollow bridge named male die thickness is 65mm.

On the premise of guaranteeing the strength, the die thickness of male die should not be too large, otherwise, the extrusion pressure will increase, it will be unfavorable to the forming and the strength.

4. The area relationship between the feeder ports is as follows:

$$S1=S2=1.35S3 \quad (1)$$

Through software simulation, it is found that S1, S2 and S3 meet the area relationship shown in Equation 2, the flow velocity tends to be consistent everywhere, the S3 value increases, the metal flow is intense and the deformation degree is bigger, the elastic offset of the die core in the radial direction will increase.

$$S1=S2=(1.2\sim1.4)\,S3 \quad (2)$$

5. The largest feeder ports diameter of feeding is 110mm.

6. The outlet of the feeder ports adopt the reaming form of 10.5 degrees. The main reason is to reduce the extrusion force. The extrusion pressure can be reduced by about 5% by adopting 5~15 degree reaming.

7. This is the obvious difference that no feeder ports are arranged on the side of the cutting plane between the twin cavities and the single cavity of the semi hollow profile. If a feeder port is set on one side of the cutting plane, it is difficult for the metal to converge.

2.5 Assembly of die and cantilever

The assembly of die and cantilever are shown in figure 5.

In a single cavity die, the joint of the cantilever in the die is usually the form of a vertical plane, which is easy to move the metal into the gap of the joint plane, the metal will be formed in the joint plane and the surface of profile will appear a raised wire or convex surface.

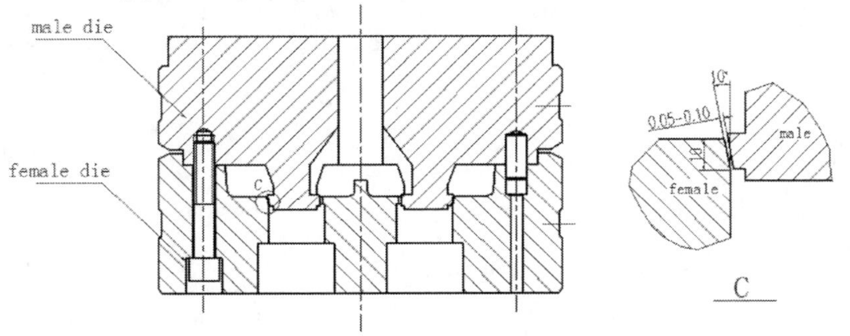

Figure5. The assembly of die and cantilever

In order to eliminate the phenomenon, and prevent the collision of cores in the assembly process with the increase of the cores, the oblique plane jointing is designed. In this way, it overcomes the shortcomings of the vertical jointing, the direction of metal flow and the jointing plane is formed into an angle, the metal will be cut so that the phenomenon of raised wire and convex surface will disappear. Thus, the bonding plane is not parallel to the direction of the metal flow to form a shearing of the metal, thereby preventing the possibility of the metal entering the gap of the joint surface. The practice shows that the effect is good.

2.6 Design of female die

The design of female die include welding chamber height, shape, structure and the choice of bearing.

The welding chamber structure and bearing as shown in figure 6.

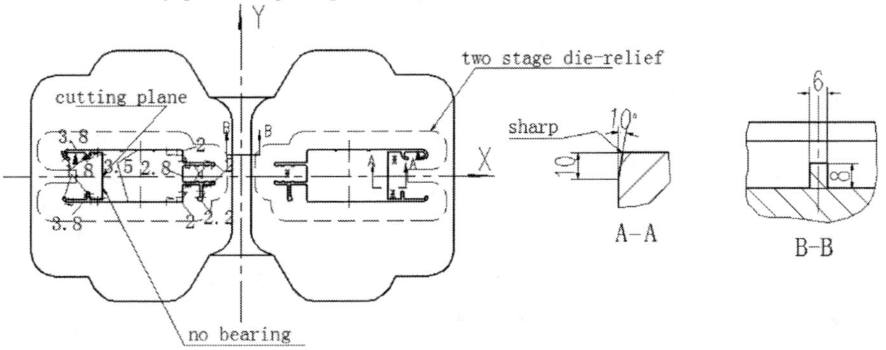

Figure6. The signal of welding chamber and the bearing

The main parameters are as follows:

1.About the welding chamber shape

The welding chamber shape is to base on the largest edge of feeder ports as the contour that ensure the metal in the welding chamber from the feeder ports that it can be not blocked on the boundary. Usually, the welding chamber contour edge must be bigger 2mm than edge of the portholes, and the piers shall be formed as far as possible at the root of the portholes to increase the strength of the die.

2.The welding chamber height is 16mm.

3.About the structure of the welding chamber

It is an important principle that the independent welding chambers are designed for the die design of multi cavities. A separating wall of 6mm in width between the welding chambers is arranged. If the partition wall is not arranged, the rigid region of metal flow is formed at the central part between the die holes, and the coarse crystal phenomenon of the corresponding section of the section bar is easy to occur, which leads to serious chromatic aberration of the section bar.

4.About the selection of bearing

For the die with twin cavities, according to the principle of selecting bearing of the single, the bearing of one die hole is selected, and the bearing of the other die hole is the same.

3 Conclusions

The die has been tested and used, the result indicates that the die has been successful at one time. Its extrusion output life of 20.3×10^{3}Kg, all indicators meet the requirements. This shows that the structure used in the case of semi hollow profiles is effective and reasonable. It can also be concluded that if a single hole extrusion is applied on the same extrusion machine, the extrusion coefficient is 111.6, which will be difficult to carry out. And smaller extrusion machine must be selected. This shows that extrusion die with twin cavities can improve production efficiency and reduce cost.

References

1. LIU Jingan. Die design, manufacture, application and maintains for aluminum profiles extrusion[M].Beijing:Metallurgical Press,1999:181～183.
2. XIE Jianxie,LIU Jingan, Die design, manufacture, application and maintains for aluminum profiles extrusion[M].Beijing:Metallurgical Press,2012:133～138
3. WANG Liwei. Optimization design of extrusion die for the bigger slenderness ratio half hollow aluminum profile[J]. Die and Mould Manufacture, 2011(4):61-64.
4. YU Mingtao,LI Fuguo.Simulation extrusion process of the sketch hollow aluminum profile based on infinite volume method[J].Die and Technology, 2008(4):40-43.
5. SUN Xuemei,ZHAO Guoqun.Fake porthole extrusion die structure design and strength analysis for cantilever aluminum alloy profiles[J].Journal of Mechanical Engineering,2013, 49(24):39～44.
6. KUANG Weihua,CHEN Biaobiao.Research on design and structure of extrusion die for cantilever aluminum profile [J].Hot Working Technology,2013,42(21):136-138.
7. DENG Rurong, Huang,Xuemei. Design of the extrusion die of semi-hollow aluminum profile[J].Light Alloy Fabrication Technology,2015,43(4):51-54.
8. Xu Yongli, Huang Shuangjian, Pang Zugao, et al.Failure analysis of extrusion die and optimization of heat treatment process for aluminum alloy circular tube [J]. Forging & Stamping Technology, 2015, 40(2):116-122.
9. Hu Dongpo, Wang Leigang, Huang Yao. Steady-state simulation and die improvement on the extrusion of prolate aluminum profile [J]. Forging & Stamping Technology, 2015, 40(4):69-73.

MATEC Web of Conferences **128**, 03004 (2017) DOI: 10.1051/matecconf/201712803004
EITCE 2017

Simulation on the Thermal Properties of Polymer Composites Reinforced by Buckypaper

AYing Zhang[1,a], ZhengHong Li[2]

[1]*Harbin University, 150086 Harbin, China*
[2]*Harbin Institute of Technology, 150001 Harbin, China*

Abstract. FLUENT was used to analyze how the bending cycles of buckypaper affects the temperature distribution, the changes of the temperature with time and the heating rate during heating. The typical temperature decreases with the increase of bending cycles of the buckypaper. The typical temperature increases with the increase of heating power. The temperature distribution of the polymer composites is more uniform with the increase of bending cycles of buckypaper. The difference of the maximum and minimum temperature of the composites increases linearly with the increase of heating power. The average temperature of the composites when reaching the stable state increase as the bending cycles of buckypaper decrease. The difference of the maximum and minimum temperature of the composites decreases with the increase of the bending cycles.

1 Introduction

CNTs have been regarded as one of the most promising reinforcement materials or functional agents for developing high performance structural and multifunctional nanocomposites [1-3]. A new approach was developed by the authors to infiltrate a preformed nanotube network or nanotube mat (often called buckypaper) with resin to produce bulk polymeric nanocomposites with a uniform CNT dispersion, well-controlled nanostructures and high CNT loading capability [4]. SWCNT-BPs can be used to fabricate high-loading CNT/thermoplastic composites with improved thermal properties [5]. With their excellent thermal conductivity, the polymer composites reinforced by the buckypaper can be used to solve the heat problems associated with advanced electronic equipment, radiators, connectors and printed circuit boards. With the effective control of nanopaper of carbon nanotubes, they can be used as good sensor and functional material. Studies on their thermal properties are less frequently reported, particularly for the thermal properties of buckypaper reinforced polymer composites analyzed by using the finite element analysis (FEA). In this study, heating model of the polymer composite reinforced by buckypaper is established to predict the thermal property of buckypaper reinforced composite.

2 Finite element models

As shown in Figure 1, the heating model of the polymer composites reinforced by the bent buckypaper under different heating conditions were developed by using the finite element program FLUENT. Effects of the bending cycles of the buckypaper on the temperature distribution and heating uniformity of the polymer composites reinforced by the bent buckypaper were investigated using finite element software FLUENT.

In Figure 1, heating the buckypaper is driven by a power source, and the cube region is the polymer matrix which is heated by the buckypaper during heating process. The temperature of the polymer matrix is increased due to the electro-heating of the buckypaper. The length, width, and the thickness of the heating model of the polymer composite reinforced by the bent buckypaper are 36 mm, 5 mm, and 10 mm respectively. The thicknesses of the buckypaper are 0.4 mm. The bending height and bending period (A) of the bent buckypaper are 6 mm and 12 mm. The objective of this research is to analyze the effect of the bending cycles of the buckypaper on the thermal conductivity of the composites using a finite element software FLUENT.

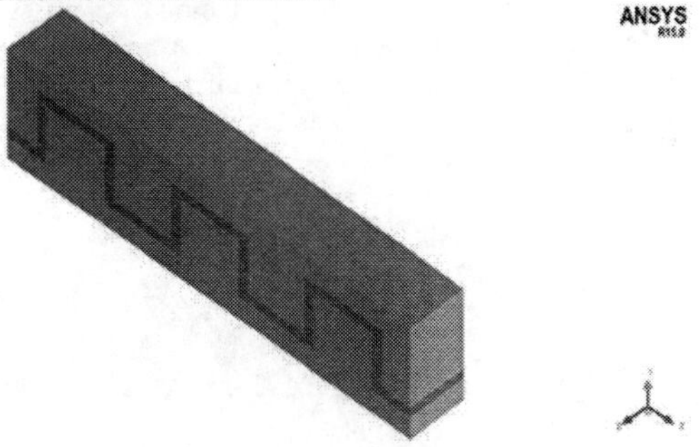

Figure 1. Model of the polymer composites reinforced by bent buckypaper

[a] Corresponding author: zaying@sina.com

DOI: 10.1051/matecconf/201712803004

The grid work is done by software ICEM, and the mesh model of the polymer composite reinforced by the bent buckypapers as shown in Figures 2.

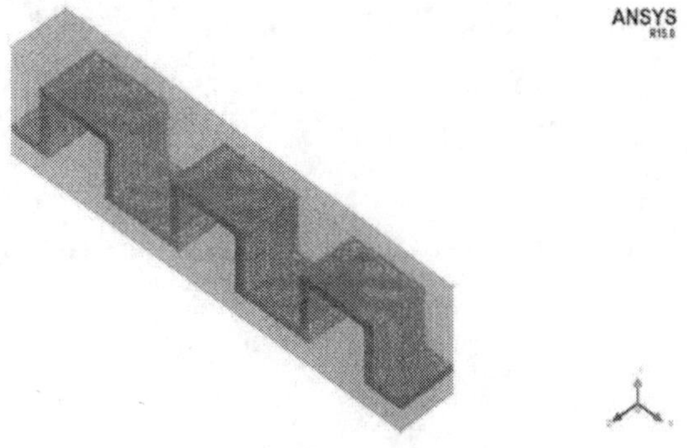

Figure 2. Mesh division model of the polymer composites reinforced by the bent buckypaper

3 Results and discussion

As shown in Table 1, the maximum, minimum and average temperature of the composites reinforced by the bent buckypaper with different bending cycles under different power along the section z=0 were calculated by the finite element software FLUENT.

Table 1. Typical temperature of composites reinforced by the bent buckypaper with different bending cycles under different power along the section z=0

Bending cycles	0.3w			0.6w		
	Tmax /K	Tmin /K	Tave /K	Tmax /K	Tmin /K	Tave /K
1	377.8	354.6	370.7	455.7	409.3	441.5
3	330.9	319.9	327.6	361.7	339.9	355.1
5	319.1	312.0	317.1	338.1	324.0	334.2

Table 1 shows that the maximum, minimum and average temperature decrease as the bending cycles of the buckypaper increase from 1 A to 3 A under the same power. As shown in Table 1, the maximum, minimum and average temperature increases as the heating power increase from 0.3 W to 0.6 W with the same bending cycle.

Figure 3 shows the temperature cloudy maps which indicate that the temperature distribution of the polymer composites reinforced by the bent buckypaper along the section z=0 is more uniform as the bending cycles of the buckypaper increase from 1 A to 3 A under the heating power of 0.3 W.

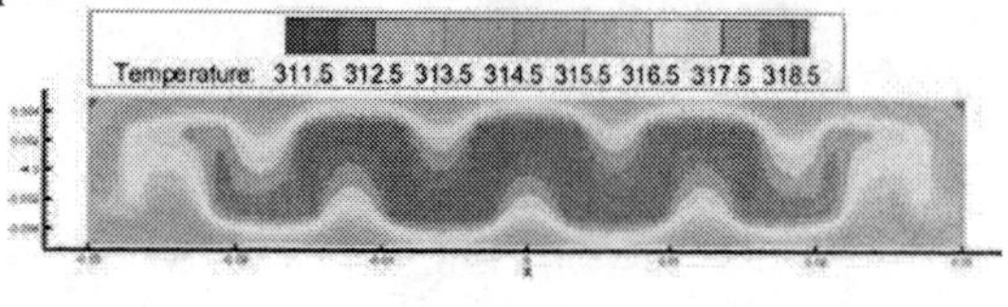

(a) 5A

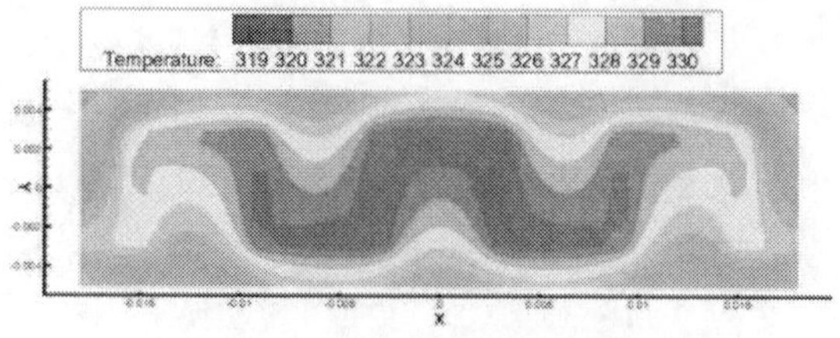

(b) 3A

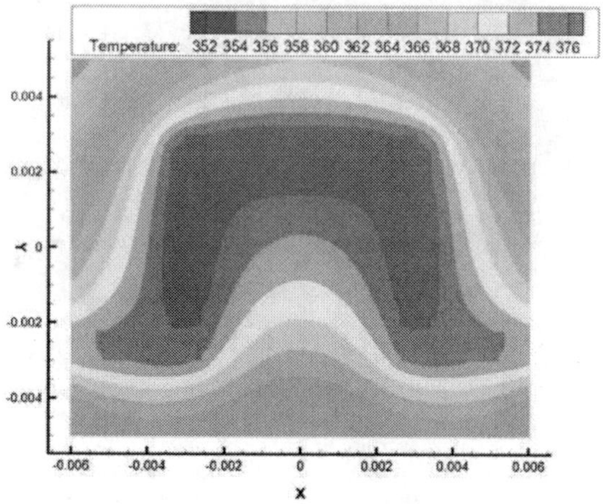

(c) 1A

Figure 3. Temperature distribution of nanocomposite with different bending cycles along the section z=0 under the heating power of 0.3w

Figure 4 shows the temperature cloudy maps which indicate that the temperature distribution of the polymer composites reinforced by the bent buckypaper along the section z=0 is more uniform as the bending cycles of the buckypaper increase from 1 A to 3 A under the power of 0.6 W.

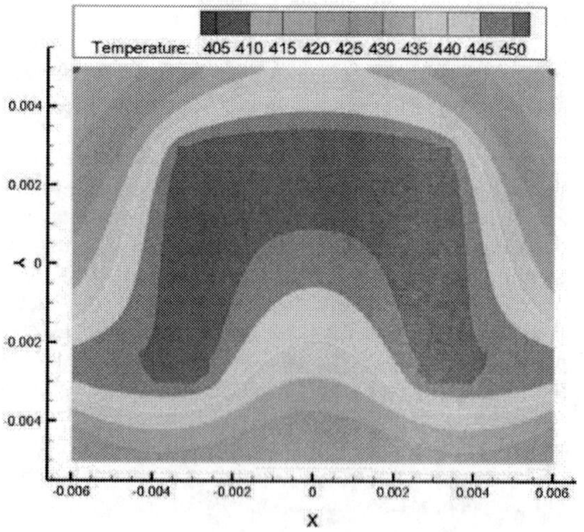

(a) 1A

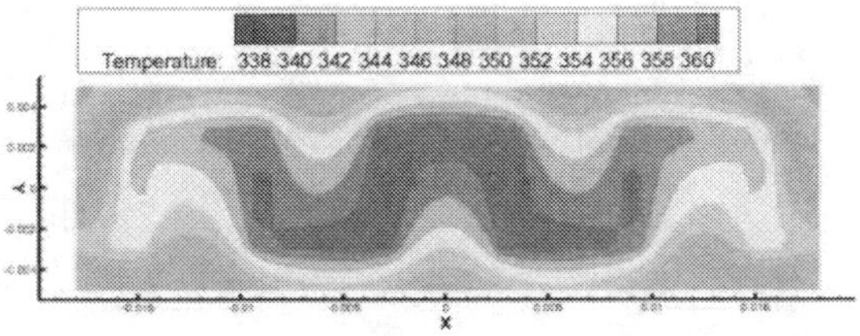

(b) 3A

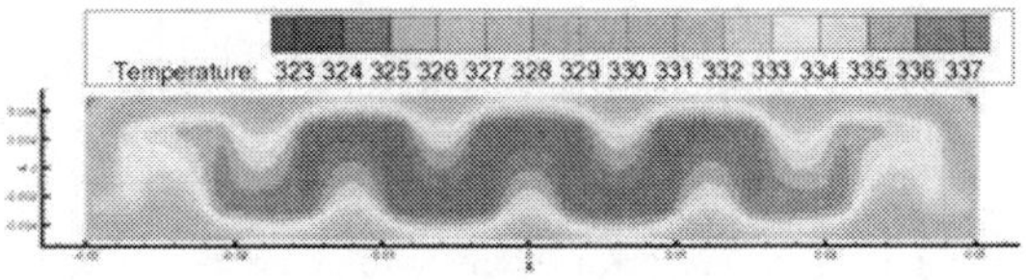

(c) 5A

Figure 4. Temperature distribution of composites reinforced by buckypaper with different bending cycles along the section z=0 under the heating power of 0.6w

Figure 3 and 4 shows the temperature cloudy maps which indicate that the temperature distribution of the polymer composites reinforced by the bent buckypaper along the section z=0 is more uniform as the bending cycles of the buckypaper increase from 1 A to 5 A.

Table 2 shows that the average thermal flow of composites reinforced by buckypaper with different bending cycles under the heating power of 0.3 W and 0.6 W along external surface. As shown in Table 2, the average thermal flow of both the buckypaper and resin decrease as the bending cycles of buckypaper increase with the same heating power.

Table 2. Average thermal flow of composites reinforced by buckypaper with different bending cycles under the heating power of 0.3 W and 0.6 W along external surface (W/m^2)

Bending cycles	0.3w		0.6w	
	Buckypaper	Resin	Buckypaper	Resin
1	748.13	641.86	1496.65	1284.06
3	287.88	250.70	501.08	575.38
5	178.10	155.77	356.33	311.68

Figure 5 shows the curve of temperature difference of composites reinforced by buckypaper with different bending cycles along the section z=0. As shown in Figure 5, the difference of the maximum and minimum temperature of the composite increases linearly with the increase of the heating power. Figure 5 shows that the difference of the maximum and minimum temperature of the composite decreases with the increase of the bending cycles of buckypaper, which indicate that the temperature distribution of the composite is more uniform.

Figure 6 shows the curve of average temperature of composites reinforced by buckypaper with different bending cycle versus time along the section z=0. Figure 6 shows that both curves of the average temperature exhibit similar trend and there are two distinct stages observed. The first stage shows that the slopes of the curves increase significantly with increasing the heating time. A fast increase of the average temperature occurs during stage I after which the slope is changed, indicating the beginning of the second stage. A progressive but slow increase of the average temperature is observed in the second stage.

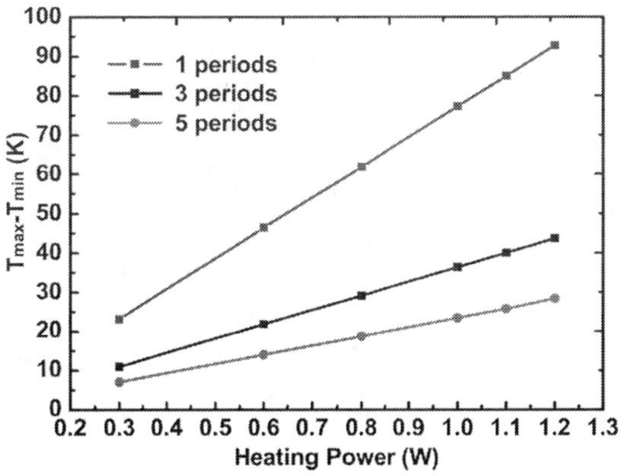

Figure 5. Curve of temperature difference of composites reinforced by buckypaper with different bending cycles along the section z=0

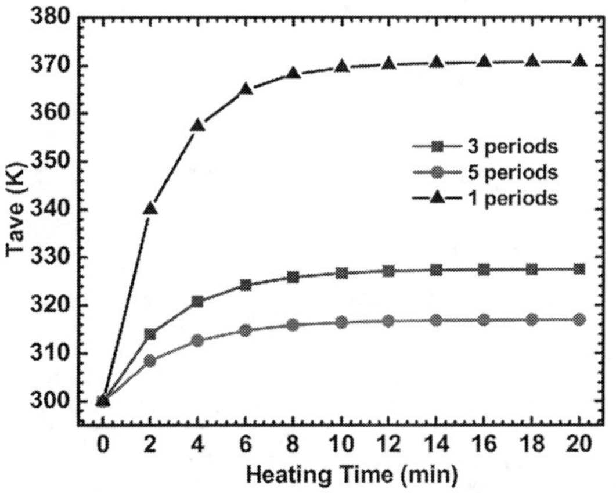

Figure 6. Curve of average temperature of composites reinforced by buckypaper with different bending cycle versus time along the section z=0

As shown in Figure 6, the heating time reaching the stable state is about 10 minutes for the polymer composites reinforced by the bent buckypaper of 5 bending cycles. The heating time reaching the stable state is about 14 minutes for the polymer composites reinforced by the bent buckypaper of 3 bending cycles. It takes longer heating time for the composites reinforced by the bent buckypaper of 1 bending cycles to reach the stable state than that of 3 and 5 bending cycles. As shown in Figure 6, the average temperature of the composites when reaching the stable state increase as the bending cycles of buckypaper decrease.

Figure 7 and 8 shows the curve of maximum and minimum temperature of composites reinforced with the bent buckypaper of different bending cycles versus time along the section z=0.

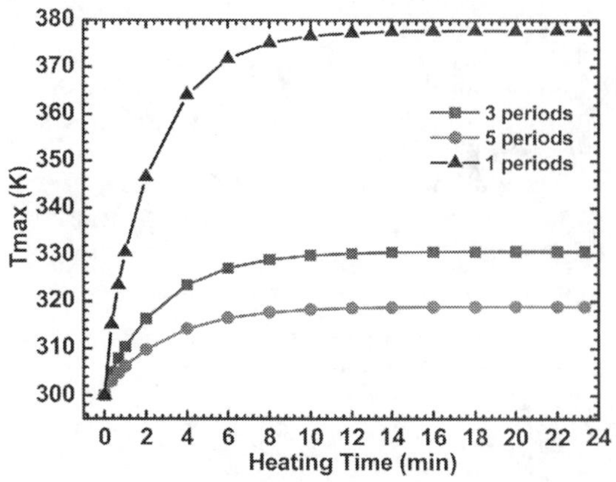

Figure 7. Curve of maximum temperature of composites reinforced with the bent buckypaper of different bending cycles versus time along the section z=0

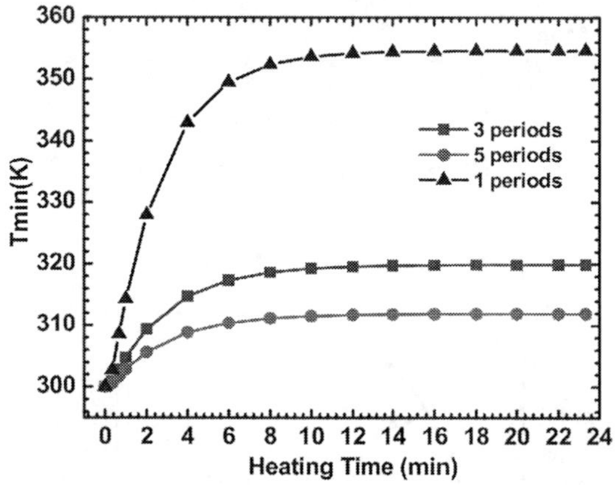

Figure 8. Curve of minimum temperature of composites reinforced with the bent buckypaper of different bending cycles versus time along the section z=0

As shown in Figure 6 to Figure 8, the maximum, minimum and average temperature of composites reinforced with the bent buckypaper of 1 bending cycles is the most highest than that of 3 and 5 bending cycles.

Table 3. Typical temperature of composites reinforced with the bent buckypaper of 1 and 3 bending cycles versus time along the section z=0

Time /s	1			3		
	T_{max} /K	T_{min} /K	T_{ave} /K	T_{max} /K	T_{min} /K	T_{ave} /K
0	300	300	300	300	300	300
120	346.6	328.0	340.0	316.3	309.4	314.0
480	375.2	352.4	368.1	329.0	318.6	325.8
960	377.7	354.5	370.6	330.7	319.8	327.4
1080	377.8	354.6	370.7	330.7	319.9	327.4
1440	377.8	354.6	370.7	330.8	319.9	327.5

Table 3 shows the typical temperature of composites reinforced with the bent buckypaper of 1 and 3 bending cycles versus time along the section z=0. As shown in Table 3 and 4, the difference of the maximum and minimum temperature of the composite decrease with the increase of the bending cycles, which indicate that the temperature distribution of the composite is more uniform.

4 Conclusions

FLUENT was used to analyze how the bending cycles of buckypaper affects the temperature distribution, the changes of the temperature with time and the heating rate during heating.

The maximum, minimum and average temperature decreases as the bending cycles of the buckypaper increase from 1 A to 3 A under the same power. The maximum, minimum and average temperature increases as the heating power increase from 0.3 W to 0.6 W with the same bending cycle. The temperature distribution of the polymer composites reinforced by the bent buckypaper along the section z=0 is more uniform with the increase of bending cycles of buckypaper. The average thermal flow of both the buckypaper and resin decrease as the bending cycles of buckypaper increase with the same heating power.

The difference of the maximum and minimum temperature of the composites increases linearly with the increase of the heating power. The difference of the maximum and minimum temperature of the composite decreases with the increase of the bending cycles of buckypaper, which indicate that the temperature distribution of the composite is more uniform.

The average temperature of the composites when reaching the stable state increase as the bending cycles of buckypaper decrease. The difference of the maximum and minimum temperature of the composites decrease with the increase of the bending cycles, which indicate that the temperature distribution of the composite is more uniform.

Acknowledgement

This work was financially supported by Heilongjiang Postdoctoral Scientific Research Developmental Fund (Grant No. LBH-Q16141).

References

1. R. S. Ruoff, D. C. Lorents. Carbon. 33, 7(1995)
2. E. T. Thostenson, Z. F. Ren, T. W. Chou. Compos Sci Technol, 61, 13(2001)
3. K.T. Lau, D. Hui. Compos Part B-Eng, 33, 4(2002)
4. Z. Liang, J. Gou, C. Zhang, et al. Mater Sci Eng A, 365, 1-2(2004)
5. A. M. Díez-Pascual, J. W. Guan, B. Simard, et al. Compos Part A-Appl S, 43, 6(2012)

Thermal Properties of Buckypaper Enabled Polymer Composites

AYing Zhang[1,a], ZhengHong Li[2]

[1]Harbin University, 150086 Harbin, China
[2]Harbin Institute of Technology, 150001 Harbin, China

Abstract. The heating process of the polymer composite reinforced by buckypaper was simulated with the finite element model. FLUENT was used to analyze how the thickness of buckypaper affect the temperature distribution, the changes of the temperature with time and the heating rate during heating. The maximum and average temperature of the composites decrease when the thickness of the buckypaper increase, whereas the minimum temperature on the samples have the opposite trend. The heating rate of the average temperature of the composites reinforced by the buckypaper with the thickness of 1.2 mm is faster than those of 0.4 mm and 0.8 mm. The temperature distribution of the polymer composites reinforced by the buckypaper is more uniform as the thickness of the buckypaper increase.

1 Introduction

Carbon nanotubes (CNTs) have been comprehensively studied for their excellent electrical, chemical, thermal and mechanical properties [1-4]. However, due to their nanoscale dimension and extra-large surface area, effectively dispersing SWNTs (single wall nanotubes) in a resin matrix for more than 10 wt.% is exceptionally difficult [5]. Compared with graphite films, buckypaper may exhibit a better thermal conducting performance not only in the plane but also more importantly along the thickness direction. Preparation of the polymer composite material reinforced by the nanopaper is straightforward the dispersion of carbon nanotubes could be more uniform and the structures and functional properties of carbon nanotubes can be further improved. Nanopaper and its reinforced polymer composite materials have extra functions of fire proof, lightening protection and electromagnetic interference shielding. However, previous research on the properties of buckypaper and buckypaper/polymer composites has mostly been concentrated to improve their mechanical properties and conductive properties. In this study, heating model of the polymer composite reinforced by buckypaper is established to predict the thermal property of buckypaper reinforced composite.

2 Finite element models

As shown in Figure 1, the heating model of the polymer composites reinforced by the bent buckypaper under different heating conditions were developed by using the finite element program FLUENT. In Figure 1, heating the buckypaper is driven by a power source, and the cube region is the polymer matrix which is heated by the buckypaper. The temperature of the polymer matrix is increased due to the electro-heating of the buckypaper. The length (L), width (w), and the thickness (T) of the heating model of the polymer composite reinforced by the bent buckypaper are 36 mm, 5 mm, and 10 mm respectively. The thicknesses (d) of the buckypaper are 0.4, 0.8 and 1.2 mm. The bending height (h) and bending period (A) of the bent buckypaper are 6 mm and 12 mm. The objective of this research is to analyze the effect of the thickness of the buckypaper on the thermal conductivity of the composites using a finite element software FLUENT.

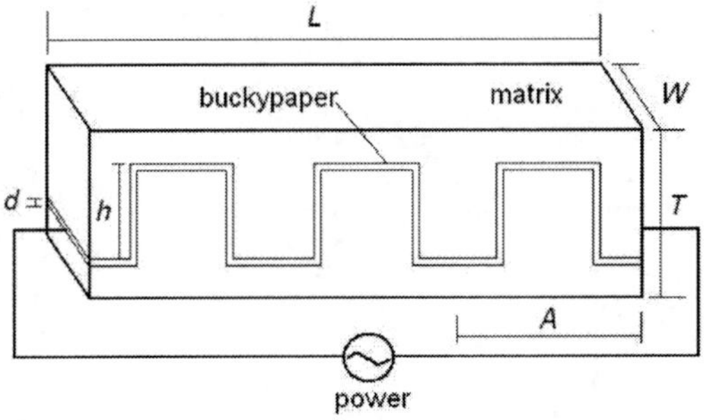

Figure 1. Sketch diagram of heating experimental device

3 Results and discussion

As shown in Figure 2, the maximum, minimum and average temperature of the buckypaper/polymer composites reaching a steady state were calculated by the finite element software FLUENT. The maximum, minimum and average temperature of the buckypaper/polymer composites varies linearly with the thickness of buckypaper.

[a] Corresponding author: zaying@sina.com

DOI: 10.1051/matecconf/201712803005

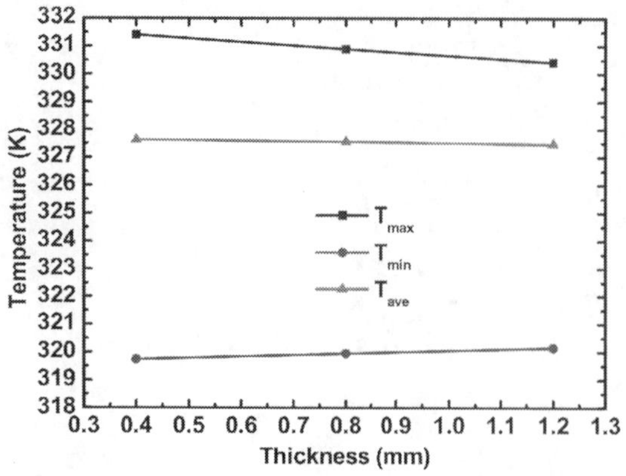

Figure 2. Temperature distribution of the buckypaper/polymer composites along the section z=0

Table 1 shows that the maximum and average temperature decrease as the thickness of buckypaper increase from 0.4 mm to 1.2 mm. Whereas, the minimum temperature on the samples have the opposite trend.

Table 1. Typical temperature of composites reinforced by buckypaper with different thickness along the section z=0

Thickness /mm	Section of z=0		
	Tmax/K	Tmin/K	Tave/K
0.4	331.40	319.74	327.63
0.8	330.90	319.95	327.57
1.2	330.42	320.15	327.47

The heating rate and the time for the buckypaper/polymer composites reaching a steady state were calculated by the finite element software FLUENT. The relationship of the average temperature as a function of time in a transient state along the section z=0 was also analyzed and the results are shown in Figure 3.

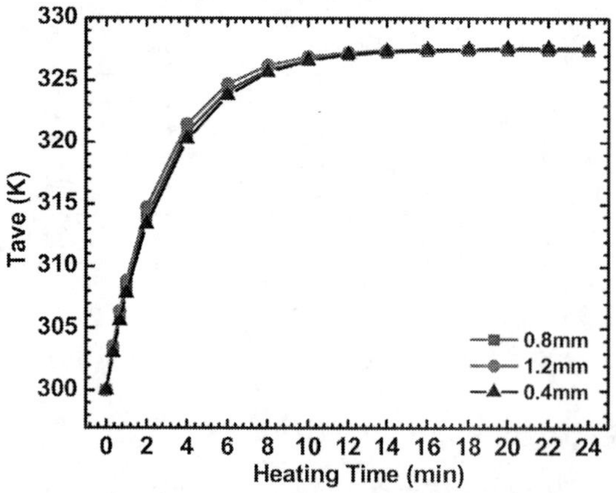

Figure 3. Curve of average temperature of composites reinforced with bending buckypaper of different thickness versus time along the section z=0

Figure 3 shows that both curves of the average temperature exhibit similar trend and there are two distinct stages observed. The first stage shows that the slopes of the curves increase significantly with increasing the heating time. A fast increase of the average temperature occurs during stage I after which the slope is changed, indicating the beginning of the second stage. A progressive but slow increase of the average temperature is observed in the second stage. Figure 3 shows that the heating rate of the average temperature for the polymer composites reinforced by the buckypaper with the thickness of 1.2 mm is faster than those of 0.4 mm and 0.8 mm.

Figures 4 and 5 show that the maximum and minimum temperatures of the polymer composites reinforced by the buckypapers of different thickness as a function of time along the section z=0 during heating until reaching the stable state. The maximum temperature of the composites reinforced by the buckypaper with the thickness of 0.4 mm in a stable state along the section z=0 is higher than that of 1.2 mm, whereas the minimum temperature on the samples have the opposite trend.

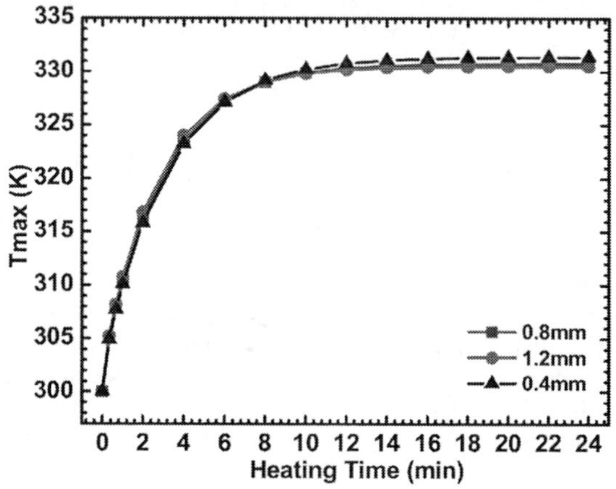

Figure 4. Curve of maximum temperature of composites reinforced with bending buckypaper of different thickness versus time along the section z=0

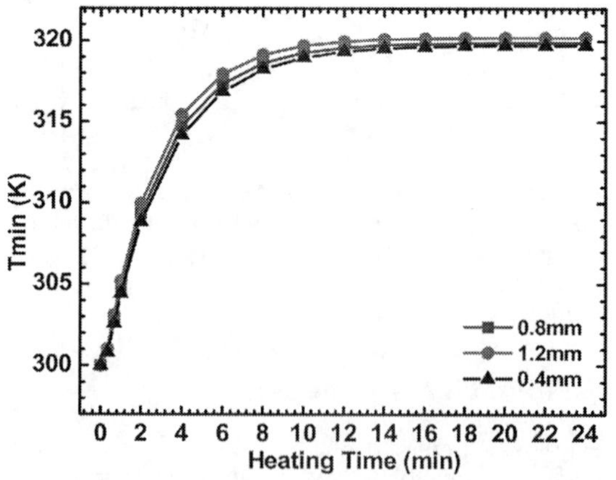

Figure 5. Curve of minimum temperature of composites reinforced with bending buckypaper of different thickness versus time along the section z=0

DOI: 10.1051/matecconf/201712803005

Figure 6 shows the temperature cloudy maps which indicate that the temperature distribution of the polymer composites reinforced by the bent buckypaper along the section z=0 is more uniform as the thickness of the buckypaper increase from 0.4 mm to 1.2 mm.

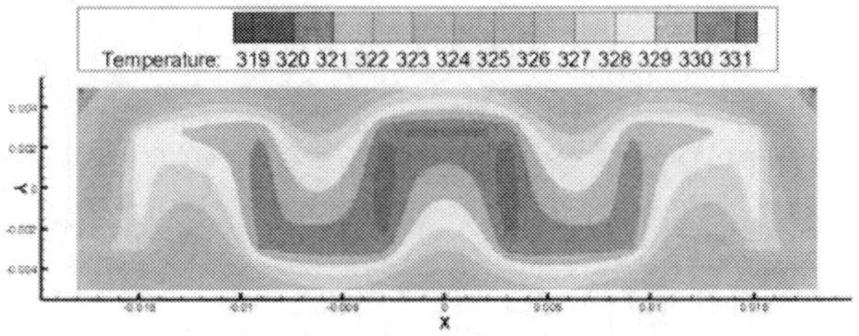

(a) d=0.4mm

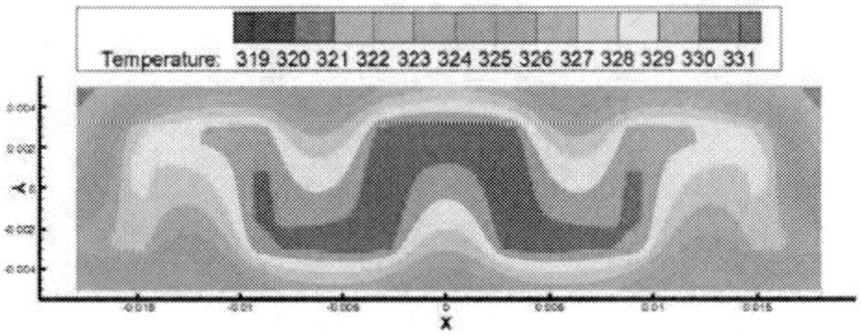

(b) d=0.8mm

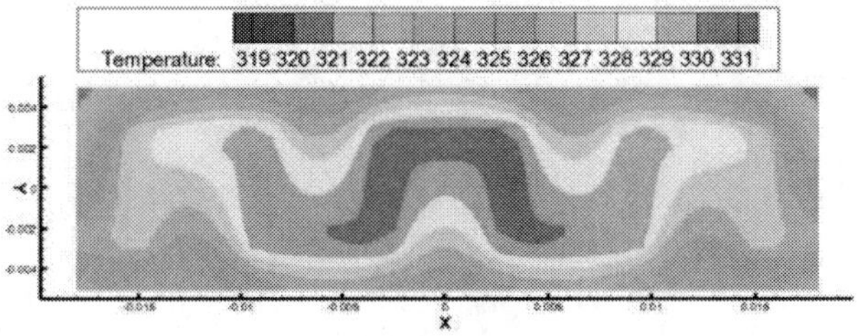

(c) d=1.2mm

Figure 6. Temperature distribution of composites reinforced with bending buckypaper of different thickness along the section z=0

Figure 7 and 8 shows that the temperature distribution of the polymer composites reinforced by the bent buckypaper with the thickness of 0.4 mm and 0.8 mm along the section z=0 during heating.

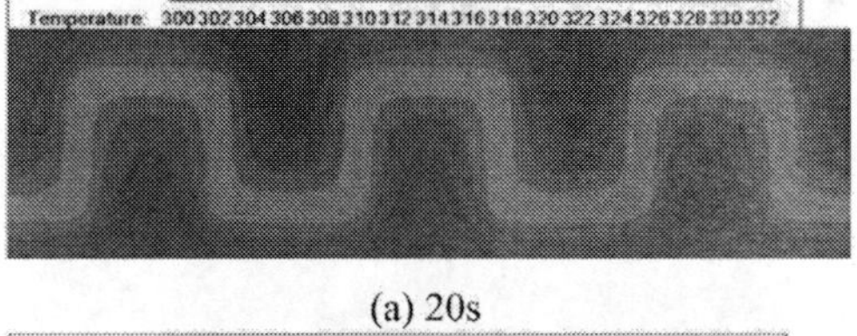

(a) 20s

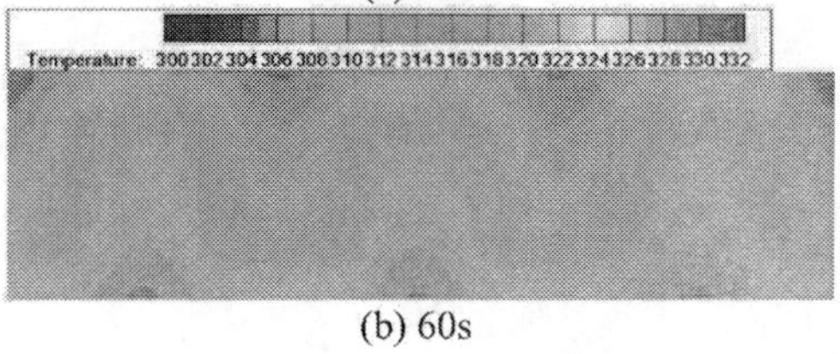

(b) 60s

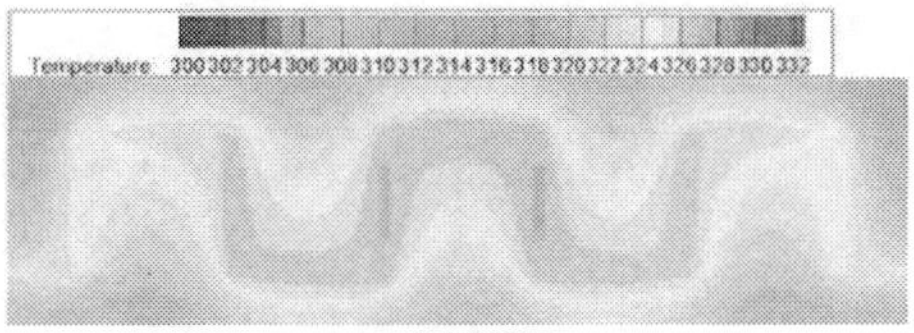

(c) 360s

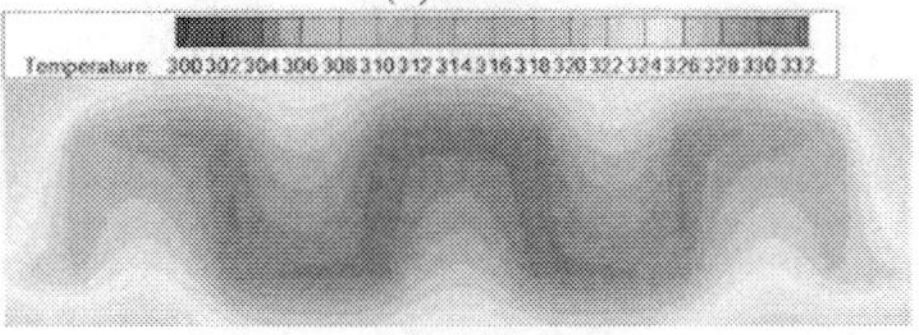

(d) 720s

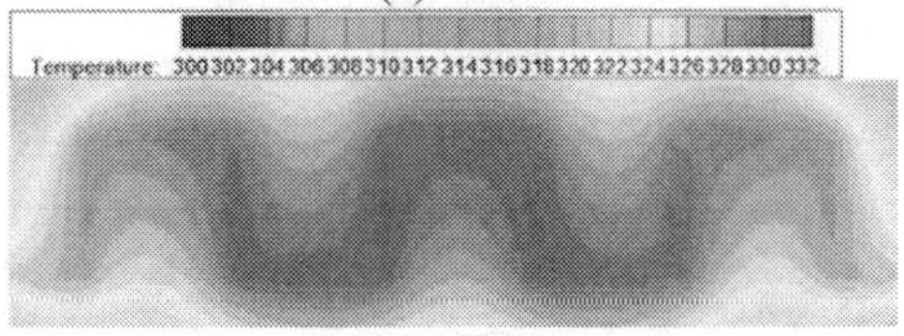

(e) 1080s

Figure 7. Temperature distribution of composites reinforced with bending buckypaper versus time with the thickness of 0.4 mm along the section z=0

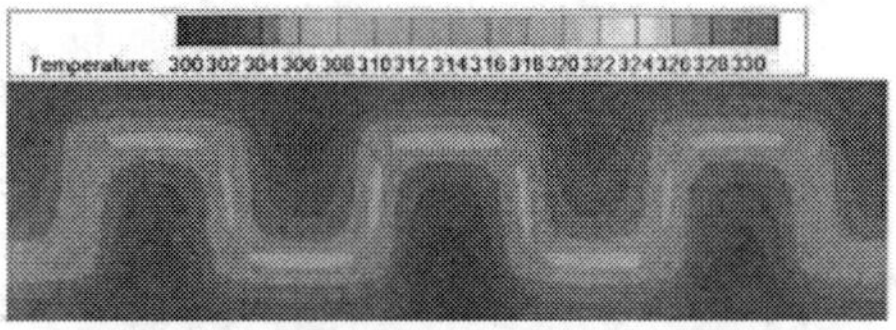

(a) 20s

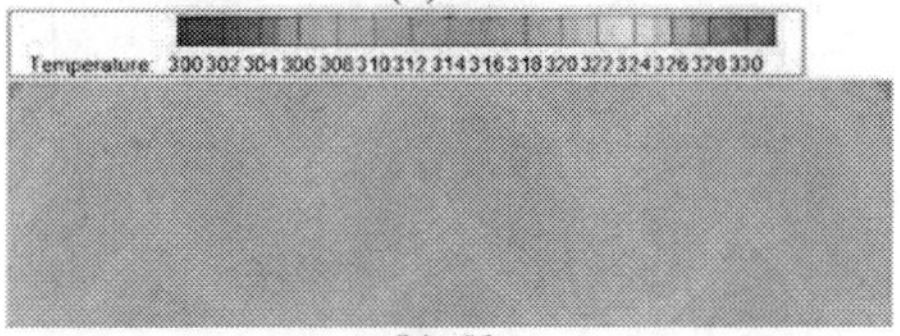

(b) 60s

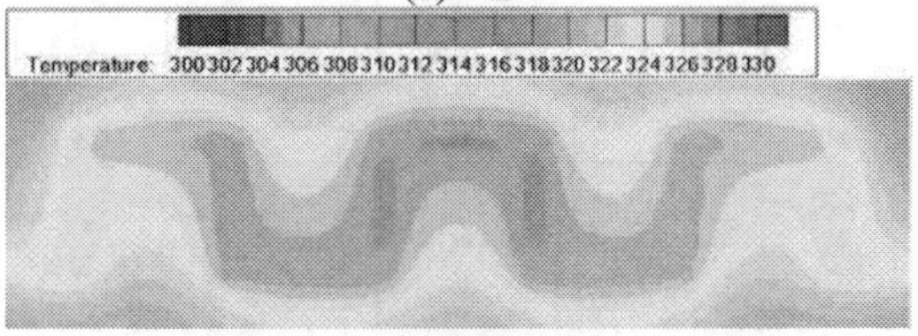

(c) 360s

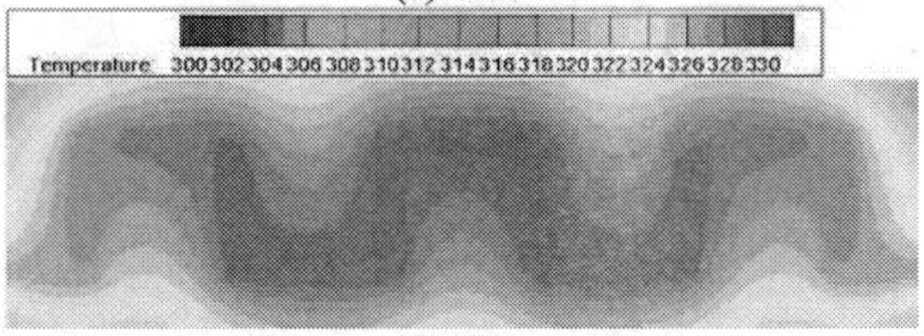

(d) 720s

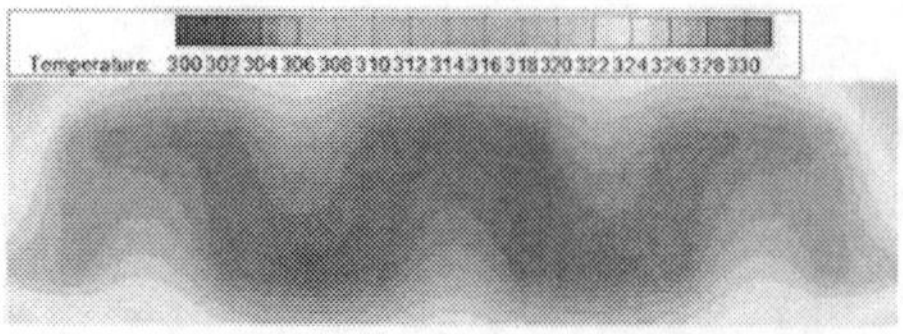

(e) 1080s

Figure 8. Temperature distribution of composites reinforced with bending buckypaper versus time with the thickness of 0.8 mm along the section z=0

As shown in Figure 7 and 8, the temperature cloudy maps indicate that the temperature distribution is more uniform as the thickness of buckypaper increase at the same heating time.

Table 2 shows the typical temperature of composites reinforced by the bent buckypaper versus time with the thickness of 0.4 mm and 0.8 mm along the section z=0.

Table 2. Typical temperature of composites reinforced by the bent buckypaper versus time with the thickness of 0.4 mm and 0.8 mm along the section z=0

Time /s	0.4mm			0.8mm		
	Tmax /K	Tmin /K	Tave /K	Tmax /K	Tmin /K	Tave /K
0	300	300	300	300	300	300
20	304.93	300.80	302.98	305.04	300.90	303.24
40	307.70	302.59	305.54	307.89	302.84	305.93
60	310.07	304.42	307.83	310.35	304.77	308.31
120	315.83	308.86	313.37	316.28	309.38	313.99
240	323.23	314.18	320.23	323.54	314.74	320.80
360	327.14	316.87	323.79	327.19	317.35	324.17
480	329.19	318.26	325.64	329.00	318.64	325.84
600	330.25	318.97	326.60	329.90	319.28	326.67
720	330.81	319.35	327.10	330.35	319.59	327.08
840	331.10	319.54	327.36	330.57	319.75	327.28
960	331.25	319.64	327.49	330.68	319.82	327.38
1080	331.33	319.69	327.56	330.74	319.86	327.43
1200	331.37	319.72	327.60	330.76	319.88	327.46
1320	331.39	319.73	327.62	330.78	319.89	327.47
1440	331.40	319.74	327.63	330.78	319.90	327.48

Table 2 show that the maximum, minimum and average temperatures of the polymer composites reinforced by the buckypapers of different thickness increase as the thickness of the buckypapers increase. As shown in Table 2, the minimum temperatures of composites increase as the thickness of buckypaper increase at the same heating time, whereas the average temperature on the samples has the opposite trend.

4 Conclusions

FLUENT was used to analyze how the thickness of buckypaper affects the temperature distribution, the changes of the temperature with time and the heating rate during heating. The maximum and average temperature of the composites decrease when the thickness of the buckypaper increase, whereas the minimum temperature on the samples have the opposite trend. The heating rate of the average temperature of the composites reinforced by the buckypaper with the thickness of 1.2 mm is faster than those of 0.4 mm and 0.8 mm. The temperature distribution of the polymer composites reinforced by the buckypaper is more uniform as the thickness of the buckypaper increase. The minimum temperature of composites increase as the thickness of buckypaper increase at the same heating time during heating, whereas the average temperature on the samples have the opposite trend, which lead to that the temperature distribution is more uniform.

Acknowledgement

This work was financially supported by Heilongjiang Postdoctoral Scientific Research Developmental Fund (Grant No. LBH-Q16141).

References

1. R. S. Ruoff, D. C. Lorents. Carbon. 33, 7(1995)
2. J. Hone, J. E. Fischer. Science, 289, 5485(2000)
3. S. Berber, Y. K. Kwon, D. Tomanek. Phys. Rev. Lett., 84, 20(2000)
4. M. A. Osman, D. Srivastava. Nanotechnolgy, 12,1(2001)
5. P. Gonnet, Z. Liang, E. S. Choi, R. S. Kadambala, C. Zhang, J. S. Brooks, B. Wang, L. Kramer. Curr. Appl. Phys., 6, 1(2006)

Microstructure and mechanical properties of 304L steel fabricated by arc additive manufacturing

Lei Ji, Jiping Lu, Changmeng Liu[a], Chenchen Jing, Hongli Fan, Shuyuan Ma

School of Mechanical Engineering, Beijing Institute of Technology, Beijing, Zhongguancun south Street, 100081, China

Abstract. For 304L large structural parts used in nuclear power, it is hard and costly to fabricate and machine traditionally. Wire arc additive manufacturing (WAAM) has low cost and high material utilization, which provides an efficient way to fabricate the large structural parts. So in this study, WAAM is used to fabricate the parts of 304L stainless steel. Through the tensile test and metallographic analysis, the mechanical properties and microstructure of the 304L stainless steel fabricated by WAAM were explored. The results indicate that with the layers depositing, the cooling rate becomes slower, the dendrites become thicker and the morphology becomes more stable. Due to the existence of dendrites, the grain boundary strengthening effect is different between the transverse direction and longitudinal direction, and resulting in anisotropy of mechanical properties. However, the mechanical properties of the parts correspond to the forged piece, which lays the foundation for future applications.

1 Introduction

As a variant of traditional 304 stainless steel, 304L is a kind of austenitic stainless steel with pretty low carbon content, which is also known as ultra-low carbon stainless steel. Because of its good corrosion resistance, formability, excellent plasticity and toughness, the 304L metal products could perform well in high temperature conditions, the fabricating performance is excellent as well [1]. Especially, 304L stainless steel is a significant structural material in nuclear power equipment [2], also it is widely used in chemical industry, furniture decoration industry and medical industry. However, for the 304L large nuclear structure, the traditional manufacturing methods are limited by the long manufacturing cycle and high cost.

The emergence of the additive manufacturing provides a new way to fabricate the structure with 304L components. As a rapid prototyping technology, Additive Manufacturing (AM) is a promising manufacturing ways building objects layer by layer [3, 4]. Based on the digital model, different metal materials or plastic and other adhesive materials could be fabricated by AM. Different with the traditional material removal processing technology, AM is a 'bottom – up' manufacturing method. Due to the innovation in the manufacturing process, it is considered to be 'an important production tool of the third industrial revolution'. Compared with the traditional manufacturing methods, The AM method can effectively save the processing time cost, reduce the amount of post-processing time, also can reduce the waste of materials and improve the utilization of materials [5].

According to the different heat sources, the current existence of the AM method consists of laser melting deposition [6, 7], wire arc additive manufacturing [8, 9], electron beam additive manufacturing[10]. Many researches have been done on the stainless steel using the AM method. Oguzhan Yilmaz et al. [11] investigated the influence of different process parameters on the macrostructure and microstructure of the deposited AISI 308LSi parts. They clarified and compared the morphology and microstructure of the parts manufactured by traditional method and pulsed current TIG-SMD methods. K Abd-Elghany et al. [12] evaluated the different properties of products fabricated by selective laser melting (SLM). They confirmed that it's possible to fabricate the parts with fine details with the low-cost 304L powder used. Zhuqing Wang et al. [13] investigated the effect of processing parameters on the mechanical properties of AISI304L stainless steel fabricated by laser-based directed energy deposition AM. They found that the tensile samples with different fabricating directions and different linear heat inputs have various mechanical strength and elongation. Beth E Carroll et al. [14] investigated the anisotropic mechanical properties of a Ti-6Al-4V part fabricated using a directed energy deposition (DED) process. They attributed the high ductility to the prevention of lack of fusion porosity in the finished component.

However, a comprehensive study that describes the 304L stainless steel fabricated by WAAM remains a gap in the existing research in the WAAM field. Compared with other AM methods, WAAM has low cost, high material utilization and high deposition rate [15]. It is suitable for large structural parts of nuclear power.

[a] Corresponding author: liuchangmeng@bit.edu.cn

 DOI: 10.1051/matecconf/201712803006

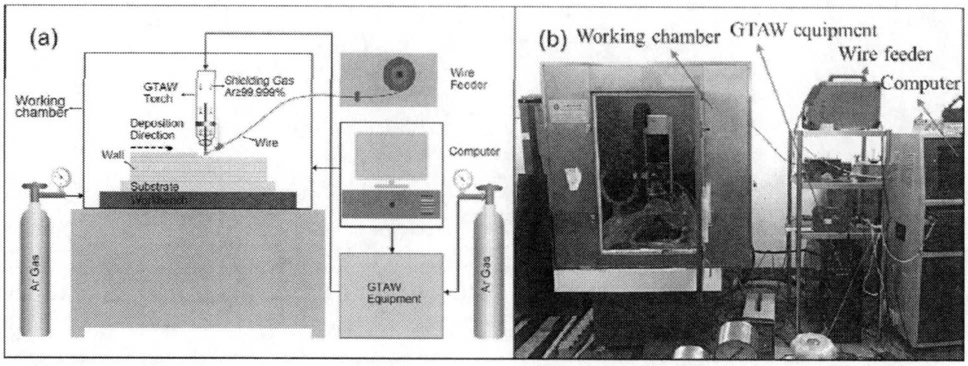

Figure 1. (a) Schematic of the experimental setup developed and (b) overview of WAAM system

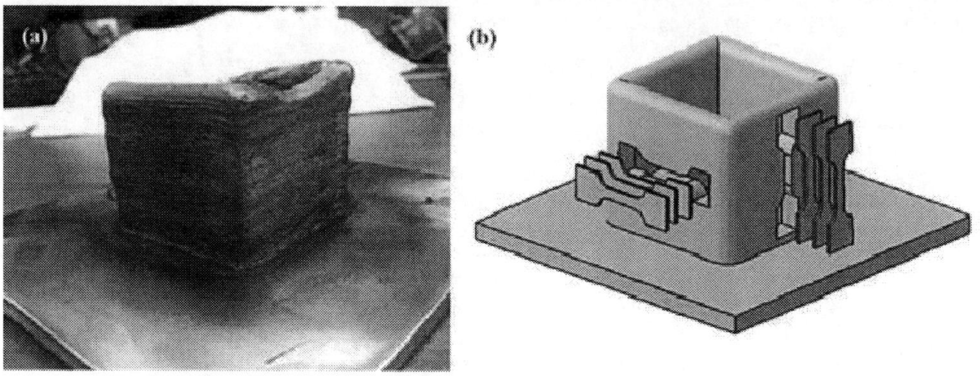

Figure 2. (a) The actual part fabricated by WAAM in this study and (b) schematic showing how the tensile specimens were extracted from the part.

So this study investigated the morphology, microstructure and mechanical properties of the components fabricated by WAAM, also clarified and compared the mechanical properties of 304L stainless steel components fabricated by different AM methods and forged standard. After analysing the result and summarizing the conclusion, it's found that the mechanical properties of the parts can satisfy the requirements of use.

2 Experimental details

The experiment of 304L stainless steel was based on the experimental setup developed for wire arc additive manufacturing (Figure 1). As the Figure 1(a) shows, the developed WAAM system mainly consists of a wire feeder, a computer, the working chamber and the GTAW equipment. The TIG welding torch is attached to a three-axis machine. The melting source used to melt the wire is provided by the GTAW machine (Dynasty 350; Miller, USA). The diameter of the 304L wire used in the experiment is 1.2mm. The entire studio environment is filled with 99.99% of the argon in case the parts are oxidized during the manufacturing process. The physical picture of the WAAM system is shown on the Figure 1(b).

The substrate used in the experiment is also 304L stainless steel, whose size is 150mm*150mm*5mm. The moving path of torch and the wire are determined by the control centre. As the material overlaps the layers on the substrate, a box-like structure with 4 walls is formed, as shown in Figure 2(a). In order to get the mechanical properties of the stainless steel, six tensile specimens were cut by wire-electrode cutting. Respectively, the first 3 specimens who is parallel to the substrate are remarked as T1, T2, T3, and the 3 specimens who is perpendicular to the substrate are remarked as L1, L2, L3, as the Figure 2(b) shows. The tensile specimens were tested on an electronic universal material testing machine (Instron 5966, Instron, Germany) at room temperature. The tensile specimen is cut in accordance with the size of Figure 3(a). Figure 3(b) shows the standard tensile specimen and the fractured tensile specimens after tensile test. Obviously, it can found that the specimen is stretched a lot compared to the standard specimen.

Table 1. Process parameters used in WAAM

Process parameters	Unit	Values
Arc current	A	280
Peak current	Ratio	30%
Deposition speed	mm/min	175
Wire-feed speed	cm/min	100
Pulse frequency	Hz	1.5

Before observing the microstructure and macro-structure of the samples, several steps need to be conducted. First, the SiC sandpaper with different fineness were used to polish the sample until the metal surface becomes flat. Then, the sample is polished by a polishing machine to get a mirror surface. Finally, according to the ratio of 1: 3: 2, respectively taking 10ml HNO3 (nitric acid), 30ml HCL (hydrochloric acid), 20ml glycerol to configure aqua regia, then etching the metallographic sample about 40 seconds. In this way, the microstructures of samples were characterized by optical microscopy (Leica DM4000M; Leica, Germany)

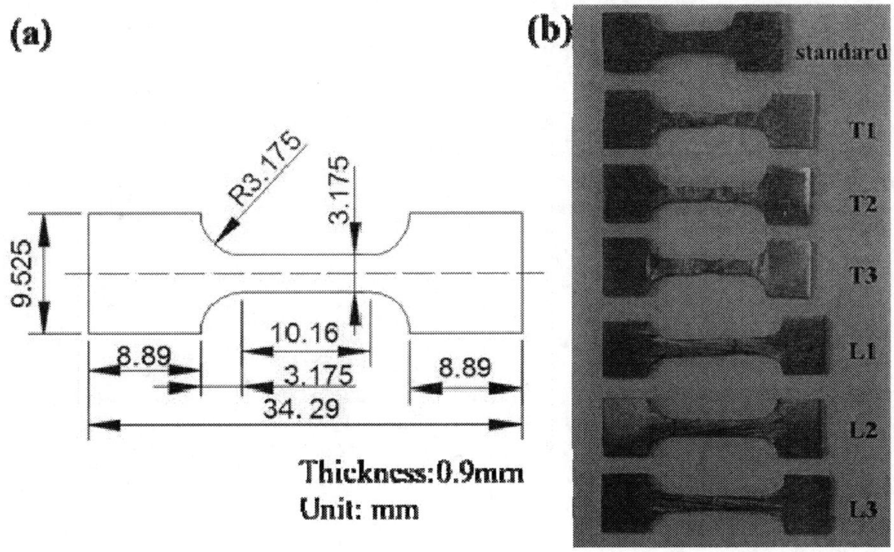

Figure 3. (a) Dimensions of tensile specimens and (b) Comparison of cracked tensile specimens and standard tensile specimens

The processing parameters used in the experiment are given in Table 1.

3 Results and Discussions

3.1. Morphology and microstructure

In order to analyse the structure of the parts fabricated by WAAM, the surface morphology and microstructure characteristics of the parts were described by observing the metallographic samples. As shown in Figure 4(a), the columnar grains on the surface were clearly visible after chemical etching. From the top of the part to the substrate, four regions (b, c, d, e) were selected to observe their characteristics of the microstructure. On the whole, the growth of the whole organization grows in a dendritic way. The Figure. 4(e) shows the junction of the substrate and the part, and the substrate is the rolled 304L stainless steel plate. Through the rolling method, the casting structure of the ingot is destroyed. The grains of the steel are refined and the defects of the microstructure are eliminated. Therefore, the rolled steel obtains a perfect structure with a dense organization. The first few layers

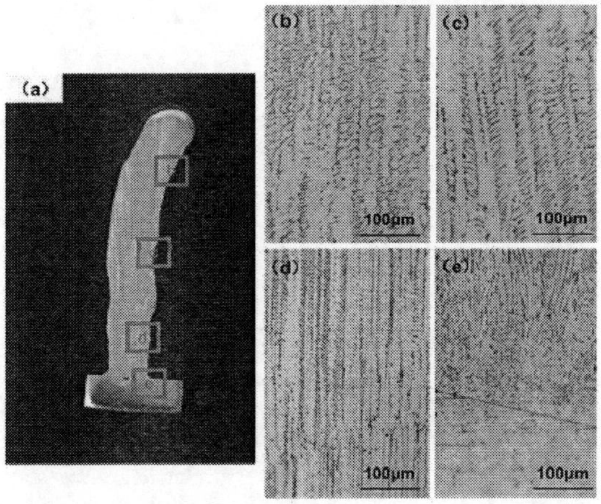

Figure 4. (a)Overview of the metallographic sample and (b, c, d, e) optical micrographs of the metallographic sample in different areas.

which is contact with the substrate are full of fine and messy dendrites. The reason why the dendrite orientation is complex and irregular is that the substrate temperature is relatively low when the parts just started melding which leads to the speeding up the cooling rate and producing more nucleation. This area can be called the transition zone. The primary dendrite arm space of this area is 4.94μm and the secondary dendrite arm space is 3.52μm. In Figure 4(d), the dendrites have a clear growth direction, showing a small columnar grain. Due to the process of grain growth is a kind of preferential growth process, the growth direction along the temperature gradient becomes obvious. In this area, the primary dendrite arm space is 8.23μm, secondary dendrite arm space is 4.98μm. As shown in Figure 4(c) and Figure 4(b), steady-state coarse austenitic columnar grains have been formed and secondary dendrites have appeared. The primary arm dendrite space is 13.59μm and 15.44μm respectively, and the secondary dendritic arm space is 8.93μm and 7.14μm respectively. Fig 5 shows the different dendritic spacing on the b, c, d, e areas.

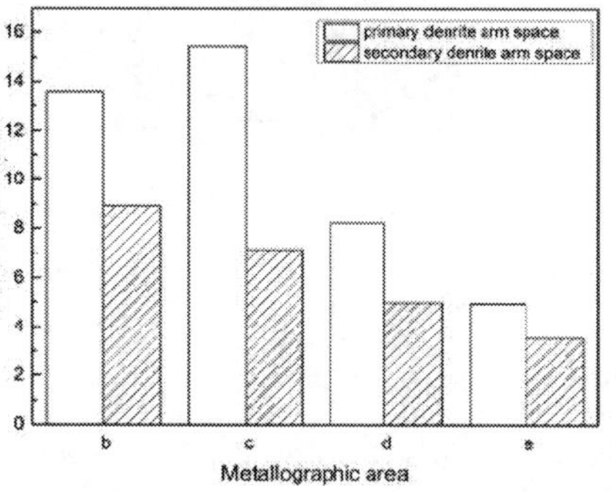

Figure 5. The different dendritic spacing on b, c, d, e areas.

From the region (e) of the substrate to the region (b) of the top, with the number of layers increasing, the heat input becomes larger and the cooling rate decreases. And the growth tendency of the grains becomes stable and single. The distribution of the organization can be seen from the schematic of Figure 6. This schematic reflects the distribution of metallographic images. The pulsed arc causes a number of molten pools formed on the substrate. When the liquid metal contacts with the low temperature substrate, the intense cooling of the liquid results in a great degree of undercooling, and the substrate with room temperature promote the non-spontaneous nucleation. So the liquid metal of this part produces a large number of nuclei and forms a layer of fine grain area manifesting as fine and messy dendrites. With the number of layers gradually increasing, the rate of cooling decreases and the direction of heat dissipation becomes apparent along the direction of accumulation of the material, the columnar grains appear parallel to each other, and the primary dendrite arm space and the secondary dendrite arm space become wider as well. At the middle position of the part, the large columnar grains appear, and the metallographic organization becomes stable. Not only the primary dendritic space and the secondary dendrites space become larger, even some three dendrites appear. This also shows that the cooling rate is pretty slow at this time. Because the direction of heat dissipation is also perpendicular to the direction of the substrate, the growth direction of the grains is along the gradient of the temperature.

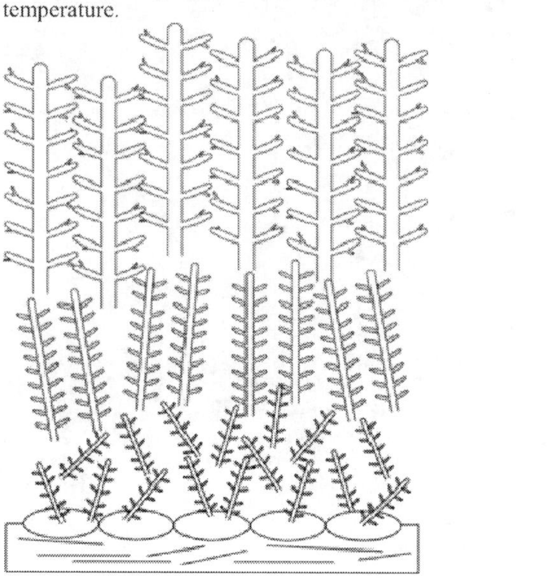

Figure 6. Schematic view of epitaxial grow of dendrites on the part fabricated by WAAM

3.2 Tensile strength

In order to obtain the mechanical properties of the parts, a tensile test was conducted to investigate the strength and elongation of the parts. Six tensile samples were fabricated to complete the test, including the transverse specimens T1, T2, T3 and the longitudinal specimens L1, L2, L3.

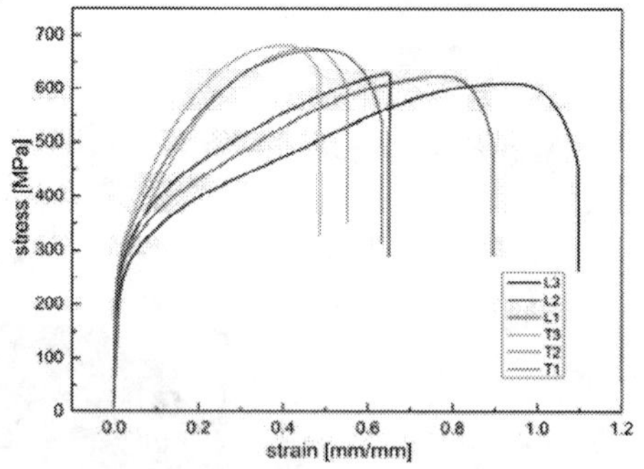

Figure 7. Stress-strain curves of the tensile specimens in longitudinal direction and transverse direction.

In general, 304L austenitic stainless steels have high ductility, low yield strength and relatively high ultimate tensile strength. Figure 7 shows the stress-strain curve of the tensile specimens. Their tensile strength, ultimate strength and elongation were measured and averaged over several samples. Overall, it is found that the performance of the series L is better than the series T. Three kinds of phenomenon were mainly found in this research. Firstly, it was clear that the parts made of

WAAM exist anisotropy in the presence of mechanical properties. As the Table 2 shows, in this study, the tensile strength and ultimate strength of transverse specimens were larger than the longitudinal specimens fabricated by WAAM, and the elongation of the transverse samples was far lower than the longitudinal samples. Besides, in the previous study, some parts produced by the methods of other additive manufacturing exist the anisotropy problem as well[13, 14]. A summary of mechanical properties of austenitic steel parts made by various AM methods, compared with forged plate[7, 16], is given in Table 2. Coincidentally, the previous study also found that the tensile strength and ultimate tensile strength of the transverse samples are greater than the longitudinal samples, and the elongation is also worse than the longitudinal samples, as the Table 2 shows. There is no doubt that this performance confirms the existence of anisotropy in the additive manufacturing methods. Compared with LMD and SLM, although these methods all belong to additive methods, the heat input of WAAM is larger than others and its cooling rate is lower. Therefore, the microstructure organization of the WAAM is coarse, which is different from the other AM ways with the laser resources. As a consequence, just like the Table 2 shows, the WAAM exhibits a lower yield strength and a lower ultimate tensile strength, but a good ductility compared with SLM and LMD. Finally, Table 2 also shows the standard values of the mechanical properties of forged 304L stainless steel. It is clear that the mechanical properties of the parts fabricated by WAAM are basically the same as forged plate. And the additive manufacturing method can effectively save the processing time cost, reduce the amount of post-processing time, also can reduce the waste of materials and improve the utilization of materials. So WAAM could have a great application prospect in the 304L large structural parts used in nuclear power.

Anisotropy is also found in previous studies, K.Zhang et al.[17] found the microstructure of SS316 components made by AM are anisotropic, they hold the view that the microstructural grains and ferrite dendrites are preferentially orientated along the highest thermal gradient, Zhuqing Wang et al.[13] fabricated the 304L parts by DED, they said that the long and narrow columnar grains growing along the build direction result in anisotropic tensile elongation properties. Combined with previous studies, the formation mechanism of anisotropic of 304L is discussed in the next.

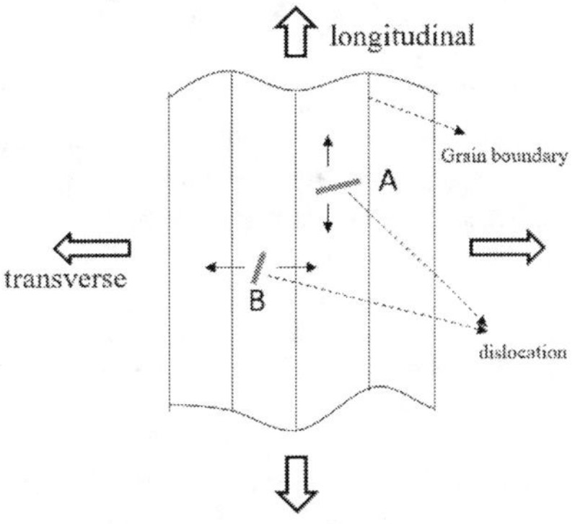

Figure 8. Schematic of grain boundary strengthening

The mechanical properties of materials are closely related to grain boundaries. Grain boundary is the interface between two adjacent grains with different space orientation, which will directly affect dislocation motion. The finer the grains are, the more grain boundaries exist, and the dislocation movement will get more resistance. Once meeting the grain boundary, the grain slippage will be end, that is to say, it is difficult to pass the boundary for the slippage. At the same time, dislocations pile up at the grain boundary, which is easy to produce stress concentration and produce cracks later. As a consequence, the plasticity is reducing.

The position of the tensile specimens used in the experiment is located in the middle section of the whole part. In this position, the microstructure is an elongated dendritic structure, and the growth direction is stable. It means that the direction is perpendicular to the substrate. As the Figure 8 shows, the transverse and longitudinal mean the direction of the tensile axis of the tensile specimens. When the loading direction is along the transverse direction, the dislocation B will appear. When the dislocation B slips along the transverse tensile direction, it's found that there is a grain boundary as a barrier. Because of the grain boundary strengthening effect, the tensile strength of the transverse direction is relatively high. On the other hand, when dislocation A slips along the longitudinal tensile direction, it is not obstructed by the grain boundary, which leads to the lower tensile strength.

Table 2. Summary of mechanical properties of 304 and 304L stainless steel fabricated by additive manufacturing compared with forged properties.

Additive manufacturing	Stainless steel alloy	Orientation	Yield strength (MPa)	Ultimate tensile strength (MPa)	Elongation (%)
LMD[13]	304L	Transverse	337	609	48.2
		Longitudinal	314	606	56.4
SLM[1]	304	Transverse	535	693	41.8
		Longitudinal	455	580	57.5
WAAM	304L	Transverse	235	678	55.6
		Longitudinal	231	622	88.1
Forged[18]	304L		≥170	≥485	≥40

 DOI: 10.1051/matecconf/201712803006

4 Conclusions

In order to investigate the microstructure and tensile strength, a 304L stainless steel part with four walls were fabricated using wire arc additive manufacturing, and compared with other additive manufacturing methods and forged standard. The main conclusions from this study are as flows:

The microstructure of 304L stainless steel parts made by WAAM is filled with a large number of dendrites, and the growth direction is along the temperature gradient. From the first layer to the top, the morphology of the dendrites changes from fine and mess to large and stable, and the primary dendrite arm space changes from 4.94μm to 13.59μm, the secondary dendrite arm space changes from 3.52μm to 8.93μm.

Through the testing and analysis of mechanical properties, it is found that the strength and elongation were at forged level and the parts can satisfy the requirements of application. Like other additive manufacturing methods, the mechanical properties also exist the anisotropy, which attributes to the effect of the grain boundary strengthening is different in different directions.

References

1. Guan K, Wang Z, Gao M, et al. Materials & Design. 50 581-586 (2013).
2. Girija S, Kamachi Mudali U. Corrosion Engineering, Science and Technology. 49 335-344 (2013).
3. Guo J, Zhou Y, Liu C, et al. Materials. 9 823 (2016).
4. Lin C-M, Tsai H-L, Cheng C-D, et al. Engineering Failure Analysis. 21 9-20 (2012).
5. Frazier WE. Journal of Materials Engineering and Performance. 23 1917-1928 (2014).
6. Wang YD, Tang HB, Fang YL, et al. Materials Science and Engineering: A. 528 474-479 (2010).
7. Wang T, Zhu YY, Zhang SQ, et al. Journal of Alloys and Compounds. 632 505-513 (2015).
8. Wu Q, Ma Z, Chen G, et al. Journal of Manufacturing Processes. 27 198-206 (2017).
9. Shi X, Ma S, Liu C, et al. Materials Science and Engineering: A. 684 196-204 (2017).
10. Gong X, Anderson T, Chou K. Manufacturing Review. 1:2 (2014).
11. Yilmaz O, Ugla AA. The International Journal of Advanced Manufacturing Technology. 89 13-25 (2016).
12. Abd-Elghany K, Bourell DL. Rapid Prototyping Journal. 18 420-428 (2012).
13. Wang Z, Palmer TA, Beese AM. Acta Materialia. 110 226-235 (2016).
14. Carroll BE, Palmer TA, Beese AM. Acta Materialia. 87 309-320 (2015).
15. Abe T, Sasahara H. Precision Engineering. 45 387-395 (2016).
16. Wang F, Williams S, Rush M. The International Journal of Advanced Manufacturing Technology. 57 597-603 (2011).
17. Zhang K, Wang S, Liu W, et al. Materials & Design. 55 104-119 (2014).
18. Standard Specification for Chromium and Chromium-Nickel Stainless Steel Plate, Sheet, and Strip for Pressure Vessels and for General Applications / Note: 2. revision 2004. 1. editorial change. Astm. 2001.

Structure and mechanical properties of TiO_2/UHMWPE nanocomposite monofilaments

Wen Wen YU, Jian Gao SHI[a], Lei WANG, Yong Li LIU, Xiao Xue CHEN

East China Sea Fisheries Research Institute, Chinese Academy Fishery Sciences, Shanghai, 200090, China

Abstract. You should leave 8 mm of space above the abstract and 10 mm after the abstract. The heading Abstract should be typed in bold 8,5-point Times. The body of the abstract should be typed in normal 8,5-point Times in a single paragraph, immediately following the heading. The text should be set to 1.15 line spacing. The abstract should be centred across the page, indented 15 mm from the left and right page margins and justified. It should not normally exceed 200 words.

1 Introduction

The ultra high molecular weight polyethylene (UHMWPE) fiber has attracted great attention due to its low density, solubility properties, and superior mechanical properties including high Young's modulus and tensile strength that are favorable for industrial applications[1-4]. Since the 1970s, UHMWPE fibers have been produced by various drawing methods such as solid state hot drawing, solid state extrusion, free growth, surface growth, and gel-spinning. Among them, one of the most successful methods of commercial introduction of high-strength, high-modulus polyethylene fiber is the process of gel-spinning. But, the apparent disadvantage of the gel-spun method is the use of organic solvents that are difficult to recycle and remove.

Melt spinning is an efficient, simple, and nonpolluting method. However, the modulus and strength of melt-spun hot drawn fibers are still much lower than those of gel-spun fiber. Producing high modulus and high strength monofilaments from PE have been one of the challenges in fishing science and technology for a very long time. Yanela Alonso [5] studied the influence of sepiolite content (1, 2, and 3 wt%) and successive drawing steps on the final properties of polyethylene/sepiolite nanocomposite fibers. They found that Young Modulus increases 17 times with drawing in pure PE fibers and 1.5 times because of the presence of sepiolite, and the strength shows similar behavior. Most of the published research has indicated that rigid fillers in composite systems, including filled polyethylene, improved mechanical properties[6-9]. And, the improvement of the mechanical properties in reinforced materials depends on the dispersed states of nano-fillers and interactions between polymer and nano-fillers.

In this paper, TiO_2/UHMWPE nanocomposite monofilament was prepared by reactive extrusion in a twin-screw extruder and melt spinning. Its morphology and thermal properties were characterized by SEM, DSC and mechanical tensile test.

2 Experimental

2.1. Materials and monofilaments preparation

UHMWPE with an density 950 kg/m^3 was supplied by Sinopec Yangzi Petrochemical Company, China. The organically modified TiO_2 was provided from Hangzhou Wanjing New Material Company, China.

TiO_2/UHMWPE hybrid was prepared by reactive extrusion in a twin-screw extruder (Jiangsu, China) at 250 ~ 280 °C from UHMWPE (dried at 80 °C for 12 h) with 3 phr organically modified SiO_2 (dried at 80 °C for 12 h). The mixing speeding is 60 rpm. The extruded strands were pelletized and dried at 80 °C for 24 h to prepare the TiO_2/UHMWPE hybrid. The TiO_2/UHMWPE hybrid was then melt-spun through a 0.5 mm diameter spinneret using a SJ-45C Fiber Spin Line equipped with two drawing roll and a collecting roll (Jiangsu, China). The drawn ratio is 24, and the diameter of TiO_2/UHMWPE nanocomposite monofilaments is about 0.35 mm.

2.2 Characterization

The microstructures of the monofilaments were examined by a JEOL 6360LA scanning electron microscope (SEM) (JEOL Ltd., Japan) operated at an acceleration voltage of 15 kV.

Differential scanning calorimetry (DSC) was applied to investigate the melting and crystallisation behaviour of the monofilaments using a DSC thermal analyser (204F1, Netzsch Instruments, Germany). The samples were scanned at a heating and cooling rate of 10 oC/min in

[a] Corresponding author: jiangaoshi666@163.com

nitrogen atmosphere. The degree of crystallinity (Xc) was calculated via the total enthalpy method, according to Eq.

$$Xc = \left(\frac{\Delta H_f^{obs}}{\Delta H_f^0}\right) \times 100 \quad (1)$$

where ΔH_f^{obs} is the observed heat of fusion values. ΔH_f^0 is the specific enthalpy of melting for 100% crystalline polymer. We used ΔH_f^0 value for HDPE 288 J/g.

The tensile properties were studied on an Electron Omnipotence Experiment Machine INSTRON-4466 (Instron Instruments, USA) at a cross-head speed of 300 mm/min according to SC/T 5005-2014 under ambient conditions. At least ten specimens were measured for each sample.

3. Results and Discussion

3.1 Morphology of TiO_2/UHMWPE nanocomposite monofilaments

Figure 1 presents the fracture surface micrographs of TiO_2/UHMWPE nanocomposite monofilaments. The nanocomposite monofilament has a smooth surface. And the SEM images of the fracture surface indicate that the TiO_2 nano particles are well dispersed throughout the polymeric matrix, which could be related to strong interactions between UHMWPE molecular chain and nano-fillers (see Figure 1).

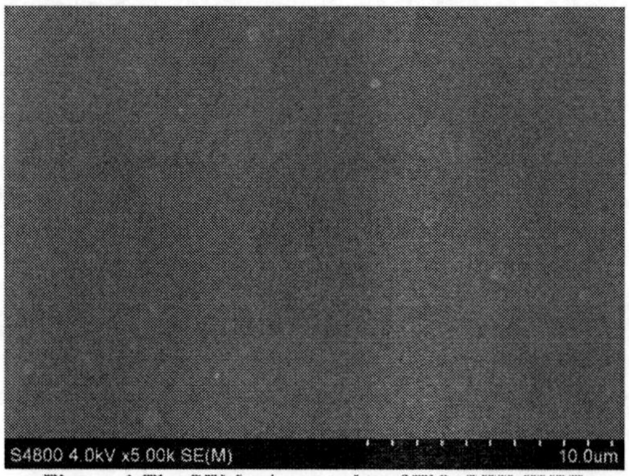

Figure 1 The SEM micrographs of TiO_2/UHMWPE nanocomposite monofilaments

3.2 Thermal analysis of TiO_2/UHMWPE nanocomposite monofilaments

Figure 2 shows the DSC heating and cooling thermograms of TiO_2/UHMWPE nanocomposite monofilaments and UHMWPE monofilaments. The DSC data are summarised in Table 1, including the melting temperature (T_m), percentage of crystallinity and crystallisation temperature (T_c). It could be noticed from Figure 2 that all monofilaments exhibit a melting peak of the PE component. And the incorporation of TiO_2 causes a increase in T_m and T_c, and reduces the degree of crystallinity of UHMWPE. The percentage of crystallinity for TiO_2/UHMWPE nanocomposite monofilaments decreases by 2.2%. This could be due to some difficulty in chain crystallization brought about by the presence of the TiO_2 in the nanocomposite monofilaments systems.

Table 1 The DSC data of UHMWPE and TiO_2/UHMWPE nanocomposite monofilaments

Samples	T_m [°C]	Percentage of crystallinity [%]	Crystallisation temperature [°C]
UHMWPE	141.2	64.9	116.7
TiO_2/UHMWPE	142.6	63.5	117.0

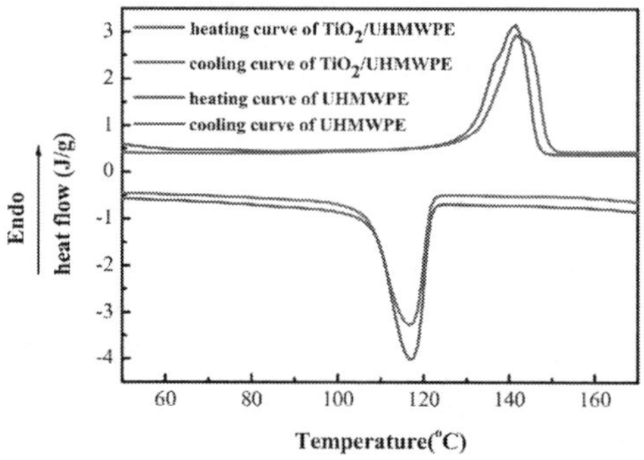

Figure 2 DSC heating cooling thermograms of UHMWPE and TiO_2/UHMWPE nanocomposite monofilaments

3.3 Tensile mechanical properties

The tensile mechanical properties of TiO_2/UHMWPE nanocomposite monofilaments are shown in Fig. 4. Compared with that of UHMWPE monofilaments, the breaking strength and knot strength of nanocomposite monofilaments increases with introducing TiO_2 content. This is probably due to the strong interaction between the UHMWPE molecular chain and nano TiO_2, which make the crack propagation blocked and passivated in the stretching process. It is noted that the TiO_2/UHMWPE nanocomposite fiber has a distinctly superior knot strength which is 32.4% higher than that of the pure UHMWPE fiber. Moreover, the breaking strength and knot breaking strength of the TiO_2/UHMWPE fiber were 7.61 cN/dtex and 8.16 cN/dtex respectively, 46.3% and 56.9% higher than the indexes for the fishing PE monofilament according to the industrial standard SC/T 5005. Elongation is a key factor in the material characteristics and the application properties, and the low elongation rate is another important property for fishing. Elongation at break decreases monotonically with the addition of nano TiO_2. This could be due to the interaction between the nano TiO_2 and UHMWPE molecular chain, and the monofilaments toughness reduces with the increase of TiO_2 content.

Table 2 The tensile mechanical properties of TiO_2/UHMWPE nanocomposite monofilaments

Samples	Breaking strength /cN·dtex-1	knot strength /cN·dtex-1	Elongation at break /%
UHMWPE monofilament	7.61	3.67	15.1
TiO_2/UHMWPE nanocomposite monofilaments	8.16	4.86	14.5

4 Conclusion

TiO_2/UHMWPE nanocomposite monofilaments were prepared successfully by melt spinning through a co-rotating screw extruder and drawing at hot water. The TiO2 nano particles are well dispersed throughout the polymeric matrix. The introduction of TiO_2 increases the melt point, wherea decreases degree of crystallinity of polyethylene. The breaking strength and knot strength of the nanocomposite monofilaments are remarkably improved upon nanofiller addition. The TiO_2/UHMWPE nanocomposite fiber has a distinctly superior knot strength which is 32.4% higher than that of the pure UHMWPE fiber.

Acknowledgements

The research work was supported by the National Key Technology R&D Program No. 2013BAD13B03 and No. 2013BAD13B02, Special Scientific Research Funds for Central Non-profit Institutes (East China Sea Fisheries Research Institute, Chinese Academy of Fishery Sciences) No. 2015T01 and the Open Foundation from Fishery Sciences in the First-Class Subjects of Zhejiang No.20160014.

References

1. Ward I M. Recent developments in the science and technology of high modulus flexible polymers[J]. Macromolecular Symposia, 1995, 100(1):1–14.
2. Huang W, Wang Y, Xia Y. Statistical dynamic tensile strength of UHMWPE-fibers[J]. Polymer, 2004, 45(11):3729-3734.
3. Du G, Wang J. The mechanical properties of surface treated UHMWPE fibers and TiO2 reinforced PMMA composite[J]. Surface & Interface Analysis, 2017.
4. Chand N, Kreuzberger S, Hinrichsen G. Influence of processing conditions on the tensile properties of unidirectional UHMWPE fibre/LDPE composites[J]. Composites, 1994, 25(9):878-880.
5. Alonso Y, Martini R E, Iannoni A, et al. Polyethylene/sepiolite fibers. Influence of drawing and nanofiller content on the crystal morphology and mechanical properties[J]. Polymer Engineering & Science, 2014, 56(8):149-149.
6. Mohammadalipour M, Masoomi M, Ahmadi M, et al. Interfacial shear strength characterization of GMA-grafted UHMWPE fiber/epoxy/nano clay hybrid nanocomposite materials[J]. Rsc Advances, 2016, 6(48):41793-41799.
7. Yu J R, Luan X N, Hu Z M, et al. Preparation and studies on the structure and properties of ultrahigh molecular weight polyethylene/nano-SiO 2 composite fibers[J]. Acta Polymerica Sinica, 2005, 1(5):764-768.
8. Yeh J T, Wang C K, Huang L K, et al. Ultradrawing and Ultimate Tenacity Properties of Ultrahigh Molecular Weight Polyethylene Composite Fibers Filled with Nanosilica Particles with Varying Specific Surface Areas[J]. Journal of Nanomaterials,2015,(2015-9-30), 2015, 2015:1-16.
9. Yeh J T, Yi D, Wang C K, et al. Ultradrawing and ultimate tenacity properties of Ultra-High Molecular Weight Polyethylene composite fibers filled with nanosilica particles with varying specific surface areas[M]// Applied System Innovation. 2016.

Influence of Material with Medium and High Molecular Weight Replacing Polyethylene on Trawl Performance

Yongli LIU, lei WANG, Wenwen YU, Jiangao SHI, Ai zhong ZHOU, Lu min WANG

East China Sea Fisheries Research Institute, Chinese Academy of Fishery Sciences,Shanghai 200090, China

Abstract. Taking single-boat trawling fishing in West Africa as the research object and maintaining the breaking strength of the original netting gear as the standard, we used medium- and high-molecular-weight materials to replace common polyethylene material in producing the trawl model. Test results showed that, under the same test conditions, the resistance of medium- and high-molecular-weight material trawls decreased by 16.80% compared with that of most of the common polyethylene material trawls. The maximum difference in the height of the net opening between the two material trawls was approximately 2.3 m. The energy consumption coefficient decreased by 23.65%.

1 Introduction

Marine fishing–trawling boats in China account for 18% of all marine fishing power-driven vessels, 25% of total power, and 48% of marine fishing yield [1] of the country. Thus, trawl fishing is significant in marine fishing in China. At present, energy saving and cost reduction are advocated. Meanwhile, the energy-saving and cost-reducing properties of netting gear are mainly evaluated based on overall resistance, height of net opening, energy consumption coefficient, power consumption [2–4], and other aspects. Currently, braided twines and other materials have been widely applied in trawl fishing abroad [5–9]. Medium- and high-molecular-weight polyethylene netting twines (new material) were used to replace common polyethylene netting twine (common material) to produce trawls that maintain the breaking strength of the original netting gear. The overall resistance, height of net opening, energy consumption coefficient, and power consumption of the two materials were compared to provide references for relevant studies on trawl fishing gear that promotes energy saving and cost reduction.

2 Materials and methods

2.1 Test instruments and equipment

The trawl model test was conducted in a fishing gear model test stilling basin with dimensions of 90 m × 6 m × 3 m. The power of the trailer drive motor was 7.5 kW × 4. The trawling speed range was 0.1–4 m/s. The microprocessor speed of the governing system had a uniform velocity of $P \leq 1\%$. The tachymeter was a light electric tachometer with accuracy of ±0.01%. The measuring range of the force sensor was 100 N with nonlinear error of 0.4% F.S.C. The net height meter was an FE-6300 type net position depth sounder with range resolution of 30 mm.

2.2 Physical and model nets

The physical prototype netting gear was produced by Weihai Haoyuntong Netting Gear Technology Co. Ltd. for single-boat trawling fishing in West Africa. The detailed parameters of the physical netting gear were as follows: The total length of the netting gear was 118 m, the net opening perimeter was 280 m, the headline length was 61.92 m, the footline length was 80.25 m, the number of net opening meshes was 56 with size of 5,000 mm, the buoyancy force was 6,066 N, the equipped sinking force was 9,330 N, and the length of the empty line was 100 m. With the criteria of maintaining the breaking strength of the original netting gear and having a "similar field" of application of the new material used to replace common material, the specification of the netting gear, size of the meshes, buoyancy force and equipped sinking force, rope accessories, and other parameters were all unchanged. According to the criteria for the prototype nets of the two types of netting twine materials in SC/T4014-1997 "Preparation of Trawl Model," two model nets were produced. The large-scale ratio of the two model nets was 20 and the small-scale ratio was 9.

2.3 Test methods

The breaking and knot-breaking strengths of the samples of each specification were measured for the common polyethylene netting twines and the new material netting twines for replacement used in prototype netting gear. The model net was tested and processed according to the criteria and data in the SC/T4011-1995 Basin Test Methods of Trawl Model [10]. The model test simulated the empty line, with the end of the line used as the tow point and the test trawling speeds divided into seven grades with the range of 2.5–5.5 kn. Every 0.5 kn was taken as a grade, and 0.35, 0.40, and 0.45 were taken as the three grades of the horizontal expansion of the model netting gear L/S (ratio of wingtip spacing and length of footline).

2.4 Conversion relation between physical and model test data

The mechanical proportional relation between physical and model net stresses was expressed as follows:

$F1 = F2 \cdot \lambda 2 \cdot \lambda'$. (1)

The conversion relation between physical and model heights of the net opening was expressed as follows:

$H1 = H2 \cdot \lambda$. (2)

In Formulas (1) and (2), λ is the large scale ratio, λ′ is the small-scale ratio, F1 is the physical net stress, F2 is the model net stress, H1 is the physical height of the net opening, and H2 is the model height of the net opening.

The calculation formula of the physical net energy consumption coefficient was expressed as

$$Ce = 3.472^{\frac{F}{H \cdot L}}. \quad (3)$$

In Formula (3), Ce [kW·h·(104 m3)−1] is the energy consumption coefficient of the physical net under a certain set trawling speed, F (kN) is the calculated resistance of the physical net under the trawling speed, H (m) is the calculated height of the net opening of the physical net under the trawling speed, and L (m) is the wingtip horizontal expansion of the physical net.

The formula for calculating the value of the physical power consumption of the simulated part of the trawl under each set trawling speed was expressed as

$P = FV$. (4)

In Formula (4), P (kW) is the consumption power of the physical net under a certain set trawling speed, F (kN) is the calculated resistance of the physical net under the trawling speed, and V (m/s) is the trawling speed of the physical net.

3 Results and analysis

3.1 Resistance of netting gear

Under the same test conditions, with the horizontal expansion L/S of 0.35, 0.40, and 0.45, the resistance rates of the two netting gears are shown in Figure 1.

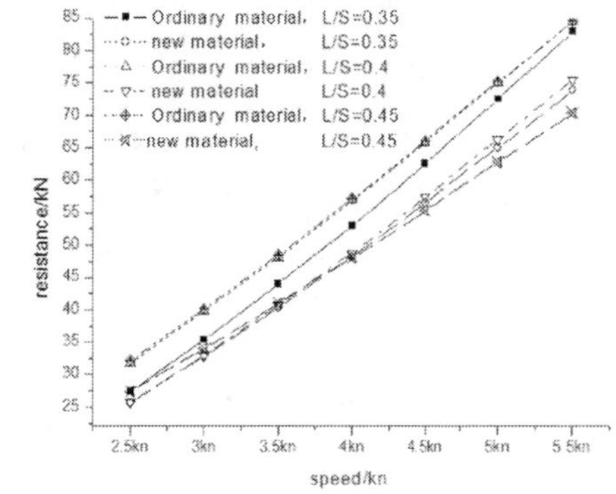

Fig. 1 Relationship curve of resistance & speed

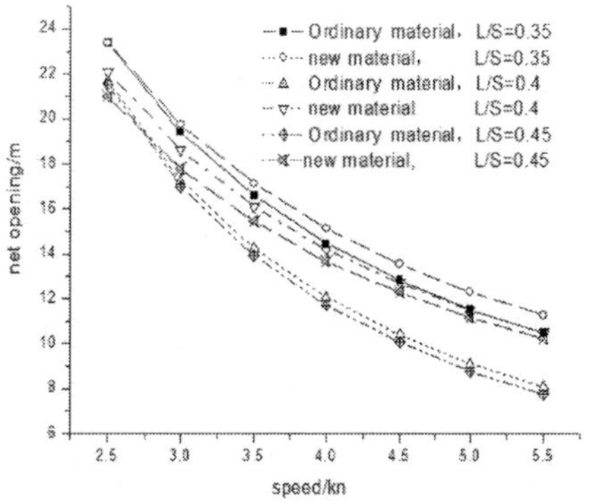

Fig. 2 Net opening under different trawling speeds

Figure 1 shows that the resistance of the netting gears increased continuously with the increase in trawling speed. The resistance of trawls of the common and new materials differed under various horizontal expansion conditions. In addition, given the same speed, the resistance was large when the horizontal expansion was large. Figure 1 also shows that, given the same speed and horizontal expansion, the resistance of trawls of the common material was larger than that of the new material. When L/S = 0.35 and trawling speed was 2.5 kn, the resistance rates of the common and new materials were 35.23 and 33.09 kN, respectively, with a difference of 6.06%. With the increase in L/S and trawling speed, the resistance of the common material trawls increased continuously and was greater than that of the new material trawls. When L/S = 0.45 and the trawling speed was 5 kn, the resistance of the common material was 16.80% more than that of the new material.

3.2 Height of net opening

When the horizontal expansion L/S was 0.35, 0.40, and 0.45, the results of the physical calculated height of the net opening of the two trawl models under different trawling speeds are presented in Figure 2.

Figure 2 shows that the height of the net opening of the two trawl models exhibited a declining trend with the increase in trawling speed. When the trawling speeds were the same, the height of the net opening of the two trawl models decreased with the increase in L/S. When

DOI: 10.1051/matecconf/201712803008

L/S of the two trawl models was the same, the height of the net opening of the netting gear of common material was lower than that of the new material under the same trawling speed. When L/S was 0.45 and the trawling speed was 5 kn, the height of the net opening of the new material was 2.3 m higher than that of the common material and increased by 24% compared with that of the common material. Studies on trawl-fishing gear model test hold that the main factors influencing the height of the net opening are perimeter of strained net opening, buoyancy force and equipped sinking force, netting resistance, length of empty line, length of netting wing, and horizontal expansion of netting gear[11]. However, the two trawl models compared in this test were the same, except for the material, thereby indicating that the net opening vertical expansion of the new material netting gear was better than that of the common material netting gear.

The net is a mobile filter that filters the water body for fishing objects during sweeping in the sea and consumes energy during the dragging process. Therefore, based on the assumption that the fishing objects are evenly distributed in the water, a better method to describe fishing efficiency is used to express the values of the energy consumed by the trawl to filter a unit of water body [12]. The energy consumption coefficients of the two trawl models of different materials are shown in Table 1. The results indicate that under the same conditions, the energy consumption coefficient of the new material was lower than that of the common material. In other words, when filtering the same volume of water body, the energy consumed by the new material trawl is smaller than that of the common material trawl. When L/S was 0.45 and the trawling speed was 3.5 kn, the energy consumption of the new material was reduced by 23.65% compared with that of the common material.

3.3 Energy consumption coefficient

Tab 1 Energy consumption coefficient under different speeds

Speed/（kn）	Energy consumption coefficient/Kw.h(104m3)-1					
	Ordinary material trawl			New material trawl		
	L/S=0.35	L/S=0.4	L/S=0.45	L/S=0.35	L/S=0.4	L/S=0.45
2.5	0.144	0.158	0.143	0.135	0.125	0.125
3.0	0.225	0.249	0.227	0.205	0.191	0.184
3.5	0.326	0.365	0.334	0.290	0.272	0.255
4.0	0.451	0.509	0.469	0.393	0.371	0.337
4.5	0.601	0.683	0.631	0.513	0.487	0.433
5.0	0.776	0.888	0.823	0.651	0.621	0.541
5.5	0.977	1.126	1.047	0.807	0.775	0.661

3.4 Power consumption

Table 2 shows the calculated values of physical net power consumption of the trawls of two materials under different trawling speeds when L/S was 0.35, 0.40, and 0.45. Under the same test conditions, the power consumption of the new material trawl was smaller than that of the common material trawl. The analysis of the model test results showed that when a 440 kW fishing boat was trawling, approximately 12% of the total rated power can be normally applied to the simulated part of the netting gear in the model test [13–15]. Table 2 also shows that, while maintaining the horizontal expansion L/S = 0.45 and the speed of 5 kn, given that the trawling time per day of the trawling fishing boat was 15 h, and based on the assumption that the fuel oil consumption rate of the diesel engine was 196 g· (kW·h) −1, approximately 100 L fuel oil can be saved.

Tab 2 Relationship curve of power consumption & speeds

Speed/（kn）	Power consumption coefficient/Kw					
	Ordinary material trawl			New material trawl		
	L/S=0.35	L/S=0.4	L/S=0.45	L/S=0.35	L/S=0.4	L/S=0.45
2.5	35.23	40.80	41.25	33.09	33.00	35.20
3.0	54.60	61.41	61.95	50.67	50.81	52.55
3.5	79.12	86.75	87.36	72.63	73.19	73.73
4.0	109.08	117.03	117.66	99.23	100.42	98.90
4.5	144.80	152.40	153.00	130.68	132.72	128.11
5.0	186.54	193.02	193.51	167.17	170.33	161.48
5.5	234.62	239.00	239.34	208.87	213.45	199.14

3 Conclusion

Based on energy saving and cost reduction as the permanent theme, the new material trawl was used to replace the common material trawl. Although the theoretical calculation of saved fuel oil volume cannot be used to precisely measure the saved fuel oil volume in practical production, the experimental results showed that the new material can reduce the netting gear resistance and improve the height of the net opening in netting gear application. In other words, the sweeping area in the sea increased and the resistance decreased, thereby reducing the fuel oil consumption and achieving energy saving and cost reduction to a certain extent.

Acknowledgements

The research work was supported by the National Key Te chnology R&D Program No. 2013BAD13B02 and Central Public-interest Scientific Institution Basal Research Fund, CAFS, No. 2017HY-ZD0605.

References

1. 2011China fishery statistics yearbook [M]. Beijing: China agricultural press, 2011.
2. Zhou A, Zhang Y, Yu Y g, et al. Experimental research on trawl performance of braided polyethylene netting twine replacing common polyethylene twisting [J] Marine fisheries, 2013, 35 (1), 98-101.
3. Zhou A, Zhang Y, Xu G, et al. Single ship towing four net-type double rig shrimp trawl model testing [J] Marine fisheries, 2014, 36(4), 364-371.
4. MATTK B, DAVID J S, RUSSELL B M. Effects of side taper on engineering and catching performances [J]. Fisheries Research, 2012, 12(134—136):73—81.
5. ANDREW S R, SIMON J. The capacity of benthos release panels to reduce the impacts of beam trawls on benthic communities[J]. Fisheries Research, 2005, 75(1—3) :73—85.
6. HEIDI M, RUNE H G, ANNA O, et a1. Resistance of aquaculture net cage materials to biting by Atlantic Cod (Gadus morhua)[J]. Aquaculture Engineering, 2009, 40(3) :126—134.
7. MALIN H, ARNE F, SVEN G L, The pontoon trap: Description and function of a seal-safe trap—net[J] . Fisheries Research, 2008, 93(3) :357—359.
8. GRAHAM K J. BROADHURST M K, MILLAR R B. Effects of codend circumference and twine diameter on selection in south. eastern Australian fish trawls[J] . Fisheries Research, 2009, 95(2—3) :341—349.
9. JOHN W V. Technological trends in capture fisheries. Ocean & Coastal Management[J]. 2001, 44(9—10) :635—651.
10. National fishery standardization technical committee, technical committee of fishery tools. SC/T4011-1995 towing model pond test method [s]. Beijing: China standard press, 1998:92—101.
11. Chen X, Xu B, Xiang Y, et al. An analysis of vertical expansion of bottom trawl network [c] //China fisheries research symposium. Suzhou: Su Zhou university press, 1997:163—170.
12. Wu Y, Yu Y, Li H, et al. A study of several issues in the trawl model test [c] // China fisheries research symposium proceedings. Suzhou: Su Zhou university press, 1997:27—36.
13. Cui J. On matching towing power and gear system for medium stern trawler[J]. Journal of Fisheries of China, 1993, 17(4) :289—296.
14. Friedman. Theory and design of fishing gear [M]. Hou H, Gao Q, translated. Beijing: china ocean press, 1988.
15. Ji X. Design and use of large mesh trawl fis hing gear[J]. Marine fisheries, 2000, 22(2):49—51.

MATEC Web of Conferences **128**, 03009 (2017) DOI: 10.1051/matecconf/201712803009
EITCE 2017

Fabrication and Characterization of 5 vol.% $(Al_2O_3)_p$ + 8 vol.% $(Al_2O_3)_f$ /A336 Hybrid Micron and Nano-Composites

Luyang Ren, Qiang Zhang, and Henry Hu*

Engineering Materials, University of Windsor, Windsor, Ontario, Canada N9B 3P4
** Corresponding author email: huh@uwindsor.ca*

Abstract. Hybrid composites are fabricated by adding two reinforcements into matrix materials so that the expected excellent properties can be achieved through the combined advantages of short fibres, and different size particles (micron or nano), which provide a high degree of design freedom. In this paper, hybrid preforms were produced with the different size reinforcement of the Al2O3 particles and short fibres. The Al-Si alloy-based hybrid composites reinforced by 5 vol. % Al2O3 particles and 8 vol. % Al2O3 fibres were fabricated by preform-squeezing casting route. The structure and performance of composite materials were studied with Transmission Electron Microscopy (TEM) and Scanning Electron Microscopy (SEM). The results show that the reinforcements, both particles and fibres, distribute homogeneously in the matrix materials, and the properties of composites are found to improve in comparison with the matrix Al-Si alloy.

1 Introduction

Metal matrix composites (MMCs) have widely been recognized to possess superior mechanical properties, such as enhanced wear resistance, high elastic modulus and yield strength, low coefficients of thermal expansion, as compared to the unreinforced monolithic metals [1-8]. With further development of metal matrix composites, their great potential has been demonstrated to be broadly used in the automobile and aerospace industries, and to fabricate various civil products as advanced materials as well. Recently, among the various types of metal matrix composites, researchers pay extra attention to aluminum or magnesium matrix composites reinforced with hybrid reinforcement in which both of particles and short fibres are employed. This is because they provide large opportunities to optimize the engineering performance of the MMCs for potential applications in the automobile industry, where a relatively low volume of reinforcement is required [9-10]. In this study, the hybrid preform with a cellular structure made by ceramic Al_2O_3 particles and fibres was fabricated. Then, the squeeze casting process was adopted to infiltrate the liquid aluminum into perform under an applied pressure. The results of preliminary microstructure analyses with both optical and Scanning Electron microscopy (SEM) show that the ceramic reinforcement including both the particles and fibres are dispersed uniformly in the matrix alloy without agglomeration and cave. The property evaluation indicates that the hybrid reinforced composite has improved elastic modulus, tensile strengths and hardness, relatively low thermal expansion coefficient in comparison to the matrix alloy.

2 Experimental Procedures

2.1 Materials

Al_2O_3 ceramic particles and Al_2O_3 short fibres were employed as the raw materials for preparation of the hybrid reinforcements. Two different sizes of the particles, 5.0 μm (named micron) and 600nm (named nano), respectively, were used for the hybrid performs for the purpose of a comparative study. The matrix alloy was A336 with the chemical composition (wt.%) of Al-12.0 Si-1.0Ni-1.0 Cu-1.0 Mg.

2.2 Hybrid Preform Preparation

Figure 1 presents the flow chart of the process for fabricating the hybrid preforms. The fabrication steps involve mixing of ceramic short fibres and particles, the introduction of binding compounds, shape formation of performs under pressure, drying and sintering. In the hybrid preform, the fibres serve as the cellular structure skeleton, and the content level of the fibre was pre-determined based on the desired amount of porosity levels of the cellular solid. Meanwhile, the particles were dispersed in the pores present in the cellular solid. The contents, sizes, and types of the ceramic reinforcement would be adjusted with the definite quantity and the shape of performs.

DOI: 10.1051/matecconf/201712803009

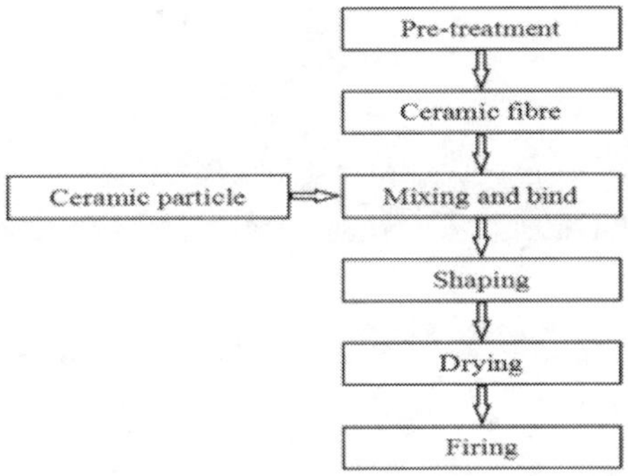

Figure 1 Flowchart Showing the Procedure for Fabricating Hybrid Perform

2.3 Composite Fabrication

Figure 2 shows the fabrication process of the composites in which a squeeze casting process was adopted. During fabrication, a hybrid perform was first preheated to 300°C. Then, molten matrix alloy at 730°C infiltrated into the preheated preform under an applied pressure of 100MPa. The pressure was maintained at the desired level for 20 seconds. After squeezing casting, a cylindrical disk of the dual-phase reinforced composite was obtained. The geometry of the disk is 0.010 m in diameter and 0.025 in thickness. In the hybrid composite, the main reinforcement phase was particles, and short fibres serve as the second reinforcement phase.

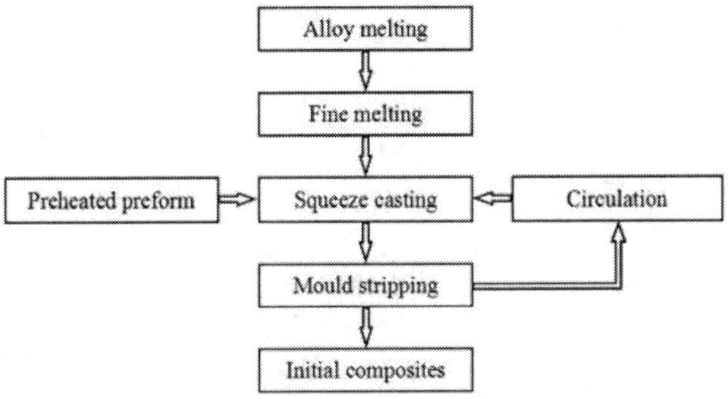

Figure 2 Flowchart Showing the Procedure for Fabricating Hybrid Composites

2.4 Microstructure

The microstructure of the new material was examined by optical microscopy and scanning electron microscopy (SEM). The alumina composites samples for optical microscopy and SEM were cut, mounted, mechanically grounded, and polished following the standard metallographic procedure. The SEM was conducted in a JEOL-200CX machine, and accelerating voltage is 200kV.

2.5 Property Evaluation

The mechanical properties of the hybrid composite were evaluated by tensile testing, which were performed at ambient temperature 300 °C, on an Instron machine equipped with computer data acquisition system. Following ASTM B557, subsize flat tensile specimens (25mm) in gage length, 6mm in width, and 6 mm in thickness) were machined from the center of the squeeze cast disc. The tensile properties, including 0.2% yield strength (YS), ultimate tensile strength (UTS), and elastic modulus, were obtained based on the average of three tests.

3. Results and Discussion

3.1 Microstructure

Figure 3 shows the hybrid preform made from the Al_2O_3 particles and fibres. Figure 4 shows the cylindrical disk of the squeeze cast hybrid reinforced Al-Si alloy-based composites.

Figure 3 A Hybrid Preform

Figure 4 Squeeze Cast Hybrid Composite

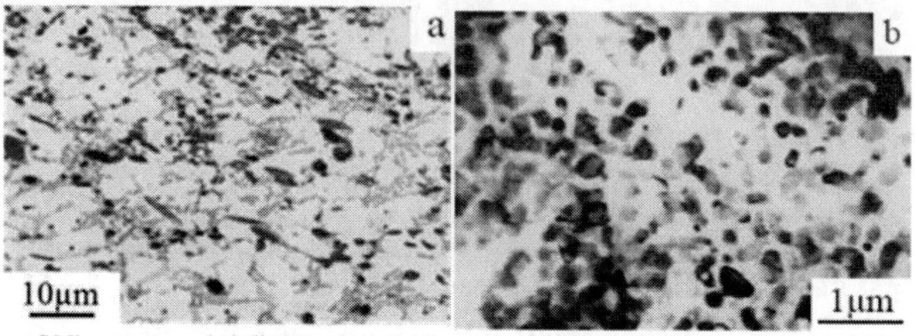

Figure 5 Microstructure of Al-Si/(8% vol. Al_2O_3 Fibres+ 5 vol. % Al_2O_3 Particles: (a) micron and (b) nano)

The microstructure of aluminum composite materials reinforced by Al_2O_3 particles and fibres is shown in Figure.5 (a, b). As shown in Figure 5 (a), the black dots are Al_2O_3 particles, and the gray areas are the matrix Al-Si alloy. Despite a large difference in the particle size, evidently, the reinforcement of the particles and fibres are dispersed uniformly without agglomeration and cavities in the matrix alloy. However, it can be seen from Figure 5 (a) and (b) that, with the same particle volume, a difference in the dispersion distance of the particle reinforcement is present in the composites. When the particle size is large (5 μm), the dispersion distance between the particles is around 1~5 μm. As the particle size decreases to the nano level (600 nm), the distance between the particles is also reduced to 80~200 nm. This observation should be attributed to the fact that, as the volume of reinforcement is constant, the number of particles are reduced with increasing the size of particles. The fewer the particles, the larger the dispersion distance which is present between the particles. It has been documented [9] that, the strength of preforms and the process parameters such as the preheated temperature of the pre-form, the pouring temperature of the matrix alloy, and the applied pressure level in the perform plus squeeze casting process, could influence the quality and performance of the composites significantly. It appears that the applied pressure during casting and infiltration enables molten matrix alloy with relatively high superheat in the preheated die to flow into the perform and wet reinforcement even with sub-micron particles involved although no wetting agents was employed. Also, because the contacting time between the molten alloy and reinforcement at relatively casting high temperature is shortened with the help of the applied pressure, no observation on severe chemical reactions between the matrix alloy and reinforcement occurred during fabrication. As a result, the microstructure of the composites is homogeneous without the porosity and reactants.

Table 1. Properties of composites and aluminum alloy and iron cast

Material		Composite	Al-Si alloy	Gray Iron 250
Density [kg·m³]		2.78	2.75	7.25~7.35
Tension strength [MPa]	RT	275	265	250
	300°C	158	131	
Hardness [HB]		138	130	215
Elasticity modulus [GPa]		96	80	311
Linear expansibility [10^{-6}/°C]	25~250°C	20.1	24.6	11.8
	25~400°C	21.4	25.7	

3.2 Mechanical property of the composites

Table 1 shows the tensile and physical properties of the hybrid composite with the reinforcement of micron (5 μm) sized 5 vol. % Al_2O_3 particles + 8 vol. % Al_2O_3 fibres in comparison with the base Al-Si alloy and cast iron. The hybrid composite exhibits improved tensile strengths over those of the matrix alloy and gray iron 250. In particular, high temperature tensile strength (158 MPa) of the composite is 20% higher than that of the matrix alloy. With almost no increase in material density, the elastic modulus of the hybrid composite shows 20% improvement over the matrix alloy despite that it is still lower than that of gray iron 250. Also, the thermal expansion of coefficient of the hybrid composite is lower than that of the matrix alloy.

4. Conclusions

1. Hybrid preforms with Al_2O_3 particles in micron or nano sizes and fibres were prepared by blending and shaping. The hybrid composites were fabricated by a squeeze casting process after the preform was infiltrated by molten Al-Si alloy under an applied pressure.

2. The results of the microstructure analyses of the hybrid composites show that the reinforcement of the particles and fibres are dispersed uniformly in the matrix alloy without agglomeration and Al_2O_3 fibres orientate random in the matrix. This observation indicates that the adopted squeeze casting process is capable of manufacturing the hybrid composites with reinforcements of different sizes and physical geometries.

3. The hybrid composite exhibits improved tensile strengths over those of the matrix alloy and gray iron 250. In particular, high temperature tensile strength (158 MPa) of the composite is 21% higher than that of the matrix alloy. With almost no increase in material density, the elastic modulus of the hybrid composite shows 20% improvement over the matrix alloy.

Acknowledgement

The authors would like to take this opportunity to thank the Natural Sciences and Engineering Research Council of Canada and the University of Windsor for supporting this work.

References

1. Zhu H., and Li Z., Wear behavior of SiC_P reinforced Al matrix composite, Mat. Mech. Eng., 20(3), 1996, 40-45.
2. Finot M., Micromechanical model of reinforcement fracture in particle-reinforced metal composites, Metall Trans, 25A (11), 1994, 2403-2406.
3. Tohgo K., and Weng G. J., A progressive damage mechanics in particle-reinforced metal-matrix composites under high triaxial tension, Trans ASME, 116(7), 1994, 414-420.
4. Yue C., Zhang Y., and Bao S., Investigations of Tribological Properties of Particle-Reinforced Aluminum Matrix Composites under Dry Sliding, Mechanical Engineering (China), 12(8), 2001, 963-962.
5. Qi H., Ding Z., Fan Y., and Jiang Z., Research on automotive brake discs of SiCp/Al composite, Acta material composite sinica, 18(1), 2001, 62-66.
6. Wang H., and Li W., Research on wear properties of aluminum matrix composites-brake materials, J. Chin. Electr. Microsc. Soc, 19(4), 2000, 551-552.
7. Bai Y., Yun H., Han E., Tan R., and Bi J., Research on properties of aluminum matrix composites, Materials protection, 36(9), 2003, 5-9.
8. Fan J., Sang J., and Zhang Y., The spatial distribution of reinforcements in aluminum matrix composites, Acta Metallurgica Sinica, 34(11), 1998, 1198-1204.
9. Hu H., Squeeze casting of Magnesium alloys and their composites. Journal of Mat. Sci., 33, 1998, 1579-1589.
10. Ye H., and Liu X., Review of recent studies in magnesium matrix composites. Journal of Mat. Sci., (39), 2004, 6153-6171.

Study on Indentation Experiments and Mechanical Behavior of RB-SiC

FAN Cheng[1,a], ZHANG Shijie[2], ZHAO Qizhi[2], ZHANG Lei[2]

[1]Jiangsu Provincial Key Labratory of Advanced Robotics & Collaborative Innovation Center of Suzhou Nano Science and Technology, Soochow University, Suzhou 215021
[2]College of Mechanical Science and Engineering, Jilin University, Changchun 130025

Abstract. In this work, we studied on the mechanical behavior of RB-SiC by the indentation experiments. The Vickers hardness tester and the laser scanning confocal microscope are used to process and observe the RB-SiC sample pieces. The indentations result shows that the hardness at the Si phase is lower than the SiC phase, thus it is easier to remove the Si than SiC. The morphology of indentations are complicated, there were no accumulation phenomenon at indentation edge. When the loading was 0.1kgf, 0.2kgf and 0.3kgf, only the radical cracking can be observed and the cracking was not obvious at Si and SiC mixed phase. Avalanche crushed phenomenon occurred when the load increased to 0.4kgf. According to the Evans' fracture toughness formula, the fracture toughness of SiC phase is about 2.5MPa·m$^{1/2}$, and the fracture toughness of Si-SiC mixed phase is bigger than 3.0 MPa·m$^{1/2}$. The critical cutting depth (d_c) of RB-SiC was calculated by empirical formula presented by T. G. Bifano, and the value is 22.54nm.

1 Introduction

RB-SiC have excellent mechanical and chemical properties, such as high hardness, high thermal conductivity, wide band gap etc. Thus, RB-SiC has been considered as one of the most promising materials for lens molds and space telescope mirror [1-3].

Because of the high hardness of the RB-SiC, it is very difficult to remove the material of RB-SiC. Many methods for processing RB-SiC were presented, such as chemical mechanical polishing [4], electro-chemical mechanical polishing [5] and plasma-assisted polishing [6]. But these methods still may leave damage and scratch on the surface. Thus, it is important to understand the mechanical behavior of RB-SiC to realize the ductile material removal. In the previous study, some research of ductile removing of glass materials [7-8] and properties of RB-SiC [9] were studied.

In this work, we studied the properties of RB-SiC on Vickers hardness, fracture toughness and critical depth by Vickers indentation experiment. This will help us know more about RB-SiC so that we can adjust the processing parameters in the future study.

2 Vickers indentation experiment

The size of sample pieces in the experiments isΦ10x8mm.The sample pieces were preprocessed on the Tegra System Modular sample preparation system (shown in Fig.1). Before processing, the samples were mounted in the epoxy resin as shown in Fig.2. Fig.3 shows the white light interferometer images of the RB-SiC surface morphology. As indicated by Fig.3, RB-SiC consists of two phases, and the distribution of the two phases is not uniform. The 'Island' is the SiC phase, and the dark part is the Si phase.

Table.1 is the experiment parameters of the indentation experiments. The Tukon 2500 full automatic Vickers hardness tester (Wilson hardness Ltd.) was used to press on three points on the sample pieces under different loads. The OLS3000 laser scanning confocal microscope (OLYMPUS Ltd.) was used to analyze the indentations.

Table1. Vickers indentation experiments

Experiments Conditions	RB-Sic
Indenter	Vickers Indenter
Load(*kgf*)	0.05,0.1,0.2,0.3,0.4
Loading time(s)	10
Holding time(s)	15
Discharging time(s)	10

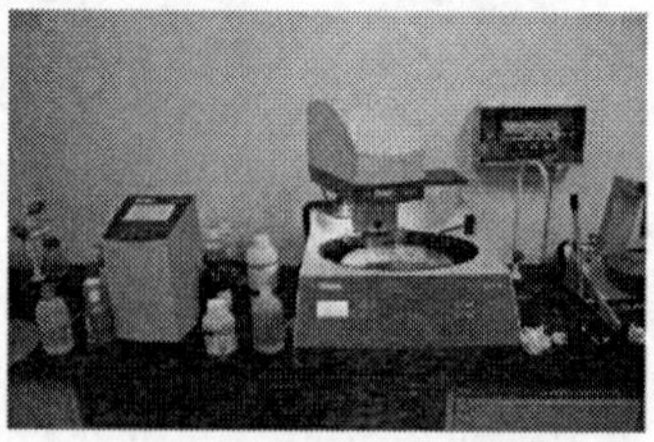

Figure.1 Tegra System Modular sample preparation system

[a] Corresponding author: chfan@suda.edu.cn

 DOI: 10.1051/matecconf/201712803010

Figure.2 Samples mounted in the epoxy resin

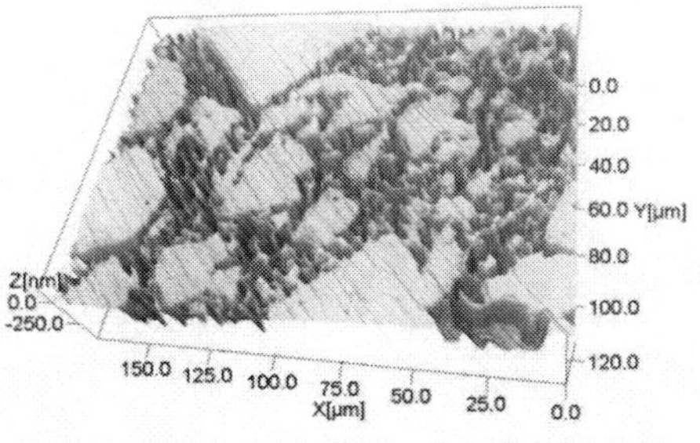

Figure.3 White light interferometer images of the RB-SiC surface morphology

3 Vickers indentation experiment

3.1. Analysis of Vickers hardness

Four arrises vertebral diamond was used as indenter in the Vickers hardness experiments. The Vickers hardness can be obtained by:

$$HV = \frac{F}{S} = \frac{2F\sin 68^{\circ}}{d^2} = 1.854\frac{F}{d^2} \quad (1)$$

where HV is the Vickers hardness(kgf/mm^2), F is the load, (kgf), S is the area of the indentation(mm^2), and d is the average length of diagonal of the indentation.

Table.2 shows the Vickers hardness of RB-SiC under different loads. According to Table 2, there is no size effect between the Vickers hardness and the load. Because there are two phases exist in RB-Si and the distribution and size of two phases are not uniform, the indenter contact different phases at each time.

Table 2. Hardness of RB-SiC under different load

Load(*kgf*)	$\overline{H}$ (*Gpa*)
0.05	19.054
0.1	23.232
0.2	19.515
0.3	25.350
0.4	20.636

For the indentation load of 0.2*kgf*, the contact area and the Vickers hardness are shown in Fig.4 and Table.3 respectively. In Fig.4(a) and (b), the indenter was pressed on the SiC phase, thus the Vickers hardness is similar as indicated in Table.3. In Fig.4(c), the indenter was pressed on the mixed phase where the particle size of SiC is small. Thus, the Vickers hardness is lower than SiC phase. We can infer that the Vickers hardness of Si is much lower than SiC. In Fig.4(d), the indentation was almost pressed on SiC phase, thus the Vickers hardness is similar to pure SiC phase.

According to the analysis above, when grinding or polishing RB-SiC, the Si phase can be removed easier than the SiC phase. As a result the 'step' structure appeared. It is quite hard to obtain high surface quality of RB-SiC.

Table.3 The Vickers hardness of different contact area under 0.2*kgf*

Contact area	*H*(Gpa)	The corresponding figure
SiC phase	27.243	Fig.4a
SiC phase	27.410	Fig.4b
Mixed phase of Si and SiC	16.465	Fig.4c
Mixed phase of Si and SiC (SiC phase over a half)	24.213	Fig.4d

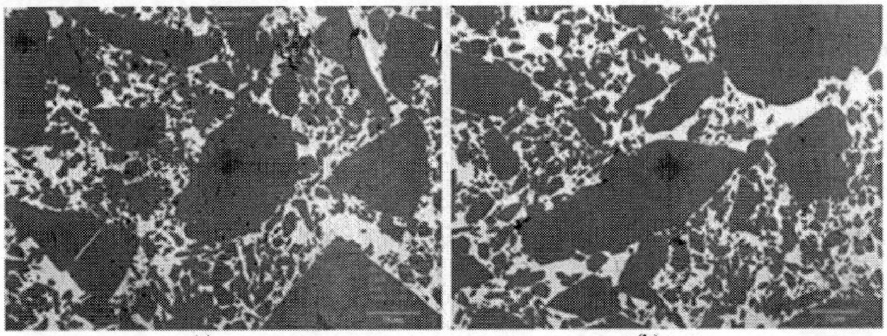

(a) (b)

DOI: 10.1051/matecconf/201712803010

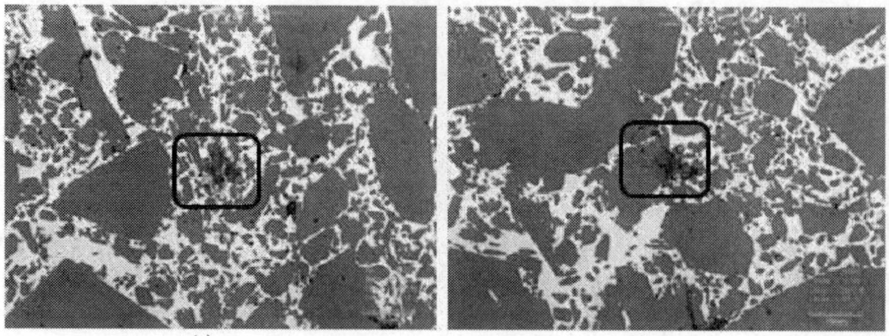

(c) (d)

Figure.4 The morphology of indentation under 0.2*kgf*

3.2 Analysis of the morphology of indentations

The general cracks of the Vickers indentation are shown in Fig.5. There are two radial cracks along the extension cord of rectangular indentation diagonal lines as shown in Fig.5(a).As shown in Fig.5(b), two radical cracks and median crack make half-penny crack. In general, half-penny crack system is considered as half round, but the reality is different from the ideal, especially under the low load. Fig.5(c) shows the radical cracks in a separate form observed from the cross section.

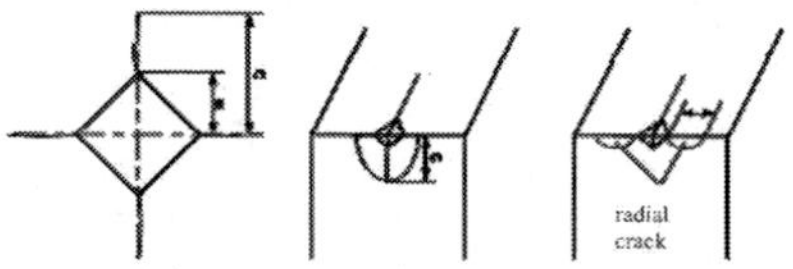

(a) (b) (c)

Figure.5 Schematic of Vickers indentation

Fig.6 shows the morphology of the indentation under different loads. The morphology is complicated, black area is the SiC phase, the white area is the the Si phase, and the distribution of two phases are not uniform. Under the low load (0.05kgf), only plastic deformation occurred. With the increasing of loads (0.1kgf, 0.2kgf and 0.3kgf), there were obvious radical cracks at the diagonal of indentation of the SiC phase, but the cracks at the Si and SiC mixed phase were shorter. No material accumulation appeared at the edges of the indentation on the mixed phase. When load increased to 0.4kgf, radical cracks could be clearly seen at the diagonal of indentation. In addition, a 'shell' like mass breakage occurred which is shown in Fig.6e. Because of the heavy load, the lateral cracks spread from subsurface to surface which results in the fall off of SiC.

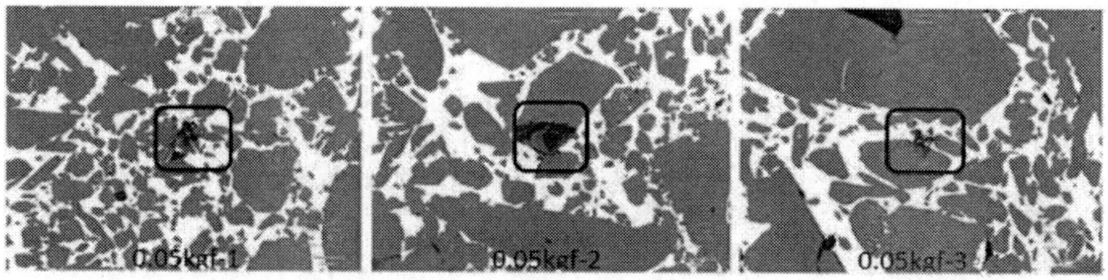

(a) 0.05kgf

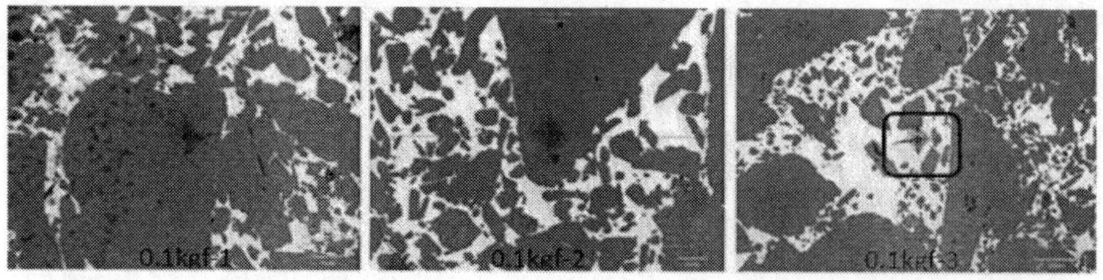

(b) 0.1kgf

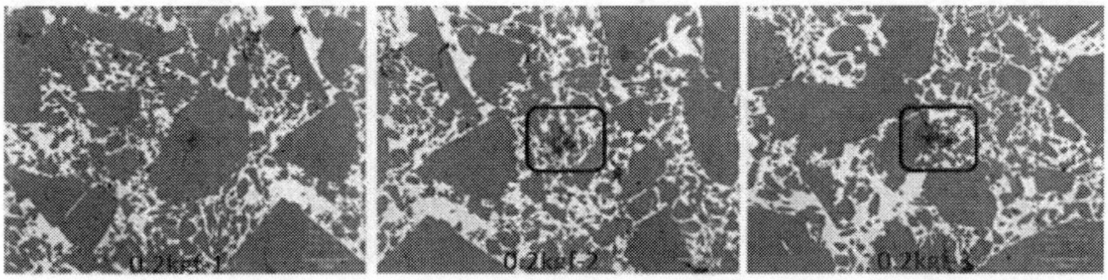

(c) 0.2kgf

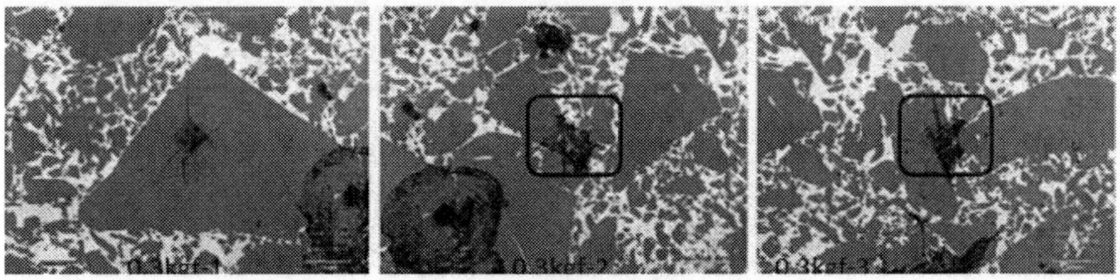

(d) 0.3kgf

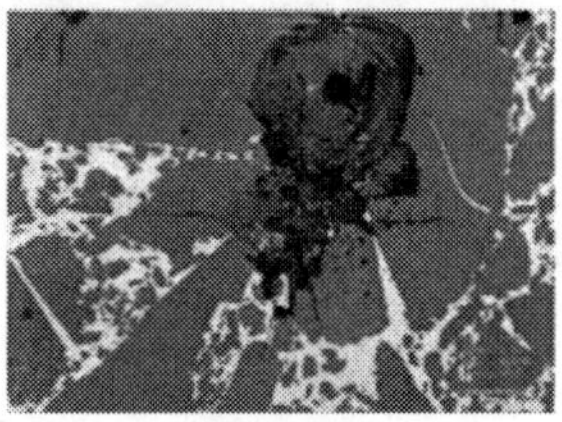

(e) 0.4kgf

Figure.6 The morphology of indentation of RB-Si

4 Fracture toughness of the indentation

The calculation of the indentation fracture toughness is mainly based on two different crack systems, one is Half - Penny Crack System, also known as the Median/Radial Crack System and the other is Palmqvist cracks System. But for RB-SiC, since its Vickers indentation cracks are complicated, it is hard to define the system it belongs to. Since the RB-SiC is a typical polycrystalline ceramic materials. Therefore, the fracture toughness formula of RB-SiC (K_{IC}) can be calculated by the equation of the fracture toughness presented by Evans[10], which gives:

$$\left(\frac{K_{IC}}{H\sqrt{a}}\right)\left(\frac{H}{E}\right)^{0.4}=10^{y} \tag{2}$$

where

$$y=-1.59-0.34x-2.02x^{2}+11.23x^{3}-24.97x^{4}+15.32x^{5} \tag{3}$$

and

$$10^{x}=\frac{c}{a} \tag{4}$$

In Eq(2), E is the elastic modulus of the material, H is the hardness, c is the half length of the crack, and a is the half length of the diagonal of the indentation. According to Eq.(2), (3) and (4), the fracture toughness is calculated and the results are shown in Table.4.

The fracture toughness of SiC phase is about 2.5MPa·m$^{1/2,}$ the fracture toughness of mixed phase is larger than 3.0MPa·m$^{1/2}$.

5 Critical depth d_c

It is necessary to calculate the critical depth so that the hard brittle material can be removed (grinding) ductile under this depth and left no cracks and damage [8-9]. T. G. Bifano[8], presented the critical depth model of the glass material by the indentation method based on the Griffith crack extension criterion, which gives:

$$d_c=a\left(\frac{E}{H_v}\right)\left(\frac{K_{IC}}{H_v}\right)^{2} \tag{5}$$

where a is a constant of system, E is the elastic modulus of the material, H_v is the hardness of the material, and K_{IC} is the fracture toughness of the material. The scanning

Table.4 The fracture toughness of RB-SiC under different load

Load(kgf)	Contact area	H(Gpa)	Length of crack(μm)	K_{IC}(MPa·m$^{1/2}$)
	SiC phase	24.94	8.812	2.606
0.1	Si phase	26.37	9.669	2.434
	SiC phase	18.39	8.111	2.657
	SiC phase	27.24	14.527	2.729
0.2	SiC phase	27.41	16.616	2.327
	Mixed phase	24.21	12.771	3.048
	SiC phase	25.97	22.903	2.205
0.3	Mixed phase	25.17	15.564	3.387
	Mixed phase	24.92	17.855	3.045

Table.5 The critical depth of RB-SiC under different load

Load(kgf)	Contact area	H(Gpa)	K_{IC}(MPa·m$^{1/2}$)	d_c(nm)
	SiC phase	24.94	2.606	21.67
0.1	Si phase	26.37	2.434	15.99
	SiC phase	18.39	2.657	56.19
	SiC phase	27.24	2.729	18.24
0.2	SiC phase	27.41	2.327	13.02
	Mixed phase	24.21	3.048	32.41
	SiC phase	25.97	2.205	13.74
0.3	Mixed phase	25.17	3.387	35.61
	Mixed phase	24.92	3.045	29.66

electron microscope is used to observe the surface, and the critical depth empirical is shown in Eq(6) when the crack of indentation surface is less than 10%.

$$d_c = 0.15\left(\frac{E}{H_v}\right)\left(\frac{K_{IC}}{H_v}\right)^2 \qquad (6)$$

After calculation, the critical depth of RB-SiC is shown in Table.5.

6 Conclusions

(1) The morphology of RB-SiC is complicated. No material accumulation appeared at the edge of the mixed phase indentation. When the load is 0.1kgf, 0.2kgf and 0.3kgf, the radical cracks appeared at SiC phase. When the load is 0.4kgf, the massive avalanche crushed phenomenon appeared.

(2) The modulus presented by Evans was used to calculate the fracture toughness under different load. The fracture toughness of SiC phase is about 2.5MPa·m$^{1/2}$, the fracture toughness of mixed phase is larger than 3.0MPa·m$^{1/2}$.

(3) The critical depth of ductile-brittle translation of RB-SiC is 22.54nm on average.

Acknowledgement

This work is supported by the Chinese National Natural Science Foundation under Grant 51505312, the Basic Research Program of Jiangsu Province under Grant BK20150330, the Chinese Postdoctoral Science Foundation under Grant 2015M571800 and National Natural Science Foundation of China under Grant 61503268.

References

1. Lee H Y, Kim D W, Sung Y J, et al. Fabrication of SiC micro-lens by plasma etching[J]. Thin Solid Films, **475(1–2)**:318-322.(2005)
2. Pang S W, Tamamura T, Nakao M, et al. Direct nano-printing on Al substrate using a SiC mold[J]. Journal of Vacuum Science & Technology B Microelectronics & Nanometer Structures, **16(3)**:1145-1149.(1998)
3. Ebizuka N, Eto H, Dai Y, et al. SiC ultralight mirror for large space telescope and for extremely huge ground-based telescope II[J]. Proceedings of SPIE - The International Society for Optical Engineering, **5487**:329-334.(2004)
4. Zhou L, Audurier V, Pirouz P, Powell JA (1997) Chemomechanical Polishing ofSilicon Carbide. Journal of the Electrochemical Society **144(6)**:L161–L163.
5. Deng H, Hosoya K, Imanishi Y, et al. Electro-chemical mechanical polishing of single-crystal SiC using CeO 2, slurry[J]. Electrochemistry Communications, **52**:5-8.(2015)
6. Yamamura K, Takiguchi T, Ueda M, et al. Plasma assisted polishing of single crystal SiC for obtaining atomically flat strain-free surface[J]. CIRP Annals - Manufacturing Technology, **60(1)**:571-574.(2011)
7. Xiang Y, Chen J, Bai M S, et al. Experimental study of brittle-ductile translation critical condition in Li2O-Al2O3-SiO2 glass-ceramic machining[J]. Journal of Applied Optics, (2014).
8. Bifano T G, Dow T A, Scattergood R O. Ductile-Regime Grinding: A New Technology for Machining Brittle Materials[J]. Journal of Engineering for Industry, **113(2)**:184-189.(1991)
9. Zhang J, Jiang D, Lin Q, et al. Properties of silicon carbide ceramics from gelcasting and pressureless

sintering[J]. Materials & Design (1980-2015), **65(20)**:12-16.(2013)
10. Evans A G, Charles E A. Fracture Toughness Determination by Indentation[J]. Journal of the American Ceramic Society, **59(7-8)**:371-372.(2006)

DOI: 10.1051/matecconf/201712803011

Study on Processing Technology and Quality of Moringa oleifera leaves with γ - Aminobutyric Acid

ZHOU Wei[1], LI Qian[1,2], GUO Changqing[3], CAO Yupo[1], PENG Shaodan[1], JING Wei[1], LI Jihua[1,*]

[1]Agricultural Products Processing Research Institute, Chinese Academy of Tropical Agricultural Sciences, Zhanjiang, Guangdong, 524001, China
[2]College of Food Science and Technology, GuangDong Ocean University, Zhanjiang, Guangdong, 524088, China;
[3]Henan Gold Moringa Biotechnology Co., Ltd., Hebi, Henan, 458000, China

Abstract. In order to obtain the high level of γ-aminobutyric acid Moringa oleifera leaves, Use 7% sodium glutamate solution to soak the fresh Moringa oleifera leaves, study effect of different treatment times and three different drying methods(hot air drying, vacuum freeze drying, shadow drying) on the formation of γ-aminobutyric acid and quality (total flavonoids, soluble sugar, amino acids, polyphenols, color)of dried Moringa oleifera leaves. The results indicated that shadow-dried Moringa oleifera leaves had the hightest retention of γ-aminobutyric acid, but its browning degree were not preferable, soluble sugar was damaged gravely, and its vulnerable to weather conditions. Vacuum freeze dried Moringa oleifera leaves had the hightest retention of flavonoids, polyphenols and amino acids. The γ-aminobutyric acid content of Vacuum freeze dried and hot air dried Moringa oleifera leaves had no much difference. Hot air dried Moringa oleifera leaves browning degree were preferable, it's had an moderate content of soluble sugar and amino acids, the short drying time is characteristics of this drying method.with the treatment time increased, the content of γ-aminobutyric acid and amino acids content first increased and then decreased. Flavonoids and polyphenols content first decreased and then increased. Soluble sugar content decreased. In summary, after soaking with 7% sodium glutamate solution for 10h, then dried by hot air drying(drying temperature of 60°C), was the most suitable way for industrial production of the high level of γ-aminobutyric acid Moringa oleifera leaves.

1 Introduction

Moringa oleifera Lam, is a species belonging to the Moringa Branch and Moringaceae family, widely distributed intropical and subtropical regions of Asia, Africa[1].The whole plant has edible value and can be useful[2].Its roots, stems, leaves, flowers, seeds, branches and barks are rich in nutrients and medicinal ingredients[3]. Studies have shown that Moringa leaves are rich in potassium, calcium, phosphorus, iron, and essential amino acids, and having antioxidant activity of vitamin C, flavonoids and polyphenols substances[3]. Moringa has antioxidant, anti-cancer, hypoglycemic and lipid-lowering and other biological activities[4-7].

γ-aminobutyric acid (GABA) is a non protein natural amino acid. It has many physiological activities, such as lowering blood pressure, anti-aging and anti-anxiety[8]. GABA in plants can be formed by L-glutamic acid or its salts under irreversible α decarboxylation catalyzed by glutamate decarboxylase (GAD) [9]. γ-aminobutyric acid can be biosynthesized by GAD, but with the increase of age and mental stress, the accumulation of GABA in the human body is very difficult. Although GABA is widely distributed, the content of GABA is very small [10]. With the immersion of exogenous amino acids as a enrichment technique,GABA biosynthetic substrates can be added not only to form hypoxic environments, to activate GAD activity, but also to promote the synthesis of large amounts of GABA [11]. Many scholars have applied exogenous amino acid soaking technology to natural products such as tea, soybean and brown rice [12-13], but there are few reports on improving the content of GABA in Moringa oleifera [14-15]. Zhao et al. [14] and others used glutamic acid as the soaking solution to increase the content of GABA in the leaves of Moringa, but did not study the effect of soaking on the quality components of Moringa oleifera. The research work needs to be further studied.

Drying is the last step in the processing of GABA Moringa leaves. Drying can reduce the moisture content of the material, effectively hinder the breeding of microorganisms within the material and the chemical reaction of water as the medium, thus significantly extending the shelf life of food and reducing the cost of storage and transportation [16]. However, different drying methods have a great influence on the quality components in the material, so it is necessary to use a suitable drying method.

Therefore, the experiment was carried out by drying at 60 ℃ oven, vacuum freeze-drying and natural drying to study the effects of three kinds of drying methods on GABA content and quality components of Moringa oleifera leaves, and to determine the best drying method.

Moringa oleifera GABA enrichment process test in Postharvest Moringa leaf as raw material, with 7% sodium glutamate (MSG) solution (D) as a solution, the best drying method was used to dry the fresh mulberry leaves after soaking. The effects of different immersion times on GABA content and quality components in Moringa lanceolata were studied. The results showed that Moringa oleifera leaves was rich in GABA, which was developed for the high content of γ-aminobutyric acid and other products lay the foundation.

2. Materials and method

2.1 Plant material

GABA Moringa leaves: fresh leaves of Moringa oleifera were bought from Henan gold M.oleifera Biological Technology Co. Ltd.

2.2 Chemical and instruments

2,4-dinitrofluorobenzen; γ-aminobutyric acid; glutamic acid; rutin gallate; Fulin phenol; chlorination Aluminum; sodium bicarbonate; sodium carbonate; potassium dihydrogen phosphate; sodium hydroxide; anhydrous sodium acetate; glacial acetic acid; N, N-dimethylformamide; anthrone and glucose.

High purity liquid chromatography Japan Shimadzu Corporation; UV1780 UV spectrophotometer Japan Shimadzu Corporation; ALPHA2-4 experimental freeze dryer Germany CHRIST company; DHG-9426A oven Shanghai Jinghong Experimental Equipment Co., Ltd; HH-4 constant temperature water bath Pots Jintan Guowang Experimental Instrument Factory; Milli-Qlntegral pure water meter France Mi Mi Bo company; pH meter METTLER TOLEDO company; color measuring instrument

2.3 Effects of different drying methods on GABA content and color of tea in Moringa oleifera leaves

The 4 groups of Moringa fresh leaves, each 50 g, were placed in the white porcelain plate, respectively by 60 °C (A) drying and vacuum freeze drying (B) and natural dried (C) drying the material, the final moisture content control in 5%.

2.4 Effects of dipping treatment on GABA content of fresh leaves of Moringa oleifera and nutritional components

The 7 groups of fresh leaves of Moringa, 20g each, were immersed in 300ml7%MSG solution (D), plastic film sealed bottle, all operations were carried out at room temperature, soaking time were 0h, 2h, 4h, 6h, 8h, 10h, 12h, remove the water after washing, steaming to about 30s. 60 °C blast drying box drying to a moisture content of around 5%, and then analyze the content of GABA after treatment of Moringa oleifera and the main quality components, using pure water as the blank control (CK), each sample was repeated 3 times.

2.5 Determination of indicators and methods

Flavonoids, Polyphenol Determination With reference to the method of Vongsak [15], the total amount of free amino acids is determined by reference to GB / T 8314-2013, the determination of soluble total sugar content by reference to the method of Wei Wei [16] et al.

GABA content of the method of determination: mobile phase: A 0.05mol / L sodium acetate buffer (pH6.8, containing 1% N, N-dimethyl formamide); B 50% acetonitrile aqueous solution (V / V) Gradient elution, flow rate 0.8ml / min, column temperature 27 °C, wavelength 360nm.

Amino acid pre-column derivatization: take the sample solution 1.0 ml placed in 10ml volumetric flask, add 0.5mol / L (pH 9.0) sodium bicarbonate 1.0ml, mixed, and then add 1% 2,4-dinitrofluorobenzene 0.25ml, the vortex oscillation uniform, in 60 °C water bath for 60min, remove and cool to room temperature, with 0.01mol / L (pH7.0) potassium dihydrogen phosphate buffer solution to the volume, with 0.45μm filter, machine.

2.6 Experimental data processing

The data were processed and analyzed by Origin 8.5 and SPSS 22.0 software. The data were analyzed by one-way ANOVA ($P < 0.05$). All the experiments were repeated three times. The experimental results were expressed as mean ± standard deviation.

3. Results and discussion

3.1 Effects of Different Drying Methods on GABA Content and Quality Components of Moringa oleifera Leaves

3.1.1 Effects of three drying methods on GABA content in Moringa oleifera leaves

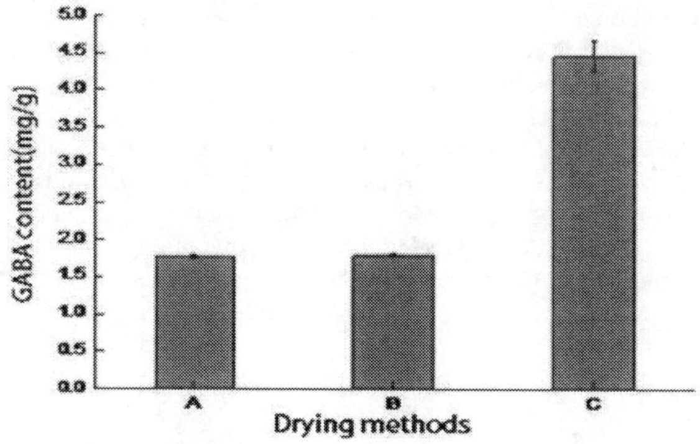

Fig.1 Effects of different drying methods on GABA content of Moringa oleifera leaves

The results of GABA content of the three kinds of drying methods are as follows: natural dryness (C)> vacuum freeze drying(B)> 60 °C blast drying(A)(Fig.1). Natural dryness is significantly higher than the other two drying methods, it may be because at room temperature during the drying process, protein hydrolase and glutamate decarboxylase and other related enzymes in an active state, glutamic acid and other amino acid content increased, thereby enhancing the Moringa oleifera Leaves GABA content.

3.1.2 Effects of Four Drying Methods on Flavonoids and Polyphenol Contents in Moringa oleifera Leaves

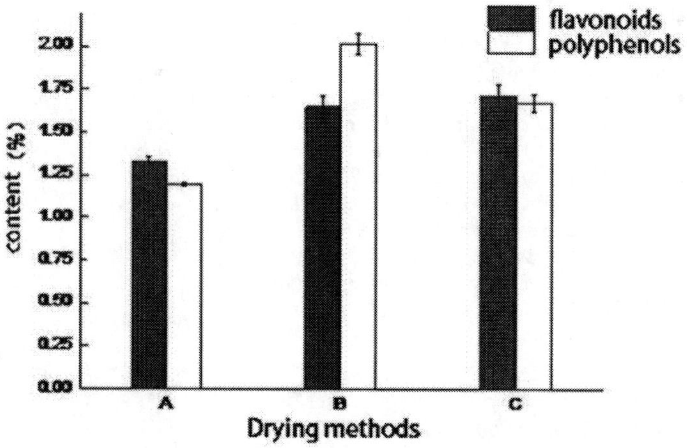

Fig.2 Effects of different drying methods on flavonoids and polyphenols content of Moringa oleifera leaves

The contents of the flavonoids from the highest to the lowest were as follows: natural drying (C) and vacuum freeze drying(B), drying at 60 °C(A), The polyphenol content from high to low are: vacuum freeze drying(B), natural drying(C), drying at 60 °C (A) (Fig.2). Vacuum Freeze Drying Moringa leaves are in a vacuum state to avoid contact with oxygen, thereby reducing the loss of oxidation. Compared with B treatment, the content of polyphenol in C was lower, the content of flavonoids was almost the same, which may be due to the enzymatic browning of phenolic substances during the long period of drying.

3.1.3 Effects of three drying methods on free amino acid and soluble total sugar content in Moringa oleifera leaves

 DOI: 10.1051/matecconf/201712803011

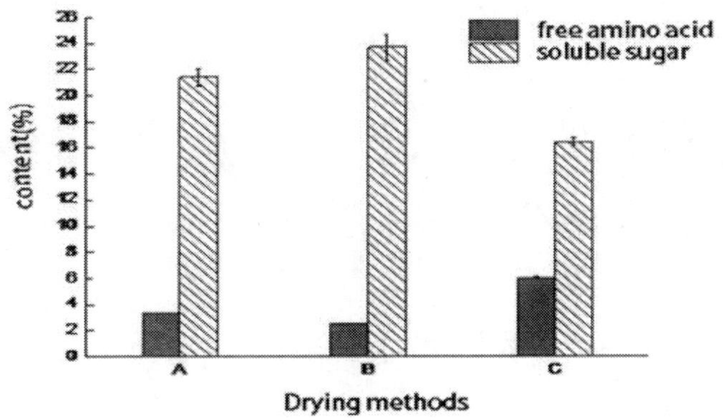

Fig.3 Effects of different drying methods on soluble sugar and amino acids content of Moringa oleifera leaves

The Moringa fresh leaves after different drying, the soluble sugar content from high to low order: vacuum freeze drying(B), 60 °C blast drying(A), natural dry(C). The free amino acid content from high to low order: natural dry(C), 60 °C blast drying(A), vacuum freeze-drying(B)(Fig.3).The free amino acids of natural dry treatment was significantly higher than that of blast drying and vacuum freeze-drying treatments, which may be related to the high content of GABA in the treatment of Moringa oleifera.The free amino acid content of vacuum freeze-drying treatment is the lowest, probably because of low temperature and low oxygen conditions, the relevant enzyme activity is inhibited, the protein is not easily hydrolyzed into amino acids. The total soluble sugar content of B was higher than that of A group and C group, the reason may be in low temperature and hypoxia conditions, total soluble sugar not prone to oxidation and Maillard reaction, and the total soluble sugars and effective retention.

3.1.4 The effect of three kinds of drying methods on the color of the tea leaves of Moringa oleifera

Table.1 Effects of different drying methods on the Moringa oleifera leaves tea color

Drying methods	Chromatic aberration			
	L*	a*	b*	-a*/b*
A	88.82	-4.04	34.75	0.116
B	88.98	-2.28	25.88	0.088
C	86.01	-5.67	50.46	0.112

For Moringa oleifera leaves, the bigger the L value, tea color brightness is better; the bigger the -a value, the soup color is green. The greater the b value, the more yellow the color of the soup; The smaller the -a/b value is, the higher the color of the soup is and the darker it is. The Moringa oleifera leaves prepared by three kinds of drying methods were soaked in boiling water, and the soup color was quantitatively analyzed . From the experimental results in Table 1, we can see that in the three drying methods, the brightness of tea is the best in B way, the L * is 88.98, followed by A and C, L * values are 88.82 and 86.01 respectively. soup color of B way brightness slightly higher than the A way, but its-a * / b * value is less than A way and B way, the highest degree of tea color and the darkest.

3.2 Effects of 7% MSG solution immersion on GABA content and quality components of fresh sprouts

3.2.1 *Effects of different immersion time on GABA content in Moringa oleifera leaves*

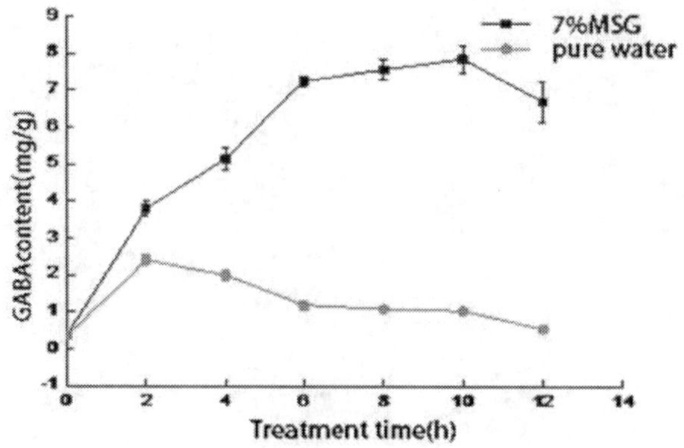

Fig.4 Effects of different treatment time on GABA content of Moringa oleifera leaves

The content of GABA in the leaves of 7% MSG solution was significantly higher than that in the pure water treatment group (blank control) within 2h ~ 12h, and the GABA content reached the maximum at 10 h in the 7% MSG solution, the blank control group reached the maximum at 2 h(Fig.4). With the prolongation of immersion time, the contents of GABA in the two treatment groups increased first and then decreased, which probably due to the excessive accumulation of GABA in Moringa oleifera leaves, leading to the activation of GABA-degrading enzymes such as succinic acid and aldehyde dehydrogenase [18], thereby producing anti-repressive effects on GABA synthesis.

3.2.2 Effects of Different Immersion Time on Contents of Polyphenols and Flavonoids in Moringa oleifera Leave

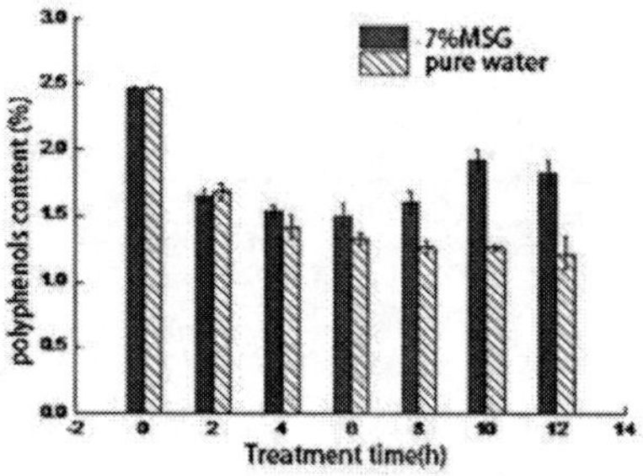

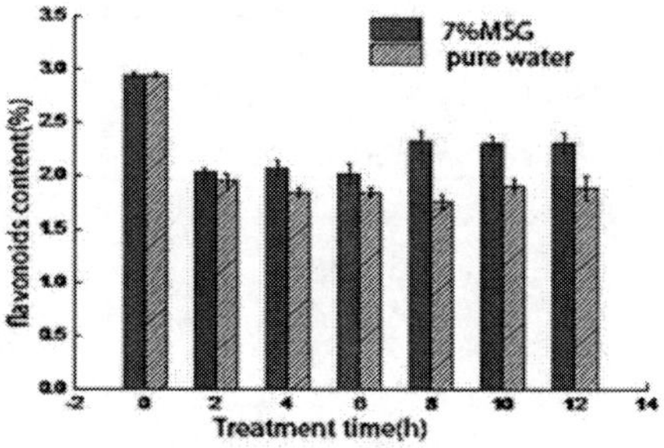

Fig.5 Effects of different treatment time on polyphenols content of Moringa oleifera leaves **Fig.6** Effects of different treatment time on flavonoids content of Moringa oleifera leaves

The content of polyphenols and flavonoids in the D treatment group was higher than that in CK treatment group under the same impregnation time(Fig.5 and Fig.6). With the prolongation of immersion time, the content of polyphenols and flavonoids in CK treatment group decreased gradually, which may be due to phenolic substances react with the reaction of oxidation and hydrolysis under the action of enzyme. The content of polyphenols and flavonoids in D treatment group decreased first and then increased, but the content of polyphenols and flavonoids varied little in the range of 1.65% ~ 1.82% and 2.01% ~ 2.31 respectively in the range of 2 ~ 12 %, Were lower than 0h treatment group. After 8 h treatment, the content of flavonoids and polyphenols increased slightly, which may be due to the excessive accumulation of GABA content of Moringa oleifera to promote the metabolism of phenolic substances, its increase in the amount of its own oxidation and dissolved loss, and thus the content of flavonoids and polyphenols increased, which remains to be further explored.

3.2.3 Effects of different immersion time on soluble total sugar and free amino acids in fresh Moringa oleifera leaves

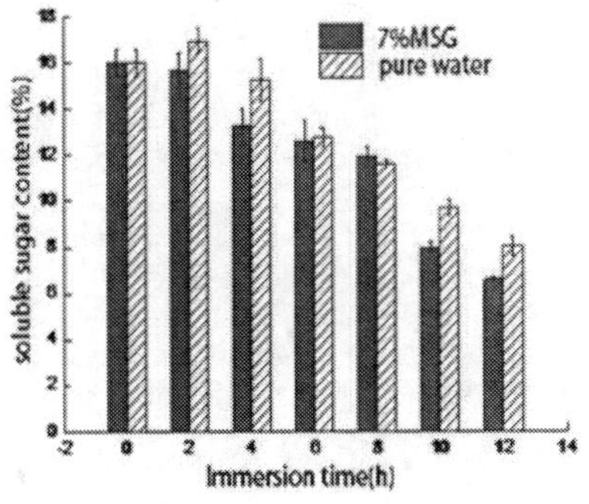

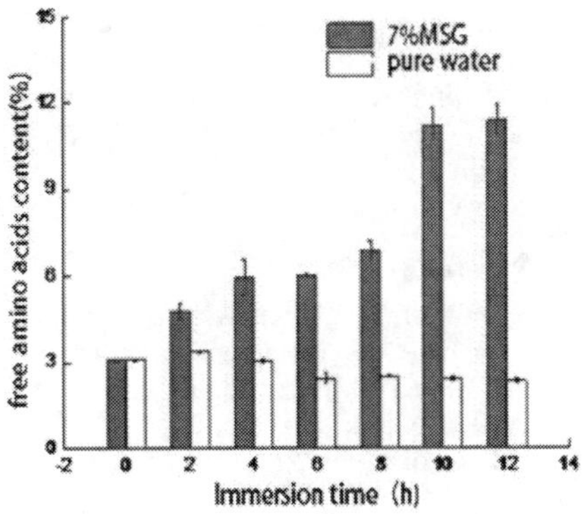

Fig.7 Effects of different immersion time on soluble sugar content of Moringa oleifera leaves **Fig.8** Effects of different immersion time on amino acids content of Moringa oleifera leaves

The same immersion time, pure water treatment group soluble total sugar content higher than 7% MSG solution treatment group is show in Fig.7. With the prolongation of immersion time, the content of soluble sugar in the two treatments showed a gradual decrease, which may be due to the oxidation and dissolution of the soluble sugar itself, and the activity of some enzymes under low oxygen condition was inhibited. And other substances difficult to hydrolysis reaction, thereby reducing the total amount of soluble sugar. With the prolongation of immersion time, the content of soluble sugar in the two treatments showed a gradual decrease, which may be due to the oxidation and dissolution of the soluble sugar itself, and the activity of some enzymes under low oxygen condition was inhibited. And other substances difficult to hydrolysis reaction, thereby reducing the total amount of soluble sugar.

With the prolongation of soaking time, CK treatment group increased first and then decreased, D treatment group showed a gradual upward trend, and tends to gentle (Fig.8), this may be related to Polyamine degradation produces GABA and beta-alanine [19]. Although The decrease in L-glutamate content is due to change to GABA , other amino acids was increased, and the total amount of free amino acids was increased. With the excessive accumulation of GABA, the GABA synthesis pathway was inhibited. GABA degrading enzyme is activated, so that the free amino acid content is reduced. After treatment with 2H, the content of free amino acids in CK treatment group began to decrease, this may have a certain relationship with the D-treated group to promote the GABA synthesis substrate, resulting in a longer increase in GABA content.

3.2.4 The effect of different immersion time on the color and odor of Moringa oleifera leaves

Table.2 Effects of different treatment time on color and smell of fresh Moringa oleifera leaves

Processing time (h)	Pure water treatment group	7% MSG treatment group
0	Green leaves, rich fragrance	Green leaves, rich fragrance
2	Leaves green, fragrant strong	Leaves green, fragrant strong
4	Leaves green, fragrance weakened	Leaves green, fragrant strong
6	Leaves green, appear qingqi	Leaves green, fragrant high
8	Leaf color dark, slightly water boring taste, Qingqi obvious	Leaves green, fragrant high
10	The leaf crease is increased, the leaves become soft, the water is stuffy, the taste is obvious, and there is sour smell	Leaves green, slightly watery taste
12	Crease red, leaves are softer, water boring serious, sour smell obvious	Crease red, leaves are softer, water boring serious, sour smell obvious

The color and odor of the fresh leaves of the two treatments changed with the immersion time are show in Tab.2. From 0 ~ 4h, the two groups of fresh leaves are green , fragrance is also more rich. When the pure water treatment group was treated for 6h, the fresh leaf smelled with qingqi gas. Since then, with the immersion time, leaf redness, crease increased, leaves become soft, water taste serious. 7% MSG solution treatment group 6h and 8h, the fresh leaves remain green, the fragrant is still obvious. Treatment 10h, the leaf color green, there is a slight water taste, but the overall effect of fresh leaves on the little impact.

4 Conclusion

There were significant differences in the quality of the three kinds of drying methods. In general, 60 °C blast drying method is the most suitable for industrial production of GABA Moringa oleifera leaves method. Under the condition of 60 °C blast drying ,the tea color brightness and soluble sugar content is higher, free amino acids was moderate, flavonoids was not the same as that of natural dry and vacuum freeze-drying. The difference of GABA content and vacuum freeze-drying was not significant. The use of 60 °C blast drying to prepare Moringa oleifera leaves, the equipment requirements are low, drying time is short, free from weather constraints, easy to control. The highest GABA content in the Moringa oleifera leaves treated with 7% MSG solution for 10 h ,and the effect was the best. The content of flavonoids, polyphenols, soluble sugar and free amino acids in the leaves of Moringa oleifera was also ideal, and the color of the fresh leaves was green after the treatment,but within the acceptable range of sensory quality. So choose 7% MSG solution and soak 10h as the preparation of high content of GABA Moringa oleifera leaves .

In summary, the fresh Moringa oleifera leaves of soaked in 7%MSG for 10h, using 60 °C blast drying treatment is a way to prepare high level of GABA Moringa oleifera leaves.

Acknowledgments

This research was supported by the Fundamental Scientific Research Funds for Chinese Academy of Tropical Agricultural Sciences (Project No. 1630122016007) and the Fundamental Scientific Research Funds for Chinese Academy of Tropical Agricultural Sciences (Project No. 1630122016011).

References

1. YUE Xiu-jie, LI Chao, FU Xiong.Preparation of Flavonoids from Moringa oleifera Leaves by Ultrasonic Wave and Its Antioxidant Activity [J]. food science and technology,2016, 37 (1).
2. Oluduro O A, Aderiye B I, Connolly J D, et al. Characterization and Antimicrobial Activity of 4-(beta-D-Glucopyranosyl-1->4-alpha-L-rhamnopyranosyloxy)-benzyl thiocarboxamide; a Novel Bioactive Compound from Moringa oleifera Seed Extract[J]. Folia Microbiologica, 2010, 55(5):422-426.
3. Fatoba T A, Faleyimu O I, Adebayo A J. Effects of Increasing Aqueous Root Extract of Moringa oleifera on Sperm Production of Albino Rats[J]. Agrosearch, 2013, 13(1):29.
4. Ogbunugafor H, Igwoezikpe M, Igwilo I, et al. In vitro and in vivo evaluation of antioxidant properties of Moringa oleifera ethanolic leaves extract and effect on serum lipid indices in rat[J]. Macedonian Journal of Medical Sciences, 2013, 5(4):397-403.
5. Nwamarah, Joy Ugo, Otitoju, et al. Effects of Moringa oleifera Lam. aqueous leaf extracts on follicle stimulating hormone and serum cholesterol in Wistar rats[J]. African Journal of Biotechnology, 2015.
6. Jung I L. Soluble extract from Moringa oleifera leaves with a new anticancer activity[J]. Plos One, 2014, 9(4):95492.
7. AbdELA, El BBS, Mahboub H D, et al. Moringa oleifera leaf extract ameliorates alloxan-induced diabetes in rats by regeneration of βcells and reduction of pyruvate carboxylase expression[J]. Biochemistry and cell biology, 2014, 92(5):413-9.
8. Tsuchiya K, Matsuda S, Hirakawa G, et al. GABA production from discolored laver by lactic acid fermentation and physiological function of fermented laver[J]. Food Preservation Science, 2011, 33(3):121-125.
9. Diana M, Quílez J, Rafecas M. Gamma-aminobutyric acid as a bioactive compound in foods: a review[J]. Journal of Functional Foods, 2014, 10(3):407-420.
10. Zhou X L, Zhao L, Technology A, et al. Physiological function of GABA and its application in food[J]. Food Industry, 2011.
11. Wang H F, Chuang S M, Hsiao C C, et al. A synergistic effect of GABA tea and copper(II) on DNA breakage in human peripheral lymphocytes[J]. Food & Chemical Toxicology, 2011, 49(4):955-962.
12. Khwanchai P, Chinprahast N, Pichyangkura R, et al. Gamma-aminobutyric acid and glutamic acid contents, and the GAD activity in germinated brown rice (Oryza sativa L.): Effect of rice cultivars[J]. Food Science and Biotechnology, 2014, 23(2): 373-379.
13. Deewatthanawong, R, Nock, J. F, Watkins, C. B. γ-Aminobutyric acid (GABA) accumulation in four strawberry cultivars in response to elevated CO2 storage[J]. Postharvest Biology & Technology, 2010, 57(2):92-96.
14. Thatchapol Chungcharoen, Somkiat Prachayawarakorn, Patcharee Tungtrakul, et al. Effects of Germination Process and Drying Temperature on Gamma-Aminobutyric Acid (GABA) and Starch Digestibility of Germinated Brown Rice[J]. Drying Technology, 2014, 32(6):742-753.
15. Vongsak B, Sithisarn P, Mangmool S, et al. Maximizing total phenolics, total flavonoids contents and antioxidant activity of Moringa oleifera, leaf extract by the appropriate extraction method[J]. Industrial Crops & Products, 2013, 44(1):566-571.
16. Wei Wei. Preparation and quality of mulberry tea with high content of GABA [D]. Southwestern University, 2014.
17. Tuin L G, Shelp B J. In situ, L-Glutamate Metabolism by Developing Soybean Cotyledons I. Metabolic Routes[J]. Journal of Plant Physiology, 1994, 143(1):1-7.
18. Shelp B J, Bozzo G G, Trobacher C P, et al. Hypothesis/review: contribution of putrescine to 4-aminobutyrate (GABA) production in response to abiotic stress[J]. Plant Science An International Journal of Experimental Plant Biology, 2012, 193-194(193-194):130-5.

Study on Hot Diaphragm Forming Process of CCF300/5228A Composites

Li Yan[a], Xuefeng An

National Key Laboratory of Advanced Composites, AVIC Composites Technology Center, Composites Company LTD of AVIC, Beijing 100095, China

Abstract. In this paper, the hot diaphragm forming process of CCF300/5228A composite was studied through self-developed hot diaphragm forming equipment. CCF300/5228A prepreg for the hot diaphragm forming process was modified. Combined the physical and chemical experiment of CCF300/5228A prepreg with modeling analysis of deformation behavior, the processing parameters of CCF300/5228A composites for hot diaphragm forming process were selected and optimized. Composites with C-shaped structure were fabricated according to the optimum parameters of hot diaphragm forming process, and final C-shaped composites could satify the requirments of design.

1 Introduction

Composites offer an attractive potential for reducing the weight of high-performance structures as consequences of their high specific strength and stiffness. At present, for the large thickness composite wing spar of aircraft and composite hat-shaped stringers, the traditional manual laying method has low efficiency and low stability. Automatic technology has been adopted in the preparation of the wing spar and composite hat-shaped stringers in foreign countries, which can improve the manufacturing efficiency and product quality by reducing the influence of human factors. In the automated manufacturing process, it is included that first composite flat pre-form is prepared by Automated Tape Laying, and then the pre-form close to the final shape is obtained by hot diaphragm forming process, last the composite pre-form is solidified by autoclave forming process.

The hot diaphragm forming process is completed at a certain temperature, and the composite flat pre-form changed with the change of curvature, and the slipping deformation of the pre-form layer occured. In order to avoid the crease and fracture of the fiber during the slipping of the layers, the deformation of the flat pre-form and the interlayer slip must be matched. Over last few years, many researchers has carried out extensive investigations on the hot diaphragm-forming process[1-8]. The hot diaphragm forming process has been successfully applied to large components such as the Boeing 777, the V22 composite stringers and the A400M wings, and it has developed into an important low-cost manufacturing technology[9-13]. However, there are few studies on the hot diaphragm forming process of thermosetting composite materials in China[14-18]. Moreover, the domestic hot diaphragm forming technology is still in the experimental stage, lacking relevant theoretical and technical basic research, and lacks the domestic prepreg system suitable for hot diaphragm forming process.

In this paper, the research on the hot diaphragm forming process of CCF300/5228A composites was carried out through self-developed hot diaphragm forming equipment. CCF300/5228A prepreg for the hot diaphragm forming process was modified. Combined the physical and chemical experiment of CCF300/5228A prepreg with modeling analysis of deformation behavior, the processing parameters of CCF300/5228A composites for hot diaphragm forming process were selected and optimized. Composites with C-shaped structure were fabricated according to the optimum parameters of hot diaphragm forming process, and final C-shaped composites could satify the requirments of design.

2 Experimental details

2.1 Materials

A high temperature carbon fiber/epoxy resin undirectional prepreg CCF300/5228A was a product of Composites Company LTD of AVIC. The diaphragms of SL700 and SL800 and other auxiliary materials were purchased from American Airtech company.

2.2 The hot diaphragm forming process

In this paper, the hot diaphragm forming process of CCF300/5228A composites was studied through the self-developed hot diaphragm forming equipment, and the hot diaphragm forming equipment and principle diagram were shown in Figure 1.

The flat pre-form was held in the hot diaphragms, which was raised or lowered with the press frame to close or leave the mold. The vacuum degree between the

[a] Corresponding author: yanli0827@163.com

DOI: 10.1051/matecconf/201712803012

double hot diaphragms was adjusted to control the degree of clamping of the diaphragm for prepreg. The hot diaphragm frame and the molding table were sealed with a sealing ring and the molding table was covered with vacuum holes. Through vacuumizing between the diaphragm and molding table, the prepreg was finally fitted with the mold. The infrared heater was controlled by the partition. At the initial stage of the process, the resin matrix was heated and softened in order to make the prereg fitted the mold. And then rmatained the temperature further and the preforming of the pre-form was completed.

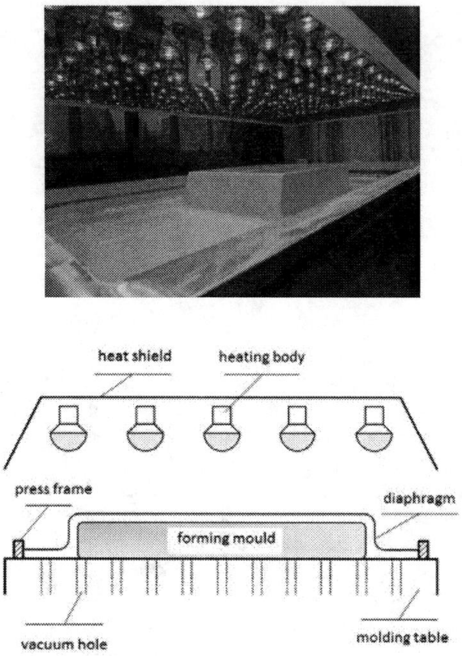

Figure 1. The hot diaphragm forming equipment and principle diagram

3 Results and discussion

3.1 CCF300/5228A prepreg for hot diaphragm forming

CCF300/5228A prereg was a high temperature curing carbon fiber/epoxy resin undirectional prepreg. Its mechanical properties, physical and chemical properties and process properties had been relatively mature. But there were certain problems to apply it to hot diaphragm forming process. It was necessary to modify the resin to meet the requirements of the hot diaphragm forming process. The DSC diagram of the 5228A resin was shown in Figure 2 and the viscosity - temperature curve of the 5228A resin was shown in Figure 3. As seen from Figure 2 and Figure 3, the initial reaction temperature of 5228A resin was 116 °C, and solidified reaction enthalpy was 436 J/g. When the lowest viscosity of the resin appeared, the temperature was around 120 °C.

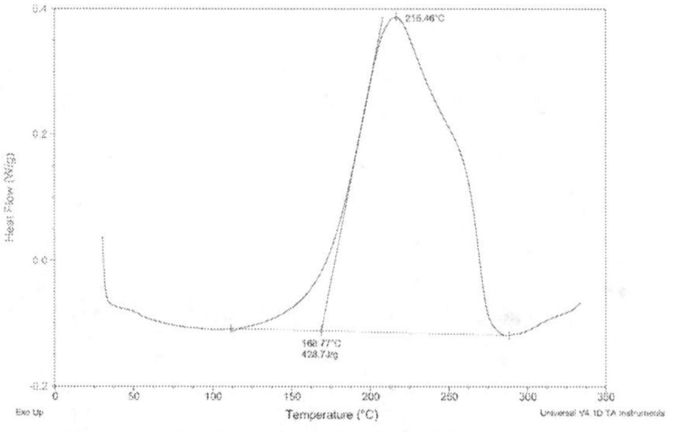

Figure 2. The DSC diagram of the 5228A resin

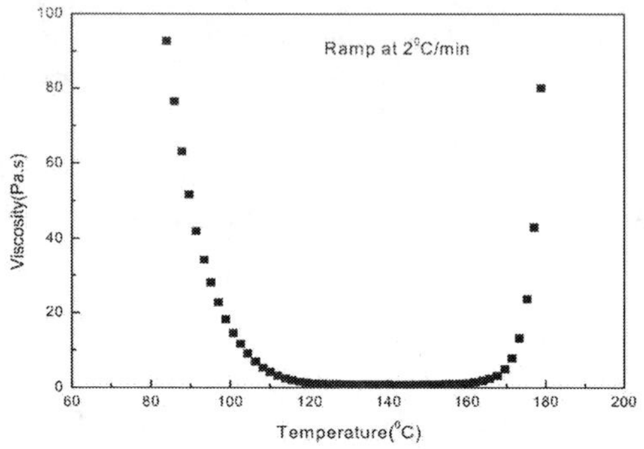

Figure 3. The viscosity - temperature curve of the 5228A resin

In order to improve the deformation and slipping ability driven by external forces, the special prereg for hot diaphragm forming process was modified on the basis of CCF300/5228A prepreg. The method to modify the prereg was improving the resin content of standard CCF300/5228A prepreg appropriately. There were more resin between layers, which was beneficial to the deformation of the inerlayers and the slipping between layersr, thus improving the overall deformation performance of the pre-form. Through the experiment, the processing parameters of CCF300/5228A for hot diaphragm forming process were determined as follows: the fiber volume fraction was 55%, the fiber surface density was 145 g/m^2, the resin surface density of prepreg was 83 g/m^2, and the weight fraction of resin was 35%.

3.2 The diaphragm for hot diaphragm forming process

The diaphragm required good ductility and high temperature resistance. The mechanical properties of the two diaphragms SL700 and SL800 were tested, and the test results were shown in Table 1.

As shown in Table 1, the elongation rate of the diaphragm SL700 was much higher than that of SL800, but SL800 had more tensile strength than SL700, according to the theory and actual test results, both SL700 and SL800 diaphragms could satisfy the requirement of hot diaphragm forming process.

DOI: 10.1051/matecconf/201712803012

Table 1. Mechanical propertites test results of diaphragms

Project	SL700		SL800	
	Tensile strength (Mpa)	Elongation (%)	Tensile strength (MPa)	Tensile strength (%)
1	35.71	819.96	44.07	502.32
2	37.83	965.13	47.40	515.57
3	36.90	1043.95	35.80	423.62
4	36.99	681.20	46.65	573.75
5	32.36	700.68	45.95	484.41
Average	35.96	842.18	43.98	499.94

3.3 Modeling analysis of deformation behavior of CCF300/5228A prereg

The research on deformation behavior of CCF300/5228A prereg for hot diaphragm forming had been done through physical and chemical tests and computational simulation. Physical and chemical experiments included DSC, DMA and rheology, and the simulation software was from the PAM-FORM of ESI company. The test results of DSC, DMA and rheology were used as simulated input of PAM-FORM. The results of simulation were shown in Figure 4.

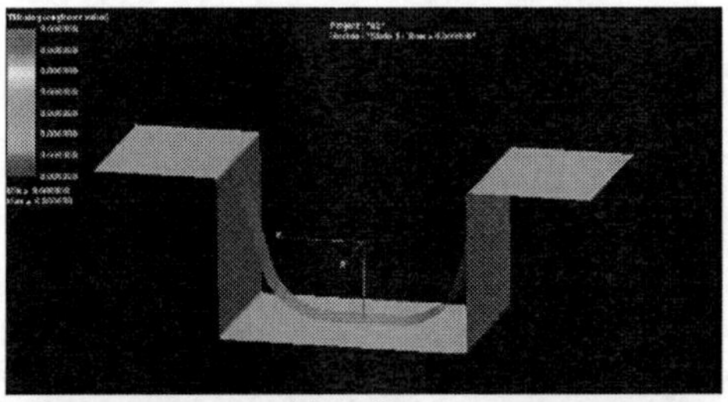

(a) t=0

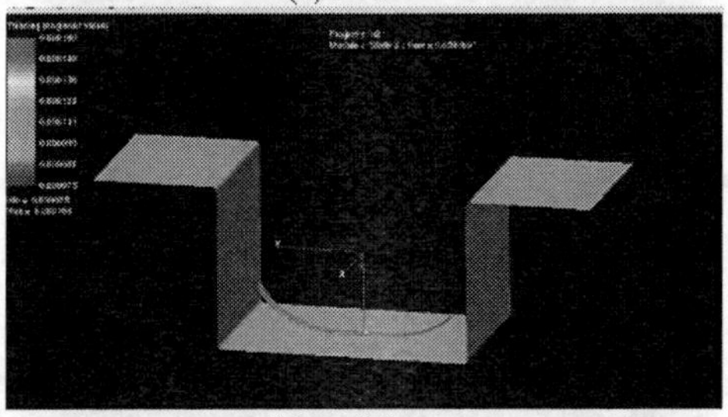

(b) t=0.5s

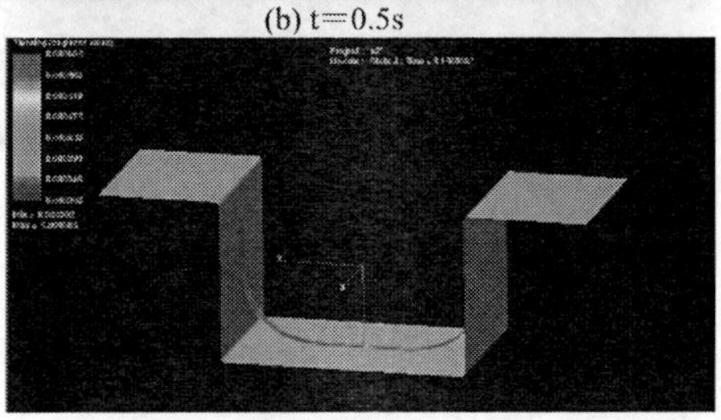

(c) t=0.15s

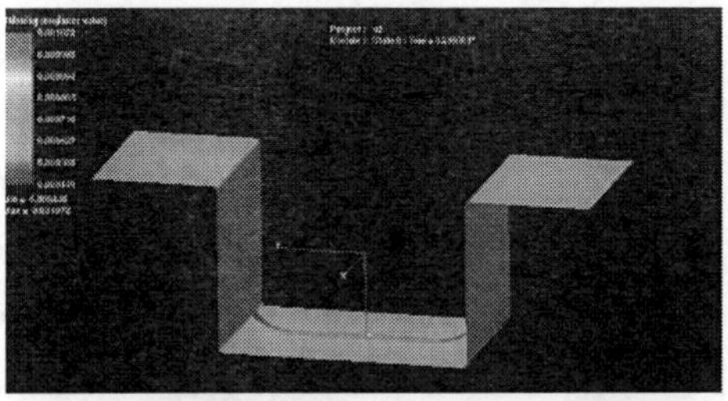

(d) t=0.25s

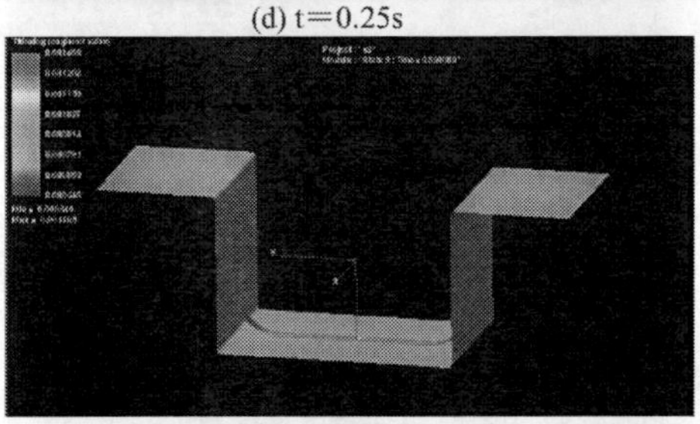

(e) t=0.35s

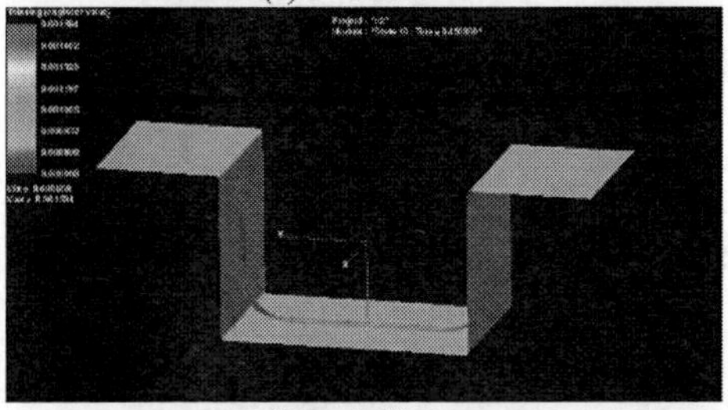

(f) t=0.45s

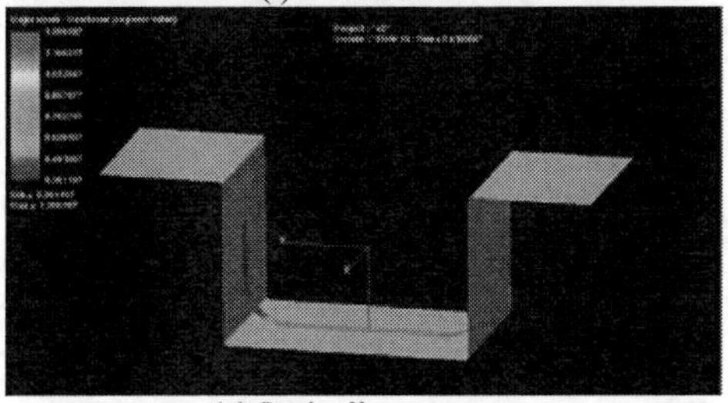

(g) Strain diagrams

Figure 4. Deformation process and strain distribution of layer with [45/90/-45/0]

(a～f: Deformation diagrams at different times, g: Strain diagrams of deformation process)

As indicated in Figure 4, in the process of hot diaphragm forming, first the bottom surface of typical specimen was fitting, and then the pre-form and the mould were gradually fitted and typed by slipping between layers to ensure that the bending angle was formed. Therefore, in the whole process of hot diaphragm forming, the bottom had a small strain, and the strain on both sides was large, which resulted in slipping between layers on the side.

3.4 Selection and preliminary optimization of parameters of hot diaphragm forming process

DOI: 10.1051/matecconf/201712803012

Table 2. Different layer deformation for typical specimen Simulated by ABQUS

Project		**layer**		
		$[45/90/-45/0/45/0/-45/0]_{4S}$	$[45/-45/90/0]_{8S}$	$[-45/90/45/0]_{8S}$
The maximal displacement	x	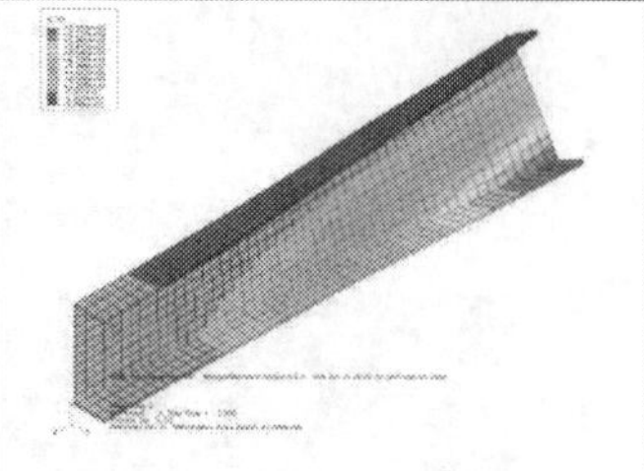 135mm	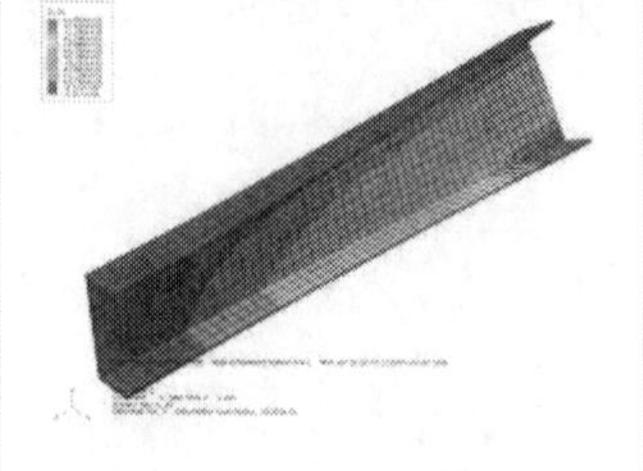 161mm	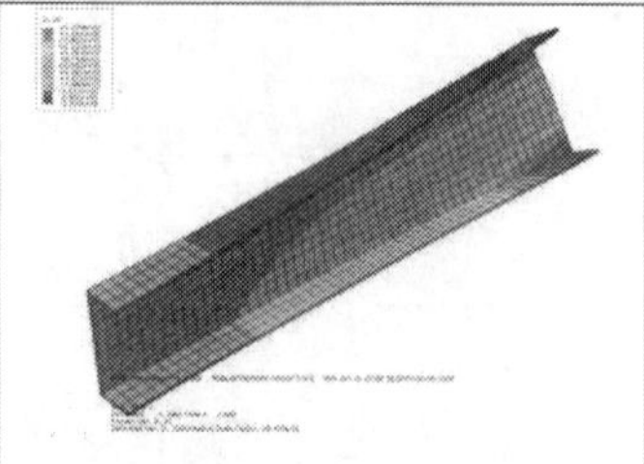 177mm
	y	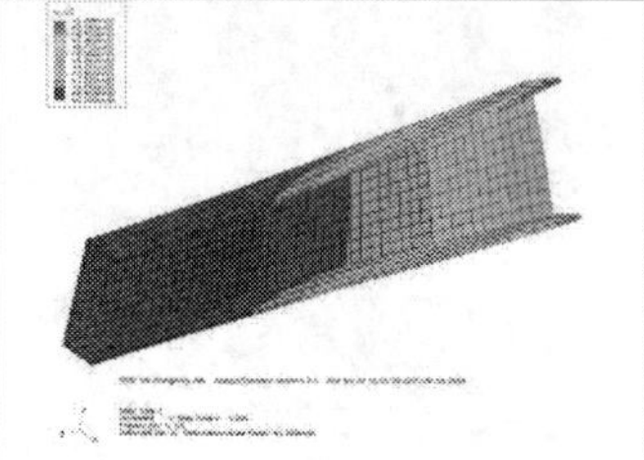 100mm	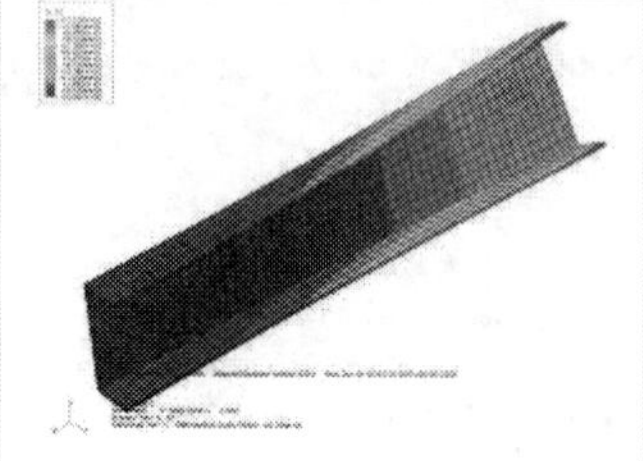 114mm	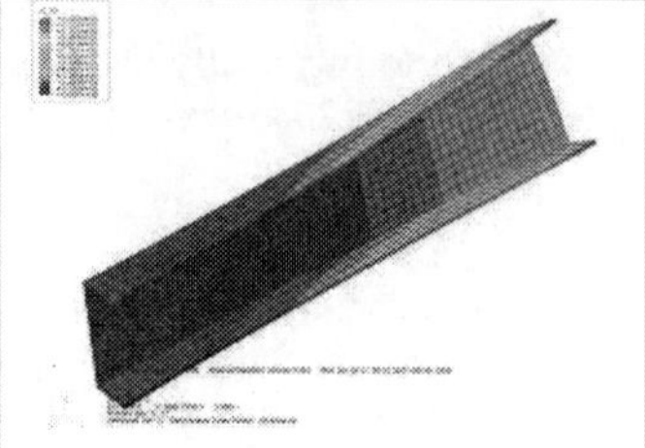 132mm
	z	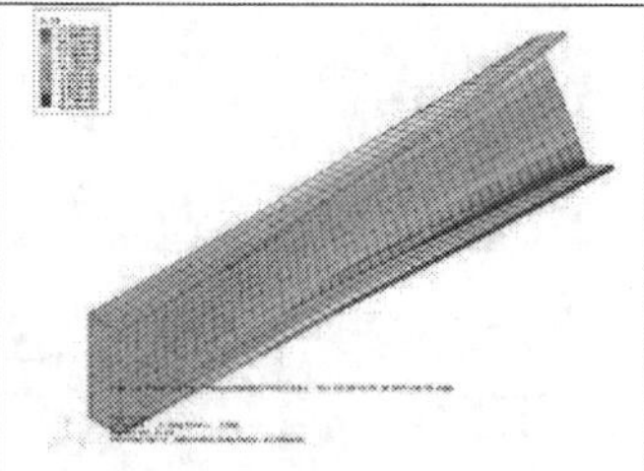 7.1mm	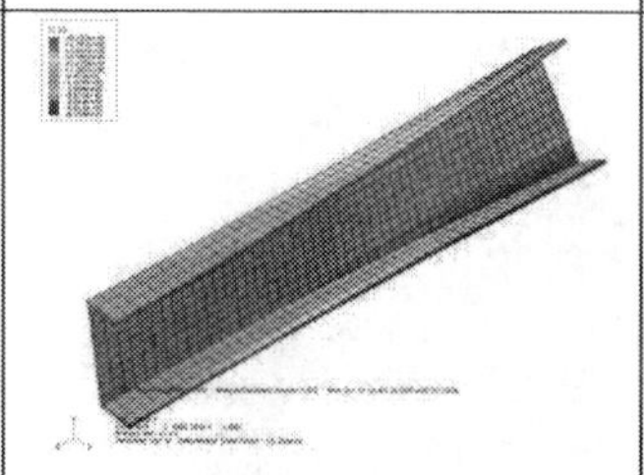 8.2mm	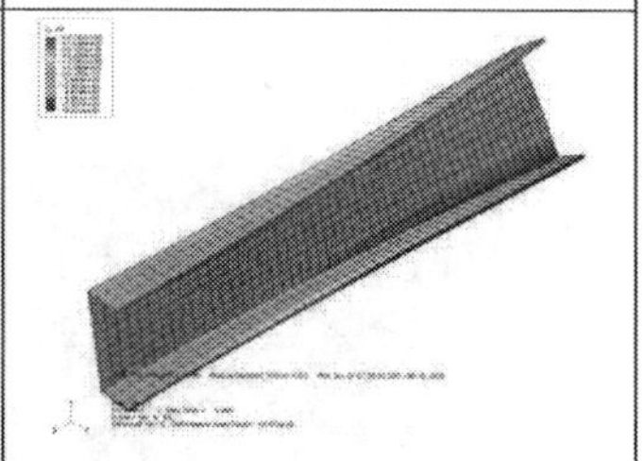 9.2mm

Table 2 showed the deformation graphs of x, y and z directions under specific loads of the typical specimen with different layers were calculated by ABUQS software. As shown in Table 2, the deformation of layer with $[45/90/-45/0/45/0/-45/0]_{4S}$ in three directions was less than layers with $[45/-45/90/0]_{8S}$ and $[-45/90/45/0]_{8S}$. The minimum deformation and stress were obtained from layer with $[45/90/-45/0/45/0/-45/0]_{4S}$. The composites with C-shaped structure prepared by this layer had larger axial stress, which could undertake the main load. Through the above analysis, it was determined that the optimal layer of typical specimen was $[45/90/-45/0/45/0/-45/0]_{4S}$.

In hot diaphragm forming process, processing temperature determined resin flowability as well as the deformability of prepreg, thus influenced the forming quality of pre-form. The best deformation temperature for CCF300/5228A prereg was 120 °C by analyzing the results of DSC and DMA. C-shaped composite spar of CCF300/5228A was fabricated at 120 °C as hot diaphragm preforming temperature and then was cured by autoclave process, and finally the spar quality could satisfy the requriment of design, as shown in Figure 5(a). In Figure 5(b), on the side of C-shaped composite spar, it appeared roughly equispaced interlayer stagger due to the smooth slipping between the fiber layers. In Figure 5(c), the fiber at the corner of composite spar had smooth transition, and there were no wrinkless on the inside of the corner and no rich resin area on the outside. That also validated the calculation results of the PAM-Form.

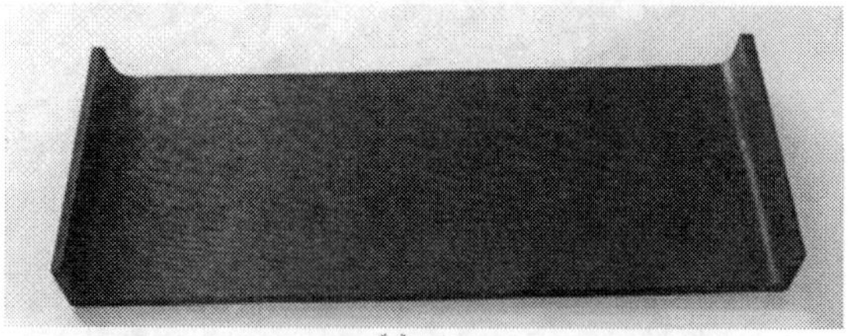

(a) spar

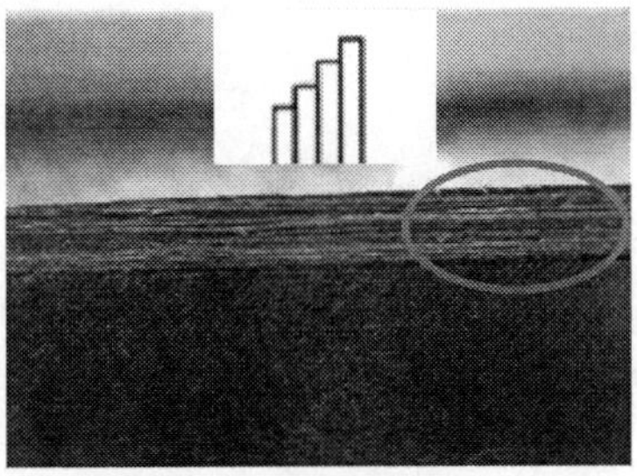

(b) interlayer slipping

(c) typical corner

Figure 5. Composites C-shaped spar of CCF300/5228A by hot diaphragm forming process

4 Conclusions

Following conclusions were drawn from this work:

(1) The processing parameters of CCF300/5228A were determined for hot diaphragm forming process as follows: the fiber volume fraction was 55%, the fiber surface density was 145 g/m^2, the resin surface density of prepreg was 83 g/m^2, and the weight fraction of resin was 35%.

(2) The test results of DSC, DMA and rheology were used as simulated input of PAM-FORM. The results of simulation was as follows: in the process of hot diaphragm forming, first the bottom surface of typical specimen was fitting, and then the pre-form and the mould were gradually fitted and typed by slipping between layers to ensure that the bending angle was formed. Therefore, in the whole process of hot diaphragm forming, the bottom had a small strain, and the strain on both sides was large, which resulted in slipping between layers on the side.

(3) The hot diaphragm forming temperature had been identified as 120 °C. On the side of C-shaped composite spar, it appeared roughly equispaced interlayer stagger due to the smooth slipping between the fiber layers. The fiber at the corner of composites spar had smooth transition, and there were no wrinkles on the inside of the corner and no rich resin area on the outside. The spar quality could satisfy the requriment of design. That also validated the calculation results of the PAM-Form.

References

1. P J Mallon, C M O'Bradaigh, R B Pipes. Compos 20(1): 48-56 (1989).
2. A J Smiley and R B Pipes. J Thermoplast Compos Mater, 1: 298-321 (1988).
3. C M O'Bradaigh, P J.Mallon. Compos Sci Technol 35: 235-255 (1989).
4. G N Labeas, V B Watiti and C V Katsiropoulos. J Thermoplast Compos Mater, 21: 353-370 (2008).
5. H Bersee, A Beukers. Compos Pt A, 33(7): 949–958 (2002).
6. S G Pantelakis, E A Baxevani. Compos Pt A, 33: 459-470 (2002).
7. J Krebs, K Friedrich, D Bhattacharyya. Compos Pt A, 29(A): 183-188 (1998).
8. K J Channer, W Cosgriff, G F Smith, et al. Plast Compos, 21: 1629-1635 (2002).
9. S Delaloye, M Niedermeir. Compos Manuf, 6(3): 135-144 (1995).
10. S G Pantelakis, E A Baxevani. Compos Part A, , 33(4): 459-470 (2002).
11. J Shen, H G Xie. Fiber Reinforced Plastics/Composites, 5: 48-54 (2006).
12. D H Liu. Fiber Composites, 2: 41-44 (2012).
13. Y L Chen. Aeronautical Manufacturing Technology, 10: 32-35 (2008).
14. Z P Kuang, L Dai, X M Wang. Beijing: china science & technology press, 613-615 (2010).
15. Z E Wu. Aeronautical Manufacturing Technology, 25: 113-116 (2009).
16. N H Yang, Y Yang, Y B Yu. Beijing: The 1st China International Congress on Composite Materials, 908-912 (2014).
17. X X Bian, Y Z Gu, J Sun, et al. Fiber Reinforced Plastics/Composites, 5: 45-50 (2013).
18. S Yao, M Li, Y Z Gu. Journal of Beijing University of Aeronautics and Astronautics, 39: 95-99 (2013).

MATEC Web of Conferences 128, 04001 (2017) DOI: 10.1051/matecconf/201712804001
EITCE 2017

Optimization on Trajectory of Stanford Manipulator based on Genetic Algorithm

Xi Han[1,a]

[1]*School of Mechanical Engineerin, University of Science and Technology Beijing, 100083 Beijing, China*

Abstract. The optimization of robot manipulator's trajectory has become a hot topic in academic and industrial fields. In this paper, a method for minimizing the moving distance of robot manipulators is presented. The Stanford Manipulator is used as the research object and the inverse kinematics model is established with Denavit-Hartenberg method. Base on the initial posture matrix, the inverse kinematics model is used to find the initial state of each joint. In accordance with the given beginning moment, cubic polynomial interpolation is applied to each joint variable and the positive kinematic model is used to calculate the moving distance of end effector. Genetic algorithm is used to optimize the sequential order of each joint and the time difference between different starting time of joints. Numerical applications involving a Stanford manipulator are presented.

1 Introduction

As modern industry advances towards intelligence and digitalization, the applications of industrial robots is becoming increasingly wider and deeper [1]. Robot manipulator is one of the most important devices among various industrial robots, which covers a diverse array of technologies from mechanical engineering, mathematical, to control theory, electronic engineering [2]. The optimization of trajectory plays a key role in the fulfillment of engineering tasks of robot manipulators, which has become a hot issue for academic and industrial research.

Atsushi et.al, who focused on the local navigation problem taking into consideration the dynamics of the robot, proposed a new technique with obstacle avoidance, called adaptive navigation. The advantages of the proposed navigation scheme are that less local information is required than in some other techniques and the navigation law is simpler and more flexible than ones using the artificial potential field methods [3]. This model has some limitations in expressing the relative motions between the end effector and the robot.

Ningyue et.al presented the ADRC controller in mobile manipulator system. A kind of dynamics decoupling control method is proposed to achieve synergy tracking between mobile platform and robotic arm. The effect of overall estimation and compensation ADRC control algorithm has on the disturbance of the model and manipulators tracking control strategy can be a good trajectory of the end-effector and mobile platforms separately controlled, and reduce the instability factor between the two coupling caused by the dynamics, reaching a higher position tracking accuracy [4]. In contrast to the previous research, this paper presented the structural relationship between the shape of manipulator and the robot body. They were not able to address the path planning problem in three-dimensional space, which is still a gap in actual industrial production. The robot mathematical model in three-dimensional space will be more complicated and contains more constrains.

Jia proposed a positive-inverse kinematics model for Stanford Manipulator, using cubic B-spline interpolation to achieve the trajectory planning of Stanford Manipulator joints [5]. But the article did not take into account the effect of the sequential order of the joint movements on the trajectory of the end effector.

Genetic algorithm (GA) was used by many researchers to solve the problem of robot path planning, which get the global optimal solution in a short time [6][7]. Dong combined the analytic method and genetic algorithm, obtaining a kinematic inverse solution with a redundant degree of freedom and achieving the optimal track planning and obstacle avoidance. The method has the characteristics of small calculation and strong adaptability [6].

Above all, the Stanford Manipulator is used as the research object in this paper, and the inverse kinematics model is established by Denavit-Hartenberg method. According to the initial posture matrix, the inverse kinematics model is used to find the initial state of each joint. In accordance with the given beginning moment, cubic polynomial interpolation is applied to each joint variable and the positive kinematic model is used to calculate the end effector path. Genetic algorithm is then used to optimize the sequential order of each joint and the time difference between different starting time of joints, with an objective function of minimizing the path of end effector.

[a] Corresponding author: hanxi1706@126.com

DOI: 10.1051/matecconf/201712804001

2 Mathematical Model of Stanford Manipulator

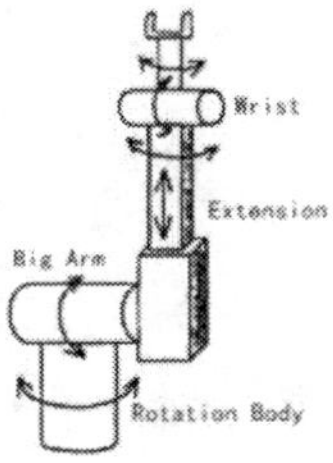

Fig 1. Model of Stanford Manipulator

0 shows that Stanford Manipulator consists of a Rotation Body, a Big Arm, an Extension Arm, Wrist and an End effector, which is made up of six joints (Five rotating joint and one locomotive joint). Each joint can express one degree of freedom. From bottom to top, the six kinematics parameters of Manipulator's joints are $\theta_1, \theta_2, d_3, \theta_4, \theta_5, \theta_6$. Obviously, end effector's position and attitude is related to the structure of Manipulator' connecting rod and kinematics parameters of Manipulator's joints. The matrix whi describes the end effector's position and attitude in reference coordinate system is expressed as follow:

$$T = [\vec{n} \quad \vec{o} \quad \vec{a} \quad \vec{p}] = \begin{bmatrix} n_x & o_x & a_x & p_x \\ n_y & o_y & a_y & p_y \\ n_z & o_z & a_z & p_z \\ 0 & 0 & 0 & 1 \end{bmatrix} \tag{1}$$

Where $\vec{n}, \vec{o}, \vec{a}$ is the end effector's attitude, $\vec{p}$ is the end effector' position, p_x, p_y, p_z is the end effector's coordinate in the datum reference coordinate system. In order to make sure the matrix of effector's position and attitude T, the coordinate systems need to be set up at every rod. The relative position and attitude between these coordinate systems can be described by homogeneous transformation.

In this passage, we set up six coordinate systems on the Stanford Manipulator, and describe their relationship by matrix. As usual, we define Matrix A as homogeneous transformation among a rod and its adjacent member. A tandem manipulator is connected by a series of rods with a drive joint. A manipulator with n degrees of freedom has n rods and n joints. The foundation rod is called rod 0. For Stanford Manipulator, it is not considered into the six rods. The rod 1 and rod 0 are connected by joint 1. The rod 2 and rod 1 are connected by joint 2, and so on. There is no joint at the end of rod 6.

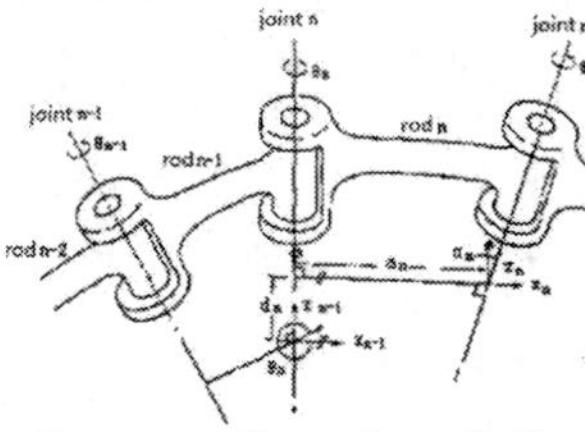

Fig 2. Coordinate transformation of adjacent connecting rod

0 shows the relationship of the adjacent coordinate system n-1and n. Firstly, the x_{n-1} axis is rotated by θ_n angle around the z_{n-1} axis. Secondly, the x_{n-1} axis moves d_n distance along the z_{n-1} axis. Thirdly, the z_{n-1} axis moves a_n distance along the rotating x_{n-1} axis, that is, x_n axis. Finally, the z_{n-1} axis is twisted by α_n angle around the x_n axis. As a result, the Matrix A is presented as follows,

$$A_n = \begin{bmatrix} cos\theta_n & -sin\theta_n & 0 & 0 \\ sin\theta_n & cos\theta_n & 0 & 0 \\ 0 & 0 & 1 & 0 \\ 0 & 0 & 0 & 1 \end{bmatrix} \begin{bmatrix} 1 & 0 & 0 & a_n \\ 0 & 1 & 0 & 0 \\ 0 & 0 & 1 & d_n \\ 0 & 0 & 0 & 1 \end{bmatrix} \begin{bmatrix} 1 & 0 & 0 & 0 \\ 0 & cos\alpha_n & -sin\alpha_n & 0 \\ 0 & sin\alpha_n & cos\alpha_n & 0 \\ 0 & 0 & 0 & 1 \end{bmatrix}$$

$$= \begin{bmatrix} cos\theta_n & -sin\theta_n & sin\theta_n sin\alpha_n & a_n cos\theta_n \\ sin\theta_n & cos\theta_n & -cos\theta_n sin\alpha_n & a_n sin\theta_n \\ 0 & sin\alpha_n & cos\alpha_n & d_n \\ 0 & 0 & 0 & 1 \end{bmatrix} \tag{2}$$

According to the structure of Stanford Manipulator, the link motion parameters is shown in 0.

Table 1 Stanford Manipulator's the link motion parameters

Joint Number	Joint Parameter	Torsional angle α	Offset
1	θ_1	-90°	0
2	θ_2	90°	d_2
3	d_3	0°	d_3
4	θ_4	-90°	0
5	θ_5	90°	0
6	θ_6	0°	0

Therefore, when the reference coordinate system is transformed to the base coordinate system, the Matrix of manipulator end effector's position and attitude can be represented as:

$$T_6 = A_1 \cdot A_2 \cdot A_3 \cdot A_4 \cdot A_5 \cdot A_6 = \begin{bmatrix} n_x & o_x & a_x & p_x \\ n_y & o_y & a_y & p_y \\ n_z & o_z & a_z & p_z \\ 0 & 0 & 0 & 1 \end{bmatrix} \tag{3}$$

To facilitate writing and reading, we denote $\sin\theta_i = s_i, \cos\theta_i = c_i$,

$$n_x = c_1[c_2(c_4c_5c_6 - s_4s_6) - s_2s_5c_6] - s_1(s_4c_5c_6 + c_4s_6) \tag{4}$$

$$n_y = s_1[c_2(c_4c_5c_6 - s_4s_6) - s_2s_5c_6] + c_1(s_4c_5c_6 + c_4s_6) \tag{5}$$

$$n_z = -s_2(c_4c_5c_6 - s_4s_6) - c_2s_5c_6 \tag{6}$$

$$o_x = c_1[-c_2(c_4c_5s_6 + s_4c_6) + s_2s_5s_6] + s_1(s_4c_5s_6 - c_4c_6) \tag{7}$$

$$o_y = s_1[-c_2(c_4c_5s_6 + s_4c_6) + s_2s_5s_6] - c_1(s_4c_5s_6 - c_4c_6) \tag{8}$$

$$o_z = s_2c_4c_5s_6 + c_2s_5s_6 + s_2s_4c_6 \tag{9}$$

$$a_x = c_1(c_2s_4s_5 + s_2c_5) - s_1s_4s_5 \tag{10}$$

$$a_y = s_1(c_2s_4s_5 + s_2c_5) + c_1s_4s_5 \tag{11}$$

$$a_z = -s_2c_4s_5 + c_2c_5 \tag{12}$$

$$p_x = c_1s_2d_3 - s_1d_2 \tag{13}$$

$$p_y = s_1s_2d_3 + c_1d_2 \tag{14}$$

$$p_z = c_2d_3 \tag{15}$$

Equations (4)-(15) is the Stanford Manipulator's

forward kinematics model, in which the position and attitude matrix T can be obtained according to the joint parameters. We can also know that the position of end effector relative to base coordinate system p_x, p_y, p_z only depends on the joint parameters θ_1, θ_2, d_3.

In industrial applications, we often design the position of end effector p_x, p_y, p_z and solve the corresponding joint parameters θ_1, θ_2, d_3. This is called inverse kinematics. For Stanford Manipulator, the inverse kinematics analytical solution is as follows,

$$\theta_1 = tan^{-1}\left(\frac{p_x}{p_y}\right) - tan^{-1}\left(\frac{d_2}{\sqrt{p_x^2 + p_y^2 - d_2^2}}\right) \tag{16}$$

$$\theta_2 = \tan^{-1}\frac{c_1 p_x + s_1 p_y}{p_z} \tag{17}$$

$$d_3 = s_2(c_1 p_x + s_1 p_y) + c_2 p_z \tag{18}$$

$$\theta_4 = tan^{-1}\frac{-s_1 a_x + c_1 a_y}{c_2(c_1 a_x + s_1 a_y) - s_2 a_z} \tag{19}$$

$$\theta_5 = tan^{-1}\frac{c_4[c_2(c_1 a_x + s_1 a_y) - s_2 a_z] + s_4[-s_1 a}{s_2(c_1 a_x + s_1 a_y) + c_2 a_z} \tag{20}$$

$$\theta_6 = tan^{-1}\frac{-c_5\{c_4[c_2(c_1 o_x + s_1 o_y) - s_2 o_z] + s_4[-s_1 o_x + c_1 o_y]\} + s_5[s_2(c_1 o_x + s_1 o_y) - c_2 o_z]}{-s_4[c_2(c_1 o_x + s_1 o_y) - s_2 o_z] + c_4(-s_1 o_x + c_1 o_y)} \tag{21}$$

3 Motion trajectory planning

From Chapter 0 we can know that the parameters of manipulator's joints $[\theta_1, \theta_2, d_3]$ can determine the position of end effector $[p_x, p_y, p_z]$. And the trajectory of end effector will be determined by the position $[p_x, p_y, p_z]$ at all moments. In trajectory planning, we solve the initial values and final values of joints' parameters by inverse kinematics according to the given corresponding initial position $[p_{x0}, p_{y0}, p_{z0}]$ and end position $[p_{xf}, p_{yf}, p_{zf}]$. Besides, the time slot from the former to the latter t_f should be specified according to the task requirements. Then, each joint parameter will be performed by polynomial interpolation operation to get smooth function $\theta(t)$. Finally, we get position-time function $p(t)$, which can accurately indicate the end effectors trajectory, by positive kinematics algebra for the smooth function $\theta(t)$.

According to mechanical knowledge, manipulator's movement should be smooth, because uneven movement will aggravate the wear of mechanical parts and cause manipulator's vibration and shock. Hence, the described trajectory function must be continuous. Its first derivative (Velocity) and even the two derivative (Acceleration) should be continuous too.

In this passage, the parameters of manipulator's joints are processed with three polynomial interpolation. So there are four constraint conditions of the joints' parameters as follows,

$$\theta(0) = \theta_0 \tag{22}$$

$$\theta(t_f) = \theta_f \tag{23}$$

$$\dot{\theta}(0) = \dot{\theta}(t_f) = 0 \tag{24}$$

The function that satisfies all of the above constraints is shown as follows,

$$\theta(t) = a_0 + a_1 t + a_2 t^2 + a_3 t^3 \tag{25}$$

The constraint is replaced by a function, and get undetermined coefficient as follows,

$$\begin{cases} a_0 = \theta_0 \\ a_1 = 0 \\ a_2 = \dfrac{3}{t_f^2}(\theta_f - \theta_0) \\ a_3 = -\dfrac{2}{t_f^3}(\theta_f - \theta_0) \end{cases} \tag{26}$$

Obviously, it is completely unnecessary to make all parameters of Manipulator's joints start changing at the same time. In the other words, there are many kinds of orders sequences between different parameter variations. With a result the trajectory of end effector will be also different. Suppose intermediate moment $t = t_m$ is inserted between starting time $t = 0$ and finishing time $t = t_f$, a part of parameters of Manipulator's joints begin changing at $t = 0$, and the others begin changing at $t = t_m$. All parameters stop at $t = t_f$ and the end effector reach the final position.

So there are serval constraint conditions of the joints' parameters which begin changing at $t = t_m$ as follows,

When $t < t_m$,

$$\theta(t) \equiv \theta_0 \tag{27}$$

When $t > t_m$, the function that satisfies all of the above constraints as (25),

The constraint conditions (22)-(24)change to (28)-(30) as follows,

$$\theta(t_m) = \theta_0 \tag{28}$$

$$\theta(t_f) = \theta_f \tag{29}$$

$$\dot{\theta}(t_m) = \dot{\theta}(t_f) = 0 \tag{30}$$

The undetermined coefficients are calculatedas follows,

$$\begin{cases} a_0 = \dfrac{\theta_0 t_f^3 - 3\theta_0 t_f^2 t_m + 3\theta_f t_f t_m^2 - \theta_f t}{(t_f - t_m)^3} \\ a_1 = \dfrac{6 t_m t_f(\theta_0 - \theta_f)}{(t_f - t_m)^3} \\ a_2 = -\dfrac{3(t_m + t_f)(\theta_0 - \theta_f)}{(t_f - t_m)^3} \\ a_3 = \dfrac{2(\theta_0 - \theta_f)}{(t_f - t_m)^3} \end{cases} \tag{31}$$

As a result, The position-time function of Manipulator's end effector $p(t)$ is a piecewise function. The movement distance of end effector is

$$L = \int_0^{t_m} \sqrt{\dot{p}_{x1}^2(t) + \dot{p}_{y1}^2(t) + \dot{p}_{z1}^2(t)dt} + \int_{t_m}^{t_f} \sqrt{\dot{p}_{x2}^2(t) + \dot{p}_{y2}^2(t) + \dot{p}_{z2}^2(t)dt} \tag{32}$$

 DOI: 10.1051/matecconf/201712804001

In this passage, the trajectory optimization objective is to find the middle moment between joint 2 and joint 3 to minimize the movement distance of end effector when the initial position $[p_{x0}, p_{y0}, p_{z0}]$ and end position $[p_{xf}, p_{yf}, p_{zf}]$ is given. Now, the concrete trajectory planning requirements for Stanford Manipulator is given as follows. The joint parameter of rotation body θ_1 will always start changing at $t = 0$, but the joint parameter of big arm θ_2 and the joint parameter of extension arm d_3 will start changing at $t = t_2$ and $t = t_3$, respectively. The three joint parameters must stop at $t = t_f$, at the same time the end effector must arrive the final position.

The solution is to get the best combination of middle moment t_2, t_3, which can make the distance of end effector from start position to final position the shortest.

4 The Proposed Genetic Algorithm

In this passage, genetic Algorithm(GA) is used for global search to find the shortest distance of end effector L and the corresponding middle moment t_2, t_3. Genetic Algorithm consists of the following functions, initialization parameters, fitness function, ranking strategy, selection, crossover and mutation probabilities. The main body of GA is shown in 0

Table 2 The main body of GA for trajectory

Input:
int generation_size;
int pop_size;
int chromo_size;
double cross_rate;
double mutate_rate;
Output:
initialization(pop_size,chromo_size);
for i=1 To generation_size
fitness(pop_size,chromo_size);
rank(pop_size, chromo_size);
selection(pop_size, chromo_size);
crossover(pop_size,chromo_size,cross_rate);
mutation(pop_size,chromo_size,mutate_rate) ;
end for

Initialization function is shown in 0. It should be noticed that the column length of population (pop) should be two times that of chromosome length (chromo_size), because there are two independent variables. pop(i, j) is equal to 0 or 1each with a fifty percent. In this case, individuals composed of arbitrary middle moment t_2, t_3 is represented as a binary code whose length is equal to two times the length of chrom_size.

Table 3 initialization function for randomly generating middle moment t_2, t_3

Function initialization(pop_size,chromo_size)
Input:
int pop_size;
int chromo_size;
int array[2] pop(pop_size, chromo_size);
Output:
for i=1 To pop_size
    for j=1 To 2×chromo_size
        pop(i, j) = round(rand);
    end for
end for

Fitness function is used to calculate population fitness (fitness_value) as 0. Each individual should be divided into two parts and converted into decimal numbers. Then, middle moment t_2, t_3 is based on the corresponding decimal numbers in the $[0, t_0]$ range. Upper limit t_0 is different from final joints stopping time t_f. The wear and vibration will be intensified if the two numbers are too close. The first half of each solution is transformed into the moment when parameters of joint 2 begins changing t_2, while the second half of each solution is transformed into the moment when parameters of joint 3 begins changing t_3. In the end of this function, t_2, t_3 is substituted into calculations to get the distance of end effector L. To facilitate the arrangement of fitness_value from small to large, fitness_value is defined to be equal to the reciprocal of L.

Table 4 fitness function for calculate fitness_value

function fitness(pop_size, chromo_size)
Input:
int pop_size;
int chromo_size;
int array[2] pop(pop_size, chromo_size);
double array t_2(pop_size);
double array t_3(pop_size);
double t_0;
double array fitness_value (pop_size);
Output:
for i=1 To pop_size
    for j = 1 To chromo_size
        if pop(i , j) == 1
            $t_2(i) = t_2(i) + 2^{j-1}$;
        end if
    end for
    for j = chromo_size+1 To 2×chromo_size
        if pop(i, j) == 1
            $t_3(i) = t_3(i) + 2^{j-chromo\_size-1}$;
        end if
    end for
    $t_2(i) = t_2(i) \times t_0/(2^{chromo\_size-1})$;
    $t_3(i) = t_3(i) \times t_0/(2^{chromo\_size-1})$;
    fitness_value=$1/L(t_2, t_3)$;
end for

The process of computing $L(t_2, t_3)$ will vary with the size of the t_2, t_3. Therefore, we need to discuss the situation separately as Figure 3.

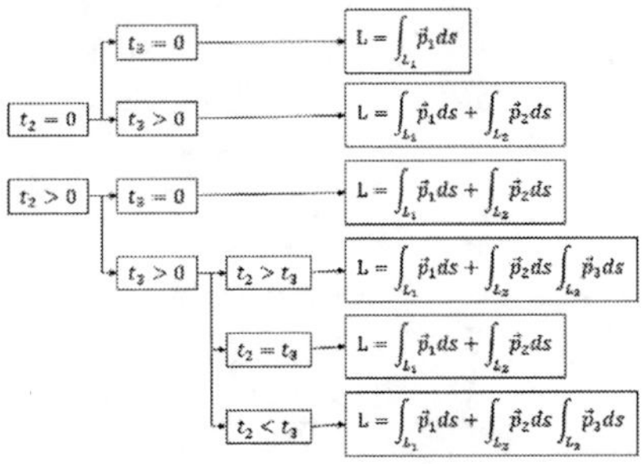

Fig 3. Multiple possibilities for computing the distance of end effector L

This paper only illustrates the process of calculating the distance of end effector L when $t_3 > t_2 > 0$. Obviously, it needs to be divided into three sections.

When $0 < t < t_2$,

$$\begin{cases} a_{10} = \theta_{10} \\ a_{11} = 0 \\ a_{12} = \frac{3}{t_f^2}(\theta_{1f} - \theta_{10}) \\ a_{13} = -\frac{2}{t_f^3}(\theta_{1f} - \theta_{10}) \end{cases} \tag{33}$$

$$\theta_1(t) = a_{10} + a_{11}t + a_{12}t^2 + a_{13}t^3 \tag{34}$$

$$\theta_2(t) = \theta_{20} \tag{35}$$

$$d_3(t) = d_{30} \tag{36}$$

$$p_{x1}(t) = \cos[\theta_1(t)]sin\theta_{20}d_{30} - \sin[\theta_1(t)]d_2 \tag{37}$$

$$p_{y1}(t) = \sin[\theta_1(t)]sin\theta_{20}d_{30} + \cos[\theta_1(t)]d_2 \tag{38}$$

$$p_{z1}(t) = cos\theta_{20}d_{30} \tag{39}$$

$$L_1 = \int_{L_1} \vec{p}_1 ds = \int_0^{t_2} \sqrt{\dot{p}_{x1}^2(t) + \dot{p}_{y1}^2(t) + \dot{p}_{z1}^2(t)dt} \tag{40}$$

When $t_2 < t < t_3$, $\theta_1(t)$ stands for Formula (34), $d_3(t)$ stands for Formula(36). The relationship between the remaining parameters and time as follows.

$$\begin{cases} a_{20} = \frac{\theta_{20}t_f^3 - 3\theta_{20}t_f^2 t_2 + 3\theta_{2f}t_f t_2^2 - \theta_{2f}}{(t_f - t_2)^3} \\ a_{21} = \frac{6t_2 t_f(\theta_{20} - \theta_{2f})}{(t_f - t_2)^3} \\ a_{22} = -\frac{3(t_2 + t_f)(\theta_{20} - \theta_{2f})}{(t_f - t_2)^3} \\ a_{23} = \frac{2(\theta_{20} - \theta_{2f})}{(t_f - t_2)^3} \end{cases} \tag{41}$$

$$\theta_2(t) = a_{20} + a_{21}t + a_{22}t^2 + a_{23}t^3 \tag{42}$$

$$p_{x2}(t) = \cos[\theta_1(t)]\sin[\theta_2(t)]d_{30} - \sin[\theta_1(t)]d_2 \tag{43}$$

$$p_{y2}(t) = \sin[\theta_1(t)]sin[\theta_2(t)]d_{30} + \cos[\theta_1(t)]d_2 \tag{44}$$

$$p_{z2}(t) = cos[\theta_2(t)]d_{30} \tag{45}$$

$$L_2 = \int_{L_2} \vec{p}_2 ds = \int_{t_2}^{t_3} \sqrt{\dot{p}_{x2}^2(t) + \dot{p}_{y2}^2(t) + \dot{p}_{z2}^2(t)dt} \tag{46}$$

When $t_3 < t < t_f$, $\theta_1(t)$ stands for Formula (34), $\theta_2(t)$ stands for Formula(42). The relationship between the remaining parameters and time as follows.

$$\begin{cases} a_{30} = \frac{d_{30}t_f^3 - 3d_{30}t_f^2 t_3 + 3d_{3f}t_f t_3^2 - d_{3f}t_3^3}{(t_f - t_3)^3} \\ a_{31} = \frac{6t_3 t_f(d_{30} - d_{3f})}{(t_f - t_3)^3} \\ a_{32} = -\frac{3(t_3 + t_f)(d_{30} - d_{3f})}{(t_f - t_3)^3} \\ a_{33} = \frac{2(d_{30} - d_{3f})}{(t_f - t_3)^3} \end{cases} \tag{47}$$

$$d_3(t) = a_{30} + a_{31}t + a_{32}t^2 + a_{33}t^3 \tag{48}$$

$$p_{x3}(t) = \cos[\theta_1(t)]\sin[\theta_2(t)]d_3(t) - \sin[\theta_1(t)]d_2 \tag{49}$$

$$p_{y3}(t) = \sin[\theta_1(t)]sin[\theta_2(t)]d_3(t) + \cos[\theta_1(t)]d_2 \tag{50}$$

$$p_{z3}(t) = cos[\theta_2(t)]d_3(t)$$

$$p_{z2}(t) = cos[\theta_2(t)]d_{30} \tag{51}$$

$$L_3 = \int_{L_3} \vec{p}_3 ds = \int_{t_3}^{t_f} \sqrt{\dot{p}_{x3}^2(t) + \dot{p}_{y3}^2(t) + \dot{p}_{z3}^2(t)dt} \tag{52}$$

Finally, the distance of end effector is calculated as follows:

$$L = L_1 + L_2 + L_3 \tag{53}$$

Ranking function sorts individuals in pop from small to large in order to facilitate selection function operation. Selection function is used to screen a new generation of populations. According to the ranking results of the pop, the probability that the N individual is selected is $P(n)$

$$P(n) = [\textstyle\sum_n^{i=1} fitness(\mathrm{i})] \Big/ [\textstyle\sum_{pop\_size}^{i=1} fitness(\mathrm{j})] \tag{54}$$

Thus, individuals with greater fitness are more likely to be selected into the next generation of individuals. At the same time, elite mechanism is utilized that individuals with the highest fitness per generation are automatically reserved for the next generation.

Crossover function selects two individuals in the new species group selected by selection function as parent individuals, and takes any point from the two extracted individuals as intersections. If their crossover probability (cross_rate) allows the two parent individuals to cross, they start at that point until all parts after that point are cross interchanged as 0.

Table 5 crossover function

```
function crossover(pop_size, chromo_size,
cross_rate)
Input:
int pop_size;
int chromo_size;
double cross_rate;
int cross_pos;
int array[2] pop(pop_size, chromo_size);
Output:
for i=1 To pop_size Step 2
    if(rand < cross_rate)
        cross_pos = round(rand×2×chromo_size);
        if or (cross_pos == 0, cross_pos == 1)
            continue;
        end if
        for j=cross_pos To 2×chromo_size
            pop(i, j) ↔ pop(i+1,j);
        end for
    end if
end for
```

Similar to B, A should first give a point that needs to mutate, and then substitute the other alleles for the gene at that point, which is usually a simple reverse operation as 0.

Table 6 mutation function

```
function mutation(pop_size, chromo_size, mutate_rate)
```

 DOI: 10.1051/matecconf/201712804001

Input:
```
int pop_size;
int chromo_size;
double mutate_rate;
int mutate_pos;
int array[2] pop(pop_size, chromo_size);
```
Output:
```
for i=1 To pop_size
    if rand < mutate_rate
        mutate_pos = round(rand×2×chromo_size);
        if mutate_pos == 0
            continue;
        end if
        pop(i,mutate_pos) = 1 - pop(i, mutate_pos);
    end if
end for
```

5 Simulation Results

All experiments were performed on MATLAB R2016a(9.0.0.341360), The operating system of the computer is 64 bit Windows10 family Chinese version, CPU is Intel(R)Core(TM)i5-4200H CPU @ 2.80GHz, RAM capacity is 4.00GB.

The 6 nodes are selected randomly in the three-dimensional space as 0 to verify the universality of the algorithm.

Table 7 Stanford Manipulator's position and joints parameters at different nodes

Node sequence	p_x	p_y	p_z	θ_1	θ_2	d_3
0	150	-100	120	-1.5708	0.6947	156.205
1	-100	150	80	-1.9656	-0.8961	128.063
2	200	100	50	-0.2717	1.2780	173.205
3	300	100	100	-0.1725	1.2259	295.804
4	-200	320	-80	-1.4210	1.3437	-355.387
5	-250	-340	-60	-1.3002	1.4198	-398.998

The algorithm parameters are set as follows,pop_size = 30, chromo_size = 10, generation_size = 300, cross_rate = 0.8, mutate_rate = 0.02. The un-optimized path indicates the distance at which all joint parameters move at the same time from the t=0 moment. Ten node sequences are used for optimization among five nodes as 0.

Table 8 experimental results in different node sequences

Node sequences	Un-optimized distance	Optimized distance	Optimum percent age	Generation of best individual	Code time
0-1	179.987	179.209	0.43%	139	97s
0-2	229.755	223.821	2.58%	137	96s
0-3	371.456	340.236	8.40%	215	92s
0-4	544.034	542.320	0.32%	218	94s
0-5	610.924	606.129	0.78%	223	99s
1-2	225.479	176.215	21.85%	141	108s
1-3	383.143	240.443	37.24%	92	113s
2-3	112.031	112.011	0.02%	295	104s
3-4	525.231	525.142	0.02%	61	84s
4-5	82.508	82.471	0.04%	245	111s

The experiments results show that the movement distance is optimized greatly by the algorithm, which is reduced by 37% compared to un-optimized condition. When the precision is set as 1/1000, the code runs from one and a half minutes to two minutes. Figure4. The comparison of un-optimized path and optimized path of Node 1-3is shown in Figure 4.

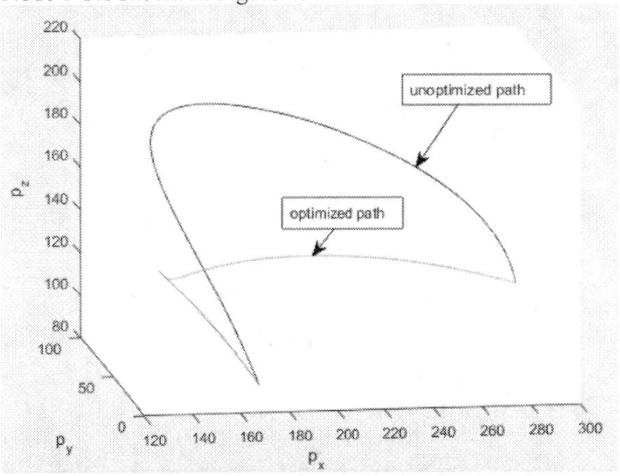

Fig 4. The comparison of un-optimized path and optimized path of Node 1-3

To investigate the influence of these parameters on the performance of the algorithm, each parameter is set in four levels as shown in 0. There is no doubt that huge computational efforts have to be performed if the algorithm is implemented under all possible combinations. To overcome this drawback, the Taguchi method of design of experiment (DOE) is used in this study, which uses orthogonal arrays to decrease the number of experiments [10]. According to the number of parameters and the number of factor levels, the orthogonal array $L_{16}(4^3)$ in 0 is selected for executing the experiments.

Table 9 Combinations of parameter values

Parameters	Factor level			
	1	2	3	4
Pop_size(p_s)	20	30	40	50
Cross_rate(c_r)	0.5	0.6	0.7	0.8
Mutate_rate(m_r)	0.02	0.03	0.05	0.1

Table 10 The orthogonal array $L_{16}(4^3)$ and experimental results

Test Numeber	Factor Level			Average results		
	p_s	c_r	m_r	Code time	Generation of best individual	The optimization distance
1	1	1	1	82s	141	176.211
2	1	2	2	80s	80	176.233
3	1	3	3	83s	68	176.211
4	1	4	4	79s	57	176.233
5	2	1	2	119s	87	176.220
6	2	2	1	120s	30	176.211
7	2	3	4	119s	106	176.211
8	2	4	3	122s	162	176.233
9	3	1	3	130s	115	176.211
10	3	2	4	146s	236	176.214
11	3	3	1	119s	79	176.211
12	3	4	2	132s	179	176.233
13	4	1	4	126s	28	176.211
14	4	2	3	58s	220	176.211
15	4	3	2	58s	140	176.211
16	4	4	1	163s	136	176.214

In different factor lever, the running time of the algorithm is between one and a half to three minutes, and the convergence of the L is stable and has no obvious fluctuation. As shown in 0, the algorithm converges to the

50th generation 50 times.

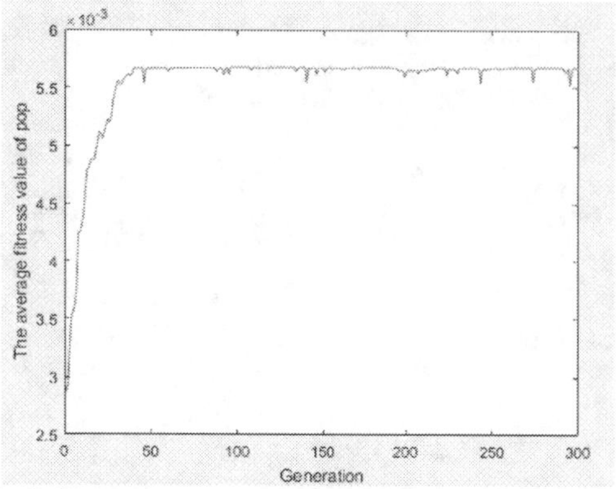

Fig 5. Convergence curve when factor level is 111

6 Conclusion

In this paper, an optimization scheme for joint motion time series is proposed on the basis of the Stanford Manipulator's mathematical model. Under the specified conditions, the minimum path of the end effector from the prescribed start point to the end point is obtained by applying the GA optimization method and performing three polynomial interpolation of the joint variables.

Genetic algorithm has good repeatability and stable solution, and is not easy to generate local optimal solution. However, the optimization effect of the algorithm is related to the predetermined position. The reason is that all joints can only reach the finishing line at the same time. In the future work, more complex joint time series constraints can be taken into consideration to provide a good optimization effect for the first and last positions.

Although the problem of obstacle avoidance is not considered in this paper, the algorithm can set up a barrier space, and then sift out all the individuals entering the barrier space in the process of population selecting. This provides some feasible direction for further research.

Refiences

1. R. Brooks, "Flesh and Machines," Pantheons Books, New York, 2002.
2. John J. Craig, "Introduction to Robotics Mechanics and Control", China Machine Press, Beijing, 2006.6.
3. Atsushi Fujimori, Peter N. Nikiforuk, and Madan M, Gupta, Adaptive Navigation of Mobile Robots with Obstacle Avoidance, IEEE Transactions on robotics and automation, 1997.8.
4. Ningyue, Liyan, and Liukeping, The Research of Mobile Manipulator Trajectory Tracking Cooperative Control based on the ADRC
5. JIA Wei-ping, The Track Project Research of Stanford Manipulator's Moving Route, Robot Technology, 2005
6. DONG Yun, YANG Tao, LI Wen. Algorithm Based on Analytical Method and Genetic Algorithm for Inverse Kinematics of Redundant Manipulator, 2012, 29(3):239-243
7. SHEN Xiao-ning, Li Sheng, GUO Yu, CHEN Qing-wei, HU Wei-li. Multi-objective Genetic Algorithm for Inverse Kinematics Problem of Redundant Manipulator[J]. Journal of System Simulation, 2008, 20(2): 399-403
8. JIA Wei-ping, The Research of Stanford Manipulator Kinematics and Compulator Simulation [D]
9. CAO Dao-you, Research and Applications Based on Improved Genetic Algorithm [D]
10. Montgomery, D.C. (2008). Design and analysis of experiments. John Wiley & Sons.

MATEC Web of Conferences 128, 04002 (2017) DOI: 10.1051/matecconf/201712804002
EITCE 2017

Evaluation and Study on Relationship between Sitting Posture and Work Efficiency

Pei Xuesheng[1,2], Tian Liyingi[2]

[1]*School of Mechatronic Engineering and Automation, Shanghai University, Shanghai, China*
[2] *School of Art and Design Henan University of Science and Technology, Luoyang , China*

Abstract. The relationship between the work efficiency and the sitting posture of the office staff was analyzed by comparing changes in operation time of different tasks at different sitting postures. Combined with the body pressure distribution experiment, the relationship of operation time at different sitting postures was concluded, which provides reference for the study on office chair design and work efficiency improvement.

1 Introduction

Most of the office staff sits during work. Sitting for a long time at work, people always feel fatigue and uncomfortable, and also feel upset mentally. Plus the comfortableness of office chairs, all the factors influence the work efficiency. However, after they change comfortable chairs with appropriate dimensions or change their postures, their work efficiency is improved unexpectedly. The work efficiency improvement due to comfortable chairs proves the statement[1-2] of ergonomics. At the same time, sitting for a long time and poor sitting postures adversely influence the human health, with an intensifying trend. Thus, the design of modern office chairs should not only improve the comfortableness but also consider the influence of the sitting posture on the work efficiency. Furthermore, the design should also sufficiently consider adjustment and correction for the sitting posture and reduce the adverse influence on human health to the maximum extent, so as to meet the human physiological needs. This needs to apply the principle and method of ergonomics and comprehensively consider the sitting posture behavior, the physical and geometric characteristics of chairs and the human-chair interaction relationship[3]. Many researches tried to improve the work efficiency by increasing the chair comfortableness. However, improvement in the comfortableness not necessarily improves the work efficiency. From different sitting postures, to verify the relationship between the sitting posture and the work efficiency, two sitting postures are adopted for testing.

There are three kinds of sitting postures, trunk bending forward, trunk straightening up and trunk bending backward. The requirement for the optimum sitting posture during office work is that the pressure it caused can be distributed in the intervertebral discs of the vertebrae in the most appropriate way and deal load it produced can be distributed in attached muscular tissues[4] in the appropriate and even way. Among these three sitting postures, trunk straightening up is the popularly required “ ideal posture ” and “ healthy posture ” . However, the research by W assem Am ir Bashir, a researcher from a Canadian hospital affiliated to the University of Aberta, with the nuclear magnetic resonance (MRD) method for the first time shows that if people sit straight up, their spine and surrounding muscles and ligament will be tensioned, which will cause chronic pain if people keep such sitting posture for a long time. This is also one of the reasons why people feel uncomfortable when sitting on a chair with a backrest at about 90 degrees[5]. When sitting for a long time, people need to adjust their postures and actions frequently, so as to eliminate abnormal pressure to the spine and to seek for the most stable and comfortable posture[6]. Thus, this paper tests the relationship between the sitting posture and the work efficiency by testing the two sitting postures, trunk straightening up and trunk bending backward.

2 Experimental process

2.1 Subjects

Twenty healthy subjects, half males and half females, aged 21-32 (25.2 years old at average), with regular work in the indoor offices, for computer operation and without medical history of spine diseases, were selected.

2.1.1 Formatting the title

The title is set in bold 14-point Arial, flush left, unjustified. The first letter of the title should be capitalised with the rest in lower case. You should leave 35 mm of space above the title and 6mm after the title.

2.1.2 Formatting author names and author affiliations

Author names should be typed in 9-point Arial. The style for the names is First Names then Last Name, with a comma after all but the last two names, which are separated by "and". Do not use academic titles.

Affiliations of authors should be typed in italic 8-point Arial. They should be preceded by a numerical superscript corresponding to the same superscript after the name of the author concerned. Please ensure that affiliations are as full and complete as possible and include the country.

2.2 Experimental design

The experiment adopts the single-factor two-level within-group design, and each subject is tested under these two fixed sitting postures. The most basic method of evaluating the relationship between the sitting posture and the work efficiency is to select suitable office chairs. Considering different heights and weights of the subjects, the chairs with adjustable height and backrest angle were chosen. The next step was to determine the sitting posture, for which the two postures, trunk straightening up and trunk bending backward, were adopted for the three experimental tasks. The last work is to set the work tasks, including typing, reading and calculating. The subjects should operate with all of these two postures and would be subjectively evaluated as to which posture is more comfortable after the test. Furthermore, the body pressure distribution of corresponding sitting postures was measured, and relevant experimental data were sorted for analysis.

2.3 Experimental facilities and testing environment

The experiment was divided into two parts, i.e. testing of the facial expression analytic system and body pressure distribution, and subjective evaluation of the subjects, which will be introduced as follows:

(1) Facial expression analytic system. Human facial expression provides massive important information for interpersonal communication. As one of the most direct communication methods, facial expression allows us to recognize the emotional state and intension of other people. However, it is extremely challenging to objectively explain the facial expression. The facial expression analytic system (Face ReaderTM) is a unique automatic facial expression analysis tool which allows users to objectively evaluate personal emotion changes. The facial expression analytic system can show whether the emotion are positive or negative while visualizing facial expression into bar charts, pie charts and continuous curve signals. It helps understand the emotional state of users in real time.

(2) The body pressure distribution of human bodies with the two sitting postures was measured with the tekscan device. The tekscan device can measure the pressure value of all points between the human body surfaces and the contact surfaces, and the tekscan pressure distribution measurement system uses the unique patent technology-the flexible film grid-type tactile pressure sensor. Due to the thin thickness of only 0.1mm and the good flexibility, the sensor provides better conditions for measuring pressure between various contact surfaces. Furthermore, pressure on any contact surface can be measured statically or dynamically, and the pressure distribution profile, various data and the pressure peak value can be displayed in real time through visual and vivid two-dimensional and three-dimensional colored images.

2.4 Experimental procedures

2.4.1Experimental preparation

(1) Researchers debugged two cameras, with one directly facing the subjects' faces, centered at nasal tips, so as to collect the subjects' expressions; and with the other one aligning at the sitting posture and operation process of the subjects, so as to verify the feasibility and accuracy of the experiment, and conduct pre-experiment for formal experimental content and do appropriate debugging.

(2) When the subjects arrived at the experimental site, they rested for 2 min before the experimenters explained the experimental purpose, method and requirements, so the subjects can understand the procedures of the whole experimental steps and followed the designed experimental steps during operation.

(3) arranged to take part in the experiment by operating with the postures of sitting upright or sitting back. Before the experiment, each subject informed the operator (responsible for recording videos of the subjects) after they were well prepared, and then started the experiment according to the sequence in the task cards after being told to start.

(4) After finishing operation with the first posture, the subjects reported to the operator and rested for 3 min, and then finished operation at the second posture with the same steps, and such procedures were repeated until the 20 subjects finished the tests.

(5) Body pressure testing. The sitting postures adopted in the experiment include sitting back and sitting upright. The subjects kept these two postures during experiment, and the body pressure distribution diagram of these two postures was obtained by the body pressure distribution testing system. Thus, the body pressure distribution borne by the chairs under these two sitting pressure can be obtained, which helps judge the comfortableness of the chairs.

3 Test results and data analysis

The experiment collected a lot of experiment video and data. The tekscan device measured body pressure distribution data, and the software of the facial expression analytic system (Face ReaderTM) processed the obtained video so as to get related experimental data[7].

3.1. Body pressure distribution test

The experiment adopts two sitting postures, sitting back and sitting upright, and tests the body pressure distribution of corresponding postures in an elaborate way, as shown in Figures 1 and 2.

From the figures, it can be seen that the maximum pressure value is 200 for each of these two sitting postures. However, the pressure distribution gradient interfaces are different that pressure distribution was concentrated surrounding two points of the ischium for the posture of sitting back, and the area with the maximum pressure value for this posture is bigger than that of the posture of sitting upright, while the leg pressure is smaller; compared with the posture of sitting back, pressure distribution and pressure gradient change of the posture of sitting upright is evener, and pressure distribution of the whole contact surface is relatively even, so people can better keep the same working state for a long time.

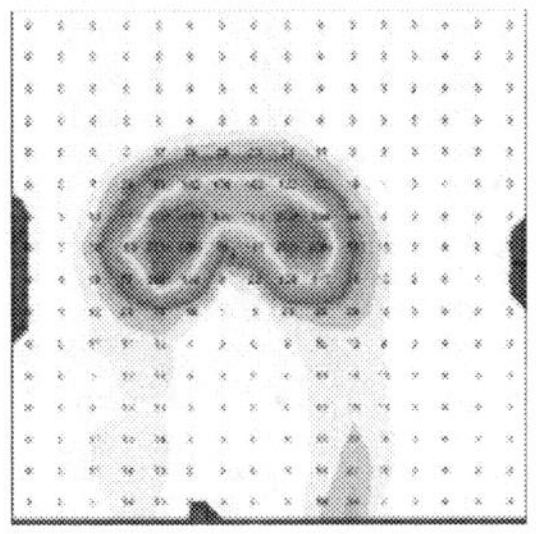

Figure 1. Body pressure distribution state at posture of sitting back.

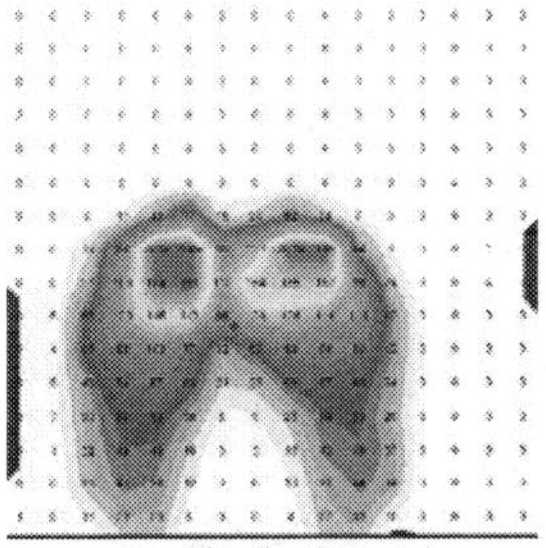

Figure 2. Body pressure distribution state at posture of sitting upright.

3.2 Task completion time statistics

As each subject operated twice during the experiment, they were divided into two parts randomly, with the first 10-person group operating sitting back firstly, while the other 10-person group operating sitting upright firstly. The time used by the subjects at both sitting postures was counted.

Table 1. Experimental time statistics

No.	First upright, then back						No.	First back, then upright					
	Sitting upright			Sitting back				Sitting back			Sitting upright		
	Typing	Reading	calculation	Typing	Reading	Calculation		Typing	Reading	Calculation	Typing	Reading	Calculation
1	252	104	124	170	98	52	2	211	131	63	169	118	42
3	254	57	30	210	32	28	5	147	53	25	194	39	26
4	211	190	98	153	179	40	7	242	99	70	213	77	29
6	360	115	81	278	81	29	10	302	141	72	249	94	47
8	221	61	71	138	48	93	12	247	53	45	240	26	35
9	255	121	70	204	103	45	13	179	65	44	151	58	40
11	272	70	141	209	81	34	14	114	81	40	110	65	25
17	231	148	60	186	135	67	15	227	58	44	214	52	34
18	143	87	38	85	97	28	16	193	89	70	170	52	38
19	137	114	49	129	82	47	20	248	124	38	204	114	29
Total time	2336	1067	762	1762	936	463	Total time	2110	894	511	1914	695	345

According to Table 1, whether for the posture of sitting back or sitting upright, all subjects used less time during the second operations. Thus, it can be seen that people's proficiency at work influences the work efficiency.

3.3 Analysis on task time

As the experiment adopts the single-factor two-level within-group design, time consumption of the first testing and the second testing for these two sitting postures was compared, the result of which showed the time consumption was the same. Thus, the time of three tasks at these two sitting postures was compared.

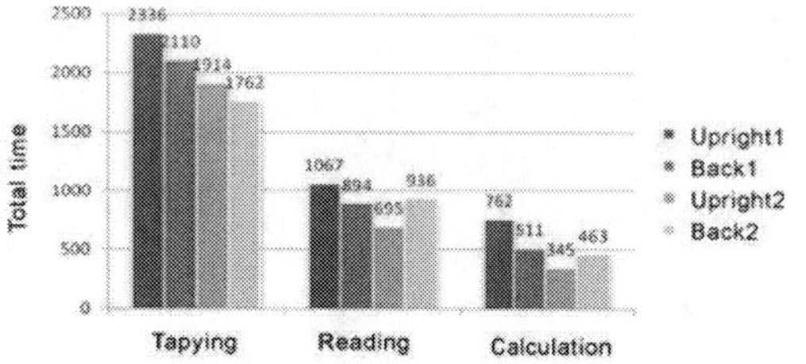

Figure 3. Bar graph of completion time of all tasks at two sitting postures.

From Figure 3, it can be seen that whether the subjects operated with the posture of sitting upright or sitting back, the time consumption of the three tasks for the posture of sitting back for the first time was less than that of the operation at the posture of sitting upright for the first time, indicating that the efficiency of people at the posture of sitting back is higher than that at the posture of sitting upright; while during operation for the second time, the subjects at the posture of sitting back were only faster in typing compared with at posture of sitting upright, while they at the posture of sitting upright were faster in reading and calculating compared with at the posture of sitting back. Through analysis, it is found that the reasons for this phenomenon include that during typing at the posture of sitting back, as the trunks bent backwards, the viewpoint height of eyes was lowered, and the sight distance was farther compared at the posture of sitting upright, so the whole field of view was broadened; in addition, the arm bending angle was bigger, so the movement scope of arms was enlarged and operation was more flexible. While when the subjects operated at the posture of sitting upright, the viewpoint height of eyes was high, and the sight distance was close, the bending angle of arms was smaller, so operation was restricted to a certain extent, and accordingly the subjects at the posture of sitting back was faster in typing. In contrast, during the experiment of "reading and calculating", why the subjects were faster at the posture of sitting upright at the second experiment was decided by the working state of the tasks. Specifically, reading needs a certain proper distance, so compared with reading at the posture of sitting upright, the sight distance of eyes was farther which influences the reading speed, and further influences the work efficiency. This can also be seen from the average values of the three tasks at these two different sitting postures.

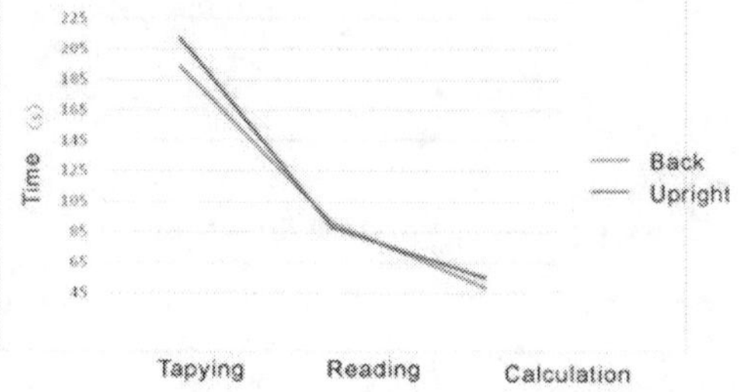

Figure 4. Task completion time at different sitting postures.

From Figure 4, it can be seen that the subjects sitting back were faster in typing and calculating compared with that sitting upright, indicating that they had higher task completion efficiency at the posture of trunk bending backward, but they were slightly slower in reading compared with that at the posture of trunk straightening up. This is decided by the operation characteristics of the tasks. In particular, the reason why the reading time at the posture of trunk bending backward was more than that at the posture of trunk straightening up is that the farther sight distance caused by the sitting posture led to the farther sight distance during reading, which influences the reading speed and further increases the reading time at the posture of trunk bending backward.

3.3 Descriptive statistics test

The facial expression analytic system (Face ReaderTM) recognized the facial expression of the 120 operating videos, and data were analyzed through software identification, from which the following icons were obtained.

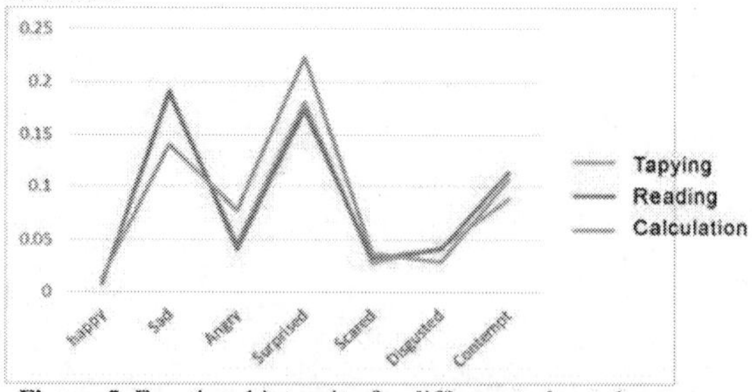

Figure 5. Emotional intensity for different tasks at the posture of sitting upright.

From Figure 5, it can be seen that the positive emotion brought by sitting upright and sitting back during calculating was surprisingly higher than that during typing and reading, indicating that different work contents can result in emotional fluctuations. Specifically, dull work with repetitive reduces people's working enthusiasm, while challenging work is more apt to cause emotional changes, and further can arouse people's working enthusiasm.

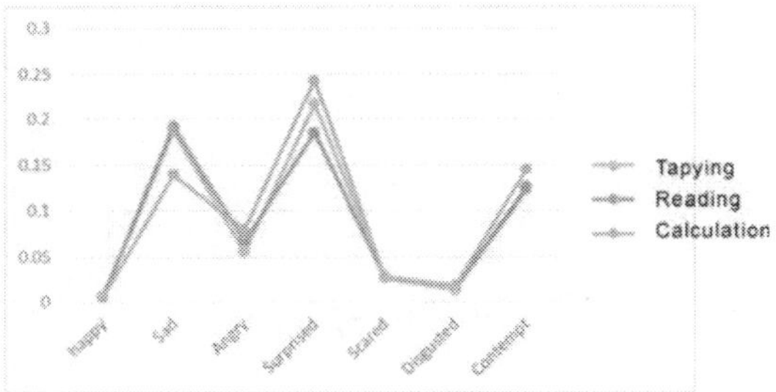

Figure 6. Emotional intensity for different tasks at the posture of sitting back.

From Figure 6, it can be seen that the positive emotional valence brought by sitting upright and sitting back during calculating was bigger than that during typing and reading, indicating that calculating gave people more positive emotional experience. However, the positive emotion caused by calculating at the beginning was truly less than that caused by reading and typing, the reason for which is that the difficult work suppresses people's working emotion at the beginning, but once approaching completion, the positive emotion will increase sharply, thus bringing the sense of joy for people.

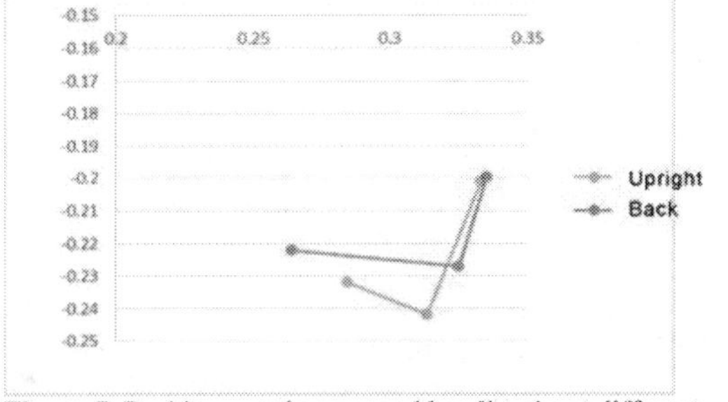

Figure 7. Positive emotion aroused by all tasks at different sitting postures.

From Figure 7, it can be seen that in the three tasks, the emotional arousal value of the posture of sitting back is the largest, indicating that the posture of sitting back causes more positive emotional experience compared with the posture of sitting upright, the reason for which is that when sitting back, the normal waists are in the curve shape of lying on side in a relax state. In this state, the gaps between the spines is normal, pressure on the intervertebral discs is tiny and even, causing hardly any thrust to the ligament, so people feel most comfortable and relaxed. Thus, in the posture of sitting back, the positive emotion is higher than that in the posture of sitting upright.

4 Shortcoming

Due to limitation in experimental task setting and random difference of the subjects, in spite of some deviation in the experimental task, the whole experimental design also has some shortcomings: (1) due to limitations of self-designed conditions of the testing personnel, there is difference which leads to deviation in the result of task completion data; (2) the operating time of each tester should be extended, the reason for which is that the less than half an hour of experimental operation time does not allow a good understanding of the difference in the work efficiency at different sitting postures during long-time work; and (3) the body pressure testing only extracted pressure distribution in the static state, rather than adopting the dynamic records.

5 Conclusion

(1) Starting from three viewpoints, the work efficiency related to the sitting posture, the office chairs and different work contents, this paper designs the experiment exploring the relationship between different sitting postures of the office staff and the work efficiency.

(2) According to the experiment, there are many factors which influence the work efficiency, including not only work contents but also the working proficiency and the operating characteristics of the work contents. The relevant data and factors obtained can help for desk and chair design in later days.

(3) Through comparison of these two sitting postures, it can be seen that for work within 10 min, the posture of sitting back can better arouse the enthusiasm of people and is favorable for the work mainly relying on arms. While for work with more than 10 min, the advantages of the posture of sitting back are only limited to the work mainly relying on arms, and the efficiency of working at the posture of sitting upright is higher for the other two tasks, which indicates that for long-time operation, it' s more appropriate to choose the posture of sitting upright for the work with requirements for the sight distance.

References

1. Liao M H, Drury C G Posture, discomfort and perfor mance in a VDT task. [J] Ergonomics, 2000,43(3):34 5-359
2. Amick III B C, Robertson M M, De Rango K. etal. Effect of office ergonomics intervention on reducing musculoskeletal symptoms. [J] Spine,2003,28(24):27 06-2711
3. Vergara M, Page A. System to Measure the Use of th e Backrest in Sitting-posture Office Tasks. [J] Applie d Ergonomics, 2002,33:1-8
4. Gutierrez E M, Hultling C, Sarasle H. Measuring Sea ting Pressure, Area, and Asymmetry in Persons with Spinal Cord Injury [J]. European Spine Journal, 2004, 13:374-379
5. Xu Ji-feng, Zhang Han-ning, Cui Tian-jian, Office C hair Design and Creation Based on Sitting Behavior. [J] Packaging Engineering, 2013,34(8):52-56
6. Li Juan, Xu Bo-chu, Lian Jifeng, Wang Chao. Seat C omfbrt Characterization by Body-seat Interflace Pres sure Distribution. [J] Mechanical Science and Techn ology for Aerospace Engineering,2014, 9 (33): 1298-1303
7. Zhao hui. Speech Emotional Recognition Fuses Faci al Expression. [J]Journal of University of Jinan (Scie nce & Technology), 2011,25(S2):1-4

MATEC Web of Conferences 128, 04003 (2017) DOI: 10.1051/matecconf/201712804003
EITCE 2017

A Novel Reliability Evaluation Method Based on RBD and AHP for Industrial Network Systems

Yongni Li [1,a], Zhenxing Li[1], Baiyi Li[1] and Song Hu[1]

[1]*CRRC QINGDAO SIFANG CO., LTD., Shandong Qingdao 266111, China*

Abstract. Since each component has different impacts on reliability of the industrial network system, a multi-layer reliability evaluation method was proposed in this paper. Firstly, in order to construct multi-layer reliability evaluation system, a framework of industrial network system was introduced based on analytic hierarchy process (AHP). Secondly, a multi-layer reliability evaluation model with weight coefficient of components was proposed based on reliability block diagram (RBD). Thirdly, the simple rule-based fuzzy judgment and risk priority number (RPN) were applied to determining weight coefficient. Last, a reliability evaluation case of the industrial network system for an electronic automatic assembly line was studied. It shows that the proposed method is more reasonable than the conventional reliability analysis method, and the reliability prediction result is consistent with the engineering practice.

1 Introduction

Reliability has become a common problem of industrial network system, and its indicator is considered as an important quality attribute, which has the same important status as technical and economic indicators such as system performance and cost. With the development of reliability engineering, the idea that reliability of product is the result of design, manufacture and management has been understood and accepted gradually. According to statistics, around 80% of the product reliability problems derive from the design stage of product, which means the design level directly influences the product reliability in practice. So, safety, reliability and efficiency of industrial network system depend on system reliability analysis, assessment, prediction and optimization during design phase.

As an important indicator of the product, reliability has got more and more attention. However, it is still difficult to evaluate the reliability of industrial network system comprehensively during design phase. Over the years, scholars all over the world have carried out a lot of fruitful research results on the problem. A series of reliability analysis methods have been put forward such as reliability block diagram(RBD)[1], binary decision diagram[2], fault tree(FT)[3], bayesian networks(BN)[4] and petri net[5,6]. As a simple, direct and efficient method, RBD has been widely applied to engineering. For example, Dr. Dou proposed reliability evaluation model of ship to air missile launching system on the basis of RBD, achieved the reliability evaluation assessment when the single shot happened[7]. Dr. Chen established reliability modeling process based on ExtendSim on the basis of RBD to solve the modeling and programming difficulties of traditional reliability method[8]. Dr. Wu studied the reliability of spacecraft solar wing system following RBD and FT[9]. Dr. Sun introduced a layered hybrid model method to analyse the reliability of the airplane control system which is based on combining RBD and generalized stochastic Petri net[10].

Though RBD can effectively build reliability model and evaluate reliability of the system, it ignores the fact that the industrial network system is a typical hybrid system integrated with parts, electrical equipment, electronic components, control components and other units, whose impacts on system reliability are different. For example, it is obvious that a server failure has a greater influence than a circuit failure on system reliability. Therefore, considering the different influence of units on system reliability is more reasonable in the construction of reliability modeling. Thereby, engineers can conveniently recognize the weak link and optimize the system reliability during design phase.

Based on the above consideration, a multi-layer reliability evaluation system was established by AHP method for the industrial network system. Then, a multi-layer reliability evaluation model with weight coefficient of units was proposed. A case proved the effectiveness of the multi-layer reliability evaluation method which meets the needs of reliability evaluation in the development process of industrial network system.

2 Overview of industrial network system

Industrial network system is a full digital, bidirectional, multi-station communication system installed in the

[a] Corresponding author: 15151853987@163.com

DOI: 10.1051/matecconf/201712804003

industrial production. It can be described that the system consists of a series of different hardware and software modules that play functions of data acquisition, data transmission, data processing and so on [11].

Industrial network system is a typical machine, electricity and control system. Any fault will result in production disruptions, even safety accidents, which will cause significant economic losses to the enterprise. As industrial 4.0 and made in China 2025 are put forward, quantities of industrial network system are rapidly increasing. Accordingly, reliability problems of industrial network system are constantly exposed and increasingly prominent. Due to the variety of parts, complex structure, high integration and so on, it is very difficult to accurately calculate the reliability of industrial network system by using the traditional reliability method. So, establishing a new reliability evaluation method that adapts to industrial network system is of great importance to improve reliability, reduce safety accidents and increase corporate profits.

3 The multi-layer reliability model

AHP is to decompose complex engineering problems from top to bottom to multiple levels and then solve the priority of each level to the upper level, so as to qualitatively and quantitatively analyze the problem or target. In this paper, system reliability model which reflects the importance of different units is constructed on the basis of AHP and RBD.

According to AHP method, industrial network system can be divided into four basic levels, namely system layer, subsystem layer, function module layer and basic module layer, as shown in figure 1. The upper layer is the target layer of next layer on reliability and the next layer is the basic unit of upper layer. The basic 4 layer can be increased or reduced in order to meet the analytic need for industrial network system with different complexity.

Every level reliability model is constructed based on RBD. For the series RBD, the reliability can be calculated as follows:

$$R_S(t) = \prod_i R_i^{w_i}(t) \quad (1)$$

where, R_s represents target reliability of the layer, t represents time, R_i represents unit i reliability of the layer, w_i represents the weight of unit i.

For parallel RBD, the reliability can be calculated as follows:

$$R_S(t) = 1 - \prod_i \left(1 - R_i^{w_i}(t)\right) \quad (2)$$

For next league or redundancy structure, reliability can be calculated by considering the impact of the weight coefficient. In theory, the weight coefficient w_i belongs to $[0, \infty)$ in the above formula.

When w_i equals to 0, R_i equals to 1 which shows that unit i has no effect on reliability for target layer. When w_i is close to ∞, R_i is close to 0 which means that unit i has a deterministic effect on reliability for target layer.

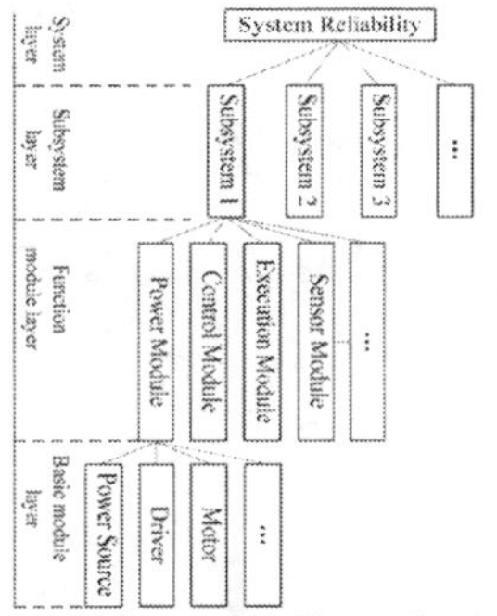

Figure 1. The multi-layer reliability evaluation system for industrial network system.

4 Weight coefficient calculating method

Weight is the most critical and difficult point when AHP method is used to analyze system reliability, that is to determine the weight coefficient in formula (1) and formula (2). AHP method needs to gain judgment matrix which can represent the relative importance of different index by experts[12]. Judgment matrix often adopts the proportional scaling method, and different proportion scales usually cause different results. Therefore, the fuzzy judgement matrix method is proposed in order to correctly evaluate system reliability by AHP in this paper. By the way, weight coefficients are able to truly reflect the relative importance of different index.

For the basic unit of each layer, index set needed to compare importance is as follows:

$$RPN = \{RPN_1, RPN_2, \dots, RPN_n\} \quad (3)$$

where, RPN_i is the risk priority number of unit i, $i = 1, 2, \dots, n$, n is total unit number. This paper calculates RPN_i by combining the risk priority number method of Criticality Analysis (CA) with the failure model frequency rate[13]. The formula is as follows:

$$RPN_i = \sum_j \alpha_{ij} \cdot OPR_{ij} \cdot ESR_{ij} \quad (4)$$

where, OPR is probability level of the failure model of the unit; ESR is the effect severe degree of the unit to target layer. α is failure model frequency rate which means ratio of the failure mode in all failure for the unit; $j = 1, 2, \cdots$ is failure model frequency number for the unit. The grading criteria of OPR and ESR are presented in table 1 and table 2, respectively.

Table 1. The grading criterion of *OPR*.

***OPR* grading level**	**Probability level**	**Probability range**
1	the lowest	$P \le 10^{-6}$
2,3	lower	$10^{-6} < P \le 10^{-4}$
4,5,6	common	$10^{-4} < P \le 10^{-2}$
7,8	higher	$10^{-2} < P \le 10^{-1}$
9,10	the highest	$P > 10^{-1}$

Table 2. The grading criterion of *ESR*.

ESR grading level	*ESR* level
1,2,3	Mild (Do not lead to people injuries, mild product damage, property loss and environmental pollution, but plan disorder)
4,5,6	Medium (Lead to medium people injuries, product damage, task delay or demotion, medium property loss and environmental pollution)
7,8	Deadly (Lead to severe people injuries, product damage, task failure, severe property loss and environmental pollution)
9,10	Disastrous (Lead to the deaths of personnel, product damage, major property loss and disastrous environmental pollution)

According to the result calculated by formula (4), RPN_i and RPN_k in index set RPN takes binary comparison. If $RPN_i > RPN_k$, let $e_{ik} = 0, e_{ki} = 0$; If $RPN_i = RPN_k$, let $e_{ik} = 0, e_{ki} = 0$; If $RPN_i < RPN_k$, let $e_{ik} = 0, e_{ki} = 1$. The binary contrast matrix on index importance is as follows:

$$E = \begin{bmatrix} e_{11} & e_{12} & \cdots & e_{1n} \\ e_{21} & e_{22} & \cdots & e_{2n} \\ \cdots & \cdots & \cdots & \cdots \\ e_{n1} & e_{n2} & \cdots & e_{nn} \end{bmatrix} = (e_{ik}) \tag{5}$$

Further, f_i (the importance ranking index of RPN_i) can be calculated as follows:

$$f_i = \sum\nolimits_k e_{ik} \tag{6}$$

Ranking f_i by value, importance degree of reliability to upper layer is get accordingly for each unit. Thus, fuzzy judgement matrix W is able to be calculated indirectly which is similar to the binary contrast matrix, as follows:

$$W = \begin{bmatrix} w_{11} & w_{12} & \cdots & w_{1n} \\ w_{21} & w_{22} & \cdots & w_{2n} \\ \cdots & \cdots & \cdots & \cdots \\ w_{n1} & w_{n2} & \cdots & w_{nn} \end{bmatrix} = (w_{ik}) \tag{7}$$

where,

$$w_{ik} = \frac{f_i - f_k}{2(\mathrm{n}-1)} + 0.5 \quad (i,k = 1,2,\ldots,\mathrm{n}) \tag{8}$$

Through this transformation, the sort index of the index is used to transform the fuzzy indirect scale which can reflect the relative importance of each index. Construct a fuzzy judgment matrix (w_{ik}), we can get the fuzzy membership degree per line. According to the nature of the fuzzy judgement matrix W, fuzzy membership of each row is able to be calculated as follows:

$$w_i = \sum\nolimits_k w_{ik} \quad (i \neq k) \tag{9}$$

where, w_i is the importance of index i to the upper layer, namely weight coefficient.

5 Case study

The reliability of the industrial network system for an electronic automatic assembly line was studied by the proposed multi-layer reliability evaluation method. The industrial network system of the electronic automatic assembly line is composed of data acquisition system, data transmission system and data processing system, as shown in figure 2.

5.1 Reliability analysis of module layer

In the case, reliability of each component is assumed to be exponential distribution and failure rate is λ. Each component parameters of failure rate, *OPR* and *ESR* are show in table 3. Failure model number of each component does not be considered to simplify the calculation. According to formula (4) and (5), the binary contrast matrix of each system in function module layer is calculated as follows:

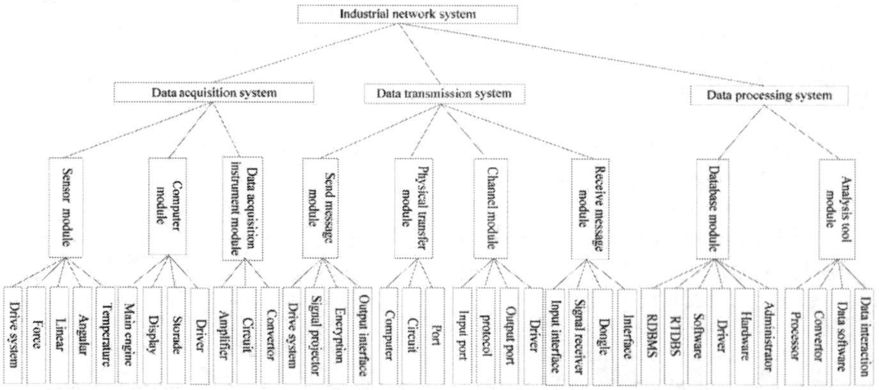

Figure 2. The multi-layer reliability evaluation system for the industrial network system of an electronic automatic assembly line.

Table 3. The failure rate, *OPR* and *ESR* of components.

DOI: 10.1051/matecconf/201712804003

Name of parts	λ (10^{-6})	*OPR*	*ESR*	Name of parts	λ (10^{-6})	*OPR*	*ESR*
Drive system	0.5	1	4	Output interface	1.5	2	1
Force	15	2	3	Computer	0.5	1	3
Linear	20	3	3	Port	2.5	1	4
Angular	1.5	1	3	Input port	15.5	3	1
Temperature	50.5	3	2	Protocol	18.5	2	4
Main engine	15.5	2	3	Output port	110.5	4	4
Display	130.5	4	1	Input interface	0.5	1	1
Storage	12.5	2	2	Signal receiver	0.5	1	1
Driver	1.5	2	1	Dongle	5.5	2	2
Amplifier	0.5	1	4	Interface	8.5	2	1
Circuit	3.5	2	3	RDBMS	5.5	2	4
Convertor	55.5	3	1	RTDBS	0.5	1	4
Signal projector	110.5	4	4	Software	23.5	3	3
Encryption	185.5	4	2	Hardware	14.5	3	1
Administrator	8.5	2	1	Processor	15.5	2	2
Data software	80.5	3	4	Data interaction	0.5	1	3

1) The binary contrast matrix of sensor module

$$E=\begin{bmatrix}0&0&0&1&0\\1&0&0&1&0\\1&1&0&1&1\\0&0&0&0&0\\1&0&0&1&0\end{bmatrix}$$

2) The binary contrast matrix of computer module

$$E=\begin{bmatrix}0&1&1&1\\0&0&0&1\\0&0&0&1\\0&0&0&0\end{bmatrix}$$

3) The binary contrast matrix of data acquisition instrument module

$$E=\begin{bmatrix}0&0&1\\1&0&1\\0&0&0\end{bmatrix}$$

4) The binary contrast matrix of send message module

$$E=\begin{bmatrix}0&0&0&1\\1&0&1&1\\1&0&0&1\\0&0&0&0\end{bmatrix}$$

5) The binary contrast matrix of physical transfer module

$$E=\begin{bmatrix}0&0&0\\1&0&1\\1&0&0\end{bmatrix}$$

6) The binary contrast matrix of channel module

$$E=\begin{bmatrix}0&0&0&1\\1&0&0&1\\1&1&0&1\\0&0&0&0\end{bmatrix}$$

7) The binary contrast matrix of receive message module

$$E=\begin{bmatrix}0&0&0&0\\0&0&0&0\\1&1&0&1\\1&1&0&0\end{bmatrix}$$

8) The binary contrast matrix of database module

$$E=\begin{bmatrix}0&1&0&1&1&1\\0&0&0&1&1&1\\1&1&0&1&1&1\\0&0&0&0&0&0\\0&0&0&1&0&1\\0&0&0&0&0&0\end{bmatrix}$$

9) The binary contrast matrix of analysis tool module

$$E=\begin{bmatrix}0&1&0&1\\0&0&0&0\\1&1&0&1\\0&0&0&0\end{bmatrix}$$

According to formula (6) ~ (8), fuzzy judgment matrix of each function module can be obtained in turn as follows:

1) Fuzzy judgment matrix of sensor module

$$W=\begin{bmatrix}0.5&3/8&1/8&5/8&3/8\\5/8&0.5&0.25&0.75&0.5\\7/8&0.75&0.5&1&0.75\\3/8&0.25&0&0.5&0.25\\5/8&0.5&0.25&0.75&0.5\end{bmatrix}$$

2) Fuzzy judgment matrix of computer module

$$W=\begin{bmatrix}0.5&5/6&5/6&1\\1/6&0.5&0.5&2/3\\1/6&0.5&0.5&2/3\\0&1/3&1/3&0.5\end{bmatrix}$$

3) Fuzzy judgment matrix of data acquisition instrument module

$$W=\begin{bmatrix}0.5&0.25&0.75\\0.75&0.5&1\\0.25&0&0.5\end{bmatrix}$$

4) Fuzzy judgment matrix of send message module

$$W=\begin{bmatrix}0.5&1/6&1/3&2/3\\5/6&0.5&2/3&1\\2/3&1/3&0.5&5/6\\1/3&0&1/6&0.5\end{bmatrix}$$

5) Fuzzy judgment matrix of physical transfer module

$$W=\begin{bmatrix}0.5&0&0.25\\1&0.5&0.75\\0.75&0.25&0.5\end{bmatrix}$$

6) Fuzzy judgment matrix of channel module

 DOI: 10.1051/matecconf/201712804003

$$W=\begin{bmatrix}0.5 & 1/3 & 1/6 & 2/3\\ 2/3 & 0.5 & 1/3 & 5/6\\ 5/6 & 2/3 & 0.5 & 1\\ 1/3 & 1/6 & 0 & 0.5\end{bmatrix}$$

7) Fuzzy judgment matrix of receive message module

$$W=\begin{bmatrix}0.5 & 0.5 & 0 & 1/6\\ 0.5 & 0.5 & 0 & 1/6\\ 1 & 1 & 0.5 & 2/3\\ 5/6 & 5/6 & 1/3 & 0.5\end{bmatrix}$$

8) Fuzzy judgment matrix of database module

$$W=\begin{bmatrix}0.5 & 0.6 & 0.4 & 0.9 & 0.7 & 0.9\\ 0.4 & 0.5 & 0.3 & 0.8 & 0.6 & 0.8\\ 0.6 & 0.7 & 0.5 & 1 & 0.8 & 1\\ 0.1 & 0.2 & 0 & 0.5 & 0.3 & 0.5\\ 0.3 & 0.4 & 0.2 & 0.7 & 0.5 & 0.7\\ 0.1 & 0.2 & 0 & 0.5 & 0.3 & 0.5\end{bmatrix}$$

9) Fuzzy judgment matrix of analysis tool module

$$W=\begin{bmatrix}0.5 & 5/6 & 1/3 & 5/6\\ 1/6 & 0.5 & 0 & 0.5\\ 2/3 & 1 & 0.5 & 1\\ 1/6 & 0.5 & 0 & 0.5\end{bmatrix}$$

According to formula (9) and above fuzzy judgment matrix, the weight coefficient of each component is evaluated. Then, reliability of each module which is shown in table 4 is obtained on the basis of series RBD when system continuously works for 1000 hours. The failure rate of each module is shown in table 5.

Table 4. Reliability of each function module.

Module name	Reliability
Sensor module	0.811
Computer module	0.792
Data acquisition instrument module	0.979
Send message module	0.539
Physical transfer module	0.991
Channel module	0.803
Receive message module	0.969
Database module	0.851
Analysis tool module	0.754

5.2 Reliability analysis of subsystem

OPR and *ESR* of each function module are shown in table 5.

Table 5. Failure rate, *OPR* and *ESR* of each function module.

Module name	λ (10^{-4})	OPR	ESR
Sensor module	2.09	4	4
Computer module	2.33	5	3
Data acquisition instrument module	0.21	3	4
Send message module	6.18	5	3
Physical transfer module	0.09	3	4
Channel module	2.19	4	5
Receive message module	0.32	3	3
Database module	1.61	4	4
Analysis tool module	2.83	5	4

Similarly, according to formula (4) ~ (8), the fuzzy judgment matrix of each subsystem can be obtained in turn as follows:

1) Fuzzy judgment matrix of data acquisition system

$$W=\begin{bmatrix}0.5 & 0.75 & 1\\ 0.25 & 0.5 & 0.75\\ 0 & 0.25 & 0.5\end{bmatrix}$$

2) Fuzzy judgment matrix of data transmission system

$$W=\begin{bmatrix}0.5 & 2/3 & 1/3 & 5/6\\ 1/3 & 0.5 & 1/6 & 2/3\\ 2/3 & 5/6 & 0.5 & 1\\ 1/6 & 1/3 & 0 & 0.5\end{bmatrix}$$

3) Fuzzy judgment matrix of data processing system

$$W=\begin{bmatrix}0.5 & 0\\ 1 & 0.5\end{bmatrix}$$

According to formula (9) and above fuzzy judgment matrix, the weight coefficient of each function module is evaluated. Then, reliability of each subsystem which shows in table 6 is obtained on the basis of series RBD when system continuously works for 1000 hours. The failure rate of each subsystem is shown in table 7.

Table 6. Reliability of each subsystem.

Subsystem name	Reliability
Data acquisition system	0.5466
Data transmission system	0.1748
Data processing system	0.7535

5.3 Reliability analysis of system

OPR and *ESR* of each function module are shown in table 5.

Table 7. Failure rate, *OPR* and *ESR* of each subsystem.

Subsystem name	λ (10^{-3})	*OPR*	*ESR*
Data acquisition system	0.604	5	4
Data transmission system	1.744	5	5
Data processing system	0.283	4	3

Similarly, according to formula (4) ~ (8), the fuzzy judgment matrix of system can be obtained in turn as follows:

$$W=\begin{bmatrix}0.5 & 0.25 & 0.75\\ 0.75 & 0.5 & 1\\ 0.25 & 0 & 0.5\end{bmatrix}$$

According to formula (9) and above fuzzy judgment matrix, the weight coefficient of each subsystem is evaluated. Then reliability of system is 0.02407 on the basis of series RBD when system continuously works for 1000 hours. Failure rate and mean time before failure of the system are 0.003727 and 268 hours respectively.

The total failure rate and mean time before failure (MTBF) of the system are 0.0009785 and 1022 hours respectively by the traditional reliability method. Statistically, from 2013 to 2016, 36-time breakdowns happened in the cumulative working 11640 hours which means mean time before failure is actually 323 hours. It is obvious that the results evaluated by method in this paper are consistent with the actual situation.

6 Conclusion

Industrial network system that is integrated with machine, electricity and control system coexist various failure modes in the long running process. It is necessary to evaluate and predict industrial network system reliability during development process in order to guarantee reliability. Therefore, a multi-layer reliability method were introduced based on RBD and AHP in this paper. In the proposed method the different influences of units on system reliability are considered. It is convenient to recognize the weak link and optimize the system reliability during design phase for engineers by using the proposed method. Through the case analysis, it shows that the method is more reasonable than the traditional reliability analysis method, and the reliability prediction result is consistent with the engineering practice.

Reference

1. X Wen, Y Shi, Z Niu. Electron. Prod. Relia. Environ. Test, **3**(2005):57-62
2. T Zhang, B Guo, Y Tan, et al. J. Syst. Eng. Electron, **27**(2005):446-448,470
3. H Yu, X Chen. J. Inst. Command. Tech. Equip, **13**(2002):37-41
4. X Hu, H Zhang, N Lin, et al. Electron. Mech. Eng, **30**(2014):22-26
5. X Qin, Z Chen. Comput. Eng, **31**(2005):33-35
6. J Cao, C Wei. J. Syst. Simul, **22**(2010):239-242
7. J Dou, W Chen, Z Zhong. J. Syst. Eng. Electron, **33**(2011):954-957
8. Z Chen, H Qi, J Wei, et al. J. Eng. Des, **18**(2011):407-411
9. J Wu, S Yan, L Xie. J. Tsinghua University, **52**(2012):15-20
10. X Sun, W Li, Z Chen. J. Shanghai Jiaotong University, **45**(2011):277-283
11. P Yan, A Che, X Tang. Comput. Integr. Manuf, **18**(2012):332-336
12. Z Peng, W Sun, *Fuzzy mathematics and its application - second edition* (2007)
13. S Zeng, *Reliability Design and Analysis*(2011)

Combining Theorem Proving and Model Checking in the Safety-Critical Software Development through Translating Event-B to SMV

Liang Sen [1,a], Luo Xiangyu[1, 2] and Chen Zuxi [1]

[1]*College of Computer Science and Technology, Huaqiao University, Xiamen, China*
[2]*Guangxi Key Laboratory of Trusted Software, Guilin University of Electronic Technology, Guilin, China*

Abstract. Model checking and theorem proving are two key vertification techniques in the formal method, but each has its advantages and disadvantages. In this paper, we first try to present the general model transformation rules from Event-B to SMV in order to realize complementary advantages, and then design the model converter of Event-B to SMV according to the rules. ProB is the only tool to implement Event-B model checking, but it lacks the real-time property verification, while nuXmv is able to verify temporal logic formulas with the real-time property for SMV models. After completing the model transformation, we use ProB and nuXmv to make the verification of LTL and CTL formulas for two equivalent models respectively. Compared to the experimental results, in solving the same problem, nuXmv has more advantages over memory consumption, time efficiency and so on than ProB, especially when the formula to be verified is very complex. Therefore, if complex verifications of system models need to be performed, it is necessary to implement the model transformation between Event-B and SMV by using our translation rules, which is of great significance for the development, design and verification of safety-critical system softwares.

1 Introduction

Formal verification method can be divided into two broad categories: model checking and theorem proving. The advantage of model checking is that it can be automated and provide counterexample paths when a specification is discovered to be false; the disadvantage is that if the system has a high degree of concurrency, there exists a state explosion problem, moreover it generally can not verify the system with infinite states. Theorem proving uses mathematical reasoning and logic inference to prove the system correctness. Its advantage is that the model to be proved is independent of system states, so it has the ability to verify the system with infinite states; the disadvantage is that this approach is generally not fully automated and requires manual interaction.

SMV (Symbolic Model Verifier) is the first model checker based on BDDs (Binary Decision Diagrams), which uses the BDD to alleviate the state explosion problem, thereby implement the symbol model checking technology [1]. For the verification of concurrent systems with finite states, it first needs to use the SMV specification language to model the system, then, the transition system described by BDDs is extracted from the model, part properties of the system is expressed in CTL (Computation Tree Logic). Finally, the search algorithm based BDDs is used to identify whether the system satisfies verified properties. If a finite state system has a given property, the True is output, else the False is output, SMV also shows counterexamples of the specification the system does not meet. SMV was originally used only to check whether a finite state system satisfies the CTL formula.

The currently widely used NuSMV [2] is the reconstruction and extension of SMV, NuSMV supports all specifications described by the CTL and LTL (Linear Temporal Logic). In addition, it integrates bounded model checking technique based on SAT. The latest version of nuXmv [3] extends from NuSMV. nuXmv is a new symbolic model checking tool that can analyze synchronous finite and infinite state systems. For the case of finite state, nuXmv is an efficient verification engine based on SAT algorithm. For the case of infinite state, it is based on SMT verification technology, tightly integrated with MathSAT5. We choose nuXmv to complete the experimental part of this paper.

B method [4] is a verification method based on theorem proving proposed on the basis of VDM and Z language. The B# method was first proposed, based on which it was created as Event-B [5]. Compared to the traditional B method, introducing event is the new feature of Event-B. The event indicates that actions are completed by triggering a state. Therefore, it is well suited for modeling periodic behavior. Event-B also

[a] Corresponding author: liangsen@hqu.edu.cn

covers the entire development cycle of software from modeling, refinement and automatic verification to code generation, so it is applicable to complex software development.

Event-B reduces the modeling difficulty by the idea of preliminary abstract modeling and layer by layer refinement. Moreover, Event-B uses the proof obligations generated by axioms and theorems to ensure the consistency among different layers. It indicates the model meets software requirements through the fully proved obligations, but it can not verify specific model properties. While SMV is suitable for system property verification, and counterexamples can be generated to adjust the model, it is difficult to make a perfect SMV model for a complex system at once, whether the model is good or bad can not be proved.

Compared with the SMV language, the Even-B modeling language is more concise and easy to understand, but it is limited to model discrete systems, and can not describe system real-time properties. Both the current version of NuSMV and nuXmv support the description and verfication of real-time systems. Combining model checking and theorem proving is a recent important trend of formal verification[6-8], however, the existing work focuses on the state explosion problem and seldom considers the complementarity of the two technologies in software engineering practice. Therefore, a practical scheme is proposed in this paper, which combines model checking and theorem proving for software development.

2 Model Structure Analysis

The formal Event-B model is based on first-order logic and typed set-theory [9], which is mainly used to describe the relationship among system components. Relatively speaking, SMV model has its own SMV input language. They are very different in terms of system modeling, but the two essentially describe the state transition of discrete systems. ProB is the only tool currently available for Event-B model checking, it is originally designed to verify program specifications written in the B language. ProB uses SICStus Prolog to execute model checking in a constrained logic programming (CLP) environment [10-11]. Because Event-B and B are similar in many ways, Event-B model checking is also supported now. In addition, it can be combined with B-Motion Studio [12] tools to realize the visual simulation and other functions in the software design process.

2.1 Event-B model structure

The core concept of Event-B formalization method is the model, a typical Event-B model contains a context that describes static system properties and an abstract machine that describes dynamic system behaviors, context and machine organize model elements into the basic model architecture [5]. Abstract machine and context have the following relationship: an abstract machine can be refined by another machine, and a context can be extended by another context, also, a machine can see a number of contexts. The relationship between machine and context is described in Figure1.

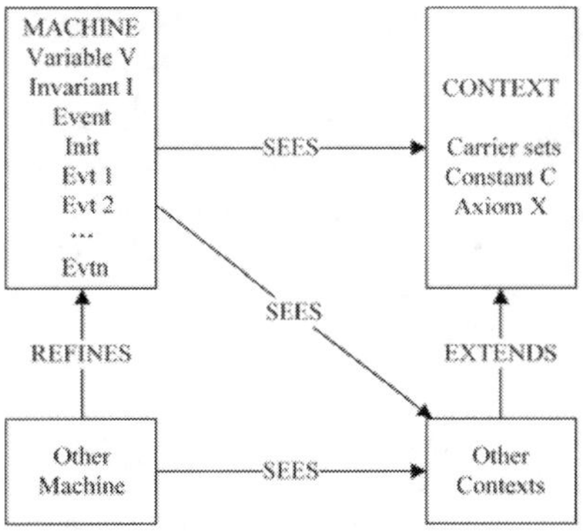

Figure 1. the relationship between machine and context

The main model elements in the context include constant, set, axiom, and theorem. constants set and constants describe the static and intrinsic attributes for the system. Axioms specify the types, attributes, and relations of constants in the form of predicate formulas, which are used as fundamental assumptions in proof obligations. Theorems contain important inferences from axioms, which is the important basis for proof obligations. It ensures the correctness of axioms and eliminates the ambiguity.

Abstract machine contains the following main elements: variable, event, invariant and theorem. Variables are used to describe system states, all dynamic system properties can be characterized by variables. Events are used to describe changes for dynamic system properties and state transitions. The function of theorems of the abstract machine is analogous to theorems of the context. Before theorems are proved, axioms and theorems in the seen context, invariants of a refined machine and the current machine have been proved.

Event has three definations, as shown in Table 1. In definition 3, the any statement defines the parameter t in event, the where statement is used to introduce the guard of event, the guard condition is the triggering condition for event, which exists in the form of predicate formula. The event is allowed to be triggered only when the guard condition is true, that is, when the constraint G (v) is satisfied, the action S (v) is executed under the then statement, where v is the system variable. S (v) may contain one or more different actions, actions describe the evolution of state variables when event is triggered. Guard conditions contain attribute restrictions for parameters, if there are no parameters in the event, the where statement is reduced to the when statement in defination 2. In definition 1, an event without parameter is used to describe the initialization event.

Table 1. Definition of event

Three possible definations for an event
Defination1: E = begin S(v) end
Defination 2: E = when G(v) then S(v) end
Defination 3: E = any t where G(t,v) then S(t,v) end

2.2 SMV model structure

SMV model is used to describe Kripke structure and specification to be verified. The Kripke structure is often called the Finite State Machine (FSM) in the SMV. The corresponding SMV program can be used as the input language for nuXmv, the SMV program is composed of modules. A module consists of name and definition, and the module definition is composed of parameters and the main body. The main body of a module is divided into three categories: Variable section, Constraint section and Specification section. The Variable section describes the state set, the Constraint section describes the transition relationships and some restrictions of the model, the Specification section describes the properties to be verified. SMV program must have at least one main module, and the main module has no formal parameter. Multiple modules can be used to describe the FSM, and then combined into a whole FSM, a typical SMV program structure is as follows:

```
MODULE main
VAR…
ASSIGN…
SPEC (or LTLSPEC,CTLSPEC)
…
MODULE…
```

There are two main categories in the Variable section: State Variable (state assignment indicates a specific state) and Input Varible (state represented by labeled relationships), they are represented by the keyword VAR or IVAR, respectively. The Variable type can be boolean, integer and enum, etc. The Constraint type can be assign, trans, init, invar and fairness, etc., respectively, using keywords ASSIGN, TRANS, INIT, INVAR, FAIRNESS as declarations. The Specification section uses the SPEC, LTLSPEC and CTLSPEC as keyword declarations, using CTL and LTL as specific property description.

3 Translation rules

After introducing composition structures of the two models, we propose a combination of Event-B theorem proving and SMV symbolic model checking for the safety-critical software development. The software model is constantly modified and perfected by formal verification technologies, the framework is shown in Figure 2.

The Event-B model design and proof obligation to be proved can be implemented by Rodin platform [13]. Rodin is a tool platform based on the Ecplise framework, which extends the advantages of open source feature and plugin scalability. With rich plugin support system, it can complete visual modeling, graphic simulation, automatic proof, model checking and so on. Models in Rodin will generate a variety of record files in the form of XML

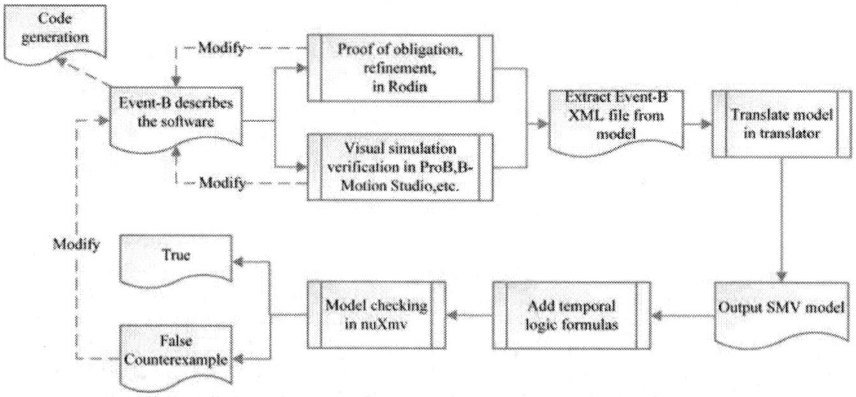

Figure 2. Development framework of safety-critical softwares

syntax, the file format includes bcc, bcm, bpo, etc. The bcc file is used to record the machine, and the bcm file is used to record the context. ProB can be used as a plugin for Rodin to support Event-B, and the implementation principle is to extract file whose suffix is .eventb from the Event-B model. It can also make model checking by the .eventb file directly in the command line version of ProB. After refinement and verification by Rodin and ProB, we can get the Event-B XML file directly from record files, the basic structure of the Event-B XML file is as follows:

```
<org.eventb.core.scMachineFile...>
    <org.eventb.core.seesContext.../>
    <org.eventb.core.scInternalContext >
    <org.eventb.core.scAxiom.../>
    <org.eventb.core.scConstant.../>
    <org.eventb.core.scInvariant.../>
    <org.eventb.core.scVariable.../>
    <org.eventb.core.scEvent>
    ...
    </org.eventb.core.scEvent/>...
</org.eventb.core.scMachineFile/>
```

Firstly we present the model translation rules of Event-B to SMV, then design a converter. The converter reads various components of Event-B model from the XML file and outputs SMV model, then we can add the verified model properties to implement model checking in nvXmv.

 DOI: 10.1051/matecconf/201712804004

3.1 Variable declaration

The process mutual exclusion as an example, B1 and B2 are the variable declaration in Event-B, and S1 is the variable declaration in SMV, the correspondence between them is shown in Figure 3. In the context description section of B1 and the machine variable declaration and definition section of B2, system property definitions are extracted. The relationships are described by sets and partitions in Event-B model, but in SMV, they are implemented by the enumeration type. For example, we can get STATE: {non_crit, wait, crit} from partition(STATE, {non_crit}, {wait}, {crit}) and proc ∈ STATE. Thereby the process proc is one of the elements in {non_crit, wait, crit}, that is, proc1: {non_crit1, wait1, crit1}; the range of integer y is 0 to 1, which is expressed as inv3 in Event-B: y ∈ 0..1, corresponding to y: 0..1 in SMV.

The two processes, proc1 and proc2 can not enter critical section at the same time, in Event-B, the invariant description inv4 :¬ (proc1 = crit1 ∧ proc2 = crit2). In SMV, the keyword INVAR is declared, then, the inv4 is equivalent to ! (proc1=crit1 & proc2=crit2).

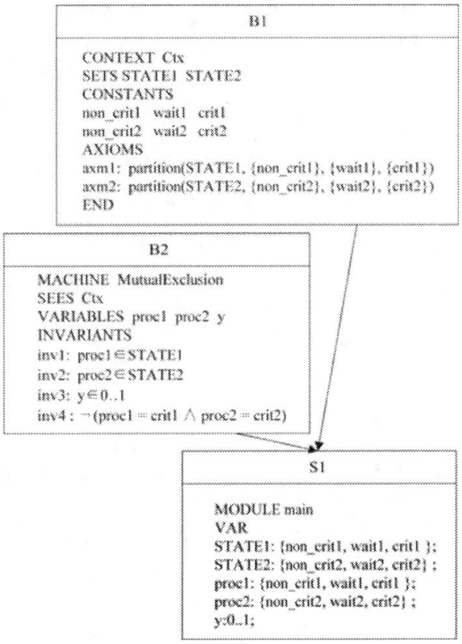

Figure 3. Correspondence between B1, B2 and S1

3.2 Variable initialization

All Event-B variables are initialized in the event INITIALISATION, as shown by B3 in Figure 4, SMV sets the initial value for each variable in the ASSIGN section: init(variable):= value, the equivalent SMV expression of B3 is shown in S2.

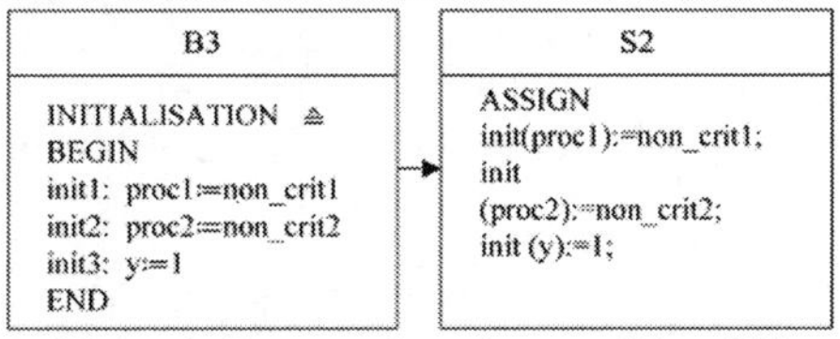

Figure 4. Correspondence between B3 and S2

3.3 State transition

For the expression of state transition, Event-B takes it as multiple Actions to be executed when the event satisfies the guard, and multiple variables may be changed in an event. For example, modeling the corresponding request event, enter event and release event for each process, the value of the mutex y also varies with process states, the details are shown as B5 and B6 in Figure 5.

The state changes of proc1 are executed in the act1 of B4, B5, and B6 respectively, meanwhile the variable y is changed in the act2 of B5, B6. In SMV, for each variable,

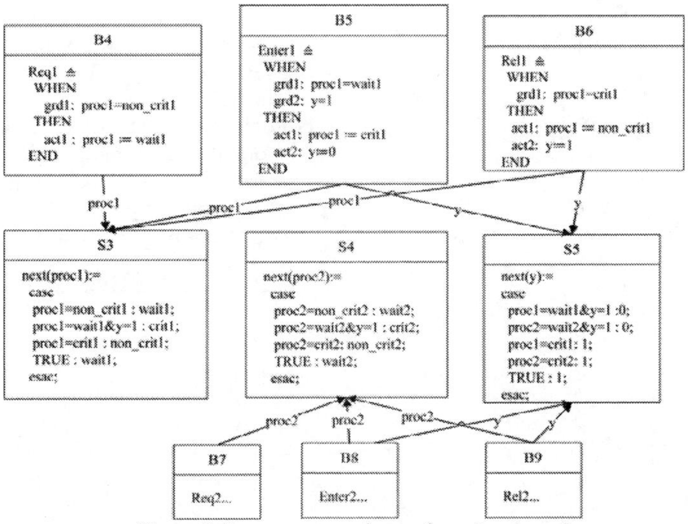

Figure 5. Event correspondence of proc1 and proc2

 DOI: 10.1051/matecconf/201712804004

the next statement describes the transitions when the precondition is satisfied, the specific format is as follows:

```
next(variable):=
    case
    cond1 : expr1;
    cond2 : expr2;
    ...
    TRUE : exprN;
  esac;
```

In Figure 5, the equivalent SMV expressions of B4, B5 and B6 of the Event-B model are presented in S3 and S5. If all conditions are not satisfied, the corresponding TRUE expression is executed in SMV. In Event-B, you can describe it directly as an event without any guard, that is, the guard of the when statement in the event definition 2 is null.

The operations of proc2 are the same as that of proc1, as shown in Figure 5, the request event, enter event and release event of proc2 correspond to B7, B8 and B9, respectively.

In addition, there is another expression of conditional choice in SMV:

```
cond_expr ? basic_expr1 : basic_expr2;
```

which is equivalent to:

```
case cond1 : expr1; TRUE : expr2; esac.
```

3.4 Basic symbol correspondence

In the basic symbolic expression, there exist intersections between Event-B and SMV. The following are semantically equivalent symbols, some are just different forms, summarized as follows in Table 2.

Table 2 Basic symbol correspondence table

Event-B	SMV
a U b	a union b
a⊄b	(a in b)&(a!=b)=FALSE
a⊈b	(a in b)=FALSE
a∈b	b:{a}
a⇔b	a<->b
a⇒b	a->b
a∧b	a&b
∀ a	A a
∃ a	E a
a≠b	a!=b
a≤b	a<=b
a≥b	a>=b
⊂	(a in b)&(a!=b)
⊆	a in b
a..b	a..b
a+b	a+b
a−b	a−b
a*b	a*b
a÷b	a÷b
a:=b	a:=b
a∉b	a is not in the enumeration of b
a∈ℕ1	a>0
a∈ℕ	a>=0
ℤ	integer
BOOL	boolean
a∨b	a | b
¬a	!a
T	TRUE
⊥	FALSE

4 Experimental comparison

At present, the model checking for Event-B model is implemented by ProB. After the model translation, we can choose nuXmv to make various temporal property verifications. ProB and nuXmv have almost common temporal logic operators of property description. In the LTL, they all support: X, G, F, U, R (V), Y, H, O, S, T, the expression about 'release' has same meaning and different keyword, that is, 'R' in ProB, 'V' in SMV. In addition, SMV has 'Z' expression, and 'Z' is basically the same as 'Y' expression. For the syntax and semantic explanations for these temporal operators, please refer to the nuXmv manual [14] or the ProB manual [15]. In the CTL, ProB supports only the verification for operator AX, EX, AF, EF, AG, EG. In addition to supporting the above CTL formula, nuXmv also supports A [p U q], E [p U q] (p and q are sub-formula). Moreover, important difference between them is that nuXmv also support the verification for real-time property, such as:

EBF m..n p, requires that there exists a path starting from a state, such that property p holds in a future time instant i, with $m \leq i \leq n$;

A [p BU m..n q], requires that for all paths starting from a state, property q holds in a future time instant i, with $m \leq i \leq n$, and property p holds in all future time instants j, with $m \leq j < i$;

Similarly, ABF m..n p, EBG m..n p, ABG m..n p, A [p BU m..n q], etc.

To sum up, the nuXmv expression is more powerful in the temporal logic expression of model checking. We still use the process mutex exclusion as a example, then select randomly 6 groups of LTL and CTL formulas to compare the performance in ProB and nuXmv. In terms of formula expression, there is a slight difference between them. In each group, the former is the formula supported by ProB, and the latter is the equivalent SMV formula.

Formula1: not{proc1 = crit1 & proc2 = crit2 ⇔ !(proc1 = crit1 & proc2 = crit2).

Formula2: XXXY{proc1 = crit1} ⇔ X(X(X(Y(proc1 = crit1)))).

Formula3: AG({proc1 = wait1} => {proc1 = crit1}) ⇔ AG(proc1 = wait1 -> proc1 = crit1).

Formula4: G({proc1 = crit1} R {proc2 = crit2}) ⇔ G(proc1 = crit1 V proc2 = crit2).

Formula5: F({proc1 = wait1} U {proc1 = crit1} ⇔ F(proc1 = wait1 U proc1 = crit1).

Formula6: EF{proc1=crit1 & proc2 = crit2 & y = 0} ⇔ EF(proc1=crit1 & proc2 = crit2 & y = 0).

The experimental results of ProB and nuXmv are shown respectively in Table 3 and table 4:

Table 3 Model checking results of ProB

Temporal formula	Memory usage(MB)	Total verification time(seconds)
Formula1	1.154	7.216
Formula2	1.796	7.449
Formula3	140.790	7.640
Formula4	1.540	7.373
Formula5	1.540	7.508
Formula6	140.775	7.520

Table 4 Model checking results of nuXmv

Temporal formula	Memory usage(MB)	Total verification time(seconds)
Formula1	8.556	0.074
Formula2	8.556	0.075
Formula3	8.556	0.064
Formula4	8.556	0.080
Formula5	8.556	0.072
Formula6	8.556	0.064

Experimental results show that, in memory consumption, nuXmv's memory occupancy is always maintained at 8.556MB, the reason is easy to find, NuXmv uses BDDs to describe state transitions, then the number of nodes of BDDs remains unchanged, thus, the memory occupancy is maintained in a stable state. ProB's memory consumption is related to formula complexity, which is consistent with the principle of model checking in the CLP environment. In terms of time consumption, nuXmv has an overwhelming advantage over ProB, the time that ProB returns verification results is rather slow. In addition, we have made lots of experimental comparisons by using various examples, then the analysis results are consistent with the above.

5 Conclusion

Model translation of Event-B to SMV combines theorem proving and symbolic model checking technique. The method not only uses the strict mathematical formula of theorem proving to guarantee systems meet the design requirements, but also takes advantage of the automated features of model checking tool and counterexample generation for error specifications. As a result, bugs or errors during the software model designment can be modified as soon as possible. The verified model is also refined and simulated by Event-B method, and then the correct software source code is generated directly, which is of great importance to the design and implementation for safety-critical softwares.

The Event-B model also includes complex functional relation, such as Total injection(↣), partial injection (⤔), total surjection (↠), etc. Direct conversion is not possible for these functional relations, thereby, for the complex system model described by Event-B, the modeler needs to modify the transformed SMV model according to the actual situation in the problem, making it more realistic. Our future work is to modify our conversion algorithm based on more instances to maximize the conversion for the two models, then reduce the workload of software design and verification process. While ensuring the reliability, correctness and security of softwares, it also greatly improves the development efficiency.

References

1. K. L. Mcmillan, Symbolic Model Checking, **38**, 161-165(1992).
2. A. Cimatti, E. Clarke, F. Giunchiglia, M. Roveri, Computer Aided Verification, **1633**, 495-499(1999).
3. R. Cavada, A. Cimatti, M. Dorigatti, A. Griggio, A.Mariotti, Computer Aided Verification, **8559**, 334-342(2014).
4. J. R. Abrial, *The B-book*(1996).
5. J. R. Abrial, *Modelling in Event-B: System and Software Engineering*(2010).
6. V. Pantelic, British Journal of Radiology, **42**, 278-280(2005).
7. K. Arkoudas, S. Khurshi, D. Marinov, M, Rinard, Lecture Notes in Computer Science, **3051**, 21-33(2003).
8. N. Shankar, Proceedings of 11th International Conference on Concurrency Theory, **1877**, 1-16(2000).
9. J. Poll, Conference of the South African Institute of Computer Scientists and Information Technologists on IT research in developing countries(2008).
10. M. Leuschel, M. Butler, International Symposium of Formal Methods Europe, 2805 ,855-874(2003).
11. M. Leuschel, M. Butler, International Journal on Software Tools for Technology Transfer, **10**, 185-203(2008).
12. L. Ladenberger, J. Bendisposto, M. Leuschel, Formal Methods for Industrial Critical Systems, 14th International Workshop (2009).
13. J. R. Abrial, M. Butler, S. Hallerstede, T. S. Hoang, F. Mehta, International Journal on Software Tools for Technology Transfer, 12, 447-466(2010).
14. nuXmv 1.1.1 User Manual, R. Cavada(2014).
15. ProB User Manual, M. Leuschel(2017).

A Practical J2EE Application Static Analysis Method Based Upon Taint Propagation

JianJun Hu[a], Qiaoyan Wen[b], DaiFei Guo[c]

State Key Laboratory of Networking and Switching Technology, Beijing University of Posts and Telecommunications, Beijing, 100876, China
Siemens Ltd., China

Abstract. Currently security audit/review for binaries is an upcoming method used to detect security vulnerabilities. In this paper we describe an efficient security audit method based on the java binaries. This method can The method in this invention can greatly reduce false positives and provides an efficient solution for automated secure auditing on binaries by only checking the exploitable security flows, especially for the scenarios which source codes are not available.

1 Introduction

Combined with java and web technology, J2EE Web applications are widely deployed in many large enterprises. These applications provide online support for enterprise business process, e-commerce activities, and information security is a crucial requirement.

According to OWASP[1] top ten and CVE[2] statistics, "Input Validation" is one of the most severe and pervasive security problems in web applications. Many famous security vulnerabilities, such as "SQL injection", "Cross-Site Scripting", "Path Traversal", "Command Injection", are caused by inefficient input validation.

For example, if programmer want to launch an operating system command, they should prepare the command string and call function exec() with the string as input. However, the command string may be controlled by the malicious user to run any OS commands, such as delete a file or open a port, etc. This kind of security vulnerability is named as "Command Injection".

There are two common approaches to address web application security issues, runtime scanning and static code review.

Runtime scanning based on web scanners [3] try to enumerate all the application data entrance point, feed them with multiple attack strings and analyze the response of the application for hints of security vulnerabilities [5]. It has several shortcomings:

-If the applications are complicated, it is hard to enumerate all the data entrance point, either by automatic crawling or manual inspection.

-Applications may have customized error message, or the inherent logic is not simply "fetch-and-show". Therefore, a lot of application vulnerabilities cannot be identified simply by request-and-response.

-If applications implement filtering mechanism that needs special crafted attack vectors to bypass, scanner cannot craft special attack vector and detect the possible vulnerabilities [5].

-The efficiency is low. Many commercial web application security scanners maintain a large database of attack vectors and try all these vectors one by one on all the data entrance points.

-The scanning may be dangerous, since scanner will test all the data entrance point, some of them may damage the application data.

Code review [6] has many advantages over the runtime scanning. All the data entrance point can be checked, the inherent application logic and filtering mechanism is recognized, and the checking process is absolutely safe [7]. However, there are several considerations about the code review:

-The efficiency: There are many kinds of security vulnerabilities and if the application is complicated, pure manual inspection is very inefficient.

-The intellectual property: The source code is intellectual property of software providers and customers always cannot get the source code to perform code review checks.

-Version problem, sometimes the source codes don't match the deployed program because of bad version management.

In this paper we propose a new approach to review based on the binaries. The review can be done with the help of automatic tools thus enhance the efficiency. Also the review is based upon the complied code, instead of source code, so there is no problem about the intellectual property.

2 Overview

The basic idea is very simple: we maintain a database of all the dangerous functions of java fundamental libraries, and

[a]hujianjun@bupt.edu.cn, [b]wqy@bupt.edu.cn, [c]Daifei.Guo@siemens.com

check whether the input of these functions can be tainted by user input.

2.1 Taint propagation introduction

Suppose we have a sample java servlet code as following:

```
private void list (HttpServletRequest request,
HttpServletResponse response)
{
  String user = request.getParameter("user");
  String password =
request.getParameter("password");
  try{
       String query = "SELECT Username, UserID,
Password
                                        FROM Users
WHERE
                    username ="" + user + "' AND
                    password ="" + password + "'";
       stmt.executeQuery(query);
  }
  ...
}
```

An experienced programmer may find the SQL injection vulnerability in the above code. The taint propagation in the above code can be illustrated in Figure 2.1:

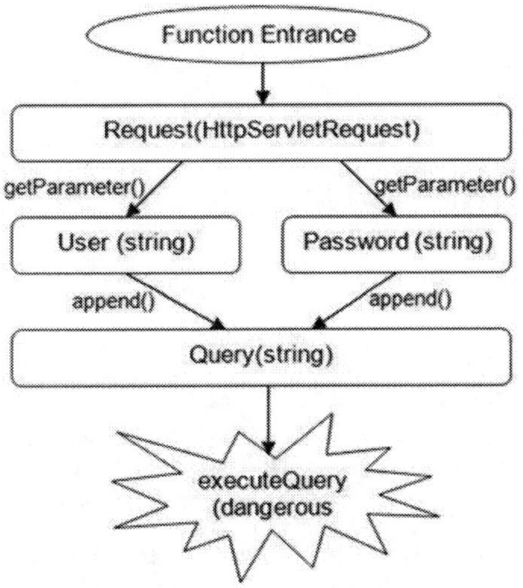

Figure 2.1 SQL injection control path

The "query" is a string variable. It is concatenated with two string variable, "user" and "password", which in turn comes from the result of calling sub-routine "request.getParameter()". Note that java language will compile string concatenation as append(). Byte code analysis will only see this function instead of concatenation. **Figure 2.2** illustrates the process of Taint Propagation.

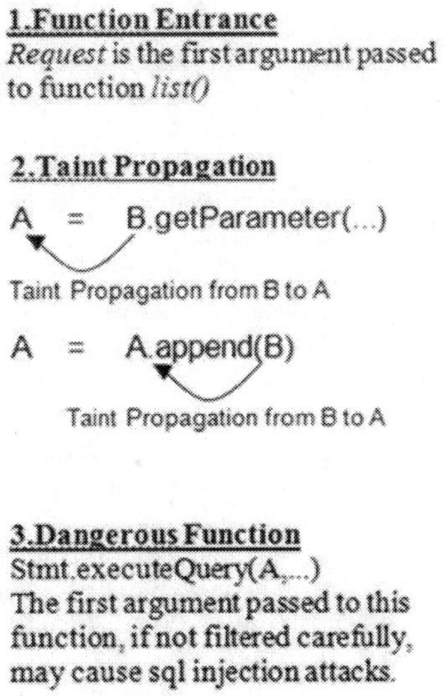

Figure 2.2 Taint Propagation process

3 Procedure

The taint propagation analysis in single function involves three key steps:

3.1 Function entrance

At the entrance of each function, we recode all the arguments with their order and type. For example, request is the first argument, of type "class HttpServletRequest".

Since java is strong typed language, if the argument type is long, int, double, etc, attacker can't inject any malicious content, so we record these arguments as UNTAINTABLE. We record other typed arguments as TAINTED.

For the entire local variable declared in the function body, we will record them as UNTAINTED. For the type of long, int, double, we will record them as UNTAINTABLE.

Now we have a table of all the variables to facilitate the following analysis, and we use a value to record the state of each variable.

Value	Meaning
-1	Untaintable
0	Untainted
1	Tainted by the first argument of the function
2	Tainted by the second argument of the function
4	Tainted by the third argument of the function
8	Tainted by the fourth argument of the function
...	...

3.2 Taint propagation

For each java byte code, we will inspect the effect of taint propagation. Since java byte code is formal language intended to be interpreted by JVM, it can easily been interpreted by our programs.

For example, declare a constant string will be compiled as LDC, when our program met with LDC, we will add a string variables tagged as "UNTAINTED".

For each sub-routine function, we will analyze arguments of the function. The taint will be propagated between the input arguments and the output argument. The detailed steps are as follows:

1) For all the input arguments,(it may include the instance class itself, because all the non-static function in java language belongs to class instance, this instance will be treated as the first argument of the function), analyze their type, if they are not int, long, double , etc, they will be tainted by all other TAINTED input arguments.

2) Analyze the function return type, if the type is taintable, it will be tainted by all the TAINTED input arguments.

Taint propagation is simulated by bitwise OR. For example: variable A's value is 4 and B's value is 10, after taint propagation, A and B all becomes 14, that means A and B are both tainted by the second, third and fourth argument in the function entrance.

Example 1: String A = A.Append(String B), This function will be compiled as String A = Append(String A, String B) .

(A, B) Before the call	(A, B) After the call
(1,0)	(1,1)
(0,0)	(0,0)
(4,1)	(5,5)

Example 2: long A = Func (String B, int C, class D)

(A, B, C, D) Before the call	(A,B,C,D) After the call
(-1,1,-1,0)	(-1,1,-1,1)
(-1,0,-1,4)	(-1,4,-1,4)
(-1,4,-1,2)	(-1,6,-1,6)

Since every function has specific inherent logic, the output may be tainted by only one of the input argument and often there is no propagation among different input arguments. We need to build the "diffusion mode" of each function to reduce the false positives and make the analysis more accurate. The "diffusion mode" can be built by firstly define all the "diffusion mode" of basic java functions, and then make diffusion analysis of the whole applications.

3.3 Dangerous Function

After the taint propagation, we will check all the sub-routine function, and check whether there is any dangerous function.

We will maintain a dangerous function list, for example:

```
<pattern>
  <className>java.sql.Statement</className>
  <methodName>executeUpdate</methodName>
  <signature>.</signature>
  <vulnParamIndex>2</vulnParamIndex>
  <category>SQL_INJECTION</category>
  <rootcause>.</rootcause>
</pattern>
<pattern>
  <className>java.sql.Statement</className>
  <methodName>executeQuery</methodName>

  <signature>(Ljava/lang/String;)Ljava/sql/ResultSet;</
signature>
  <vulnParamIndex>2</vulnParamIndex>
  <category>SQL_INJECTION</category>
  <rootcause>.</rootcause>
</pattern>
```

"VulnParamIndex" stands for the position of argument, that if tainted by user input, will cause security problems. "className", "methodName" and "signature" are used to match the exact function. Many functions have multiple form of argument list declaration, so we simply use "." to match all of them.

In the example above, the executeQuery is a dangerous function, if the second argument is tainted, we will record this as a finding.

We can extend our signature database with other famous third party libraries. For example, for the famous ORM library hibernate2, we have the following signatures:

No	Dangerous Function	Argument Position
1	Net.sf.hibernate.Session.delete	1
2	Net.sf.hibernate.Session.iterate	1
3	Net.sf.hibernate.Session.find	1
4	Net.sf.hibernate.Session.createQuery	1
5	Net.sf.hibernate.Session.createSQLQuery	1

Also user can define their customized dangerous functions.

3.4 Taint propagation in multiple functions

Large application always has layered architecture, complex dataflow and well encapsulation. The main body of the application may only call the encapsulating function without calling dangerous function in our predefined database directly. So the analysis result of each function must be correlated together to construct the full attack path. For example:

```
Func1(String call1arg1, String call1arg2){
  ...
  Func2(o, m, call1arg1 + call1arg2, n);
}
Func2(String call2arg1, int call2arg2, String call2arg3, int
call2arg4){
  ...
  Func3(call2arg3);
}
Func3(String call3arg1){
  ...
  Stmt.executeQuery(call3arg1);
}
```

DOI: 10.1051/matecconf/201712804005

The Func2 encapsulating Func3, which encapsulating dangerous function executeQuery(). If all the other code only call Func2 without direct calling stmt.executeQuery, such as Func1, and the argument call1arg1 can be tainted by user inputs, we may fail to recognize Func1 as a security violation.

The solution is simple: we will analyze the application recursively and populate our dynamic list of dangerous function.

For the example code before, the check process is as follows:

1) The first run, it finds Func3 with vulnerable argument 1, and adds Func3 to dangerous function list;

2) After the first run, the list is dirty and updated, so it needs to run again and recheck the application.

3) The second run, it finds Func2 with vulnerable argument 3, and adds Func2 to dangerous function list;

4) After the second run, the list is dirty and updated, so it needs to run again.

5) The third run, it finds Func1 with the vulnerable argument 1 and 2, and adds Func1 to dangerous function list;

6) …

7) The list is not dirty, the check is finished.

8) From the list, the full attack path is constructed, that is Func3 Func2 Func1.

Note that Func1, Func2, Func3 does not necessarily need to be in the same java class.

By above solution, we provide a practical and effective method to detect these possible vulnerabilities in J2EE web applications. It has been implemented as an independent application. It successfully finds all the vulnerabilities detected by manual inspection, and with great efficiency.

4 Conclusion

The method described in this paper can greatly reduce false positives and provides an efficient solution for automated secure auditing on binaries by only checking the exploitable security flows. And it greatly improves the efficiency of code review process.

Since it will simulate the data flow and function calling network, it is theoretically zero false negative. We have tested it on several realworld applications, and it successfully covers all the vulnerabilities found by other means. This solution also has the advantages such as no need for source codes, and it will construct the full attack path for the identified vulnerabilities.

Acknowledgements

We are grateful to a number of readers whose comments have substantially improved the paper, and the anonymous reviewers. Thanks especially to Beijing university of Posts and Telecommunications and Siemens Ltd., China.

References

1. OWASP: The Open Web Application Security Project, https://www.owasp.org/index.php/Category:OWASP_Top_Ten_Project
2. CVE: Common Vulnerabilities and Exposures, https://cve.mitre.org/.
3. Elizabeth Fong, Vadim Okun, "Web Application Scanners: Definitions and Functions", hawaii international conference on system sciences, 2007
4. Marco Vieira, Nuno Antunes, Henrique Madeira, "Using web security scanners to detect vulnerabilities in web services", dependable systems and networks, 2009
5. Nidal Khoury, Pavol Zavarsky, Dale Lindskog, Ron Ruhl, "An Analysis of Black-Box Web Application Security Scanners against Stored SQL Injection", international conference on social computing, 2012
6. Tor Stalhane, Cat Kutay, Hiyam Alkilidar, Ross Jeffery, "Teaching the process of code review", australian software engineering conference, 2004
7. Panagiotis Louridas, "Static code analysis", IEEE Software, page 58-61, 2006

MATEC Web of Conferences 128, 04006 (2017) DOI: 10.1051/matecconf/201712804006
EITCE 2017

Investigation and Analysis on the Construction Situation of "Three Links and Two Platforms" of Education for Nationalities in Yunnan Province in China

Zhao Zhilin[1], Gan Jianhou[2,a]

[1]*College of Tourism and Geographical Sciences and College of Adult Education, Yunnan Normal University, Kunming, Yunnan, China*
[2]*Key Laboratory of Educational Informatization for Nationalities, Yunnan Normal University, Kunming, Yunnan, China*

Abstract. "Three Links and Two Platforms", which refers to schools links to ICTs, high-quality resource of class links to ICTs, people links to ICTs, public service platform for educational resources and public service platform for educational management, has played a crucial role in improving the educational equality in minority areas in Yunnan province and in realizing the sharing of high-quality educational resources. This research mainly adopts method of document investigation, which has investigated the construction situation of "Three Links and Two Platforms" in eight ethnic autonomous prefectures in Yunnan province in China including Chuxiong Yi Nationality Autonomous Prefecture, etc. The results show that the average value of the construction of "Three Links" is 63.55%、14.75% and 9.00% respectively. "Two Platforms" mainly focus on public service platform for educational resources and public service platform for the construction of educational statistics, and the informatization of national education in Yunnan province should be improved greatly.

1 Introduction

In 2012, Conference on National Educational Informatization presented that in the period of "the 12th Five-Year Plan", we should focus on the construction of "Three Links and Two Platforms", accelerating the educational informatization and improving the educational development in rural areas as well as remote and border areas. "Three Links"refers to Campus Links to ICTs (Information and Communication Technologies), high-quality resource of Class Links to ICTs, People Links to ICTs, and "Two Platforms" refers to public service platform for educational resources and public service platform for educational management. "Three Links and Two Platforms", the important content of China's National Educational Informatization Plan (2011-2020), has played active role in reforming and optimizing classroom teaching methods, increasing quality and efficiency of education and teaching, improving educational equality and accelerating educational modernization.

Located in frontier region of southwest in China, with complex terrain and a number of ethnic groups, the development of economy and education of Yunnan province is relatively slow. "Three Links and Two Platforms" has played a unique and important role in promoting educational equality in ethnic areas in Yunnan province and realizing wide sharing of high-quality educational resources, improving nationalities education quality and building learning-oriented society, promoting the reform of nationalities education concept and cultivating innovative talents. It is also the motivation and support of the accomplishment of the modernization of nationalities education in Yunnan province. Therefore, Yunnan province put the equipment of education informatization into supervision and evaluation index system for education research of County-level People's Government and put the construction and equipment situation of "three links two platform" into the key content of evaluating governments' resumptions. In particular, Yunnan province requires all ethnic autonomous prefectures to take full advantage of modern information technology, and pay attention to the deep integration of information technology and education. According to Three-year Plan for Informatization of Basic Education in Yunnan Province (2013-2015), until 2015, Yunnan province would have network teaching and learning environment, network learning spaces would cover all kinds of education and the high-quality educational resources would benefit to all minorities.

This research mainly focuses on the investigation of the construction situation of "Three Links and Two Platforms" in minority areas in Yunnan province in China. The result is not only helpful for Electrification Center of Yunnan Province to formulate educational resources construction program in minority areas, but also provide research references to accelerating the overall development of education in minority areas in Yunnan province.

2 Research objects and methods

2.1 Research objects

[a] Corresponding author: 1318581165@qq.com; cjyzhaozhilin@163.com

Sixth census in Yunnan province shows that in the actual registered populations, minorities has a population of 15.337 million, accounting for 33.37% of the total. Thus, Yunnan province always attaches great importance to the nationalities education. The minorities in Yunnan province mainly live in Chuxiong Yi Autonomous Prefecture, Honghe Hani and Yi Autonomous Prefecture, Wenshan Zhuang and Miao Autonomous Prefecture, Xishuangbanna Dai Autonomous Prefecture, Dali Bai Autonomous Prefecture, Dehong Dai and Jingpo Autonomous Prefecture, Nujiang of the Lisu Autonomous Prefecture and Diqing Tibetan Autonomous Prefecture. The total areas of these eight autonomous prefectures almost take the half of the area of Yunnan province, and the main minorities are Yi nationality, Bai nationality, Hani nationality and Dai nationality. This research mainly investigates the practical application situation of "Three Links and Two Platforms" in the education bureau of Chuxiong City, Mengzi City, Wenshan City, Jinghong City, Dali City, Mang City, Lushui County and Shangri-La City.

2.2 Research methods

This research mainly adopts method of document investigation, which has investigated the construction situation of "Three Links and Two Platforms" in those eight ethnic autonomous prefectures in Yunnan province. The contents include visiting web portal of Yunnan Electronic Education, consulting "presentation of educational informatization" during 2011-2015, acquiring basic data of educational informatization of autonomous prefectures in "the percentage of network access in school", "the percentage of network access in class", "the percentage of network access of computer room in school" and "the percentage of link between teachers".

3 Result and analysis

Informatization of basic education is the footstone of improving the information quality of students in minority areas, and the most important thing to accelerate educational informatization in minority areas in Yunnan province. Minority areas in Yunnan province need to accelerate infrastructure construction of informatization of basic education, realize the four-level educational network system between province, state (city), county (city, district) and school, increase the number of computer for each students in every one hundred students in middle and primary schools, and equip more multimedia distance learning facilities for national middle and primary schools. In order to thoroughly implement Development Plan of Educational Informatization in Yunnan Province (2013-2015) and Three-year Plan for Informatization of Basic Education in Yunnan Province (2013-2015), all autonomous prefectures in Yunnan province take the construction of "Three Links and Two Platforms" as the main task of educational information construction. For this purpose, State Bureau of Educations such as Chuxiong are strengthening management of school education information and construction of school network and focus on the construction of "Three Links and Two Platforms" of educational informatization.

3.1 Investigation and analysis of "Three Links"

According to monthly report of work progress of educational informatization of all autonomous prefectures in July 2015, educational informatization in Yunnan province is still faced with some special difficulties and prominent problems, and the gap between the overall development level and national average level still exist, as illustrated in Table 1.

Table 1. Basic Statistics of educational information construction in major minority areas in Yunnan province

Major minority areas in Yunnan province in China	The percentage of Schools links to ICTs	The percentage of class links to ICTs	The percentage of network access of computer room in school	The percentage of teachers links to ICTs
Chuxiong	83.9%	10%~20%	20%~30%	1%~10%
Honghe	40%~50%	10%~20%	30%~50%	No statistics
Wenshan	70%	25.78%	30%~50%	10%~20%
Xishuang banna	89.8%	22.2%	58.6%	1%~10%
Dali	75.09%	10%~20%	20%~30%	0
Dehong	60%	<10%	54.6%	0
Nujiang	31.6%	<10%	15%~20%	1%~10%
Diqing	53%	10%~20%	15%~20%	42%
Average	63.55%	14.75%	34.78%	9.00%

Data sources: Electrification Center of Yunnan Province; Report on the work progress of educational informatization in Yunnan province in July 2014 by Yunnan Provincial Department of Education

In order to act in the spirits of the Fifth Plenary Session of the 18th CPC Central Committee and accelerate to popularize information technology in primary and middle schools, the Ministry of Education decided to implement the project, "Schools Links to ICTs" in primary and middle schools and issued Notice on Implication of "Schools Links to ICTs" Project in Primary and Middle Schools in 2000. The goal of this project was that 90% primary and middle schools in China which are independently established can have access to the internet in 5-10 years. However, as is shown in Table 1, the proportion of "Schools Links to ICTs" (the proportion of access to campuses) in Xishuangbanna Dai Autonomous Prefecture is the highest, 89.8% and the lowest, Nujiang Lisu Autonomous Prefecture, 31.6%, which is lower than the goal of 90%. It was obvious that there were unbalanced allocation of basic resources in "Schools Links to ICTs". In the construction of high-quality resource of "Class Links to ICTs", 2922 compulsory education schools in Yunnan Province had built campus network by July 2014, accounting for 15.4% of the total number of compulsory education schools. The average value of "the proportion of access to class" in minority autonomous prefectures was 14.75%, which was equal to the overall construction situation of the high-quality resource of "Class Links to ICTs" in Yunnan Province but it is still very low. Work

Points of Education Informatization in 2015 of Ministry of Education required 50% teachers and 30% students who were at least senior high school students could have real-name network learning space and the network learning space would be applied intensively in education and teaching. At present, Yunnan Provincial Audio-Visual Education Center only counts the proportion of "People Links to ICTs" of teachers, except that the proportion in Diqing Tibetan Autonomous Prefecture basically meet the standards, and the proportion for most teachers in other autonomous prefectures is not more than 10%. Schools in Dali Bai Autonomous Prefecture and Dehong Dai and Jingpo Autonomous Prefecture haven't built the "People Links to ICTs", indicating that the construction and application of network learning space, "People Links to ICTs", in Yunnan Province has been in the initial stage.

3.2 Research analysis of "Two Platforms"

On the basis of National Public Platform of Educational Resources, Yunnan Province relies on the high-quality education resources of "Yunnan Distance Education Network", actively explores the resource sharing mechanism of "enterprises compete to offer, government assess to enter and schools self-determine to adopt", and vigorously promotes the exploration and research of teachers training, resources sharing, interactive teaching and other aspects. In 2014, Yunnan built the Yunnan Public Platform of Education Resources (YunJiao Cloud for short) so as to achieve the joint construction and sharing of Yunnan Province's quality education resources and meet the urgent needs of teachers and students in Yunnan Province toward quality education resources. In the meantime, YunJiao Cloud can effectively spread the advanced teaching ideas and methods, which helps solve the problem of "lack of teachers and few teaching materials" in many poor schools in Yunnan remote minority areas, comprehensively improve the teaching quality and promote the balanced development of education. As is shown in Table 2, according to the data of Yunnan Public Platform of Education Resources, by November 17, 2015, the total number of registration of minority autonomous prefectures is 92,957, accounting for 40.10% in the province; the total number of uploading teaching resources is 451 and the download times of resources is close to 200,000. The download times of resources in Chuxiong Yi Autonomous Prefecture ranks first in the province. According to the number of registered users, resources to be uploaded and download inYunJiao Cloud, it can be seen that the resource utilization of Yunnan minority autonomous prefectures is still in the early stage of resources sharing and the number of joint resources is very small.

Table 2. Statistics of public platforms of educational resources in Yunnan main ethnic regions

Minority areas	Number of registered users		Number of uploading resources		Number of downloading resources	
	Number	Ranking in Yunnan	Number	Ranking in Yunnan	Number	Ranking in Yunnan
Chuxiong	21,584	4	112	6	107,329	1
Honghe	22,008	3	16	13	29,386	7
Wenshan	16,333	8	93	7	12,930	12
Xishuangbanna	7,056	11	22	12	4,249	14
Dali	16,991	7	152	4	33,878	4
Dehong	5,685	13	47	10	6,654	13
Nujiang	1,129	17	7	16	2,718	16
Diqing	2,171	16	2	17	1,545	17
Total number	92,957		451		198,689	
Total number of Yunnan Province	231,818		1,416		404,697	
Proportion in Yunnan Province	40.10%		31.85%		49.10%	

Source: Yunnan Public Platform of Education Resources [EB / OL], Key Laboratory of Education Informatization for Nationalities (Yunnan Normal University), Ministry of Education, China

In China, speeding up education management informatization, well building the National Public Service Platform of Education Management and having a comprehensive command of the dynamic data of conditions for setting up schools in students, teachers and schools across the country is of great significance to improve the education service, support the scientific decision-making and strengthen the education management. The construction of Yunnan Education Data Center has made great strides and education management information system has been run smoothly since 2014, including "Management Information System for Primary and middle School Students' Status", "Students Financial Management Information System", "Vocational School Student Management Information System", "Campus Security Management Information System" and other management systems. At the same time, the minority autonomous prefectures also actively built and run their public platform of educational resources according to their situations. For example, Work Points for National Pilot Urban Construction of Information Benefiting People in Wenshan pointed out the digitization for Students' Status files management would reach 100% and the public service for education management should be finished by the end of 2016; public platform of educational resources in Honghe had already been officially launched and run and in 2013, the online management for primary and middle school students 'status had been completed in Nujiang through which the information of the primary and middle school students in Nujiang, and had been input in Management

DOI: 10.1051/matecconf/201712804006

Information System for National Primary and Middle School Students' Status and Management System of Academic Proficiency Examination in Yunnan Province.

4 Conclusions

In summary, the "Three Links and Two platforms" is the core objective and key project of the construction for national education informatization during the "Twelfth Five-Year Plan" in China. In Yunnan Province, eight ethnic autonomous prefectures have implemented the related work of "Three Links and Two Platforms". The construction and application of "Three Links" have been in the early stage. In the construction of "Two Platforms", YunJiao Cloud, as the main public platform of educational resources in Yunnan Province, has attracted more than 90,000 students from ethnic autonomous prefectures to register on, and the education resources has been downloaded nearly 20 million times. Furthermore, the public service platform of educational management should consist of three subsystems: information system for educational management, supporting system for educational decision-making and information system for education evaluation. Yunnan ethnic regions are mainly in the transition stage from information system for educational management to supporting system for educational decision-making and information system for education evaluation.

Acknowlegement

This work was supported by the National Soft Science Project of China under Grant No. 2013GXS4D149, Education Humanities and Social Sciences Research Project of Ministry of Education in China under Grant No. 12YJCZH053 and Yunnan Science and Technology Development Strategy and Policy Research Project in China under Grant No. 2014RD029.

References

1. Zhu Zhiting, Guan Jueqi. Construction Framework of "Network Learning Space: People Access to ICTs". China Educational Technology, **10,** (2013).
2. Yunnan Provincial Bureau of Statistic. Data Bulletin of Yunnan's Sixth National Census [Z].2011-05-09.
3. Yunnan Provincial Audio - Visual Education Center. Notice on the Yunnan Provincial Progress of Education Informationization of Yunnan Education in July, 2014 [Z]. 2014-07-30.
4. Yunnan Public Platform of Education Resources [EB/OL].
5. Yan Qichao, Zhou Xuehe. Education of Ethnic Minorities in Xinjiang from the Angle of Three Links & Two Platforms. China Educational Technology, **9,** (2014).
6. Wang Ane. Technological Changes Education: Research on the Construct Model of the Informatization Environment in the Border Ethnic Schools of Yunnan, Chengdu, Southwest University, (2014).
7. Zhu Jingjing. Research on Sharing Strategy of Cultural Informationization Resources between Schools and Community in Frontier Nationality Areas of Yunnan Province. Chengdu, Southwest University (2014).
8. Jiao Jianli. An Informal Talk on "Two Platforms" of "Three Accesses and Two Platforms". China Information and Technology, 11, (2013).
9. Wei Jian. The Culture, "Fusion· Harmony", Leads the Construction of Schools with Ethnic Characteristics. China Nationalities Education, **1**, (2015).
10. Chu Zhuwu, Mo Hongmei, An Analysis of Ethnic Cultural Construction in the Early Period of New China. Journal of Beijing University of Nationalities, **5,** (2012)

MATEC Web of Conferences 128, 04007 (2017) DOI: 10.1051/matecconf/201712804007
EITCE 2017

Measurement Method and Principle for Thoracic Impedance Graph

Zhao Hui, Kuang Shi-jiang[a], He Bai-qing, Wang Zi-min and Cheng Xiao-ling

Department of Electronic Engineering, Nanchang Institute of Technology, Nanchang 330044, China

Abstract. Thoracic impedance graph is an impedance change curve measured on the surface of the human chest. It reflects indirectly the volume change of the heart and large vessels in the thorax, and it includes rich information about physiological activities and pathological changes. Thoracic impedance graph is measured using the four-electrode method in this article. Thoracic impedance change is transformed to the voltage change by means of the high frequency current I_0, with a constant root-mean-square (rms) current. The voltage change which is directly proportional to thoracic impedance change can be obtained through the amplification, detection and calibration. The direct proportional relationship between the thoracic impedance change and volume change of the blood vessels is deduced by means of the thoracic parallel impedance model.

1 Introduction

Thoracic impedance graph, also known as Impedance cardiograph, is the impedance change curve measured on the chest surface. Because the thoracic impedance graph indirectly reflects the volume changes of the heart and large vessels within the thorax, thus it is closely related to the cardiovascular physiological activity and pathological changes, it carries rich information on the cardiovascular activity. The valuable measurement results for the clinical diagnosis and treatment can be obtained by using the thoracic impedance graph. It is widely used to measure the cardiac function and to monitor the hemodynamic changes clinically[1-4]. This article will discuss the measurement method and principle of thoracic impedance graph through the aspect of electricity.

2 Measurement method of the thoracic impedance graph

Thoracic impedance graph is generally measured using the four-electrode method. There are two ways for the placement of electrodes: Kubicek's four-ring electrode method and Sramek's eight-point electrode method[5-6].

2. 1 Kubicek's four-ring electrode method

As shown in Fig.1, where I_1 and I_2 are the current electrodes, E_1 and E_2 are the voltage detection electrodes, which are all thin silver-plated copper ring or disposable aluminum foil. E_1 is located at lower neck, and E_2 is located at the lower edge of the thoracic xiphoid. The inner distance between the current and voltage electrodes is greater than 3.0 cm. The high frequency current I_0, with a constant root-mean-square (rms) current, is fed into the body through I_1 and I_2, and the voltage signal between E_1 and E_2 is sent to the impedance detection circuit.

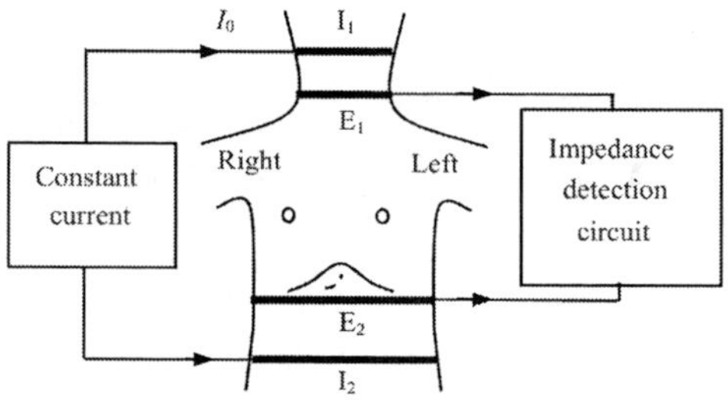

Fig.1. Kubicek's four-ring electrode method

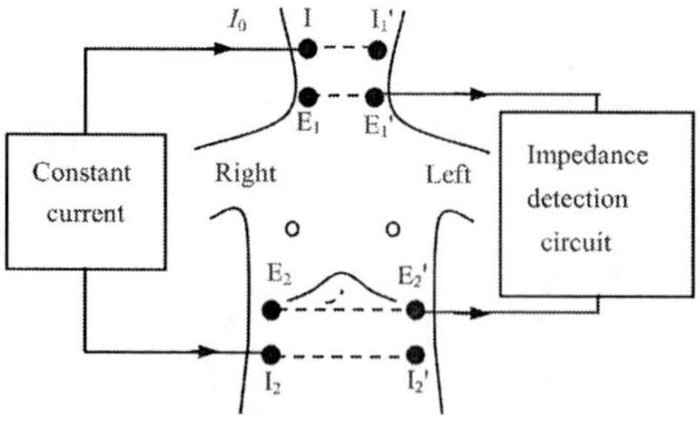

Fig.2. Sramek's eight-point electrode method

2. 2 Sramek's eight-point electrode method

From the above, we can see that the ribbon ring electrodes need to go around the neck and chest in

[a] Corresponding author: 270689016@qq.com.cn

Kubicek's method. In the case of long-term monitoring, the patient will feel uncomfortable, and it is not suitable for monitoring the chest and stomach during the surgery. Thus Sramek proposed the eight-point electrode method to measure the thoracic impedance graph, and its method of electrode placement is shown in Fig. 2.

The eight-point electrode method is actually another form of the four-electrode method. I_1, I_1', I_2, I_2' are the current electrodes, among which I_1 and I_1' are connected, and I_2 and I_2' are connected. The high frequency current I_0, with a constant root-mean-square (rms) current, is fed into the human chest through I_1, I_1', I_2, I_2'. E_1, E_1' and E_2, E_2' are the voltage detection electrodes, among which E_1 and E_1' are connected, and E_2 and E_2' are connected. These dot electrodes are disposable Ag/AgCl electrodes. Among which E_1 and E_1' are located at the lower neck, and E_2 and E_2' are located at the lower xiphoid, and E_2', I_2' and E_2, I_2 are located in the front left and right axillary position of the chest, respectively. The inner distance between the current and voltage electrodes is greater than 3.0 cm.

3 Block diagram of circuit composition of measuring the thoracic impedance graph

Fig. 3 is the block diagram of the circuit for measuring the thoracic impedance graph. It mainly includes the high frequency oscillator, constant current output circuit, four ring electrodes, high frequency amplifier, linear peak detection, low frequency amplifier and differential circuit. The high frequency current I_0 is fed into the human chest through current electrodes I_1 and I_2. The voltage signals corresponding to the basic impedance (Z_0), impedance change (ΔZ), impedance differential (dZ/dt) can be obtained, respectively, after the impedance modulation signal generated between E_1 and E_2 is processed through the high frequency amplifier, linear peak detection, low frequency amplifier and differential circuit.

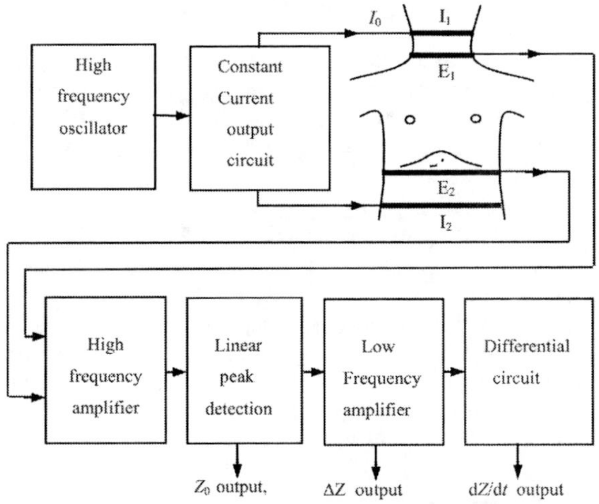

Figure 3. The block diagram of the circuit composition of measuring the thoracic impedance graph

4 Transform of the thoracic impedance change into the voltage change

The human thorax is a volume conductor which shows certain impedance towards the high frequency current, in which the constant part is the basic impedance (Z_0). The blood volume of the blood vessels in thorax will change constantly with the intermittent ejection of the heart, and a corresponding impedance change (ΔZ) will occur at the chest surface. As shown in Fig.1, when the high frequency current I_0 passes through the thorax, a high frequency voltage U is generated between the detection electrodes (E_1 and E_2), i.e.

$$U = U_0 + \Delta U \quad (3\text{-}1)$$

Where U_0 reflects the base impedance (Z_0), and ΔU reflects the impedance change (ΔZ). It is assumed that the total impedance (Z) between the detection electrodes (E_1 and E_2) can be expressed as

$$Z = Z_0 + \Delta Z \quad (3\text{-}2)$$

Since the root-mean-square (rms) current (I_0) fed into the chest is the constant in the measurement, the voltage U between E_1 and E_2 can be expressed as

$$U = I_0 (Z_0 + \Delta Z) = I_0 Z_0 + I_0 \Delta Z = U_0 + \Delta U \quad (3\text{-}3)$$

From Equation (3-3), we can lead to respectively:

$$U_0 = I_0 Z_0 \quad \Delta U = I_0 \Delta Z \quad (3\text{-}4)$$

The above equations show that U_0 is proportional to the base impedance (Z_0), and ΔU is proportional to thoracic impedance change (ΔZ). Thus the U_0 and ΔU can reflect the basic impedance and thoracic impedance change, respectively.

5 Thoracic parallel impedance model

Suppose that the human thorax is a cylindrical volume conductor [Fig. 4(a)], and the aorta is a flexible duct, which is located in the center of thorax. Fig. 4(b) shows the equivalent parallel circuit of thoracic impedance [7].

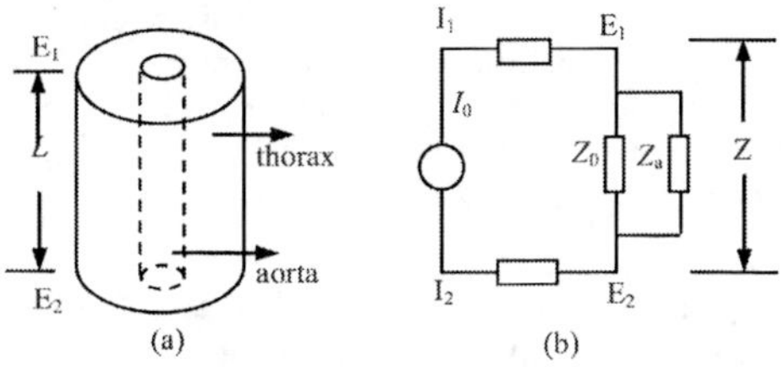

Figure4. Thoracic parallel impedance model

It is assumed that the L is the distance between the voltage electrodes (E_1 and E_2), S_{a0} is the cross-sectional area of the aorta in the basic state, and Z_0 is the thoracic impedance excluding the aorta. Z_{a0} is the impedance of the aorta in the basic state. The total impedance (Z_1) between E_1 and E_2 is the total impedance of Z_0 and Z_{a0} in parallel, that is

$$Z_1 = \frac{Z_0 Z_{a0}}{Z_0 + Z_{a0}} \quad (4\text{-}1)$$

When the heart ejects the blood and the volume of the aorta expand, the impedance of the aorta changes from Z_{a0} to Z_a, then the total impedance becomes

$$Z_2 = \frac{Z_0 Z_a}{Z_0 + Z_a} \quad (4\text{-}2)$$

From equations (4-1) and (4-2), the impedance change (ΔZ) before and after the expansion of the aorta can be obtained,

$$\Delta Z = Z_2 - Z_1 = \frac{Z_0 Z_a}{Z_0 + Z_a} - \frac{Z_0 Z_{a0}}{Z_0 + Z_{a0}}$$

$$= \frac{Z_0^2 (Z_a - Z_{a0})}{(Z_0 + Z_a)(Z_0 + Z_{a0})} \quad (4\text{-}3)$$

Since $Z_0 << Z_{a0}$, $Z_0 << Z_a$, the above equation (4-3) can be approximated into

$$\Delta Z \approx \frac{Z_0^2 (Z_a - Z_{a0})}{Z_a Z_{a0}} = Z_0^2 (\frac{1}{Z_{a0}} - \frac{1}{Z_a}) \quad (4\text{-}5)$$

According to the law of resistance, Z_{a0} and Z_a in the above equations can be expressed as, respectively

$$Z_{a0} = \frac{\rho L}{S_{a0}} = \frac{\rho L^2}{S_{a0} L} = \frac{\rho L^2}{V_{a0}} \quad (4\text{-}6a)$$

$$Z_a = \frac{\rho L}{S_a} = \frac{\rho L^2}{S_a L} = \frac{\rho L^2}{V_a} \quad (4\text{-}6b)$$

The ρ in the above equations is the resistivity of the blood. $V_{a0}=S_{a0}L$, $V_a=S_aL$, which are the volumes of the aorta before and after the expansion, respectively. Substituting the equation (4-6) into the equation (4-5), after rearranging we can get

$$\Delta Z = -\frac{Z_0^2}{\rho L^2} \Delta V \text{ or } \Delta V = -\frac{\rho L^2}{Z_0^2} \Delta Z \quad (4\text{-}7)$$

The above equation is called Nyboer's Impedance Change Equation[7]. In this equation, $\Delta V=V_{a0}-V_a$, because the volume (V_{a0}) of the aorta before the expansion is smaller than the volume (V_a) after the expansion, the negative sign is introduced in the equation (4-7), which is indicating that the impedance decreases when the volume of the blood vessel expands. It can be shown from the equation (4-7) that the impedance change of the blood vessel is numerically proportional to its volume change, that is, the impedance change of the blood vessel can indirectly reflect the law of its volume change. Thus this lays the theoretical basis for the measurement of the thoracic impedance graph.

6 Relation between the thoracic impedance change and chest circumference

Suppose that U_0 and U_1 are the voltages of the aorta in the basal and expanded state respectively, and j_b is the current density of the blood. The currents of the blood vessel in the basal and expanded state can be denoted respectively as:

$$I_{b0} = j_b S_{b0}, \quad I_b = j_b S_{b1}$$

In terms of Ohm's law ($Z=U/I$), the impedances (Z_{a0}) and (Z_a) of the aorta in the basal and expanded states can also be expressed respectively as

$$Z_{a0} = U_0 / j_b S_{a0}, \quad Z_a = U_1 / j_b S_{a1}$$

Substituting them into the equation (4-5) yields

$$\Delta Z = \frac{Z_0^2 \cdot j_b}{U_1 U_0} \cdot (U_1 S_{b0} - U_0 S_{b1}) \quad (5\text{-}1)$$

Here $U_1 \approx U_0$. Substituting it into equation (5-1) obtains

$$\Delta Z \approx \frac{Z_0^2 \cdot j_b}{U_0} \cdot (S_{b0} - S_{b1}) \quad (5\text{-}2)$$

Suppose that ρ_t and j_t are the average resistivity and current density of the thoracic tissue, respectively. The blood current density j_b can be expressed as $j_b = \rho_t j_t / \rho_b$[8]. Substituting it into equation (5-2) yields

$$\Delta Z = -\frac{\rho_t}{\rho_b} \cdot \frac{Z_0^2 \cdot j_t}{U_0} \cdot \Delta S \quad (5\text{-}3)$$

Where $S_{b0} - S_{b1} = -\Delta S$. U_0 can be denoted as $U_0 = I_0 Z_0$ (I_0 is the frequency current I_0 injecting into the thorax). Substituting it into the equation (5-3) obtains

$$\Delta Z = -\frac{\rho_t}{\rho_b} \cdot \frac{Z_0 \cdot j_t}{I_0} \cdot \Delta S \quad (5\text{-}4)$$

The numerator and denominator in the equation (5-4) both are multiplied by the length L,

$$\Delta Z = -\frac{\rho_t}{\rho_b} \cdot \frac{Z_0 \cdot j_t}{I_0 L} \cdot \Delta S L \quad (5\text{-}5)$$

Here $\Delta SL = \Delta V$. Substituting it into equation (5-5) yields

$$\Delta Z = -\frac{\rho_t}{\rho_b} \cdot \frac{Z_0 \cdot j_t}{I_0 L} \cdot \Delta V \quad (5\text{-}6)$$

It shows that thoracic impedance change ΔZ is directly proportional to the current density j_t in the thorax.

If S_t denotes the cross-sectional area of the thorax, the average current density in the thorax can be expressed as $j_t = I_0 / S_t$. Substituting it into equation (5-6) gives

$$\Delta Z = -\frac{\rho_t}{\rho_b} \cdot \frac{Z_0}{S_t L} \cdot \Delta V \quad (5\text{-}7)$$

Where the S_t can be denoted as $S_t = C_t^2 / 4\pi$ (C_t is the chest circumference). Substituting it into equation (5-7) obtains

$$\Delta Z = -\frac{4\pi \rho_t}{\rho_b} \cdot \frac{Z_0}{C_t^2 L} \cdot \Delta V \quad (5\text{-}8)$$

According to Sramek's formula[6], the distance L between two voltage electrodes (E_1, E_2) on the chest surface can be approximately expressed as $L=0.168H$ (H is the body height). Substituting it into the equation (5-8) yields

$$\Delta Z \approx -\frac{24\pi \rho_t}{\rho_b} \cdot \frac{Z_0}{C_t^2 H} \cdot \Delta V \quad (5\text{-}9)$$

This is a equation of the thoracic impedance change including the chest circumference[8]. The equation (5-9) shows that the thoracic impedance change (ΔZ) is directly proportional to the volume change ΔV of the blood vessel, and to the ratio (Z_0/H)of the basal impedance to the body height, while it is inversely proportional to the square of the chest circumference (C_t^2).

References:

1. A. P. DeMarzo. Using impedance cardiography to detect asymptomatic cardiovascular disease in

prehypertensive adults with risk factors [J]. High Blood Press Cardiovasc Prev., 20(2): 61-67, 2013.

2. Morris R, Sunesara I, Rush L, et al. Maternal hemodynamics by thoracic impedance cardiography for normal pregnancy and the postpartum period [J]. 123(2 Pt 1): 318-324, 2014.
3. Heinink TP, Lund JN, Williams JP. Accuracy of impedance cardiography for evaluating trends in cardiac output [J]. Br J Anaesth. 115(2): 322-323, 2015.
4. Xia H, Liu G. Practical Cardiac Function [M]. Beijing: China Medical Science and Technology Press, 70-147, 259-260, 1993.
5. Kubicek WG, Karnegis JN, Patterson RP, et al. Development and evaluation of impedance cardiac output system. Aerospace Med. [J], 37(12): 1208-1212, 1966.
6. Sramek BB, Rose DM and Miyamoto A. Strove volume equation with a linear base impedance model and its accuracy, as compared to thermodilution and magnetic flowmeter techniques in humans and animals [C]. Proceeding of 6th ICEBI, Zadar, Yugoslavia, 38-41, 1983.
7. Lu Jing-Xin. Electrical impedance plethysmography of human body. Bei Jing,China: Science publishing company, 17-21, 1987.
8. Xiao Qiu-Jin, Wang Zhen, Kuang Ming-Xing, et al. Thoracic impedance change equation deduced on the basis of parallel impedance model and Ohm's law [J]. Med. Phys., 39(2): 1042-1045, 2012.

An Improved Sequential Smoothing Particle Filtering Method

Shijie Cao*

University of Electronic Science and Technology of China, 2006 Xiyuan Ave, West Hi-Tech Zone

Abstract. In order to cope with the challenges of non-cooperative targets such as stealth targets to modern radar, especially when traditional threshold detection and tracking methods can hardly detect fast-moving stealth targets, technological innovation has long been required. In this paper we have proposed a new algorithm which can reduce computational cost and improve tracking accuracy. Firstly, the number of particles in the traditional particle filter is reduced and a small number of sampling points are derived from the possible distribution of the target to be tracked, each given a proper weight. Then, the transformed sampling points are sequentially smoothed. And finally, the target positions are estimated. The simulation results show that the proposed algorithm is more accurate than the traditional particle filter algorithm and has lower computational complexity. In the case when SNR is between 0dB to 15dB, a total of 100 Monte Carlo simulations are carried out, obtaining a high detection probability. The detection probability of the improved algorithm is higher than that of the existing particle filter at 7dB. Also, the computational cost is lower than the existing particle filter algorithm. **Keywords:** Smoothing, Particle Filter, Tracking

1 Introduction

Military combat technologies, equipment and combat methods have been improving with the development of social progress and continuous innovation. Having experienced several local wars and regional conflicts since the 90s, many countries and regions in the world are developing and improving military equipment to adapt to the new and complicated environment of modern war. Among them, the radar is an important "radio detection and ranging" instrument, making use of the reflected waves from the target echo to extract information including distance, angle, speed and so on [1]. In a word, in modern warfare, the strategic radar technology is significant.

In recent decades, due to the application of digital electronic computers and the emergence of new theory, new technologies and devices, the development of radar technology has undergone a fundamental change [2]. Along with these changes, the main threats to modern radar come from many aspects such as radiation-absorbent materials and stealth technology, anti-radiation missiles, integrated electronic interference, rapid ultra-low altitude penetration and so on. In order to cope with the challenges of non-cooperative targets such as stealth targets to modern radar, passive location and tracking methods are booming [3]. And a key problem in passive system signal detection technology is the detection and tracking of weak maneuvering targets [4, 5].

The term weak especially refers to the low reflection cross-sectional area of the radar, generates from low detectable targets with weak electromagnetic reflections. These targets include stealth aircrafts, missiles, small ships, and so on [6]. When these targets are irradiated with electromagnetic waves, the relative intensity of the reflected waves are significantly reduced compared with traditional radar targets. The resulting echo signals are very weak and the signal to noise ratios are also very low, which can reduce the detection range of an ordinary single base radar by one third or even half [7, 8]. At the same time, these typical weak targets tend to have very high mobility. Target maneuvering refers to the phenomenon when the change of the original movement of the target go beyond what the filter model can track, which can usually cause model mismatch. The combination of the weak target echo and the maneuverability of the motion not only shortens the detection range of the traditional radar, but also greatly reduces the sensitivity of the detection [9]. Therefore, the traditional threshold detection and tracking method for the weak maneuvering target is not at an advantage. As a result, technological innovations have been imminent at hand.

2 Problem Formulation

Several hypotheses about the target must be satisfied before it can be tracked. The target is in uniform media space, the state and density of which is time invariant. In addition, the target state can be described by a finite state space hidden Markov model. Moreover, the model's parameters are known. Based on the above assumptions, the detection and tracking process can be summarized and illustrated as figure 1.

[a] Corresponding author: caoshijie2015@gmail.com

DOI: 10.1051/matecconf/201712804008

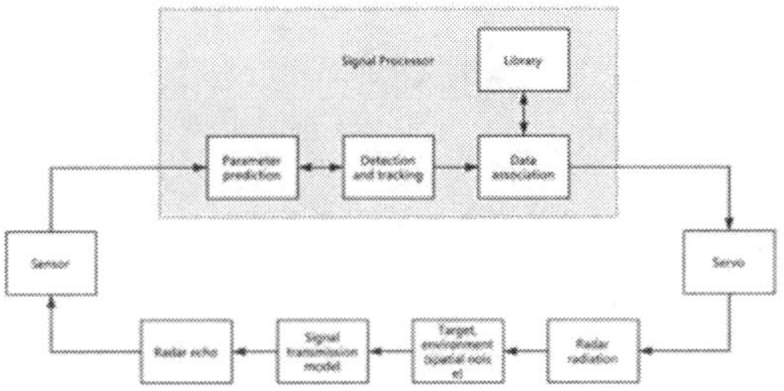

Figure 1. Overview of the processing workflow

At moment k, given the state vector X_k, the observation vector Y_k and the value of target state $Y_0, \dots Y_k$, it is desirable to estimate the value of the hidden state X_k. The state vector of the target is $X_k = [x_k, \dot{x}_k, y_k, \dot{y}_k, I_k]^T$. $\dot{x}_k$ shows the rate of change of the variable x_k, I_k indicates the signal amplitude at moment k. If $\dot{x}_k = 0$, the model is a uniform motion model. Otherwise if $\dot{x}_k \neq 0$, it is a motion model with acceleration. The state vector changes according to the state update model, which is described by the following equation:

$$X_k = F(X_{k-1}, W_k) \tag{1}$$

Where F is the state transition matrix, which is a set of specific stochastic processes that describe the system state noise. The state-transition matrix is

$$F = \begin{bmatrix} F_s & 0 & 0 \\ 0 & F_s & 0 \\ 0 & 0 & 1 \end{bmatrix} \tag{2}$$

where

$$F_s = \begin{bmatrix} 1 & T \\ 0 & 1 \end{bmatrix} \tag{3}$$

and T is the sampling period.

Given the state vector, the observation vector conforms to a certain posterior distribution and the state vector and the observation vector can be written as follows:

$$X_k = g(X_{k-1}) + W_k \tag{4}$$

$$Y_k = h(X_k) + V_k \tag{5}$$

Where g and h are known functions, W_k and V_k are additive independent additive noise sequences with known probability density function.

3 Algorithms

In this paper, an improved sequential smoothing particle filtering(ISS-PF) algorithm is proposed, which aims to reduce the computational consumption. Firstly, the number of particles in the traditional particle filter is reduced, and a small number of sampling points are derived from the proposed distribution of the target. Then, by introducing different weights for each sampling point, after the transformation of the sampling point for smoothing, real-time correction of the filter error ensures that the final output can achieve the target location estimation.

3.1 Sampling Points

First, calculate the mean and covariance of the proposed distribution and use them as the basis for the distribution of the sampling points.

$$\mu_X = \sum xP(x) \tag{6}$$

$$COV(X, Y) = E[(X - \mu_X)(Y - \mu_Y)] \tag{7}$$

Where μ is the mean of the proposed distribution. $COV(X, Y)$ is the covariance of the two variables.

The mean of the proposed distribution is chosen as the first sampling point, and two sets of sampling points are symmetrically selected on both sides of the first sampling point. Furthermore, the distribution of the sampling points conforms to the following constraint equations:

$$1 = \sum_i w_i^m \tag{8}$$

$$\mu = \sum_i w_i^m f(\xi_i) \tag{9}$$

$$\Sigma = \sum_i w_i^c (f(\xi_i) - \mu)(f(\xi_i) - \mu)^{\mathrm{T}} \tag{10}$$

$$COV(x, y) = \frac{\sum (x - \bar{x})(y - \bar{y})}{n} \tag{11}$$

Where w_i^m and w_i^c are the weights of the mean and variance of the first two equations. $f(\xi_i)$ stands for an arbitrary non-linear function and ξ_i stands for the i th sampling point.

3.2 Weights of the Sampling Points

For convenience, define

$$\lambda = \alpha^2(n + \kappa) - n \tag{12}$$

The means and variances of all the sampling points in step one are given different weights so that the weights of all the sampling points add up to one, and the formula should satisfy:

$$\xi_i = \begin{cases} \mu + \left[\sqrt{(n + \lambda)\Sigma}\right]_i, i = 1, 2, \dots, n \\ \mu - \left[\sqrt{(n + \lambda)\Sigma}\right]_{i-n}, i = n + 1, n + 2, \dots, 2n \end{cases} \tag{13}$$

Where the subscript i indicates that the i th column vector of the matrix is selected. This process is equivalent to scaling the covariance matrix with a constant, taking the square root of the matrix and ensuring the symmetry of the sampling points and their weights by adding and subtracting the square root from the mean.

The weight of the mean of the point ξ_0 is:

$$W_0^m = \frac{\lambda}{n+\lambda} \tag{14}$$

The weight of the variance of the point ξ_0 is:

$$W_0^c = \frac{\lambda}{n+\lambda} + 1 - \alpha^2 + \beta \tag{15}$$

The weights of the mean of the remaining points are the same as the covariance, as described in the following equation:

$$W_i^m = W_i^c = \frac{1}{2(n+\lambda)} \quad i = 1, 2, \ldots, 2n \tag{16}$$

3.3 Sequential Smoothing

The sample points are transformed by non-linear function, and the transformed points are smoothed sequentially. First, select a state point as the center so that the other points fall within the area of a circle of radius r and make sure that the distribution of these sampling points consistent with the distribution of the posterior probability of the particle filter:

$$\hat{p}(dx_k|y_{0:k-1}) = \frac{1}{N}\sum_{i=1}^{N} \delta_{\xi_n^i} dx_n \tag{17}$$

According to the following formula on the sampling points before and after the time to estimate the location of the weighted average

$$K(x_0, x_i) = \exp\left(-\frac{(x_0-x_i)^2}{2b^2}\right) \tag{18}$$

$$\hat{f}(x_0) = \frac{\sum_{i=1}^{N} K_{r_i}(x_0,x_i) f(x_i)}{\sum_{i=1}^{N} K_{r_i}(x_0,x_i)} \tag{19}$$

$$r_i = r_0 \frac{(f(x_i)-\mu)^2}{\Sigma} \tag{20}$$

Where $K(x_0, x_i)$ represents the weight value of the smoothing operation, $\hat{f}(x_0)$ represents the current estimated point of the continuous probability density function of x, r means the smooth window radius and only the point within the interval will participate in the smoothing calculation.

3.4 Resampling

After the smoothing procedure, the proposed algorithm then calculates the mean and variance of the smoothed sampling points, re-estimates the proposed distribution based on the mean and variance after smoothing, and resamples from the smoothed distribution function.

The above four steps are repeated until the amount for sequential filtering is sufficient, then the filtering result is outputted.

4 Simulation Results

The maneuvering targets move in a square area of $1000m \times 1000m$ with non-linear motions. The sequential time is 30 frames. Set the maximum speed variation to $2m/s^2$. The maximum speed for a target is $100m/s$. The initial position for the target is $[4.2m, 124.5m]$ and the initial speed for the target is $[1.2m/s, 1.5m/s]$. The Monte Carlo simulation is set to 100 times. The power of the noise is $\sigma^2 = 1/2$. The defined signal-to-noise ratio is the logarithm of the square-sum of the mean of the signal amplitude to noise power, varying from $0dB$ to $20dB$.

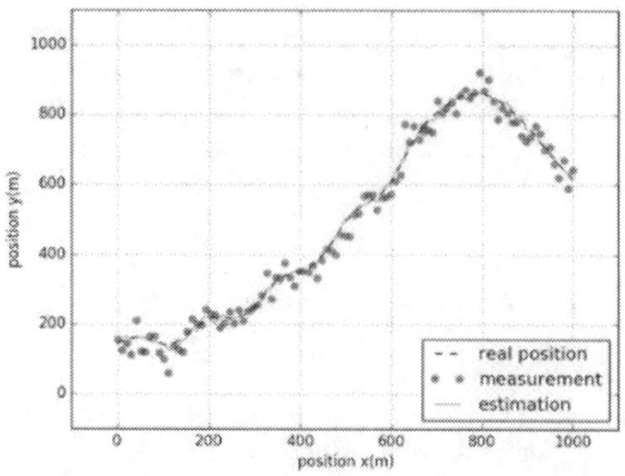

Figure 2. Trajectory track with ISS-PF

Figure 1 shows the resulting trajectory, which is obtained by filtering a group of noisy measurements with ISS-PF. Figure 1 also compares the tracking trajectory and the real track of the weak maneuvering target. Although there are unavoidable errors in a controllable range, especially in the target maneuvering position, the tracking accuracy is high enough to avoid large shifts of the estimation result.

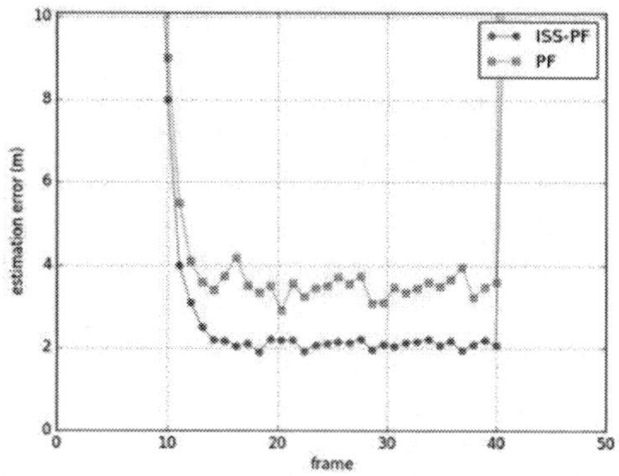

Figure 3. Tracking estimation error

As shown in figure 2, the estimation error is derived by calculating the mean square error along the tracking process. The result shows that ISS-PF algorithm can generally achieve less estimation error of the track than the traditional particle filter algorithm.

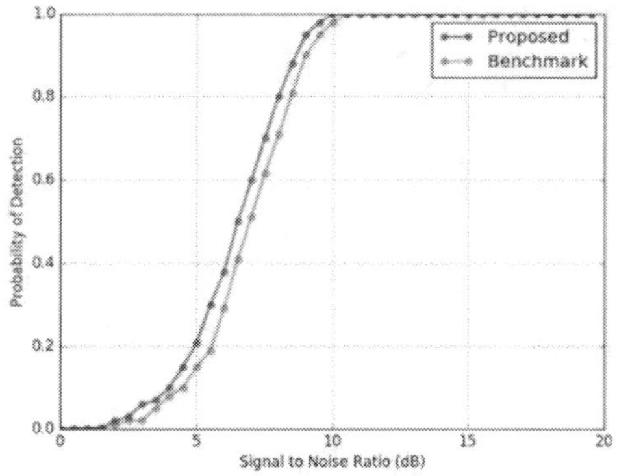

Figure 4. Detection probability comparison

We notice that with the gaining of signal-to-noise ratio, the rise of the detection probability of traditional particle filter is generally slower. On the other hand, the optimized ISS-PF target tracking algorithm can achieve enough detection probability at 6dB. When the signal-to-noise ratio is above 9dB, the detection probability can reach more than 90%, and the system can work robustly. Especially when the signal-to-noise ratio is less than 5dB, the detection probability of the optimized ISS-PF target tracking algorithm is obviously higher than that of the traditional particle filter algorithm.

Table 1. Detection time comparison of the algorithms

Detection time (seconds every 10 simulations)		
Detection Probability	**Traditional Particle Filter**	**Proposed ISS-PF Algorithm**
0.2	402.7803	41.4901
0.4	272.1028	21.2624
0.6	141.4242	10.5848
0.8	30.7465	3.5967
1.0	10.0683	1.3499

It can be found that the ISS-PF algorithm proposed in this paper is much less costly than the traditional particle filter method in the same simulation environment after reasonable optimization and improvements.

5 Conclusion

Summing up, the algorithm of optimization and improvement in this paper can realize the effective tracking and detection of weak maneuvering targets and reduce the overall cost of the system. It can be seen that the advantage of the proposed algorithm in this paper lies in the availability of using less particles to obtain effective estimates. In the case of insufficient system computing resources, high real-time requirements and low accuracy requirements, the ISS-PF algorithm proposed in this paper has some advantages. And in the same condition, the algorithm, compared with traditional target detection and tracking algorithms, shows a superior detection and state estimation performance, especially concerning the detection time.

References

1. Risfic B, Arulampalam S, Gordon N. Beyond the kalman filter - Book Review[J]. Aerospace & Electronic Systems Magazine IEEE, 2004, 19(7):37-38.
2. Davey S J, Rutten M G, Cheung B. A comparison of detection performance for several Track-Before-Detect algorithms[C]. International Conference on Information Fusion. IEEE, 2008:1-8.
3. Bandiera F, Besson O, Orlando D, et al. GLRT-Based Direction Detectors in Homogeneous Noise and Subspace Interference[J]. Signal Processing IEEE Transactions on, 2007, 55(6):2386-2394.
4. Vo B N, Vo B T, Mahler R P S. Closed-Form Solutions to Forward–Backward Smoothing[J]. IEEE Transactions on Signal Processing, 2012, 60(1):2-17.
5. Vo B T, Clark D, Vo B N, et al. Bernoulli Forward-Backward Smoothing for Joint Target Detection and Tracking[J]. IEEE Transactions on Signal Processing, 2011, 59(9):4473-4477.
6. Moral P D, Jacod J, Protter P. The Monte-Carlo method for filtering with discrete-time observations[J]. Probability Theory & Related Fields, 2001, 120(3):346-368.
7. Moral P D, Doucet A, Jasra A. On Adaptive Resampling Procedures for Sequential Monte Carlo Methods[J]. Bernoulli, 2012, 18(1):252-278.
8. Davey S J, Rutten M G, Cheung B. A Comparison of Detection Performance for Several Track-before-Detect Algorithms[C] International Conference on Information Fusion. IEEE, 2007:1-8.
9. Orlando D, Ricci G, Bar-Shalom Y. Track-Before-Detect Algorithms for Targets with Kinematic Constraints[J]. IEEE Transactions on Aerospace & Electronic Systems, 2011, 47(3):1837-1849.

The Design of Nonlinear Chirp Based on the DSP Builder Technique

Dong Zhang[1], Shou-liang Yang[1, a], Yang Zhang [2]

[1]*Engineering Research Center of New Energy Storage Devices and Applications, Chongqing University of Arts and Sciences, Chongqing 402160, P. R. China*
[2]*Chongqing Preschool education College, Chongqing 404047, P. R. China)*

Abstract. This paper, by analyzing the function Chirp, studies the software design and realization of the function. It offers a design plan based on the nonlinear Chirp signal of DSP Builder technique and designs the signal generator of the nonlinear Chirp based on the design flow of Matlab/Simulink/DSP Builder/QuartusII. It also conducts simulation verification using the development software Matlab/Simulink and QuartusII, proving that the design can well realize the signal source Chirp. The experiment proves that the DSP Builder technique can modify the starting frequency, bandwidth and the frequency resolution of linear frequency modulation signals by changing the programming parameters. The method is proved to be simple in designing, convenient in modification, low in cost and it doesn't involve any programming; therefore, it is easy to realize.

1 Introduction

The non-linear FM pulse signals are the ones whose instantaneous frequencies change with the time, i.e., the sine waves whose instantaneous frequencies change with the time in a range1.They are widely used in such fields as communication, radar, sonar for their wonderful bandwidth efficiency[2]3.The study of the realization of the wireless fuze signals Chirp in FPGA is significant for the research of wireless fuze system4. The test of stress waves based on the theory of chirp signals is widely used in engineer quality nondestructive testing. A large number of experiments have proved that the testing instruments developed on the basis of the study are effective in engineer testing.

Most of the Chirp signal sources commonly used in the current market are designed with the dedicated chips DDS[5]5[7]. They have wide output frequency and excellent high frequency performance. But they cannot meet the requirements for the fixed signal wave forms, functions and controlling modes produced by the dedicated DDS chips. Therefore, it is desirable to integrate one or several DDS core circuits and the other parts on a FPGA by using a programmable logic device. In this way, programming can be done on the chip and will be highly flexible and reconfigurable.

2 Math model analysis of Chirp signals

2.1 Chirp mathematical expression

The instantaneous frequencies of Chirp change with the time, i.e., it is a time function. Its math expression is as follows.

$$x(t) = \cos(2\pi \cdot f(t) \cdot t + \theta_0) \tag{1}$$

The Chirp functions can be divided into two types: linear chirp function and nonlinear chirp function according to the gradation rules of the Chirp output frequencies corresponding to the sampling time. The following two diagrams show the two chirp functions.

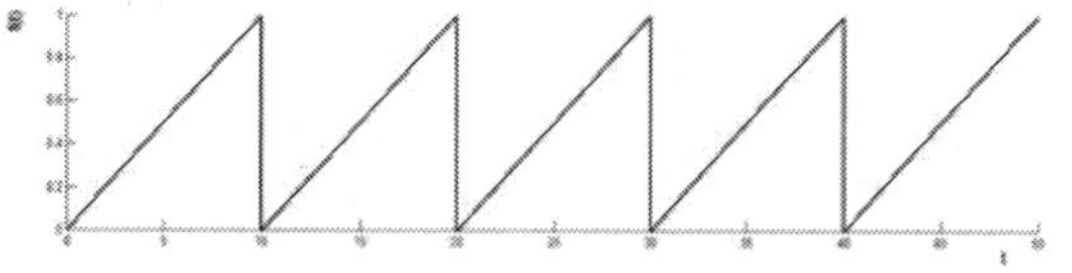

Fig1. linear chirp function

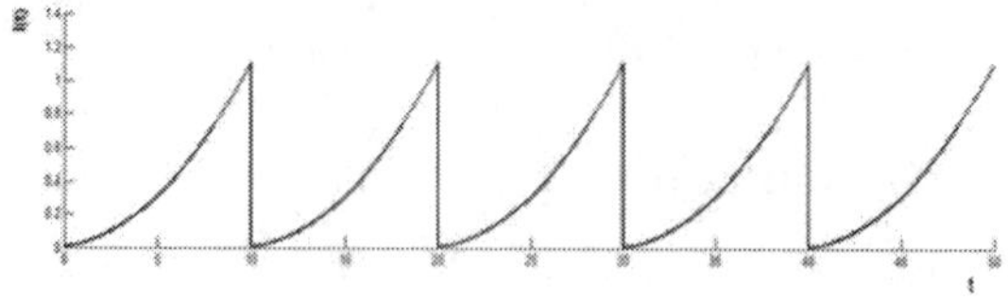

Fig2. Non-linear chirp function

From Fig.1 and Fig.2, we can generalize the closed system $f-t$ relation of Chirp function's frequency output and the time as follows:

For the linear Chirp function, the relationship expression in a continuous time domain can be:

[a] Corresponding author: slyang@cqwu.edu.cn

$$f_{out} = \kappa t + f_0 \quad (2)$$

In equation 2, κ is a constant, f_0 is the initial output frequency, t means the continuous time. The relationship expression in a discrete time domain is:

$$f_{out} = \kappa n + f_0 \quad (3)$$

In equation 3, κ is a constant, f_0 is the initial output frequency, n is a sampling site.

For the non-linear Chirp function, the relationship expression in a continuous time domain is:

$$f_{out} = f(t) + f_0 \quad (4)$$

In equation 4, $f(t)$ is nonlinear functions, f_0 is the initial output frequency; t is continuous time。In discrete time domain, there is relation formula:

$$f_{out} = f(n) + f_0 \quad (5)$$

In equation 5, $f(n)$ $f(t)$ is nonlinear functions, f_0 is the initial output frequency; n is a sampling site.

For nonlinear (Nonlinear) chirp functions, it is actually the quadratic function of the instantaneous frequency of signals, which can be expressed as a function:

$$f(t) = f_1 + f_2 t + (f_3/2)t^2 \quad (6)$$

In equation 6, f_1 is the static (fixed, initial etc) frequency, f_2 is the Doppler frequency, and f_3 is the conversion rate. When f_3 is 0, secondary FM signals are degraded into linear FM signals, so the sine and cosine signals and linear FM signals are the specials cases of secondary FM signals.

2.2 Phase-amplitude analysis

After the digitization of ADC, the expression of the quadratic frequency modulation signal is (sampling frequency f_0):

$$x[n] = \cos(2\pi(f_1 + \frac{f_2}{f_0}n + \frac{f_3}{2f_0}n^2)\frac{n}{f_0} + \theta_0) \quad (7)$$

By equation 7, it can be seen that the instantaneous phase:

$$\theta[n] = 2\pi(\frac{f_1}{f_0}n + \frac{f_2}{f_0^2}n^2 + \frac{f_3}{2f_0^3}n^3) + \theta_0 \quad (8)$$

In order to simplify equation 8, if

$$y_1[n] = \frac{f_1}{f_0}n + \frac{f_2}{f_0^2}n^2 + \frac{f_3}{2f_0^3}n^3$$

$$y_2[n] = y_1[n] - y_1[n-1] = \frac{2f_2}{f_0^2}n + \frac{3f_3}{2f_0^3}n^2 - \frac{3f_3}{2f_0^3}n + \frac{f_1}{f_0} - \frac{f_2}{f_0^2} + \frac{f_3}{2f_0^3}$$

$$y_3[n] = y_2[n] - y_2[n-1] = \frac{3f_3}{f_0^3}n + \frac{2f_2}{f_0^2} - \frac{3f_3}{f_0^3}$$

$$y_3[n] - y_3[n-1] = \frac{3f_3}{f_0^3}$$

Thus:

$$y_3[n] = c_3 + y_3[n-1] \quad (9)$$

$$y_2[n] = y_3[n] + y_2[n-1] \quad (10)$$

$$y_1[n] = y_2[n] + y_1[n-1] \quad (11)$$

Supposing $y_3[n]$ initial state is c_2, $y_2[n]$ initial state is c_1, $y_1[n]$ initial state is 0, thus $y_3[n] = c_3 n + c_2$

$$y_2[n] = \sum_{i=1}^{n}(c_3 i + c_2) + c_1 = c_3\frac{n(n+1)}{2} + c_2 n + c_1 \quad (12)$$

$$y_1[n] = \sum_{i=1}^{n} y_2[i] = \sum_{i=1}^{n}(c_3\frac{i(i+1)}{2} + c_2 i + c_1) \quad (13)$$

$$= \frac{c_3}{6}n^3 + (\frac{c_2}{2} + \frac{c_3}{2})n^2 + (\frac{c_3}{3} + \frac{c_2}{2} + c_1)n$$

Supposing:

$$Addr[n] = y_1[n] + c_0 \quad (14)$$

Thus:

$$Addr[n] = \frac{c_3}{6}n^3 + (\frac{c_2}{2} + \frac{c_3}{2})n^2 + (\frac{c_3}{3} + \frac{c_2}{2} + c_1)n + c_0 \quad (15)$$

The sine function values from $0 \square 2\pi$ are divided into N parts, and the amplitude values on the points are stored in ROM. Then the phase values ωT are accumulated with a phase accumulator to figure out the current phase value and the current amplitude value is worked out by looking up ROM. The system chart is shown in Fig3.

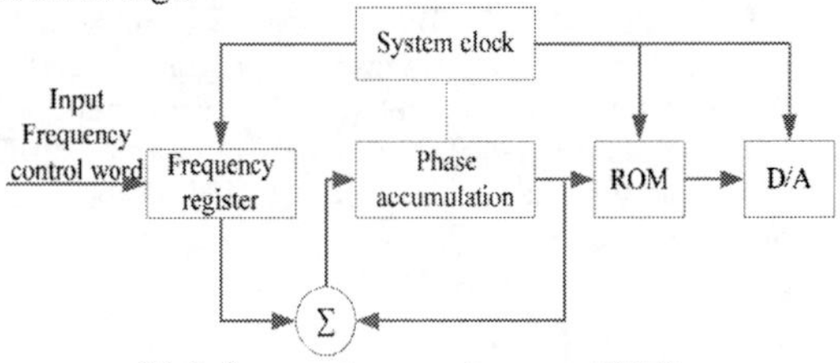

Fig3. System structure diagram of DDS

By searching ROM, the current amplitude can be worked out; then the output signals in table lookup by taking $Addr[n]$ as the address signal can be shown as follows:

$$x[n]=\cos(2\pi\frac{Addr[n]}{2^N})=\cos(2\pi\frac{\frac{c_3}{6}n^3+(\frac{c_2}{2}+\frac{c_3}{2})n^2+(\frac{c_3}{3}+\frac{c_2}{2}+c_1)n+c_0}{2^N}) \tag{16}$$

Compare with

$$x[n]=\cos(2\pi(f_1+\frac{f_2}{f_0}n+\frac{f_3}{2f_0^2}n^2)\frac{n}{f_0}+\theta_0),$$

$$\theta_0=2\pi\frac{c_0}{2^N},\quad f_1=(c_1+\frac{c_2}{2}+\frac{c_3}{3})\frac{f_0}{2^N},$$

$$f_2=(c_2+c_3)\frac{f_0^2}{2^{N+1}},\quad f_3=c_3\frac{f_0^3}{3\cdot 2^N}.$$

The equivalent is:

$c_0=\theta_0\frac{2^N}{2\pi}$, c_0 is phase control word;

$c_1=f_1\frac{2^N}{f_0}-f_2\frac{2^N}{f_0^2}+0.5f_3\frac{2^N}{f_0^3}$, c_1 is frequency control word;

$c_2=2f_2\frac{2^N}{f_0^2}-3f_3\frac{2^N}{f_0^3}$, c_2 is Doppler frequency control word;

$c_3=3f_3\frac{2^N}{f_0^3}$, c_3 is Doppler change rate control word.

3 The algorithm realization

DSP Builder is a system-level (or algorithm level) design instrument provided by Altera. It is constructed on several software instruments and connects two design instruments: system level and RTL level. Therefore, it can bring the superiority of two instruments to their greatest play. It can help the designer fulfill the DSP design on the basis of FPGA6. Besides the graphic system modeling, DSP Builder can also achieve most design and simulation systematically, until the design document is downloaded on the DSP development board. According to equation 9, the model is set up using DSP Builder module under Matlab\Simulink89. The model is shown in the following figure 4.

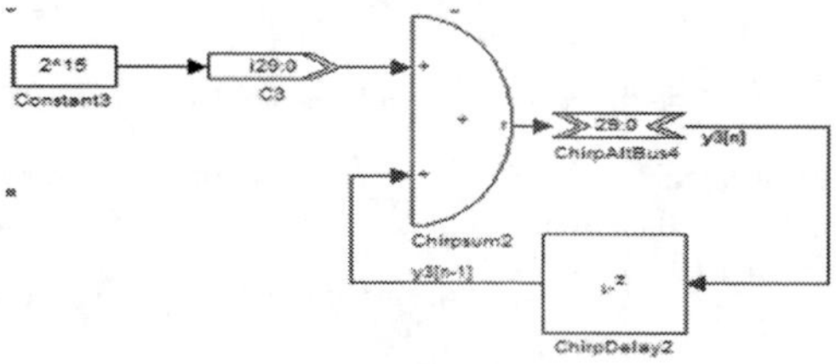

Fig4. Model of y3(n)

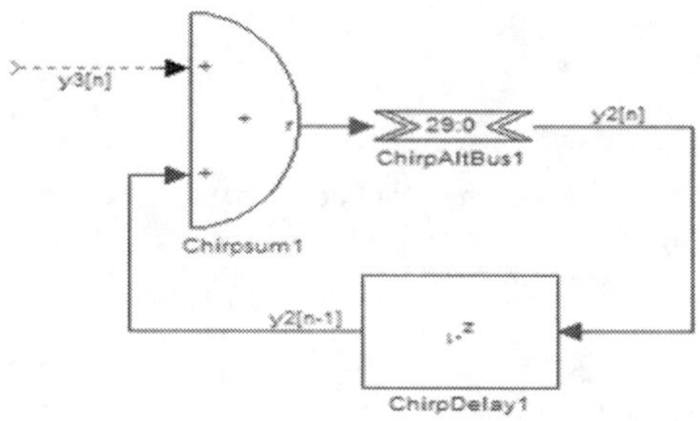

Fig5. Model of y2(n)

In Figure 4, the chirpsum2 is addition module, chirpDelay2 is Delay module, Implementation function of $y_3[n]=c_3+y_3[n-1]$. According to equation 10, Under Matlab\Simulink, the model is built with DSP Builder module, and the model is shown in the figure 5.

In Figure 5, chirpsum1 is addition module, chirpDelay1 is Delay module, Implementation function of $y_2[n]=y_3[n]+y_2[n-1]$.

According to equation 11, Under Matlab\Simulink, the model is built with DSP Builder module, and the model is shown in the figure 6:

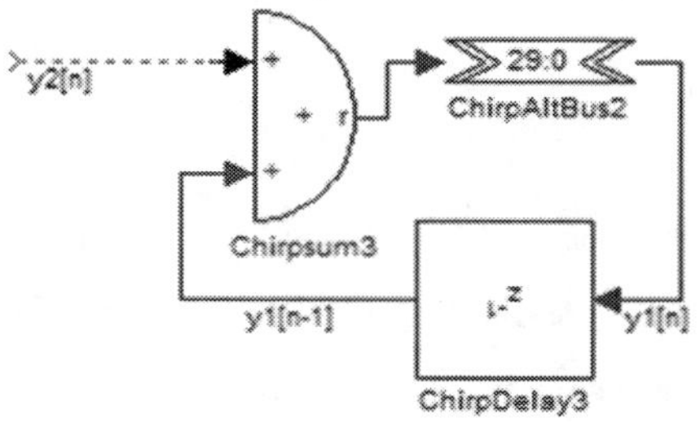

Fig6. Model of y1(n)

In Figure 6, chirpsum3 is a add-module and chirpDelay3 is a postponement module, which can realize the function in $y_1[n]=y_2[n]+y_1[n-1]$. According to equation 14, In order to realize the phase to amplitude conversion function, the model is built with DSP Builder module under matlab\simulink, and the model is shown in the Fig7.

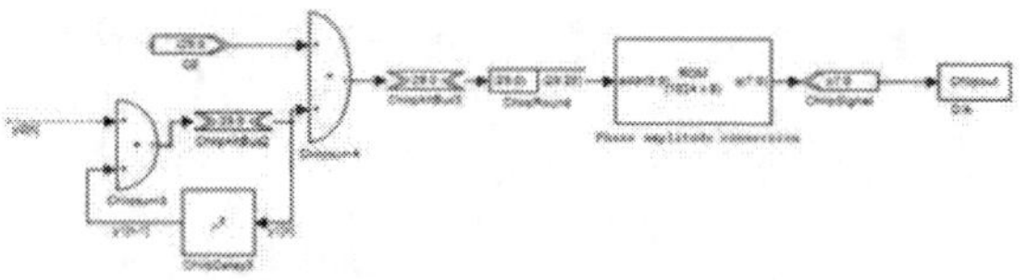

Fig7. Phase amplitude conversion circuit

4 Simulation analysis

After the simulation in Matlab/Simulink is ensured to be correct, the chirp signal model is transformed into VHDL language document using the Signal Compiler in DSP Builder so that it can be realized in FPGA. Figure 8 shows the result of the timing sequence simulation

DOI: 10.1051/matecconf/201712804009

conducted in QuartusII. Figure 9 shows the waves tested by embedded logic analyzer. It indicates that its waves are similar to the simulation waves of Matlab/Simulink and it confirms the correctness of the design.

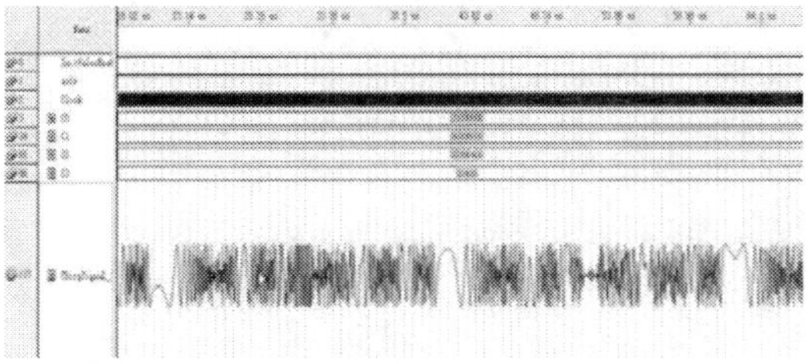

Figure 8 Timing simulation diagram in QuartusII

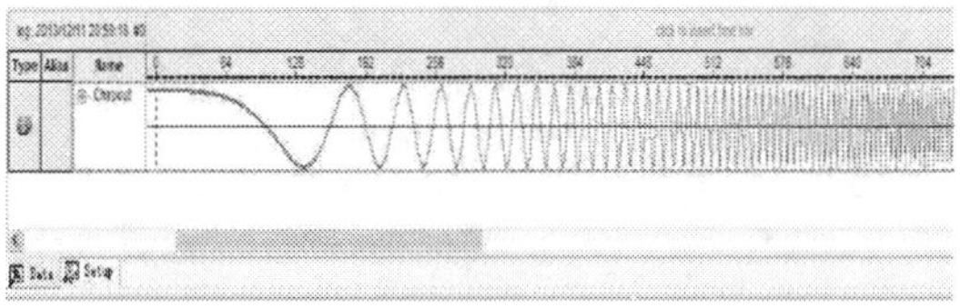

Figure 9 waveform measured by embedded logic analysis

5 Experimental Result

After the system is set up, the pin of FGPA is configured. Then it is translated and edited and the engineer document downloads the document •sof to the FPGA chips in the experiment box through the download cable. In this way, the Chirp signal generator is designed. The output side of the generator is tested with the Oscilloscope. Part of its waves are shown in figure 10.

Figure 10 Chirp waveform observed by oscilloscope

From the figure 10 we can find that the frequencies of the Chirp signals designed in the way change obviously with the time, are considerably controllable and has good continuity in phases. Their functions and indicators are: 1) they can be used to generate sine waves with fixed frequencies and used in nonlinear FM; 2) the word length of the accumulator is 30, the output of the phase accumulator used to search ROM is 10 and the output word length of ROM is 8.

6 Conclusion

The paper studies the design plan of nonlinear FM pulse signals based on the technique DSP-Builder. It has simple system circuit, is extremely controllable and can be programmed repeatedly. Meanwhile, the design based on FPGA is highly readable and portable; therefore, it has good application prospect.

Acknowledgment

This work was supported by the Science Foundation of Chongqing Committee of Education of China (No: KJ1711280)

Reference

1. JI Guoqing, Feng Chunhuan. The Implementation of Chirp Signal Based on DDS. Electronics R & D.2015,09: 6-8
2. JIN Xue-zhe, QI Fei-tao, GAO Qing-yun, QIN Shi-cai. A Wide-Band Chirp-DDS and Its Implementation on FPGA3. Microelectronics.2003, Vol.33, NO.4:365-368
3. Zheng Yang, He Cunfu, Wu Bin. Chirp signal and its application in ultrasonic guided wave inspection . Chinese Journal of Scientific Instrument. Vol.34 No.3 2013, 552-558
4. Jiang Wen-gang . Signal Generation and Data Acquisition Design of Chirp Radar Based on FPGA. Electronics Quality. No 8,2013,20-23
5. WANG Kang-jia, LIU Shi-wei, SUN Pan-dian. Two Ways for Design of Arbitrary Waveform Signal Generator Based on Matlab/DSP Builder. Modern Electronics Technique. Vol.34 No.3, Feb.2011,179-184
6. SUN Ming, LIN Jun, CHEN Zu-bin, YU Sheng-bao. he producing system of chirp signal based on DDS . Journal of Foshan University (Natural Science Edition). Vol.22 No.4 2004, 22-24
7. DONG Liang, WANG Min,HAO Longfei,DONG Jiang. Design of Chirp Signal Source Based on DSP Builder. Modern Electronics Technique. 2009, 16: 92-94, 99
8. XU Jingjing, LI Guolin, HU Min. Design of Chirp signal of radio fuze based on DDS. Chinese Journal of Naval Aeronautical and Astronautical University. 2006, 1: 134-136
9. Sheng Yuanyuan, Liu Yicheng,Zheng Gongming. Research of chirp signal realization method based on DDS Technology. Petroleum Tubular Goods & Instruments. 2008,01,78-79,77

Simplified Casing Program for Development Wells in Mahu Well Block

Zongyu Lu[1], Weifeng Chen[1], Sihao Li[2], and Yingjin Zhang[2,a]

[1]*Engineering and Technology Research Institute of Xinjiang Oil Field Co, Karamay 834000, China*
[2]*National Engineering Laboratory of Petroleum Drilling Technology, Leak Resistance & Sealing Technology Research Department, Yangtze University, Wuhan 430100, China*

Abstract. In the Mahu well block of Junggar basin, the complex formation has many sets of pressure system. Especially, the formation with microcracks in the middle layer is loose and the pressure bearing capacity is low. Lost circulation is prone to occur in this layer. At present, high investment and long drilling period were the main problems in the exploration and development process. The geostress 3D model of Mahu well block was established by means of logging and drilling data. The model provided the three-pressure profiles of Mahu well block for casing program optimization and safety drilling. Each well could be optimized the intermediate casing setting position. The intermediate casing was saved 160 meters long. The total of drilling speed was improved 5 times compared with the past drilling process. Slim hole drilling technology raised ROP 51.96% higher, and the average drilling period is shorten to 24.83 days.

1 Introduction

Mahu well block with complex lithology in Xinjiang Junggar basin of China is a new oil & gas reserves and production oilfield. The important technical items for development wells are focused in the simplifying casing program. There are many sets of pressure system, and the middle layer contains microcracks. The sandstone layer is the loose conglomerate cementation, which has a weak capacity of bearing pressure. The drilling wells is prone to leakage[1,2]. There are thick gravel layers in the deep strata. The rock strength is higher and the rate of penetration (ROP) is low. The pressure coefficient of the abnormally high-pressure formations was 1.74, such as the Triassic Bkq Formation. The well control risks are higher. The above factors lead to the Mahu well block drilling process are being the situations of difficulty, high risk and long period[3].

In order to reduce the cost, the study of simplifying casing program was carried out by choosing the right drill bit and drilling fluid system. A reasonable casing program for the well block was formed, which avoided lost circulation, well blowout, borehole collapse, pipe sticking and other engineering accidents. The smoothly safety of drilling operations reduced significantly the project costs[4].

2 Influencing factors of casing program design

2.1 Stratigraphic lithology

In the past, during drilling operation, lost circulation in the Jurassic Bdw formation and Triassic Bjt formation in Mahu well block had been occured. The main reason is that the Jurassic Bdw formation contains a large number of microcracks, and that the bottom formation of the conglomerate layer is loose. Although the lithology of the Bjt formation is dominated by mudstone, the layer's is low, because there are two sets of sandstone layers at the top and middle location[5].

2.2 Formation pressure evaluation

2.2.1 Formation pore pressure

The pore pressure in Mahu well block is analysed by the theory of undercompaction according to logging data[6]. The pore pressure is almost identical to each well. The strata above Triassic are the normal pressure system. Triassic Bjt formation is a pressure transition zone. The formation from Triassic Krmy to Bkq is an abnormally high-pressure layer. The target layer pore pressure of Bkq formation is differences. The pore pressure equivalent density is between 1.40 g/cm^3 ~ 1.75 g/cm^3. The Bkq formation was prone to overflow, well-kick and other complex conditions during drilling well[7].

2.2.2 Formation fracture pressure

The minimum horizontal principal stress can be used as a fracture pressure, especially for fractured formation[8-10]. The minimum horizontal principal stress model of Mahu

[a] Corresponding author: zhangyingjin@yangtzeu.edu.cn

well block is established by the geostress model combined the well logging method with the effective stress ratio method.

There is a low-fracture-pressure condition in the bottom formation of the Jurassic Bdw and the Bjt formation. The equivalent density of the minimum horizontal principal stress is about 1.50 g/cm^3. In Cretaceous and Triassic strata, the minimum horizontal principal stress is relatively high, and equivalent density of Bkq formation is 1.70g/cm^3~1.90g/cm^3.

2.2.3 Three formation pressure profiles

The three-pressure profiles of Mahu well block were established by well logging, mud logging and drilling data[11].

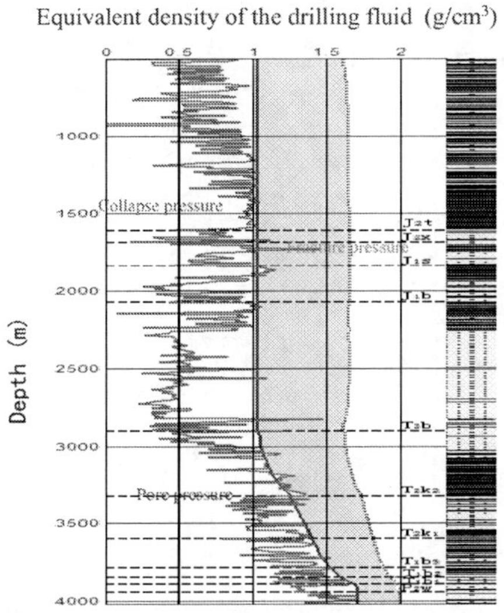

Figure 1. Three-pressure profiles of Mahu well block

From figure 1, the strata above Triassic are normal pressure system, and the formation from Triassic Krmy to Bkq formation is an abnormal high-pressure stratigraphy, which is very prone to well-kick, overflow and even more seriously complex situations[12]. The strata above the Jurassic Bdw formation are dominated by sandstone-mudstone. The collapse pressure is increasing according to the well depth. The borehole wall stability is weakened. The stability of the wellbore at the bottom of the Bdw formation is stabilized. The collapse pressure of Triassic strata formation is synchronized with the increase in formation pore pressure. The security density window of Triassic formation narrows gradually, especially the security density window in the lower strata of the Triassic Bkq formation is the smallest (Figure 1).

1.3 Rock mechanics characteristic

The rock mechanical characteristic profiles Mahu well block[13] are set up. The rock mechanical parameters of stratum are fluctuated greatly because of the varied lithology (Table 1).

Table 1. Rock mechanical parameters

Formation	*Compressive strength /MPa*	*Internal friction angle/°*	*PDC bit drillability*	*Cone bit drillability*
Tgl	10~50	26~38	0.5~3.5	0.5~6
Bdw	60~90	38~41	5~9	5~9
Bjt	20~40	38~32	2~4	4~6
Krmy	30~60	35~38	3~4.5	5~7
Bkq	25~70	35~43	3.2~4.5	3.8~8

3 Disadvantage of previous casing program

3.1 Difficult points in drilling operation

From the formation pressure and rock mechanical characteristic, the difficulties during drilling engineering in Mahu well block are the following:

- The Jurassic and Triassic formation are prone to lost circulation, pipe sticking and other complex situations;
- The target layer of Bkq formation is an abnormally high-pressure formation. The security drilling fluid density window is narrow and the drilling fluid type is difficult to optimize.
- The bottom of Jurassic system is a set of thick gravel beds. The rock strength is grave. The bit optimization is difficult.
- The low drilling speed of previous wells restricts the economical and efficient development of Mahu well block.

3.2 Present situation of casing program

Before 2016, the main third spud section structure is shown in Table 2. The previous casing program has the following problems:

- The middle-deep wells with the normal pore pressure system formation, three-spudding casing program was too single. The drilling speed is too slow to reduce drilling costs.
- The bit type was almost cone bit, which was not better adapt to the underground environment. The drilling complex situations was prone to provide lower penetration.
- The improper handling method of drilling fluid was prone to leakage and other complex collapse conditions.

Table 2. Present situation of casing program.

Spudding	Bit diameter (mm)	Drilling depth (m)	Casing diameter (mm)	Casing depth (m)
First	444.5	500	339.73	500
Second	311.15	3140	244.84	3140
Third	215.9	Design depth	139.7	Design depth

4 Optimized casing program

The casing program of oil production wells was optimized from conventional-size three-spudding structure to slim hole three-spudding structure. The horizontal wells adopted slim hole three-spudding structure, and the completion method of horizontal wells was simplified(Figure 2). Anti-sloughing drilling fluid system was adopted to the formation characteristics of the Mahu well block for safe and efficient drilling operation.

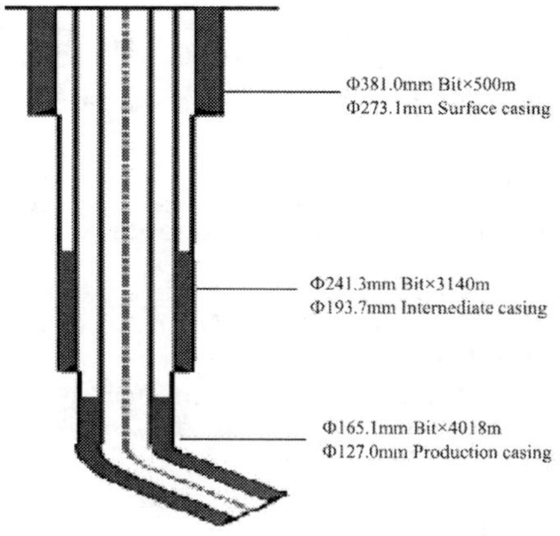

Figure 2. Casing program of straight well/directional well

Figure 2 shows the slim hole three-spudding structure of oil production wells. First spudding is designed to seal the superficial layer for refrainment from the loosed and collapsed formation, and for equipment the well-control blowout preventer on the wellhead. Second spudding is designed to seal two sets of pore pressure system in the corresponding well section. The cement slurry is back to the depth of 2540m. Third spudding is designed to create safety drilling conditions. The cement slurry is back to the depth of 3276m.

5 Matching technology for the optimized casing program

5.1 Anti-sloughing drilling fluids

The experimental analysis of hydration swelling indicated that the unstable layers of the Mahu well block are Sgh formation, Bjt formation, Krmy formation and Bkq formation. The rock sample has the same linear expansion rate in 2 hours as the bentonite in 16 hours. The low rate of rock expansion shows that the rock is unstable when it touches water. That is to say, the initial expansion is faster, but the hydration expansion will gradually slow down. Clay minerals in Mahu well block contain the weak swelling ingredient. A large number of strong water sensitive disperse minerals in rock sample is lower. The linear swelling rate of rock sample is low, but the roller recovery is low too. The formation belongs to weak expansion and strongly dispersed layer. Drilling fluid should be optimized to improve the ability of restraining dispersion for the expansion formation.

The synergistic inhibition of drilling fluid system can be enhanced the ability of restraining dispersion for the expansion formation by triadic coordination inhibitor. The average roller recovery of the ternary synergistic controlled drilling fluid system has been improved to about 90%. The inhibition of hydration swelling in the sediments of the Mahu well block is not obvious. This is mainly related to the hydrodynamic characteristics of the volcanic strata [14,15]. (Table 3)

Table 3. *Ternary synergistic suppression* water-based drilling fluid preferred formula

Recipe number	Formula
M-3-1	4% Soil pulp +0.3% FA367+2% SMP-2 +2% SPNH + 1% Redul + 0.3% CaO +0.3% KOH + 10% OS-80 +1%SIAT +3%KCl +4%PHT+1% Graphite powder + Barite
M-3-2	4% Soil pulp +0.3%FA367+2%SMP-2+2% SPNH +1% Redul +0.3%CaO +0.3% KOH +10% OS-80+1%MFG +3% KCl +4%PHT+1% Graphite powder + Barite
M-3-1	4% Soil pulp +0.3%FA367+2%SMP-2+2% SPNH +1% Redul+0.3%CaO+ 0.3% KOH +10% OS-80+1%JXL-B+ 3% KCl +4% PHT +1% Graphite powder + Barite

5.2 Bit optimization

Rock mechanics is the main factor affected the rock breaking efficiency. According to the established rock mechanical characteristics section (Table 1), the sizes and types bit series for Mahu well block is optimized. The optimization method is combined the drilling bit optimization model with the best efficiency drill bit used in the reference area. Table 4 show rsults of bit optimization for Mahu well block.

Table 4. Results of bit optimization

Spudding	Recommended bit type
First	ST115G,SKG124
Second	FX56DX3(DBS), SF56H3(DBS), S519, MS1952SS, FR1965, M935T
Third	SF54VH3(DBS), SF44VH3(DBS), FR1643S, MS1643SS, BTM115AE

5.3 Application of simplified casing program

The effect of the casing program optimization and the increasing drilling speed technology is remarkable on the slim hole drilling in Mahu well block. The slim hole average ROP was 8.13m/h, increased 51.96% compared to the previous wells. The average drilling period of the slim hole was 55.7days, saved 24.83days than the previous wells. (Table 5)

Table 5. Comparison of optimization effects

	Drilling period (d)	**Average ROP (m/h)**
Previous wells	80.53	5.53
Slim hole wells	55.7	8.13

6 Conclusions

According to the bottom of Jurassic and Triassic leakage and deep mudstone sloughing characteristics, the main ideas are to prevent leakage, control formation dispersion and expansion, and realize the safety drilling. The ternary synergistic suppression drilling fluid system is proposed. The system combines with three steps of hydration-physical, chemical plugging and stress support. Jurassic formation is characterized by deep grey and gray silty mudstone. The rigid PDC drill with 5 blades and 16mm teeth is selected to ensure the safety and fast drilling in the bottom of the thick gravel layer. According to the geological environment of Mahu well block, the three-pressure profiles of Mahu well block were established for the optimized casing program. The borehole size of each spudding is reduced. The slim hole average ROP was 8.13m/h, increased 51.96% compared to the previous wells. The average drilling period of the slim hole was 55.7 days, saved 24.83days than the previous wells. The drilling cycle is reduced and the drilling speed is improved.

Acknowledgement

The authors wish to acknowledge the National Program on General Program of National Natural Science Foundation of China (Contract No. 51474036 and 51204024) for the financial support.

References

1. Drilling Handbook (Second Edition), drilling handbook compilation group, petroleum industry press, **9** (2013).
2. Reservoir geology. Mark, D., Zuo Bai Ke, petroleum industry press, **1** (2012).
3. Guan Zhichuan, Ke Ke, Su Kanhua. The design method of deepwater drilling well structure. petroleum drilling techniques, **39**, (2011): 16-21.
4. Ceng Wei, Wei Qiang, Zhu Xiujuan, et al. Rapid drilling technology for Yingshan formation in Longgang area. drilling and production technology, **34** (2011): 28-31.
5. Yu Jin, Liu Peng, Wu Yicheng, et al. Optimized well structure and drilling fluid technology in the northern block of burning mountain oilfield. Xinjiang Petroleum Science and technology, **2** (2013): 6-8.
6. Yang Yukun. Technique actuality on hole structure design of unconventional series casing and its application foreground in zhungeer basin. Drilling& production technology, **28** (2005): 1-3.
7. Fan Zhaobin, first, Qi, Yang Shijun. Leak prevention, plugging and pressure control drilling technology for complex igneous rocks in Junggar basin. natural gas industry, **31** (2011): 88-92.
8. Ai Guicheng. Potassium calcium based cationic drilling fluid technology. petroleum drilling and production technology, **29** (2007): 87-88.
9. Su Peidong, Qin Qirong, Huang Runqiu. Current situation and Prospect of reservoir fracture prediction. Journal of Southwest Petroleum University, **27** (2005): 14-17.
10. Yang Zhibin, Hu Yongzhang, Zhong Jingmin, et al. Influence of engineering geological factors on drilling speed increase. fault block oil and gas field, **17** (2010), 363-365.
11. Halal A S, Warling D J, Wagner R R. *Minimum Cost Casing Design*. Oil Well, (1996).
12. Hills J O. *Design of Casing Programs, Drilling and Production Practice*. American Petroleum Institute, (1939).
13. Jeffrey L. Didas. *Pipeline Casings - Management of Pipeline Casing Issues*. NACE, **9520** (2017)
14. Bleier R. Selecting a Drilling Fluid. Journal of Petroleum Technology; (USA), **42** (1990): 832-834.
15. Sampey J A, Cottingham R. *Computer Analysis Of Drilling Fluids*, Society of Petroleum Engineers, (1980).

 DOI: 10.1051/matecconf/201712804011

Improving co-running program's performance on CMP

Dawei Tian[1], Hongkui Li[2,a], Wenhui Niu[2], Ying Deng[2], Fujian Li[2]

[1]*State Grid Shandong Electric Power Company, 250001 Jinan, Shandong Province, China*
[2]*State Grid Shandong Heze Electric Power Company, 274000 Heze, Shandong Province, China*

Abstract. Chip multi-processor (CMP) has become the most common processor in the current cluster and desktop computer, and it is also the current development direction. On CMP, programs usually co-running with each other. However, programs commonly interfere with each other. Some time the interference takes big effect, which cause serious drop down of performance. In order to avoid the serious performance interference, programs should be scheduled reasonably to different socket to improve the program's performance and system's utilization. In this paper we propose a new scheduling method to realize a more reasonable scheduling. We do not only consider the LLC miss rate, but also consider the LLC reference of the programs. By the information of LLC reference and LLC miss rate, we schedule programs to different sockets, which realize a reasonable scheduling. The experiment result show that making use of the scheduling method proposed by our paper, program's performance can improve 4%, because the performance improve is realized by on-chip resource, which is a big contribution.

1 Introduction

Chip multi-processor (CMP) has become the most common processor in the current cluster and desktop computer, and it is also the current development direction [1, 2]. A great deal of work is directed at the scheduling of on-chip processors in an effort to improve program performance and system resource utilization.

On CMP, programs usually co-running with each other. However, programs commonly interfere with each other [3]. Some times the interference takes a little effect, which do little effect to program's performance. Some time the interference takes big effect, which cause serious drop down of performance [4]. Meanwhile, for programs co-running on CMP, serious performance dropdown is not expected.

In order to avoid the serious performance interference, programs should be scheduled reasonably to different socket to improve the program's performance and system's utilization [5]. How to schedule the programs is the problem should be deeply explored. The past work uses the last level cache (LLC), they schedule programs to different socket with evenly allocate the LLC miss rate [6], but they do not consider the LLC reference.

In this paper we propose a new scheduling method to realize a more reasonable scheduling. We do not only consider the LLC miss rate, but also consider the LLC reference of the programs. By the information of LLC reference and LLC miss rate, we schedule programs to different sockets, which realize a reasonable scheduling. The scheduling Algorithm consist of two components: the decision module and the scheduling module.

In the decision module, we use micro-architecture events LLC reference and LLC miss rate to do the decision. The value of LLC reference and LLC miss rate are composing to a complex value, and then a program queue with the complex value from small to big are obtained. Then the schedule decision can be make, resulting in the complex value of the two socket are basically same

In the scheduling module, we schedule the programs to the appropriate execution environment. The basic operation of *taskset* is used for our scheduling. we use *taskset* to bind programs to the object process core, then we can change OS scheduling to our schedule with in decision module.

The experiment result show that making use of the scheduling method proposed by our paper, compared with operating system scheduling, program's performance can be improved by 4%, because the performance improve is realized by on-chip resource, which is a big contribution.

2 Related work

There are many related work on CMP scheduling for program's performance and system's utilization.

Zhuravlev et al. [6] found that compared with the cache space contention, memory controller contention, memory bus contention and prefetching hardware contention contribute more to the performance of program. Then predict that it is necessary to minimize the total number of miss rate. Then they use LLC miss rate as the index, which is evenly distribute in each socket.

[a] Corresponding author: dkzxzdh@163.com

SDC [7] is first used for predict the cache contention between threads. It's basic idea is to model the program's LRU stack positions in the LLC and the extra miss produced by other program's contention.

Xie et al. [8] use the animalistic classification to classify program. They classify programs by the interference to each other when co-running on one socket. Then programs can be classified with: turtle (low LLC ref), sheep (low miss rate, insensitive to the number of cache ways), rabbit (low miss rate, sensitive to the number of cache ways) and devil (high miss rate, easy to the hurt co-running programs).

Knauerhase et al. [9] propose contention-aware scheduling algorithm based on LLC miss rate. The hypothesis that the miss rate should explain contention contradicted the models based on stack- distance profiles

Qureshi et al. [10] use Utility Cache Partitioning to predict each program's number of hits and misses for all possible number of ways allocated to the program in the cache. Then thse cache is partitioned with the aim of minimizing the number of cache misses for the co-running programs.

2 Scheduling Algorithm

The scheduling algorithm consist of two components: the decision module and the scheduling module. In the decision module, we use micro-architecture events LLC reference and LLC miss rate to do the decision. In the scheduling module, we schedule the programs to the appropriate execution environment. The flow chart as in Figure 1.

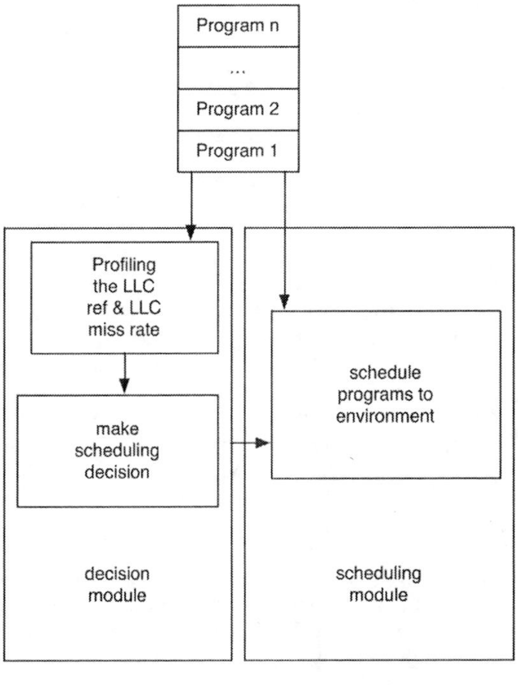

Figure 1. The flow chart of resource isolation method.

2.1 Decision module

In this module, related events of every programs should be profiled, and these events is the input of the decision module. The LLC ref and LLC miss rate can be obtained on-line via common profiling tools such as *perf* [11]. This procedure can be accomplished on-line or off-line.

The function of decision module is to decide which program should be scheduled to the separate socket. This part is the core content of our paper. Because the scheduling plan has directly effect to the program's performance.

If the scheduling plan is good, programs has litte contention for LLC and memory resource, then the program's performance will be good. If the scheduling plan is not good, programs has serious contention for LLC and memory resource, then the program's performance will be bad. The input of the decision module is the events of every programs, including LLC ref and LLC miss rate. The output of the decision module is the scheduling strategy of the programs. The decision module obeys the pseudo-code below.

Pseudo-code of the decision module

```
for i = 1 to n do
    collect the LLC ref and LLC miss rate information of the program
    normalize ref[i], miss[i]
end for
for i = 1 to n do
    complex[i]= ref[i]*0.2 + miss[i]*0.8
    reorder programs from small to big by complex
    schedule programs to different socket according to complex[i]
end for
```

Figure 2. Pseudo-code of the decision module

According this pseudo-code, first we profile program's LLC ref and LLC miss rate by performance profiling tool perf, we profile 108 instructions of every program. Then we normalize the LLC ref and LLC miss rate. The method is take the biggest value of LLC ref and LLC miss rate as 1 separately, and the other value of LLC ref and LLC miss rate is a value between [0,1]. Then calculate the complex value according the pseudo-code, and reorder the programs according the value of complex value. After that we can get a queue with the complex value from small to big. Then the schedule decision can be make. We put the smallest complex value and the biggest complex value into the first socket, then put the second smallest complex value and the second biggest complex value into the second socket, then put the third smallest complex value and the third biggest complex value into the first socket, and so on. At last, all the programs can be scheduled to the two sockets, and the complex value of the two socket are basically same. The above is our decision module.

2.2 Scheduling module

The scheduling module do the implementation of scheduling programs to the object environment. For the operating system, programs are schedule to two sockets evenly. That is, the OS do not consider other thing such as interference, the OS consider only load balance []. For

 DOI: 10.1051/matecconf/201712804011

example, there are four programs need schedule, the OS will schedule the first program to the first socket, then schedule the second program to the second socket, then schedule the third program to the first socket, then schedule the forth program to the second socket. However, the work in our paper can improve program's performance by considering interference. In decision module, all programs are planed to schedule to the two sockets, and the complex value of the two socket are basically same. In the scheduling module, the basic Linux command *taskset* is used to realize the schedule. According the strategy in decision module, we use *taskset* to bind programs to the object process core, then we can change OS scheduling to our schedule with in decision module.

3 Experiment

Our experiments are executed on a NUMA server, which with two socket and 4 core on each socket. The detail server information is in TABLE 1. We select programs from SPEC CPU2006. The SPEC CPU2006 benchmark is SPEC's industry-standardized, CPU-intensive benchmark suite, stressing a system's processor, memory subsystem and compiler. The programs as workloads are in TABLE 2. The LLC reference and LLC miss rate event collected by *perf* are listed in TABLE 3.

We compare our decision module with the OS scheduler to illustrate the advantage or our method. The OS scheduler scheduling programs according load balance. However, our method scheduling programs not only according load balance, but also according the interference of programs.

Table 1. Server configuration

CPU	Intel Xeon E5620
core	4 cores@2.13G
L1 caches	32K
L2 caches	256K
L3 caches	4M
Threads per core	1 thread
Sockets	2
Memory	8GB, DDR3

Table 2. Workloads

Workloads	Program
Workload 1	410, 416, 429, 444
Workload 2	445, 450, 453,482

Table 3. Collected events

Item	Events
LLC reference	last level cache reference
LLC miss rate	last level cache miss

We use two workloads for our experiment, Figure 3 shows the program's performance with different strategy, and the baseline is the program's performance when program running alone on a server. The programs in the first workload is 410, 416, 429, 444. It is shown by the OS scheduling strategy that the performance of the program is 95% of that when program running alone. But by our scheduling strategy, program's performance is 98% of the performance when program running alone. It is because compared with OS scheduling, our scheduling strategy can not only deal with the load balance, but also deal with the interference between programs running on one socket. Sadly, the OS scheduling can not do contribute on dealing with program's interference running on one socket. However, for this workload, both the two scheduling strategy do not result in serious performance drop down of programs. It is because of the characteristic of programs. These programs (expect 429) have relative little LLC ref and LLC miss rate value, meaning they have little contention on on-chip share resource. Which is means when these programs co-running on one socket, they have little interference and little performance download. But for workload 2, it is different.

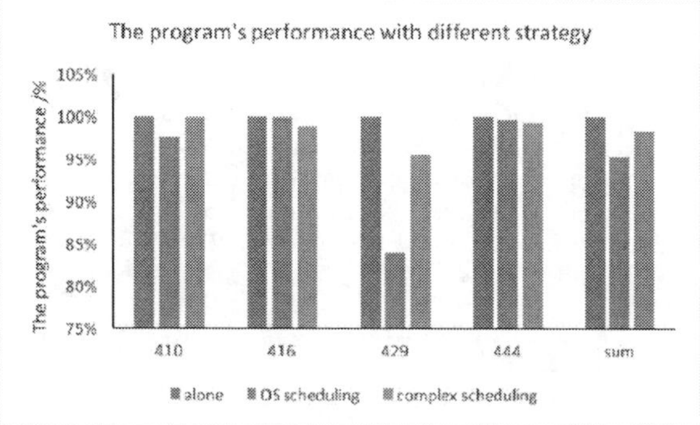

Figure 3. Program's performance with different strategy (workload 1)

Figure 4 shows the program's performance with different strategy of workload 2, and the baseline is the program's performance when program running alone on a server. The programs in the second workload is 445, 450, 453,482. It is shows by the OS scheduling strategy, program's performance is 94% of the performance when program running alone. But by our scheduling strategy, program's performance is 99% of the performance when program running alone. For workload 2, when using the OS scheduling strategy, the average program's performance drop down relative serious, it is because in workload 2, both 450 and 482 have relative large event on LLC ref and LLC miss rate value, which means they have sharp contention on on-chip share resource. when these programs co-running on one socket, they have serious interference and serious performance drop down. So for workload 2 when using the OS scheduling strategy, program 450 and 482 are co-running on one socket, which resulting in performance drop down.

 DOI: 10.1051/matecconf/201712804011

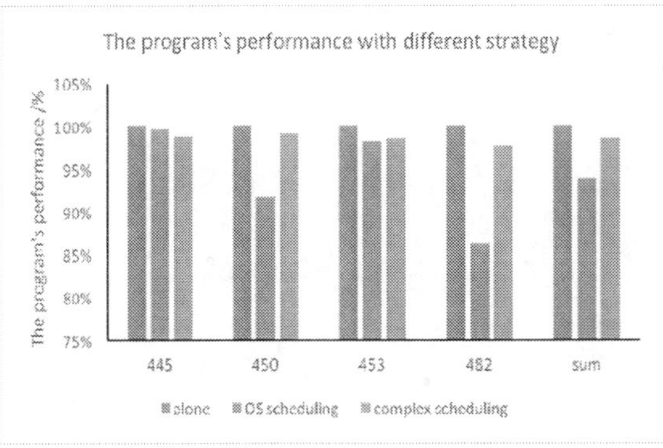

Figure 4. Program's performance with different strategy (workload 2)

4 Conclusion

In this paper we propose a new scheduling method to realize a more reasonable scheduling. By the information of LLC reference and LLC miss rate, we schedule programs to different sockets, which realize a reasonable scheduling. The scheduling Algorithm consist of two components: the decision module and the scheduling module.

In the decision module, we use micro-architecture events LLC reference and LLC miss rate to do the decision. The value of LLC reference and LLC miss rate are compose to a complex value, and then a program queue with the complex value from small to big are obtained. Then the schedule decision can be make, resulting in the complex value of the two socket are basically same

In the scheduling module, we schedule the programs to the appropriate execution environment. The basic operation of *taskset* is used for our scheduling. we use *taskset* to bind programs to the object process core, then we can change OS scheduling to our schedule with in decision module.

The experiment result show that making use of the scheduling method proposed by our paper, compared with operating system scheduling, program's performance can be improved by 4%, because the performance improve is realized by on-chip resource, which is a big contribution.

References

1. C. Dhruba, G. Fei, K. Seongbeom, et al. Predicting inter-thread cache contention on a chip multi-processor architecture[C]. 11th International Symposium on High-Performance Computer Architecture, 2005: 340-351.
2. K. Seongbeom, C. Dhruba, S. Yan. Fair cache sharing and partitioning in a chip multiprocessor architecture[C]. Proceedings of the 13th International Conference on Parallel Architectures and Compilation Techniques, 2004: 111-122.
3. Y. Jiang, X. Shen, C. Jie, et al. Analysis and approximation of optimal co-scheduling on chip multiprocessors[C]. 2008 International Conference on Parallel Architectures and Compilation Techniques, 2008: 220-229.
4. K. Rob, B. Paul, H. Barbara, et al. Using OS observations to improve performance in multicore systems[J]. IEEE MICRO, 2008(28):0272-1732.
5. L. Wang, R. Wang, C. Fu, et. al. Interference-aware Program Scheduling for Multicore Processors[C]. ICA3PP 2013, 201312: 436-445.
6. S.Zhuravlev, S. Blagodurov, A. Fedorova. Addressing Shared Resource Contention in Multicore Processors via Scheduling[C]. Fifteenth International Conference on Architectural Support for Programming Languages and Operating Systems (ASPLOS '10), New York, USA: ACM, 2010: 129-141
7. D. Chandra, F. Guo, S. Kim, and Y. Solihin. Predicting Inter- Thread Cache Contention on a Chip Multi-Processor Architecture. In HPCA '05: Proceedings of the 11th International Symposium on High- Performance Computer Architecture, pages 340–351, 2005.
8. Y. Xie and G. Loh. Dynamic Classification of Program Memory Behaviors in CMPs. In Proc. of CMP-MSI, held in conjunction with ISCA-35, 2008.
9. R., P. Brett, B. Hohlt, T. Li, and S. Hahn. Using OS Observations to Improve Performance in Multicore Systems. IEEE Micro, 28(3):54–66, 2008.
10. M. K. Qureshi and Y. N. Patt. Utility-based cache partitioning: A low- overhead, high-performance, runtime mechanism to partition shared caches. In MICRO 39: Proceedings of the 39th Annual IEEE/ACM International Symposium on Microarchitecture, pages 423–432, 2006.
11. https://perf.wiki.kernel.org/index.php/Main_Page

A Method of Initial Velocity Measurement for Rocket Projectile

Jiancheng Zhang[1], Tianle Zhang[2], Zhengyu Cai[3]

[1]School of Electronic and Optical Engineering, Nanjing University of Science and Technology, 210094, Nanjing, China
[2]School of Electronic and Optical Engineering, Nanjing University of Science and Technology, 210094, Nanjing, China
[3]School of Electronic and Optical Engineering, Nanjing University of Science and Technology, 210094, Nanjing, China

Abstract. In this paper, a novel method is proposed to measure the initial velocity of the rocket based on STFT (the short-time Fourier transform) and the WT (wavelet transform). The radar echo signal processing procedure involves the following steps: sampling process, overlapping windows, wavelet decomposition and reconstruction, computing FFT (Fast Fourier Transform) and spectrum analysis, power spectrum peak detection. Then, according to the peak of the detection power spectrum, the corresponding Doppler frequency is obtained. Finally, on the basis of the relationship between Doppler frequency and instantaneous velocity, the V-T curve is drawn in MATLAB to obtain the initial velocity of the rocket muzzle.

1 Introduction

With the development of weapon system, people have higher requirements on the performance of weapon system. As an important indicator of weapon characteristics and trajectory characteristics, the velocity and acceleration of ammunition are widely used in the research of weapon system. Therefore, the initial velocity of muzzle is of great significance to the development of weapon system and the development of ballistics theory. In this paper, we present a new method for initial velocity measurement by combining STFT with wavelet transform.

2 Radar echo signal model

The radar echo signal of the rocket is usually considered as stationary random signal in a short time and the instantaneous Doppler frequency is time-varying [1]. Thence the echo signal model of the rocket can be expressed as formula (1).

$$x(t)=\sum_{i=1}^{n}a_i\sin(2\pi f_i t+\varphi)+\sum_{i=1}^{n}\rho_\omega\delta(i) \qquad (1)$$

Where f_i is the frequency of the ith signal; a_i is the amplitude of the ith signal; $\rho_\omega\delta(i)$ is the ith noise signal.

Therefore, the core of signal processing is how to extract the Doppler frequency that the radial velocity corresponds to from the radar echo signal of the rocket. In order to extract the time-varying characteristic of echo signal, we take advantage of the method of the time-frequency analysis to describe the echo signal of the rocket. Time-frequency analysis methods primarily include the following sections: the short-time Fourier transform, wavelet transform, WVD (wigner-ville distribution) transformation, fractional Fourier transform, polynomial phase transformation, Dechirp transform method, and so on [2]. This paper aims at proposing a new design method for processing radar signal that combine STFT with wavelet transform. By overlaying the window with the advantage of high magnitudes of the Blackman window in the time domain, it is possible to extract useful information that is missed at the edge of the window.

3 Radar echo signal analysis

3.1 The short-time Fourier transform

In practice, the procedure for computing STFT is to divide a longer time signal into shorter segments of equal length and then compute the Fourier transform separately on each shorter segment [3]. Then we usually plot the changing spectra as a function of time.

In the discrete time case, the data to be transformed could be broken up into chunks or frames (which usually overlap each other, to reduce artifacts at the boundary). Each chunk is Fourier transformed, and the complex result is added to a matrix, which records magnitude and phase for each point in time and frequency. The formula can be delivered as

$$X(m,\omega)=\sum_{n=-\infty}^{\infty}x[n]w[n-m]e^{-j\omega n} \qquad (2)$$

In formula (2), where $x[n]$ is the signal function, $w[n]$ is the window function, m and ω are discrete and quantized respectively. $X(m,\omega)$ is the Fourier Transform of $x[n]w[n-m]$.

[1] Corresponding author: jiancheng_z@163.com

3.2 Wavelet de-noising

Wavelet transform is a new transform analysis method, which inherits and develops the idea of localized STFT, and overcomes the shortcomings of window size not changing with frequency. It is an ideal tool for signal time-frequency analysis and processing [4]. In the continuous time case, continuous wavelet transform can be expressed as

$$W_{\varphi}f(a,b)=\frac{1}{\sqrt{|a|}}\int_{-\infty}^{+\infty}f(t)\varphi^{*}\left(\frac{t-b}{a}\right)dt \tag{3}$$

Where a (a ∈ R, a ≠ 0) is scale factor and denotes the stretch and shrink of the frequency, b is time shift factor.

$$\varphi_{a,b}(t)=\frac{1}{\sqrt{|a|}}\varphi\left(\frac{t-b}{a}\right) \tag{4}$$

The above-mentioned formula (4) is wavelet mother function.

In our design, wavelet transform is utilized to remove part of the noise signal.

3.3 Power spectrum estimation algorithm

In a short time, the radar echo signal of the rocket belongs to stationary random signal, therefore we adopt the method of power spectrum estimation in signal processing [5]. This power spectrum estimation algorithm is based on the Fourier Transform, and there are two methods to realize this algorithm. The detailed theoretical analyses would be showed as follows.

During signal processing, the periodogram is an estimate of the spectral density of a signal [6]. Assume that the random signal is $x(n)$, we intercept N points of $x(n)$ and it is denoted as $x_N(n)$. Then computing DFT (Discrete Fourier Transform) for $x_N(n)$ and its corresponding spectrum is expressed as $X_N(k)$.

$$X_N(k)=\sum_{n=0}^{N-1}x_N(n)e^{-j\omega kn} \tag{5}$$

Where $\omega=\frac{2\pi}{N}$, $n=0,1,2\ldots.N-1$. For discrete signals, the power spectrum estimation value is expressed as

$$\hat{P}_{PER}(k)=\frac{1}{N}|X_N(k)|^2 \tag{6}$$

The other method is the autocorrelation power spectrum estimation. We can obtain the autocorrelation function for $x_N(n)$, and it is expressed as

$$\hat{r}(m)=\frac{1}{N}\sum_{n=0}^{N-1}x(n+k)x^{*}(n),k=0,1,2,\ldots,M \tag{7}$$

The power spectrum estimation is expressed as

$$\hat{P}_{BT}(\omega)=\sum_{m=-M}^{M}\hat{r}(m)e^{-j\omega m},\ |M|\leq N-1 \tag{8}$$

When $M<<N-1$, $\hat{P}_{BT}(\omega)$ makes the signal smooth and improves the method of the periodogram. When $M=N-1$, the periodogram is a special case of the autocorrelation power spectrum estimation.

4 ALGORITHM DESCRITION

4.1 Signal processing process

The data used in this paper are collected by the Doppler velocimetry radar of the 35GHz continuous wave system and the sampling frequency is 0.25MHz. The process of signal processing involves the following steps:

(1) The discrete radar echo signal of the rocket are divided into 200 segments and the length of each segment is 1024.

(2) According to the Mallat algorithm, the db12 wavelet is selected to filter each segment of the signal, then utilize the method of the tower decomposition and reconstruction to obtain the approximate component of the signal [7].

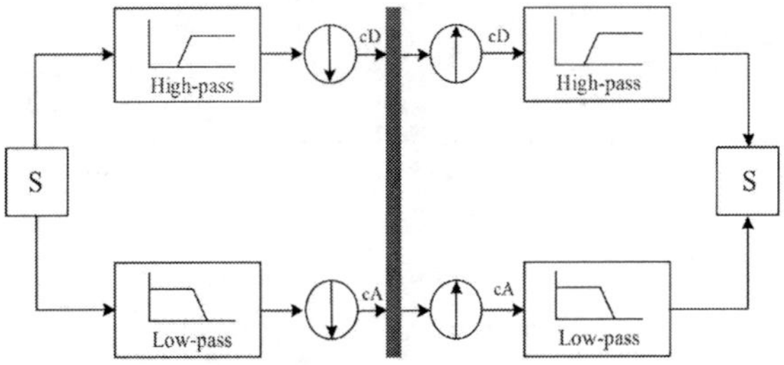

Figure 1. Realization of the Mallat algorithm.

Figure 1 shows the procedure of the whole decomposition and reconstruction. But in our paper, we just need to gain low frequency wavelet coefficient. That would be explained detailly in Figure 2.

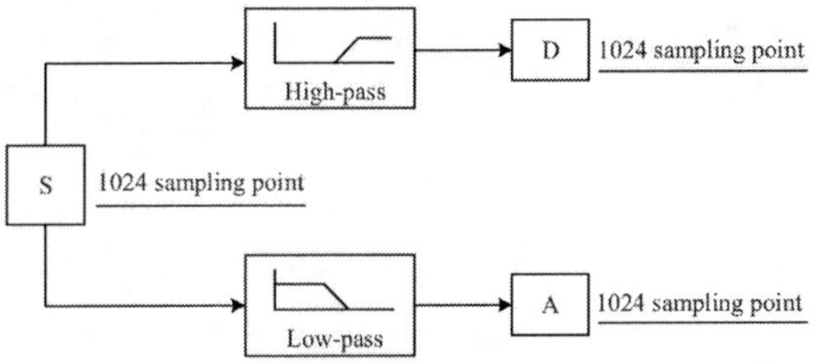

Figure 2. Obtaining the low frequency wavelet coefficient.

The db12 wavelet is selected to compute DWT (Discrete Wavelet Transform) for the approximate component of the signal, then we take the method of wavelet threshold denoising to process low frequency wavelet coefficient, which is depicted as cA in Figure 1. The db12 wavelet is a kind of Daubechies wavelet, it is used to decompose and refactor signals or as a filter [8]. It would be showed in detail in Figure 3.

DOI: 10.1051/matecconf/201712804012

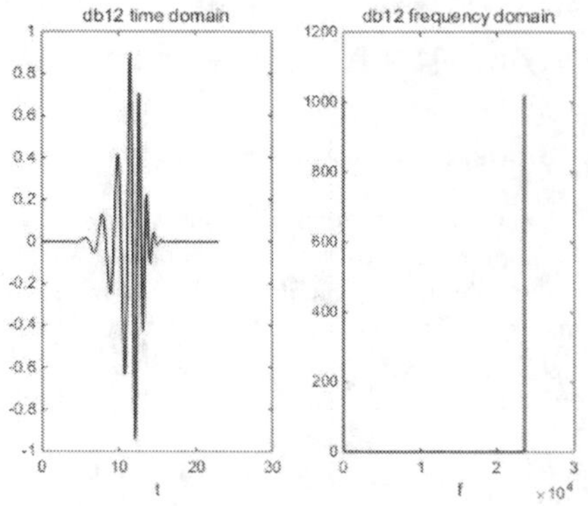

Figure 3. Db12 wavelet.

(3) Each segment of the signal computes 1024 point FFT transformation, and detecting the peak value of the power spectrum to obtain corresponding Doppler frequency and instantaneous velocity. Moving the sliding window back 512 points and circular 200 times. Finally, a power spectrum waterfall diagram that contains 200 groups signal is drawn in MATLAB. That would be showed in detail in Figure 4.

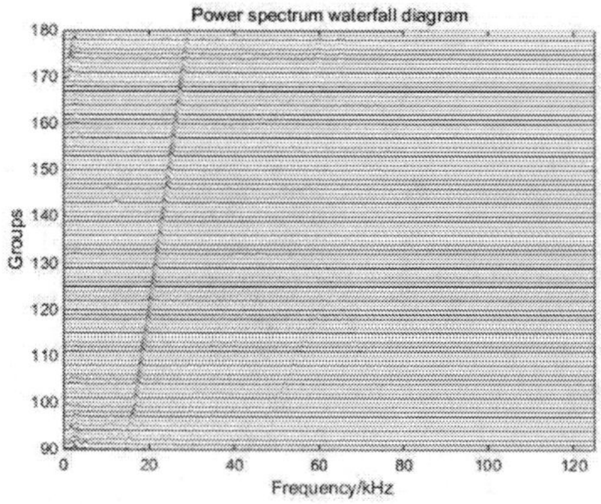

Figure 4. Power spectrum waterfall diagram.

(4) In this paper, the frequency of the radar transmit signal is 35GHz, it is expressed as f_1. The sampling frequency is 0.25MHz, it is expressed as f_s. For discrete signals, the actual frequency is expressed as

$$f = \frac{nf_s}{N} \tag{9}$$

Where n is the position of the sampling point ; N is the length of a window, in this paper, the length of a window is 1024. The instantaneous velocity can be computed by the classical equation:

$$v = \frac{\lambda f_d}{2} \tag{10}$$

Where $f_d = \frac{df_s}{N}$, $\lambda = \frac{c}{f_1}$.

The involved symbols in (10) are explained as follow

f_d: the Doppler frequency,

d: the position of the sampling point that the peak of the power spectrum corresponding,

λ : the wavelength of the radar transmit signal in free space,

c: the speed of the electromagnetic wave in free space.

According to the relationship between the Doppler frequency and instantaneous velocity of the rocket, we fitting V-T curve in MATLAB by using the method of least squares. It is showed in Figure 5.

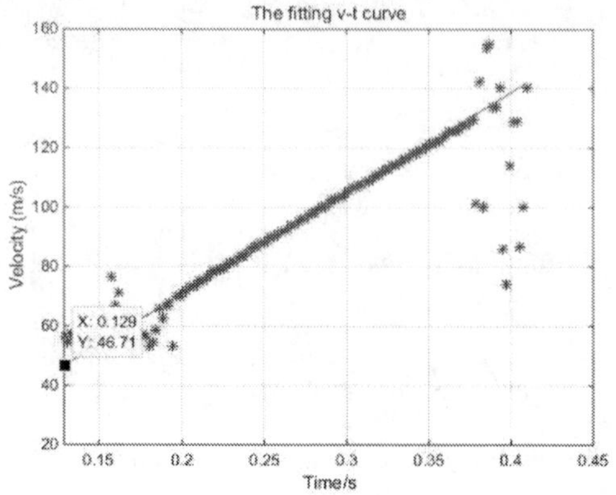

Figure 5. The fitting V-T curve.

Finally, we briefly show the process of signal processing with a flow chart in MATLAB. That is showed in detail in Figure 6.

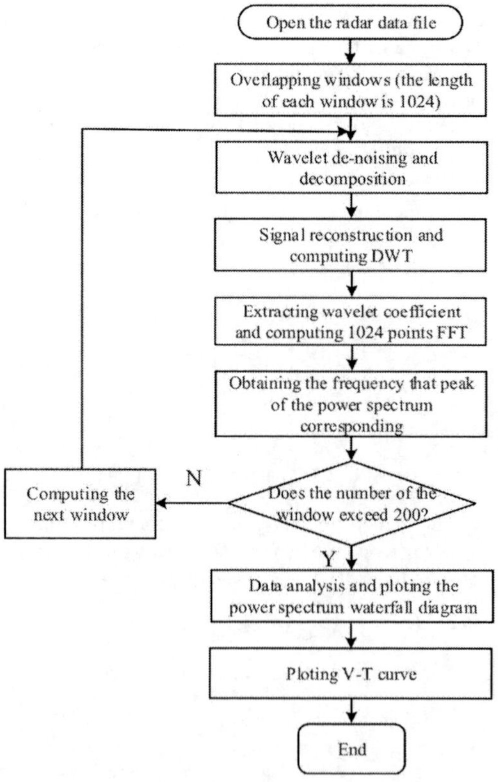

Figure 6. The flow chart of the signal processing

4.2 Data analysis

We can obtain the instantaneous velocity of the rocket from the Figure 5, the data would be showed in detail in Table 1.

Table 1. Initial velocity fitting data.

Time/s	0.129	0.131	0.133	0.135	0.137	0.139
Velocity(m/s)	46.71	47.99	48.71	49.41	50.11	50.82
Time/s	0.141	0.143	0.145	0.147	0.149	0.152
Velocity(m/s)	51.51	52.21	52.91	53.61	54.32	55.02
Time/s	0.154	0.156	0.158	0.160	0.162	0.164
Velocity(m/s)	55.72	56.43	57.12	57.83	58.53	59.23
Time/s	0.166	0.168	0.169	0.172	0.174	0.176
Velocity(m/s)	59.93	60.63	61.34	62.04	62.74	63.44

From the above table, it shows that the instantaneous velocity of the rocket is 46.71m/s when the time is 129 ms and 47.99 m/s when time is 131ms. And on the basis of the muzzle vibration test, the time that this rocket went out of the muzzle is 130 ms. Finally， in order to get the instantaneous velocity when time is 130 ms, we take the average of these two instantaneous velocity value. The result shows that the instantaneous velocity of the rocket is 47.35 m/s when the time is 130ms.Therefore, we can draw a conclusion that the initial velocity of the rocket is 47.35 m/s when this rocket went out of the muzzle.

5 Conclusion

A novel method of initial velocity measurement of the rocket is proposed in this paper. This algorithm has a low calculation and is more suitable for the radar signal. The result of the actual signal processing verify that the proposed method achieves better estimation accuracy than the traditional spectrum analysis, and the segment of useful information that related to the target can be extracted effectively in the low SNR (Signal Noise Ratio) conditions.

Acknowledgment

The authors would like to thank the members of Radar Signal Processing Laboratory of Nanjing University of Science and Technology for their help to this paper.

References

1. J. Flamant; N. Le Bihan; P. Chainais, "Spectral analysis of stationary random bivariate signals," in IEEE Transactions on Signal Processing , vol.PP, no.99, pp.1-1.
2. B. Wu, K. Li, M. Yang and C. H. Lee, "A study on sampling of STFT modifications in time and frequency domains for DNN-based speech dereverberation,"2016 Asia-Pacific Signal and Information Processing Association Annual Summit and Conference (APSIPA), Jeju, 2016, pp. 1-4.
3. F. Qifeng, C. Guoqing and S. Zibo, "Application of wavelet de-noising method in vibration signal analysis of elevator car," 2016 13th International Conference on Ubiquitous Robots and Ambient Intelligence (URAI), Xi'an, 2016, pp. 610-614.
4. Y. Zhao, L. Zhang, J. Hu and T. Liao, "Mallat Wavelet Filter Coefficient Calculation," 2013 International Conference on Computational and Information Sciences, Shiyang, 2013, pp. 963-965.
5. P. Balakrishnan, M. M. Hasan and K. A. Wahid, "An Efficient Algorithm for Daubechies Lifting Wavelets Using Algebraic Integers," in Canadian Journal of Electrical and Computer Engineering, vol. 37, no. 3, pp. 127-134, Summer 2014.
6. Zheng Cheng gong, Chen Xi and Huang Zhen, "A comprehensive analysis on Doppler frequency and Doppler frequency rate characterization for GNSS receivers," 2016 2nd IEEE International Conference on Computer and Communications (ICCC), Chengdu, 2016, pp. 2606-2610.
7. Y. Zhao, L. Zhang, J. Hu and T. Liao, "Mallat Wavelet Filter Coefficient Calculation," 2013 International Conference on Computational and Information Sciences, Shiyang, 2013, pp. 963-965.
8. P. Balakrishnan, M. M. Hasan and K. A. Wahid, "An Efficient Algorithm for Daubechies Lifting Wavelets Using Algebraic Integers," in Canadian Journal of Electrical and Computer Engineering, vol. 37, no. 3, pp. 127-134, Summer 2014.

Research on Collaborative Acquisition of Multidimensional Massive Web Based on Fusion Credibility

ZHANG Ya-juan[1,a], HE Wen-qing[2]

[1]Railway Telecommunication Department, Hunan Technical College of railway high-speed, China
[2]CNOOC Zhuhai Natural Gas Co., Ltd., China

Abstract. In the era of rapid development of Internet technology and people's growing social needs, web information collection has been successfully applied to the major search engines and search areas. In this paper, the mass information collection is regarded as the dynamic task allocation problem based on the co-operation of the package. A multi-dimensional computer resource model is proposed, which uses the heuristic algorithm of the mutation to match the heuristic algorithm. Conditional cost objective function is optimized, so that the whole system in the process of dynamic changes, the time and cost are as small as possible. Finally, the experimental results show that the algorithm can meet the different user requirements on the basis of maximizing the total cost of the system.

1 Introduction

In the massive web page information collection task allocation problem, the concern is often how to divide the task, such as: Web division, regional division, domain name division, and then according to the size of the distribution of the corresponding physical nodes, few based on crawling nodes Self-attribute allocation method. Therefore, this paper proposes a multi-dimensional computer resource model which integrates the credibility, and then uses the mutation-matching heuristic algorithm to dynamically allocate the task. By optimizing the cost objective function with multiple constraints solving, making the whole system in the process of dynamic changes, the time and cost are as small as possible.

2 Basic concept

Dynamic task allocation problem is the core research problem of various kinds of complex collaborative systems in engineering project and practical application. During the operation of this kind of system, because of the external environment and some of the internal resources of the internal constraints, in the face of each task project And the unexpected situation, the system requirements will change accordingly, and the time cost and cost overhead will also change, seriously affect the stability of the entire system, the implementation of efficiency and overall cost, in order to solve these problems, the system needs to constantly Task sequence allocation and redistribution operation, this process is the dynamic task allocation, in a sense, this dynamic task allocation problem is an uncertain environment interdependent task allocation of the decision-making problem, also known as multi-objective decision Problem [1,2,3].

Multi-objective decision-making problem: Let the system have m objective functions: $f_1(x), f2(x), \ldots, f_m(x)$ and n decision variables composed of vector: $x=(x_1, x_2, \ldots, x_n)^T$. If these goals require the largest (or minimum), and the solution to meet the constraints of k constraints, the mathematical model Can be expressed as follows:

$$Z=F(X)=\begin{bmatrix} \max(\min) f_1(X) \\ \max(\min) f_2(X) \\ \vdots \\ \max(\min) f_m(X) \end{bmatrix} \tag{1}$$

$$s.t. \quad \phi(X)=\begin{bmatrix} \varphi_1(X) \\ \varphi_2(X) \\ \vdots \\ \varphi_k(X) \end{bmatrix} \le G=\begin{bmatrix} g_1 \\ g_2 \\ \vdots \\ g_k \end{bmatrix} \tag{2}$$

Equation (1) shows that there are m objective functions that need to be optimized. Equation (2) shows that there are k constraints that need to be satisfied.

2 The proposed technique

2.1 Multi-Dimensional computer resource model with fusion credibility

In the actual project implementation process, the demand is always changing, the number of tasks is dynamic, the resources required for each task is also uncertain, so we

[a] ZHANG Ya-juan: zhangyajuan2017@sina.com

DOI: 10.1051/matecconf/201712804013

assume that the project demand for the machine m_j is d_i. Then the vector $D=\{d_1,d_2,\ldots,d_n\}$ indicates the project's demand for all types of machines. Under the influence of the dynamic execution of the project, the value of each element in D is uncertain. In this paper, the Gaussian distribution model is used to simulate the stochastic problem of demand change in the process of actual project implementation [5, 6].

The value of each element in the vector $D=\{d_1,d_2,\ldots,d_n\}$ is different, assuming that $d_1',d_2',\ldots,d_n'$ represents the value of each element in D, then the set $D'=d_1'*d_2'*\ldots*d_n'$ represents the Cartesian product of the set, then the relation between the set D and the set D' Can be formalized as:

$$D\in D' \text{ and } \sum_{D\in D'} p(D)=1 \tag{3}$$

At this point, when the number of reserved machines is $N_{j,i}^b$, the number of machines actually used during the operation of the project is $N_{j,i}^u(D)$, and the number of machines that may be attached is $N_{j,i}^a(D)$ for the specific requirements D mentioned above. Then the relationship between the three can be formalized as:

$$D=N_{j,i}^u+N_{j,i}^a(D),\ N_{j,i}^u(D)\le N_{j,i}^e \tag{4}$$

According to the universal collection fee standard, the total cost of the user needs to be paid in the case where the current demand is D:

$$C(D)=\sum_{t_i\in T}\sum_{m_i\in M} c_{j,i}{}^{[b]}N_{j,i}^{[b]} + \sum_{D\in D'}\sum_{t_i\in T}\sum_{m_i\in M} P(D)(c_{j,i}{}^{[u]}N_{j,i}^{[u]}(D)+c_{j,i}{}^{[a]}N_{j,i}^{[a]}(D)) \tag{5}$$

In the dynamic task allocation, because the actual operation of the project will inevitably change the task, the machine node without feedback, node crashes and other factors, in order to better maintain the stability of the system to enhance the system's efficiency and task execution rate. We also consider the cost of the time also need to consider the cost of time. Therefore, in this paper, when we optimize the dynamic task allocation model of fusion confidence, we first set a time threshold of the project itself, under which the cost is minimized, which ensures the actual project operation time Overhead, but also to achieve the purpose of minimizing the cost.

The optimization of the dynamic task allocation method for fusion confidence is carried out by using the maximal minimum method to convert the total cost of the target function $C(D)$ and the total time T_{total} to the single objective optimization problem which only optimize the total cost of $C(D)$. To the target function total time T_{total} set a threshold, the original constraints remain unchanged, respectively, the reserve phase, the use of stages and additional stages of the machine price, the number of machines used in each stage, processing time.

Minimize:

$$C(D)=\sum_{t_i\in T}\sum_{m_i\in M} c_{j,i}{}^{[b]}N_{j,i}^{[b]} + \sum_{D\in D'}\sum_{t_i\in T}\sum_{m_i\in M} P(D)(c_{j,i}{}^{[u]}N_{j,i}^{[u]}(D) + c_{j,i}{}^{[a]}N_{j,i}^{[a]}(D)) \tag{6}$$

$$s.t.\quad N_{j,i}^u(D)\le N_{j,i}^b, t_i\in T, \mathrm{m}_i\in M, D\in D' \tag{7}$$

$$\sum_{t_i\in T} n_{j,i}^{cpu}(N_{j,i}^u(D)+N_{j,i}^a(D))\le \max\nolimits_j^{cpu} \tag{8}$$

$$\sum_{t_i\in T} n_{j,i}^{m}(N_{j,i}^u(D)+N_{j,i}^a(D))\le \max\nolimits_j^{m} \tag{9}$$

$$\sum_{t_i\in T} n_{j,i}^{br}(N_{j,i}^u(D)+N_{j,i}^a(D))\le \max\nolimits_j^{br} \tag{10}$$

$$N_{j,i}^b, N_{j,i}^u(D), N_{j,i}^a(D)\in Z, \quad \mathrm{t}_i\in T, m_i\in M, D\in D' \tag{11}$$

$$T_{total}=T(r)+T(a) \tag{12}$$

$$T_{total}\le T_{value} \tag{13}$$

Equation (7) indicates that the number of machines used when demand D cannot be greater than the total number of machines reserved. Equation (8) ~ (10) indicates that when the demand is D, the total amount of resources used in the use phase and the reservation phase cannot be greater than the maximum amount of resources of the machine. Equation (11) indicates that the number of machines used at each stage is a nonnegative integer. Equation (12) ~ (13) indicates that the total processing time cannot be greater than the threshold T_{value} we set.

2.2 A heuristic task allocation algorithm for mutation priority matching

Variation of the priority match Heuristic algorithm is described as follows:

(1) Selecting a node from all the used physical node sequences;

(2) Determine whether the confidence of the physical node Confidence value is greater than the set threshold;

a. Less than, to perform all the tasks of its revocation, back to the queue to be executed in the task sequence, continue to traverse the next has been used in the physical node sequence;

b. Not less than, to determine the physical nodes of multiple dimensions (CPU, memory, network bandwidth, etc.) can meet the requirements of the current task. Meet the requirements, the current task will be assigned to the physical node; do not meet the requirements, back to (1), continue to implement;

(3) If all of the used physical nodes cannot meet the requirements of the current task, then select the first from the list of physical nodes that are not used;

(4) To determine the physical nodes of multiple dimensions (CPU, memory, network bandwidth, etc.) can meet the requirements of the current task;

a. To meet the requirements, the current task will be assigned to the physical node;

b. Does not meet the requirements, then continue to traverse the current unused physical node sequence until you find the physical node to meet the requirements of the current task assigned to the physical node;

(5) Repeat the above steps until all tasks have been assigned.

3 Experiment results

Experiment 1 The number of physical nodes is fixed, and the relationship between the number of user requirements and the total cost is simulated.

Set the number of physical nodes to be 30, the number of physical nodes required for users is 1 to 60, the reservation phase, the use phase, the additional phase of the price were 3 Yuan, 8 Yuan, 15 Yuan. The values of each variable are shown in Table 1.

Table 1. Experimental variable value table.

Variable name	Variable value
Reserve physical nodes	30
User desired physical nodes	1-60
Reserve price	3
Use price	8
Additional price	15

Then, according to the above table the value of each variable and the formula (6) ~ (13) can be obtained, the reserve phase, the use of stages and additional stages of the cost of the situation shown in Table 2 below.

Table 2. The stage of the experiment, the stage of the use, the stage of the additional stage.

	d_1: 1~30	d_2: 30~60
Reserve phase	30*3	30*3
Use phase	d_1*8	30*8
Additional phase	0(No additional)	(d_2-30) *15

The results of Matlab simulation experiment 1 are shown in Fig 1.

From the experimental results in Figure 2 shows that the number of fixed physical nodes in the fixed, with the number of users need to increase the number of physical nodes, the reserve stage of the cost remains unchanged; the use of stage costs first increase in the demand exceeds The cost of the additional phase is always zero when the number of reserved physical nodes is greater than or equal to the user's demand. When the user's demand exceeds the reserve number, the additional cost increases; the total cost is always on the rise.

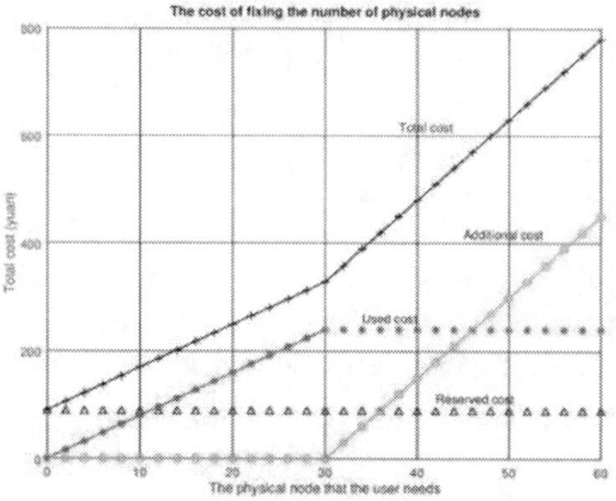

Figure 1. Fixed total cost changes when reserving physical nodes.

Experiment 2 The total number of physical nodes required by the user is the same, and the relationship between the number of physical nodes and the total cost is simulated.

Set the total demand for 50 physical nodes, the number of physical nodes reserved for the 1 to 150, the reserve phase, the use of stage, the additional phase of the price were 3 Yuan, 8 Yuan, and 15 Yuan. The values of each variable are shown in Table 3.

Table 3. Experimental variable value table.

Variable name	Variable value
Reserve physical nodes	1-150
User desired physical nodes	50
Reserve price	3
Use price	8
Additional price	15

Then, according to the value of each variable in Table 3 and the formulas (6) ~ (13) in Section 2.1, the cost of the reserve phase, the use stage and the additional stage are shown in Table 4 below.

Table 4. The stage of the experiment, the stage of the use, the stage of the additional stage.

	d_1: 1~50	d_2: 50~1500
Reserve phase	d_1*3	d_2*3
Use phase	d_1*8	50*8
Additional phase	50*15-(d_1*3+d_1*8)	0(No additional)

DOI: 10.1051/matecconf/201712804013

The results of Matlab simulation experiment 2 are shown in Fig 2.

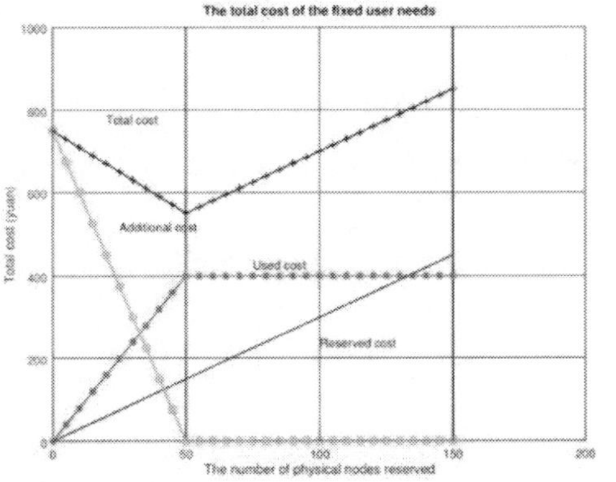

Figure 2. Fixed total cost changes when the user is required.

4 Conclusion

Based on the self-attribute of the computer, the multi-dimensional computer resource model is established. At the same time, in order to consider the timeliness of the physical node in practical application, the concept of credibility is put forward, and this constraint condition Integrated into the computer resource model, can better adapt to the dynamic changes in the system. The simulation results show that the proposed algorithm can meet the needs of users in a limited time range, and the total cost is the smallest.

References

1. Jadidi O, Zolfaghari S, Cavalieri S. International Journal of Production Economics. A new normalized goal programming model for multi-objective problems: A case of supplier selection and order allocation, 148(1):158-165(2014).
2. Choudhary D, Shankar R. Computers & Industrial Engineering. A goal programming model for joint decision making of inventory lot-size, supplier selection and carrier selection, 71(1):1-9(2014).
3. Jadidi O, Cavalieri S, Zolfaghari S. Applied Mathematical Modelling. An Improved Multi-Choice Goal Programming Approach for Supplier Selection Problems, 39(14):4213-4222(2014).
4. Luo J, Lan C E. Journal of Guidance Control & Dynamics. Determination of weighting matrices of a linear quadratic regulator, 18(6):1462-1463(2015).
5. Ejsmont W. Statistics & Probability Letters. A characterization of the normal distribution by the independence of a pair of random vectors, 114:1-5(2016).
6. Qun-ying. Acta Mathematicae Applicatae Sinica. Laws of the Iterated Logarithm for ρ -mixing Random Variables with Normal Distribution, 2:385-394(2016).

Design of a Distributed Food Traceability Platform and Its Application in Food Traceability at Guangdong Province

Haibiao luo, Yin Li, Dongcheng Liu, Yunxiong Ouyang, Feng Yuan

Institute of Software Application Technology, Guangzhou & Chinese Academy of Sciences, Guangzhou 511458, China

Abstract. Food traceability is an important measure to secure food safety. This paper designed a food traceability platform based on distribution framework and implemented it in Guangdong province. The platform can provide traceability service, production and management service for food enterprise, provide forward and backward traceability of the whole cycle of food production and circulation, and provide various methods of food traceability for public. One characteristic of the platform is that it opens up the data flow among production, circulation and supervising departments, and builds a unified commodity circulation data pool. Based on the flow data pool, not only the production and circulation information of the food product can be traced, but also its inspection and quarantine information. Another characteristic of the platform is that its database and data interface were developed based on the fool electronic traceability standards formulated by the National Food and Drug Administration. Its interface standardization and compatibility with other food traceability platforms can thus be guaranteed. The platform is running at Guangdong province for key supervising products of Infant formula foods (including milk powder, rice flour, farina, etc), editable oil and liquor. The public can use the Guangdong food traceability portal, mobile APP, Wechat or the self-service terminals in the supermarkets to trace food products by scanning or input its traceability code or its product code and verify its authenticity. It will help to promote consumer confidence in food safety.

1 Introduction

Food security issue has become an important social problem worldwide. From the outburst of bovine spongiform encephalopathy (BSE) at the end of last century in Europe [1], detection of melamine in milk in China in 2008, to the horse meat incident in France in 2013[2], as well as the bird flu, the illegal cooking oil, the Sudan red and other food security incidents [3], all highlight the gravity of the food security situation. In 2015 a first ever estimates of the global burden of foodborne diseases by World Health Organization (WHO) [4] show almost 1 in 10 people fall ill every year from eating contaminated food and 420 000 die as a result, children under 5 account for almost one third of deaths. World health statistics conducted by WHO [5] show that more than 100 countries are transitioning rapidly towards a greater proportion of deaths from noncommunicable diseases and injuries. In 22 under-developed countries, 70% or more of years of life lost (due to premature deaths) are still caused by infectious diseases and related conditions. Meanwhile, in 47 countries (mostly high-income), noncommunicable diseases and injuries cause more than 90% of years of life lost. These fully testify that food security is a very severe situation worldwide. Building food traceability systems, monitoring, managing and tracing food from farm to food production, processing and circulation in the market, is deem as an important method to guarantee food security and prevent food borne diseases [6-10].

Therefore countries in the world develop various food traceability systems. The first was beef products traceability and management system [11] built by European Union (EU) in 1997. And the opinion of traceability management was first proposed at that time. In 2002, EU further expanded the scope of traceability to all the food sold in EU. The US proposed "risk management from farm to table" [12] and asked food corporations to build food traceability system. Japan started to trace beef products at 2003 [13]. These food traceability system formed new non-tariff barriers to trade in effect. To answer the new changes in food security management and food trade, Australia, New Zealand, Canada and other countries developed traceability management of animal husbandry related products. China started to explore and study food traceability system since 2000 [14-16]. At first port commodity was chosen to experiment and then extended to cow, sheep, vegetables, etc.

The EAN•UCC system [17] proposed by EAN International and America Uniform Code Council is the most popular food track and trace system, and has been applied widely by EU and the US to traceability system of food, drink, meat and other products. The EAN•UCC system mainly include 3 parts: coding system, data carrier (bar code, for instance) and data exchange

[a] Corresponding author: luohaibiao@gz.iscas.ac.cn

 DOI: 10.1051/matecconf/201712804014

(Electronic Data Interchange, EDI for instance). Through the EAN•UCC system, every step of the food supply chain can be effectively marked and information among steps can be transmitted, interchanged and managed. Food therefore can be tracked and traced in efficient and effective ways. Netherlands built a comprehensive production chain management system called Integrale Keten Beheersing (IKB) [19], which is a quality detection and control system to ensure all important activities in production chains under control. The British government built the Cattle Tracing system (CTS) [20-21] to register cattle births and report cattle deaths and movements. The Australia's National Live Stock Identification System, NLIS [22] record livestock movements from its birth to slaughter by its permanent id system. Australia further established the Efficient Consumer Response Australia (ECRA) based on GS1 standards [23] to trace food, drinks and other products' supply chain. Canada first built the Canadian Livestock Tracking System (CLTS) [25] to track supply chain of livestock, especially cow. After its success, CLTS was further extended to track agricultural products and resulted in National Agriculture and Food Traceability System (NAFTS) [26].

In China, there are many food traceability systems. The largest is the State food (product) Safety Traceability platform 28, which was established by GS1 China [27] and started to collect product codes since 2007. Currently the total number of the traceable products in the platform is 71225540. The Public Service Platform of State Food Industry Corporation Credit [29] aims to improve public trust for Chinese food corporations by developing food industry credit system and evaluating corporation credit. It also provides food product traceability service for 6 infant formula milk powder manufactories. Reclamation of Agricultural Product Quality Safety Net [30] provides tracking and tracing service of agricultural products of 5 provinces. In addition, local governments also build their own food traceability systems. In Sichuan province, Agricultural Product Quality Safety Platform [31] was set up to record supply chain information of agricultural products (tea, lemon, mutton and some fruits), from source of raw materials, processing, inspection of finished products, logistics channel, to retail information electronically. Anhui Food Safety Traceability Platform [32] developed food traceability system of whole chain from raw materials to retail of infant formula milk powder, meat products, dairy products, edible vegetable oil and liquor. Shanghai Food Safety Traceability Platform [33] also built a traceability system of the whole chain of from raw material to retail of cereals, fruits, edible vegetable oil, livestock products, aquatic product, vegetable and dairy products based on Internet of Things technology. It works with local food supervision departments to import product supervision information. There are more food traceability systems developed by food corporations themselves or industry associations. For example, Bee Product Association built a bee product traceability system [34] aiming to promote transparency of bee product and improve consumer's trust. Yili Milk Corporation established a traceability system [35] that records every step of milk production process from cow breeding, logistics of product to retail. Pork Quality Traceability system [36] provide traceability information to the public by Personal Digital Assistant (PDA) and mobile communication technology.

In conclusion, at present most food traceability system can only trace food production process including raw materials and manufacturing of one or a few food products. Their main purpose is for quality control and to satisfy food quality regulations. Product circulation and retail processes usually involve other corporations who will not report their product circulation information without large enough benefits or strong forces from outside. Government food supervision departments normally won't open their data to other parties. Therefore, most food traceability systems cannot provide product circulation information and inspection and quarantine information from government supervision departments.

Data structure and interfaces of food traceability system have not been standardized by state regulations and standards until recently the State Food and Drug administration issued a serials of standards [37-44] for food safety electronic traceability systems.

The food traceability platform proposed in this paper has the following characteristics:

(1) From paper research results, the food traceability platform designed in this paper is one of the few platforms that can provide traceability not only throughout the whole production and circulation chain process, but also inspection and quarantine information from government supervision departments.

(2) The platform has built a Unified Merchandise Circulation Data Pool (UMCDP), in which manufacturing enterprises, circulation enterprises, supervision departments could record product information of the whole production and circulation process based on electronic product code, traceability code and manufacturing time.

Based on UMCDP, platform users, including consumers, can trace not only product's normal information such as manufacturer, production date and address, but also its inspection and quarantine information. It promotes transparency of this product's supervision, which is usually rare to be seen but most requested by consumers to ensure the food product's quality and security.

Based on UMCDP, the platform can provide big data analysis of the whole food supply and circulation chain for enterprises of the food corporations, while most food traceability system can only provide food production information.

(3) The platform designs its food traceability information data structure, internet of things information service interfaces and Internet of Things Name Service interfaces based on the latest standards specified by the State Food and Drug administration to ensure standardization and universality.

(4) Most traceability systems are built based on the product coding rule of corporation itself or industry specification. The platform in this paper developed a multi-industry food traceability coding, separation, parsing and transforms mechanism. A unified IOT identification id can be created for various products based

on this mechanism and achieve traceability for all the domestic food products.

2 Material and Methods

2.1 Food Traceability Requirements for the Whole Production and Circulation Cycle of Food

The whole production and circulation cycle of food can be divided into raw material phase, production phase, finished-product left factory phase, delivery and circulation phase, and sales terminal phase. It's required to collect data from all the phases. For big corporations, the data collection work is usually done by their own ERP system. For small corporations, a SaaS service provided by the platform in this paper can be used.

Table 1. Required management information in a full cycle of food production.

A full cycle	mm
Raw	Supplier、incoming inspection, in storage time, etc
Production	During production and manufacture phase, key information of production, inspection record, finished-product information, storage information, etc
finished-product	Information about leaving factory, delivery, distributor
Circulation	Information about left factory, in storage, out of storage
Retail Terminal	Traceability code, product bar code, sale time, etc

Normally liquor, edible cooking oil, infant formula foods have one or multiple identification information of Electronic Product Codes (EPC), production date or production batch, box code or traceability code. The traceability code is the only identity label for a merchandise item. The carrier of the traceability code can be two-dimension QR code, RFID or NFC. The manufacturer or distributor must report the complete product package information including quantity, manufactory date, box code or traceability code. The circulation enterprises or catering enterprises must report the package information of products when they are bought or sold. The platform provides three methods to track and trace a product: EPC + production date, box code or traceability code.

2.2 Regulations and Standards

This platform was designed according to regulations of GB/T 22003-2008 Food safety management systems-requirements for bodies providing audit and certification of food safety management systems[37-38], Standard system for food and drug administration information[39] and Standard system for Internet of Things of the state key food (product) quality and safety traceability [40].

Data structure of the food safety electronic traceability identification information was designed according to Standard for data structure of food safety traceability identification [41]. This standard designs food traceability coding structure including The Global Language of Business (GS1), Electronic Product code (EPC) and China Food Safety Trace (CFST).

Database service interface was designed according to Standard for Interfaces of Internet of Things Information Service Database of Food Safety Electronic Traceability (IOTIS) [42] that designs the database interfaces through which food safety traceability applications interchange data and events through internet. In this paper, IOTIS interfaces are provided to food corporations to upload required data.

Electronic traceability name service was designed according to Standard of Internet of Things Name Service for Food Electronic Traceability (IOTNS) [43] that designs the system architecture of internet of things name service, terminal user query interface, IOTNS query interface and IOTNS registration interface. IOTNS is composed of coding service and IOT name service. Coding service is to decode the identification information uploaded by users. IOT name service is to decode IOT web address uploaded by users.

Internet of things discovery service was designed according to Standard of Internet of Things Discovery Service for Food Electronic Traceability (IOTDS) [44]. When information of a single merchandise item is located at different IOTIS, the address of this item can be achieved by IOTDS.

2.3 System Design

The system architecture of Guangdong Province Food Safety Traceability Platform is showed at figure. 1. Distributed architecture is chosen to build the distributed traceability center, on which the Corporation Traceability Data Interchange Service Module, Production & Operation Supervision Module, Public Traceability Service Module. In the Corporation Traceability Data Interchange Service Module, SaaS platform was built for corporations to deploy data upload and interchange service or connect with its own ERP system or a third party traceability system. Based on IOT technology, data can be uploaded and integrated from phases of manufacture, circulation and retail. To the public, supervision departments and other food industry partners, various terminals including web portals, mobile APPs, self-service terminals, are provided to serve food traceability requests.

2.4 Architecture of System Functioning

The main components of the system functioning are food traceability service and food traceability data center.

1) Food traceability service: mainly corporation traceability data interchange service, production & operation supervision service, public query service. The corporation traceability data interchange service covers the business requirements of production and circulation corporations. It provides management functions for events of production and circulation.

 DOI: 10.1051/matecconf/201712804014

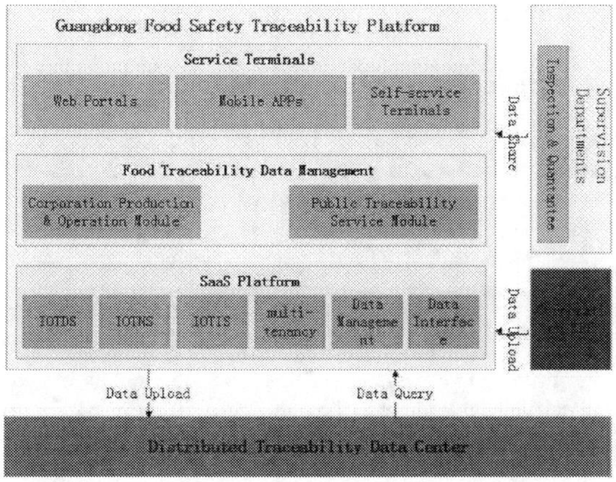

Figure 1. System of Framework

Production & operation supervision service serves various levels of supervision departments and provide them food product management and supervision functions including corporation information management, product information management, product flow tracking, emergency operation, recall operation, risk prediction.

Public query service is to serve consumers and the public the product query request and provide genuine product manufacture information, delivery information, sales information, inspection information. The public can report quality and safety issues in the query terminals.

2) Food traceability data center: composed of two parts, basic data and business data. The basic data includes corporation information and production information which are produced during corporation and product registration. Business data includes production, circulation, inspection, retail information. The center provides interfaces for data upload, data interchange and data decoding.

2.5 SaaS Platform for Multi-tenancy

The platform has to serve various corporations with different business needs. Therefore it is crucial to be able to provide customization of software service based on tenancy. Tenancy is referred to the same group of users who have common demands for the platform [45]. The user rents software packages based on tenancy unit. The platform provides SaaS service to multi-tenancy and share human labor and device resource among tenants to lower the cost. The key technology to multi-tenancy is the multi-tenancy customization. The platform applied Metadata Driven Component-based Software Development method [46] to customize multi-tenancy.

The core of multi-tenancy customization based on Component-based Software Development method (CBSD) is extension point, by which business logics, interface logics and data entities of different tenancy can be substituted to build customized software. The business component can contain multi extension points and include extended functions for other components.

Metadata driven method is to develop generalization programs based on metadata, in which entity relationship showed at figure 2 is defined. MetaType defines metadata type and builds hierarchical structure by recursive parentType. MetaItem defines the metadata. Based on different metadata type, various business logics can be defined. For customization requests such as menu, business logic, entity and internationalization, the type of metadata can be defined correspondingly. Configuration of mutil-tenancy is stored as metadata. As deployment of a tenancy, addition, deletion or substitution of a present tenancy configuration metadata can build a new tenancy configuration.

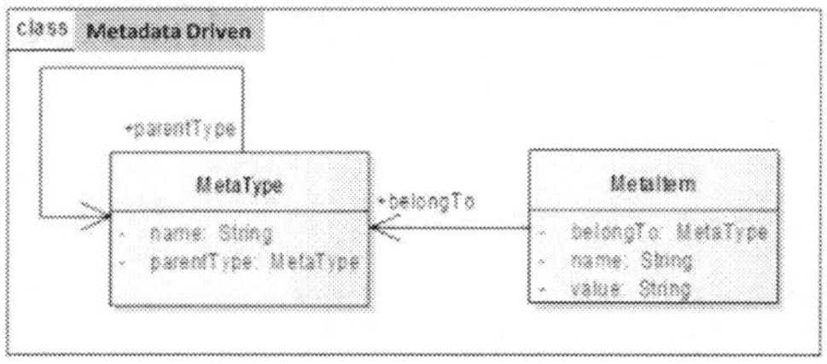

Figure 2. Metadata driven entity relationship

2.6 Service Framework based on IOT Technology

The platform designs the service framework based on IOT technology and follows IOTIS specification as shown in figure 3. The service framework has unified interfaces that food corporations upload and interchange their data through their own ERP system or ERP system provided by the SaaS service in the platform.

Traceability data are stored in corporation database as well as the traceability data center of this platform. The query address of all traceability data are registered in the traceability data center. Therefore, the province level platforms (Guangdong and Jiangsu Food Safety Traceability Platforms) are responsible for traceability query address. The state level food safety traceability platforms are responsible for the IP resolution of the query address.

This platform is a first attempt in the state to communicate query information between province level food traceability platforms. And it is also one of the first few food traceability platforms to specify the interfaces and data structures according to the latest food safety electronic traceability standards.

2.7 Unified Merchandise Circulation Data Pool

The platform records data from production, circulation, retail and supervisions and build a Unified Merchandise Circulation Data Pool (UMCDP), in which products are recorded and linked by product code, traceability code and production date.

By tracking retail state of the product, one can quickly find out counterfeit products if the total number of products be sold by retailers and in circulation state is higher than the number of production.

UMCDP data can also be used to analysis the market based on data from production, circulation and retail corporations and provide a more complete picture of the product flow situation.

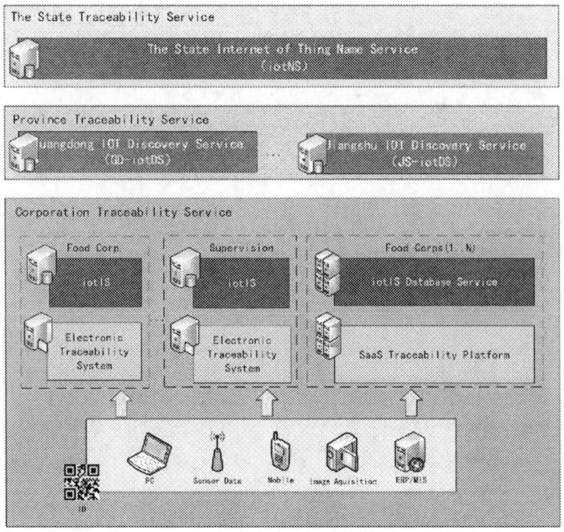

Figure 3. Framework of Internet of Things Service

2.8 Public Traceability Service Terminals

The food product query channels provided to the public are a web portal, public WeChat platform, mobile app and self-service terminals placed at supermarkets. Consumers can scan the product code or traceability code of the product using an APP, WeChat scanner, barcode scanner of the self-service terminals, or input the codes by hands in one of the terminals to get feedback of product information including product photo, place of origin, expiration date, inspection information, etc. If there is a safety or quality issue, one can report the issue through any of the terminals to supervision departments and relevant corporations.

3 Results and Discussions

3.1. Application at Guangdong Province

Guangdong Food Safety Traceability Platform was launched in 05/06/2016 and started to collect data from food corporations and supervision departments. The public traceability terminals were launched at the same time.

The web portal of the platform is: http://spsy.gdfda.gov.cn/. Public WeChat applet and mobile APPs for Android and Apple OS can be downloaded by searching Guangdong Food Traceabilityat the APP markets or from the web portal.

By the end of 12/31/2016, there were 883 food manufacturers, 36047 circulation and retail corporations, 4283 restaurants registered in the platform and started to report data regularly. There were 18497 domestic and imported products, 350 million traceability data, 122261 pieces of inspection reports. At the same time, public awareness of this platform has been growing. The APPs has been downloaded more than 100 thousand times and 400 thousand product queries through different terminals.

3.2 Traceability Service for the Public

Figure 4 shows the query results from the public WeChat applet. After scanning the QR code of a product, the front page of scanning result is shown in Fig. 4., from which one can see the name of the product, expiration date and traceability index. The traceability index is the result of the inspection report, expiration date and UMCDP data analysis results. In most cases, the index will be "good" in green. But if the inspection report is disqualified, the expiration date has passed, or UMCDP analysis indicates possible counterfeit the index will show warning information.

Figure 4. Query Page of a good product by WeChat applet "Guangdong Food Traceability"

Figure 5. Query Page of a disqualified product by WeChat applet "Guangdong Food Traceability"

At the bottom of the product page, there are four buttons (from left to right): product information, inspection & quarantine, material information, circulation information. The product information page shows the product image and detail product information. Inspection & quarantine page contains inspection report issued by the local food supervision departments. The report is a pdf file and can be downloaded to learn the inspection detail. The material information page shows the detail information about the manufacturers. The circulation page shows the circulation corporations the product has gone through.

In an actual event that a food product was found disqualified during random inspections, the platform automatically received the inspection report and the traceability index was changed to "warning" in red and a sentence "The product's random inspection failed to pass, please be caution to buy" was shown below the warning sign.

4 Conclusion

This paper designed a food traceability platform for Guangdong province. It's built on distributed traceability data center where corporation data management, supervision service and public query service were established. SaaS platform were developed to support corporations, especially small corporations to build their food traceability system on it. Data will be collected from production, circulation, retail and supervision departments according to the latest state standards for food safety electronic traceability system. All traceability data enter into a data pool that links data from different parties together. The platform designs its food traceability information data structure, internet of things information ser-vice interfaces and Internet of Things Name Service interfaces based on the latest standards specified by the State Food and Drug administration to ensure standardization and universality. Unified IOT identification for varieties of product codes can help lower the communication barriers. Currently, the Guangdong Food Safety Traceability Platform can communicate with Jiangsu Food Safety Traceability Platform and the State food (product) Safety Traceability platform for food product query out of province.

Various query terminals have been developed to satisfy different needs. Within half of year after its launch, 350 million traceability data have been recorded and more than 400 thousand queries have been made. It indicates that there is urgent need within the public to trace food product information. It also means that there is serious trust issue for food industry. Hopefully, the food traceability system can increase the credit of food product and improve the trust.

Acknowledgements

This research was financially supported by the National Sci-tech Support Plan 2015BAK36B02 and 2015BAK36B06, Guangzhou Sci-tech Plan 201610010092 and 201604020101.

References

1. C.B. Xue, P.Y. Wang, J. Zhao., et al. J. of Food Safety & Quality **7**(7) 2815-2820 (2016)
2. H. Xie, L.I. Jun-Min, Food Res. & Dev. **34**(22) 122-125 (2013)
3. J. Y. Lin, Q. X. Zeng, Modern Food Sci. & Tech. **22**(4) 189-192 (2006)
4. WHO, In children under five who estimates nearly a third of food borne disease deaths worldwide http://www.who.int/mediacentre/news/releases/2015/foodborne-disease-estimates/en/ [2015-12-3]
5. WHO, World Health Statistics 2014: Large gains in life expectancy http://www.who.int/mediacentre/news/releases/2014/world-health-statistics-2014/en/ [2014-05-15].
6. S. Kinoshita, Systems Control & Information. **0** 133-139 (2006)
7. R. Ward, D. V. Bailey, R. Jensen, Int. Food & Agri. Man. Rev. **08**(2) (2005)
8. Y. C. Choe, J. Park, M. Chung, Inf. Syst. Frontiers., **11**(2) 167-179 (2009)
9. L. U. Opara, F. Mazaud. Outlook on Agri. **30**(4) 239-247 (2001)
10. L. U. Opara, Agri. Eng. Int.: The CIGR e-journal. (2004)
11. G. Lu. Comp. Appl. & Soft. **27**(1) 20-22 (2010)
12. E. H. Golan, B. Krissoff, F. Kuchler, Agri. Econ. Reports (2004)
13. K. Sugiura, T. Onodera, Veterinaria Italiana **44**(3) 519-519 (2008)
14. L. Lin,Stand. Sci. **4**:55-60 (2009)
15. X. S. Tong, Y. Wu, Log. Eng. & Man. **32**(1) 126-128 (2010)
16. Y. L. Fei, X. F. Xiao, X. M. Wu, China Collective Economy **1** 84-85 (2011)
17. D. C. Bulterman, IEEE Computer Society Press, 2001.
18. T. Yue, Int. Conf. on E-Bus. and E-Gov. IEEE 1-3 (2011)
19. E. Kanis, A. F. Groen, K. H. D. Greef, J. of Agri. & Env. Ethics **16**(2) 137-162 (2003)
20. D. M. Green, R. R. Kao, Veterinary Record **161**(13) 439-43 (2007)
21. CTS online. https://www.gov.uk/cattle-tracing-online
22. Australia's National Live Stock Identification System. https://www.nlis.com.au/
23. Australia GSI, Australia serving up safety and traceability http://www.ferret.com.au/c/GS1-Australia (2010)
24. S. Kress, Australia Key Iss. & Cha. Sup. Cha. Man. An Int. J. in Print **8** 873-901 (2011)
25. Canadian Livestock Tracking System Services http://www.canadaid.com/CLTSServices.html
26. National Agriculture and Food Traceability System (NAFTS) http://www.ats-sea.agr.gc.ca/trac/sys-eng.htm
27. GS1 China http://www.ancc.org.cn/
28. The State food (product) Safety Traceability platform http://www.chinatrace.org/
29. The Public Service Platform of State Food Industry Corporation Credit http://www.foodcredit.org.cn/zs/zhuisu.html
30. Reclamation of Agricultural Product Quality Safety

DOI: 10.1051/matecconf/201712804014

Net http://www.safetyfood.gov.cn/
31. Sichuan Agricultural Product Quality Safety Platform http://www.scfoodsafe.cn/
32. Anhui Food Safety Traceability Platform http://www.ahspy.cn
33. Shanghai Food Safety Traceability Platform http://www.shfda.org/
34. Bee Product Association built a bee product traceability system http://www.china-bee.org.cn
35. J. Cheng, Food Tech. **3** 3-3 (2008)
36. B. H. Xiong, Y. T. Fu, Z. H. Lin, Chinese Agri. Sci. **42**(1) 230-237 (2009)
37. The state administration of food and drug administration, http://www.sda.gov.cn/WS01/CL0087/171362.html **39** [2017-04-01]
38. The state administration of food and drug administration, GB/T 22003-2008 Food safety management systems-requirements for bodies providing audit and certification of food safety management systems (2009)
39. The state administration of food and drug administration, CFDAB/T 0101-2014 Standard system for food and drug administration information (2014)
40. The state administration of food and drug administration, Standard system for Internet of Things of the state key food (product) quality and safety traceability (Not released)
41. The state administration of food and drug administration, Standard for data structure of food safety traceability identification (Not released)
42. The state administration of food and drug administration, Standard for Interfaces of Internet of Things Information Service Database of Food Safety Electronic Traceability (IOTIS) (Not released)
43. The state administration of food and drug administration, Standard of Internet of Things Name Service for Food Electronic Traceability (IOTNS) (Not released)
44. The state administration of food and drug administration, Standard of Internet of Things Discovery Service for Food Electronic Traceability (IOTDS) (Not released)
45. H. L. Lin, Y. B. Han, Chinese J. of Comp. **33**(10) 1881-1895 (2010)
46. Y. Li, F. Yuan, H. Wu, Comp. Eng. & App. **51**(9) 22-29 (2015)
47. X. Yang, J. Cao, App. Math. Mod. **34**(11)3631-3641 (2010)
48. Y. Sun, W. Li, J. Ruan, Comm. in Theo. Phy. **58**(5) 697-703 (2012)

MATEC Web of Conferences 128, 04015 (2017) DOI: 10.1051/matecconf/201712804015
EITCE 2017

Finger vein recognition based on convolutional neural network

Gesi Meng, Peiyu Fang, Bao Zhang

Computer Science, University of Posts and Telecommunications, Beijing, China
Computer Science, University of Posts and Telecommunications, Beijing, China
Automation, North China Electric Power University, Beijing, China

Abstract. Biometric Authentication Technology has been widely used in this information age. As one of the most important technology of authentication, finger vein recognition attracts our attention because of its high security, reliable accuracy and excellent performance. However, the current finger vein recognition system is difficult to be applied widely because its complicated image pre-processing and not representative feature vectors. To solve this problem, a finger vein recognition method based on the convolution neural network (CNN) is proposed in the paper. The image samples are directly input into the CNN model to extract its feature vector so that we can make authentication by comparing the Euclidean distance between these vectors. Finally, the Deep Learning Framework Caffe is adopted to verify this method. The result shows that there are great improvements in both speed and accuracy rate compared to the previous research. And the model has nice robustness in illumination and rotation.

1 Introduction

Biometric recognition technology has a long development history. At present, there are so many categories of biometric technologies such as fingerprint, face, iris, speech and other features. Although these biological features are unique, accessible, widespread and can be regarded as markers of human identity, some challenges still exist [1]. In recent years, it has been proved that the error rate (ERR) of finger vein recognition can reach 0.0009% under certain conditions [2]. At the same time, finger vein identification also has the following advantages: (1) It is a non-contact biometric identification method without finger touch, so it is easy to be accepted by the user. (2) Finger vein belongs to human's internal characteristics, and it can not be copied and embezzled. (3) It has been proved by medical science that finger vein is unique. (4) Each of us has ten fingers. If there is a sudden condition, we can use other fingers instead.

In the traditional finger vein recognition, the main processes are: ROI extracting, filtering, noise reducing, image enhancing, feature extracting and distance matching. However, it takes a long time in computing in the pre-processing stage, and different image sources are suitable for different processing methods. So this paper proposed the finger vein recognition system based on convolutional neural network(CNN) [3], it can solve the problem of illumination change, scale transformation and image rotation, leading to an excellent performance on finger vein recognition.

2 Related Works

The traditional methods of finger vein recognition mainly focus on the extraction of ROI and the representation of feature vectors. In 2010, Yang proposed interphalangeal joint prior method to get ROI segment and calculated feature vector by steerable filter. Then the nearest neighbour classifier is used to identify individual, and the accuracy has reached 98.7% [4]. Later, Guan made improvements. He combined it with filters to remove noise, then used two direction weighted(2D)2LDA methods to represent feature vector. However, the accuracy hadn't been achieved as expected, only 94.69% [5]. Based on the above research, Yang raised a more detailed method. In the pre-process stage, elimination, noise reduction, image enhancement, size and brightness normalization are executed. Finally, the accuracy rate reached 100% through the template matching [6]. However, it can not be a perfect method because these complex processing steps take a long time. After four years, Gupta adopted a new approach to get feature by multi-scale matched filtering and line tracking, then he got 4.47% err [7]. Although some achievements have been made by conventional approaches, the robustness of them is not enough in both noise and misalignment. Therefore, we need to find a more suitable and efficient method.

In recent years, with the development of artificial intelligence, scholars have made an attempt to apply machine learning method into finger vein recognition. Wu and Liu made an experiment based on Principal Component Analysis and neuro-fuzzy system(ANFIS) and achieved high accuracy of 99%, but the execution time is 45.0s [8]. In addition, Kuan-Quan extracted finger vein vectors by Gaussian filter and local binary pattern, and then it reached 98.75% accuracy rate by improved SVM method [9]. However, this method lacks robustness because of the low accuracy in the middle and small finger. In this paper, a new approach using CNN for finger-vein biometric identification was proposed, which reached a high accuracy and speed rate.

3 The proposed approach

Inspired by the visual nerve mechanism, CNN is designed by biologists Hubel and Wiesel in their early research and it's an extension of the multilayer perceptron [10]. It has the advantages of rotation invariance, position invariance and scale invariance because of its three characteristics: local receptive field, weight sharing and pooling.

3.1 Proposed finger vein recognition system

The finger vein recognition system proposed in this paper is shown in Figure 1. In the registration phase, we capture the image of the finger vein by the device and get the region of interest(ROI), and then extract the feature vector through the CNN. In the authentication phase, we use the same method to get the image and its feature vector. Then we calculated the Euclidean distance [11] between the two vectors obtained above. If this distance is less than the threshold, it can be considered that two images comes from the same person and the authentication is successful, otherwise failed. The value of threshold is obtained by plenty of experiments in which we compare the Euclidean distance between intra-class and inter-class and choose a proper threshold as a judgment standard. And its value can be adjusted flexibly according to the practical applications, which makes it stricter for acceptation or rejection.

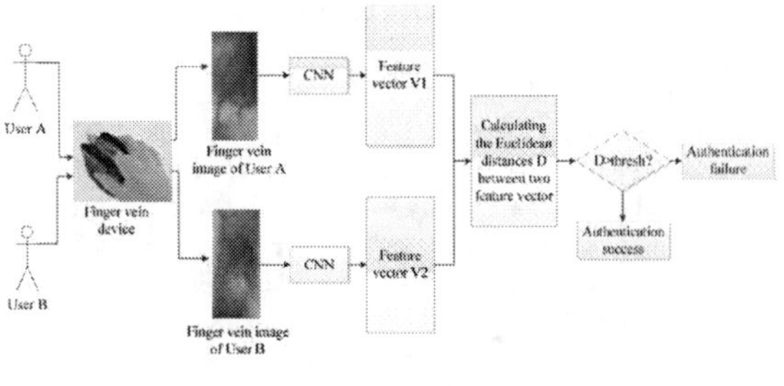

Figure 1. Finger vein recognition system

3.2 Proposed CNN Architecture

In the finger vein recognition system mentioned above, one of the most critical parts is using CNN to extract features, and how to extract the most representative and robust feature vector is the focus of our research. The finger vein image has the characteristics of location invariance and compositionality and the vein lines distribution of different people are similar. And then the CNN model can be trained by inputting a large number of images so that it gets the ability to extract the most representative vector. Also, the feature vectors of new images can be extracted by this already trained model. Therefore, training the CNN to get the most suitable model to extract finger vein features vectors is extremely important.

The most typical structure of AlexNet contains eight layers with weights, the first five is convolutional and the remaining three are fully-connected [12]. The AlexNet is relatively complex and it has higher dimension in the last three full connection layers which is not suitable for training in small data sets. Therefore, the AlexNet needs to be cut properly. At present, there is no rule to set the values of some parameters such as the number of layers, convolution kernel size, sliding step size and so on. After observation, we found the background of finger vein picture is not complicated and colourful, and the mainly differences between different pictures are reflected in the distribution and brightness of vein lines. In order to extract features as fast as possible, it need to reduce the dimensions of three full connection layers. Secondly, our purpose is to make the Euclidean distances as large as possible for the different persons, and as small as possible for the same person. In that case, we take a cost function called Softmax Loss [13]. In order to get the proper parameters of the fully connection layers, we did a lot of experiments and designed a CNN shown in Table 1. The input dimension is 256 * 256 pixels and the output dimension is 64 * 1 pixels.

Table 1. Proposed CNN model structure.

Layer	Layer Type	Size	Output Shape
1	Conv+Relu	96, 11*11, stride: 4	(96,62,62)
1	Max Pooling	3*3, stride: 2	(96,31,31)
1	Norm LRN		(96,31,31)
2	Conv+ReLU	256, 5*5, stride: 1	(256,31,31)
2	Max Pooling	3*3, stride:2	(256,15,15)
2	Norm LRN		(256,15,15)
3	Conv+ReLU	384, 3*3, stride: 1	(384,15,15)
4	Conv+ReLU	384, 3*3, stride: 1	(384,15,15)
5	Conv+ReLU	256, 3*3, stride: 1	(256,15,15)
5	Max Pooling	3*3, stride: 2	(256,7,7)
6	Fully Connection	1024 hidden units	1024
7	Fully Connection	128 hidden units	128
8	Fully Connection	64 hidden units	64
9	SoftmaxWithLoss		

4 Experimental work and results

4.1 Experimental data

In this experimental, the finger vein image database was obtained from the DataTang [14]. And it consists of 64 subjects with 15 samples each for finger, which were captured in three months and 5 images per month. The original size of the captured image is 376*328 pixels. In order to enrich the samples and make the network more robust in illumination and rotation, we added random illumination and slight rotation in the 960 pictures, which is closer to the real application scenarios. Finally, we got 4800 images. In the whole images, we took the 39 images from each subject randomly as training samples. 6 images were used as the testing samples and the remaining 30 images were validation samples, and each image was numbered.

 DOI: 10.1051/matecconf/201712804015

4.2 Experimental process

An open source deep learning framework—Caffe is adopted in the experiment, which has a clear and efficient architecture [15]. This experiment was carried out in CPU environment. First, all images in training set and testing set are numbered separately, and marked with different labels according to their categories. Then we need to convert format of the images form jpg to lmdb by the tools in Caffe which is helpful to reduce the overhead time of IO.

Besides, in order to speed up the convergence of Loss, we calculate the average of the pixel value of the training image by Caffe tools. Before each picture is put into the network, its pixel value must subtract the average to make the data smaller. In this experiment, the amount of data is relatively small and the number of model layers is large. If we just use the random initial value to training the CNN, the Loss doesn't converge and the desired effect cannot be achieved. Therefore, we fine tuned this CNN based on the previous trained caff model. The parameters of each layer were taken as the initial value of the network, then Loss can converge.

In order to avoid overfitting, the weight is reduced by a smaller factor called weight_decay in each iterate. It means a penalty is added in the total weights to keep the weight smaller. So we set the weight_decay value to 0.01. In the SGD optimization [16], the gradient can not be too large or too small. In the former case, there is no decline for the Loss as the iteration number increases; And the latter one will make it difficult to find a fast descent direction to change the Loss. In this paper, the learning rate is adjusted continuously through experiments, and finally is set to 0.001. To realistically and vividly describe the process of extracting features in CNN, we visualized the results of the forth convolution layer in Figure 2. It can be seen that the extracted feature image is smooth and it has the characters of low correlation, irregular structure and less noise, which prove that CNN is suitable to extract finger vein features.

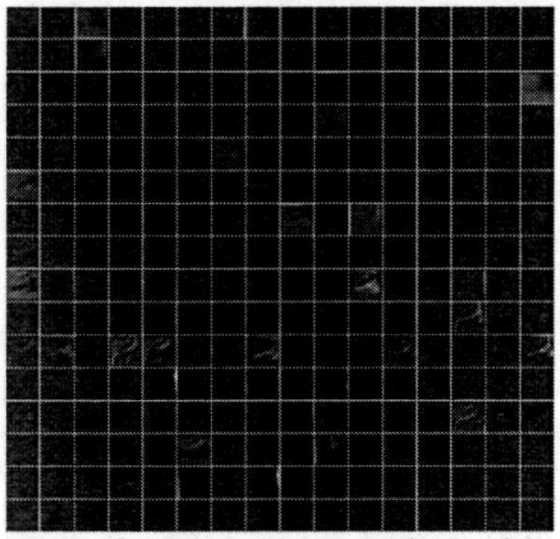

Figure 2. The extracted feature of the fourth layer

4.3 Experimental Results Analysis

4.3.1 Evaluate the extracted features

In the previous CNN training process, in order to increase the contrast between the background and vein lines, the original images were equalized. After the training, we set the 0.25 as threshold value to determine whether authentication is successful by observing the Euclidean distance between intra-class and inter-class in the test set (shown in Figure 3.1). According to this threshold, we made a test in the validation set as is shown in Figure 3.2. Unfortunately, the performance was poor, which was judged as a serious overfitting in train set.

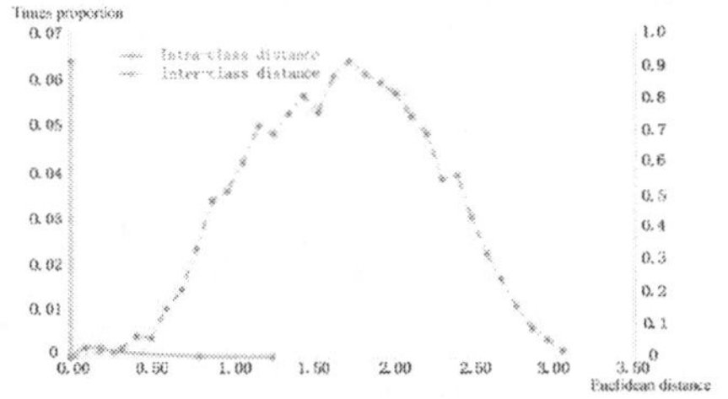

(1) Test set

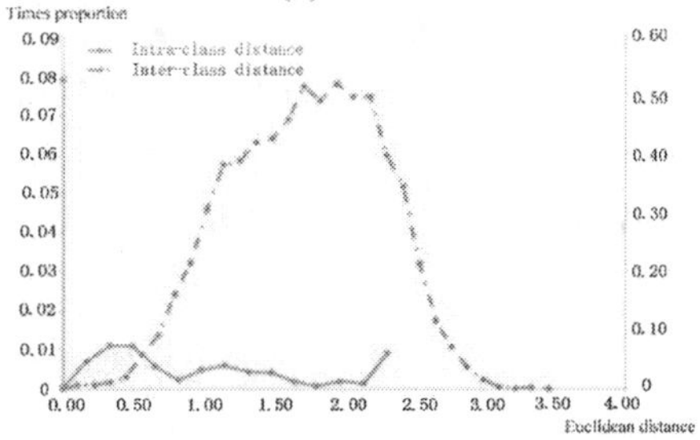

(2) Validation set

Figure 3. Distance distribution in the previous experiments

Then we picked out those pictures according to the false rejection and false acceptance and found that most pictures contain large chunks of white or black areas which is shown in Figure 4. Therefore, equalization is the reason to cause these errors.

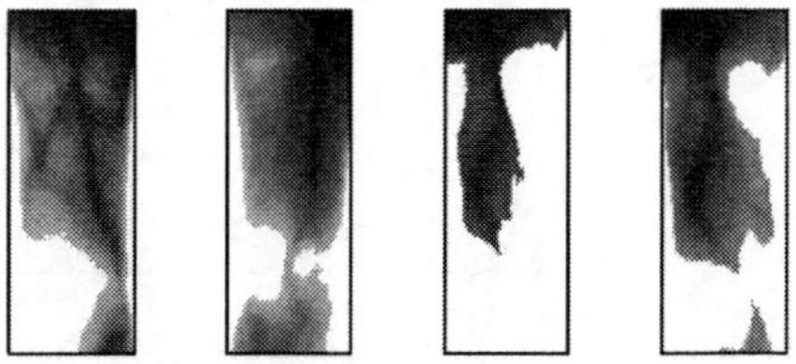

Figure 4. Error images in validation set

So we cancelled the step equalization and directly resized the image to 256*256 pixels, and input them into the CNN for training. Finally, we got the Euclidean distance distribution between intra-class and inter-class in the test set and validation set which are separately shown in Figure 5.1 and Figure 5.2. It is easy to distinguish whether two feature vectors belong to the same person in test set and validation set when the threshold of Euclidean distance is 1.49. The ROC curve is drawn according to different thresholds, as is shown in Figure 6. It can be seen that when the threshold is set to be 1.24, both FRR and FAR achieve the ideal value. The equal error rate is 0.21%. According to the experimental results, this network has better ability to extract finger vein features and can effectively distinguish the distance between intra-class and inter-class.

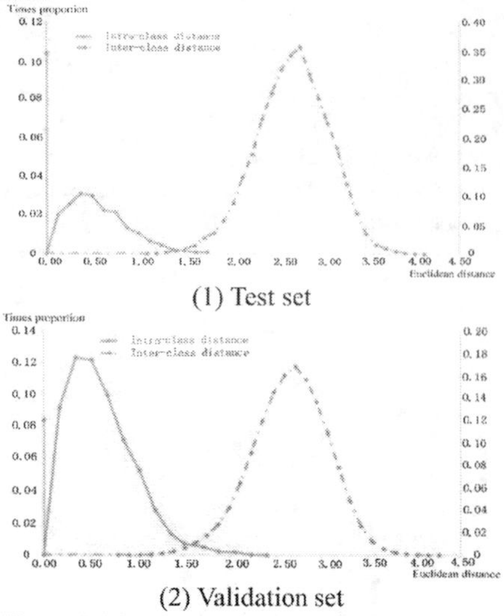

(1) Test set

(2) Validation set

Figure 5. Distance distribution in final experiments

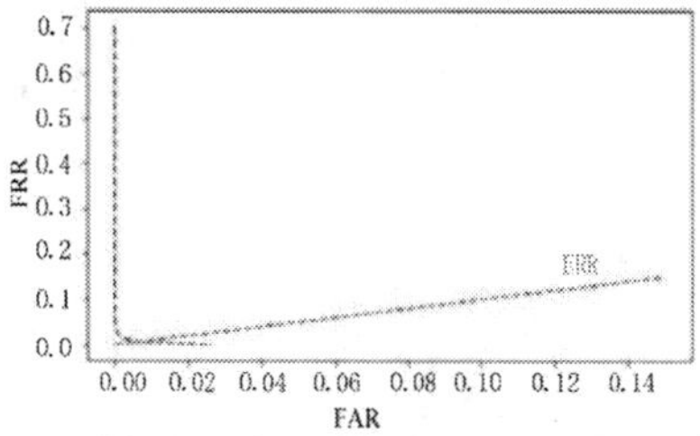

Figure 6. Visualization of the fourth convolution layer

4.3.2 Comparison Between CNN and Other Methods

A new finger vein recognition system is proposed in this paper. Particularly, the feature vectors of finger vein images are extracted by CNN. Through the experiment, we can see that this method is outstanding both in speed and accuracy. The Table 2 shows the performance comparison between the CNN and the traditional method. It can be seen that there is no complex pre-processing procedures for images. Therefore, CNN is not only faster when extracting features, but also more accurate. Most importantly, it has a stronger robustness in rotation and illumination.

5 Conclusion

Finger vein, as an evidence of authentication, has a wide application prospects. However, finger vein images must be processed by various complex algorithms in most of the current finger vein authentication systems. The speed and robustness of this kind of system need to be improved. So in this paper, we proposed a new finger vein authentication system in which the ROI of captured images are directly input to CNN to extract the feature vector, then we judged success or failure of the authentication according to the Euclidean distance between two vectors. Finally, through experiments and analysis, this method shows a good performance in practical application. In the future, we hope to train a better network based on a larger data set to improve the technology of finger vein technology.

Table 2. The comparison between the traditional method and CNN

Reference	Produce	Accuracy	ERR
Liu et al, 2010 [17]	ROI Detection Image Enhancement → Normalization →Manifold learning for image sequence → Construct manifold model library →Image manifold distance for recognition	97.80	0.8%
Wenming et al,2011 [6]	Background → Elimination → Noise reduction → Image enhancement →Brightness → Normalization → Median filter → Vein location and direction coding	100%	0.44%
Wu and Liu 2011 [8]	PCA → LDA → SVM → Adaptive neuro-fuzzy inference system(ANFIS)	98%	-
Perez Vega etal,2014 [18]	Sobel detector → Enhancement filter → Personalized Best Bit Map	-	27.56%
Song Dong ,2015 [19]	Multi-Orientation Weighted Symmetric Local Graph Structure. →Dimensionality Reduction. → the Extreme Learning Machine classifier.	90.9%	-
Shan Juan Xie, 2015 [20]	Guided Filter → Single scale retinex algorithm → Propsed GFSSR	-	1.56%
This paper	Extract feature vector by CNN → Recognition	99.4%	0.21%

References

1. Vacca J R. Biometric Technologies and Verification Systems[M]. Butterworth-Heinemann, 2007.
2. Kulkarni S, Raut D R. Finger Vein Recognition[J]. IOSR Journal of Electrical and Electronics Engineering (IOSR-JEEE), 2014: 32-36.
3. Bichler O. CONVOLUTIONAL NEURAL NETWORK:, WO/2016/030230[P]. 2016.
4. Yang J, Li X. Efficient Finger Vein Localization and Recognition[C]// International Conference on Pattern Recognition. IEEE, 2010:1148-1151.
5. Guan F, Wang K, Yang Q. A study of two direction weighted (2D)2LDA for finger vein recognition[C]// International Congress on Image and Signal Processing. IEEE, 2011:860-864.
6. Yang W, Rao Q, Liao Q. Personal Identification for Single Sample Using Finger Vein Location and Direction Coding[C]// International Conference on Hand-Based Biometrics. IEEE, 2011:1-6.

7. Gupta P, Gupta P. An accurate finger vein based verification system[J]. Digital Signal Processing, 2015, 38:43-52.
8. Wu J D, Liu C T. Finger-vein pattern identification using principal component analysis and the neural network technique[J]. Expert Systems with Applications, 2011, 38(5):5423-5427.
9. Wang K Q, Khisa A S, Wu X Q, et al. Finger vein recognition using LBP variance with global matching[C]// International Conference on Wavelet Analysis and Pattern Recognition. IEEE, 2012:196-201.
10. Hubel D H, Weisel T N. Wiesel, T.N.: Receptive fields, binocular interaction and functional architecture in cat's visual cortex. J. Physiol. (London) 160, 106-154[J]. 1962, 160.
11. Breu H, Gil J, Kirkpatrick D, et al. Linear time Euclidean distance transform algorithms[J]. IEEE Transactions on Pattern Analysis & Machine Intelligence, 2002, 17(5):529-533.
12. Yuan Z W, Zhang J. Feature extraction and image retrieval based on AlexNet[C]// Eighth International Conference on Digital Image Processing. 2016:100330E.
13. Liu W, Wen Y, Yu Z, et al. Large-Margin Softmax Loss for Convolutional Neural Networks[J]. 2016.
14. http://www.datatang.com
15. Jia, Yangqing, Shelhamer, et al. Caffe: Convolutional Architecture for Fast Feature Embedding[J]. 2014:675-678.
16. Neyshabur B, Salakhutdinov R, Srebro N. Path-SGD: Path-Normalized Optimization in Deep Neural Networks[J]. Computer Science, 2015.
17. Liu Z et al. Finger vein recognition with manifold learn- ing. Journal of Network and Computer Applications. 2010; 33(3):275–82.
18. Perez Vega A, Travieso CM, Alonso JB. Biometric personal identi cation system based on patterns created by nger veins. 2014 International Work Conference on Bio-inspired Intelligence (IWOBI), IEEE. 2014.
19. Dong S, Yang J, Chen Y, et al. Finger Vein Recognition Based on Multi-Orientation Weighted Symmetric Local Graph Structure[J]. Ksii Transactions on Internet & Information Systems, 2015, 9(10):4126-4142.
20. Xie S J, Lu Y, Yoon S, et al. Intensity Variation Normalization for Finger Vein Recognition Using Guided Filter Based Singe Scale Retinex.[J]. Sensors, 2015, 15(7):17089-17105.

MATEC Web of Conferences **128**, 04016 (2017) DOI: 10.1051/matecconf/201712804016
EITCE 2017

Ensuring the Fairness of program's performance on CMP

Qilong Wang, Jun Gao, Guangsong Hou, Hongkui Li[a], Ke Xu

State Grid Shandong Heze Electric Power Company, 274000 Heze, Shandong Province, China

Abstract. On CMP, programs commonly interference with each other. But for programs co-running on CMP, serious performance dropdown is not expected. With the growth of the program's size, program's contention for limited shared resources in the system will become increasingly intense, and the resulting impact on system performance will be even more pronounced. How to allocate and share limited shared resources among programs is a very important problem. In this paper we propose a new method to ensure the fairness of program's performance on CMP. The share resource CPU and memory are included in our study. Meanwhile, the Linux resource management tool Cgroups is used to realize our idea. By the resource we profiled and the tool support, we realize a reasonable resource dividing method to ensure the fairness of program's performance. The reasonable resource dividing method include three Engine. The experiment result show that making use of the fairness resource dividing method proposed by our paper, compared with operating system scheduling, program's performance difference can be largely reduced.

1 Introduction

With the development of integrated circuit technology, chip multi-processor (CMP) has become the most common processor in the current cluster and desktop computer, and it is also the current development direction [1, 2].

On CMP, programs commonly interference with each other [3]. Some times the effect of interference is little, which do little effect to program's performance. Some time the interference takes big effect, which cause serious drop down of performance [4,5]. Further more, for programs co-running on CMP, serious performance dropdown is not expected.

On the CMP, cores typically share the last level cache, DRAM controllers, memory bus bandwidth, etc. With the growth of the program's size, program's contention for limited shared resources in the system will become increasingly intense, and the resulting impact on system performance will be even more pronounced. How to allocate and share limited shared resources among programs is a very important problem. In order to alleviate this problem, in addition to increasing the availability of shared resources, a scheduling algorithm that can share the shared resources among programs in a fair and efficient manner is also critical. Among all kinds of shared resources, CPU and memory have the greatest impact on program's performance.

If a scheduling policy exists to allocate the shared resources fairly and efficiently among multiple parallel threads, it can mitigate the negative impact of contention for shared resources, thereby improving system performance. Therefore, the allocation and scheduling of shared resources in CMP systems has become a hot issue to be studied.

In this paper we propose a new method to ensure the fairness of program's performance on CMP. The share resource CPU and memory are included in our study. Meanwhile, the Linux resource management tool Cgroups is used to realize our idea. By the resource we profiled and the tool support, we realize a reasonable resource dividing method to ensure the fairness of program's performance. The reasonable resource dividing method include three Engine.

The first is the profiling engine, in the profiling engine, the resource usage information of every programs are profiled. The resource profiled are CPU and memory. We top program's resource usage of CPU and memory and transfer the information to the planning engine.

The second is the planning engine, the function of the planning engine is to decide how to divide CPU and memory resource to all the programs, with the aim of making program's performance almost the same. The input of the planning engine is the information of CPU and memory resource usage passed from the profiling engine, and the output of the planning engine is is the size of CPU and memory resource should be applied for all the programs.

The third is the implement engine, we use Cgroups to realize the implement engine. The input of the implement engine is the output of the planning engine. The data of the size of CPU and memory are used to set the size of Cgroups control groups. After that, programs can be running in it's own execution environment.

The experiment result show that making use of the fairness resource dividing method proposed by our paper,

[a] Corresponding author: dkzxzdh@163.com

 DOI: 10.1051/matecconf/201712804016

compared with operating system scheduling, program's performance difference can be largely reduced.

2 Related work

There are some related work on the fairness of program's performance on CMP. Mutlu et al. [6] propose a shared DRAM controller, with the aim of both improve program's performance and the QoS of programs. Zhou et al. [7] introduces a model to analyze the perfor- mance impact of cache sharing, and proposes a mechanism of cache sharing management to provide performance fairness for concurrently executing applications.

3 Fairness resource dividing method

The fairness resource dividing method consist of three engines: the profiling engine is use to profiling program's basic information on CPU and memory, the planning engine is used to do the resource assignment plan, and the implement engine is used to divide CPU and memory resource to programs. Figure 1 shows the flow chart.

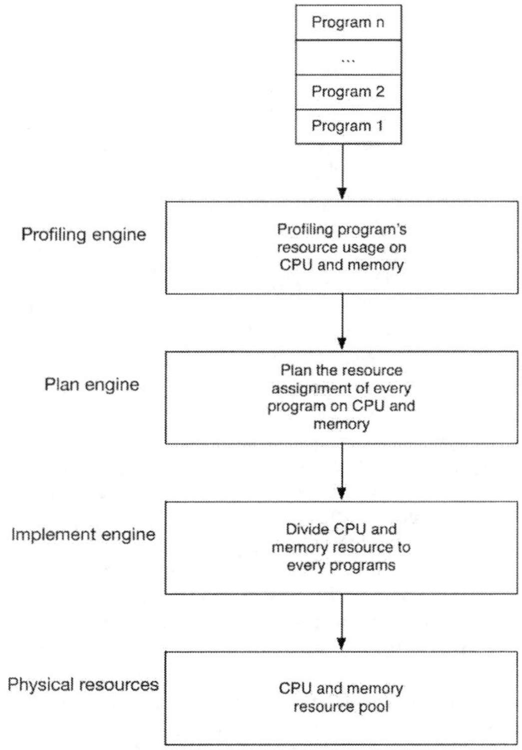

Figure 1. The flow chart of the fairness resource dividing method

3.1 The profiling engine

In the profiling engine, the resource usage information of every programs are profiled. The resource profiled are CPU and memory. The general performance profiling tools can be used to accomplish the task. In our paper we use Linux tool Top. We top program's resource usage of CPU and memory and transfer the information to the planning engine. This procedure can be accomplished on-line. Then the profiling result is the input of the planning engine.

3.2 The planning engine

The function of the planning engine is to decide how to divide CPU and memory resource to all the programs, with the aim of making program's performance almost the same. This part is very important for our fairness resource dividing method, which directly resulting in program's performance.

The first step is to decide the number of programs can be running on one server, so we calculate the number of programs based on the pseudo-code in Figure 2.

Pseudo-code of caculating the number of program running on one server

```
cpu_sum=cpu[p1]
mem_sum=mem[p1]
for i = p1 to pn do
    cpu_sum=cpu_sum+cpu[i+1];
    mem_sum=mem_sum+mem[i+1];
    if cpu_sum >cpu_usage
    {
    num_pro=i
    break;
    }
    if mem_sum >mem_usage
    {
    num_pro=i
    break;
    }
end for
```

Figure 2. Pseudo-code of calculating the number of program running on one server

In the pseudo-code, we sum the program's usage of CPU from p1 until the cpu_sum more than the CPU size of serve, meanwhile, we sum the program's usage of memory from p1 until the mem_sum more than the memory size of server. It is means once one of the CPU or memory resource is bigger than the size of CPU or memory, we will not add on new program. Then we can make sure the number of the program running on one server, which is pi. Then the programs which can not scheduled on this server will be scheduled onto the next server.

The input of the planning engine is the information of CPU and memory resource usage passed from the profiling engine, and the output of the planning engine is is the size of CPU and memory resource should be applied for all the programs. The output of the planning engine can be calculated obey the formula below.

Assume that there are n programs running on one server. There are p1, p2, ..., pn respectively. The CPU resource usage of these program when running alone are Cp1, Cp2, ..., Cpn, respectively, and the memory resource usage of these program when running alone are Mp1, Mp2, ..., Mpn, respectively.

Then the CPU resource calculate method should obey formula (1). And the memory resource calculate method should obey formula (2).

$$C_{pi-schedule} = \frac{C_{pi}}{C_{p1} + C_{p2} + \ldots + C_{pn}} \times C_{server} \quad (1)$$

$$M_{pi-schedule} = \frac{M_{pi}}{M_{p1} + M_{p2} + \ldots + M_{pn}} \times M_{server} \quad (2)$$

In formula (1), pi is the number of the program, C_{pi} is the resource usage of program pi when it running alone on a server. C_{server} is the total CPU resource of the server. $C_{pi-schedule}$ is the size of the CPU resource when program pi is scheduled along with other programs.

In formula (2), M_{pi} is the memory resource usage of program pi when it running alone on a server. M_{server} is the total memory resource of the server. $M_{pi-schedule}$ is the size of the memory resource when program pi is scheduled along with other programs.

By the algorithm above, the size of CPU and memory resource divided for the programs can be calculate properly.

3.3 The implement engine

In the implement engine, Linux resource management tool Cgroups play a very important role, Cgroups is used to realize the implement engine. The input of the implement engine is the output of the planning engine. The data of the size of CPU and memory are used to set the size of Cgroups control groups, then the program's execution environment can be created. After that, programs can be running in it's own execution environment.

By making use of this method, all programs can be running under proper resource, ensuring the fairness of every programs.

4 Experiment

Our experiments are executed on a NUMA server, which with two socket and 4 core on each socket. The detail server information is in TABLE 1. We select programs from SPEC CPU2006 and NAS Parallel Benchmarks (NPB). The SPEC CPU2006 benchmark is SPEC's industry-standardized, CPU-intensive benchmark suite, stressing a system's processor, memory subsystem and compiler. The NPB are a set of benchmarks targeting performance evaluation of highly parallel supercomputers. The programs as workloads are in TABLE 2.

We compare the program's performance under fairness resource dividing method with program's performance when running alone.

Table 1. Server configuration

CPU	Intel Xeon E5620
core	4 cores@2.13G
L1 caches	32K
L2 caches	256K
L3 caches	4M
Threads per core	1 thread
Sockets	2
Memory	8GB, DDR3

Table 2. Workloads

Workloads	program
Workload 1	410, cg.C.8
Workload 2	445, 450, 453, ft.C.4
Workload 3	445, mg.C.8

We use three workloads for our experiment, Figure 3 shows the program's performance with different strategy, and the baseline is the program's performance when program running alone on a server. The programs in the first workload is 410, cg.C.8, we decide the number of program based on the idea in Figure 2. It is shows by the OS scheduling strategy, the performance difference of two programs is 8%, but by our fairness resource dividing method, ther performance difference of two programs is only 5%. It is because compared with OS scheduling, our scheduling can realize more fairness. By making use of Cgroups, the CPU and memory resource can be divided to all programs fairnessly. However, by OS scheduling, when programs running together on one server, the will competing the CPU and memory resource. Then the resource size can not be used very fairness by all programs. It is because different programs have different competitive power. Programs with a bigger competitive power will take over more resource, then the program's performance will be better. Programs with a smaller competitive power will take over little resource, then the program's performance will be poor. The competitive power is very complex, it is related the program's resource access pattern, coding method etc.

Figure 4 shows the program's performance with different strategy for workload 2, and the baseline is the program's performance when program running alone on a server. The programs in the second workload is 445, 450, 453, ft.C.8. It is shows by the OS scheduling strategy, the biggest performance difference of programs is 53%, but by our fairness resource dividing method, the biggest performance difference of programs is only 9%.

Figure 5 shows the program's performance with different strategy for workload 3, and the baseline is the program's performance when program running alone on a server. The programs in the second workload is 445, mg.C.8. It is shows by the OS scheduling strategy, the biggest performance difference of programs is 8%, but by our fairness resource dividing method, the biggest performance difference of programs is only 2%.

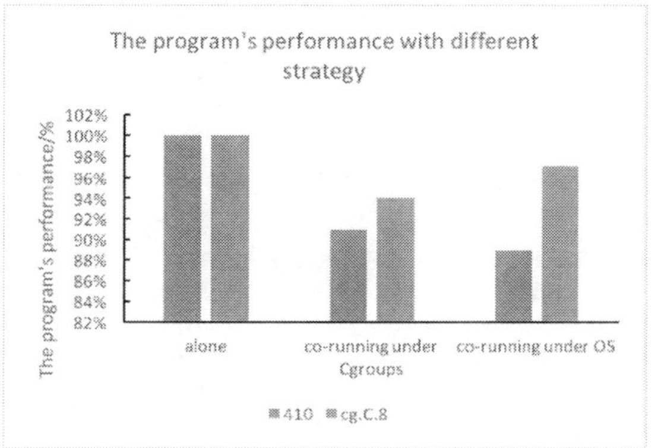

Figure 3. Program's performance with different strategy (workload 1)

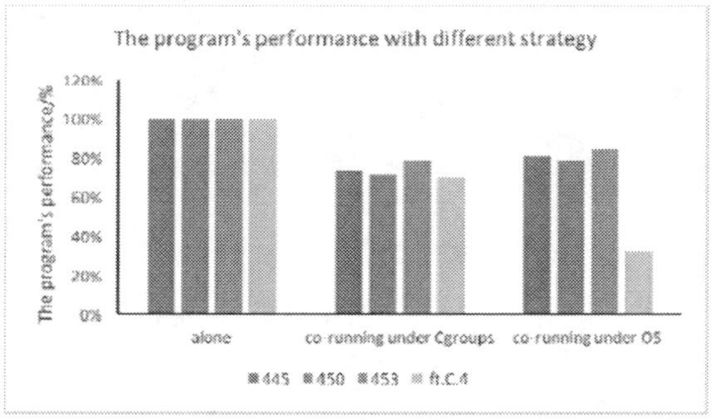

Figure 4. Program's performance with different strategy (workload 2)

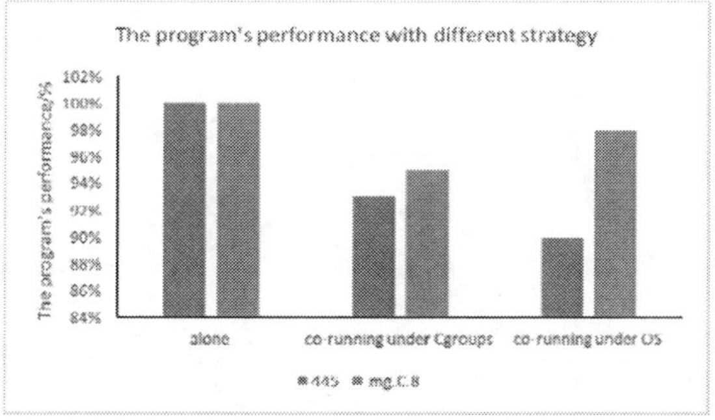

Figure 5. Program's performance with different strategy (workload 3)

5 Conclusion

In this paper we realize a reasonable resource dividing method to ensure the fairness of program's performance on CMP. The share resource CPU and memory are included in our study. Meanwhile, the Linux resource management tool Cgroups is used to realize our idea. The reasonable resource dividing method include three Engine.

The first is the profiling engine, in the profiling engine, the resource usage information of every programs are profiled. The resource profiled are CPU and memory. We top program's resource usage of CPU and memory and transfer the information to the planning engine.

The second is the planning engine, the function of the planning engine is to decide how to divide CPU and memory resource to all the programs, with the aim of making program's performance almost the same. The input of the planning engine is the information of CPU and memory resource usage passed from the profiling engine, and the output of the planning engine is is the size of CPU and memory resource should be applied for all the programs.

The third is the implement engine, we use Cgroups to realize the implement engine. The input of the implement engine is the output of the planning engine. The data of the size of CPU and memory are used to set the size of Cgroups control groups. After that, programs can be running in it's own execution environment.

The experiment result show that making use of the fairness resource dividing method proposed by our paper, compared with operating system scheduling, program's performance difference can be largely reduced.

References

1. C. Dhruba, G. Fei, K. Seongbeom, et al. Predicting inter-thread cache contention on a chip multi-processor architecture[C]. 11th International Symposium on High-Performance Computer Architecture, 2005: 340-351.
2. K. Seongbeom, C. Dhruba, S. Yan. Fair cache sharing and partitioning in a chip multiprocessor architecture[C]. Proceedings of the 13th International Conference on Parallel Architectures and Compilation Techniques, 2004: 111-122.
3. Y. Jiang, X. Shen, C. Jie, et al. Analysis and approximation of optimal co-scheduling on chip multiprocessors[C]. 2008 International Conference on Parallel Architectures and Compilation Techniques, 2008: 220-229.
4. K. Rob, B. Paul, H. Barbara, et al. Using OS observations to improve performance in multicore systems[J]. IEEE MICRO, 2008(28):0272-1732.
5. L. Wang, R. Wang, C. Fu, et. al. Interference-aware Program Scheduling for Multicore Processors[C]. ICA3PP 2013, 201312: 436-445.
6. O. Mutlu, T. Moscibroda. Parallelism-aware batch scheduling: Enhancing both performance and fairness of shared DRAM systems[J]. ACM SIGARCH Computer Architecture News, 2008(36): 63-74
7. X. Zhou, W. Chen, and W. Zheng. Cache sharing manage- ment for performance fairness in chip multiprocessors. In PACT, pages 384–393, Sept. 2009.

 DOI: 10.1051/matecconf/201712804017

Resistance requirements of threshold switching selectors in 1S1R crossbar array

Chenglong Lin[a], Gaosheng Li, Xueqing Jia

College of Electronic Science, National University of Defense Technology (NUDT), Changsha 410073, China

Abstract. Leakage current suppression ability of threshold switching selectors is important for the high-density crossbar array of resistive random access memory (RRAM). Nevertheless, incompatibility of selector with paired RRAM element will lead to serious problems during operation. This paper investigates the ON-/OFF- resistance requirements of threshold switching selectors with simulation in 1Mb array. Results show that OFF-resistance needs to be higher than certain value while ON-resistance needs to be lower than some value to make sure successful operation. In addition, it presents the method determining the appropriate resistance range in detail. It aims at proposing guideline for fabricating and choosing adequate threshold switching selectors before integrating with RRAM element economically.

1 Introduction

Resistive random access memory (RRAM) is one of the most promising candidates for next generation non-volatile memory. A two-terminal simple structure allows highly geometry scalability and fabrication in crossbar arrays. However, leakage current of crossbar RRAM array is one of the main obstacles for the high-density memory application. It can be effectively tackled by the addition of necessary nonlinearity to the RRAM by integrating a highly nonlinear and bidirectional selector device. This topology is known as the 1S1R architecture [1-3].

To date, selectors based on various mechanisms are proposed and mainly two kinds of I-V characteristics are observed for reported devices. Therein, Threshold switching selectors are widely concerned because of large nonlinearity and large drive current in the ON-state, including ovonic threshold switch (OTS) [4-6], metal-insulator transition switch(MIT) [7,8], field-assisted super-linear threshold switch (FAST) [9,10] and threshold vacuum switch (TVS) [11]. As figure 1, during forward voltage sweeps, it maintains high-resistive state (OFF-state) before threshold voltage (Vth) is achieved. When applied voltage surpasses threshold voltage, an abrupt and reversible transition occurs to conductive state (ON-state). During reverse sweeps, it transits to OFF-state after applied voltage is less than hold voltage (Vhold).

To investigate the impact of selector characteristics on the 1S1R crossbar array performance, IMEC compare various selectors and demonstrate that threshold voltage and ON-state resistance (Rs_on) are crucial parameters [12]. In addition, they studied the impact of resistance ratio of RRAM on the read performance of 1S1R array. They took nonlinearity of tunneling selector into consideration [13]. Nevertheless the concrete resistance of selectors was neglected and they will lead to considerable effect to the array size and power consumption. As a result, it is essential to bring up the resistance requirements of selector before integrating the selector with RRAM. Meanwhile, it is economic and time-saving for fabricating an adequate threshold switching selector.

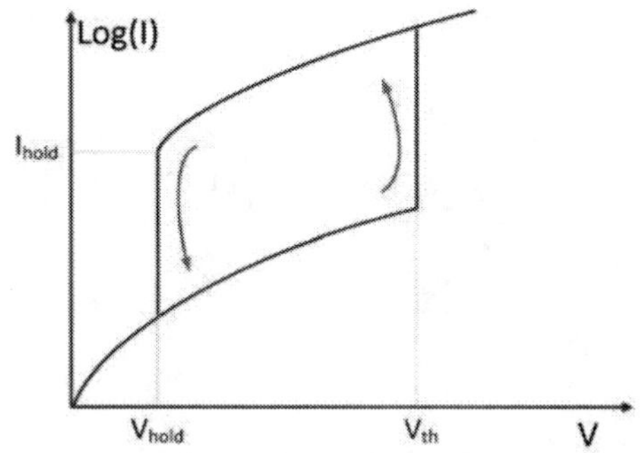

Figure 1 Schematic behavior of threshold switching selectors in voltage sweeps.

This paper is organized as follows. The simulation settings are presented in Section 2. The impact of ON- and OFF- resistance on array performance is analyzed in Section 3. In Section 4, appropriate ON- and OFF-resistance is determined. The conclusion is given in Section 5.

2 Simulation Setup

[a] Corresponding author: 505185732@qq.com

2.1 Array configuration

The schematic of the simulated crossbar array is shown in figure 2 with fixed 1-Mb capacity (1024x1024). The word-lines (WL) perpendicularly intersect with bit-lines (BL) in a crossbar array with 1S1R cells built at the junctions. All RRAM elements and selector are identical without considering variability. Simulation is implemented using the worst case scenario for different read and write operation modes (Table I). The selected cell is located at the farthest distance from voltage source and ground. 1/2 bias schemes are adopted for single-bit read and write operation. Default line resistance is fixed at 5Ω/cell.

Table I Worst Case Data Pattern

Read HRS	Read LRS	Set	Reset
SEL: HRS WLHS: LRS BLHS: LRS NS: LRS	SEL: HRS WLHS: LRS BLHS: HRS NS: LRS	SEL: HRS WLHS: LRS BLHS: LRS NS: LRS	ALL LRS

Figure-of-merit (FOM) for read or write operation can be evaluated by read margin (RM), write margin (WM), read power (Pr) and write power (Pw). Read margin is defined as the ratio of readout disparity between HRS and LRS states over readout of LRS state. Write margin is defined as the ratio of voltage drop on selected RRAM over applied voltage. Read power and write power is the total power consumption of array in read and write process respectively.

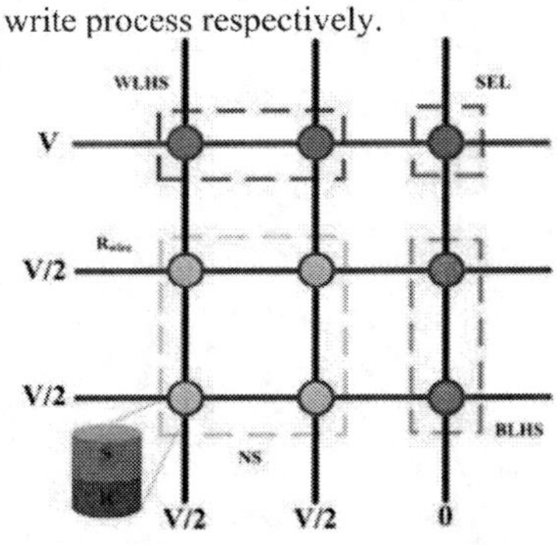

Figure 2 Schematic of 2-D cross-point array. SEL: selected cell. WLHS: WL half-selected cell. BLHS: BL half-selected cell. NS: non-selected cell. R_{wire}=5Ω/cell.[12]

2.2 RRAM Model

The RRAM device is described using a parameterized template with fixed behaviour. As in figure 3, RRAM device can switch between a high-resistance (HRS) and a low-resistance state (LRS) by applying opposite voltage. For simplicity, both LRS and HRS are assumed being ohmic, where RHRS and RLRS are fixed at 500 kΩ and 50 kΩ respectively. It leads HRS/LRS resistance ratio equals to 10, which represents a typical resistance ratio for HfO_x-based RRAM device [14]. The parameterized RRAM has symmetrical set and reset voltages of ±1.5V. Nonetheless, unintentional switching of practical devices occurs occasionally when applied voltage is less than write voltage. Disturb voltage is defined to determine the maximum voltage drop on the RRAM element, beyond which the element state may change unintentionally. At this stage, default disturb voltage value is set to 1.0V.

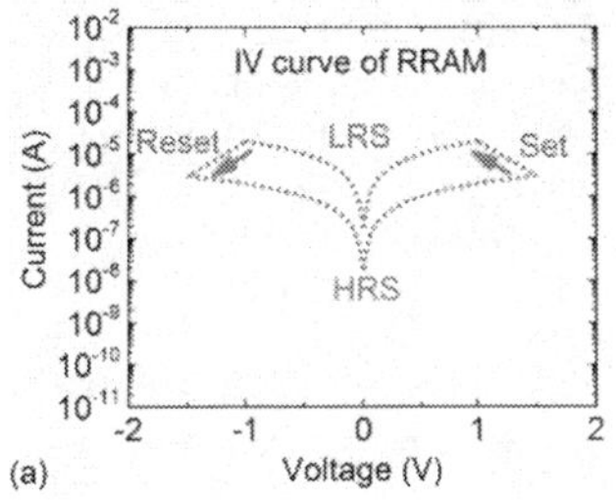

Figure 3 Schematic I-V curve of RRAM element

2.3 Selector Model

Figure 1 represents a typical threshold switching selector behavior. Three parameters are employed to describe the threshold switching selectors, namely threshold voltage (Vth), OFF-resistance (Rs_off) and ON-resistance (Rs_on). For simplicity, in our model, OFF-state and ON-state are regarded as linear. The nonlinearity (NL) of selectors is defined as OFF-/ON- resistance ratio ranging from 1e3 to 1e5. In this case, once the selector is turned to ON-state, it will keep this state till the applied voltage is removed.

3 Analysis of Impact of ON- and OFF-resistance on array performance

Firstly, it is inevitable to generate adversary effect on array performance if resistance of selector cannot meet the requirements. When the array is prepared to operate, all the selectors are in OFF state. At this point, applied voltage will lead to large leakage current if OFF resistance is not high enough. While considering the line resistance, leakage current increases voltage drop on line, leading to the voltage/current loss. Then voltage on the farthest selected cell (as in table I) is not sufficient to turn on the selector, resulting in failed operation. When larger applied voltage is inflicted to solve the problem, voltage drop on unselected cell adjacent to the apply port may surpass the threshold voltage to switch on the selector, increasing leakage current and power consumption, even leading to false operation. Hence, it can be determined that in an array with certain size and threshold voltage of selectors, OFF-resistance of selectors cannot be less than some value lest for adversary effect on performance.

Secondly, during set/reset operations, although OFF-resistance is adequate to turn on the farthest selector, there may be other problems. For example, RRAM splits the voltage with selector in ON-state. If the ON-resistance is rather large leading to less voltage drop on RRAM, it still fails to switch the RRAM. In addition, during read operation, large ON-resistance will reduce the read margin, increasing difficulty of discriminating the HRS and LRS of RRAM. Then it can be determined that ON-resistance of selectors cannot be less than some value. In addition, most voltage will drop on RRAM after paired selector turned on. If threshold voltage of selector

 DOI: 10.1051/matecconf/201712804017

is much larger than disturb voltage of RRAM, then voltage drop on RRAM may surpass the disturb voltage. In order to avoid above-mentioned situation, ON-resistance of selectors should be adequate to make sure the appropriate voltage division.

As a conclusion, OFF-resistance must be larger than certain value and ON-resistance must be less than some value to make sure smooth read/write operation. Meanwhile, in order to prevent false write during read, ON-resistance must be also larger than some value. Corresponding simulation process of 1/2 bias scheme is as follows: 1) fixing the threshold voltage, reset simulation determine the required minimum OFF-resistance and corresponding maximum ON-resistance; 2) based on the results of step 1), read simulation verify the read margin of the minimum OFF-resistance and corresponding maximum ON-resistance, determine the maximum ON-resistance; 3) read simulation determine the minimum ON-resistance to assure the voltage drop on RRAM less than disturb voltage with voltage division; 4) changing the threshold voltage and repeating above process.

4 Appropriate ON- and OFF- Resistance

4.1 Minimum OFF-resistance determination

In order to explore minimum OFF-resistance, simulation of reset process is implemented as follows: 1) fixing the threshold voltage, determining the maximum applied voltage less than double threshold voltage lest unselected selectors are switched on; 2) assuming the ON-resistance as 1 ohm, then all voltage will drop on the RRAM after paired selector is turned on, determining the minimum OFF-resistance and corresponding maximum ON-resistance by iterative calculation; 3) changing the OFF-resistance larger than minimum OFF-resistance, calculating corresponding maximum ON-resistance.

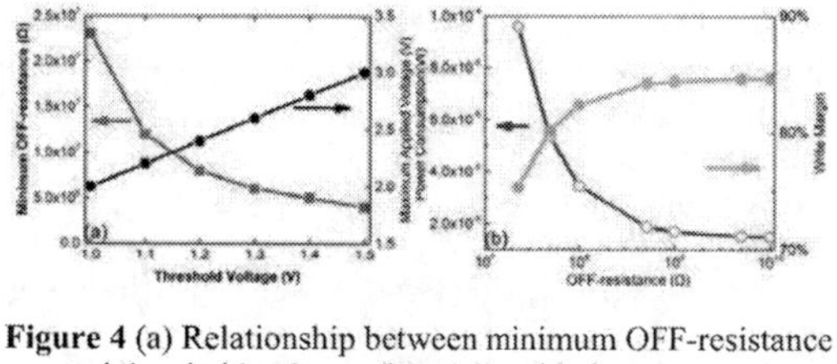

Figure 4 (a) Relationship between minimum OFF-resistance and threshold voltage; (b) relationship between reset performance and OFF-resistance

As can be seen from figure 4(a), minimum OFF-resistance decreases with the increasing threshold voltage. It can be deduced that with the increase of threshold voltage, bearable applied voltage increases. Then according to the analysis in section 3, larger applied voltage will reduce the requirement of minimum OFF-resistance. Although there is larger leakage current and voltage decay, larger applied can make sure enough voltage drop on the selected cell to operate. As a result, once the OFF-resistance is larger than the critical one, reset operation can be successfully implemented. In addition, according to figure 4(b), if threshold voltage is fixed as 1.0V, relationship between array performance and OFF-resistance is analyzed. Larger OFF-resistance leads to lower leakage current and less power consumption. In addition, most of the voltage can drop on the selected cell, increasing write margin. This is in accordance with the instinct that larger OFF-resistance is better.

4.2 Maximum ON-resistance determination

Simulation of reset process can be utilized to evaluate the required maximum OFF-resistance, but also to deduce corresponding maximum ON-resistance because ON-resistance will affect the voltage division after selector turns on. As can be seen from the figure 5, under fixed threshold voltage, maximum ON-resistance increases with increasing OFF-resistance and level off finally. When maximum applied voltage corresponding to respective threshold voltage is applied, larger OFF-resistance will reduce leakage current and voltage decay. Then voltage drop on the selected cell increases and larger ON-resistance can also make sure that the voltage division on the RRAM is sufficient to switch. However, with further increase of OFF-resistance, leakage current cannot be reduced obviously. As a result, voltage drop on the selected cell cannot increase and maximum ON-resistance cannot increase as well. In addition, when threshold voltage decreases, applied voltage can be reduced then probability of false writing is lower during read operation.

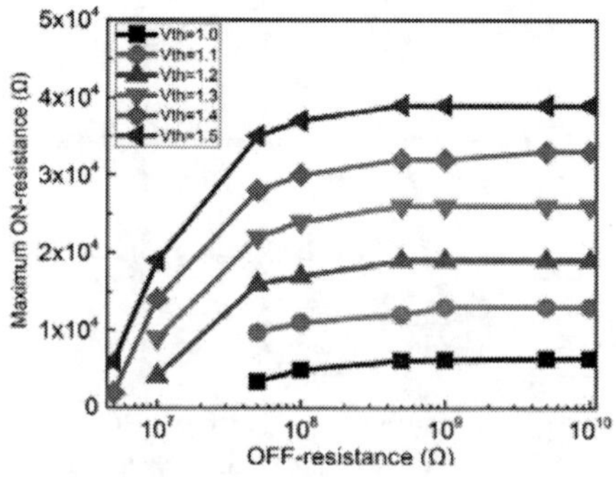

Figure 5 Relationship between maximum ON-resistance and OFF-resistance and threshold voltage

5 Conclusion

ON-/OFF-resistance of threshold switching selectors severely affect array operation and performance. Controlling impacts of the appropriate resistance range is proved to be essential before integrating selector and RRAM element. In this work, we analyse the possible impact of ON-/OFF-resistance of selectors. Meanwhile, we propose a method to determine minimum and maximum ON-resistance and OFF-resistance in crossbar array. Results show that threshold switching selectors must satisfy the requirements of minimum OFF-resistance and maximum ON-resistance. This proposes guideline for fabrication and option of appropriate selectors.

References

1. G. W. Burr, R. S. Shenoy, K. Virwani, P. Narayanan, A.Padilla, B. Kurdi and H. Hwang, J. Vac. Sci. Technol. B, **32**, 4 (2014)
2. B. Govoreanu, L. Zhang and M. Jurczak, Int. Conference on IC Design & Technology (ICICDT) (2015)
3. A. Chen, IEEE Trans. Electron Devices **62**, 9 (2015)
4. K. Yunmo, B. Kyungjoon and H. Hyunsang, IEEE Symp. VLSI Technol. (2016)
5. H. Yang, M. Li, W. He, Y. Jiang, K. G. Lim, W. Song, V. Y. Zhuo, C. C. Tan, E. K. Chua, W. Wang, Y. Yang and R. Ji, IEEE Symp. VLSI Technol. (2015)
6. M. Lee, D. Lee, S. Cho, J. Hur, S. Lee, D. H. Seo and D. Kim, Nat. comm. **4**, 2629 (2013)
7. K. Zhang, B. Wang, F. Wang, Y. Han, X. Jian, H. Zhang and H. S. P. Wong, IEEE Electron Device Lett. **37**, 8 (2016)
8. E. Cha, J. Woo, D. Lee, S. Lee and J. Song, IEEE Int. Electron Devices Meeting (IEDM) (2013)
9. S. H. Jo, T. Kumar, S. Narayanan, W. D. Lu and H. Nazarian, IEEE Int. Electron Devices Meeting (IEDM) (2014)
10. S. H. Jo, T. Kumar, S. Narayanan and H. Nazarian, IEEE Trans. Electron Devices **62**, 11 (2015)
11. C. H., Ho, H, Huang, M. Lee, C. Hsu, T. Lai, W. Chiu, M. Lee, T, Chou, I. Yang, M. Chen, C. Wu, K. Chiang, Y. Yao, C. Hu, F.Yang, IEEE Int. Electron Devices Meeting (IEDM) (2012)
12. L. Zhang, S. Cosemans, D. J. Wouters, G. Groeseneken, M. Jurczak and B. Govoreanu, IEEE Trans. Electron Devices **62**, 10 (2015)
13. L. Zhang, S. Cosemans, and D. J. Wouters, IEEE Electron Device Lett. **36**, 6 (2015)
14. L. Zhang, S. Cosemans, D. J.Wouters and G. Groeseneken, IEEE Int. Memory Workshop (IMW) (2014)

DOI: 10.1051/matecconf/201712804018

Design and Implementation of the Automatic Assessment System for the Command and Control Specialty in Ships

Hao Zhang[1,2,a], Zheng-yi Wang[2] and Wei Yin[1]

[1]*Dalian Naval Academy of the PLA, 1160018 Dalian, China*
[2]*Naval Command College, 210016 Nanjing, China*

Abstract. On the basis of analyzing the actual demand of automated assessment system for the command and control specialty in ships, the thought of the overall design of automated assessment system for the command and control specialty in ships is given, and the concrete realization methods of the user login module, test paper operation module and system maintenance module are studied and demonstrated. The proposed design idea and implementation method of automated assessment system for the command and control specialty in ships is scientific, efficient and practical, and provides reference for the exploitation of automated assessment system for the command and control specialty in ships.

1 Introduction

Currently, The construction of automated assessment system for the command and control specialty in ships lags. The automated assessment system used in troops have the shortcomings of poor objectivity of schema, low degree of intelligence, and poor completeness of functional. Thus it is difficult to meet the practical needs of the talent training and assessment of the forces in the new period [1-3]. In order to resolve the shortage of the current system and improve the assessment efficiency of professional ability of command and control specialty in troops, the high validity, strong extensibility and good open automated assessment system for the command and control specialty in ships is studied, designed and implemented by using the advanced theory and method of system engineering theory, object-oriented programming technology and relational database and so on.

2 Demand Analysis

There are two main tasks of the automated assessment system for the command and control specialty in ships, one is to provide more convenient means to collect the questions, and the other one is to organize, edit and print the test paper flexibility according to the requirement of the question and the user. In the process of management and use of the question bank system, the most important is the autonomy and flexibility of the question bank system, which can be embodied in the following three aspects.

2.1 Independent initialization of the question bank

Users have the right to create a new question bank. There are major defects of part of the question bank which selling on the market, such as not built a new question bank or the user has no right to modify the attribute of the test questions which stored in the question bank. This problems will restrict the authority of the system. The administrator would like to create a new question bank, or add and change the attributes and classification scheme according to demand.

2.2 Independent maintenance of the question bank

Users have the right to add, modify and delete the test questions. The test questions which sold in the market have no scalability and openness. Therefore, the users have no complete control over the question bank [4]. The question bank such as the above will not be able to keep up with the times and will be aging and losing vitality in a relatively short time. For the automation assessment system for the command and control specialty in ships, faculty members clearly want to have the right to control, including the entry, the deletion and the change of the test questions and so on.

2.3 Flexibly call for the question bank

Users will be able to extract the test questions from the question bank on their own. Although the question bank system on the market have this basic function, but the selectivity is not available for the user, so it can't meet the needs of specific specialty, and most of the system does not allow the modification of generated test paper and have poor compatibility. For the command and control

[a] Corresponding author: zhanghao_zhh_81@126.com

specialty in ships, each assessment will have different emphases, so the assessment system must meet the assessment requirements.

3 The overall design

3.1 Overall design

According to the demand analysis of the automated assessment system for the command and control specialty in ships, the overall technology roadmap of system is shown in figure 1. The system has three modules: user login module, test paper operation module and system maintenance module.

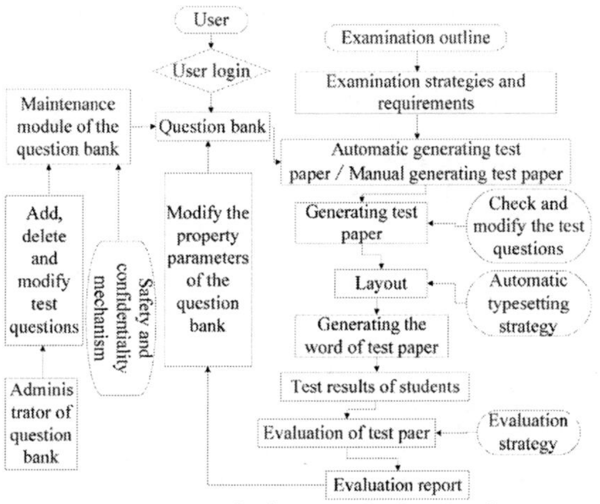

Figure 1. Below the figure. Technology Roadmap.

3.2 User login module design

The system can set different permissions for users of all access systems, and can divide users into three categories: administrators, experts and assessment objects. The first type is the administrator, who has the highest authority. The administrator not only has full access to the test module and system maintenance module, but also can read other users' information and modify the user's rights. The second category is experts, who have full access to test paper operating modules and system maintenance modules, but cannot access other user information. The third category is the assessment object, which can only browse the generated test paper or answer sheet when accessing the question bank system, but unable to carry out generating paper and operating on the test questions and the question bank.

3.3 Design of test paper operation module

The test paper operation module is divided into the generating paper sub-module and the paper analysis sub-module.

3.3.1 Generating paper

Generating paper can be divided into manual generating paper and automatic generating paper. After the user enter to generating paper module, the user needs to input the requirements of generating paper according to the requirement of the exam outline and exam strategy, and system will form the constraint matrix on the basis of the above requirement. If the user selects the automatic generating paper, the system will generate the test paper by calling the random function method in the question bank. If the user selects the manual generating paper, the system will retrieve the test questions in the question bank for the user to select, and the system will automatically generate the test paper after the user has chosen to complete the test.

3.3.2 Test paper analysis

It consists of historical analysis and test questions feedback. After the completion of the examination, the faculty members can use the question bank system to analyze the test paper, the analysis results will be saved in the form of statistics of the question bank system. At the same time, the property of the test questions will be feedback to question bank in the form of a certain parameter.

3.4 System maintenance module design

The system maintenance module is divided into question bank operation sub-module and test questions operation sub-module. The question bank operation is the user who have the authority of administrators and teachers to design the storage scheme as well as attribute name and attribute values of test questions according to their own needs, so as to realize the personalized and flexibility design of question bank. The test questions operation is the user who have the authority of administrators and teachers to have right to operate and edit all the test questions in the question bank, so as to update the test questions in time.

4 Implementation of functional module technology

4.1 Create application objects

4.1.1 Create workspace

In PowerBuilder, click the New icon in the toolbar to pop the New dialog box. Select the Workspace tab in the dialog box, then select the Workspace tab and click the OK button. In the save dialog box that pops up, input the filename to save and select the saved path, and finally click the save button.

4.1.2 Create new application objects

Click the New icon in the toolbar, pop the New dialog box, select the Application item on the Target tab, and click the OK button. Input the name of the application object, the name of the application library, and the name of the target object in the pop-up dialog box, and click the Finish button.

4.1.3 Connect to the database

Write the following statement in the Open event of the current application:

```
// Profile Tiku
SQLCA.DBMS = "ODBC"
SQLCA.AutoCommit = False
SQLCA.DBParm = "Connectstring='DSN=tiku'"
connect using sqlca;
if Sqlca.Sqlcode <> 0 Then
   MessageBox
   Return
End if
Open (w_userlogin)
```

4.2 Create a database

Click the DB Profile icon in the toolbar, and select ODB ODBC → Utilities → Create ASA → Database in the pop-up dialog box. Double-click the selected item and pop up the dialog box. In this dialog, fill in the database information, including User ID, Password, Database Name and other attribute information.

Once the database have been created, and then the tables can be created. This database includes five kinds of tables: user information table, test questions type table, test paper table, examinee answer table, auxiliary coding table. There are two ways to create a table, one is that visually creates tables and the other one is that creates tables with SQL statements.

4.3 Implementation of functional modules

The required windows for the command and control system and combat use in ships are as follows.The creation methods and procedures of these windows are described in detail as follows.

4.3.1 Create the main menu window

The main menu window is the basis of many windows in the command and control system and combat use in ships, and some of the subsequent windows can be inherited from it. The function of the main menu window is to implement the main menu in the question bank system, which can enter the corresponding window by clicking the menu items in the main menu. In the PowerBuilder toolbar, click on the New icon and select the window item in the PB Object page. After creating the window, you can set properties window, such as the title of the window in the General page and settings window size in the Other page, etc. Finally, use the w_main name to store the window.

4.3.2 Specific implementation of user login module

(1) Create a user login window

The main function of the user login window is to determine whether the visitor is the user of the question bank of the command and control system and combat use in ships, and what privileges the user has. The Name of the first single line editor in the window pane is set as sle_user, and the Name of the second single-row editor is set as sle_password. Write the following code in the Clicked event of the "user login" button:

```
string ls_user,ls_password
ls_user=trim(sle_user.text)
select password
into :ls_password
from user1
where id= :ls_user;
ls_password = trim(ls_password)
if sle_user.text='' or sle_password.text= '' then
   messagebox
   return
end if
if trim(sle_password.text)=ls_password then
   open(w_main)
   close(parent)
else
   messagebox
end if
```

In the Clicked event of the "register" button, the following code is written:

```
open(w_newuser)
close(parent)
```

(2) Create a user registration window

The user registration window is set up for new users who are not authorized to visit the command and control system and combat use in ships for the first time. In the window, the new user need to fill out personal information and their required permissions, if registered the users of faculty, the right registration code should be needed to fill in a registration code, otherwise the registration failure. After the creation of the window, and then save the window with the name of w_newuser1, and w_newuser2. Create a function of wf_save (), which is used to save the User's User name, password, and other personal information in the User information table (User). [5] the code is as follows:

```
if dw_1.update ( )=1 then
   commit;
else
   rollback;
   return
end if   // save data
if isnull (ib_emp_pic) false then
   string ls_code
   ls_code=dw_1.getitemstring(1,"em_code")
   updatelob employees set picture=:ib_emp_pic
   where em_code=:ls_code;
   if sqlca.sqlnrows<=0 then
      messagebox
      return
   end if
```

In user registration window 2, write the following code in the Clicked event of the cb_zhuce "register" button:

```
wf_save ( )
messagebox
open(w_userlogin)
close(parent)
```

4.3.3 Specific implementation of the test paper module

Test paper operation module is the most important module in the command and control system and the operational use in ships, which contains four windows: automatic generating test paper window, manual generating test paper window, extraction test paper window and statistical analysis window.

(1) create automatic generating test paper window

The main function of automatic generating test window is to set up the test information according to the test requirement, and the system will automatically generate the test paper after given the attribute parameters.

(2) create manual generating test paper window

The main function of manual generating of test paper window is to browse the question bank according to the questions or chapters, and manually select the appropriate questions to form the test paper.

(3) create extract test paper window

The test paper generated by the automatic generating test paper window and manually generated test paper window will be stored in the test paper table of the database. The main functions of the extract test paper window is selecting the generated test paper in the database, and browse the test questions in the test paper.

(4) create statistical analysis window

The statistical analysis window is set up to analyze the situation of the examination after completing the examination. In the statistical analysis window, the OLE control is used to draw the statistical table and the chart. It is used to transmit a computer application to another application information by adopting remote procedure calls. The user can not only save an object by using OLE, but also can deal directly with the server application object.

4.3.4 Implementation of system maintenance module

The system maintenance module is the main ways for administrators and teachers to manage and update the question bank. The main functions include the entry and maintenance of the test questions. Because of the different of the contents and properties in each topic, each topic separately create up the input and maintenance window, the module contains eight windows: choice question entry window, fills-in-the-blanks entry window, true or false entry window, essay entry window, choice question maintenance window, fills-in-the-blanks maintenance window, true or false maintenance windows, essay maintenance window. This is to select the choice question entry window as an example to introduce its concrete implementation method.

In the choice question entry window, the user who have the authority of the administrator and faculty can input the questions and their attributes, including the question number, title, option, answer, difficulty and chapter. The code is written in the CloseQuery event of this window as follows [6] :

```
long ll_backvalue
if (dw_1.modifiedcount()+dw_1.deletedcount()<>0) then
    ll_backvalue=messagebox
    if ll_backvalue=3 then
        messagebox.returnvalue=1
    elseif ll_backvalue=1 then
        cb_save.triggerevent(clicked!)
    else
    end if
end if
```

Create a function of wf_save (), which has no arguments or return values. The function of this function is to store the user's entry test questions and their property information into the database selection table (TopicSelect). The specific code is as follows:

```
if dw_1.updata( )=1 then
    commit;
else
    rollback;
    return
end if
long ll_row
ll_row=w_newselect.dw_1.retrieve( )
string ls_code
ls_code=dw_1.getitemstring(1,"ts_code")
long ll_findnum
ll_findnum=w_newselect.dw_1.find("ts_code='"&+ls_code+"'",1,ll_row)
w_newselect.dw_1.scrolltorow(ll_findnum)
```

Write the following code in the "input" button's Clicked event:

```
wf_save()
dw_1.reset()
dw_1.insertrow(0)
dw_1.setfocus()
```

References

1. Xiu Z H, Zhang H, *Command and control system in ships and operational use* (Tide Press, 2014)
2. Luo L, Liu Z, The key technologies of the future command and control system of the naval vessel, Modern Defense Technology, 31, 5 (2003)
3. Xu J, Xia H C, Match analysis model and simulation of shipborne C2 system and combat task, Command Control & Simulation, 32, 5 (2010)
4. Jeffrey D, Ullman, Jennifer W, *A first course in database systems* (1999)
5. Li H J, Liu C R, *Case development of PowerBuilder* (Electronic Industry Press, 2009)
6. Yin H X, Zhang W M, *PowerBuilder practical course* (Electronic Industry Press, 2009)

 DOI: 10.1051/matecconf/201712804019

Design and Implementation of Terminal Logistics Distribution System Based on IOS Platform

Yufeng Zhuang[1] and Rong Huang[1,a]

[1]*Logistics Department of Automation School, Beijing University of Posts and Telecommunications, Beijing, China*

Abstract. The logistics companies often face inefficient distribution and a multitude of customer complaints on the shopping festival. This paper will find out the existing terminal logistics distribution problems, and put forward some suggestions for improvement according to these problems. Combined with the suggestions, an application for the optimization of terminal logistics distribution based on IOS is designed and developed. The application can mainly be divided into order module, map navigation module and communication module. Couriers login the application, process the orders by using bar code technology and get the best solution of delivery by the map. It can improve the distribution efficiency and customer satisfaction to some extent.

1 Introduction

In 1998, China's first online transaction was completed, which marks the beginning of a new era of e-commerce in China. By 2012, the amount of online transactions in China is more than 10 trillion RMB [1]. As the online shopping is becoming more and more popular, the express industry has also developed rapidly. According to the statistics, in 2014, the amount of the national parcels was 13.96 billion, with a growth rate of 51.9% [2]. This shows that the express industry is growing rapidly and it plays an increasing important role in our daily life.

However, the express industry has also exposed a lot of problems, especially the "last mile" problem. According to the statistics of the State Post Bureau, 40930 consumer complaints were received in February 2012, of which 39783 were related to express delivery, accounting for 97.2% [3] of the total amount of complaints. Data show that express delays and delivery services are the two main complaints, accounting for 40.2%, 33% respectively. Thus, the problem of express delay is the most prominent. While in the express delivery process, the time of terminal logistics distribution accounts for a considerable proportion of the whole time of express delivery, so it is particularly important to improve the efficiency of terminal logistics distribution.

With the development of mobile Internet, smart phones have become popular. Google issued a report on the use of smart phones and the survey showed that China's smartphone penetration rate reached 44% in 2015. The express industry should also follow the trend of the times and provide users with more efficient, more convenient, more flexible terminal delivery services by using intelligent mobile terminals.

Based on the background analysis above, this paper focuses on the problems in the distribution of the terminal logistics. And then constructive suggestions will be made to reduce the time or distance of delivery in order to improve the distribution efficiency, reduce logistics costs, and improve the customer satisfaction. At last, an application will be established, which can provide express queries as well as route planning.

2 The system design

As the figure 1 shows, the system is divided into two parts: IOS mobile terminal and the server. Logistics distribution station administrators and couriers use different devices to access the LeanCloud background cloud server through the network, and carry out the operation of the relevant database. Logistics distribution station administrators login the background system, and then they can view the message, communicate with the couriers, and deal with the emergency situations. The courier can login IOS mobile terminal by using the username and password. He can scan the express lists, and display the locations of the orders on the map, and then the system will plan the best path to help the courier improve delivery efficiency.

3 The mobile terminal design

This chapter mainly includes the analysis and solutions of the "last mile" problem, functional requirements analysis and business process design, and database design.

[a] Corresponding author: rongerhuang@126.com

DOI: 10.1051/matecconf/201712804019

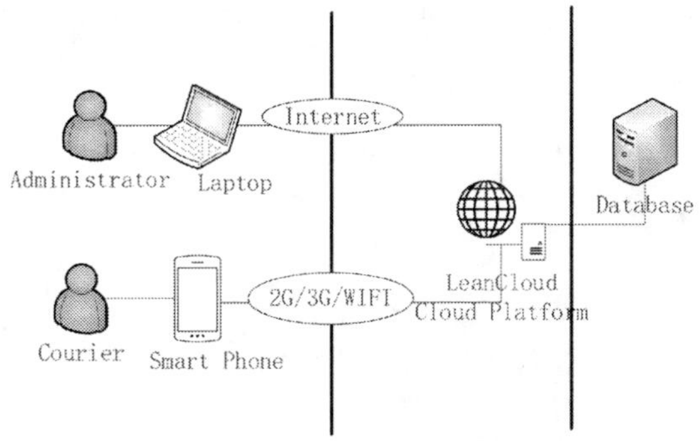

Figure 1. The system design

3.1 The "last mile" problem and the solutions

Through the analysis, there are three main problems in terminal logistics distribution:

- The service of logistics delivery is bad.
- Logistics delivery efficiency is low.
- The communication in the logistics delivery is impeded.

According the problems, evaluation and feedback system can be established to improve the service of couriers. It shows that good logistics delivery services can greatly improve customer satisfaction [4]. Meanwhile, electronic maps are applied for route planning. Data show that advanced information technologies, such as GIS technology and GPS technology, can improve the efficiency of logistics delivery and save costs [5]. What's more, more functions are added for better communication between couriers and customers.

3.2 Functional requirements analysis and business process design

According the analysis above, we can design the main functions of the application, which is shown in figure 2:

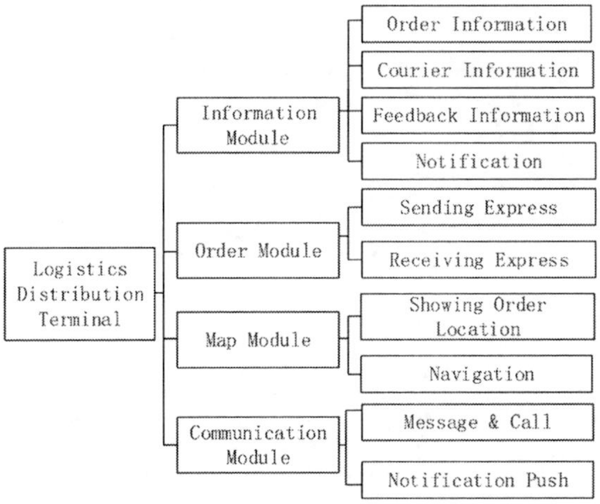

Figure 2. System functional module diagram

The application is mainly divided into four modules, the order module, the map module, the communication module and the basic information module. The order module has two functions which are receiving the express and delivering the express. The courier can use the application to scan the express lists to get the details of the orders and then the information will be added to the application. At the same time when the courier receives the express, new information of the order will be added into the database by scanning the bar code and filling in the express list. The map module can display all orders' addresses, plan the best path and navigate. The communication module can enable the couriers to communicate quickly with the distribution station and other couriers, and receive the push from the distribution station. The basic information module can maintain information, including the order information, the courier information, the evaluation information, pushes and so on.

This application mainly relates to the delivering phase and receiving phase in the general logistics delivery process. This application will refine the business process of the delivering phase and the receiving phase, and effectively improve the efficiency of the terminal logistics distribution. The figure 3 shows the delivering phase in the logistics delivery process.

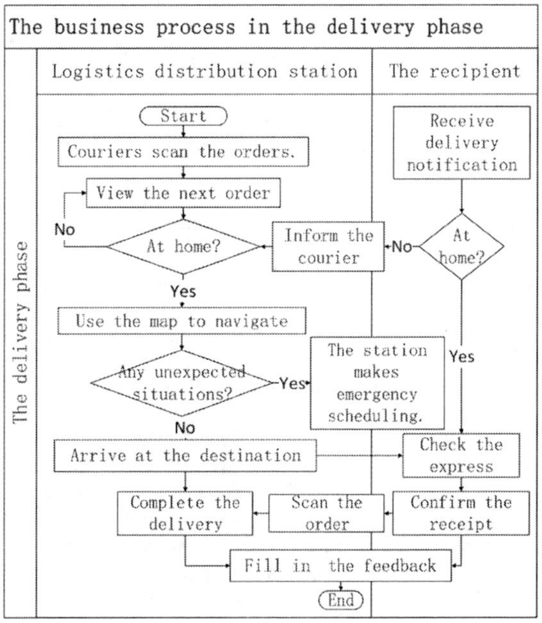

Figure 3. The delivering flowchart

3.3 Database design

This application uses a third-party server called LeanCloud for data storage. The database mainly consists of four tables, which are the order table, the courier table, the evaluation table and the push table. The order table includes the order number, the recipient's phone number and address, the sender's phone number and address, the status of the order and the attributes of the express, such

 DOI: 10.1051/matecconf/201712804019

as weight, payment method, and so on. The courier table includes the courier number, the username, password and mobile phone number. The evaluation table includes the order number, the courier number, and the scores. The push table includes the push number and the push content. The relational data model is shown as the figure 4:

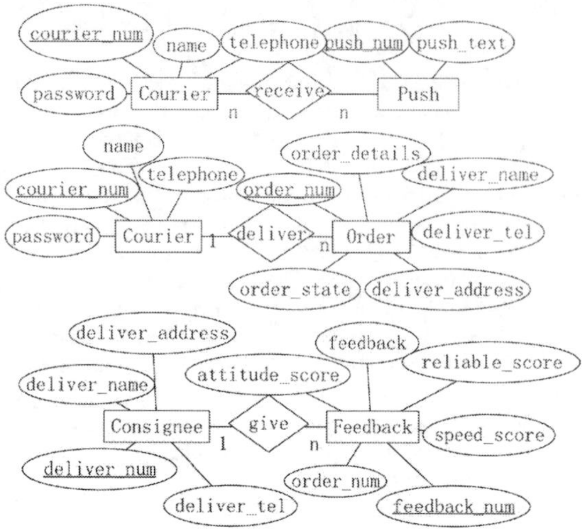

Figure 4. The ER diagram

4 The implementation of the mobile terminal

4.1 The order module

The order module can display the specific information of the order by scanning the bar code of the express list. When the courier completes the delivery, he needs to scan the express list to update the order state. After that the courier needs to invite the consignee evaluate the courier's services. The evaluation and feedback will be kept in the database, which standardize the courier's behaviours for better services to the public.

In the barcode scanning part, I use the third-party open source software called Zbar. Click on the 'Add' button, the system will automatically focus on the bar code by using camera, and the bar code number will appear in the text box below. According to the bar code, the system will connect to the database to query the order. The order details will be displayed on the mobile phone.

Figure 5 and figure 6 following show the effect.

4.2 The map module

In the map module, the electronic map can show the courier's current position and the locations of all orders. The specific address information will be shown on the label above the pin when the courier clicks on one of the pins on the map. When the courier clicks on the label, the application will automatically jump to the AMAP. The courier need not input the starting point and the end point. The system will default to the current position as a starting point, and the address on the label as the end point. The map will provide multiple driving routes. After the courier chooses one of them, the map will begin to navigate. Figure 7 and figure 8 show the effect of the map module:

Figure 5. The effect picture of the barcode scanning part

DOI: 10.1051/matecconf/201712804019

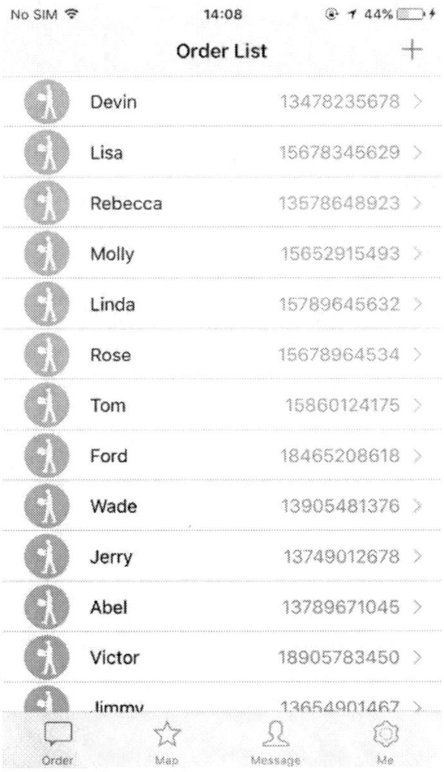

Figure 6. The effect picture of the order module

Figure 7. The first effect picture of the map module

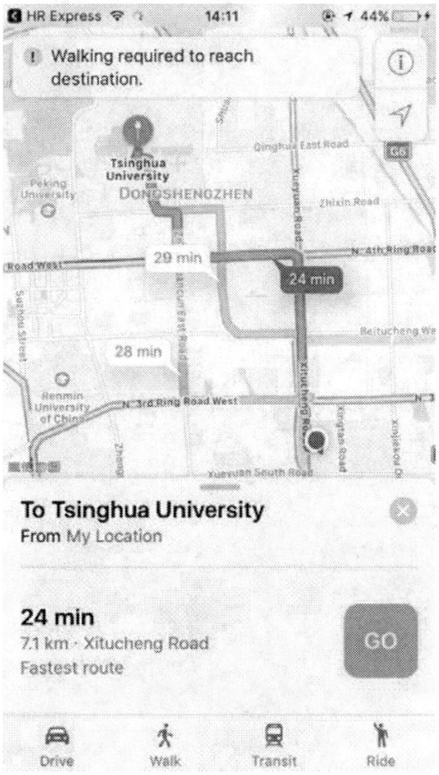

Figure 8. The second effect picture of the map module

4.3 The communication module

The communication module is used in two cases, one is that the courier can view the message from the logistics distribution station through the mobile terminal, and the courier can make a choice according to the message. For example, some recipients cannot accept the express temporarily. The courier can deliver the express next time when he sees the notification.

Another is that the courier can use the functions of telephone and SMS to save time when the courier encounters unexpected situations.

Figure 9 and figure 10 show the effect of the module.

4.4 The basic information module

The basic information module is mainly about the maintenance of some basic information including historical orders, feedbacks, pushes, courier information and so on.

Couriers can see and modify their basic information in this module, including username and password. At the same time, the courier can view the orders and the evaluations of the orders that he has already delivered.

The effect is as figure 11 shows.

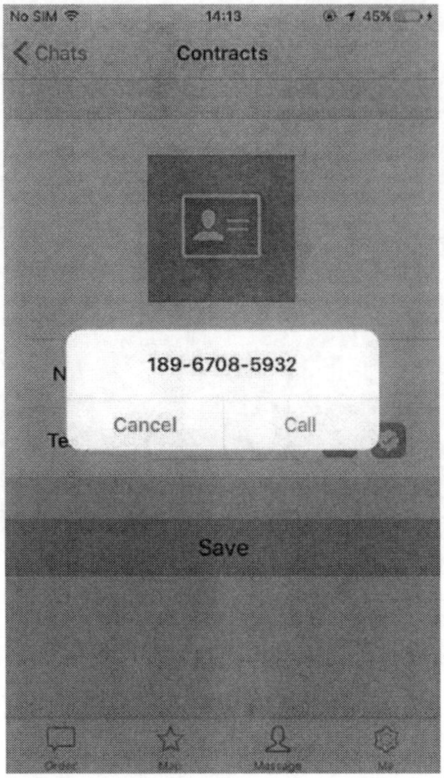

Figure 9. The effect picture of the communication module

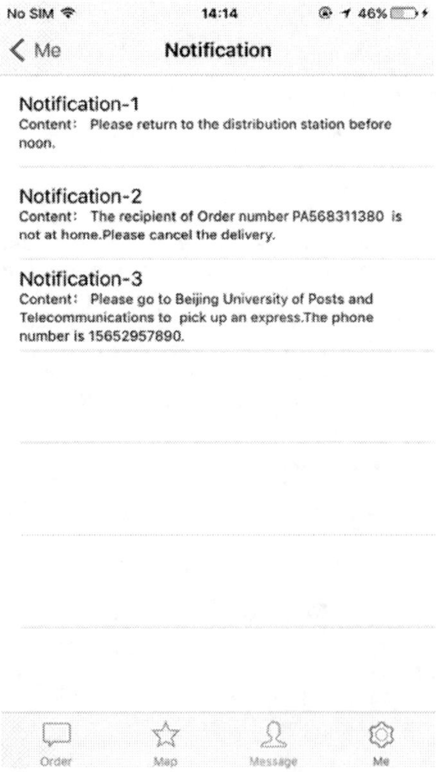

Figure 10. The effect picture of the notification part

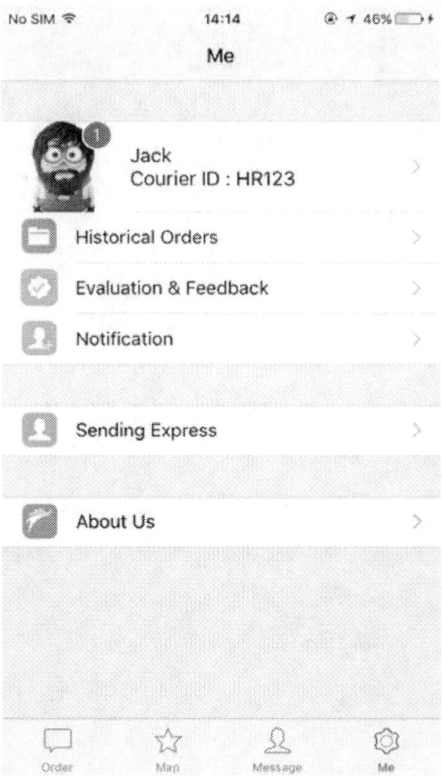

Figure 11. The effect picture of the basic information module

5 Conclusion

This paper mainly analyses the problems existing in the terminal logistics distribution, and puts forward some effective solutions according to these problems. According to these solutions, an application will be designed based on IOS platform which can provide express queries as well as route planning. The courier can effectively improve distribution efficiency and service quality by using the app.

After the test, the actual operation of this application is consistent with the expected effect. At the same time, the business logic is correct and the interaction is good. Facts have proved that it can be applied in practical work. Meanwhile, the design also needs to be improved in the daily work.

Acknowledge

I would like to thank my tutor, Professor Zhuang Yufeng. Mr. Zhuang made a lot of constructive suggestions to help me improve my paper. The teacher's rigorous work attitude and open mind have given me a lot of inspiration and encouragement, so that I can complete the paper successfully.

References

1. L. Kang, *Research on Community Logistics Distribution System in Y Company Based on Electronic Business Platform* (Nanchang University, 2014)
2. Z.Q. Yang, *Research on the Multi-objective Vehicle Routing Optimization in Urban Express Distribution* (Harbin Institute of Technology, 2015)
3. L.F. Xiao, *Research on Commom Distribution Model for End of Logistics in B2C E-Commerce* (Jinan University, 2013)
4. S. Holdorf, H.D. Haasis, G. Lacorata, 8th Int. Conf. on Software, Knowledge, Infromation Management and Applications (SKIMA), 1-6 (2014)
5. Y. Dai, B.S. Zhong, Logistics Technology, **11**, 121-123(2004)

DOI: 10.1051/matecconf/201712804020

Research on Test System for Disease Aided Diagnosis

Wei CHEN[a], Zhangxiong WEN, Lin CHEN and Fengwen SUN

School of Electrical Engineering and Intelligentization, Dongguan University of Technology, 523808 Dongguan, Guangdong Province, P.R.China

Abstract. A real-time multi parameter acquisition system is designed in this paper. Sensors collect physiological parameter data. The parameters are transmitted to the main processor module via a wireless sensor network. The main processor processes the data. The results reflect the current physiological condition of the monitored person.If the physiological condition is abnormal, alarm measures will be initiated to inform the monitor. Wavelet analysis method is used to denoise data. The wavelet transform and least squares support vector machines are used to predict the information, and the model is corrected by the statistical results of the measured data. Experiments show that the modified method is effective.

1 Introduction

People pay more and more attention to the condition of health in daily life. Many people are in a state of sub-health now. For some elderly people, physical functioning and limb flexibility are falling. Real time monitoring is needed to prevent common geriatric diseases, such as stroke, asthma, coronary heart disease and some other chronic diseases.

Health management originally originated in the United States, Canada and so on. These western countries carried out the public disease prevention service firstly. People with different health conditions have different health needs. Health management performs different tests, analyses and assessments for different people. Health management provides professional health advice and services to the population and proposes appropriate health management plans. Health management can coordinate individual and social actions, and then carry out systematic management according to various risk factors. At present, the object of health management is limited, in addition to high-income groups in China. Most of the residents have no sense of health management, especially the young workers who work hard in the city. So the public awareness is still very low[1].

The occurrence and development of diseases, especially chronic diseases, can be interfered. From the point of view of health management, everyone experiences the process from health to disease. Generally it is from the health state, to a low risk state, and then to a high risk state, and then to the onset of disease, and finally is the clinical state. The course of chronic disease can be very long. It usually takes a few years or more years, or even decades. But one thing in common is that they are preventable and controllable. Chronic diseases change in a longer process and are not easily detected. However, the risk factors of disease can be found through the examination and analysis of health management system. People can carry out targeted prevention before the disease formation.

Health management can prevent and control the occurrence and development of disease. It can also reduce the cost of medical treatment and improve the quality of life. Health management helps people carry out health management education, improve people's health management consciousness and level, and understand the related threat health factors in life. We can continue to improve our health through intervention, testing, evaluation, and information collection.

The two important links in health management are the collection and detection of health information. Health management can only be carried out effectively according to the adjustment of the data obtained from the collection and testing of health information

In this paper, a portable device is designed to monitor the physiological parameters of human body in real time. These parameters include pulse rate, oxygen, body temperature, and so on. ZigBee technology is used to realize data communication in the network. The system is based on the self formed wireless sensor network. Sensors are worn on the observer. The terminal node collects the physiological parameters of the monitored person. Parameters are transmitted to the coordinator in real time. The coordinator sends data to the master processor via the interface. The system facilitates real-time perception of physical parameters of the body.

The premise of finding a disease is to obtain accurate physiological information. In physiological signal analysis, the useful signals are usually low frequency signals or some relatively stationary signals, while the noise signals usually show high frequency

[a] Corresponding author: grace_chen@163.com

DOI: 10.1051/matecconf/201712804020

signals. In this paper, the method of removing noise from physiological signals is studied, and the noise and interference signals contained in physiological parameters are effectively suppressed by using wavelet transform.

The physiological parameters of the monitoring object are analyzed, and the hidden slow changes are found. It can predict the disease of the monitoring object and notify observers in time to prevent it. In this paper, comprehensive prediction method is adopted to realize the analysis of multiple physiological parameters of human body. Statistical method is used to analyze the actual data, which is used to correct the prediction results so as to improve the prediction accuracy.

2 System Overall Design

Physiological parameter acquisition is realized by sensor module. The collected data is transmitted to the Zigbee terminal node. The terminal node transmits the coordinator to the coordinator after the network is completed, and realizes the wireless transmission of data[2]. After receiving the physiological parameters sent by the Zigbee terminal node, the Zigbee coordinator sends it to the upper computer for data processing. The structure of system is shown in Figure 1.

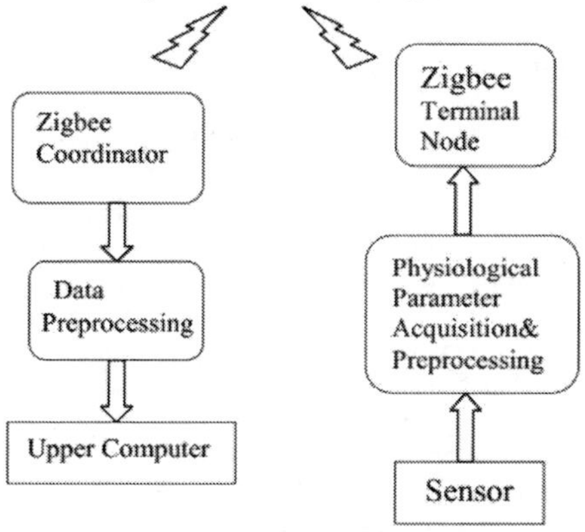

Figure 1. System Overall Structure.

The architecture of the upper computer software consists of three parts: the acquisition end, the display interface and the storage end.

The data acquisition process at the acquisition end is: data reception, identity authentication, data acquisition and data transmission.

Some of the details of the acquisition process are as follows:

(1) The acquisition end of physiological parameters uses C# to develop multi thread program, and the acquisition end asynchronously receives data through the serial port. If the data is read by the serial port, the data is parsed. When the string conforms to the agreed string format, asynchronous calls are made to the parsed data. The data will be saved to the database, and the line graph can be automatically drawn from the display interface of the main interface.

(2) When the physiological parameter data is collected, the the acquisition end of user creates the thread.Functions are constructed in the singleton mode to complete the new and start of the thread.

(3) The opening and closing of the serial port is realized by the way of asynchronous delegate, and the time interval of the acquisition can be chosen as one of "05 seconds", "30 seconds", "1 minutes" and "10 minutes".

(4) When the physiological parameters are imported into the acquisition system in the form of Excel, the Excel is opened by COM, and the data can be reached along the COM port. After the data is collected, the data line graph is redrawn.

The display interface is not only the operation interface of the whole software, but also the broken line display of physiological parameters. There is an operation selection on the display interface. To make the interface look more friendly, the left side of the main form interface is designed to display graphical small interface, the right side of the design is the operation of other users. When the user selects different physiological parameters, the left side of the small interface changes line graph. In the small interface, three physiological parameters are as follows: oxygen unit is%, body temperature unit is degrees Celsius and pulse rate units are units / min..

Some of the details of the display interface are designed as follows:

(1) In the small parameter display interface, the X axis is the number of measurements, and the Y axis is the measured data. When the new data is collected, move the old data forward a bit by using an asynchronous delegate call firstly, and then filled with new data to the bottom, then redraw the data line chart based on the current data. When drawing, the logical coordinate points are converted to the drawing coordinate point. The Y axis of the drawing coordinate point is from top to bottom, and the X axis is the offset to the left or to the right.

(2) The user operation is divided into software settings, view log entries, import data, export data and four physiological parameters selection, the software settings items and view log entries are used as actions to jump to the interface of another form

(3) A form interface is not enough to complete all the functions, so you need to create another two forms. In the new form interface, there are serial selection, serial access and closing items, baud rate entries, database selection, collection interval selection, and another new form has log information .

(4) The export and import of data are implemented using the COM call.

(5) The physiological parameter selection uses the Radio Button control. The conversion of physiological parameters is achieved through the Click event of the control. After the Radio Button is selected, the data line graph is redrawn immediately.

(6) The software settings item and the log entries also use the Button (button) control's Click event, which automatically jumps out of the form interface and log interface.

(7) In the form interface, the opening and closing of serial ports are Click events using Button (button) control, and are implemented asynchronously. The serial selection, baud rate, and collection interval selections use the

ComboBox (drop-down combo box) control. The database selection is used to select the database where the data is stored.

The storage end is divided into two parts, one is the data stored in the Access 2010 database[3]. The other part is data storage to the Excel table. The difference is that the data is stored automatically when it is stored in the database, and the Excel table is selected by the user himself[4].

3 Denoising of Physiological Signals Based on Wavelet Analysis

The traditional design of physiological signal denoising uses filter design, but the denoising accuracy is difficult to satisfy. In recent years, denoising and recognition algorithms are mainly wavelet transform, adaptive filter and other methods. The basic idea of these algorithms is converting the signal into the frequency domain, partial inhibition of noise signals, and ECG signal recognition in the main frequency range; or denoising and recognition by using mathematical morphology and combined with the characteristics of ECG signal. Although these algorithms can guarantee better denoising effect and higher recognition accuracy, the algorithm is complex and difficult to meet the requirement of real-time signal processing.

The research in this paper is aimed at the actual needs of the project. This paper chooses wavelet analysis as the basic algorithm, because wavelet analysis has the characteristics of multi-resolution. Multi-resolution time-frequency domain analysis can focus on any signal details, and wavelet analysis has been successfully applied in many fields. This system adopts wavelet lifting, because it is a fast wavelet transform, which can greatly reduce the amount of computation; the weighted threshold shrinkage method is improved in this system, because it improves the denoising effect; the system uses intermediate denoising results combined with difference method. Denoising and recognition algorithm are combined to reduce computation complexity. The algorithm has the advantages of less computation and simple structure, so it is easy to implement by FPGA, and can meet the requirements of real-time processing of monitoring equipment.

4 Research on Monitoring Information Prediction

Prediction uses time as independent variable, uses monitoring data as dependent variable, and establishes a functional relation between monitoring information and time. The prediction uses the monitoring data at each moment, and uses regression model to predict the future physiological parameters.

Due to the shortage of existing monitoring information forecasting methods, this paper combines wavelet decomposition and least squares support vector machines to study prediction techniques to improve accuracy. Wavelet analysis has the characteristic of multi-resolution.

Support vector machines (SVM) have the advantages of small sample, nonlinear, high dimension, avoiding local minimum point and avoiding over learning phenomenon.Least squares support vector machine instead of inequality constraints with equality constraints. The algorithm can be transformed into linear equations, which choose less parameters than the standard support vector machine method ,and no longer need to specify the precision of convergence criterion. The utility model has the advantages of simple operation, fast solving speed and high precision. The mathematical model is constructed by the combination of wavelet decomposition and least squares support vector regression. Then the model is used to predict the monitoring signal.

The original parameter sequence is decomposed into approximation signal and detail signal by wavelet decomposing. The forecasting model of approximation signal and detail signal can be establised. After getting the prediction value of the approximate signal and the detail signal, inverse wavelet transform is used on the prediction value of each part, and then the final prediction result is obtained.

The prediction process is broadly divided into the following steps: firstly, the monitoring data is normalized, which is to normalize the monitoring data before establish the prediction model, in order to reduce the computational complexity of numerical training process; secondly,wavelet decomposition is used to monitoring data normalized sequences in order to obtain the decomposed sequence of each layer ; the third is to construct training samples of each layer data after wavelet decomposition; the fourth is to calculate parameter of the model; parameters of training samples and the fourth step is then established with the third step training model; forecast model and forecast the trained data of each layer wavelet decomposition the inverse wavelet transform; the prediction results and data layer; anti normalization is to forecast model output data back Normalization operations are used to obtain the final prediction results.

then the trained prediction model is used to predict the data of each layer after wavelet decomposition; inverse wavelet transform is used to prediction results of each layer ; fnally, data inverse normalization is used, which is inverse normalization operation of the output data from the prediction model, and the final prediction results are obtained.

5 Using Statistical Methods for Correction

For the designed system, we use the statistical results of the measured data to correct the model.

Take the temperature test as an example to illustrate the effectiveness of the method. The system is tested with different temperatures. Test results are statistically calculated in the table, the difference between the test value and the standard value, and the relative law is analyzed.

After more than 100 measurements and statistics, some results are shown in Figure 2, Figure 3, Figure 4.

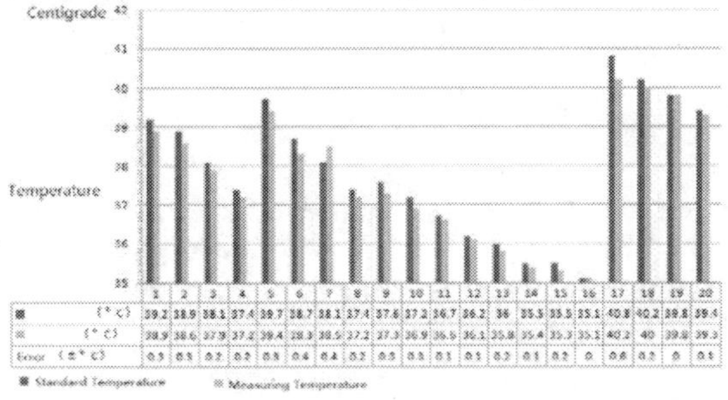

Figure 2. Comparison of Temperature.

From the 20 samples measured in Figure 2, it can be seen that the difference between the measured value and the standard temperature is maximum at 0.6 °C when in a high temperature state. The remaining temperature difference mainly falls at 0.1°C -0.3 °C , and in a fever state, the temperature difference is larger.

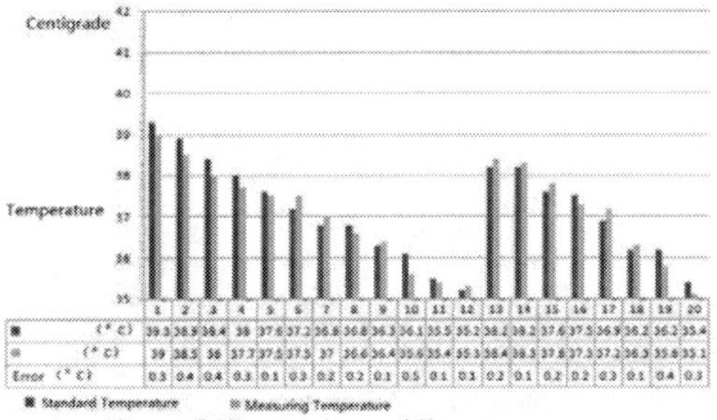

Figure3. Comparison of Temperature.

From the 20 samples measured in Figure 3, it can be seen that the difference between the measured value and the standard temperature is maximum at 0.5 °C when in a lown temperature state. The remaining temperature difference mainly falls at 0.1°C -0.4 °C.

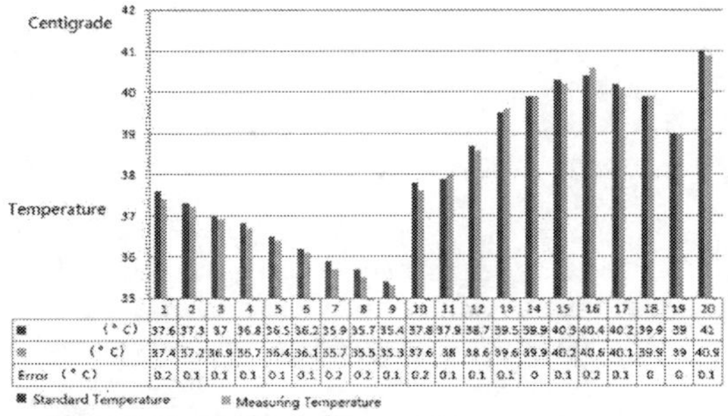

Figure4. Comparison of Temperature.

From the 20 samples measured in Figure 4, it can be seen that the difference between the measured value and the standard temperature is maximum at 0.4 °C when in a high temperature state. The remaining temperature difference mainly falls at 0.1°C -0.3 °C. Compare Figure 4 and Figure 2. The difference between them is that Figure 4 is mainly in the state of rising temperature, and Figure 2 is mainly in the process of temperature drop.

By comparing the above values, the difference between the measured and the standard values can be obtained. In general, the data measured by the electronic probe is lower than the standard data. When the temperature is high, which is greater than 38 °C, the error of temperature probe is larger relatively.

Most of the errors are at 0.1 degrees C, 0.2 degrees C, 0.3 degrees C, and 0.4 degrees C . As the temperature decreases, the temperature error reduces slowly°C.When the body temperature is lower than 38 °C, the error is concentrated at± 0.1 °C and±0.2 °C.

The system adopts two times Fitting Correction System model. When the standard temperature is greater than or equal to 38°C, the temperature error measured by the temperature probe is± 0.2 °C .The error is ±0.1°C when the temperature is lower than 38 °C. Therefore, after the model is corrected, the measurement accuracy is improved.

6 Summary

A real-time physiological parameter acquisition system is designed in this paper. The data is denoised by wavelet analysis, and wavelet decomposition and least squares support vector machines are used to predict the information. The model is corrected by statistical results, and the accuracy of the results is improved.

Acknowledgment

This research was financially supported as follows:
Guangdong science and technology project 2015A010103023;
Dongguan social science and technology development project 2013108101009.

References

1. Hong Jingchun, Community health education in the prevention and treatment of chronic diseases [J], Contemporary medicine, 12 :161-162 (2015)
2. Yang Xiuyu,Design of multi physiological parameter acquisition and management system [D],Beijing Jiaotong University(2015)
3. Shi Xingjia, Wang Binghong, Access 2010 database application basic tutorial(Tsinghua University press, Beijing(2013)
4. Lei Lei, Wang Li,etc,Establishment of pain patient information management system using Access2010 database [J], Chinese Journal of pain medicine, 22) :927-931(2016)

 DOI: 10.1051/matecconf/201712805001

Experimental Verification of New Function Theories of Particles (1)- Experimental Verification of New Kinetic Energy Theorem of Rigid Body Fixed Axis Rotation

Yong YANG[a], Wei-Ping ZHAO, Xiao-Gang GUO and Zheng-Qiang JING

Tongchuan Vocational Technology College, Shaanxi Radio and Television University, Tongchuan, Shaanxi, China

Abstract. Sliding friction torque does dissipative work on the force-bearer, transforming the kinetic energy of the bearer into internal energy and others of the bearer. Sliding friction countertorque does dissipative work on the applying body, transforming the kinetic energy of the bearer into internal energy and others of the applying body. In the experiment, the dissipative work done by sliding friction torque on the bearer is measured and calculated, the increase value of the internal energy of the bearer is measured and calculated, and the increase value of the internal energy of the applying body is measured and calculated. The consistency between their respective dissipative work and their respective internal energy increase value is compared.

1 Introduction

Conservative force (torque) or non-conservative force (torque) can do non-dissipative work to transfer mechanical energy, and non-conservative force (torque) can also do dissipative work to transform mechanical energy into other forms of energy. Non-conservative force (torque) does dissipative work, and non-conservative reacting force (torque) does the equivalent dissipative work also at the same time. This is a law of motion energy transformation of matter. This natural law is perceptually recognized [1], theoretically proved [2], explored and concluded [3]. Based on energy transformation and conservation laws, Newton's laws of motion, work characteristics of conservative force (torque) and non-conservative force (torque), a new kinetic energy theorem of particle, a new kinetic energy theorem of particle system, a new function principle of particle system and a new kinetic energy theorem of rigid body fixed axis rotation are derived. These 4 new theorems and principles constitute new function theory [4].

2 Prediction of the new kinetic energy theorem of rigid body fixed axis rotation

The new kinetic energy theorem of rigid body fixed axis rotation is a reflection of the new function theory, expressed as follows.

In differential expression:

$$dA_{cm} + dA_{ncmi} + dA_{ncmd} + dA_{ncrmd} = d(\frac{1}{2}J\omega^2) \quad (1)$$

In integral expression:

$$A_{cm} + A_{ncmi} + A_{ncmd} + A_{ncrmd} = \frac{1}{2}J\omega^2 - \frac{1}{2}J\omega_0^2 \quad (2)$$

The meaning is that during a rigid body fixed axis rotation process there are two parts of non-dissipative work: A_{cm} (infinitesimal), work done by all conservative external acting torque on the rigid force-bearer, and A_{ncmi} (infinitesimal), implicated work done by all non-conservative acting torque on the rigid force-bearer. There are two parts of dissipative work: A_{ncmd} (infinitesimal), dissipative work done by all non-conservative acting torque on the rigid force-bearer, and A_{ncmd} (infinitesimal), dissipative work done by all non-conservative reacting torque on the rigid bearer. The sum of these 4 parts of work is equal to the increment (infinitesimal) of the kinetic energy of the rigid body fixed axis rotation.

From the expressions of the new kinetic energy theorem of rigid body fixed axis rotation, we can see that the rotational kinetic energy increment of fixed axis rotation rigid body is determined by the sum of 4 terms of non-dissipative work and dissipative work. So, let the earth's surface be inertial system S, a rigid body for a research object be No. 0, rigid body No.0 with rotary inertia J_0 to rotating axis *oz* rotate around the fixed axis *oz*, and the direction of angular speed ω of the fixed axis rotation rigid body be the reference positive direction of the fixed axis *oz*. Rigid body No.0 in fixed axis rotation is under the effect of *m* applying rigid bodies. These *m* applying rigid bodies are in turn No. $j(j=1,2,\cdots,m)$, their rotary inertias to fixed axis *oz* are in turn J_j.

[a] Corresponding author: 1393806366@qq.com

Scene 1: The resultant conservative torque $M_{(cm)0}$ does non-dissipative work on the fixed axis rotation rigid body. Implicated work $dA_{(ncmi)}= M_{(ncm)0j}\cdot d\theta_j$ done by static friction torque $M_{(ncm)0j}$ on the fixed axis rotation rigid body is also dissipative work and can change kinetic energy of the rigid force-bearer fixed axis rotation. This is a law described by the classical kinetic energy theorem of rigid body fixed axis rotation and has been verified [5].

Scene 2: If the fixed axis rotation rigid body is only under the effect of the non-conservative torque $M_{(ncm)0j}$, non-conservative torque $M_{(ncm)0j}$ would generally do both implicated work A_{ncmi} and dissipative work A_{ncmd} on the rigid force-bearer J_0. Non-conservative countertorque $M_{(ncm)j0}$ does dissipative work $A_{(ncrmd)j}$ on the applying rigid body J_j also at the same time. The dissipative work done by non-conservative torque and non-conservative countertorque is related to both the non-conservative torque on the rigid force-bearer and the relative angular displacement $d\theta_{0j}$ and $d\theta_{j0}$ of the force-bearing point relative to the applying point.

That is, under the condition of

$$\begin{cases} \mathbf{M}_{(cm)0} = \sum_{j=1}^{m} \mathbf{M}_{(cm)0j} \equiv 0 & (3) \\ dA_{cm} = \mathbf{M}_{(cm)0} \cdot d\boldsymbol{\theta}_0 \equiv 0 & (4) \end{cases}$$

Form (1) and (4), we can obtain

$$\begin{cases} dA_{ncmd} = dA_{ncrmd} = \frac{1}{2}[-dA_{ncmi} + d(\frac{1}{2}J\omega^2)] & (5) \\ dA_{ncmd} = \sum_{j=1}^{m} \frac{1}{2}\mathbf{M}_{(ncm)0j} \cdot d\boldsymbol{\theta}_{0j} & (6) \\ dA_{ncrmd} = \sum_{j=1}^{m} dA_{(ncrmd)j} = \sum_{j=1}^{m} \frac{1}{2}\mathbf{M}_{(ncrm)j0} \cdot d\boldsymbol{\theta}_{j0} & (7) \\ dA_{ncmi} = \sum_{j=1}^{m} \mathbf{M}_{(ncm)0j} \cdot d\boldsymbol{\theta}_j & (8) \end{cases}$$

From (5), we can see that the sliding friction torque does dissipative work and the sliding friction countertorque does equivalent dissipative work at the same time. Both transform the kinetic energy of rigid body J_0 into non-mechanical energy of respective force-bearers. If wear is neglected, rigid body J_0 for the research object will be regarded as a thermodynamic system. When the thermodynamic system in an adiabatic process ($dQ_0=0$), we can, based on the first law of thermodynamics $dQ_0=dU+dA$, obtain

$$\begin{cases} dQ = dU + dA, dQ_0 = 0 & (9) \\ dU_0 = -dA_{ncmd} = -\sum_{j=1}^{m} \frac{1}{2}\mathbf{M}_{(ncm)0j} \cdot d\boldsymbol{\theta}_{0j} & (10) \\ dU_0 = -dA_{ncmd} = -dA_{ncrmd} = \sum_{j=1}^{m} dU_j & (11) \end{cases}$$

That is, in an adiabatic process, the sliding friction torque does dissipative work and the sliding friction countertorque does equivalent dissipative work at the same time. Both transform the kinetic energy of rigid body J_0 into internal energy increment infinitesimals dU_0 and dU_j of respective force-bearers. From (10) and (11), we can obtain

$$dU_0 = \sum_{j=1}^{m} dU_j = -\sum_{j=1}^{m} \frac{1}{2}\mathbf{M}_{(ncm)0j} \cdot d\boldsymbol{\theta}_{0j} \qquad (12)$$

In the adiabatic process with wear neglected, dissipative work done by all sliding friction torque on rigid body J_0 transformed into total infinitesimal dU_0 of internal energy increment of rigid body J_0, is equal to dissipative work done by all sliding friction countertorque on applying rigid body J_j transformed into internal energy increment infinitesimal $\sum_{j=1}^{m} dU_j$ of rigid body J_j.

This is the prediction of the new kinetic energy theorem of rigid body fixed axis rotation on numerical relation that in the adiabatic process with wear neglected, all sliding friction torque and all sliding friction countertorque do dissipative work on their respective force-bearers and transform the kinetic energy of rigid body J_0 into internal energy increment infinitesimal of their respective force-bearers. This prediction needs experimental verification.

3 The experiment devices and principle

3.1 The experiment devices

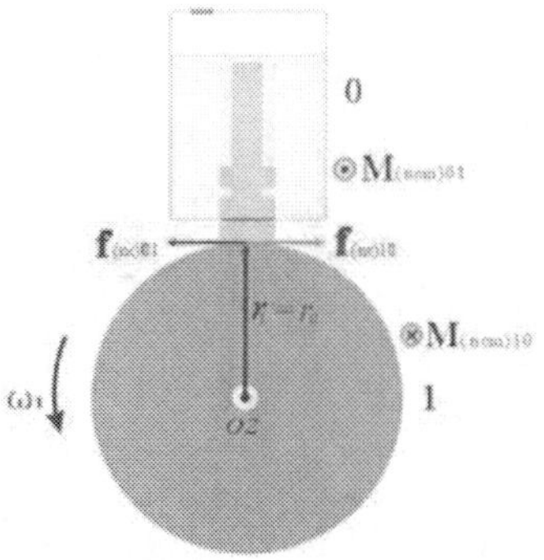

Figure 1. Two friction pairs

As shown in Figure 1, a cylindrical iron flywheel as the rotating friction pair is mounted at the left end of a single-phase motor shaft; another fixed combined friction pair composed of brass bolt, transparent hard plastic bottle and water is supported just above the iron flywheel cylinder. When the motor drives the iron flywheel to rotate synchronously, sliding friction occurs between flywheel cylindrical surface and the lower surface of the brass bolt of the fixed combined friction pair. A reduction gear box is installed at the right end of the motor shaft. The output end of the reduction gear box is connected with a rotary counter used to record revolution of rotary friction pair flywheel. Dynamometer, electronic scales, alcohol thermometer, calorimeter, infrared thermometer are necessary.

3.2 The verification experiment principle

In the process of rigid body fixed axis rotation, the direction of sliding friction torque vector $\mathbf{M}_{(ncm)0j}$ is opposite to the direction of relative angular displacement vector $d\theta_{0j}$ of the force-bearing point relative to the applying point. From (10) and (11), we obtain

$$\begin{aligned} dA_{ncmd} &= \sum_{j=1}^{m}\frac{1}{2}\mathbf{M}_{(ncm)0j}\cdot d\boldsymbol{\theta}_{0j} \\ &= \sum_{j=1}^{m}\frac{1}{2}(M_{(ncm)0j}\mathbf{k})\cdot(-\mathbf{k}d\theta_{0j}) \\ &= \sum_{j=1}^{m}(-\frac{1}{2})M_{(ncm)0j}d\theta_{0j} \\ &= dA_{ncmd} \end{aligned} \quad (13)$$

Substituting (13) into (12) obtains

$$\begin{aligned} dU_0 &= -\sum_{j=1}^{m}-(\frac{1}{2}M_{(ncm)0j}d\theta_{0j}) \\ &= \sum_{j=1}^{m}dU_j \end{aligned} \quad (14)$$

That is, for single direction fixed axis rotation rigid body in the process of sliding friction without wear, internal energy increment infinitesimal is equal to the negative value of total infinitesimal of dissipative work done by sliding friction torque, or equal to internal energy increment infinitesimal of applying rigid bodies transformed from dissipative work done by all sliding friction countertorque on all applying rigid bodies.

In integral expression is

$$\begin{aligned} \Delta U_0 &= -\sum_{j=1}^{m}-(\frac{1}{2}M_{(ncm)0j}\Delta\theta_{0j}) \\ &= \sum_{j=1}^{m}\Delta U_j \end{aligned} \quad (15)$$

In the experiment, the internal energy increment of rigid bodies J_0 and J_j can be measured and calculated on the basis of the following formulas.

$$\Delta U_0 = m_0 c_0 (T_{01} - T_{00}) \quad (16)$$

$$\Delta U_j = m_j c_j (T_{j1} - T_{j0}) \quad (17)$$

The dissipative work done by the sliding friction torque on rigid body J_0 can be measured and calculated on the basis of the following formulas.

$$-A_{ncmd} = \sum_{j=1}^{m}\frac{1}{2}M_{(ncm)0j}\Delta\theta_{0j} = -dA_{ncmd} \quad (18)$$

$$M_{(ncm)0j} = f_{0j}r_0 \quad (19)$$

$$\Delta\theta_{0j} = 2\pi|n_{0j}| \quad (20)$$

In the experiment, when the cylindrical flywheel as the rotary friction pair starts rotating around a fixed axis with a stationary state, sliding friction occurs once the fixed friction pair into contact with the flywheel cylindrical surface, and the flywheel stops rotating after number of turns. Based on the new kinetic energy theorem of rigid body fixed axis rotation, dissipative work done by sliding friction torque and sliding friction countertorque on their respective force-bearing friction pairs can be calculated, and internal energy increment of two friction pairs during friction can be measured.

As the research object, the number of the fixed friction pair is 0. The number of the rotating friction pair flywheel, as the applying rigid body of friction torque, is 1. The number of the earth is 3.

In the whole process of rigid body No.0 under friction, only the sliding friction torque $M_{(ncm)01}$ does dissipative work A_{ncmd} and implicated work A_{ncmi} on rigid body No.0. No other torque does work on rigid body No. 0.

From (18), (19) and (20), we obtain

$$\begin{aligned} -A_{ncmd} &= \sum_{j=1}^{1}\frac{1}{2}M_{(ncm)0j}\Delta\theta_{0j} \\ &= \frac{1}{2}M_{(ncm)01}\Delta\theta_{01} \\ &= \frac{1}{2}f_{01}r_0(2\pi|n_{01}|) \\ &= -A_{ncmd} \\ &= \Delta U_0 \\ &= \Delta U_1 \end{aligned} \quad (21)$$

(21) Is a calculation expression of dissipative work done by sliding friction torque and sliding friction countertorque on their respective force-bearing friction pairs, or a calculation expression of the theoretical value of internal energy of force-bearing friction pairs transformed from mechanical energy of rigid body No.0 as the research object with deformation energy consumption neglected.

$$\begin{aligned} A_{ncmi} &= \sum_{j=1}^{1}M_{(ncm)0j}\Delta\theta_j \\ &= M_{(ncm)01}\Delta\theta_1 \\ &= 2\pi n_1 f_{01}r_0 \end{aligned} \quad (22)$$

(22) Is a calculation expression that sliding friction torque does implicated work A_{ncmi} on rigid body No.0, and transfers mechanical energy of applying rigid body No.1 into mechanical energy of rigid body No.0, as the source of mechanical energy of rigid body No.0.

3 Experiment procedure

a. Mass m_0 and specific heat c_0 of combined friction pair No.0 and the positive pressure N_{01} on friction surface are measured and recorded. Sliding friction coefficient μ_{01} is checked and recorded. Sliding friction f_{01} is calculated. Mass m_1 and radius r_1 of friction pair No.1 are measured and recorded. Specific heat c_1 is checked and recorded. Ambient temperature 298 k.

b. According to Fig.1, the experimental devices are assembled with 220V three-hole power socket.

c. Initial temperature T_{00} of combined friction pair No.0 is measured with the alcohol thermometer and recorded. Initial temperature T_{10} of friction pair No.1 is measured with calorimeter. Rotary counter is reset.

d. The power plug of single-phase motor is into the power socket. The motor is started.

Table 1. Non-mechanical energy and internal energy increment transformed to friction pair No.0 (SI system)

No.	$f_{(nc)01}$	$r_0=r_1$	$M_{(ncm)01}$	$\lvert n_{01}\rvert = n_1$	$-A_{ncmd}$	m_0	c_0	T_{00}-273.1	T_{01}-273.1	ΔU_0	E_r
1	2	0.0375	0.075	2000	471.00	0.138	2038.1	25.5	27.1	450.01	0.0446
2	2	0.0375	0.075	2100	494.55	0.138	2038.1	24.8	26.5	478.14	0.0332
3	2	0.0375	0.075	2200	518.10	0.138	2038.1	24.7	26.5	506.26	0.0228

Table 2. Non-mechanical energy and internal energy increment transformed to friction pair No.1 (SI system)

No.	$-A_{ncrmd}= -A_{ncmd}$	m_1	c_1	T_{10}-273.1	T_{11}-273.1	ΔU_1	E'_r
1	471.00	0.602	444	25.8	27.5	454.390	0.0353
2	494.55	0.602	444	24.8	26.6	481.118	0.0272
3	518.10	0.602	444	25.1	27.0	507.847	0.0198

e. Attention to the running condition of friction pair is taken. The speed control knob can be used to adjust rated output power of the motor.
f. When the rotary counter is up to 2000 revolutions, the motor is stopped.
g. A thermal insulation pad is put at the contact surface of two friction pairs, and temperature T_{01} of combined friction pair No.0 is measured and recorded. The final average temperature T_{11} of friction pair No.1 is measured, calculated and recorded.
h. The experimental data are handled.

The relative errors in the tables

$$E_r = \frac{|A_{ncmd}| - \Delta U_0}{|A_{ncmd}|} \quad (23)$$

$$E'_r = \frac{|A_{ncrmd}| - \Delta U_1}{|A_{ncrmd}|} \quad (24)$$

4 Experimental matters needing attention

It is the value of dissipative work done by sliding friction torque on the research object, the value of internal energy increment of the research object and the equivalent relation between the two values that are measured in this verification experiment. Unlike traditional, only the value of work done by sliding friction torque on a single force-bearer is calculated, and the total value of internal energy increment of two parties in mutual friction is measured[6], as well as the equivalent relation between the two values. The work done by sliding friction countertorque on the single applying body is placed to the sliding friction torque.

For the contact sliding friction between the rigid bodies, thermal transmission between friction bodies has great influence on the experimental results [7]. Therefore, material making two friction pairs with approximately equal heat capacity, better heat transfer and similar thermal conductivity is selected. So, two friction pairs with the same initial temperature can obtain the same internal energy increment in the sliding friction process, and temperature difference always close to zero has little influence on heat transfer between them. The energy transformed from sliding friction is kept in their friction bodies as far as possible.

At the same time, there is heat transfer between two friction pairs and the environment matters also. In order to reduce experimental errors, the difference between the final temperature of friction pair and the ambient temperature in each experiment is not too much. The temperature difference in this experiment was within the range of 3K.

5 Conclusions

From Table 1 and Table 2, we can see, the value of dissipative work done by a pair of sliding friction torque on their respective force-bearing friction pairs is equal to the value of internal energy increment of the friction pairs in the error range. The new kinetic energy theorem of rigid body fixed axis rotation can reflect a law of the nature.

References

1. Y. Yang, Journal of Shaanxi Normal University (Natural Science Edition),30, 24-26 (2002)
2. Y. Yang, Journal of Shaanxi Normal University (Natural Science Edition),33,12-15,292 (2005)
3. Y. Yang, Manufacturing Automation,12,126-128 (2009)
4. Y. Yang, *Proceedings of the 2015 International Conference on Advanced Material Engineering*, 65-83 (2015)
5. X. C. Ren, Y. Q. Wang, N. G. Yang, Journal of Yan'an University (Natural Sciences), 20 (1) ,49-50(2001)
6. Y. L. Ma, Journal of Yanbei Teachers College,12(3),70-71(1996)
7. C.G. Cui , P. Y. Tian , Y. Tian, Lubrication Engineering,42(3):23-27,10(2017)

MATEC Web of Conferences **128**, 05002 (2017) DOI: 10.1051/matecconf/201712805002
EITCE 2017

Survey of optimization methods for BIW lightweight design

WANG Zheyun[1, a]

[1]*School of Automotive Engineering, Dalian University of Technology, Dalian 116024, P.R. China*

Abstract. The body lightweight is important to the vehicle design and development, which has become one of the main research subjects in vehicle industries and research institutes. This paper systematically expounds the background and significance of the lightweight design of automobile, and systematically expatiates the implementation method of the light weight of the vehicle from the fields of lightweight materials, body structural optimization design, molding technology and new connecting technologies. The present situation of domestic and foreign research on lightweight design is introduced at the same time. On this basis, this paper establishes the process of multidisciplinary lightweight design of vehicles, and applies a variety of simulation and modeling tools into this process. The experiment results show the effectiveness and efficiency of the method

1 Introduction

Energy consumption and pollutant emission is serious, and the car's energy consumption is especially large. Lightweight design can have great effect on reducing energy consumption and pollutant. At the same time, body-in-white (BIW) lightweight can improve the performance of auto parts, i.e. brake performance security performance and so on. In this paper, it's mainly about the Lightweight design of the body-in-white.

The body was an important part to the whole vehicle. Most of the vehicle body was made up of stamping parts, which had a complex structure and was composed of many parts. The body occupies almost 60% of the investment cost, whose mass occupies about 30-40% of the whole vehicle. In no-live load condition, about 70% of the vehicle's gas consumption was expended on the vehicle body. Therefore, the body lightweight was important to the vehicle lightweight, also it was one of the main research subjects in vehicle industry [1] [2].

2 Lightweight Design Methods

In order to achieve the purpose of weight loss, researchers constantly explore the vehicle lightweight methods and technologies in the development of new vehicles. Although the method of weight reduction is diverse, it is generally summarized as follows.

2.1 High-strength lightweight materials

2.1.1 High strength steel

Baogang and Taigang have produced the third-generation high strength steel, with a tensile strength and ductility of 20% GPA and 30% GPA, respectively. They have also cooperating with First Automotive Works, Shanghai Automotive Industry Corporation, China Automotive Engineering Research Institute and other units to carry out the evaluation research of applicability.

2.1.2 Aluminum alloy

Audi launches Audi A2, whose white body adopts the second generation ASF technology, using simple extrusion parts as far as possible and a lot of laser welding technology. The aluminum joint connection was also changed to adhesive connection. Jaguar's new XJ applies a single shell structure to steel bodies and connects parts of the body by self-piercing riveting and bonding techniques. On the basis of summing up the advantages of ASF technology and monomer construction technology, Honda and General Company have developed the Honda Insight and general Precept by giving full play to the role of aluminum alloy.

2.1.3 Magnesium alloy

There are more than 100 kinds of magnesium alloy parts in the strong automotive countries like Europe and North America. The three largest automotive groups in the United States, general motors, Ford and Chrysler employ more than 45, 30 and 20 magnesium alloy components, respectively. Chen from Zhejiang University studied the NVH performance of automotive magnesium alloy materials and performed an acoustic optimization design for the magnesia dashboard, which reduced the dashboard quality by 3.6kg [3].

2.1.4 Non-metallic materials

Automotive fiber composites mainly include carbon fiber reinforced polymer (CFRP) and glass fiber reinforced plastic (GFRP). The density of CFRP is 1380Kg/m3, about 1/6 to 1/5 of steel. Audi has introduced fiber reinforced plastic (FRP) round springs, which reduced the weight of each A4 front suspension system from 2.66kg to 1.53kg, more than 40% weight loss than in the steel spring [4]. In March, 2013, Daimler's new GL-class SUV equipped its six-cylinder diesel engine with the world's first plastic engine bracket. Compared with the previous aluminum stent, plastic stent has a better acoustic properties and thermal insulation performance, as well as lighter quality and better carrying capacity [5].

2.2 Body structure optimization

Through the structural lightweight design, the corresponding material, the optimal structure and size are used in the appropriate location of the car structure, so that each part of the material can perform the maximum load and energy absorption. An optimized body structure can improve material utilization, reduce vehicle weight, reduce material costs and achieve energy saving, emission reduction, and reducing consumption at the same time.

2.2.1 Topology optimization and size optimization

In engineering, topology optimization and shape optimization are combined together to determine the optimum structure. In the development of new material automotive components, topology optimization method is used to obtain the structural contour of the component, and then the dimensional optimization method is used to obtain the specific structure of the component.

Zhu et.al applied the topology optimization technology into the automotive gearbox shell structure design based on variable-density method, which improves the strength, stiffness, natural frequency and control structure quality through static and dynamic topology optimization considering the constraints of the manufacturing process [6]. Zhou et.al conducted the bus body lightweight design based on topology optimization and sensitivity analysis, with a body mass reduction of 362 kg [7].

2.2.2 Shape optimization

Shi et.al used SFE-CONCEPT software to establish the model of the white body parameters and optimization of the model. The optimized model is basically unchanged in the context of the performance, with the quality of BIW reduced by 12Kg, and a weight loss rate of 4.5% [8].

2.2.3 Multi-objective multidisciplinary optimization

The multi-objective optimization problem was first put forward by Pareto in 1896. He concluded the multi-objective optimization problem from the point of view of economic balance. While lightening the vehicle, the following requirements must be met: vibration, noise and ride comfort (Noise Vibration Harshness); stiffness, strength and crashworthiness requirements of the entire vehicle; reliability, etc. Therefore, many scholars have applied the research methods of multi-objective algorithms to the design of automotive lightweight [9] [10].

After taking into consideration the dashboard collision performance and NVH performance and lightweight performance, Wang et.al established a multi-discipline multi-objective optimization design model [11]. Under the frontal collision condition, the vehicle occupant protection system is designed with the multi-objective optimization method to improve the vehicle occupant protection system by Gu et.al [12]. Considering the lightweight, bus stiffness and intensity, rolling safety and other factors, Su et.al carried out the multi-objective optimization design of the bus body frame and the experiments at the same time [13]. The bus body weight decreased 2.7% to ensure the vehicle body rigidity and strength performance.

2.3 Application of new technologies

2.3.1 Laser tailor welded blanks

Azuma and others have studied the formability of tailor welded blanks. The results show that the formability of tailor welded blanks is related to the orientation of welds and the main strain.

2.3.2 Continuous variable panel technology

Compared with TWB technology, TRB technology eliminates welding process, thus reducing production cost. In addition, the TRB plate has no welding seam, so the component has the advantages of high connection strength, good uniformity and good shock resistance. The board surface with TRB technology is smooth and beautiful, and can be widely used in automobile body outer panel. Ford Focus B column was produced by TRB technology.

2.3.3 Tailor Rolling Tube - TRT

TRT is a new technology formed on the basis of TRB technology and hydraulic forming technology. It can realize the strength design of parts, prolong the life of parts and simplify the production process. TRT technology can be used in the production of A, B column, sub frame and other components.

2.3.4 Thermoforming Technology

There were over 210 thermal forming steel production lines worldwide, and more and more models were being used in thermoforming technology. Hot forming technology is applied in the A column, B column, C column, sill, front and rear anti-collision beam, roof side beam, backplane channel and so on.

2.3.5 Hydraulic forming and gas forming technology

DOI: 10.1051/matecconf/201712805002

FAW and the Harbin Institute of Technology cooperated on the model of the engine sub frame. In addition, Baogang has also introduced hydraulic to form the production line and produce some prototypes.

2.4 New connection technology

2.4.1 Laser welding

It is mainly used for welding thin materials and welding speed, welding process of heat conduction, laser radiation heating surface. Surface heat through the heat transfer oriented internal diffusion by controlling the pulse width and energy, peak power and repetition frequency parameter to form the specific melting pool in the 1970s.

2.4.2 Self-piercing riveting

SPR technology was first applied to Audi A8, which was then subsequently applied to Jaguar, XJ, Audi, new 5 series, Audi TT and other models. The self-piercing riveting technology can not only realize the connection of the same material plate, but also realize the connection of dissimilar materials and plates with different thickness.

2.4.3 Pressure connection technique

At present, the pressure connection technology has been applied to Audi, A6, Passat, POLO, new Golf-5 and other models. Although the price of pressure connection is low compared to SPR technology, and the strength of the connection position is also low, which limits the application of the pressure connection technique.

3 Multidisciplinary optimization lightweight design process

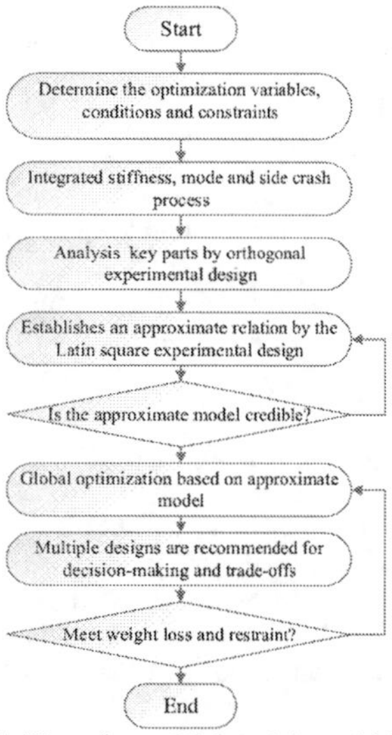

Figure 1. Flow chart of lightweight multidisciplinary optimization design.

Based on the above analysis of BIW lightweight design methods, this paper proposed a Multidisciplinary optimization lightweight design process. Fig.1 shows the flow chart of lightweight multidisciplinary design optimization for a domestic car. This chapter focuses on the design variables (factors), response and level determination. At the same time, the parametric integration of stiffness, modal and side collision is implemented by Isight, and the experimental design analysis is carried out. According to the process, for the optimization design in this paper, we must first define the calculation conditions, constraints, and determine the factors and their level. Secondly, factors and horizontal orthogonal test table by the orthogonal experimental design method of orthogonal experiment are formed. Using the orthogonal table, this paper integrates stiffness and modal, side collision calculation file by Isight and submit the calculated arch for further analysis of sample points. Global optimization algorithms are designed based on the approximate models.

4. Simulation and modeling tools

In our experiments, we select twenty-one parts' thickness and eleven kinds of material from the BIW design example as design variables. The design tasks considered in this case study determine these design variables step by step to minimize the weight while satisfying multidisciplinary constraints such as static stiffness, vibration characteristics, low/high speed crash, and Noise Vibration Harshness (NVH) analysis. The following table shows the optimization process for vehicle lightweight design by using different simulation modeling tools [14] [15].

Table 1. Modeling and simulation tools for BIW optimization design process

Subject	Content	Tools
Finite element modeling and verification	Modeling and verification of BIW stiffness, modal and side impact by finite element method	Nastran Pam
Simulation process integration and parameterization	Integrated the simulation models of various disciplines and parameterize the input and output	Isight
Sampling analysis of experimental design	Design the experimental matrix and analyze the key parameters and sensitivities	Isight/ Nastran Pam
Establish an approximate (alternative) model	Replace the time-consuming simulation in optimization by an efficient and accurate approximation model	Isight
Global multidisciplinary optimization	Find the global optimal solution based on the approximate model	Isight
Verification and tradeoff of optimization results	verify the optimization results by finite element, balance by multiple criteria	Nastran PamCr ash

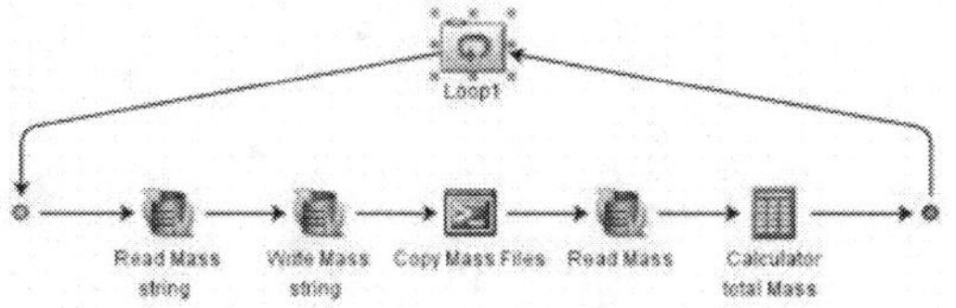

Figure 2. Flow GUI of Isight simulation platform

Fig.2 shows the Graphical User Interface (GUI) of Isight, which provides a comprehensive selection of parallelized optimization techniques that can be applied to a variety of problems. By applying the optimization methods and software, the simulation time is reduced from 8 hours to 2 hours.

5 Conclusion and future work

This paper systematically expounds the background and significance of the lightweight design of automobile, and systematically expatiates the implementation way of the light weight of the vehicle from the fields of lightweight materials, structural optimization design and molding technology. The present situation of domestic and foreign research on lightweight design is described at the same time. On this basis, this paper establishes a process of lightweight multidisciplinary design of white body, and applies a variety of simulation and modeling tools into this process. The experiment results show the effectiveness and efficiency of the methods.

Reference

1. A.V. Londhe. A systematic approach for weight reduction of BIW panels through optimization, SAE Technical Paper, 2010-01-0389.
2. Y.W. Lee. A Study on the improvement of the structural joint stiffness for Aluminium BIW, SAE Technical Paper, (1997). 970583.
3. Chen Xinrui, Investigation on NVH performance of automotive magnesium alloy and acoustic optimization design for magnesium dash [D], Zhejiang University, 2011.
4. Jenne, M., et al. "Improved Mechanical Preload Measurement of Bolted Joints for Light Weight Design with CFRP Components." ASME 2015 International Mechanical Engineering Congress and Exposition. American Society of Mechanical Engineers, 2015.
5. http://ae-plus.com/technology/basf-designs-plastic-engine-mount-for-daimler.
6. ZHU, Jian-feng, et al. "Structural topology optimization based design of automotive transmission housing structure." Journal of Jilin University (Engineering and Technology Edition) 3 (2013): 004.
7. Wei, Z. H. O. U. "Research on the lightweight design of bus body based on topology optimization and sensitivity analysis." Journal of Hefei University of Technology (Natural Science) 4 (2013): 006.
8. Yuze, SHI Guohong CHEN Yong YANG, and JIANG Xin SONG Zhengchao. "BIW Architecture Multidisciplinary Light Weight Optimization Design." Journal of Mechanical Engineering 8 (2012): 019.
9. Karande, Prasad, and Shankar Chakraborty. "Application of multi-objective optimization on the basis of ratio analysis (MOORA) method for materials selection." Materials & Design 37 (2012): 317-324.
10. Su, Ruiyi, Liangjin Gui, and Zijie Fan. "Multi-objective optimization for bus body with strength and rollover safety constraints based on surrogate models." Structural and Multidisciplinary Optimization 44.3 (2011): 431-441.
11. Wang, Ping, and Guangqiang Wu. "Multidisciplinary design optimization of vehicle instrument panel based on multi-objective genetic algorithm." Chinese Journal of Mechanical Engineering 26.2 (2013): 304-312.
12. Gu, Xianguang, et al. "Multiobjective optimization design for vehicle occupant restraint system under frontal impact." Structural and Multidisciplinary Optimization 47.3 (2013): 465-477.
13. Gu, Xianguang, et al. "Multiobjective optimization design for vehicle occupant restraint system under frontal impact." Structural and Multidisciplinary Optimization 47.3 (2013): 465-477.
14. Y. Qu. 2013. Stiffness evaluation method of BIW with sensitivity coefficients, SAE Technical Paper, 2013-01-0975.
15. Nomura, S. Murakami, H. Kuroda, K. Tanaka, R. Ramoo, P. Kosarek, M. Parthasarathy and R. Chandaroy. 2003. Improvement of BIW NVH characteristics using a concurrent design optimization approach, SAE Technical Paper, 2003-01-1596.

MATEC Web of Conferences **128**, 05003 (2017) DOI: 10.1051/matecconf/201712805003
EITCE 2017

Effect of bevel angle of three-layer parallel plate on hydrodynamic performances of otter-board

Lei WANG, Lu Min WANG, Yu ZHANG, Ai Zhong ZHOU, Yong Li LIU, Wen Wen YU, Xun ZHANG[a]

Key Laboratory of Oceanic and Polar Fisheries, Ministry of Agriculture; East China Sea Fisheries Research Institute, Chinese Academy of Fishery Sciences, Shanghai 200090, China

Abstract. The effect of bevel angle of three-layer parallel plate of otter-board on hydrodynamic performances is investigated by model wind tunnel test. Four otter-board models are designed with four different bevel angles (8 °, 10 ° , 12° and 14 °) , and tested under the wind speed 28 m / s in wind tunnel. Model experiment is conducted to obtain the drag coefficients C_x, the lift coefficient C_y, the pitch moment coefficient C_m, the center of pressure coefficient C_p and calculated the lift-drag ratio C_y/C_x. The result shows that the maximum lift coefficient and the maximum lift-drag ratio of the otter-board model with a bevel angle 12 degree is higher, there is 2.598(α=65°) and 2.607(α=37.5°); For comparison in stability of otter-board, the stability of the otter-board model with the bevel angle 8 degree is better by the comparative analysis of C_m and C_p, the absolute value of C_m is 0.174 and the minimum variation coefficient of C_p is 4.37%. The results can offer reference for the structural optimization design of trawl otter-board.

1 Introduction

Trawl doors is an important member of fishing gear for spread of trawl. The merits of otter-board hydrodynamic performance can be measured by the lift coefficient of the trawl door, the drag coefficient of the trawl door and pitching moment coefficient of the trawl door [1]. By optimizing the structure of otter-board may improve hydrodynamic performance of the otter-board, and reducing the energy consumption of fishing vessels [2-3]. Currently, extensive studies on otter-board hydrodynamic performance had been conducted in the US, Japan, Norway and other countries [4-9]; In China, researchers have studied the relevant hydrodynamic performance of otter-board early since 1980s, and the series of optimization studies on otter-board structure is still necessary [10-15]. With the development of offshore fishing, higher requirements on the otter-board design is put forward, hydrodynamic performance improvement of otter-board will be the focus of future research. This article is part of the series of tests, which analyze the hydrodynamic performance of otter-board with the bevel angle of three-layer parallel plate changing.

2 2 Material and Methods

2.1 Design and manufacture of otter-board model

Test model of otter-board with three parallel plates is designed in different bevel angle of the three parallel plates. Ensuring the premise of other parameters in common, the design of model structure has been simplified based on the test objectives and requirements, while, only the bevel angle of three parallel plates changes. The structure and parameters of the model are illustrated in figure 1.

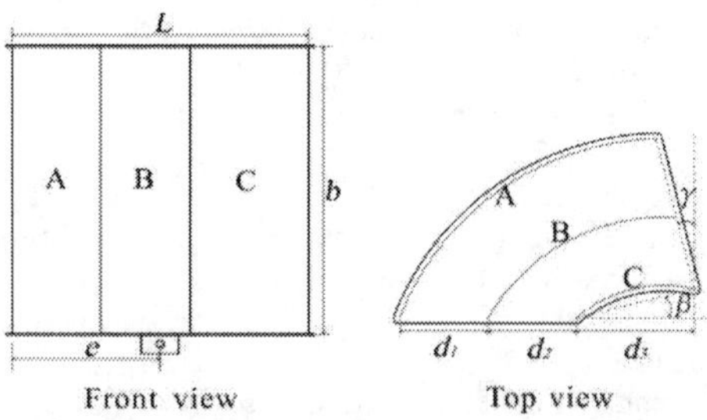

Figure 1 Structure and parameters of otter-board

Note: *L*: chord; *b*: span; *e*: distance between fulcrum and front end of model; A, B, C: parallel plate; *γ*: bevel angle; *β*: angle of front plate; d_1: horizontal distance between A and B; d_2: horizontal distance between B and C; d_3: projected length of C.

For four otter-board test models, the aspect ratio is fixed at 1.0, model's area is 0.250m2, the corresponding distance between plate A-B-C and each projected length of plate C are same, when the bevel angle of three parallel plates changes four angle (8, 10, 12 and 14), the curvature of the plate C is 12%, the specific parameters in table 1, four otter-board models are numbered 1, 2, 3, 4 respectively. Models are made of steel with painted

[a] Corresponding author: zhangxun007@hotmail.com

 DOI: 10.1051/matecconf/201712805003

surfaces (figure 2).

Table 1 Introductions for dimension and structure parameters of four otter-board models

No.	L/m	b/m	λ	S/m^2	e/m	d_1= d_2/m	d_3/m	γ=β	δ
1	0.50	0.50	1.0	0.250	0.25	0.15	0.20	8°	0.12
2	0.50	0.50	1.0	0.250	0.25	0.15	0.20	10°	0.12
3	0.50	0.50	1.0	0.250	0.25	0.15	0.20	12°	0.12
4	0.50	0.50	1.0	0.250	0.25	0.15	0.20	14°	0.12

Note: b: span; L: chord; $\lambda = b / L$, aspect ratio; $S = L \cdot b$; e: distance between fulcrum and front end of model; d_1: horizontal distance between A and B; d_2: horizontal distance between B and C; d_3: projected length of C; γ: bevel angle; β: angle of plate C; δ: curvature of plate C.

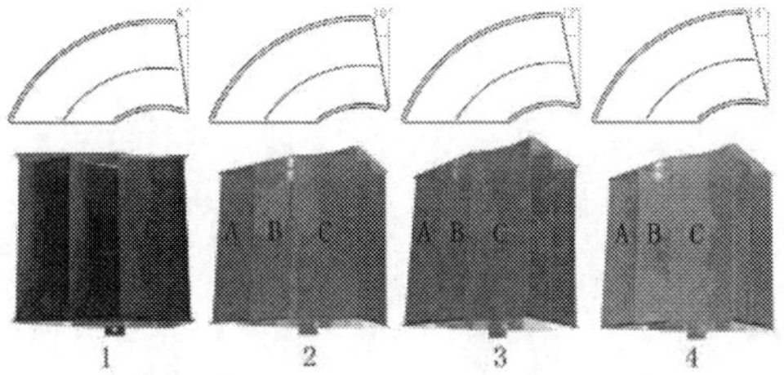

Figure 2 Four otter-board models and top view of design

Note: A, B, C: parallel plate.

2.2 Test facility

Wind tunnel for this test is Nanjing University of Aeronautics and Astronautics NH-2 wind tunnel, the tunnel is closed reflux wind tunnel with double string test section, this experiment is carried out in a small test section, the main technical performance of the small test section: 6 m (length) ×3 m (width) ×2.5 m (height), import cross-sectional area 7.18 m^2, the maximum wind speed is 90m / s, the minimum steady wind speed is 5 m / s.

The dynamometer test uses six-component mechanical tower - Balances to measure, test model installation is shown in figure 3.

Test data acquisition and processing system used is made up by the pre-amplifier and four networked computer system.

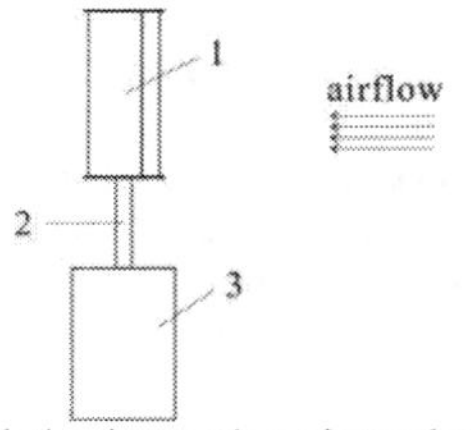

Figure 3 Installation instruction of otter-board model in wind tunnel

Note: 1.otter-board model 2.model connection 3.six-component force balance

2.3 Test method

2.3.1 Parameter definition of test model

Test models need to be installed on the wind tunnel in six-component balance mechanical base according to the order, angle of attack of model rotates by the 0 ° -70 ° when the wind speed reaches 28m / s (room temperature 20 °C),wherein the angle of attack in the range 0 ° -50 °, 2.5 ° intervals to record a measurement data point, after the attack angle 50 °, each measurement interval of 5 ° to record data points, there are 25 sets of data totally, including the drag coefficient C_x, the lift coefficient C_y, the pitch moment coefficient C_m and the center of pressure coefficient C_p.

The relevant parameters of models in the wind tunnel test section are defined as shown in figure 4. In figure 4, O is torque reference point, which is the punch of the model at the bottom. During the test, the resistance of the model is provided by the force of balance along the X-axis direction, the lift is provided by the force of balance along the Z-axis direction, and the pitch moment is provided by the M_y of balance along the Z-axis direction.

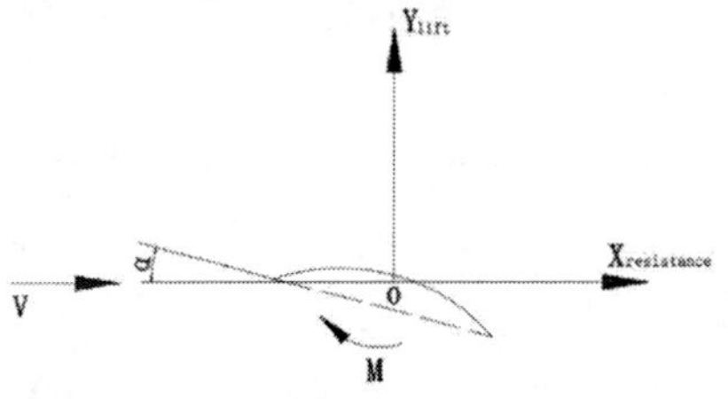

Figure 4 Parameter definition diagram of test model in wind tunnel

For this test, Wind speed V=28m/s, when the Reynolds number $R_e = VL/\upsilon = 0.93\times10^6$ (coefficient of viscosity $\upsilon = 15\times10^6$ m^2·s^{-1}) [10].

2.3.2 Parameter definition of test measurement

 DOI: 10.1051/matecconf/201712805003

Three components: lift Y, drag X, pitching moment M (around the fulcrum), while the distance from the center of pressure to the front-end otter-board $d=e-(M/N)$ [12], (N is the normal force).

Lift coefficient $C_y = \frac{Y}{\rho V^2 S/2}$ [3]; drag coefficient $C_x = \frac{X}{\rho V^2 S/2}$; pitch moment coefficient $C_m = \frac{M}{\rho V^2 SL/2}$; center of pressure coefficient $C_p = \frac{d}{L}$.

Air density ρ=1.225 kg/m^3 in above formula; S is otter-board area (m^2); L is the otter-board chord length (m).

All the experimental data have been carried out the stent disturbance correction which is completed by the method of taking out light pole directly.

3 Results and Discussion

3.1 Drag coefficient and lift coefficient

Data from the experiment includes the drag coefficient C_x, the lift coefficient C_y, the pitch moment coefficient C_m and the center of pressure coefficient C_p. C_y / C_x is the lift-drag ratio, which is an important factor to determine the merits of otter-board hydrodynamic performance. Otter-board with excellent hydrodynamic properties will get higher lift-drag ratio and better stability, what can be analyzed by comparing the pitching moment coefficient C_m stencil and the center of pressure coefficient C_p[1-3]. The test data is divided and made C_x-α, C_y-α and C_y / C_x-α graph shown in figure 5 for analyzing the differences of hydrodynamic properties of four otter-board models clearly.

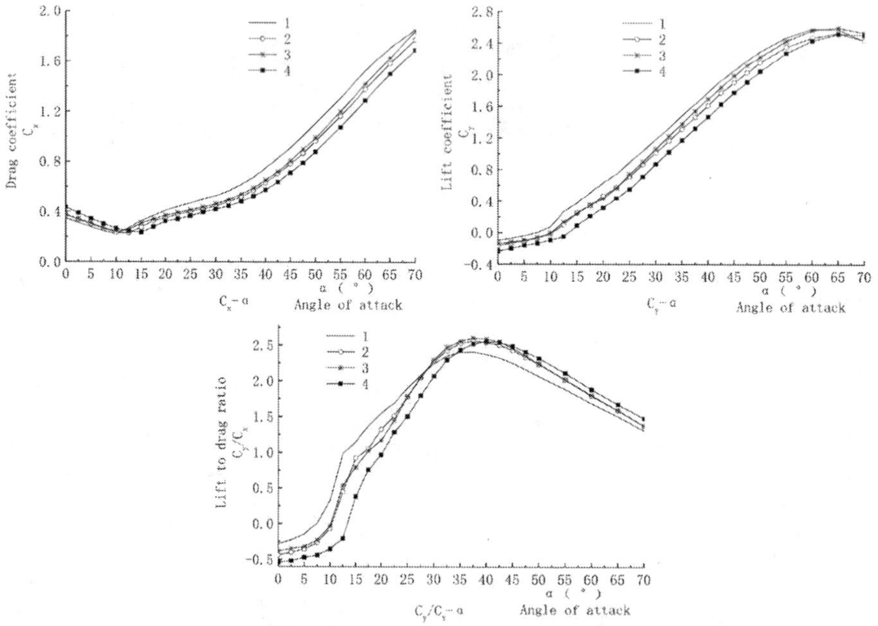

Figure 5 The changing curve comparison of C_x(a), C_y(b) and C_y/C_x(c) along with the angle of attack α

In figure 5, graph C_x-α and C_y-α show the variation curve of drag coefficient C_x and lift coefficient of four models while the angle of attack α changed. The relationship between C_x and α is proportional, No.1 otter-board model with the bevel angle of 8°has the higher drag coefficient. The maximum lift coefficient C_y of No. 3 model is higher, there is 2.598 (α= 65 °), and the maximum lift coefficient of No. 1 and No. 2 otter-board model are 2.583 (α = 60 °) and 2.527 (α = 65 °) , the maximum lift coefficient C_y of No. 4 model is the lowest, there is 2.519 (α= 65 °).

3.2 Lift-drag ratio

The lift-drag ratio can be more intuitive to analysis the hydrodynamic performance of otter-board, and the otter-board with higher lift-drag ratio gets the better operational efficiency. In figure 5, the curve C_y / C_x-α indicates that the lift-drag ratio C_y / C_x of No. 1 otter-board model with the bevel angle of 8°is higher at the angle of attack α<27.5 °, and the maximum lift-drag ratio is 2.411 (α= 37.5 °), the maximum lift-drag ratio of No. 2 and No. 4 model is 2.564 (α= 37.5 °) and2.555 (α= 40 °), respectively; however, the maximum lift-drag ratio C_y / C_x of No. 3 otter-board model with the bevel angle of 12°is higher than the other three models, there is 2.607(α= 37.5 °).

3.3 Stability of otter-board

Pitching moment, also known as longitudinal moment, what is the component along the horizontal axis of the moment of force that is generated by the aerodynamic acting on the otter-board to the center of gravity of model, and the pitching moment coefficient C_m is usually converted for analysis and comparison instead. Pitching moment can be divided into upper and lower pitching moment, what are usually distinguished by positive and negative, its absolute value represents the level of pitching moment, and the pitching moment coefficient tending to 0 represents the more excellent stability of otter-board generally, in practice, comparing the absolute value C_m corresponding to the operation angle of attack of otter-board may determine the stability level of otter-board. For comparison, it is assumed to select the angle of attack corresponding to the maximum lift-drag ratio C_y/C_x [16], when the absolute value of C_m corresponded is shown in table 2. The absolute value of C_m of No.1 model is 0.174, so the stability of No.1 otter-board model is better.

Table 2 Parameters of four otter-board for stability analysis

No.	Angle corresponding to the maximum lift – drag ratio α	$\lvert C_m \rvert$	Variable coefficient of C_p
1	37.5°	0.174	4.37%
2	37.5°	0.194	4.70%
3	37.5°	0.183	5.17%
4	40°	0.191	4.99%

The stability of otter-board can be measured by the center of pressure coefficient C_p, and it is generally compared by analyzing the coefficient of variation of C_p within the range of angle around 5 ° of the angle of attack corresponding to the maximum lift-drag ratio, the smaller the coefficient, the better the stencil stability [17]. Data Calculated is shown in table 2, the minimum variation coefficient of C_p is 4.37%, and it also means the stability of No.1 otter-board model is better.

4 Conclusion

The test study concludes that designing the bevel angle of otter-board plates appropriately can improve the lift coefficient of the otter-board. When the bevel angel of three parallel plates of otter-board is designed in 8°or 12°, the otter-board has the higher maximum lift coefficient. It is also needed to pay attention to adjust the lift -drag ratio and stability of the otter-board, test shows that the maximum lift-drag ratio of otter-board model with the bevel angle of 12°is higher than the other three models, and the stability of the otter-board model with the bevel angle of 8°is better. Data and conclusions of this study can provide a reference for the design of otter-board.

Acknowledgements

This work is financially supported by the National Key Technology R&D Program (No. 2013BAD13B05).

References

1. Guo G X, Liu TY, Huang X H, Gu F L. Theory and Practice of trawl doors Kinetic [M]. Guangdong Science and Technology Publications, 2008.
2. Zhou Y Q. Mechanics of fishing gear [M]. China Agriculture Publications, 2001.
3. Chen X Z, Huang X C. Theory and method of gear model test [M]. Shanghai Science and Technology Publications, 2011.
4. Sala A, Prat J, Antonijuan J, Lucchetti A. Performance and impact on the seabed of an existing- and an experimental-otter board: Comparison between model testing and full-scale sea trials [J]. Fisheries Research, 2009, 100(2): 156-166.
5. Takahashi Y, Fujimori Y, Hu F X, Shen X L, Kimura N. Design of trawl otter boards using computational fluid dynamics [J]. Fisheries Research, 2015, 161: 400-407.
6. Shen X L, Hu F X, Kumazawa T, Shiode D, Tokai T. Hydrodynamic characteristics of a hyper-lift otter board with wing-end plates [J]. Fisheries Science, 2015, 81(3): 433-442.
7. Broadhurst M K, Sterling D J, Millar R B. Modifying otter boards to reduce bottom contact: Effects on catches and efficiencies of triple-rigged penaeid trawls [J]. Fisheries Management and Ecology, 2015, 22(5): 407-418.
8. Fukuda K, Hu F X, Tokai T, Matuda K. Effect of Aspect Ratio on Lift and Drag Coefficients of Cambered Plates [J]. Nippon Suisan Gakkaishi, 2000, 66(1): 97-103.
9. Park C D, Matuda K, Hu F X. Effects of Dihedral and Sweepback Angles on Lift and Drag of the Cambered Otter Board [J]. Nippon Suisan Gakkaishi, 1996, 62(6): 920-927.
10. Zhang X, Wang J H, Wang M Y, Yu Y F, Xu, B. S. Hydrodynamic characteristics of rectangular cambered V type otter board-- Ⅰ : Relationship between cambered ratio of fairwater fin and hydrodynamic characteristics of otter board [J]. Journal of Fishery Sciences of China, 2004, 11(z1): 5-8.
11. Wang J H, Wang M Y, Zhang X, Yu Y F, Xu B S. Hydrodynamic characteristics of rectangular cambered V type otter board-- Ⅱ : Effects of aspect ratio, slotted position and slotted width on hydrodynamic characteristics of otter board [J]. Journal of Fishery Sciences of China, 2004, S1: 9-13.
12. Wang M Y, Wang J H, Zhang X, Yu Y F, Xu B S. Hydrodynamic characteristics of vertical V type otter board [J]. Journal of Fisheries of China, 2004, 3: 311-315.
13. Li C C, Liang Z L, Huang L Y, Zhou W F, Sun P, Wang L. Hydrodynamic study on a vee type otter board of small trawl vessels [J]. Marine Sciences, 2013, 11: 69-73.
14. Wang L, Wang L M, Feng C L, Zhang X, Shi J G, Zhang Y, Liu Y L, Yu W W. Influence of vane dimension on hydrodynamic performances of single slotted cambered otter board [J]. Fishery Modernization, 2015, 6: 55-60.
15. Wang L, Wang L M, Yu W W, Feng C L, Shi J G, Liu Y L, Zhang X. Influence of deflector angular variation on hydrodynamic performances of single slotted cambered otter board [C]. Conference: International Forum on Energy, Environment and Sustainable Development, 2016, 75: 530-535.
16. Yang L. Hydrodynamic characteristics of slotted

circular plate [J]. Fisheries Science and Technology, 1996, 2: 38-41.
17. Yang L. Hydrodynamic characteristics of double - plate circular plate [J]. Fisheries Science and Technology, 1996, 5: 42-44.

MATEC Web of Conferences **128**, 05004 (2017)
EITCE 2017
DOI: 10.1051/matecconf/201712805004

Effect of deflector angle on hydrodynamic performances of a double-slotted cambered otter-board

Lei WANG, Lu Min WANG, Jian Gao SHI, Yu ZHANG, Yong Li LIU, Wen Wen YU, Xun ZHANG[a]

Key Laboratory of Oceanic and Polar Fisheries, Ministry of Agriculture; East China Sea Fisheries Research Institute, Chinese Academy of Fishery Sciences, Shanghai 200090, China

Abstract. The effect of deflector angle on hydrodynamic performances of a double-slotted cambered otter-board is investigated using engineering models in a wind tunnel. Three different angle combinations (35°-30°, 30°-25°and 25°-20°) are evaluated at a wind speed of 28 m/s. Parameters measured included: drag coefficient C_x, lift coefficient C_y, pitch moment coefficient C_m, center of pressure coefficient C_p , over a range of angle of attack (0° to 70°). These coefficients are used in analyzing the differences in the performance among the three otter-board models. Results shows that the maximum lift coefficient C_y of the otter-board model with the angle combination (35°-30°) of two deflectors is the highest (2.160 at α=55°). The maximum C_y/C_x of the otter-board with the angle combination (25°-20°) is the highest (3.842 at α=2.5°). A comparative analysis of C_m and C_p shows that the stability of otter-board model with the angle combination (25°-20°) is better in pitch, and the stability of otter-board model with the angle combination (30°-25°) is better in roll. The findings of this study can offer useful reference data for the structural optimization of otter-boards for trawling.

1 Introduction

Trawl doors are an important part of fishing gear for the spreading of a trawl. The merits of the hydrodynamic performance of otter-boards can be measured on the basis of the lift coefficient of the trawl door, the drag coefficient of the trawl door, and the pitching moment coefficient of the trawl door [1]. Optimizing the structure of otter-boards may improve the hydrodynamic performance of the otter-board and reduce the energy consumption of fishing vessels [2-3]. Extensive studies on the hydrodynamic performance of otter-boards have been conducted in the United States, Japan, Norway, and other countries [4-9]. In China, researchers have studied the relevant hydrodynamic performance of otter-boards since the early 1980s, including the hydrodynamic performance and optimization of different otter-boards with various structure types. The development of offshore trawler fleets has increased globally in recent decades, raising the demand for improved otter-board designs. Accordingly, improvements in the hydrodynamic performance of otter-boards has become a major research interest. Some studies have shown that the slit in otter-boards can reduce the resistance and improve the stability of otter-boards [10-15]. The following study investigates the importance of the angle of the deflector within the otter-board. We describe an experiment using model otter-boards (n=3 designs) in a wind tunnel in which we measured various hydrodynamic coefficients for a range of angles of attack. The results are relevant as a reference for the study of the structural parameters of the main-panel of otter-boards.

2 Material and Methods

2.1 Design and manufacture of otter-board model

The otter-boards evaluated in this study are double-slit curved structures comprising two deflectors and one main-panel (figure 1). This simplified design is selected in order to meet objectives and requirements of the study. Only the angle of two deflectors are modified.

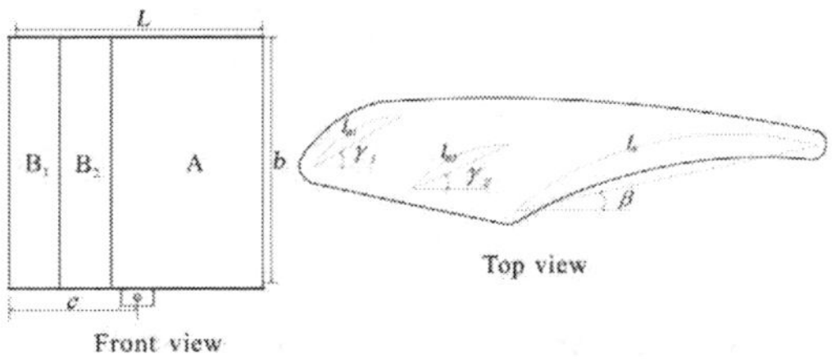

Figure 1 Structure and parameters of otter-board

Note: L: chord; b: span; e: distance between fulcrum and the front end of model; B_1, B_2: deflector; A: main-panel; γ_1, γ_2: angle of deflector; β: angle of main-panel; l_{B1}, l_{B2}: arc length of deflector; l_A: arc length of main-panel

Each of models has an aspect ratio of 1.0, surface area of 0.25 m^2, and are identical in many structural parameters and dimensions (table 1). The curvature of the deflector

[a] Corresponding author: zhangxun007@hotmail.com

and main panels is 12% and is consistent in all models. The only parameter that varied between the models is the angle of two deflectors (γ_1, γ_2). The models are made of steel with painted surfaces (figure 2).

Table 1 Descriptive characteristics of the three model otter boards evaluated in this study.

No.	L/m	b/m	λ	S/m^2	e/m	γ_1	γ_2	β	l_{B1}	l_{B2}	l_A
1	0.50	0.50	1.0	0.25	0.25	35°	30°	6°	0.127	0.120	0.313
2	0.50	0.50	1.0	0.25	0.25	30°	25°	6°	0.127	0.120	0.313
3	0.50	0.50	1.0	0.25	0.25	25°	20°	6°	0.127	0.120	0.313

Note: L: chord; b: span; λ: aspect ratio (b/L); S : surface area ($L{\cdot}b$); e: distance between fulcrum and the front end of model; γ_1, γ_2: angle of deflector; β: angle of main-panel; l_{B1}, l_{B2}: arc length of deflector; l_A: arc length of main-panel.

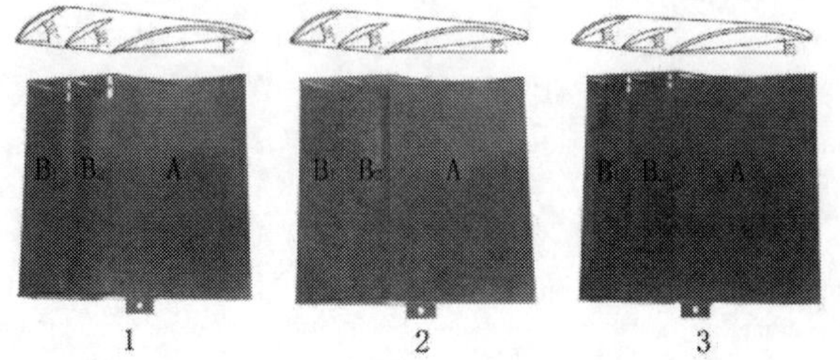

Figure 2 Three otter-board models evaluated in this study.

Note: A: main-panel; B_1, B_2: deflector.

2.2 Test facility

The wind tunnel used for this experiment is the NH-2 wind tunnel located at Nanjing University of Aeronautics and Astronautics, China. The tunnel is a closed reflux wind tunnel with a double-string test section. The experiment is conducted in a small test section. Dimensions of the test section are 6 m (length) × 3 m (width) × 2.5 m (height). The cross-sectional area is 7.18 m^2. The minimum and maximum wind speeds of the tunnel are 5 m/s and 90 m/s, respectively. Figure 3 illustrates the experimental setup inside the wind tunnel. The model otter-boards are attached to a dynamometer compromising a six-component mechanical tower-balance to measure forces in all directions. The data acquisition and processing system used is composed of a pre -amplifier and a four -networked computer system.

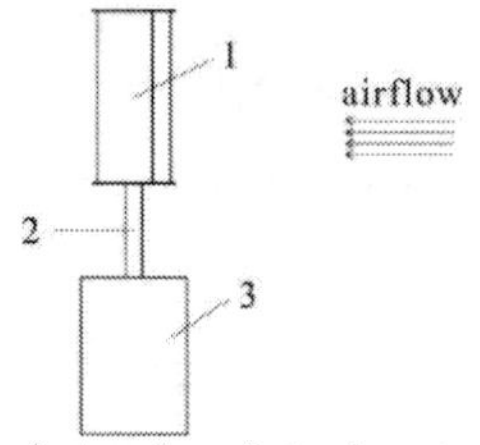

Figure 3 Installation instruction of otter-board model in wind tunnel

Note: 1. otter-board model 2 .model connection 3.six-component force balance

2.3 Test method

2.3.1 Parameter definition of test model

Test models need to be installed on the wind tunnel in six-component balance mechanical base according to the order, angle of attack of model rotates by the 0 ° -70 ° when the wind speed reaches 28m / s (room temperature 20 °C),wherein the angle of attack in the range 0 ° -50 °, 2.5 ° intervals to record a measurement data point, after the attack angle 50 °, each measurement interval of 5 ° to record data points, there are 25 sets of data totally, including the drag coefficient C_x, the lift coefficient C_y, the pitch moment coefficient C_m and the center of pressure coefficient C_p.

The relevant parameters of models in the wind tunnel test section are defined as shown in figure 4. In figure 4, O is torque reference point, which is the punch of the model at the bottom. During the test, the resistance of the model is provided by the force of balance along the X-axis direction, the lift is provided by the force of balance along the Z-axis direction, and the pitch moment is provided by the M_y of balance along the Z-axis direction.

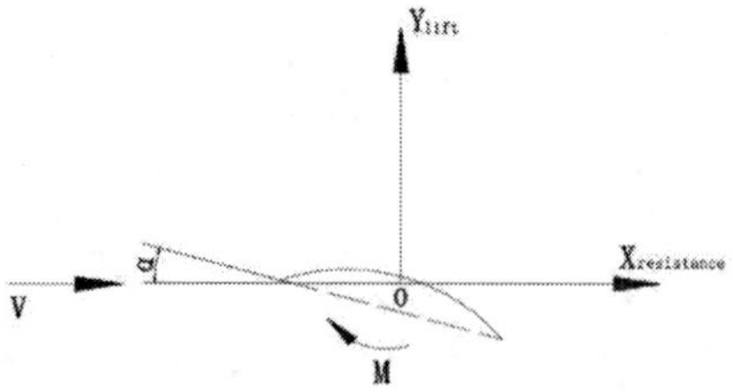

Figure 4 Parameter definition diagram of test model in wind tunnel

For this test, Wind speed V=28m/s, when the Reynolds number $R_e=VL/\upsilon=0.93\times10^6$ (coefficient of viscosity $\upsilon=15\times10^6$ m^2·s^{-1}) [10].

2.3.2 Parameter definition of test measurement

Three components: lift Y, drag X, pitching moment M (around the fulcrum), while the distance from the center of pressure to the front-end otter-board $d=e-(M/N)$ [12], (N is the normal force).

Lift coefficient $C_y = \frac{Y}{\rho V^2 S/2}$ [3]; drag coefficient $C_x = \frac{X}{\rho V^2 S/2}$; pitch moment coefficient $C_m = \frac{M}{\rho V^2 SL/2}$; center of pressure coefficient $C_p = \frac{d}{L}$.

Air density ρ=1.225 kg/m^3 in above formula; S is otter-board area (m^2); L is the otter-board chord length (m).

All the experimental data have been carried out the stent disturbance correction which is completed by the method of taking out light pole directly.

3 Results and Discussion

3.1 Drag coefficient and lift coefficient

Data from the experiment includes the drag coefficient C_x, the lift coefficient C_y, the pitch moment coefficient C_m, and the center of pressure coefficient C_p. The lift–drag ratio is computed (C_y / C_x), which is an important factor for determining the merits of the hydrodynamic performance of otter-boards. An otter-board with excellent hydrodynamic properties can achieve higher lift–drag ratio and improved stability; such performance can be analyzed by comparing the pitching moment coefficient C_m stencil and the center of pressure coefficient C_p . The test data are divided into groups, yielding C_x-α, C_y-α and C_y / C_x-α graphs shown in figure 5. These graphs are used for analyzing the differences in the hydrodynamic properties of the three otter-board models.

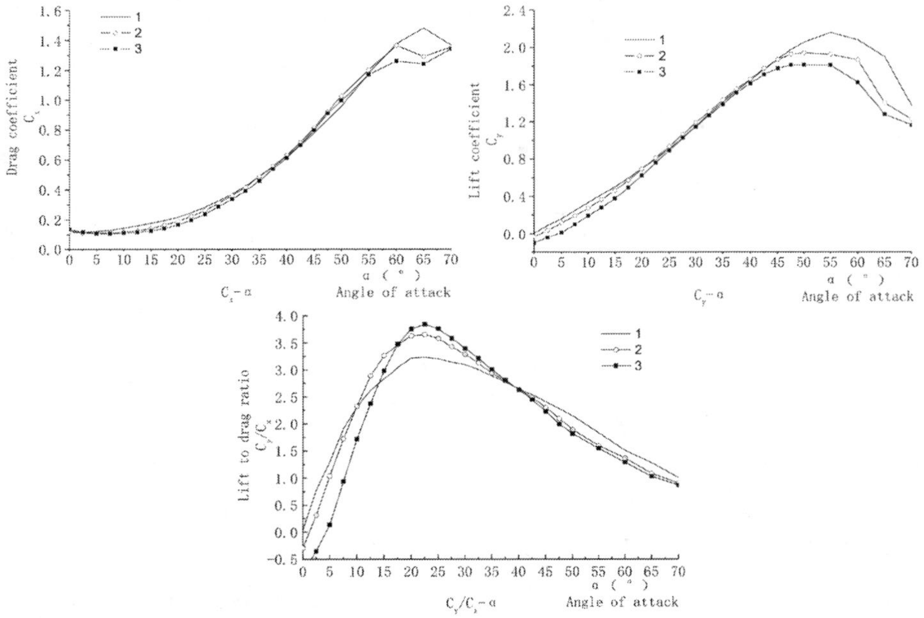

Figure 5 Hydrodynamic properties of three otter-board models across a range of angle of attack

In figure 5, C_x-α and C_y-α graphs show the variation curve of the drag and lift coefficient of the three models while the angle of attack α changes. The relationship between C_x and α is proportional totally. The maximum lift coefficients C_y of No. 1, No. 2, and No. 3 otter-board models are 2.160 (α = 55°), 1.942 (α = 50 °), and 1.812 (α = 50 °), respectively. It shows that the maximum lift coefficients becomes larger as the angle of two deflectors increasing.

3.2 Lift-drag ratio

In figure 5, the maximum lift–drag ratios of No.3 model with a small angle of two deflectors is 3.842 (α = 22.5 °), and the maximum lift–drag ratios of No. 1 and No. 2 models are 3.234 (α = 22.5 °) and 3.655 (α = 22.5°), respectively. The increasing of two deflectors' angle may result in a lower maximum lift–drag ratio.

3.3 Stability of otter-board

Pitching moment can be divided into upper and lower pitching moments, what are usually distinguished by positive and negative values, Positive means the otter-board tilts backward, and negative means tilts forward. Its absolute value represents the level of pitching moment; and the pitching moment coefficient tending to zero represents the more excellent stability of otter-board. In practice, comparing the absolute value C_m corresponding to the operation angle of attack of otter-board may determine the stability level of otter-board. For comparison, the angle of attack corresponding to the maximum lift–drag ratio C_y/C_x

is selected [16]. The corresponding absolute value of C_m is shown in table 2. The absolute value of C_m of No. 3 model is 0.144, so hence, the stability of No. 3 otter-board model is better in pitch.

Table 2 Parameters of three otter-board for stability analysis

No.	Angle corresponding to the maximum lift –drag ratio α	$\lvert C_m \rvert$	Variable coefficient of C_p
1	22.5°	0.287	10.12%
2	22.5°	0.180	5.49%
3	22.5°	0.144	8.13%

The stability in roll of otter-board can be measured according to the center of pressure coefficient C_p; and the way of comparison is analyzing the coefficient of variation in C_p within the range of angle approximately 5° of the angle of attack corresponding to the maximum lift–drag ratio; a smaller coefficient results in the improved stability [17]. The calculated data is shown in table 2. The minimum variation coefficient of C_p is 5.49%; this value also means that the stability of No. 2 otter-board model is better in roll of otter-board.

4 Conclusion

Test analysis shows that the angle combination of two deflectors has a point for equilibrating the hydrodynamic performances of otter-board, results from this experiment suggest that a better angle combination of two deflectors should be 30° and 25°, thereby yielding has a higher lift coefficient and higher lift–drag ratio on average, and the stability in roll and pitch of otter-board is also better comparatively. The data and conclusions of this study can provide a reference for the design of otter-board.

Acknowledgements

This work is financially supported by the National Key Technology R&D Program (No. 2013BAD13B05).

References

1. Guo G X, Liu TY, Huang X H, Gu F L. Theory and Practice of trawl doors Kinetic [M]. Guangdong Science and Technology Publications, 2008.
2. Zhou Y Q. Mechanics of fishing gear [M]. China Agriculture Publications, 2001.
3. Chen X Z, Huang X C. Theory and method of gear model test [M]. Shanghai Science and Technology Publications, 2011.
4. Sala A, Prat J, Antonijuan J, Lucchetti A. Performance and impact on the seabed of an existing- and an experimental-otter board: Comparison between model testing and full-scale sea trials [J]. Fisheries Research, 2009, 100(2): 156-166.
5. Takahashi Y, Fujimori Y, Hu F X, Shen X L, Kimura N. Design of trawl otter boards using computational fluid dynamics [J]. Fisheries Research, 2015, 161: 400-407.
6. Shen X L, Hu F X, Kumazawa T, Shiode D, Tokai T. Hydrodynamic characteristics of a hyper-lift otter board with wing-end plates [J]. Fisheries Science, 2015, 81(3): 433-442.
7. Broadhurst M K, Sterling D J, Millar R B. Modifying otter boards to reduce bottom contact: Effects on catches and efficiencies of triple-rigged penaeid trawls [J]. Fisheries Management and Ecology, 2015, 22(5): 407-418.
8. Fukuda K, Hu F X, Tokai T, Matuda K. Effect of Aspect Ratio on Lift and Drag Coefficients of Cambered Plates [J]. Nippon Suisan Gakkaishi, 2000, 66(1): 97-103.
9. Park C D, Matuda K, Hu F X. Effects of Dihedral and Sweepback Angles on Lift and Drag of the Cambered Otter Board [J]. Nippon Suisan Gakkaishi, 1996, 62(6): 920-927.
10. Zhang X, Wang J H, Wang M Y, Yu Y F, Xu, B. S. Hydrodynamic characteristics of rectangular cambered V type otter board-- Ⅰ: Relationship between cambered ratio of fairwater fin and hydrodynamic characteristics of otter board [J]. Journal of Fishery Sciences of China, 2004, 11(z1): 5-8.
11. Wang J H, Wang M Y, Zhang X, Yu Y F, Xu B S. Hydrodynamic characteristics of rectangular cambered V type otter board-- Ⅱ: Effects of aspect ratio, slotted position and slotted width on hydrodynamic characteristics of otter board [J]. Journal of Fishery Sciences of China, 2004, S1: 9-13.
12. Wang M Y, Wang J H, Zhang X, Yu Y F, Xu B S. Hydrodynamic characteristics of vertical V type otter board [J]. Journal of Fisheries of China, 2004, 3: 311-315.
13. Li C C, Liang Z L, Huang L Y, Zhou W F, Sun P, Wang L. Hydrodynamic study on a vee type otter board of small trawl vessels [J]. Marine Sciences, 2013, 11: 69-73.
14. Wang L, Wang L M, Feng C L, Zhang X, Shi J G, Zhang Y, Liu Y L, Yu W W. Influence of vane dimension on hydrodynamic performances of single slotted cambered otter board [J]. Fishery Modernization, 2015, 6: 55-60.
15. Wang L, Wang L M, Yu W W, Feng C L, Shi J G, Liu Y L, Zhang X. Influence of deflector angular variation on hydrodynamic performances of single slotted cambered otter board [C]. Conference: International Forum on Energy, Environment and Sustainable Development, 2016, 75: 530-535.
16. Yang L. Hydrodynamic characteristics of slotted circular plate [J]. Fisheries Science and Technology, 1996, 2: 38-41.
17. Yang L. Hydrodynamic characteristics of double - plate circular plate [J]. Fisheries Science and Technology, 1996, 5: 42-44.

Investigation on Mechanical Properties' Anisotropy of Rod Units in Lattice Structures Fabricated by Selective Laser Melting

Chenchen Jing[1], Yong Zhou[1], Jiping Lu[1,a], Hongli Fan[1], Lei Ji and Penglin Li[1]

[1]*School of Mechanical Engineering, Beijing Institute of Technology, 100081 Beijing, China*

Abstract. Lattice structure with high strength and low mass using selective laser melting (SLM) has been a hot topic. However, there are some problems in the fabrication of lattice structure by SLM. Rod unit is the basic component of lattice structure and its performance affects the whole structure. It is necessary to investigate the influence of selective laser melting on rod unit's mechanical properties. A series of rod units with different inclination angle and diameter were fabricated by SLM in this research. And the mechanical properties of these units were measured by tensile test. The results show that the rod units with different diameters and inclination angles have good mechanical properties and show no difference. It is a good news for lattice structure designing for there is no necessary to consider the mechanical properties' anisotropy of rod units.

1 Introduction

In the aerospace, military, automotive, medical and other fields, the significance of the lightweight of components has become more and more important, which can help reduce the amount of spending [1,2]. Lattice structure has become a hot spot to study, as it not only provides good mechanical properties, but also greatly reduces the weight of parts [3–6]. However, complex shape of lattice structure makes the traditional way of processing very difficult. At present, proven methods of three-dimensional lattice structures' manufacturing include Investment casting [7], Deformation forming [8], Woven metal textiles [9], Non-woven metal textiles [9] and so on [10,11]. These methods are complex, costly and low in material utilization [12]. However, additive manufacturing technology can shed light on solving this problem [11].

Additive manufacturing refers to a technique that fabricates part layer by layer which can manufacture parts with any complex geometries theoretically [13]. Selective laser melting (SLM) is one of the additive manufacturing technique [14]. The SLM process begins with splitting a component into layers, and fuses the powder selectively by a laser power to make this fully melted powder combined with former layer. Finally it can get a fully dense part [15–18]. This method makes it possible to fabricate very complex lattice structures [19]. Chunze Yan et al. [3,20] have fabricated an advanced lightweight 316L stainless steel cellular lattice structures and a king of gyroid cellular lattice structures via SLM. Sajad Arabnejad et al. [21] have fabricated high-strength porous biomaterials using SLM.

However, there are some problems in the fabrication of lattice structure. The lattice structure can be seen as a series of rod elements. The SLM process can compromise the quality of these rod units. Layer-by-layer build-up makes the parts have the characteristic of anisotropy, which makes the mechanical properties of the parts inconsistent in all directions [22–24]. In addition, the SLM process also makes the portion which is close to the horizontal poor quality and rougher [25]. The influence of the angle between the rod and the build direction on the lattice structure is caused by the principle of SLM method, which arouses great research significance.

To investigate the influence of inclination angle and diameter on mechanical properties of rod unit, a group of Ti-6Al-4V rod unit structure samples were designed and manufactured by SLM with necessary support. The mechanical properties were analysed by tensile test. The results show that the rod units with different diameters and inclination angles have good mechanical properties and show no difference. It is a good news for lattice structure designing for there is no necessary to consider the mechanical properties' anisotropy of rod units.

2 Methods and Material

2.1 Sample designing

In this research, a group of rod unit structures were designed. The structure consists of two plates and a rod, and the rod is sandwiched between the two plates. Fig. 1 is an illustration of the samples with a rod length of 14mm, a plate length of 10mm, a width of 8mm, and the thickness of the plate equal to the strut diameter. The

[a] Corresponding author: jipinglu@bit.edu.cn

inclination of the rod is shown in Figure 1, and it is 4 mm from the substrate in the horizontal direction. It is used for tensile test in order to investigate the mechanical properties of the rod unit. In this group, 35 sets of tensile specimens with different combination of inclination angle θ (0-90 degree, in increments of 15 degree,) and strut diameter D (0.50-2.00mm, in 0.25mm increments) were set. After the tensile specimens were manufactured completely, they were cut by electrical discharge machining. The design parameters of all the samples are shown in Table 1.

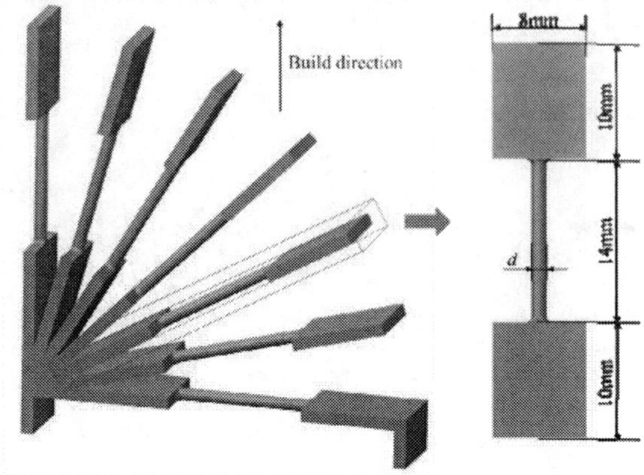

Figure 1. Detail of the sample structure

Table 1. Sample's design parameter.

Inclination angle (θ/degree)	Design diameter (*D*/mm)				
0	1.00	1.25	1.50	1.75	2.00
15	1.00	1.25	1.50	1.75	2.00
30	1.00	1.25	1.50	1.75	2.00
45	1.00	1.25	1.50	1.75	2.00
60	1.00	1.25	1.50	1.75	2.00
75	1.00	1.25	1.50	1.75	2.00
90	1.00	1.25	1.50	1.75	2.00

2.2 Sample manufacturing and tensile tests

The specimens were fabricated by EOSINT M 280 (EOS GmbH, Germany) (Figure 2) using Ti6Al4V. Titanium (Ti) alloys have high specific strength, strong resistance to creep and great corrosion resistance [26]. Due to the good mechanical characters, Ti and its alloys are becoming more important in material field, and widely used in aerospace field, military field, biomaterial field, etc. [23,27,28]. The process parameters are in optimal setup. The samples exerted the necessary support at a smaller inclination when fabricating.

The samples were cut into individual tensile specimens by electrical discharge machining after fabricated. Tensile tests were carried on INSTRON5966. Three samples were used in every group. The tensile tests were conducted with reference to ASTME-E8/E8M-15a [29].

Figure 2. The picture of EOSINT M 280

3 Results & Discussion

The fabricated samples were shown in Figure 3. In order to ensure consistent cross-sectional area of the samples, necessary support was added when printing. As can be seen from Figure 3, the rod unit diameter is uniform, and there is no significant difference. Each sample was cut into individual tensile specimens by electrical discharge machining for tensile testing. Figure 4 shows the stress-strain curves of the rod elements at each angle (0-90 degrees, in 15 degrees increments) when the design diameter of the rod is 1.50mm. It can be seen that the inclination angle of the rod elements has little influence on the mechanical properties, and so do the other rod units of the diameter. Figure 5 shows the stress-strain curves of the rod elements with different diameters (1.00-2.00mm, in 0.25mm increments) and same inclination angle (15 degree). It can be seen that the diameter of the rod element does not have a great effect on its mechanical properties and the same is true for other inclination angles.

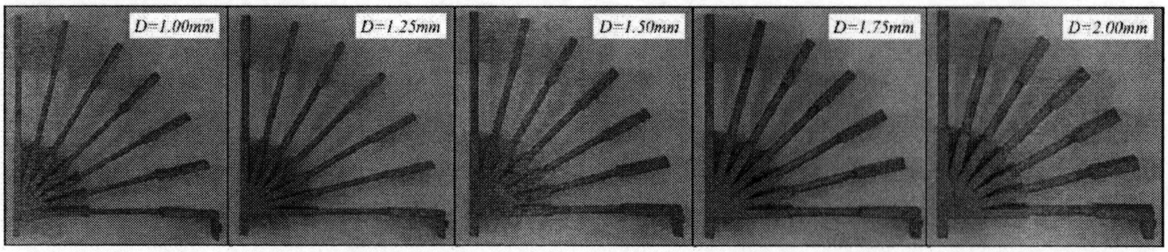

Figure 3. Ti-6Al-4V samples manufactured by SLM for rod diameter of 1.00-2.00mm in increments of 0.25mm

The yield strength (YS) and tensile strength (TS) of each rod units were summarized (Table 2) and were shown in Figure 6, where the solid line represents the tensile strength (TS) and the dash line indicates the yield strength (YS). The tensile strength and yield strength of all rod units is about 1100MPa and 1000Mpa respectively with no significant difference with the inclination angle and diameter change. It can be concluded that the inclination and diameter have no significant impacts on the mechanical properties of the rod element.

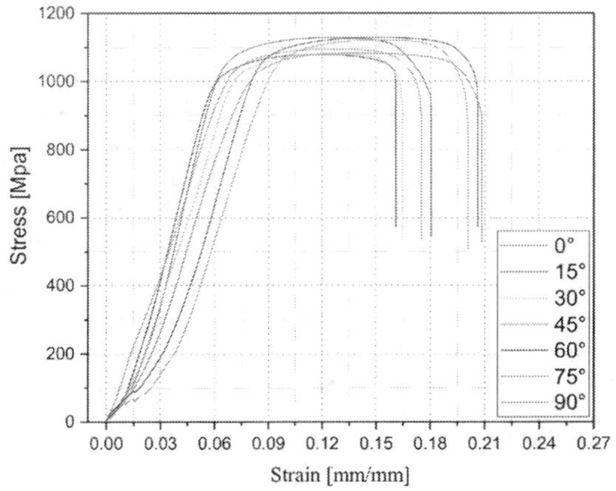

Figure 4. Stress-strain response of the Ti-6Al-4V rod units manufactured by SLM with diameter of 1.50mm

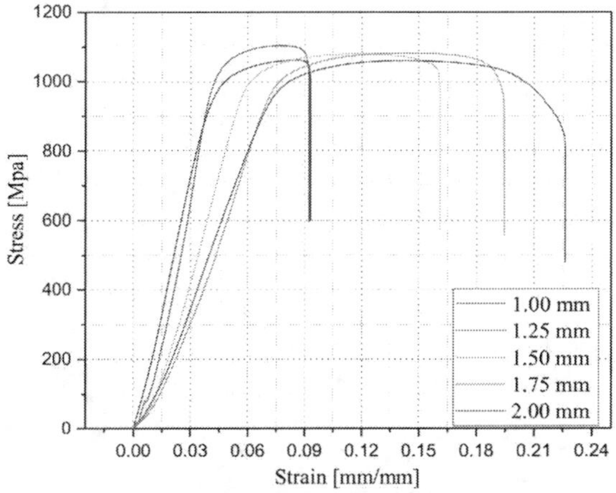

Figure 5. Stress-strain response of the Ti-6Al-4V rod units manufactured by SLM with inclination angle of 15 degree

The mechanical property of Ti-6Al-4V is directly determined by their microstructure [30-32]. There are three important factors affect the mechanical property including the size of β grains, the β grain orientation and the lamellar α microstructure. In the sample manufactured by SLM, the anisotropy of mechanical properties primarily depends on the deference of the β grain orientation [31]. For the small rod unit of lattice structure, the molten pool is very tiny, and the cooling rate is high. It leads to a small size of the β grains and the lamellar α microstructure. Thus the rod unit's tensile strength is up to 1100Mpa and yield strength is about 1000Mpa. And the effect of grain orientation is relatively weakened. Therefore, there is no obvious anisotropy of mechanical properties in rod units. The results of the experiment are meaningful to the designer, for they can ignore the anisotropy of mechanical properties when designing lattice structure.

Table 2. The tensile strength (TS/Mpa) and yield strength (YS/Mpa) of the sample

Inclination angle/degree		Diameter/mm				
		1.00	**1.25**	**1.5**	**1.75**	**2**
0	TS	1225	1109	1127	1105	1184
	YS	1113	1004	1008	1016	950
15	TS	1104	1062	1080	1078	1061
	YS	1011	911	980	986	919
30	TS	1122	1087	1079	1105	1101
	YS	1043	1034	1011	978	1012
45	TS	1076	1119	1102	1083	1073
	YS	1006	1020	998	997	987
60	TS	1094	1074	1127	1114	1062
	YS	1008	925	1037	1020	951
75	TS	1146	1043	1122	1107	1094
	YS	1063	934	1001	1007	987
90	TS	1147	1108	1076	1100	1072
	YS	1039	995	923	992	985

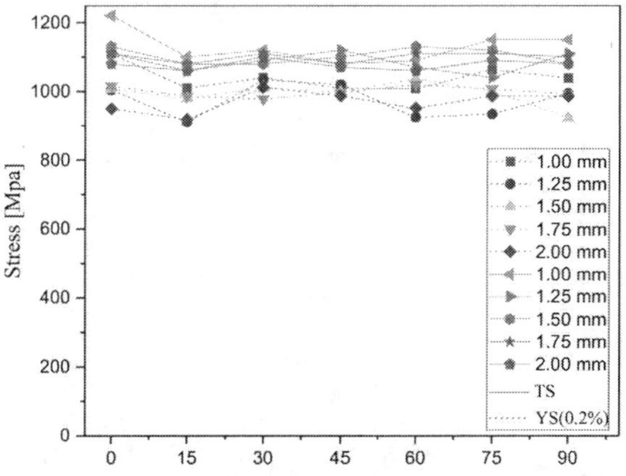

Figure 3. Influence of Inclination on Tensile Strength (TS) (Solid line) and Yield Strength (YS) (Dash line) of the rod units manufactured by SLM

4 Conclusion

To investigate the influence of selective laser melting on rod unit's mechanical properties, a group of samples with different inclination angle and diameter were manufactured. The tensile tests were carried to estimate the tensile strength (TS) and yield strength (YS). It can be concluded that the rod units fabricated by SLM exhibits good mechanical properties and the tensile strength is up to 1100Mpa and yield strength is about 1000Mpa. And there is no obviously difference with the inclination angle

DOI: 10.1051/matecconf/201712805005

and diameter change. It is a good news for designer for they can ignore the mechanical properties' anisotropy of rod units when they design the lattice structure.

References

1. C. Beyer, D. Figueroa, J. Manuf. Sci. Eng. 138 (2016) 121014.
2. H. Alsalla, L. Hao, C. Smith, Materials Science & Engineering A. 669 (2016) 1–6.
3. C. Yan, L. Hao, A. Hussein, P. Young, D. Raymont, Mater. Des. 55 (2014) 533–541.
4. H. Nakajima, Fabrication, Prog. Mater. Sci. 52 (2007) 1091–1173.
5. A.G. Evans, J.W. Hutchinson, N.A. Fleck, M.F. Ashby, H.N.G. Wadley, Prog. Mater. Sci. 46 (2001) 309–327.
6. S.K. Moon, Y.E. Tan, J. Hwang, Y.J. Yoon, Int. J. Precis. Eng. Manuf. - Green Technol. 1 (2014) 223–228.
7. Wang J, Evans A G, Dharmasena K, et al. International Journal of Solids & Structures, 2003, 40(25):6981-6988.
8. G.W. Kooistra, H.N.G. Wadley, Materials & Design , 28 (2007) 507–514.
9. D.T. Queheillalt, H.N.G. Wadley, 53 (2005) 303–313.
10. H.N.G. Wadley, N.A. Fleck, A.G. Evans, 63 (2003) 2331–2343.
11. P. Li, Z. Wang, N. Petrinic, C.R. Siviour, Materials Science & Engineering A, 614 (2014) 116–121.
12. M.G. Rashed, M. Ashraf, R.A.W. Mines, P.J. Hazell, Mater. Des. 95 (2016) 518–533.
13. S.L. Sing, J. An, W.Y. Yeong, F.E. Wiria, J. Orthop. Res. 34 (2016) 369–385.
14. X. Shi, S. Ma, C. Liu, Q. Wu, Opt. Laser Technol. 90 (2017) 71–79.
15. S.L. Sing, W.Y. Yeong, F.E. Wiria, J. Alloys Compd. 660 (2016) 461–470.
16. L.E.E. Loh, Z.H.H. Liu, D.Q.Q. Zhang, M. Mapar, S.L.L. Sing, C.K.K. Chua, W.Y.Y. Yeong, Virtual Phys. Prototyp. 9 (2014) 11–16.
17. G. Casalino, S.L. Campanelli, N. Contuzzi, A.D. Ludovico, Opt. Laser Technol. 65 (2015) 151–158.
18. E. Yasa, J. Deckers, J.-P. Kruth, M. Rombouts, J. Luyten, Virtual Phys. Prototyp. 5 (2010) 89–98.
19. M. Cloots, K. Kunze, P.J. Uggowitzer, K. Wegener, Mater. Sci. Eng. A. 658 (2016) 68–76.
20. C. Yan, L. Hao, A. Hussein, D. Raymont, Int. J. Mach. Tools Manuf. 62 (2012) 32–38.
21. S. Arabnejad, R. Burnett Johnston, J.A. Pura, B. Singh, M. Tanzer, D. Pasini, Acta Biomater. 30 (2016) 345–356.
22. L. Thijs, F. Verhaeghe, T. Craeghs, J. Van Humbeeck, J.P. Kruth, Acta Mater. 58 (2010) 3303–3312.
23. L.Y. Chen, J.C. Huang, C.H. Lin, C.T. Pan, S.Y. Chen, T.L. Yang, D.Y. Lin, H.K. Lin, J.S.C. Jang, Mater. Sci. Eng. A. 682 (2017) 389–395.
24. L. Facchini, E. Magalini, P. Robotti, A. Molinari, S. Höges, K. Wissenbach, Rapid Prototyp. J. 16 (2010) 450–459.
25. M. Mazur, M. Leary, M. McMillan, S. Sun, D. Shidid, M. Brandt, Elsevier Ltd, 2017.
26. Boyer R R. Materials Science & Engineering A, 1996, 213(1–2):103-114.
27. S. Zhang, Q. Wei, L. Cheng, S. Li, Y. Shi, Mater. Des. 63 (2014) 185–193.
28. C.N. Elias, M.A. Meyers, R.Z. Valiev, S.N. Monteiro J. Mater. Res. Technol. 2 (2013) 340–350.
29. ASTM Int., Standard Test Methods for Tension Testing of Metallic Materials 1, Astm. (2015) 1–27.
30. W. Jia, L. Ma, Y. Tang, Q. Le, L. Fu, Mater. Des. 103 (2016) 171–182.
31. X. Shi, S. Ma, C. Liu, Q. Wu, J. Lu, Y. Liu, W. Shi, Mater. Sci. Eng. A. 684 (2017) 196–204.
32. Y.Z. Zhu, S.Z. Wang, B.L. Li, Z.M. Yin, Q. Wan, P. Liu, Mater. Des. 55 (2014) 456–462.

The baffle influence on sound radiation characteristics of a plate

Liu Bao[1,a], Sun Yuchen[2] and Wang Deshi[1]

[1]*Naval University of Engineering, 430033 Wuhan, China*

Abstract. The acoustic radiation characteristics of the baffle plates and unbaffle plates are calculated and compared by single-layer potential and double-layer potential. Based on the boundary integral equation, the sound pressure integral equation of the baffle and the baffle are deduced respectively. According to the boundary compatibility condition, the sound pressure and the vibration velocity of the plates are obtained. Further, the dynamic equation of the structure is substituted into the vibration equation in the form of the baffle plate and the baffle plate. The sound pressure difference and the displacement of a plate surface are in the form of the vibration mode superposition and the acoustic radiation impedance of the double integral form is obtained, which determines vibration mode coefficient and sound radiation parameters. The effect of the baffle on the acoustic radiation characteristics of the thin plate is analyzed by comparing the acoustic radiation parameters with the simple and simple rectangular plate in water.

1 Introduction

Many of the structures used in engineering can be treated as a finite plate approximately, and the acoustic radiation characteristics such as sound efficiency and sound power are widely concerned by engineers. When analyzing the acoustic radiation characteristics of a thin plate, a simple rectangular plate is usually used as the solution model. Not only because of the simple vibration pattern of simple-supported rectangular thin plate, it is convenient to use analytic solution to express its surface vibration velocity and sound radiation characteristic parameters, and its analytical solution can be compared with numerical calculation method such as finite element method to reveal the structural sound radiation general rule.

In the early study, the acoustic radiation characteristics of the simply supported rectangular thin plate are usually placed on an infinite baffle. Only the single-layer potential is needed to be calculated, and the integral term exhibits weak singularity, which can simplify the computational complexity. In the 1960s, Maidanik[1] first proposed the approximate equation of the acoustic radiation resistance of a simple rectangular plate, which provided a theoretical basis for later researchers. Wallace[2] then used the integral of the far field sound intensity to deduce a series of approximate integral equations of acoustic radiation resistance, and successfully solved the modal sound radiation power of the structure with an critical frequency. Heckl[3] uses Fourier transform to study the acoustic radiation problem of the plate in the wavenumber segment. Leppington[4] obtained several approximate equations to solve the vibration mode efficiency of the large wavenumber domain, but the above scholars neglected the influence of crossmodal on the sound power. To this end, using the modal radiation efficiency and taking into account the coupling between the modals, Snyder and Tanaka[5] calculated the low-frequency structural sound power. Li and Gibeling[6-7] used the integral transformation method to transform the acoustic radiation resistance from the quadratic integral form into the form of double integral and successfully transformed into a form of single integral, and obtained the self-radiation resistance, mutual-radiation resistance. For the acoustic radiation problem of underwater plate, because the need to consider the role of fluid on the structure, it can be attributed to the sound and vibration coupling problem. Crighton[8-9] analyzes the acoustic radiation of infinite plate in water under point excitation. Leibowitz[10] proposed a method for calculating the acoustic properties of finite plates in water. M.L.Rumerman[11] studied the effect of water load presence on the sound radiation efficiency. B.E. Sandman[12] further validated the correctness of the theory of plate vibration and acoustic radiation under fluid loading by experiments.

However, in the actual project, the infinite baffle is not present, so there is the need to study the sound properties of unbaffled plates. Williams[13] used the fast Fourier transform (FFT) to give the sound pressure of the simply supported thin plate in the air by the iterative operation. However, the convergence of the acoustic radiation impedance in high-order modes is poor. Atalla[14] calculated the sound characteristics of an unbaffled plate in air under any boundary conditions using Kirchhoff-Helmholtz integral equation, but ignores the impact of pressure fluctuations on both sides of the plate resulting in large error in high frequency.

[a] Corresponding author: lbao_miao@163.com

Oppenheimer and Dubrowsky[15] used experiments to modify the acoustic radiation parameters of baffled plates to match unbaffled plates and gave empirical formulas for the acoustic radiation of an unbaffled plate.

In this paper, the acoustic radiation characteristics of the baffled and unbaffled plates are analyzed. The sound pressure integral equations of the baffled and unbaffled plates are deduced by the boundary integral equation, and sound pressure and velocity in double integral form are obtained according to boundary compatibility condition. Further, the structural dynamic equation is substituted into the sound pressure equation of the baffled and unbaffled plates. Through expanding sound pressure difference and the displacement of plates in the form of the vibration mode superposition, the acoustic radiation impedance in the double integral form is obtained to solve the vibration modal coefficient, and determine the sound radiation characteristics. The effect of the baffle on the acoustic radiation characteristics to a plate is analyzed by comparing the acoustic radiation parameters with the simply rectangular plate in water.

2 Plate dynamics equations and fundamentals of acoustics

The acoustic radiation characteristics of simply supported rectangular thin plates are studied in this paper. The density of the plate is ρ_S , its dimensions are $a \times b$. There is an excitation force $F(x, y)$ of angular frequency ω which is perpendicular to the plate shown in figure 1. From the classical dynamics, the transverse vibration equation of the thin plate is shown as

$$B\nabla^4 w(x,y) - \bar{m}\omega^2 w(x,y) = F(x,y) + \Delta p(x,y) \quad (1)$$

where $B = Eh^3/12(1-\nu^2)$ is the bending stiffness of the plate, E is Yong's modulus, h is the plate thickness and ν is Poisson's ratio. $\bar{m} = \rho_S h$ indicates the mass in an unit area.

The displacement of a simple rectangular plate can be expressed as a superposition of the following vibration modes:

$$w(x,y) = \sum_{m=1}^{\infty}\sum_{n=1}^{\infty} A_{mn}\phi_{mn}(x,y) \quad (2)$$

where A_{mn} is the modal velocity amplitude and $\phi_{mn}(x,y)$ is the modal shape function which can be expressed as $\phi_{mn}(x,y) = \sin(m\pi x/a)\sin(n\pi y/b)$ for simply supported plate. Set $L_m = m\pi / a$ and $L_n = n\pi / b$, then $\varphi_{mn}(x, y) = \sin(L_m x)\sin(L_n y)$ .External forces can also be expressed as follows similarly:

$$F(x,y) = \sum_{m=1}^{\infty}\sum_{n=1}^{\infty} F_{mn}\phi_{mn}(x,y) \quad (3)$$

where F_{mn} is the modal force amplitude and $\Delta p(x,y)$ is the difference between the sound pressure on the upper and lower surfaces of the plate shown as

$$\Delta p(x,y) = p^-(x,y) - p^+(x,y) \quad (4)$$

where $p^-(x,y)$ is the sound pressure acting on the lower surface of the plate, $p^+(x,y)$ is the sound pressure acting on the higher surface of the plate.

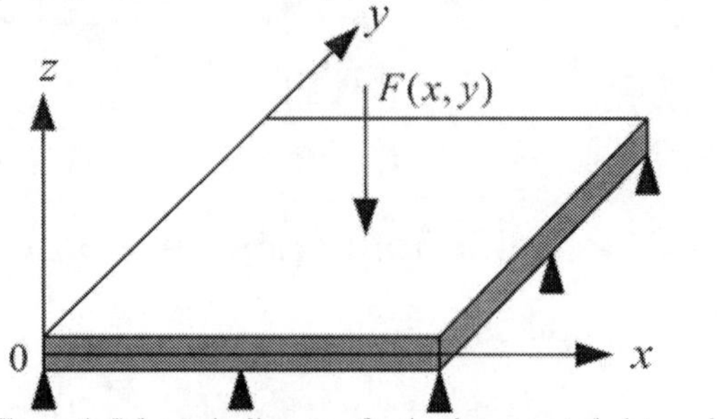

Figure 1. Schematic diagram of a simply supported plate and associated coordinate system

The sound pressure of the plate in the medium satisfies the classical Helmholtz integral equation, expressed as

$$\nabla^2 p(x, y) + k^2 p(x, y) = 0 \quad (5)$$

where $p(x, y)$ is the sound pressure at any point in the medium , k is the wave number, c is the velocity of sound. Based on Euler equation, the compatibility condition is:

$$\frac{\partial p(x, y)}{\partial z}\Big|_{z=\pm\frac{h}{2}} = \rho_f \omega^2 w(x, y) \quad (6)$$

where ρ_f is the density of the medium

Using the Kirchhoff-Helmholtz integral formula to an infinite space of a bounding plate structure, the sound pressure at any point in the space can be expressed as

$$C(M_0)p(M_0) = -\int_S j\omega\rho_f v(M)G(M, M_0)dS + \int_S p(M)\frac{\partial G}{\partial n_M}(M, M_0)dS \quad (7)$$

where $C(M_0)$ is the sound pressure coefficient. When M_0 located outside the structure, $C(M_0)$ is taken as 1, when M_0 located on the smooth structure, $C(M_0)$ is taken as $1/2$ .The first and second terms on the right side of the equation are called single-layer potential and double-layer potential respectively. n_M denotes the outer normal direction of the structural surface, and $G(M, M_0)$ is Green function in free space, satisfying the following equation:

$$\nabla^2 G(M, M_0) + k^2 G(M, M_0) = \delta(x - x_0)\delta(y - y_0)\delta(z - z_0) \quad (8)$$

where δ is Delta function, $G(M, M_0)$ is Green function in free space shown as

$$G(M, M_0) = \frac{e^{-ikr}}{4\pi r} \quad (9)$$

where $r = \sqrt{(x'-x)^2 + (y'-y)^2 + z'^2}$ means the distance between (x', y', z') in space and (x, y, z) on the plate. Using two-dimensional Fourier integral transformation to

DOI: 10.1051/matecconf/201712805006

the above formula, the Green's function can be expressed as:

$$G(M, M_0) = \frac{j}{8\pi^2} \cdot \int_{-\infty}^{+\infty}\int_{-\infty}^{+\infty} \frac{e^{jk_x(x-x_0)}e^{jk_y(y-y_0)}e^{jk_z|z-z_0|}}{k_z}\mathrm{d}k_x\mathrm{d}k_y \tag{10}$$

where k_x 、 k_y is the Fourier variations in the two-dimensional wavenumber space, $k_z=\sqrt{k^2-k_x^2-k_y^2}$, k_z adopts the following form:

$$\begin{cases} k_z = \sqrt{k^2 - k_x^2 - k_y^2}, & k^2 \geq k_x^2 + k_y^2 \\ k_z = j\sqrt{k_x^2 + k_y^2 - k^2}, & k^2 \leq k_x^2 + k_y^2 \end{cases} \tag{11}$$

The normal direction of the upper and lower surfaces of the thin plate is opposite, and for this purpose the uniform direction of Green function is defined as positive direction of z axial. The coordinates are shown in figure 2.

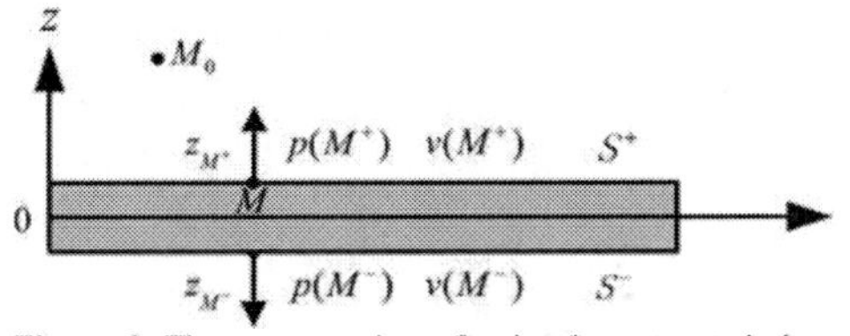

Figure 2. The cross section of a simply supported plate

3 The calculation of a baffled plate

For a baffled plate, since in Eq. (7) $\partial G/\partial n_M = 0$, the sound pressure generated at a point **r** above the plate is equal to the integral of the points on the plate.

$$p(M_0) = \frac{i\omega\rho_f}{2\pi}\int_0^a\int_0^b v(M)\frac{e^{-ikr'}}{r'}\mathrm{d}S \tag{12}$$

Substituting the above formula into Eq. (1), one obtains

$$B\nabla^4 w(x, y) - \overline{m}\omega^2 w(x, y) = F(x, y) - \frac{\omega^2\rho_f}{2\pi}\int_0^a\int_0^b w(M)\frac{e^{-ikr'}}{r'}\mathrm{d}S \tag{13}$$

Seen from Eq. (2), the deflection of the rectangular plate can be expressed as a linear superposition of the vibration mode, so Eq. (13) can be transformed into

$$\sum_{m=1}^{\infty}\sum_{n=1}^{\infty} A_{mn}[B(L_m^4 + 2L_m^2L_n^2 + L_n^4) - \omega^2\overline{m}]\varphi_{mn}(x, y) = F - \frac{\omega^2\rho_f}{2\pi}\sum_{m=1}^{\infty}\sum_{n=1}^{\infty} A_{mn}\int_0^a\int_0^b \varphi_{mn}(x', y')\frac{e^{-ikr'}}{r'}\mathrm{d}x'dy' \tag{14}$$

Take Fourier inverse transformation to the above equation

$$abA_{pq}(BL_{pq}^4 - \omega^2\overline{m}) + 4i\omega\rho_f c\sum_{m=1}^{\infty}\sum_{n=1}^{\infty} Z_{pqmn} = 4\int_0^a\int_0^b F\varphi_{pq}(x, y)\mathrm{d}xdy \tag{15}$$

where $L_{mn}^2 = L_m^2 + L_n^2$.

$$Z_{pqmn} = \frac{k}{2\pi}\int_0^a\int_0^b\int_0^a\int_0^b \varphi_{mn}(x', y')\varphi_{pq}(x, y)\frac{e^{-ikr'}}{r'}dx'dy'dxdy$$

is defined as the radiation impedance of (pq, mn).

Through coordinate transformation, Suppose $u = \frac{x - x'}{a}$, $u = \frac{x'}{a}$, $v = \frac{y - y'}{b}$, $v' = \frac{y'}{b}$, Z_{pqmn} can be transformed into a double integral form

$$Z_{pqmn} = \begin{cases} \frac{ik}{2\pi}\int_0^1\int_0^1 J_{pm}(u)M_{qn}(v)\Omega(u, v)\,\mathrm{dudv} & m + p = 2, 4, 6, \cdots \quad n + q = 2, 4, 6, \cdots \\ 0 & m + p = 1, 3, 5, \cdots or \quad n + q = 1, 3, 5, \cdots \end{cases} \tag{16}$$

where $M_{qn}(v) = \int_0^{1-u} \sin p\pi(u + u')\sin m\pi u'du'$,

$J_{qn}(v) = \int_0^{1-u} \sin q\pi(v + v')\sin n\pi v'dv'$,

$\Omega(u, v) = \frac{e^{[-\mathrm{i}ka(u^2+b^2v^2/a^2)^{1/2}]}}{(u^2 + b^2v^2/a^2)^{1/2}}$.

The transformed acoustic radiation impedance is substituted into Eq.(15), a matrix form can be expressed as

$$(K + i\omega R - \omega^2 M)A = F \tag{17}$$

where K is stiffness matrix, $K_{pqmn} = BL_{pq}^4\delta_{pm}\delta_{qn}$, R is impedance matrix, $R_{pqmn} = 4i\omega\rho_f cZ_{pqmn}$, M is mass matrix, $M_{pqmn} = ab\overline{m}\delta_{pm}\delta_{qn}$, F is external force array, $F = 4\int_0^a\int_0^b F\varphi_{pq}(x, y)\mathrm{d}xdy$ .Since the mass matrix and stiffness matrix are known, and the acoustic radiation matrix can be obtained by the double integral operation, the matrix of the vibration mode coefficients can be obtained by the inverse operation of the matrix which can calculate the surface vibration velocity and sound radiation power.

4 The calculation of an unbaffled plate

In order to calculate the sound pressure at M_0 , the position of point M_0 needs to be determined. The Green function in Eq. (10) can be expressed as:

$$\begin{cases} e^{-jk_z(z-z_0)}, & z_0 \geq 0 \\ e^{jk_z(z-z_0)}, & z_0 \leq 0 \end{cases} \tag{18}$$

For any point M_0 in space, Eq. (7) can be discretized as:

$$C(M_0)p(M_0) = \int_{S^+} -\frac{\partial G}{\partial z_{M^+}}(M^+, M_0)p(M^+)\mathrm{d}S^+ + \int_{S^-}\frac{\partial G}{\partial z_{M^-}}(M^-, M_0)p(M^-)\mathrm{d}S^- + j\omega\rho_f\int_{S^+} v(M^+) G(M^+, M_0)\mathrm{d}S^+ - j\omega\rho_f\int_{S^-} v(M^-)G(M^-, M_0)\mathrm{d}S^- \tag{19}$$

In the formula, $p(M^+)$ 、 $v(M^+)$ represents the sound

pressure and the velocity of point M^+ in the upper surface, and $p(M^-)$ 、 $v(M^-)$ represents the sound pressure and the velocity of point M^- in the lower surface. When the plate is quite thin, the single-layer potential disappears

$$\int_{S^+} v(M^+)G(M^+, M_0)dS^+ - \int_{S^-} v(M^-)G(M^-, M_0)dS^- = 0 \quad (20)$$

$\frac{\partial G}{\partial z_{M^+}}(M^+, M_0)$ and $\frac{\partial G}{\partial z_{M^-}}(M^-, M_0)$ can be expressed as the same approximately in thin plate, then Eq.(19) can reduced to

$$\frac{1}{2}p(M_0) = \int_S \frac{\partial G}{\partial z_M}(M, M_0)\Delta p(M)dS \quad (21)$$

Substituting Eq.(1) into the above formula, the sound pressure expression of M_0 is

$$C(M_0)p(M_0) = \int_S \frac{\partial G(M, M_0)}{\partial z_M} \cdot [B\nabla^4 w(x, y) - \bar{m}\omega^2 w(x, y) - F(x, y)]dS \quad (22)$$

By the Euler formula, deriving on both sides of the above equation, one obtains

$$\rho_f \omega^2 C(M_0)w(x, y) = \int_S \frac{\partial^2 G(M, M_0)}{\partial z_M \partial z_{M_0}} \cdot [B\nabla^4 w(x, y) - \bar{m}\omega^2 w(x, y) - F(x, y)]dS \quad (23)$$

The equation for the plate surface displacement is established. Expand vibration modes on the items of displacement $w(x, y)$ and external force F

$$\rho_f \omega^2 \sum_{m=1}^{\infty}\sum_{n=1}^{\infty} A_{mn}\varphi_{mn}(x, y) = \int_S \{\sum_{m=1}^{\infty}\sum_{n=1}^{\infty}[B(L_m^4 + 2L_m^2 L_n^2 + L_n^4) -\omega^2\bar{m}\omega^2]A_{mn} - F_{mn}\}\varphi_{mn}(x, y)\frac{\partial^2 G(M, M_0)}{\partial z_M \partial z_{M_0}}dxdy \quad (24)$$

For the point force acting on (x_0, y_0), F_{mn} can be expressed as

$$F_{mn} = \frac{4F_0}{S}\phi_{mn}(x_c, y_c) \quad (25)$$

where F_0 is the magnitude of the force. Using the orthogonality of the vibration modes, Eq.(24) can be reduced to:

$$\rho_f \omega^2 \frac{S}{4} A_{pq} = \sum_{m=1}^{\infty}\sum_{n=1}^{\infty}[\bar{m}(\omega_{mn}^2 - \omega^2)A_{mn} - F_{mn}]\beta_{pqmn} \quad (26)$$

where $\omega_{mn}^2 = (B/\bar{m})[(m\pi/a)^2 + (n\pi/b)^2]^2$ represents the square of the first natural frequency of the simply supported rectangular plate

$$\beta_{pqmn} = \int_S \int_S \phi_{pq}(x_0, y_0)\phi_{mn}(x, y)\frac{\partial^2 G(M, M_0)}{\partial z_M \partial z_{M_0}}dx_0 dy_0 dxdy$$

Exchanging the order of the structural surface integral, β_{pqmn} can be expressed as:

$$\beta_{pqmn} = \frac{j}{8\pi^2}\int_{-\infty}^{\infty}\int_{-\infty}^{\infty} k_z \tilde{\phi}_{pq}^*(k_x, k_y)\tilde{\phi}_{mn}(k_x, k_y)dk_x dk_y \quad (27)$$

where $\tilde{\phi}_{pq}^*$ is the conjugate complex form of $\tilde{\phi}_{pq}$, $\tilde{\phi}_{mn}$ is the Fourier transform of ϕ_{mn} defined by:

$$\tilde{\varphi}_{mn} = ab\pi^2 mn \frac{[(-1)^m e^{jk_x a} - 1]}{a^2k_x^2 - m^2\pi^2}\frac{[(-1)^n e^{jk_y b} - 1]}{b^2k_y^2 - n^2\pi^2} \quad (28)$$

when m, p are the same as odd or even as well as n, q, β_{pqmn} is not equal to zero. Using the symmetry of β_{pqmn}, further simplification can be made as follows:

$$\beta_{pqmn} = \frac{2jS^2}{pqmn\pi^6}\int_0^{\infty}\int_0^{\infty}\frac{k_z}{(a^2k_x^2/n^2\pi^2 - 1)(a^2k_x^2/p^2\pi^2 - 1)} \cdot \frac{(1-(-1)^p\cos k_x a)(1-(-1)^q\cos k_y b)}{(b^2k_y^2/q^2\pi^2 - 1)(b^2k_y^2/m^2\pi^2 - 1)}dk_x dk_y \quad (29)$$

When the elements β_{pqmn} are determined, A_{mn} can be solved by the formula (26), the matrix form is expressed as:

$$\bar{m}\beta\,\Omega A - \frac{1}{4}\rho_f \omega^2 S A = \beta F \quad (30)$$

where β is the matrix for the formed matrix, Ω is expressed as:

$$\Omega = \begin{bmatrix} \omega_{11}^2 - \omega^2 & 0 & \cdots & 0 \\ 0 & \omega_{12}^2 - \omega^2 & \cdots & \vdots \\ \vdots & \vdots & \ddots & 0 \\ 0 & \cdots & 0 & \omega_{mn}^2 - \omega^2 \end{bmatrix}$$

Referring to the definition of acoustic radiation impedance in above section, the acoustic radiation impedance of the unbaffled plate is defined as

$$Z_{pqmn} = j\omega\rho_f(\frac{S}{4})^2\beta_{pqmn}^{-1} \quad (31)$$

5 Numerical Analysis

Set length $a = 1\text{m}$, width $b = 1.2\text{m}$, thickness $h = 0.01\text{m}$, the sound speed $c = 1400\text{m/s}$ in the water, regardless of board damping, and reference sound power $W_f = 10^{-12}W$. In the center of the plate excited by a normal excitation force, the amplitude is 1N. The pictures below show the comparison of the sound radiation power, mean square velocity and sound radiation efficiency of the plate.

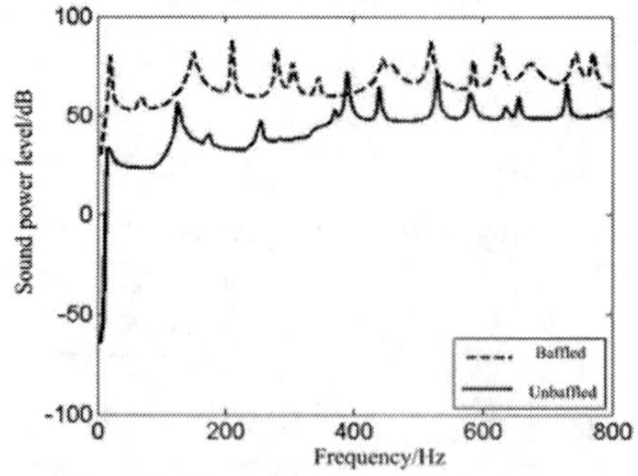

Figure 3. The comparison of the sound power

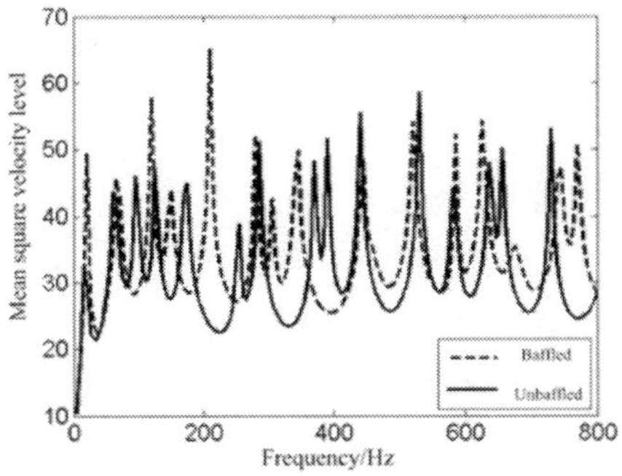

Figure 4. The comparison of the mean square velocity

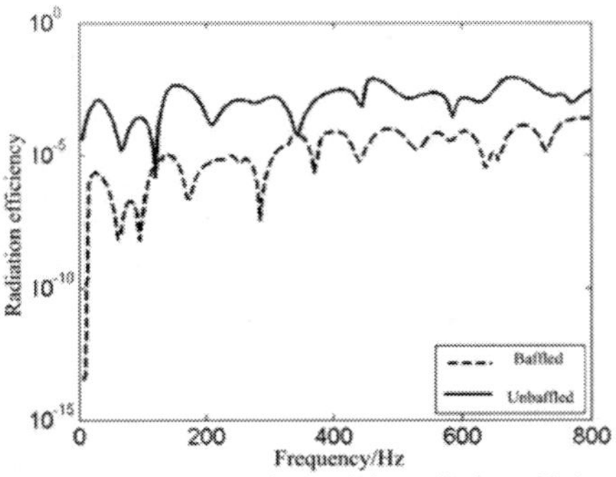

Figure 5. The comparison of the radiation efficiency

The figure above shows that the presence of the baffle causes the acoustic radiation impedance to be different, which causes the change of resonance frequency of the structure. The existence of the baffle causes the resonance frequency of the structure to be further reduced, and the sound radiation power of the structure is increased. This is due to the existence of the baffle, that the flat surface compresses one side medium which can not flow to the other side medium, resulting in structural vibration energy being more effectively converted into sound energy, thereby increasing the energy of acoustic radiation.So at the same frequency, the radiation power and efficiency of a baffled plate are higher than the unbaffled plate. The radiation from the baffled plate is similar to that of the monopole, and the acoustic radiation of the unbaffle plate is similar to that produced by the dipole. The acoustic radiation resistance of the baffled plate is higher than that of the unbaffled plate, and the acoustic resistance is equivalent to the additional mass on the surface of the structure. Therefore, it can be seen from the figure that the mean square velocity of the baffle plate is lower than that of the unbaffled one.

6 Conclusion

By using the boundary integral equation, the formulas of the acoustic radiation of the baffled plate and the unbaffled one are established respectively. Their respective acoustic radiation impedances are analyzed, and the radiated sound power, mean square velocity and the radiation efficiency of them are compared. It can be concluded that:

(1) The presence of the baffle causes the sound radiation power and efficiency of the structure to be improved, similar to the conversion of the structure of the dipole radiation to the monopole radiation;

(2) The presence of the baffle also changes the resonance frequency of structures in heavy medium, resulting in a reduced resonant frequency of the structure;

(3) In general, the mean square velocity of the baffled plate is lower than the unbaffled one.

References

1. Maidanik G. Response of Ribbed Panels to Reverberant Acoustic Field . Journal of the Acoustical Society of America, **34**(6), 809-826 (1962).
2. Wallace C E. Radiation resistance of a rectangular panel. Journal of the Acoustical Society of America, **51**(3), 946-952(1972).
3. Heckl M . Radiation from plane sound sources. Acustica. **37**, 155-166(1977).
4. Leppington F G, Broadbent E G, Heron K H. Acoustic radiation from rectangular panels with constrained edges. Proceedings of Royal Society London A, **393**, 67-84(1984).
5. Syder S, Tanaka N . Calculating total acoustic power output using modal radiation efficiencies. Journal of the Acoustical Society of America, **97**, 1702-1709(1995).
6. Li W L, Gibeling H J. Determination of the mutual radiation resistances of a rectangular plate and their impact on the radiated sound power. Journal of Sound and Vibration, **229**(5) , 1213-1233(2000).
7. Li W L, Gibeling H J. An analytical solution for the self and mutual radiation resistance efficiency . Journal of Sound and Vibration, **245**(1) ,1-16(2001).
8. Crighton D G. Force and moment admittance of plates under arbitrary fluid loading . Journal of Sound and Vibration, **20**, 209-218(1972).
9. Crighton D G. Approximations to the admittances and free wavenumbers of fluid-loaded panels. Journal of Sound and Vibration, **68**, 15-33(1980) .
10. Leibowitz R C . Methods for computing fluid loading and the vibratory response of fluid-loaded finite rectangular plates subject to turbulence excitation-option 3. NSRDC Rep, 2976C(1971).
11. Rumerman M L. The effect of loading on radiation efficiency. Journal of the Acoustical Society of America, **111**(1), 75-79 (2002).
12. Sandman B E. Fluid-loaded vibration of an elastic plate carrying a concentrated mass. Journal of the Acoustical Society of America,**61**(6), 1503-1510(1977).
13. Williams EG. Numerical evaluation of the radiation from unbaffled, finite plates using the FFT. Journal

of the Acoustical Society of America, **74**(1), 343-347 (1983).

14. Atalla N, Nicolas J, Gauthier C. Acoustic radiation of an unbaffled vibrating plate with general elastic boundary conditions. J. Acoust. Soc. Am., **99**(3) , 1484-1494(1996).
15. Oppenheimer C H, Dubrowsky S . A radiation efficiency for unbaffled plates with experimental validation . J. Acoust. Soc. Am., **199**(3), 473-489(1997).

MATEC Web of Conferences 128, 05007 (2017) DOI: 10.1051/matecconf/201712805007
EITCE 2017

Effect of combined tensile, bending and torsion deformation on medium carbon steel wire

Marina Polyakova[1,a], Aleksandr Gulin[1] and Eduard Golubchik[1]

[1]*Nosov Magnitogorsk state technical university, Materials Processing Department, 38 Lenin Avenue, Magnitogorsk, Russia*

Abstract. Such schemes of plastic deformation as bending, torsion, tension, compression etc. are considered to be the basic schemes for metal processing methods. Each of these types of deformation has specific influence on microstructure and mechanical properties of the processed metal. For the optimal result of plastic deformation impact on metal structure and properties the mechanism of plastic processing should follow the definite requirements. The effect of different kinds of deformation on medium carbon steel wire was studied using several methods: scanning electron microscopy, atomic force microscopy, dynamic hardness testing. The obtained results can be used in the design of combined methods of deformation processing of carbon steel.

1 Introduction

The main tendency in the development and design of effective engineering processes in metallurgy is considered to be the creation of new technological systems with little quantity of operations, without wastes and manual management. But at the same time improving the labour efficiency and essential increase of product quality are of high importance. Application of such technologies simplifies the structure of production process, changes the essence of technological operations and as a result decreases the quantity of equipment, material and energy sources necessary for the production [1 – 4]. At the same time it is obvious that continuous technological processes are more preferable from this point of view. Hence the competitiveness of the manufacturing process depends to high extent on the implementation the continuous technological processes at the industrial enterprises.

The technological process of metal ware production is the multioperation one and the only one operation is detected as the basic operation during which the transformation of the workpiece size and material occurs. Such kinds of deformation as tension, compression, bending and twisting form the basics of different types of metal deformational processing because they change properties and microstructure of the processed metal in a wide range. It is the perspective way for new technological processes design to combine different kinds of deformation in order to obtain the metal product with definite level of properties. But this combination have to be ground on the basic operation of the technological process. Drawing is the basic operation for wire production during which wire is processed by tension and compression. When designing the new method of combined deformation it is necessary to study the peculiarities of influence of different kinds of deformation on the wire properties [5 – 7].

Alternating bending is widely used in different metal processing technologies as intermediate operation (winding, rewinding) as independent operation (sheet stamping, descaling, flattening). In some cases alternating bending can be used as the metal processing technique with specific effect on metal structure and properties without changing the shape of the product. Distinguishing from other kinds of deformation where the total strain is limited by the workpiece sizes the total strain and the workpiece length at alternating bending practically are not limited but at the same time the process efficiency can be rather high. The influence of alternating bending on carbon steel wire and ropes properties is studied in [8 - 12]. Analytical models which can be used for prediction the effects of nonlinear bending of wires are presented in [12]. The obtained results can be used in practice of technologies design for manufacturing wire with different cross-sections from different materials.

Another kind of deformation which has a great effect on metal properties is torsion [13 - 18]. It is the kind of deformation when each element of the workpiece goes around the horizontal axis. Twisting is the basic operation in rope manufacturing so the study of metal properties after twisting is important in order to get this kind of metal product with high quality level. Torsion is characterized by very complicated stress-strain state which is maximum on the surface and tends to zero in the center of the steel wire. Due to the basics of metal resistance theory the transversal lines on the surface of the round workpiece after it is twisted remain plane, diameters of the cross-sections and the distances between them do not change. At the same time the rectangular net

[a] Corresponding author: m.polyakova-64@mail.ru

changes to the net with parallelograms. Hence, the stress state of the twisted round workpiece is considered to be the pure shear. Another factor which is necessary to take into consideration is that torsion influences the microstructure changing of carbon steel wire depending on the carbon content [15, 16]. Experimentally it was proved that after twisting strength of the wire increased [18]. So choosing the proper modes of torsion deformation one can improve toughness and durability of the carbon steel wire.

Drawing is the main technological process for wire production. It is well known that the deformation scheme during the drawing process is characterized by longitudinal and radial stresses. Such technological parameters as die approach, bearing parts of die, drawing speed effect the mechanical properties, microstructure and texture of the processed steel wire [19 - 26]. At the same time carbon content significantly influences the properties of carbon steel wire at drawing. But drawing is considered to be rather conservative process. At present time drawing has already exhausted its resources for improving the processed metal properties by changing deformation parameters or drawing speed. So it is necessary to design new methods based on the combination of different kinds of deformation which will be very effective for production steel wire with high level of mechanical properties [27 - 29]. This way is connected with the necessity to study the peculiarities of carbon steel wire microstructure formation after different kinds of deformation.

2 Materials and methods

In order to estimate the possibilities of the technological constraints of the combined plastic deformation for medium carbon steel wire, the research group carried out complex research work on investigation the processing modes' impact on microstructure and mechanical properties formation [30 – 32]. The wire made of medium carbon steel wire containing 0.5 % C (0.5 %C - 0.2 %Si - till 0.6 %Mn - till 0.25 %Cu - till 0.08 %As - till 0.25 %Ni - till 0.040 %S - till 0.035 % %P - till 0.25 %Cr - in wt. %) 3.45 mm in diameter was chosen for the experiments. This carbon steel wire is used for a wide range of engineering components. The aim of the investigation was to identify the effect of different types of plastic deformation (reduction and elongation, bending) and their combination with torsion on medium carbon steel wire.

The deformation ratio by drawing was chosen 37% depending on the medium carbon steel wire mechanical properties in as-received state. Bending deformation was applied on steel wire while going along the moving line of the 4-roll system with rolls 90 mm in diameter. Torsion deformation was 150 rpm (revolutions per minute). The combination of drawing with torsion and bending was arranged by the laboratory setup [33].

Atomic force microscopy was exercised in non-contact mode. A stiff cantilever was oscillated in the attractive regime, meaning that the tip was quite close to the sample, but not touching it. The forces between the tip and sample are quite low, on the order of pN (10^{-12} N). The detection scheme is based on measuring changes to the resonant frequency or amplitude of the tungsten cantilever as the interaction between the tip and sample dampen the oscillation. In order to obtain AFM images the cantilever moved along the line directly and reversly. Then it moves to the next line. The quantity of scanning points was chosen in a such way which made it possible to study the peculiarities of the carbon steel wire surface.

Scanning electron-microscope analysis of the wire in the as received state (after drawing) and after combined deformation was carried out on the electron microscope JEOL JSM-6490 LV with accelerating voltage 30 kV in conditions of Nano Steel Research Studies Institute of Nosov Magnitogorsk state technical university. Samples for metallographic examination were prepared from the deformed wire by polishing and etching the cross-section and observed at the surface of the sample.

Microhardness was measured by Dynamic ultramicrodurometer DUH-211S. Dynamic hardness is determined by measuring an indentation depth, instead of by measuring the diagonal lengths of an indentation. Due to ISO standard (ISO14577-1), it provides for the method of requesting the following material parameters from the relation of test force and indentation depth. Martens hardness (HMT) is measured under applied test force. Martens hardness is determined from the values given by the force/indentation depth curve during the increasing of the test force, preferably after reaching the specified test force. Martens hardness includes the plastic and elastic deformation, thus this hardness value can be calculated for Vickers indenter, triangular indenter with 115° tip angle (Berkovich indenter). Martens hardness, determined from the slope of the increasing force / indentation depth curve (HM_S). This hardness (HM_S) has the advantage of avoiding the zero-point determination for homogeneous materials. Indentation hardness (H_{it}) is a measure of the resistance to permanent deformation or damage. A simple function may be derived for a perfect Vickers geometry indenter, or for a Vickers indenter where the projected area function is known. In this case measurements of hardness, H_{IT} are related to the Vickers Hardness numbers, HV*, by a scaling factor.

3 Results and discussion

Results of AFM of carbon steel wire after different kids of deformation processing is shows in Figure 1. Using computer visualization 2D-images were obtained. At 2D-visualisation each point on the surface $Z = f(x, y)$ is identified by the definite colour depending on the point height (z-coordinate).

Microstructure of medium carbon steel wire consists of ferrite-carbide composition and low quantity of structured free ferrite which is located separately along the boundaries of pearlite colonies (Figure 2). This is characteristic to such carbon content in steel. The microstructure is uniform.

After drawing one can observe that cementite plates become curved in both directions (Figure 2, a, b).

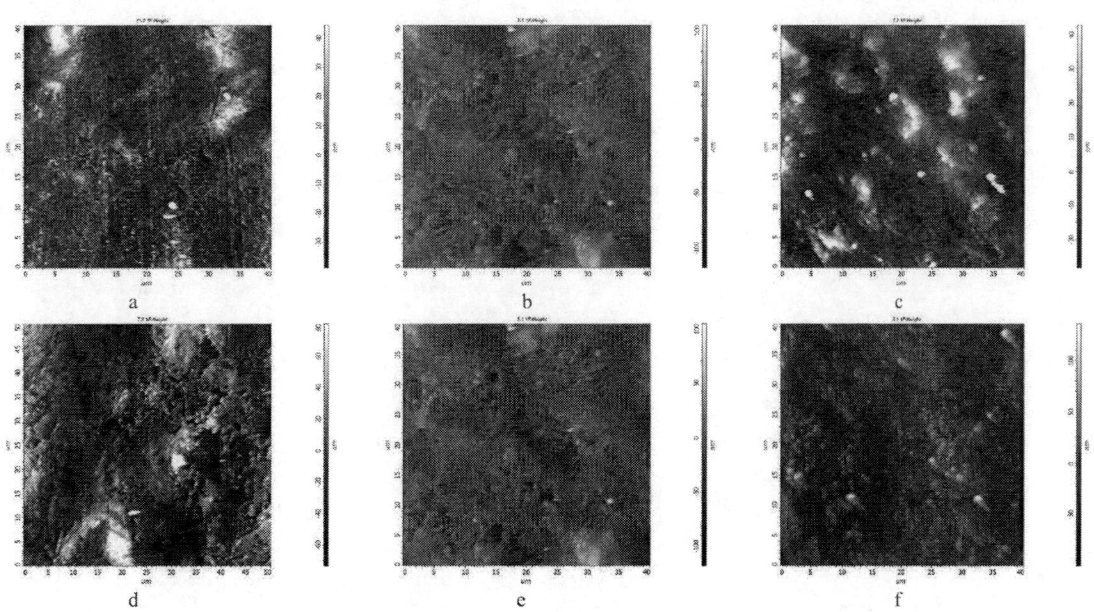

Figure 1. AFM of medium carbon steel wire after drawing (a, d), drawing with bending (b, e) and drawing with bending and torsion (c, f) (a-c – transverse cross-section, d-f – longitudinal cross-section)

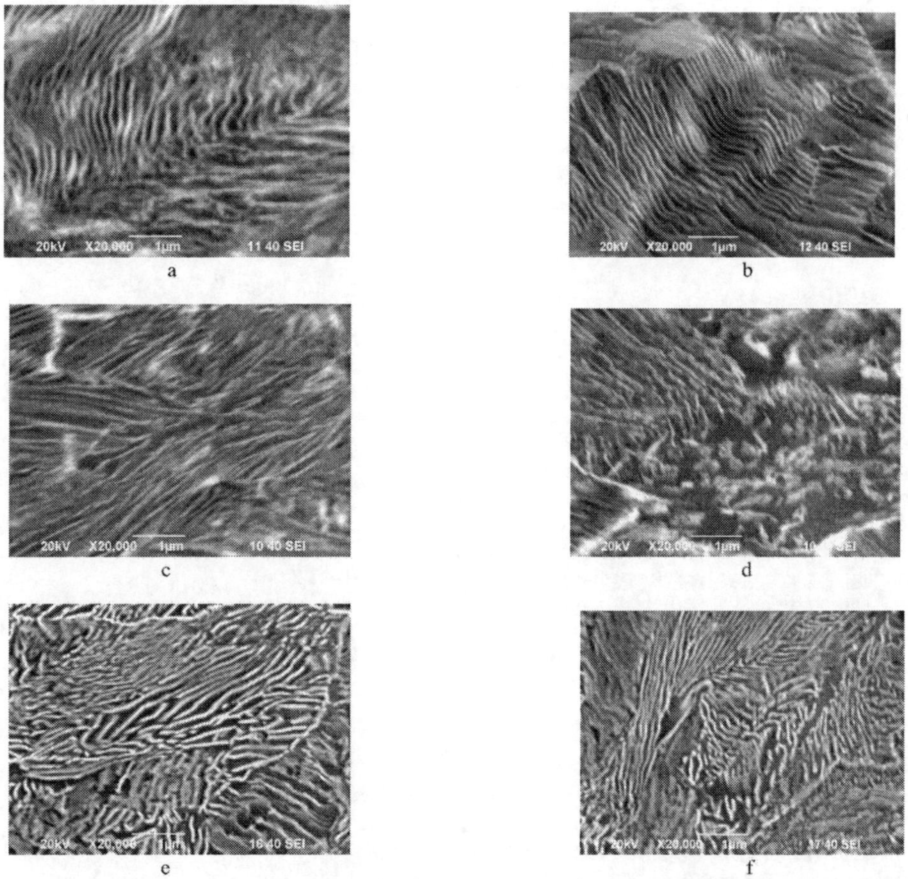

Figure 2. Deformation and crashing of cementite plates after drawing (a, b), drawing with bending (c, d) and drawing with bending and torsion (e, f) (a, c, e – longitudinal cross-section, b, d, f – transverse cross-section)

Combination of drawing with bending leads to crashing the cementite plates (Figure 2, c, d) which becomes drastically after drawing with bending and torsion (Figure 2, e, f). This can be explained by the metal complex deformation processing in such deformation action. Such microstructure changes of medium carbon steel wire prove the results of dynamic hardness testing (Figure 3).

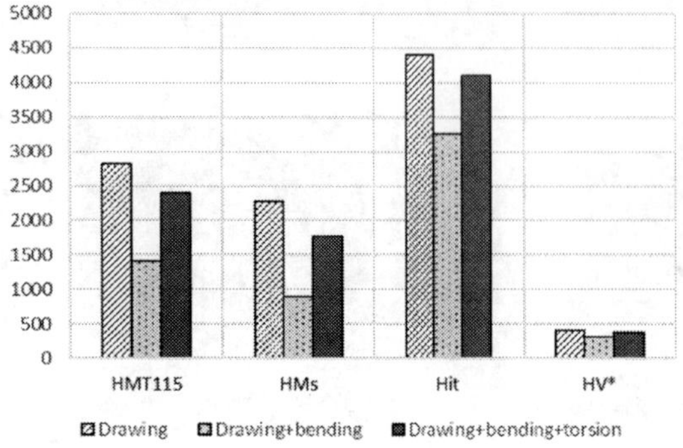

Figure 3. Dynamic hardness parameters of medium carbon steel wire after different kinds of deformation processing

As a result of combination of different kinds of deformation on medium carbon steel wire one can see the decrease of all dynamic hardness parameters. It can be explained that after such kind of deformation the medium carbon steel wire becomes more ductile but at the same time its strength does not decrease so much as compared with drawing (see Figure 3). Such peculiarities of mechanical properties which medium carbon steel wire possesses after combined deformation processing can be very useful for practical application in cable manufacturing.

4 Conclusions

Improving properties of carbon steel wire is the important item for investigations. The aim of practical interests is the combination of drawing as the basic operation in wire manufacturing with other kinds of deformation. The presented investigation shows the effect of different deformational processing on the medium carbon steel wire microstructure and dynamic hardness changing. As a result of combined deformational processing the medium carbon steel wire becomes more ductile as compared with it after drawing. Experimental results of the peculiarities of medium carbon steel wire after different kinds of combined deformational processing can be used in wide range of practical applications where it is used both as a finished product and as an intermediate workpiece.

References

1. H-S. Park, N-H. Tran. Int J Adv Manuf Tech. **56** (9-12) 1159-1165 (2011).
2. H-S Park, N-H. Tran. Int J Control, Automation and Systems. **10** (4) 806-816 (2012).
3. M.B. Sokol. J of Business and Psychology. **8** (3) 277-296 (1994).
4. N. Kim, J.H. Pae. J of the Academy of Marketing Science. **35** (2) 259-269 (2007).
5. Saunders, J. Nutting. Met Sci. **18** (12) 571-575 (1984)
6. Verpoest, B.D. Notohardjono, E. Aernoudt. ASTM Spec Tech Publ. 361-377 (1985)
7. M. Zelin, R.M. Shemenski. Conf. Proc. Wire Assoc. Int., Inc.: Wire Expo. 1-14 (2006)
8. R. Kruzel. Metalurgija. **52** (1) 93-95 (2013)
9. G. Oplatka. Proc 9th Cong Mater Test. 44-48 (1986)
10. D. Abel. Wire. **52** (1) 24-25 (2002)
11. M. Di Ludovico, G.P. Lignola, A. Prota, E. Cosenza. ACI Struct J. **107** (4) 390-399 (2010)
12. S. Baragetti. Meccanica. **41** 443-458 (2006)
13. Blackmore. Wire J Int. **39** (4) 98-102 (2006)
14. J. Hajduk. Arch Budowy Masz. **32** (3-4) 161-173 (1985)
15. N. Guo, B. Song, B-S. Wang, Q. Liu. Acta Metall. Sin. **28** (6) 707-714 (2015)
16. C. Cordier-Robert, B. Forfert, B. Bolle, J-J. Fundenberger, A.Tidu. J Mater Sci. **43** 1241-1248 (2008)
17. B. Goes, A. Martin-Meizoso, J. Gil-Sevillano, I. Lefever, E. Aernoudt. Eng Frac Mech. **60** (3) 255-272 (1998)
18. F. Knap. Wire World Int. **29** (4) 94-96 (1987)
19. R.L. Plaut, A.F. Padilha, N.B. Lima, C. Herrera, A.F.Filho, L.H.Yoshimura. Mater Sci and Eng A, **499** 337-341 (2000)
20. F. Fang, X-j. Hu, B-m. Zhang, Z-h. Xie, J-q. Jiang. Mater Sci and Eng A. **583** 78-83 (2013)
21. J. Adamczyk, M. Suliga, J.W. Pilarczyk, M. Burdek. Arch Metal and Mater **57** (4) 1105-1110 (2012)
22. J.W. Pilarczyk, J. Krnac, J. Adamczyk, B. Golis. Conf. Proc. Annu. Conf. Wire Assoc. Int. (2011)
23. J. Krnac, R. Wludzik, J.W. Pilarczyk, R. Kruzel. Conf. Proc. Wire Assoc. Int., Inc. – Wire Cable Tech. Symp., Annu. Conf. 163-176 (2009)
24. M. Zidani, S. Maessaoudi, T. Baudin, D. Solas. M.H. Mathon. Int J Mater Form **3** 7-11 (2010)
25. M. Suliga. Arch Metal and Mater **57** (4) 1021-1030 (2012)
26. Nemec, B. Golis, J.W. Pilarczyk, R. Budzik, W. Waszkielewicz. Conf. Proc. Wire Assoc. Int., Inc.: Wire Expo 182-197 (2006)
27. M. Zelin, R.M. Shemenski. 2006 Conference Proceedings of the Wire Association International. 1-4 (2006).
28. M. Chukin, A. Korchunov, M. Polyakova, D. Emaleeva. Steel in Translation. **40** (6) 595-597 (2010).
29. M. Polyakova, E. Golubchik, Yu. Efimova, A. Gulin. Key Eng Mater. **724** 77-86 (2017).
30. Calliari I., Brunelli K., Polyakova M., Gulin A., Golubchik E. 5th Int Conf TMP 2016.
31. M.V. Chukin, M.A. Polyakova, A.E. Gulin. Steel in Translation. **46** (8) 548-551 (2016).
32. M. Polyakova, I. Calliari, A. Gulin. Key Eng Mater. **716** 201-207 (2016).

33. M. Polyakova, M. Chukin, E. Golubchik, A. Gulin, RU Patent 130,525. (2013)

DOI: 10.1051/matecconf/201712805008

Study on Assembly Precision Reliability Assessment for Industrial Sensing Devices

Tian Fan [1,a], Wei Tao[1], Hanxian Hu[1] and Wei Liu[1]
CRRC QINGDAO SIFANG CO., LTD., Shandong Qingdao 266111, China

Abstract. This paper investigates the method of assembly precision reliability assessment for industrial sensing devices. The part variation is formulated by small displacement torsor. The assembly error model is developed through the approach of pose transformation matrix, then the error transfer between the parts is analyzed and the assembly error is calculated. The concept of assembly precision reliability is proposed. Monte Carlo simulation is adopted to calculate the reliability, after that the procedure of assembly precision reliability is determined. Case study of a laser sensor is provided therefore the effectiveness of the proposed models is verified.

1 Introduction

Assembly precision is a crucial technique target for industrial sensing devices. As the devices play important role in industrial network system, and different devices can be used to measure diverse physical quantities, such as length, distance, vibration, speed. Meanwhile, assembly precision of industrial sensing devices has an important impact on the measuring precision. Therefore, the study on assembly precision reliability assessment for industrial sensing devices has potential value of engineering application.

Manufacturing error and assembly error are gradually introduced and accumulated in assembly process, which eventually affect the assembly precision reliability of the devices. Therefore, the study of assembly precision reliability assessment should be based on the propagation and accumulation analysis of error sources.

Some methods of assembly error transfer commonly used include Stream of Variation (SoV)1, state space method1 2, multi-body system theory4, etc. In the early, Mantripragada5 presented a state transition model of assembly and concepts from control theory to model variation propagation and control during assembly. Also, a systematic study regarding assembly variation modeling in automobile assemblies is conducted at the University of Michigan. HU1 developed a methodology to evaluate the dimensional variation propagation in a multi-station compliant assembly system based on linear mechanics and a state space representation. Literature25 developed process state space model based on SoV. Liu7 adopted SoV and Statistical Process Control (SPC) methodologies respectively to analyze the variation reduction for multistage manufacturing processes. Yu8 established a geometric error propagation model by the theory of multi-body system and homogeneous transformation method (HTM). Tan, et al8 investigated surface variation of compliant Parts, and developed a comprehensive approach of geometrical covariance modeling. The industrial robot flexible assembly technology for the plane drilling and riveting was presented in literature9. Tang11 introduced a new geometric error modeling approach for multi axes system (MAS) based on SoV, especially for multi-axis precision stage. Cao12 investigated a vibration propagation model based on key point.

Many researches have been done in the field of mechanical precision reliability. Literature8 took reliability as the index of machining precision, and proposed the method of precision assignment based on reliability analysis. Besides, response surface method was adopted to calculate precision reliability in this paper. Based on the theory of mechanical precision design and mechanical reliability design, Song established the model of machine tool transmission precision reliability, and studied the main factors affecting the transmission precision of CNC machine tools13.

Reliability theory has been widely applied in the field of mechanical structure and precision, while there is still no general assembly precision reliability evaluation system that can be used for industrial sensing devices. In this paper, combined with the actual need of Laser sensor assembly, the product assembly error transfer model is established and reliability assembly precision is evaluated. The model proposed considers part dimension, product structure, assembly error and other factors systematically. The study in this paper can provide an effective theoretical method for the assembly precision reliability for industrial sensing devices.

2 Assembly Error Transfer Model

[a] Corresponding author: 1064272117@qq.com

DOI: 10.1051/matecconf/201712805008

Assembly is the process of connecting parts together by mechanical connection mode. During assembly, error is transferred and accumulated through joint surface. In this section, part error is presented by unified expression and assembly error transfer model is established based on the HTM.

2.1 Part variation

In this paper, small displacement torsor(SDT) is presented to describe the part variation as this representation can be conveniently transformed into a transfer matrix form, then the relationship between the error and the target precision is obtained through the transformation of HTM.

Parts variation includes direction error along x, y and z axes and orientation error about the x, y and z axes, which can be expressed as error vector. For a part G, error vector consists of small linear shift along the axes of a point g on the part G and small angular shift about the axes of the whole part:

$$\begin{cases} \mathbf{G}(g)=\left[\Delta X_g(G) \quad \Delta Y_g(G) \quad \Delta Z_g(G)\right]^{\mathrm{T}} \\ \mathbf{G}'=\left[\Delta\alpha(G) \quad \Delta\beta(G) \quad \Delta\theta(G)\right]^{\mathrm{T}} \end{cases} \tag{1}$$

Where $\mathbf{G}(g)$ represents position error vector of the part; $\mathbf{G}'$represents the direction error vector of the part; $\Delta X_g(G)$, $\Delta Y_g(G)$, $\Delta Z_g(G)$ represent small translational displacement along the axes of the point g on part G, respectively; $\Delta\alpha(G)$, $\Delta\beta(G)$, $\Delta\theta(G)$ represent small rotational displacement about the axes of part G.

2.2 Assembly Error Transfer Model

2.2.1 Transformation matrix

Position and orientation transformation of parts under different coordinate system can be expressed by HTM:

$$\mathbf{F} = Rot(\alpha,\ \beta,\ \theta)\ Trans(a,b,c) = \begin{bmatrix} 1 & 0 & 0 & 0 \\ 0 & \cos\alpha & -\sin\alpha & 0 \\ 0 & \sin\alpha & \cos\alpha & 0 \\ 0 & 0 & 0 & 1 \end{bmatrix} \begin{bmatrix} \cos\beta & 0 & \sin\beta & 0 \\ 0 & 1 & 0 & 0 \\ -\sin\beta & 0 & \cos\beta & 0 \\ 0 & 0 & 0 & 1 \end{bmatrix} \begin{bmatrix} \cos\theta & -\sin\theta & 0 & 0 \\ \sin\theta & \cos\theta & 0 & 0 \\ 0 & 0 & 1 & 0 \\ 0 & 0 & 0 & 1 \end{bmatrix} \begin{bmatrix} 1 & 0 & 0 & a \\ 0 & 1 & 0 & b \\ 0 & 0 & 1 & c \\ 0 & 0 & 0 & 1 \end{bmatrix} \tag{2}$$

Where *Trans* is translation transformation; a, b, c is translational displacement along the x, y, z axes during coordinate transformation respectively; *Rot* is rotation transformation; α, β, θ is rotational displacement about the x, y, z axes during coordinate transformation respectively.

When assembly error exists, there will be small translational displacement along the x, y, z axes and small rotational displacement about the x, y, z axes during coordinate transformation; Ignoring second and third order components in formula (2), the error transformation matrix can be obtained

$$\Delta\mathbf{F} = \begin{bmatrix} 1 & -\sin\Delta\gamma & \sin\Delta\beta & \Delta a \\ \sin\Delta\gamma & 1 & -\sin\Delta\alpha & \Delta b \\ -\sin\Delta\beta & \sin\Delta\alpha & 1 & \Delta c \\ 0 & 0 & 0 & 1 \end{bmatrix} = \begin{bmatrix} 1 & -\Delta\gamma & \Delta\beta & \Delta a \\ \Delta\gamma & 1 & -\Delta\alpha & \Delta b \\ -\Delta\beta & \Delta\alpha & 1 & \Delta c \\ 0 & 0 & 0 & 1 \end{bmatrix} \tag{3}$$

And transformation matrix can be written as

$$\mathbf{F}' = \Delta\mathbf{F}\cdot\mathbf{F} \tag{4}$$

2.2.2 Construction of Assembly Error Transfer Coordinate System

The assembly error propagation can be described as error transfer between joint surfaces in the assembly process. Joint surface refers to a surface on a part which has joint relationship with a surface on another part during the assembly process. Joint surface has a variety of types, such as plane, cylinder, cone, sphere, etc. Among these, planar surface (shown as the join surface between part 1 and part 2 in Fig.1) and cylindrical surface (shown as the join surface between part 2 and part 3 in Fig.1) are the most common features[14].

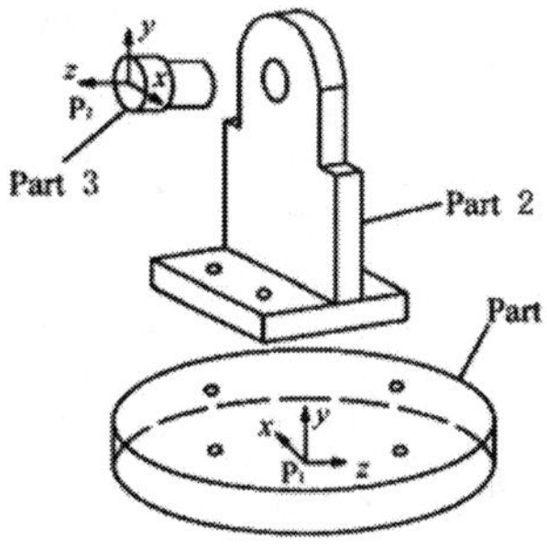

Figure 1. Schematic diagram of parts assembly

2.2.3 Calculation of Assembly Error Transfer

During the assembly error transfer model building, the first step is to establish the error transfer coordinate system. As for a machine, if there are t parts to be assembled, we need to establish t+1 coordinate systems, including the global reference coordinate system defined as P_0, the target coordinate system defined as P_t, the error transfer coordinate between parts defined as P_1, P_2,... P_{t-1}.

As for a middle part I, its position and orientation transformation relationship between coordinate system P_i and P_{i-1} can be represented as:

$$\begin{cases} \mathbf{U}_{i-1}^{i_m}=\mathbf{V}_i\mathbf{U}_{i_m} \\ \mathbf{U}_{i-1}^{\prime i_m}=(\Delta\mathbf{M}_i+\Delta\mathbf{N}_i)\mathbf{V}_i\mathbf{U}_{i_m} \end{cases} \tag{5}$$

Where $\mathbf{U}_{i_m}$ is the ideal coordinate vector of point m on part i under P_i; $\mathbf{V}_i$ is position and orientation transformation matrix of point j between the two adjacent coordinate systems; $\mathbf{U}_{i-1}^{i_m}$ is the ideal coordinate vector of point m on part i under P_{i-1}; $\Delta\mathbf{M}_i$ is position and orientation transformation matrix of manufacturing error; $\Delta\mathbf{N}_i$ is position and orientation transformation matrix of assembly error; $\mathbf{U}_{i-1}^{\prime i_m}$ is the actual coordinate vector of point m on part i under P_{i-1}.

DOI: 10.1051/matecconf/201712805008

According to Eq. (5), combined with a series of position and orientation transformation matrix, the normal coordinate vector and the actual coordinate vector of point I on the target part t under P_t, P_{t-1}, V_{N-2}, $P_{t-2} \ldots P_0$ can be obtained:

$$\begin{cases} \mathbf{U}_o^{t_i} = \mathbf{V}_1 \mathbf{V}_2 \cdots \mathbf{V}_{t-1} \mathbf{V}_t \mathbf{U}_{t_i} \\ \mathbf{U}_o^{'t_i} = (\Delta\mathbf{M}_1 + \Delta\mathbf{N}_1)\ \mathbf{V}_1 (\Delta\mathbf{M}_2 + \Delta\mathbf{N}_2)\ \mathbf{V}_2 \cdots\ (\Delta\mathbf{M}_{t-1} + \Delta\mathbf{N}_{t-1})\ \mathbf{V}_{t-1} (\Delta\mathbf{M}_t)\ \mathbf{V}_t \mathbf{U}_{t_i} \end{cases} \tag{6}$$

The difference between the actual coordinate value and the ideal coordinate value of the point I in the global coordinate system is the error vector of the target part, denoted by $\Delta\mathbf{U}_o^{t_i}$:

$$\Delta\mathbf{U}_o^{t_i} = \mathbf{U}_o^{'t_i} - \mathbf{U}_o^{t_i} \tag{7}$$

3 Analysis of assembly precision reliability

3.1 Definition of Assembly Precision Reliability

Assembly precision reliability refers to the probability that products meet the design requirements under regular assembly condition. Assumes that the calculation of the actual assembly precision is ΔS, the range of the target assembly precision is between ΔS_- and ΔS_+ . If $\Delta S_- \le \Delta S \le \Delta S_+$, the actual precision meets the known requirement. Otherwise doesn't meet the requirement. Set the sample size L (to ensure the sampling accuracy, L should be large enough), l is the number that sample meets the requirement. The assembly precision reliability can be obtained as:

$$R = \frac{l}{L} \cdot 100\% \tag{8}$$

3.2 Calculation of Assembly Precision Reliability Based on Monte Carlo Simulation Method

On the basis of the definition of assembly precision reliability, Monte Carlo simulation method is adopted to calculate the precision reliability data in this paper.

The error sources that affect the assembly precision are considered as random variables, then the probability distribution and parameters of the known error sources are obtained. Therefore, the assembly precision reliability can be solved by Monte Carlo simulation. The solution steps are as follows:

Step 1: Set the calculation object and specified precision reliability according to the actual requirement.

Step 2: Establish the assembly error transfer model of industrial sensing devices based on the assembly structure of the object. Therefore the actual value of assembly error can be calculated.

Step 3: Determine whether the actual error of the analysis object is within the specified limits. If the actual error is within the prescribed range, the effective simulation number needs to be increased once; otherwise, the number keeps unchanged. When the judgment is completed, return to Step 2 to continue the next round of calculations until the number of simulation reaches L.

Step 4: Output the result of assembly precision reliability.

The assembly precision reliability is an important indicator to evaluate the assembly quality of devices, and its calculation results can be used as a quantitative index to assess the assembly precision of industrial sensing devices.

4 Case Study

In this section, the proposed methodology is illustrated with an example of a laser sensor, the parts and basic dimensions of which is shown in Fig.2. Assumes that all parts of the sensor are at the given location in non-operating mode, dimensional tolerance of which is ±0.05mm, geometric tolerance is 0.01mm. The target of the assembly precision is that the reliability of direction error of working part in each direction has to be not less than 95%.

Lower surface on the base of the base is treated as global benchmark surface. The origin of each coordinate system is shown in Table 1, and each coordinate system is parallel to the global coordinate system P0.

The data in Table 2 shows that the mean deviation of the direction tends to accumulate during assembly.

The direction error reliability in x, y and z directions is 96.52%, 95.36% and 94.37%, respectively, calculated by MATLAB simulation. The results show the direction error of x and y is in accord with the requirement of assembly precision, while the precision of z direction is not satisfied with the requirement. According to the state variables calculated, the error state of the drilling machine can be estimated and predicted.

The difficulty of achieving different precision is different. When setting the target precision value of assembly, it is necessary to weigh the difficulty, cost and function realization, and so on. As for the assembly precision not conforming to the requirements, taking higher manufacture precision and other measures can reduce the assembly error of the parts.

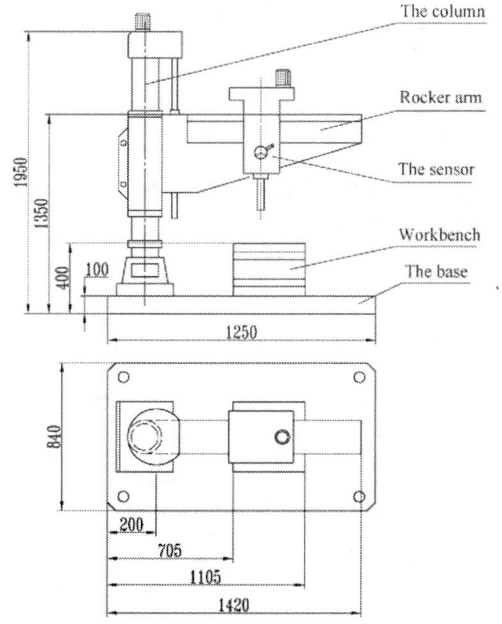

Fig.2 A frame model of a laser sensor

Table.1 The origin of coordinate system with respect to the global coordinate system/mm

	x	y	z
P_0	0	0	0
P_1	420	150	100
P_2	420	150	1350
P_3	420	1262.5	1350
P_4	420	1262.5	650

Table.2 Mean of direction error of the parts during assembly

	The base	The column	Rocker arm	The sensor
α /rad	-0.00328	0.00175	0.00236	0.00278
β /rad	0.00192	0.00143	0.00201	0.00257
θ /rad	0.00273	0.00230	0.00279	0.00280

5 Conclusion

In this paper, the assembly error model is established by the position and orientation transformation matrix. Besides, the definition and the numerical calculation method of assembly precision reliability are given, which provides a theoretical basis for the reliability analysis of assembly precision. Through the assembly process analysis of a laser sensor, the validity of the method above is verified.

In the future study, we can further develop the sensitivity analysis of various error sources, and realize the optimization and improvement of the assembly precision by the reasonable allocation of the tolerances.

References

1. S Hu, Y Koren. CIRP ANN-MANUF TECHN, **46** (1997) :1-6
2. J Jin, J Shi. J MANUF SCI E-T ASME, **121**(1999):756-762
3. Y Ding, D Ceglarek, J Shi. JUSFA, (2000): 23-26
4. J Chen. INT J MACH TOOL MANU, **35**(1995): 593-605
5. R Mantripragada, D Whitney. IEEE T ROBOTIC AUTOM, **15**(1999): 124-140
6. S Zhou, Q Huang, J Shi. EEE T ROBOTIC AUTOM, **19**(2003): 296-309
7. J Liu. QUAL RELIAB ENG INT, **26**(2010): 645-661
8. Z Yu, Z Liu, Y Ai, et al. CHIN J MECH ENG, **49**(2013): 142-151
9. C Tan, D Hou. Transactions of University of Aeronautics and Astronautics, **3**(2014)
10. J Shen, W Tian. J NANJING U AERONAUT ASTRONAUTICS, **46**(2014): 181-189
11. H Tang, J Duan, S Lan, et al. INT J MACH TOOL MANU, **92**(2015):41-51
12. Y Cao, B Li, J Guan, et al. P I MECH ENG B-J ENG, **229**(2015): 1164-1179
13. J Song, H Liu, D Yuan, et al. CHIN MECH ENG, **7**(2011): 785-789
14. Yi G, et al. J. Zhejiang Univ, **40**(2006): 921-926

Effect of Tool-Path on Morphology and Mechanical Properties of Ti-6Al-4V Fabricated by Wire and Arc Additive Manufacturing

Jie Fu[1], Kun Qiu[2,a], Lin Gong[1], Changmeng Liu[1], Qianru Wu[1], Jiping Lu[1], Hongli Fan[1]

[1]*School of Mechanical Engineering, Beijing Institute of Technology, Beijing, Zhongguancun south Street, 100081, China*
[2]*School of Mechanical Engineering, Beijing Polytechnic, Beijing, 100176, China*

Abstract. Ti-6Al-4V components are widely used in aerospace industry. However, it's not economic to manufacture them in traditional subtractive methods. Wire and arc additive manufacturing (WAAM) is a promising alternative technology for fabricating it efficiently and economically. Tool-path planning strategy is a very important step in WAAM process. This paper investigated the influence of the lap way between layers and layers in tool-path on the Ti-6Al-4V samples fabricated by WAAM. It has been found that the lap way between layers and layers in tool-path do influence the forming quality and especially mechanical properties of the fabricated samples. Samples have different surface quality (smooth or undulating) and defects inside or on the surface of the components. The highest and smallest ultra tensile strength of the fabricated samples are respectively 907.86 MPa, 684.82 MPa. But it has few effect on the grains of the fabricated samples, and they all have cross-sectional columnar grains.

1 Introduction

Wire and arc additive manufacturing (WAAM) is a promising technology in the aerospace industry manufacturing titanium alloy parts. As a method of additive manufacturing, it can fabricate any complex component with near net shape and without any mold, while saving materials, reducing manufacturing costs and shortening the production cycle. Compared with other additive manufacturing methods, such as Selective Laser Melting (SLM), Electron Beam Direct Manufacturing (EBDM), it fabricates the component with higher forming efficiency and lower costs. So it has grained more and more attention in the last decades [1-4].

Gas Tungsten Arc Welding (GTAW) [5] and Plasma Arc Welding (PAW) [6] are the two main methods of WAAM. Compared with PAW, GTAW is simple to control, has less process parameters, and the arc in the deposition process is relatively stable, make it easy to improve and research.

In the deposition process, many factors have an impact on the forming quality. Jun Xiong et al. [7] used a parabolic model, a cosine model, and a circular model to simulate the cross section profile of the welding in the WAAM, and select the deposit spacing as two thirds of the welding width. His experiments found that the ratio of wire feed rate to welding speed greatly influence the shape of the welding profile. Donghong Ding et al. [8] proposed a new multi-bead overlapping model for WAAM which set the deposit spacing to 0.738 times welding width and the fabricated components have a smoother surface. In addition to the deposit spacing, tool-path planning is also an important part of the impact of forming surface quality. There are now five main tool-path used in the WAAM process: raster, zigzag, contours, and continuous[9]. The zigzag tool-path is the most popular method used in WAAM process, and many papers have already researched it [10, 11]. But for the lap way between layers and layers, there are few researches.

Thus, the aim of this paper is to investigate the effect of the lap way between layers and layers on the morphology and mechanical properties of the Ti-6Al-4V samples fabricated by GTAW.

2 Experiment

The additive manufacturing equipment used in this study was assembled by Beijing Institute of Technology as shown in **Figure 1**. It can be divided into four parts: control system, wire feeding system, argon protection system and welding machine as shown in .Control system controls welding machine arc switch, wire feeder switch and machine movement. The wire feeding system controls the wire feeding speed. Argon protection system to transport argon, protect the workpiece, to avoid oxidation of titanium alloy at high temperatures. Welding machine is responsible for providing arc and controls peak current, pulse frequency, peak time ratio, base-to-peak current ratio and other parameters.

The components will be fabricated on the Ti-6Al-4V titanium alloy substrates with the size of 150mm×50mm ×5mm. The process parameters used in the deposition process is shown in **Table 1**.

[a] Corresponding author: gonglin@bit.edu.cn

Four kinds of tool-path were used in this experiment as shown in **Figure 2** and the direction was also marked on it. They are all made up of zigzag paths. Their difference lies in the lap way between layers and layers. The first and third tool-path schemes are the same for repeated scaninng, the difference is that one is mainly for the side wire feeding, one for the front and back feeding to testing the influence of the wire-feeding directions as shown in **Figure 2**a&c [12]. The layer is interlaced with the previous layer in the second tool-path scheme as show in **Figure 2**b. Each layer is moved 3 mm outward in the horizontal direction. The tool-path between the layers are symmetrical in the fourth tool-path scheme as shown in **Figure 2**d. The first three scheme do not require arc failure in the scanning process, and the fourth scheme requires arcing and arc failure at each layer. Each scheme has ten layers.

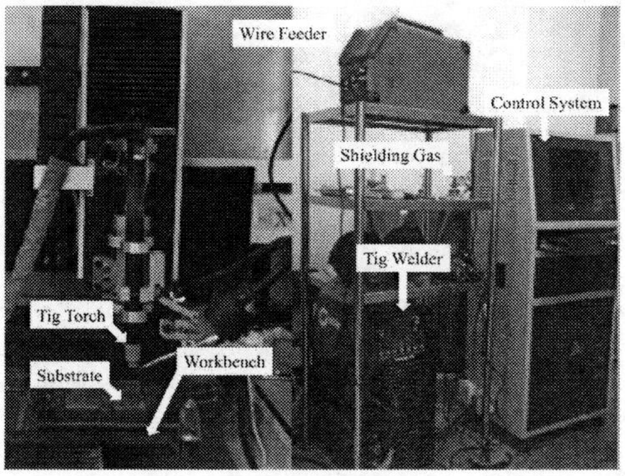

Figure 1 Experimental Equipment

Table 1 Deposition parameters used in this study

Parameter name	Unit	Values
Wire feed speed	mm/min	1000
Peak current	A	260
Pulse frequency	Hz	1.8
Peak time ratio	%	40
Base-to-peak current ratio	%	5
Scanning speed	mm/min	360
Layer thickness	mm	1.1
Deposit spacing	mm	5.5
Wire feed angle	°	45
Electrode to workpiece distance	mm	8

After forming process, three tensile specimens perpendicular to the weldings were obtained in the horizontal plane of each sample by wire-cutting techniques. Static tensile tests at room temperature were carried out on an INSTRON 5966 material testing machine. The max load capacity of it is 10kN and the drive type is powerful motors. The strain is acquired by video-extensometer. The cross-head displacement speed was 0.01mm/s.

The samples for microstructural characterization were be obtained from XZ plane by wire-cutting techniques. The samples were firstly polished with SiC paper (180, 360, 600, 1000, 2000), then etching for 20s using a solution consisting of 2% HF (hydrofluoric acid) and 6% HNO3 (nitric acid). All the grains size were determined by ImageJ software.

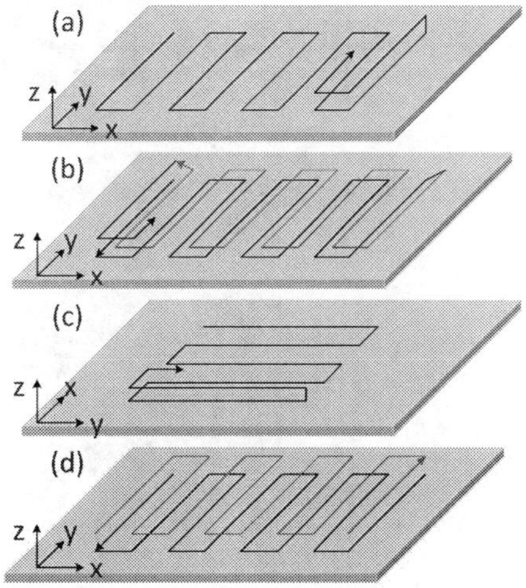

Figure 2 The four tool-path used in the experiment

3 Results

3.1 Macrostructure

The four fabricated samples are shown in **Figure 3**. In general, four samples were successfully formed. The molten pool was arranged in an orderly manner like fish scales. There is also a phenomenon that can not be ignored, from one side of the welding to the other side, the molten pool size gradually becomes larger or smaller especially in **Figure 3**c. Samples A, D are free of defects and their surface are flat. Samples B, C have a defect on the surface. Samples B, D appear splashing.

The contours of the upper and lower sides of the four samples are shown in **Figure 4**. It can be seen from the figure: the sample A, C contour fluctuation degree of the largest, the sample D is the most smooth. It shows that the lap way between layers and layers do influence the forming quality.

As the tool-path is zigzag, during the scanning process, when the torch gun scan to the turning point, the heat accumulation, the temperature rise, resulting in increased molten pool size. when scanning long welding, the temperature gradually decreased, the molten pool size changes small, therefore from one side of the welding to the other side, the molten pool size gradually becomes larger or smaller, resulting in lateral contours fluctuate up and down, as shown in **Figure 5**. So the lateral contours of sample A&C fluctuate up and down, followed by the sample B, and sample D is the most smooth. Because the tool-path between the layers are symmetrical in the fourth scheme, the tool-path between layers and layers form a complementary, eliminating fluctuations in the lateral profile, forming a smooth side profile.

DOI: 10.1051/matecconf/201712805009

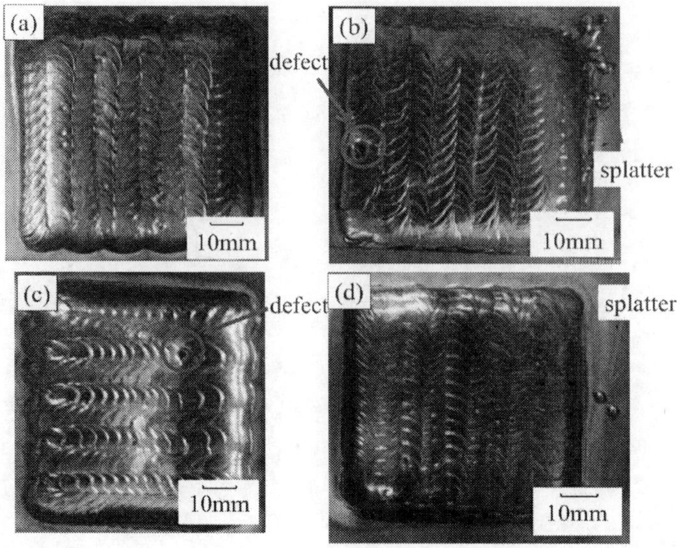

Figure 3 The fabricated samples, correspond to the tool-path shown in **Figure 2**. (a) sample A, (b) sample B, (c) sample C, sample D.

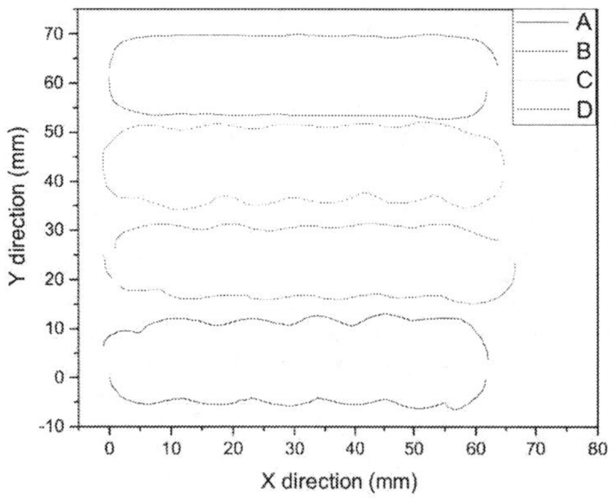

Figure 4 The contours of the upper and lower sides of the four samples

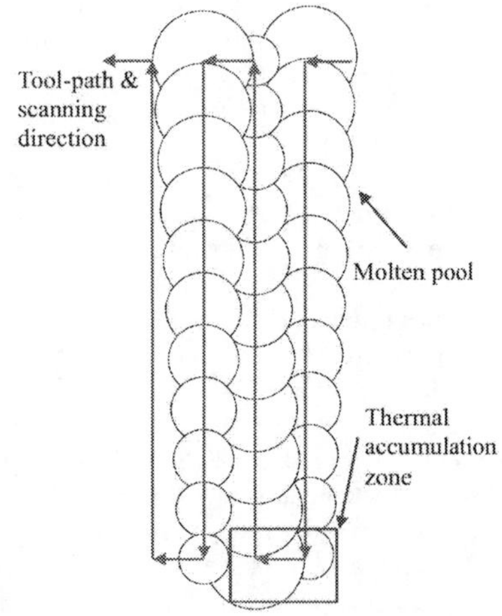

Figure 5 The schematic of the formation of molten pool size

3.2 Grains and Morphology

The macrostructure of the fabricated samples is shown in **Figure 6**. It's obvious that the bottom part (substrate) of the four samples are equiaxed grains, and the forming parts are formed into columnar grains throughout the samples. The average width of the columnar grains from each sample is 0.664mm, 0.946mm, 0.899mm, 1.371mm. The columnar grains of each sample are not significantly different in shape and size. It indicates that the tool-path has few effect on the macrostructure of the fabricated samples.

Sample A, C, D appeared not obvious defects, sample B appeared lots of defects and holes. The differences of the z coordinate between the highest point and the lowest point of the cross section profile of each sample stabilized part are 3.371mm, 0.943mm, 1.267mm, 1.962mm.

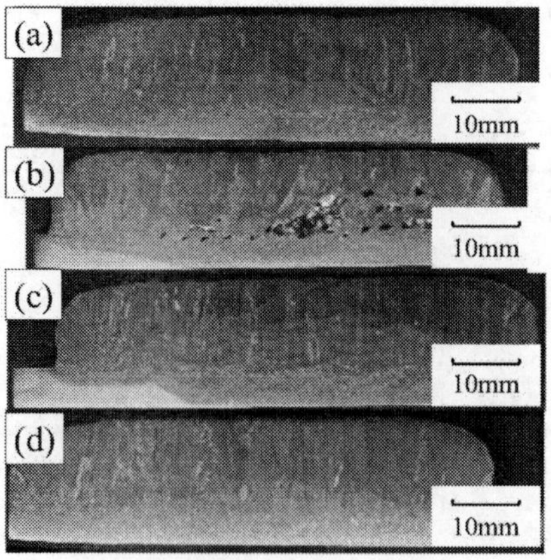

Figure 6 Macrostructure of the fabricated samples: all columnar grains throughout the samples

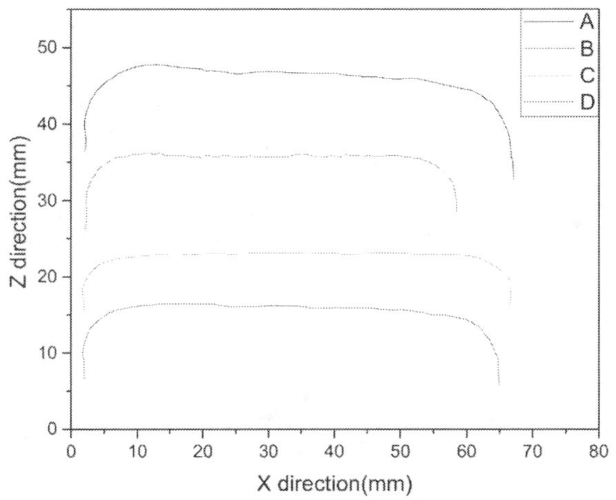

Figure 7 The contours of the cross section of the fabricated samples.

4 Mechanical properties

The results of the static tensile tests at room temperature are shown in Figure 9. From sample A to D, the average ultra tensile strength (UTS) of each sample is: 907.86 MPa, 876.82 MPa, 791.75 MPa, 684.82 MPa. the average strain of each sample is 5.93%, 11.74%, 10.91%, 8.37%. Sample A has the highest ultra tensile strength, while sample B has the highest strain, and the strength and strain of sample D are the worst.

The tensile results of the sample A&C shows that the wire-feeding direction influence the mechanical properties of the fabricated samples. The tensile results of the samples indicate that tool-path influence the UTS and strain of the fabricated samples in WAAM process.

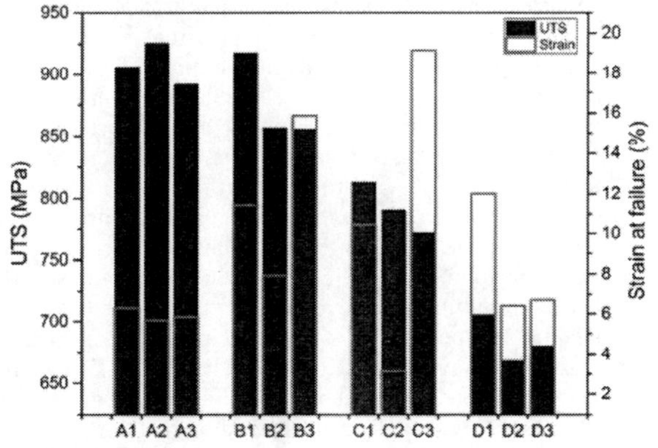

Figure 8 Ultimate tensile strength and strain of the sample fabricated by WAAM.

5 Conclusion

In this paper, the influences of tool-path on the fabricated samples in WAAM process was investigated. Sample B shows splatter outside and defects, holes inside. Sample C shows defect outside and has fluctuating sides. Although sample D has a very smooth surface, it has splatter outside and has the worst mechanical properties. Sample A performed well in all respects except in side profile, but this is not a disadvantage, it meets the requirements of forming quality.

The results of this paper shows that the lap way between layers and layers do influence the morphology and mechanical properties of the Ti-6Al-4V samples fabricated by GTAW. The simpler the lap way, the better performance of the fabricated samples.

References

1. Williams SW, Martina F, Addison AC, Ding J, Pardal G, Colegrove P. Mater Sci Technol, **641–7**, 32 (2016).
2. Ding D, Pan Z, Cuiuri D, Li H. Int J Adv Manuf Technol. **465–81**, 81 (2015).
3. Baufeld B, Biest O V D, Dillien S. Metallurgical & Materials Transactions A. **1917-1927**, 8 (2010).
4. Wu Q, Ma Z, Chen G, et al. Journal of Manufacturing Processes, **198-206**, 27 (2017).
5. Wang, F., Williams, S., Colegrove, P., & Antonysamy, A. A. Metallurgical & Materials Transactions A. **968-977**, 2 (2013),.
6. Martina F, Mehnen J, Williams S W, et al. Journal of Materials Processing Technology. **1377-86**, 6 (2012).
7. Xiong J, Zhang G, Gao H, et al. Robotics and Computer Integrated Manufacturing. **417-423**, 2 (2013).
8. Ding D, Pan Z, Cuiuri D, et al. Robotics & Computer Integrated Manufacturing, **101-110**, C (2015).
9. Ding D H, Pan Z X, Dominic C, et al. Springer International Publishing, **437-450**, (2015).
10. Park S C, Choi B K. K.: Computer-Aided Design, 17-25, 1 (2000).
11. Tarabanis K A, Rajan V T, Srinivasan V. Rapid Prototyping Journal, **231-241**,5 (2001).
12. Fu J, Gong L, Zhang Y, et al. Applied Sciences, **227**, 3 (2017).

Reform and Practice of Multimedia Technology and Application for Applied Undergraduates

Zhong jiaming[1], Zhu geng[2]

[1]*Xiangnan University, Chenzhou 423000, China*
[2]*School of computer and network security, Dongguan University of technology, Dongguan 523808, China;*

Abstract: According to the characteristics of applied undergraduate talents, this article demonstrates the characteristics of Multimedia Technology and Application course, analyzes the teaching reform of the course in several aspects such as content of the course, practical teaching, teaching methods, assessment and evaluation, and analyzes and discusses the tasks and processes of the course design in detail.

1 Introduction

As Chinese economy has entered into New Normal, the structural contradiction of our higher education is more typical and homogeneity-oriented. In regard to this, the third committee of Ministry of Education has proposed to promote local universities' transformation into developing applied talents, and to improve the economic and social development abilities and innovation-driven development abilities in service area of universities. To develop applied talents, it is important to understand and grasp the characteristics of applied undergraduate talents. They should have a certain degree of depth and width of knowledge and obtain a complete, systematic, scientific and professional knowledge system, which allow them to meet academic standards of undergraduate education according to Higher Education Law of the People's Republic of China. As for ability and quality requirements, high-quality applied talents should not only have certain practical abilities and strong innovation ability, but also have high professional qualities and certain scientific and humanistic qualities [1-3].

2 Characteristics of Multimedia Technology and Application course

Multimedia technology is a new technology and course which is formed by the inter-infiltration and integration of computer technology, communication technology and modern information technology. Today, it has been applied to all aspects of society, economy and science, and as a result, brings tremendous changes to people's life, view and production activities. Therefore, it is significant for modern university students to learn and acquire the basic theories, methods and standards of multimedia technology. Multimedia Technology and Application course is an important general course for popularizing the application of information technology, which aims to improve students' comprehensive abilities on collecting, manufacturing and designing multimedia such as planar static/ dynamic pictures, audios, videos and animations [4]. Based on characteristics of applied undergraduate talents, the teaching of multimedia technology courses should neither be considered as operating media materials with software tools nor pure theories learning, but should make students understand, learn and obtain the basic concepts, theories and methods of multimedia technology, grasp all kinds of medias and media processing technologies, acquire data compression techniques and relevant international standards on multimedia data compression, understand and obtain hardware and software basics of multimedia technology and achieve multimedia information management technology. Finally, through learning the course, students will obtain the basic theories and practical technologies of multimedia technology, hold its development direction as well as be armed with the basic knowledge and abilities to utilize multimedia technology. In detail, contents of the course include: teaching students various multimedia development tools and designing techniques such as PHOTOSHOP planar image design, FLASH animation design, AUTHORWARE dynamic demonstration system, audio recording and processing and PREMIERE video recording and editing; at the same time, enhancing students' various processing abilities of collecting, processing and composing multimedia materials [5]. By improving actual and practical abilities, students will meet businesses' requirements of basic techniques and methods on photo processing and advertising designing and manufacturing, etc. Furthermore, it provides material designing and knowledge supports for multimedia database designing and related application systems developing.

3 Teaching reform and practice of Multimedia Technology and Application course

3.1 Reform of course's contents

Multimedia technology is a comprehensive technology with multi-crossed disciplines, thus, the course aims to let students achieve the skeleton of multimedia technology and comprehensively and systematically introduce the principles and applications of multimedia technology on the basis of new achievement of multimedia technology. It not only focuses on introducing theories, methods and standards, but also gives considerations on discussions of specific techniques and examples of solving practical issues; it not only describes mature theories and techniques, but also introduce the new development of relevant areas of multimedia technology. During teaching the course, it should pay attention to the basic techniques of multimedia, explain various medias and its processing techniques data compression techniques and information management techniques in detail and multimedia's hardware and software techniques in short. There are different requirements of teaching contents and teaching hours for computer major and non-computer major. Students major in computer have higher requirements on theoretical depth and technological innovation while those of non-computer major put more emphasis on application design ability, but different teaching modules can be worked out for options of students from different majors and having different requirements. Adjustment of teaching hours will be determined in accordance with the importance and practicability of the contents of teaching modules, requirements of students, targets of course construction and other factors. Table 1 shows specific arrangements.

Table 1 Arrangements of teaching modules of the course

No.	Teaching modules	Computer major	Non-computer major	Notes of allocation
1	Overview of multimedia technology	12	4	Professional students need deeper theoretical supports.
2	PHOTOSHOP designing	4	10	Non-professional students pay more attention to application designing.
3	FLASH animation designing and programming	12	8	Add code programming for professional students.
4	AUTHORWARE designing	2	6	Non-professional students pay more attention to application designing.
5	Video composition processing	2	4	Limited by experimental conditions

3.2 Reform of practical teaching

Multimedia technology has rich contents which is both strong theoretical and strong practical. In order to deepen students' understanding of the course's knowledge and improve their abilities to solve practical issues, practical teaching should be strengthened. Curriculum Design is an experimental course of the Multimedia Technology and Application course, which mainly develops students' developing and designing abilities of multimedia projects and is an important way to develop applied talents. It needs to utilize various designing methods in theoretical courses to connect different multimedia designing software in series and finally generates a payable video document by multiplayer mode and connecting software developing processes.

Because there needs a lot of work to develop multimedia application system and demonstration system, it is difficult to complete the work by only one person. Thus, it usually be done by a team formed by several people, which is in favor of allowing different students to play more important roles in system development and to adapt to real environment of social software development better. There are often 5 to 8 people in a team. The design topic is chosen by teachers or the team leader according to designing requirement. Each member should have his or her independent design direction and sub-topic. Everyone has different design content so that they can take the opportunity to show their design talents. Topics often include landscape, folk-custom, sports, figures, food, etc. which is in favor of picture collecting, animation manufacturing and lines designing, etc. For example, a team taking "Chinese food on the tip of the tongue" as its topic, each member should design sub-topics with different cuisines such as Hunan Cuisine, Guangdong Cuisine, Beijing Cuisine or other local cuisines. In general, it does not recommend students to design topics like history, politics or religions because it is hard to collect relevant materials and they are sensitive. Design mainly reflects students' abilities of image processing, animation designing and line designing, and the end products should be beautiful images, humous languages or appreciation-deserving animations. Table 2 shows specific division of work for team members.

Table 2 Division of work for Curriculum Design team members

Role	Team leader	Team member	Tester
Task	Choose topics, plan and divide work	Design one's own sub-topic independently	Test images, audios and videos
Requirements	Know the whole process of	Know multimedia design	Test bugs and problems of

 DOI: 10.1051/matecconf/201712805010

	development, have communication ability, be able to solve key technical issues	methods, write files	the design of each other
Number of members	1-2	5-8	5-8

In the process of project design, working out the general idea and unifying the style should be the first step. Team members should collect pictures (with unified size and photographic style) needed by the task from actual environment other than from others on the internet. We emphasize the originality of works and materials. If a student uses more than 30% of pictures of others in his work, the work will be negative or disqualified. By using PHOTOSHOP CS, pictures will be tailored into unified sizes (e.g. 800*600 pixels) as animations require and will be used in follow-up work after finishing PS, deformation and other treatment. With previous processed pictures and designed lines, animations or demonstration systems will be produced by FLASH or AUTHORWARE, i.e. in the form of PS+FLASH or PS+AUTHORWRE, or video systems will be developed by integrating the three. FLASH is recommended to design animation because it provides good effects on lines and motion design though it has bigger technical difficulties. AUTHORWRE is comparatively simple but there exist compatibility issues between AUTHORWRE and other software files. For example, files issued by FLASH should be reduced on version 7.0, or pictures cannot be displayed when it plays in AUTHORWRE. It demands each member to collect no less than 10 pictures of which at least 8 should be PS processed, and animation made by each member should be not less than 20 seconds and the whole team's animation should be not less than 2 minutes. Then, students test video files of each other and put forward the reviews of correction. According to these reviews, students adjust the content or rhythm of videos, then bub their own videos and add them into video files. Works should contain pictures, words and sounds, some of which without sounds will not get high opinions. Each member has independent demonstration file and team leader connect them in series into one file. Team leader or major contributor are responsible for connecting disperse works of each member into a complete and organic animation file in accordance with storyline. And the final work should be an independent file (in form of SWF or EXE) which can be displayed in cross platforms directly.

At last, each member should write at least 4 pages of project documents, i.e. Final Report of Project, or he fails the exam. File writing ability is another important ability except design ability. Software companies have high requirement for files, so students are necessary to obtain the ability. Each member introduces his design idea and procedures and software processing procedure based on his design, and inserts some pictures in the file for comparison. Then, team leader compiles each member's files to a complete and organic file other than simply overlaps them, and adds the introduction of the project and the work distribution chart of each member to the first page of the file, indicating completing work of each member and tips of the major contributor. According to students' videos, files and the work distribution chart, teacher gives every student an individual score, not a score for a team, so that students in a team will get scores of different levels based on their own contribution and completing works.

3.3 Reform of teaching methods

This course combines theory teaching with practice teaching and focuses on heuristic education, which begins with basic concepts, then step by step, highlighting difficult and key points. In particular, it introduces new knowledge and trends of the subject to improve teaching qualities and provide more information. In class, teachers use PPT and general outline of the course, experimental guidance, electronic teaching plan, multimedia courseware and other teaching resources.

Contents of Multimedia Technology and Application course decide it a course with strong operability and practicality. Picture processing, animation design, demonstration system design and other contents can only be completed with related software which is not suitable for traditional paper teaching and exams [6]. Therefore, multimedia online teaching, network experimental environment and online test environment are the necessary hardware and software environment of the course. Online multimedia teaching software and system, online experimental and working platform and online test system are three significant tasks for reform of online teaching. Multimedia classes and labs connect students' dormitory ends and other public ends and teaching material webs through campus LAN to construct a campus online teaching platform, and realize interactive teaching through distance online teaching, broadcasting teaching in computer room and teachers and students' online dialogue and answering questions and so on. In addition, teaching discussion can also be done on EMAIL, QQ, WeChart and other public communication platforms, which construct a good teaching communication environment without any expense [7].

3.4 Reform of assessment and evaluation

Exams of the course includes written exam (close-book exam) and online exam. Final score is composed of three parts: daily performance score (30%), online exam score (30%) and final exam score (40%). Daily performance score includes: attendance, assignments, quizzes, online work, etc. Close-book exam mainly evaluates students' understanding of basic concepts, theories and methods and operating status of relevant software. Online exam mainly evaluates actual application of software. Assignments and experimental designs are main ways of practice for students, and electronic file is the main form. Traditional paper work has not met requirements of the course, and paper-free and electronic solution is its trends. Today, multimedia material processing and design demands experimental platforms to provide PHOTOSHOP CS4-6,

FLASH CS4, AUTHORWARE 7.02 and other multimedia design software, and offer video design cases for students' reference and imitation. Based on the purpose of teaching experiment, it provides corresponding design software and basic multimedia materials, and asks students to learn necessary operating methods and make multimedia design documents and works which meet the experimental requirements through software and material processing. Students should be good at operating software, process materials fast and make appreciation-deserving design works. High requirements for practical and design ability make students devote enough time to the course, or their works cannot be perfect and they fail exams.

In order to avoid simplification of exams and standardization of answers, environment and contents of exams also need to be reformed. Except that some questions of basic theory have the same answers, other design questions demand students give different solutions by playing their own individuality. Students should add their personal information such as names to image processing and animation design, which permits students to cheat by copying files and avoids design files being destroyed by virus from U Disk at the same time. Exams are held through campus LAN and test documents are issued on online platform. The same or different computer rooms can issue different exam paper. Students submit exam documents to network server through network terminals. After that, students' exam documents on terminals are deleted automatically which does not affect follow-up exams.

4 Summary

Multimedia Technology and Application is an important compulsory course. As a key component of practical teaching, Course Design is in favor of developing students' practical ability and innovation ability. Research on teaching practice for many years indicates that the closer topics of Course Design to the requirements of multimedia technology from society, the more motivation students have. Teaching has a pressing need to improve students' social adaptive capability and tris hard to cultivate applied talents of multimedia design that society needs [8] .

Acknowledgements

This study is supported by Hunan science and technology program(NO:2014SK3229), 2013 Hunan province ordinary university teaching reform project (xiangjiangtong[2013]NO:223)(based on cyberspace "management information system" inquiry teaching research and practice),China, "Educational Reform and Research Project in 2015" (1E150534) of Dongguan University of Technology.

References

1. Q.H. Shi, A.P. Wang Aiping, Educational Development Research, pp34-37, 21(2008)
2. G.Y. Qian, G. Wang, L.Q. Xu, China University Teaching, pp54-56, 9(2005)
3. S.Q. Sun, Y.A.Gu, Modern Education Management, pp72-75, 9(2012)
4. Y.X. Mao, Z.Z. Cang Zhizhi, Multimedia Technology and Application, pp12-25, (Beijing: The People's Posts and Telecommunications Press, 2011)
5. Y.Z. Zhong, Fundamentals and Applications of Multimedia Computer Technology, pp12-25, (Beijing: Higher Education Press, 2012)
6. B. Zhou, Journal of XiangNan University, pp82-85, 2(2016)
7. X. Huang, Computer Knowledge and Technology, pp5522-5523, 24,(2013)
8. B.H. Xue, Journal of Xiangnan University, pp116-120, 4(2016)

Recognition of Aircraft Engine Sound Based on GMM-UBM Model

Shuai Yuan[1], Chengli Sun [2,*], Haoge Yang [2]

[1]*Science and Technology on Avionics Integration Laboratory,Shanghai, China*
[2]*Information School, Hangkong University, Nanchang, China*
[*]*Corresponding author*

Abstract—Gaussian mixture model-universal background model (GMM-UBM) is a commonly-used speaker recognition technology, and which has achieved good effect for detection speaker's sound. In this paper, we explore GMM-UBM method for use with abnormal aircraft engine sound detection. We designed a GMM-UBM based aircraft engine sound recognition system, which extracts MFCC feature parameters and trains the GMM-UBM models using maximum a posteriori (MAP) adaptive algorithm. Experimental results show the GMM-UBM based aircraft engine sound recognition system can achieve higher recognize rate in real-word aircraft engine sound test.
Keywords: Speaker Recognition; GMM-UBM; MFCC; Abnormal sound detection; MAP

1 Introduction

In daily life conditions, we often need to recognize many kinds of environmental sound. Sound recognition technology has been successfully used in the bio-medicine, agriculture, public security, astronomy and many other fields. Sound recognition also plays important role in Aircraft field. Aircraft engine sound signal contains a lot of important information, which makes the aircraft engine sound signal recognition being a very important tool for engine status diagnosis [1-2].

There are many research works are conducted in sound recognition community. Harma.M proposed an audio monitoring system using in the office environment [3]. They combine the tone and spectrum centroid features to detect the events occurred in the office. In [4], an audio classification system for detecting crime in the elevator is reported. Their system uses GMM models to classify and identify alarm sounds events. In literature [5], Ntalampiras et al. use mel- frequency cepstrum coefficient (MFCC), MPEG-7, and CB-TEO feature to detect dangerous sound events occurred in subway station. In [6], Cheng Qingyun employs GMM method to identify two kinds of abnormal sounds in office environment. In [7], Zhou proposed to construct feature set including MFCC and logarithmic domain subband energy. They use Adboost algorithm to select effective features to detect conference room sound event. In [8, 9], the researchers developed an audio monitoring system that uses MFCC and short-term energy as sound event characteristics. GMMs were used as recognition models to detect abnormal sound events in the elevator environment. Theoretically, the engine sound signal recognition are the same as the speech recognition, therefore the speech recognition technology can be explored for aircraft engine sound recognition. However, as aircraft engine sound acquisition is difficult, few aircraft engine sound processing research literatures are reported until now.

In this paper, a GMM-UBM based model is used to identify the engine sound, we use MFCC as sound features, and GMM-UBM models is trained by MAP optimization algorithm. The system can effectively recognize abnormal engine sound only require few data.

2 Engine Sound Recognition System Based on GMM-UBM

2.1 Universal Background Model

GMM-UBM is a high order GMM, it can reduce the variation of speaker utterance differences [10]. GMM is a linear weighted combination of a certain number of Gaussian probability density functions. The M-order Gaussian mixture model GMM uses the linear combination of M single Gaussian distributions to describe the distribution of frame features in the feature space:

$$p(x \mid \lambda) = \sum_{i=1}^{M} w_i b_i(x), \quad (1)$$

where X is a D-dimensional eigenvector, w_i is the weight for each Gaussian density function which should satisfy the following condition:

$$\sum_{i=1}^{M} w_i = 1. \quad (2)$$

The Gaussian distribution function $b_i(x)$, can be expressed as:

$$b_i(x) = \frac{1}{(2\pi)^{D/2}|\Sigma_i|^{1/2}} \exp\{-\frac{1}{2}(x-\mu)'\Sigma_i^{-1}(x-\mu)\}, \quad (3)$$

where μ is the mean vector and Σ is the covariance matrix. Thus, a complete Gaussian mixture model can be expressed as

$$\lambda = \{w_i, \mu_i, \Sigma_i\}_{i=1,2,\cdots m}. \quad (4)$$

GMM learning generally use the classic EM (Expectation-maximization) algorithm. According to the maximum likelihood estimation criterion, the likelihood of GMM model can be expressed as:

$$\log p(x|\lambda) = \sum_{t=1}^{T} \log p(x_t|\lambda) \quad (5)$$

According to EM algorithm, the weight, mean and variance of the *i*-th GMM model can be calculated by

$$w_i' = \frac{1}{n}\sum_j^n p(i|x_j,\lambda) \quad (6)$$

$$\mu_i' = \frac{\sum_j^n x_j p(i|x_j,\lambda)}{\sum_j^n p(i|x_j,\lambda)} \quad (7)$$

$$\sigma_i' = \frac{\sum_j^n (x_j-\mu_i')^2 p(i|x_j,\lambda)}{\sum_j^n p(i|x_j,\lambda)}. \quad (8)$$

The posterior probability of the i-th GMM model is

$$p(i|x_j,\lambda) = \frac{w_i p_i(x_t|\lambda_i)}{\sum_k^M w_k p_k(x_t|\lambda_k)}. \quad (9)$$

Speaker adaptation schemes should ideally be effective for small amounts of speaker-specific adaptation data and converge to a true speaker dependent estimate when a large amount of data is available. Most GMM-based speaker recognition systems are trained using maximum a posteriori (MAP) estimation [11].

For a particular Gaussian mean, with prior mean μ_0, the estimate is

$$\mu' = \frac{\tau\mu_0 + \sum_{t=1}^T \gamma(t)o_t}{\tau + \sum_{t=1}^T \gamma(t)}, \quad (10)$$

where τ is a meta-parameter which gives the bias between the ML estimate of the mean from the data, and the prior mean o_t is the adaptation vector at time *t* from a *T* length set and $\gamma(t)$ is the probability of this Gaussian at time t. Usually, values of τ is often set between two and twenty.

Speaker recognition technology can be transferred into a sound recognition problem, so the sound recognition can be built based on GMM [12-19]. For a given sound feature vector $\{X_t\}$, t=1,2,..., T, assuming we have K classes of aircraft engine sound which is different from each other, the purpose of sound recognition is to find the class of sound k, whose corresponding GMM model k obtain the largest posterior probability P(k/X).

2.2 Engine sound recognition system architecture

Figure 1 shows the GMM-UBM based aircraft engine sound recognition system. In the training phase, after pre-process the engine sound data, we extract the MFCC feature of the engine sound. Then the UBM model is trained via EM learning algorithm. Finally, each individual GMM model is obtained using MAP of the UBM with the aircraft engine sound data. In the recognition phase, the matched likelihood is calculated used the variation between the output scores of GMM and UBM

$$S = \frac{1}{T}\sum_{t=1}^{T}[\log p_i(X_t|\lambda_{TAR}) - p_i(X_t|\lambda_{UBM})], \quad (11)$$

where X_t is the eigenvector of a certain frame of audio to be recognized, λ_{TAR} and λ_{UBM} represent the target sound model and the UBM model, respectively.

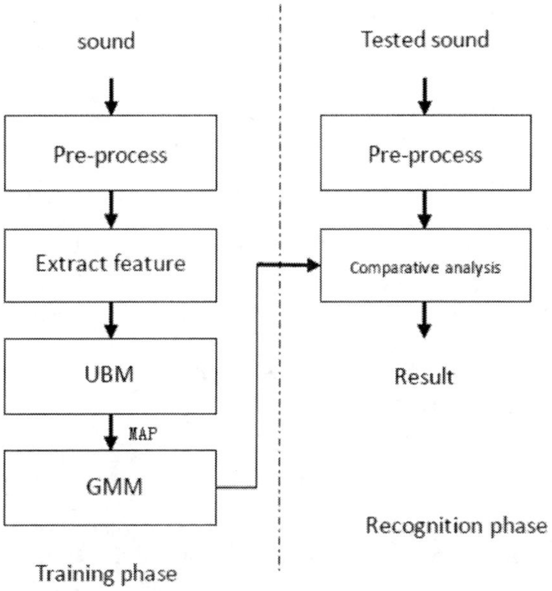

Figure 1. GMM-UBM based aircraft engine sound recognition system.

3 Experimental results and analysis

The aircraft engine sound database used for experiments contains a number of aircraft engine sounds from Civil Aviation Boeing 727 and Military Fighter F-15. In the training phase, we selected 61 engine audio for UBM training, including 12 start-up audio, 8 stop audio, 30 normal operation audio and 11 crash audio, the total length of the sound is 388s. the test sound are 6 start-up, 6 stop, 29 normal and 11 crash audio clips. MAP is made using 332s length audio. In the test phase, the test engine sound include engine start sound, stop sound, run sound and some engine crash sound. The total length of the engine sound used in the experiment is 1474s, containing of engine starting sound 347s, stop sound 205s, the normal operation sound 629s, and crash sound 293s. All the sound data sampling frequency is 16 KHz, monaural recording, 16bit format. The sound features are MFCC coefficients. Recognition rate is used for evaluation the performance of sound recognition system.

$$\text{recognition rate}=\frac{\text{number of right}}{\text{total number of samples}}\times 100\%$$

3.1 The effect of mixture number on performance

Firstly, we compare the effect of different mixture component on the recognition performance. We use the 12 dimensional MFCC characteristic parameters. It can be seen from the experimental results that the best average recognition is achieved when the mixture number is 256. when increase the number of mixture components, the recognition rate is also increases, but when the mixture number increase to a certain value, the recognition rate no longer increases.

Table 1. Recognition performance with the increase of mixture number

	Recognition rate					
Mixedness	8	16	32	64	128	256
Start-up	0.333	0.500	0.500	0.666	0.666	0.666
Stop	0.666	0.666	0.666	0.833	0.833	0.833
Normal	0.896	0.965	0.965	1.000	1.000	0.862
Crash	0.636	0.727	1.000	1.000	1.000	1.000

3.2 The effect of different MFCC coefficients on performance

Standard MFCC coefficient only represent static coefficient feature. In this experiment, we will evaluate the combination of standard and dynamic MFCC feature. Let ΔMFCC be the first-order differential coefficient, and ΔΔMFCC be the second-order differential coefficient. ΔMFCC and ΔΔMFCC reflect the dynamic characteristics. It can be seen from Table 2 that the recognition rate of theΔΔMFCC and ΔMFCC can significantly improve recognition performance of the start-up sound, which is due to the dynamic characteristics of the start-up sound. In the experiments, we can see that HMFCC (the combination of static and dynamic coefficients) can improve system performance. For the normal and crash sounds, the HMFCC feature can obtain the 100% recognition rate.

	Recognition rate				
Feature	MFCC	ΔMFCC	ΔΔMFCC	MFCC-ΔMFCC	HMFCC
Start-up	0.333	0.333	0.500	0.500	0.666
Stop	0.500	0.500	0.500	0.666	0.833
Normal	0.311	0.172	0.276	0.965	1.000
Crash	0.166	0.273	0.273	0.818	1.000

From above experiments we can see that increase the number of mixture components, recognition rate can improve as well, but when it reaches a certain value, the recognition rate began to decline. This is because the GMM model is a generative mode which relies on the amount of training data. The higher the mixture order is, the more complex the model will be. The amount of data in this experiment is relatively small. If the mixture number increases too much, it will result in excessive fitting problem and the GMM model performance become deteriorate.

4 Conclusion

In this paper, a GMM-UBM based aircraft engine sound recognition system is presented. This system can work well in little limited data case. Experimental results show that the recognition system with the combination of dynamic and static MFCC features could achieve higher recognition rate. In future research work, we will investigate incorporating more prior knowledge about the aircraft engine sound into the framework, such as the sound continuity property, sound duration property, to further improve the robustness and accuracy for the proposed system. We also interest in applying DNN (Deep Neural Networks) for aircraft engine sound recognition.

Acknowledgment

This work was supported by China's Aviation Science fund (No. 20145556011).

References

1. Chenlei. Sound Recognition Technology for Helicopter Using Vector Quantization [D]. Shandong Univerdity.2014.
2. Leida. Study on Prediction of Health Status of Civil Aviation Engine Based on Intelligent Learning Model[D]. Harbin Institute of Technology.2013.
3. Harma E, McKinney F, Skowronek J.Automatic Surveillance of the Acoustic activity in our Living Environment.Proc.IEEE Internation Conference on Multimedia and Expo.DigitalSignaoProcess.Netherlands,2005,152-152.
4. Radhakrishnan R,Divakaran A.Systematic Acquisition of Audio Classes for Elevator Surveillance.SPIE Image and Video Communications and Processing.San Jose,CA,USA,2005,64-17.
5. Ntalampiras S, Potamitis I, Fakotakis N. An Adaptive Framework for Acoustic Monitoring of Potential

Hazards. EURASIP Journal on Audio, Speech, and Music Processing.2009. 2: 1-15
6. Qingyun Cheng. Research on Two Kinds of Abnormal Sound Recognition in Office Environment Based on GMM[D]. Anhui University.2016.
7. Zhou X, Zhuang X, Liu M, Tang H, Hasegawa-Johnson M, HMM-based Acoustic Event Detection with AdaBoost Feature Selection. Lecture Notes in Computer Science. 2008. 4625: 345-353.
8. Jianjie Ye. Design and Implementation of Supervised and Staged Abnormal Sound Detection System[D]. South China University of Technology.2014.
9. Xiaoyun LV, Hongxia Wang. Research on Abnormal Audio Recognition Algorithm Based on MFCC and GMM [D]. Southwest Jiaotong University.2010.
10. Bingxi wang, Qudan, Pengxuan. Practical Fundamentals of Speech Recognition[M]. Beijing:National Defense Industry Press,2005.1.
11. Zhengping Zhang. Research on Continuous Adaptive Algorithm Based on GMM-UBM Speaker Model[J]. Communication Power Technology,2016.33(2).
12. Akinori Ito,Akihito Aiba.Dectetion of Abnormal Sound Using Multi-stage GMM for Surveillance Microphone.International Conference on Information Assurance and Security.2009.
13. Ntalampiras S, Potamitis I, Fakotakis N. An Adaptive Framework for Acoustic Monitoring of Potential Hazards. EURASIP Journal on Audio, Speech, and Music Processing.2009. 2: 1-15.
14. S Bou-Ghazale, J H L Hansen.A comparative study of Traditional and Newly Proposed Feature for Recognition of Speech under Stress[J].IEEE Trans on Speech and Audio Processing,2000;8(4):429-442.
15. J H L Hansen,M A Clements.Source Generator Equalization and Enhancement of Spectral Properties for Robust Speech Recognition in Noise and Stress[J]. IEEE Trans on Speech and Audio Processing,1995;3(5):407-415.
16. B D Womack,J H L Hansen.N-Channel Hidden Markove Models for Combined Stressed Speech Classification and Recognition[J].IEEE Trans on Speech and Audio Processing,1999;7 (6):668-677.
17. P. kenny, G. Boulianne, P. Ouellet,and P. Dumouchel. Joint factor analysis versus eigenchannels in speaker recognition[J]. IEEE Trans on Speech and Audio Processing.2007;15 (4):1435-1447.
18. T. Hasan, John H. L. Hansen. A study on Universal Background Model training in Speaker Verification[J]. IEEE Trans. Audio Speech Lang. Process. September 2011, Vol. 19, 7, pp. 1890 – 1899.
19. C J Leggetter, P C Woodland. Maximum Likelihood Linear Regression for Speaker Adaptation of Continuous Density Hidden Markov Model[J]. Computer Speech and Language,1995

An Innovative Cellular Automata Technique for Mapping Cracking Pattern of Airport Pavement

Fucheng Yin[1], Guangchun Zhou[2], Edward Guo[3], Shuang Zhang[1, a]

[1]*Data Recovery Key Laboratory of Sichuan Province, Neijiang Normal University, Neijiang 641100, Sichuan, P.R. China;*
[2]*School of Civil Engineering, Harbin Institute of Technology, China, 150090;*
[3]*America, RSA, Atlantic City, 08405*

Abstract. In this study, an innovative cellular automata (CA) technique was proposed for mapping cracking pattern of the airport pavement. The CA technique was developed to establish a numerical model describing the effect of boundary condition of pavement on zones (CA cells) within the pavement. A state function was used to describe the state values in the cells within the CA lattice. The correction coefficient principle is used as the criterion of zone similarity and the corresponding technique is proposed to find similar zones within and between pavements. Three pavement models, HRS, MRS and LRS, tested in FAA, USA, are set as the base pavements to map the cracking patterns of pavements with different sizes from the base pavements. The mapped cracking patterns of unseen pavements are empirically verified by referring to the relative experimental models.

1 Introduction

In the current research, three issues on structural engineering have been raised:

The first one is about the existing conventional analytical methods. In some cases, for example, for masonry and reinforced concrete as well as other complex and composite structures, an accurate prediction of structural response/behavior could not be achieved as long as global parameters of structural properties are used; besides, these structures have obvious variation in physics and configuration properties, which is generally treated as random factor. However, is the variation really totally random? In other words, is there any determinative content included in the random factor? If yes, how do we extract and model it?

The second one is about the existing experiment or test. As is well-known, no experiment is perfect, because the experimental error corresponding to the real situation is unavoidable. The problem is that these experimental data with error have not been fully used in the current analytical methods and design codes. Besides, these experimental data certainly include some useful information which is not discovered at present.

The third one is that artificial intelligence (AI) techniques are more and more applied to the civil engineering. These AI techniques such as neural networks, cellular automata, genetic algorithm and support vector can deal with highly non-linear and multi-parameter engineering problems efficiently. The question is, to what extent can AI techniques be better than traditional analytical techniques to use experimental data or to make analytical techniques closer to the real situation?

This study involves in the first and third issues related to airport pavements. The developed CA technique for mapping the cracking pattern of the pavement is based on two concepts(stiffness corrector and zone similarity) and two criteria (the criterion for matching similar zones within and between pavements and the criterion for mapping/compositing the cracking pattern of a pavement based on the tested cracking pattern of the pavement). Thus, it realizes a CA modeling method as well as the corresponding technique for directly mapping the cracking pattern of pavement from the tested results.

2 The CA Technique for Mapping Cracking Pattern of Pavement

The CA technique for mapping cracking pattern of pavement is based on the concept of zone similarity which actually came from a tested data mining [Zhou, 2003]. From the curves of ratios between the tested and FEA displacements at various measured points on the wall panel, it was found that these ratios approach to their individual stable values after the load reaches a certain level. Hence, these stable ratios were defined as the stiffness/strength correctors because they could be used to modify the global parameters of structural properties, such as the elastic modulus, so as to improve the FEA accuracy of the wall panels. Furthermore, from the contour plots of the correctors, it was found that the corrector distribution patterns in some zones are similar. It was conceptually verified that this zone similarity is

[a] Corresponding author: zhangshuanghua1@126.com

related to similar boundary types and similar locations of zones. Thus, the concept of zone similarity and the criterion for matching similar zones within and between wall panels was proposed; the details can be found in References [1] and [2].

Cellular Automata is an artificial intelligent technique based on a discrete space-time lattice, introduced by von Neumann (1966). There are four parts in a CA model: the physical environment, the state of a cell, the neighborhoods of a cell and a local transition rule (Sarkar, 2000; Maerivoet and Moor, 2005). Fig. 1 shows two common CA models, the von Neumann model and the Moore model, and they have four and eight neighborhoods for a cell, respectively. These two models have been applied to model airport pavements as follows.

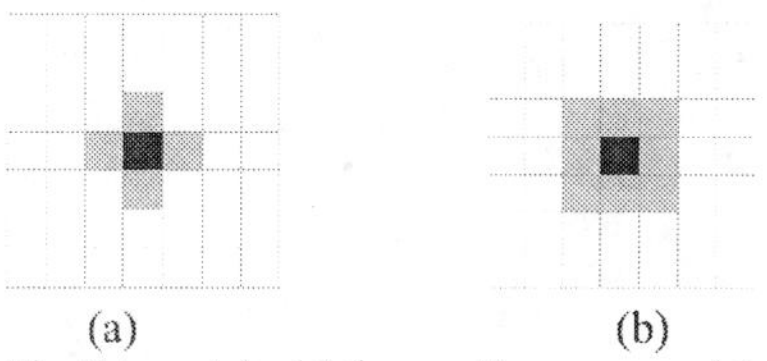

(a) (b)

Fig. 1. The CA models: (a) the von Neumann model; (b) the Moore model

Fig. 1 is also used to represent the CA model of a pavement, in which a cell indicates a zone. For the state values of individual zones within a pavement, they can be calculated by Eq. (1) of the von Neumann model or Eq. (2) of the Moore model (Zhou, G. C. et al, 2002). The transition functions in Eq. (1) and Eq. (2) propagate the boundary effect into individual zones within the wallet.

$$\begin{aligned}
L_{i,j} &= L_{i,j-1} + \eta\left(1 - L_{i,j-1}\right) && (i = 1,2,\mathrm{L}\ ,M; j = 1,2,\mathrm{L}\ ,N)\\
R_{i,j} &= R_{i,j+1} + \eta\left(1 - R_{i,j+1}\right) && (i = 1,2,\mathrm{L}\ ,M; j = N,N-1,\mathrm{L}\ ,1)\\
B_{i,j} &= B_{i-1,j} + \eta\left(1 - B_{i-1,j}\right) && (i = M,M-1,\mathrm{L}\ ,1; j = 1,2,\mathrm{L}\ ,N)\\
T_{i,j} &= T_{i+1,j} + \eta\left(1 - T_{i+1,j}\right) && (i = M,M-1,\mathrm{L}\ ,1; j = N,N-1,\mathrm{L}\ ,1)
\end{aligned} \tag{1}$$

$$\begin{aligned}
LT_{i,j} &= LT_{i-1,j-1} + \eta\left(1 - LT_{i-1,j-1}\right) && (i = 1,2,\mathrm{L}\ ,M; j = 1,2,\mathrm{L}\ ,N)\\
RT_{i,j} &= RT_{i-1,j+1} + \eta\left(1 - RT_{i-1,j+1}\right) && (i = 1,2,\mathrm{L}\ ,M; j = N,N-1,\mathrm{L}\ ,1)\\
LB_{i,j} &= LB_{i+1,j-1} + \eta\left(1 - LB_{i+1,j-1}\right) && (i = M,M-1,\mathrm{L}\ ,1; j = 1,2,\mathrm{L}\ ,N)\\
RB_{i,j} &= RB_{i+1,j+1} + \eta\left(1 - RB_{i+1,j+1}\right) && (i = M,M-1,\mathrm{L}\ ,1; j = N,N-1,\mathrm{L}\ ,1)
\end{aligned} \tag{2}$$

where

$L_{i,j}$, $R_{i,j}$, $B_{i,j}$, $T_{i,j}$, $LT_{i,j}$, $RT_{i,j}$, $LB_{i,j}$ and $RB_{i,j}$ are the state values of a zone (i, j) on the wallet calculated by the transition functions, which indicate the effect of the left, right, bottom, top, top-left, top-right, bottom-left and bottom-right boundaries on the zone respectively;

$L_{i,0}$, $R_{i,N+1}$, $B_{0,j}$, $T_{M+1,j}$, $LT_{M+1,0}$, $RT_{M+1,N+1}$, $LB_{0,0}$, and $RB_{0,N+1}$ are the input initial values for the transition functions in Eq. (1) and Eq. (2); they are the load types defined as follows: 0.0 for a free edge, 0.2 for a simply supported edge and 0.4 a fixed edge;

η is the transition coefficient which is equal to 0.2;

M and N are the numbers of rows and columns of divided zones, respectively.

The state value $S_{i,j}$ of each cell is closely related to its four or eight adjacent cells and defined as the average effect from its four or eight neighborhoods, which is shown in Eq. (3) and Eq.(4).

$$S_{i,j} = \frac{L_{i,j} + R_{i,j} + B_{i,j} + T_{i,j}}{4} \qquad (i = 1,2\mathrm{L}\ ,M; j = 1,2,\mathrm{L}\ ,N) \tag{3}$$

$$S_{i,j} = \frac{L_{i,j} + R_{i,j} + B_{i,j} + T_{i,j} + LT_{i,j} + RT_{i,j} + LB_{i,j} + RB_{i,j}}{8} \qquad (i = 1,2\mathrm{L}\ ,M; j = 1,2,\mathrm{L}\ ,N) \tag{4}$$

The past research results (Zhou, 2003) indicate that the cracking pattern/mode of wall panel is governed by the configuration of the structure, that is to say, the cracking mode of wall panel is closely related to the resulting effect of its boundary types and dimension. This just satisfies the CA function which can propagates the boundary constraint effect into individual zones within the wall panel. Therefore, a CA transition function and the corresponding formula are used to express the state of a zone. This state value reflects the effect of the boundaries and zone locations on the zone. In other words, this state value quantifies the effect of the structural configuration on the zone. Hence, a cellular automata technique for automatically and mechanically matching similar zones was developed. This CA criterion for matching similar zones needs to calculate 8 difference values corresponding to 8 different orientations of two zones with their neighborhoods, as shown in Fig. 2. Then the minimum one in the eight difference values is determined as a so-called ratio between two zones. Similarly, N so-called ratios are obtained for a zone on a panel to N zones divided on the other panel. Again, the minimum one in these N so-called ratios is determined. Finally, two zones corresponding to the minimum value among N values are defined as similar zones.

Correction coefficient, which ranges from -1 to 1, is an index about the corrective degree between two variables. The closer the correction coefficient approaches to 1, the better the linear relationship between the two variables is. Accordingly we can estimate the

DOI: 10.1051/matecconf/201712805012

zone similarity between the new plate and the base plate by calculating the correction coefficients of corresponding zones in the two plates. In order to estimate the zone similarity between the new plate and the base plate, we use the Moore neighborhood model, which is expressed as follows:

$$\overline{S}_{i,j}^{new} = \frac{1}{9}\sum_{u=-1}^{1}\sum_{v=-1}^{1} S_{i+u,j+v}^{new} \quad (1)$$

$$\overline{S}_{m,n}^{base} = \frac{1}{9}\sum_{u=-1}^{1}\sum_{v=-1}^{1} S_{m+u,n+v}^{base} \quad (2)$$

$$E_{i,j\to new}^{m,n\to base} = \underset{m=1,n=1}{\overset{M,N}{MAX}} \frac{\sum_{u=-1}^{1}\sum_{v=-1}^{1}(S_{i+u,j+v}^{new}-\overline{S}_{i,j}^{new})(S_{m+u,n+v}^{base}-\overline{S}_{m,n}^{base})}{\sqrt{\sum_{u=-1}^{1}\sum_{v=-1}^{1}(S_{i+u,j+v}^{new}-\overline{S}_{i,j}^{new})^2}\sqrt{\sum_{u=-1}^{1}\sum_{v=-1}^{1}(S_{m+u,n+v}^{base}-\overline{S}_{m,n}^{base})^2}} \quad (3)$$

Where $E_{i,j\to new}^{m,n\to base}$ is the maximum correction coefficients of corresponding zones in the new plate and the base plate; i , j are zone position in the new plate, respectively; m , n are zone position in the base plate, respectively; $S_{m,n}^{base}$ is state values of the base plate; $\overline{S}_{i,j}^{new}$ is average state value of any zone and all its neighborhood zones in the new plate; $\overline{S}_{m,n}^{base}$ is the average state value of any zone and all its neighborhood zones in the base plate.

We can get the maximum correction coefficients of corresponding zones in the new plate and the base plate from Eq. (3-3) – Eq. (3-5); then the zone (m , n) in the base plate can be defined as the similar zone of the zone (i , j) in the new plate.

Once similar zones are matched, the rule for identifying the cracking zones within the pavement can be proposed as follows: if two zones are similar zones under the same loading, these two zones have the same behavior, in other words, if a zone is cracked, then, its similar zone is also cracked.

By summarizing all the results above, a CA technique for mapping the cracking pattern of the pavement can be formed as shown in Fig. 4: the first step is to use the proposed CA modeling method, mesh both unseen and the tested pavements to get their CA lattices, and then the cracking pattern of the tested pavement is projected to its CA lattice; the second step is to use the CA rule for matching similar zones and match similar zones between the two pavements; the third step is to use the rule for identifying cracking zones to map the cracking pattern of the unseen pavement.

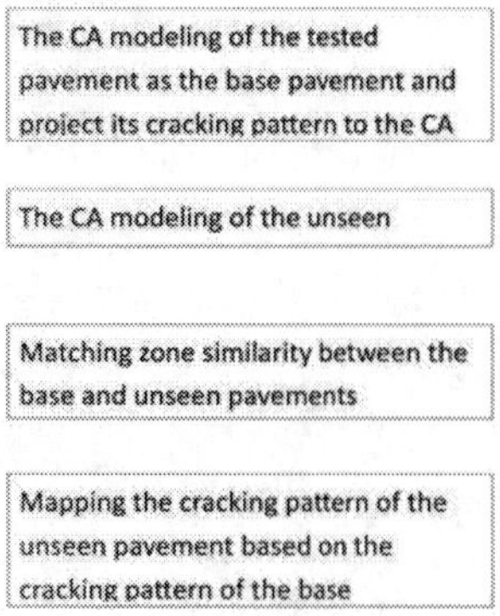

Fig. 4. Procedure of CA technique for mapping cracking pattern of pavement

3 Case Study on Mapping Cracking Pattern of Pavement

In the following some examples of concrete pavements are presented to validate the CA technique proposed in this study. Three examples are the pavements tested in NAPTF, FAA ().

Example: The pavement HRS is taken as the base pavement to map the cracking patterns of a smaller and a larger unseen pavements. Similarly, the smaller and larger pavements are all the same with the base pavement except for their lengths and widths. The mapped results are shown in Fig. 7.

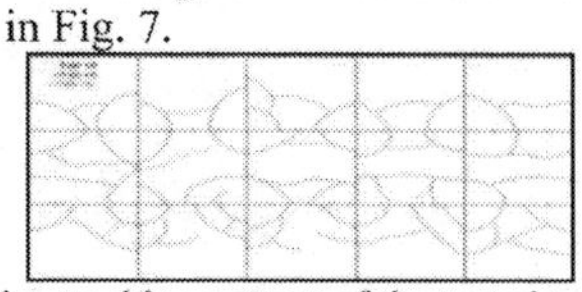

Fig. 5 The cracking pattern of the tested pavement

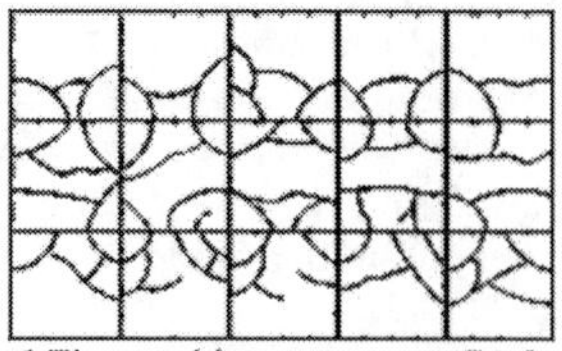

Fig. 6 The cracking pattern on CA lattice

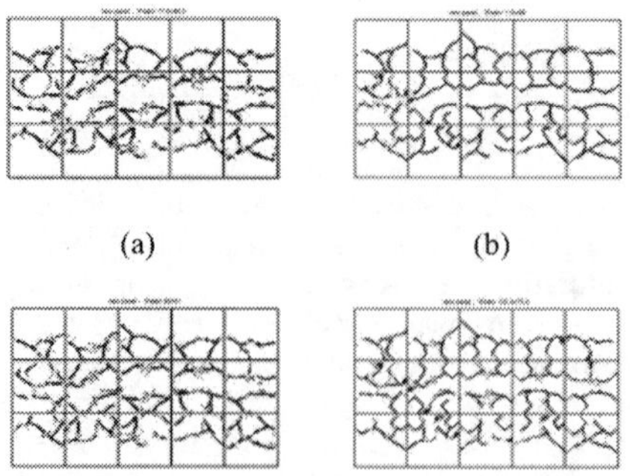

(a) (b)

(b) (d)

Fig. 7 The mapped cracking patterns of two unseen pavements from Pavement HRS

(a) The CA technique needs further improvement because we do not know how accurately it reflects real performance of pavements.(b)The thickness needs further modeling in the CA numerical mode of pavement.(c)The configuration of pavement needs further modeling in the CA numerical mode of pavement.

The six examples show that two new concepts, two rules, one CA modeling method and one CA technique for mapping the cracking pattern of the structure are valid.

Because all these contents are quite new, they certainly have some problems to be further studied, as shown on the screen. But the results achieved in this study are significant, I think.

First the CA technique we have developed can save research funds; in my study on masonry wall panels, at least 40% fund could have been saved if the CA technique had been used.

Second, the CA technique can obtain more knowledge and comprehension on the problems from the test data.

Third, the CA technique can be directly used by design engineers besides researchers.

4 Conclusions

The proposed CA technique for mapping cracking pattern of pavement 1.Provides a new way in which the failure/cracking pattern of a pavement is directly "predicted", only based on the failure/cracking pattern of the base pavement.2.Could considerably save research fund for test, because a few typical tested pavements could be used to produce the "test results" of unseen pavements.3.Explores the new application of the existing experimental data of full-scale structural models.4.The pattern matching techniques using cellular automata, developed in this study, can replace the conventional finite element analysis and are capable of predicting the failure patterns of laterally-loaded masonry wall panels with various boundary conditions.5.The boundary condition and the variation in masonry properties at various locations within the panel, as discussed in the authors' previous publications, play a key role in determining the failure patterns of laterally-loaded masonry panels. 6.The CA technique introduced in this paper can be used as reference for analysis and design of masonry panels more confidently.7.Techniques developed in this paper can be used as an artificial experimental environment replacing some of the physical tests for masonry panels, which could be very expensive.

Acknowledgments

This work presented in this paper is supported by The Sichuan Province Department of Science and Technology under Grant 14ZA0243; The authors would like to thank Harbin Institute of Technology, China, the FAA and the SRA, USA, for their supports to this project. This research has been supported financially by the Yoh Foundation, USA.

References

1. Anthony, T.C., Goh et al. (1995). "Estimation of lateral wall movements in braced excavations using neural networks." Can. Geotech. J., 32, 1059-1064
2. Arslan, A., and Ince, R. (1996). "Neural network-based design of edge-supported reinforced concrete slabs." Structural Engineering Review, 8(4), 329-335
3. Ashraf, M., Elazouni et al. (1997). "Estimating resource requirements at conceptual stage using neural networks." Journal of Computing in Civil Engineering, 11(4)
4. Chen, S., and Shan, K. (1992). ''Neural networks in dynamic analysis of bridges.'' Proc., 8th Annual Conference of Computing in Civil Engineering, ASCE, 1058–1065
5. Drysdale, R.G., and Hamid, A.A. (1984). "Tension failure criteria for plain concrete masonry." Journal of Structural Engineering, ASCE, 110(2), 228-244
6. Flood, I. and Kartam N. (1994). "Neural networks in civil engineering. I: Principles and understanding. II: Systems and application". Journal of Computing in Civil Engineering, 8(2)
7. Garrett, J.H., Jr., Ghaboussi, J., Wu, X., and Ranjithan, S. (1992). ''Neural networks and their application to civil engineering.'' Expert systems in civil engineering-Knowledge representation, R. H. Allen, ed., Expert Systems Committee of ASCE, New York
8. Ghaboussi, J., Garrett, J.H., Jr., and Wu, X. (1991). ''Knowledge-based modeling of material behavior with neural networks.'' J. Eng. Mech., 117(1), 132-153
9. Haykin, S. (1994). "Neural networks: a comprehensive foundation." New York, Macmillan
10. Hsu, D.S., Yeh, I.C., and Lian, W.T. (1993). ''Artificial neural damage detection of existing structure.'' Proc., 3rd ROC and Japan Seminar on Natural Hazards Mitigation, Tainan, 423-436
11. Larry, M. et al. (1997). "Finite-element mesh generation using self-organizing neural networks." Microcomputers in Civil Engineering, 12, 233-250
12. Liu, L.P., Tang, D.X., and Zhai, X.M. (2006). "Failure criteria for grouted concrete block masonry under biaxial compression." Advances in Structural Engineering, 9(2), 229-239
13. Mathew, A., Kumar, B., Sinha, B.P., and Pedreschi, R.F. (1999). "Analysis of masonry panel under biaxial bending using ANNs and CBR." Journal of Computing in Civil Engineering, 170-177
14. Mukherjee, A. et al. (1996). "Prediction of buckling load of columns using artificial neural networks." Journal of Structural Engineering, 122(11)
15. Rafiq, M.Y., Bugmann, G., and Easterbrook, D.J. (1998). "Artificial neural networks for modelling some of the activities of the conceptual stage of the design process." ASCE Computing Congress, 1998
16. Sarkar, P. (2000). "A brief history of cellular automata." ACM Comput. Surveys, 32(1), 80-107
17. Smith, M. (1994). "Neural networks for statistical modeling." Van Nostrand Reinhold, NY, 235
18. Maerivoet, S., and Moor, B.D. (2005). "Cellular automata models of road traffic." Physics Reports, 419, 1-64

19. Tsai, C.H., and Hsu, D.S. (1997). ''Reinforced concrete structural damage diagnosis by using artificial neural network.'' Proc., Intelligent Information System, IEEE Computer Society, Los Alamitos, Calif., 149-155
20. Tsai, C.H., and Hsu, D.S. (2002). "Diagnosis of reinforced concrete structural damage base on displacement time history using the back-propagation neural network technique." Journal of Computing in Civil Engineering, 16(1), 49-58
21. Von Neumann, J. (1966). Theory of Self Reproducing Automata, Burks, A., ed., University of Illinois Press, Champaign, Ill. 305-317
22. Zhou, G.C. (2002). "Application of stiffness/strength corrector and cellular automata in predicting response of laterally loaded masonry panels." Ph.D. thesis, University of Plymouth, U.K
23. Zhou, G.C., Rafiq, M.Y., Bugmann, G.C., and Easterbrook, D.J. (2006). "Cellular automata model for predicting the cracking pattern of laterally loaded masonry wall panels." Journal of Computing in Civil Engineering, 20(6), 400-409
24. Zhou, G.C., Rafiq, M.Y., Easterbrook, D.J. and Bugmann, G.C. (2003). "Application of cellular automata in modeling laterally loaded masonry panel boundary effects." Masonry Int., 16(3), 104-114

Factory-like Optimum Drilling Design of Cluster Well in Jimsar Well Block

Yingbiao Liu[1], Wenbo Zhang[1], Han Lin[2], and Zhongxi Zhu[2,a]

[1]Engineering and Technology Research Institute of Xinjiang Oil Field Co, Karamay 834000, China
[2]National Engineering Laboratory of Petroleum Drilling Technology, Leak Resistance & Sealing Technology Research Department, Yangtze University, Wuhan 430100, China

Abstract. The deep heavy oil reservoir of Jimsar well block, which located in Xinjiang oilfield, was developed by cluster well in 2016. In view of the ground environment, long open hole section and poor wellbore stability, the scheme which based on the research of factory-like wellsite platform deployment, well trajectory design and reservoir protection, was designed and carried out in the block. Firstly, the platform was divided into different control regions according to the anti-collision requirement. Secondly, truck-mounted drilling rig and civil power were applied to the factory-like drilling. Thirdly, well track was designed to be three parts: straight, increase and steady. The design can improve the proportion of composite drilling footage. Fourthly, the method of plane scanning and normal surface scanning was adopted to ensure the safety of downhole trajectory. Finally, the natural polymer drilling fluid system and drilling fluid reuse system were used to protect environment and reduce drilling cost. The results show that the maximum reducing time of single drill rig is 32.5 day, and the penetration rate of whole platform is increasing continuously.

1 Introduction

The deep heavy oil reservoir of Wutonggou formation in Jimsar Well Block is located in Xinjiang oilfield. The buried depth of the block is about 1500m~1700m[1-2]. Before 2015, the single well deployment was mainly adopted, there was no obviously economic benefit from middle and deep heavy oil reservoir in this block. In 2016, in order to protect the farm, grassland and environment, reduce the land acquisition area, the cluster wells should be deployed[3-7].

The difficulties of factory-like drilling in Jimusar Well Block are mainly concentrated on platform layout, drilling cost reduction, wellbore trajectory calculation method, anti-collision technology, and so on. The main researches are as follows[8-9]:

- The open hole section of the wells is long and the borehole wall of this section is unstable. The formation above Xsy is mainly pelite with strong water sensitivity, and liable to cause wellbore shrinkage and collapse.
- The cluster well track of factory-like drilling is very tight, so that giving rise to collision risk. The spacing of the platform well is 5m and some wells' angle is equal or lesser than 15 degree. It is easy to drift in azimuth and difficult to control well trajectory.
- Factory-like drilling is a relatively advanced drilling operation model, which involves various of specialties and complex related technologies.

2 Optimum design of factory-like wellsite platform

2.1 Deployment of factory-like wellsite platform

According to the wellhead position, well hole axis trend, drilling target and distribution of well control area, the platform with 43 wells is divided into three different control areas to avoid the occurrence of cross orbit in the different control areas, and to reduce the overall risk of anti-collision10. The platform is designed as double rows platform with 5m wellhead spacing and 60m rows spacing (Figure 1).

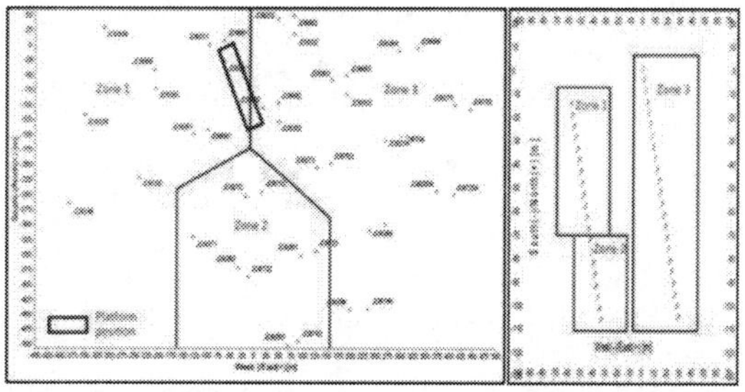

Figure 1. Control area distribution of platform and wellheads deployment in the platform

2.2 Equipment of factory-like drilling

[a] Corresponding author: zhuzhongxi@yangtzeu.edu.cn

DOI: 10.1051/matecconf/201712805013

In order to realize factory-like drilling and rapid movement of drilling rig, ZJ20(Figure 2) rig is equipped to achieve the overall movement of the platform. Some power equipment in the wellsite use the civilian electricity to reduce exhaust emissions of diesel engines. To reduce the times of peripheral equipment moving and save the drilling time, extension electric cables are used instead of the power system, extension outlet pipe are used instead of the tank circulatory system movement and extension high-pressure ground pipeline instead of drilling pump movement (Figure 3).

Figure 2. Drilling rig employed ZJ20 mounted series vehicle

Figure 3. Extended drilling fluid high pressure pump pipeline and outlet pipeline

3 Well trajectory optimization design

The well profile is mainly composed of three-section: straight, increase and steady. Very few well, which are unable to meet the demand of the anti-collision by adjusting the wellhead location, kick off point and build rate, are adopted by the five-section profile: vertical, increase, steady, fall and second steady (Figure 4). The design improved the proportion of composite drilling footage.

In order to reduce the risk of collision in vertical section, the large displacement wells begin to build angle from 430m to 720m, and the small displacement wells move down the kick off point. Compound drilling is applied in steady section to improve the ROP, so that the one trip drilling can be accomplished

By the method of target danger zoning, exchanging the wellhead positions and kick off points, adjusting build rate, etc. Anti-collision requirements of all wells can be met (Figure 5 and Figure 6).

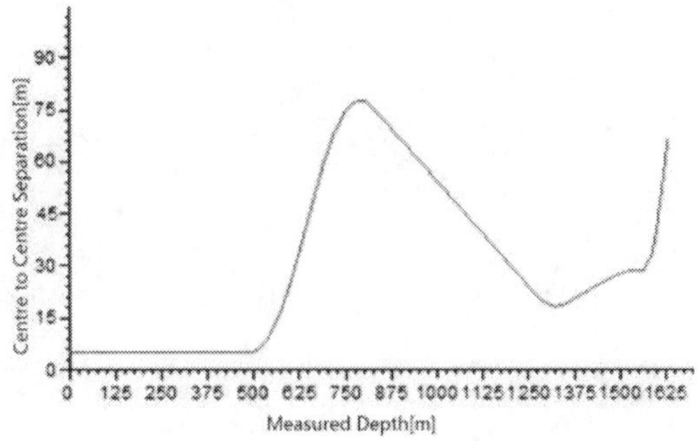

Figure 4. Well trajectory design (five-section profile)

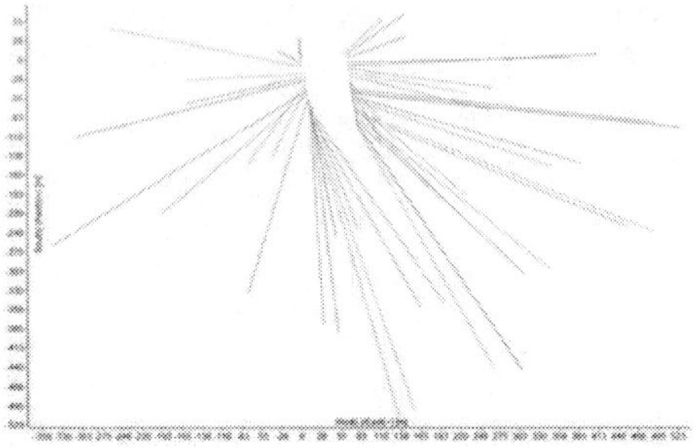

Figure 5. Horizontal projection view of the platform wells trajectory

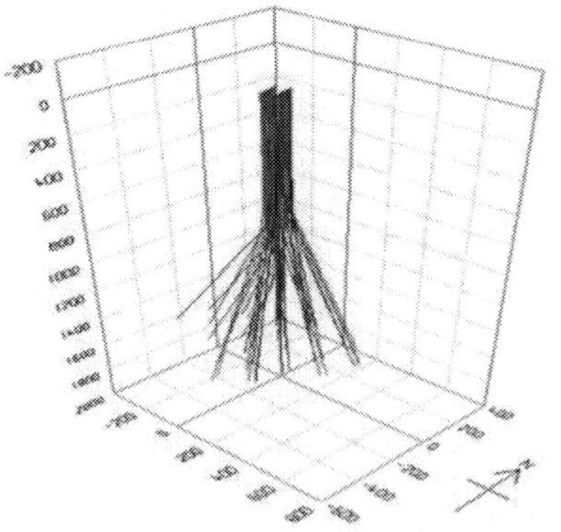

Figure 6. 3D projection view of the platform wells

The plane scanning method and normal surface scanning method show that the minimum distance of the well trajectory is greater than 5m and the separation coefficients is greater than 1.5. The design can ensure the drilling safety along the downhole trajectory (Figure 7 and Figure 8).

During the second opening interval, screw drill tools and PDC bits were used to prevent deviation in straight section. Build angle also from second open. The step laid the firm foundation of borehole trajectory anti-collision. In the process of building angle section, the error ellipsoid anti-collision method was adopted to avoid the close borehole collision through real-time data scanning.

DOI: 10.1051/matecconf/201712805013

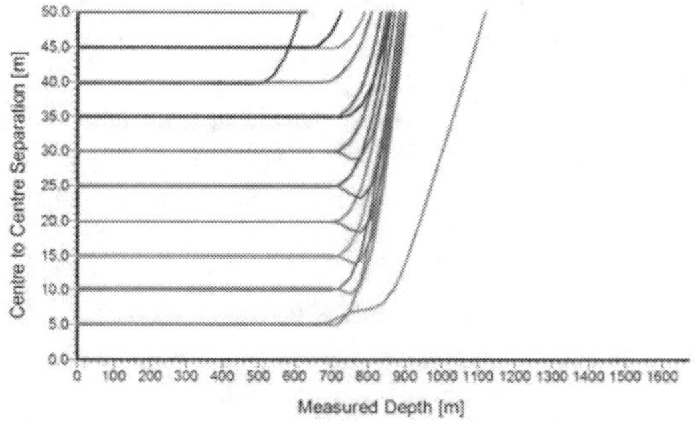

Figure 7. Scanning distance consequence between platform adjacent wells

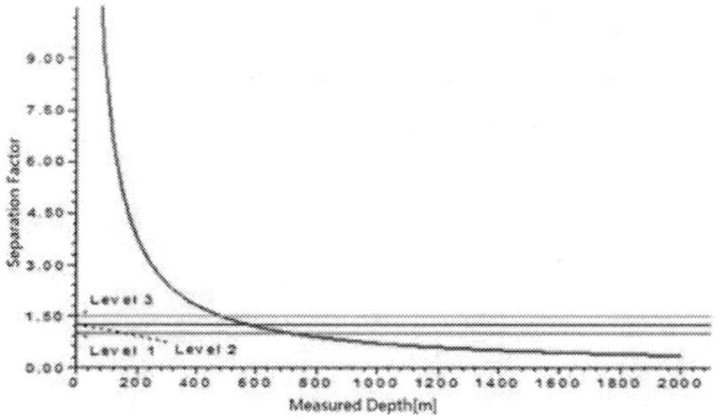

Figure 8. Vertical separation coefficient of straight wells

4 Environmental protection drilling fluid systems

Natural polymer drilling fluid system was adopted in Jimsar well block, whose treatment agent is all-natural high polymer, such as guar gum, konjac gum, sesbania gum, starch, or other vegetable gum, It's non-fluorescence and easily biodegradable. On the premise of satisfying drilling engineering requirements such as mudstone inhibition, etc., it will not pollute the surrounding environment of the wellsite. Its reservoir protection mechanism is as follow:

- Natural raw material treatment agent is easy to degrade.
- White asphalt is used as a good oil and gas protective agent for shielding temporary plugging.
- The microemulsion formed by the cloud point effect of the polyol can helpfully protect the oil and gas reservoirs.
- The alcohol can be adsorbed on the pore surface of the oil and gas zone or oil water interface, thus reducing the interfacial tension and the water-locked phenomenon.

The recovery test of mud pool was carried out in view of the environmental protection performance of natural polymer drilling fluid. The test results show that plants can grow in the mud pool after backfilling, which proved that the natural high polymer drilling fluid was non-toxic, harmless, and no pollution to the environment, so that achieved the purpose of environmental protection (Figure 9).

(a) Before recovery

(b) After recovery

Figure 9. Recovery situation of in mud tank

Because factory-like drilling adopts batch operation, the drilling fluid can be reused in many wells to reduce drilling cost. Drilling requirements, drilling fluid parameters and properties can be adjusted by adding proper drilling fluid additive at different opening. These methods improve drilling fluid reuse rate. By the simple operation, easily maintenance and transform, it is convenient and quick to achieve the reuse of drilling fluid at different opening. The highest reuse rate of drilling fluid is up to 51.2%.

5 Application results of factory-like drilling operation

The largest drilling time saved by single rig is 32.5 days since May 2016. Through the factory-like operation model, the total time of drilling and cementing have been reduced greatly. The penetration of the whole platform is continuously improved by optimizing each process (Figure 10).

DOI: 10.1051/matecconf/201712805013

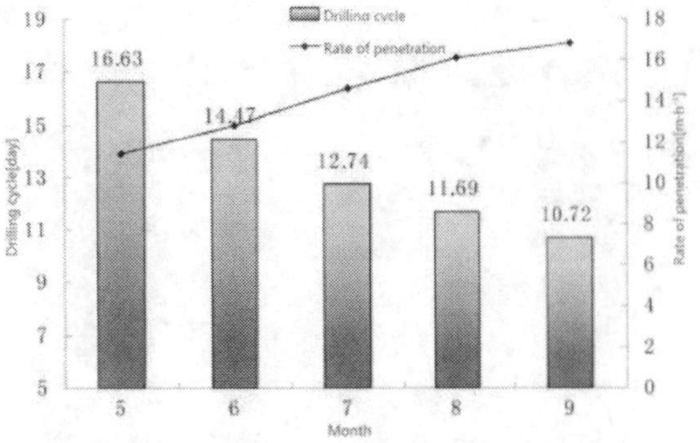

Figure 10. Drilling technical index statistics

6 Conclusions

Considering the overall anti-collision needs of platform wells, the platform with 43 wells is divided into three different control areas, designed into double rows platform with wellhead spacing of 5m and row spacing of 60m. The well site is equipped with ZJ20 truck-mounted rig and civil power supply, which can reduce exhaust emissions and save transportation time. Most wells' profile is mainly composed of three-section, in order to improve the proportion of composite drilling footage. Few wells use five-section profile. Through plane scanning and normal surface scanning, the minimum distance of the well trajectory is designed greater than 5m and the separation coefficients is designed greater than 1.5. The design can ensure the safe drilling along the downhole trajectory. The natural polymer drilling fluid system is adopted to reduce environmental pollution. The drilling fluid reuse process system is established, which improves drilling fluid reuse efficiency and reduces drilling cost. The largest drilling time saved by single rig is 32.5day, and the penetration rate of the whole platform is continuously increasing month by month.

Acknowledgement

The authors wish to acknowledge the National Program on General Program of National Natural Science Foundation of China (Contract No. 51474036 and 51204024) for the financial support.

References

1. Zhang Li-hua, Zhang Guo-bin, Li Jing, Wei Meng-zhou, Shi Xin-qin. Evaluation of reservoir of Permain Wutonggou Formation in JI 7 area. Foreign logging technology, **5** (2014): 39-41.
2. Song Wei. Research of reservoir characteristics of Permain Wutonggou Formation in JI 7 area of Jimusar sag. Yangtze University, (2012)
3. Devine M D, Lesso W G. Models for the Minimum Cost Development of Offshore Oil Fields. INFORMS, (1972).
4. Lilien G L. A Note on Offshore Oil Field Development Problems and Suggested Solutions. Management Science, **20** (1973): 536-539.
5. Frair L, Devine M. Economic Optimization of Offshore Petroleum Development. Management Science, **21** (1975): 1370-1379.
6. Dogru S. Selection of Optimal Platform Locations. Spe Drilling Engineering, **2** (1987): 382-386.
7. Copp E A. Technical Change and Petroleum Drilling Costs. Land Economics, **50** (1974): 120-126.
8. Wang Xin, Zhang Lei. Drilling and Completion Technique of Shallow Heavy Oil Horizontal Well in Xinjiang Oilfield. Domestic and foreign energy, **13** (2008): 38-42.
9. Kang Xiu-fa, Tong Chang-hai, Huang Feng, Jia Yao-hui, Song Ming-hui. Drilling technique suitable for exploit-ing super heavy oil reservoir. Special oil and gas reservoirs, **S1** (2000): 28-30+58.

MATEC Web of Conferences 128, 05014 (2017)
EITCE 2017

DOI: 10.1051/matecconf/201712805014

Multiple Synergistic Drilling Fluid System Application in Aihu Oilfield

Yingbiao Liu[1], Zongyu Lu[1], Wenhui Dang[1], and Zhongxi Zhu[2,a]

[1]Engineering and Technology Research Institute of Xinjiang Oil Field Co, Karamay 834000, China
[2]National Engineering Laboratory of Petroleum Drilling Technology, Leak Resistance & Sealing Technology Research Department, Yangtze University, Wuhan 430100, China

Abstract. The unstable layer of Aihu oilfield is characterized by strong hydration dispersion and weak expansion. The theory of multiple synergistic wall stabilization was applied to improve synergistic efficiency of the drilling fluid. The recipe of multiple synergistic drilling fluid is worked out. The multiple synergistic drilling fluid was evaluated by analysing the rheology, filtration, wall building, inhibition for the borehole & the weak layers. The inhibition and rheology of the tested drilling fluid system is as good as anti-temperature performance. The ternary-inhibitive drilling fluid system is superior to the binary-inhibitive drilling fluid system. The ternary-inhibitive contained in the multiple synergistic drilling fluid system enhances the ability of water dispersion inhibition. The application of Aihu oilfield shows that the multiple synergistic drilling fluid has satisfied the requirements of low filtration and slight wall expansion.

1 Introduction

It is necessary to study the physicochemical properties and the mineral composition of the collapsible formation. The results offer the drilling engineers to solve the instability of the borehole wall and to improve the speed of drilling operation effectively. X ray diffraction technique is applied to determine the mineral composition and physicochemical properties of the rock samples from the groups of Sgh, Bjt, Krmy, Bkq and Urho in Aihu oilfield[1-4].

The collapsible strata of Aihu oilfield contains weak swelling clay minerals which are water sensitive dispersive minerals. Although it is difficult to expand, it is very easy to disperse[5].

Comprehensive experimental evaluation of the instable layers in Aihu oilfield shows that the clay minerals have the characteristics of weak swelling and strong water sensitive disperse. The clay minerals have the low activity and the little linear swelling rate. So the drilling fluid should be mainly aimed to avoiding the cuttings dispersion and preventing rock from expansion[6-8].

2 Optimization of drilling fluid inhibitor

2.1 Evaluation of inhibitive ability of inhibitors

The hot roll experiment and recovery experiment were done on the mudstone. The inhibitive ability of various inhibitors on hydration dispersion and swelling of mudstone was evaluated under the condition of inhibitors interaction[9-11]. The single agent of inorganic salts (KCl, NaCl, or $CaCl_2$) were optimized the dosage range of the inhibitors. And the single agent of organic salts (Weigh2, Weigh3, OS-80, or OS-100), organic polymer (SIAT), silicone series (LYG, FMS-1, or MFG) were optimized the dosage range.

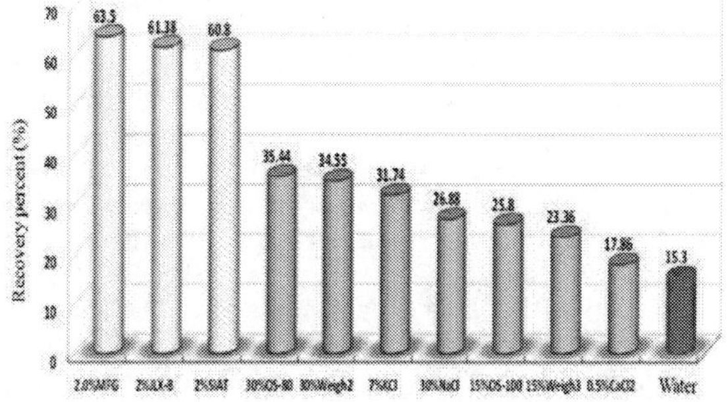

Figure 1. Hot rolling recovery of mudstone under the action of various inhibitors

As shown in figure 1, the inhibitive capacity of the optimum dosage of inhibitor on the dispersity of mudstone is, followed the order of large to small, 2% MFG > 2% JLX-B > 2% SIAT > 30% Weigh2 (OS-80) > 7% KCl > 30% NaCl > 15% Weigh3 (OS-100) > 0.5% $CaCl_2$。

The results show that organic inhibitors with the certain molecular weight have some advantages in inhibiting the dispersion of shale.

[a] Corresponding author: zhuzhongxi@yangtzeu.edu.cn

DOI: 10.1051/matecconf/201712805014

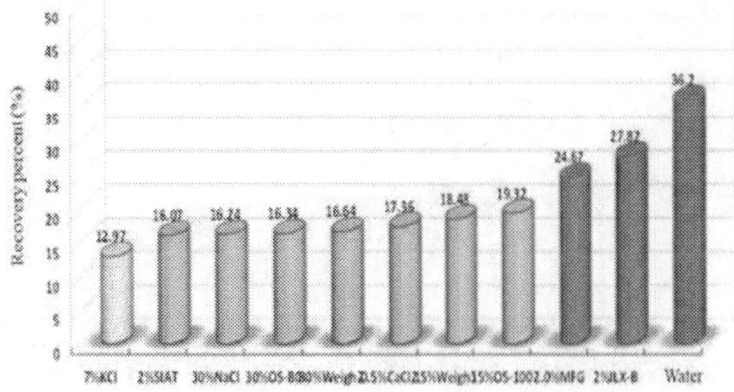

Figure 2. Linear expansion rates of mudstone under the action of various inhibitors

As shown in figure 2, the inhibitive capacity of the optimum dosage of inhibitor on the swelling of the shale is, followed the order of large to small, 7% KCl > 2% SIAT > 30% NaCl > 30% Weigh2 (OS-80) > 0.5% $CaCl_2$ > 15% Weigh3 (OS-100) > 2% MFG > 2% JLX-B。

Therefore, the results of experiments shows that one drilling fluid inhibitor is difficult to meet two aspects of inhibiting clay requirements: hydration expansion and hydration dispersity. So the dominated contradiction should be selected according to the actual needs of the formation. If the need to suppress dispersion of the clay is dominated, organic inhibitors with a certain molecular weight should be selected. Conversely, if the need to inhibit the expansion of the clay is dominated, inorganic salt should be chosen as the main inhibitor.

2.2 Optimization of inhibitors

Laboratory test of 7% KCl, 0.5% $CaCl_2$, 30% weigh2, 15% weigh3, 2% SIAT, 2% JLX-B and 2% MFG for the instable formation in Aihu oilfield are given the order of inhibitory. The inhibitive ability of drilling fluid is related to the type of drilling fluids. That is to say, the oil base drilling fluids or the water base drilling fluids are sensitive to the inhibitory. Many drilling fluid researchers have already explicitly noted that inorganic salts, organic acids, salts and polymer inhibitors have different inhibitory effects on the hydration expansion and hydration dispersity of clay. Organic inhibitors with a certain molecular weight such as silicones (MFG); polymers (JLX-B) and polyamines (SIAT), have very high inhibition of the hydration dispersing ability to the shale formation. However, the ability of restraining the swelling of the shale formation is ordinary for the inorganic salts of KCl or the organic polyamine of SIAT.

3 Mechanism of multiple synergistic drilling fluid

Because of the single inhibitor is limited to the inhibition of the target formation, it is necessary to study multiple synergistic inhibitor formulation according to the target formation characteristics. The aim is to improve the drilling fluid system's ability to control the unstable target formation. Based on the multiple synergistic theory, the mechanism of multiple synergistic inhibitors was studied. The results provided a theoretical basis for the design of multiple synergistic inhibitors to Aihu oilfield[11].

3.1 Mechanism of synergistic inhibitors

The shale contains clay minerals and non-clay minerals. The basic reason for hydration dispersion and hydration expansion of shale is the clay minerals particles' dispersion and swelling. It is the key to inhibit the dispersion and expansion of shale.

The ways of inhibiting shale from hydrating include the following aspects:

Firstly, compress the clay minerals particles' thickness of double electric layers and reducing the clay minerals particles' repulsion of double electric layers.

Secondly, apply the insert layer Mosaic effect to increase electrostatic attraction.

Thirdly, utilize the adsorption package to maintain the integrity of the clay minerals particles.

Finally, reduce water activity and cutting down water entry.

Multiple synergistic inhibitors are based on the above considerations. The inhibitive mechanism of multiple synergistic inhibitors was verified through experiments. Multiple synergistic inhibitor formulations are further confirmed whether the inhibitors have the above-mentioned mechanisms of action.

3.2 Study on the formula of multiple synergistic inhibitor

According to inhibitor type and the lithologic character of stratum in Aihu oilfield, the experimental study on the optimization of multiple synergistic inhibitor formulations have been carried out. The evaluation and screening results are presented in the above text. Six inhibitors such as inorganic salts of KCl, organic salts of weigh2 (OS-80), organic salts of weigh3 (OS-100), organic silicon of MFG, Polymeric alcohol of JLX-B and organic amine of SIAT, were used in the experiments. According to the chemical action mechanism and the type of treatment agent, six inhibitors are divided into three categories: inorganic salt inhibitor, organic salts inhibitor and organic polymer inhibitor. It is shown in Table 1.

Table 1. List of experimental inhibitors

Category	Inhibitor
Inorganic salt inhibitors	KCl
Organic salts inhibitors	Weigh2 (OS-80) Weigh3 (OS-100)
Organic polymer inhibitors	Amines (SIAT) Organosilicon (MFG) Polymeric alcohol (JLX-B)

The experimental process is recommended to divide up into three kinds of combination way: inorganic Salt + organic salt, inorganic salt + organic polymer, organic salt + organic polymer. Three kinds form a binary synergistic inhibitor formula. Meanwhile, the experimental process is recommended the way of inorganic salt + organic salt + organic polymer to form a ternary synergistic inhibitor formula.

During the evaluation experiment of inhibitor, two steps were carried out:

a) Using the above inhibitors and their optimum dosage, the formulation of "binary synergy" and "ternary synergy" were formed and evaluated the inhibiting ability.

b) Combined the formed inhibitor formulation with the base slurry of drilling fluid, the inhibiting ability of multiple synergistic inhibitor drilling fluid system was evaluated. The base slurry of drilling fluid formula is as follows: 4% basic mud +0.3% FA367 +2% SMP-2+2% SPNH+0.8% Redul+ 0.3% CaO+0.3% KOH + 4% PHT+1% graphite powder.

According to the experimental scheme, a series of experiments were conducted. The preliminary formula of multiple synergistic inhibitors was obtained to cater to the unstable formation of Aihu oilfield. The preliminary formula is shown in table 2.

Table 2. The preliminary formula

Formation	Preliminary formula of multiple synergistic inhibitors
Sgh	7%KCl+2%JLX-B(MFG)
Bjt	
Krmy	7%KCl+30%Weigh2+2%JLX-B(MFG)
Bkq	7%KCl+2%JLX-B(MFG)
Urho	

4 Optimization and evaluation of drilling fluid system

The inhibitor dosage was the best single agent contraposed the clay of the formation. The basic formula of multiple synergistic inhibitors for Aihu formation was required to further optimization for each inhibitor amount in the binary synergistic inhibitor or ternary synergistic inhibitor drilling fluid. The formula of multiple synergistic inhibition of drilling fluid system are evaluated to the corresponding drilling fluid system rheology, filtration, wall inhibition.

The best multiple synergistic inhibition of drilling fluid formula is 4% soil slurry + 0.3% FA367 +2% SMP-2 + 2% SPNH + 1% Redul + 0.3% CaO + 0.3% KOH + multiple inhibitors + 4% PHT + 1% graphite powder + barite.

4.1 Optimization scheme

In the optimization experimental process, only one inhibitor's amount is adjusted, the other inhibitors are kept the amount unchanged. The amount of the selected inhibitor when the property of drilling fluid system changes abruptly is the perfect amount. Then the selected inhibitor maintains the perfect amount and adjusts the amount of other inhibitors, and so on. So it can form a formula of the performance of the drilling fluid system. The perfect drilling fluid system.

4.2 Optimization of binary synergistic inhibitor amount

Through the above optimized schemes (shown in Table 3), the formula of binary synergy inhibitive water-based drilling fluid has been obtained: 4% basic mud + 0.3% FA367 + 2% SMP-2 + 2% SPNH + 1% Redul + 0.3% CaO + 0.3% KOH + 1% MFG + 3% KCl + 4% PHT + 1% graphite powder + barite.

Table 3. Optimization schedule of binary synergistic inhibitor

KCl (%)	MFG (%)
7	2
5	1.5
3	1

4.3 Optimization of adding amount of ternary synergistic inhibitor

The results of binary synergistic inhibitor optimization shows that compound inhibitors are more conducive to the performance of their respective advantages. So ternary synergistic inhibitor is employed according to the optimization result of binary synergistic inhibitor drilling fluid system. The optimization research of ternary synergistic inhibitor drilling fluid system was continued.

The different amounts of organic salt are screened out on the base of the optimized binary synergistic inhibitor formula. The compound inhibitors or ternary synergistic inhibitors are evaluated the rheological properties, filtration, wall forming and inhibition capacity. The schedule of organic salt OS-80 dosage experiments is shown in Table 4.

Table 4. Schedule of organic salt OS-80 dosage adding in the binary synergistic inhibitor

Dosage of OS-80	ρ g/cm³	Φ 600	Φ 300	FlAPI (mL)	Rate of recovery %	Rate of expansion %
10%	1.63	102	55	3.4	94.16	15.7
15%	1.63	86	44	3.6	92.4	15.55
20%	1.62	75	36	3.6	94.6	15.22

From Table 4, the binary synergistic inhibitor drilling fluid system is increased the inhibition by the organic salt OS- 80. The rheological properties of the corresponding system or ternary synergistic inhibitors system can be further improved with the increasing amount of organic salt 0S-80. The recovery rate of shale has been improved by the he ternary synergistic inhibitors system compared with binary synergistic inhibitors drilling fluid system. The linear expansion rate also increases slightly. It indicates that the inhibitive ability of ternary synergistic inhibitors drilling fluid system has increased the inhibition of drilling fluid for Aihu oilfield. Considering the performance and economic rationality of drilling fluid, the amount of 0S-80 added to organic salt is 10%. Therefore, ternary synergistic inhibition water base drilling fluid system has been formed.

The optimized formula of binary and ternary synergistic inhibition water base drilling fluid has been obtained. Multiple synergistic inhibitor drilling fluid system has been carried out.

The plastic viscosity and dynamic shear force of the binary synergistic drilling fluid with density of 1.63g/cm^3 before hot roll are 49Pa and 3.5Pa respectively. The plastic viscosity and dynamic shear force after hot roll are 52 and 4.5Pa respectively. The water loss of API is 3.6ml and the water loss of HTHP is 12ml before and after the hot roll. It shows that the binary synergistic drilling fluid system has good rheological and temperature resistance properties. The binary synergistic drilling fluid system can meet the requirements of filtration and wall forming performance. At the same time, the average cutting recovery rate of the binary synergistic drilling fluid system is about 85%, and the linear expansion rate of binary synergistic drilling fluid system is about 13.5%.

The plastic viscosity and dynamic shear force of the ternary synergistic drilling fluid with density of 1.63g/cm^3 before hot roll are 47Pa and 4Pa respectively. The plastic viscosity and dynamic shear force after hot roll are 52 and 3Pa respectively. The water loss of API is 3.4ml, and the water loss of HTHP is 11.2ml before and after the hot roll. It shows that the ternary synergistic drilling fluid system also has good rheological and temperature resistance properties. The ternary synergistic drilling fluid system can also meet the requirements of filtration and wall forming performance like as the binary synergistic drilling fluid system. At the same time, the average cutting recovery rate of the ternary synergistic drilling fluid system is about 94%. It shows that the ternary synergistic drilling fluid system has the better ability of enhancing hydration and dispersing inhibition than binary synergistic drilling fluid system. The linear expansion rate of ternary synergistic drilling fluid system is about 15.7%. The improvement is not obvious because the formation of Aihu oilfield belongs to the strong dispersed and weakly swelling formation.

5 Conclusions

The drilling fluid of Aihu oilfield should mainly focus on improving the restraining ability and decreasing the expansion of formation. Using inorganic salt + organic salt, inorganic salt + organic polymer, or organic salt + organic polymer, the binary synergistic inhibitor formula is formed. The ternary synergistic inhibitor formula is formed by inorganic salt + organic salt + organic polymer way. The basic recipe of multiple synergistic inhibitor that suits to the target layer in Aihu oilfield can cater to the requirement of the sensitive formation. The dosage of different inhibitors that consist in the multiple synergistic inhibitor can further improve the inhibitor of the drilling fluid. The ideal multiple synergistic inhibitor using in Aihu formation are formed. According evaluating the rheology, filtration wall inhibition and inhibition ability of multiple synergistic drilling fluid, the demand of the sensitive formation is met.

Acknowledgement

The authors wish to acknowledge the National Program on General Program of National Natural Science Foundation of China (Contract No. 51474036 and 51204024) for the financial support.

References

1. Drilling manual Compiling group, *Drilling manual (Second Edition)*, Petroleum Industry Press (2013)
2. Zoback M D. *Reservoir geomechanics*, Cambridge University Press, (2007)
3. Xiangyu Fan, Geological environment description of complex drilling, Petroleum Industry Press, (2012)
4. Tongtai Xu, Zhongju Zhao. Drilling fluid and completion fluid technology abroad in early twenty-first Century, Petroleum Industry Press, (2004).
5. Jingjie Zhao. Drilling fluid leakage prevention and anti-sloughing drilling fluid technology for TK1040 well in Tahe Oilfield. West-China Exploration Engineering, **22** (2010): 67-70.
6. Changchun Su, Chunwen Liu. Drilling leak prevention and plugging technology in D block, Burma. Petroleum Drilling Techniques, **5** (2010): 18-21.
7. Fuhua Chun, Zhenlu Wei. Research and application of a new drilling leak proof and plugging agent[J]. Drilling Fluid & Completion Fluid, **3** (2006): 42-44.
8. Shizhong Fan, Jienian Yan, Dachen Zhou. *Drilling fluid, completion fluid and reservoir protection technology*. Petroleum University Press, (1996): 232-302.
9. Xiaofeng Zou, Xinlai Du. Techniques and methods for improving borehole stability. China well and rock salt, **44** (2013): 25-27.
10. Jienian Yan. *Drilling fluid technology*, Beijing: China University of Petroleum press, (2006): 57-77.
11. Xiaohua Yang. Progress in research and application of drilling fluid additives in China in recent 5 years. Oilfield Chemistry, **26** (2009): 210-216.

Fault Diagnosis for Constant Deceleration Braking System of Mine Hoist based on Principal Component Analysis and SVM

Juan-Juan Li[1], Liang Hu[1], Guo-Ying Meng[1,a], Guang-Ming Xie[2], Ai-Ming Wang [1], Shuai Wang [1] and Yi-Fan Jia[1]

[1]*School of Mechanical Electronic and Information Engineering, China University of Mining and Technology (Beijing), Beijing 100083, China*
[2]*College of Engineering, Peking University, Beijing 100871, China*

Abstract. Based on AMESim simulation platform, the pressure-time curve of constant deceleration braking system is obtained in this paper firstly, by simulating three typical faults of brake, the spring stiffness decrease, the brake shoe friction coefficient decrease and brake leaking. Then pressure data on the curve for each time are seen as a variable and the curve is chosen as the fault sample, analysed by the method of Principal Component Analysis (PCA). Last, principal components or sum of variance contribution rates more than 95% are selected as sample eigenvalues and Support Vector Machine (SVM) is used for fault diagnosis. Diagnosis results show that all testing faults can be identified accurately, which indicates SVM model has an extremely excellent ability to identify faults. To further verify the performance of SVM for fault identification, BP neural network is established to compare. The result shows that SVM model is more accurate than BP neural network in fault recognition.

1 Preface

As the key equipment in the production process, connection between the mine ground and underground, the mine hoist undertakes the important task to lift coal or ore, down materials and elevate personnel or equipment [1]. Braking system of the hoist is the final barrier to ensure safe operation. Its braking performance directly affects safety and reliability of hoist. Thus, fault diagnosis of the brake has become a hot spot of research.

According to uncertain problems in the fault diagnosis of hoist, the literature [2] proposes a fault diagnosis method based on ontology and Bayesian network. The literature [3] extracts feature vectors by wavelet packet of 3 layers and reconstruction method, takes results of neural network recognition as independent evidence, and judges based on evidence theory of synthesis. The literature [4] presents a multi-class classification algorithm based on ordering binary tree SVM for fault diagnosis. Also, there are other methods for fault diagnosis like SVM [5], the genetic algorithm to optimize the BP neural network [6], SOM neural network method [7], particle swarm optimization [8] and so on. Effective results of fault diagnosis can be gotten by adapting methods mentioned above on some certain conditions, but in those methods, there are still some problems that parameters can't be accurately gotten, or can't represent the general characteristics of the braking system [9]. For example, online monitoring of the friction coefficient still has no mature feasible solution [10]; the signal linearity and zero drift problem of brake pressure sensors are difficult to solve because of its long-term load. In order to overcome deficiencies of methods mentioned above, this paper presents a brand-new method which extracts principal components from pressure-time curve of the brake system as characteristic parameters and uses the method SVM for fault diagnosis.

2 Principal Component Analysis

Principal Component Analysis (PCA) adapts the thought of dimension reduction which converts multiple index to a few comprehensive index. PCA is a statistical procedure that uses an orthogonal transformation to convert a set of observations of possibly correlated variables into a set of values of linearly uncorrelated variables called principal components, keeping the total variance of variables constant during the transformation. This transformation is defined in such a way that the first principal component has the largest variance, the second principal component corresponding to the second largest variance, and so on. The way of saving lower order principal component and ignoring the higher can maintain the main features of data, which can achieve the purpose of dimension reduction. The flowchart of principal component analysis is shown in Figure 1.

[a] Guo-Ying Meng: mgy@cumtb.edu.cn

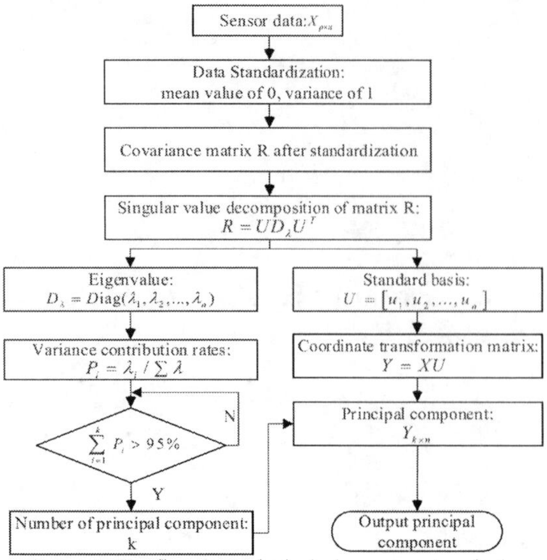

Figure 1. The flowchart of principal component analysis.

3 Support Vector Machine

3.1 Introduction of Support Vector Machine

Support Vector Machine (SVM), a machine learning algorithm, is developed on the basis of the statistical theory. The main idea of SVM is to establish a classification hyperplane, maximizing two types of intervals. SVM is the approximate realization of the structural risk minimization principle.

When linear classification, the classification face, $(w \cdot x) + b = 0$, is defined on the place farthest away from two groups of samples. Then the solving optimal hyperplane problem can be transformed into its dual problem by using the Lagrangian optimization technique, or

$$\begin{cases} \max Q(a) = \sum_{i}^{I} \alpha_i - \frac{1}{2} \sum_{i=1}^{I} \sum_{j=1}^{I} \alpha_i \alpha_j y_i y_j (x_i x_j) \\ \text{s.t.} \ \sum_{i=1}^{I} \alpha_i y_j = 0, \qquad \alpha_i \geq 0 \end{cases} \quad (1)$$

Where (x_i, y_i) is the sample needed to classify; I is the number of samples; $\alpha_i \geq 0\ (i = 1,2, ..., I)$ is Lagrange multiplier.

Equation (1) is the quadratic function optimization subject to an inequality. Suppose its optimum solution is $X_{p\times n}$ (sensor data), the optimal W^* and classification threshold b^* could be found. The optimal classification function, Equation (2), can be found.

$$f(x) = \mathrm{sgn}\left[\sum_{i=1}^{I} \alpha_i^* y_i (x x_i) + b^*\right] \quad (2)$$

When nonlinear classification, linearly inseparable samples in lower dimensional space are usually mapped to the linearly separable space of higher dimension, where the optimal hyperplane is constructed. The way of constructing the optimal hyperplane in the higher dimensional space is similar to linearly separable SVM, that is, dot product in the higher dimensional space is replaced by kernel function $K(x_i, x_j)$ subject to Mercer. Finally, the optimal classification function is the Equation (3).

$$f(x) = \mathrm{sgn}[W^* \emptyset(x) + b^*] = \mathrm{sgn}\left[\sum_{i=1}^{I} \alpha_i^* y_i K(x_i, x) + b^*\right] \quad (3)$$

The flowchart of SVM is shown in the Figure 2.

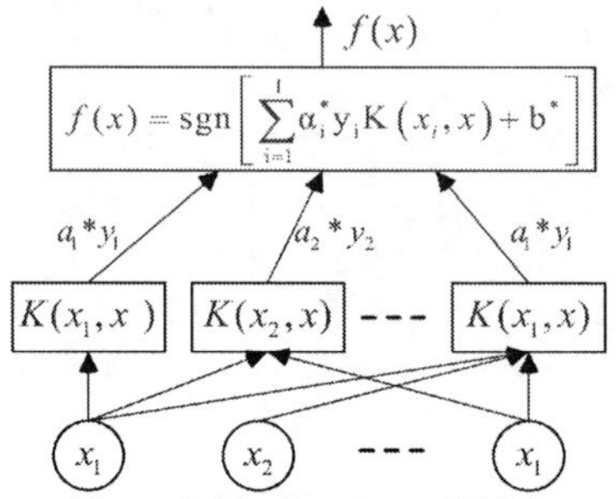

Figure 2. The flowchart of SVM.

3.2 Support Vector Machine Multiclass Classification

Support Vector Machine is originally designed for binary classification problems, but when processing multiclass classification problems, the SVM multiclass classifier is needed to construct. There are two common ways to construct the SVM multiclass classifier, direct method and the indirect. Direct method is to directly modify the object function, combining parameter solution of multiple classification faces into an optimization problem, by solving the optimization problem, "one time" to realize classification. Because of the high computational complexity, the high difficulty to realize, direct method is only suitable for simple problems. Indirect method is mainly to realize construction of multiple classifiers by combining multiple binary classifiers. The common ways of indirect method are "one versus one (1-V-1)", "one versus rest (1-V-R)" and Hierarchical Support Vector Machine (H-SVM).

3.2.1 "1-V-1" Multiclass Classification

One SVM classifier is needed to be designed between any two groups of samples, so k(k-1)/2 classifiers are needed for k-class samples. After classifying an unknown sample x by (k-1)/2 classifiers, which category the unknown sample x belongs to is defined by which the largest number of votes in k-class samples.

3.2.2 "1-V-R" Multiclass Classification

Classifying a type of samples into one class, the rest into one another class, k SVM classifiers can be constructed to k-class samples. The unknown sample belongs to the

DOI: 10.1051/matecconf/201712805015

class which has the maximum classification function value.

3.2.3 Hierarchical Support Vector Machine

H-SVM is the method that firstly all categories are divided into two subclasses, and then the subclass is further divided into two secondary subclasses, and so on, until a separate category so far.

4 Fault Simulation and Diagnosis

In the working process of mine hoist, the performance of its brake inevitably degenerates gradually until the brake fails, because of its brake springs, brake cylinders, pistons and rings working under the long-term high load condition. In this paper, we will simulate and diagnose three typical faults of brake, the spring stiffness decrease, the brake shoe friction coefficient decrease and brake leaking. The flowchart of fault simulation and diagnosis is shown in Figure 3.

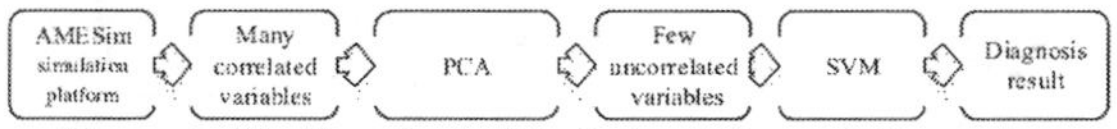

Figure 3. The flowchart of fault simulation and diagnosis.

4.1 Simulating Samples of Faults

Taking the matching constant deceleration braking system JKMD4.5X4 of mine hoist E141A as the research object, a fault simulation model of the system is built based on AMESim simulation platform [10]. Only considering the overloaded working condition, simulation time is set to 10s, including 1-2s for energy accumulator charging, 2-5s for brake releasing, 5-8s for constant deceleration braking, and 8-10s for system pressure relief; besides, the sampling frequency is set to 100HZ. Pressure data from 5-8.2s are collected as a group of fault data; besides, each type of faults is simulated by 30 groups of data. The pressure-time curve of the brake system is gotten by simulating three typical faults, as is shown respectively in the Figure 4, Figure 5 and Figure 6.

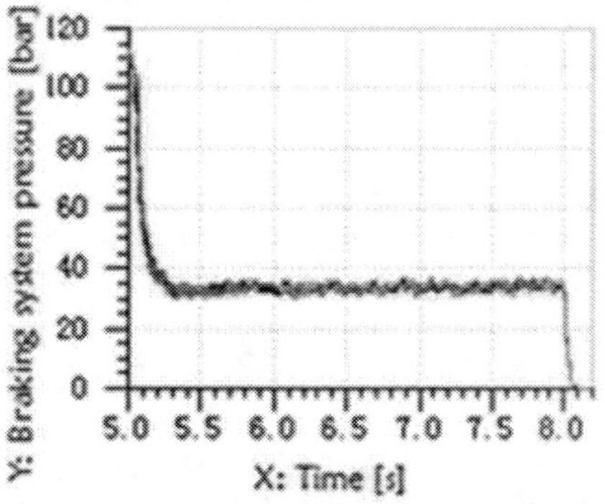

Figure 4. Braking system pressure in different spring stiffness.

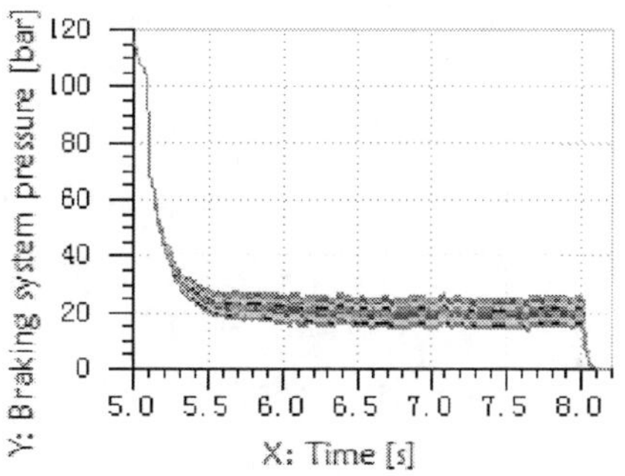

Figure 5. Braking system pressure in different brake shoe friction coefficient.

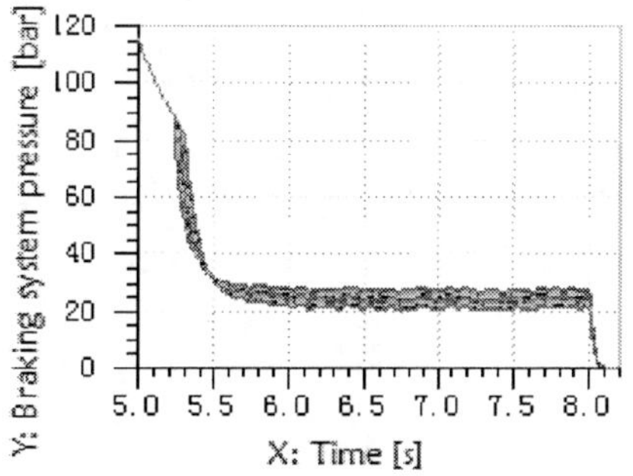

Figure 6. Braking system pressure in different leakage.

4.2 Extracting Sample Eigenvalues of Fault Samples

From 30 groups of data, 25 groups are selected randomly for training samples, the remaining 5 groups for test samples. Thus, for three typical faults, there are 75 groups of 320-dimensional (acquisition time of 3.2s, sampling frequency of 100HZ) training data and 15 groups of 320-dimensional test data. Data are seen as a variable in each dimension, which means each group of data can be viewed as the sample consisting of 320 variables, then analysed by the method of PCA. Besides, principal components or sum of variance contribution rates more than 95% are selected as sample eigenvalues. In this paper, the first five principal components are selected as eigenvalues. After normalization processing, eigenvalues and fault types from part of training samples and test samples are shown respectively in the Table 1 and Table 2.

Table 1. SVM training samples.

Sample number	SVM training input					SVM training output	Corresponding fault
	P1	P2	P3	P4	P5		

1	0.6893	-0.9687	-0.8108	0.1625	-0.8115	-1	The brake shoe friction coefficient decrease
2	0.7704	-0.8557	-0.5879	0.1314	0.1379	-1	
3	0.6777	-0.9845	-0.8408	0.1659	-0.9119	-1	
…	…	…	…	…	…	…	
26	-0.1823	0.9381	-0.8849	-0.6818	0.1901	0	The spring stiffness decrease
27	0.0784	0.7384	-0.4693	0.3522	0.3064	0	
28	0.0335	0.7671	-0.5333	0.212	0.2971	0	
…	…	…	…	…	…	…	
73	-0.6325	-0.2598	0.9486	0.0567	0.1852	1	Brake leaking
74	-0.6726	-0.2671	0.954	0.0562	0.1787	1	
75	0.1868	-0.0968	0.8477	0.0295	0.2844	1	

Table2. SVM test samples.

Sample number	SVM test input					Corresponding fault
	P1	P2	P3	P4	P5	
1	0.8283	-0.7775	-0.4394	0.1114	0.705	The brake shoe friction coefficient decrease
2	0.8166	-0.7911	-0.4609	0.1128	0.6902	
…	…	…	…	…	…	
6	-0.1615	0.92	-0.8506	-0.5873	0.2053	The spring stiffness decrease
7	0.0113	0.7816	-0.5654	0.1365	0.29	
…	…	…	…	…	…	
11	-0.1708	-0.1709	0.8906	0.0504	0.2495	Brake leaking
12	-0.208	-0.1783	0.8951	0.0518	0.2451	

4.3 Construction of the SVM classifier and testing results

In this paper, the toolbox called "libsvm" is used for SVM fault diagnosis, which is developed by the C.J Lin, the professor of National Taiwan University. Because the type of kernel function and model parameters have a great impact on model performance, RBF kernel function, most widely used in SVM, is chosen in this paper, using cross-validation method for seeking the optimum parameter c (penalty factor) and parameter g (variance of RBF kernel function) , then training model by the optimum parameter. After completing the training, the data are inputted for test and then the test result is gotten as is shown in the Figure 7.

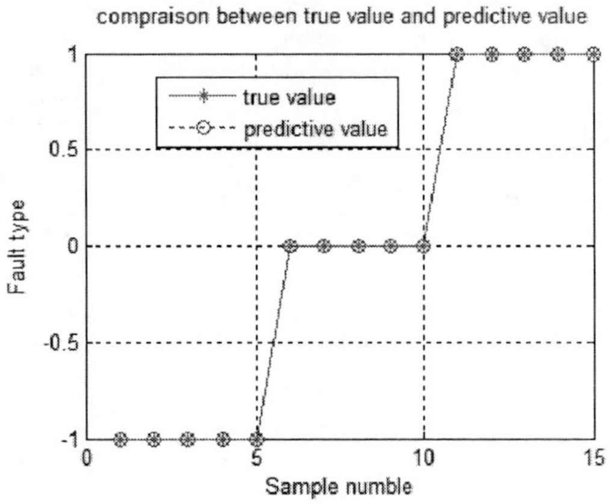

Figure 7. The result of SVM diagnosis.

As can be seen from the Figure 7, all testing faults can be identified accurately, the mean square error of 0, which indicates SVM model has an extremely excellent ability to identify the fault.

To further verify the performance of SVM for fault identification, BP neural network is established to compare [11]. The result of BP neural network diagnosis is shown in the Figure 8.

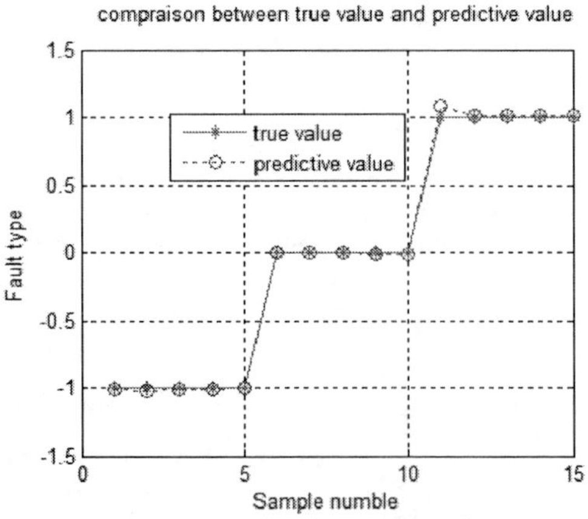

Figure 8. The result of BP neural network diagnosis.

As can be seen from the Figure 8, the diagnosed fault of 1-5 samples is the friction coefficient decrease, 6-10 samples for the spring stiffness decrease, 11-15 samples for brake leaking, which indicates diagnosed faults are consistent with testing faults. The BP neural network diagnosis also can identify the fault, but its mean square error of 0.0025. That is, SVM model is more accurate than BP neural network in fault recognition.

DOI: 10.1051/matecconf/201712805015

5 Conclusion

Based on AMESim simulation platform, the pressure-time curve of constant deceleration braking system is obtained in this paper firstly, by simulating three typical faults of brake, the spring stiffness decrease, the brake shoe friction coefficient decrease and brake leaking. Then pressure data on the curve for each time are seen as a variable and the curve is chosen as the fault sample, analysed by the method of Principal Component Analysis (PCA). Last, principal components or sum of variance contribution rates select more than 95% are selected as sample eigenvalues and Support Vector Machine (SVM) is used for fault diagnosis. Diagnosis results show that all testing faults can be identified accurately, which indicates SVM model has an extremely excellent ability to identify the fault. To further verify the performance of SVM for fault identification, BP neural network is established to compare. The result shows that SVM model is more accurate than BP neural network in fault recognition.

6 Funding

The authors are grateful to the National key research and development plan, "Basic theory and key technology of coal mine deep well construction and hoist". (Grant No.2016YFC0600900)

References

1. Bo Du, Bu-Bin Zhang, Hai-Ping Feng, Mining & Processing Equipment, **44**, 1-7 (2016)
2. Juan-Li Li, Zhao-Jian Yang, Journal of Vibration, Measurement & Diagnosis, **33,** 993-997 (2013)
3. Zheng-You Wang, Ji-Lin Liu, Journal of China Coal Society, **28**,650-654 (2003)
4. Ying Wang, Ya-Li Gao, Jian-Wei Ma, Mining & Processing Equipment, **39**, 46-48(2011)
5. Xiao-Hui Guo, Xiao-Ping Ma, Journal of China University of Mining & Technology, **35**, 813-817 (2006)
6. Qiang Zhang, Nan Hu, Hong-Feng Li. Journal of Liaoning Technical University(Natural Science), **35**, 155 -159 (2016)
7. Geng-Yun Zhang, Mining & Processing Equipment, **39**, 48-52 (2011)
8. Jing-Yan Liu, Fu-Zhong Wang, Yu-Dong Li, Control Engineering of China, **23**, 294-298 (2016)
9. Rui Lian, Zheng-Guo Xu, Jian-Gang Lu, Safety in Coal Mines, **44**, 131-133 (2013)
10. Juan-Juan Li, Liang Hu, Guo-Ying Meng, Guang-Ming Xie et al, Industry and Mine Automation, **43**, 55-60 (2017)
11. Juan-Juan Li, Ai-Ming Wang, Guo-Ying Meng, et al, Fault Diagnosis in Braking System of Mine Hoist Based on Monent Characteristics, (to be published)

 DOI: 10.1051/matecconf/201712805016

Measurement of Argon emission spectral of ICP plasma using a diagnostic system based on photomultiplier tubes array

Weifeng Liu[1,2], Yiyong Yang[1,2,*], Chuankun Han[1,2], Jia Cheng[3] and Linhong Ji[3]

[1]*School of Engineering and Technology, China University of Geosciences (Beijing), Beijing 10083, China*
[2]*Key Laboratory of Deep Geodrilling Technology, Ministry of Land and Resources, Beijing 100083, China*
[3]*Department of Mechanical Engineering, Tsinghua University, Beijing 100084, China*

Abstract. Optical emission spectroscopy (OES) is one of the most important diagnostic tools in plasma physics. A self-built spectroscopic diagnostic system, owning temporal and spatial resolution, has been constructed using photo multiplier tubes (PMTs) array, spectrometer and other parts. The problem of superposition between inlet plane of bundle fiber and the focal plane of the spectrometer is analyzed and solved. In addition, the synchronization regulation of output of PMTs has been completed. This system is installed on an inductively coupled (ICP) plasma chamber in order to study the Argon (Ar) emission spectrum generated from typical radio frequency (RF) and pulse discharges. The test results show that the intensity of Ar emission spectrum increases with the power and pressure, but increase less with the flow and current ratio. Under pulse discharge condition, the intensity of spectrum does not change with the frequency, neither does the broadening of spectrum with time.

1 Introduction

In order to understand the plasma chemistry, various plasma process diagnostic tools such as OES and Langmuir probe have been developed to quantify the concentration of reactive species in the plasma[1]. Because it is non-intrusive, inexpensive, and can be easily incorporated into an existing plasma reactor, the OES quickly gains popularity in the microelectronics industry for monitoring the plasma processing. Optical emission spectroscopy (OES) has been proved to be a powerful technique in plasma diagnostics [4–7]. There are mainly two kinds of OES methods, one is measurement of the spectrum of certain wavelengths by PMT and slit [2-5], the other is using two-dimensional detector arrays such as charge coupled device (CCD) or intensified charge-coupled device (iCCD) camera to provide the spatial multi-channel spectrum of a range of wavelengths[6,7]. The CCDs own various advantages including their subtle detector dimension, high sensitivity, and significant signal to noise ratio. However, the readout period is often longer and the time resolution is usually several KHz, which make the CCD or iCCD has stringent restrictions on the time response of the emission spectral measurement. In many cases, the readout time (~0.5 s) is much longer than the typical time constant of the plasma evolution; hence, temporal variation of the intensity is hardly to be obtained directly by using the spectroscopic system with a CCD or iCCD camera.

In this paper, we analyzed the development of a novel spectroscopic measurement system based on PMTs array. We successfully constructed the measurement system to measure the spatially and temporally resolved intensity of plasma light emissions from ICP Ar RF discharge and pulse discharge.

2 Spectroscopic system

2.1 Spectroscopic system

Figure 1 shows the schematic overview of the spectroscopic measurement system based on PMTs array. Emissions from an ICP plasma chamber formed from Argon gas are collimated by convex lenses and introduced to the measurement system by the inlet optical fibers with inlet core diameter of 2 mm. The other ends of the optical fibers are bundled in a one-dimensional vertical array fixed on a six-degree-of-freedom (6-D) adjusting mount. And the one-dimensional vertical array is coupled with the entrance slit of a Czerny-Turner spectrometer (Horiba iHR550) by the 6-D adjusting mount.

* Corresponding author: yangyy@cugb.edu.cn

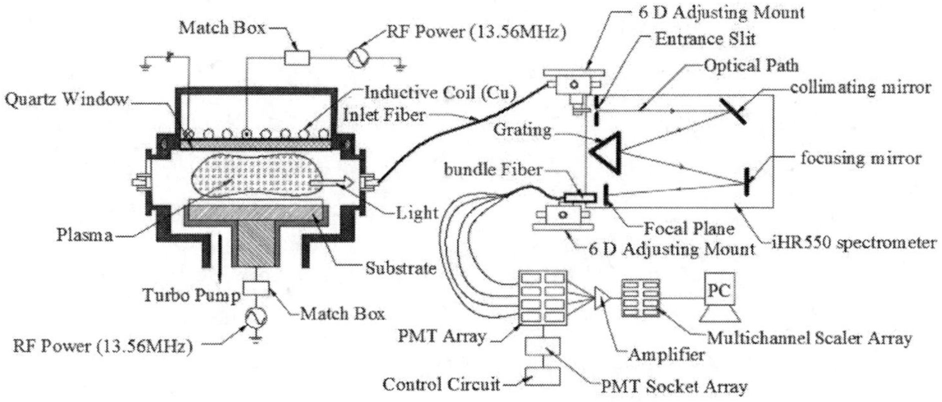

Fig.1. Schematic overview of the spectroscopic measurement system

The spectrometer has a focal length of 550 mm and equips three gratings of 1200, 1800 and 2400 grooves/mm respectively. The light from the ICP plasma chamber go into the spectrometer and then focus on the focal plane of the spectrometer outlet. Like the inlet fiber with the entrance slit, we also adjust the bundle fiber fixed on a 6-D adjusting mount to couple the inlet plane of the bundle fiber with the focal plane of the spectrometer. The inlet plane of the bundle fiber is comprised of 30×30 fibers and the outlet is comprised of 30 fibers. And each of these 30 fibers corresponds to every row of the 30×30 fibers of inlet plane. Eight of the 30 fibers are inserted into eight PMTs (HAMAMATSU R928), and each of them equips a high voltage socket (HAMAMTSU CC238). The PMTs convert the light signal from the 8 PMTs into eight channel electronic signals, and then the electronic signals are amplified by two preamplifiers (Stanford Research Systems, SR445A-350 MHz preamplifier, 4-channel). Every channel signal amplified is collected by a multichannel scaler (MCS, ORTEC), and then analyzed by a PC software.

2.2 Focal plane adjustment

In order to measure the spectrum accurately, the inlet plane of the bundle fibers must be coincided with the focal plane of the spectrometer. We design a fixture to fix the inlet plane of the bundle fibers on a 6-D adjusting mount, by which the inlet plane can be moved to coincide with the focal plane. As the focal plane is still, the inlet plane is moveable by the adjusting mount. Assuming the focal plane in a fixed coordinate OXYZ and the inlet plane in a mobile coordinate O'X'Y'Z' as shown in Figure 2. When the inlet plane is coincided with the focal plane, the coordinate OXYZ equals to the coordinate O'X'Y'Z'.

Except to adjust the inlet plane to coincide with the focal plane, the outlet plane of inlet fiber also should be coincided with the entrance silt of spectrometer. To obtain a higher resolution, the entrance silt should be narrow enough. Similarly, there are 6 degrees between outlet plane and entrance silt. Therefore, the vertical fiber array 1mm×10mm of inlet plane remains to be modulated to coincide with the entrance silt to allow most of the light into the spectrometer. We also use a 6-D adjusting mount to achieve that.

2.3 Performance evaluation

Accurate evaluations of total system performances, such as sensitivity, signal-to-noise (S/N) ratio, magnification are essential for appropriate usage of the spectroscopic system. Optical system setup and calibration are carried out by using sharp spectrum from laser or lamp emissions. A stable Hg lamb is employed to establish initial alignment of the optical components so as to minimize the unexpected noise signal. As the output of each PMT varies, the uniformity of the output in light intensity measurement must be assured. At first, we turn the grating of spectrometer to a fixed wavelength, and then we move the X axis of the adjustment mount to make the light reflected on the focal plane aim at the central vertical array fiber in the inlet plane of bundle fibers. After that, we insert the out fiber corresponding to the central vertical array fiber into one of the 8 PMTs in turn. Moreover, we adjust the control voltage of the control circuit and discriminator voltage of the multichannel scaler simutaneously to obtain almost same output of the eight PMTs. During the measurement process, the dark signal from surrounding evironment could enter into the system and lead to a noise signal influencing the correct signal of light. Therefore, the discriminator should be selected carefully to filter the noise from the signal. In our measurement system, due to the weak dark signal, we choose the voltage value when the signal counter is maximum as the discriminator voltage value. The last verified value of control voltage, discriminator voltage and signal counters corresponding to the eight PMTs are listed in Table 1 in details. After the initial arrangement, we make the system calibration at He-Ne laser wavelength and then confirm that the system meets our requirement.

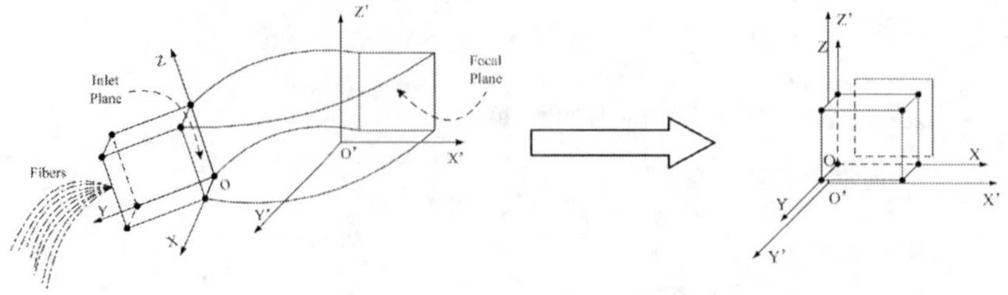

Fig.2. The coordinate of focal plane and inlet plane of bundle fibers

Table 1. Control voltage, discriminator voltage and signal counters corresponding to the eight PMTs

PMT No.	1	2	3	4	5	6	7	8
Disc. Vol. [a]	-0.037	-0.04	-0.043	-0.049	-0.043	-0.049	-0.052	-0.052
Control Vol. [b]	4.05	4.49	4.15	3.96	4.25	4.24	4.2	4.6
Counts/a.u.	13250	13462	13617	13000	13258	13389	13520	13538
ΔCounts [c]	-129.25	82.75	237.75	-379.25	-121.25	9.75	140.75	158.75
%	-0.98%	0.61%	1.75%	-2.92%	-0.91%	0.07%	1.04%	1.17%

[a] Discriminator voltage
[b] Control voltage
[c] Δ Counts is the difference value between each PMT's value and the average value of the eight PMTs' value.

3 Experimental performance and discussion

3.1 ICP RF discharge

In the study of low temperature ICP argon plasma, 1s and 2p levels of argon atoms are often focused by researchers and processing engineers. Argon atom 1s level has higher density and more energy, which can have a great influence on active particles produced in plasma chemical reaction[8]. Due to the strong radiative transition from 2p to 1s, 2p level is very important for researching the argon plasma radiation properties[8]. In our ICP rf Argon discharge process, the pressure is 20mTorr and the flow is 200sccm, hence the corona model is valid for analyzing the process. The reason is that other collisional processes are trivial and the density of metastables is too low to make a significant contribution to the excitation of the excited species under these conditions[9-11]. In a corona model for these levels, we have the electron-impact excitation from the ground-state atom,

$$Ar(gs) + e \rightarrow Ar(2p_1) + e \qquad (1)$$

and the spontaneous radiation,

$$Ar(2p_1) \rightarrow Ar(1s_2) + h\nu \qquad (2)$$

The symbol gs denotes the ground state, 1s and 2p denote the Paschen 1s and 2p levels, e is for an electron and $h\nu$ is for a photon.

The emission intensity, I , from the excited state $2p_1$ is given by

$$I = A_{Ar(2p1)} \cdot n_{Ar(2p1)} = n_e \cdot n_{gs} \cdot Q_{exc} \qquad (3)$$

The symbol A is the Einstein coefficient, n is the density and Q_{exc} denotes the excitation rate coefficient[11].

Usually, strong emission lines from the Paschen $2p_1$ can be observed easily with wavelength of 750.4 nm. Therefore, we choose the intensity of this wavelength to observe its variation with the various process parameters, such as pressure, flow, power and current ratio. The current ratio is ratio of the current of inside coil to the sum current of the both inside and outside coil. Under a low pressure (<100mTorr), the broadening of the wavelength profile is mainly the instrument broadening as the Doppler broadening and Stark broadening is too low to be observed. We get the intensity of each wavelength by fitting the data from the eight MCSs corresponding to the eight PMTs. The intensity variation under different process conditions is shown in Figure 3 from (a) to (d).

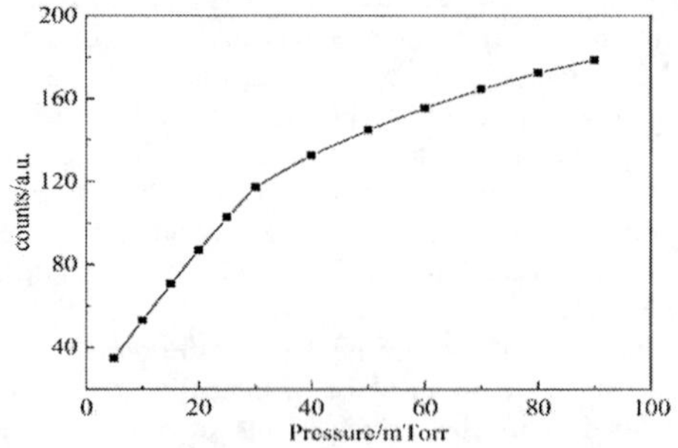

(a)

DOI: 10.1051/matecconf/201712805016

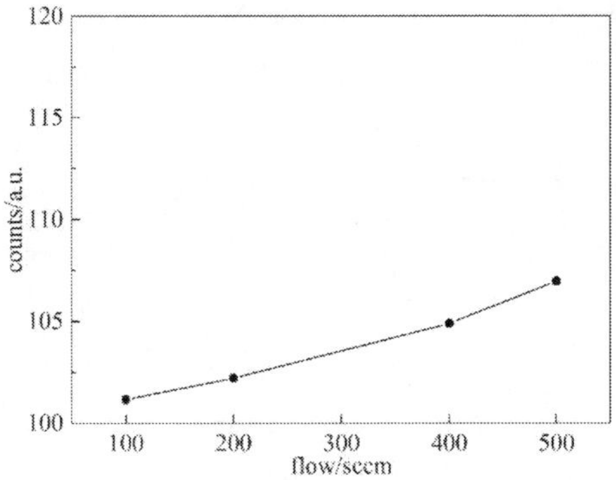

(b)

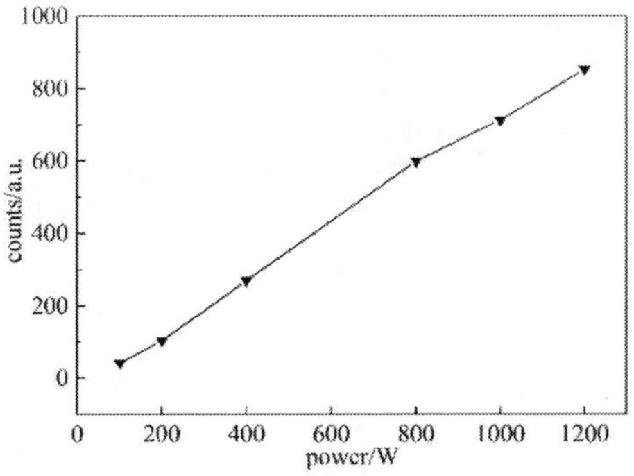

(c)

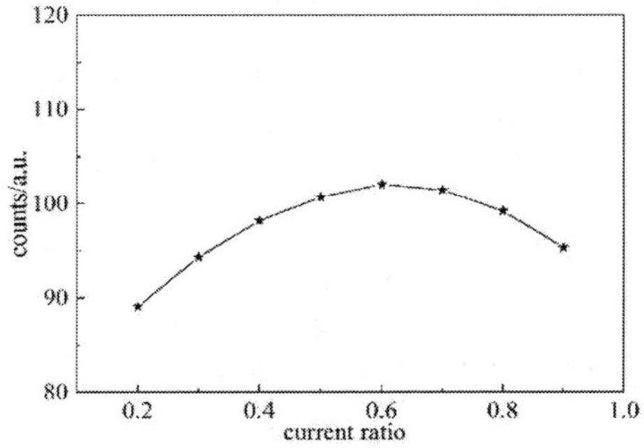

(d)

Fig.3. Intensity of various process conditions

It can be seen from figure 3 that with the increase of processing parameters, the intensity also increases except with the current ratio. As the current ratio increases, the intensity increases firstly and then decreases. And the intensity reaches to maximum value when the current ratio equals to 0.6. Although the intensity almost increases with the process parameters, it barely increases with the gas flow and evidently increases with the pressure and power, especially with power. The reasion lies in the fact that the pressure mainly affects the electronic temperature and power mainly affects electronic density. So while the pressure and power increase, the intensity is also increased due to the increase of electronic temperature and electronic density. With the increase of gas flow, the intensity will increase with the density of Argon gas increases while the pressure is stable. Besides, the variation of coil current ratio merely changes the distribution of plasma in space, which affect the light flux flow into the measurement system. When the current ratio is among 0.5 ~ 0.7, the plasma distribution in the chamber is uniform, and the measured value of light intensity is higher as a consequence.

3.2 ICP pulse discharge

During the pulse discharge, there exists a nonlinear function relation between the any process function R and discharge power P, as is shown below.

$$\langle R[P(t)]\rangle \neq R(\langle P(t)\rangle) \qquad \left(\langle X\rangle = \frac{1}{\tau}\int_0^{\tau} X dt\right) \tag{4}$$

The symbol τ is pulse period, X is a arbitrary function, $P(t)$ is loaded pulse power and angle brackets show the time average value. The significance of equation (4) is that the average value of process function R does not equal to the value of process function under the time average power. As the equation (4) is nonlinear, the time average processing means inadequacy to depict the key parameters of pulse plasma, such as electronic temperature and density. Therefore, in order to research the pulse discharge plasma, the evolution of the plasma parameters should contain the time dimension. Due to the difficulty to obtain the change of plasma parameters with time, CCD or iCCD is not a suitable tool. However, the PMT has a good time sensitivity to get the light intensity of plasma, and can be used to analyze the light intensity variation with the process parameters. We get the results of the light intensity changes with three different pulse frequencies, as is shown in figure 4 from (a) to (c). And we also obtain the light intensity changes of No.1-8 PMT with time, as is shown in figure 5.

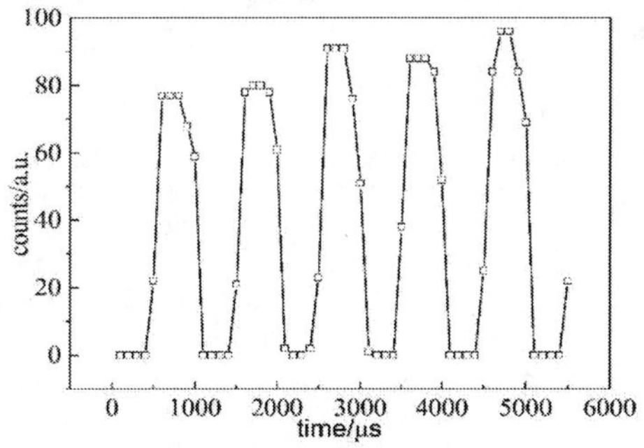

(a)

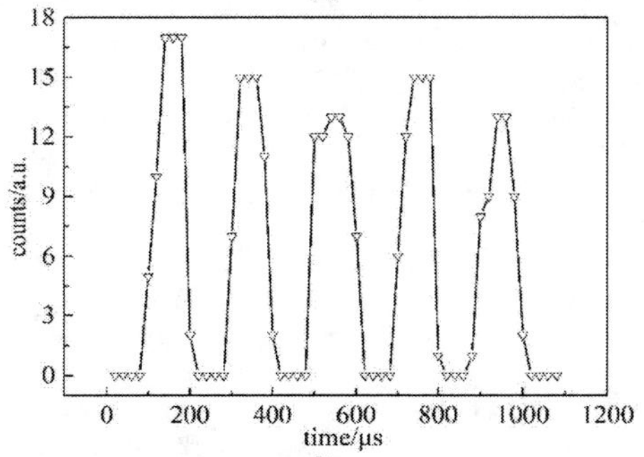

(b)

DOI: 10.1051/matecconf/201712805016

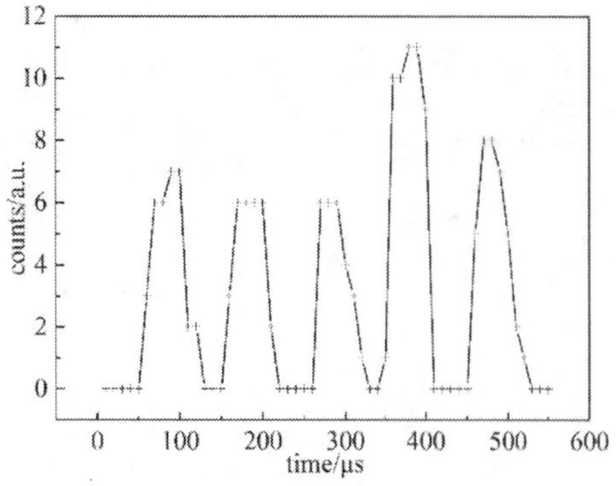

(c)

Fig.4. Intensity change of various pulse frequencies

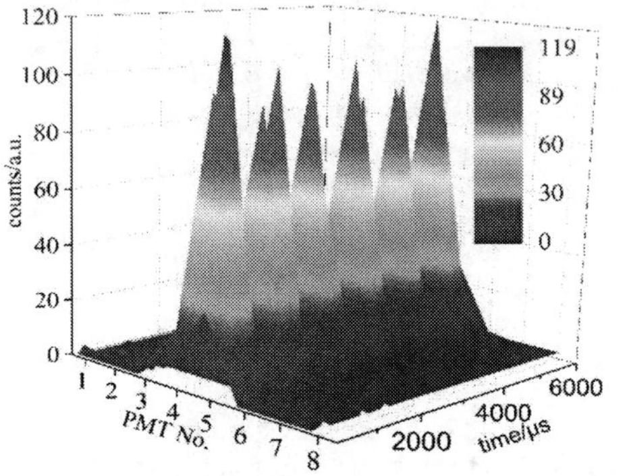

Fig.5. Intensity change of No.1-8 PMT with time increase

Figure 4(a) to 4(c) show that the light intensity varies with the pulse cycle. But the light intensity per 1 millisecond is nearly unchanged when the pulse frequency changes. This is because the change of pulse frequency only changes the number of discharge, which does not affect the light intensity. Increasing the duty ratio of pulse means that the pulse on time is increased, which leads to the improvement of the total light intensity of a pulse cycle. However, when the pulse frequency is constant, changing the duty ratio does not alter the intensity per unit time. Figure 5 shows the intensity change of No.1-8 PMT with a time range of 0s to 6ms. Because of the instrument broadening, the light intensity profile is a Gaussian function distributing among the focal plane of spectrometer and is obtained by the eight vertical array fibers. Figure 5 shows that when the pulse discharge power is loaded by phase step, the light intensity does not change by phase step. Since the light intensity has a relation with plasma parameters, the results in figure 5 show that the plasma parameters evolution is nonlinear during the transient discharge process. Non-stable pulse power supply in pulse discharge steady state leads to unstable collecting spectral intensity, which will also affect the plasma parameters in steady state.

4 Conclusion

A measuring system consisted of photo multiplier tubes (PMTs) array, spectrometer and other parts has been developed. And the position of inlet plane of bundle fiber and the focal plane of the spectrometer have been analyzed under two different coordinates and are adjusted to coincide with each other. The output synchronization calibration of the eight PMTs also has been completed. After that, the Ar emission spectrum intensity from typical rf and pulse discharges are collected by this system. The measurement results show that the intensity of Ar emission spectrum increases with the power and pressure but increase less with the gas flow and current ratio. The intensity of the pulsed discharge is almost unchanged with the frequency. Since the light intensity of the pulsed discharge has a relation with plasma parameters, the results show that the plasma parameters evolution is nonlinear during the transient discharge process. For the spectrum broadening in low pressure is too narrow to be observed. The broadening is mainly the instrument broadening. However, the spectrum broadening in high pressure discharge is the convolution of Doppler broadening and Stark broadening and is wide enough to be observed, so we can make use of this system to obtain the spectrum profile so as to analyze the ion temperature, which will be our further work.

The authors thank Profess Pu Yikang of Tsinghua University for his help in the experiment and data analysis. This work is financially supported by National Science and Technology Major Project (2011ZX02403-4-3).

References

1. E. Karakas, V. M. Donnelly, and D. J. Economou, J. Appl. Phys. **21**, 870-876 (2013)
2. M. B. Chowdhuri, J. Ghosh, R. Manchanda et al. Rev. Sci. Instrum. **85**, 11E411-11E411-3 (2014)
3. S. Kamio, N. Suzuki, Q. H. Cao et al. Rev. Sci. Instrum. **83**, 083103 (2012)
4. R. M. Lan, X. F. Liu, X. R. Yao, W.K. Yu, G.J. Zhai, J. Optoelectronics. Laser, **26**, 2175-2179 (2015)
5. T. H. Chung, H. R. Kang, M. K. Bae, Phys. Plasmas **19**, 113502 (2012)
6. Y. Chen, Z.G. Guo and X.M. Zhu, J. Phys. D: Appl. Phys. **40**, 5112-5116 (2007)
7. G. Avaria, O. Cuadrado, J. Moreno, C. Pavez, L. Soto, J. Phys.: Conf. Ser. **720**, 012041 (2016)
8. U. Fantz, Plasma Sources Sci. Technol. **15**, S137–S147(2006)
9. J. B. Boffard, C. C. Lin, C. A. J. Phys. D: Appl. Phys. **37**, R143–61 (2004)
10. V. M. Donnelly, J. Phys. D: Appl. Phys. **37**, R217–36 (2004)
11. J. T. Gudmundsson, E. G. Thorsteinsson, Plasma Sources Sci Technol. **16**, 399-412 (2007)

Individual Drilling Bit Design and Optimization in Mahu Area

Wenbo Zhang[1], Wenhui Dang[1], Weifeng Chen[1], and Yingjin Zhang[2,a]

[1]*Engineering and Technology Research Institute of Xinjiang Oil Field Co, Karamay 834000, China*
[2]*National Engineering Laboratory of Petroleum Drilling Technology, Leak Resistance & Sealing Technology Research Department, Yangtze University, Wuhan 430100, China*

Abstract. There are three sets of gravels in Mahu region. The gravels formation is characterized by high heterogeneity, high abrasiveness and poor drillability. It is so difficult to optimize bit that restrict seriously the overall exploration and development process. The compressive strength, internal friction angle, and drillability of the formation are tested to check the rock mechanical characteristic profile established by logging data. The individual bit design is carried out by the 3D simulation technology. A new PDC bit type is designed to form the drill bit series for Mahu area. Single PDC bit increases 90% of the drilling footage. The trip average footage is improved 3.45 times, the horizontal section average penetration increased 34.8%. The technical achievements have greatly improved economic development benefits of Mahu region by improving drilling speed and saving drilling costs.

1 Introduction

Three sets of gravels are developed in the Jurassic and Triassic sections of Mahu region. The lateral lithologic variation is large and the vertical interlayer is more. The gravel rock particle size is uneven. The particle size is generally 20mm-50mm and the biggest size is up to 80mm-90mm. the total gravels' thickness is up to 600m-850m(Figure 1). Soft and hard strata is interbedded, strong heterogeneity and high grinding. The effect of cone bit and conventional PDC bit is not ideal. The average penetration is only 1.8m/h-3.7m/h and the footage of single bit is only 132m-319m. Optimizating drill bit is very difficult[1].

Figure 1. Core of gravels in Mahu area

2 Evaluation of rock mechanics characteristics

Rock mechanics is the main factor affecting the breaking rock efficiency of bit[2,3]. The rock mechanics parameters can be obtained by the two methods: one is the experimental method of underground core, another is to calculate through the logging data[4-5]. The experiment method is more precise and expensive but not easy to get the core of all strata, according to the formation strength of mechanical property and longitudinal wave velocity (or time). So the calculation method is more popular. There is a certain relationship among the amount of principle, which can realize continuous prediction of underground rock mechanics parameters by using logging data[6-8]. Experimental results of uniaxial compression deformation of rock is shown in Table 1. Experiment of rock three axis deformation evaluation is shown in Table 2.

Table 1. Experimental results of uniaxial compression deformation of rock

Well name	Rock Mark	Rock description	UCS (MPa)	YM (GPa)	PR
Ma1	1	Sandstone	34.045	6.966	0.2
	2	Glutenite	11.785	4.255	0.156
Ma2	3	Conglomerate	32.659	9.984	0.129
Ma18	4	Conglomerate	14.014	9.794	0.168

Table 2. Experimental results of three axial compression deformation of rock

Well name	Rock Mark	TCS (MPa)	YM (GPa)	PR
Ma1	1	78.016	10.754	0.13
	2	61.854	7.881	0.13
Ma2	3	91.045	17.165	0.1
Ma18	4	72	25.444	0.1

Drillability is defined as the difficulty of rock fragmentation. It is generally used to measure the ability of rock to resist the crushing of bits at the bottom hole. It

[a] Corresponding author: zhangyingjin@yangtzeu.edu.cn

is a comprehensive expression of formation resistance to drilling. The rock drillability is one of the most important parameters to optimize bits and drilling parameters[9, 10]. The experimental results of rock drillability is shown in Table 3.

Table 3. Results of rock drillability test

Well name	Drillability		ITT (us/ft)	Density (g/cm^3)
	Cone	*PDC*		
Ma1	4.61	4.12	72.74	2.55
Ma18	6.46	5.21	68.02	2.51
	6.48	5.12	66.19	2.56
Ma158	6.61	5.34	69.20	2.53

The hardness of rocks is the ability of rocks to resist the intrusion or intrusion of other surfaces[11]. The experimental data are shown in Table 4.

Table 4. Results of rock hardness test

Well name	Hardness (MPa)	Level of hardness
Ma1	1002.676	5
Ma18	1308.254	5
	1597.916	6
Ma158	1499.240	5

The rock mechanical characteristics section of Mahu well area is set up combination the laboratory test data with logging data. The formation rock mechanical parameters are influenced by lithology(Figure 2).

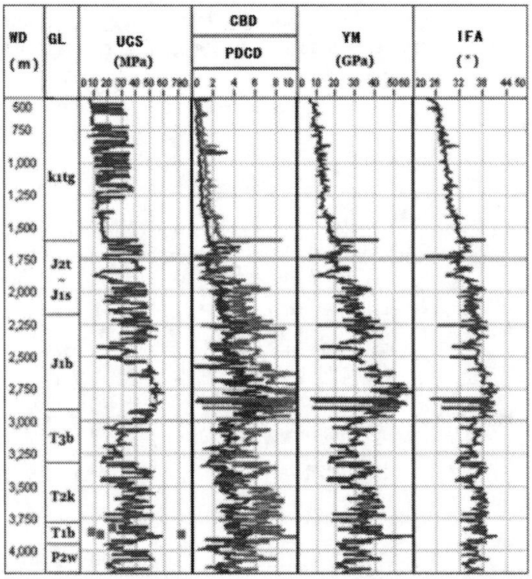

Figure 2. Rock mechanics parameter profile of Mahu area

3 Individual design of PDC bit through 3D simulation technology

The two-dimensional surface design technology cannot achieve the PDC drill surface design. The PDC tooth three-dimensional space positioning parameter design, and the three-dimensional simulation technology can solve this difficult problem well. The 3D simulation technology is to establish the digital model of virtual borehole wall, the drill bit motion mode, the simulation of bit working stress state and the state of PDC teeth cutting into the formation. The potential problem of the bit is analysed by the 3D simulation technology. The finite element method is applied to predict engineering strength and stress in the individual design of PDC bit.

The individual design of PDC bit realized by 3D simulation technology is divided into two stages:

➢ The three-dimensional entity simulation technology is applied to each part of the drill bit according to the design plan. Then, all the 3D component models are assembled into a virtual drill model according to their mutual assembly relation. The size and structure of the interference are corrected in time.

➢ The movement simulation technology is used to simulate the rotation of the drill bit. The drill bit and wall is defined to simulate the actual working process and to check the work force of the bit in the borehole. The efficiency of drilling work process of strata in is ensured and all the bit parts do not interfere the teeth of PDC into the formation. Calculating the cutting area of the PDC teeth in the axial direction, the effect of the drill bit on the formation is determined (Figure 3).

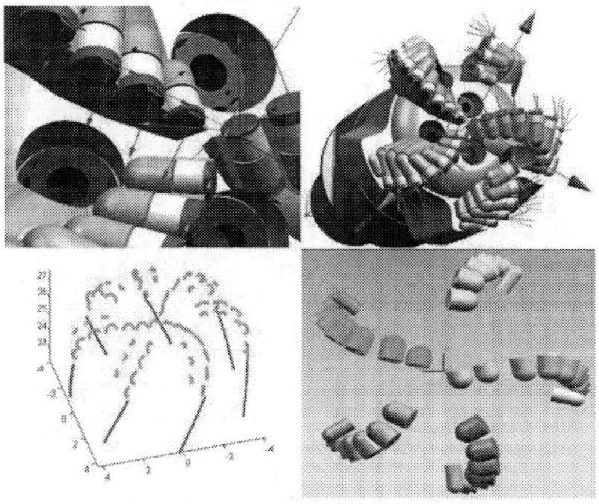

Figure 3. Simulation of teeth and sketch of gear

4 Finite element analysis of material strength

4.1 Physical properties of materials

In the static strength analysis of the lower body of the drill bit, the material attributes to be defined: the material of the drill bit is 40CrNiMo, Young's Modulus is 210GPa, Poisson's ratio is 0.3, and density is 7800kg/m^3.

4.2 Finite element analysis

Firstly, unit selection and mesh generation are performed. It is crucial that the finite element is analysed and calculated, the reasonable unit type and shape is selected, and the grid is arranged. The tetrahedral with 10 nodes element is chosen when the unit mesh is divided for the because of the tetrahedral 10 nodes element with higher stiffness and higher computational accuracy.

Considering the operation time and accuracy, the unit size is 10, and the free meshing unit is adopted. At the same time, the software automatically sets relatively dense grids in the lower part of the drill bit, such as holes and corners. The sparse grids are arranged in areas where the stress changes gently. In this way, two requirements of accuracy and efficiency can be satisfied simultaneously. A finite element model of the lower body of the drill bit is generated. The finite element model consists of element 52070 and node 83017, as shown in Figure 4.

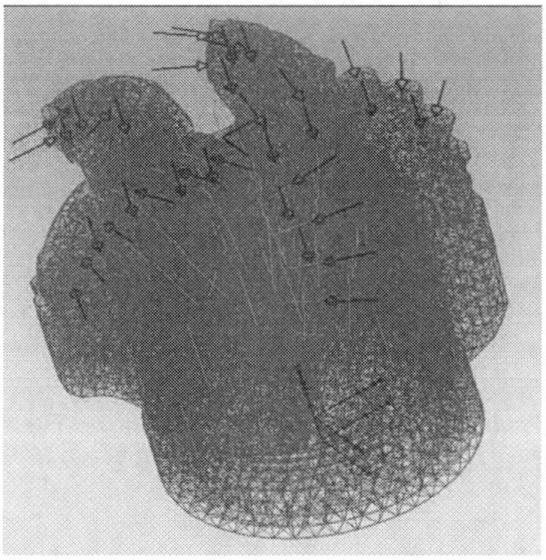

Figure 4. Finite element analysis of the drill bit

4.3 Static strength analysis

The static strength mainly focuses on the structural strength analysis of the object when it is subjected to the maximum load at short time. For the lower part of the drill bit, the worst condition of the lower part of the drill bit is that the drill bit is stopped at the bottom of the drill hole. At this point, the maximum torque of the turntable will be loaded on the lower part of the drill bit. The lower part of the drill bit is held up while working underground. The reason is mainly due to the downhole falling blocks or the high eating depth of teeth. Therefore, the status loading process is analyzed when the drill bit is stopped.

A boundary constraint is applied to the joint of the lower part of the drill bit. The torque and drilling pressure on the cutting teeth of the lower part of the drill bit are loading. The model of 215.9mm SF54VH3 bit's normal working torque is 3000N.m. The rig sets the safe working torque of the turntable is 15,000N.m. Considering the impact inertia and safety factor, the loading torque on the lower part of the drill is 20000N.m; The maximum drilling force of bit is 12t; The cutting torque and the load distribution is mainly affected by the loading force. Subsequently, the solver is performed (Figure 5, Figure 6 and Figure 7).

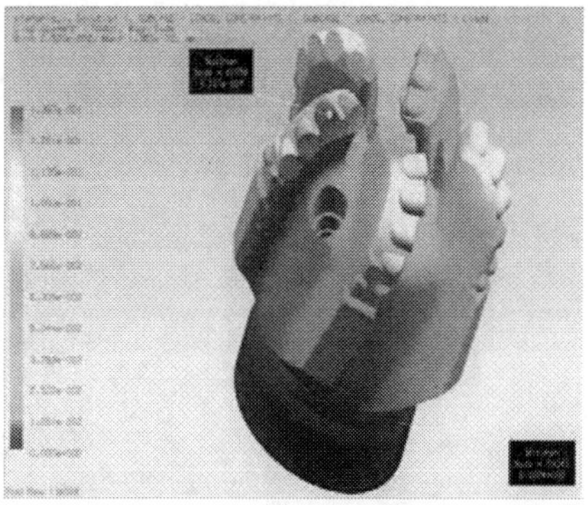

Figure 5. Displacement nephogram of drill bit-deformation

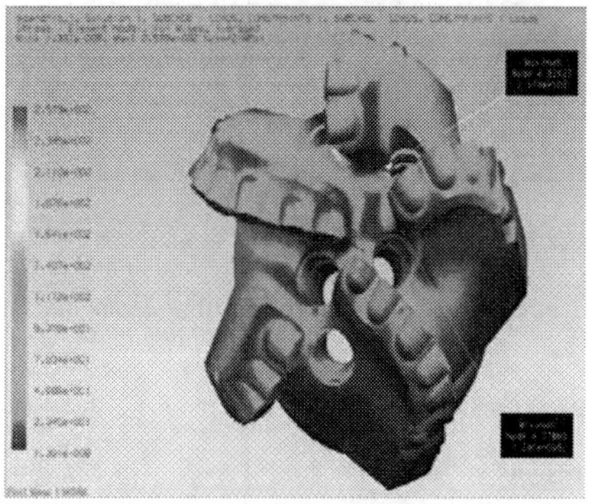

Figure 6. Nephogram of bit stress analysis

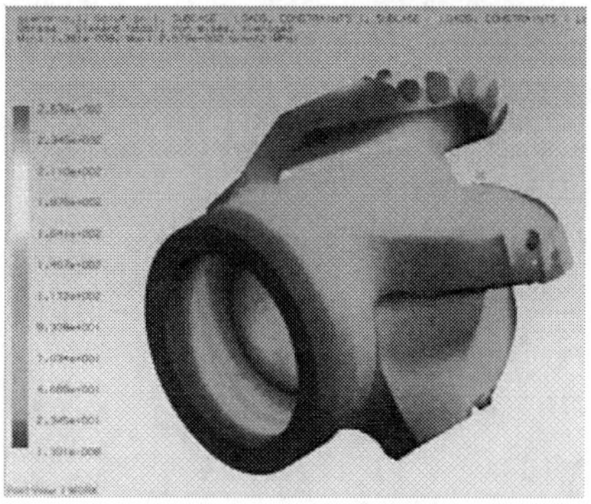

Figure 7. Strength check of drill lower body

4.4 Individual design result of PDC bit

According to the rock mechanics of Mahu region and PDC bit design of 3D simulation technology, the individual PDC bits are designed for the gravels of Mahu region.

The drill bit of SF65DH3 is featured by the assembly of high performance H3 teeth, 6 blades and 2 rows tooth bit, front teeth angle of 18~25degrees, rear teeth 15 ~20 degrees, 13mm and 16mm composited film and mixed teeth arrangement. The high content of sand and gravel layer, medium-hard formation are adapted to the steel body bits, 6 big channels hydraulic design. Mud proof coating, anti-deviation and diameter protection are designed too.

The drill bit of SF54VH3 is featured by the 5 blades with 13mm H3 teeth of composite high abrasion resistance, the low angle of 10-18deg, the flow straight wing, 5 nozzles hydraulic optimization. Mud proof coating, anti-deviation and diameter protection are designed as the bit of SF65DH3.

5 Application

The new type of PDC bit 99 wells are used in Mahu area. Actual average ROP of whole wells is 7.24m/h, 31% higher than before, as is shown in Figure 8. The average drilling cycle is 54.2 days. The self-designed PDC bit achieves that the speed of a single PDC bit is 1.79 to 1.9 times than Smith bit.

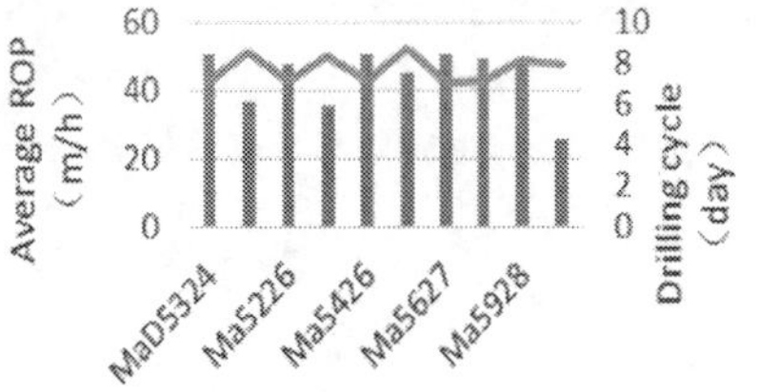

Figure 8. Technical statistics of drilling index of Mahu area

6 Conclusions

The gravels of Jurassic and Triassic in Mahu region is thick. The lithologic lateral and vertical variation is large. The gravel rock particle size is uneven, soft and hard interbedded strata, strong heterogeneity and high grinding. The cone bit and conventional PDC bit are not ideal to use.

The rock mechanical parameters of experiments are tested, such as the compressive strength, internal friction angle and drillability. The new designed type of PDC SF65DH3 and SF56VH3 through three-dimensional simulation technology successfully applied in Mahu region.

7 Nomenclature

WD: Well Depth
GL: Geological Layering
UCS: Unconfined Compressive Strength
TCS: Triaxial Compressive Strength
CBD: Cone Bit Drillability
PDCD: Polyerystalline Diamond Cutter Drillability
PR: Poisson Ratio
YM: Young Modulus
IFA: Internal Friction Angle
ITT: Interval Transit Time

Acknowledgement

The authors wish to acknowledge the National Program on General Program of National Natural Science Foundation of China (Contract No. 51474036 and 51204024) for the financial support.

References

1. Jianhua Huo, Lei Zhang, Jun Wu, Xincai You. Reservoir characteristics and controlling factors of the west slope of Baikouquan glutenite reservoir in Mahu depression. Xinjiang Petroleum Geology, **1**(2017): 1-6.
2. Haitao Wang. Fast drilling technology research and circum Mahu area of Xinjiang Oilfield. Yangtze University, (2015).
3. Fei Xin, Junping Wang, Jian Wang. Application of drilling technology in Xinjiang oilfield with the Western circum Mahu. Inner Mongolia petrochemical industry, **40**(2014): 74-77.
4. Minghe Yang, Weixuan Li, Yingbiao Liu. Fast drilling technology applied in sag slope zone of depressed Mahu. Petrochemical Industry Application, **33**(2014): 23-26.
5. Hui Zhang, Deli Gao. Research on general method of bit selection. Journal of China University of Petroleum: Natural Science Edition, **29**(2005): 45-49.
6. Wenbin Chen, Hao cheng. Research on Optimization Algorithm of drill bit in adjacent well. Information Technology, **7**(2009): 128-130.
7. SINOR L A, POWERS J R, WARREN T M. The effect of PDC cutter density, back rate, size, and speed on performance. IADC/SPE 39306, (1998).
8. G. Mensa-Wilmot, B. Mikhail. Innovative Design Processes and Technologies Improve PDC Bit Performance in Harsh Drilling Environments. SPE103983, (2006).
9. Yufeng Liu. Optimization of PDC bit by parametric analysis. Fault-Block Oil-Gas Field, **4**(2009): 121-123.
10. Deyong Zou, Yonghong Chen. Determination of rock drillability using acoustic time difference data. Petroleum drilling and production technology, **18**(1996): 27-30.
11. Jung S J, Prisbrey K, Wu G. Prediction of rock hardness and drillability using acoustic emission signatures during indentation. International Journal of Rock Mechanics & Mining Sciences & Geomechanics Abstracts, **31**(1994): 561-567.

 DOI: 10.1051/matecconf/201712805018

Research and Implementation of Instrument System on a Light-Duty Electric Aircraft Simulator

Feng Tian, Yonggang Sun[a], Guanglei Meng and Yongtao Yu

School of Automation, Shenyang Aerospace University, Shenyang 110136, China

Abstract. Considering the demands of the instrument system on a light-duty electric aircraft simulator, a semi-physical simulation instrument system, which is based on virtual reality and microcontroller technologies, is designed and implemented. Meanwhile, some key technologies are discussed and a general development method is put forward in this paper. After being completed, this simulated instrument system is connected with the flight-computing system to test its performances. The results show that it has real effect, stable operation and real time response. In practice, the instrument system not only meets the demands of the light-duty electric aircraft simulator, but also can be seen as a certain reference to develop the instrument system of other aircraft simulators.

1 Introduction

Flight simulator is a ground equipment to simulate the conditions of aircraft's flight. The simulation of instrument is essential to a semi-physical flight simulator or a pure virtual flight simulator because it affects the performance of flight simulation and the coverage of training tasks. The instrument system is also one of important technical indexes to determine the fidelity of flight simulator system [1]. Virtual instrument technology possesses the features of short development cycle, fine fidelity and reusability, so it has distinct advantages in the field of instrument simulation [2]. Meanwhile, microcontroller, with the features of easy design, is used to collect and process signals in this system. Combining the virtual instrument technology and microcontroller technology, this paper discussed the related design methods of a semi-physical simulation instrument system.

2 The design of the instrument system

2.1 The framework of the instrument system

As shown in Figure 1, the system structure mainly includes the software and hardware parts. Specially, the software part includes some aeronautical instruments such as altimeter, airspeed meter, vertical speedometer, side-slip angle indicator, magnetic compass and central integrated instrument because they are all necessary to the light-duty electric aircraft simulator. The hardware mainly implements the collection, processing and transmission of operation signal. To realize data exchange between the software and the hardware parts, serial communication technology is adopted in this system. It is clearly known that the inputs of the instrument system are the flight data and the dashboard operation signals, and the outputs are the display information of the virtual instrument and the status of the panel indicator.

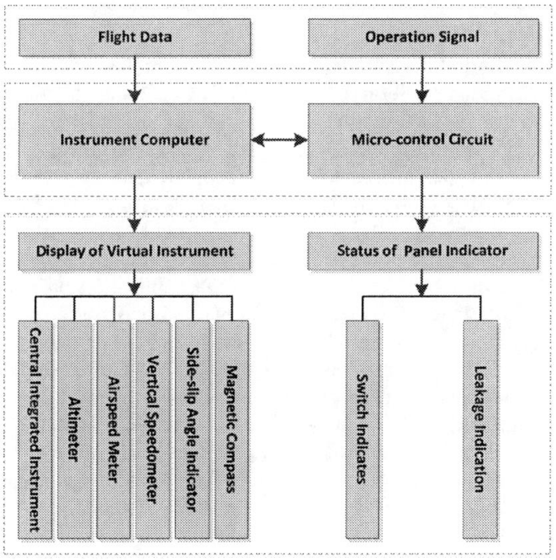

Figure 1. The Framework of Instrument System

2.2 Software development of the instrument system

2.2.1 Introduction to the development platforms

[a] Yonggang Sun: sunyonggangwangyi@163.com

The software of this instrument system is designed with GL Studio and VC++ 6.0 platforms. GL Studio is a professional instrument simulation software launched by United States DISTI company, and it is able to be used to create real-time, two-dimensional or three-dimensional graphical interface on Windows or Linux operating system [3]. The 3.2 version GL Studio includes a design window and a control window. In the design window, users can design instrument models with various graphic elements such as rectangle, circle and sphere. The control window contains coding area, interface setting options and the tree structure of GL Studio objects which created by users [4]. The behaviors of instrument objects can be realized by calling GL Studio library functions. Meanwhile, code generator in the control window can transform a GL Studio file into C++ or Open GL source codes, and the codes can be further compiled and debugged on Visual C++ 6.0 platform to generate an application program.

In addition, GL Studio provides two development modes, namely standalone mode and component mode. The standalone mode file can be used to create an application program. While the component file can only be embedded into a standalone file to take effect [5]. According to the practical requirements, users can chose different modes to design virtual instrument system on GL Studio platform.

2.2.2 Development steps

On the GL Studio platform, the development of virtual instrument system is generally divided into two steps, namely the establishment of instrument model and the realization of instrument objects' behaviors. The instrument model can be built by GL Studio graphical editor, or other graphics editing software [6]. The behaviors of instrument objects can be realized by calling GL Studio library functions. The actions of library functions such as rotation, sliding and characters display can meet the general demands of virtual instrument.

In order to maintain the independence, integrity and flexibility in the process of developing instrument objects, all objects are designed with component mode. After all instrument components are completed, they are all loaded in a standalone file to generate the application program. In the standalone file, the position, size, and attitude of all components can be adjusted for layout. This development method is not only easy to realize the reuse of instrument components, but also obtain the aim of multi-person cooperation [7]. In particular, the flow charts for developing virtual instrument on GL Studio platform is shown in Figure 2, in which the (1) is about component mode and the (2) is concerning standalone mode.

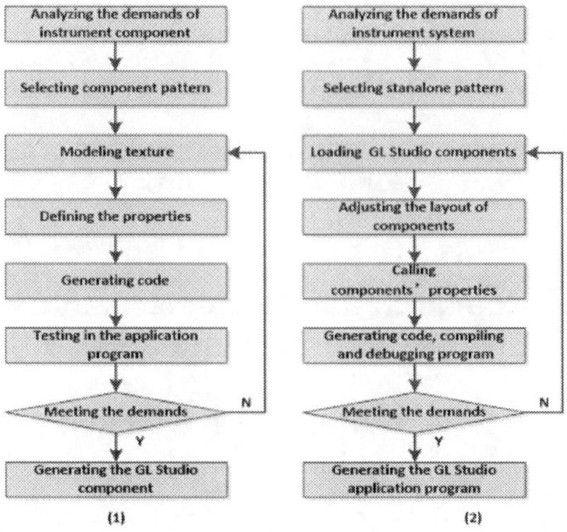

Figure 2. The Flow Chart of Developing Virtual Instrument

2.2.3 Model establishment and behavior realization of the instrument components

The aeronautical instruments required in this system include the central integrated instrument, the altimeter, the airspeed meter, the vertical speedometer, the side-slip angle indicator and the magnetic compass. In this section, three representative instrument components (the altimeter, the airspeed meter and the central integrated instrument) are analyzed and implemented because the principle of designing the others is similar to these.

According to the actual instrument appearance, use the GL Studio tool to build the model of instruments, and then analyse the mathematical features which indicates the movement characteristics of instrument. Generally, to realize the instrument behaviors, the flight data transmitted into instrument components are transformed into angle value or the object's dimension in logical units defined by GL Studio [8].

(1) Altimeter component

The altimeter component is as Figure 3, and it has two pointers and a text box. The long pointer denotes the height range of 0~999 meter, the short pointer represents the height range of 0~5000 meter, and the text box displays the atmospheric pressure.

Figure 3. Altimeter Component

For the altimeter component, the long pointer, short pointer and text box (which actually are the member objects of the Altimeter component object) are respectively named Long_Pointer, Short_Pointer and Pressure_Text. The methods which control the behaviors of the altimeter's pointers and the text box are defined as Alt_Pointers(const float & value) and Alt_Text(const float& value), respectively. According to the scale attributes of altimeter shown in Figure 4 and Figure 5, the formula (1) gives the value of rotation angle for the long pointer, and the formula (2) denotes the angle value of the short pointer.

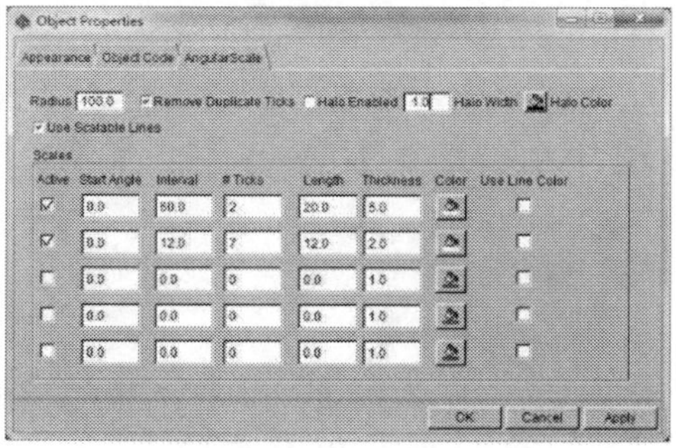

Figure 4. The Scale Attribute for the Altimeter's Long Pointer

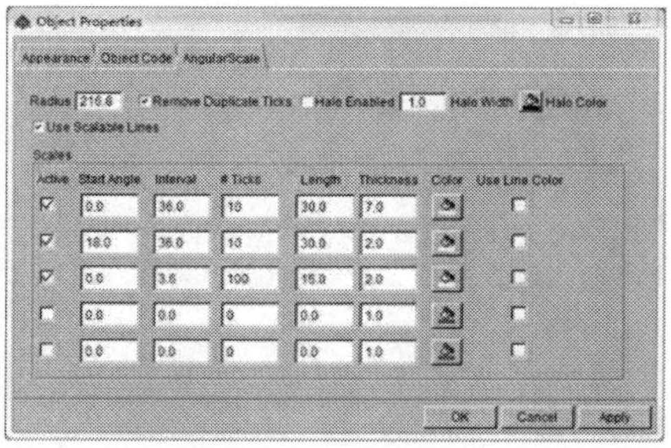

Figure5. The Scale Attribute for the Altimeter's Short Pointer

$$Long\_Angle = Alt\_Value \times 0.36 \quad (1)$$

$$Short\_Angle = Alt\_Value \times 0.012 \quad (2)$$

Where Alt_Value represents the real height value, Long_Angle and Short_Angle respectively denotes the rotation angle of the long pointer and short pointer. Considering the two formulas above, the codes to realize the altimeter's behaviors are added as follows.

```
//controlling the movement of the altimeter's pointers
Alt_Pointers(const float & value)
{
  float   Long_Angle, Short_Angle;
  Long_Angle=value *0.36;
  Short_Angle=value*0.012;
  // controlling the rotary movement of the long pointer
  Long_Pointer->DynamicRotate(Long_Angle,Z_AXIS);
  //controlling the rotary movement of the short pointer
  Short_Pointer->DynamicRotate(Short_Angle,Z_AXIS);
}
```

```
//controlling the display of the text box
Alt_Text (const float& value)
{
  //defining a character array to store string
  Char AirPressureChar[64];
  //transforming value into string
  sprintf(AirPressureChar,"%d",value);
  //displaying the string to in the text box
  Pressure_Text ->String(AirPressureChar);
}
```

Where DynamicRotate(float angle, axis) is to set rotation around X, Y or Z axis by angle, and String(char* s) is used to set the ASCII string that is to be displayed in the text. However, it should be noted that the two methods are all from GL Studio library.

(2) Airspeed meter component and its behavioral realization

As shown in Figure 6, the airspeed meter has only one pointer to denote the speed range of 0~220 (Km/s). The pointer is named as Pointer and the method is defined as Speed_Pointer(const float& value). Figure 7 displays the airspeed meter's scale attribute, which determines the rotation angle of the pointer as formula (3).

Figure 6. Airspeed Meter Component

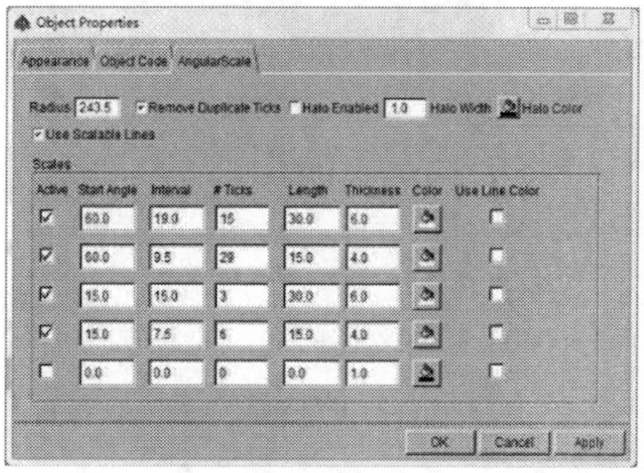

Figure 7. The Scale Attribute for the Airspeed Meter's Pointer

$$SpeedAngle = \begin{cases} Value \times 0.5 & 0 \le Value < 30 \\ Value \times 1.5 - 30 & 30 \le Value < 60 \\ Value \times 0.9 - 54 & 60 \le Value \le 220 \end{cases} \quad (3)$$

Where Value is the speed value transmitted to the airspeed meter and SpeedAngle represents the angle value. For the above mathematical features, the codes is added in the airspeed meter's method as follows.

```
//controlling the movement of the airspeed meter's
//pointer
Speed_Pointer (const float& value)
{
  //rotation angle of the pointer
  float SpeedAngle;
  //transforming the speed value into the rotation angle
  if(0<=value&&value<=30)
  {
    SpeedAngle=value*0.5;
  }
  if(30<value&&value<60)
  {
    SpeedAngle=value*1.5-30;
  }
  if(60<=value)
  {
    SpeedAngle=value*1.9-54;
  }
  // controlling the clockwise movement of the pointer
  Pointer->DynamicRotate(
  -SpeedAngle, Z_AXIS);
}
```

(3) Central integrated instrument component

The central integrated instrument component is shown in Figure 8, and it contains many subordinate components. Here only two subordinate indicators (the throttle indicator and the voltage indicator) are analyzed and implemented.

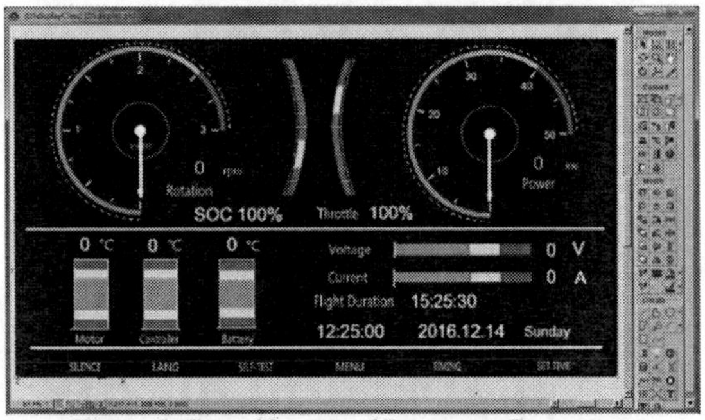

Figure 8. Central Integrated Instrument Component

It can be shown from Figure 9 that the throttle indicator consists of a cambered progress bar and a text box. The progress bar is composed with ten different parallelogram objects. The green part implies that the throttle's state is normal, the yellow part indicates prompt state and the red part represents warning state. For a created GL Studio object, its member method Visibility() can control the visibility of itself, so it is utilized to control the visibility of the respective parallelogram objects in this component. Meanwhile, the throttle value is used to define the number of the parallelogram objects whose state are to be visible. The object names of the ten parallelograms from bottom to top are respectively named Green1, Green2, Green3, Green4, Green5, Green6, Yellow7, Yellow8, Red9 and Red10, and the method that controls the visibility of the parallelograms is defined as Throttle_Display(const oat& value). The parts of the codes are given as follows, and the "..." represents the omitted codes which can be obtained via the similar principle.

```
//Control the throttle indicator
Throttle_Display (const float& value)
{
  ...
  //according to the value, Green1, Green2, Green3 and
  //Green4 are visible. Green5, Green6, Yellow7,
  //Yellow8, Red9 and Red10 are invisible.
  If(30<value&&value<=40)
   {
     Green1->Visibility(true);
     Green2->Visibility(true);
     Green3->Visibility(true);
     Green4->Visibility(true);
     Green5->Visibility(false);
     Green6->Visibility(false);
     Yellow7->Visibility(false);
     Yellow8>Visibility(false);
     Red9->Visibility(false);
     Red10->Visibility(false);
   }
   ...
}
```

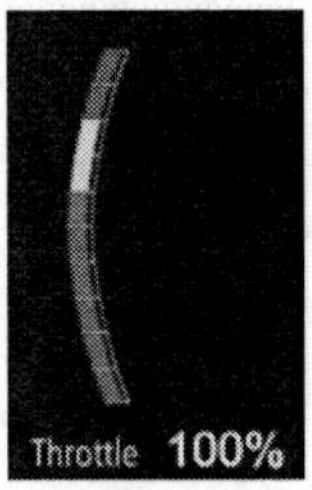

Figure 9. Throttle Indicator **Figure 10.** Voltage Indicator

As shown in Figure 10, the voltage indicator mainly consists of a slide bar, a pointer and a text box. Its specifications are given in Table 1.

Table 1. The Specifications of Voltage Indicator

Color	Green	Yellow	Red
Voltage(V)	0~220	220~320	320~420

The width of the slide bar is 420. Obviously, the voltage specifications shown in the above table matches the width of the slide bar, and the mathematical characteristic of the movement for the voltage indicator's pointer can be obtained as the formula (4).

$$X\_Position = Voltage\_Value \quad (4)$$

Where X_Position represents the pointer's position in the X-axis direction of the slide bar and Voltage_Value is the real voltage value which is to be displayed on the

DOI: 10.1051/matecconf/201712805018

slide bar. The pointer is named Voltage_Pointer and the method that controls the pointer is defined as Voltage_Display(const float& value). The codes are as follows.

```
//Control the voltage indicator
Voltage_Display(const float& value)
{
  //Controlling the pointer moves in the positive X axis
  //direction of the sliding bar
  Voltage_Pointer>DynamicTranslate(value,0,0,false);
}
```

Where DynamicTranslate(float x, float y, float z, bool relative = false) can be utilized to set the dynamic translation to the specified value for all axes (in logical units), and parameter x, y and z respectively means the new dynamic translation for the X axis, Y axis and Z axis.

2.3 Hardware design of the instrument system

The hardware circuit structure shown in Figure 11 mainly include a signal conversion module, a microprocessor module and a serial communication module.

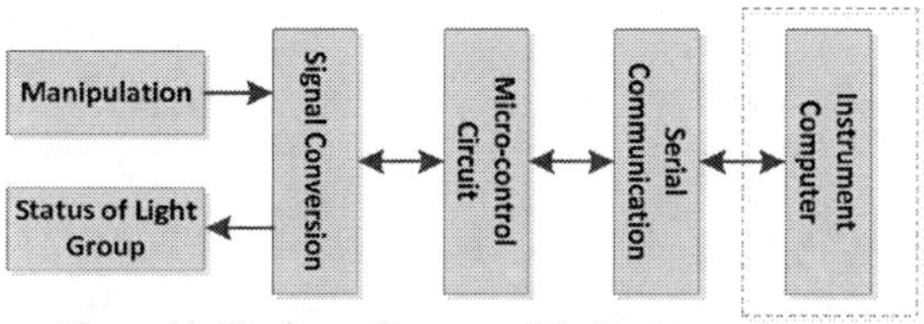

Figure 11. Hardware Structure of the Instrument System

Considering the demands of this instrument system. The STC90C52 microcontroller is used to collect and process the operation signals. Meanwhile, the serial communication module is designed with RS-232 standard to realize the data transmission between instrument computer and microcontroller. In fact, the hardware circuit not only meets the needs, but also reduces the development costs.

3 System integration and test

After all instrument components is finished, the primary task is to create a standalone file, then all the components can be loaded into it. Meanwhile, the position, size, and attitude of all the components can be adjusted for layout. Moreover, in the built-in method caclulate(double time), all component objects' behaviors can be realized by calling library functions.

In the standalone file, the central integrated instrument component object is named CentralPanel, the altimeter object is AltPanel and the airspeed meter object is AirspeedPanel, respectively. The parts of the codes are as follows, and there INFO is a struct variable saving the flight data.

```
caclulate(double time)
{
  // Do not remove (for normal operations)
objects->Group::Calculate(time);
...
//transmitting altitude value to the altimeter
AltPanel-> Alt_Pointers (INFO.Altitude);
//transmitting atmospheric pressure value to the
//altimeter
AltPanel-> Alt_Text (INFO.AirPressure);
//transmitting speed value to the airspeed meter
AirspeedPanel->Speed_Pointer (INFO.AirSpeed);
//transmitting throttle value to the central integrated
//instrument component
CentralPanel-> Throttle_Display(INFO.Throttle);
//transmitting voltage value to the central integrated
//instrument component
CentralPanel-> Voltage_Display(INFO.Voltage);
...
}
```

To test the system's performance, the simulated instrument system is connected with flight-computing computer. The UDP protocol is adopted to realize network communication between the instrument system and the flight-computing system because it has the remarkable advantages for its fast transmission speed, and fine real-time [9]. Through repeatedly debugging and testing, the requirements of the instrument system is reached well, and the operating effect is shown in Figure 12.

Figure 12. The Operating Effect of the Instrument System

4 Conclusions

After the instrument system is connected with the flight-computing computer, the performance of the system is tested and the results show that it not only possess real effect, stable operation, but also has fine fidelity and good reusability. The practice has showed that this instrument system meets the demands of the light-duty electric aircraft simulator.

References

1. H.Wang, Y.Qiu, Microcomputer Information, **25**, 180, (2011).

2. Y.Wu, T.Yu, J.Zhang, F.Yu, J.Liu, Measurement & Control Technology, **1**, 140, (2015).
3. Q.Xu, Z.Ouyang, R.Zhu, Ship Electronic Engineering, **28**, 152, (2008).
4. Y.Zhao, Z.Li, Electronic Design Engineering, **24**, 35, (2016).
5. Y.Xu, F.Yang, Instrumentation and Measurement, **27**, 76, (2008).
6. Y.Sun, L.Wang, J.Chen, System Simulation Technology, **11**,151, (2015).
7. J.Xu, G.Li, H.Zhao, S.Fan, Aerospace Control, **28**, 70, (2010).
8. G.Liu, Z.Li, Microcomputer Information, **26**, 110, (2010).
9. H.Chen, J.Wu and X.Huang, Measurement & Control Technology, **32**, 89, (2013).

AUTHOR INDEX

An Xuefeng 233
Bai-qing He 270
Bao Liu 353
Bi Chunyu 132
Bing Jia 67
Cai Zhengyu 290
Cao Shijie 274
Changqing Guo 226
Chen Debao 172
Chen Lizhen 91
Chen Weifeng 282, 403
Chen Xuemei 137
Chen Zhixin 86
Cheng Fan 220
Cheng Jia 398
Chunmei Wu 13
Dandan Ma 33
Dang Wenhui 389, 403
Deng Rurong 190
Deng Ying 286
Desheng Liu 33
Deshi Wang 353
Du XueLiang 45
Duan Xuliang 159
Fan Di 113
Fan Hongli 203, 349, 368
Fan Tian 364
Fang Peiyu 305
Fang Zhijun 168
Fei Qiou 181
Fengwen Sun 328
Fu Jie 368
Fu YongGang 91
Fu Zhen 164
Gao Jun 310
Gao SHI Jian 209
Geng Zhu 372
Golubchik Eduard 359
Gong Lin 368
Gong-chang Ren 141
Guilin Li 13
Gulin Aleksandr 359
Guo Dai Fei 262
Guo Edward 380
Han Chuankun 398
Han Xi 238
He Ling 152
Hongbo Liu 49
Hou Guangsong 310
Hu Hanxian 364
Hu Henry 216
Hu Jian Jun 262
Hu Liang 393
Hu Shachang 105
Hu Song 250
Hua Xiaopeng 144
Huang Rong 322
Huang Xin 45
Huang Xuemei 190
Hui Zhao 24, 270
Ji Lei 203, 349
Ji Linhong 398
Ji Yalin 148
Jia Xueqing 314
Jia Yifan 137
Jia Yi-Fan 393
Jia Zhen 100
Jiaming Zhong 372
Jiang Chengzhi 1
Jiang Yunfei 91
Jianhou Gan 266
Jihua Li 226
Jihui Wang 67
Jin Li 95
Jing Chenchen 203, 349
Jinshuai Yang 95
Jiping Lu 349
Juan Li 76
Lei Zhang 220
Li Baiyi 250
Li Chenxu 81
Li Fujian 286
Li Gaosheng 314
Li Haiying 109
Li Hongkui 286, 310
Li Jianguo 181
Li Juan-Juan 393
Li Liu Yong 209, 340
Li Penglin 349
Li Sihao 282
Li Tianli 1, 5, 105
Li Yin 298
Li Yongni 250
Li Yu 177
Li ZhengHong 195, 199
Li Zhenxing 250
Liang Yanlei 177
Liang Yizeng 185
Lin Chen 328
Lin Chenglong 314
Lin Han 385
Lin Liqun 86
Lin Meng 132
Lin Wen-Feng 54
Ling-zhi Li 156
Liu Changmeng 203, 368
Liu Dongcheng 298
Liu Hengyan 59
Liu Pengfei 132
Liu QingBin 45

AUTHOR INDEX

Liu Wei 364
Liu Weifeng 398
Liu Xiaoshuang 168
Liu Yingbiao 385, 389
Liu Yong Li 345
Liu Yongli 212
Liyingi Tian 245
Lu Jiping 203, 368
Lu PengFei 152
Lu Zongyu 282, 389
Luo ChangShou 125
Luo Haibiao 298
Luo Mingqi 37, 41
Lutie Xu 49
Lv Yafei 59
Ma Shuyuan 203
Ma Wei-Dong 54
Meishan Li 33
Meng Gesi 305
Meng Guanglei 407
Meng Guo-Ying 393
Meng Zhang 49
Ming-xing Kuang 24
Mu Jiong 159
Niu Jigao 81
Niu Wenhui 286
Ouyang Yunxiong 298
Pan Baijun 121
Polyakova Marina 359
Qian Li 226
Qiu Kun 368
Qizhi Zhao 220
Ren Luyang 216
Sen Liang 256
Shaodan Peng 226
Shaowei Wang 13
Shi Boqiang 181
Shi Jian Gao 212, 345
Shi Song 148
Shi Xiaoli 81
Shi-jiang Kuang 24, 270
Shijie Zhang 220
Shu Dai Jia 19
Song Jiancheng 109
Song Xinli 132
Song Yufei 28
Su Zhida 132
Sun Chengli 9, 376
Sun Sufen 125
Sun Yonggang 407
Tang Dan 113
Tang Jiachen 181
Tao Wei 364
Tian Dawei 286
Tian Feng 407
Tong Wen 95
Tu Shilong 121
Wan Fucheng 71
Wang Ai-Ming 393
Wang Bin 28
Wang DongLin 45
Wang HuiRong 91
Wang Lei 209, 212, 340, 345
Wang Lu Min 212, 340, 345
Wang Mantao 159
Wang Qilong 310
Wang Rujie 181
Wang Shuai 393
Wang Tuo 37, 41
Wang Zheng-yi 318
Wang Zhongsheng 181
Wei Chen 328
Wei Hou 128
Wei Huayu 5
Wei Jing 226
Wei Ping 54
Wei Qin 76
Wei Qingfeng 125
Wei Zhou 226
Weibo Yu 49
Wei-Ping Zhao 332
Wen Qiaoyan 262
Wen Yu Wen 209, 212, 340, 345
Wen-qing He 294
Wu Guoyang 132
Wu JunNing 45
Wu Lehui 172
Wu Qianru 368
Xi Zhenghao 168
Xia Jianhua 71
Xiangyu Luo 256
Xiao Feng 113
Xiao-Gang Guo 332
Xiao-ling Cheng 270
Xie Guang-Ming 393
Xie Min 54
Xiong Wei 59
Xu Chunhua 81
Xu Ke 310
Xu Li-Xing 54
Xu Sen 144
Xu Yongli 59
Xue Chen Xiao 209
Xue Zhuocheng 109
Xuesheng Pei 245
Xueyan Lan 13
Xu-hui Lan 156
Ya-juan Zhang 294
Yan Li 1, 5, 105, 233
Yan Nan 19

AUTHOR INDEX

Yang Haoge 376
Yang Shou-liang 278
Yang Wenchuan 164
Yang Yiyong 398
Yi Wang 95
Yin Fucheng 380
Yin Wei 318
Yong Yang 332
Yong-ming Guo 156
Yu Yang 132
Yu Yongtao 407
Yuan Feng 298
Yuan Shuai 9, 376
Yuan Yingchun 28
Yuchen Sun 353
Yue Liu 33
Yue-xina Yang 141
Yuheng Zhang 128
Yupo Cao 226
Zhang AYing 195, 199
Zhang Bao 305
Zhang Bo 177
Zhang Dong 278
Zhang Hao 318
Zhang Jiancheng 290
Zhang Jiyue 1, 5, 105
Zhang Qiang 216
Zhang Shuang 380
Zhang Tianle 290
Zhang Tianlu 137
Zhang Wenbo 385, 403
Zhang Xi 137
Zhang Xiangxiang 168
Zhang Xiaojie 1, 5, 105
Zhang Xun 340, 345
Zhang Yang 278
Zhang Yingjin 282, 403
Zhang Yu 340, 345
Zhangxiong Wen 328
Zhanqiang Liu 95
Zheng-Qiang Jing 332
Zhenshan Wang 67
Zheyun Wang 336
Zhilin Zhao 266
Zhong Zhou Ai 340
Zhou Ai zhong 212
Zhou Bin 37, 41
Zhou Guangchun 380
Zhou Liya 28
Zhou Qing 152
Zhou Rui 100
Zhou Yong 349
Zhu Zhongxi 385, 389
Zhuang Yufeng 322
Zi-min Wang 24, 270
Zoua Feng 172
Zuo Wen 164
Zuxi Chen 256